P9-DWP-644

COMPANIES DISCUSSED IN THIS BOOK
(CONTINUED)

DATE DUE

NO 15 '96			
MO 4 '97			
FE 24 '98			

DEMCO 38-296

Illinois Tool Works
In-Store Advertising
Incomnet, Inc.
Interco, Inc.
International Finance Corpor
ITT Corporation
J. M. Smucker Co.
Janney Montgomery Scott
Japan Airlines (JAL)
Jiffy Lube
Jugtown Mountain Smokeho
Kawasaki Heavy Industries
Kimberly-Clark
Kohlberg Kravis Roberts (KK
Laventhol & Horwath
Lincoln Savings and Loan of
Liquid Paper Corporation
Manufacturers Hanover Cor
Matsushita Electric Industrial
May Department Stores
MCA
Mellon Bank Corp.
Midwest Express
Minera Escondida Limitada
Minnetonka Labs
MNC Corporation
Morgan Stanley
National Westminster Bank
NCR
Northwest Airlines
Norwest Corp.
Noxell
Payco American
Petex, Inc.
Philip Morris
Phillips Petroleum Company
Phoenix-Hecht
Pinkerton's

rporation of America
ties, Inc.

ation

Loan Association

Co.
rities
Western Digital Corporation
Yasoda Trust and Banking Company

BASIC MANAGERIAL FINANCE

THIRD EDITION

LAWRENCE J. GITMAN
SAN DIEGO STATE UNIVERSITY

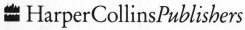 HarperCollins*Publishers*

Riverside Community College
Library
APR '93   4800 Magnolia Avenue
Riverside, California 92506

To all teachers of finance,
with the hope that this text will enhance
their ability to communicate effectively an understanding
of managerial finance to their students, our future
business leaders

Sponsoring Editor: Suzy Spivey
Development Editor: Ann Torbert
Project Coordination, Text and Cover Design: York Production Services
Production Manager: Michael Weinstein
Compositor: York Graphic Services, Inc.
Printer and Binder: R.R. Donnelley & Sons Company
Cover Printer: The Lehigh Press, Inc.

For permission to use copyrighted material, grateful acknowledgment is made to the copyright holders on pg. S-1, which are hereby made part of this copyright page.

Basic Managerial Finance, Third Edition
Copyright © 1992 by Lawrence J. Gitman

All rights reserved. Printed in the United States of America. No part of this book may be used or reproduced in any manner whatsoever without written permission, except in the case of brief quotations embodied in critical articles and reviews. For information address HarperCollins Publishers Inc., 10 East 53rd Street, New York, NY 10022.

Library of Congress Cataloging-in-Publication Data

Gitman, Lawrence J.
    Basic managerial finance/Lawrence J. Gitman.—3rd ed.
      p. cm.
    Includes index.
    ISBN 0-06-500166-4
    1. Business enterprises—Finance. 2. Corporations—Finance.
I. Title.
HG4026.G59 1992
658.15—dc20
                                                   91-40342
                                                     CIP

92 93 94 95 9 8 7 6 5 4 3 2 1

BRIEF CONTENTS

DETAILED CONTENTS

TO THE INSTRUCTOR

Basic Managerial Finance has been carefully developed and revised to provide a stimulating first exposure to the basic concepts and practices of managerial finance. It is intended for use in the first undergraduate managerial finance course at both two-year and four-year schools. In addition, the text works well in technical and continuing education courses in finance offered through management development and adult education programs and seminars.

The text's streamlined, straightforward, and easily understandable approach blends a traditional accounting orientation with modern valuation techniques. Numerous examples and illustrations clarify basic concepts. A variety of pedagogical aids are included to catch student interest and make learning the material easier and more enjoyable.

MAJOR CHANGES IN THE THIRD EDITION

The third edition of *Basic Managerial Finance* represents a significant revision of the text. In addition to the customary updating to reflect the changing financial marketplace, four major changes were incorporated into this edition: improved organization and coverage, greater emphasis on practice, more contemporary coverage, and better pedagogy.

Improved Organization and Coverage

The text's flexible organizational structure was carefully designed to assure a smooth transition from accounting to managerial finance topics. It is structured around the corporate balance sheet, with linkages to share price. Various financial decisions are examined as they relate to the balance sheet and in terms of their impact on return, risk, and share price. Although the book is intended to be read as a continuum, almost any chapter can be taken out of sequence and studied as a self-contained unit. Since each instructor has particular topic preferences, the book's coverage is intentionally both extensive and flexible.

The text's organization and coverage have been improved in this edition by restructuring it to contain six (rather than seven) parts. The first three are devoted to the firm's environment and short-term operations, and the final three parts are concerned with long-term financial topics. The following organizational and coverage changes have been made in this edition:

■ The book now presents new material on mergers, LBOs, divestitures, and failure (formerly Chapter 20) as Chapter 17, the final chapter in Part Five on long-term financial decisions. This organization more correctly places the material with the chapters on capital budgeting and other long-term financial decisions.

■ A new chapter on investment banking has been added. This chapter (Chapter 18) is included as the first chapter in Part Six on sources of long-term financing. It describes the important role played by investment bankers in issuing and selling the firm's new securities, and it lays the groundwork for the discussion of specific long-term financing sources in the chapters that follow.

■ Finally, the international material (formerly Chapter 21) has been integrated throughout the text. This material now appears as the final section in 13 of the text's 21 chapters. Integration of the international material represents the most logical way to structure coverage of this important dimension of managerial finance. This approach better meets the requirements of the American Assembly of Collegiate Schools of Business (AACSB). The international sections (and related end-of-chapter materials) are marked with a multinational globe symbol, ⬤.

Greater Emphasis on Practice

Every chapter in this edition includes three or more real-company events. New chapter opening vignettes and boxed examples in each chapter expose the student to the experiences of a broad cross-section of firms. A list of the companies discussed appears on the front endpapers.

More Contemporary Coverage

I have added discussion of the important current and emerging issues, instruments, and techniques affecting the practice of financial management. Attention to the real-world practice of managerial finance assures the students' exposure to a state-of-the-art—rather than historic—view of managerial finance. Contemporary topics covered in this edition include:

■ The role of ethics in managerial finance (Chapter 1)
■ The savings and loan crisis (Chapter 2)
■ Implications of Europe 1992 (Chapter 2)
■ The statement of cash flows (Chapter 3)
■ Automated clearinghouses (Chapter 8)
■ Materials requirement planning (MRP) and just-in-time (JIT) inventory systems (Chapter 9)

■ The recent merger wave, modern merger terminology, leveraged buyouts (LBOs), and popular defenses for fighting hostile takeovers (Chapter 17)

■ Financial engineering and investment banking in the future (Chapter 18)

■ Extendable notes and putable bonds (Chapter 19)

■ Payment-in-kind (PIK) preferreds (Chapter 20)

■ Use of voting rights as a defense against hostile mergers (Chapter 20)

Better Pedagogy

The pedagogy in this edition has been significantly improved. Six areas of strengthened pedagogy are noteworthy:

■ **Chapter-opening vignettes:** To capture students' attention, each chapter begins by relating timely real-company events to one or more of the chapter's concepts. Students are introduced to large companies such as General Electric, Matsushita Electric, Quaker Oats, and Sears, as well as to smaller firms such as Albany Ladder, Buford Television, Hilltop Trading Company, and Incomnet.

■ **Thematic boxes:** Over 40 boxed items (2 per chapter) appear throughout the text to provide practical insights. Each is keyed to one of four themes: ethics in finance, small business, careers in finance, and finance in action. The *ethics boxes* address ethical concerns and practices of financial managers; *small business boxes* highlight some of the unique issues and problems involved in the financial management of small businesses; *career boxes* provide insight into various finance careers; and *finance in action boxes* describe actual company situations that demonstrate text concepts and illustrate practice.

■ **Calculator keystrokes:** Calculator keystrokes are now incorporated into all discussions and examples involving use of time-value techniques. Students are assumed to have one of the least expensive and most popular calculators—the Texas Instruments BA-35. Although the use of financial tables to make such calculations continues to be discussed, the inclusion of calculator keystrokes allows students to use this technology to improve speed and accuracy when making financial computations.

■ **Marginal equation captions:** Throughout the book, equations are labeled and captioned in the margin when they first appear, to help students locate and remember important equations.

■ **Summary tied to learning objectives:** The summary at the end of each chapter is presented as a numbered list that corresponds directly to the six chapter-opening learning objectives. Each learning objective is restated in the summary and followed by a brief paragraph that summarizes the material that fulfills the objective. This feature clearly links each chapter's learning goals to the material presented.

■ **Integrative chapter-end cases:** At the end of each chapter (except the first) is a brief integrative case that ties together the key concepts introduced in the chapter. These cases provide students with the means to use the chapter material to formulate and solve realistic business problems. (Solutions to the cases are included in the acetate transparencies package, described on page xvii.)

Each chapter of the textbook also retains the proven pedagogical devices of earlier editions to stimulate and enhance student interest and learning. These are:

■ **Learning objectives:** Action-oriented learning objectives preview and guide the students' understanding of the chapter material.

■ **Practical examples:** Over 100 well-marked practical examples in the text demonstrate potentially troublesome concepts. Quite often the reason for using a particular approach is given along with the demonstration. Reviewers of this and earlier editions have remarked that the examples contribute greatly to both teaching and learning this material well.

■ **Marginal glossary:** New terms introduced and defined in the text appear in bold type, and their definitions are shown as a running glossary in the margins of the text pages. Each term is also included in the end-of-text glossary.

■ **Questions:** Ten to fifteen questions are provided to serve as a review by which students can test their understanding of the chapter's content.

■ **Problems:** Because I am a strong believer in the use of many problems during all phases of the first finance course, at whatever level it is taught, a comprehensive set of problems, containing more than one problem for each concept or technique, is included. These problems assure students multiple self-testing opportunities and give instructors a wide choice of assignable material. A short description at the beginning of each problem identifies the concept that the problem has been designed to test. Some of the end-of-chapter problems are captioned as "integrative" since they tie together related topics. In addition, a disk symbol, ■ , appears in the margin next to all problems that can be solved using the *BMF Problem-Solver*—a menu-driven personal computer program (described below) that accompanies the textbook. For those problem types that can be worked using the *BMF Tutor*—a self-testing problem generating software program (also described below)—a symbol, ⌨ , appears in the margin.

■ **End-of-text appendixes:** Included at the end of the textbook are a number of appendixes useful to students. Appendix A includes brief descriptions of 20 career opportunities in managerial finance and financial services. Appendix B gives instructions for using the *BMF Disk*—the *BMF Tutor* and the *BMF Problem-Solver*. Appendix C is a complete set of financial tables for percentage rates between 1 and 50 percent. (Also included in the book for the student's convenience is a removable, laminated future- and present-value table card.) Finally, answers to selected end-of-chapter problems appear in Appendix D; these answers help students evaluate their progress in preparing detailed problem solutions.

IMPORTANT CONTENT IMPROVEMENTS IN THE THIRD EDITION

A large number of important but less sweeping changes have been made in the third edition. They are summarized below.

■ **Chapter 1** on finance and the financial manager has new examples of marginal analysis and wealth maximization, and includes discussions of the emergence of the large private corporation, and the role of ethics in finance.

■ **Chapter 2** on the firm and its operating environment has been reorganized to begin with a discussion of the basic forms of business organization. It includes an improved discussion of corporate tax rates (including a corporate tax rate schedule), discusses the treatment of corporate interest and dividend income, and describes the recent savings and loan crisis.

■ **Chapter 3** on financial statements, depreciation, and cash flow has a new schematic of the firm's cash flow that is consistent with the statement of cash flows and develops and discusses the statement of cash flows using a step-by-step approach.

■ **Chapter 4** on financial statement analysis has been refined and tightened, and earnings per share (EPS) has been added to the discussion of profitability ratios.

■ **Chapter 6** on financial planning includes a new discussion of coping with uncertainty in the cash budget.

■ **Chapter 7** on working capital fundamentals contains new and streamlined discussions of net working capital and the associated trade-off between profitability and risk.

■ **Chapter 8** on cash and marketable securities has a discussion of the firm's operating cycle, presents an improved discussion of the cash conversion cycle and its management, and contains updated discussions of popular cash management techniques and marketable securities.

■ **Chapter 9** on accounts receivable and inventory has been reorganized and presents a new accounts receivable decision model that eliminates fixed costs. The chapter also includes discussions of the materials requirement planning (MRP) and just-in-time (JIT) inventory systems.

■ **Chapter 10** on sources of short-term financing now includes a separate and improved discussion of short-term loan interest computations.

■ **Chapter 11** on time value of money now contains improved algebraic notation, introduces and demonstrates calculator use to simplify financial computations, and includes many new end-of-chapter problems.

■ **Chapter 12** on risk, return, and valuation has been streamlined and clarified and now discusses popular stock valuation approaches after, rather than before, presenting the zero and constant growth models.

■ **Chapter 13** on the cost of capital contains an improved discussion of the calculation and application of the weighted marginal cost of capital (WMCC).

▰▰ **Chapter 15** on capital budgeting techniques demonstrates calculator use throughout, contains an improved discussion of the IRR calculation for mixed streams of cash inflows, and includes brief discussions of scenario analysis and divisional costs of capital.

▰▰ **Chapter 16** on capital structure and dividend policy includes improved discussions of the optimal capital structure, the relevance of dividend policy, and the accounting aspects of stock dividends.

▰▰ **Chapter 17** on mergers, LBOs, divestitures, and failure has been completely revised to fully reflect popular terminology and new techniques and methods of corporate restructuring. It includes numerous real-company events related to the recent merger wave, has an expanded discussion of leveraged buyouts (LBOs), and describes a number of hostile takeover defenses.

▰▰ **Chapter 18,** a completely new chapter on investment banking, provides an overview of the long-term fund-raising process (including venture capital), the role of the investment banker, compensating investment bankers, initial public offerings, selling additional common stock, and recent trends in the investment banking industry.

▰▰ **Chapter 19** on long-term debt and leasing contains an improved discussion of collateralized term loans, describes extendable notes and putable bonds, contains a completely new discussion, framework, and demonstration of bond-refunding decisions, and includes an improved discussion of the lease-versus-purchase decision.

▰▰ **Chapter 20** on preferred and common stock now describes payment-in-kind (PIK) preferreds, discusses voting rights in light of recent takeover activity, and emphasizes the use of stock rights primarily by smaller corporations.

▰▰ **Chapter 21** on convertibles, warrants, and options contains a new example of the logic underlying the purchase of a put option.

SUPPLEMENTAL MATERIALS

A number of additional materials are available to aid and enrich the teaching and learning process.

For Instructors

Instructor's Manual

The comprehensive *Instructor's Manual* enables the professor to use the text easily and effectively in the classroom. Prepared by Marlene G. Bellamy and myself, the manual includes for each chapter an overview of topics, a chapter outline, reference to the *BMF Disk*, teaching suggestions, suggested *Study Guide* problems, and detailed answers and solutions to all text questions, problems, and integrative cases. Great care has been taken to ensure the accuracy of all answers and solutions.

Lecture Notes

Prepared by Thomas J. Liesz of Western State College (CO), this new instructional aid provides approximately 20 pages of lecture notes per chapter. Developed from my own lecture notes, this supplement is bound, perforated, and three-hole-punched for convenient use. Each page of lecture notes is laid out in an open format as a transparency master. The notes not only summarize the chapter material but also contain additional information, examples, and problems with solutions that can be used in the classroom to reinforce more quantitative and challenging material. In addition, references to the transparency acetates available with the textbook enable instructors to more easily integrate them into their lectures.

Test Bank
(Both in Printed and Computer Software Disk Form)
A significantly revised and accurate test bank containing more than 2,000 multiple-choice questions and 100 problems with worked-out solutions has been developed by Hadi Salavitibar of SUNY–New Paltz. It is available in a separate test-bank manual as well as on TestMaster, a highly acclaimed microcomputerized test-generation system with full word-processing capabilities. It produces customized tests and allows instructors to scramble questions and/or add new ones. TestMaster is available free to adopters for the IBM and compatibles.

Acetate Transparencies
A set of 100 transparency acetates of key exhibits, and solutions to all end-of-chapter cases is available free to adopters. The *Instructor's Manual* includes a complete list of the available transparencies.

For Students

Study Guide
The student review manual, *Study Guide to accompany Basic Managerial Finance*, Third Edition, authored by Thomas M. Krueger of the University of Wisconsin-La Crosse and D. Anthony Plath of the University of North Carolina at Charlotte, has been completely revised. Each chapter of the study guide contains a chapter summary and chapter outline, a programmed self-test, helpful hints, exercises with detailed solutions, and a summary of equations and techniques. Where appropriate, discussions and problems are keyed to both the *BMF Tutor* and the *BMF Problem-Solver*.

Free BMF Disk
Included with each new copy of the book is the *BMF Disk*, a computer disk for use with IBM PCs and compatible microcomputers. The disk contains two different sets of routines: the *BMF Tutor* and the *BMF Problem-Solver*, both written in Turbo Pascal™, so that they may be transferred easily to other computers with little or no difficulty. The *Tutor* provides students with numerous self-testing opportunities. The *Problem-Solver* helps students perform the often time-consuming computations required in managerial finance. Both parts of the *BMF Disk* are described in further detail below.

BMF Tutor Developed by John Hansen, Robert Bush, and George Flowers, all of Houston Baptist University, the *BMF Tutor*—a *new* software package—extends self-testing opportunities beyond those included at the ends of specified chapters. Use of the *Tutor* helps students recognize and solve various types of managerial finance problems presented throughout the text. Its applicability throughout the text and study guide is always keyed by the tutor symbol shown above.

Over 100 different problem *types* can be easily accessed through user friendly menus. All problems of each type are constructed by random number generation, thereby providing an inexhaustible supply of problems, with little chance of repetition. The *Tutor* gives immediate feedback with detailed solutions, provides tutorial assistance, and for convenience includes text page references. The broad problem areas addressed by the *BMF Tutor* include financial ratios, time value of money, valuation, cost of capital, and capital budgeting. Instructions for use are included in Appendix B.

BMF Problem-Solver   Also on the *BMF Disk* is the *BMF Problem-Solver*, a collection of financial computation routines specifically developed and revised by Frederick Rexroad to accompany this textbook. The *Problem-Solver* includes 7 short programs, presented in a menu-driven format. They aid the student's learning by providing a fast and easy method for performing necessary financial computations. The broad topic areas cover financial ratios, cash budgets, time value of money, bond and stock valuation, cost of capital, capital budgeting cash flows, and capital budgeting techniques. Applicability of the problem-solver throughout the textbook and the study guide is always keyed by a printed disk symbol like that shown above. Each routine on the problem-solver includes page references to the text discussion of the techniques being applied. A detailed description of how to use the problem-solver is given in Appendix B.

ACKNOWLEDGMENTS

Many people have made significant contributions to this edition as well as to earlier editions. Without their classroom experience, guidance, and advice, this book could not have been written or revised. Receiving continual feedback from colleagues, students, and practitioners helps me create a truly teachable textbook. If you or your students are moved to write me about any matters pertaining to this text package, please do. I welcome constructive criticism and suggestions for the book's further improvement.

HarperCollins obtained the experienced advice of a large group of excellent reviewers. I appreciate their many suggestions and criticisms, which strongly influenced various aspects of this volume. My special thanks go to the following people, who reviewed all or part of the manuscripts for earlier editions:

Allen S. Anderson

Brian Belt

Robert A. Benson

Holland Blades

Louis E. Bonanni

Paul J. Corr

Thomas P. Czubiak

Samir P. Dagher

Alberto Davila

Anthony N. Duruh

Fred J. Ebeid

Keith Wm. Fairchild

Brigitte Lea Jacob

Alvin Kelly

Theodore T. Latz

John L. Lohret

Ilhan Meric   Abu Selimuddin
Clifford D. Mpare   Edwin C. Sims
Dimitrios Pachis   Jean L. Souther
Janice L. Pitera   Alice Steljes
Ralph A. Pope   Bev S. Stevenson
Howard L. Puckett   A.M. Tuberose
J.J. Quinn   Dean R. Vickstrom
Mary Ann Rafa   John Washecka
David K. Risley   Loren Weishaar

The following people provided extremely useful reviews and input to the third edition.

Dwight Anderson, *Louisiana Tech University*
Stephen L. Avard, *East Texas State University*
Maurice P. Corrigan, *Post College*
David R. Durst, *University of Akron*
Stephen Elliott, *Northwest State University of Louisiana*
George W. Gallinger, *Arizona State University*
Raj Guttha, *Bloomsburg State University*
Linda C. Hittle, *San Diego State University*
Jim Hopkins, *Morningside College*
Martin I. Lowy, *Harrisburg Area Community College*
Douglas M. Patterson, *Virginia Polytechnic Institute*
Eugene O. Poindexter, *West Georgia College*
Daniel H. Raver, *Geneva College*
George W. Trivoli, *Jacksonville State University*
Richard Wiedemann, *Rancho Santiago College*
Richard H. Yanow, *North Adams State College*

I am especially indebted to D. Anthony Plath of the University of North Carolina at Charlotte for his help in preparing the first draft of Chapter 18 and to Mehdi Salehizadeh of San Diego State University for revising the international finance material. Special thanks is due Thomas M. Krueger and D. Anthony Plath for their splendid assistance in preparing the opening vignettes and theme boxes as well as for revising the *Study Guide*. Thanks is also due Marlene G. Bellamy for her outstanding work in revising the *Instructor's Manual* and Appendix A on career opportunities. Thanks to Hadi Salavitibar for his useful feedback and excellent work in revising the *Test Bank*. In addition I greatly appreciate the support of my colleagues at San Diego State University.

I also wish to thank John Hansen, Robert Bush, and George Flowers for developing the *BMF Tutor* and Fred Rexroad for developing and revising the *BMF Problem-Solver*. A special word of thanks goes to Thomas J. Liesz for his useful feedback and first-class work in preparing the *Lecture Notes*. I also appreciate the help of Michael D. Joehnk of Arizona State University.

The staff of HarperCollins—particularly Suzy Spivey and Meg Holden—deserve thanks for their professional expertise, creativity, enthusiasm, and commitment to this text. Thanks is also due project editor Susan Bogle, of York Production Services, for efficiently and effectively managing the text's production. A special word of thanks goes to development editor Ann Torbert for her help with the development and production of this book.

Finally, my wife, Robin, and our children, Zachary and Jessica, have played most important parts in patiently providing the support and understanding I needed during the writing of this book. To them I will be forever grateful.

Lawrence J. Gitman

TO THE STUDENT

Dear Student,

Twenty-five years ago I took my first finance course. It was tough! The blending of basic accounting with new and more quantitative financial concepts challenged my classmates and me. Although the text we used was the most popular at that time, it seemed boring and abstract. It presented concepts confusingly and failed to relate them to actual business practice. You may have already had a similar experience in your studies. I hope not.

I wrote this text for you. My objective was to convey the important concepts and practices of managerial finance in an interesting and understandable fashion. As I wrote and revised, I constantly kept in mind the unnecessary difficulty I had in my first finance course. Based on feedback from students and reviewers, I feel that this text meets my objective. If it does, you should find your first exposure to managerial finance an enjoyable educational experience. If it doesn't, I apologize and hope that you will not give up on the study of finance. I didn't! In either case, you will find the *Study Guide to Accompany Basic Managerial Finance*, Third Edition, helpful in studying this subject.

I sincerely hope you enjoy learning the basics of managerial finance and earn an "A" in the course. Best of luck!

Sincerely,

Lawrence J. Gitman

BASIC MANAGERIAL FINANCE

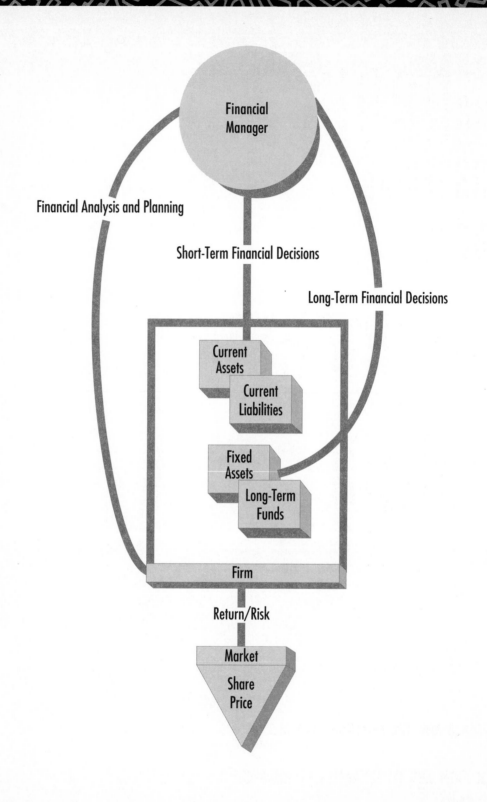

INTRODUCTION TO MANAGERIAL FINANCE

CHAPTER 1

FINANCE AND THE FINANCIAL MANAGER

After studying this chapter, you should be able to:

1 Define finance and describe its major areas and opportunities.

2 Describe the managerial finance function and differentiate managerial finance from the closely related disciplines of economics and accounting.

3 Justify the wealth maximization goal of the financial manager and explain the effect of the agency issue and the role of ethics on the achievement of this goal.

4 Identify the key activities of the financial manager within the firm.

5 Recognize the importance of the international dimension and the major factors influencing the financial operations of multinational companies.

6 Understand the text's approach to the key managerial finance concepts, tools, and techniques.

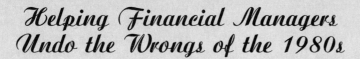

Helping Financial Managers Undo the Wrongs of the 1980s

" Financial managers who earlier had been acquiring debt . . . were seeking ways to shed it. "

Charles Masson, director of the restructuring group at Salomon Brothers, labored in obscurity through the 1980s. While his investment-banking colleagues made headlines using borrowed money to buy companies, Masson assisted companies overloaded with debt. Headlines and wealth bypassed him.

Undisciplined companies allowed momentum found on Wall Street to overwhelm their financial discipline. In the 1970s and 1980s, diversification was the rage, resulting in companies merging without apparently considering the financial worth of such expansions. Many firms bought businesses they knew little about. Firms became so diverse that managers lost focus of the goal of maximizing share price. High levels of unpaid accounts, bloated inventories, and empty plants reduced the value of these firms. For a fee, investment bankers helped selling firms to spin off earlier acquisitions and buying firms to finance new acquisitions using borrowed funds.

All too soon the economy weakened and companies that loaded up on debt during the period of merger mania were struggling to make interest payments. Financial managers who earlier had been acquiring debt to finance takeovers were seeking ways to shed it. As merger mania died, Masson was sought by corporations, business schools, and other financial institutions.

Leveraged buyouts (LBOs) had allowed managers to acquire their firms with a relatively low personal investment. Masson and others began offering financial managers de-leveraged buyout (DBO) packages. With these, financial managers are faced with talking holders of debt into either reducing interest payments or accepting stock for debt. Lenders must be convinced that the firm's core business is healthy but that its coffers are being robbed by the high debt payments. At the same time, shareholders—often management itself—must be convinced that the cost savings will spell the difference between making a profit or facing bankruptcy. During 1990, every big brokerage house set up or expanded its divisions which help companies restructure loans.

Financial managers face the task of choosing the financing that works the best for them—the combination that results in the lowest cost per dollar of financing. It is estimated that $150 billion of debt will have to be restructured during the 1991–1995 period. The impact on share price arising from Charles Masson's de-leveraged buyout technique will be debated for a longer time.

The financial manager plays an extremely important role in the operation and success of a business. All key employees of any business organization, however large or small, should understand the duties and activities of its financial manager. Developing such an understanding begins with some basic questions: What is finance? What career opportunities exist in the field of finance? What is the managerial finance function, and what are the goals and activities of the financial manager? Answering these basic questions sets the stage for discussion of the basic concepts, tools, and techniques of managerial finance.

FINANCE AS AN AREA OF STUDY

The field of finance is broad and dynamic. It directly affects the lives of every person and every organization, financial or nonfinancial, private or public, large or small, profit-seeking or not-for-profit. Many areas of finance can therefore be studied, and a large number of career opportunities are available.

What Is Finance?

finance The art and science of managing money.

Finance can be defined as the art and science of managing money. Virtually all individuals and organizations earn or raise money and spend or invest money. Finance is concerned with the process, institutions, markets, and instruments involved in the transfer of money among and between individuals, businesses, and governments.

Major Areas and Opportunities in Finance

The major areas of finance can be summarized by reviewing the career opportunities in finance. These opportunities can, for convenience, be divided into two broad categories: financial services and managerial finance.

Financial Services

financial services
The area of finance concerned with design and delivery of advice and financial products.

Financial services is the area of finance concerned with the design and delivery of advice and financial products to individuals, business, and government. It is one of the fastest growing areas of career opportunity in our economy. Financial services includes banking and related institutions, personal financial planning, investments, and real estate and insurance. Exciting career opportunities available in each of these areas are described briefly in Table 1.1.

Table 1.1   Career Opportunities in Financial Services

Opportunity	Brief description
Banking and related institutions	Banks, savings and loan associations, savings banks, finance companies, and credit unions all offer challenging career opportunities for those trained in financial services. Because of the many services offered by these institutions, a wide choice of careers is available. Loan officers handle installment, commercial, real estate, and/or consumer loans. Trust officers administer trust funds for estates, foundations, and business firms. Many of these institutions have begun to offer new services in insurance brokerage, real estate, and personal financial planning.
Personal financial planning	Career opportunities for personal financial planners have increased dramatically in recent years, largely due to increasingly complicated tax laws, new investment vehicles, and a relaxed regulatory environment. Financial institutions, brokerage firms, insurance companies, and consulting firms are all interested in hiring individuals who can provide sound advice to consumers regarding the management of their personal financial affairs.
Investments	Careers in investments include working as a securities broker or as a securities analyst in a brokerage firm, insurance company, or other financial institution. Investment specialists are involved in analyzing securities and constructing portfolios that will achieve their clients' objectives. Related opportunities to work in investment banking, which involves developing and marketing security offerings for corporate and government issuers, are also available.
Real estate and insurance	Real estate is a field with varied career opportunities. Careers include real estate mortgage banker, property manager, broker, appraiser, developer, and lender. There are also highly rewarding career opportunities for insurance specialists, such as sales agents, statisticians, and underwriters. Insurance companies also need personnel well-trained in finance to help them manage their vast investment portfolios.

Managerial Finance

Managerial finance is concerned with the duties of the financial manager in the business firm. **Financial managers** actively manage the financial affairs of many types of business—financial and nonfinancial, private and public, large and small, profit-seeking and not-for-profit. They perform such varied tasks as budgeting, financial forecasting, cash management, credit administration, investment analysis, and funds procurement. In recent years the changing economic and regulatory environments have increased the importance and complexity of the financial manager's duties. As a result many top executives in industry and government have come from the finance area.

managerial finance
Concerns the duties of the financial manager in the business firm.

financial manager
Actively manages the financial affairs of any type of business.

The Study of Managerial Finance

An understanding of the concepts, tools, and techniques presented throughout this text will fully acquaint you with the financial manager's activities and decisions. As you study, you will learn about career opportunities in managerial finance. Appendix A of the text provides a summary of career opportunities in managerial finance and financial services. I hope that this first exposure to the exciting field of finance will provide the foundation and initiative for further study and possibly even a future career.

THE MANAGERIAL FINANCE FUNCTION

Since most business decisions are measured in financial terms, the financial manager plays a key role in the operation of the firm. People in all areas—accounting, manufacturing, marketing, personnel, research, and so forth—need a basic understanding of the managerial finance function. To gain this understanding, we will now look at the organizational role of the finance function and its relationship to economics and accounting.

An Organizational View

The size and importance of the managerial finance function depend on the size of the firm. In small firms the finance function is generally performed by the accounting department. As a firm grows, the importance of the finance function typically results in the evolution of a separate department. It is usually linked directly to the company president or chief executive officer (CEO) through a vice-president of finance, commonly called the chief financial officer (CFO). Figure 1.1 is an organizational chart showing the structure of the finance activity within a typical medium-to-large-size firm. Reporting to the vice-president of finance are the treasurer and the controller. The **treasurer** is commonly responsible for handling financial activities. These include financial planning and fund raising, managing cash, making capital expenditure decisions, managing credit activities, and managing the investment portfolio. The **controller** typically handles the accounting activities, such as tax management, data processing, and cost and financial accounting. The activities of the treasurer, or financial manager, are the primary concern of this text.

treasurer The officer responsible for the firm's financial activities.

controller The officer responsible for the firm's accounting activities.

Relationship to Economics

The field of finance is closely related to economics. Since every business firm operates within the economy, the financial manager must understand the country's economic framework. He or she must be alert to the

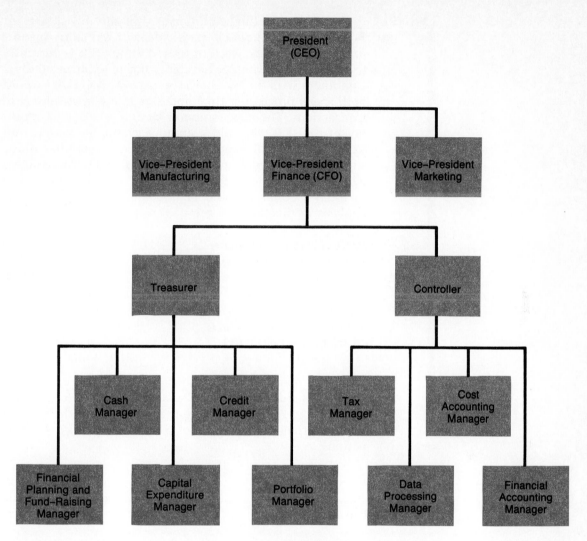

Figure 1.1   **Organization of the Finance Function**

The treasurer and controller typically report to the vice-president of finance (CFO), who reports to the company president or chief executive officer (CEO). The treasurer commonly handles financial activities and the controller handles accounting activities.

consequences of varying levels of economic activity and changes in economic policy. The financial manager must also be able to use economic theories as guidelines for efficient business operation. The primary economic principle used in managerial finance is **marginal analysis,** the principle that financial decisions should be made and actions taken only when the added benefits exceed the added costs. Nearly all financial decisions ultimately come down to an assessment of their marginal benefits and marginal costs. A basic knowledge of economics is therefore necessary to understand both the environment and the decision techniques of managerial finance.

marginal analysis
States that financial decisions should be made and actions taken only when added benefits exceed added costs.

EXAMPLE   Amy Chen is a financial manager for Strom Department Stores—a large chain of upscale department stores operating primarily in the western United States. She is currently trying to decide whether to replace one of the firm's on-line computers with a new, more sophisticated one that would both speed processing time and handle a larger volume of transactions. The new computer would require a cash outlay of $80,000. The old computer could be sold to net $28,000. The total benefits from the new computer (measured in today's dollars) would be $100,000. The benefits over a similar time period from the old computer (measured in today's dollars) would be $35,000. Applying marginal analysis to this data we get:

Benefits with new computer	$100,000	
Less: Benefits with old computer	35,000	
(1) Marginal (Added) benefits		$65,000
Cost of new computer	$80,000	
Less: Proceeds from sale of old computer	28,000	
(2) Marginal (Added) costs		52,000
Net benefit [(1) − (2)]		$13,000

Since the marginal (added) benefits of $65,000 exceed the marginal (added) costs of $52,000, the purchase of the new computer to replace the old one is recommended. The firm will experience a net gain of $13,000 as a result of this action.

Relationship to Accounting

The firm's finance (treasurer) and accounting (controller) activities are typically within the control of the financial vice-president (CFO), as shown in Figure 1.1. These functions are closely related and generally overlap. Indeed, managerial finance and accounting are not often easily distinguishable. In small firms the controller often carries out the finance function; in large firms many accountants are intimately involved in various finance activities. However, there are two basic differences between finance and accounting. One relates to the emphasis on cash flows and the other to decision making.

Emphasis on Cash Flows

accrual method
Recognizes revenue at the point of sale and recognizes expenses when incurred.

The accountant's primary function is to develop and provide data for measuring the performance of the firm, assessing its financial position, and paying taxes. Using certain standardized and generally accepted principles, the accountant prepares financial statements that recognize revenue at the point of sale and expenses when incurred. This approach is commonly referred to as the **accrual method.**

The financial manager, on the other hand, places primary emphasis on *cash flows*, the intake and outgo of cash. He or she maintains the firm's solvency by analyzing and planning its cash flows. The firm's cash flows must allow it to satisfy its obligations and acquire the assets needed to achieve its goals. The financial manager uses this **cash method** to recognize revenues and expenses only with respect to actual inflows and outflows of cash.

cash method
Recognizes revenues and expenses only with respect to actual inflows and outflows of cash.

A simple analogy may help to clarify the basic difference in viewpoint between the accountant and the financial manager. If we consider the human body as a business firm in which each pulsation of the heart represents a transaction, the accountant's primary concern is *recording* each of these pulsations as sales revenues, expenses, and profits. The financial manager is primarily concerned with whether the resulting flow of blood through the arteries reaches the cells and keeps the various organs of the whole body functioning. It is possible for a body to have a strong heart but cease to function due to the development of blockages or clots in the circulatory system. Similarly, a firm may be profitable but still may fail due to an insufficient flow of cash to meet its obligations as they come due.

EXAMPLE   Thomas Yachts, a small yacht dealer, in the calendar year just ended sold one yacht for $100,000; the yacht was purchased during the year at a total cost of $80,000. Although the firm paid in full for the yacht during the year, at year end it has yet to collect the $100,000 from the customer. The accrual-based accounting view and the cash-flow-oriented financial view of the firm's performance during the year are given by the following income and cash flow statements, respectively.

Accounting View

Income statement Thomas Yachts for the year ended 12/31	
Sales revenue	$100,000
Less: Costs	80,000
Net profit	$ 20,000

Financial View

Cash flow statement Thomas Yachts for the year ended 12/31	
Cash inflow	$ 0
Less: Cash outflow	80,000
Net cash flow	($80,000)

Whereas in an accounting sense the firm is quite profitable, it is a financial failure in terms of actual cash flow. Thomas Yachts' lack of cash flow resulted from the uncollected account receivable of $100,000. Without adequate cash inflows to meet its obligations the firm will not survive, regardless of its level of profits.

The example above shows that accrual accounting data do not fully describe the circumstances of a firm. Thus the financial manager must look beyond financial statements to obtain insight into developing or existing problems. The financial manager, by concentrating on cash flow, should be able to avoid insolvency and achieve the firm's financial goals. Of course, while both accountants and financial managers are aware of each others' concerns and methods, the primary emphasis of accountants is on accrual methods and the primary emphasis of financial managers is on cash flow methods.

Decision Making

We come now to the second major difference between finance and accounting: decision making. The accountant devotes the majority of his or her attention to the collection and presentation of financial data. The financial manager evaluates the accountant's statements, develops additional data, and makes decisions based on his or her assessment of the associated returns and risks. The accountant's role is to provide consistently developed and easily interpreted data about the firm's past, present, and future operations. The financial manager uses these data, either in raw form or after certain adjustments and analyses, as an important input to the decision-making process. Of course, this does not mean that accountants never make decisions or that financial managers never gather data; but the primary focuses of accounting and finance are distinctly different.

GOAL OF THE FINANCIAL MANAGER

In the case of corporations, the owners of a firm are normally distinct from its managers. The goal of the financial manager should be to achieve the objectives of the firm's owners, its stockholders. In most cases, if the managers are successful in this endeavor, they will also achieve their own financial and professional objectives. In the sections that follow we evaluate profit maximization and describe the relationship of profit and risk to wealth maximization. We discuss the *agency issue* related to potential conflicts between the goals of stockholders and the actions of management, and finally consider the role of ethics.

Maximize Profit?

Some people believe that the owner's objective is always to maximize profits. To achieve the goal of profit maximization the financial manager takes only those actions that are expected to make a major contribution to the firm's overall profits. Thus, for each alternative being considered, the financial manager would select the one expected to result in the highest monetary return. For corporations, profits are commonly measured in terms of **earnings per share (EPS).** These represent the amount earned during the period—typically a quarter (3 months) or a year—on each outstanding share of common stock. EPS are calculated by dividing the period's total earnings available for the firm's common stockholders—the firm's owners—by the number of shares of common stock outstanding.

earnings per share (EPS) The amount earned during the period on each outstanding share of common stock.

EXAMPLE   Nick Bono, the financial manager of Harper's Inc., a major manufacturer of fishing gear, is attempting to choose between two alternative investments, X and Y. Each is expected to have the following earnings-per-share effects over its three-year life.

	Earnings per share (EPS)			
Investment	Year 1	Year 2	Year 3	Total for years 1, 2, and 3
X	$1.40	$1.00	$ .40	$2.80
Y	.60	1.00	1.40	3.00

Based on the profit-maximization goal, investment Y would be preferred over investment X. It results in higher earnings per share over the three-year period ($3.00 EPS for Y is greater than $2.80 EPS for X).

Profit maximization fails for a number of reasons: It ignores (1) the timing of returns, (2) cash flows available to stockholders, and (3) risk.

Timing

Because the firm can earn a return on funds it receives, *the receipt of funds sooner as opposed to later is preferred.* In our example, investment X may be preferred due to the greater EPS it provides in the first year. This is true in spite of the fact that the total earnings from investment X are smaller than those from Y. The greater returns in Year 1 could be reinvested in order to provide greater future earnings.

Cash Flows

A firm's earnings do *not* represent cash flows available to the stockholders. Owners receive returns either through cash dividends paid them or by selling their shares for a higher price than initially paid. A greater EPS does not necessarily mean that dividend payments will increase, since the payment of dividends results solely from the action of the firm's board of directors. Furthermore, a higher EPS does not necessarily translate into a higher stock price. Firms sometimes experience earnings increases without any correspondingly favorable change in stock price. Only when earnings increases are accompanied by increased current and/or expected cash flows would a higher stock price be expected.

Risk

risk The chance that actual outcomes may differ from those expected.

Profit maximization disregards not only cash flow but also **risk**—the chance that actual outcomes may differ from those expected. A basic premise in managerial finance is that a trade-off exists between return (cash flow) and risk. *Return and risk are in fact the key determinants of share price, which represents the wealth of the owners in the firm.* Cash flow and risk affect share price differently: Higher cash flow is generally associated with a higher share price. Higher risk tends to result in a lower share price since the stockholder must be compensated for the greater risk. In general, stockholders are **risk-averse**—that is, they want to avoid risk. Where risk is involved, stockholders expect to earn higher rates of return on investments of higher risk and vice versa.

risk-averse Seeking to avoid risk.

EXAMPLE   Midwestern Distillers, a manufacturer of bourbon and blended whiskeys, is interested in expanding into one of two new product lines—gin or vodka. Because competition and availability of vodka is significantly affected by political events, it is viewed as a higher-risk line of business than is gin. Today's cost of entering either of these markets is $45 million. The expected annual cash inflows from each product line is expected to average $9 million per year over the next 10 years, as shown in column 2 of the following table.

Product line	Risk (1)	Average annual cash inflows (2)	Required rate of return (3)	Present value of cash inflows[a] (4)
Gin	Lower	$9 million	12%	$50.9 million
Vodka	Higher	9 million	15	45.2 million

[a]These values were found using present-value techniques, which will be fully explained and demonstrated in Chapter 11.

In order to be compensated for taking risk, the firm must earn a higher rate of return on the higher-risk vodka than on the lower-risk gin line. The firm's required rate of return for each line is shown in column 3 of the preceding table. Applying present-value techniques—quantitative financial techniques that are presented in Chapter 11—we can find the present value (today's value) of the average annual cash inflows over the 10 years for each product line as shown in column 4 of the table.

Three important observations can be made: (1) Because the firm's stockholders are *risk-averse,* they must earn a higher rate of return on the higher-risk vodka line than on the lower-risk gin line. (2) Although the vodka line and the gin line have the same expected annual cash inflows, the vodka line's *greater risk causes its cash flows to be worth less* today than the gin line's cash flows ($45.2 million for vodka versus $50.9 million for gin). And (3) while both product lines appear attractive since their benefits (present value of cash inflows) exceed the $45 million cost, the gin alternative would be preferred ($50.9 million for gin and only $45.2 million for vodka). It should be clear from this example that differences in risk can significantly affect the value of an investment and therefore the wealth of an owner.

Maximizing Shareholder Wealth

The goal of the financial manager is to maximize the wealth of the owners for whom the firm is being managed. The wealth of corporate owners is measured by the share price of the stock. The share price, in turn, is based on the timing of returns (cash flows), their magnitude, and their risk. When considering each financial decision alternative or possible action in terms of its impact on the share price of the firm's stock, financial managers should accept only those actions that are expected to increase share price. (Figure 1.2 depicts this process.) Since share price represents the owners' wealth in the firm, share-price maximization is consistent with owner-wealth maximization. Note that *return (cash flows) and risk are the key decision variables in the wealth maximization process.*

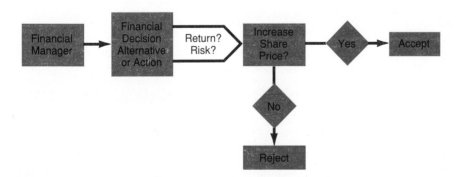

Figure 1.2   **Financial Decisions and Share Price**

The financial manager, when evaluating decision alternatives or potential actions, must consider both return and risk and their expected impact on share price. Actions expected to increase share price should be accepted.

ETHICS IN FINANCE

Don't Say "Sell Taj Mahal"

In addition to corporate managers, respected securities analysts have the greatest influence on share price. The word "sell" is perhaps the most terrorizing word stock analysts can include in a stock recommendation. One of the options open to the firm faced with a negative analyst recommendation is that of retaliating by choking off or impeding the flow of information to the analyst.

The most widely publicized instance of company reprisal involved Marvin Roffman, a former analyst at Philadelphia-based Janney Montgomery Scott. The firm generates a significant portion of its revenues through public offerings of stocks and bonds. Mr. Roffman alleged that he was fired after issuing an unflattering report on billionaire Donald Trump's Taj Mahal casino. He asserted that Janney Montgomery Scott was concerned about being bypassed in subsequent initial public offerings. This incident, which has been proven true, illustrates the worst-case scenario of corporations using their power to unethically extract desirable recommendations from analysts.

The firing of analysts making negative recommendations is uncommon. In most cases, the punishment inflicted is more subtle. The analyst's telephone calls are not returned, financial information arrives late, and professional reputation is called into question. At a minimum, corporate public relations officers may want to withhold comment until the exact problem and a solution have been identified.

Nevertheless, investors have a right to timely information, whether it is good or bad. In fact, corporate PR officials who are members of the nation's primary public relations association must adhere to a Code of Ethics, which covers financial matters. The Code calls on its members to make full and timely disclosure of corporate information and to make it available on an equal basis. Corporations are to report the facts to all, regardless of how a specific analyst has interpreted the company's data in the past.

Source: Adam Shell, "Coping when an analyst says 'Sell!'"
Public Relations Journal, July 1990, pp. 9–10.

The Agency Issue

The control of the modern corporation is frequently placed in the hands of professional nonowner managers. We have seen that the goal of the financial manager should be to maximize the wealth of the owners of the firm. Thus management can be viewed as *agents* of the owners who have hired them and given them decision-making authority to manage the firm for the owners' benefit. Technically, any manager owning less than 100 percent of the firm is to some degree an agent of the other owners.

In theory, most financial managers would agree with the goal of owner wealth maximization. In practice, however, managers are also concerned with their personal wealth, job security, lifestyle, and perquisites (benefits such as country club memberships, chauffeured limousines, and posh offices, all provided at company expense). Such concerns may make managers reluctant or unwilling to take more than moderate risk if they perceive that too much risk might result in a loss of job and damage to personal wealth. The result of such a "satisficing" approach (a compromise between satisfaction and maximization) is a less-than-maximum return and a potential loss of wealth for the owners.

Agency Costs

From this conflict of owner and personal goals arises what has been called the **agency problem**—the likelihood that managers may place personal goals ahead of corporate goals. In order to prevent or minimize agency problems, stockholders incur **agency costs.** These are the costs of monitoring management behavior, insuring against dishonest acts of management, and giving management the financial incentive to act in a fashion consistent with share price maximization. Today more firms are tying management compensation to the firm's performance. This incentive appears to motivate managers to operate in a manner reasonably consistent with stock price maximization. Much of the evidence suggests that share price maximization—the focus of this book—is the primary goal of most firms.

agency problem The likelihood that managers may place personal goals ahead of corporate goals.

agency costs The costs borne by stockholders to prevent or minimize agency problems.

Emergence of the Large Private Corporation

Agency problems and their associated costs have in recent years spurred the emergence of the **large private corporation**—a major corporation whose shares are not publicly traded and that relies heavily on debt as its key source of financing. Corporations such as RJR Nabisco, Goodyear, and Foodmaker have "gone private," using sophisticated transactions such as mergers, takeovers, leveraged buyouts (LBOs), and stock repurchases (which are described in detail in later chapters, particularly Chapter 17). These transactions in effect replace existing equity (ownership) with large amounts of debt. The restructured firms are closely managed and monitored by **active investors**—persons or institutions with a major equity or debt interest in the firm. This situation minimizes agency problems by eliminating corporate waste and more closely aligning management and owner interests. The result is the achievement of greater value.

large private corporation A major corporation whose shares are not publicly traded and that relies heavily on debt as its key source of financing.

active investors Persons or institutions with a major equity or debt interest in a firm.

Evidence of the superiority of these restructured corporations is believed to be reflected in the far-above-market prices paid for them in the transactions that take them private. Although the jury is still out with respect to long-run success, the large private corporation appears to be emerging as an attractive vehicle for corporate ownership and control.

The Role of Ethics

In recent years the legitimacy of actions taken by government officials, businesses, individuals, and even religious leaders have received major media attention. Examples include Senator Alan Cranston's lobbying on behalf of Charles Keating, whose self-dealing with depositor funds resulted in the failure of Lincoln Savings and Loan of California; Volvo's misleading automobile advertisements; Michael Milken's conviction for insider-trading activities; and televangelist Jim Bakker's personal and financial indiscretions. Clearly these and other similar actions have raised the question of **ethics**—standards of conduct or moral judgment. Today society in general and the financial community in particular—primarily due to the notable financial offenders such as Keating and Milken—are developing and enforcing ethical standards. The goal of these standards is to motivate business and market participants to adhere to both the letter and the spirit of laws and regulations in all aspects of business and professional practice.

ethics Standards of conduct or moral judgment.

Opinions
A recent opinion survey of business leaders, business school deans, and members of Congress showed that 94 percent of the over 1,000 respondents felt that the business community is troubled by ethical problems.[1] In addition, only 32 percent of the respondents felt that this issue had been overblown by the media and political leaders. Most striking was the survey's finding that 63 percent of respondents felt that a business firm actually strengthens its competitive position by maintaining high ethical standards. Respondents to the survey believed that the best way to encourage ethical business behavior is for firms to adopt a business code of ethics. They rated legislation as the least effective way.

Considering Ethics
Robert A. Cooke, a noted ethicist, suggests the following questions be used to assess the ethical viability of a proposed action:[2]

1 ▪ Is the action . . . arbitrary or capricious? Does it unfairly single out an individual or group?

2 ▪ Does the action . . . violate the moral or legal rights of any individual or group?

3 ▪ Does the action . . . conform to accepted moral standards?

4 ▪ Are there alternative courses of action that are less likely to cause actual or potential harm?

Clearly, considering such questions prior to taking action can help to assure its ethical viability.

---

[1] *Ethics in American Business* (New York: Touche Ross), December 1987.
[2] "Business Ethics: A Perspective," in *Arthur Anderson Cases on Business Ethics*, September 1988, p. 2.

Today more and more firms are directly addressing the issue of ethics by establishing corporate ethics policies and guidelines and by requiring employee compliance with them. Frequently employees are required to sign a formal pledge to uphold the firm's ethics policies. Such policies typically apply to employee actions in dealing with all corporate constituents—other employees, customers, vendors, creditors, owners, regulators, and the public at large. Many companies require employees to participate in ethics seminars and training programs that convey and demonstrate corporate ethics policy. Role playing and case exercises are sometimes used to give employees hands-on experience in effectively dealing with potential ethical dilemmas.

Ethics and Share Price

The implementation of a pro-active ethics program is expected to enhance corporate value. An ethics program can produce a number of positive benefits: reduce potential litigation and judgment costs, maintain a positive corporate image, build shareholder confidence, and gain the loyalty, commitment, and respect of all the firm's constituents. Such actions, by maintaining and enhancing cash flow and reducing perceived risk (as a result of greater investor confidence), are expected to positively affect the firm's share price. *Ethical behavior is therefore viewed as necessary for achievement of the firm's goal of owner wealth maximization.*

KEY ACTIVITIES OF THE FINANCIAL MANAGER

The financial manager's activities, all of which are aimed at achieving the goal of owner wealth maximization, can be related to the firm's basic financial statements. His or her primary activities are (1) performing financial analysis and planning; (2) making investment decisions; and (3) making financing decisions. Figure 1.3 relates each of these financial activities to the firm's **balance sheet,** which shows the firm's financial position at a given point in time. It is important to note that although investment and financing decisions can be conveniently viewed in terms of the balance sheet, these decisions are made on the basis of their cash flow effects. This emphasis on cash flow will become clearer in Chapter 3 as well as in later chapters.

balance sheet
Record that shows the firm's financial position at a given point in time.

Performing Financial Analysis and Planning

Financial analysis and planning is concerned with (1) transforming financial data into a form that can be used to monitor the firm's financial condition; (2) evaluating the need for increased (or reduced) productive capacity; and (3) determining what additional (or reduced) financing is required. These functions encompass the entire balance sheet as well as the firm's income statement and other financial statements. Although

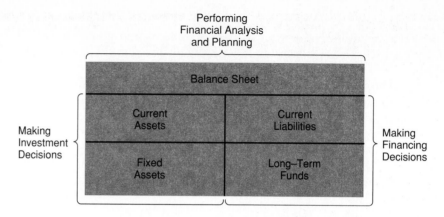

Figure 1.3   **Key Activities of the Financial Manager**
The financial manager's key activities—(1) financial analysis and planning,
(2) making investment decisions, and (3) making financing decisions—can
be related to the firm's balance sheet.

this activity relies heavily on accrual-based financial statements, its
underlying objective is to assess the firm's historic as well as future cash
flows.

Making Investment Decisions

The financial manager's investment decisions determine both the mix
and the type of assets found on the firm's balance sheet. This activity is
concerned with the left-hand side of the balance sheet. *Mix* refers to the
number of dollars of current and fixed assets. Once the mix is established, the financial manager must attempt to maintain certain optimal
levels of each type of current asset. He or she must also decide which are
the best fixed assets to acquire and know when existing fixed assets
need to be modified, replaced, or liquidated. These decisions are important in that they affect the firm's success in achieving its goals.

Making Financing Decisions

Financing decisions deal with the right-hand side of the firm's balance
sheet and involve two major areas. First, the most appropriate mix of
short-term and long-term financing must be established. A second and
equally important concern is which individual short-term or long-term
sources of financing are best at a given point in time. Many of these
decisions are dictated by necessity. However some require an in-depth
analysis of the available financing alternatives, their costs, and their
long-run implications. Again, it is the effect of these decisions on the
firms' goal achievement that is most important.

S M A L L   B U S I N E S S

Offering Reader's Digest and Other Small Businesses to the Public

All publicly held businesses at one time were owned by a single individual or group of individuals. The original owners receive their reward for years of inspiration and perspiration when the stock is sold to the public. The monetary value of an initial public offering (IPO) underlies the need for effective financial management at this juncture in a business's existence. Faulty planning, asset misuse, and capital structure mismanagement will increase investors' perception of risks and reduce their profit expectations. Lower offering prices will result, reducing the wealth of the entrepreneurs.

The initial public offering market accelerated in 1990 and then crashed. Reader's Digest was the largest IPO of 1990. Pinkerton's, the security service, and Safeway Foods were a couple of other household names put on the auction block. On July 19, 1990, a record six new stocks were sold to the public. Although low by recent standards, a total of $10.2 billion was raised through 1990's 221 IPOs.

Iraq's invasion of Kuwait and the deteriorating U.S. economy, however, spotlighted the vulnerability of young companies to tough times. At In-Store Advertising, share prices declined over 80 percent after the company released a post-IPO report of unexpectedly lower earnings. The prospect of greater risks and lesser returns reduced interest in IPOs. In fact, only 75 IPOs were expected in 1991, due to investor apprehension and owner unwillingness to sell a business amid "depressed" prices.

Source: Anne Newman, "IPOs crash to earth after a stellar start," *The Wall Street Journal*, January 2, 1991, p. R21.

INTERNATIONAL DIMENSION: INTRODUCTION

In recent years, as world markets have become significantly more interdependent, international finance has become an increasingly important element in the management of **multinational companies (MNCs).** These firms, being based in the United States, Western Europe, and Japan, as well as many other countries, have international assets and operations in foreign markets. They draw part of their total revenue and profits from such markets. The basics of managerial finance presented in this text are applicable to the management of MNCs. However, certain factors unique to the international setting tend to complicate the financial

multinational companies (MNCs) Firms that have international assets and operations in foreign markets and draw part of their total revenue and profits from such markets.

Table 1.2   **International Factors and Their Influence on MNCs' Operations**

Factor	Firm A (Domestic)	Firm B (MNC)
Foreign ownership	All assets owned by domestic entities	Portions of equity of foreign investments owned by foreign partners, thus affecting foreign decision making and profits
Multinational financial markets	All debt and equity structures based on the domestic financial market	Opportunities and challenges arise from the existence of different financial markets where debt and equity can be issued
Multinational accounting	All consolidation of financial statements based on one currency	The existence of different currencies and of specific translation rules influence the consolidation of financial statements into one currency
Foreign exchange risks	All operations in one currency	Changes in foreign exchange markets can affect foreign revenues and profits as well as overall value of the firm

management of multinational companies. A simple comparison between a domestic U.S. firm (firm A) and a U.S.-based MNC (firm B), as illustrated in Table 1.2, can give an indication of the influence of some of the international factors on MNCs' operations. Clearly, differences in the ownership structure, financial markets, accounting procedures, and currency exchange rates create both challenges and opportunities for the financial manager of the multinational firm.

Sections similar to this one, titled "International Dimension" and marked with a globe symbol (🌍), are included as the final section in a number of subsequent chapters. These sections should provide a good understanding of the additional considerations required by the financial manager operating in today's international marketplace.

AN OVERVIEW OF THE TEXT

The text's organization is structured around the corporate balance sheet, with linkages to share price. The activities of the financial manager are described in six separate but related parts:

Part 1: Introduction to Managerial Finance

Part 2: Financial Analysis and Planning

Part 3: Short-Term Financial Decisions

Part 4: Basic Long-Term Financial Concepts

Part 5: Long-Term Financial Decisions

Part 6: Sources of Long-Term Financing

The activities of the financial manager in each of the areas listed above are presented in relation to the firm's balance sheet. The book gives primary attention to both return and risk factors and their potential impact on the owner's wealth, as reflected by share value. This framework is depicted in Figure 1.4 which relates each part of the text to the share-price-oriented decision framework.

Keyed to various parts of the text is the *Basic Managerial Finance (BMF) Disk*, a menu-driven computer disk for use with IBM PCs and

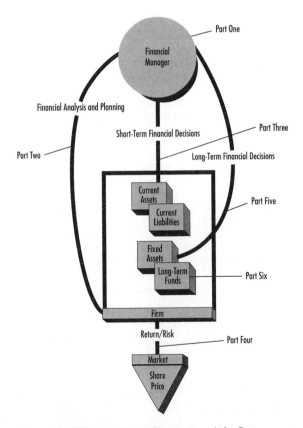

Figure 1.4   Basic Framework and Organization of the Text

This text is organized around the balance sheet, with primary attention given to both return and risk factors and their potential impact on share value. Each of the six parts of the text can be keyed to this model.

compatible microcomputers. The disk contains two different sets of routines: The *BMF Tutor* and the *BMF Problem-Solver*. *BMF Tutor* is a user-friendly program that provides self-testing opportunities in the more quantitative chapters. It gives immediate feedback with detailed solutions, provides tutorial assistance, and for convenience includes text page references. Problems with which the *BMF Tutor* can be used are marked with a ⌨ . *BMF Problem-Solver* can be used as an aid in performing many of the routine financial calculations and procedures presented in this text. For convenience, a disk symbol, �adisk , is used to identify those text discussions and end-of-chapter problems that can be solved with the *BMF Problem-Solver*. A detailed discussion of how to use the *BMF Disk*—both the *Tutor* and the *Problem-Solver*—is included in Appendix B at the end of the book.

SUMMARY

1   **Define finance and describe its major areas and opportunities.** Finance, the art and science of managing money, affects the lives of every person and every organization. Major opportunities in finance exist in financial services—banking and related institutions, personal financial planning, investments, and real estate and insurance—and in managerial finance, which is concerned with the duties of the financial manager in the business firm.

2   **Describe the managerial finance function and differentiate managerial finance from the closely related disciplines of economics and accounting.** In large firms the managerial finance function might be handled by a separate department headed by the vice-president of finance (CFO), to whom the treasurer and controller report. In small firms the finance function is generally performed by the accounting department. Managerial finance is closely related to the disciplines of economics and accounting. It is a form of applied microeconomics and differs from accounting by concentrating on cash flows and decision making rather than accrual concepts and gathering and presenting data.

3   **Justify the wealth maximization goal of the financial manager and explain the effect of the agency issue and the role of ethics on the achievement of this goal.** The goal of the financial manager is to maximize the owners' wealth (dependent on stock price) rather than profits, because profit maximization ignores the timing of returns, does not directly consider cash flows, and ignores risk. Because risk and return are the key determinants of share price, both must be assessed by the financial manager when evaluating decision alternatives or actions. Agency problems resulting from managers placing personal goals ahead of corporate goals can be minimized by incurring agency costs or taking the corporation private. In addition, positive ethical practices by the firm and its managers are believed necessary for achieving the firm's goal of owner wealth maximization.

4   **Identify the key activities of the financial manager within the firm.** The three key activities of the financial manager are (1) performing financial analysis and planning, (2) making investment decisions, and (3) making financing decisions.

 5   **Recognize the importance of the international dimension and the major factors influencing the financial operations of multinational companies.** Although basic managerial finance concepts, tools, and techniques are applicable to international operations, multinational companies (MNCs) face additional unique factors in their foreign activities. Differences in the ownership structure, financial markets, accounting procedures, and currency exchange rates create both challenges and opportunities for the financial manager of the MNC.

6 **Understand the text's approach to the key managerial finance concepts, tools, and techniques.** The text is divided into six major parts. It relates the activities of the financial manager to the firm's balance sheets, giving primary attention to both return and risk and their potential impact on the firm's value. The *Basic Managerial Finance (BMF) Disk*, a menu-driven computer disk containing two different routines keyed to the text, can be used to extend self-testing opportunities and as an aid in performing many of the routine financial calculations and procedures presented in this text.

QUESTIONS

1—1   What is *finance?* Explain how this field affects the lives of everyone and every organization.

1—2   What is the *financial services* area of finance? Briefly describe each of the following areas of career opportunity:
   a. Banking and related institutions
   b. Personal financial planning
   c. Investments
   d. Real estate and insurance

1—3   Describe the field of *managerial finance.* Compare and contrast this field with financial services.

1—4   How does the finance function evolve within the business firm? What financial activities does the treasurer, or financial manager, perform in the mature firm?

1—5   Describe the close relationship between finance and economics, and explain why the financial manager should possess a basic knowledge of economics. What is the primary economic principle used in managerial finance?

1—6   What are the major differences between accounting and finance with respect to:
   a. Emphasis on cash flows?
   b. Decision making?

1—7   Briefly describe three basic reasons why profit maximization fails to be consistent with wealth maximization.

1—8   What is *risk?* Why must risk as well as return be considered by the financial manager when evaluating a decision alternative or action?

1—9   What is the goal of the financial manager? Discuss how one measures achievement of this goal.

1—10   What is the *agency problem?* What are *agency costs,* and why do firms incur them?

1—11   Describe the emergence of the *large private corporation* and explain its rationale. How does it help eliminate potential agency problems?

1—12   Why has corporate ethics become so important in recent years? How are corporations addressing the issue of ethics? What relationship is believed to exist between ethics and share price?

1—13   What are the three key activities of the financial manager? Relate them to the firm's balance sheet.

1—14   List and briefly describe the four major international factors that influence the operations of multinational companies (MNCs) and create both challenges and opportunities for their financial managers.

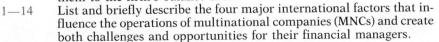

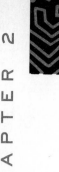

CHAPTER 2

THE FIRM AND ITS OPERATING ENVIRONMENT

After studying this chapter, you should be able to:

1 Describe the basic legal forms of business organization and their respective strengths and weaknesses.

2 Understand the fundamentals of corporate taxation of ordinary income and capital gains, and the role of S corporations.

3 Identify the key participants in financial transactions, and identify the basic activities and changing role of the major financial institutions.

4 Understand the relationship between institutions and markets, and the basic function and operation of the money market, capital markets, and major securities exchanges.

5 Discuss the fundamentals of interest rates and required returns—their role, the term structure, and risk and rates of return.

6 Recognize the impact that differing legal forms of business, taxation, and financial markets can have on the financial management of a multinational company.

Controlled Mayhem:
Life as a Securities Trader

❝ On good days, Wilner can leave the exchange $22,000 richer. . . . However, he has lost as much as $51,000 in a single trading session. ❞

Ask many people to describe the way in which securities are exchanged in the financial markets, and sooner or later someone will tell you about distinguished, silver-haired and gray-suited gentlemen talking in hushed tones over lunch in posh Manhattan restaurants with mahogany paneling on the walls. In truth, however, securities trading occurs in noisy, vibrant, and chaotic places that are far different from the buttoned-down offices of New York's old-line investment banking firms.

Just ask Michael Wilner and Daniel Uslander, the 35-year-old co-founders of Hilltop Trading Company. In just three years, these young entrepreneurs have built Hilltop into one of the largest independent commodity brokers on the New York Mercantile Exchange. The firm has 20 employees and makes $2 million in annual gross commissions. As commodity brokers, Wilner and Uslander buy and sell a particular type of security known as a futures contract. As a small firm, Hilltop specializes in trading just one kind of futures contracts—energy futures—that call for the future sale and delivery of crude oil, natural gas, propane, and heating oil.

In normal times, the trading pit is a blur of activity. Traders shout instructions to one another. Telephones ring constantly. Messengers run between the telephones and the traders to exchange information. In addition, the price of energy futures contracts can fluctuate dramatically. On particularly good days, Wilner can leave the exchange $22,000 richer than when he arrived. However, he has lost as much as $51,000 in a single trading session.

In this chapter, you will learn about different markets in which securities are traded and the various types of financial institutions that operate in these markets. In addition, you will explore how interest rates are established within the economy, and how these rates affect the value of securities. You will find each of these concepts important if, like Wilner and Uslander, you someday decide to test your own skills and abilities by trading securities in financial markets.

A firm operates not as an isolated entity but in a close and dynamic interrelationship with the government and various financial intermediaries and markets. Forms of business organization, business taxation, financial institutions, financial markets, and interest rates are all key aspects of the firm's operating environment. In this chapter we will study these important aspects in order to understand how they both limit and create opportunities for the financial manager.

BASIC FORMS OF BUSINESS ORGANIZATION

The three basic legal forms of business organization are the *sole proprietorship*, the *partnership*, and the *corporation*. The sole proprietorship is the most common form of organization. However, the corporation is by far the dominant form with respect to receipts and net profits. Corporations are given primary emphasis in this text.

Sole Proprietorships

sole proprietorship
A business owned by one person and operated for his or her own profit.

A **sole proprietorship** is a business owned by one person who operates it for his or her own profit. About 75 percent of all business firms are sole proprietorships. The typical sole proprietorship is a small firm, such as a neighborhood grocery, auto-repair shop, or shoe-repair business. Typically the proprietor, along with a few employees, operates the proprietorship. He or she normally raises capital from personal resources or by borrowing and is responsible for all business decisions. The sole proprietor has **unlimited liability,** which means that his total wealth, not merely the amount originally invested, can be taken to satisfy creditors. The majority of sole proprietorships are found in the wholesale, retail, service, and construction industries. The key strengths and weaknesses of sole proprietorships are summarized in Table 2.1.

unlimited liability
The condition of a sole proprietorship (or general partnership) allowing the owner's total wealth to be taken to satisfy creditors.

partnership A business owned by two or more persons and operated for profit.

Partnerships

articles of partnership The written contract used to formally establish a business partnership.

A **partnership** consists of two or more owners doing business together for profit. Partnerships, which account for about 10 percent of all businesses, are typically larger than sole proprietorships. Finance, insurance, and real estate firms are the most common types of partnership. Public accounting and stock brokerage partnerships often have large numbers of partners.

Most partnerships are established by a written contract known as the **articles of partnership.** In a *general* (or *regular*) *partnership*, all the partners have unlimited liability. In a **limited partnership,** one or more partners can be designated as having limited liability as long as at least

limited partnership
A partnership in which one or more partners has limited liability as long as at least one partner has unlimited liability.

Table 2.1   **Strengths and Weaknesses of the Basic Forms of Business Organization**

| | Legal form | | |
	Sole proprietorship	Partnership	Corporation
Strengths	• Owner receives all profits (as well as losses) • Low organizational costs • Income taxed as personal income of proprietor • Secrecy • Ease of dissolution	• Can raise more funds than sole proprietorships • Borrowing power enhanced by more owners • More available brain power and managerial skill • Can retain good employees • Income taxed as personal income of partners	• Owners have *limited liability*, which guarantees they cannot lose more than invested • Can achieve large size due to marketability of stock (ownership) • Ownership is readily transferable • Long life of firm—not dissolved by death of owners • Can hire professional managers • Can expand more easily due to access to financial markets • Receives certain tax advantages
Weaknesses	• Owner has *unlimited liability*—total wealth can be taken to satisfy debts • Limited fund-raising power tends to inhibit growth • Proprietor must be jack-of-all-trades • Difficult to give employees long-run career opportunities • Lacks continuity when proprietor dies	• Owners have *unlimited liability* and may have to cover debts of other less financially sound partners • When a partner dies, partnership is dissolved • Difficult to liquidate or transfer partnership • Difficult to achieve large-scale operations	• Taxes generally higher since corporate income is taxed and dividends paid to owners are again taxed • More expensive to organize than other business forms • Subject to greater government regulation • Employees often lack personal interest in firm • Lacks secrecy since stockholders must receive financial reports

one partner has unlimited liability. A *limited partner* is normally prohibited from being active in the management of the firm. Strengths and weaknesses of partnerships are summarized in Table 2.1.

Corporations

A **corporation** is an artificial being created by law. Often called a "legal entity," a corporation has the powers of an individual in that it can sue and be sued, make and be party to contracts, and acquire property in its

corporation An intangible business entity created by law.

own name. Although only about 15 percent of all businesses are incorporated, the corporation is the dominant form of business organization. It accounts for nearly 90 percent of business receipts and 80 percent of net profits. Since corporations employ millions of people and have many thousands of shareholders, their activities affect the lives of everyone. Although corporations are involved in all types of business, manufacturing corporations account for the largest portion of corporate business receipts and net profits. The key strengths and weaknesses of large corporations are summarized in Table 2.1. It is important to recognize that there are many small private corporations in addition to the large corporations emphasized throughout this text. For many small corporations there is no access to financial markets, and the requirement that the owner co-sign a loan moderates limited liability.

The major parties in a corporation are the stockholders, the board of directors, and the president. Figure 2.1 depicts the relationship among these parties. The **stockholders** are the true owners of the firm by virtue of their equity in preferred and common stock. They vote periodically to elect the members of the board of directors and to amend the firm's corporate charter. The **board of directors** has the ultimate authority in guiding corporate affairs and in making general policy. The directors include key corporate personnel as well as outside individuals who typically are successful business persons and executives of other major organizations. Outside directors for major corporations are typically paid an annual fee of $10,000 to $20,000 or more. The **president or chief executive officer (CEO)** is responsible for managing day-to-day operations and carrying out the policies established by the board. He or she is required to report periodically to the firm's directors. The separation of owners and managers in a large corporation, shown by the dashed horizontal line in Figure 2.1, can result in the *agency problem* described in Chapter 1.

stockholders The true owners of the firm by virtue of their equity in the form of preferred and common stock.

board of directors Group elected by the firm's stockholders and having ultimate authority to guide corporate affairs and make general policy.

president or chief executive officer (CEO) Corporate official responsible for managing the firm's day-to-day operations.

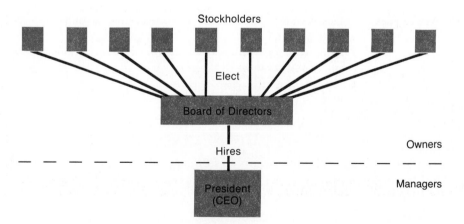

Figure 2.1   The General Organization of a Corporation
The stockholders are the owners of the firm. They elect the board of directors, who establish policies and hire the president, or chief executive officer (CEO), to manage the firm and implement their policies. The separation of owners and managers in the large corporation can result in an *agency problem*.

FINANCE   IN   ACTION

A Change at Equitable Life

The particular organizational form that a business adopts can play an important role in the firm's ability to raise outside capital—even long after the business is established. For example, consider the current state of affairs within the Equitable Life Assurance Society of the U.S., the nation's third largest insurance company. Organized under New York state law as a mutual company since 1918, Equitable has no shareholders or common equity. As a mutual firm, the company is owned by its policyholders.

This mutual organizational form offers both advantages and disadvantages to Equitable's managers. One major advantage is that managerial decisions are subject to much less public scrutiny. A mutual organization does not face financial analysts snooping around in its financial statements. Nor does it have an annual shareholders' meeting at which managers must stand up in front of the firm's angry owners and defend their actions.

At the same time, mutual organizations can't sell stock when they need to raise additional funds. In late 1990, Equitable's managers announced that the firm desperately needed to raise about $500 million to bolster its weak equity base. To raise this sum, Equitable reported that it would sacrifice the peace and quiet provided by its mutual organizational structure to become a publicly held corporation. The firm hoped to sell a 25 percent stake to outside investors.

Why did Equitable plan to wait over a year to sell equity, when it needed the cash much sooner? To avoid those nosey financial analysts as long as possible. In 1989, Equitable posted a $29 million loss, and the firm expected to post a similar loss in 1990. In addition, Equitable holds an excessive portfolio of troubled investments in junk bonds and real estate. Waiting over a year to sell stock would give Equitable's managers time to do some financial housecleaning—by writing off the value of worthless assets from the firm's balance sheet—before inviting the public to examine its financial statements and invest new equity in the firm.

Source: Larry Light, "Equitable can no longer afford the quiet life," *Business Week*, December 24, 1990, p. 21.

BUSINESS TAXATION

Businesses, like individuals, must pay taxes on their income. The actual rates of taxation differ depending upon the form of business organization. Income can be subject to either individual or corporate income taxes. The income of sole proprietorships and partnerships is taxed as the income of the individual owners. Corporate income is subject to corporate taxes. Regardless of their legal form, all businesses can earn two types of income—ordinary and capital gains. Both types of income are treated the same for tax purposes under current law. Because the corporation is financially dominant in our economy, *emphasis here is given to corporate taxation.* A special type of corporate, tax-reporting entity is the S corporation, which we will also discuss.

Ordinary Income

ordinary income
Income earned though the sale of a firm's goods or services.

The **ordinary income** of a corporation is income earned through the sale of its goods or services. Ordinary income is currently taxed subject to the rates depicted in the corporate tax rate schedule given in Table 2.2.

EXAMPLE   Western Manufacturing, Inc., a small producer of kitchen utensils, has before-tax earnings of $250,000. The tax on these earnings can be found using the tax rate schedule given in Table 2.2.

$$\text{Total taxes due} = \$22,250 + [.39 \times (\$250,000 - \$100,000)]$$
$$= \$22,250 + (.39 \times \$150,000)$$
$$= \$22,250 + \$58,500 = \underline{\underline{\$80,750}}$$

The firm's total taxes on its before-tax earnings are therefore $80,750. If the firm had earned only $20,000 before taxes, its total tax liability would have been $3,000 [$0 + (.15 × $20,000)].

Table 2.2   **Corporate Tax Rate Schedule**

Range of taxable income	Base tax	+	Tax calculation (Rate × amount over base bracket)
$ 0 to $ 50,000	$ 0	+	(15% × Amount over $ 0)
50,000 to 75,000	7,500	+	(25 × Amount over 50,000)
75,000 to 100,000	13,750	+	(34 × Amount over 75,000)
100,000 to 335,000[a]	22,250	+	(39 × Amount over 100,000)
Over $335,000	113,900	+	(34 × Amount over 335,000)

[a]Because corporations with taxable income in excess of $100,000 must increase their tax by the lesser of $11,750 or 5 percent of the taxable income in excess of $100,000, they will end up paying a 39 percent tax on taxable income between $100,000 and $335,000. The 5 percent surtax that raises the tax rate from 34 percent to 39 percent causes all corporations with taxable income above $335,000 to have an *average tax rate* of 34 percent, as can be seen in Table 2.3.

Table 2.3   Pretax Income, Tax Liabilities, and Average Tax Rates

Pretax income (1)	Tax liability (2)	Average tax rate [(2) ÷ (1)] (3)
$ 50,000	$ 7,500	15.00%
75,000	13,750	18.33
100,000	22,250	22.25
200,000	61,250	30.63
335,000	113,900	34.00
500,000	170,000	34.00
1,000,000	340,000	34.00
2,500,000	850,000	34.00

Average Tax Rates

The **average tax rate** paid on the firm's ordinary income can be calculated by dividing its taxes by its taxable income. The average tax rate ranges from 15 to 34 percent, reaching 34 percent when taxable income equals or exceeds $335,000. The average tax rate paid by Western Manufacturing, Inc., in our preceding example was 32.3 percent ($80,750 ÷ $250,000). Table 2.3 presents the firm's tax liability and average tax rate for various levels of pretax income; as income increases, the rate approaches and finally reaches 34 percent.

average tax rate A firm's taxes divided by its taxable income.

Marginal Tax Rates

The **marginal tax rate** represents the rate at which additional income is taxed. In the current corporate tax structure, the marginal tax rate on income up to $50,000 is 15 percent; from $50,000 to $75,000 it is 25 percent; from $75,000 to $100,000 it is 34 percent; for income between $100,000 and $335,000 it is 39 percent; and for income in excess of $335,000 it is 34 percent. To simplify calculations in the text, *a fixed 40 percent tax rate is assumed to be applicable to ordinary corporate income.*

marginal tax rate The rate at which additional income is taxed.

EXAMPLE   If Western Manufacturing's earnings go up to $300,000, the marginal tax rate on the additional $50,000 of income will be 39 percent. The company will therefore have to pay additional taxes of $19,500 (.39 × $50,000). Total taxes on the $300,000, then, will be $100,250 ($80,750 + $19,500). To check this figure using the tax rate schedule in Table 2.2, we would get a total tax liability of $22,250 + [.39 × ($300,000 − $100,000)] = $22,250 + $78,000 = $100,250. This is the same value obtained by applying the marginal tax rate to the added income and adjusting the known tax liability.

Interest and Dividend Income

In the process of determining taxable income, any *interest received* by the corporation is included as ordinary income and therefore taxed at the firm's applicable tax rates. *Dividends received* on common and preferred stock held in other corporations, and representing less than 20 percent ownership in them, on the other hand, are subject to a 70 percent exclusion for tax purposes.[1] Because of the dividend exclusion only 30 percent of these **intercorporate dividends** are included as ordinary income. The tax law provides this exclusion in order to avoid *triple taxation*—the first and second corporations are taxed on income prior to paying the dividend, and the dividend recipient must include the dividend in his or her taxable income. This feature in effect provides some relief by eliminating most of the potential tax liability from the dividend received by the second (and any subsequent) corporations.

intercorporate dividends Dividends received by one corporation on common and preferred stock held in other corporations.

EXAMPLE   Checker Industries, a major manufacturer of molds for the plastics industry, during the year just ended received $100,000 in interest on bonds it held and $100,000 in dividends on common stock it owned in other corporations. The firm is subject to a 40 percent marginal tax rate and is eligible for a 70 percent exclusion on its intercorporate dividend receipts. The after-tax income realized by Checker from each of these sources of investment income is found as follows:

	Interest income		Dividend income
(1) Before-tax amount	$100,000		$100,000
Less: Applicable exclusion	0	(.70 × $100,000) =	70,000
Taxable amount	$100,000		$ 30,000
(2) Tax (40%)	40,000		12,000
After-tax amount [(1) − (2)]	$ 60,000		$ 88,000

As a result of the 70 percent dividend exclusion, the after-tax amount is greater for the dividend income than for the interest income. Clearly the dividend exclusion enhances the attractiveness of stock investments relative to bond investments made by one corporation in another corporation.

---

[1]The exclusion is 80 percent if the corporation owns between 20 and 80 percent of the stock in the corporation paying it dividends; 100 percent of the dividends received are excluded if it owns more than 80 percent of the corporation paying it dividends. For convenience, here we are assuming the ownership interest in the dividend-paying corporation is less than 20 percent.

Tax-Deductible Expenses

When calculating their taxes, corporations are allowed to deduct operating expenses, such as advertising expense, sales commissions, and bad debts as well as interest expense. The tax-deductibility of these expenses reduces their after-tax cost, making them less costly than they might at first appear. The following example illustrates the benefit of tax-deductibility.

EXAMPLE   Companies X and Y each expect in the coming year to have earnings before interest and taxes of $200,000. Company X during the year will have to pay $30,000 in interest. Company Y has no debt and therefore will have no interest expense. Calculation of the earnings after taxes for these two firms, which pay a 40 percent tax on ordinary income, are shown below.

	Company X	Company Y
Earnings before interest and taxes	$200,000	$200,000
Less: Interest expense	30,000	0
Earnings before taxes	$170,000	$200,000
Less: Taxes (40%)	68,000	80,000
Earnings after taxes	$102,000	$120,000
Difference in earnings after taxes	$18,000	

The data demonstrate that while Company X had $30,000 more interest expense than Company Y, Company X's earnings after taxes are only $18,000 less than those of Company Y ($102,000 for Company X versus $120,000 for Company Y). This difference is attributable to the fact that Company X's $30,000 interest expense deduction provided a tax savings of $12,000 ($68,000 for Company X versus $80,000 for Company Y). This amount can be calculated directly by multiplying the tax rate by the amount of interest expense (.40 × $30,000 = $12,000). Similarly, the $18,000 *after-tax cost* of the interest expense can be calculated directly by multiplying one minus the tax rate times the amount of interest expense [(1 − .40) × $30,000 = $18,000].

The tax-deductibility of certain expenses can be seen to reduce their actual (after-tax) cost to the profitable firm. Note that *interest is a tax-deductible expense, whereas dividends are not.* Because dividends are not tax-deductible, their after-tax cost is equal to the amount of the dividend. Thus a $30,000 cash dividend would have an after-tax cost of $30,000.

Capital Gains[2]

capital gain The
amount by which the sale
price of an asset exceeds
the asset's initial pur-
chase price.

If a firm sells a capital asset such as stock held as an investment for
more than its initial purchase price, the difference between the sale
price and the purchase price is called a **capital gain.** For corporations,
capital gains are added to ordinary corporate income and taxed at the
regular corporate rates, with a maximum marginal tax rate of 39 percent. To simplify the computations presented in later chapters of the
text, as for ordinary income, *a 40 percent tax rate is assumed to be applicable to corporate capital gains.*

EXAMPLE   The Loos Company, a manufacturer of pharmaceuticals,
has operating earnings of $500,000. It has just sold for
$40,000 a capital asset initially purchased two years ago for
$36,000. Since the asset was sold for more than its initial
purchase price, there is a capital gain of $4,000 ($40,000 sale
price − $36,000 initial purchase price). The corporation's
taxable income will total $504,000 ($500,000 ordinary income + $4,000 capital gain). Since this total is above
$335,000, the capital gain will be taxed at the 34 percent
rate, resulting in a tax of $1,360 (.34 × $4,000).

S Corporations

S corporation A tax-
reporting entity whose
earnings are taxed not
as a corporation but as
the incomes of its stock-
holders, thus avoiding
double taxation.

double taxation
Occurs when the once-
taxed earnings of a cor-
poration are distributed
as cash dividends to its
stockholders, who are
then taxed on these divi-
dends.

Subchapter S of the Internal Revenue Code permits corporations meeting specified requirements, and having 35 or fewer stockholders, to
elect to be taxed like partnerships. That is, income is normally taxed as
direct personal income of the shareholders, regardless of whether it is
actually distributed to them. The **S corporation** is a tax-reporting entity
rather than a tax-paying entity. The key advantage of this form of organization is that the stockholders receive all the organizational benefits
of a corporation while escaping the *double taxation* normally associated
with the distribution of corporate earnings. (**Double taxation** results
when the already once-taxed earnings of a corporation are distributed
as cash dividends to stockholders, who must pay taxes on these dividends.) S corporations do not receive other tax advantages accorded
regular corporations.

FINANCIAL INSTITUTIONS

financial institution
An intermediary that
channels the savings of
individuals, businesses,
and governments into
loans or investments.

Financial institutions are intermediaries that channel the savings of
individuals, businesses, and governments into loans or investments.

---

[2]To simplify the discussion, only capital assets are considered here. The full tax treatment
of gains and losses on depreciable assets is presented as part of the discussion of capital-
budgeting cash flows in Chapter 14.

Many financial institutions directly or indirectly pay savers interest on deposited funds. Others provide services for which they charge depositors (for example, the service charges levied on checking accounts). Some financial institutions accept savings and lend their money to their customers; others invest customers' savings in earning assets such as real estate or stocks and bonds; and still others both lend money and invest savings. Financial institutions are required by the government to operate within established regulatory guidelines.

Key Participants in Financial Transactions

The key suppliers and demanders of funds are individuals, businesses, and governments. The savings of individual consumers placed in certain financial institutions provide these institutions with a large portion of their funds. Individuals not only supply funds to financial institutions but also demand funds from them in the form of loans. However, the important point here is that individuals as a group are the *net suppliers* for financial institutions: They save more money than they borrow.

Business firms also deposit some of their funds in financial institutions, primarily in checking accounts with various commercial banks. Firms, like individuals, also borrow funds from these institutions. As a group, business firms, unlike individuals, are *net demanders* of funds: They borrow more money than they save.

Governments maintain deposits of temporarily idle funds, certain tax payments, and social security payments in commercial banks. They do not borrow funds directly from financial institutions. However, by selling their securities to various institutions, governments indirectly borrow from them. The government, like business firms, is typically a *net demander* of money: it borrows more than it saves.

Major Financial Institutions

The major financial institutions in the U.S. economy are commercial banks, savings banks, savings and loans, credit unions, life insurance companies, pension funds, and mutual funds. These institutions attract funds from individuals, businesses, and governments, combine them, and perform certain services to make attractive loans available to individuals and businesses. They may also make some of these funds available to fulfill various government demands. Table 2.4 provides brief descriptions of the major financial institutions.

Changing Role of Financial Institutions

Passage of the **Depository Institutions Deregulation and Monetary Control Act of 1980 (DIDMCA)** signaled the beginning of the "financial services revolution" that continues to change the nature of financial insti-

Depository Institutions Deregulation and Monetary Control Act of 1980 (DIDMCA) Eliminated interest-rate ceilings on all accounts and permitted certain institutions to offer new types of accounts and services.

Table 2.4   **Major Financial Institutions**

Institution	Brief description
Commercial bank	Accepts both demand (checking) and time (savings) deposits. Also offers negotiable order of withdrawal (NOW) accounts, which are interest-earning savings accounts against which checks can be written. In addition, currently offers money market deposit accounts, which pay interest at rates competitive with other short-term investment vehicles. Makes loans directly to borrowers or through the financial markets.
Savings bank	Similar to commercial banks except that it may not hold demand (checking) deposits. Obtains funds from savings, NOW, and money market deposit accounts. Generally lends or invests funds through financial markets, although some residential real estate loans are made to individuals. Located primarily in New York, New Jersey, and the New England states.
Savings and loan	Similar to a savings bank in that it holds savings deposits, NOW accounts, and money market deposit accounts. Also raises capital through the sale of securities in the financial markets. Lends funds primarily to individuals and businesses for real estate mortgage loans. Some funds are channeled into investments in the financial markets.
Credit union	A financial intermediary that deals primarily in transfer of funds between consumers. Membership is generally based on some common bond, such as working for a given employer. Accepts members' savings deposits, NOW account deposits, and money market deposit accounts. Lends the majority of these funds to other members, typically to finance automobile or appliance purchases or home improvements.
Life insurance company	The largest type of financial intermediary handling individual savings. Receives premium payments that are placed in loans or investments to accumulate funds to cover future benefit payments. Lends funds to individuals, businesses, and governments or channels them through the financial markets to those who demand them.
Pension fund	Set up so that employees of various corporations or government units can receive income after retirement. Often employers match the contributions of their employees. Money is sometimes transferred directly to borrowers, but the majority is lent or invested via the financial markets.
Mutual fund	A type of financial intermediary that pools funds of savers and makes them available to business and government demanders. Obtains funds through sale of shares and uses proceeds to acquire bonds and stocks issued by various business and governmental units. Creates a diversified and professionally managed portfolio of securities to achieve a specified investment objective, such as liquidity with a high return. Hundreds of funds, with a variety of investment objectives, exist. Money market mutual funds, which provide competitive returns with very high liquidity, are currently quite popular.

financial supermarket An institution at which the customer can obtain a full array of financial services.

tutions. This act eliminated interest-rate ceilings on all accounts and permitted certain institutions to offer new types of accounts and services. It thus intensified competition and blurred traditional distinctions among these institutions. The acquisition by Prudential Insurance of Bache & Co. and by American Express of Shearson, Lehman, and Hutton, both brokerage firms, is testimony to this revolution. What is evolving is the **financial supermarket,** at which a customer can obtain a

ETHICS IN FINANCE

Financial Managers Should Know Better

For the most part, the actions of managers within the financial services industry are ethical, legal, and demonstrate good business judgment. Unfortunately, however, exceptions can occur, and when they do, it's front-page news.

It was a financial tragedy when Silverado Savings and Loan Association of Denver, Colorado, collapsed in 1988. The collapse left taxpayers with a $1 billion bill for management's mistakes. What was noteworthy about this particular event was that Neil Bush, son of President George Bush, served as an outside director at Silverado before its collapse. Although directors are supposed to supervise the actions of senior managers, Bush minimized his role in the thrift's collapse by arguing in 1990, "I never pretended to be an expert on the savings and loan business."

A federal judge expressed little sympathy for Mr. Bush's professed ignorance. The judge ordered that Bush be disciplined for not disclosing to his fellow board members that he maintained a personal relationship with two key Silverado borrowers, and that he stood to profit personally from decisions by Silverado's board to extend credit to these borrowers.

Source: "Most of business," *Time Magazine,* December 31, 1990, p. 50.

full array of financial services, such as checking, savings, brokerage, insurance, retirement, and estate planning. An example of the financial supermarket is Sears, Roebuck and Company's "Sears Financial Network." In addition to its credit and insurance (Allstate) and home mortgage (Sears Mortgage) operations, Sears now owns a national real estate brokerage firm (Coldwell Banker), a major stock brokerage firm (Dean Witter), and a West Coast savings and loan (Allstate Savings and Loan). It offers all these financial services in a growing number of "Financial Network Centers" housed within its retail stores.

The role of financial institutions is undergoing further change as a result of the "savings & loan (S&L) crisis" of the late 1980s. The crisis was caused by a number of factors including (1) enhanced competition stimulated by DIDMCA, (2) plummeting oil and real estate prices in the "oil patch" (oil-producing areas of the country), (3) poor regulation by S&L authorities, and (4) the illegal and unethical acts of officers of some major S&Ls. The failures of numerous S&Ls resulted in the Bush administration's thrift bailout plan. This plan—the cost of which is of course being borne by taxpayers—is aimed at resolving the S&L crisis by providing needed financing and more restrictive regulation and enforcement of the nation's S&Ls. As a result, future crises will be avoided. Also as a result, further blurring of the lines of distinction between banks, S&Ls, and other financial institutions is expected. Clearly, a single type of full-service financial institution is evolving.

FINANCIAL MARKETS

financial markets
Provide a forum in which suppliers of funds and demanders of loans and investments can transact business directly.

Financial markets provide a forum in which suppliers of funds and demanders of loans and investments can transact business directly. Whereas the loans and investments of institutions are made without the direct knowledge of the suppliers of funds (savers), suppliers in the financial markets know where their funds are being lent or invested.

The Relationship between Institutions and Markets

Financial institutions actively participate in the financial markets as both suppliers and demanders of funds. Figure 2.2 depicts the general flow of funds through and between financial institutions and financial markets; private placement transactions are also shown. The suppliers and demanders of funds may be domestic or foreign. Because of the importance to the firm of the two key financial markets—the money market and the capital market—the next two sections of this chapter are devoted to these topics.

The Money Market

money market A financial relationship created between suppliers and demanders of *short-term funds*.

marketable securities Short-term debt instruments issued by government, business, and financial institutions.

The **money market** is created by a financial relationship between suppliers and demanders of *short-term funds*, which have maturities of one year or less. The money market is not an actual organization housed in some central location, such as a stock market. Most money market transactions are made in the form of **marketable securities**—short-term debt instruments, such as U.S. Treasury bills, commercial paper, and negotiable certificates of deposit issued by government, business, and financial institutions, respectively. (Marketable securities are described in Chapter 8.)

The money market exists because certain individuals, businesses, governments, and financial institutions have temporarily idle funds. Rather than leave the funds idle, they wish to place them in some type of liquid asset or short-term, interest-earning instrument. At the same time, other individuals, businesses, governments, and financial institutions find themselves in need of seasonal or temporary financing. The money market thus brings together these suppliers and demanders of short-term liquid funds.

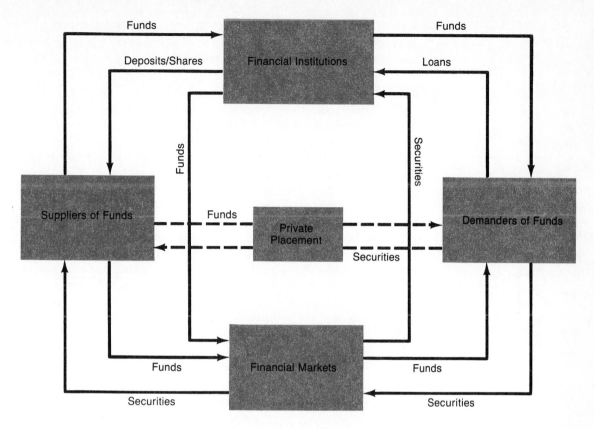

Figure 2.2   Flow of Funds for Financial Institutions and Markets

Financial institutions and financial markets as well as private placements are the mechanisms used to transfer funds between individuals, business, and government suppliers and demanders. These mechanisms allow savings to be converted into investment.

The Capital Market

The **capital market** is a financial relationship created by a number of institutions and arrangements that allows the suppliers and demanders of *long-term funds*—funds with maturities of more than one year—to make transactions. Included among long-term funds are securities issues of business and government. The backbone of the capital market is formed by the various *securities exchanges* that provide a forum for debt and equity transactions. The smooth functioning of the capital market is important to the long-run growth of business.

capital market A financial relationship created by institutions and arrangements, allowing suppliers and demanders of *long-term funds* to make transactions.

Key Securities
Major securities traded in the capital market include bonds (long-term debt) and both common and preferred stock (equity, or ownership). **Bonds** are long-term debt instruments used by business and government to raise large sums of money, generally from a diverse group of lenders. *Corporate bonds* typically pay interest *semiannually* (every six

bond Long-term debt instrument used by businesses and government to raise large sums of money.

months) at a stated *coupon interest rate,* have an initial *maturity* of from 10 to 30 years, and have a *par,* or *face, value* of $1,000 that must be repaid at maturity. Bonds are described in detail in Chapter 19.

EXAMPLE   Lakeview Industries, a picture tube manufacturer, has just issued a 12 percent coupon interest rate, 20-year bond with a $1,000 par value that pays interest semiannually. Investors who buy this bond receive the contractual right to (1) $120 annual interest (12% coupon interest rate × $1,000 par value) distributed as $60 at the end of each six months (½ × $120) for 20 years and (2) the $1,000 par value at the end of year 20.

common stock
Collectively, units of ownership interest, or equity, in a corporation.

dividends   Periodic distributions of earnings to the owners of stock in a firm.

preferred stock   A special form of ownership having a fixed periodic dividend that must be paid prior to payment of any common stock dividends.

Shares of **common stock** are units of ownership interest, or equity, in a corporation. Common stockholders expect to earn a return by receiving **dividends**—periodic distributions of earnings—or by realizing gains through increases in share price. **Preferred stock** is a special form of ownership that has features of both a bond and common stock. Preferred stockholders are promised a fixed periodic dividend that must be paid prior to payment of any dividends to the owners of common stock. In other words, preferred stock has "preference" over common stock. Preferred and common stock are described in detail in Chapter 20.

primary market
Financial market in which securities are initially issued.

secondary market
Financial market in which preowned securities are traded.

investment banker
A financial intermediary who purchases securities from corporations and governments and sells them to the public in the *primary market.*

Primary and Secondary Markets

All securities, whether in the money or capital markets, are initially issued in the **primary market.** This is the only market in which the corporate or government issuer is directly involved in the transaction and receives direct benefit from the issue—that is, the company actually receives the proceeds from the sale of securities. Once the securities begin to trade among individual, business, government, or financial institution savers and investors, they become part of the **secondary market.** The primary market is the one in which "new" securities are sold; the secondary market can be viewed as a "used" or "preowned" securities market. The **investment banker,** discussed in detail in Chapter 18, acts as a financial intermediary ("middleman") who purchases new securities from corporations and governments and sells them to the public in the primary market.

securities exchanges
The marketplace in which firms can raise funds through the sale of new securities and in which purchasers can resell securities.

efficient market
Market that allocates funds to their most productive uses as a result of competition among wealth-maximizing investors.

Major Securities Exchanges

As we noted earlier, **securities exchanges** provide the marketplace in which firms can raise funds through the sale of new securities. They also enable purchasers of securities to maintain liquidity by being able to easily resell them when necessary. In addition they create **efficient markets** which allocate funds to the most productive uses. This is especially true for securities that are actively traded on major exchanges where the competition among wealth-maximizing investors determines and publicizes prices that are believed to be close to their true value.

Many people call securities exchanges "stock markets," but this label is somewhat misleading because bonds, common stock, preferred stock, and a variety of other investment vehicles are all traded on these exchanges. The two key types of securities exchange are the organized exchange and the over-the-counter exchange.

Organized Securities Exchanges

Organized securities exchanges are tangible organizations that act as *secondary markets* where outstanding securities are resold. Organized exchanges account for over 72 percent of *total* shares traded. The dominant organized exchanges are the New York Stock Exchange (NYSE) and the American Stock Exchange (AMEX), both headquartered in New York City. There are also regional exchanges, such as the Midwest Stock Exchange (in Chicago) and the Pacific Stock Exchange (in San Francisco).

Most exchanges are modeled after the New York Stock Exchange, which accounts for over 80 percent of the shares traded on organized exchanges. To make transactions on the "floor" of the New York Stock Exchange, an individual or firm must own a "seat" on the exchange. There are a total of 1,366 seats on the NYSE. Most are owned by brokerage firms. In order to be listed for trading on an organized stock exchange, a firm must file an application for listing and meet a number of requirements. Trading is carried out on the floor of the exchange through an *auction process*. The goal of trading is to fill *buy orders* (orders to purchase securities) at the lowest price and to fill *sell orders* (orders to sell securities) at the highest price, thereby giving both purchasers and sellers the best possible deal. Once placed, an order to either buy or sell can be executed in minutes, thanks to sophisticated telecommunication devices. Information on the daily trading of securities is reported in various media, including financial publications such as *The Wall Street Journal*.

organized securities exchanges Tangible organizations on whose premises outstanding securities are resold.

The Over-the-Counter Exchange

The **over-the-counter (OTC) exchange** is not an organization but an intangible market for the purchase and sale of securities not listed by the organized exchanges. Active traders in this market are linked by a sophisticated telecommunications network. Unlike the auction process on the organized securities exchanges, the prices at which securities are traded in the OTC market result from both competitive bids and negotiation. The OTC, in addition to creating a *secondary* (resale) *market* for outstanding securities, is a *primary market* in which new public issues are sold. The OTC accounts for nearly 28 percent of *total* shares traded.

over-the-counter (OTC) exchange Not an organization, but an intangible market for the purchase and sale of securities not listed by the organized exchanges.

INTEREST RATES AND REQUIRED RETURNS

Financial institutions and markets create the mechanism through which funds flow between savers (funds suppliers) and investors (funds demanders). When funds are lent, the cost of borrowing the funds is the **interest rate.** When funds are invested to obtain an ownership (or eq-

interest rate When funds are lent, the cost of borrowing funds.

required return The cost paid by the demander of funds to the owner of an equity interest in a firm.

uity) interest—as in stock purchases—the cost to the demander is commonly called the **required return.** In both cases the supplier is compensated for providing funds. Generally, the lower the interest rate or required return, the greater the flow of funds from savers to investors, and therefore the greater the economic growth and vice versa.

The Term Structure of Interest Rates

term structure of interest rates The relationship between the time to maturity and the interest rate or rate of return on similar-risk securities.

yield The annual rate of interest earned on a security purchased on a given day and held to maturity.

yield curve A graph that shows the term structure of interest rates.

For any class of similar-risk securities, the **term structure of interest rates** relates the interest rate or rate of return to the time to maturity. The annual rate of interest earned on a security purchased on a given day and held to maturity is called its **yield.** At any point in time the relationship between the yield and the remaining time to maturity can be represented by a **yield curve.** In other words, the yield curve is a graphic depiction of the term structure of interest rates.

Figure 2.3 shows three yield curves for all U.S. Treasury securities—one at May 22, 1981, a second at October 30, 1987, and a third at Sep-

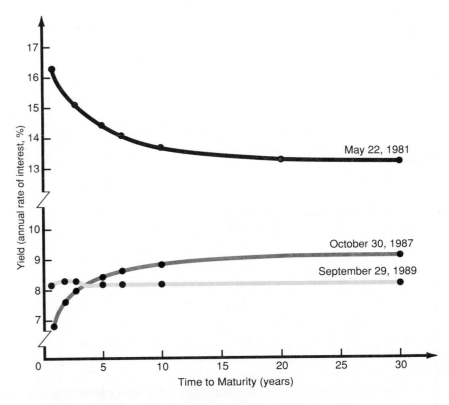

Figure 2.3   Yield Curves for U.S. Treasury Securities at Three Points in Time
The May 22, 1981, yield curve was downward-sloping, reflecting an expected long-run decline in interest rates. On October 30, 1987, the upward-sloping yield curve reflected an expected increase in interest rates. On September 29, 1989, the flat yield curve reflected an expectation of stable interest rates.

Source: Data from *Federal Reserve Bulletin*, June 1981, p. A25; January 1988, p. A24; and December 1989, p. A24.

tember 29, 1989. It can be seen that both the position and the shape of the yield curves change over time. The May 22, 1981, curve was *downward-sloping*, reflecting expected lower future interest rates. On October 30, 1987, the yield curve was *upward-sloping*, reflecting the expectation of higher future rates. And on September 29, 1989, the curve was *flat*, indicating a stable expectation—future interest rates similar to current interest rates.

Risk and Return[3]

A positive relationship exists between risk and return. After assessing the risk embodied in a given asset, investors tend to make those investments that are expected to provide a return commensurate with the risk involved. The actual return earned on an investment will affect investors' subsequent actions—whether they sell, hold, or buy additional assets. In addition, most investors look to certain types of assets to provide the desired range of risk-return behaviors.

Actual and Expected Return

The **actual return** on an investment is measured as a percentage return on the initial price or amount invested. Equation 2.1 presents the basic expression for calculating actual return.

$$\text{Return} = \frac{\text{ending value} - \text{initial value} + \text{cash received}}{\text{initial value}}$$

Basically the equation expresses the sum of the change in value and any cash received as a percentage of the initial value. This method of calculating investment return is commonly applied over annual periods or expressed as an annual rate of return.[4]

actual return   The percentage return on the initial price or amount invested.

Equation 2.1
Formula for calculating actual return

EXAMPLE   Roberta's Gameroom, a high-traffic video arcade, wishes to determine the actual rate of return on two of its video machines, Starman and Avenger. Starman was purchased exactly one year ago for $20,000 and currently has a market value of $21,500. During the year it generated $800 of after-tax cash receipts. Avenger was purchased four years ago, and its value at the beginning and end of the year just completed declined from $12,000 to $11,800. During the year it generated $1,700 of after-tax cash receipts. Substituting into Equation 2.1, the annual rate of return for each video machine is calculated.

[3]Detailed discussions of risk and return and their linkage to value are included in Chapter 12.

[4]The measurement of return over longer periods of time using present value techniques is presented in Chapters 13 and 15. For now this single time period measure is assumed.

Starman

$$\text{Return} = \frac{\$21,500 - \$20,000 + \$800}{\$20,000} = \frac{\$2,300}{\$20,000} = \underline{\underline{11.5\%}}$$

Avenger

$$\text{Return} = \frac{\$11,800 - \$12,000 + \$1,700}{\$12,000} = \frac{\$1,500}{\$12,000} = \underline{\underline{12.5\%}}$$

Although the value of Avenger declined during the year, its relatively high cash flow caused it to earn a higher rate of return than that earned by Starman during the same period. Clearly, it is the combined impact of changes in value and cash flow measured by the rate of return that is important.

The return calculated using Equation 2.1 is typically an actual rather than an expected return. When estimating **expected return,** the decision maker must forecast the ending value and cash receipts, thus introducing an element of risk or uncertainty as to the real outcome.

expected return
The sum of the forecast change in an investment's value and any expected cash receipts expressed as a percentage of the initial amount invested.

risk-return trade-off
The expectation that for accepting greater risk, investors must be compensated with greater returns.

The Basic Trade-off

A **risk-return trade-off** exists such that investors must be compensated for accepting greater risk with the expectation of greater returns.[5] Figure 2.4 illustrates the typical relationship between risk and return for several popular securities. Clearly, higher returns (costs to the issuer) are expected with greater risk. Financial managers must attempt to keep revenues up and costs down, but they must also consider the risks associated with each investment and financing alternative. Decisions will ultimately rest on an analysis of the impact of risk and return on share price.

INTERNATIONAL DIMENSION: THE ENVIRONMENT

Three important aspects of the international environment that provide both challenges and opportunities to an MNC's financial management are legal forms of business, taxes, and financial markets.

Legal Forms of Business

In many countries outside the United States, operating a foreign business as a subsidiary or affiliate can take two forms, both similar to the U.S. corporation. In German-speaking nations, the two forms are the *Aktiengesellschaft* (A.G) or the *Gesellschaft mit beschrankter Haftung*

---

[5]The risk-return trade-off is discussed in detail in Chapter 12, where certain refinements are introduced to explain why investors are actually rewarded with higher returns for taking only certain types of "nondiversifiable" or inescapable risks.

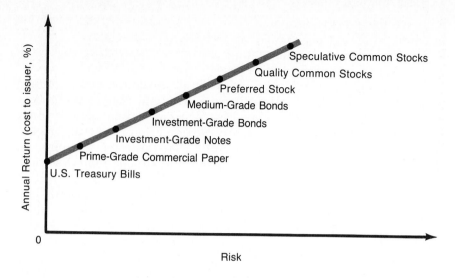

Figure 2.4   **Risk-Return Profile for Popular Securities**

The greater the risk of a given security, the higher the expected return (cost to the issuer). Low-risk securities include U.S. Treasury bills and prime-grade commercial paper; high-risk securities include all types of common stocks.

(GmbH). In many other countries the similar forms are a *Société Anonyme* (S.A.) or a *Société à Responsabilité Limitée* (S.A.R.L.). The A.G. or the S.A. is the most common form, but the GmbH and the S.A.R.L. enjoy much greater freedom and require fewer formalities for formation and operation.

Establishing a business in a form such as the S.A. can involve most of the provisions that govern a U.S.-based corporation. To operate in many foreign countries, especially in most of the less-developed nations, it is often essential to enter into joint-venture business agreements. A **joint venture** is a partnership under which the participants have contractually agreed to contribute specified amounts of money and expertise in exchange for stated proportions of ownership and profit. In foreign countries, U.S.-based firms often find it beneficial to form partnerships with private investors or with government-based agencies of the host country. The governments of numerous countries, such as Brazil, Colombia, Mexico, and Venezuela in Latin America as well as Indonesia, Malaysia, the Philippines, and Thailand in East Asia, have in recent years instituted new laws and regulations governing MNCs. The basic rule introduced by most of these nations requires that the majority ownership (i.e., at least 51 percent of the total equity) of MNCs' joint-venture projects be held by domestically based investors. In other regions of the world, MNCs, especially those based in the United States and Japan, will face new challenges and opportunities, particularly in terms of ownership requirements and mergers. Three regions providing these challenges and opportunities in the near future are Western Europe as it approaches the end of 1992 (discussed below)

joint venture A partnership under which the participants agree to contribute specified amounts of money and expertise for stated proportions of ownership and profit.

and both Eastern Europe and the Soviet Union (and Republics) as they attempt to adopt more market-based economic principles.

The existence of joint-venture laws and restrictions has certain implications for the operation of foreign-based subsidiaries. First of all, majority foreign ownership may result in a substantial degree of management and control by host-country participants. Managerial policies and procedures normally pursued by MNCs in day-to-day operations may change for the worse as a result. Next, foreign ownership may result in disagreements among the partners as to the exact distribution of profits and the portion to be set aside for reinvestment. Moreover, operating in foreign countries, especially on a joint-venture basis, can entail problems regarding the actual remission of profits. In the past, the governments of Argentina, Brazil, Nigeria, and Thailand, among others, have imposed ceilings not only on the repatriation (return) of capital by MNCs but also on profit remittances by these firms back to the parent companies. The shortage of foreign exchange is usually cited as the motivating factor by these governments. Finally, from a "positive" point of view, it can be argued that to operate in many of the less-developed countries, it would be beneficial for MNCs to enter into joint-venture agreements, given the potential risks stemming from political instability in the host countries. This issue will be addressed in detail in subsequent discussions.

Taxes

Multinational companies, unlike domestic firms, have financial obligations—as well as opportunities—in foreign countries. One of their basic responsibilities is international taxation—a complex issue because national governments follow a variety of tax policies. In general, from the point of view of a U.S.-based MNC, several factors must be taken into account.

First, the *level* of foreign taxes needs to be examined. Among the major industrial countries, corporate tax rates do not vary too widely. Many less industrialized nations set relatively moderate rates, partly as an incentive for attracting foreign capital inflows. Certain countries, meanwhile, including the Bahamas, Switzerland, Liechtenstein, the Cayman Islands, and Bermuda, are known for their "low" tax levels. These nations typically have no withholding taxes on *intra-MNC dividends*, which are dividends paid by a foreign subsidiary of a MNC to the parent company.

Next, there is a question of how to define *taxable income.* Some countries tax profits as received on a cash basis. Others tax profits earned on an accrual basis. Differences can also exist in treatments of noncash charges, such as depreciation, amortization, and depletion. Finally, the existence of tax agreements between the United States and other governments can influence not only the total tax bill of the parent MNC, but also its international operations and financial activities. Effective January 1, 1988, for example, the U.S. Treasury terminated a 1948 tax treaty with the Netherlands Antilles, affecting about $32 billion of debt issued by U.S.-based MNCs. Under this treaty, debt issued there was exempt from a 30 percent withholding tax imposed by the United States.

Tax rates and rules applied to the global earnings of their own multinationals vary among different home countries. Moreover, tax rules are subject to frequent modifications. In the United States, for instance, the Tax Reform Act of 1986 resulted in certain changes affecting the taxation of U.S.-based MNCs. Special provisions apply to tax deferrals by MNCs on foreign income; operations set up in American possessions, such as the U.S. Virgin Islands, Guam, and American Samoa; capital gains from the sale of stock in a foreign corporation; and withholding taxes. Furthermore, MNCs (both American and foreign) can be subject to national as well as local taxes. As an example, a number of individual state governments in the United States have in recent years introduced new measures in the form of special **unitary tax laws.** These tax the multinationals on a percentage of their *total* worldwide income rather than, as is generally accepted elsewhere, on their earnings arising within the jurisdiction of each respective state government. As a part of their response to unitary tax laws, some multinationals have already pressured a number of state governments into abolishing the laws. In addition, some MNCs have relocated their investments away from those states that continue to apply such laws. For updated details on various countries' tax laws, consult relevant publications by international accounting firms.

unitary tax laws
Laws in some U.S. states that tax multinationals on a percentage of their *total* worldwide income.

As a general practice, the U.S. government claims jurisdiction over *all* the income of an MNC, wherever earned. (Special rules apply to foreign corporations conducting business in the United States.) However, it may be possible for a multinational company to take foreign income taxes as a direct credit against its U.S. tax liabilities. The following simple example illustrates one way of accomplishing this objective.

EXAMPLE   American Enterprises, a U.S.-based MNC that manufacturers heavy machinery, has a foreign subsidiary that earns $100,000 before local taxes. All of the after-tax funds are available to the parent in the form of dividends. The applicable taxes consist of a 35 percent foreign income tax rate, a foreign dividend withholding tax rate of 10 percent, and a U.S. tax rate of 34 percent.

Subsidiary income before local taxes	$100,000
Foreign income tax at 35%	− 35,000
Dividend available to be declared	$ 65,000
Foreign dividend withholding tax at 10%	− 6,500
MNC's receipt of dividends	$ 58,500

Using the so-called *grossing up procedure,* the MNC will add the full before-tax subsidiary income to its total taxable income. Next, the U.S. tax liability on the grossed-up income is calculated. Finally, the related taxes paid in the foreign country are applied as a credit against the additional U.S. tax liability.

Additional MNC income		$100,000
U.S. tax liability at 34%	$34,000	
Total foreign taxes paid to be used as a credit ($35,000 + $6,500)	− 41,500	− 41,500
U.S. taxes due		0
Net funds available to the parent MNC		$ 58,500

Since the U.S. tax liability is less than the total taxes paid to the foreign government, *no additional U.S. taxes are due* on the income from the foreign subsidiary. In our example if tax credits were not allowed, then "double taxation" by the two authorities, as shown below, would have resulted in a substantial drop in the overall net funds available to the parent MNC.

Subsidiary income before local taxes	$100,000
Foreign income tax at 35%	− 35,000
Dividend available to be declared	$ 65,000
Foreign dividend withholding tax at 10%	− 6,500
MNC's receipt of dividends	$ 58,500
U.S. tax liability at 34%	− 19,890
Net funds available to the parent MNC	$ 38,610

The preceding example clearly demonstrates that the existence of bilateral tax treaties and the subsequent application of tax credits can significantly enhance the overall net funds available to MNCs from their worldwide earnings. Consequently, in an increasingly complex and competitive international financial environment, international taxation is one of the variables that multinational corporations should fully utilize to their advantage.

Financial Markets

Euromarket The international financial market that provides for borrowing and lending currencies outside their country of origin.

During the last two decades the **Euromarket**—which provides for borrowing and lending currencies outside their country of origin—has grown quite rapidly. The Euromarket provides multinational companies with an "external" opportunity to borrow or lend funds with the additional feature of less government regulation. The importance of this market, as well as the international product markets, is expected to be greatly affected by *Europe 1992*. Before discussing the Euromarket we therefore take a brief look at this major event.

Europe 1992

The European Economic Community (EC or, as also referred to, EEC) has been in existence since 1959. It has a current membership of 12 nations. With a total population estimated at more than 350 million and an overall gross national income paralleling that of the United States, the EC is a significant global economic force. Now, due to a series of major economic, monetary, financial, and legal provisions set forth by the member countries during the 1980s, the Community is to be further transformed and turned into a *single* market by year-end 1992. This transformation is commonly called **Europe 1992.** Although the EC has managed to reach agreements on most of these provisions, debates continue on certain other aspects (some key), including those related to automobile production and imports, monetary union, taxes, and work-ers' rights.

> **Europe 1992** The transformation of the European Economic Community (EC) into a single market by year-end 1992.

It is generally believed that the EC can expect to enjoy enhanced economic growth rates for much of the 1990s and perhaps beyond. The new Community will offer both challenges and opportunities to a variety of players, including multinational firms. MNCs, especially those based in the United States, will face heightened levels of competition when operating inside the EC. As more of the existing restrictions and regulations are eliminated, for instance, U.S. multinationals will have to face other MNCs. Some, such as the larger and perhaps more efficient firms resulting from mergers, will come from within the Community. Others, including the giants from Japan, could challenge the U.S. MNCs in a manner similar to that already done in the U.S. market.

U.S. companies can benefit from a single European market, but only if they are prepared. They must offer the correct mix of products to a collection of varied consumers and be ready to take advantage of a variety of currencies (including the EC's own, the *European Currency Unit, ECU*) as well as financial markets and instruments (such as the emerging Euro-equities). They must staff their operations with the appropriate combination of local and foreign personnel and, when necessary, enter into joint ventures and strategic alliances.

Growth of the Euromarket

Several reasons can be offered to explain why the Euromarket has grown so large. First, beginning in the early 1960s, the Russians wanted to maintain their dollar earnings outside the legal jurisdiction of the United States, mainly due to the Cold War. Second, the consistently large U.S. balance of payments deficits helped "scatter" dollars around the world. Third, the existence of specific regulations and controls on dollar deposits in the United States, including interest rate ceilings imposed by the government, helped send such deposits to places outside the United States.

One aspect of the Euromarket is the so-called **offshore centers.** Certain cities or states around the world—including London, Singapore, Bahrain, Nassau, Hong Kong, and Luxembourg—are considered major offshore centers for Euromarket business. The availability of communication and transportation facilities, along with the importance of language, costs, time zones, taxes, and local banking regulations, are among the main reasons for the prominence of these centers.

> **offshore centers** Certain cities or states that have achieved prominence as major centers for Euromarket business.

Major Participants

The Euromarket is still dominated by the U.S. dollar. However, activities in other major currencies, including Deutsche mark, Swiss franc, Japanese yen, British pounds sterling, French franc, and the European Currency Unit (ECU), have in recent years grown much faster than those denominated in the U.S. currency. Similarly, while American banks and other financial institutions continue to play a significant role in the global markets, financial giants from Japan and Europe have become major participants in Euromarkets. At the end of 1989, for example, nine of the top ten largest banks in the world as measured in terms of total assets were based in Japan.

Following the oil price increases by the Organization of Petroleum Exporting Countries (OPEC) in 1973–1974 and 1979–1980, massive amounts of dollars have been placed in various Euromarket financial centers. International banks, in turn, as part of the so-called *redistribution* of "oil money," have been lending to different groups of borrowers. Although developing countries have become a major borrowing group in recent years, the industrialized nations continue to borrow actively in international markets. Included in the latter group's borrowings are the funds obtained by multinational companies. The multinationals use the Euromarket to raise additional funds as well as to invest excess cash. Both Eurocurrency and Eurobond markets are extensively used by MNCs. Further details on MNCs' Euromarket activities are presented later.

SUMMARY

1　　**Describe the basic legal forms of business organization and their respective strengths and weaknesses.**　The basic forms of business organization are the sole proprietorship, the partnership, and the corporation. Although there are more sole proprietorships than any other form of business organization, the corporation is dominant in terms of business receipts and net profits. Limited liability and the resulting ability to market its ownership are major strengths of the corporation that differentiate it from sole proprietorships and partnerships. The keys strengths and weaknesses of each form of business organization are summarized in Table 2.1.

2　　**Understand the fundamentals of corporate taxation of ordinary income and capital gains, and the role of S corporations.**　Corporations are subject to corporate tax rates applicable to both ordinary income (after deducting allowable expenses) and capital gains, which are sales proceeds received in excess of an asset's initial purchase price. The average tax rate paid by a corporation ranges from 15 to 34 percent. (For convenience, we assume a 40 percent marginal tax rate in this book.) Certain provisions in the tax code such as intercorporate dividend exclusions and tax-deductible expenses provide corporate taxpayers with opportunities to reduce their taxes. In addition S corporations—small corporations meeting specified IRS requirements—can elect to be taxed as partnerships.

3　　**Identify the key participants in financial transactions, and identify the basic activities and changing role of the major financial institutions.**　Financial institutions, such as banks, savings and loans, and mutual funds, channel the savings of various individuals, businesses, and governments into the hands of demanders of these funds. Their role is changing as the era of the "financial supermarkets," where a customer can obtain a full array of financial services, is being ushered in by recent legislation. The role of each of the major financial institutions is briefly described in Table 2.4.

4   **Understand the relationship between institutions and markets, and the basic function and operation of the money market, capital markets, and major securities exchanges.**   The financial markets—the money and capital market—provide a forum in which suppliers and demanders of loans and investments can transact business directly. Financial institutions actively participate in the financial markets as both suppliers and demanders of funds. In the money market, short-term debt instruments are traded. In the capital market, long-term debt (bonds) and equity (common and preferred stock) transactions are made. The backbone of the capital market is the securities exchanges. The organized exchanges are the dominant exchanges providing secondary (resale) markets for securities. The over-the-counter (OTC) exchange is both the primary market in which new public issues are sold and a secondary market for outstanding securities.

5   **Discuss the fundamentals of interest rates and required returns—their role, the term structure, and risk and rates of return.**   The flow of funds between savers (suppliers) and investors (demanders) is regulated by the interest rate or required return. The term structure of interest rates reflects the relationship between the interest rate, or rate of return, and the time to maturity. Yield curves can be downward-sloping, upward-sloping, or flat, reflecting lower, higher, or stable future interest rate expectations, respectively. Since investors must be compensated for taking risk, they expect higher returns for greater risk. Each type of security offers a range of risk-return trade-offs.

6   **Recognize the impact that differing legal forms of business, taxation, and financial markets can have on the financial management of a multinational company.**   Setting up operations in foreign countries can entail special problems due to, among other things, the legal form of business organization chosen, the degree of ownership allowed by the host country, and possible restrictions and regulations on the return of capital and profits. Taxation of multinational companies is a complex issue due to the existence of varying tax rates, differing definitions of taxable income, measurement differences, and tax treaties. For U.S. MNCs it may be possible to take foreign taxes as a direct credit against U.S. tax liabilities. Europe 1992, the transformation of the European Economic Community into a single market by year-end 1992, is expected to greatly affect international financial as well as product markets. The existence and expansion of dollars held outside the United States have contributed in recent years to the development of a major international financial market, the Euromarket. The large international banks, developing and industrialized nations, and multinational companies participate as borrowers and lenders in this market.

QUESTIONS

2—1   What are the three basic forms of business organization? Which form is most common? Which form is dominant in terms of business receipts and net profits? Why?

2—2   Briefly define ordinary income and capital gains and describe the tax treatments of each. What is the *average tax rate?* What is the *marginal tax rate?*

2—3   Describe the *intercorporate dividend* exclusion. What benefit results from the tax-deductibility of certain corporate expenses? Compare and contrast the tax treatment of corporate interest and dividend payments.

2—4   What role do financial institutions play in our economy? Who are the key participants in these transactions? Indicate who are net suppliers (savers) and who are net demanders (borrowers).

2—5   Briefly describe each of the following financial institutions:
   a. Commercial banks
   b. Savings and loans
   c. Life insurance companies
   d. Mutual funds

2—6   Describe the changing role of financial institutions and explain how "financial supermarkets" fit into the evolving institutional environment. What effect, if any, has the "savings and loan (S&L) crisis" had on the evolution of the financial supermarket?

2—7   What are financial markets and what role do they play in our economy? What relationship exists between financial institutions and financial markets?

2—8   What is the *money market?* Where is it housed? How does it differ from the capital market?

2—9   What is the *capital market?* What are *primary* and *secondary* markets? What role do securities exchanges play in the capital market?

2—10   How does the over-the-counter exchange operate? How does it differ from the organized securities exchanges?

2—11   What is the *term structure of interest rates*, and how does it relate to the *yield curve?* For a given class of similar-risk securities, what expectation causes the yield curve to be downward-sloping, upward-sloping, or flat?

2—12   How are actual and expected returns measured, and what is the difference between them? What is meant by the *risk-return trade-off?*

2—13   What is a *joint venture?* Why is it often essential to use this arrangement? What effect do joint venture laws and restrictions have on the operation of foreign-based subsidiaries?

2—14   From the point of view of a U.S.-based MNC, what key tax factors need to be considered? What are *unitary tax laws?*

2—15   What is *Europe 1992* and why is it important? Discuss the major reasons for the growth of the Euromarket. What is an *offshore center?* Name the major participants in the Euromarket.

PROBLEMS

2—1   **(Liability Comparisons)**   Marilyn Smith has invested $25,000 in the Research Marketing Company. This firm recently declared bankruptcy and has $60,000 in unpaid debts. Explain the nature of payments, if any, by Ms. Smith in each of the following situations.
   a. The Research Marketing Company is a sole proprietorship owned by Ms. Smith.
   b. The Research Marketing Company is a 50–50 partnership of Ms. Smith and Arnold Jones.
   c. The Research Marketing Company is a corporation.

2—2   **(Corporate Taxes)**   Kim Supply, Inc., is a small corporation acting as the exclusive distributor of a major line of sporting goods. During 1992 the firm earned $92,500 before taxes.
   a. Calculate the firm's tax liability using the corporate tax rate schedule given in Table 2.2.

b. How much is Kim Supply's 1991 after-tax earnings?

c. What was the firm's average tax rate, based on your findings in **a**?

d. What is the firm's marginal tax rate, based on your findings in **a**?

2—3   **(Average Corporate Tax Rates)**   Using the corporate tax rate schedule given in Table 2.2, perform the following:

a. Calculate the tax liability, after-tax earnings, and average tax rates for the following levels of corporate earnings before taxes: $10,000; $80,000; $300,000; $500,000; $1.5 million.

b. Plot the average tax rates (measured on the y-axis) against the pretax income levels (measured on the x-axis). What generalization can be made concerning the relationship between these variables?

2—4   **(Marginal Corporate Tax Rates)**   Using the corporate tax rate schedule given in Table 2.2, perform the following:

a. Find the marginal tax rate for the following levels of corporate earnings before taxes: $15,000; $60,000; $90,000; $200,000; $400,000; $1 million.

b. Plot the marginal tax rates (measured on the y-axis) against the pretax income levels (measured on the x-axis). Explain the relationship between these variables.

2—5   **(Interest versus Dividend Income)**   Stork Distributors, Inc., during the year just ended had pretax earnings from operations of $490,000. In addition during the year it received $20,000 in interest on bonds it held in Zorn Manufacturing and received $20,000 in common stock dividends on its 5 percent interest in Tong Industries, Inc. Stork is in the 40 percent tax bracket and is eligible for a 70 percent dividend exclusion on its Tong Industries stock.

a. Calculate the firm's tax on its operating earnings only.

b. Find the tax and after-tax amounts resulting from the interest received on the Zorn Manufacturing bonds.

c. Find the tax and after-tax amounts resulting from the dividends received on the Tong Industries, Inc., common stock.

d. Compare, contrast, and discuss the after-tax amounts resulting from the bond interest and dividend receipts calculated in **b** and **c**.

e. What is the firm's total tax liability for the year?

2—6   **(Interest versus Dividend Expense)**   The Randy Company expects earnings before interest and taxes to be $40,000 for this period. Assuming an ordinary tax rate of 40 percent, compute the firm's earnings after taxes and earnings available for common stockholders (earnings after taxes and preferred stock dividends, if any) under the following conditions:

a. The firm pays $10,000 in interest.

b. The firm pays $10,000 in preferred stock dividends.

2—7   **(Capital Gains Taxes)**   Waters Manufacturing is considering the sale of two nondepreciable assets, X and Y. Asset X was purchased for $2,000 and will be sold today for $2,250. Asset Y was purchased for $30,000 and will be sold today for $35,000. The firm is subject to a 40 percent tax rate on capital gains.

a. Calculate the amount of capital gain, if any, realized on each of the assets.

b. Calculate the tax on the sale of each asset.

2—8   **(Capital Gains Taxes)**   The table below contains purchase and sale prices for the nondepreciable capital assets of a major corporation. The firm paid taxes of 40 percent on capital gains.

Asset	Purchase price	Sale price
A	$ 3,000	$ 3,400
B	12,000	12,000
C	62,000	80,000
D	41,000	45,000
E	16,500	18,000

a. Determine the amount of capital gain realized on each of the five assets.

b. Calculate the amount of tax paid on each of the assets.

2—9   (Yield Curve) A firm wishing to evaluate interest rate behavior has gathered yield data on five U.S. Treasury securities, each having a different maturity and all measured at the same point in time. This data is summarized below.

U.S. Treasury security	Time to maturity	Yield (%)
A	1 year	12.6
B	10 years	11.2
C	6 months	13.0
D	20 years	11.0
E	5 years	11.4

a. Draw the yield curve associated with the data given above.

b. Describe the resulting yield curve in a, and explain the general expectations embodied in it.

2—10   (Term Structure of Interest Rates) The following yield data for a number of highest-quality corporate bonds existed at each of the three points in time noted.

Time to maturity (years)	Yield (%)		
	5 years ago	2 years ago	Today
1	9.1	14.6	9.3
3	9.2	12.8	9.8
5	9.3	12.2	10.9
10	9.5	10.9	12.6
15	9.4	10.7	12.7
20	9.3	10.5	12.9
30	9.4	10.5	13.5

a. On the same set of axes, draw the yield curve at each of the three points in time given.

b. Label each curve in a as to its general shape (downward-sloping, upward-sloping, flat).

c. Describe the general interest rate expectation existing at each of the three points in time.

2—11   **(Actual Return)**   For each of the following investments, calculate the rate of return earned over the unspecified time period.

Investment	Beginning-of-period value ($)	End-of-period value ($)	Cash receipts during period ($)
A	800	1,100	−100
B	120,000	118,000	15,000
C	45,000	48,000	7,000
D	600	500	80
E	12,500	12,400	1,500

2—12   **(Actual Return)**   Alex Williams wishes to estimate his returns during the past year on a number of securities he owns. Using the data summarized in the table below, find the actual return Alex would have earned during the year had he purchased the securities at the beginning price and sold them at the ending price.

Security	Cash dividends or interest received ($)	Market price Beginning ($)	Market price Ending ($)
A	2.00	30.00	34.00
B	0.00	25.00	27.00
C	2.50	17.50	16.00
D	1.00	86.00	89.50
E	3.00	63.50	54.00

2—13   **(Actual and Expected Return)**   The following data describe the actual return inputs as well as the expected returns on five securities for the year just ended.

Security	Cash dividends or interest received ($)	Market price Beginning ($)	Market price Ending ($)	Expected return (%)
A	4.50	22.50	21.00	15
B	2.00	17.00	19.00	20
C	0.00	64.00	67.50	8
D	1.50	25.00	26.50	12
E	3.20	30.00	26.00	10

   a. Calculate the actual return on each security for the year just ended.

   b. Evaluate each security's actual return in view of the expected return.

   c. If you owned each of the securities, what action, if any, would you take in view of your findings in **b**?

CASE

Finding Expected Investment Returns at Olive Industries

Dorothy Kline, a financial analyst at Olive Industries, wants to estimate the rate of return for two similar-risk investments—X and Y. Kline's research indicates that the immediate past returns will act as reasonable estimates of future return. A year earlier, investment X had a market value of $20,000 and investment Y, of $55,000. During the year, investment X generated cash flow of $1,500 and investment Y, of $6,800. The current market values of investments X and Y are $21,000 and $55,000, respectively.

Required

   a. Calculate the expected returns on investments X and Y using the most recent year's data.

   b. Assuming that the two investments are equally risky, which one should Kline recommend? Why?

CHAPTER 3

FINANCIAL STATEMENTS, DEPRECIATION, AND CASH FLOW

CHAPTER OBJECTIVES

After studying this chapter, you should be able to:

1 Describe the purpose and basic components of the stockholders' report.

2 Identify the format and key components of the income statement and the balance sheet, and interpret these statements.

3 Recognize the purpose and basic content of the statement of retained earnings and the statement of cash flows.

4 Understand the effect of depreciation on cash flow, the depreciable value and life of an asset, and the methods used to depreciate assets for tax purposes.

5 Discuss the firm's cash flows and develop and interpret the statement of cash flows.

6 Describe the key differences between purely domestic and international financial statements—particularly consolidation, translation of individual accounts, and international profits.

"Why the sudden interest in electronic tax filing? It's a real dollars-and-cents, cash flow thing."

The Electric Tax Collector

In 1988, the state of Indiana started a trend by becoming the first state in the nation to require electronic income tax payments from corporate taxpayers. By 1990, another 14 states had followed the Hoosier State's lead, and in the next few years, analysts predict that over half of all state governments will require corporate tax payments via electronic funds transfer (EFT).

Why the sudden interest in electronic tax payments? "It's a real dollars-and-cents, cash flow thing" explains Richard Sessions, manager of cash and banking at Quaker Oats Company in Chicago. Since electronic funds transfer payments reach state coffers after a single day's lag, tax revenue flows far more quickly to the government in EFT states than in states using the mail to collect taxes.

From the corporate taxpayer's perspective, however, electronic tax payments aren't entirely painless. The major problem taxpayers face with EFT taxes is deciphering various state formatting requirements that spell out how and when to forward tax information and taxes due to different taxing authorities. The problem is particularly challenging for firms that do business in a number of states, because different states use different standards.

To help businesses solve this problem and generate a bit of new cash flow in the process, Chicago's Harris Bank and the First National Bank of Chicago recently launched a service that takes the burden of electronic tax filing off the hands of harried corporate executives. For a reasonable fee, these banks format tax information and wire-transfer state tax payments for their corporate depositors. The Quaker Oats Company became one of the first customers at Harris Bank to sign up for the new service. Quaker's management team recognized that as more and more states switch to electronic tax collection, formatting problems will worsen.

In an increasingly technical world, good financial managers in both the public and private sectors of the economy need an expanding repertoire of technical skills. Managers must be able to read and interpret financial statement data, use these data to complete a variety of tax forms, and make decisions that enhance organizational cash flows. For state taxing authorities, one way to boost cash flow is to require electronic tax collection. For Harris Bank and First National Bank of Chicago, helping depositors prepare electronic tax returns improves corporate cash flow.

Every corporation has many and varied uses for the standardized records and reports of its financial activities. Periodically, reports must be prepared for regulators, creditors (lenders), owners, and management. Regulators, such as federal and state securities commissions, enforce the proper and accurate disclosure of corporate financial data. Creditors use financial data to evaluate the firm's ability to meet scheduled debt payments. Owners use corporate financial data in assessing the firm's financial condition and in deciding whether to buy, sell, or hold its stock. Management is concerned with regulatory compliance, satisfying creditors and owners, and monitoring the firm's performance.

The guidelines used to prepare and maintain financial records and reports are known as **generally accepted accounting principles (GAAP).** These accounting practices and procedures are authorized by the accounting profession's rule-setting body, the **Financial Accounting Standards Board (FASB).** In the sections that follow we will examine the most important of the various corporate documents that depend upon the application and interpretation of these fundamental accounting principles.

THE STOCKHOLDERS' REPORT

Publicly held corporations are those whose stock is traded on either an organized securities exchange or the over-the-counter exchange. These corporations are required by the **Securities and Exchange Commission (SEC)**—the federal regulatory body that governs the sale and listing of securities—and by state securities commissions to provide their stockholders with an annual **stockholders' report.** This report summarizes and documents the firm's financial activities during the past year. It begins with a letter to the stockholders from the firm's president or chairman of the board and is followed by the key financial statements. In addition, other information about the firm is often included.

The Letter to Stockholders

The **letter to stockholders** is the primary communication from management to the firm's owners. Typically the first element of the annual stockholders' report, it describes the events considered to have had the greatest impact on the firm during the year. In addition, the letter generally discusses management philosophy, strategies, and actions as well as plans for the coming year and their anticipated effects on the firm's financial condition. Figure 3.1 includes excerpts from the letter to the stockholders of Phillips Petroleum Company, from its 1989 stockholders' report. The letter summarizes key national and company events

generally accepted accounting principles (GAAP) The practice and procedure guidelines used to prepare and maintain financial records and reports.

Financial Accounting Standards Board (FASB) The accounting profession's rule-setting body.

publicly held corporations Corporations whose stock is traded on either an organized securities exchange or the over-the-counter exchange.

Securities and Exchange Commission (SEC) The federal regulatory body that governs the sale and listing of securities.

stockholders' report Annual report that summarizes and documents for stockholders the firm's financial activities during the past year.

letter to stockholders Typically the first element of the annual stockholders' report and the primary communication from management to the firm's owners.

Fellow Shareholders:

As our cover suggests, energy development *can* take place in harmony with the environment. Achieving this harmony will be the greatest challenge we face as a company and as an industry in the 1990s. To have the public support needed in our business, we'll need to find more ways to reduce the environmental impact of our actions. And we'll have to gain better public understanding of what we do and why our work is vital to society.

Key events in 1989 show why:

- In March, a tanker ran aground in Alaska. It spilled millions of gallons of crude oil in one of the nation's most scenic areas.

- Congress began consideration of a sweeping new Clean Air Act, legislation that would impose greater costs on society by restricting industrial activity and requiring consumers to change long-established patterns of behavior.

- And in August, an action by the California Coastal Commission blocked oil and gas production from the offshore Point Arguello field, the most significant oil discovery in the United States during the 1980s.

Phillips has a major interest in the Point Arguello field, and because of the regulatory stalemate, we felt it essential to reduce the value of our offshore California assets by $423 million ($280 million after taxes) in December. This writedown caused substantial negative results for the fourth quarter.

1989: Accomplishment and Tragedy

Our company's accomplishments in 1989, significant in many respects, were overshadowed by the tragic explosion and fire in October at the Houston Chemical Complex.

During 1989, both the Point Arguello writedown and the Houston explosion had a negative impact on net income, which was $219 million, or 90 cents a share, for the year, compared with $650 million, or $2.72 a share, in 1988.

Higher worldwide oil prices and higher worldwide natural gas production in 1989 were beneficial to our exploration and production operations. But these gains were more than offset by lower earnings in our downstream businesses.

A major positive development during the year was the further reduction of our total debt by $869 million. At year-end, total debt was $4 billion, down from a 1985 peak of $8.6 billion, and we are looking into refinancing alternatives to reduce interest costs.

1990 and Beyond: Seeking Superior Value

Looking ahead to 1990 and beyond, we're encouraged by the outlook for stability in oil prices, and we plan to spend 20 percent more this year on exploration and production than in 1989. Much of our success in the future will depend on our ability to increase oil and gas production—as well as replacing the reserves that we produce, a goal we've met in each of the past three years.

We believe that natural gas will gain recognition as a premium fuel in the 1990s. We're drilling more wells and expanding production to take full advantage of our extensive supplies.

In our refining, marketing and chemical businesses, we intend to build on our strong integration; that is, our ability to convert the raw materials we produce into high-value products. With lower economic growth expected for the next year or two, our marketing objectives are to make and sell more premium fuel, to continue consolidating into our most profitable markets, and to increase the number of high-volume company-operated service stations.

Our chemicals business continues to grow, although profit margins have dropped recently from record levels. We expect further growth and are continuing to invest in areas where we have particular strength.

Our overall mission as a company remains unchanged: To enhance the value of your investment as a shareholder. Our shareholders realized a total return of 35 percent in 1989 and 44 percent the year before. In carrying out our mission, we remain dedicated to a safe working environment, high standards of ethical conduct and a constantly improving record of environmental performance.

For the Board of Directors,

C. J. Silas
Chairman and Chief
Executive Officer

Glenn A. Cox
President and Chief
Operating Officer

March 12, 1990

Figure 3.1   **Excerpt from Phillips Petroleum Company's 1989 Letter to Stockholders**

The letter to stockholders is the first element of an annual report. It describes the key events—both positive and negative—considered to have had the greatest impact on the firm during the year. The letter also discusses management philosophy, strategies, and actions as well as plans for the coming year and their anticipated effects on the firm's financial condition.

during the year ended December 31, 1989, and discusses the outlook for 1990 and beyond.

Financial Statements

Following the letter to stockholders will be, at minimum, the four key financial statements required by the Securities and Exchange Commission (SEC). Those statements are (1) the income statement, (2) the balance sheet, (3) the statement of retained earnings, and (4) the statement of cash flows. The annual corporate report must contain these statements for at least the three most recent years of operation (two years for balance sheets). Historical summaries of key operating statistics and ratios for the past five to ten years are also commonly included with the financial statements. (Financial ratios are discussed in Chapter 4.)

Other Features

The stockholders' reports of most widely held corporations also include discussions of the firm's activities, new products, research and development, and the like. Most companies view the annual report not only as a requirement, but also as an important vehicle for influencing owners' perceptions of the company and its future outlook. Because of the information it contains, the stockholders' report may affect expected risk, return, stock price, and ultimately the viability of the firm.

BASIC FINANCIAL STATEMENTS

Our chief concern in this section is to understand the factual information presented in the four required corporate financial statements. The financial statements from the 1992 stockholders' report of a hypothetical firm, the Elton Corporation, are presented and briefly discussed below.

Income Statement

The **income statement** provides a financial summary of the firm's operating results during a specified period. Most common are income statements covering a one-year period ending at a specified date, ordinarily December 31 of the calendar year. (Many large firms, however, operate on a 12-month financial cycle, or *fiscal year*, that ends at a time other than December 31.) In addition, monthly statements are typically prepared for use by management, and quarterly statements must be made available to the stockholders of publicly held corporations.

Table 3.1 presents Elton Corporation's income statement for the year ended December 31, 1992. The statement begins with *sales revenue*—the total dollar amount of sales during the period—from which the *cost*

income statement
Provides a financial summary of the firm's operating results during a specified period.

Table 3.1   **Elton Corporation Income Statement ($000) for the Year Ended December 31, 1992**

Sales revenue		$1,700
Less: Cost of goods sold		1,000
Gross profits		$ 700
Less: Operating expenses		
Selling expense	$ 80	
General and administrative expense	150	
Depreciation expense	100	
Total operating expense		330
Operating profits		$ 370
Less: Interest expense[a]		70
Net profits before taxes		$ 300
Less: Taxes (rate = 40%)		120
Net profits after taxes		$ 180
Less: Preferred stock dividends		10
Earnings available for common stockholders		$ 170
Earnings per share (EPS)[b]		$ 1.70

[a]Interest expense includes the interest component of the annual financial lease payment as specified by the Financial Accounting Standards Board (FASB).
[b]Calculated by dividing the earnings available for common stockholders by the number of shares of common stock outstanding ($170,000 ÷ 100,000 shares = $1.70 per share).

of goods sold is deducted. The resulting *gross profits* of $700,000 represents the amount remaining to satisfy operating, financial, and tax costs after meeting the costs of producing or purchasing the products sold. Next *operating expenses,* which includes sales expense, general and administrative expense, and depreciation expense, is deducted from gross profits.[1] The resulting *operating profits* of $370,000 represents the profit earned from producing and selling products; it does not consider financial and tax costs. (Operating profit is often called *earnings before interest and taxes* or *EBIT.*) Next, the financial cost—interest expense—is subtracted from operating profits in order to find *net profits (or earnings) before taxes.* After subtracting $70,000 in 1992 interest, Elton Corporation had $300,000 of net profits before taxes.

After the appropriate tax rates have been applied to before-tax profits, taxes are calculated and deducted to determine *net profits (or earnings) after taxes.* Elton Corporation's net profits after taxes for 1992 were $180,000. Next, any preferred stock dividends must be subtracted from net profits after taxes to arrive at *earnings available for common stockholders.* This is the amount earned by the firm on behalf of the common stockholders during the period. Dividing earnings available for common stockholders by the number of shares of common stock outstanding results in *earnings per share (EPS).* EPS represents the

---

[1]Depreciation expense can be, and frequently is, included in manufacturing costs—cost of goods sold—in order to calculate gross profits. Depreciation is shown as an expense in this text in order to isolate its impact on cash flows.

ETHICS   IN   FINANCE

Financial Statement Preparation Within the Federal Government

Audited financial statements provide a formal record of business activities over a period of time, offer a means by which managers document their progress in meeting organizational goals, and prescribe a systematic framework for organizing and recording business revenue and costs. In short, audited financial statements help managers monitor and control the financial resources for which they are accountable.

Examining the lack of financial responsibility present in many recent projects managed by the federal government—including the savings and loan disaster, NASA's embarrassing failure in launching the Hubble space telescope, and the ever-expanding cost of the Stealth bomber—it probably comes as no surprise that the federal government is not required to prepare audited financial statements. But this may soon change.

Bills introduced in both the Senate and the House of Representatives in 1990 would require the government and its largest agencies to appoint a chief financial officer as well as prepare audited financial statements on an annual basis. Audits would be conducted by the Inspectors General, the Comptroller General, or an independent outside auditing firm.

It sounds like a proposal that should be passed into law immediately, right? According to Jared Burden, counsel for the House Government Operations Committee, "You're not going to see a law coming from this for several months, and probably not in this Congress." Do you think that Congress has an ethical responsibility to improve financial accountability within government?

Source: Lori Calabro, "Closing in on a federal CFO," CFO Magazine, October 1990, p. 16.

amount earned during the period on each outstanding share of common stock. In 1992 Elton Corporation earned $170,000 for its common stockholders, which represents $1.70 for each outstanding share. (The earnings per share amount rarely equals the amount, if any, of common stock dividends paid to shareholders.)

Balance Sheet

The **balance sheet** presents a summary statement of the firm's financial position at a given point in time. The statement balances the firm's *assets* (what it owns) against its financing, which can be either *debt*

balance sheet
Summary statement of the firm's financial position at a given point in time.

current assets
Short-term assets, expected to be converted into cash within one year or less.

current liabilities
Short-term liabilities, expected to be converted into cash within one year or less.

(what it owes) or *equity* (what was provided by owners). Elton Corporation's balance sheets on December 31 of 1992 and 1991, respectively, are presented in Table 3.2. They show a variety of asset, liability, and equity accounts. An important distinction is made between short-term and long-term assets and liabilities. The **current assets** and **current liabilities** are *short-term* assets and liabilities. This means that they are expected to be converted into cash within one year or less. All other assets and liabilities, along with stockholders' equity, which is assumed to

Table 3.2   **Elton Corporation Balance Sheets ($000)**

	December 31	
Assets	**1992**	**1991**
Current assets		
Cash	$ 400	$ 300
Marketable securities	600	200
Accounts receivable	400	500
Inventories	600	900
Total current assets	$2,000	$1,900
Gross fixed assets (at cost)		
Land and buildings	$1,200	$1,050
Machinery and equipment	850	800
Furniture and fixtures	300	220
Vehicles	100	80
Other (includes certain leases)	50	50
Total gross fixed assets (at cost)	$2,500	$2,200
Less: Accumulated depreciation	1,300	1,200
Net fixed assets	$1,200	$1,000
Total assets	$3,200	$2,900
Liabilities and stockholders' equity		
Current liabilities		
Accounts payable	$ 700	$ 500
Notes payable	600	700
Accruals	100	200
Total current liabilities	$1,400	$1,400
Long-term debt	$ 600	$ 400
Total liabilities	$2,000	$1,800
Stockholders' equity		
Preferred stock	$ 100	$ 100
Common stock—$1.20 par, 100,000 shares outstanding in 1992 and 1991	120	120
Paid-in capital in excess of par on common stock	380	380
Retained earnings	600	500
Total stockholders' equity	$1,200	$1,100
Total liabilities and stockholders' equity	$3,200	$2,900

have an infinite life, are considered *long-term*, or *fixed*, since they are expected to remain on the firm's books for one year or more.

A few points about Elton Corporation's balance sheets need to be highlighted. As is customary, the assets are listed beginning with the most liquid down to the least liquid. Current assets therefore precede fixed assets. *Marketable securities* represents very liquid short-term investments such as U.S. Treasury bills or certificates of deposit, held by the firm. Because of their highly liquid nature, marketable securities are frequently viewed as a form of cash. *Accounts receivable* represent the total monies owed the firm by its customers on credit sales made to them. *Inventories* include raw materials, work-in-process (partially finished goods), and finished goods held by the firm. The entry for *gross fixed assets* is the original cost of all fixed (long-term) assets owned by the firm.[2] *Net fixed assets* represents the difference between gross fixed assets and *accumulated depreciation*—the total expense recorded for the depreciation of fixed assets. (The net value of fixed assets is called their *book value*.)

Like assets, the liabilities and equity accounts are listed on the balance sheet from short-term to long-term. Current liabilities includes: *accounts payable*, amounts owed for credit purchases by the firm; *notes payable*, outstanding short-term loans, typically from commercial banks; and *accruals*, amounts owed for services for which a bill may not or will not be received. (Examples of accruals include taxes due the government and wages due employees.) *Long-term debt* represents debt for which payment is not due in the current year. *Stockholders' equity* represents the owners' claims on the firm. The *preferred stock* entry shows the historic proceeds from the sale of preferred stock ($100,000 for Elton Corporation). Next, the amount paid in by the original purchasers of common stock is shown by two entries—common stock and paid-in capital in excess of par on common stock. The *common stock* entry is the **par value** of common stock, an arbitrarily assigned per-share value used primarily for accounting purposes. **Paid-in capital in excess of par** represents the amount of proceeds in excess of the par value received from the original sale of common stock. The sum of the common stock and paid-in capital accounts divided by the number of shares outstanding represents the original price per share received by the firm on a single issue of common stock. Elton Corporation therefore received $5.00 per share [($120,000 par + $380,000 paid-in capital in excess of par) ÷ 100,000 shares] from the sale of its common stock. Finally, **retained earnings** represents the cumulative total of all earnings retained and reinvested in the firm since its inception. It is important to recognize that retained earnings *are not cash*, but rather have been utilized to finance the firm's assets.

Elton Corporation's balance sheets in Table 3.2 show that the firm's total assets increased from $2,900,000 in 1991 to $3,200,000 in

par value   Per-share value arbitrarily assigned to an issue of common stock.

paid-in capital in excess of par   The amount of proceeds in excess of the par value received from the original sale of common stock.

retained earnings   The cumulative total of all earnings retained and reinvested in the firm since its inception.

---

[2]For convenience the term *fixed assets* is used throughout this text to refer to what, in a strict accounting sense, is captioned "property, plant, and equipment." This simplification of terminology permits certain financial concepts to be more easily developed.

1992. The $300,000 increase was due primarily to the $200,000 increase in net fixed assets. The asset increase in turn appears to have been financed primarily by an increase of $200,000 in long-term debt. Better insight into these changes can be derived from the statement of cash flows, which we will discuss shortly.

Statement of Retained Earnings

statement of retained earnings Reconciles the net income earned, and any cash dividends paid, with the change in retained earnings between the start and end of a given year.

The **statement of retained earnings** reconciles the net income earned during a given year, and any cash dividends paid, with the change in retained earnings between the start and end of that year. Table 3.3 presents this statement for Elton Corporation for the year ended December 31, 1992. A review of the statement shows that the company began the year with $500,000 in retained earnings and had net profits after taxes of $180,000. From this amount it paid a total of $80,000 in dividends, resulting in year-end retained earnings of $600,000. Thus the net increase for Elton Corporation was $100,000 ($180,000 net profits after taxes minus $80,000 in dividends) during 1992.

Statement of Cash Flows

statement of cash flows Provides a summary of the firm's operating, investment, and financing cash flows, over a certain period.

The **statement of cash flows** provides a summary of the cash flows over the period of concern, typically the year just ended. The statement, which is sometimes called a "source and use statement," provides insight into the firm's operating, investment, and financing cash flows. It reconciles them with changes in its cash and marketable securities during the period of concern. Elton Corporation's statement of cash flows for the year ended December 31, 1992, is presented in Table 3.10 on page 81. However, before we look at the preparation of this statement, it is helpful to understand various aspects of depreciation.

DEPRECIATION

depreciation The systematic charging of a portion of the costs of fixed assets against annual revenues over time.

Business firms are permitted to systematically charge a portion of the costs of fixed assets against annual revenues. This allocation of historic cost over time is called **depreciation.** For tax purposes, the depreciation

Table 3.3   **Elton Corporation Statement of Retained Earnings ($000) for the Year Ended December 31, 1992**

Retained earnings balance (January 1, 1992)		$500
Plus: Net profits after taxes (for 1992)		180
Less: Cash dividends (paid during 1992)		
Preferred stock	($10)	
Common stock	(70)	(80)
Retained earnings balance (December 31, 1992)		$600

of corporate assets is regulated by the Internal Revenue Code, which experienced major changes under the *Tax Reform Act of 1986*. Because the objectives of financial reporting are sometimes different from those of tax legislation, a firm often will use different depreciation methods for financial reporting than those required for tax purposes. (An observer should thus not jump to the conclusion that a company is attempting to "cook the books" simply because it keeps two different sets of records.) Tax laws are used to accomplish economic goals such as providing incentives for corporate investment in certain types of assets, whereas the objectives of financial reporting are of course quite different.

Depreciation for tax purposes is determined using the **Accelerated Cost Recovery System (ACRS).**[3] For financial reporting purposes a variety of depreciation methods are available. Before discussing the methods of depreciating an asset, we must understand the relationship between depreciation and cash flows, the depreciable value of an asset, and the depreciable life of an asset.

Accelerated Cost Recovery System (ACRS)   System used to determine the depreciation of assets for tax purposes.

Depreciation and Cash Flows

The financial manager is concerned with cash flows rather than net profits as reported on the income statement. To adjust the income statement to show *cash flow from operations,* all noncash charges must be *added back* to the firm's *net profits after taxes.* **Noncash charges** are expenses that are deducted on the income statement but do not involve an actual outlay of cash during the period. Depreciation, amortization, and depletion allowances are examples. Since depreciation expenses are the most common noncash charges, we shall focus on their treatment; amortization and depletion charges are treated in a similar fashion.

noncash charges Expenses deducted on the income statement that do not involve an actual outlay of cash during the period.

The general rule for adjusting net profits after taxes by adding back all noncash charges is expressed as follows:

Cash flow from operations = net profits after taxes + noncash charges

Equation 3.1 Formula for determining cash flow from operations

Applying Equation 3.1 to the 1992 income statement for Elton Corporation presented earlier in Table 3.1 yields a cash flow from operations of $280,000 due to the noncash nature of depreciation:

Net profits after taxes	$180,000
Plus: Depreciation expense	100,000
Cash flow from operations	$280,000

(This value is only approximate since not all sales are made for cash and not all expenses are paid when they are incurred.)

---

[3]This system was first established in 1981 with passage of the *Economic Recovery Tax Act.* The *Tax Reform Act of 1986* revised this system, which is sometimes referred to as the "new" or "modified" accelerated cost recovery system (ACRS). For convenience, the new system is called "ACRS" throughout this text.

F I N A N C E   I N   A C T I O N

Depreciation Expenses on Trial at Liquid Paper

Although most businesses would like to depreciate all of the assets they own, the IRS can be picky when it comes to allowable depreciation deductions. Depreciation reduces tax revenue, because noncash depreciation expenses reduce taxable income reported by businesses to the IRS.

So what does it take to claim a legal depreciation deduction for a particular asset? The asset in question must have (1) an identifiable market value, and (2) a finite useful life that can be measured accurately. These requirements sound simple enough—at least until you start to apply them to actual business assets.

Take the case of Liquid Paper Corporation's quest to depreciate the white goop it manufactures to cover up typing mistakes. Liquid Paper claimed that the unpatented "secret formula" in its correction fluid had a known useful life. The IRS argued that the life of unpatented technology was unknowable. Accordingly, the IRS used a little white-out of its own to remove this depreciation deduction on Liquid Paper's tax return.

The case went to tax court, where Liquid Paper officials were able to demonstrate that the life of their trade secret was easy to define. The firm showed that technological advances in typewriter technology, such as the introduction of the microcomputer and word processing software in the business world, would destroy 95 percent of the market for correction fluid by 1995. The court agreed. Liquid Paper won back its depreciation deduction for the secret formula contained in its correction fluid.

Source: Patrick J. Sweet, "Technology need not be patented to be depreciated," *Taxation for Accountants*, August 1990, p. 110

Depreciation and other noncash charges shield the firm from taxes by lowering taxable income. Some people do not define depreciation as a source of funds. However, it is a source of funds in the sense that it represents a "nonuse" of funds. Table 3.4 shows the Elton Corporation's income statement prepared on a cash basis as an illustration of how depreciation shields income and acts as a nonuse of funds. Ignoring depreciation, except in determining the firm's taxes, results in cash flow from operations of $280,000—the value obtained above. Adjustment of the firm's net profits after taxes by adding back noncash charges such as depreciation will be used on many occasions in this text to estimate cash flow.

Table 3.4   **Elton Corporation Income Statement Calculated on a Cash Basis ($000) for the Year Ended December 31, 1992**

Sales revenue		$1,700
Less: Cost of goods sold		1,000
Gross profits		$ 700
Less: Operating expenses		
Selling expense	$ 80	
General and administrative expense	150	
Depreciation expense (noncash charge)	0	
Total operating expense		230
Operating profits		$ 470
Less: Interest expense		70
Net profits before taxes		$ 400
Less: Taxes (from Table 3.1)		120
Cash flow from operations		$ 280

Depreciable Value of an Asset

Under the basic ACRS procedures, the depreciable value of an asset (the amount to be depreciated) is its *full* cost including outlays for installation. No adjustment is required for expected salvage value.

EXAMPLE   Elton Corporation acquired a new machine at a cost of $38,000, with installation costs of $2,000. Regardless of its expected salvage value, the depreciable value of the machine is $40,000: ($38,000 cost + $2,000 installation cost).

Depreciable Life of an Asset

The time period over which an asset is depreciated—its **depreciable life**—can significantly affect the pattern of cash flows. The shorter the depreciable life, the more quickly the cash flow created by the depreciation write-off will be received. Given the financial manager's preference for faster receipt of cash flows, a shorter depreciable life is preferred to a longer one. However, the firm must abide by certain Internal Revenue Service (IRS) requirements for determining depreciable life. These ACRS standards, which apply to both new and used assets, require the taxpayer to use as an asset's depreciable life the appropriate ACRS **recovery period**, except in the case of certain assets depreciated under the *alternative depreciation system.*[4] There are six ACRS recovery periods— 3, 5, 7, 10, 15, and 20 years—excluding real estate. As is customary, the

depreciable life Time period over which an asset is depreciated.

recovery period The appropriate depreciable life of a particular asset as determined by ACRS.

---

[4]For convenience, the depreciation of assets under the *alternative depreciation system* is ignored in this text.

Table 3.5   **First Four Property Classes under ACRS**

Property class (recovery period)	Definition
3-year	Research and experiment equipment and certain special tools.
5-year	Computers, typewriters, copiers, duplicating equipment, cars, light-duty trucks, qualified technological equipment, and similar assets.
7-year	Office furniture, fixtures, most manufacturing equipment, railroad track, and single-purpose agricultural and horticultural structures.
10-year	Equipment used in petroleum refining or in the manufacture of tobacco products and certain food products.

property classes (excluding real estate) are referred to in accordance with their recovery periods, as 3-year, 5-year, 7-year, 10-year, 15-year, and 20-year property. The first four property classes—those routinely used by business—are defined in Table 3.5.

Depreciation Methods

For *tax purposes,* using ACRS recovery periods, assets in the first four property classes are depreciated by the double-declining balance (200%) method using the half-year convention and switching to straight line when advantageous. Although tables of depreciation percentages are not provided by law, the *approximate percentages* (i.e., rounded to nearest whole percent) written off each year for the first four property classes are given in Table 3.6 on page 74. Rather than using the percentages in the table, the firm can either use straight-line depreciation over the asset's recovery period with the half-year convention or use the alternative depreciation system. For purposes of this text, we will use the ACRS depreciation percentages given in Table 3.6, since they generally provide for the fastest write-off and therefore the best cash flow effects for the profitable firm.

Because ACRS requires use of the half-year convention, assets are assumed to be acquired in the middle of the year. Therefore only one-half of the first year's depreciation is recovered in the first year. As a result, the final half year of depreciation is recovered in the year immediately following the asset's stated recovery period. In Table 3.6 the depreciation percentages for an *n*-year class asset are given for $n + 1$ years. For example, a 5-year asset is depreciated over 6 recovery years. (*Note:* The percentages in Table 3.6 have been rounded to the nearest whole percentage in order to simplify calculations while retaining realism.)

For *financial reporting purposes* a variety of depreciation methods—straight-line, double-declining balance, and sum-of-the-years'-digits—can be used.[5] Since primary concern in managerial finance centers on cash flows, *only tax depreciation methods will be utilized throughout this textbook*. The application of the tax depreciation percentages given in Table 3.6 can be demonstrated by a simple example.

EXAMPLE   Elton Corporation acquired, for an installed cost of $40,000, a machine having a recovery period of five years. Using the applicable percentages from Table 3.6, the firm calculated the depreciation in each year as shown below.

Year	Cost (1)	Percentages (from Table 3.6) (2)	Depreciation [(1) × (2)] (3)
1	$40,000	20%	$ 8,000
2	40,000	32	12,800
3	40,000	19	7,600
4	40,000	12	4,800
5	40,000	12	4,800
6	40,000	5	2,000
Totals		100%	$40,000

Column 3 shows that the full cost of the asset is written off over six recovery years.

ANALYZING THE FIRM'S CASH FLOW

The *statement of cash flows*, briefly described earlier, summarizes the firm's cash flow over a given period of time. Because it can be used to capture historic cash flow, the statement is developed in this section. First, however, we need to discuss cash flow through the firm and the classification of sources and uses.

The Firm's Cash Flows

Figure 3.2 illustrates the firm's cash flows. Note that both cash and marketable securities, which because of their highly liquid nature are considered the same as cash, represent a reservoir of liquidity that is increased by cash inflows and decreased by cash outflows. Also note

---

[5]For a review of these depreciation methods as well as other aspects of financial reporting, see any recently published financial accounting text.

Table 3.6   **Rounded Depreciation Percentages by Recovery Year Using ACRS for First Four Property Classes**

	Percentage by recovery year[a]			
Recovery year	3-year	5-year	7-year	10-year
1	33%	20%	14%	10%
2	45	32	25	18
3	15	19	18	14
4	7	12	12	12
5		12	9	9
6		5	9	8
7			9	7
8			4	6
9				6
10				6
11				4
Totals	100%	100%	100%	100%

[a]These percentages have been rounded to the nearest whole percent in order to simplify calculations while retaining realism. In order to calculate the *actual* depreciation for tax purposes, be sure to apply the actual unrounded percentages or directly apply double-declining balance (200%) depreciation using the half-year convention.

that the firm's cash flows have been divided into (1) operating flows, (2) investment flows, and (3) financing flows. The **operating flows** are cash flows—inflows and outflows—directly related to production and sale of the firm's products and services. These flows capture the income statement and current account transactions (excluding notes payable) occurring during the period. **Investment flows** are cash flows associated with purchase and sale of both fixed assets and business interests. Clearly, purchase transactions would result in cash outflows whereas sales transactions would generate cash inflows. The **financing flows** result from debt and equity financing transactions. Borrowing and repaying either short-term debt (notes payable) or long-term debt would result in a corresponding cash inflow or outflow. Similarly the sale of stock would result in a cash inflow, whereas the repurchase of stock or payment of cash dividends would result in a financing outflow. In combination, the firm's operating, investment, and financing cash flows during a given period will increase, decrease, or leave unchanged the firm's cash and marketable securities balances.

operating flows Cash flows directly related to production and sale of the firm's products and services.

investment flows Cash flows associated with purchase and sale of both fixed assets and business interests.

financing flows Cash flows that result from debt and equity financing transactions.

Classifying Sources and Uses of Cash

The statement of cash flows in effect summarizes the sources and uses of cash during a given period. (Table 3.7 classifies the basic sources and uses of cash.) For example, if a firm's accounts payable increased by

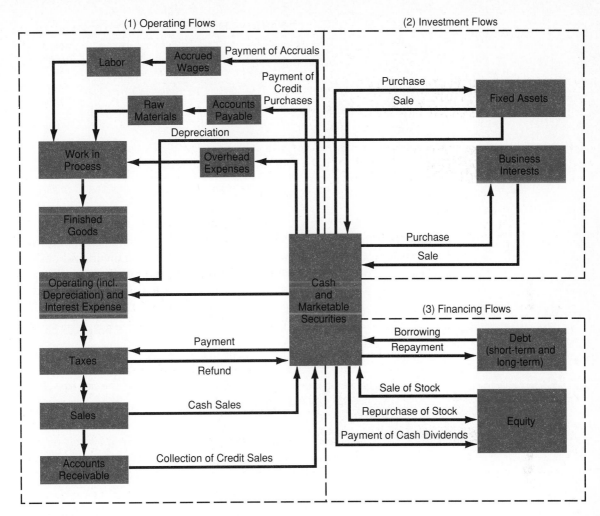

Figure 3.2   **The Firm's Cash Flows**

The firm's cash flows can be broken into (1) operating flows, (2) investment flows, and (3) financing flows. Operating flows are directly related to production and sale of the firm's products and services. Investment flows are associated with purchase and sale of both fixed assets and business interests. Financing flows result from debt and equity financing transactions.

$1,000 during the year, this change would be a *source of cash*. If the firm's inventory increased by $2,500, the change would be a *use of cash*, meaning that an additional $2,500 was tied up in inventory.

A few additional points should be made with respect to the classification scheme in Table 3.7:

1 ████ A *decrease* in an asset, such as the firm's cash balance, is a *source of cash flow* because cash is released for some purpose, such as adding to inventory. On the other hand, an *increase* in the firm's cash balance is a *use of cash flow* since the cash must be drawn from somewhere.

Table 3.7   **The Sources and Uses of Cash**

Sources	Uses
Decrease in any asset	Increase in any asset
Increase in any liability	Decrease in any liability
Net profits after taxes	Net loss
Depreciation and other noncash charges	Dividends paid
Sale of stock	Repurchase or retirement of stock

2 ▬▬ Earlier, Equation 3.1 and the related discussion explained why depreciation and other noncash charges are considered cash inflows, or sources of cash. Adding noncash charges back to the firm's net profits after taxes gives cash flow from operations:

Cash flow from operations =
                net profits after taxes + noncash charges

Note that a firm can have a *net loss* (negative net profits after taxes) and still have positive cash flow from operations when depreciation during the period is greater than the net loss. In the statement of cash flows, net profits after taxes (or net losses) and noncash charges are therefore treated as separate entries.

3 ▬▬ Because depreciation is treated as a separate source of cash, only *gross* rather than *net* changes in fixed assets appear on the statement of cash flows. This treatment avoids the potential double counting of depreciation.

4 ▬▬ Direct entries of changes in retained earnings are not included on the statement of cash flows. Instead, entries for items that affect retained earnings appear as net profits or losses after taxes and cash dividends.

Developing the Statement of Cash Flows

The statement of cash flows can be developed in three steps: (1) prepare a statement of sources and uses of cash, (2) obtain needed income statement data, and (3) properly classify and present relevant data from steps 1 and 2. With this three-step procedure, we can use the financial statements for Elton Corporation presented in Tables 3.1 and 3.2 to demonstrate the preparation of its December 31, 1992, statement of cash flows.

Statement of Sources and Uses of Cash
A three-step procedure can be used to prepare a statement of sources and uses of cash.

Step 1:   Calculate the balance sheet changes in assets, liabilities, and stockholders' equity over the period of concern. (*Note:* Calculate the *gross* fixed asset change for the fixed asset account along with any change in accumulated depreciation.)

Step 2:   Using the classification scheme in Table 3.7, classify each change calculated in Step 1 as either a source (S) or a use (U). (*Note:* An increase in accumulated depreciation would be classified as a source, whereas a decrease in accumulated depreciation would be a use. Changes in stockholders' equity accounts are classified in the same way as changes in liabilities— increases are sources and decreases are uses.)

Step 3:   Separately sum all sources and all uses found in Steps 1 and 2. If this statement is prepared correctly, *total sources should equal total uses.*

Application of the three-step procedure to prepare a statement of sources and uses of cash is demonstrated in the following example.

EXAMPLE   Elton Corporation's balance sheets in Table 3.2 can be used to develop its statement of sources and uses of cash for the year ended December 31, 1992.

> Step 1:   The key balance sheet entries from Elton Corporation's balance sheets in Table 3.2 are listed in a stacked format in Table 3.8. Column 1 lists the account name, and columns 2 and 3 give the December 31, 1992 and 1991 values, respectively, for each account. In column 4 the change in the balance sheet account between December 31, 1991, and December 31, 1992, is calculated. Note that for fixed assets, both the gross fixed asset change of +$300,000 and the accumulated depreciation change of +$100,000 are calculated.

> Step 2:   Based on the classification scheme from Table 3.7 and recognizing that changes in stockholders' equity are classified in the same way as changes in liabilities, each change in column 4 of Table 3.8 is listed as either a source in column 5 or a use in column 6.

> Step 3:   The sources and uses in columns 5 and 6, respectively, of Table 3.8 are totaled at the bottom. Since total sources of $1,000,000 equal total uses of $1,000,000, it appears that the statement has been correctly prepared.

Obtaining Income Statement Data

Three important inputs to the statement of cash flows must be obtained from an income statement for the period of concern. These inputs are (1) net profits after taxes, (2) depreciation and any other noncash charges,

Table 3.8   Elton Corporation Statement of Sources and Uses of Cash ($000)
                                         for the Year Ended December 31, 1992

| Account (1) | Account balance December 31 (from Table 3.2) | | Change [(2) − (3)] (4) | Classification | |
	1992 (2)	1991 (3)		Source (5)	Use (6)
Assets					
Cash	$ 400	$ 300	+$100		$ 100
Marketable securities	600	200	+ 400		400
Accounts receivable	400	500	− 100	$ 100	
Inventories	600	900	− 300	300	
Gross fixed assets	2,500	2,200	+ 300		300
Accumulated depreciation[a]	1,300	1,200	+ 100	100	
Liabilities					
Accounts payable	700	500	+ 200	200	
Notes payable	600	700	− 100		100
Accruals	100	200	− 100		100
Long-term debt	600	400	+ 200	200	
Stockholders' equity					
Preferred stock	100	100	0		
Common stock at par	120	120	0		
Paid-in capital in excess of par	380	380	0		
Retained earnings	600	500	+ 100	100	
			Totals	$1,000	$1,000

[a]Because accumulated depreciation is treated as a deduction from gross fixed assets, an increase in it is classified as a source; any decrease would be classified as a use.

and (3) cash dividends paid on both preferred and common stock. Net profits after taxes and depreciation typically can be taken directly from the income statement. Dividends may have to be calculated using the following equation:

Equation 3.2
Formula for finding dividends paid

Dividends = net profits after taxes − change in retained earnings

The value of net profits after taxes can be obtained from the income statement, and the change in retained earnings can be found in the statement of sources and uses of cash or can be calculated using the beginning- and end-of-period balance sheets. The dividend value could be obtained directly from the statement of retained earnings, if available.

EXAMPLE   For the Elton Corporation the values of net profits after taxes and depreciation for 1991 can be found on its income statement presented earlier in Table 3.1.

Net profits after taxes ($000)	$180
Depreciation ($000)	$100

Substituting the net profits after taxes value of $180,000 and the increase in retained earnings of $100,000 from Elton Corporation's statement of sources and uses of cash for the year ended December 31, 1992, given in Table 3.8, into Equation 3.2, we find the 1992 cash dividends to be:

$$\text{Dividend (\$000)} = \$180 - \$100 = \$80$$

Note that the $80,000 of dividends calculated above could have been drawn directly from Elton's statement of retained earnings, given in Table 3.3.

Classifying and Presenting Relevant Data

The relevant data from the statement of sources and uses of cash along with the net profit, depreciation, and dividend data obtained from the income statement can be used to prepare the statement of cash flows. Two steps are required to complete this process.

Step 1: Classify relevant data into one of three categories:

1. Cash flow from operating activities

2. Cash flow from investment activities

3. Cash flow from financing activities

These three categories are consistent with the operating, investment, and financing cash flows depicted in Figure 3.2. Table 3.9 lists the items that would be included in each category on the statement of cash flows. In addition the source of each data item is noted.

Step 2: List relevant data in a fashion consistent with the order of the categories and data items listed in Table 3.9. All sources as well as net profits after taxes and depreciation would be treated as positive values—cash inflows. All uses, any losses, and dividends paid would be treated as negative values—cash outflows. The items in each category—operating, investment, and financing—should be totaled and these three totals added to get the "net increase (decrease) in cash and marketable securities" for the period. As a check, this value should reconcile with actual change in cash and marketable securities for the year, which can be obtained from either the beginning- and end-of-period balance sheets or the statement of sources and uses of cash for the period.

EXAMPLE   The relevant data developed for Elton Corporation for 1992 can be combined using the two-step procedure above to create its statement of cash flows. Applying these steps, we would get the resulting statement presented in Table 3.10. Based on this statement, the firm experienced a $500,000 increase in cash and marketable securities during 1992. Looking at Elton Corporation's December 31, 1991

Table 3.9   Categories and Sources of Data Included
                                       in the Statement of Cash Flows

Categories and data items	Data source S/U = Statement of sources and uses of cash I/S = Income statement
Cash Flow from Operating Activities	
Net profits (losses) after taxes	I/S
Depreciation and other noncash charges	I/S
Changes in all current assets other than cash and marketable securities	S/U
Changes in all current liabilities other than notes payable	S/U
Cash Flow from Investment Activities	
Changes in gross fixed assets	S/U
Changes in business interests	S/U
Cash Flow from Financing Activities	
Changes in notes payable	S/U
Changes in long-term debt	S/U
Changes in stockholders' equity other than retained earnings	S/U
Dividends paid	I/S

and 1992 balance sheets in Table 3.2 or its statement of sources and uses of cash in Table 3.8, we can see that the firm's cash increased by $100,000 and its marketable securities increased by $400,000 between December 31, 1991, and December 31, 1992. The $500,000 net increase in cash and marketable securities from the statement of cash flows therefore reconciles with the total change of $500,000 in these accounts during 1992. The statement is therefore believed to have been correctly prepared.

Interpreting the Statement

The statement of cash flows allows the financial manager and other interested parties to analyze the firm's past and possibly future cash flow. The manager should pay special attention to both the major categories of cash flow and the individual items of cash inflow and outflow in order to assess whether any developments have occurred that are contrary to the company's financial policies. In addition, the statement can be used to evaluate the fulfillment of projected goals. Specific links between cash inflows and outflows cannot be made using this statement, but it can be used to isolate inefficiencies. For example, increases in accounts receivable and inventories resulting in major cash outflows may, respectively, signal credit or inventory problems.

Table 3.10   Elton Corporation Statement of Cash Flows ($000)
                          for the Year Ended December 31, 1992

Cash Flow from Operating Activities

Net profits after taxes	$ 180	
Depreciation	100	
Decrease in accounts receivable	100	
Decrease in inventories	300	
Increase in accounts payable	200	
Decrease in accruals	(100)[a]	
Cash provided by operating activities		$780
Cash Flow from Investment Activities		
Increase in gross fixed assets	($300)	
Changes in business interests	0	
Cash used for investment activities		(300)
Cash Flow from Financing Activities		
Decrease in notes payable	($100)	
Increase in long-term debts	200	
Changes in stockholders' equity[b]	0	
Dividends paid	(80)	
Cash provided by financing activities		20
Net increase in cash and marketable securities		$500

[a]As is customary, parentheses are used to denote a negative number, which in this case is a cash outflow.
[b]Consistent with this data item in Table 3.9, retained earnings are excluded here since their change is actually reflected in the combination of the net profits after taxes and dividend entries.

In addition, the financial manager can prepare and analyze a statement of cash flows developed from projected, or pro forma, financial statements. This approach can be used to determine whether planned actions are desirable in view of the resulting cash flows.

EXAMPLE   Analysis of Elton Corporation's statement of cash flows in Table 3.10 does not seem to indicate the existence of any major problems for the company. Its $780,000 of cash provided by operating activities plus the $20,000 provided by financing activities was used to invest an additional $300,000 in fixed assets and to increase cash and marketable securities by $500,000. The individual items of cash inflow and outflow seem to be distributed in a fashion consistent with prudent financial management. The firm seems to be growing since (1) less than half of its earnings ($80,000 out of $180,000) was paid to owners as dividends, and (2) gross fixed assets increased by three times the amount of historic cost written off through depreciation expense ($300,000 increase in gross fixed assets versus $100,000 in depreciation expense). Major cash inflows were realized by decreasing inventories and increasing accounts payable. The major outflow of cash was to increase cash and marketable securities by $500,000 and thereby improve liquidity. Other inflows and outflows of Elton Corporation tend to support the fact that the firm was well managed financially during the period. *An understanding of the basic financial principles presented throughout this text is a prerequisite to the effective interpretation of the statement of cash flows.*

INTERNATIONAL DIMENSION: FINANCIAL STATEMENTS

Several features distinguish domestically oriented financial statements and internationally based reports. Among these are the issues of consolidation, translation of individual accounts within the financial statements, and overall reporting of international profits.

Consolidation

At the present time the rules in the United States require the consolidation of financial statements of subsidiaries according to the percentage of ownership by the parent of the subsidiary. Table 3.11 illustrates this point. As indicated, the regulations range from requiring a one-line income-item reporting of dividends, to a pro rata inclusion of profits and losses, to a full disclosure in the balance sheet and income statement. (When ownership is less than 50 percent, since the balance sheet and thus the subsidiary's financing do not get reported, it is possible for the parent MNC to have off-balance-sheet financing.)

Translation of Individual Accounts

Unlike domestic items in financial statements, international items require translation back into U.S. dollars. Since December 1982 all finan-

Table 3.11   **United States Rules for Consolidation of Financial Statements**

Percentage of beneficial ownership by parent in subsidiary	Consolidation for financial reporting purposes
0–19%	Dividends as received
20–49%	Pro rata inclusions of profits and losses
50–100%	Full consolidation[a]

[a]Consolidation may be avoided in the case of some majority-owned foreign operations if the parent can convince its auditors that it does not have control of the subsidiaries or if there are substantial restrictions on the repatriation of cash.

Source: Rita M. Rodriguez and E. Eugene Carter, *International Financial Management*, 3rd ed. (Englewood Cliffs, NJ: Prentice-Hall, 1984), p. 492.

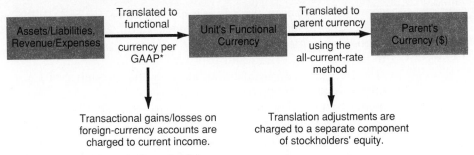

Figure 3.3   **Details of FASB No. 52**

Under FASB No. 52, financial statement accounts are first translated using GAAP into the country's functional currency, which is then translated using the all-current-rate method into the parent firm's currency. The first translation can result in transaction (cash) gains or losses, and the second can result in translation (accounting) adjustments.

cial statements of U.S. multinationals have to conform to Statement No. 52 issued by the Financial Accounting Standards Board (FASB). The basic rules of FASB No. 52 are given in Figure 3.3.

Under **FASB No. 52,** the *current rate method* is implemented in a two-step process. First, each entity's balance sheet and income statement are *measured* in terms of their functional currency by using generally accepted accounting principles (GAAP). That is, before financial statements are submitted to the parent for consolidation foreign-currency elements are translated by each subsidiary into the **functional currency.** This is the currency of the economic environment in which an entity primarily generates and expends cash, and in which its accounts are maintained.

The second step, as shown in Figure 3.3, is to use the **all-current-rate method** to translate the functional-currency–denominated financial statements into the parent's currency. This method requires the translation of all balance sheet items at the closing rate and all income statement items at average rates.

Each of these steps can result in certain gains or losses. The first step can lead to transaction (cash) gains or losses, which, whether realized or not, are charged directly to net income. The second step can result in translation (accounting) adjustments, which are excluded from current income. Instead, they are disclosed and charged to a separate component of stockholders' equity.

FASB No. 52
Statement requiring U.S. MNCs first to convert financial statement accounts of foreign subsidiaries into their *functional currency* and then to translate them into the parent firm's currency using the *all-current-rate method.*

functional currency
The currency in which a business entity primarily generates and expends cash and in which its accounts are maintained.

all-current-rate method   The method by which the functional-currency–denominated financial statements of an MNC's subsidiary are translated into the parent company's currency.

International Profits

Prior to January 1976, the practice for most U.S. multinationals was to utilize a special account called the *reserve account* to show "smooth" international profits. Excess international profits due to favorable exchange fluctuations were deposited in this account. Withdrawals were made during periods of high losses stemming from unfavorable exchange movements. The overall result was to display a smooth pattern in an MNC's international profits.

Between 1976 and 1982, however, the existence of *FASB No. 8* required that both transaction gains or losses and translation adjustments be included in net income, with the separate disclosure of only the aggregate foreign exchange gain or loss. This requirement caused highly visible swings in the reported net earnings of U.S. multinationals. Under FASB No. 52, only certain transactional gains or losses are reflected in the income statement. Overall, assuming a positive income flow for a subsidiary, the income statement risk will be positive and will be similarly enhanced or reduced by an appreciation or depreciation of the functional currency.

SUMMARY

1   **Describe the purpose and basic components of the stockholders' report.** The annual stockholders' report, which publicly held corporations are required to provide to their stockholders, summarizes and documents the firm's financial activities during the past year. It includes, in addition to the letter to stockholders and various subjective and factual information, four key financial statements: (1) the income statement, (2) the balance sheet, (3) the statement of retained earnings, and (4) the statement of cash flows.

2   **Identify the format and key components of the income statement and the balance sheet, and interpret these statements.** The income statement summarizes operating results during the period of concern by subtracting costs, expenses, and taxes from sales revenue in order to find the period's profits. The balance sheet summarizes the firm's financial position at a given point in time by balancing the firm's assets (what it owns) against its financing, which can be either debt (what it owes) or equity (what was provided by owners). The statement makes an important distinction between short-term (current) and long-term assets and liabilities.

3   **Recognize the purpose and basic content of the statement of retained earnings and the statement of cash flows.** The statement of retained earnings reconciles the net income earned during a given year, and any cash dividends paid, with the change in retained earnings between the start and end of that year. The statement of cash flows provides a summary of the cash flows over the period of concern, typically the year just ended. The statement provides insight into the firm's operating, investment, and financing cash flows, and reconciles them with changes in its cash and marketable securities during the period of concern.

4   **Understand the effect of depreciation on cash flow, the depreciable value and life of an asset, and the methods used to depreciate assets for tax purposes.** Depreciation, or the allocation of historic cost, is the most common type of corporate noncash expenditure. To estimate cash flow from operations, depreciation and any other noncash charges are added back to net profits after taxes. The depreciable value of an asset and its depreciable life are determined using the Accelerated Cost Recovery System (ACRS) standards set out in the federal tax code. ACRS groups assets (excluding real estate) into six property classes based on length of recovery period—3, 5, 7, 10, 15, and 20 years—and can be applied over the appropriate period using a schedule of yearly depreciation percentages for each period.

5 **Discuss the firm's cash flows, and develop and interpret the statement of cash flows.** The cash flow of a firm over a given period of time can be summarized in the statement of cash flows which is broken into operating, investment, and financing flows. The statement can be developed in three steps: (1) prepare a statement of sources and uses of cash, (2) obtain needed income statement data, and (3) properly classify and present relevant data from steps 1 and 2. The "net increase (decrease) in cash and marketable securities" found in the statement should reconcile with the actual change in cash and marketable securities during the period. Interpretation of the statement of cash flows requires an understanding of basic financial principles and involves evaluation of both the major categories of cash flow and the individual items of cash inflow and outflow.

6 **Describe the key differences between purely domestic and international financial statements—particularly consolidation, translation of individual accounts, and international profits.** Certain regulations that apply to international operations tend to complicate the preparation of foreign-based financial statements. Rulings in the United States require the consolidation of financial statements of subsidiaries according to the percentage of ownership by the parent in the subsidiary. Individual accounts of subsidiaries must be translated back into U.S. dollars using the procedures outline in FASB No. 52. This standard also requires that only certain transactional gains or losses from international operations be included in the U.S. parent's income statement.

QUESTIONS

3—1 What are *generally accepted accounting principles (GAAP)?* Who authorizes GAAP? What role does the *Securities and Exchange Commission (SEC)* play in the financial reporting activities of corporations?

3—2 Describe the basic contents, including the key financial statements, included in the stockholders' reports of publicly held corporations.

3—3 What basic information is contained in each of the following financial statements? Briefly describe each.
   a. Income statement
   b. Balance sheet
   c. Statement of retained earnings

3—4 In what sense does depreciation act as cash inflow? How can a firm's after-tax profits be adjusted to determine cash flow from operations?

3—5 Briefly describe the first four Accelerated Cost Recovery System (ACRS) property classes and recovery periods. Explain how the depreciation percentages are determined using the ACRS recovery periods.

3—6 Describe the overall cash flow through the firm in terms of (a) operating flows, (b) investment flows, and (c) financing flows.

3—7 List and describe *sources of cash* and *uses of cash.* Discuss why a decrease in cash is a source and an increase in cash is a use.

3—8 Describe the three-step procedure used to develop a statement of sources and uses of cash. How are changes in fixed assets and accumulated depreciation treated on this statement?

3—9 What three inputs to the statement of cash flows are typically obtained from an income statement for the period of concern? Explain how the income statement and statement of sources and uses of cash can be used to determine dividends for the period of concern. What other methods can be used to obtain the value of dividends?

3—10 Describe the general format of the statement of cash flows, and review the two steps involved in preparing the final statement. How can the accuracy of the final statement balance, "net increase (decrease) in cash and marketable securities," be conveniently verified?

3—11   How is the statement of cash flows interpreted and used by the financial manager and other interested parties?

3—12   State the rules for consolidation of foreign subsidiaries. Under FASB No. 52, what are the translation rules for financial statement accounts?

PROBLEMS

3—1   **(Reviewing Basic Financial Statements)** The income statement for the year ended December 31, 1992, the balance sheets for December 31, 1992 and 1991, and the statement of retained earnings for the year ended December 31, 1992, for Gold Equipment Company are given below and on page 87. Briefly discuss the form and informational content of each of these statements.

Income statement
Gold Equipment Company
for the year ended December 31, 1992

Sales revenue		$600,000
Less: Cost of goods sold		460,000
Gross profits		$140,000
Less: Operating expenses		
General and administrative expense	$30,000	
Depreciation expense	30,000	
Total operating expense		60,000
Operating profits		$ 80,000
Less: Interest expense		10,000
Net profits before taxes		$ 70,000
Less: Taxes		27,100
Earnings available for common stockholders		$ 42,900
Earnings per share (EPS)		$2.15

Balance sheets
Gold Equipment Company

	December 31	
Assets	**1992**	**1991**
Cash	$ 15,000	$ 16,000
Marketable securities	7,200	8,000
Accounts receivable	34,100	42,200
Inventories	82,000	50,000
Total current assets	$138,300	$116,200
Land and buildings	$150,000	$150,000
Machinery and equipment	200,000	190,000
Furniture and fixtures	54,000	50,000
Other	11,000	10,000
Total gross fixed assets	$415,000	$400,000
Less: Accumulated depreciation	145,000	115,000
Net fixed assets	$270,000	$285,000
Total assets	$408,300	$401,200

Liabilities and stockholders' equity		
Accounts payable	$ 57,000	$ 49,000
Notes payable	13,000	16,000
Accruals	5,000	6,000
Total current liabilities	$ 75,000	$ 71,000
Long-term debt	$150,000	$160,000
Stockholders' equity		
Common stock equity (20,000 shares outstanding)	$110,200	$120,000
Retained earnings	73,100	50,200
Total stockholders' equity	$183,300	$170,200
Total liabilities and stockholders' equity	$408,300	$401,200

Statement of retained earnings
Gold Equipment Company
for the year ended December 31, 1992

Retained earnings balance (January 1, 1992)	$50,200
Plus: Net profits after taxes (for 1992)	42,900
Less: Cash dividends (paid during 1992)	(20,000)
Retained earnings balance (December 31, 1992)	$73,100

3—2   **(Financial Statement Account Identification)** Mark each of the accounts listed in the table below as follows:
a. In column (1) indicate in which statement—income statement (IS) or balance sheet (BS)—the account belongs.
b. In column (2) indicate whether the account is a current asset (CA), current liability (CL), expense (E), fixed asset (FA), long-term debt (LTD), revenue (R), or stockholders' equity (SE).

Account name	(1) Statement	(2) Type of account
Accounts payable	————	————
Accounts receivable	————	————
Accruals	————	————
Accumulated depreciation	————	————
Administrative expense	————	————
Buildings	————	————
Cash	————	————
Common stock (at par)	————	————
Cost of goods sold	————	————
Depreciation	————	————
Equipment	————	————
General expense	————	————
Interest expense	————	————
Inventories	————	————

Land	_____	_____
Long-term debt	_____	_____
Machinery	_____	_____
Marketable securities	_____	_____
Notes payable	_____	_____
Operating expense	_____	_____
Paid-in capital in excess of par	_____	_____
Preferred stock	_____	_____
Preferred stock dividends	_____	_____
Retained earnings	_____	_____
Sales revenue	_____	_____
Selling expense	_____	_____
Taxes	_____	_____
Vehicles	_____	_____

3—3   **(Income Statement Preparation)** Use the *appropriate items* from those listed below to prepare in good form Driscoll Corporation's income statement for the year ended December 31, 1992.

Item	Values ($000) at or for year ended December 31, 1992
Accounts receivable	$350
Accumulated depreciation	205
Cost of goods sold	285
Depreciation expense	55
General and administrative expense	60
Interest expense	25
Preferred stock dividends	10
Sales revenue	525
Selling expense	35
Stockholders' equity	265
Taxes	rate = 40%

3—4   **(Income Statement Preparation)** Mary Hernandez, a self-employed Certified Public Accountant (CPA), on December 31, 1992, completed her first full year in business. During the year she billed $160,000 in business. She had two employees, a bookkeeper and a clerical assistant. In addition to her *monthly* salary of $3,500, she paid annual salaries of $22,000 and $16,000, respectively, to the bookkeeper and the clerical assistant. Employment taxes and benefit costs for health insurance, etc., for Ms. Hernandez and her employees totaled $15,800 for the year. Expenses for office supplies, including postage, totaled $4,800 for the year. In addition, Ms. Hernandez spent $7,500 during the year on travel and entertainment associated with client visits and new business development. Lease payments for the office space rented (a tax-deductible expense) were $1,250 *per month*. Depreciation expense on the office furniture fixtures was $7,200 for the year. During the year,

Ms. Hernandez paid interest of $7,500 on the $55,000 borrowed to start the business. She paid an average tax rate of 30 percent during 1992.

a. Prepare an income statement for Mary Hernandez, CPA, for the year ended December 31, 1992.

b. How much cash flow from operations did Mary realize during 1992?

c. Evaluate her 1992 financial performance.

3—5 **(Calculation of EPS and Retained Earnings)**   Zach, Inc. ended 1992 with net profit *before* taxes of $218,000. The company is subject to a 40 percent tax rate and must pay $32,000 in preferred stock dividends prior to distributing any earnings on the 85,000 shares of common stock currently outstanding.

a. Calculate Zach, Inc.'s 1992 earnings per share (EPS).

b. If the firm paid common stock dividends of $.80 per share, how many dollars would go to retained earnings?

3—6 **(Balance Sheet Preparation)**   Use the *appropriate items* from those listed in the table below to prepare in good form Kowalski Corporation's balance sheet at December 31, 1992.

Item	Value ($000) at December 31, 1992
Accounts payable	$ 220
Accounts receivable	450
Accruals	55
Accumulated depreciation	265
Buildings	225
Cash	215
Common stock (at par)	90
Cost of goods sold	2,500
Depreciation expense	45
Equipment	140
Furniture and fixtures	170
General expense	320
Inventories	375
Land	100
Long-term debt	420
Machinery	420
Marketable securities	75
Notes payable	475
Paid-in capital in excess of par	360
Preferred stock	100
Retained earnings	210
Sales revenue	3,600
Vehicles	25

3—7 **(Initial Sale Price of Common Stock)**   OK Industries has one issue of preferred stock and one issue of common stock outstanding. Given OK's stockholders' equity account below, determine the original price per share at which the firm sold its single issue of common stock.

Stockholders' equity ($000)	
Preferred stock	$ 125
Common stock ($.75 par, 300,000 shares outstanding)	225
Paid-in capital in excess of par on common stock	2,625
Retained earnings	900
Total stockholders' equity	$3,875

3—8   **(Financial Statement Preparation)** The balance sheet for Todd Enterprises for December 31, 1991, is given below. Following the statement is information relevant to Todd's 1992 operations. Using the data presented:

a. Prepare in good form an income statement for Todd Enterprises for the year ended December 31, 1992. Be sure to show earnings per share (EPS).

b. Prepare in good form a balance sheet for Todd Enterprises for December 31, 1992.

Balance sheet ($000)
Todd Enterprises
December 31, 1991

Assets		Liabilities and stockholders' equity	
Cash	$ 40	Accounts payable	$ 50
Marketable securities	10	Notes payable	80
Accounts receivable	80	Accruals	10
Inventories	100	Total current liabilities	$140
Total current assets	$230	Long-term debt	$270
Gross fixed assets	$890	Preferred stock	$ 40
Less: Accumulated depreciation	240	Common stock ($.75 par, 80,000 shares)	60
Net fixed assets	$650	Paid-in capital in excess of par	260
Total assets	$880	Retained earnings	110
		Total stockholders' equity	$470
		Total liabilities and stockholders' equity	$880

Relevant information
Todd Enterprises

1. Sales in 1992 were $1,200,000.

2. Cost of goods sold equals 60 percent of sales.

3. Operating expenses equals 15 percent of sales.

4. Interest expense is 10 percent of the total beginning balance of notes payable and long-term debts.

5. The firm pays 40 percent taxes on ordinary income.

6. Preferred stock dividends of $4,000 were paid in 1992.

7. Cash and marketable securities are unchanged.

8. Accounts receivable equals 8 percent of sales.

9. Inventory equals 10 percent of sales.

10. The firm acquired $30,000 of additional fixed assets in 1992.

11. Total depreciation expense in 1992 was $20,000.

12. Accounts payable equals 5 percent of sales.

13. Notes payable, long-term debt, preferred stock, common stock, and paid-in capital in excess of par remain unchanged.

14. Accruals are unchanged.

15. Cash dividends of $119,000 were paid to common stockholders in 1992.

3—9   **(Statement of Retained Earnings)** Colton Cosmetics began 1992 with a retained earnings balance of $928,000. During 1992 the firm earned $377,000 after taxes. From this amount preferred stockholders were paid $47,000 in dividends. At year-end 1992 the firm's retained earnings totaled $1,048,000. The firm had 140,000 shares of common stock outstanding during 1992.
  a. Prepare a statement of retained earnings for the year ended December 31, 1992, for Colton Cosmetics. (*Note:* Be sure to calculate and include the amount of common stock dividends paid in 1992.)
  b. Calculate the firm's 1992 earnings per share (EPS).
  c. How large a per share cash dividend did the firm pay on common stock during 1992?

3—10   **(Cash Flow)** A firm had earnings after taxes of $50,000 in 1992. Depreciation charges were $28,000, and a $2,000 charge for amortization of a bond discount was incurred. What was the firm's cash flow from operations during 1992?

3—11   **(Depreciation)** On January 1, 1992, Antex Corporation acquired two new assets. Asset A was research equipment costing $17,000 and having a three-year recovery period. Asset B was duplicating equipment having an installed cost of $45,000 and a five-year recovery period. Using the ACRS depreciation percentages in Table 3.6 on page 74, prepare a depreciation schedule for each of these assets.

3—12   **(Depreciation and Cash Flow)** A firm in the third year of depreciating its only asset, originally costing $180,000 and having a five-year ACRS recovery period, has gathered the following data relative to the given year's operations.

Accruals	$ 15,000
Current assets	120,000
Interest expense	15,000
Sales revenue	400,000
Inventory	70,000
Total costs before depreciation, interest, and taxes	290,000
Tax rate on ordinary income	40%

  a. Use the *relevant data* above to determine the *cash flow from operations* for the current year.
  b. Explain the impact that depreciation, as well as any other noncash charges, has on a firm's cash flows.

3—13   **(Classifying Sources and Uses)** Classify each of the following items as a source (S) or a use (U) of funds, or as neither (N).

Item	Change ($)	Item	Change ($)
Cash	+100	Accounts receivable	−700
Accounts payable	−1,000	Net profits	+600
Notes payable	+500	Depreciation	+100
Long-term debt	−2,000	Repurchase of stock	+600
Inventory	+200	Cash dividends	+800
Fixed assets	+400	Sale of stock	+1,000

3—14   **(Finding Dividends Paid)** Vent Manufacturing's net profits after taxes in 1992 totaled $186,000. The firm's year-end 1992 and 1991 retained earnings on its balance sheet totaled $812,000 and $736,000, respectively. How many dollars, if any, in dividends did Vent pay in 1992?

3—15   **(Preparing a Statement of Cash Flows)** Given the balance sheets and selected data from the income statement of Raney Russell Company below and on page 93:

a. Prepare the firm's statement of cash flows for the year ended December 31, 1992.

b. Reconcile the resulting "net increase (decrease) in cash and marketable securities" with the actual change in cash and marketable securities for the year.

c. Interpret the statement prepared in **a.**

Balance sheets
Raney Russell Company

Assets	December 31 1992	December 31 1991
Cash	$ 1,500	$ 1,000
Marketable securities	1,800	1,200
Accounts receivable	2,000	1,800
Inventories	2,900	2,800
Total current assets	$ 8,200	$ 6,800
Gross fixed assets	$29,500	$28,100
Less: Accumulated depreciation	14,700	13,100
Net fixed assets	$14,800	$15,000
Total assets	$23,000	$21,800

Liabilities and stockholders' equity		
Accounts payable	$ 1,600	$ 1,500
Notes payable	2,800	2,200
Accruals	200	300
Total current liabilities	$ 4,600	$ 4,000
Long-term debt	$ 5,000	$ 5,000
Common stock	$10,000	$10,000
Retained earnings	3,400	2,800
Total stockholders' equity	$13,400	$12,800
Total liabilities and stockholders' equity	$23,000	$21,800

Income statement data (1992)	
Depreciation expense	$ 1,600
Net profits after taxes	1,400

3—16   **(Preparing a Statement of Cash Flows)** Using the 1992 income statement and the 1992 and 1991 balance sheets for Gold Equipment Company, given in Problem 3–1:
a. Prepare the firm's statement of cash flows for the year ended December 31, 1992.
b. Reconcile the resulting "net increase (decrease) in cash and marketable securities" with the actual change in cash and marketable securities for the year.
c. Interpret the statement prepared in **a**.

CASE

Analyzing Ace Software's Cash Flows

Charles Hart, formerly a practicing CPA, founded, owns, and operates Ace Software—a company that develops and markets cost accounting software to the construction industry. Charles just received his firm's 1992 income statement, balance sheet, and statement of retained earnings, shown below along with the 1991 balance sheet. While he is quite pleased to have achieved record earning of $48,000 in 1992, he is concerned about the firm's cash flows. Specifically, he is finding it more and more difficult to pay the firm's bills in a timely manner. In order to gain insight into these cash flow problems, Charles is planning to have the firm's 1992 statement of cash flows prepared and evaluated.

Income statement ($000)
Ace Software
for the year ended December 31, 1992

Sales revenue		$1,550
Less: Cost of goods sold		1,030
Gross profits		$ 520
Less: Operating expenses		
Selling expense	$150	
General and administrative expense	270	
Depreciation expense	11	
Total operating expense		431
Operating profits		$ 89
Less: Interest expense		29
Net profits before taxes		$ 60
Less: Taxes (20%)		12
Net profits after taxes		$ 48

Balance sheets ($000)
Ace Software

	December 31	
Assets	**1992**	**1991**
Current assets		
Cash	$ 12	$ 31
Marketable securities	66	82
Accounts receivable	152	104
Inventories	191	145
Total current assets	$421	$362
Gross fixed assets	$195	$180
Less: Accumulated depreciation	63	52
Net fixed assets	$132	$128
Total assets	$553	$490

Liabilities and stockholders' equity		
Current liabilities		
Accounts payable	$136	$126
Notes payable	200	190
Accruals	27	25
Total current liabilities	$363	$341
Long-term debt	$ 38	$ 40
Total liabilities	$401	$381
Stockholders' equity		
Common stock (100,000 shares at		
$0.20 par value)	$ 20	$ 20
Paid-in capital in excess of par	30	30
Retained earnings	102	59
Total stockholders' equity	$152	$109
Total liabilities and stockholders' equity	$553	$490

Statement of retained earnings ($000)
Ace Software
for the year ended December 31, 1992

Retained earnings balance (January 1, 1992)	$ 59
Plus: Net profits after taxes (for 1992)	48
Less: Cash dividends on common stock (paid during 1992)	(5)
Retained earnings balance (December 31, 1992)	$102

Required

    a. Use the financial data presented to prepare Ace Software's statement of cash flows for the year ended December 31, 1992.

    b. Evaluate the statement prepared in **a** in light of Ace's current cash flow difficulties.

    c. Based on your evaluation in **b**, what recommendations might you offer Charles?

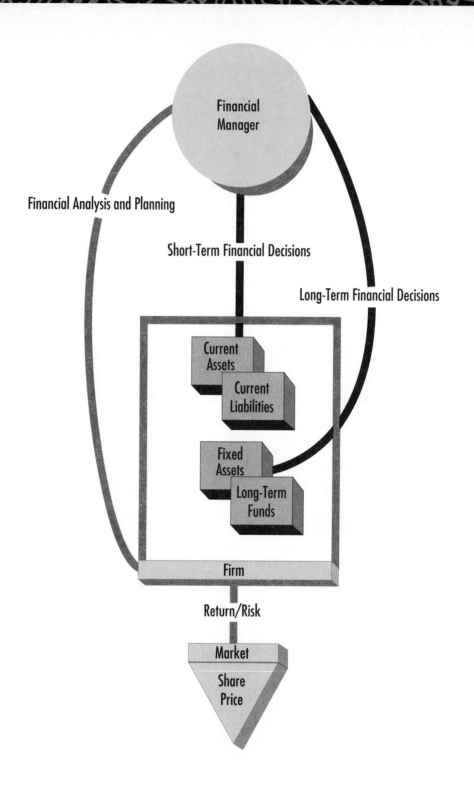

FINANCIAL ANALYSIS AND PLANNING

CHAPTER 4

FINANCIAL STATEMENT ANALYSIS

After studying this chapter, you should be able to:

1 Understand the parties interested in performing financial ratio analysis and the common types of ratio comparisons.

2 Describe some of the cautions that should be considered when performing financial ratio analysis.

3 Use popular ratios to analyze a firm's liquidity and the activity of inventory, accounts receivable, accounts payable, fixed assets, and total assets.

4 Assess the firm's debt position as well as its ability to meet the payments associated with debt.

5 Evaluate a firm's profitability relative to sales, asset investment, owners' equity investment, and share value.

6 Use the DuPont system and a summary analysis of a large number of ratios to evaluate a firm's financial status and make appropriate recommendations.

Kathy Braun's Prescription for Ailing Western Digital Corporation

❝The firm's financial statements show unsold inventory, high labor costs, and low-tech consumer products with small profit margins.❞

In the next few years, Kathy Braun has a great deal of work to do. As the executive vice president in charge of all business operations at Western Digital Corporation, Braun faces a number of vexing problems in the highly competitive computer industry. As one of the firm's senior managers, it's her job to solve these problems.

Western Digital manufactures hard-disk drives, the mass storage devices found on most new microcomputers. The firm posted an impressive track record in the 1980s, moving from near bankruptcy in 1978 to record earnings of $46 million in 1987. Sustaining this financial performance into the 1990s won't be easy.

In 1989, Western Digital's earnings fell 29 percent, to $24.2 million, and sales revenue rose just 8 percent, to $1.07 billion. The company has been slow to introduce new products, and the financial results for 1990 were expected to show a disappointing loss.

So what's the problem at Western Digital? A quick look at the firm's financial statements shows a dangerous level of unsold inventory, above-average labor costs, and excessive dependence on low-technology consumer products that generate small profit margins for the firm.

What's the solution? Braun has prepared a strategy to address each of Western Digital's financial problems. First, she plans to write down on the firm's balance sheet the value of aging inventory that remains unsold. This action will reduce Western Digital's profits in the short run. But it will ultimately improve the firm's efficiency in transforming inventory into sales and reduce the firm's net investment in inventory. Second, Braun is slashing labor costs by eliminating full-time positions within the firm. Third, she is changing Western Digital's business strategy by developing low-margin products such as PC add-in boards for networking and graphic applications. To improve corporate profits, she is focusing on products that combine several different computer components into a single modular unit. These products yield a significantly higher gross profit margin for Western Digital.

Braun used financial statement analysis, the topic of this chapter, to locate, diagnose, and recommend a treatment for ailing Western Digital Corporation.

In the preceding chapter we studied the format, components, and primary purpose of each of the firm's four basic financial statements. The information contained in these statements is of major significance to shareholders, creditors, and managers, all of whom regularly need to have relative measures of the company's operating efficiency and condition. *Relative* is the key word here since the analysis of financial statements is based on the knowledge and use of *ratios* or *relative values*.

THE USE OF FINANCIAL RATIOS

ratio analysis
Involves the methods of calculating and interpreting financial ratios in order to assess the firm's performance and status.

Ratio analysis involves the methods of calculating and interpreting financial ratios in order to assess the firm's performance and status. The basic inputs to ratio analysis are the firm's income statement and balance sheet for the periods to be examined. However, before proceeding further we need to describe the various interested parties and the types of ratio comparisons.

Interested Parties

Ratio analysis of a firm's financial statements is of interest to shareholders, creditors, and the firm's own management. Both present and prospective shareholders are interested in the firm's current and future level of risk and return. As will be explained in Chapter 12, these two dimensions directly affect share price. The firm's creditors are primarily interested in the short-term liquidity of the company and in its ability to make interest and principal payments. A secondary concern of creditors is the firm's profitability; they want assurance that the business is healthy and will continue to be successful. Management, like stockholders, must be concerned with all aspects of the firm's financial situation. Thus it attempts to operate in a manner that will result in financial ratios that will be considered favorable by both owners and creditors. In addition, management uses ratios to monitor the firm's performance from period to period. Any unexpected changes are examined in order to isolate developing problems.

Types of Comparisons

Ratio analysis is not merely the application of a formula to financial data in order to calculate a given ratio. More important is the *interpretation* of the ratio value. To answer such questions as, Is it too high or too low? Is it good or bad?, a meaningful standard or basis for comparison is needed. Two types of ratio comparisons can be made: cross-sectional and time-series.

Cross-Sectional Analysis

Cross-sectional analysis involves the comparison of different firms' financial ratios at the same point in time. The typical business is interested in how well it has performed in relation to its competitors. If the competitors are also corporations, their reported financial statements should be available for analysis. Often the firm's performance will be compared to that of the industry leader, and the firm may uncover major operating differences, which, if changed, will increase efficiency. Another popular type of comparison is to industry averages. These figures can be found in the *Almanac of Business and Industrial Financial Ratios, Dun & Bradstreet's Key Business Ratios, Business Month, FTC Quarterly Reports, Robert Morris Associates Statement Studies,* and other sources such as industry association publications.[1] A sample from one available source of industry averages is given in Table 4.1.

cross-sectional analysis The comparison of different firms' financial ratios at the same point in time.

Table 4.1   **Industry Average Ratios for Selected Lines of Business[a]**

Line of business (number of concerns reporting)	Quick ratio (X)	Current ratio (X)	Current liabilities to net worth (%)	Current liabilities to inventory (%)	Total liabilities to net worth (%)	Fixed assets to net worth (%)	Collection period (days)	Sales to inventory (X)	Total assets to sales (%)	Sales to net working capital (X)	Accounts payable to sales (%)	Return on sales (%)	Return on total assets (%)	Return on net worth (%)
Crude oil and	3.2	5.2	6.0	92.7	10.5	16.8	29.2	59.7	112.6	7.6	4.7	21.0	7.8	14.8
natural gas	1.1	1.7	22.9	295.7	42.6	51.5	62.8	21.7	214.3	2.8	11.9	6.8	2.1	3.7
(2285)	0.6	0.9	72.9	596.0	141.4	113.0	121.9	9.5	352.2	1.1	29.3	(8.1)	(3.8)	(7.0)
Crude oil	1.4	2.1	9.1	212.0	33.4	92.1	14.2	75.0	101.1	24.1	2.4	36.3	27.9	54.2
pipelines	0.7	1.5	21.6	465.9	100.2	110.0	27.4	46.6	143.9	10.9	3.8	28.1	16.5	31.3
(79)	0.2	1.0	43.6	721.3	174.6	247.2	35.1	26.1	238.5	3.9	7.4	16.6	6.8	15.4
Department	2.5	6.3	14.3	28.1	17.2	6.0	6.2	6.2	37.4	6.7	2.8	3.9	7.6	15.7
stores	1.3	3.7	32.3	50.1	55.1	18.2	24.1	4.5	49.2	3.8	4.8	1.7	3.3	6.6
(1892)	0.4	2.1	76.8	77.9	146.3	52.1	52.6	3.2	69.0	2.5	7.7	0.3	0.6	1.2
Grocery	1.4	4.3	19.5	32.0	32.0	21.5	1.1	25.2	12.4	32.6	1.3	2.9	12.2	28.3
stores	0.6	2.2	46.6	70.3	83.2	50.9	2.3	17.3	18.0	16.9	2.4	1.4	6.0	13.1
(2183)	0.3	1.3	110.8	117.6	197.8	111.5	6.2	11.8	28.2	9.4	4.0	0.4	1.7	4.5
Petroleum	1.2	2.2	27.3	108.4	62.3	58.0	21.1	20.1	37.0	25.9	4.6	6.1	9.0	22.3
refining	0.8	1.5	59.1	187.3	133.6	119.6	33.3	13.7	48.4	12.6	7.9	3.3	5.1	12.0
(231)	0.5	1.1	106.6	299.3	218.6	173.1	50.7	9.2	92.8	6.5	11.3	0.9	1.3	5.2
Specialized	1.9	3.4	29.8	76.3	42.5	17.5	29.9	19.1	35.7	13.1	3.0	9.4	13.0	1.1
industrial	1.0	1.8	75.6	143.1	110.3	38.8	50.0	8.0	49.8	6.0	5.7	3.7	5.8	1.6
machinery	0.6	1.2	176.8	234.0	223.0	79.8	71.0	4.7	72.0	3.3	10.3	1.1	12.4	4.4
(756)														

[a]These values are given for each ratio for each line of business. The center value is the median, and the values immediately above and below it are the upper and lower quartiles, respectively.
Source: Values for 1989 provided courtesy of Dun & Bradstreet Business Credit Services, Murray Hill, NJ.

---

[1]Cross-sectional comparisons of firms operating in several lines of business are difficult to perform. The use of weighted-average industry average ratios based on the firm's product line mix or, if data are available, analysis of the firm on a product-line basis can be performed to analyze a multiproduct firm.

The comparison of a particular ratio to the standard is made in order to isolate any *deviations from the norm*. Many people mistakenly believe that in the case of ratios for which higher values are preferred, as long as the firm being analyzed has a value in excess of the industry average, it can be viewed favorably. However, this "bigger is better" viewpoint can be misleading. Quite often a ratio value that has a large but positive deviation from the norm can be indicative of problems. These may, upon more careful analysis, be more severe than had the ratio been below the industry average.[2] It is therefore important for the analyst to investigate *significant deviations to either side* of the industry standard.

The analyst must also recognize that ratio comparisons resulting in large deviations from the norm reflect only the *symptoms* of a problem. Further analysis of the financial statements coupled with discussions with key managers is typically required to isolate the *causes* of the problem. Once this is accomplished, the financial manager must develop prescriptive actions for eliminating such causes. The fundamental point is that *ratio analysis merely directs the analyst to potential areas of concern; it does not provide conclusive evidence as to the existence of a problem.*

EXAMPLE   In early 1993 Marie Sanchez, the chief financial analyst at Dwiggins Manufacturing, a producer of refrigeration equipment, gathered data on the firm's financial performance during 1992, the year just ended. She calculated a variety of ratios and obtained industry averages for use in making comparisons. One ratio she was especially interested in was inventory turnover, which reflects the speed with which the firm moves its inventory from raw materials through production into finished goods and to the customer as a completed sale. Generally, higher values of this ratio are preferred, since they indicate a quicker turnover of inventory. Dwiggins Manufacturing's calculated inventory turnover for 1992 and the industry average inventory turnover were, respectively:

	Inventory turnover, 1992
Dwiggins Manufacturing	14.8
Industry average	9.7

Marie's initial reaction to these data was that the firm had managed its inventory significantly better than the av-

---

[2]Similarly, in the case of ratios for which "smaller is better," one must be as concerned with calculated values that deviate significantly *below* the norm, or industry average, as with values that fall above it. Significant deviations, regardless of the side of the norm, require further investigation by the analyst.

erage firm in the industry. The turnover was in fact nearly 53 percent faster than the industry average. Upon reflection, however, she felt there could be a problem, since a very high inventory turnover could also mean very low levels of inventory. In turn, the consequence of low inventory could be excessive stockouts (insufficient inventory). Marie's review of other ratios and discussions with persons in the manufacturing and marketing departments did in fact uncover such a problem: The firm's inventories during the year were extremely low as a result of numerous production delays that hindered its ability to meet demand and resulted in lost sales. What had initially appeared to reflect extremely efficient inventory management was actually the symptom of a major problem.

Time-Series Analysis

Time-series analysis is applied when a financial analyst evaluates performance over time. Comparison of current to past performance, using ratio analysis, allows the firm to determine whether it is progressing as planned. Developing trends can be seen by using multiyear comparisons, and knowledge of these trends should assist the firm in planning future operations. As in cross-sectional analysis, any significant year-to-year changes can be evaluated to assess whether they are symptomatic of a major problem. The theory behind time-series analysis is that the company must be evaluated in relation to its past performance, developing trends must be isolated, and appropriate action taken to direct the firm toward immediate and long-run goals. Time-series analysis is often helpful in checking the reasonableness of a firm's projected (pro forma) financial statements. A comparison of *current* and *past* ratios to those resulting from an analysis of *projected* statements may reveal discrepancies or overoptimism.

time-series analysis
Evaluation of the firm's financial performance over time using financial ratio analysis.

Combined Analysis

The most informative approach to ratio analysis is one that combines cross-sectional and time-series analyses. A combined view permits assessment of the trend in the behavior of the ratio in relation to the trend for the industry. Figure 4.1 depicts this type of approach using the average collection period ratio of Alcott Oil Company, a small manufacturer of lubricating oil, over the years 1989–1992. Generally, lower values of this ratio, which reflects the average amount of time it takes the firm to collect bills, are preferred. A look at the figure quickly discloses that (1) Alcott Oil's effectiveness in collecting its receivables is poor in comparison to the industry, and (2) there is a trend toward longer collection periods. Clearly Alcott Oil needs to shorten its collection period.

Some Words of Caution

Before discussing specific ratios, we should consider the following cautions:

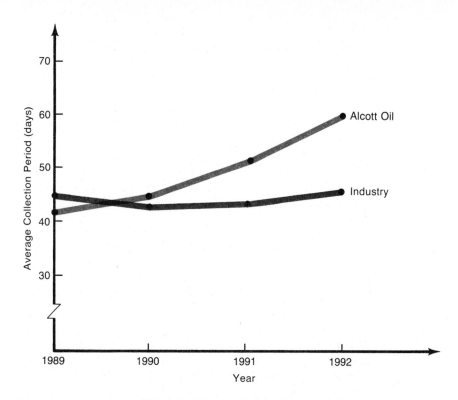

Figure 4.1   **Combined Cross-Sectional and Time-Series View
of Alcott Oil Company's Average Collection Period, 1989–1992**

Combining cross-sectional and time-series analysis permits assessment of
the trend in the behavior of the ratio in relation to the trend for the
industry. Alcott Oil's collection of receivables is poor both in comparison
to the industry and in its trend.

1 ▦   A single ratio does not generally provide sufficient information
       from which to judge the overall performance of the firm. Only
       when a group of ratios is used can reasonable judgments be
       made. If an analysis is concerned only with certain specific as-
       pects of a firm's financial position, one or two ratios may be
       sufficient.

2 ▦   The financial statements being compared should be dated at the
       same point in time during the year. If not, the effects of seasonal-
       ity may produce erroneous conclusions and decisions. For exam-
       ple, comparison of the inventory turnover of a toy manufacturer
       at the end of June with its end-of-December value can be mis-
       leading. The relatively high inventory at the end of June would
       result in a low inventory turnover, whereas at year-end the low
       inventory balance would result in a very high inventory turn-
       over. Clearly the seasonal impact of the December holiday sell-
       ing season would make the firm's inventory management falsely

appear to have greatly improved. Erroneous conclusions such as this can be avoided by comparing results for June of the current year to June of the prior year, December to December, and so forth.

3 ▰▰▰ It is preferable to use audited financial statements for ratio analysis. If the statements have not been audited, there may be no reason to believe that the data contained in them reflect the firm's true financial condition.

4 ▰▰▰ The financial data being compared should have been developed in the same way. The use of differing accounting treatments—especially relative to inventory and depreciation—can distort the results of ratio analysis, regardless of whether cross-sectional or time-series analysis is used.

5 ▰▰▰ When we compare the ratios of one firm to another or a firm to itself over time, results can be distorted due to inflation. Inflation can cause the book values of inventory and depreciable assets to greatly differ from their true (replacement) values. Additionally, inventory costs and depreciation write-offs can differ from their true values, thereby distorting profits. These inflationary effects typically have greater impact the larger the differences in the ages of the assets of the firms being compared. Without adjustment, inflation tends to cause older firms (older assets) to appear more efficient and profitable than newer firms (newer assets). Clearly, care must be taken when comparing ratios of older to newer firms or a firm to itself over a long period of time.

Groups of Financial Ratios

Financial ratios can for convenience be divided into four basic groups or categories: liquidity ratios, activity ratios, debt ratios, and profitability ratios. Liquidity, activity, and debt ratios primarily measure risk; profitability ratios measure return. In the near-term, the important elements are liquidity, activity, and profitability, since these provide the information critical to the short-run operation of the firm. (If a firm cannot survive in the short run, we need not be concerned with its longer-term prospects.) Debt ratios are useful primarily when the analyst is sure the firm will successfully weather the short run.

As a rule, the necessary inputs to an effective financial analysis include, at minimum, the income statement and the balance sheet. The 1992 and 1991 income statements and balance sheets for Alcott Oil Company are presented in Tables 4.2 and 4.3, respectively, to demonstrate calculation of the ratios presented in the remainder of this chapter.

Table 4.2   Alcott Oil Company Income Statements ($000)

	For the years ended December 31	
	1992	1991
Sales revenue	$3,074	$2,567
Less: Cost of goods sold	2,088	1,711
Gross profits	$ 986	$ 856
Less: Operating expenses		
Selling expense	$ 100	$ 108
General and administrative expenses	194	187
Lease expense[a]	35	35
Depreciation expense	239	223
Total operating expense	$ 568	$ 553
Operating profits	$ 418	$ 303
Less: Interest expense	93	91
Net profits before taxes	$ 325	$ 212
Less: Taxes (rate = 29%)[b]	94	64
Net profits after taxes	$ 231	$ 148
Less: Preferred stock dividends	10	10
Earnings available for common stockholders	$ 221	$ 138
Earnings per share (EPS)[c]	$ 2.90	$ 1.81

[a]Lease expense is shown here as a separate item rather than included as interest expense and amortization as specified by the FASB for financial reporting purposes. The approach used here is consistent with tax reporting rather than financial reporting procedures.
[b]The 29 percent tax rate for 1992 results from the fact that the firm has certain special tax write-offs that do not show up directly on its income statement.
[c]Calculated by dividing the earnings available for common stockholders by the number of shares of common stock outstanding—76,262 in 1992 and 76,244 in 1991. Earnings per share in 1992: ($221,000 ÷ 76,262 = $2.90); in 1991: ($138,000 ÷ 76,244 = $1.81).

▓ ANALYZING LIQUIDITY

liquidity A firm's ability to satisfy its short-term obligations as they come due.

The **liquidity** of a business firm is measured by its ability to satisfy its short-term obligations *as they come due*. Liquidity refers to the solvency of the firm's *overall* financial position—the ease with which it can pay its bills. The three basic measures of liquidity are (1) net working capital, (2) the current ratio, and (3) the quick (acid-test) ratio.

Net Working Capital

net working capital
A measure of liquidity, calculated by subtracting current liabilities from current assets.

Net working capital, although not actually a ratio, is commonly used to measure a firm's overall liquidity. It is calculated as follows:

Net working capital = current assets − current liabilities

Table 4.3   **Alcott Oil Company Balance Sheets ($000)**

Assets	December 31	
	1992	1991
Current assets		
Cash	$ 363	$ 288
Marketable securities	68	51
Accounts receivable	503	365
Inventories	289	300
Total current assets	$1,223	$1,004
Gross fixed assets (at cost)[a]		
Land and buildings	$2,072	$1,903
Machinery and equipment	1,866	1,693
Furniture and fixtures	358	316
Vehicles	275	314
Other (includes financial leases)	98	96
Total gross fixed assets (at cost)	$4,669	$4,322
Less: Accumulated depreciation	2,295	2,056
Net fixed assets	$2,374	$2,266
Total assets	$3,597	$3,270

Liabilities and stockholders' equity		
Current liabilities		
Accounts payable	$ 382	$ 270
Notes payable	79	99
Accruals	159	114
Total current liabilities	$ 620	$ 483
Long-term debts (includes financial leases)[b]	$1,023	$ 967
Total liabilities	$1,643	$1,450
Stockholders' equity		
Preferred stock—cumulative 5%, $100 par, 2,000 shares authorized and issued[c]	$ 200	$ 200
Common stock—$2.50 par, 100,000 shares authorized, shares issued and outstanding in 1992: 76,262; in 1991: 76,244	191	190
Paid-in capital in excess of par on common stock	428	418
Retained earnings	1,135	1,012
Total stockholders' equity	$1,954	$1,820
Total liabilities and stockholders' equity	$3,597	$3,270

[a]In 1992, the firm has a six-year financial lease requiring annual beginning-of-year payments of $35,000. Four years of the lease have yet to run.
[b]Annual principal repayments on a portion of the firm's total outstanding debt amount to $71,000.
[c]The annual preferred stock dividend would be $5 per share (5% × $100 par), or a total of $10,000 annually ($5 per share × 2,000 shares).

The net working capital for Alcott Oil in 1992 is

$$\text{Net working capital} = \$1,223,000 - \$620,000 = \$603,000$$

This figure is *not* useful for comparing the performance of different firms, but is quite useful for internal control.[3] A time-series comparison of the firm's net working capital is often helpful in evaluating its operations.

Current Ratio

current ratio A measure of liquidity, calculated by dividing the firm's current assets by its current liabilities.

The **current ratio,** one of the most commonly cited financial ratios, measures the firm's ability to meet its short-term obligations. It is expressed as follows:

$$\text{Current ratio} = \frac{\text{current assets}}{\text{current liabilities}}$$

The current ratio for Alcott Oil in 1992 is

$$\frac{\$1,223,000}{\$620,000} = 1.97$$

A current ratio of 2.0 is occasionally cited as acceptable, but acceptability of the value depends on the industry in which a firm operates. For example, a current ratio of 1.0 would be considered acceptable for a utility but might be unacceptable for a manufacturing firm. The more predictable a firm's cash flows, the lower the acceptable current ratio. Since Alcott Oil is in a business with a relatively predictable annual cash flow, its current ratio of 1.97 should be quite acceptable.

It is useful to note that whenever a firm's current ratio is 1.0, its net working capital is zero. If a firm has a current ratio of less than 1.0, it will have negative net working capital. Net working capital is useful only in comparing the liquidity of the same firm over time. It should not be used to compare the liquidity of different firms; the current ratio should be used, instead, for that purpose.

Quick (Acid-Test) Ratio

quick (acid-test) ratio A measure of liquidity, calculated by dividing the firm's current assets minus inventory by current liabilities.

The **quick (acid-test) ratio** is similar to the current ratio except that it excludes inventory which is generally the least liquid current asset. The quick ratio is calculated as follows:

$$\text{Quick ratio} = \frac{\text{current assets} - \text{inventory}}{\text{current liabilities}}$$

---

[3]To make cross-sectional as well as better time-series comparisons, *net working capital as a percent of sales* can be calculated. For Alcott Oil in 1992 this ratio would be 19.6 percent ($603,000 ÷ $3,074,000). In general, the larger this value, the greater the firm's liquidity, and vice versa. Because of the relative nature of this measure, it is often used to make liquidity comparisons.

The quick ratio for Alcott Oil in 1992 is

$$\frac{\$1,223,000 - \$289,000}{\$620,000} = \frac{\$934,000}{\$620,000} = 1.51$$

A quick ratio of 1.0 or greater is occasionally recommended, but, as with the current ratio, an acceptable value depends largely on the industry. The quick ratio provides a better measure of overall liquidity only when a firm's inventory cannot easily be converted into cash. If inventory is liquid, the current ratio is a preferred measure of overall liquidity.

ANALYZING ACTIVITY

Activity ratios are used to measure the speed with which various accounts are converted into sales or cash. Measures of liquidity are generally inadequate because differences in the composition of a firm's current assets and liabilities can significantly affect the firm's "true" liquidity. For example, consider the current portion of the balance sheets for firms A and B in the following table:

activity ratios
Measure the speed with which various accounts are converted into sales or cash.

Firm A			
Cash	$ 0	Accounts payable	$ 0
Marketable securities	0	Notes payable	10,000
Accounts receivable	0	Accruals	0
Inventories	20,000	Total current liabilities	$10,000
Total current assets	$20,000		

Firm B			
Cash	$ 5,000	Accounts payable	$ 5,000
Marketable securities	5,000	Notes payable	3,000
Accounts receivable	5,000	Accruals	2,000
Inventories	5,000	Total current liabilities	$10,000
Total current assets	$20,000		

Both firms appear to be equally liquid since their current ratios are both 2.0 ($20,000 ÷ $10,000). However, a closer look at the differences in the composition of current assets and liabilities suggests that *firm B is more liquid than firm A*. This is true for two reasons: First, firm B has more liquid assets in the form of cash and marketable securities than firm A, which has only a single and relatively illiquid asset in the form of inventories. Second, firm B's current liabilities are in general more flexible than the single current liability—notes payable—of firm A.

It is therefore important to look beyond measures of overall liquidity to assess the activity (liquidity) of specific current accounts. A number of ratios are available for measuring the activity of the most important current accounts, which include inventory, accounts receivable, and accounts payable. The activity (efficiency of utilization) of fixed and total assets can also be assessed.

Inventory Turnover

inventory turnover
Measures the activity, or liquidity, of a firm's inventory.

Inventory turnover commonly measures the activity, or liquidity, of a firm's inventory. It is calculated as follows:

$$\text{Inventory turnover} = \frac{\text{cost of goods sold}}{\text{inventory}}$$

Note that since inventory is measured at cost, cost of goods sold rather than sales is used in the numerator for consistency. Applying this relationship to Alcott Oil in 1992 yields

$$\text{Inventory turnover} = \frac{\$2,088,000}{\$289,000} = 7.2$$

The resulting turnover is meaningful only when compared with that of other firms in the same industry or to the firm's past inventory turnover. An inventory turnover of 20.0 would not be unusual for a grocery store, whereas a common inventory turnover for an aircraft manufacturer would be 4.0.

average age of inventory The average length of time inventory is held by the firm.

Inventory turnover can easily be converted into an **average age of inventory** by dividing it into 360—the number of days in a year.[4] For Alcott Oil, the average age of inventory would be 50.0 days (360 ÷ 7.2). This value can also be viewed as the average number of days' sales in inventory.

Average Collection Period

average collection period The average amount of time needed to collect accounts receivable.

The **average collection period,** or average age of accounts receivable, is useful in evaluating credit and collection policies.[5] It is arrived at by dividing the average daily sales[6] into the accounts receivable balance:

---

[4]Unless otherwise specified, a 360-day year consisting of twelve 30-day months is assumed throughout this text. This assumption allows some simplification of the calculations used to illustrate key concepts.

[5]A discussion of the evaluation and establishment of credit and collection policies is presented in Chapter 9.

[6]The formula as presented assumes, for simplicity, that all sales are made on a credit basis. If such is not the case, *average credit sales per day* should be substituted for average sales per day.

$$\text{Average collection period} = \frac{\text{accounts receivable}}{\text{average sales per day}}$$

$$= \frac{\text{accounts receivable}}{\dfrac{\text{annual sales}}{360}}$$

The average collection period for Alcott Oil in 1992 is

$$\frac{\$503,000}{\dfrac{\$3,074,000}{360}} = \frac{\$503,000}{\$8,539} = 58.9 \text{ days}$$

On the average it takes the firm 58.9 days to collect an account receivable.

The average collection period is meaningful only in relation to the firm's credit terms. If, for instance, Alcott Oil extends 30-day credit terms to customers, an average collection period of 58.9 days may indicate a poorly managed credit or collection department, or both. Of course, the lengthened collection period could be the result of an intentional relaxation of credit-term enforcement by the firm in response to competitive pressures. If the firm had extended 60-day credit terms, the 58.9-day average collection period would be acceptable. Clearly, additional information would be required in order to draw definitive conclusions about the effectiveness of the firm's credit and collection policy.

Average Payment Period

The **average payment period,** or average age of accounts payable, is calculated in the same manner as the average collection period:

average payment period The average amount of time needed to pay accounts receivable.

$$\text{Average payment period} = \frac{\text{accounts payable}}{\text{average purchases per day}}$$

$$= \frac{\text{accounts payable}}{\dfrac{\text{annual purchases}}{360}}$$

The difficulty in calculating this ratio stems from the need to find annual purchases—a value not available in published financial statements. Ordinarily, purchases are estimated as a given percentage of cost of goods sold. If we assume that Alcott Oil's purchases equaled 70 percent of its cost of goods sold in 1992, its average payment period is

$$\frac{\$382,000}{\dfrac{.70 \times \$2,088,000}{360}} = \frac{\$382,000}{\$4,060} = 94.1 \text{ days}$$

The above figure is meaningful only in relation to the average credit terms extended to the firm. If Alcott Oil's suppliers, on the average, have extended 30-day credit terms, an analyst would give it a low credit rating. If the firm has been generally extended 90-day credit terms, its credit would be acceptable. Prospective lenders and suppliers of trade credit are especially interested in the average payment period, since it provides them with a sense of the bill-paying patterns of the firm.

Fixed Asset Turnover

fixed asset turnover
Measures the efficiency with which the firm has been using its *fixed*, or earning, assets to generate sales.

The **fixed asset turnover** measures the efficiency with which the firm has been using its *fixed*, or earning, assets to generate sales. It is calculated by dividing the firm's sales by its net fixed assets:

$$\text{Fixed asset turnover} = \frac{\text{sales}}{\text{net fixed assets}}$$

The fixed asset turnover for Alcott Oil in 1992 is

$$\frac{\$3,074,000}{\$2,374,000} = 1.29$$

This means the company turns over its net fixed assets 1.29 times a year. Generally, higher fixed asset turnovers are preferred since they reflect greater efficiency of fixed asset utilization.

Total Asset Turnover

total asset turnover
Indicates the efficiency with which the firm uses *all* its assets to generate sales.

The **total asset turnover** indicates the efficiency with which the firm uses *all* its assets to generate sales. Generally, the higher a firm's total asset turnover, the more efficiently its assets have been used. This measure is probably of greatest interest to management since it indicates whether the firm's operations have been financially efficient. Total asset turnover is calculated as follows:

$$\text{Total asset turnover} = \frac{\text{sales}}{\text{total assets}}$$

The value of Alcott Oil's total asset turnover in 1992 is

$$\frac{\$3,074,000}{\$3,597,000} = 0.85$$

The company therefore turns its assets over .85 times a year.

ANALYZING DEBT

The *debt position* of the firm indicates the amount of other people's money being used in attempting to generate profits. In general, the financial analyst is most concerned with long-term debts; these commit the firm to paying interest over the long run as well as eventually repaying the principal borrowed. Since the claims of creditors must be satisfied prior to the distribution of earnings to shareholders,[7] present and prospective shareholders pay close attention to degree of indebtedness and ability to repay debts. Lenders are also concerned about the firm's degree of indebtedness and ability to repay debts, since the more indebted the firm, the higher the probability that the firm will be unable to satisfy the claims of all its creditors. Management obviously must be concerned with indebtedness because of the attention paid to it by other parties and in the interest of keeping the firm solvent.

In general, the more debt a firm uses in relation to its total assets, the greater its **financial leverage.** Financial leverage is the magnification of risk and return introduced through the use of fixed-cost financing such as debt and preferred stock. In other words, the more fixed-cost debt, or financial leverage, a firm uses, the greater will be its risk and return. The concept of financial leverage is developed in Chapter 5. Attention is given here to the use of financial debt ratios to externally assess the degree of corporate indebtedness and the ability to meet fixed payments associated with debt.

financial leverage The magnification of risk and return introduced through the use of fixed-cost financing.

Debt Ratio

The **debt ratio** measures the proportion of total assets financed by the firm's creditors. The higher this ratio, the greater the amount of other people's money being used in an attempt to generate profits. The ratio is calculated as follows:

debt ratio Measures the proportion of total assets financed by the firm's creditors.

$$\text{Debt ratio} = \frac{\text{total liabilities}}{\text{total assets}}$$

The debt ratio for Alcott Oil in 1992 is

$$\frac{\$1,643,000}{\$3,597,000} = .457 = 45.7\%$$

This indicates that the company has financed 45.7 percent of its assets with debt. The higher this ratio, the more financial leverage a firm has.

Times Interest Earned Ratio

The **times interest earned ratio** measures the ability to make contractual interest payments. The higher the value of this ratio, the better able the firm is to fulfill its interest obligations. Times interest earned is calculated as follows:

times interest earned ratio Measures the firm's ability to make contractual interest payments.

$$\text{Times interest earned} = \frac{\text{earnings before interest and taxes}}{\text{interest}}$$

---

[7]The law requires that creditors' claims be satisfied prior to those of the firm's owners. This makes sense, since the creditor is providing a service to the owners and should not be expected to bear the risks of ownership.

Applying this ratio to Alcott Oil yields the following 1992 value:

$$\text{Times interest earned} = \frac{\$418,000}{\$93,000} = 4.5$$

The value of earnings before interest and taxes is the same as the figure for operating profits shown in the income statement given in Table 4.2. The times interest earned ratio for Alcott Oil seems acceptable. As a rule, a value of at least 3.0—and preferably closer to 5.0—is suggested.

Fixed-Payment Coverage Ratio

fixed-payment coverage ratio Measures the firm's ability to meet all fixed-payment obligations.

The **fixed-payment coverage ratio** measures the firm's ability to meet all fixed-payment obligations, such as loan interest and principal, lease payments, and preferred stock dividends. Like the times interest earned ratio, the higher this value, the better. Principal payments on debt, scheduled lease payments, and preferred stock dividends[8] are commonly included in this ratio. The formula for the fixed-payment coverage ratio is as follows:

Fixed-payment coverage ratio =

$$\frac{\text{earnings before interest and taxes + lease payments}}{\text{interest + lease payments + [(principal payments + preferred stock dividends)} \times [1/(1 - T)]]}$$

where T is the corporate tax rate applicable to the firm's income. The term $1/(1 - T)$ is included to adjust the after-tax principal and preferred stock dividend payments back to a before-tax equivalent consistent with the before-tax values of all other terms. Applying the formula to Alcott Oil's 1992 data yields the following value:

Fixed-payment coverage ratio =

$$\frac{\$418,000 + \$35,000}{\$93,000 + \$35,000 + [(\$71,000 + \$10,000) \times [1/(1 - .29)]]}$$
$$= \frac{\$453,000}{\$242,000} = 1.9$$

Since the earnings available are nearly twice as large as its fixed-payment obligations, the firm appears able to safely meet the latter.

Like the times interest earned ratio, the fixed-payment coverage ratio measures risk. The lower the ratio the greater the risk to both lenders and owners, and vice versa. This risk results from the fact that if the firm were unable to meet scheduled fixed payments, it could be driven into bankruptcy. An examination of the ratio therefore allows owners, creditors, and managers to assess the firm's ability to handle additional fixed-payment obligations such as debt.

---

[8]Although preferred stock dividends, which are stated at the time of issue, can be "passed" (not paid) at the option of the firm's directors, it is generally believed that the payment of such dividends is necessary. This text therefore treats the preferred stock dividend as a contractual obligation, to be paid as a fixed amount, as scheduled.

ETHICS   IN   FINANCE

Did First Executive Corporation Go Too Far?

Financial managers often go to great lengths to protect the book value of shareholders' equity, because higher equity capital implies lower leverage, and lower leverage signals less risk. As an example, consider the recent actions of First Executive Life Insurance Corporation. In order to avoid a significant deterioration in the value of First Executive's equity capital in 1990, the insurance company may have understated the amount of write-downs it is required to show when customers surrender their life insurance policies to the firm.

A little bit of background information will help to clarify the issues. When a life insurer sells a policy, the firm does not immediately expense the costs of acquiring the policy, such as advertising, processing, and selling costs. Instead, the insurer spreads these costs over the life of the policy. When customers redeem policies before their scheduled maturity dates, however, insurers must write off all remaining acquisition costs immediately.

In First Executive's case, customers surrendered $3.1 billion in life insurance during the first nine months of 1990. The company expensed only $83 million in deferred acquisition costs for this period. In contrast, the insurer wrote down $180 million in acquisition costs in 1989, when only $1 billion in life insurance was surrendered.

What might motivate the firm to postpone a significant expenditure for deferred acquisition costs? According to one of its major creditors, Yasoda Trust and Banking Company, if First Executive's net worth falls by $321 million in 1990, the firm must begin repaying $275 million in principal to the bank. At present, First Executive can't meet even its scheduled interest payments. The life insurer recently appealed to its bankers to reschedule the company's loan payments.

This state of affairs raises a number of interesting questions for astute financial analysts. First, do First Executive's financial statements accurately reflect the condition of the firm? Second, will the firm's bankers turn a sympathetic ear to the firm's requested debt restructuring? Third, will the SEC approve of First Executive's "creative" accounting practices? Finally, did the firm go too far in trying to protect the book value of the firm's equity capital?

Source: Kathleen Kerwin, "First Executive finds itself between a rock and a hard audit," *Business Week*, December 24, 1990, p. 22.

ANALYZING PROFITABILITY

There are many measures of profitability. Each relates the returns of the firm to its sales, assets, equity, or share value. As a group, these measures allow the analyst to evaluate the firm's earnings with respect to a given level of sales, a certain level of assets, the owners' investment, or share value. Without profits a firm could not attract outside capital. Moreover, present owners and creditors would become concerned about the company's future and attempt to recover their funds. Owners, creditors, and management pay close attention to boosting profits due to the great importance placed on earnings in the marketplace.

Common-Size Income Statements

common-size income statement   An income statement in which each item is expressed as a percentage of sales.

A popular tool for evaluating profitability in relation to sales is the **common-size income statement.** On this statement each item is expressed as a percentage of sales, thus enabling the relationship between sales and specific revenues and expenses to be easily evaluated. Common-size income statements are especially useful in comparing the performance for a particular year with that for another year. Two frequently cited ratios of profitability that can be read directly from the common-size income statement are: (a) the gross profit margin and (b) the net profit margin. These are both discussed below.

Common-size income statements for 1992 and 1991 for Alcott Oil are presented in Table 4.4. An evaluation of these statements reveals

Table 4.4   **Alcott Oil Company Common-Size Income Statements**

	For the years ended December 31	
	1992	**1991**
Sales revenue	100.0%	100.0%
Less: Cost of goods sold	67.9	66.7
(a) Gross profit margin	32.1%	33.3%
Less: Operating expenses		
Selling expense	3.3%	4.2%
General and administrative expenses	6.3	7.3
Lease expense	1.1	1.3
Depreciation expense	7.8	8.7
Total operating expense	18.5%	21.5%
Operating profits	13.6%	11.8%
Less: Interest expense	3.0	3.5
Net profits before taxes	10.6%	8.3%
Less: Taxes	3.1	2.5
(b) Net profit margin	7.5%	5.8%

that the firm's cost of goods sold increased from 66.7 percent of sales in 1991 to 67.9 percent in 1992, resulting in a decrease in the gross profit margin from 33.3 to 32.1 percent. However, thanks to a decrease in operating expenses from 21.5 percent in 1991 to 18.5 percent in 1992, the firm's net profit margin rose from 5.8 percent of sales in 1991 to 7.5 percent in 1992. The decrease in expenses in 1992 more than compensated for the increase in the cost of goods sold. A decrease in the firm's 1992 interest expense (3.0 percent of sales versus 3.5 percent in 1991) added to the increase in 1992 profits.

Gross Profit Margin

The **gross profit margin** indicates the percentage of each sales dollar remaining after the firm has paid for its goods. The higher the gross profit margin the better, and the lower the relative cost of merchandise sold. Of course, the opposite case is also true, as the Alcott Oil example shows. The gross profit margin is calculated as follows:

gross profit margin
Indicates the percentage of each sales dollar left after the firm has paid for its goods.

$$\text{Gross profit margin} = \frac{\text{sales} - \text{cost of goods sold}}{\text{sales}} = \frac{\text{gross profits}}{\text{sales}}$$

The value for Alcott Oil's gross profit margin for 1992 is

$$\frac{\$3,074,000 - \$2,088,000}{\$3,074,000} = \frac{\$986,000}{\$3,074,000} = 32.1\%$$

This value is shown on line (a) of the common-size income statement in Table 4.4.

Net Profit Margin

The **net profit margin** measures the percentage of each sales dollar remaining after all expenses, including taxes, have been deducted. The higher the firm's net profit margin, the better. The net profit margin is a commonly cited measure of the corporation's success with respect to earnings on sales. "Good" net profit margins differ considerably across industries. A net profit margin of 1 percent or less would not be unusual for a grocery store, while a net profit margin of 10 percent would be low for a retail jewelry store. The net profit margin is calculated as follows:

net profit margin
Measures the percentage of each sales dollar remaining after all expenses, including taxes, have been deducted.

$$\text{Net profit margin} = \frac{\text{net profits after taxes}}{\text{sales}}$$

Alcott Oil's net profit margin for 1992 is

$$\frac{\$231,000}{\$3,074,000} = 7.5\%$$

This value is shown on line (b) of the common-size income statement in Table 4.4.

Return on Investment (ROI)

return on investment (ROI) Measures the overall effectiveness of management in generating profits with its available assets.

The **return on investment (ROI),** which is often called the firm's *return on total assets*, measures the overall effectiveness of management in generating profits with its available assets. The higher the firm's return on investment, the better. The return on investment is calculated as follows:

$$\text{Return on investment} = \frac{\text{net profits after taxes}}{\text{total assets}}$$

Alcott Oil's return on investment in 1992 is

$$\frac{\$231,000}{\$3,597,000} = 6.4\%$$

This value, which seems acceptable, could have been derived using the DuPont system of analysis, which will be described in a subsequent section.

Return on Equity (ROE)

return on equity (ROE) Measures the return earned on the owners' (both preferred and common stockholders') investment in the firm.

The **return on equity (ROE)** measures the return earned on the owners' (both preferred and common stockholders') investment in the firm. Generally, the higher this return, the better off are the owners. Return on equity is calculated as follows:

$$\text{Return on equity} = \frac{\text{net profits after taxes}}{\text{stockholders' equity}}$$

This ratio for Alcott Oil in 1992 is

$$\frac{\$231,000}{\$1,954,000} = 11.8\%$$

The above value, which seems to be quite good, could also have been derived using the DuPont system of analysis, to be described below.

Earnings per Share (EPS)

The firm's *earnings per share (EPS)* are generally of interest to present or prospective stockholders and management. The earnings per share represent the number of dollars earned on behalf of each outstanding share of common stock. They are closely watched by the investing public and are considered an important indicator of corporate success. Earnings per share, as noted in Chapter 1, are calculated as follows:

$$\text{Earnings per share} = \frac{\text{earnings available for common stockholders}}{\text{number of shares of common stock outstanding}}$$

The value of Alcott Oil's earnings per share in 1992 is

$$\frac{\$221,000}{76,262} = \$2.90$$

The figure represents the dollar amount *earned* on behalf of each share outstanding. It does not represent the amount of earnings actually distributed to shareholders.

Price/Earnings (P/E) Ratio

Though not a true measure of profitability, the **price/earnings (P/E) ratio** is commonly used to assess the owners' appraisal of share value.[9] The P/E ratio reflects the amount investors are willing to pay for each dollar of the firm's earnings. The level of the price/earnings ratio indicates the degree of confidence (or certainty) that investors have in the firm's future performance. The higher the P/E ratio, the greater the investor confidence in the firm's future. The P/E ratio is calculated as follows:

price/earnings (P/E) ratio Reflects the amount investors are willing to pay for each dollar of the firm's earnings.

$$\text{Price/earnings (P/E) ratio} = \frac{\text{market price per share of common stock}}{\text{earnings per share}}$$

If Alcott Oil's common stock at the end of 1992 was selling at $32\frac{1}{4}$ (i.e., $32.25), using the *earnings per share (EPS)* of $2.90 from the income statement in Table 4.2, the P/E ratio at year-end 1992 is

$$\frac{\$32.25}{\$2.90} = 11.1$$

This figure indicates that investors were paying $11.10 for each $1.00 of earnings.

A COMPLETE RATIO ANALYSIS

As indicated in the chapter, no single ratio is adequate for assessing all aspects of the firm's financial condition. Two popular approaches to a complete ratio analysis are (1) the DuPont system of analysis and (2) the summary analysis of a large number of ratios. Each of these approaches has merit. The DuPont system acts as a *search technique* aimed at finding the key areas responsible for the firm's financial performance. The summary analysis approach tends to view *all aspects* of the firm's financial activities in order to isolate key areas of responsibility.

---

[9]Use of the price/earnings ratio to estimate the value of the firm is included as part of the discussion of popular approaches to common stock valuation in Chapter 12.

DuPont System of Analysis

DuPont system of analysis System used to dissect a firm's financial statements and assess its financial condition.

The **DuPont system of analysis** has for many years been used by financial managers as a structure for dissecting the firm's financial statements in order to assess its financial condition. The DuPont system merges the income statement and balance sheet into two summary measures of profitability: return on investment (ROI) and return on equity (ROE). Figure 4.2 depicts the basic DuPont system with Alcott Oil's 1992 monetary and ratio values. The upper portion of the chart summarizes the income statement activities; the lower portion summarizes the balance sheet activities.

The DuPont system first brings together the *net profit margin,* which measures the firm's profitability on sales, with its *total asset turnover,* which indicates how efficiently the firm has used its assets to generate sales. In the **DuPont formula,** the product of these two ratios results in the *return on investment (ROI):*

DuPont formula Relates the firm's net profit margin and total asset turnover to its return on investment (ROI).

$$ROI = \text{net profit margin} \times \text{total asset turnover}$$

Substituting the appropriate formulas into the equation and simplifying results in the formula given earlier,

$$ROI = \frac{\text{net profits after taxes}}{\text{sales}} \times \frac{\text{sales}}{\text{total assets}} = \frac{\text{net profits after taxes}}{\text{total assets}}$$

If the 1992 values of the net profit margin and total asset turnover for Alcott Oil, calculated earlier, are substituted into the DuPont formula, the result is

$$ROI = 7.5\% \times 0.85 = 6.4\%$$

As expected, this value is the same as that calculated directly in an earlier section. The DuPont formula allows the firm to break down its return into a profit-on-sales and an efficiency-of-asset-use component. Typically, a firm with a low net profit margin has a high total asset turnover, which results in a reasonably good return on investment. Often, the opposite situation exists.

The second step in the DuPont system employs the **modified DuPont formula.** This formula relates the firm's return on investment (ROI) to the return on equity (ROE). The latter is calculated by multiplying the return on investment by the **equity multiplier,** which is the ratio of total assets to stockholders' equity:

modified DuPont formula Relates the firm's return on investment (ROI) to its return on equity (ROE) using the *equity multiplier.*

equity multiplier The ratio of the firm's total assets to stockholders' equity.

$$ROE = ROI \times \text{equity multiplier}$$

Substituting the appropriate formulas into the equation and simplifying results in the formula given earlier,

$$ROE = \frac{\text{net profits after taxes}}{\text{total assets}} \times \frac{\text{total assets}}{\text{stockholders' equity}}$$

$$= \frac{\text{net profits after taxes}}{\text{stockholders' equity}}$$

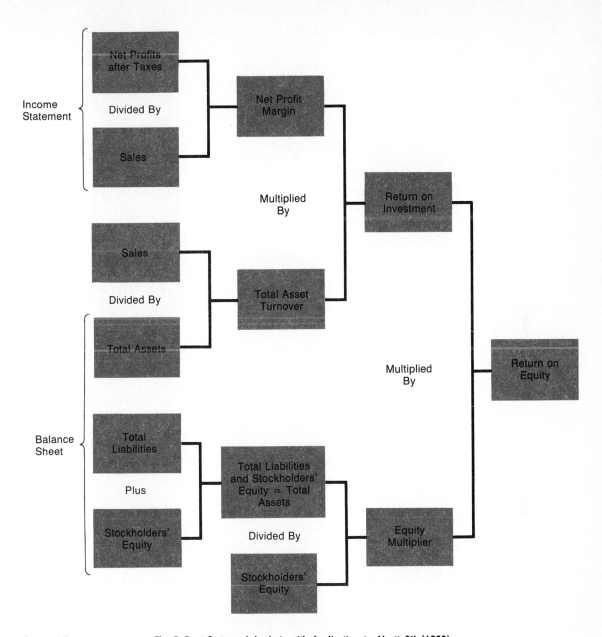

Figure 4.2   **The DuPont System of Analysis with Application to Alcott Oil (1992)**
The DuPont system of analysis creates a structure used to dissect the firm's income statement and balance sheet in order to assess its financial condition. The system focuses on return on investment (ROI) and return on equity (ROE).

Use of the equity multiplier to convert the ROI to the ROE reflects the impact of leverage (use of debt) on owners' return. Substituting the values for Alcott Oil's ROI of 6.4%, calculated earlier, and Alcott's equity multiplier of 1.84 ($3,597,000 total assets ÷ $1,954,000 stockholders' equity) into the modified DuPont formula yields

$$ROE = 6.4\% \times 1.84 = 11.8\%$$

The 11.8 percent ROE calculated using the modified DuPont formula is the same as that calculated directly.

The considerable advantage of the DuPont system is that it allows the firm to break its return on equity into a profit-on-sales component (net profit margin), an efficiency-of-asset-use component (total asset turnover), and a use-of-leverage component (equity multiplier). The total return to the owners can be analyzed in light of these important dimensions. As an illustration, let's look ahead to the ratio values summarized in Table 4.5 on page 124. Alcott Oil's net profit margin and total asset turnover increased between 1991 and 1992 to levels above the industry average. In combination, improved profit on sales and better asset utilization resulted in an improved return on investment (ROI). Increased investment return coupled with the increased use of debt reflected in the increased equity multiplier (not shown) caused the owners' return (ROE) to increase. Simply stated, it is clear from the DuPont system of analysis that the improvement in Alcott Oil's 1992 ROE resulted from greater profit on sales, better asset utilization, and the increased use of leverage.

 ## Summarizing All Ratios

The 1992 ratio values calculated earlier and the ratio values calculated for 1990 and 1991 for Alcott Oil, along with the industry average ratios for 1992, are summarized in Table 4.5. The table shows the formula used to calculate each ratio. Using these data, we can discuss the four key aspects of Alcott's performance—(1) liquidity, (2) activity, (3) debt, and (4) profitability—on a cross-sectional and time-series basis.

Liquidity
The overall liquidity of the firm seems to exhibit a reasonably stable trend. It has been maintained at a level that is relatively consistent with the industry average in 1992. The firm's liquidity seems to be good.

Activity
Alcott Oil's inventory appears to be in good shape. Its inventory management seems to have improved, and in 1992 it performed at a level above that of the industry. The firm may be experiencing some problems with accounts receivable. The average collection period seems to have crept up to a level above that of the industry. Alcott also appears to be slow in paying its bills; it is paying nearly 30 days later than the industry average. Payment procedures should be examined to make sure that the company's credit standing is not adversely affected. While overall liquidity appears to be good, some attention should be given to the management of accounts receivable and payable. Alcott's fixed asset turnover and total asset turnover reflect sizable declines in the efficiency of fixed and total asset utilization between 1990 and 1991. Although in 1992 the total asset turnover rose to a level considerably above the industry average, it appears that the pre-1991 level of efficiency has not yet been achieved.

ETHICS IN FINANCE

Finance Professionals Are Accountable for Their Actions

In the medical profession, physicians are held accountable by patients for the quality of service they provide. Failure to render competent professional advice often results in an expensive malpractice lawsuit. Like medical doctors, financial managers and accountants are also held responsible for their actions, and dereliction of professional duty can spell litigation, damage claims, and even bankruptcy.

The early 1990s witnessed the dawn of open hunting season on the accounting industry. In November 1990, the partnership of Laventhol & Horwath (L & H) filed bankruptcy in the wake of numerous malpractice suits. The best-known case against the firm involved a $184 million damage claim brought by angry creditors of television evangelist Jim Bakker and his failed PTL ministry for Laventhol's role as auditor to the PTL. Another claim involved a $40 million judgment against Laventhol for its role as auditor for the bankrupt Grabill Corporation of Chicago.

L & H is not the only target of angry creditors. The PTL suit also names accounting firm Deloitte & Touche as a co-defendant. Ernst & Young (E & Y), a third large accounting firm, currently faces a $560 million suit brought by the Federal Deposit Insurance Corporation over E & Y's role in auditing a failed Dallas savings and loan association. In each of these cases, creditors and investors seek damages from auditors because these firms are the only participants in failed business transactions with any cash left.

These events contain an important message for individuals contemplating careers as financial managers: competence, integrity, and sound judgment are necessary ingredients for a successful future. Financial managers must be able to read and interpret accounting data, and make decisions that reflect an honest understanding of financial statement relationships. Anything less represents a dereliction of professional responsibility, and in today's litigious environment, this can signal the end of a promising career.

Source: Joseph Weber, "Behind the fall of Laventhol," *Business Week*, December 24, 1990, p. 54.

Debt

Alcott Oil's indebtedness increased over the 1990–1992 period and is currently at a level above the industry average. Although the increase in the debt ratio could be cause for alarm, the firm's ability to meet interest and fixed-payment obligations improved from 1991 to 1992 to a level that outperforms the industry. The firm's increased indebtedness

Table 4.5

Summary of Alcott Oil Company Ratios (1990–1992, including 1992 industry averages)

| | | Year | | | Industry average 1992[c] | Evaluation[d] | | |
| | | 1990[a] | 1991[b] | 1992[b] | | Cross-sectional 1992 | Time-series 1990–1992 | Overall |
Ratio	Formula							
Liquidity								
Net working capital	current assets − current liabilities	$583,000	$521,000	$603,000	$427,000	good	good	good
Current ratio	$\dfrac{\text{current assets}}{\text{current liabilities}}$	2.04	2.08	1.97	2.05	OK	OK	OK
Quick (acid-test) ratio	$\dfrac{\text{current assets} - \text{inventory}}{\text{current liabilities}}$	1.32	1.46	1.51	1.43	OK	good	good
Activity								
Inventory turnover	$\dfrac{\text{cost of goods sold}}{\text{inventory}}$	5.1	5.7	7.2	6.6	good	good	good
Average collection period	$\dfrac{\text{accounts receivable}}{\text{average sales per day}}$	43.9 days	51.2 days	58.9 days	44.3 days	poor	poor	poor
Average payment period	$\dfrac{\text{accounts payable}}{\text{average purchases per day}}$	75.8 days	81.2 days	94.1 days	66.5 days	poor	poor	poor
Fixed asset turnover	$\dfrac{\text{sales}}{\text{net fixed assets}}$	1.50	1.13	1.29	1.35	OK	OK	OK
Total asset turnover	$\dfrac{\text{sales}}{\text{total assets}}$	0.94	0.79	0.85	0.75	OK	OK	OK

Ratio	Formula	Year 1990[a]	Year 1991[b]	Year 1992[b]	Industry average 1992[c]	Cross-sectional 1992	Time-series 1990–1992	Overall
Debt								
Debt ratio	$\dfrac{\text{total liabilities}}{\text{total assets}}$	36.8%	44.3%	45.7%	40.0%	OK	OK	OK
Times interest earned ratio	$\dfrac{\text{earnings before interest and taxes}}{\text{interest}}$	5.6	3.3	4.5	4.3	good	OK	OK
Fixed-payment coverage ratio	$\dfrac{\text{earnings before interest and taxes + lease payments}}{\text{int. + lease payments} + [(\text{prin.} + \text{pref. div}) \times [1/(1 - T)]]}$	2.4	1.4	1.9	1.5	good	OK	good
Profitability								
Gross profit margin	$\dfrac{\text{gross profit}}{\text{sales}}$	31.4%	33.3%	32.1%	30.0%	OK	OK	OK
Net profit margin	$\dfrac{\text{net profits after taxes}}{\text{sales}}$	8.8%	5.8%	7.5%	6.4%	good	OK	good
Return on investment (ROI)	$\dfrac{\text{net profits after taxes}}{\text{total assets}}$	8.3%	4.5%	6.4%	4.8%	good	OK	good
Return on equity (ROE)	$\dfrac{\text{net profits after taxes}}{\text{stockholders' equity}}$	13.1%	8.1%	11.8%	8.0%	good	OK	good
Earnings per share (EPS)	$\dfrac{\text{earnings available for common stockholders}}{\text{number of shares of common stock outstanding}}$	$3.26	$1.81	$2.90	$2.26	good	OK	good
Price/earnings (P/E) ratio	$\dfrac{\text{market price per share of common stock}}{\text{earnings per share}}$	10.5	10.0	11.1	12.5	OK	OK	OK

[a]Calculated from data not included in the chapter.
[b]Calculated using the financial statements presented in Tables 4.2 and 4.3.
[c]Obtained from sources not included in this chapter.
[d]Subjective assessments based on data provided.

125

in 1991 apparently caused a deterioration in its ability to pay debt adequately. However, Alcott has evidently improved its income in 1992 so that it is able to meet its interest and fixed-payment obligations in a fashion consistent with the average firm in the industry. In summary, it appears that although 1991 was an off year, the company's ability to pay debts in 1992 adequately compensates for the increased degree of indebtedness.

Profitability

Alcott's profitability relative to sales in 1992 was better than that of the average company in the industry, although it did not match the firm's 1990 performance. While the *gross* profit margin in 1991 and 1992 was better than in 1990, it appears that higher levels of operating and interest expenses in 1991 and 1992 caused the 1992 *net* profit margin to fall below that of 1990. However, Alcott's 1992 net profit margin is quite favorable when compared to the industry average. The firm's return on investment, return on equity, and earnings per share behaved in a fashion similar to its net profit margin over the 1990–1992 period. Alcott appears to have experienced either a sizable drop in sales between 1990 and 1991 or a rapid expansion in assets during that period. The owners' return, as evidenced by the exceptionally high 1992 level of return on equity, seems to suggest that the firm is performing quite well. In addition, although the firm's shares are selling at a price/earnings (P/E) multiple below that of the industry, some improvement occurred between 1991 and 1992. The firm's above-average returns—net profit margin, ROI, ROE, and EPS—may be attributable to its above-average risk as reflected in its below-industry-average P/E ratio.

In summary, it appears that the firm is growing and has recently undergone an expansion in assets, this expansion being financed primarily through the use of debt. The 1991–1992 period seems to reflect a phase of adjustment and recovery from the rapid growth in assets. Alcott's sales, profits, and other performance factors seem to be growing with the increase in the size of the operation. In short, the firm appears to have done quite well in 1992.

SUMMARY

1   **Understand the parties interested in performing financial ratio analysis and the common types of ratio comparisons.** Ratio analysis allows present and prospective stockholders and lenders and the firm's management to evaluate the firm's financial performance and status. It can be performed on a cross-sectional or a time-series basis. Cross-sectional analysis involves comparisons of different firms' financial ratios at the same point in time. Time-series analysis measures a firm's performance over time.

2   **Describe some of the cautions that should be considered when performing financial ratio analysis.** Cautions in ratio analysis include: (1) a single ratio does not generally provide sufficient information; (2) financial statements being compared should be dated at the same point in time during the year; (3) only audited financial statements should be used; (4) data should be checked for consistency of accounting treatment; and (5) inflation and different asset ages can distort ratio comparisons.

3   **Use popular ratios to analyze a firm's liquidity and the activity of inventory, accounts receivable, accounts payable, fixed assets, and total assets.**   The liquidity, or ability of the firm to pay its bills as they come due, can be measured by the firm's net working capital, its current ratio, or its quick (acid-test) ratio. Activity ratios measure the speed with which various accounts are converted into sales or cash. The activity of inventory can be measured by its turnover, that of accounts receivable by the average collection period, and that of accounts payable by the average payment period. Fixed and total asset turnovers can be used to measure the efficiency with which the firm has used its fixed and total assets to generate sales. Formulas for these liquidity and activity ratios are summarized in Table 4.5.

4   **Assess the firm's debt position as well as its ability to meet the payments associated with debt.**   Financial debt ratios measure both the degree of indebtedness and the ability to pay debts. A commonly used measure of debt position is the debt ratio. The ability to pay contractual obligations such as interest, principal, lease payments, and preferred stock dividends can be measured by times interest earned and fixed-payment coverage ratios. Formulas for these debt ratios are summarized in Table 4.5.

5   **Evaluate the firm's profitability relative to sales, asset investment, owners' equity, investment, and share value.**   Measures of profitability can be made in various ways. The common-size income statement, which shows all items as a percentage of sales, can be used to determine gross profit margin and net profit margin. Other measures of profitability include return on investment, return on equity, earnings per share, and the price/earnings ratio. Formulas for these profitability ratios are summarized in Table 4.5.

6   **Use the DuPont system and a summary analysis of a large number of ratios to evaluate a firm's financial status and make appropriate recommendations.**   The DuPont system of analysis is a search technique aimed at finding the key areas responsible for the firm's financial performance. It allows the firm to break the return on equity into a profit-on-sales component, an efficiency-of-asset-use component, and a use-of-leverage component. The structure of the DuPont system of analysis is depicted in Figure 4.2. By summarizing a large number of ratios, the financial analyst can assess all aspects of the firm's activities in order to isolate key areas of responsibility.

QUESTIONS

4—1   With regard to financial ratio analyses of a firm, how do the viewpoints held by the firm's present and prospective shareholders, creditors, and management differ? How can these viewpoints be related to the firm's fund-raising ability?

4—2   How can ratio analysis be used for *cross-sectional* and *time-series* comparisons? Which type of comparison would be more common for internal analysis? Why?

4—3   When performing cross-sectional ratio analysis, to what types of deviations from the norm should the analyst devote primary attention? Explain why.

4—4   Financial ratio analysis is often divided into four areas: *liquidity* ratios, *activity* ratios, *debt* ratios, and *profitability* ratios. Describe and differentiate each of these areas of analysis from the others. Which is of the greatest relative concern to present and prospective creditors?

4—5   Why is net working capital useful only in time-series comparisons of overall liquidity whereas the current and quick ratios can be used for both cross-sectional and time-series analyses?

4—6   In order to assess the reasonableness of the firm's average collection period and average payment period ratios, what additional information is needed in each instance? Explain.

4—7   What is *financial leverage*? What ratio can be used to measure the degree of indebtedness? What ratios are used to assess the ability of the firm to meet fixed payments associated with debt?

4—8   What is a *common-size income statement*? Which two ratios of profitability are found on this statement? How is the statement used?

4—9   How can a firm's having a high gross profit margin and a low net profit margin be explained? To what must this situation be attributable?

4—10   Define and differentiate between return on investment (ROI), return on equity (ROE), and earnings per share (EPS). Which measure is probably of greatest interest to owners? Why?

4—11   What is the *price/earnings (P/E) ratio*? How does its level relate to the degree of confidence (or certainty) of investors in the firm's future performance? Is the P/E ratio a true measure of profitability?

4—12   Three areas of analysis or concern are combined in the *DuPont system of analysis*. What are these concerns, and how are they combined to explain the firm's return on equity (ROE)? Can this formula yield useful information through cross-sectional or time-series analysis?

4—13   Describe how you would approach a complete ratio analysis of the firm on both a cross-sectional and a time-series basis by summarizing a large number of ratios.

PROBLEMS

4—1   **(Liquidity Management)**   The Bently Corporation's total current assets, net working capital, and inventory for each of the past four years are given below.

Item	1989	1990	1991	1992
Total current assets	$16,950	$21,900	$22,500	$27,000
Net working capital	7,950	9,300	9,900	9,600
Inventory	6,000	6,900	6,900	7,200

a. Calculate the firm's current and quick ratios for each year. Compare the resulting time series of each measure of liquidity (i.e., net working capital, the current ratio, and the quick ratio).

b. Comment on the firm's liquidity over the 1989–1992 period.

c. If you were told that the Bently Corporation's inventory turnover for each year in the 1989–1992 period and the industry averages were as follows, would this support or conflict with your evaluation in **b**? Why?

Inventory turnover	1989	1990	1991	1992
Bently Corporation	6.3	6.8	7.0	6.4
Industry average	10.6	11.2	10.8	11.0

4—2   **(Inventory Management)** The Pearson Company has sales of $4 million and a gross profit margin of 40 percent. Its *end-of-quarter inventories* are as follows:

Quarter	Inventory
1	$ 400,000
2	800,000
3	1,200,000
4	200,000

a. Find the average quarterly inventory and use it to calculate the firm's inventory turnover and the average age of inventory.
b. Assuming the company is in an industry with an average inventory turnover of 2.0, how would you evaluate the activity of Pearson's inventory?

4—3   **(Accounts Receivable Management)** An evaluation of the books of Bowman Supply Company, shown in the following table, gives the end-of-year accounts receivable balance, which is believed to consist of amounts originating in the months indicated. The company had annual sales of $2.4 million. The firm extends 30-day credit terms.

Month of origin	Amounts receivable
July	$ 3,875
August	2,000
September	34,025
October	15,100
November	52,000
December	193,000
Year-end accounts receivable	$300,000

a. Use the year-end total to evaluate the firm's collection system.
b. If the firm's peak selling season is from July to December, how would this affect the validity of your conclusion above? Explain.

4—4   **(DuPont System of Analysis)** Boswell Industries has the following ratio data on its own business and its industry:

Boswell	1990	1991	1992
Equity multiplier	1.75	1.75	1.85
Net profit margin	.059	.058	.049
Total asset turnover	2.11	2.18	2.34

Industry averages			
Equity multiplier	1.67	1.69	1.64
Net profit margin	.054	.047	.041
Total asset turnover	2.05	2.13	2.15

a. Use the preceding information to construct the *DuPont system of analysis* for both Boswell and the industry.

b. Evaluate Boswell (and the industry) over the three-year period.

c. In which areas does Boswell require further analysis? Why?

 4—5 **(Debt Analysis)** The Center City Bank is evaluating the Tiley Corporation, which has requested a $4,000,000 loan, in order to assess the firm's financial leverage and financial risk. Based on the debt ratios for Tiley, along with the industry averages and Tiley's recent financial statements, evaluate and recommend appropriate action on the loan request.

Balance sheet
Tiley Corporation
December 31, 1992

Assets	
Current assets	
Cash	$ 1,000,000
Marketable securities	3,000,000
Accounts receivable	12,000,000
Inventories	7,500,000
Total current assets	$23,500,000
Gross fixed assets (at cost)[a]	
Land and buildings	$11,000,000
Machinery and equipment	20,500,000
Furniture and fixtures	8,000,000
Gross fixed assets	$39,500,000
Less: Accumulated depreciation	13,000,000
Net fixed assets	$26,500,000
Total assets	$50,000,000

Liabilities and stockholders' equity	
Current liabilities	
Accounts payable	$ 8,000,000
Notes payable	8,000,000
Accruals	500,000
Total current liabilities	$16,500,000
Long-term debt (includes financial leases)[b]	$20,000,000
Stockholders' equity	
Preferred stock (25,000 shares, $4 dividend)	$ 2,500,000
Common stock (1 million shares at $5 par)	5,000,000
Paid-in capital in excess of par value	4,000,000
Retained earnings	2,000,000
Total stockholders' equity	$13,500,000
Total liabilities and stockholders' equity	$50,000,000

[a]The firm has a four-year financial lease requiring annual beginning-of-year payments of $200,000.
[b]Required annual principal payments are $800,000.

Income statement
Tiley Corporation
for the year ended December 31, 1992

Sales revenue		$30,000,000
Less: Cost of goods sold		21,000,000
Gross profits		$ 9,000,000
Less: Operating expenses		
Selling expense	$3,000,000	
General and administrative expenses	1,800,000	
Lease expense	200,000	
Depreciation expense	1,000,000	
Total operating expense		6,000,000
Operating profits		$ 3,000,000
Less: Interest expense		1,000,000
Net profits before taxes		$ 2,000,000
Less: Taxes (rate = 40%)		800,000
Net profits after taxes		$ 1,200,000

Industry averages	
Debt ratio	0.51
Times interest earned ratio	7.30
Fixed-payment coverage ratio	1.85

4—6   **(Common-Size Statement Analysis)** A common-size income statement for the Tiley Corporation's 1991 operations is presented below. Using the firm's 1992 income statement presented in Problem 4-5, develop the 1992 common-size income statement and compare it to the 1991 statement. Which areas require further analysis and investigation?

Common-Size income statement
Tiley Corporation
for the year ended December 31, 1991

Sales revenue ($35,000,000)		100.0%
Less: Cost of goods sold		65.9
Gross profits		34.1%
Less: Operating expenses		
Selling expense	12.7%	
General and administrative expenses	6.3	
Lease expense	0.6	
Depreciation expense	3.6	
Total operating expense		23.2
Operating profits		10.9%
Less: Interest expense		1.5
Net profits before taxes		9.4%
Less: Taxes (rate = 40%)		3.8
Net profits after taxes		5.6%

 4—7   **(Cross-Sectional Ratio Analysis)** Use the financial statements provided below for Delta Equipment Company for the year ended December 31, 1992, along with the industry average ratios on page 133, to:
a. Prepare and interpret a ratio analysis of the firm's 1992 operations.
b. Summarize your findings and make recommendations.

Income statement
Delta Equipment Company
for the year ended December 31, 1992

Sales revenue		$600,000
Less: Cost of goods sold		460,000
Gross profits		$140,000
Less: Operating expenses		
General and administrative expenses	$30,000	
Depreciation expense	30,000	
Total operating expense		60,000
Operating profits		$ 80,000
Less: Interest expense		10,000
Net profits before taxes		$ 70,000
Less: Taxes		27,100
Net profits after taxes (Earnings available for common stockholders)		$ 42,900
Earnings per share (EPS)		$ 2.15

Balance sheet
Delta Equipment Company
December 31, 1992

Assets

Cash	$ 15,000
Marketable securities	7,200
Accounts receivable	34,100
Inventories	82,000
Total current assets	$138,300
Net fixed assets	$270,000
Total assets	$408,300

Liabilities and stockholders' equity

Accounts payable	$ 57,000
Notes payable	13,000
Accruals	5,000
Total current liabilities	$ 75,000
Long-term debt	$150,000
Stockholders' equity	
Common stock equity (20,000 shares outstanding)	$110,200
Retained earnings	73,100
Total stockholders' equity	$183,300
Total liabilities and stockholders' equity	$408,300

Ratio	Industry average, 1992
Net working capital	$125,000
Current ratio	2.35
Quick ratio	.87
Inventory turnover[a]	4.55
Average collection period[a]	35.3 days
Fixed asset turnover	1.97
Total asset turnover	1.09
Debt ratio	.300
Times interest earned ratio	12.3
Gross profit margin	.202
Net profit margin	.091
Return on investment (ROI)	.099
Return on equity (ROE)	.167
Earnings per share (EPS)	$3.10

[a]Based on a 360-day year and on end-of-year figures.

4—8   **(Financial Statement Analysis)** The financial statements of the Robin Manufacturing Company for the year ended December 31, 1992, are given below and on page 134.

Income statement
Robin Manufacturing Company
for the year ended December 31, 1992

Sales revenue	$160,000
Less: Cost of goods sold	106,000
Gross profits	$ 54,000
Less: Operating expenses	
Selling expense	$ 16,000
General and administrative expenses	10,000
Lease expense	1,000
Depreciation expense	10,000
Total operating expense	$ 37,000
Operating profits	$ 17,000
Less: Interest expense	6,100
Net profits before taxes	$ 10,900
Less: Taxes	4,360
Net profits after taxes	$ 6,540

Balance sheet
Robin Manufacturing Company
December 31, 1992

Assets	
Cash	$ 500
Marketable securities	1,000
Accounts receivable	25,000
Inventories	45,500
Total current assets	$ 72,000
Land	$ 26,000
Buildings and equipment	90,000
Less: Accumulated depreciation	38,000
Net fixed assets	$ 78,000
Total assets	$150,000

Liabilities and stockholders' equity	
Accounts payable	$ 22,000
Notes payable	47,000
Total current liabilities	$ 69,000
Long-term debt	$ 22,950
Common stock	31,500
Retained earnings	26,550
Total liabilities and stockholders' equity	$150,000

a. Use the preceding financial statements to complete the following table. Assume that the industry averages given in the table are applicable for both 1991 and 1992.

Robin Manufacturing Company ratio analysis

Ratio	Industry average	Actual 1991	Actual 1992
Current ratio	1.80	1.84	_____
Quick ratio	.70	.78	_____
Inventory turnover[a]	2.50	2.59	_____
Average collection period[a]	37 days	36 days	_____
Debt ratio	65%	67%	_____
Times interest earned ratio	3.8	4.0	_____
Gross profit margin	38%	40%	_____
Net profit margin	3.5%	3.6%	_____
Return on investment	4.0%	4.0%	_____
Return on equity	9.5%	8.0%	_____

[a]Based on a 360-day year and on end-of-year figures.

b. Analyze Robin Manufacturing Company's financial condition as it relates to (1) liquidity, (2) activity, (3) debt, and (4) profitability. Summarize the company's overall financial condition.

4—9   **(Integrative—Complete Ratio Analysis)** Given the financial statements, historical ratios, and industry averages below and on page 136 calculate the Reid Company's financial ratios for the most recent year. Analyze its overall financial situation from both a cross-sectional and a time-series viewpoint. Break your analysis into an evaluation of the firm's liquidity, activity, debt, and profitability.

Income statement
Reid Company
for the year ended December 31, 1992

Sales revenue		$10,000,000
Less: Cost of goods sold		7,500,000
Gross profits		$ 2,500,000
Less: Operating expenses		
Selling expense	$300,000	
General and administrative expenses	650,000	
Lease expense	50,000	
Depreciation expense	200,000	
Total operating expense		1,200,000
Operating profits		$ 1,300,000
Less: Interest expense		200,000
Net profits before taxes		$ 1,100,000
Less: Taxes (rate = 40%)		440,000
Net profits after taxes		$ 660,000
Less: Preferred stock dividends		50,000
Earnings available for common stockholders		$ 610,000
Earnings per share (EPS)		$3.05

Balance sheet
Reid Company
December 31, 1992

Assets		
Current assets		
Cash		$ 200,000
Marketable securities		50,000
Accounts receivable		800,000
Inventories		950,000
Total current assets		$ 2,000,000
Gross fixed assets (at cost)[a]	$12,000,000	
Less: Accumulated depreciation	3,000,000	
Net fixed assets		$ 9,000,000
Other assets		$ 1,000,000
Total assets		$12,000,000

Liabilities and stockholders' equity	
Current liabilities	
Accounts payable[b]	$ 900,000
Notes payable	200,000
Accruals	100,000
Total current liabilities	$ 1,200,000
Long-term debts (includes financial leases)[c]	$ 3,000,000
Stockholders' equity	
Preferred stock (25,000 shares, $2 dividend)	$ 1,000,000
Common stock (200,000 shares at $3 par)[d]	600,000
Paid-in capital in excess of par value	5,200,000
Retained earnings	1,000,000
Total stockholders' equity	$ 7,800,000
Total liabilities and stockholders' equity	$12,000,000

[a]The firm has an eight-year financial lease requiring annual beginning-of-year payments of $50,000. Five years of the lease have yet to run.
[b]Annual credit purchases of $6,200,000 were made during the year.
[c]The annual principal payment on the long-term debt is $100,000.
[d]On December 31, 1992, the firm's common stock closed at $27½ (i.e., $27.50).

Historical and industry-average ratios
Reid Company

Ratio	1990	1991	Industry average, 1992
Net working capital	$760,000	$720,000	$1,600,000
Current ratio	1.40	1.55	1.85
Quick ratio	1.00	.92	1.05
Inventory turnover	9.52	9.21	8.60
Average collection period	45.0 days	36.4 days	35.0 days
Average payment period	58.5 days	60.8 days	45.8 days
Fixed asset turnover	1.08	1.05	1.07
Total asset turnover	0.74	0.80	0.74
Debt ratio	0.20	0.20	0.30
Times interest earned ratio	8.2	7.3	8.0
Fixed-payment coverage ratio	4.5	4.2	4.2
Gross profit margin	0.30	0.27	0.25
Net profit margin	0.067	0.067	0.058
Return on investment (ROI)	0.049	0.054	0.043
Return on equity (ROE)	0.066	0.073	0.072
Earnings per share (EPS)	$1.75	$2.20	$1.50
Price/earnings (P/E) ratio	12.0	10.5	11.2

CASE

Assessing Metal Manufacturing's Current Financial Position

Bonnie White, an experienced budget analyst at Metal Manufacturing Company, has been charged with assessing the firm's financial performance during 1992 and its financial position at year-end 1992. In order to complete this assignment, she gathered the firm's 1992 financial statements which are presented below and on page 138. In addition, Bonnie obtained the firm's ratio values for 1990 and 1991 along with the 1992 industry average ratios (also applicable to 1990 and 1991). These are presented in the table on page 138.

Income statement ($000)
Metal Manufacturing Company
for the year ended December 31, 1991

Sales revenue		$5,075,000
Less: Cost of goods sold		3,704,000
Gross profits		$1,371,000
Less: Operating expenses		
Selling expense	$650,000	
General and administrative expenses	416,000	
Depreciation expense	152,000	
Total operating expense		1,218,000
Operating profits		$ 153,000
Less: Interest expense		93,000
Net profits before taxes		$ 60,000
Less: Taxes (rate = 40%)		24,000
Net profits after taxes		$ 36,000

Balance sheets ($000)
Metal Manufacturing Company

	December 31	
Assets	**1992**	**1991**
Current assets		
Cash	$ 25,000	$ 24,100
Accounts receivable	805,556	763,900
Inventories	700,625	763,445
Total current assets	$1,531,181	$1,551,445
Gross fixed assets	$2,093,819	$1,691,707
Less: Accumulated depreciation	500,000	348,000
Net fixed assets	$1,593,819	$1,343,707
Total assets	$3,125,000	$2,895,152

Liabilities and stockholders' equity		
Current liabilities		
Accounts payable	$ 230,000	$ 400,500
Notes payable	311,000	370,000
Accruals	75,000	100,902
Total current liabilities	$ 616,000	$ 871,402
Long-term debts	$1,165,250	$ 700,000
Total liabilities	$1,781,250	$1,571,402
Stockholders' equity		
Preferred stock	$ 50,000	$ 50,000
Common stock (at par)	100,000	100,000
Paid-in capital in excess of par value	193,750	193,750
Retained earnings	1,000,000	980,000
Total stockholders' equity	$1,343,750	$1,323,750
Total liabilities and stockholders' equity	$3,125,000	$2,895,152

Historical ratios
Metal Manufacturing Company

Ratio	1990	1991	1992	Industry average
Current ratio	1.7	1.8		1.5
Quick ratio	1.0	0.9		1.2
Inventory turnover (times)	5.2	5.0		10.2
Average collection period	50 days	55 days		46 days
Fixed asset turnover (times)	3.2	3.5		4.1
Total asset turnover (times)	1.5	1.5		2.0
Debt ratio	45.8%	54.3%		24.5%
Times interest earned	2.2	1.9		2.5
Gross profit margin	27.5%	28.0%		26.0%
Net profit margin	1.1%	1.0%		1.2%
Return on investment	1.7%	1.5%		2.4%
Return on equity	3.1%	3.3%		3.2%

Required

    a. Calculate the firm's 1992 financial ratio values and fill them in the table above.

    b. Analyze the firm's current financial position from both a cross-sectional and a time-series viewpoint. Break your analysis into an evaluation of the firm's liquidity, activity, debt, and profitability.

    c. Summarize the firm's overall financial position based on your findings in **b.**

CHAPTER 5

BREAKEVEN ANALYSIS AND LEVERAGE

CHAPTER OBJECTIVES

After studying this chapter, you should be able to:

1 Relate operating leverage, financial leverage, and total leverage to the firm's income statement.

2 Discuss the role of breakeven analysis and the calculation and graphic depiction of the operating breakeven point in terms of units, dollars, and cash.

3 Describe the chief limitations inherent in the use of breakeven analysis.

4 Measure the degree of operating leverage and discuss its relationship to fixed costs and business risk.

5 Calculate the degree of financial leverage, graphically compare financing plans, and discuss financial risk.

6 Discuss the degree of total leverage and describe its relationship to operating leverage, financial leverage, and total risk.

❝ As an avid golfer who once considered a professional golfing career, Bates jumped at the chance to work for one of the sport's greatest legends. ❞

From the Fairway to Finance

Sometimes, after a great deal of hard work and a little bit of luck, the perfect job opportunity comes along. That's the way it worked out for Jack Bates, a 30-year-old graduate of Florida Southern College. After college, Bates was working for a local accounting firm, gaining business experience and looking for the right opportunity to move into a management position. One day in 1984 a friend called to tell him about a job opening in nearby North Palm Beach, working in the controller's area for Golden Bear International, Inc. Golfers will quickly connect the name to golfing superstar Jack Nicklaus. In fact, Golden Bear represents an S corporation formed in 1962 to manage Nicklaus' nonplaying business affairs.

As an avid high school golfer who once considered a professional golfing career, Bates jumped at the chance to go to work for one of the sport's greatest legends. Within weeks, he was working as controller in Golden Bear's golf-services division. Today, at the ripe old age of 30, he is the treasurer and chief financial officer for the entire corporation.

How did Bates achieve his dream? Sure, he had good fortune working on his side, and the fact that he was a low handicap player didn't exactly hurt his chances in the interview. But his success is attributable to much more than luck. When Bates first joined Golden Bear, the firm was in need of help. It faced two major problems. Nicklaus' former business managers had allowed the firm to wander in a variety of directions, from oil-and-gas partnerships to a home security company. In addition, the firm was deep in debt from a series of ventures to develop private golf communities, and much of this debt carried Nicklaus' personal guarantee.

Bates worked to solve both of these problems. First, he assisted the firm's executive committee in consolidating and refocusing Golden Bear's businesses around core, golf-related activities. Second, he designed and implemented a strategy to reduce the firm's debt burden. Between 1986 and 1989, Bates used the firm's positive cash flow to retire close to $200 million in debt.

Today, Golden Bear is healthy and growing. Profits have increased a whopping 700 percent since 1986. In addition, Golden Bear is practically debt-free, and Nicklaus no longer provides a personal guarantee when the firm does decide to borrow. While Bates may never achieve success on the PGA tour, he definitely scored well in the boardroom.

B reakeven analysis and leverage are two closely related concepts that can be used to evaluate various aspects of the firm's return and risk. *Breakeven analysis* is a popular technique used to measure the firm's returns (profits) against various cost structures and levels of sales. **Leverage** results from the use of fixed-cost assets or funds to magnify returns to the firm's owners. Generally, increases in leverage result in increased return and risk, whereas decreases in leverage result in decreased return and risk.

leverage The use of fixed-cost assets or funds to magnify returns to the firm's owners.

TYPES OF LEVERAGE

The three basic types of leverage can best be defined with reference to the firm's income statement. In the general income statement format in Table 5.1, the portions related to the firm's operating leverage, financial leverage, and total leverage are clearly labeled. *Operating leverage* is concerned with the relationship between the firm's sales revenue and its earnings before interest and taxes, or EBIT. (EBIT is a descriptive label for *operating profits*.) *Financial leverage* is concerned with the relationship between the firm's earnings before interest and taxes (EBIT) and its common stock earnings per share (EPS). *Total leverage* is concerned with the relationship between the firm's sales revenue and the earnings per share (EPS). It is important to recognize that the demonstrations of these three forms of leverage that follow are *not* routinely used by financial managers for decision-making purposes. But first, before we examine the three leverage concepts separately in detail, it is important to understand various aspects of breakeven analysis.

Table 5.1   General Income Statement Format and Types of Leverage

Operating leverage	Sales revenue	
	Less: Cost of goods sold	
	Gross profits	
	Less: Operating expenses	
	Earnings before interest and taxes (EBIT)	Total leverage
Financial leverage	Less: Interest	
	Net profits before taxes	
	Less: Taxes	
	Net profits after taxes	
	Less: Preferred stock dividends	
	Earnings available for common stockholders	
	Earnings per share (EPS)	

BREAKEVEN ANALYSIS

breakeven analysis (cost-volume-profit) analysis Concept used (1) to determine the level of operations necessary to cover all operating costs and (2) to evaluate the profitability associated with various levels of sales.

Breakeven analysis, which is sometimes called **cost-volume-profit analysis,** is used by the firm (1) to determine the level of operations necessary to cover all operating costs and (2) to evaluate the profitability associated with various levels of sales. To understand breakeven analysis, we must analyze further the firm's costs.

Types of Costs

fixed costs Costs that are a function of time, not sales volume.

variable costs Costs that vary directly with sales and that are a function of volume rather than time.

The three types of costs are depicted graphically in Figure 5.1. **Fixed costs** are a function of time, not sales volume, and are typically contractual. These costs require the payment of a specified amount in each accounting period. Rent, for example, is a fixed cost. **Variable costs** vary directly with sales and are a function of volume rather than time. Production and delivery costs are variable costs. **Semivariable costs** are partly fixed and partly variable. One example of semivariable costs might be sales commissions, which may be fixed for a certain volume of sales and then increase to higher levels for higher volumes.

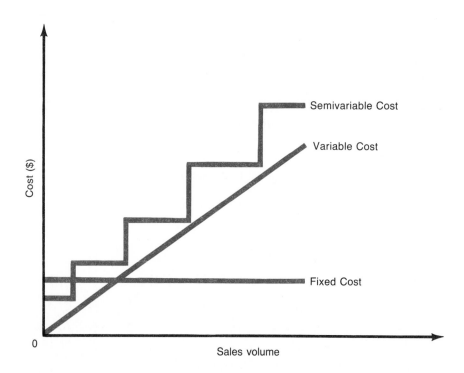

Figure 5.1   **Types of Costs**

Costs may be fixed, variable, or semivariable. Fixed costs are a function of time, not sales volume; variable costs vary with sales; and semivariable costs are partly fixed and partly variable.

Table 5.2   **Operating Leverage, Costs, and Breakeven Analysis**

	Item	Algebraic representation
Operating leverage	Sales revenue	$P \times Q$
	Less: Fixed operating costs	$- FC$
	Less: Variable operating costs	$-(VC \times Q)$
	Earnings before interest and taxes	EBIT

Finding the Operating Breakeven Point

The firm's **operating breakeven point** is the level of sales necessary to cover all operating costs. At the operating breakeven point, earnings before interest and taxes, or EBIT, equals zero.[1] The first step in finding the operating breakeven point is to divide the cost of goods sold and operating expenses into fixed and variable operating costs. The top portion of Table 5.1 can then be recast as shown in the left-hand side of Table 5.2. With this framework, the firm's operating breakeven point can be developed and evaluated.

operating breakeven point   The level of sales necessary to cover all operating costs.

The Algebraic Approach
Using the following variables, we can represent the operating portion of the firm's income statement as shown in the right-hand portion of Table 5.2.

$$P = \text{sale price per unit}$$

$$Q = \text{sales quantity in units}$$

$$FC = \text{fixed operating cost per period}$$

$$VC = \text{variable operating cost per unit}$$

Rewriting the algebraic calculations in Table 5.2 as a formula for earnings before interest and taxes yields Equation 5.1:

$$\text{EBIT} = (P \times Q) - FC - (VC \times Q)$$

Equation 5.1
Formula for EBIT

Simplifying Equation 5.1 yields

$$\text{EBIT} = Q \times (P - VC) - FC$$

Equation 5.2
Simplified formula for EBIT

As noted above, the operating breakeven point is the level of sales at which all fixed and variable operating costs are covered—that is, the

[1]Quite often the breakeven point is calculated so that it represents the point where *all operating and financial costs* are covered. Our concern in this chapter is not with this overall breakeven point.

level at which EBIT equals zero. Setting EBIT equal to zero and solving Equation 5.2 for *Q* yields

Equation 5.3
Formula for the operating breakeven point

$$Q = \frac{FC}{P - VC}$$

Q is the firm's operating breakeven point. Let us look at an example.

EXAMPLE   Assume that Cindy's Posters, a small poster retailer, has fixed operating costs of $2,500, its sale price per unit (poster) is $10, and its variable operating cost per unit is $5. Applying Equation 5.3 to these data yields

$$Q = \frac{\$2,500}{\$10 - \$5} = \frac{\$2,500}{\$5} = 500 \text{ units}$$

At sales of 500 units the firm's EBIT should just equal zero.

In the example, the firm will have positive EBIT for sales greater than 500 units and negative EBIT, or a loss, for sales less than 500 units. We can confirm this by substituting values above and below 500 units, along with the other values given, into Equation 5.1.

The Graphic Approach

Figure 5.2 presents in graph form the breakeven analysis of the data in the example above. The firm's operating breakeven point is the point at

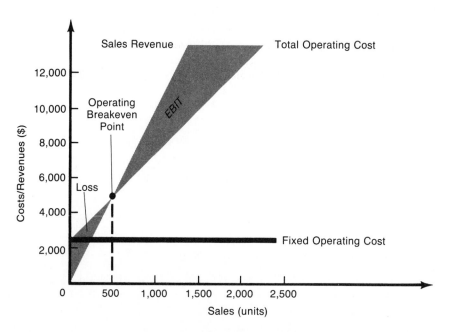

Figure 5.2   **Graphic Operating Breakeven Analysis**

The operating breakeven point of 500 units is the level of sales at which total operating cost, which is the sum of fixed and variable operating costs, equals sales revenue. EBIT is positive above the operating breakeven point, and a loss occurs below it.

Table 5.3   **Sensitivity of Operating Breakeven Point to
                            Increases in Key Breakeven Variables**

Increase in variable	**Effect on operating breakeven point**
Fixed operating cost (*FC*)	Increase
Sale price per unit (*P*)	Decrease
Variable operating cost per unit (*VC*)	Increase

Note: Decreases in each of the variables shown would have the opposite effect from that indicated on the breakeven point.

which its *total operating cost,* or the sum of its fixed and variable operating costs, equals sales revenue. At this point EBIT equals zero. The figure shows that a loss occurs when the firm's sales are *below* the operating breakeven point. In other words, for sales of less than 500 units, total operating costs exceed sales revenue and EBIT is less than zero. For sales levels *greater than* the breakeven point of 500 units, sales revenue exceeds total operating costs and EBIT is greater than zero.

Changing Costs and the Operating Breakeven Point

A firm's operating breakeven point is sensitive to a number of variables: fixed operating costs (*FC*), the sale price per unit (*P*), and the variable operating cost per unit (*VC*). The effects of increases or decreases in each of these variables can be readily assessed by referring to Equation 5.3. The sensitivity of the breakeven sales volume (*Q*) to an *increase* in each of these variables is summarized in Table 5.3. As might be expected, the table indicates that an increase in cost (*FC* or *VC*) tends to increase the operating breakeven point, whereas an increase in the sale price per unit (*P*) will decrease the operating breakeven point.

EXAMPLE   Assume that Cindy's Posters wishes to evaluate the impact of (1) increasing fixed operating costs to $3,000, (2) increasing the sale price per unit to $12.50, (3) increasing the variable operating cost per unit to $7.50, and (4) simultaneously implementing all three of these changes. Substituting the appropriate data into Equation 5.3 yields the following:

(1) Operating breakeven point $= \dfrac{\$3,000}{\$10 - \$5} = 600$ units

(2) Operating breakeven point $= \dfrac{\$2,500}{\$12.50 - \$5} = 333\frac{1}{3}$ units

(3) Operating breakeven point $= \dfrac{\$2,500}{\$10 - \$7.50} = 1,000$ units

(4) Operating breakeven point $= \dfrac{\$3,000}{\$12.50 - \$7.50} = 600$ units

FINANCE   IN   ACTION

It's a Crime That This Idea Isn't Profitable

It may be a grim statistic, but it is a fact. Drug arrests and tougher sentencing requirements have sent America's prison population soaring by 51 percent since 1986, although prison capacity increased just 30 percent during this period. For private security company Wackenhut Corp., headquartered in Coral Gables, Florida, this grim statistic signals a golden business opportunity. Or does it?

Wackenhut is quietly becoming a leader in building, managing, and operating private prison facilities. With rising crime rates, overcrowding in public prisons, and government budgets stretched to the breaking point, Wackenhut sees private correctional facilities as the next growth industry in the United States. And at present, the market stands wide open. Private prisons house just 1 percent of the total prison population, divided among just three firms.

So what's the catch? Private prisons generate plenty of sales growth, but very little income. At Wackenhut, prison management contributes $26 million in sales, but no earnings. Corrections Corporation of America, Wackenhut's leading competitor, turned its first profit of $1.6 million on $36.7 million in sales during 1990—after seven full years in the prison management business.

Why is it so difficult to make money in this business? The answer lies in the industry's revenue and cost characteristics. Significant overhead expenses, such as marketing, training, and administrative labor costs, elevate breakeven points so that it becomes extremely difficult to earn profits in small- and medium-size prisons. As prison size expands to the point where operating revenues exceed total costs, security problems multiply. As a consequence, private prisons represent a great growth industry, but there's very little money to be made there.

Source: Gail DeGeorge, "Wackenhut is out to prove that crime does pay," *Business Week,* December 17, 1990, p. 95.

Comparing the resulting operating breakeven points to the initial value of 500 units, we can see that, as noted in Table 5.3, the cost increases (actions 1 and 3) raise the breakeven point (600 units and 1,000 units, respectively), whereas the revenue increase (action 2) lowers the breakeven point to $333\frac{1}{3}$ units. The combined effect of increasing all three variables (action 4) results in an increased breakeven point of 600 units.

Other Approaches to Breakeven Analysis

Two other popular approaches to breakeven analysis are (1) measuring the breakeven point in terms of dollars and (2) determining the cash breakeven point. Each of these approaches is briefly described below.

Breakeven in Dollars

When a firm has more than one product, it is useful to calculate the breakeven point in terms of dollars rather than units. The use of a dollar breakeven point is especially important for firms that have a variety of products, each selling at a different price. Assuming that the firm's product mix remains relatively constant, the breakeven point can be calculated in terms of dollars by using a contribution margin approach. The **contribution margin** in this case will be defined as the percent of each sales dollar that remains after satisfying variable operating costs. Utilizing the following notation, we can define the firm's dollar operating breakeven point:

contribution margin
The percent of each sales dollar that remains after satisfying variable operating costs.

TR = total sales revenue in dollars

TVC = total variable operating costs paid to achieve TR dollars of sales

FC = total fixed operating costs paid during the period in which TR dollars of sales are achieved

In the case of a single-product firm, using the notation presented earlier, $TR = P \times Q$ and $TVC = VC \times Q$.

The variable operating cost per dollar of sales can be represented as $TVC \div TR$. Subtracting $TVC \div TR$ from 1 will yield the contribution margin, which reflects the per-dollar contribution toward fixed operating costs and profits provided by each dollar of sales:

$$\text{Contribution margin} = 1 - \frac{TVC}{TR}$$

Equation 5.4
Formula for the contribution margin

Dividing the contribution margin into the fixed operating costs, FC, yields the dollar (of sales) breakeven point, D.

$$D = \frac{FC}{\left(1 - \dfrac{TVC}{TR}\right)}$$

Equation 5.5
Formula for the dollar breakeven point

Let us look at the following example.

EXAMPLE   Assume that during a period SC Industries, a small producer of motor casings, has total fixed operating costs of $100,000, total sales of $800,000, and total variable operating costs of $600,000. Applying Equation 5.5 to these data yields

$$D = \frac{\$100,000}{\left(1 - \dfrac{\$600,000}{\$800,000}\right)} = \frac{\$100,000}{.25} = \$400,000$$

Assuming the firm's product mix does not change, at a $400,000 sales level the firm will break even on its operation. At that point its EBIT will equal zero.

Cash Breakeven Analysis

cash breakeven analysis A technique used to find the operating breakeven point when certain noncash charges make up a portion of the firm's fixed operating costs.

Under certain conditions it is sometimes useful to perform a **cash breakeven analysis.** This technique is used to find the operating breakeven point when certain noncash charges, such as depreciation, constitute an important portion of the firm's fixed operating costs. Any charges of this type that are included as part of the firm's fixed costs must be deducted when preparing the cash analysis. If they are not, the presence of such charges tends to overstate the firm's breakeven point. Assuming that the firm has certain noncash charges, NC, included in its fixed operating costs, we can rewrite Equation 5.3 for the cash operating breakeven point as shown in Equation 5.6:

Equation 5.6
Formula for the cash operating breakeven point

$$\text{Cash operating breakeven point} = \frac{FC - NC}{P - VC}$$

EXAMPLE   Assume that Cindy's Posters (see example on page 144) had included in its fixed operating costs of $2,500, $1,500 of depreciation. Substituting this information (FC = $2,500 and NC = $1,500) along with the firm's $10 per unit sale price (P) and $5 per unit variable operating cost (VC) into Equation 5.6 yields the following:

$$\text{Cash operating breakeven point} = \frac{\$2,500 - \$1,500}{\$10 - \$5} = \frac{\$1,000}{\$5}$$

$$= 200 \text{ units}$$

The firm's cash operating breakeven point is therefore 200 units. This point is considerably below the 500-unit operating breakeven point calculated earlier using accounting data.

Although the cash breakeven analysis provides a convenient mechanism for assessing the level of sales necessary to meet cash operating costs, it is not a substitute for detailed cash plans. Chapter 6 provides a discussion of more formal techniques for analyzing and budgeting cash flows.

Limitations of Breakeven Analysis

Although breakeven analysis is widely used by business, it has a number of inherent limitations. First it assumes that the firm faces linear, or nonvarying, sales revenue and total operating cost functions. Generally, however, this is not the case: Neither the firm's sales price per unit nor

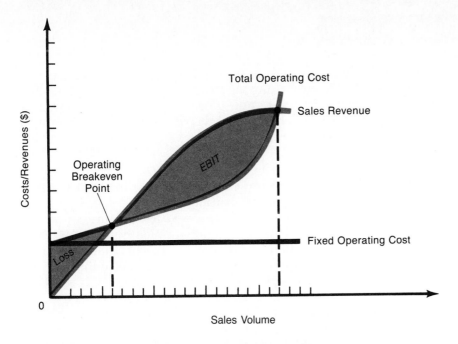

Figure 5.3   A Nonlinear Operating Breakeven Analysis

Nonlinear (curved) breakeven analysis reflects the fact that the firm faces
varying sales revenue and total operating cost functions. This occurs since
the sales price generally decreases with increasing sales volume and cost
per unit generally increases with increasing sales volume.

its variable cost per unit is independent of sales volume. The sales price
per unit generally decreases with increasing sales volume; the cost per
unit generally increases with increasing sales volume, thereby resulting
in *curved*, rather than straight (linear), revenue and cost functions. Figure 5.3 shows a graphic operating breakeven analysis using nonlinear
sales revenue and total operating cost functions. Recognition of these
curved functions may complicate the analysis and result in solutions
different from those obtained using linear revenue and cost functions.

A second limitation of breakeven analysis is the difficulty of breaking semivariable costs into fixed and variable components. Still another
limitation occurs in the application of breakeven analysis to multiproduct firms. Due to the difficulty of allocating costs to products, special
and more sophisticated multiproduct breakeven models must be used
to determine breakeven points for each product line.

Finally, the short-term—typically one year—time horizon of
breakeven analysis often limits its use. A large outlay in the current
financial period could significantly raise the firm's breakeven point,
while the benefits may occur over a period of years. Expenses for advertising and research and development (R and D) are examples of such
outlays. Clearly, all of these potential limitations must be considered
when applying breakeven analysis.

OPERATING LEVERAGE

operating leverage
The potential use of *fixed operating costs* to magnify the effects of changes in sales on the firm's EBIT.

Operating leverage results from the existence of *fixed operating costs* in the firm's income stream. Using the structure presented in Table 5.2, we can define **operating leverage** as the potential use of *fixed operating costs* to magnify the effects of changes in sales on the firm's earnings before interest and taxes (EBIT). The following example illustrates how operating leverage works.

EXAMPLE   Using the data presented earlier for Cindy's Posters (sale price, P = $10 per unit; variable operating cost, VC = $5 per unit; fixed operating cost, FC = $2,500), Figure 5.4 presents the operating breakeven chart originally shown in Figure 5.2. The additional notations on the chart indicate that as the firm's sales increase from 1,000 to 1,500 units (Q_1 to Q_2), its EBIT increases from $2,500 to $5,000 ($EBIT_1$ to $EBIT_2$). In other words, a 50 percent increase in sales (1,000 to 1,500 units) results in a 100 percent increase in EBIT. Table 5.4 includes the data for Figure 5.4 as well as relevant data for a 500-unit sales level. We can illustrate two cases using the 1,000-unit sales level as a reference point.

Case 1:   A 50 percent *increase* in sales (from 1,000 to 1,500 units) results in a 100 percent *increase* in earnings before interest and taxes (from $2,500 to $5,000).

Case 2:   A 50 percent *decrease* in sales (from 1,000 to 500 units) results in a 100 percent *decrease* in earnings before interest and taxes (from $2,500 to $0).

From the above example we see that operating leverage works in both directions. When a firm has fixed operating costs, operating leverage is present. An increase in sales results in a more-than-proportional

Table 5.4   **The EBIT for Various Sales Levels**

		Case 2		Case 1
		−50%		+50%
Sales (in units)		500	1,000	1,500
Sales revenue[a]		$5,000	$10,000	$15,000
Less: Variable operating costs[b]		2,500	5,000	7,500
Less: Fixed operating costs		2,500	2,500	2,500
Earnings before interest and taxes (EBIT)		$ 0	$ 2,500	$ 5,000
		−100%		+100%

[a]Sales revenue = $10/unit × sales in units.
[b]Variable operating costs = $5/unit × sales in units.

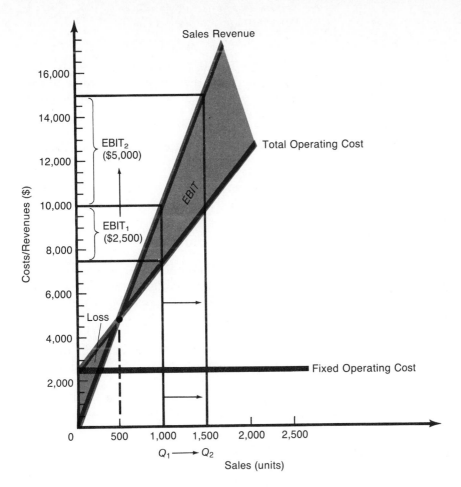

Figure 5.4   Breakeven Analysis and Operating Leverage
The breakeven chart can be used to demonstrate operating leverage. As sales increase by 50 percent from 1,000 units (Q_1) to 1,500 units (Q_2), EBIT increases by 100 percent from $2,500 (EBIT$_1$) to $5,000 (EBIT$_2$).

increase in earnings before interest and taxes. A decrease in sales results in a more-than-proportional decrease in earnings before interest and taxes.

Measuring the Degree of Operating Leverage (DOL)

The **degree of operating leverage (DOL)** is the numerical measure of the firm's operating leverage. It can be derived using the following equation:[2]

degree of operating leverage (DOL) The numerical measure of the firm's operating leverage.

[2]The degree of operating leverage also depends on the base level of sales used as a point of reference. The closer the base sales level used is to the operating breakeven point, the greater the operating leverage. *Comparison of the degree of operating leverage of two firms is valid only when the base level of sales used for each firm is the same.*

Equation 5.7
Formula for the degree of operating leverage (DOL)

$$DOL = \frac{\text{percentage change in EBIT}}{\text{percentage change in sales}}$$

Whenever the percentage change in EBIT resulting from a given percentage change in sales is greater than the percentage change in sales, operating leverage exists. This means that as long as DOL is greater than 1, there is operating leverage.

EXAMPLE   Applying Equation 5.7 to cases 1 and 2 in Table 5.4 yields the following results:[3]

$$\text{Case 1: } \frac{+100\%}{+50\%} = 2.0$$

$$\text{Case 2: } \frac{-100\%}{-50\%} = 2.0$$

Since the result is greater than 1, operating leverage exists. For a given base level of sales, the higher the value resulting from applying Equation 5.7, the greater the degree of operating leverage.

A more direct formula for calculating the degree of operating leverage at a base sales level, Q, is shown in Equation 5.8, using the symbols given on page 143.

Equation 5.8 Direct formula for the degree of operating leverage (DOL)

$$\text{DOL at base sales level } Q = \frac{Q \times (P - VC)}{Q \times (P - VC) - FC}$$

EXAMPLE   Substituting $Q = 1,000$, $P = \$10$, $VC = \$5$, and $FC = \$2,500$ into Equation 5.8 yields the following result:

$$\text{DOL at 1,000 units} = \frac{1,000 \times (\$10 - \$5)}{1,000 \times (\$10 - \$5) - \$2,500}$$

$$= \frac{\$5,000}{\$2,500} = 2.0$$

The use of the formula results in the same value for DOL (2.0) as that found using Table 5.4 and Equation 5.7.[4]

---

[3]Because the concept of leverage is *linear*, positive and negative changes of equal magnitude will always result in equal degrees of leverage when the same base sales level is used as a point of reference. This relationship holds for all types of leverage discussed in this chapter.

[4]When total sales in dollars—instead of unit sales—are available, the following equation in which TR = dollar level of base sales and TVC = total variable operating costs in dollars can be used:

$$\text{DOL at base dollar sales } TR = \frac{TR - TVC}{TR - TVC - FC}$$

This formula is especially useful for finding the DOL for multiproduct firms. It should be clear that since in the case of a single-product firm $TR = P \times Q$ and $TVC = VC \times Q$, substitution of these values into Equation 5.8 results in the equation given here.

Fixed Costs and Operating Leverage

Changes in fixed operating costs affect operating leverage significantly. Firms can sometimes incur fixed operating costs rather than variable operating costs, and at other times may be able to substitute one type of cost for the other. For example, a firm could make fixed-dollar lease payments, rather than payments equal to a specified percentage of sales, or it could compensate sales representatives with a fixed salary and bonus rather than with a pure percent-of-sales commission. The effects of changes in fixed operating costs on operating leverage can best be illustrated by continuing our example.

EXAMPLE   Assume that Cindy's Posters is able to exchange a portion of its variable operating costs (by eliminating sales commissions) for fixed operating costs (by increasing sales salaries). This exchange results in a reduction in the variable operating cost per unit from $5 to $4.50 and an increase in the fixed operating costs from $2,500 to $3,000. Table 5.5 presents an analysis similar to that given in Table 5.4 using these new costs. Although the EBIT of $2,500 at the 1,000-unit sales level is the same as before the shift in operating cost structure, Table 5.5 shows that by shifting to greater fixed operating costs, the firm has increased its operating leverage.

With the substitution of the appropriate values into Equation 5.8, the degree of operating leverage at the 1,000-unit base level of sales becomes

$$\text{DOL at 1,000 units} = \frac{1,000 \times (\$10 - \$4.50)}{1,000 \times (\$10 - \$4.50) - \$3,000}$$

$$= \frac{\$5,500}{\$2,500} = 2.2$$

Comparing this value to the DOL of 2.0 before the shift to more fixed costs, we see that the higher the firm's fixed operating costs relative to variable operating costs, the greater the degree of operating leverage.

Business Risk

Because leverage works in two ways, a shift toward more fixed costs increases business risk. Stated simply, **business risk** is the risk to the firm of being unable to cover operating costs. In the foregoing examples the increase in business risk can be demonstrated by comparing the operating breakeven points before and after the shift. Before the shift, the firm's operating breakeven point is 500 units [$2,500 ÷ ($10 − $5)]. After the shift the operating breakeven point is 545 units [$3,000 ÷ ($10 − $4.50)]. Clearly the firm must achieve a higher level of sales in

business risk The risk to the firm of being unable to cover operating costs.

Table 5.5   **Operating Leverage and Increased Fixed Costs**

		Case 2		Case 1
			−50%	+50%
Sales (in units)		500	1,000	1,500
Sales revenue[a]		$5,000	$10,000	$15,000
Less: Variable operating costs[b]		2,250	4,500	6,750
Less: Fixed operating costs		3,000	3,000	3,000
Earnings before interest and taxes (EBIT)		−$250	$ 2,500	$ 5,250
			−110%	+110%

[a]Sales revenue was calculated as indicated in Table 5.4.
[b]Variable operating costs = $4.50/unit × sales in units.

order to meet increased fixed operating costs. On the positive side, however, higher operating leverage causes EBIT to increase more for a given increase in sales. When considering fixed operating cost increases, the financial manager must weigh the increased business risk associated with greater operating leverage against the expected increase in returns.

FINANCIAL LEVERAGE

financial leverage
The potential use of fixed financial costs to magnify the effects of changes in EBIT on the firm's EPS.

Financial leverage results from the presence of *fixed financial costs* in the firm's income stream. Using the framework in Table 5.1, we can define **financial leverage** as the potential use of *fixed financial costs* to magnify the effects of changes in earnings before interest and taxes (EBIT) on the firm's earnings per share (EPS). The two fixed financial costs that may be found on the firm's income statement are (1) interest on debt and (2) preferred stock dividends. These charges must be paid regardless of the amount of EBIT available to pay them. The following example illustrates how financial leverage works.

EXAMPLE   Pedros, a small Mexican food company, expects earnings before interest and taxes of $10,000 in the current year. It has a $20,000 bond with a 10 percent (annual) coupon rate of interest and an issue of 600 shares of $4 (annual dividend per share) preferred stock outstanding. It also has 1,000 shares of common stock outstanding. The annual interest on the bond issue is $2,000 (.10 × $20,000). The annual dividends on the preferred stock are $2,400 ($4.00/share × 600 shares). Table 5.6 presents the earnings per share corresponding to levels of earnings before interest and taxes of

Table 5.6 **The EPS for Various EBIT Levels**

	Case 2		Case 1
	−40%		+40%
EBIT	$6,000	$10,000	$14,000
Less: Interest (*I*)	2,000	2,000	2,000
Net profits before taxes (*NPBT*)	$4,000	$ 8,000	$12,000
Less: Taxes (*T* = .40)	1,600	3,200	4,800
Net profits after taxes (*NPAT*)	$2,400	$ 4,800	$ 7,200
Less: Preferred stock dividends (*PD*)	2,400	2,400	2,400
Earnings available for common (*EAC*)	$ 0	$ 2,400	$ 4,800
Earnings per share (EPS)	$\frac{\$0}{1,000} = \$0$	$\frac{\$2,400}{1,000} = \$2.40$	$\frac{\$4,800}{1,000} = \$4.80$
	−100%		+100%

$6,000, $10,000, and $14,000, assuming the firm is in the 40 percent tax bracket. Two situations are illustrated in the table.

Case 1: A 40 percent *increase* in EBIT (from $10,000 to $14,000) results in a 100 percent *increase* in earnings per share (from $2.40 to $4.80).

Case 2: A 40 percent *decrease* in EBIT (from $10,000 to $6,000) results in a 100 percent *decrease* in earnings per share (from $2.40 to $0).

The effect of financial leverage is such that an increase in the firm's EBIT results in a more-than-proportional increase in the firm's earnings per share, whereas a decrease in the firm's EBIT results in a more-than-proportional decrease in EPS.

Measuring the Degree of Financial Leverage (DFL)

The **degree of financial leverage (DFL)** is the numerical measure of the firm's financial leverage. It can be computed in a fashion similar to that used to measure the degree of operating leverage. The following equation presents one approach for obtaining DFL.[5]

degree of financial leverage (DFL) The numerical measure of the firm's financial leverage.

---

[5]This approach is valid only when the base level of EBIT used to calculate and compare these values is the same. In other words, *the base level of EBIT must be held constant in order to compare the financial leverage associated with different levels of fixed financial costs.*

Equation 5.9
Formula for the degree of financial leverage (DFL)

$$DFL = \frac{\text{percentage change in EPS}}{\text{percentage change in EBIT}}$$

Whenever the percentage change in EPS resulting from a given percentage change in EBIT is greater than the percentage change in EBIT, financial leverage exists. This means that whenever DFL is greater than 1, there is financial leverage.

EXAMPLE Applying Equation 5.9 to cases 1 and 2 in Table 5.6 yields

$$\text{Case 1: } \frac{+100\%}{+40\%} = 2.5$$

$$\text{Case 2: } \frac{-100\%}{-40\%} = 2.5$$

In both cases, the quotient is greater than 1, and financial leverage exists. The higher this value, the greater the degree of financial leverage.

A more direct formula for calculating the degree of financial leverage at a base level of EBIT is given by Equation 5.10, using the notation from Table 5.6. Note that in the denominator the term, $\frac{1}{1-T}$, converts the after-tax preferred stock dividend to a before-tax amount for consistency with the other terms in the equation.

Equation 5.10
Direct formula for the degree of financial leverage (DFL)

$$DFL \text{ at base level EBIT} = \frac{EBIT}{EBIT - I - \left(PD \times \dfrac{1}{1-T}\right)}$$

EXAMPLE Substituting EBIT = $10,000, I = $2,000, PD = $2,400, and the tax rate (T = .40) into Equation 5.10 yields the following result:

DFL at $10,000 EBIT =

$$\frac{\$10,000}{\$10,000 - \$2,000 - \left(\$2,400 \times \dfrac{1}{1 - .40}\right)}$$

$$= \frac{\$10,000}{\$4,000} = 2.5$$

Notice that the formula given in Equation 5.10 provides a more direct method for calculating the degree of financial leverage than the approach illustrated using Table 5.6 and Equation 5.9.

Graphic Comparison of Financing Plans

Financing plans can be compared graphically by plotting them on a set of EBIT–EPS axes. This approach can be illustrated with an example.

EXAMPLE   The key characteristics of the financing plan presented earlier, referred to as plan A, and a new financing plan, plan B, are summarized below:

Type of financing	Plan A	Plan B
Debt	$20,000 of 10% interest	$10,000 of 10% interest
Annual interest	.10 × $20,000 = $2,000	.10 × $10,000 = $1,000
Preferred stock	600 shares of $4 dividend	300 shares of $4 dividend
Annual dividend	600 × $4 = $2,400	300 × $4 = $1,200
Common stock Number of shares	1,000	1,750

These two plans can be illustrated graphically. Like all plans of this type, they can be plotted as a *straight line* on a set of EBIT–EPS axes. Two EBIT–EPS coordinates, or plotting points, are needed for each plan. These coordinates can be drawn from Table 5.6 for plan A, but we need to calculate two coordinates for plan B. The EPS associated with EBIT values of $10,000 and $14,000, respectively, are calculated for plan B in Table 5.7. It can be seen that for plan B a 40 percent increase in the firm's EBIT will result in a 57 percent increase in EPS. Applying Equation 5.10 to these values yields

$$\text{DFL at \$10,000 EBIT} = \frac{\$10,000}{\$10,000 - \$1,000 - \left(\$1,200 \times \dfrac{1}{1 - .40}\right)}$$

$$= \frac{\$10,000}{\$7,000} = 1.4$$

Plan B's degree of financial leverage of 1.4, when compared to the *DFL* of 2.5 calculated earlier for plan A, indicates that plan B has a lower degree of financial leverage than plan A.

The three EBIT–EPS coordinates from Table 5.6 for plan A and the two coordinates derived in Table 5.7 for plan B are summarized below:

Table 5.7   Calculation of Plan B's EBIT–EPS Coordinates

	+40%	
EBIT	$10,000	$14,000
$-I$	1,000	1,000
NPBT	$ 9,000	$13,000
$-$Taxes $(T = .40)$	3,600	5,200
NPAT	$ 5,400	7,800
$-PD$	1,200	1,200
EAC	$ 4,200	$ 6,600
EPS	$\dfrac{\$4,200}{1,750} = \$2.40$	$\dfrac{\$6,600}{1,750} = \$3.77$
	+57%	

	Coordinates	
Plan	EBIT	EPS
A	$ 6,000	$0.00
	10,000	2.40
	14,000	4.80
B	$10,000	$2.40
	14,000	3.77

With these coordinates, the two financing plans are presented graphically in Figure 5.5.

As Figure 5.5 illustrates, the slope of plan A is steeper than that of plan B. This indicates that plan A has more financial leverage than plan B. This result is as expected, since the degree of financial leverage (DFL) is 2.5 for plan A and 1.4 for plan B. The higher the DFL, the greater the leverage a plan has, and the steeper its slope when plotted on EBIT–EPS axes.

Financial Breakeven Point

financial breakeven point The level of EBIT necessary for the firm to just cover all fixed financial costs.

In our example, the point of intersection of each plan with the EBIT axis represents the amount of earnings before interest and taxes necessary for the firm to just cover all fixed financial costs—that is, the point at which EPS = $0. This point of intersection can be thought of as a **financial breakeven point,** since it represents the level of EBIT necessary for the firm to just cover all fixed financial costs. The breakeven EBIT for plan A is $6,000; for plan B it is $3,000. In other words, earnings before interest and taxes of less than $6,000 with plan A or less than $3,000 with plan B will result in a loss, or negative EPS.

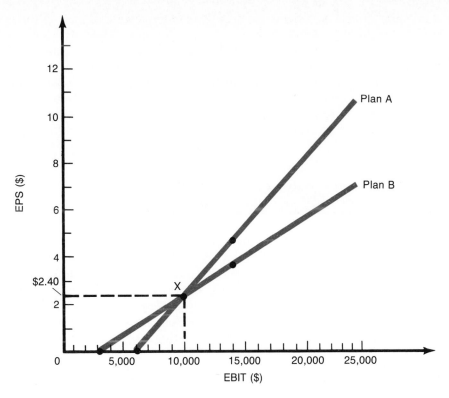

Figure 5.5   **A Graphic Presentation of Alternate Financing Plans**
Because the slope of Plan A is steeper than that of Plan B, Plan A has more
financial leverage. In addition, Plan A has a higher financial breakeven
point ($6,000) than Plan B ($3,000). At EBIT below the $10,000 indifference
point Plan B is preferred; above $10,000 EBIT Plan A is preferred.

Indifference Point

The point labeled *X* in Figure 5.5 represents the **indifference point** between plan A and plan B. It indicates that at a level of EBIT of $10,000,
EPS of $2.40 would result under both plans. At levels of EBIT below
$10,000, plan B results in higher levels of EPS. At levels of EBIT above
$10,000, plan A results in higher levels of EPS. The usefulness of this
type of analysis is discussed in Chapter 16.

indifference point
On a graphed compari-
son of two financing
plans, the point at which,
for a given EBIT, EPS is
the same for both plans.

Financial Risk

Increasing financial leverage results in increasing risk. Increased financial payments require the firm to maintain a higher level of EBIT in
order to break even. **Financial risk** is the risk to the firm of being unable
to cover financial costs. If the firm cannot cover these financial payments, it can be forced out of business by creditors whose claims remain

financial risk The risk
to the firm of being un-
able to cover financial
costs.

unsettled.[6] On the positive side, higher financial leverage causes EPS to increase more for a given increase in EBIT. Financial leverage is often measured using various debt ratios (Chapter 4). These ratios indicate the relationship between the funds on which fixed financial charges must be paid and the total funds invested in the firm. When considering the increased use of debt or preferred stock financing, the financial manager must weigh the increased financial risk associated with greater financial leverage against the expected increase in returns.

TOTAL LEVERAGE: THE COMBINED EFFECT

total leverage The potential use of fixed costs, *both operating and financial,* to magnify the effect of changes in sales on the firm's EPS.

The combined effect of operating and financial leverage on the firm's risk can be assessed using a framework similar to that used to develop the individual concepts of leverage. This combined effect, or **total leverage,** can be defined as the potential use of *fixed costs, both operating and financial,* to magnify the effect of changes in sales on the firm's earnings per share (EPS). Total leverage can therefore be viewed as the total impact of the fixed costs on the firm's operating and financial structure.

EXAMPLE   Health Cereal, a small cereal company, expects sales of 20,000 units at $5 per unit in the coming year and must meet the following: variable operating costs of $2 per unit; fixed operating costs of $10,000; interest of $20,000; and preferred stock dividends of $12,000. The firm is in the 40 percent tax bracket and has 5,000 shares of common stock outstanding. Table 5.8 presents the levels of earnings per share (EPS) associated with the expected sales of 20,000 units and with sales of 30,000 units.

The table illustrates that as a result of a 50 percent increase in sales (20,000 to 30,000 units), the firm would experience a 300 percent increase in earnings per share (from $1.20 to $4.80). Although not shown in the table, a 50 percent decrease in sales would, conversely, result in a 300 percent decrease in earnings per share. The linear nature of the leverage relationship accounts for the fact that sales changes of equal magnitude in opposite directions result in earnings-per-share changes of equal magnitude in the corresponding direction. At this point it should be clear that whenever a firm has fixed costs—operating or financial—in its structure, total leverage will exist.

---

[6]Preferred stockholders do not have the power to force liquidation if their claims remain unpaid. The problem with not paying preferred stock dividends is that then the common stockholders can receive no dividends.

Table 5.8   **The Total Leverage Effect**

	+50%			
Sales (in units)	20,000	30,000		
Sales revenueª	$100,000	$150,000	DOL =	
Less: Variable operating costsᵇ	40,000	60,000		
Less: Fixed operating costs	10,000	10,000	$\frac{+60\%}{+50\%} = 1.2$	
Earnings before interest and taxes (EBIT)	$ 50,000	$ 80,000		
	+60%			DTL =
Less: Interest	20,000	20,000		
Net profits before taxes	$30,000	$60,000		$\frac{+300\%}{+50\%} = 6.0$
Less: Taxes (40%)	12,000	24,000		
Net profits after taxes	$18,000	$36,000	DFL =	
Less: Preferred stock dividends	12,000	12,000		
Earnings available for common	$ 6,000	$24,000	$\frac{+300\%}{+60\%} = 5.0$	
Earnings per share (EPS)	$\frac{\$6,000}{5,000} = \$1.20$	$\frac{\$24,000}{5,000} = 4.80$		
	+300%			

ªSales revenue = $5/unit × sales in units.
ᵇVariable operating costs = $2/unit × sales in units.

Measuring the Degree of Total Leverage (DTL)

The **degree of total leverage (DTL)** is the numerical measure of the firm's total leverage. It can be obtained in a fashion similar to that used to measure operating and financial leverage. The following equation presents one approach for measuring DTL.[7]

$$DTL = \frac{\text{percentage change in EPS}}{\text{percentage change in sales}}$$

Whenever the percentage change in EPS resulting from a given percentage change in sales is greater than the percentage change in sales, total leverage exists. This means that as long as the DTL is greater than 1, there is total leverage.

degree of total leverage (DTL) The numerical measure of the firm's total leverage.

Equation 5.11
Formula for the degree of total leverage (DTL)

---

[7]This approach is valid only when the base level of sales used to calculate and compare these values is the same. In other words, *the base level of sales must be held constant in order to compare the total leverage associated with different levels of fixed costs.*

FINANCE IN ACTION

Fly the Nervous Skies of America West

When fear of recession strikes the economy, you can almost feel the impact on heavily leveraged companies. At America West Airlines, the ninth largest domestic airline with sales of $993.4 million and profits of $20 million in 1989, the feeling produces nervousness.

As an airline, America West faces substantial operating leverage due to the high proportion of fixed operating expenses in the firm's total cost structure. In addition, America West uses a significant amount of financial leverage to keep its planes in the air. At the end of 1989, the firm's long-term debt totaled $625 million; stockholders' equity stood at only $96 million.

In the early months of 1990, America West pursued an aggressive expansion strategy fueled with additional borrowing. Then in August, Iraq seized Kuwait, and the price of aviation fuel rose from 60 to 90 cents per gallon in eight short weeks. This unexpected jump in the price of fuel elevated America West's operating leverage to unprecedented levels. Fuel costs represent a semi-variable cost to the airline, because the cost of gasoline necessary to complete a scheduled flight does not depend on the number of passengers the flight carries. Hence, fuel costs do not vary with sales revenue.

Given America West's significant leverage, the firm's earnings expectations plummeted upon news of the Iraqi invasion. Before the invasion, analysts expected the firm to earn $1.00 per share in 1990 and $1.21 in 1991. After the invasion, these estimates were revised to a loss of $0.24 per share in 1990, and earnings of only $0.17 per share in 1991. As the Gulf crisis unfolded, America West shareholders bid its stock price down from $9.00 per share to $5.75, making it even more difficult for the firm to reduce its financial leverage by issuing new equity. Further financial deterioration resulted in America Wests' filing for bankruptcy in mid 1991.

Source: Henry Dubroff, "On a wing and a prayer," *CFO Magazine*, November 1990, p. 32.

EXAMPLE   Applying Equation 5.11 to the data in Table 5.8 yields

$$\text{DTL} = \frac{+300\%}{+50\%} = 6.0$$

Since this result is greater than 1, total leverage exists. The higher the value, the greater the degree of total leverage.

A more direct formula for calculating the degree of total leverage at a given base level of sales, Q, is given by Equation 5.12, which uses the same notation presented earlier:

DTL at base sales level $Q =$

$$\frac{Q \times (P - VC)}{Q \times (P - VC) - FC - I - \left(PD \times \dfrac{1}{1 - T}\right)}$$

Equation 5.12
Direct formula for the
degree of total
leverage (DTL)

EXAMPLE   Substituting $Q = 20{,}000$, $P = \$5$, $VC = \$2$, $FC = \$10{,}000$, $I = \$20{,}000$, $PD = \$12{,}000$, and the tax rate ($T = .40$) into Equation 5.12 yields the following result:

DTL at 20,000 units $=$

$$\frac{20{,}000 \times (\$5 - \$2)}{20{,}000 \times (\$5 - \$2) - \$10{,}000 - \$20{,}000 - \left(\$12{,}000 \times \dfrac{1}{1 - .40}\right)}$$

$$= \frac{\$60{,}000}{\$10{,}000} = 6.0$$

Clearly, the formula used in Equation 5.12 provides a more direct method for calculating the degree of total leverage than the approach illustrated using Table 5.8 and Equation 5.11.

The Relationship of Operating, Financial, and Total Leverage

Total leverage reflects the combined impact of operating and financial leverage on the firm. High operating and high financial leverage will cause total leverage to be high. The opposite will also be true. The relationship between operating and financial leverage is *multiplicative* rather than *additive*. The relationship between the degree of total leverage (DTL) and the degrees of operating (DOL) and financial (DFL) leverage is given by Equation 5.13.

$$DTL = DOL \times DFL$$

Equation 5.13
Formula depicting the
relationship between
the degrees of total,
operating, and
financial leverage

EXAMPLE   Substituting the values calculated for DOL and DFL, shown on the right-hand side of Table 5.8, into equation 5.13 yields

$$DTL = 1.2 \times 5.0 = 6.0$$

The resulting degree of total leverage (6.0) is the same value as was calculated directly in the preceding examples.

Total Risk

In a relationship similar to those between operating leverage and business risk, and financial leverage and financial risk, total leverage reflects the total risk of the firm. The firm's **total risk** is therefore the firm's risk of being unable to cover both operating and financial costs.

total risk   The risk to the firm of being unable to cover both operating and financial costs.

With increasing costs—especially fixed operating and financial costs—comes increasing risk, since the firm will have to achieve a higher level of sales just to break even. If a firm is unable to meet these costs, it could be forced out of business by its creditors. On the positive side, higher total leverage causes EPS to increase more for a given increase in sales. When considering fixed operating or financial cost increases, the financial manager must weigh the increased risk associated with greater leverage against the expected increase in returns.

SUMMARY

1   **Relate operating leverage, financial leverage, and total leverage to the firm's income statement.**   Operating leverage is concerned with the relationship between a firm's sales and its earnings before interest and taxes (EBIT). Financial leverage is concerned with the relationship between the firm's EBIT and its earnings per share (EPS). Total leverage is concerned with the relationship between the firm's sales and its EPS.

2   **Discuss the role of breakeven analysis and the calculation and graphic depiction of the operating breakeven point in terms of units, dollars, and cash.**   Breakeven analysis is used both to determine the level or sales necessary to cover all operating costs and to evaluate profitability. Below the operating breakeven point, the firm experiences a loss. Above the operating breakeven point, the firm's earnings before interest and taxes (EBIT) are positive. Cost increases raise the breakeven point and sales price increases lower it, and vice versa. The breakeven point can be found in terms of units of sales, dollars of sales, or on a cash basis.

3   **Describe the chief limitations inherent in the use of breakeven analysis.**   Breakeven analysis suffers from a number of limitations, chief among which are the assumption of linearity, the difficulty of classifying costs, problems caused by multiproduct situations, and the short-term nature of the typical time horizon.

4   **Measure the degree of operating leverage and discuss its relationship to fixed costs and business risk.**   Operating leverage is the potential use of fixed operating costs by the firm to magnify the effects of changes in sales on earnings before interest and taxes (EBIT). The higher the fixed operating costs, the greater the operating leverage. The degree of operating leverage (DOL) at a specified level of sales can be calculated using a tabular approach or by formula. The firm's business risk is directly related to its degree of operating leverage.

5   **Calculate the degree of financial leverage, graphically compare financing plans, and discuss financial risk.**   Financial leverage is the potential use of fixed financial costs by the firm to magnify the effects of changes in earning before interest and taxes (EBIT) on earnings per share (EPS). The higher the fixed financial costs—typically interest on debt and preferred stock dividends—the greater the financial leverage. The degree of financial leverage (DFL) at a specified level of earnings before interest and taxes can be calculated using a tabular approach or by formula. Financing plans can be graphed on a set of EBIT–EPS axes. The steeper the slope of the financing plan, the higher its degree of financial leverage. The level of EBIT at which EPS just equals zero is the financial breakeven point. The firm's financial risk is directly related to its degree of financial leverage.

6   **Discuss the degree of total leverage and describe its relationship to operating leverage, financial leverage, and total risk.** The total leverage of the firm is the potential use of fixed costs—both operating and financial—to magnify the effects of changes in sales on earnings per share. The higher these fixed costs, the greater the total leverage. The degree of total leverage (DTL) at a specified level of sales can be measured using a tabular approach or by formula. It can also be found by multiplying the degree of operating leverage (DOL) by the degree of financial leverage (DFL). The firm's total risk is directly related to its degree of total leverage.

QUESTIONS

5—1   What is meant by the term *leverage?* How do operating leverage, financial leverage, and total leverage relate to the income statement?

5—2   Define and differentiate between fixed costs, variable costs, and semi-variable costs. Which of these costs is the key element creating leverage?

5—3   Define and differentiate between each of the following operating breakeven points:
   a. Breakeven in *units*
   b. Breakeven in *dollars*
   c. *Cash* breakeven

5—4   How do changes in fixed operating costs, the sale price per unit, and the variable operating cost per unit affect the firm's *operating breakeven point?*

5—5   One of the key limitations of breakeven analysis is the assumption of linear sales revenue and total operating cost functions. Why might these functions actually be curved? What are some other limitations of breakeven analysis?

5—6   What is meant by *operating leverage?* What causes it? How is the *degree of operating leverage (DOL)* measured?

5—7   What is the relationship between operating leverage and business risk? How is each of these related to the operating breakeven point and risk-return trade-off?

5—8   What is meant by *financial leverage?* What causes it?

5—9   What is the *degree of financial leverage (DFL)?* What two methods can be used to calculate the DFL?

5—10   Why must financial managers assess the firm's degree of financial leverage? Why is this measure important in evaluating various financing plans?

5—11   What is the relationship between financial leverage and financial risk? How is each of these related to the financial breakeven point and risk-return trade-off?

5—12   What is the general relationship among operating leverage, financial leverage, and the total leverage of the firm? Do these types of leverage complement each other? Why, or why not?

PROBLEMS

5—1   **(Breakeven Point–Algebraic)** Marilyn Cosgrove wishes to estimate the number of pairs of shoes she must sell at $24.95 per pair in order to break even. She has estimated fixed operating costs of $12,350 per year and variable operating costs of $15.45 per pair. How many pairs of shoes must Marilyn sell in order to break even on operating costs?

5—2   **(Breakeven Point–Algebraic and Graphic)** Sting Industries sells its single product for $129.00 per unit. The firm's fixed operating costs are $473,000 annually and its variable operating costs are $86.00 per unit.

a. Find the firm's operating breakeven point.

b. Label the x-axis "Sales (units)" and the y-axis "Costs/Revenues ($)" and then graph the firm's sales revenue, total operating cost, and fixed operating cost functions on these axes. In addition, label the operating breakeven point and the areas of loss and profit (EBIT).

5—3   **(Breakeven Analysis)** Doug Mills is considering opening a record store. He wants to estimate the number of records he must sell in order to break even. The records will be sold for $6.98 each, variable operating costs are $5.23 per record, and annual fixed operating costs are $36,750.

a. Find the operating breakeven point.

b. Calculate the total operating costs at the breakeven volume found in **a**.

c. If Doug estimates that at a minimum he can sell 2,000 records *per month*, should he go into the record business?

d. How much EBIT would Doug realize if he sells the minimum 2,000 records per month noted in **c**?

5—4   **(Breakeven Point–Changing Costs/Revenues)** Hi-Tek Press publishes the *Video Yearbook*. Last year the book sold for $10 with variable operating cost per book of $8 and fixed operating costs of $40,000. How many books must be sold this year to achieve the breakeven point for the stated operating costs, given the following different circumstances?

a. All figures remain the same as last year.

b. Fixed operating costs increase to $44,000; all other figures remain the same as last year.

c. The selling price increases to $10.50; all costs remain the same as last year.

d. Variable operating cost per book increases to $8.50; all other figures remain the same.

e. What conclusions about the operating breakeven point can be drawn from your answers?

5—5   **(Breakeven Comparisons)** Given the following price and cost data for each of the three firms M, N, and O, answer the questions below.

	M	**N**	**O**
Sale price per unit	$ 18.00	$ 21.00	$ 30.00
Variable operating cost per unit	6.75	13.50	12.00
Fixed operating cost	45,000	30,000	90,000

a. What is the operating breakeven point *in units* for each firm?

b. Compute the *dollar* operating breakeven point.

c. Assuming $10,000 of each firm's fixed operating costs are depreciation, compute the *cash* operating breakeven point for each firm.

d. How would you rank these firms in terms of their risk?

5—6   **(EBIT Sensitivity)** The Harlow Company sells its finished product for $9 per unit. Its fixed operating costs are $20,000 and the variable operating cost per unit is $5.

    a. Calculate the firm's earnings before interest and taxes (EBIT) for sales of 10,000 units.
    b. Calculate the firm's EBIT for sales of 8,000 and 12,000 units, respectively.
    c. Calculate the percentage change in sales (from the 10,000-unit base level) and associated percentage changes in EBIT for the shifts in sales indicated in **b**.

5—7   **(Degree of Operating Leverage)** The Withers Design Group has fixed operating costs of $380,000, variable operating costs per unit of $16, and a selling price of $63.50 per unit.
    a. Calculate the operating breakeven point in units and sales dollars.
    b. Calculate the firm's EBIT at 9,000, 10,000, and 11,000 units, respectively.
    c. Using 10,000 units as a base, what are the percentage changes in units sold and EBIT as sales move from the base to the other sales levels used in **b**?
    d. Use the percentages computed in **c** to determine the degree of operating leverage (DOL).
    e. Use the formula for degree of operating leverage to determine the DOL at 10,000 units.

5—8   **(Degree of Operating Leverage—Graphic)** Zandy, Inc. has fixed operating costs of $72,000, variable operating costs of $6.75 per unit, and a selling price of $9.75 per unit.
    a. Calculate the operating breakeven point in units.
    b. Compute the degree of operating leverage (DOL) for the following unit sales levels: 25,000, 30,000, 40,000. Use the formula given in the chapter.
    c. Graph the DOL figures you computed in **b** (on the y-axis) against sales levels (on the x-axis).
    d. Compute the degree of operating leverage at 24,000 units; add this point to your graph.
    e. What principle is illustrated by your graph and figures?

5—9   **(EPS Calculations)** Fleet Corporation has $60,000 of 16-percent (annual interest) bonds outstanding, 1,500 shares of preferred stock paying an annual dividend of $5 per share, and 4,000 shares of common stock outstanding. Assuming the firm has a 40 percent tax rate, compute earnings per share (EPS) for the following levels of EBIT:
    a. $24,600
    b. $30,600
    c. $35,000

5—10   **(Degree of Financial Leverage)** Central Canning Company has EBIT of $67,500. Interest costs are $22,500 and the firm has 15,000 shares of common stock outstanding. Assume a 40 percent tax rate.
    a. Use the degree of financial leverage (DFL) formula to calculate the DFL for the firm.
    b. Using a set of EBIT–EPS axes, plot Central Canning's financial plan.
    c. Assuming the firm also has 1,000 shares of preferred stock paying a $6.00 annual dividend per share, what is the DFL?
    d. Plot the financing plan including the 1,000 shares of $6.00 preferred stock on the axes used in **b**.
    e. Briefly discuss the graph of the two financing plans.

5—11   **(DFL and Graphic Display of Financing Plans)** Western Oil Corporation has a current capital structure consisting of $250,000 of 16 percent (annual interest) debt and 2,000 shares of common stock. The firm pays taxes at the rate of 40 percent.

      a. Using EBIT values of $80,000 and $120,000, determine the associated earnings per share (EPS).

      b. Using $80,000 of EBIT as a base, calculate the degree of financial leverage (DFL).

      c. Graph the firm's current financing plan on a set of EBIT–EPS axes.

      d. Rework parts **a** and **b** assuming the firm has $100,000 of 16 percent (annual interest) debt and 3,000 shares of common stock.

      e. Graph the financing plan in **d** on the same axes used in **c**, and discuss the relationship between financial leverage and the graphic display of the two financing plans.

5—12   **(Total Breakeven)** Magowan Manufacturing produces small motors. Their fixed operating costs are $20,000, variable operating costs are $18 per unit, and the motors sell for $23 each. Magowan has $50,000 in 10 percent (annual interest) bonds and 20,000 shares of common stock outstanding. The firm is in the 40 percent tax bracket.

      a. What is Magowan's operating breakeven point in units?

      b. What is Magowan's financial breakeven point?

      c. What is Magowan's total (i.e., both operating and financial costs) breakeven point?

5—13   **(Integrative—Multiple Leverage Measures)** Musk Oil Cosmetics produces skin-care products, selling 400,000 bottles a year. Each bottle produced has a variable operating cost of $.84 and sells for $1.00. Fixed operating costs are $28,000. The firm has annual interest charges of $6,000, preferred dividends of $2,000, and a 40 percent tax rate.

      a. Calculate (1) the operating breakeven point in units and (2) the total (including both operating and financial costs) breakeven point in units.

      b. Use the degree of operating leverage (DOL) formula to calculate DOL.

      c. Use the degree of financial leverage (DFL) formula to calculate DFL.

      d. Use the degree of total leverage (DTL) formula to calculate DTL. Compare this to the product of DOL and DFL calculated in **b** and **c**.

5—14   **(Integrative—Leverage and Risk)** Firm J has sales of 100,000 units at $2.00 per unit, variable operating costs of $1.70 per unit, and fixed operating costs of $6,000. Interest is $10,000 per year. Firm R has sales of 100,000 units at $2.50 per unit, variable operating costs of $1.00 per unit, and fixed operating costs of $62,500. Interest is $17,500 per year. Assume that both firms are in the 40 percent tax bracket.

      a. Compute the degree of operating, financial, and total leverage for firm J.

      b. Compute the degree of operating, financial, and total leverage for firm R.

      c. Compare the relative risks of the two firms.

      d. Discuss the principles of leverage illustrated in your answers.

CASE

Evaluating Newton Electronics' Financing Plans

Newton Electronics, a large consumer electronics manufacturer, needs to raise $10,000,000 to pay for the final phase of a major plant expansion. The firm currently has $50,000,000 of 12 percent (annual interest) bonds and 10,000,000 shares of common stock outstanding. After lengthy investigation, the firm's financial analysts have isolated the following two financing plans.

1 ▮▮▮▮ Bonds: Sell $10,000,000 of 12 percent (annual interest) bonds.

2 ▮▮▮▮ Stock: Sell 1,000,000 shares of common stock at an average price of $10 per share.

The firm's analysts expect its earnings before interest and taxes (EBIT) to average about $30,000,000 annually. The firm is subject to a 40 percent tax rate.

Required

a. Use EBIT of $30,000,000 as a point of reference to determine the degree of financial leverage (DFL) under each financing plan.

b. Plot the two financing plans on a set of EBIT–EPS axes. From the graph estimate (1) the financial breakeven point for each plan and (2) the indifference point between them.

c. Based on your graph in **b**, over what range of EBIT would each plan be preferred?

d. Assuming the firm's objective is to maximize its earnings per share (EPS), which plan would you recommend? Why?

FINANCIAL PLANNING

Checking the Financial Level at Jiffy Lube

((Sales depend on convenience, and revenue depends on the number of cars the outlet can attract.))

The fast-lube trade was one of the most rapidly growing industries during the 1990s. Over 4,000 outlets pump sales in excess of $1 billion. Many outlets are owned by franchisees. Jiffy Lube, the largest franchiser, provides insight to the financial pros and cons of franchise ownership.

Demand plays a crucial role in determining the feasibility of a franchise. Sales depend on convenience, and revenue depends on the number of cars the outlet can attract. Industry guidelines recommend attention to accessibility of location and to the demographic profile of potential customers. A good location is on the going-home side of a road with a maximum 35-mile-per-hour speed limit and 25,000 "pass-bys" a day. A good customer base consists of 20,000 people, with a $20,000 median income, within a 3-mile radius.

Gross profits are approximately $15 per car, based upon a $24 gross sale less $9 product cost. At a rate of 5 cars per hour, an 8-hour shift should be able to handle 40 cars per service bay. A primary financial question is whether the average daily contribution of $600 ($15 × 40) is sufficient to cover other typical expenses found on a lube-shop income statement, including salaries, utilities, insurance, advertising, and franchise fees.

The single-purpose nature of the building is a critical aspect of the outlet's fixed assets. Drive-through service bays and full-service basements are the industry norm. Automalls, which include sellers of auto parts, insurance, car washes, mufflers, and auto repairs, are frequently developed to enhance sales.

As with all retail businesses, cash flow is of paramount importance. One quick-lube advantage is that cash or credit cards are the normal payment mode, reducing receivables. Unfortunately, quick lube franchises generally start off in a negative cash position, paying several thousand dollars for the right to use the franchiser's name and services. The percentage of funds that can be borrowed to purchase or build an outlet tends to be low, reflecting the single-purpose nature of the fixed assets. In addition, most franchise operators must make a personal guarantee to the lender. Financial planning is necessary to provide for the fluid management of a Jiffy Lube franchise before and after the first oil change.

financial planning is an important aspect of the firm's operation and livelihood since it provides road maps for guiding, coordinating, and controlling the firm's actions in order to achieve its objectives. Two key aspects of the financial planning process are *cash planning* and *profit planning*. Cash planning involves the preparation of the firm's cash budget. Without adequate cash—regardless of the level of profits—any firm could fail. Profit planning is usually done by means of pro forma financial statements, which show anticipated levels of profits, assets, liabilities, and equity. Cash budgets and pro forma statements not only are useful for internal financial planning but also are routinely required by present and prospective lenders. Before studying the preparation and use of these statements, we examine the relationship between long-run and short-run financial plans.

THE FINANCIAL PLANNING PROCESS

financial planning process Planning that begins with long-run financial plans that in turn guide short-run plans and budgets.

The **financial planning process** begins with long-run, or strategic, financial plans that in turn guide the formulation of short-run, or operating, plans and budgets. Generally, the short-run plans and budgets implement the firm's long-run strategic objectives. Although the major emphasis in this chapter is on short-run financial plans and budgets, a few comments on the long-run plans are appropriate here.

Long-Run (Strategic) Financial Plans

long-run (strategic) financial plans Planned long-term financial actions and the anticipated financial impact of those actions.

Long-run (strategic) financial plans are planned long-term financial actions and the anticipated financial impact of those actions. Such plans tend to cover periods ranging from two to 10 years. The use of five-year strategic plans, which are periodically revised as significant new information becomes available, is common. Generally, firms that are subject to high degrees of operating uncertainty, relatively short production cycles, or both tend to use shorter planning horizons. Long-run financial plans consider proposed fixed-asset outlays, research and development activities, marketing and product development actions, and major sources of financing. Also included would be termination of existing projects, product lines, or lines of business; repayment or retirement of outstanding debts; and any planned acquisitions. Such plans tend to be supported by a series of annual budgets and profit plans.

Short-Run (Operating) Financial Plans

short-run (operating) financial plans Planned short-term financial actions and the anticipated financial impact of those actions.

Short-run (operating) financial plans are planned short-term financial actions and the anticipated financial impact of those actions. These plans most often cover a one- to two-year period. Key inputs include the

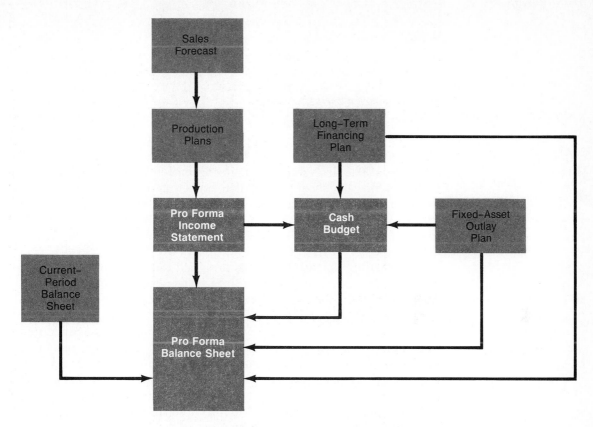

Figure 6.1   **The Short-Run (Operating) Financial Planning Process**

The key input to the short-run (operating) financial planning process is the sales forecast. It is used to develop production plans that take into account lead (preparation) times and include estimates of the required types and quantities of raw materials. These estimates are input to the pro forma income statement and cash budget, which with additional data are used to prepare the pro forma balance sheet.

sales forecast and various forms of operating and financial data. Key outputs include a number of operating budgets, the cash budget, and pro forma financial statements. The short-run financial planning process, from the initial sales forecast through the development of the cash budget and pro forma income statement and balance sheet, is presented in the flow diagram in Figure 6.1.

From the sales forecast are developed production plans that take into account lead (preparation) times and include estimates of the required types and quantities of raw materials. Using the production plans, the firm can estimate direct labor requirements, factory overhead outlays, and operating expenses. Once these estimates have been made, the firm's pro forma income statement and cash budget can be prepared. With the basic inputs—pro forma income statement, cash budget, fixed-asset outlay plan, long-term financing plan, and current-period balance sheet—the pro forma balance sheet can finally be developed. Throughout the remainder of this chapter we will concentrate on the key outputs of the short-run financial planning process: the cash budget, the pro forma income statement, and the pro forma balance sheet.

CASH PLANNING: CASH BUDGETS

cash budget (cash forecast) Financial projection of the firm's short-term cash surpluses or shortages.

The **cash budget,** or **cash forecast,** allows the firm to plan its short-term cash needs. The firm gives particular attention to planning for surplus cash and for cash shortages. A firm expecting a cash surplus can plan short-term investments (marketable securities). A firm expecting shortages in cash must arrange for short-term financing (notes payable). The cash budget gives the financial manager a clear view of the timing of the firm's expected cash inflows and outflows over a given period.

Typically, the cash budget is designed to cover a one-year period, although any time period is acceptable. The period covered is normally divided into smaller time intervals. The number and type of intervals depend on the nature of the business. The more seasonal and uncertain a firm's cash flows, the greater the number of intervals. Since many firms are confronted with a seasonal cash flow pattern, the cash budget is quite often presented on a monthly basis. Firms with stable patterns of cash flow may use quarterly or annual time intervals. If a cash budget is developed for a period greater than one year, fewer time intervals may be warranted due to the difficulty and uncertainty of forecasting sales and other related cash items.

The Sales Forecast

sales forecast The prediction of the firm's sales over a given period, based on external or internal data.

The key input to the short-run financial planning process and therefore any cash budget is the firm's **sales forecast.** This is the prediction of the firm's sales over a given period and is ordinarily furnished to the financial manager by the marketing department. On the basis of the forecast, the financial manager estimates the monthly cash flows that will result from projected sales receipts and from production-related, inventory-related, and sales-related outlays. The manager also determines the level of fixed assets required and the amount of financing, if any, needed to support the forecast level of production and sales. The sales forecast may be based on an analysis of external or internal data, or on a combination of the two.

External Forecasts

external forecast A sales forecast based on the relationships between the firm's sales and certain key external economic indicators.

An **external forecast** is based on the relationships that can be observed between the firm's sales and certain key external economic indicators such as the gross national product (GNP), new housing starts, or disposable personal income. Forecasts containing these indicators are readily available. The rationale for this approach is that since the firm's sales are often closely related to some aspect of overall national economic activity, a forecast of economic activity should provide insight into future sales.

Internal Forecasts

Internal forecasts are based on a buildup, or consensus, of sales forecasts through the firm's own sales channels. Typically, the firm's salespeople in the field are asked to estimate the number of units of each type of product they expect to sell in the coming year. These forecasts are collected and totaled by the sales manager, who may adjust the figures using his or her own knowledge of specific markets or of the salesperson's forecasting ability. Finally, adjustments may be made for additional internal factors, such as production capabilities.

internal forecast A sales forecast based on a consensus of forecasts through the firm's own sales channels.

Combined Forecasts

Firms generally use a combination of external and internal forecast data in making the final sales forecast. The internal data provide insight into sales expectations. The external data provide a means of adjusting these expectations to take into account general economic factors. The nature of the firm's product also often affects the mix and types of forecasting methods used.

Preparing the Cash Budget

The general format of the cash budget is presented in Table 6.1. We will discuss each of its components individually.

Cash Receipts

Cash receipts includes all items from which cash inflows result in any given financial period. The most common components of cash receipts are cash sales, collections of accounts receivable, and other cash receipts.

cash receipts All cash inflows during a given financial period.

Table 6.1   **The General Format of the Cash Budget**

	Jan.	Feb.	. . .	Nov.	Dec.
Cash receipts					
Less: Cash disbursements	____	____	. . .	____	____
Net cash flow					
Add: Beginning cash	____ ↗	____ ↗	. . . ↗	____ ↗	____
Ending cash					
Less: Minimum cash balance	____	____	. . .	____	____
Required total financing			. . .		
Excess cash balance			. . .		

EXAMPLE   Halley Company, a defense contractor, is developing a cash budget for October, November, and December. Halley's sales in August and September were $100,000 and $200,000, respectively. Sales of $400,000, $300,000, and $200,000 have been forecast for October, November, and December, respectively. Historically, 20 percent of the firm's sales have been for cash, 50 percent have generated accounts receivable collected after one month, and the remaining 30 percent have generated accounts receivable collected after two months. Bad-debt expenses (uncollectible accounts) have been negligible.[1] In December, the firm will receive a $30,000 dividend from stock in a subsidiary. The schedule of expected cash receipts for the company is presented in Table 6.2. It contains the following items.

Forecast sales This initial entry is *merely informational*. It is provided as an aid in calculating other sales-related items.

Cash sales The cash sales shown for each month represent 20 percent of the total sales forecast for that month.

Collections of A/R These entries represent the collection of accounts receivable (A/R) resulting from sales in earlier months.

Lagged one month These figures represent sales made in the preceding month that generated accounts receivable collected in the current month. Since 50 percent of the current month's sales are collected one month later, the collections of accounts receivable with a one-month lag shown for September, October, November, and December represent 50 percent of the sales in August, September, October, and November, respectively.

Lagged two months These figures represent sales made two months earlier that generated accounts receivable collected in the current month. Since 30 percent of sales are collected two months later, the collections with a two-month lag shown for October, November, and December represent 30 percent of the sales in August, September, and October, respectively.

Other cash receipts These are cash receipts expected to result from sources other than sales. Items such as interest received, dividends received, proceeds from the sale of equipment, stock and bond sale proceeds, and lease receipts may show up here. For Halley Company, the only cash receipt is the $30,000 dividend due in December.

Total cash receipts This figure represents the total of all the cash receipt items listed for each month in the cash

---

[1]Normally it would be expected that the collection percentages would total slightly less than 100 percent to reflect the fact that some of the accounts receivable would be uncollectible. In this example the sum of the collection percentages is 100 percent (20% + 50% + 30%), which reflects the fact that all sales are assumed to be collected since bad debts are said to be negligible.

Table 6.2   **A Schedule of Projected Cash Receipts for Halley Company ($000)**

	Aug.	Sept.	Oct.	Nov.	Dec.
Forecast sales	$100	$200	$400	$300	$200
Cash sales (.20)	$ 20	$ 40	$ 80	$ 60	$ 40
Collections of A/R:					
Lagged one month (.50)		50	100	200	150
Lagged two months (.30)			30	60	120
Other cash receipts					30
Total cash receipts			$210	$320	$340

receipt schedule. In the case of Halley Company, we are concerned only with October, November, and December; the total cash receipts for these months are shown in Table 6.2.

Cash Disbursements

Cash disbursements include all outlays of cash in the period covered. The most common cash disbursements are:

> **cash disbursements**
> All cash outlays by the firm during a given financial period.

Cash Purchases

Payments of Accounts Payable

Payments of Cash Dividends

Rent (and Lease) Payments

Wages and Salaries

Tax Payments

Fixed-Asset Outlays

Interest Payments

Principal Payments (Loans)

Repurchases or Retirements of Stock

It is important to recognize that *depreciation and other noncash charges are NOT included in the cash budget* because they merely represent a scheduled write-off of an earlier cash outflow. The impact of depreciation, as noted in Chapter 3, is reflected in the level of cash outflow represented by the tax payments.

EXAMPLE   Halley Company has gathered the following data needed for the preparation of a cash disbursements schedule for the months of October, November, and December.

Purchases   The firm's purchases represent 70 percent of sales. Ten percent of this amount is paid in cash, 70 percent is paid in the month immediately following the month of purchase, and the remaining 20 percent is paid two months following the month of purchase.[2]

Cash dividends   Cash dividends of $20,000 will be paid in October.

Rent payments   Rent of $5,000 will be paid each month.

Wages and salaries   The firm's wages and salaries can be estimated by adding 10 percent of its monthly sales to the $8,000 fixed-cost figure.

Tax payments   Taxes of $25,000 must be paid in December.

Fixed-asset outlays   New machinery costing $130,000 will be purchased and paid for in November.

Interest payments   An interest payment of $10,000 is due in December.

Principal payments (loans)   A $20,000 principal payment is also due in December.

Repurchases or retirements of stock   No repurchase or retirement of stock is expected during the October–December period.

The firm's cash disbursements schedule, based on the data above, is presented in Table 6.3. Some items in Table 6.3 are explained in greater detail below.

Purchases   This entry is *merely informational*. The figures represent 70 percent of the forecast sales for each month. They have been included to facilitate the calculation of the cash purchases and related payments.

Cash purchases   The cash purchases for each month represent 10 percent of the month's purchases.

Payments of A/P   These entries represent the payment of accounts payable (A/P) resulting from purchases in earlier months.

Lagged one month   These figures represent purchases made in the preceding month that are paid for in the current month. Since 70 percent of the firm's purchases are paid for one month later, the payments lagged one month shown for September, October, November, and December represent 70 percent of the August, September, October, and November purchases, respectively.

Lagged two months   These figures represent purchases made two months earlier that are paid for in the current month. Since 20 percent of the firm's purchases are paid for two months later, the payments lagged two months for October, November, and December represent 20 percent of the August, September, and October purchases, respectively.

---

[2]Unlike the collection percentages for sales, the total of the payment percentages should equal 100 percent since it is expected that the firm will pay off all of its accounts payable. In line with this expectation, the percentages for Halley Company total 100 percent (10% + 70% + 20%).

Table 6.3   **A Schedule of Projected Cash Disbursements for Halley Company ($000)**

	Aug.	Sept.	Oct.	Nov.	Dec.
Purchases (.70 × sales)	$70	$140	$280	$210	$140
Cash purchases (.10)	$ 7	$ 14	$ 28	$ 21	$ 14
Payments of A/P:					
Lagged one month (.70)		49	98	196	147
Lagged two months (.20)			14	28	56
Cash dividends			20		
Rent payments			5	5	5
Wages and salaries			48	38	28
Tax payments					25
Fixed-asset outlays				130	
Interest payments					10
Principal payments					20
Total cash disbursements			$213	$418	$305

Wages and salaries These values were obtained by adding $8,000 to 10 percent of the *sales* in each month. The $8,000 represents the salary component; the rest represents wages.

    The remaining items on the cash disbursements schedule are self-explanatory.

Net Cash Flow, Ending Cash, Financing, and Excess Cash

A firm's **net cash flow** is found by subtracting the cash disbursements from cash receipts in each period. By adding beginning cash to the firm's net cash flow, we can find the **ending cash** for each period. Finally, subtracting the desired minimum cash balance from ending cash yields the **required total financing** or the **excess cash balance.** If the ending cash is less than the minimum cash balance, *financing* is required. Such financing is typically viewed as short-term and therefore represented by notes payable. If the ending cash is greater than the minimum cash balance, *excess cash* exists. Any excess cash is assumed invested in a liquid, short-term, interest-paying vehicle and therefore included in marketable securities.

EXAMPLE   Table 6.4 presents Halley Company's cash budget, based on the cash receipt and cash disbursement data already developed for the firm. Halley's end-of-September cash balance was $50,000. The company wishes to maintain as a reserve for unexpected needs a minimum cash balance of $25,000.

net cash flow The mathematical difference between the firm's cash receipts and its cash disbursements in each period.

ending cash The sum of the firm's beginning cash and its net cash flow for the period.

required total financing Amount of funds needed by the firm if the ending cash for the period is less than the desired minimum cash balance.

excess cash balance The amount available for investment by the firm if the period's ending cash is greater than the desired minimum cash balance.

Table 6.4   **A Cash Budget for Halley Company ($000)**

	Oct.	Nov.	Dec.
Total cash receipts[a]	$210	$320	$340
Less: Total cash disbursements[b]	213	418	305
Net cash flow	$ (3)	$(98)	$ 35
Add: Beginning cash	50	47	(51)
Ending cash	$ 47	$(51)	$(16)
Less: Minimum cash balance	25	25	25
Required total financing[c]	—	$ 76	$ 41
Excess cash balance[d]	$ 22	—	—

[a]From Table 6.2.
[b]From Table 6.3.
[c]Values are placed in this line when the ending cash is less than the minimum cash balance since in this instance financing is required. These amounts are typically financed short-term and therefore are represented by notes payable.
[d]Values are placed in this line when the ending cash is greater than the minimum cash balance since in this instance an excess cash balance exists. These amounts are typically assumed invested short-term and therefore are represented by marketable securities.

For Halley Company to maintain its required $25,000 ending cash balance, it will need to borrow $76,000 in November and $41,000 in December. In the month of October the firm will have an excess cash balance of $22,000, which can be held in an interest-earning marketable security. The required total financing figures in the cash budget refer to *how much will have to be owed at the end of the month;* they do *not* represent the monthly changes in borrowing.

The monthly changes in borrowing as well as excess cash can be found by further analyzing the cash budget in Table 6.4. In October the $50,000 beginning cash, which becomes $47,000 after the $3,000 net cash outflow is deducted, results in a $22,000 excess cash balance once the $25,000 minimum cash is deducted. In November the $76,000 of required total financing results from the $98,000 net cash outflow less the $22,000 of excess cash from October. The $41,000 of required total financing in December results from reducing November's $76,000 of required total financing by the $35,000 of net cash inflow during December. Summarizing, the financial activities for each month would be as follows:

October: Invest $22,000 of excess cash.

November: Liquidate $22,000 of excess cash and borrow $76,000.

December: Repay $35,000 of amount borrowed.

Evaluating the Cash Budget

The cash budget provides the firm with figures indicating the expected ending cash balance. These can be analyzed to determine whether a cash shortage or surplus is expected to result in each of the months covered by the forecast. Halley Company can expect a surplus of $22,000 in October, a deficit of $76,000 in November, and a deficit of $41,000 in December. Each of these figures is based on the internally imposed requirement of a $25,000 minimum cash balance and represents the total balance at the end of the month.

The excess cash balance in October can be invested in marketable securities. The deficits in November and December will have to be financed—typically, by short-term borrowing (notes payable). Since it may be necessary for the firm to borrow up to $76,000 for the three-month period evaluated, the financial manager should be sure that a line of credit is established or some other arrangement made to assure the availability of these funds. The manager will usually request or arrange to borrow more than the maximum financing indicated in the cash budget. This is necessary due to the uncertainty of the ending cash values, which are based on the sales forecast and other forecast values.

Coping with Uncertainty in the Cash Budget

In addition to carefully preparing sales forecasts and other estimates included in the cash budget, the financial manager frequently copes with the statement's uncertainty by preparing several cash budgets— one based on a pessimistic forecast, one based on the most likely forecast, and a third based on an optimistic forecast.[3] An evaluation of these cash flows allows the financial manager to determine the amount of financing necessary to cover the most adverse situation. The use of several cash budgets, each based on differing assumptions, should also give the financial manager a sense of the riskiness of alternatives so that he or she makes more intelligent short-term financial decisions. The sensitivity (or "what if") analysis approach is often used to analyze cash flows under a variety of possible circumstances. Computers and spreadsheet programs such as Lotus 1-2-3, Excel, and Quattro are commonly used to greatly simplify the process of performing sensitivity analysis.

EXAMPLE   Table 6.5 presents the summary results of the Halley Company's cash budget prepared for each month of concern using a pessimistic, most likely, and optimistic estimate of cash receipts and cash disbursements. The most likely estimate is based on the expected outcomes presented earlier in Tables 6.2 through 6.4; the pessimistic and optimistic out-

---

[3]The term *uncertainty* is used here to refer to the variability of the cash flow outcomes that may actually occur. A thorough discussion of risk and uncertainty is presented in Chapter 12.

Table 6.5   **A Sensitivity Analysis of Halley Company's Cash Budget ($000)**

	October			November			December		
	Pessi-mistic-	Most likely	Opti-mistic	Pessi-mistic	Most likely	Opti-mistic	Pessi-mistic	Most likely	Opti-mistic
Total cash receipts	$160	$210	$285	$ 210	$320	$410	$ 275	$340	$422
Less: Total cash disbursements	200	213	248	380	418	467	280	305	320
Net cash flow	$ (40)	$ (3)	$ 37	$(170)	$ (98)	$ (57)	$ (5)	$ 35	$102
Add: Beginning cash	50	50	50	10	47	87	(160)	(51)	30
Ending cash	$ 10	$ 47	$ 87	$(160)	$ (51)	$ 30	$(165)	$ (16)	$132
Less: Minimum cash balance	25	25	25	25	25	25	25	25	25
Required total financing	$ 15	—	—	$ 185	$ 76	—	$ 190	$ 41	—
Excess cash balance	—	$ 22	$ 62	—	—	$ 5	—	—	$107

comes are based on the worst and best possible outcomes, respectively. During the month of October, Halley will need a maximum of $15,000 of financing; at best it will have a $62,000 excess cash balance available for short-term investment. During November, its financing requirement will be between $0 and $185,000. It could experience an excess cash balance of $5,000 during November. The December projections reflect maximum borrowing of $190,000 with a possible excess cash balance of $107,000. By considering the extreme values reflected in the pessimistic and optimistic outcomes, Halley Company should be better able to plan cash requirements. For the three-month period, the peak borrowing requirement under the worst circumstances would be $190,000, an amount considerably greater than the most likely estimate of $76,000 for this period.

PROFIT PLANNING: PRO FORMA STATEMENT FUNDAMENTALS

pro forma statements Projected financial statements—income statements and balance sheets.

The profit-planning process centers on the preparation of **pro forma statements,** which are projected, or forecast, financial statements—income statements and balance sheets. The preparation of these statements requires a careful blending of a number of procedures to account for the revenues, costs, expenses, assets, liabilities, and equity resulting from the firm's anticipated level of operations. The basic steps in this process were shown in the flow diagram presented in Figure 6.1. The financial manager frequently uses one of a number of simplified approaches to estimate the pro forma statements. The most popular are based on the belief that the financial relationships reflected in the firm's historical (past) financial statements will not change in the coming period. The commonly used approaches are presented in subsequent discussions.

Two inputs are required for preparing pro forma statements using the simplified approaches: (1) financial statements for the preceding year and (2) the sales forecast for the coming year. A variety of assumptions must also be made when using simplified approaches. The company we will use to illustrate the simplified approaches to pro forma preparation is Metcalfe Manufacturing Company, which manufactures and sells one product. It has two basic models—model X and model Y. Although each model is produced by the same process, each requires different amounts of raw material and labor.

Past Year's Financial Statements

The income statement for the firm's 1992 operations is given in Table 6.6. It indicates that Metcalfe had sales of $100,000, total cost of goods sold of $80,000, and net profits after taxes of $7,650. The firm paid $4,000 in cash dividends, leaving $3,650 to be transferred to retained earnings. The firm's balance sheet at the end of 1992 is given in Table 6.7.

Table 6.6   **An Income Statement for Metcalfe Manufacturing Company for the Year Ended December 31, 1992**

Sales revenue		
Model X (1,000 units at $20/unit)	$20,000	
Model Y (2,000 units at $40/unit)	80,000	
Total sales		$100,000
Less: Cost of goods sold		
Labor	$28,500	
Material A	8,000	
Material B	5,500	
Overhead	38,000	
Total cost of goods sold		80,000
Gross profits		$ 20,000
Less: Operating expenses		10,000
Operating profits		$ 10,000
Less: Interest expense		1,000
Net profits before taxes		$ 9,000
Less: Taxes (.15 × $9,000)		1,350
Net profits after taxes		$ 7,650
Less: Common stock dividends		4,000
To retained earnings		$ 3,650

Table 6.7   **A Balance Sheet for Metcalfe Manufacturing Company**
(December 31, 1992)

Assets		Liabilities and equities	
Cash	$ 6,000	Accounts payable	$ 7,000
Marketable securities	4,000	Taxes payable	300
Accounts receivable	13,000	Notes payable	8,300
Inventories	16,000	Other current liabilities	3,400
Total current assets	$39,000	Total current liabilities	$19,000
Net fixed assets	51,000	Long-term debts	$18,000
Total assets	$90,000	Stockholders' equity	
		Common stock	$30,000
		Retained earnings	$23,000
		Total liabilities and stockholders' equity	$90,000

Sales Forecast

Like the cash budget, the key input for the development of pro forma statements is the sales forecast. The sales forecast by model for the coming year, 1993, for the Metcalfe Company is given in Table 6.8. This forecast is based on both external and internal data. The unit sale prices of the products reflect an increase from $20 to $25 for model X and from $40 to $50 for model Y. These increases are required to cover the firm's anticipated increases in the cost of labor, material, overhead, and operating expenses.

◼• ▎ PREPARING THE PRO FORMA INCOME STATEMENT

A simple method for developing a pro forma income statement is to use the **percent-of-sales method.** It forecasts sales and then expresses the

Table 6.8   **1993 Sales Forecast**
for Metcalfe Manufacturing Company

Unit sales	
Model X	1,500
Model Y	1,950
Dollar sales	
Model X ($25/unit)	$ 37,500
Model Y ($50/unit)	$ 97,500
Total	$135,000

E T H I C S   I N   F I N A N C E

A Cold Winter in Moline

Deere & Co., the world's largest manufacturer of farm equipment, is headquartered on John Deere Road in Moline, Illinois. In recent years, Moline's economy had been hurt as Deere exported manufacturing facilities to Canada, France, South Africa, and Argentina, as well as other sections of the United States.

Then, in December 1990, Deere & Co. posted a 28 percent decline in fiscal fourth-quarter net income. Furthermore, a slowdown in sales of farm and construction equipment caused Deere to forecast significantly diminished sales of both of its core operations.

These gloomy predictions were announced simultaneously with a report indicating that fiscal-year sales of farm equipment had actually risen 5 percent, and total sales had risen 3 percent, from the previous year. And, although down, quarterly earnings had been 98 cents a share. Finally, earnings posted by Deere's financial services division were expected to offset losses in the manufacturing divisions.

Nonetheless, financial managers at Deere, like those everywhere, must prepare their company for the future. Recognizing that it is easier, both emotionally and financially, to plan less production and add overtime as conditions warrant, Deere announced plans to slash output by 20 percent by repeated plant closings of a week or two. Fortunately for its employees, the decision was announced early in December, which allowed workers to adjust Christmas spending plans. Yet, there was very little to cheer about as Moline settled in for a cold winter.

Source: Robert Rose, "Deere net fell 28% in its 4th quarter as sales rose 3%," *The Wall Street Journal,* December 5, 1990, p. B2.

cost of goods sold, operating expenses, and interest expense as a percentage of projected sales. The percentages used are likely to be the percentage of sales for these items in the immediately preceding year. For the Metcalfe Manufacturing Company, these percentages are:

percent-of-sales method Method for developing the pro forma income statement that expresses the cost of goods sold, operating expenses, and interest expense as a percentage of projected sales.

$$\frac{\text{Cost of goods sold}}{\text{Sales}} = \frac{\$80,000}{\$100,000} = 80.0\%$$

$$\frac{\text{Operating expenses}}{\text{Sales}} = \frac{\$10,000}{\$100,000} = 10.0\%$$

$$\frac{\text{Interest expense}}{\text{Sales}} = \frac{\$1,000}{\$100,000} = 1.0\%$$

Table 6.9   **A Pro Forma Income Statement,
Using the Percent-of-Sales Method,
for Metcalfe Manufacturing Company
for the Year Ended
December 31, 1993**

Sales revenue	$135,000
Less: Cost of goods sold (.80)	108,000
Gross profits	$ 27,000
Less: Operating expenses (.10)	13,500
Operating profits	$ 13,500
Less: Interest expense (.01)	1,350
Net profits before taxes	$ 12,150
Less: Taxes (.15 × $12,150)	1,823
Net profits after taxes	$ 10,327
Less: Common stock dividends	4,000
To retained earnings	$ 6,327

The dollar values are from the 1992 income statement (Table 6.6).

Applying these percentages to the firm's forecast sales of $135,000, developed in Table 6.8, and assuming the firm will pay $4,000 in common stock dividends in 1993, results in the pro forma income statement in Table 6.9. The expected contribution to retained earnings is $6,327, representing a considerable increase over $3,650 in the previous year.

Considering Types of Costs and Expenses

The technique used to prepare the pro forma income statement in Table 6.9 assumes that all the firm's costs are *variable*. This means that the use of the historical (1992) ratios of cost of goods sold, operating expenses, and interest expense to sales assumes that for a given percentage increase in sales, the same percentage increase in each of these expense components will result. For example, as Metcalfe's sales increased by 35 percent (from $100,000 in 1992 to $135,000 projected for 1993), its cost of goods sold also increased by 35 percent (from $80,000 in 1992 to $108,000 projected for 1993). Based on this assumption, the firm's net profits before taxes also increased by 35 percent (from $9,000 in 1992 to $12,150 projected for 1993).

In the approach just illustrated, the broader implication is that since the firm has no fixed costs, it will not receive the benefits often resulting from them.[4] Therefore, the use of past cost and expense ratios generally tends to understate profits when sales are increasing and

---

[4]The potential returns as well as risks resulting from use of fixed (operating and financial) costs to create "leverage" are discussed in Chapter 5. The key point to recognize here is that when the firm's revenue is *increasing*, fixed costs can magnify returns.

overstate profits when sales are decreasing. Clearly, if the firm has fixed operating and financial costs, when sales increase these costs do not change. The result is increased profits. When sales decline, these costs, by remaining unchanged, tend to lower profits. The best way to adjust for the presence of fixed costs when using a simplified approach for pro forma income statement preparation is to break the firm's historical costs into *fixed* and *variable components* and make the forecast using this relationship.

EXAMPLE   The Metcalfe Manufacturing Company's last-year (1992) and pro forma (1993) income statements, which are broken into fixed- and variable-cost components, are given below.

Metcalfe Manufacturing's Income Statements

	Last year (1992)	Pro forma (1993)
Sales revenue	$100,000	$135,000
Less: Cost of goods sold		
Fixed cost	40,000	40,000
Variable cost (.40 × sales)	40,000	54,000
Gross profits	$ 20,000	$ 41,000
Less: Operating expenses		
Fixed expense	5,000	5,000
Variable expense (.05 × sales)	5,000	6,750
Operating profits	$ 10,000	$ 29,250
Less: Interest expense (all fixed)	1,000	1,000
Net profits before taxes	$ 9,000	$ 28,250
Less: Taxes (.15 × net profits before taxes)	1,350	4,238
Net profits after taxes	$ 7,650	$ 24,012

By breaking Metcalfe's costs and expenses into fixed and variable components, we get a more accurate projection of the firm's pro forma profit. Had the firm treated all costs as variable, its pro forma (1993) net profits before taxes would equal 9 percent of sales, just as was the case in 1992 ($9,000 net profits before taxes ÷ $100,000 sales). As shown in Table 6.9, by assuming *all* costs are variable the net profits before taxes would have been $12,150 (.09 × $135,000 projected sales) instead of the $28,250 of net profits before taxes obtained above by using the firm's fixed-cost–variable-cost breakdown.

The preceding example should make it clear that when using a simplified approach to pro forma income statement preparation, it is advisable to consider first breaking down costs and expenses into fixed and variable components. For convenience, the pro forma income statement prepared for Metcalfe Manufacturing Company in Table 6.9 was based on the assumption that all costs were variable—which is *not* likely to be the case. Therefore, Metcalfe's projected profits were understated using the percent-of-sales method.

▪▫▪ PREPARING THE PRO FORMA BALANCE SHEET

judgmental approach Method for developing the pro forma balance sheet in which the values of certain accounts are estimated while others are calculated, using the firm's external financing as a "plug" figure.

A number of simplified approaches are available for preparing the pro forma balance sheet. Probably the best and most popular is the judgmental approach.[5] Under the **judgmental approach** for developing the pro forma balance sheet, the values of certain balance sheet accounts are estimated while others are calculated. When this approach is applied, the firm's external financing is used as a balancing, or "plug," figure. To apply the judgmental approach in order to prepare Metcalfe Manufacturing Company's 1993 pro forma balance sheet, a number of assumptions must be made:

1 ▪▪▪ A minimum cash balance of $6,000 is desired.

2 ▪▪▪ Marketable securities are assumed to remain unchanged from their current level of $4,000.

3 ▪▪▪ Accounts receivable will on average represent 45 days of sales. Since Metcalfe's annual sales are projected to be $135,000, accounts receivable should average $16,875 ($\frac{1}{8} \times$ $135,000). (Forty-five days equals one-eighth of a year: $45/360 = \frac{1}{8}$.)

4 ▪▪▪ The ending inventory should remain at a level of about $16,000, of which 25 percent (approximately $4,000) should be raw materials, while the remaining 75 percent (approximately $12,000) should consist of finished goods.

5 ▪▪▪ A new machine costing $20,000 will be purchased. Total depreciation for the year will be $8,000. Adding the $20,000 acquisition to the existing net fixed assets of $51,000 and subtracting the depreciation of $8,000 will yield net fixed assets of $63,000.

6 ▪▪▪ Purchases are expected to represent approximately 30 percent of annual sales, which in this case would be approximately $40,500 (.30 × $135,000). The firm estimates it can take 72 days on average to satisfy its accounts payable. Thus accounts payable should equal one-fifth (72 days ÷ 360 days) of the firm's purchases, or $8,100 ($\frac{1}{5} \times$ $40,500).

7 ▪▪▪ Taxes payable are expected to equal one-fourth of the current year's tax liability, which would equal $455 (one-fourth of the tax liability of $1,823 shown in the pro forma income statement presented in Table 6.9).

---

[5]The judgmental approach represents an improved version of the often discussed *percent-of-sales approach* to pro forma balance sheet preparation. Because the judgmental approach requires only slightly more information and should yield better estimates than the somewhat naive percent-of-sales approach, it is presented here.

8 ■■■ Notes payable are assumed to remain unchanged from their current level of $8,300.

9 ■■■ No change in other current liabilities is expected. They will remain at the level of the previous year: $3,400.

10 ■■■ The firm's long-term debt and its common stock are expected to remain unchanged, at $18,000 and $30,000, respectively, since no issues, retirements, or repurchases of bonds or stocks are planned.

11 ■■■ Retained earnings will increase from the beginning level of $23,000 (from the balance sheet dated December 31, 1992, in Table 6.7) to $29,327. The increase of $6,327 represents the amount of retained earnings calculated in the year-end 1993 pro forma income statement in Table 6.9.

A 1993 pro forma balance sheet for the Metcalfe Manufacturing Company based on these assumptions is presented in Table 6.10. A **"plug" figure**—called the **external funds required**—of $8,293 is needed to bring the statement into balance. This means that the firm will have to obtain about $8,293 of additional external financing to support the increased sales level of $135,000 for 1993. When this approach is used, under certain circumstances a negative external funds requirement might result. It would indicate that the firm's financing is in excess of its needs. Funds would therefore be available for repaying debt, repurchasing stock, or increasing the dividend to stockholders. Analysts sometimes use the judgmental approach to pro forma preparation as a technique for estimating financing needs, but for our purposes the approach is used to prepare the pro forma balance sheet.

external funds required ("plug" figure) The amount of external financing needed to bring the pro forma balance sheet into balance under the judgmental approach.

Table 6.10

A Pro Forma Balance Sheet, Using the Judgmental Approach, for Metcalfe Manufacturing Company (December 31, 1993)

Assets			Liabilities and equities	
Cash		$ 6,000	Accounts payable	$ 8,100
Marketable securities		4,000	Taxes payable	455
Accounts receivable		16,875	Notes payable	8,300
Inventories			Other current liabilities	3,400
Raw materials	$ 4,000		Total current liabilities	$ 20,255
Finished goods	12,000		Long-term debts	$ 18,000
Total inventory		16,000	Stockholders' equity	
Total current assets		$ 42,875	Common stock	$ 30,000
Net fixed assets		$ 63,000	Retained earnings	$ 29,327
Total assets		$105,875	Total	$ 97,582
			External funds required[a]	$ 8,293
			Total liabilities and stockholders' equity	$105,875

[a]The amount of external funds needed to force the firm's balance sheet to balance. Due to the nature of the judgmental approach, the balance sheet is not expected to balance without some type of adjustment.

EVALUATION OF PRO FORMA STATEMENTS

It is difficult to forecast the many variables involved in pro forma statement preparation. As a result, analysts—including investors, lenders, and managers—frequently use the techniques presented here in order to make rough estimates of pro forma financial statements. Although the growing use of personal computers and electronic spreadsheets is streamlining the financial planning process, simplified approaches to pro forma preparation are expected to remain popular. An understanding of the basic weaknesses of these simplified approaches is therefore important. Equally important is the ability to effectively use pro forma statements to make financial decisions.

Weaknesses of Simplified Approaches

The basic weaknesses of the simplified pro forma approaches shown in the chapter lie in two assumptions: (1) that the firm's past financial condition is an accurate indicator of its future and (2) that certain variables, such as cash, accounts receivable, and inventories, can be forced to take on certain "desired" values. These assumptions are questionable, but due to the ease of the calculations involved, the use of these approaches is quite common.

Other simplified approaches exist. Most are based on the assumption that certain relationships among revenues, costs, expenses, assets, liabilities, and equity will prevail in the future. For example, in preparing the pro forma balance sheet, all assets, liabilities, *and* equity are often increased by the percentage increase expected in sales. The financial analyst must know the techniques that have been used in preparing pro forma statements in order to judge the quality of the estimated values and thus the degree of confidence he or she can have in them.

Using Pro Forma Statements

In addition to estimating the amount, if any, of external financing required to support a given level of sales, pro forma statements also provide a basis for analyzing in advance the level of profitability and overall financial performance of the firm in the coming year. Using pro forma statements, the financial manager, as well as lenders, can analyze the firm's sources and uses of cash as well as various aspects of performance, such as liquidity, activity, debt, and profitability. Sources and uses can be evaluated by preparing a pro forma statement of cash flows. Various ratios can be calculated from the pro forma income statement and balance sheet to evaluate performance.

F I N A N C E   I N   A C T I O N

Tying Interest Expense to Sales at Escondida

When creating pro forma financial statements, financial managers typically assume interest rates to be fixed or tied to sales increases through a designated change in the amount of debt financing. However, in the case of the Chilean copper mine called Escondida, there is a direct link between sales and interest payments. An international consortium of banks extended a total of $1.1 billion in return for interest based on shipping tonnage and copper prices.

Minera Escondida Limitada was able to attract creditors to this innovative type of financing because of some unique aspects of the mineral content of its properties. Early samples of concentrate gathered at the mine were so high in copper that the cost of production was projected to be only 40 cents per pound. Escondida is required to fully make scheduled interest payments as long as copper prices exceed $.60 per pound. If copper prices drop below this level, each creditor will receive only a prorated share of available revenues. In addition, the International Finance Corporate, an affiliate of the World Bank, and the Chilean government guaranteed the loan.

Banks in Japan, Germany, and Finland will be repaid based on sales of the mine's copper concentrate. Smelters in these countries supported financing of the venture so that they would have the first option to buy copper concentrate. In return, the banks required that all sales contracts be for a 12-year sales period, which matches the duration of the loans. As a result of the financial arrangements, Escondida has abnormally long contracts, smelters have a source of quality copper, and the creditors have a source of return.

Source: "Escondida: Tying financing to copper sales," *Corporate Risk Management*, January 1991, p. 12.

After analyzing the pro forma statements, the financial manager can take steps to adjust planned operations in order to achieve short-run financial goals. For example, if profits on the pro forma income statements are too low, a variety of pricing or cost-cutting actions, or both, might be initiated. If the projected level of accounts receivable on the pro forma balance sheet is too high, changes in credit policy may avoid this outcome. Pro forma statements are therefore of key importance in solidifying the firm's financial plans for the coming year.

SUMMARY

1   **Understand the financial planning process, including the role of and interrelationship between long-run (strategic) financial plans and short-run (operating) plans.**   The two key aspects of the financial planning process are cash planning and profit planning. Cash planning involves the cash budget or cash forecast. Profit planning relies on preparation of the pro forma income statement and balance sheet. Long-run (strategic) financial plans act as a guide for preparing short-run (operating) financial plans. Long-run plans tend to cover periods ranging from two to 10 years and are updated periodically.

2   **Describe the key inputs to and key outputs from short-run (operating) financial plans.**   Key inputs to short-run (operating) plans are the sales forecast and various forms of operating and financial data. Key outputs include operating budgets, the cash budget, and the pro forma financial statements.

3   **Discuss the cash planning process, the role of sales forecasts, and the procedures for preparing, evaluating, and coping with uncertainty in the cash budget.**   The cash planning process uses the cash budget, which is based upon a sales forecast, to estimate short-term cash surpluses and shortages. The cash budget is typically prepared for a one-year period divided into months. It lists cash receipts and disbursements for each period in order to calculate net cash flow. Ending cash is estimated by adding beginning cash to the net cash flow. By subtracting the desired minimum cash balance from the ending cash, the financial manager can determine required total financing (typically represented by notes payable) or the excess cash balance (typically included in marketable securities). To cope with uncertainty in the cash budget, sensitivity analysis is frequently used.

4   **Develop, prepare, and evaluate a pro forma income statement using the percent-of-sales method.**   A pro forma income statement can be developed by calculating past percentage relationships between certain cost and expense items and the firm's sales and then applying these percentages to forecasts. This process can be improved upon by first breaking down costs and expenses into fixed and variable components.

5   **Develop, prepare, and evaluate a pro forma balance sheet using the judgmental approach.**   A pro forma balance sheet can be estimated using the judgmental approach. Under this simplified technique, the values of certain balance sheet accounts are estimated, while others are calculated, using the firm's external financing as a balancing, or "plug," figure.

6   **Describe the weaknesses of the simplified approaches to pro forma preparation, and describe the common uses of pro forma financial statements.**   The use of simplified approaches for pro forma statement preparation, although quite popular, can be criticized for assuming the firm's past condition is an accurate predictor of the future and for assuming that certain variables can be forced to take on desired values. Pro forma statements are commonly used by financial managers and lenders to analyze in advance the firm's level of profitability and overall financial performance. Based on their analysis, financial managers adjust planning operations to achieve short-run financial goals.

QUESTIONS

6—1   What is the *financial planning process?* Define, compare, and contrast *long-run (strategic) financial plans* and *short-run (operating) financial plans.*

6—2   Which three statements result as part of the short-run (operating) financial planning process? Describe the flow of information from the sales forecast through the preparation of these statements.

6—3   What is the purpose of the *cash budget?* The key input to the cash budget is the sales forecast. What is the difference between *external* and *internal* forecast data?

6—4   Briefly describe the basic format of the cash budget, beginning with forecast sales and ending with required total financing or excess cash balance.

6—5   How can the two bottom lines of the cash budget be used to determine the firm's short-term borrowing and investment requirements?

6—6   What is the cause of uncertainty in the cash budget? What technique can be used to cope with uncertainty?

6—7   What is the purpose of *pro forma financial statements?* Which of the pro forma statements must be developed first? Why?

6—8   Briefly describe the pro forma income statement preparation process using the *percent-of-sales method.* What are the strengths and weaknesses of this simplified approach?

6—9   Describe the *judgmental approach* for simplified preparation of the pro forma balance sheet. Contrast this with the more detailed approach shown in Figure 6.1.

6—10   What is the significance of the balancing ("plug") figure, *external funds required,* used with the judgmental approach for preparing the pro forma balance sheet?

6—11   What are the two key weaknesses of the simplified approaches to pro forma statement preparation? In spite of these weaknesses, why do these approaches remain popular?

6—12   How may the financial manager wish to evaluate pro forma statements? What is his or her objective in evaluating these statements?

PROBLEMS

6—1   **(Cash Receipts)** A firm has actual sales of $65,000 in April and $60,000 in May. It expects sales of $70,000 in June and $100,000 in July and in August. Assuming that sales are the only source of cash inflows and that half of these are for cash and the remainder are collected evenly over the following two months, what are the firm's expected cash receipts for June, July, and August?

6—2   **(Cash Budget—Basic)** The Quick Digital Company had sales of $50,000 in March and $60,000 in April. Forecast sales for May, June, and July are $70,000, $80,000, and $100,000, respectively. The firm has a cash balance of $5,000 on May 1 and wishes to maintain a minimum cash balance of $5,000. Given the following data, prepare and interpret a cash budget for the months of May, June, and July.

(1) Twenty percent of the firm's sales are for cash; 60 percent are collected in the next month, and the remaining 20 percent are collected in the second month following sale.

(2) The firm receives other income of $2,000 per month.

(3) The firm's actual or expected purchases, all made for cash, are $50,000, $70,000, and $80,000 for the months of May through July, respectively.

(4) Rent is $3,000 per month.

(5) Wages and salaries are 10 percent of the previous month's sales.

(6) Cash dividends of $3,000 will be paid in June.

(7) Payment of principal and interest of $4,000 is due in June.

(8) A cash purchase of equipment costing $6,000 is scheduled in July.

(9) Taxes of $6,000 are due in June.

6—3   **(Cash Budget—Advanced)**   The actual sales and purchases for Advanced Appliance Company for September and October 1992, along with its forecast sales and purchases for the period November 1992 through April 1993, follow.

Year	Month	Sales	Purchases
1992	September	$210,000	$120,000
1992	October	250,000	150,000
1992	November	170,000	140,000
1992	December	160,000	100,000
1993	January	140,000	80,000
1993	February	180,000	110,000
1993	March	200,000	100,000
1993	April	250,000	90,000

The firm makes 20 percent of all sales for cash and collects on 40 percent of its sales in each of the two months following the sale. Other cash inflows are expected to be $12,000 in September and April, $15,000 in January and March, and $27,000 in February. The firm pays cash for 10 percent of its purchases. It pays for 50 percent of its purchases in the following month and for 40 percent of its purchases two months later.

Wages and salaries amount to 20 percent of the preceding month's sales. Rent of $20,000 per month must be paid. Interest payments of $10,000 are due in January and April. A principal payment of $30,000 is also due in April. The firm expects to pay cash dividends of $20,000 in January and April. Taxes of $80,000 are due in April. The firm also intends to make a $25,000 cash purchase of fixed assets in December.

a. Assuming that the firm has a cash balance of $22,000 at the beginning of November, determine the end-of-month cash balances for each month, November through April.

b. Assuming that the firm wishes to maintain a $15,000 minimum cash balance, determine the monthly total financing requirements or excess cash balances.

c. If the firm were requesting a line of credit to cover needed financing for the period November to April, how large would this line have to be? Explain your answer.

6—4   **(Cash Flow Concepts)**   The table at the top of page 195 lists financial transactions that the Ballou Company will be undertaking in the next planning period. For each transaction check the statement or statements that will be affected immediately.

6—5   **(Multiple Cash Budgets—Sensitivity Analysis)**   Patterson's Parts Store expects sales of $100,000 during each of the next three months. It will make monthly purchases of $60,000 during this time. Wages and salaries are $10,000 per month plus 5 percent of sales. Patterson's expects to make a tax payment of $20,000 in the next month and a $15,000 purchase of fixed assets in the second month and to receive $8,000 in cash from the sale of an asset in the third month. All sales and

Transaction	Statement		
	Cash budget	Pro forma income statement	Pro forma balance sheet
Cash sale			
Credit sale			
Accounts receivable are collected			
Asset with five-year life is purchased			
Depreciation is taken			
Amortization of goodwill is taken			
Sale of common stock			
Retirement of outstanding bonds			
Fire insurance premium is paid for the next three years			

purchases are for cash. Beginning cash and the minimum cash balance are assumed to be zero.

a. Construct a cash budget for the next three months.

b. Patterson's is unsure of the sales levels, but all other figures are certain. If the most pessimistic sales figure is $80,000 per month and the most optimistic is $120,000 per month, what are the monthly minimum and maximum ending cash balances the firm can expect for each of the one-month periods?

c. Briefly discuss how the data in **a** and **b** can be used by the financial manager to plan for his or her financing needs.

6—6   **(Pro Forma Income Statement)** The marketing department of Hartman Manufacturing estimates that its sales in 1993 will be $1.5 million. Interest expense is expected to remain unchanged at $35,000, and the firm plans to pay $70,000 in cash dividends during 1993. Hartman Manufacturing's income statement for the year ended December 31, 1992, on page 196, followed by a breakdown of the firm's cost of goods sold and operating expenses into its fixed- and variable-cost components.

a. Use the *percent-of-sales method* to prepare a pro forma income statement for the year ended December 31, 1993.

b. Use the *fixed- and variable-cost data* to develop a pro forma income statement for the year ended December 31, 1993.

c. Compare and contrast the statements developed in **a** and **b**. Which statement will likely provide the better estimates of 1993 income? Explain why.

Income statement
Hartman Manufacturing Company
for the year ended December 31, 1992

Sales revenue	$1,400,000
Less: Cost of goods sold	910,000
Gross profits	$ 490,000
Less: Operating expenses	120,000
Operating profits	$ 370,000
Less: Interest expense	35,000
Net profits before taxes	$ 335,000
Less: Taxes (rate = 40%)	134,000
Net profits after taxes	$ 201,000
Less: Cash dividends	66,000
To retained earnings	$ 135,000

Fixed- and variable-cost breakdown
Hartman Manufacturing Company
for the year ended December 31, 1992

Cost of goods sold	
Fixed cost	$210,000
Variable cost	700,000
Total cost	$910,000
Operating expenses	
Fixed expenses	$ 36,000
Variable expenses	84,000
Total expenses	$120,000

 6—7 **(Pro Forma Balance Sheet—Basic)** May Cosmetics wishes to prepare a pro forma balance sheet for December 31, 1993. The firm expects 1993 sales to total $3,000,000. It has the following information:

(1) A minimum cash balance of $50,000 is desired.

(2) Marketable securities are expected to remain unchanged.

(3) Accounts receivable represent 10 percent of sales.

(4) Inventories represent 12 percent of sales.

(5) A new machine costing $90,000 will be acquired during 1993. Total depreciation for the year will be $32,000.

(6) Accounts payable represent 14 percent of sales.

(7) Accruals, other current liabilities, long-term debt, and common stock are expected to remain unchanged.

(8) The firm's net profit margin is 4 percent and it expects to pay out $70,000 in cash dividends during 1993.

(9) The December 31, 1992, balance sheet is given below.

Balance sheet
May Cosmetics
December 31, 1992

Assets		Liabilities and equities	
Cash	$ 45,000	Accounts payable	$ 395,000
Marketable securities	15,000	Accruals	60,000
Accounts receivable	255,000	Other current liabilities	30,000
Inventories	340,000	Total current liabilities	$ 485,000
Total current assets	$ 655,000	Long-term debt	$ 350,000
Net fixed assets	600,000	Common stock	$ 200,000
Total assets	$1,255,000	Retained earnings	$ 220,000
		Total liabilities and stockholders' equity	$1,255,000

a. Use the *judgmental approach* to prepare a pro forma balance sheet dated December 31, 1993, for May Cosmetics.

b. How much, if any, additional financing will be required by May Cosmetics in 1993? Discuss.

c. Could May Cosmetics adjust its planned 1993 dividend in order to avoid the situation described in **b**? Explain how.

6—8   **(Pro Forma Balance Sheet)** Widget Tool has 1992 sales of $10 million. It wishes to analyze expected performance and financing needs for 1994—two years ahead. Given the following information, answer questions **a** and **b**.

   (1) The percent of sales for items that vary directly with sales are as follows:
   Accounts receivable, 12 percent
   Inventory, 18 percent
   Accounts payable, 14 percent
   Net profit margin, 3 percent
   (2) Marketable securities and other current liabilities are expected to remain unchanged.
   (3) A minimum cash balance of $480,000 is desired.
   (4) A new machine costing $650,000 will be acquired in 1993 and equipment costing $850,000 will be purchased in 1994. Total depreciation in 1993 is forecast as $290,000 and in 1994 $390,000 of depreciation will be taken.
   (5) Accruals are expected to rise to $500,000 by the end of 1994.
   (6) No sale or retirement of long-term debt is expected.
   (7) No sale or repurchase of common stock is expected.
   (8) The dividend payout of 50 percent of net profits is expected to continue.
   (9) Sales are expected to be $11 million in 1993 and $12 million in 1994.
   (10) The December 31, 1992, balance sheet appears below.

Balance sheet
Widget Tool
December 31, 1992
($000)

Assets		Liabilities and equities	
Cash	$ 400	Accounts payable	$1,400
Marketable securities	200	Accruals	400
Accounts receivable	1,200	Other current liabilities	80
Inventories	1,800	Total current liabilities	$1,880
Total current assets	$3,600	Long-term debt	$2,000
Net fixed assets	$4,000	Common equity	$3,720
Total assets	$7,600	Total liabilities and stockholders' equity	$7,600

   a. Prepare a pro forma balance sheet dated December 31, 1994.
   b. Discuss the financing changes suggested by the statement prepared in **a**.

6—9   **(Integrative—Pro Forma Statements)** The Clancey Daughters Corporation wishes to prepare financial plans. Use the financial statements below and the other information provided to prepare the financial plans.
   a. Prepare a pro forma income statement for the year ended December 31, 1993, using the *percent-of-sales method*.
   b. Prepare a pro forma balance sheet dated December 31, 1993, using the *judgmental approach*.
   c. Analyze these statements and discuss the resulting external funds required.

Income statement
Clancey Daughters Corporation
for the year ended December 31, 1992

Sales revenue	$800,000
Less: Cost of goods sold	600,000
Gross profits	$200,000
Less: Operating expenses	100,000
Net profits before taxes	$100,000
Less: Taxes (rate = 40%)	40,000
Net profits after taxes	$ 60,000
Less: Cash dividends	20,000
To retained earnings	$ 40,000

Balance sheet
Clancey Daughters Corporation
December 31, 1992

Assets		Liabilities and equities	
Cash	$ 32,000	Accounts payable	$100,000
Marketable securities	18,000	Taxes payable	20,000
Accounts receivable	150,000	Other current liabilities	5,000
Inventories	100,000	Total current liabilities	$125,000
Total current assets	$300,000	Long-term debt	$200,000
Net fixed assets	$350,000	Common stock	$150,000
Total assets	$650,000	Retained earnings	$175,000
		Total liabilities and stockholders' equity	$650,000

The following financial data are also available:
(1) The firm has estimated that its sales for 1993 will be $900,000.
(2) The firm expects to pay $35,000 in cash dividends in 1993.
(3) The firm wishes to maintain a minimum cash balance of $30,000.
(4) Accounts receivable represent approximately 18 percent of annual sales.
(5) The firm's ending inventory will change directly with changes in sales in 1993.
(6) A new machine costing $42,000 will be purchased in 1993. Total depreciation for 1993 will be $17,000.
(7) Accounts payable will change directly in response to changes in sales in 1993.
(8) Taxes payable will equal one-fourth of the tax liability on the pro forma income statement.
(9) Marketable securities, other current liabilities, long-term debt, and common stock will remain unchanged.

CASE

Preparing Metal Manufacturing's 1993 Pro Forma Financial Statement

In order to improve its competitive position, Metal Manufacturing is planning to implement a major plant modernization program. Included will be construction of a state-of-the-art manufacturing facility that will cost $400 million in 1993 and is expected to lower the variable cost per ton of steel. Bonnie White, an experienced budget analyst, has been charged with preparing a forecast of the firm's 1993 financial position assuming construction of the proposed new facility. She plans to use the 1992 financial statements presented earlier on pages 137 and 138 along with the key projected financial data summarized in the following table.

Key projected financial data (1993)
Metal Manufacturing Company
($000)

Data item	Value
Sales revenue	$6,500,000
Minimum cash balance	$25,000
Inventory turnover (times)	7.0
Average collection period	50 days
Fixed assets purchases	$400,000
Dividend payments	$20,000
Depreciation expense	$185,000
Interest expense	$97,000
Accounts payable increase	20%
Accruals and long-term debt	Unchanged
Preferred and common stock, notes payable	Unchanged

Required

a. Use the historic and projected financial data provided to prepare a pro forma income statement for the year ended December 31, 1993. (*Hint:* Use the *percent-of-sales method* to estimate all values *except* for depreciation expense and interest expense, which have been estimated by management and included in the table above.)

b. Use the historic and projected financial data provided along with relevant data from the pro forma income statement prepared in **a** above to prepare the pro forma balance sheet at December 31, 1993. (*Hint:* Use the *judgmental approach.*)

c. Will Metal Manufacturing Company need to raise *external funds* in order to finance construction of the proposed facility? Explain.

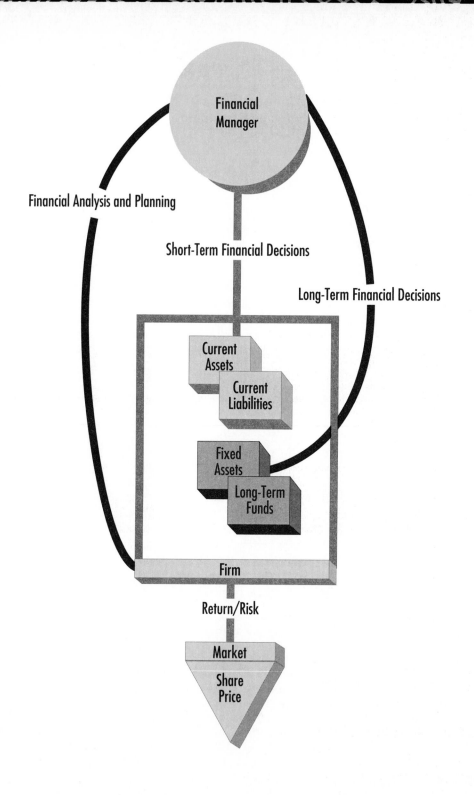

SHORT-TERM FINANCIAL DECISIONS

CHAPTER 7

WORKING CAPITAL FUNDAMENTALS

After studying this chapter, you should be able to:

1 Define net working capital using both the common and alternate definitions and discuss its implications.

2 Discuss the trade-off between profitability and risk as it relates to changing levels of current assets and current liabilities.

3 Use changes in the asset mix and changes in the financing mix to demonstrate the trade-off between profitability and risk.

4 Explain how the firm's funds requirements, when viewed over time, can be broken into a permanent component and a seasonal component.

5 Describe, in terms of profitability and risk, the aggressive strategy and the conservative strategy for determining the firm's financing mix.

6 Discuss financing strategies that trade off the high profitability and risk effects of aggressive strategies and the lower profitability and risk effects of conservative strategies.

“ In return for $1 in salary, Schwartz was given control of Incomnet. ”

Managing Working Capital for Profitable Growth at Incomnet

During 1982, Incomnet, Inc., began tracking used auto parts for auto repair shops in California. Five years later, the company's annual sales were $1.2 million. Despite $13 million in financing from banks, suppliers, and investors over this period, the company had never come close to reporting a profit. In fact, the prior year's income statement reported a net loss of $4 million.

Concerned about his investment, one investor, Sam Schwartz, met with Incomnet management in January 1988. In return for $1 in salary, Schwartz was given control of Incomnet.

Mr. Schwartz paved the way to company success by applying some basic principles to managing Incomnet's working capital. He arranged for detailed reports on cash, sales, accounts receivable, inventory, installations, and overhead expenses. The reports were on Schwartz's desk every Monday morning at 9:00 a.m. Schwartz plotted asset and income numbers in order to isolate any trends that deviated from expectations.

With these guidelines in place, Schwartz examined his working capital. Inventory accounts were bloated by unsalable inventory. Accounts receivable were so old that many customers were bankrupt or could not be located. By writing off these and other items, current assets declined from $1.3 million to $180,000.

Even when receivables were collected, the average collection period was a dismal 110 days. Yet, many customers stated they couldn't manage without Incomnet's service. Recognizing customers' dependence, Schwartz started requiring monthly payment, in advance. As a result, monthly cash flow rose $110,000.

Schwartz also cut back on expenses. Eliminating some "perks," bringing all 30 employees under one roof, cutting excess research and development expenditures, and improving efficiency resulted in an increase in net working capital of $2.1 million, from a negative $1.6 million to a positive $500,000.

Though sales initially declined, the size of Incomnet's net loss also declined in 1988. The following year, Incomnet reported a profit on sales that was twice that of any other year. Sam Schwartz is betting that controlled working capital growth will lead to positive net income at Incomnet during the 1990s.

short-term financial management
Management of current assets and current liabilities.

A n important responsibility of the financial manager is overseeing the firm's day-to-day financial activities. This area of finance, known as **short-term financial management,** is concerned with management of the firm's current assets and current liabilities. In U.S. manufacturing firms, current assets currently account for about 40 percent of total assets; current liabilities represent about 26 percent of total financing. It is therefore not surprising that short-term financial management is one of the most important activities of the financial manager. The goal is to manage each of the firm's current assets and current liabilities in order to achieve a balance between profitability and risk that contributes to the firm's value. In this chapter we give attention to the basic relationship between current assets and current liabilities. In following chapters we will consider the individual current accounts.

NET WORKING CAPITAL

working capital
Current assets, which represent the portion of investment that circulates from one form to another in the ordinary conduct of business.

operating cycle The recurring transition of a firm's working capital from *cash to inventories to receivables* and back to *cash.*

The firm's current assets, commonly called **working capital,** represent the portion of investment that circulates from one form to another in the ordinary conduct of business. This idea embraces the recurring transition from *cash* to *inventories* to *receivables* and back to cash that forms the **operating cycle** of the firm. As a cash substitute, *marketable securities* are considered part of working capital.

Current liabilities represent the firm's short-term financing since they include all debts of the firm that come due (must be paid) in one year or less. These debts usually include amounts owed to suppliers (*accounts payable*), banks (*notes payable*), and employees and governments (*accruals*), among others.

The Common Definition and Its Implications

net working capital
The difference between the firm's current assets and its current liabilities; alternatively, the portion of the firm's current assets financed with long-term funds.

As noted in Chapter 4, **net working capital** is commonly defined as the difference between the firm's current assets and its current liabilities. When the current assets exceed the current liabilities, the firm has *positive net working capital*. In the less common case, when current assets are less than current liabilities, the firm has *negative net working capital*. In general, the more a firm's current assets cover its short-term obligations (current liabilities), the better able it will be to pay its bills as they come due. The conversion of current assets from inventory to receivables to cash provides the source of cash used to pay the current liabilities, which represent a use of cash.

The cash outlays for current liabilities are relatively predictable. When a debt is incurred, the firm generally learns when the corresponding bill will be due. For instance, when merchandise is purchased on credit, the terms extended by the seller require payment by a known point in time. What is difficult to predict are the cash inflows—that is, the conversion of the current assets to more liquid forms. The more predictable its cash inflows, the less net working capital a firm needs. Because they are unable to match cash inflows to outflows with certainty, most firms need current assets that more than cover outflows for current liabilities. Let us look at an example.

EXAMPLE   Berenson Company, a sausage manufacturer, has the current position given in Table 7.1. All $600 of the firm's accounts payable, plus $200 of its notes payable and $100 of accruals, are due at the end of the current period. The $900 in outflows is certain; how the firm will cover these outflows is not certain. The firm can be sure that $700 will be available since it has $500 in cash and $200 in marketable securities, which can easily be converted into cash. The remaining $200 must come from the collection of accounts receivable, the sale of inventory for cash, or both.[1] However, the firm cannot be sure when either the collection of an account receivable or a cash sale will occur. Generally, the more accounts receivable and inventories on hand, the greater the probability that some of these items will be converted into cash.[2] Thus a certain level of net working capital is often recommended to ensure the firm's ability to pay bills. Berenson Company has $1,100 of net working capital (current assets minus current liabilities, or $2,700 − $1,600), which will most likely be sufficient to cover its bills. Its current ratio of 1.69 (current assets divided by current liabilities, or $2,700 ÷ $1,600) should provide sufficient liquidity as long as its accounts receivable and inventories remain relatively active.

Table 7.1   **The Current Position of Berenson Company**

Current assets		Current liabilities	
Cash	$ 500	Accounts payable	$ 600
Marketable securities	200	Notes payable	800
Accounts receivable	800	Accruals	200
Inventories	1,200	Total	$1,600
Total	$2,700		

---

[1] A sale of inventory for credit would show up as a new account receivable, which could not be easily converted into cash. Only a *cash sale* will guarantee the firm that its bill-paying ability during the period of the sale has been enhanced.

[2] Note that levels of accounts receivable or inventory can be too high, reflecting certain management inefficiencies. Acceptable levels for any firm can be calculated. The efficient management of accounts receivable and inventory is discussed in Chapter 9.

FINANCE   IN   ACTION

Company Relationship Accounts

A critical partner in the firm's working capital strategy is its bank. Beyond offering short-term loans, banks help manage the flow of money into a firm's coffers. Rapid check clearing will add dollars to the cash accounts. These funds can, in turn, be used to pay suppliers of materials and capital.

Banks frequently attempt to make money by charging new and higher fees for services. Credit cards, certified checks, and stop-payment orders are among the services that banks target for special fees. Firms may combat these fees by establishing "relationship accounts" at Chase Manhattan and other banks. By keeping combined balances in checking and savings accounts and CDs, firms may qualify for such benefits as waived annual fees on credit cards and discounts on certified checks and stop-payment orders.

The minimum balances range from $5,000 to $25,000. The irony lies in the fact that these services are designed to increase the firm's cash on hand, but simultaneously make a certain portion of the firm's cash and marketable securities a fixed investment. Making matters more trying for the financial manager, banks commonly pay interest on only 88 percent of the entire balance. The portion is known as the "investable balance," reflecting the Federal Reserve's requirement to keep the other 12 percent on reserve.

Firms that fall below the minimum balance are charged a special fee. (In the case of BayBank Boston, for example, there is a thirty-five cent fee per transaction.) Such charges arise precisely when the firm is trying to marshall its cash to get back above the limit.

Source: Suzanne Woolley, "Banks make a statement with fatter fees," *Business Week*, February 18, 1991, pp. 138–39.

An Alternate Definition of Net Working Capital

net working capital
The portion of the firm's current assets financed with long-term funds; alternatively, the difference between the firm's current assets and its current liabilities.

As an alternative to its earlier definition, **net working capital** can be defined as the portion of the firm's current assets financed with long-term funds. This definition can best be illustrated by a special type of balance sheet. Its vertical axis is a dollar scale on which all the major items on the firm's regular balance sheet are indicated. As the special balance sheet for Berenson Company presented in Figure 7.1 shows, the firm has current assets of $2,700, fixed assets of $4,300, total assets of $7,000, current liabilities of $1,600, long-term debts of $2,400 ($4,000 − $1,600), and stockholders' equity of $3,000 ($7,000 − $4,000). The firm's

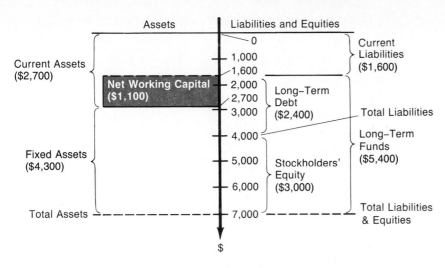

Figure 7.1   A Special Balance Sheet for Berenson Company
This special balance sheet with a dollar scale on the vertical axis
demonstrates that Berenson Company's net working capital of $1,100 can
be viewed as the portion of current assets financed with long-term funds
(long-term debt plus stockholders' equity).

long-term funds—the sum of long-term debt and stockholders' equity—
equal $5,400. The portion of Berenson's current assets that have been
financed with long-term funds equals $1,100. It is labeled "net working
capital" in Figure 7.1. Since current liabilities represent the firm's
sources of short-term funds, as long as current assets exceed current
liabilities, the amount of the excess must be financed with longer-term
funds. The usefulness of this alternate definition of net working capital
will become more apparent later in the chapter.

long-term funds The
sum of the firm's long-
term debt and stockhold-
ers' equity.

THE TRADE-OFF BETWEEN PROFITABILITY AND RISK

A trade-off exists between a firm's profitability and its risk. **Profitability,** in this context, is the relationship between revenues and costs. A
firm's profits can be increased in two ways: (1) by increasing revenues
or (2) by decreasing costs. **Risk,** in the context of short-term financial
decisions, is the probability that the firm will be unable to pay its bills
as they come due. A firm that cannot pay its bills as they come due is
said to be **technically insolvent.** The risk of becoming technically insolvent is commonly measured using either the current ratio or the
amount of net working capital. In this chapter the latter measure is
used. It is generally assumed that *the greater the firm's net working capital, the lower its risk.* In other words, the more net working capital, the
more liquid the firm, and therefore the *lower its risk of becoming technically insolvent.* We will now discuss the effects of changes in current

profitability The relationship between reve-
nues and costs.

risk The probability
that a firm will be unable
to pay its bills as they
come due.

technically insolvent
Describes a firm that is
unable to pay its bills as
they come due.

Table 7.2   **Effects of Changing Ratios on Profits and Risk**

Ratio	Change in ratio	Effect on profit	Effect on risk
<u>Current assets</u> Total assets	Increase Decrease	Decrease Increase	Decrease Increase
<u>Current liabilities</u> Total assets	Increase Decrease	Increase Decrease	Increase Decrease

assets and in current liabilities on the firm's profitability-risk trade-off separately prior to combining them.

Changes in Current Assets

The effects of changing the level of the firm's current assets on its profitability-risk trade-off can be demonstrated using the ratio of current assets to total assets. This ratio indicates the *percentage of total assets* that is current. Assuming that the level of total assets remains unchanged, the effects of an increase or decrease in this ratio on both profitability and risk are summarized at the top of Table 7.2[3]. When the ratio increases, profitability decreases. The reason is that current assets are less profitable than fixed assets. Fixed assets are more profitable because they add more value to the product than that provided by current assets. Without the fixed assets, the firm could not produce the product.

The risk effect, however, decreases as the ratio of current assets to total assets increases. The increase in current assets increases net working capital, thereby reducing the risk of technical insolvency. In addition, as you go down the asset side of the balance sheet, the risk associated with the assets increases. Investment in cash and marketable securities is less risky than investment in accounts receivable, inventories, and fixed assets. Accounts receivable investment is less risky than investment in inventories and fixed assets. Investment in inventories is less risky than investment in fixed assets. The nearer an asset is to cash, the less risky it is. It is generally easier to turn receivables into the more liquid asset cash than it is to turn inventory into cash. As another example, fixed assets are long-term investments, and newer, more efficient, machines and facilities can quickly make the firm's fixed assets relatively inefficient or obsolete. The opposite effects on profit and risk result from a decrease in the ratio of current assets to total assets.

---

[3]The level of total assets is assumed *constant* in this and the following discussion in order to isolate the effect of changing asset and financing mixes on the firm's profitability and risk.

EXAMPLE The balance sheet for Berenson Company presented in Figure 7.1 is shown in Table 7.3 with the initial as well as a second asset mix. Assume the firm earns 2 percent annually on its current assets and 15 percent annually on its fixed assets. As noted in the evaluation in Table 7.3, the initial asset mix results in a ratio of current to total assets of .386, an annual profit on total assets of $699, and net working capital of $1,100. If the firm shifts its asset mix by investing $300 more in fixed assets (and thus $300 less in current assets), current and fixed assets will be as shown in Table 7.3. After the shift the ratio of current to total assets drops to .343, annual profits on total assets increase by $39 to $738, and net working capital drops by $300 to $800. Clearly, a decrease in the ratio resulted in higher profits ($39 increase) and higher risk (liquidity is reduced by $300 from net working capital of $1,100 to $800). These shifts support our earlier conclusions concerning the profitability-risk trade-off as related to changes in current assets.

Changes in Current Liabilities

The effects of changing the level of the firm's current liabilities on its profitability-risk trade-off can be demonstrated using the ratio of current liabilities to total assets. This ratio indicates the percentage of total

Table 7.3 **Evaluation of a Shift in Berenson's Current Assets**

Balance sheet				
Assets				
	Initial	**After shift**	**Liabilities and equity**	
Current assets	$2,700	$2,400	Current liabilities	$1,600
Fixed assets	4,300	4,600	Long-term funds	5,400
Total	$7,000	$7,000	Total	$7,000

Evaluation

Initial assets

Ratio of current to total assets = $2,700 ÷ $7,000   = .386

Profit on total assets = (2% × $2,700) + (15% × $4,300) = $699

Net working capital = $2,700 − $1,600   = $1,100

After shift in assets

Ratio of current to total assets = $2,400 ÷ $7,000   = .343

Profit on total assets = (2% × $2,400) + (15% × $4,600) = $738

Net working capital = $2,400 − $1,600   = $800

Effect of shift on profit = $738 − $699   = +$39

Change in net working capital = $800 − $1,100   = −$300 assets that has been financed with current liabilities. Assuming that total assets remain unchanged, the effects on both profitability and risk of an increase or decrease in the ratio are summarized at the bottom of Table 7.2. When the ratio increases, profitability increases; the firm uses more of the less expensive current-liability financing and less long-term financing. Current liabilities (accounts payable, notes payable, and accruals) are less expensive because only notes payable have a cost. (Notes payable represent only about 20 percent of a manufacturer's current liabilities.) The other current liabilities are basically debts on which the firm pays no charge or interest.

Risk also increases as the ratio of current liabilities to total assets increases. The increase in current liabilities decreases net working capital, thereby increasing the risk of technical insolvency. The opposite effects on profit and risk result from a decrease in the ratio.

EXAMPLE   The balance sheet for Berenson Company is shown with the initial as well as a second financing mix in Table 7.4. Assume that the firm's current liabilities cost 3 percent annually to maintain and that the average cost of long-term funds is 11 percent. As noted in the evaluation in Table 7.4, the initial financing mix results in a ratio of current liabilities to total assets of .229, an annual cost of total financing of

Table 7.4   **Evaluation of a Shift in Berenson's Current Liabilities**

	Balance sheet		
		Liabilities and equity	
Assets		**Initial**	**After shift**
Current assets	$2,700	Current liabilities $1,600	$1,900
Fixed assets	4,300	Long-term funds 5,400	5,100
Total	$7,000	Total $7,000	$7,000

Evaluation
Initial financing
   Ratio of current liabilities to total assets = $1,600 ÷ $7,000 =   .229
   Cost of total financing = (3% × $1,600) + (11% × $5,400)   = $642
   Net working capital = $2,700 − $1,600   = $1,100
After shift in financing
   Ratio of current liabilities to total assets = $1,900 ÷ $7,000 =   .271
   Cost of total financing = (3% × $1,900) + (11% × $5,100)   = $618
   Net working capital = $2,700 − $1,900   = $800

   Effect of shift on profit[a] = −$618 − (−$642)   = +$24
   Change in net working capital = $800 − $1,100   = −$300

[a]The minus sign preceding the $618 and $642 values reflects the fact that they are costs.

$642, and net working capital of $1,100. If the firm shifts its financing mix by using $300 more current-liability financing (and thus $300 less in long-term financing), current liabilities and long-term funds will be as shown in Table 7.4. After the shift the ratio of current liabilities to total assets rises to .271, the annual cost of total financing decreases by $24 to $618, and net working capital drops to $800. Clearly, an increase in the ratio resulted in higher profits ($24 increase due to a decrease in financing cost) and higher risk (liquidity is reduced by $300 from net working capital of $1,100 to $800). This supports our earlier conclusions concerning the profitability-risk trade-off as related to changes in current liabilities.

Combined Effects of Changes

In the preceding examples, the effects of a decrease in the ratio of current assets to total assets and the effects of an increase in the ratio of current liabilities to total assets were illustrated. Both changes were shown to increase the firm's profits and, correspondingly, its risk. Logically, then, the *combined effect* of these actions should also increase profits and increase risk (decrease net working capital).

EXAMPLE Table 7.5 illustrates the results of combining the changes in current assets and current liabilities demonstrated in Tables 7.3 and 7.4. The values in Table 7.5 show that the combined effect of the two shifts illustrated earlier is an increase in annual profits of $63 and a decrease in net working capital (liquidity) of $600. The trade-off here is obvious; the firm has increased its profitability by increasing its risk.

Table 7.5   **The Combined Effects of Changes in Berenson's Current Assets and Current Liabilities**

Change	Change in profits	Change in net working capital
Decrease in ratio of current to total assets	+$39	−$300
Increase in ratio of current liabilities to total assets	+$24	−$300
Combined effect	+$63	−$600

DETERMINING THE FIRM'S FINANCING MIX

One of the most important decisions that must be made with respect to current assets and liabilities is how current liabilities will be used to finance current assets. The amount of current liabilities available is limited by the dollar amount of purchases in the case of accounts payable, by the dollar amount of accrued liabilities in the case of accruals, and by the amount of seasonal borrowing considered acceptable by lenders in the case of notes payable. Lenders make short-term loans to allow a firm to finance seasonal buildups of accounts receivable or inventory. *They generally do not lend short-term money for long-term uses.*[4]

The firm's financing requirements can be separated into a permanent and a seasonal need. The **permanent need,** which consists of fixed assets plus the permanent portion of the firm's current assets, remains unchanged over the year. The **seasonal need,** which is attributable to certain temporary current assets, varies over the year. The relationship between current and fixed assets and permanent and seasonal funds requirements can be illustrated graphically with the aid of a simple example.

permanent need

Financing requirements for the firm's fixed assets plus the permanent portion of the firm's current assets, which remain unchanged over the year.

seasonal need

Financing requirements for temporary current assets, which vary over the year.

EXAMPLE   Berenson Company's estimate of current, fixed, and total asset requirements on a monthly basis for the coming year is given in columns 1, 2, and 3 of Table 7.6. Note that the relatively stable level of total assets over the year reflects, for convenience, an absence of growth by the firm. Columns 4 and 5 present a breakdown of the total requirement into its permanent and seasonal components. The permanent component (column 4) is the lowest level of total assets during the period; the seasonal portion is the difference between the total funds requirement (i.e., total assets) for each month and the permanent funds requirement.

By comparing the firm's fixed assets (column 2) to its permanent funds requirement (column 4), we can see that the permanent funds requirement exceeds the firm's level of fixed assets. This result occurs because *a portion of the firm's current assets is permanent,* since they are apparently always being replaced. The size of the permanent component of current assets is $800 for Berenson Company. This value represents the base level of current assets that remains on the firm's books throughout the entire year. This value can also be found by subtracting the level of fixed assets from the permanent funds requirement ($13,800 − $13,000 = $800). The relationships presented in Table 7.6 are depicted graphically in Figure 7.2 on page 214.

---

[4]The rationale for, techniques of, and parties to short-term business loans are discussed in detail in Chapter 10. The primary sources of short-term loans to businesses—commercial banks—make these loans *only for seasonal or self-liquidating purposes* such as temporary buildups of accounts receivable or inventory.

Table 7.6   **Estimated Funds Requirements for Berenson Company**

Month	Current assets (1)	Fixed assets (2)	Total assets[a] [(1) + (2)] (3)	Permanent funds requirement[b] (4)	Seasonal funds requirement [(3) − (4)] (5)
January	$4,000	$13,000	$17,000	$13,800	$3,200
February	3,000	13,000	16,000	13,800	2,200
March	2,000	13,000	15,000	13,800	1,200
April	1,000	13,000	14,000	13,800	200
May	800	13,000	13,800	13,800	0
June	1,500	13,000	14,500	13,800	700
July	3,000	13,000	16,000	13,800	2,200
August	3,700	13,000	16,700	13,800	2,900
September	4,000	13,000	17,000	13,800	3,200
October	5,000	13,000	18,000	13,800	4,200
November	3,000	13,000	16,000	13,800	2,200
December	2,000	13,000	15,000	13,800	1,200
Monthly Average[c]				$13,800	$1,950

[a]This represents the firm's total funds requirement.
[b]This figure represents the minimum total asset requirement.
[c]Found by summing the monthly amounts for the 12 months and dividing the resulting totals by 12.

There are a number of strategies for determining the appropriate mix of short-term (current liability) and long-term financing. The three basic strategies—(1) the aggressive strategy, (2) the conservative strategy, and (3) a trade-off between the two—are discussed below in terms of both cost and risk considerations. In these discussions the alternate definition that defines *net working capital* as *the portion of current assets financed with long-term funds* is applied.

AN AGGRESSIVE FINANCING STRATEGY

An **aggressive financing strategy** results in the firm financing at least its seasonal needs, and possibly some of its permanent needs, with short-term funds. The balance is financed with long-term funds. This strategy can be illustrated graphically.

aggressive financing strategy Strategy by which the firm finances at least its seasonal needs, and possibly some of its permanent needs, with short-term funds and the majority of its permanent needs with long-term funds.

EXAMPLE   Berenson Company's estimate of its total funds requirements (i.e., total assets) on a monthly basis for the coming year is given in column 3 of Table 7.6. Columns 4 and 5 divide this requirement into permanent and seasonal components.

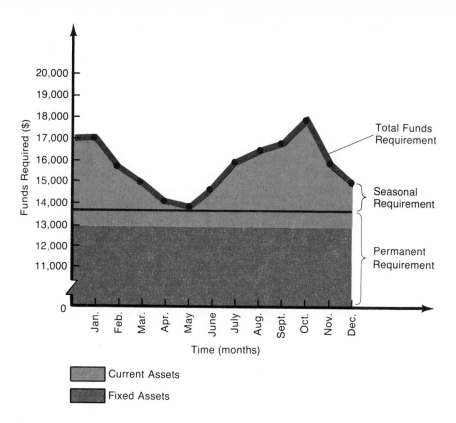

Figure 7.2   Berenson Company's Estimated Funds Requirements
Berenson Company's total funds requirement varies over the year. It
consists of a permanent component, which includes fixed assets and the
permanent portion of current assets, and a seasonal component
attributable to temporary current assets.

An aggressive strategy may finance the permanent portion of the firm's funds requirement ($13,800) with long-
term funds and finance the seasonal portion (ranging from
$0 in May to $4,200 in October) with short-term funds. Much
of the short-term financing may be in the form of *trade credit*
(i.e., accounts payable). The application of this financing
strategy to the firm's total funds requirement is illustrated
graphically in Figure 7.3.

Cost Considerations

Under the aggressive strategy, Berenson's average short-term borrowing (seasonal funds requirement) is $1,950; average long-term borrow-
ing (permanent funds requirement) is $13,800. (See columns 4 and 5 of
Table 7.6.) If the annual cost of short-term funds needed by Berenson is
3 percent and the annual cost of long-term financing is 11 percent, the
total cost of the financing strategy is estimated as follows:

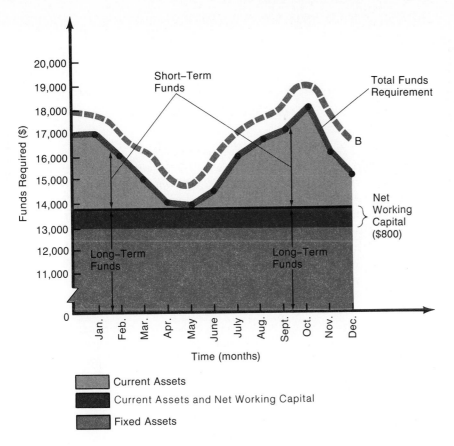

Figure 7.3   **Applying the Aggressive Strategy
to Berenson Company's Funds Requirements**

Under the aggressive financing strategy Berenson Company would finance
its permanent need of $13,800 with long-term funds and finance its
seasonal needs with short-term funds. This strategy results in $800 of net
working capital ($13,800 long-term financing − $13,000 fixed assets).

Cost of short-term financing =   3% × $ 1,950 = $ 58.50
Cost of long-term financing = 11% ×   13,800 =   1,518.00
Total cost $1,576.50

The total annual cost of $1,576.50 will become more meaningful when
compared to the cost of various other financing strategies. The relatively low cost of short-term financing results from using a high amount
of free trade credit (a topic discussed in Chapter 10).

Risk Considerations

The aggressive strategy operates with minimum net working capital
since only the permanent portion of the firm's current assets is being
financed with long-term funds. For Berenson Company, as shown in

F I N A N C E   I N   A C T I O N

Competition Between the Debt-Laden and Debt-Free

Conservative and aggressive uses of debt financing may be found within many industries. Differences occur even in highly cyclical industries such as retailing and textiles, with winners being determined by general economic conditions. After keeping its debt below $1.0 billion during the 1980s, May Department Stores registered a debt offering of $1.0 billion in mid-1991. Proceeds were to be used to buy assets of distressed competitors at bargain-basement prices. Among the debt-laden whose assets May could pick from were Federated Department Stores, Carter Hawley Hale, and R. H. Macy.

In the textile industry, Burlington Industries' privatization drained cash from most capital projects. Though Burlington asserts that the company is now more efficient, there is an absence of funds to finance projects in which the efficiency could be employed. Conversely, the smaller Springs Industries, one of Burlington's competitors, was able to spend $118 million on plant improvements in 1990.

Even in noncyclical industries, the aggressive use of debt may lead to failure. Charter Medical, the largest private chain of psychiatric hospitals, took on $1.7 billion of debt after a prosperous period. Shortly thereafter, corporations and insurance companies began to clamp down on costs. Cash flow per bed fell, losses ensued, and liabilities exceeded assets. Community Psychiatric Centers, which is about one fourth the size of Charter Medical, remained comparatively debt-free during the same period. And, in mid-1991, Community Psychiatric offered to buy Charter for $1.1 billion.

Source: Anne Fisher, "Don't be afraid of the big bad debt," *Fortune*, April 22, 1991, p. 121.

Figure 7.3, the level of net working capital is $800, which is the amount of permanent current assets ($13,800 permanent funds requirement − $13,000 fixed assets = $800).

The aggressive financing strategy is risky. Not only is the net working capital at a minimum, but also the firm must draw as heavily as possible on its short-term sources of funds to meet seasonal fluctuations in its requirements. If its total requirement turns out to be, say, the level represented by dashed curve B in Figure 7.3, the firm may find it difficult to obtain longer-term funds quickly enough to satisfy short-term needs. This aspect of risk associated with the aggressive strategy results from the fact that a firm has only a limited amount of short-term borrowing capacity. If it draws too heavily on this capacity, unexpected needs for funds may become difficult to satisfy.

A final aspect of risk associated with the aggressive strategy's maximum use of short-term financing is the fact that changing short-term interest rates can result in significantly higher borrowing costs as the short-term debt is refinanced. With long-term financing, a more stable rate and less frequent refinancing needs result in greater certainty and less risk.

A CONSERVATIVE FINANCING STRATEGY

The most **conservative financing strategy** should be to finance all projected funds needs with long-term funds and use short-term financing for an emergency or an unexpected outflow of funds. It is difficult to imagine how this strategy could actually be implemented, since the use of short-term financing tools, such as accounts payable and accruals, is virtually unavoidable. In illustrating this strategy, the spontaneous short-term financing provided by payables and accruals will be ignored.

conservative financing strategy Strategy by which the firm finances all projected funds needs with long-term funds and uses short-term financing only for emergencies or unexpected outflows.

EXAMPLE   Figure 7.4 shows graphically the application of the conservative strategy to the total funds requirement for Berenson Company given in Table 7.6. Long-term financing of $18,000, which equals the firm's peak need (during October), is used under this strategy. Therefore all the funds required over the one-year period, including the entire $18,000 forecast for October, are financed with long-term funds.

Cost Considerations

In the preceding example the annual cost of long-term funds was 11 percent per year. Since the average long-term financing balance under the conservative financing strategy is $18,000, the total cost of this strategy is $1,980 or (11% × $18,000). Comparing this figure to the total cost of $1,576.50 using the aggressive strategy indicates the greater expense of the conservative strategy. The reason for this higher expense is apparent if we examine Figure 7.4. The area above the total funds requirement curve and below the long-term funds, or borrowing, line represents the level of funds not actually needed but for which the firm is paying interest. In spite of the fact that the financial manager will invest these excess funds in some type of marketable security so as partially to offset their cost, it is highly unlikely that the firm can earn more on such funds than their interest cost.

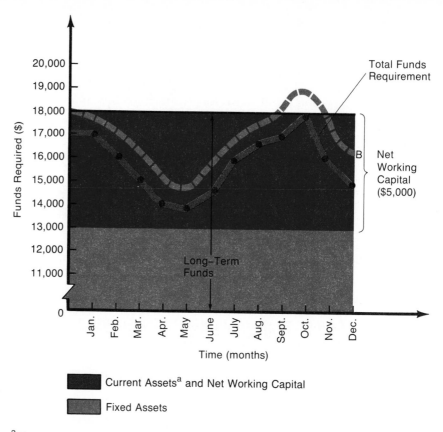

Figure 7.4   Applying the Conservative Strategy
                         to Berenson Company's Funds Requirements

Under the conservative financing strategy Berenson Company would finance all projected funds requirements, including the entire $18,000 forecast for October, with long-term funds. This strategy results in $5,000 of net working capital ($18,000 long-term financing − $13,000 fixed assets).

Risk Considerations

The $5,000 of net working capital ($18,000 long-term financing− $13,000 fixed assets) associated with the conservative strategy should mean a very low level of risk for the firm.[5] The firm's risk should also be lowered by the fact that the strategy does not require the firm to use any

---

[5]The level of net working capital is constant throughout the year since the firm has $5,000 in current assets that will be fully financed with long-term funds. Because the portion of the $5,000 in excess of the scheduled level of current assets is assumed to be held as marketable securities, the firm's current asset balance will increase to this level.

of its limited short-term borrowing capacity. In other words, if total required financing actually turns out to be the level represented by the dashed line B in Figure 7.4, sufficient short-term borrowing capacity should be available to cover the unexpected needs and avoid technical insolvency. In addition, the need to frequently refinance high levels of short-term financing, possibly at high rates, is avoided, thereby further lowering risk.

Conservative versus Aggressive Strategy

Unlike the aggressive strategy, the conservative strategy requires the firm to pay interest on unneeded funds. The lower cost of the aggressive strategy therefore makes it more profitable than the conservative strategy. However, the aggressive strategy involves much more risk. For most firms a trade-off between the extremes represented by these two strategies should result in an acceptable financing strategy.

A TRADE-OFF FINANCING STRATEGY

Most firms employ a **trade-off financing strategy,** a compromise between the high-profit, high-risk aggressive strategy and the low-profit, low-risk conservative strategy. One of the many possible trade-offs in Berenson Company's case is described in the following example.

trade-off financing strategy A compromise financing strategy between the aggressive financing strategy and the conservative financing strategy.

EXAMPLE   After careful analysis, Berenson Company has decided on a financing plan based on an amount of permanent financing equal to the midpoint of the minimum and maximum monthly funds requirements for the period. An examination of column 3 of Table 7.6 reveals that the minimum monthly funds requirement is $13,800 (in May) and the maximum monthly funds requirement is $18,000 (in October). The midpoint between these two values is $15,900 [($13,800 + $18,000) ÷ 2]. Thus the firm will use $15,900 in long-term funds each month and will raise any additional funds required from short-term sources. The breakdown of long- and short-term funds under this plan is given in Table 7.7.

Column 3 in Table 7.7 shows the amount of short-term funds required each month. These values were found by subtracting $15,900 from the total funds required each month, given in column 1. For March, April, May, June, and December, the level of total funds required is less than the level of long-term funds available; therefore, no short-term funds are needed. Figure 7.5 presents graphically the trade-off strategy (line 3) described in Table 7.7 along with the plans based on the aggressive (line 1) and the conservative (line 2) strategies, respectively. Line 3 represents the $15,900 financed with long-term funds; the seasonal needs above that amount are financed with short-term funds.

Table 7.7   **A Financing Strategy Based on a Trade-off between Profitability and Risk for Berenson Company**

Month	Total assets[a] (1)	Long-term funds[b] (2)	Short-term funds (3)
January	$17,000	$15,900	$1,100
February	16,000	15,900	100
March	15,000	15,900	0
April	14,000	15,900	0
May	13,800	15,900	0
June	14,500	15,900	0
July	16,000	15,900	100
August	16,700	15,900	800
September	17,000	15,900	1,100
October	18,000	15,900	2,100
November	16,000	15,900	100
December	15,000	15,900	0
Monthly Average[c]		$15,900	$ 450

[a]This represents the firm's total funds requirement from column 3 of Table 7.6.
[b]Found by taking the average of the minimum monthly funds requirement of $13,800 (in May) and the maximum monthly funds requirement of $18,000 (in October)—[(($13,800 + $18,000) ÷ 2 = $15,900)].
[c]Found by summing the monthly amounts for the 12 months and dividing the resulting totals by 12.

Cost Considerations

Under the trade-off strategy Berenson's average short-term borrowing is $450, and average long-term borrowing is $15,900. (See columns 2 and 3 of Table 7.7.) With the cost of short-term financing at 3 percent and the cost of long-term financing at 11 percent, the total cost of this financing strategy is estimated as follows:

$$\text{Cost of short-term financing} = 3\% \times \$ \quad 450 = \$ \quad 13.50$$
$$\text{Cost of long-term financing} = 11\% \times \quad 15,900 = \underline{\quad 1,749.00}$$
$$\text{Total cost} \qquad\qquad \underline{\underline{\$1,762.50}}$$

The total financing cost under the trade-off strategy is therefore $1,762.50.

Risk Considerations

As Figure 7.5 shows, the trade-off strategy results in $2,900 of net working capital ($15,900 long-term financing − $13,000 fixed assets). This is less risky than the aggressive strategy but more risky than the conserva-

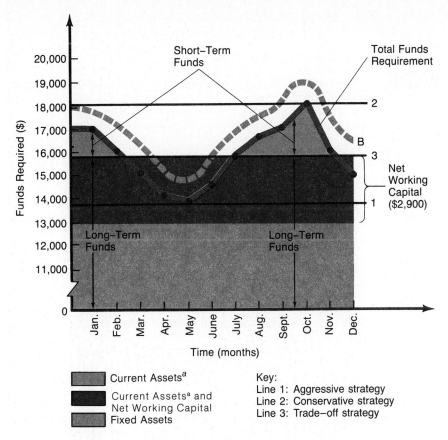

The current assets above the total funds requirements line and below the long–term financing line (line 3) are excess current assets created under the trade–off strategy by investment of excess long–term funds in marketable securities.

Figure 7.5   Three Alternative Financing Strategies for Berenson Company
Under the trade-off financing strategy, represented by Line 3, Berenson would finance $15,900 of its funds need with long-term funds and the remaining seasonal needs with short-term funds. This strategy results in $2,900 of net working capital ($15,900 long-term financing − $13,000 fixed assets).

tive strategy. Under the trade-off strategy, if the total funds requirement is actually at the level represented by dashed line B in Figure 7.5, the likelihood that the firm will be able to obtain additional short-term financing is good, since a portion of its short-term financing requirements is actually being financed with long-term funds. Under this strategy the risk of having to refinance frequently at possibly higher interest rates falls between that of the aggressive and conservative strategies.

SUMMARY

1   **Define net working capital using both the common and alternate definitions and discuss its implications.** Net working capital is defined as the difference between current assets and current liabilities, or, alternatively, as the portion of a firm's current assets financed with long-term funds. Firms maintain net working capital in order to provide a cushion between cash outflows and inflows. Generally the higher the firm's net working capital, the better able it will be to pay its bills as they come due.

2   **Discuss the trade-off between profitability and risk as it relates to changing levels of current assets and current liabilities.**   Profitability, in this context, is the relationship between revenues and costs. Risk, in the context of short-term financial decisions, is the probability that a firm will become technically insolvent—unable to pay its bills as they come due. Net working capital is often used to measure this risk. In general, the more liquid a firm is, the higher its net working capital and the lower its risk of technical insolvency. The firm typically will trade less profitability for less risk, and vice versa.

3   **Use changes in the asset mix and changes in the financing mix to demonstrate the trade-off between profitability and risk.**   Assuming a constant level of total assets, the higher a firm's ratio of current assets to total assets, the less profitable the firm, and the less risky it is. The converse is also true. With constant total assets, the higher a firm's ratio of current liabilities to total assets, the more profitable and more risky the firm is. The converse of this statement is also true.

4   **Explain how the firm's funds requirements, when viewed over time, can be broken into a permanent component and a seasonal component.**   Financing requirements can be forecast and broken down into permanent and seasonal needs. The permanent need is attributable to fixed assets and the permanent portion of current assets, whereas the seasonal need is attributable to the existence of certain temporary current assets.

5   **Describe, in terms of profitability and risk, the aggressive strategy and the conservative strategy for determining the firm's financing mix.**   The aggressive strategy for determining an appropriate financing mix is a high-profit, high-risk financing strategy under which the firm finances at least its seasonal needs, and possibly some of its permanent needs, with short-term funds and the majority of its permanent needs with long-term funds. The conservative strategy is a low-profit, low-risk financing strategy under which all funds requirements—both permanent and seasonal—are financed with long-term funds. Short-term financing is saved for emergencies or unexpected outflows.

6   **Discuss financing strategies that trade off the high profitability and risk effects of aggressive strategies and the lower profitability and risk effects of conservative strategies.**   Trade-off strategies result in a compromise between the high-profit, high-risk aggressive strategy and the low-profit, low-risk conservative strategy. As a result, some seasonal needs are financed with long-term funds. The more seasonal needs financed with long-term funds, the lower the profit and risk, and vice versa.

QUESTIONS

7—1   Why is *short-term financial management* one of the most important and time-consuming activities of the financial manager? What are the two most common definitions of *net working capital?*

7—2   What relationship would you expect there to be between the predictability of a firm's cash inflows and its required level of net working capital?

7—3   How are net working capital, liquidity, and the risk of technical insolvency related?

7—4   Why is an increase in the ratio of current to total assets expected to decrease both profits and risk as measured by net working capital?

7—5   How can changes in the ratio of current liabilities to total assets affect profitability and risk?

7—6   How would you expect an increase in a firm's ratio of current assets to total assets and a decrease in its ratio of current liabilities to total assets to affect profit and risk? Why?

7—7   What is the basic premise of the *aggressive strategy* for meeting a firm's funds requirements? What are the effects of this strategy on the firm's profitability and risk?

7—8   What is the *conservative strategy* for financing funds requirements? What kind of profitability-risk trade-off is involved?

7—9   If a firm has a constant funds requirement throughout the year, which, if any, of the three financing strategies—aggressive, conservative, or trade-off—is preferable? Why?

7—10   As the difference between the cost of short-term and long-term financing becomes smaller, which financing strategy—aggressive or conservative—becomes more attractive? Would the aggressive or the conservative strategy be preferable if the costs were equal? Why?

PROBLEMS

7—1   **(Changing Level of Current Assets)** Bonnie Bowl Products had the following levels of assets, liabilities, and equity:

Assets		Liabilities and equity	
Current assets	$ 5,000	Current liabilities	$ 3,000
Fixed assets	12,000	Long-term debt	6,000
Total	$17,000	Equity	8,000
		Total	$17,000

The company annually earns approximately 4 percent on its current assets and 14 percent on its fixed assets.

a. Calculate the firm's initial values of (1) the ratio of current to total assets, (2) annual profits on total assets, and (3) net working capital.

b. If the firm were to *shift $2,000 of current assets to fixed assets*, find the values of (1) the ratio of current to total assets, (2) annual profits on total assets, and (3) net working capital.

c. If the firm were to *shift $2,000 of fixed assets to current assets*, find the values of (1) the ratio of current to total assets, (2) annual profits on total assets, and (3) net working capital.

d. Summarize your finds in **a, b,** and **c** in tabular form and discuss the impact of shifts in the asset mix on profits and risk.

7—2   **(Changing Level of Current Liabilities)** Mullhollan Smelting had the following levels of assets, liabilities, and equity:

Assets		Liabilities and equity	
Current assets	$18,000	Current liabilities	$ 9,000
Fixed assets	32,000	Long-term debt	22,000
Total	$50,000	Equity	19,000
		Total	$50,000

The firm's current liabilities cost approximately 5 percent annually to maintain, and the average annual cost of its long-term funds is 16 percent.

a. Calculate the firm's initial values of (1) the ratio of current liabilities to total assets, (2) the annual cost of financing, and (3) net working capital.

b. If the firm were to *shift $5,000 of current liabilities to long-term funds,* find the value of (1) the ratio of current liabilities to total assets, (2) the annual cost of financing, and (3) net working capital.

c. If the firm were to *shift $5,000 of long-term funds to current liabilities,* find the value of (1) the ratio of current liabilities to total assets, (2) the annual cost of financing, and (3) net working capital.

d. Summarize your findings in **a, b,** and **c** in tabular form and discuss the impact of shifts in the asset mix on profits and risk.

7—3   **(Liquidity, Risk, and Return—Basic)**   Last year, the NRC Corporation had the following balance sheet:

Assets		Liabilities and equity	
Current assets	$ 6,000	Current liabilities	$ 2,000
Fixed assets	14,000	Long-term funds	18,000
Total	$20,000	Total	$20,000

The firm estimated it earned 10 percent annually on current assets, current liabilities cost 14 percent annually, fixed assets earned 25 percent annually, and long-term funds cost 16 percent annually.

For the coming year, calculate the expected annual profits on total assets, annual financing costs, and net working capital under the following different circumstances:

a. There are no changes.

b. The firm shifts $1,000 from current assets to fixed assets and $500 from long-term funds to current liabilities.

c. Discuss the changes in annual profits and risk illustrated by **a** and **b.**

7—4   **(Liquidity, Risk, and Return—Advanced)**   The Badger Company had the following balance sheet at the end of last year:

Assets		Liabilities and equity	
Current assets	$ 30,000	Current liabilities	$ 15,000
Fixed assets	90,000	Long-term funds	105,000
Total	$120,000	Total	$120,000

a. Calculate the annual profits on total assets, annual financing costs, and net working capital if the firm (1) expects to earn annually 8 percent on current assets and 20 percent on fixed assets, current liabilities cost 12 percent annually, and long-term funds cost 16 percent annually; and (2) expects to earn annually 10 percent on current assets and 20 percent on fixed assets, current liabilities cost 3 percent annually, and long-term funds cost 15 percent annually.

b. The firm wishes to decrease net working capital by $10,000. This could be accomplished by either decreasing current assets or by increasing current liabilities. Under each circumstance above— a(1) and a(2)—would this goal be more profitably accomplished by decreasing current assets or by increasing current liabilities? Explain.

7—5   **(Permanent versus Seasonal Funds Requirements)** Mintex Corporation's current, fixed, and total assets for each month of the coming year are summarized in the table below:

Month	Current assets (1)	Fixed assets (2)	Total assets [(1) + (2)] (3)
January	$15,000	$30,000	$45,000
February	22,000	30,000	52,000
March	30,000	30,000	60,000
April	18,000	30,000	48,000
May	10,000	30,000	40,000
June	6,000	30,000	36,000
July	9,000	30,000	39,000
August	9,000	30,000	39,000
September	15,000	30,000	45,000
October	20,000	30,000	50,000
November	22,000	30,000	52,000
December	20,000	30,000	50,000

a. Divide the firm's monthly total funds requirements (total assets) into a permanent and a seasonal component.

b. Find the monthly average (1) permanent and (2) seasonal funds requirements using your findings in a.

7—6   **(Annual Loan Cost)** What is the average loan balance and the annual loan cost, given an annual interest rate on loans of 15 percent, for a firm with total monthly borrowings as follows?

Month	Amount	Month	Amount
January	$12,000	July	$6,000
February	13,000	August	5,000
March	9,000	September	6,000
April	8,000	October	5,000
May	9,000	November	7,000
June	7,000	December	9,000

7—7   **(Aggressive versus Conservative)** Dynabase Tool has forecast its total funds requirements for the coming year as follows:

Month	Amount	Month	Amount
January	$2,000,000	July	$12,000,000
February	2,000,000	August	14,000,000
March	2,000,000	September	9,000,000
April	4,000,000	October	5,000,000
May	6,000,000	November	4,000,000
June	9,000,000	December	3,000,000

a. Divide the firm's monthly funds requirement into (1) a *permanent* and (2) a *seasonal* component and find the monthly average for each of these components.
b. Describe the amount of long-term and short-term financing used to meet the total funds requirement under (1) an *aggressive strategy* and (2) a *conservative strategy*. Assume that under the aggressive strategy, long-term funds finance permanent needs and short-term funds are used to finance seasonal needs.
c. Assuming short-term funds cost 12 percent annually and the cost of long-term funds is 17 percent annually, use the averages found in **a** to calculate the total cost of each of the strategies described in **b.**
d. Discuss the profitability-risk trade-offs associated with the aggressive strategy and the conservative strategy.

7—8   **(Aggressive versus Conservative)** Marbell International has forecast its seasonal financing needs for the next year as follows:

Month	Seasonal requirement	Month	Seasonal requirement
January	$ 0	July	$700,000
February	300,000	August	400,000
March	500,000	September	0
April	900,000	October	200,000
May	1,200,000	November	700,000
June	1,000,000	December	300,000

Assuming that the firm's permanent funds requirement is $4 million, calculate the total annual financing costs using the aggressive strategy and the conservative strategy, respectively. Recommend one of the strategies under the following conditions:
a. Short-term funds cost 9 percent annually and long-term funds cost 15 percent annually.
b. Short-term funds cost 10 percent annually and long-term funds cost 13 percent annually.
c. Both short-term and long-term funds cost 11 percent annually.

7—9   **(Testing Assumptions)**   LSB, Inc. has seasonal financing needs that
         vary from zero to $2 million. For each separate condition in **a** through
         f, would the condition tend to move the firm toward an aggressive
         financing strategy or toward a conservative financing strategy?
         a. The difference between short-term and long-term financing costs
             has decreased.
         b. The average seasonal financing need is $400,000.
         c. The average seasonal financing need is $1.8 million.
         d. The long-term financing cost is much higher than the short-term
             cost.
         e. The firm has a high proportion of its assets in current assets.
         f. Sales are very difficult to predict.

7—10   **(Aggressive, Conservative, and Trade-off)**   Ideas Enterprises expects
         to need the following amounts of funds next year:

Month	Amount	Month	Amount
January	$10,000	July	$10,000
February	10,000	August	9,000
March	11,000	September	8,000
April	12,000	October	8,000
May	13,000	November	9,000
June	11,000	December	9,000

         a. What is the average amount of funding needed during the year?
         b. If annual short-term financing costs 8 percent and long-term fi-
             nancing costs 20 percent, what will be the total financing costs for
             the aggressive and conservative financing strategies, respectively?
         c. If the firm finances $10,000 with long-term financing, what will be
             the total financing cost?

7—11   **(Aggressive versus Conservative—No Seasonality)**   Snyder Supply
         has financing needs of $250,000 per month forecast for every month of
         the coming year. The annual cost of short-term financing is 12 percent
         and the annual cost of long-term financing is 14 percent.
         a. What are the total annual costs of the aggressive and conservative
             financing strategies, respectively?
         b. Which strategy is preferable? Why?

CASE

Kent Company's Choice of Financing Strategies

Miriam Hirt, the CFO of Kent Company, carefully developed the following estimates of the firm's total funds requirements for the coming year.

Month	Total funds	Month	Total funds
January	$1,000,000	July	$6,000,000
February	1,000,000	August	5,000,000
March	2,000,000	September	5,000,000
April	3,000,000	October	4,000,000
May	5,000,000	November	2,000,000
June	7,000,000	December	1,000,000

In addition, Miriam expects short-term financing costs of about 10 percent and long-term financing costs of about 14 percent during the coming year. She has developed the three possible financing strategies described below.

Strategy 1—Aggressive: Finance seasonal needs with short-term funds and permanent need with long-term funds.

Strategy 2—Conservative: Finance an amount equal to the peak need with long-term funds and use short-term funds only in an emergency.

Strategy 3—Trade-off: Finance $3,000,000 with long-term funds and finance the remaining funds requirements with short-term funds.

Required

    a. Divide Kent's monthly funds requirements into (1) a *permanent* and (2) a *seasonal* component and find the monthly average for each.

    b. For each of the three possible financing strategies, determine (1) the amount of long-term and short-term financing required and (2) the total annual cost of each strategy.

    c. Assuming the firm expects its current assets to total $4 million throughout the year, determine the average amount of net working capital under each financing strategy. (*Hint:* Current liabilities equal average short-term financing.)

    d. Discuss the profitability-risk trade-off associated with each financing strategy. Which strategy would you recommend to Miriam Hirt for Kent Company? Why?

CHAPTER 8

CASH AND MARKETABLE SECURITIES

CHAPTER OBJECTIVES

After studying this chapter, you should be able to:

1 Discuss the motives for holding cash and marketable securities, and describe the three basic strategies for managing the cash conversion cycle in order to minimize financing needs.

2 Define *float*, including its three basic components, and explain the firm's major objective with respect to the levels of collection float and disbursement float.

3 Describe popular collection and disbursement techniques and the role of strong banking relationships in cash management.

4 Understand the basic characteristics of marketable securities and the trade-off involved in timing purchase decisions.

5 List and briefly describe the key features of the popular marketable securities, including government issues and nongovernment issues.

6 Explain how a multinational firm can use either hedging or certain adjustments in its operations in order to protect its undesirable cash and marketable securities exposures against changing relationships between currencies.

"As the U.S. economy skidded into a recession . . . the Japanese economy also began to sputter."

You Can Never Be Too Rich or Too Thin, But You Can Have Too Much Cash

Over the last 20 years, the world of corporate finance has become a truly global environment, where interest-rate changes in Germany affect the sale of automobiles in Detroit, and Detroit's auto sales influence the value of the Japanese yen. As the U.S. economy skidded into a recession in mid-1990, the Japanese economy also began to sputter. In 1990 alone, Japanese stock prices fell 41 percent, wiping out $1.8 trillion in value, and by the end of the year, Japanese interest rates were rising sharply.

In this weak economic environment, you'd expect Japanese corporations to enter a period of retrenchment, hoping to cover their capital losses and wait for lower interest rates before considering any significant business expansion. That's exactly what many of Japan's small- and medium-sized businesses did. But some top-name, multinational Japanese corporations discovered a slightly different way to cope with global recession—they went on a buying spree.

In December 1990, Japan's Matsushita Electric Industrial Company agreed to pay $6.13 billion *in cash* to acquire American entertainment giant MCA. The acquisition was made possible by the Japanese firm's enormous $15 billion cash reserve. Matsushita wasn't the only Japanese multinational flush with cash. At the end of 1990, Toyota Motor Corporation showed a $15.9 billion cash balance, and Hitachi Limited held $15.8 billion in cash reserves.

Financial managers at these three firms consider this much cash a problem. Shareholders and creditors expect these corporations to earn acceptable rates of return on the funds they have invested, and financial managers won't obtain much of a return by holding cash. Accordingly, firms with substantial cash resources look to invest these reserves in higher-yielding projects. Matsushita's managers are planning $3.2 billion in additional investment beyond their MCA acquisition. Toyota's spending plans call for $4.2 billion worth of new expenditures. Hitachi has similar investment plans. If Matsushita writes a $6.1 billion check to MCA's shareholders, and then spends another $3.2 billion on new investment, that leaves only . . . $5.7 *billion* to worry about!

C ash and marketable securities are the most liquid of the firm's assets. **Cash** is the ready currency to which all liquid assets can be reduced. **Marketable securities** are short-term interest-earning money market instruments used by the firm to obtain a return on temporarily idle finds. Together cash and marketable securities act as a pool of funds that can be used to pay bills as they come due and to meet any unexpected outlays.

cash The ready currency to which all liquid assets can be reduced.

marketable securities Short-term interest-earning money market instruments used to obtain a return on temporarily idle funds.

CASH AND MARKETABLE SECURITY BALANCES

Because the rate of interest applied by banks to checking accounts is relatively low, firms tend to use excess bank balances to purchase marketable securities. The firm must therefore determine the appropriate balances for both cash and marketable securities in order to reduce the risk of technical insolvency to an acceptable level. The desired balances are determined by carefully considering the motives for holding them. The higher they are, the lower the risk of technical insolvency, and vice versa.

Motives for Holding Cash and Near-Cash Balances

There are three motives for holding cash and **near-cash (marketable security)** balances. Each motive is based on two underlying questions: (1) What is the appropriate degree of liquidity to maintain? and (2) What is the appropriate distribution of liquidity between cash and marketable securities?

near-cash Marketable securities, viewed the same as cash because of their high liquidity.

Transactions Motive
A firm maintains cash balances to satisfy the **transactions motive,** which is to make planned payments for items such as materials and wages. If cash inflows and cash outflows are closely matched, transaction cash balances can be smaller.

transactions motive A motive for holding cash or near-cash—to make planned payments for items needed for operations.

Safety Motive
Balances held to satisfy the **safety motive** are invested in highly liquid marketable securities that can be immediately transferred from securities to cash. Such securities protect the firm against being unable to satisfy unexpected demands for cash.

safety motive A motive for holding cash or near-cash—to protect the firm against being unable to satisfy unexpected demands for cash.

Speculative Motive
At times, firms invest in marketable securities in excess of needs to satisfy the safety motive, as well as in long-term instruments. A firm may do so because it currently has no other use for certain funds, or because it wants to be able to quickly take advantage of unexpected

speculative motive
A motive for holding cash or near-cash—to put unneeded funds to work or to be able to quickly take advantage of unexpected opportunities.

opportunities that may arise. These funds satisfy the **speculative motive**, which is the least common of the three motives.

Estimating Cash Balances

Management's goal should be to *maintain levels of transactional cash balances and marketable securities investments that contribute to improving the value of the firm*. If levels of cash or marketable securities are too high, the profitability of the firm will be lower than if more optimal balances were maintained. This concept was examined in the last chapter in the profitability-risk trade-off discussion. Firms can use either quantitative models or subjective approaches to determine appropriate transactional cash balances. Quantitative cash balance models are beyond the scope of this text. A subjective approach might be to maintain a transactional balance equal to 10 percent of the following month's forecast sales. If the forecast amount of sales for the following month is $500,000, the firm would maintain a $50,000 (.10 × $500,000) transactional cash balance.

The Level of Marketable Securities Investment

In addition to earning a positive return on temporarily idle funds, the marketable securities portfolio serves as a safety stock of cash that can be used to satisfy unexpected demands for funds. The level of the safety stock is the difference between management's desired liquidity level and the level of transactional cash balances determined by the firm. For example, if management wishes to maintain $70,000 of liquid funds and a transactional balance of $50,000 is desired, a $20,000 ($70,000 − $50,000) safety stock of cash would be held as marketable securities. The firm may use as safety stocks its pre-arranged short-term borrowing power (known as a line of credit, which is discussed in Chapter 10) instead of a portfolio of marketable securities, or a combination of such borrowing power and marketable securities.

THE EFFICIENT MANAGEMENT OF CASH

Cash balances and safety stocks of cash are significantly influenced by the firm's production and sales techniques and by its procedures for collecting sales receipts and paying for purchases. These influences can be better understood through analysis of the firm's operating and cash conversion cycles.[1] By efficiently managing these cycles, the financial

---

[1]The conceptual model used in this part to demonstrate basic cash management strategies was developed by Lawrence J. Gitman in "Estimating Corporate Liquidity Requirements: A Simplified Approach," *The Financial Review*, 1974, pp. 79–88, and refined and operationalized by Lawrence J. Gitman and Kanwal S. Sachdeva in "A Framework for Estimating and Analyzing the Required Working Capital Investment," *Review of Business and Economic Research*, Spring 1982, pp. 35–44.

manager can maintain a low level of cash investment and thereby contribute toward maximization of share value.

The Operating Cycle

The **operating cycle (OC)** of a firm is defined as the amount of time that elapses from the point when the firm inputs material and labor into the production process (i.e., begins to build inventory) to the point when cash is collected from the sale of the finished product that contains these production inputs. The cycle is made up of two components: the average age of inventory and the average collection period of sales. The firm's operating cycle (OC) is simply the sum of the *average age of inventory (AAI)* and the *average collection period (ACP)*:

$$OC = AAI + ACP$$

The concept of the operating cycle can be illustrated using a simple example.

EXAMPLE   RIF Company, a producer of paper dinnerware, sells all its merchandise on credit. The credit terms require customers to pay within 60 days of a sale. The firm's calculations reveal that, on average, it takes 85 days to manufacture, warehouse, and ultimately sell a finished good. In other words, the firm's average age of inventory (AAI) is 85 days. Calculation of the average collection period (ACP) indicates that it is taking the firm, on average, 70 days to collect its accounts receivable. Substituting AAI = 85 days and ACP = 70 days into Equation 8.1, we find RIF's operating cycle to be 155 days (85 days + 70 days). It is graphically depicted above the time line in Figure 8.1.

The Cash Conversion Cycle

A company is usually able to purchase many of its production inputs (i.e., raw materials and labor) on credit. The time it takes the firm to pay for these inputs is called the *average payment period (APP)*. The ability to purchase production inputs on credit allows the firm to partially (or maybe even totally) offset the length of time resources are tied up in the operating cycle. The total number of days in the operating cycle less the average payment period for inputs to production represents the **cash conversion cycle (CCC)**:

$$CCC = OC - APP$$
$$= AAI + ACP - APP$$

A continuation of the RIF Company example illustrates this concept.

EXAMPLE   The credit terms extended the firm for raw material purchases currently require payment within 40 days of a purchase, and employees are paid every 15 days. The firm's cal-

---

operating cycle (OC)
The amount of time that elapses from when the firm begins to build inventory to when cash is collected from sale of the resulting finished product.

Equation 8.1
Expression for calculating the operating cycle

cash conversion cycle (CCC)   The amount of time the firm's cash is tied up between the payment for production inputs and receipt of payment from the sale of the resulting finished product.

Equation 8.2
Expression for calculating the cash conversion cycle

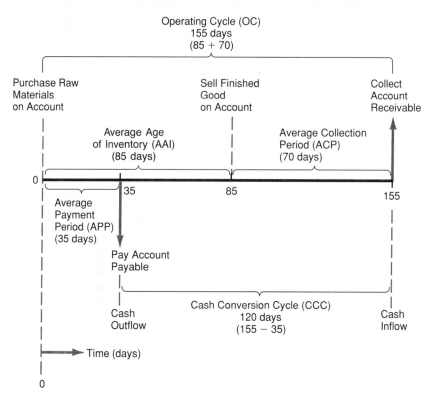

Figure 8.1   RIF Company's Operating and Cash Conversion Cycles
The RIF Company's *operating cycle* of 155 days results from the fact that items are in inventory for an average of 85 days and it takes an average of 70 days to collect accounts receivable. The firm's *cash conversion cycle* of 120 days results from the fact that cash inflow occurs on day 155 at the end of the operating cycle and cash outflow occurs on day 35, which is the end of the average payment period.

culated weighted average payment period for raw materials and labor is 35 days, which represents the average payment period (APP). Substituting RIF Company's 155-day operating cycle (OC), found in the preceding example, and its 35-day average payment period (APP) into Equation 8.2 results in its cash conversion cycle (CCC):

$$CCC = OC - APP$$

$$= 155 - 35 = 120 \text{ days}$$

RIF Company's cash conversion cycle is graphically depicted below the time line in Figure 8.1. There are 120 days between the *cash outflow* to pay the accounts payable (on day 35) and the *cash inflow* from the collection of the account receivable (on day 155). During this period—the cash conversion cycle—the firm's money is tied up.

Managing the Cash Conversion Cycle

A *positive* cash conversion cycle, as in the case of RIF Company in the above example, means that the firm must obtain financing (i.e., borrow) to support the cash conversion cycle. This should be obvious from the above discussion since the cash conversion cycle is the difference between the number of days resources are tied up in the operating cycle and the average number of days the firm can delay making payment on the production inputs purchased on credit.

Ideally, a firm would like to have a *negative* cash conversion cycle. A negative CCC means the average payment period (APP) exceeds the operating cycle (OC) (see Equation 8.2). Manufacturing firms usually will not have negative cash conversion cycles unless they extend their average payment periods an unreasonable length of time (a topic further discussed later). Nonmanufacturing firms are more likely to have negative cash conversion cycles; they generally carry smaller, faster-moving inventories and often sell their products for cash. As a result, these firms have shorter operating cycles. These operating cycles may be shorter than the firm's average payment periods, thereby resulting in negative cash conversion cycles. When a firm's cash conversion cycle is negative, the firm should benefit by being able to use the financing provided by the suppliers of its production inputs to help support aspects of the business other than just the operating cycle.

When the cash conversion cycle is positive (the more common case), the firm needs to pursue strategies to minimize the CCC without causing harm to the company in the form of lost sales or the inability to purchase on credit. The basic strategies that should be employed by the firm to manage the cash conversion cycle are as follows:

1 ▪▪ Turn over inventory as quickly as possible, avoiding stockouts (depletions of stock) that might result in a loss of sales.

2 ▪▪ Collect accounts receivable as quickly as possible without losing future sales due to high-pressure collection techniques. Cash discounts, if they are economically justifiable, may be used to accomplish this objective.

3 ▪▪ Pay accounts payable as late as possible without damaging the firm's credit rating, but take advantage of any favorable cash discounts.[2]

The effects of each of these strategies are described in the following paragraphs using the RIF Company data. The costs of implementing each proposed strategy are ignored; in practice these costs would be measured against the calculated savings in order to make the appropriate strategic decision.

---

[2]A discussion of the variables to consider when determining whether to take cash discounts appears in Chapter 10. A cash discount is often an enticement to pay accounts payable early in order to effectively reduce the purchase price of goods. Strategies for the use of accruals as a free source of short-term financing are also discussed in Chapter 10.

Efficient Inventory-Production Management

One strategy available to RIF is to increase inventory turnover. To do so, the firm can increase raw materials turnover, shorten the production cycle, or increase finished goods turnover. Regardless of which of these approaches is used, the result will be a reduction in the amount of financing required—that is, the cash conversion cycle will be shortened.

EXAMPLE   If RIF Company manages to increase inventory turnover by reducing the average age of inventory from the current level of 85 days to 70 days—a reduction of 15 days—the effect on the firm can be estimated as follows. Suppose RIF currently spends $12 million annually on operating cycle investments. The daily expenditure is $33,333 (i.e., $12 million ÷ 360 days). Since the operating cycle is reduced 15 days, $500,000 (i.e., $33,333 × 15) of financing can be repaid. If RIF pays 10 percent for its financing, the firm will reduce financing costs and thereby increase profit by $50,000 (.10 × $500,000) as a result of managing inventory more efficiently.

Accelerating the Collection of Accounts Receivable

Another means of reducing the cash conversion cycle (and the financing need) is to speed up, or accelerate, the collection of accounts receivable. Accounts receivable, like inventory, tie up dollars that could otherwise be used to reduce financing or be invested in earning assets. Let us consider the following example.

EXAMPLE   If RIF Company, by changing its credit terms, is able to reduce the average collection period from the current level of 70 days to 50 days, it will reduce its cash conversion cycle by 20 days (70 days − 50 days) to 100 days (CCC = 120 days − 20 days = 100 days). Again, assume that $12 million is spent annually—$33,333 daily—to support the operating cycle. By improving the management of accounts receivable by 20 days, the firm will require $666,666 less in financing. With an interest rate of 10 percent, the firm is able to reduce financing costs and thereby increase profits by $66,666 (.10 × $666,666).

Stretching Accounts Payable

stretching accounts payable Paying the firm's bills as late as possible without damaging its credit rating.

A third strategy is **stretching accounts payable**—that is, paying its bills as late as possible without damaging its credit rating. Although this approach is financially attractive, it raises an important ethical issue: clearly, a supplier would not look favorably on a customer who purposely postponed payment.[3]

---

[3]The resolution of this ethical issue is not further addressed in this text. Suffice it to say that although the use of various techniques to slow down payments is widespread due to its financial appeal, it may not be justifiable on purely ethical grounds.

EXAMPLE   If RIF Company can stretch the payment period from the current average of 35 days to an average of 45 days, its cash conversion cycle will be reduced to 110 days (CCC = 85 days + 70 days − 45 days = 110 days). Once more, if operating cycle expenditures total $12 million annually, stretching accounts payable 10 additional days will reduce the firm's financing need by $333,333 [($12 million ÷ 360) × 10 days]. With an interest rate of 10 percent, the firm can reduce its financing costs and thereby increase profits by $33,333 (.10 × $333,333).

Combining Cash Management Strategies

Firms typically do not attempt to implement just one cash management strategy; they attempt to use them all to reduce their financing needs. Of course, when implementing these policies, firms should take care to avoid having a large number of inventory stockouts, to avoid losing sales due to the use of high-pressure collection techniques, and to not damage the firm's credit rating by overstretching accounts payable. Using a combination of these strategies would have the following effects on RIF Company.

EXAMPLE   If RIF simultaneously decreased the average age of inventory by 15 days, sped the collection of accounts receivable by 20 days, and increased the average payment period by 10 days, its cash conversion cycle would be reduced to 75 days, as shown here.

Initial cash conversion cycle		120 days
Reduction due to:		
1. Decreased inventory age 85 days to 70 days =	15 days	
2. Decreased collection period 70 days to 50 days =	20 days	
3. Increased payment period 35 days to 45 days =	10 days	
Less: Total reduction in cash conversion cycle		45 days
New cash conversion cycle		75 days

The 45-day reduction in RIF Company's cash conversion cycle means that it can reduce its financing needs. If annual expenditures for operations are $12 million, then financing can be reduced by $1.5 million [($12 million ÷ 360 days) × 45 days]. If the company pays 10 percent interest on its financing, then it is able to save $150,000 (i.e., .10 × $1,500,000) through improved management of the cash conversion cycle.

CASH MANAGEMENT TECHNIQUES

Financial managers have at their disposal a variety of cash management techniques that can provide additional savings. These techniques are aimed at minimizing the firm's financing requirements by taking advantage of certain imperfections in the collection and payment systems. Assuming that the firm has done all it can to stimulate customers to pay promptly and to select vendors offering the most attractive and flexible credit terms, certain techniques can further speed collections and slow disbursements. These procedures take advantage of the "float" existing in the collection and payment systems.

Float

float Funds dispatched by a payer that are not yet in a form that can be spent by the payee.

In the broadest sense, **float** refers to funds that have been dispatched by a payer (the firm or individual *making* payment) but are not yet in a form that can be spent by the payee (the firm or individual *receiving* payment). Float also exists when a payee has received funds in a spendable form but these funds have not been withdrawn from the account of the payer. Delays in the collection-payment system resulting from the transportation and processing of checks are responsible for float. With electronic payment systems as well as deliberate action by the Federal Reserve system, it seems clear that in the foreseeable future float will virtually disappear. Until that time, however, financial managers must continue to understand and take advantage of float.

Types of Float

collection float The delay between the time a payer deducts a payment from its checking account ledger and the time the payee actually receives the funds in a spendable form.

Currently business firms and individuals can experience both collection and disbursement float as part of the process of making financial transactions. **Collection float** results from the delay between the time that a payer or customer deducts a payment from its checking account ledger and the time that the payee or vendor actually receives these funds in a spendable form. Thus collection float is experienced by the payee and is a delay in the receipt of funds. **Disbursement float** results from the lapse between the time that a firm deducts a payment from its checking account ledger (disburses it) and the time that funds are actually withdrawn from its account. Disbursement float is experienced by the payer and is a delay in the actual withdrawal of funds.

disbursement float The lapse between the time a firm deducts a payment from its checking account ledger (disburses it) and the time funds are actually withdrawn from its account.

Components of Float

Both collection float and disbursement float have the same three basic components:

mail float The delay between the time a payer mails a payment and the time the payee receives it.

1 ▬▬ **Mail float:** The delay between the time that a payer places payment in the mail and the time that it is received by the payee.

processing float The delay between the receipt of a check by the payee and its deposit in the firm's account.

2 ▬▬ **Processing float:** The delay between the receipt of a check by the payee and the deposit of it in the firm's account.

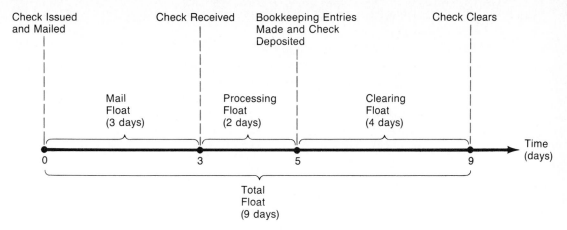

Figure 8.2   **Float Resulting from a Check Issued and Mailed by the Payer Company to the Payee Company**

On a check issued by the payer company to the payee company it takes 3 days (mail float) to reach the payee. The payee then takes 2 days (processing float) to process the check and deposit it in its account where it takes 4 days (clearing float) to clear the banking system and become spendable funds. A total of 9 days (total float) therefore results from this transaction.

3 ▬ **Clearing float:** The delay between the deposit of a check by the payee and the actual availability of the funds. This component of float is attributable to the time required for a check to clear the banking system.

> **clearing float** The delay between the deposit of a check by the payee and the actual availability of the funds.

Figure 8.2 illustrates the key components of float resulting from a check issued and mailed by the payer company to the payee company on day zero. The entire process required a total of nine days: three days' mail float; two days' processing float; and four days' clearing float. To the payer company, the delay is disbursement float; to the payee company, the delay is collection float.

Collection Techniques

The firm's objective is not only to stimulate customers to pay their accounts as promptly as possible but also to convert their payments into a spendable form as quickly as possible—in other words, to *minimize collection float.* A variety of techniques aimed at *speeding up collections,* and thereby reducing collection float, are available.

Concentration Banking

Firms with sales outlets throughout the country often designate certain offices as collection centers for given geographic areas. Customers in these areas send their payments to these sales offices, which in turn deposit the receipts in local banks. At certain times, or on a when-needed basis, funds are transferred by wire from these regional banks to a concentration, or disbursing, bank. Bill payments are dispatched from there.

Concentration banking is used to reduce collection float by shortening the mail and clearing float components. Mail float is reduced because regionally dispersed collection centers bring the collection point closer to the point from which the check is sent. Clearing float should also be reduced, since the payee's regional bank is likely to be in the same Federal Reserve district or the same city as the bank on which the check is drawn; it may even be the same bank. A reduction in clearing float will, of course, make funds available to the firm more quickly.

concentration banking A collection procedure in which payments are made to regionally disbursed collection centers, then deposited in local banks for quick clearing.

EXAMPLE   Suppose Style, Inc., a hair products manufacturer, could go to concentration banking and reduce its collection period by 3 days. If the company normally carried $10 million in receivables and that level equaled a 30-day supply, cutting 3 days from the collection process would result in a $1 million decline in receivables [(3 ÷ 30) × $10,000,000]. Given a 10 percent opportunity cost, the gross annual benefits (profits) of concentration banking would amount to $100,000 (.10 × $1,000,000). Clearly, assuming no change in risk, so long as total annual costs (*incremental* administrative costs and bank service fees, and the opportunity cost of holding specified minimum bank balances) are less than the expected annual benefits of $100,000, Style, Inc.'s proposed program of concentration banking should be implemented.

Lockboxes

lockbox system A collection procedure under which payers send payments to a nearby post office box from which the firm's bank empties and deposits payment checks in its account several times daily.

Another method used to reduce collection float is the **lockbox system,** which differs from concentration banking in several important ways. Instead of mailing payment to a collection center, the payer sends it to a post office box that is emptied by the firm's bank one or more times each business day. The bank opens the payment envelopes, deposits the checks in the firm's account, and sends a deposit slip (or, under certain arrangements, a computer file) indicating the payments received, along with any enclosures, to the collecting firm. Lockboxes normally are geographically dispersed, and the funds, when collected, are wired from each lockbox bank to the firm's disbursing bank.

The lockbox system is superior to concentration banking because it reduces processing float as well as mail and clearing float. The receipts are immediately deposited in the firm's account by the bank so that processing occurs after, rather than before, funds are deposited in the firm's account. This allows the firm to use the funds almost immediately for disbursing payments. Additional reductions in mail float may also result since payments do not have to be delivered but are picked up by the bank at the post office.

EXAMPLE   Davidson Products, a manufacturer of disposable razors, has annual credit sales of $6 million, which are billed at a constant rate each day. It takes about 4 days to receive customers' payments at corporate headquarters. It takes another day for the credit department to process receipts and deposit them in the bank. A cash management consultant has told Davidson that a lockbox system would shorten the mail float from 4 days to 1½ days and completely eliminate the processing float. The lockbox system would cost the firm $8,000 per year. Davidson currently earns 12 percent on investments of comparable risk. The lockbox system would free $58,333 of cash [($6 million ÷ 360 days) × (4 days mail float + 1 day processing float − 1½ days mail float)] that is currently tied up in mail and processing float. The gross annual benefit would be $7,000 (.12 × $58,333). Since the $7,000 gross annual benefit is less than the $8,000 annual cost, Davidson should *not* use the lockbox.

Direct Sends

To reduce clearing float, firms that have received large checks drawn on distant banks, or a large number of checks drawn on banks in a given city, may arrange to present these checks directly for payment to the bank on which they are drawn. Such a procedure is called a **direct send.** Rather than depositing these checks in its collection account, the firm arranges to present the checks to the bank on which they are drawn and receive immediate payment. The firm can use Express Mail or private express services to get the checks into a bank in the same city or to a sales office where an employee can take the checks to the bank and present them for payment. In most cases the funds will be transferred via wire into the firm's disbursement account.

direct send A collection procedure in which the payee presents payment checks directly to the banks on which they are drawn.

Deciding whether to use direct sends is relatively straightforward. If the benefits from the reduced clearing time are greater than the cost, the checks should be sent directly for payment rather than cleared through normal banking channels.

EXAMPLE   If a firm with an opportunity to earn 10 percent on its idle balances can, through a direct send, make available $1.2 million 3 days earlier than would otherwise be the case, the benefit of this direct send would be $1,000 [.10 × (3 days ÷ 360 days) × $1,200,000]. If the cost of achieving this 3-day reduction in float is less than $1,000, the direct send would be recommended.

Other Techniques

A number of other techniques can be used to reduce collection float. One method commonly used by firms that collect a fixed amount from customers on a regular basis, such as insurance companies, is the preauthorized check. A **preauthorized check (PAC)** is a check written against a customer's checking account for a previously agreed-upon amount by the firm to which it is payable. Because the check has been legally authorized by the customer, it does not require the customer's signature. The payee merely issues and then deposits the PAC in its account. The check clears through the banking system just as if it were written by the customer and received and deposited by the firm.

preauthorized check A check written by the payee against a customer's checking account for a previously agreed-upon amount.

FINANCE IN ACTION

Postal Service Regulations and Mail Float

There are times in the world of finance when seemingly insignificant events can have major financial consequences. Take, for example, the 1990 revision in the U.S. Postal Service's delivery standards. Since 1970, the Post Office has published the length of time—overnight, two days, and three days—it should take to move mail around the country. This schedule represents the delivery standard.

In 1990, the Postal Service decided to lengthen its delivery standards in order to save money. It hoped to reduce transportation and labor costs by moving more mail by truck rather than by plane. The change may have dramatic consequences for some financial managers that depend on lockbox operations to speed the collection of cash.

Phoenix-Hecht, a cash management consulting firm located in North Carolina, measured mail delivery times between New York City, northern New Jersey, and southern Connecticut, where delivery standards changed from overnight to two days. The firm estimated that the increase in mail float attributable to the change is approximately six hours per day. For a $300 million company with daily cash flow of $1 million, the annual cost of the lengthened delivery schedule—measured in terms of interest income lost—is $20,000. If this seems like a small sum, remember that it represents the approximate annual salary of a new college graduate beginning a career as a management trainee.

Are there ways to get around the Postal Service's action? Firms can refine their lockbox operations and establish more collection points in areas where a high volume of credit sales occur. Alternatively, businesses can apply for their own Zip Code, which speeds the flow of mail to them through the postal system. There's one small catch, however. Before the Post Office will assign a unique corporate Zip Code, managers must be able to demonstrate weekly mail volume in excess of 15,000 individual items.

Source: Pete Costigan, "Will new mail delivery standards affect lockbox operations?" *CFO Magazine,* December 1990, p. 36.

depository transfer check (DTC) An unsigned check drawn on one of the firm's bank accounts and deposited into its account at a concentration or major disbursement bank.

A method used by firms with multiple collection points to move funds is the depository transfer check. A **depository transfer check (DTC)** is an unsigned check drawn on one of the firm's bank accounts and deposited into its account at another bank—typically a concentration or major disbursing bank. Once the DTC has cleared the bank on which it is drawn, the actual transfer of funds is completed. Most firms currently transmit deposit information via telephone rather than by mail to their concentration banks, which then prepare and deposit DTCs into the firm's accounts.

Firms frequently use wire transfers to reduce collection float by quickly transferring funds from one bank account to another. **Wire transfers** are telegraphic communications that, via bookkeeping entries, remove funds from the payer's bank and deposit them into the payee's bank. Wire transfers can eliminate mail and clearing float and may provide processing float reductions as well. They are sometimes used instead of DTCs to move funds into key disbursing accounts, although a wire transfer is more expensive than a DTC.

Another popular method of accelerating cash inflows involves the use of **ACH (automated clearinghouse) debits.** These are preauthorized electronic withdrawals from the payer's account. A computerized clearing facility (called an automated clearinghouse, or ACH) makes a paperless transfer of funds between the payer and payee banks. An ACH settles accounts among participating banks. Individual depositor accounts are settled by respective bank balance adjustments. ACH transfers clear in one day, in most cases reducing mail, processing, and clearing float.

wire transfers Telegraphic communications that, via bookkeeping entries, remove funds from the payer's bank and deposit them in the payee's bank.

ACH (automated clearinghouse) debits Preauthorized electronic withdrawals from the payer's account which are then transferred to the payee's account via a settlement among banks by the automated clearinghouse.

Disbursement Techniques

The firm's objective relative to accounts payable is not only to pay its accounts as late as possible but also to slow down the availability of funds to suppliers and employees once the payment has been dispatched—in other words, to *maximize disbursement float*. A variety of techniques aimed at *slowing down disbursements,* and thereby increasing disbursement float, are available.

Controlled Disbursing

Controlled disbursing involves the strategic use of mailing points and bank accounts to lengthen mail float and clearing float, respectively. When the date of postmark is considered the effective date of payment by the supplier, the firm may be able to lengthen the mail time associated with disbursements. It can place payments in the mail at locations from which it is known they will take a considerable amount of time to reach the supplier. Typically, small towns not close to major highways and cities provide excellent opportunities to increase mail float.

The widespread availability of computers and data on check clearing times allows firms to develop disbursement schemes that maximize clearing float on their payments. These methods involve assigning payments going to vendors in certain geographic areas to be drawn on specific banks from which maximum clearing float will result.

controlled disbursing The strategic use of mailing points and bank accounts to lengthen mail float and clearing float, respectively.

Playing the Float

Playing the float is a method of consciously anticipating the resulting float, or delay, associated with the payment process. Firms often play the float by writing checks against funds not currently in their checking

playing the float A method of consciously anticipating the resulting delay associated with the payment process and using it to keep funds in an interest-earning form for as long as possible.

accounts. They are able to do this because they know a delay will occur between the deposit of checks by suppliers and the actual withdrawal of funds from their checking accounts. It is likely that the firm's bank account will not be drawn down by the amount of the payments for a few additional days. Although the ineffective use of this practice could result in problems associated with "bounced checks," many firms use float to stretch out their accounts payable.

Firms play the float in a variety of ways—all of which are aimed at keeping funds in an interest-earning form for as long as possible. For example, one way of playing the float is to deposit a certain proportion of a payroll or payment into the firm's checking account on several successive days *following* the actual issuance of a group of checks. This technique is commonly referred to as **staggered funding.** If the firm can determine from historic data that only 25 percent of its payroll checks are cashed on the day immediately following the issuance of the checks, then only 25 percent of the value of the payroll needs to be in its checking account one day later. The amount of checks cashed on each of several succeeding days can also be estimated, until the entire payroll is accounted for. Normally, however, to protect itself against any irregularities a firm will place slightly more money in its account than is needed to cover the expected withdrawals.

Overdraft Systems, Zero-Balance Accounts, and ACH Credits

Firms that aggressively manage cash disbursements will often arrange for some type of overdraft system or a zero-balance account. In an **overdraft system,** if the firm's checking account balance is insufficient to cover all checks presented against the account, the bank will automatically lend the firm enough money to cover the amount of the overdraft. The bank, of course, will charge the firm interest on the funds lent and will limit the amount of overdraft coverage. Such an arrangement is important for a business that actively plays the float.

Firms can also establish **zero-balance accounts**—checking accounts in which zero balances are maintained. Under this arrangement, each day the bank will notify the firm of the total amount of checks presented against the account. The firm then transfers only that amount—typically from a master account or through liquidation of a portion of its marketable securities—into the account. Once the corresponding checks have been paid, the account balance reverts to zero. The bank, of course, is paid for this service.

ACH (automated clearinghouse) credits are frequently used by corporations for making direct bank deposits of payroll into the payees' (employees') accounts. Disbursement float is sacrificed with this technique because ACH transactions immediately draw down the company's payroll account on payday. The benefit of ACH credits is that employees enjoy convenience, which the firm hopes generates enough goodwill to justify its loss of float.

The Role of Strong Banking Relationships

Establishing and maintaining strong banking relations is one of the most important elements in an effective cash management system.

staggered funding Depositing a certain proportion of a payroll or payment into the firm's checking account on several successive days *following* the actual issuance of checks.

overdraft system Automatic coverage by the bank of all checks presented against the firm's account, regardless of the account balance.

zero-balance account A checking account in which a zero balance is maintained and the firm is required to deposit funds to cover checks drawn on the account only as they are presented for payment.

ACH (automated clearinghouse) credits Deposits of payroll directly into the payees' (employees') accounts.

Banks have become keenly aware of the profitability of corporate accounts. In recent years banks have developed a number of innovative services and packages designed to attract various types of businesses. No longer are banks simply a place to establish checking accounts and secure loans; instead, they have become the source of a wide variety of cash management services. For example, banks are selling sophisticated information-processing packages to commercial clients. These packages are designed to help financial managers maximize day-to-day cash availability and facilitate short-term investing.

Today most bank services are offered to corporations on a direct-fee basis, but some of the depository functions are still paid for with deposit balances rather than direct charges. Banks prefer the "compensating balance" approach—giving credit against bank service charges for amounts maintained in the customer's checking account. This approach fosters deposit growth and provides a foundation for the future growth of bank earnings. Of course, bank services should be used only when the benefits to be derived from them are greater than their costs.

MARKETABLE SECURITIES

Marketable securities are short-term, interest-earning, money market instruments that can easily be converted into cash.[4] Marketable securities are classified as part of the firm's liquid assets. The securities most commonly held as part of the firm's marketable securities portfolio are divided into two groups: (1) government issues and (2) nongovernment issues. Before describing the popular government and nongovernment marketable securities, we discuss the basic characteristics of marketable securities and making purchase decisions. Table 8.1 summarizes the key features and recent yields for the marketable securities described in the following sections.

Characteristics of Marketable Securities

The characteristics of marketable securities affect the degree of their salability. To be truly marketable, a security must have two basic characteristics: (1) a ready market and (2) safety of principal (no likelihood of loss in value).

A Ready Market

The market for a security should have both breadth and depth in order to minimize the amount of time required to convert it into cash. The **breadth of a market** is determined by the number of participants (buyers). A broad market is one that has many participants. The **depth of a market** is determined by its ability to absorb the purchase or sale of a

breadth of a market
A characteristic of a ready market, determined by the number of participants (buyers) in the market.

depth of a market A characteristic of a ready market, determined by its ability to absorb the purchase or sale of a large dollar amount of a particular security.

[4]As explained in Chapter 2, the *money market* results from a financial relationship between the suppliers and demanders of short-term funds, that is, marketable securities.

Table 8.1   **Features and Recent Yields on Popular Marketable Securities**

Security	Issuer	Description	Initial maturity	Risk and return	Yield on April 24, 1991[a]
Government Issues					
Treasury bills	U.S. Treasury	Issued weekly at auction. Sold at a discount. Strong secondary market.	91 and 182 days, occasionally 1 year	Lowest, virtually risk free.	5.69%
Treasury notes	U.S. Treasury	Stated interest rate. Interest paid semiannually. Strong secondary market.	1 to 7 years	Low, but slightly higher than U.S. Treasury bills.	5.73
Federal agency issues	Agencies of federal government	Not an obligation of U.S. Treasury. Strong secondary market.	3 months to 10 years	Slightly higher than U.S. Treasury issues.	6.13[b]
Nongovernment Issues					
Negotiable certificates of deposit (CDs)	Commercial banks	Represent specific cash deposits in commercial banks. Amounts and maturities tailored to investor needs. Large denominations. Good secondary market.	1 month to 3 years	Higher than U.S. Treasury issues and comparable to commercial paper.	6.10
Commercial paper	Corporation with a high credit standing	Unsecured note of issuer. Large denominations.	3 to 270 days	Higher than U.S. Treasury issues and comparable to negotiable CDs.	6.11

[a]Yields obtained for 3-month maturities of each security.
[b]Federal National Mortgage Association (FNMA) issue maturing in July 1991.
Source: *The Wall Street Journal*, April 25, 1991, pp. C16, C19, C21.

large dollar amount of a particular security. It is therefore possible to have a broad market that has no depth. Thus 100,000 participants each willing to purchase 1 share of a security is less desirable than 1,000 participants each willing to purchase 2,000 shares. Although both breadth and depth are desirable, in order for a security to be salable it is much more important for a market to have depth.

Safety of Principal (No Likelihood of Loss in Value)
There should be little or no loss in the value of a marketable security over time. Consider a security recently purchased for $1,000. If it can be sold quickly for $500, does that make it marketable? No. According to the definition of marketability, the security not only must be salable quickly, but also must be salable for close to the $1,000 initially in-

Table 8.1 continued   **Features and Recent Yields on Popular Marketable Securities**

Security	Issuer	Description	Initial maturity	Risk and return	Yield on April 24, 1991[a]
Nongovernment Issues					
Banker's acceptances	Banks	Results from a bank guarantee of a business transaction. Sold at discount from maturity value.	30 to 180 days	Slightly lower than CDs and commercial paper but higher than U.S. Treasury issues.	5.90
Eurodollar deposits	Foreign banks	Deposits of currency not native to the country in which the bank is located. Large denominations. Active secondary market.	1 day to 3 years	Highest, due to less regulation of depository banks and some foreign exchange risk.	6.25
Money market mutual funds	Professional portfolio management companies	Professionally managed portfolios of marketable securities. Provide instant liquidity.	None— depends on wishes of investor	Vary, but generally higher than U.S. Treasury issues and comparable to CDs and commercial paper.	6.05[c]
Repurchase agreements	Bank or security dealer	Bank or security dealer sells specific securities to firm and agrees to repurchase them at a specific price and time.	Customized to purchaser's needs	Generally slightly below that associated with the outright purchase of the security.	—

[c]Value Line Money Market Fund with an average maturity of 90 days.

vested. This aspect of marketability is referred to as **safety of principal.** Only securities that can be easily converted into cash without any appreciable reduction in principal are candidates for short-term investment.

safety of principal
The ease of salability of a security for close to its initial value.

Making Purchase Decisions

A major decision confronting the business firm is when to purchase marketable securities. This decision is difficult because it involves a trade-off between the opportunity to earn a return on idle funds during the holding period and the brokerage costs associated with the purchase and sale of marketable securities.

EXAMPLE   Assume that a firm must pay \$35 in brokerage costs to purchase and sell \$4,500 worth of marketable securities yielding an annual return of 8 percent that will be held for one month. Since the securities are to be held for $1/12$ of a year, the firm will earn interest of .67 percent ($1/12 \times 8\%$) or \$30 (.0067 × \$4,500). Since the interest return is less than the \$35 cost of the transaction, the firm should *not* make the investment. This trade-off between interest returns and brokerage costs is a key factor in determining when and whether to purchase marketable securities.

Government Issues

The short-term obligations issued by the federal government and available as marketable security investments are Treasury bills, Treasury notes, and federal agency issues.

Treasury Bills

Treasury bills U.S. Treasury obligations issued weekly on an auction basis, having varying maturities, generally under one year, and virtually no risk.

Treasury bills are obligations of the U.S. Treasury that are issued weekly on an auction basis. The most common maturities are 91 and 182 days, although bills with one-year maturities are occasionally sold. Treasury bills are sold by competitive bidding. Because they are issued in bearer form, there is a strong *secondary (resale) market*. The bills are sold at a discount from their face value (the face value being received at maturity). The smallest denomination of a Treasury bill currently available is \$10,000. Since Treasury bills are issues of the U.S. government, they are considered to be virtually risk-free. For this reason, and because of the strong secondary market for them, Treasury bills are one of the most popular marketable securities. The yields on Treasury bills are generally lower than those on any other marketable securities due to their virtually risk-free nature.

Treasury Notes

Treasury notes U.S. Treasury obligations with initial maturities of between one and seven years, paying interest at a stated rate semiannually, and having virtually no risk.

Treasury notes have initial maturities of between one and seven years. Due to the existence of a strong secondary market, they are quite attractive marketable security investments. They are generally issued in minimum denominations of \$5,000, carry a coupon interest rate, and pay interest semiannually. A firm that purchases a Treasury note with less than one year left to maturity is in the same position as if it had purchased a marketable security with an initial maturity of less than one year. Due to their virtually risk-free nature, Treasury notes generally have a low yield relative to other securities with similar maturities.

Federal Agency Issues

federal agency issues Low-risk securities issued by government agencies but not guaranteed by the U.S. Treasury, having short maturities, and offering slightly higher yields than comparable Treasury issues.

Certain agencies of the federal government issue their own debt. These **federal agency issues** are not part of the public debt, are not a legal obligation of the U.S. Treasury, and are not guaranteed by the U.S. Treasury. Regardless of their lack of direct government backing, the issues of government agencies are readily accepted as low-risk securi-

S M A L L   B U S I N E S S

Treasury Securities and the Houston Clerk of Courts Office

Finding appropriate short-term investments for idle cash balances isn't always an easy task, as Jesse Clark, the federal clerk of court in Houston, Texas, recently learned. Mr. Clark opened his mail in early 1991 and discovered a $400 million check from Michael Milken, the former head of junk bond trading at Drexel, Burnham, Lambert, Inc. The check represented payment to the federal government to settle civil charges brought against Milken by the Securities and Exchange Commission.

Although the $400 million will eventually be distributed among the victims of illegal securities transactions executed by Drexel, Burnham, Lambert, for now the money is resting safely in Treasury bills. Mr. Clark selected these short-term securities because they provide maximum safety and liquidity. Not all observers agree that this is the best use of Milken's former money.

Some money managers argue that Treasury securities are a bit *too* conservative. They believe that the settlement proceeds should be divided among a variety of high-quality investments such as commercial paper, corporate bonds, and even common stock. Mr. Clark, on the other hand, believes that safety of principal is the most important objective for the clerk of courts office.

The federal government apparently agrees with him. Although Milken's case was tried in New York, the settlement check ended up in Texas because the New York federal judge in charge of the case admired Clark's system of investing only in safe, stodgy Treasury securities. Besides, how would the victims of Milken's high-risk investments feel if the government invested their damage claims in some of the very same securities that Milken himself used to defraud them in the first place?

Source: Christi Harlan and John Dorfman, "A Houston court clerk is playing it safe with Milken's money," *The Wall Street Journal*, January 9, 1991, p. C-1.

ties, since most purchasers feel they are implicitly guaranteed by the federal government. Agency issues generally have minimum denominations of $5,000 and are issued either with a stated interest rate or at a discount. Agencies commonly issuing short-term instruments include the Bank for Cooperatives (BC), the Federal Home Loan Banks (FHLB), the Federal Intermediate Credit Banks (FICB), the Federal Land Banks (FLB), and the Federal National Mortgage Association (FNMA). Most agency issues have short maturities and offer slightly higher yields than U.S. Treasury issues having similar maturities. Agency issues have a strong secondary market, which is most easily reached through government security dealers.

Nongovernment Issues

A number of additional marketable securities are issued by banks or businesses. Due to the slightly higher risks associated with them, these nongovernment issues typically have slightly higher yields than government issues with similar maturities. The principal nongovernment marketable securities are negotiable certificates of deposit, commercial paper, banker's acceptances, Eurodollar deposits, money market mutual funds, and repurchase agreements.

Negotiable Certificates of Deposit (CDs)

negotiable certificates of deposit (CDs) Negotiable instruments representing specific cash deposits in commercial banks, having varying maturities and yields based on size, maturity, and prevailing money market conditions.

Negotiable certificates of deposit (CDs) are negotiable instruments representing the deposit of a certain number of dollars in a commercial bank. The amounts and maturities are normally tailored to the investor's needs. Average maturities of 30 days are quite common. A good secondary market for CDs exists. Normally the smallest denomination for a negotiable CD is $100,000. (Nonnegotiable CDs can be purchased for smaller amounts.) The yields on CDs are initially set on the basis of size, maturity, and prevailing money market conditions. They are typically above those on U.S. Treasury issues and comparable to the yields on commercial paper with similar maturities.

Commercial Paper

commercial paper A short-term, unsecured promissory note issued by a corporation with a high credit standing.

Commercial paper is a short-term, unsecured promissory note issued by a corporation with a very high credit standing.[5] These notes are issued, generally in multiples of $100,000, by all types of firms and have initial maturities of anywhere from 3 to 270 days. They can be sold directly by the issuer or through dealers. The yield on commercial paper typically is above that paid on U.S. Treasury issues and is comparable to that available on negotiable CDs with similar maturities.

Banker's Acceptances

banker's acceptances Short-term, low-risk marketable securities arising from bank guarantees of business transactions.

Banker's acceptances arise from a short-term credit arrangement used by businesses to finance transactions, especially those involving firms in foreign countries or firms with unknown credit capacities. The purchaser, to assure payment to the seller, requests its bank to issue a *letter of credit* on its behalf, authorizing the seller to draw a *time draft*—an order to pay a specified amount at a specified time—on the bank in payment for the goods. Once the goods are shipped, the seller presents a

---

[5]The role of commercial paper from the point of view of the issuer is included in the discussion of the various sources of short-term financing available to business in Chapter 10.

time draft along with proof of shipment to its bank. The seller's bank then forwards the draft with appropriate shipping documents to the buyer's bank for acceptance and receives payment for the transaction. The buyer's bank may either hold the acceptance to maturity or sell it at a discount in the money market. If sold, the size of the discount from the acceptance's maturity value and the amount of time until the acceptance is paid determine the purchaser's yield.

As a result of its sale, the banker's acceptance becomes a marketable security that can be traded in the marketplace. The initial maturities of banker's acceptances are typically between 30 and 180 days; 90 days is most common. A banker's acceptance is a low-risk security because at least two, and sometimes three, parties may be liable for its payment at maturity. The yields on banker's acceptances are generally slightly below those on negotiable CDs and commercial paper, but generally higher than those on U.S. Treasury issues with similar maturities.

Eurodollar Deposits

Eurodollar deposits are deposits of currency that are not native to the country in which the bank is located. London is the center of the Eurodollar market. Other important centers are Paris, Frankfurt, Zurich, Nassau (Bahamas), Singapore, and Hong Kong. Nearly 75 percent of these deposits are in the form of U.S. dollars. The deposits are negotiable, usually pay interest at maturity, and are typically denominated in units of $1 million. Maturities range from overnight to several years, with most of the money in the 1-week to 6-month maturity range. Eurodollar deposits tend to provide yields above nearly all other marketable securities, government or nongovernment, with similar maturities. These higher yields are attributable to (1) the fact that the depository banks are generally less closely regulated than U.S. banks and are therefore more risky, and (2) some foreign exchange risk may be present. An active secondary market allows Eurodollar deposits to be used to meet all three motives for holding cash and near-cash balances.

Eurodollar deposits Negotiable deposits of currency not native to the country in which the bank is located.

Money Market Mutual Funds

Money market mutual funds, often called *money funds*, are professionally managed portfolios of marketable securities such as those described earlier. Shares or interests in these funds can be easily acquired—often without paying any brokerage commissions. A minimum initial investment of as low as $500, but generally $1,000 or more, is required. Money funds provide instant liquidity, much like a checking or savings account. In exchange for investing in these funds, investors earn returns that are comparable to or higher than—especially during periods of high interest rates—those obtainable from most other marketable securities. Due to the high liquidity, competitive yields, and often low transactions costs, these funds have achieved significant growth in size and popularity in recent years.

money market mutual funds Professionally managed portfolios of various popular marketable securities.

Repurchase Agreements

A **repurchase agreement** is not a specific security. It is an arrangement whereby a bank or security dealer sells specific marketable securities to a firm and agrees to repurchase the securities at a specific price at a

repurchase agreement An agreement whereby a bank or security dealer sells a firm specific securities and agrees to buy them back at a specific price and time.

specified point in time. In exchange for the tailor-made maturity date provided by this arrangement, the bank or security dealer provides a return slightly below that obtainable through outright purchase of similar marketable securities. The benefit to the purchaser is the guaranteed repurchase, and the tailor-made maturity date ensures that the purchaser will have cash at a specified point in time. The actual securities involved may be government or nongovernment issues. Repurchase agreements are ideal for marketable securities investments made to satisfy the transactions motive.

 INTERNATIONAL DIMENSION: CASH MANAGEMENT

Because the revenues and costs of a multinational company are based on different foreign currencies, it must protect itself against changing relationships between them. In its international cash management, the firm can protect against changing relationships between currencies either by hedging them or by making certain adjustments in its operations. Each of these two approaches is examined here.

Hedging Strategies

hedging strategies
Techniques used to offset the risk of changing relationships between currencies.

Hedging strategies are techniques used to offset the risk of changing relationships between currencies. In international cash management these strategies include actions such as borrowing or lending in different currencies, and undertaking contracts in the forward, futures, or options markets. Table 8.2 provides a brief summary of some of the major hedging tools available to MNCs.

Adjustments in Operations

In responding to currency fluctuations, MNCs can give some protection to international cash flows through appropriate adjustments in assets and liabilities. Two routes are available to a multinational company. The first centers on the operating relationships that a subsidiary of an MNC maintains with *other* firms—*third parties*. The firm can reduce its liabilities if the currency is appreciating, or it can reduce its financial assets if the currency is depreciating. Which it does depends on management's expectation of the local currency's position. For example, if a U.S.-based MNC with a subsidiary in Mexico expects the Mexican currency to *appreciate* in value relative to the U.S. dollar, local customers' accounts receivable would be *increased* and accounts payable would be reduced if at all possible. Because the dollar is the currency in which the MNC parent will have to prepare consolidated financial statements, the net result in this case would be to favorably increase the Mexican subsidiary's resources in local currency. If the Mexican currency were, instead, expected to *depreciate*, the local customers' accounts receivable

Table 8.2   **Major Hedging Tools Available to MNCs**

Tool	Description	Impact on risk
Borrowing or lending	Borrowing or lending in different currencies to take advantage of interest rate differences and currency appreciation/depreciation.	Can be used to offset exposures in existing assets/liabilities and in expected revenues/expenses.
Forward contract	"Tailor-made" contracts representing an *obligation* to buy/sell, with the amount, rate, and maturity agreed upon between the two parties.	Can eliminate risk of loss but locks out any potential gain.
Futures contract	Standardized contracts offered on organized exchanges; same basic tool as a forward contract, but less flexible due to standardization; more flexibility due to secondary market access.	Can also eliminate risk of loss, plus position can be nullified, creating possible gain.
Options	Tailor-made or standardized contracts providing the *right* to buy or to sell an amount of the currency, at a particular price, during a specified time period.	Can eliminate risk of loss and retain unlimited potential gain.

Note: The participants in the above activities include MNCs, financial institutions, and brokers. The organized exchanges include Amsterdam, Chicago, London, New York, Philadelphia, and Zurich, among others.

would be *reduced* and accounts payable would be increased, thereby reducing the Mexican subsidiary's resources in the local currency.

The second route focuses on the operating relationship a subsidiary has with its parent or with other subsidiaries within the same MNC. In dealing with currency fluctuations, a subsidiary can rely on *intra-MNC accounts*. Specifically, undesirable currency exposures can be corrected to the extent that the subsidiary can take the following steps:

1 ■■■ In appreciation-prone countries, intra-MNC accounts receivable are collected as soon as possible, and payment of intra-MNC accounts payable is delayed as long as possible.

2 ■■■ In devaluation-prone countries, intra-MNC accounts receivable are collected as late as possible, and intra-MNC accounts payable are paid as soon as possible.

Again using the example of a Mexican subsidiary, the net result of step 1 or step 2 would be the potential increase or decrease of that subsidiary's resources in the Mexican currency, depending on whether that currency is appreciating or depreciating relative to the parent MNC's main currency, the U.S. dollar.

From a *global* point of view and as far as an MNC's consolidated intracompany accounts are concerned, the manipulation of such accounts by one subsidiary can produce the opposite results for another subsidiary or the parent firm. For example, suppose an MNC has subsidiaries in Brazil and Mexico. If the Brazilian subsidiary anticipates appreciation of that country's currency relative to that of Mexico, it can manipulate its accounts along the lines just discussed (i.e., collect Brazilian accounts receivable as soon as possible and delay paying its Mexican accounts payable for as long as possible). The result for the MNC will be exchange gains for the Brazilian subsidiary but losses for the Mexican one. The exact degree and direction of the actual manipulations, however, may depend on the tax status of each country. The MNC obviously would want to have the exchange losses in the country with the higher tax rate. Finally, changes in intra-MNC accounts can also be subject to restrictions and regulations put forward by the respective host countries of various subsidiaries.

SUMMARY

1　**Discuss the motives for holding cash and marketable securities, and describe the three basic strategies for managing the cash conversion cycle in order to minimize financing needs.**　The three motives for holding cash and near-cash (marketable security) balances are: (1) the transactions motive, (2) the safety motive, and (3) the speculative motive. The efficient management of cash is affected by the firm's operating and cash conversion cycles. Ideally, management wants to minimize the length of these cycles without jeopardizing profitability. The three basic strategies for managing the cash conversion cycle in order to achieve this objective are (1) turning over inventory as quickly as possible, (2) collecting accounts receivable as quickly as possible, and (3) paying accounts payable as late as possible without damaging the firm's credit rating.

2　**Define *float*, including its three basic components, and explain the firm's major objective with respect to the levels of collection float and disbursement float.**　Float refers to funds that have been dispatched by a payer (the firm or individual *making* payment) but are not yet in a form that can be spent by the payee (the firm or individual *receiving* payment). Both collection and disbursement float have the same three basic components—(1) mail float, (2) processing float, and (3) clearing float. The firm's major objective with respect to float is to minimize collection float and maximize disbursement float within reasonable limits.

3　**Describe popular collection and disbursement techniques and the role of strong banking relationships in cash management.**　Popular collection techniques include concentration banking, lockboxes, direct sends, preauthorized checks (PACs), depository transfer checks (DTCs), wire transfers, and ACH (automated clearinghouse) debits. Disbursement techniques include controlled disbursing, playing the float, overdraft systems, zero-balance accounts, and ACH credits. Establishing and maintaining strong banking relationships is crucial for effective cash management.

4　**Understand the basic characteristics of marketable securities and the trade-off involved in timing purchase decisions.**　Marketable securities allow the firm to earn a return on temporarily idle funds. For a security to be considered marketable, it must have a ready market that has both breadth and depth. Furthermore, the risk associated with the safety of principal must be quite low. The decision to purchase marketable securities depends on the trade-off between the return earned during the holding period and the brokerage costs associated with purchasing and selling the securities.

5▪   **List and briefly describe the key features of the popular market-able securities, including government issues and nongovernment issues.**   Government-issue marketable securities are Treasury bills, Treasury notes, and federal agency issues. Nongovernment issues include negotiable certificates of deposit (CDs), commercial paper, banker's acceptances, Eurodollar deposits, money market mutual funds, and repurchase agreements. Table 8.1 summarizes the key features and recent yields for each of these marketable securities.

6▪   **Explain how a multinational firm can use either hedging or certain adjustments in its operations in order to protect its undesirable cash and marketable securities exposures against changing relationships between currencies.**   The multinational firm can use hedging, which is a technique for offsetting the risk of changing relationships between currencies. It involves borrowing and lending in different currencies and undertaking contracts in the forward, futures, or options markets. Another method of responding to currency fluctuations involves making adjustments in operations—specifically assets and liabilities. This approach involves either manipulating accounts receivable and accounts payable from and to third parties or relying on intra-MNC accounts.

QUESTIONS

8—1   List and describe the three motives for holding cash and near-cash (marketable securities). Which are the most common motives?

8—2   What is management's goal with respect to the management of cash and marketable securities?

8—3   What is the firm's *operating cycle*? What is the *cash conversion cycle*? Compare and contrast them. What is the firm's objective with respect to each of them?

8—4   What are the *key strategies* with respect to inventory, accounts receivable, and accounts payable for the firm that wants to manage its cash conversion cycle efficiently?

8—5   If a firm reduces the average age of its inventories, what effect might this action have on the cash conversion cycle? On the firm's total sales? Is there a trade-off between average inventory and sales? Give reasons for your answer.

8—6   Define *float* and describe its three basic components. Compare and contrast collection and disbursement float and state the financial manager's goal with respect to each of these types of float.

8—7   Briefly describe the key features of each of the following collection techniques.
   a. Concentration banking
   b. Lockboxes
   c. Direct sends
   d. Preauthorized checks (PACs)
   e. Depository transfer checks (DTCs)
   f. Wire transfers
   g. ACH (automated clearinghouse) debits

8—8   Briefly describe the key features of each of the following disbursement techniques.
   a. Controlled disbursing
   b. Playing the float
   c. Overdraft systems
   d. Zero-balance accounts
   e. ACH (automated clearinghouse) credits

8—9   Describe the role of strong banking relationships in the cash management process. How should available bank services be evaluated?

8—10   What two characteristics are deemed essential for a security to be marketable? Which aspect of a market for a security is more important—breadth or depth? Why?

8—11   For each of the following government-based marketable securities, give a brief description emphasizing maturity, liquidity, risk, and return.
     a. Treasury bill
     b. Treasury note
     c. Federal agency issue

8—12   Describe the basic features—including maturity, liquidity, risk, and return—of each of the following nongovernment marketable securities.
     a. Negotiable certificate of deposit (CD)
     b. Commercial paper
     c. Banker's acceptance
     d. Eurodollar deposit

8—13   Briefly describe the basic features of the following marketable securities and explain how they both involve other marketable securities.
     a. Money market mutual fund
     b. Repurchase agreement

 8—14   Discuss the steps to be followed in adjusting a subsidiary's accounts relative to *third parties* when that subsidiary's local currency is expected to appreciate in value in relation to the currency of the parent MNC.

 8—15   Outline the changes to be undertaken in *intra-MNC accounts* if a subsidiary's currency is expected to depreciate in value relative to the currency of the parent MNC.

PROBLEMS

8—1   **(Cash Conversion Cycle)** Wilderness Products is concerned about managing cash in an efficient manner. On the average, inventories have an average age of 90 days and accounts receivable are collected in 60 days. Accounts payable are paid approximately 30 days after they arise. The firm spends $30 million on operating cycle investments each year, at a constant rate. Assuming a 360-day year:
     a. Calculate the firm's operating cycle.
     b. Calculate the firm's cash conversion cycle.
     c. Calculate the amount of financing required to support the firm's cash conversion cycle.
     d. Discuss how management might be able to reduce the cash conversion cycle.

8—2   **(Cash Conversion Cycle)** Gerald & Company has an inventory turnover of 12, an average collection period of 45 days, and an average payment period of 40 days. The firm spends $1 million on operating cycle investments each year. Assuming a 360-day year:
     a. Calculate the firm's operating cycle.
     b. Calculate the firm's cash conversion cycle.
     c. Calculate the amount of financing required to support the firm's cash conversion cycle.
     d. If the firm's operating cycle were lengthened, without any change in its average payment period (APP), how would this effect its cash conversion cycle and financing need?

8—3   **(Comparison of Cash Conversion Cycles)** A firm turns its inventory, on average, every 105 days. Its accounts receivable are collected, on the average, after 75 days, and accounts payable are paid an average of 60 days after they arise. Assuming a 360-day year, what changes will occur in the cash conversion cycle under each of the following circumstances?

a. The average age of inventory changes to 90 days.
b. The average collection period changes to 60 days.
c. The average payment period changes to 105 days.
d. The circumstances in **a, b,** and **c** occur simultaneously.

8—4   **(Changes in Cash Conversion Cycles)** A firm is considering several plans that affect its current accounts. Given the five plans and their probable results in the following table, which one would you favor? Explain.

Plan	Change		
	Average age of inventory	**Average collection period**	**Average payment period**
A	+30 days	+20 days	+5 days
B	+20 days	−10 days	+15 days
C	−10 days	0 days	−5 days
D	−15 days	+15 days	+10 days
E	+5 days	−10 days	+15 days

8—5   **(Changing Cash Conversion Cycle)** Barnstead Industries turns its inventory 8 times each year, has an average payment period of 35 days, and has an average collection period of 60 days. The firm's total annual outlays for operating cycle investments are $3.5 million. Assuming a 360-day year:

a. Calculate the firm's operating and cash conversion cycles.
b. Calculate the firm's daily cash operating expenditure. How much financing is required to support its cash conversion cycle?
c. Assuming the firm pays 14 percent for its financing, by how much would it increase its annual profits by *favorably* changing its current cash conversion cycle by 20 days?

8—6   **(Multiple Changes in Cash Conversion Cycle)** Hubbard Corporation turns its inventory 6 times each year; it has an average collection period of 45 days and an average payment period of 30 days. The firm's annual operating cycle investment is $3 million. Assuming a 360-day year:

a. Calculate the firm's cash conversion cycle, daily cash operating expenditure, and the amount of financing required to support its cash conversion cycle.
b. Find the firm's cash conversion cycle and financing requirement in the event that it makes the following changes simultaneously.
  (1) Shortens the average age of inventory by 5 days.
  (2) Speeds the collection of accounts receivable by an average of 10 days.
  (3) Extends the average payment period by 10 days.
c. If the firm pays 13 percent for its financing, by how much, if anything, could it increase its annual profit as a result of the changes in **b**?
d. If the annual cost of achieving the profit in **c** is $35,000, what action would you recommend to the firm? Why?

8—7   **(Float)** Breeland Industries has daily cash receipts of $65,000. A recent analysis of its collections indicated that customers' payments were in the mail an average of 2½ days. Once received, the payments are processed in 1½ days. After payments are deposited, it takes an average of 3 days for these receipts to clear the banking system.
   a. How much collection float (in days) does the firm currently have?
   b. If the firm's opportunity cost is 11 percent, would it be economically advisable for the firm to pay an annual fee of $16,500 in order to reduce collection float by 3 days? Explain why or why not.

8—8   **(Concentration Banking)** Tal-Off Corporation sells to a national market and bills all credit customers from the New York City office. Using a continuous billing system, the firm has collections of $1.2 million per day. Under consideration is a concentration banking system that would require customers to mail payments to the nearest regional office to be deposited in local banks.
   Tal-Off estimates that the collection period for accounts will be shortened an average of 2½ days under this system. The firm also estimates that *annual* service charges and administrative costs of $300,000 will result from the proposed system. The firm can earn 14 percent on equal-risk investments.
   a. How much cash will be made available for other uses if the firm accepts the proposed concentration banking system?
   b. What savings will the firm realize on the 2½-day reduction in the collection period?
   c. Would you recommend the change? Explain your answer.

8—9   **(Lockbox System)** Orient Oil feels a lockbox system can shorten its accounts receivable collection period by 3 days. Credit sales are $3,240,000 per year, billed on a continuous basis. The firm has other equally risky investments with a return of 15 percent. The cost of the lockbox system is $9,000 per year.
   a. What amount of cash will be made available for other uses under the lockbox system?
   b. What net benefit (cost) will the firm receive if it adopts the lockbox system? Should it adopt the proposed lockbox system?

8—10   **(Direct Send—Single)** Lorca Industries of San Diego, California, just received a check in the amount of $800,000 from a customer in Bangor, Maine. If the firm processes the check in the normal manner, the funds will become available in 6 days. To speed up this process, the firm could send an employee to the bank in Bangor on which the check is drawn to present it for payment. Such action will cause the funds to become available after 2 days. If the cost of the direct send is $650 and the firm can earn 11 percent on these funds, what recommendation would you make? Explain.

8—11   **(Direct Sends—Multiple)** Ricor Enterprises just received four sizable checks drawn on various distant banks throughout the United States. The data on these checks is summarized in the table on the following page. The firm, which has a 12 percent opportunity cost, can lease a small business jet with pilot to fly the checks to the cities of the banks on which they are drawn and present them for immediate payment. This task can be accomplished in a single day—thereby reducing to one day the funds availability from each of the four checks. The total cost of leasing the jet with pilot and other incidental expenditures is $4,500. Analyze the proposed action and make a recommendation.

Check	Amount	Number of days until funds are available
1	$ 600,000	7 days
2	2,000,000	5
3	1,300,000	4
4	400,000	6

8—12   **(Controlled Disbursing)** A large Midwestern firm has annual cash disbursements of $360 million made continuously over the year. Although annual service and administrative costs would increase by $100,000, the firm is considering writing all disbursement checks on a small bank in Idaho. The firm estimates this will allow an additional 1½ days of cash usage. If the firm earns a return on other equally risky investments of 12 percent, should it change to the distant bank? Why, or why not?

8—13   **(Playing the Float)** Tollfree Enterprises routinely funds its checking account to cover all checks when written. A thorough analysis of its checking account discloses that the firm could maintain an average account balance 25 percent below the current level and adequately cover all checks presented. The average account balance is currently $900,000. If the firm can earn 10 percent on short-term investments, what, if any, annual savings would result from maintaining the lower average account balance?

8—14   **(Payroll Account Management)** Clearview Window has a weekly payroll of $250,000. The payroll checks are issued on Friday afternoon each week. In examining the check-cashing behavior of its employees, the firm has found the following pattern:

Number of business days[a] since issue of check	Percentage of checks cleared
1	20%
2	40
3	30
4	10

[a]Excludes Saturday and Sunday.

Given this information, what recommendation would you make to the firm with respect to managing its payroll account? Explain.

8—15   **(Zero-Balance Account)** Danzig Industries is considering establishment of a zero-balance account. The firm currently maintains an average balance of $420,000 in its disbursement account. As compensation to the bank for maintaining the zero-balance account, the firm will have to pay a monthly fee of $1,000 and maintain a $300,000 noninterest-earning deposit in the bank. The firm currently has no other deposits in the bank. Evaluate the proposed zero-balance account and make a recommendation to the firm assuming it has a 12 percent opportunity cost.

8—16   **(Marketable Securities Purchase Decisions)**   To purchase and sell $25,000 in marketable securities, a firm must pay $800. If the marketable securities have a yield of 12 percent annually, recommend purchasing or not if:

a. The securities are held for one month.
b. The securities are held for three months.
c. The securities are held for six months.
d. The securities are held for one year.

CASE

Mexicali Furniture's Cash Management Efficiency

In January 1993, Marie Chen was named treasurer of Mexicali Furniture—a manufacturer of contemporary Spanish furniture. She began to familiarize herself with the firm by studying its operating and cash conversion cycles.

Ms. Chen found that Mexicali's average payment period was 30 days. She consulted industry data, which showed that the average payment period for the industry was 39 days. Investigation of six similar furniture manufacturers revealed that their average payment period was also 39 days.

Next, Chen studied the production cycle and inventory policies. The average inventory age was 110 days. Chen determined that the industry standard as reported in a survey done by *Furniture Age*, the trade association journal, was 83 days.

Ms. Chen discovered that the firm's average collection period was 60 days. The trade association and six similar furniture manufacturers' average were found to be 45 days—25 percent lower than Mexicali's.

Mexicali Furniture was spending an estimated $26,500,000 per year on its operating cycle investments. Chen considered this expenditure level to be the minimum she could expect the firm to disburse during 1993. Her concern was whether the firm's cash management was as efficient as it could be. She knew that the company paid 15 percent for its financing. For this reason she was concerned about the financing cost resulting from any inefficiencies in the management of Mexicali's cash conversion cycle.

Required

a. Assuming a constant rate for purchases, production, and sales throughout the year, what are Mexicali's existing operating cycle (OC), cash conversion cycle (CCC), and financing need?

b. If Chen can optimize operations according to industry standards, what would its operating cycle (OC), cash conversion cycle (CCC), and financing needs be under these more efficient conditions?

c. In terms of financing requirements, what is the cost of Mexicali Furniture's operational inefficiency?

CHAPTER 9

ACCOUNTS RECEIVABLE AND INVENTORY

After studying this chapter, you should be able to:

1 Discuss the key aspects of credit selection, including the five C's of credit, obtaining credit information, analyzing credit information, and credit scoring.

2 Understand how to isolate and measure the key variables and use them to make both credit standard and credit term decisions.

3 Explain the key features of collection policy, including aging accounts receivable, the basic trade-offs, and the types of collection techniques.

4 Understand the types of inventory, differing viewpoints about inventory level, inventory as an investment, and the relationship between inventory and accounts receivable.

5 Describe the common techniques for managing inventory, including the ABC system, the basic economic order quantity (EOQ) model, the reorder point, the materials requirement planning (MRP) system, and the just-in-time (JIT) system.

6 Identify the key concerns and strategies that multinational companies need to consider in order to effectively manage credit and inventory when exporting and selling in foreign markets.

*((As the saying goes
. . . (It's not a sale
until you collect the
money.)))*

Collecting Sales Dollars
at Albany Ladder

Albany Ladder's financial services manager, Jim Ullery, faced a dilemma. The firm's drive for market share in the construction equipment industry made it necessary to extend credit early and often. Yet most of its customers were carpenters, roofers, and small contractors who seldom borrow money from the bank for business purposes. Consequently, Albany Ladder's customers lacked a history of responsibly paying debt. As the saying goes among collection agents, "It's not a sale until you collect the money." Jim Ullery needed to learn how to collect debts early and often.

Albany Ladder's management decided not to use a collection agency. They believed that an agency could create ill will and that its costs were too high, providing a return of only 12 cents on the dollar. Instead, Ullery developed an aggressive credit policy that relied on diligence and empathy. The diligence aspect is reflected in Albany's program of telephone calls, short memos, formal letters, and offerings to negotiate to resolve a past-due account.

In Ullery's view, Albany Ladder's collection strength is based upon the firm's willingness to empathize with the customer. The firm offers to cosign bank loans and seeks an understanding of why a contractor cannot pay. Phrases such as "pulling together" and "help each other" are included in collection letters. Telephone contacts begin 35 days after the sale, and if calls fail to produce payment, collection letters are sent 60 days after the sale. The letters are customized with the name of the owner or receiving agent and are produced on high quality printers to indicate that Albany Ladder means business. They are sent by return-receipt-requested mail, to eliminate the excuse that the letter didn't arrive. (And if a letter is not accepted and signed for by its recipient, Ullery's five-year-old daughter addresses the envelope to increase the likelihood of its being accepted the next time!) The collection letter appeals to the honesty and reputation of the customer. It requests urgency but offers a grace period: payment is due immediately but the firm promises not to take further action for a specified period.

The result of Ullery's letter is that 25 percent of those who buy on credit pay in full within a month of receiving it, 30 percent wait longer, and 35 percent negotiate other terms. Although 10 percent never do pay, the success of the collection process has reduced the number of collection letters sent. Only 1 percent of Albany Ladder's total sales are written off as uncollectible—which is very low considering the industry and the firm's generosity with credit.

In order to keep current customers and attract new ones, most manufacturing concerns must extend credit and maintain inventories. *Accounts receivable* represent the extension of credit by the firm to its customers. *Inventory*, or goods on hand, is a necessary current asset that permits the production-sale process to operate with a minimum of disturbance. Accounts receivable and inventory are the dominant current assets held by most firms. For the average manufacturer, together they account for about 79 percent of *current assets* and about 34 percent of *total assets.* The firm's financial manager generally has direct control over accounts receivable; he or she must act as a "watchdog" and adviser in matters concerning inventory, which is generally under the direct control of the firm's manufacturing department. In the following sections we will examine the important aspects of accounts receivable followed by a brief discussion of inventory.

CREDIT SELECTION

The accounts receivable of a manufacturer typically represent about 37 percent of its *current assets* and about 16 percent of its *total* assets. They are most often directly controlled by the firm's financial manager through involvement in the establishment and management of (1) **credit policy,** which includes determining credit selection, credit standards, and credit terms, and (2) collection policy. Here we discuss credit selection; in the following sections we look at credit standards, credit terms, and collection policy.

A firm's **credit selection** activity involves deciding whether to extend credit to a customer and how much credit to extend. Appropriate *sources of credit information* and *methods of credit analysis* must be developed. Each of these aspects of credit policy is important to the successful management of accounts receivable. First we look at the five C's of credit, which are the traditional focus of credit investigation.

credit policy The determination of credit selection, credit standards, and credit terms.

credit selection The decision whether to extend credit to a customer and how much credit to extend.

The Five C's of Credit

Credit managers often use the **five C's of credit** to determine an applicant's creditworthiness. They analyze these five dimensions—character, capacity, capital, collateral, and conditions—as follows:

five C's of credit The five key dimensions—character, capacity, capital, collateral, and conditions—used by credit managers in their analysis of an applicant's creditworthiness.

1 ▪▪ *Character:* The applicant's record of meeting past obligations—financial, contractual, and moral. Past payment history as well as any pending or resolved legal judgments against the applicant would be used to evaluate its character.

2 ▪▪ *Capacity:* The applicant's ability to repay the requested credit. Financial statement analysis (see Chapter 4) with particular

emphasis on liquidity and debt ratios is typically used to assess the applicant's capacity.

3 ▰ *Capital:* The financial strength of the applicant as reflected by its ownership position. Analysis of the applicant's debt relative to equity and its profitability ratios are frequently used to assess its capital.

4 ▰ *Collateral:* The amount of assets the applicant has available for use in securing the credit. The larger the amount of available assets, the greater the chance a lender will recover its funds if the applicant defaults. A review of the applicant's balance sheet, asset value appraisals, and any legal claims filed against the applicant's assets can be used to evaluate its collateral.

5 ▰ *Conditions:* The current economic and business climate as well as any unique circumstances affecting either party to the credit transaction. For example, if the lender has excess inventory of the item the applicant wishes to purchase on credit, it may be willing to sell on more favorable terms or to less creditworthy applicants. Analysis of general economic and business conditions, as well as special circumstances that may affect the applicant or lender, is performed in order to assess conditions.

The credit manager typically gives primary attention to the first two C's—character and capacity—since they represent the most basic requirements for extending credit to an applicant. Consideration of the last three C's—capital, collateral, and conditions—is important in structuring the credit arrangement and making the final credit decision, which is affected by the credit manager's experience and judgment.

Obtaining Credit Information

When a business is approached by a customer desiring credit terms, the credit department typically begins the evaluation process by requiring the applicant to fill out various forms which request financial and credit information and references. Working from the application, the firm obtains additional information from other sources. If the firm has previously extended credit to the applicant, it will have its own information on the applicant's payment history. The major external sources of credit information are as follows:

Financial Statements
With the credit applicant's financial statements for the past few years, the firm can analyze the applicant firm's liquidity, activity, debt, and profitability positions.

Dun & Bradstreet
The largest mercantile credit-reporting agency in the United States.

Dun & Bradstreet, Inc.
Dun & Bradstreet is the largest mercantile credit-reporting agency in the United States. It provides subscribers with a reference book con-

Key to Ratings

	Estimated Financial Strength		Composite Credit Appraisal			
			High	Good	Fair	Limited
5A	$50,000,000	and over	1	2	3	4
4A	$10,000,000 to	49,999,999	1	2	3	4
3A	1,000,000 to	9,999,999	1	2	3	4
2A	750,000 to	999,999	1	2	3	4
1A	500,000 to	749,999	1	2	3	4
BA	300,000 to	499,999	1	2	3	4
BB	200,000 to	299,999	1	2	3	4
CB	125,000 to	199,999	1	2	3	4
CC	75,000 to	124,999	1	2	3	4
DC	50,000 to	74,999	1	2	3	4
DD	35,000 to	49,999	1	2	3	4
EE	20,000 to	34,999	1	2	3	4
FF	10,000 to	19,999	1	2	3	4
GG	5,000 to	9,999	1	2	3	4
HH	Up to	4,999	1	2	3	4

DUN & BRADSTREET
Credit Services
DB a company of
The Dun & Bradstreet Corporation

Figure 9.1   The Key to Dun & Bradstreet's Ratings
The rating key used in the *Dun & Bradstreet Reference
Book* indicates both the estimated financial strength and
a composite credit appraisal for each rated firm. A rating
of 2A3 would indicate an estimated financial strength
between $750,000 and $999,999 and a *fair* credit
appraisal.

taining credit ratings and keyed estimates of overall financial strength
for virtually millions of U.S. and Canadian firms. The key to the D & B
ratings is shown in Figure 9.1. For example, a firm rated 2A3 would
have estimated financial strength (net worth) in the range of $750,000 to
$999,999 and would have a *fair* credit appraisal. For an additional
charge, subscribers can obtain detailed reports on specific companies.

Credit Interchange Bureaus
Firms can obtain credit information through the National Credit Inter-
change System, a national network of local credit bureaus that exchange information. The reports obtained through these exchanges contain factual data rather than analyses. A fee is usually levied for each
inquiry.

Direct Credit Information Exchanges
Another means of obtaining credit information is through local, regional, or national credit associations. Often, an industry association
maintains certain credit information that is available to members. Another method is to contact other suppliers selling to the applicant and
ask what its payment patterns are like.

Bank Checking

It may be possible for the firm's bank to obtain credit information from the applicant's bank. However, the type of information obtained will most likely be vague, unless the applicant helps the firm obtain it. Typically, an estimate of the firm's cash balance is provided. For instance, it may be found that a firm maintains a "high five-figure" balance.

Analyzing Credit Information

credit analysis The evaluation of credit applicants.

Firms typically establish set procedures for use in **credit analysis**—the evaluation of credit applicants. Often the firm not only must determine the creditworthiness of a customer but also must estimate the maximum amount of credit the customer is capable of supporting. Once this is done, the firm can establish a **line of credit,** the maximum amount the customer can owe the firm at any point in time. Lines of credit are established to eliminate the necessity of checking a major customer's credit each time a large purchase is made. We now consider procedures for analyzing credit information and the economic considerations involved in such analyses.

line of credit The maximum amount a credit customer can owe the lending firm at any one time.

Procedures

A credit applicant's financial statements and accounts payable ledger can be used to calculate its "average payment period." This value can be compared to the credit terms currently extended the firm. For customers requesting large amounts of credit or lines of credit, a thorough ratio analysis of the firm's liquidity, activity, debt, and profitability should be performed using the relevant financial statements. A time-series comparison (discussed in Chapter 4) of similar ratios for various years should uncover any developing trends. The *Dun & Bradstreet Reference Book* can be used for estimating the maximum line of credit to extend. Dun & Bradstreet suggests no more than 10 percent of a customer's "estimated financial strength."

One of the key inputs to the final credit decision is the credit analyst's *subjective judgment* of a firm's creditworthiness. Experience provides a "feel" for the nonquantifiable aspects of the quality of a firm's operations. The analyst will add his or her knowledge of the character of the applicant's management, references from other suppliers, and the firm's historic payment patterns to any quantitative figures developed to determine creditworthiness. He or she will then make the final decision whether to extend credit to the applicant, and what amount of credit to extend. Often these decisions are made not by one individual but by a credit review committee.

Economic Considerations

Regardless of whether the firm's credit department is evaluating the creditworthiness of a customer desiring credit for a specific transaction or that of a regular customer in order to establish a line of credit, the basic procedures are the same. The only difference is the depth of the analysis. A firm would be unwise to spend $100 to investigate the creditworthiness of a customer making a one-time $40 purchase, but $100 for a credit investigation may be a good investment in the case of a customer expected to make credit purchases of $60,000 annually. Clearly, the firm's credit selection procedures must be established on a sound economic basis that considers the costs and benefits of obtaining and analyzing credit information.

Credit Scoring

Consumer credit decisions, because they involve a large group of similar applicants, each representing a small part of the firm's total business, can be handled using impersonal, computer-based credit decision techniques. One popular technique is **credit scoring.** This procedure results in a score reflecting an applicant's overall credit strength, derived as a weighted average of the scores obtained on a variety of key financial and credit characteristics. Credit scoring is often used by large credit card operations such as oil companies and department stores. This technique can best be illustrated by an example.

credit scoring   The ranking of an applicant's overall credit strength, derived as a weighted average of scores on key financial and credit characteristics.

EXAMPLE   Paula's Stores, a major regional department store chain, uses a credit scoring model to make its consumer credit decisions. Each credit applicant fills out and submits a credit application to the company. The application is reviewed and scored by one of the company's credit analysts, and then the relevant information is entered into the computer. The rest of the process, including making the credit decision, generating a letter of acceptance or rejection to the applicant, and dispatching the preparation and mailing of a credit card, is automated.

Table 9.1. demonstrates the calculation of Herb Consumer's credit score. The firm's predetermined credit standards are summarized in Table 9.2. The cutoff credit scores were developed to accept the group of credit applicants that will result in a positive contribution to the firm's share value. In evaluating Herb Consumer's credit score of 80.25 in light of the firm's credit standards, Paula's would decide to *extend standard credit terms* to him (80.25 > 75).

The attractiveness of credit scoring should be clear from the above example. Unfortunately, most manufacturers sell to a diversified group of different-sized businesses, not to individuals. The statistical characteristics necessary for applying credit scoring to decisions regarding *mercantile credit*—credit extended by business firms to other business firms—rarely exist. In the following discussion we concentrate on the basic concepts of mercantile credit decisions, which cannot easily be expressed in quantifiable terms.

Table 9.1   **Credit Scoring of Herb Consumer by Paula's Stores**

Financial and credit characteristics	Score (0 to 100) (1)	Predetermined weight (2)	Weighted score [(1) × (2)] (3)
Credit references	80	.15	12.00
Home ownership	100	.15	15.00
Income range	70	.25	17.50
Payment history	75	.25	18.75
Years at address	90	.10	9.00
Years on job	80	.10	8.00
	Total	1.00	Credit score 80.25

Key: Column 1: Scores assigned by analyst or computer using company guidelines on the basis of data presented in credit application. Scores range from 0 (lowest) to 100 (highest). Column 2: Weights based on the company's analysis of the relative importance of each financial and credit characteristic in predicting whether or not a customer will pay an account. The sum of these weights must be 1.00.

CHANGING CREDIT STANDARDS

credit standards The minimum requirements for extending credit to a customer.

The firm's **credit standards** are the minimum requirements for extending credit to a customer. Our concern here is how restrictive a firm's overall policy is. Understanding the key variables that must be considered when a firm is contemplating relaxing or tightening its credit standards will give a general idea of the kinds of decisions involved.

Key Variables

The major variables that should be considered when evaluating proposed changes in credit standards are (1) sales volume, (2) the investment in accounts receivable, and (3) bad debt expenses. Let us examine each in more detail.

Table 9.2   **Credit Standards for Paula's Stores**

Credit score	Action
Greater than 75	Extend standard credit terms.
65 to 75	Extend limited credit; if account is properly maintained, convert to standard credit terms after one year.
Less than 65	Reject application.

Sales Volume

Changing credit standards can be expected to change the volume of sales. If credit standards are relaxed, sales are expected to increase; if credit standards are tightened, sales are expected to decrease. Generally, increases in sales affect profits positively, whereas decreases in sales affect profits negatively.

Investment in Accounts Receivable

Carrying, or maintaining, accounts receivable involves a cost to the firm. This cost is the forgone earnings opportunities resulting from tying up funds in accounts receivable. Therefore, the higher the firm's investment in accounts receivable, the greater the carrying cost, and vice versa. If the firm relaxes its credit standards, the volume of accounts receivable increases and so does the firm's carrying cost (investment). This change results from increased sales and longer collection periods due to slower payment on average by credit customers. The opposite occurs if credit standards are tightened. Thus a relaxation of credit standards is expected to affect profits negatively due to higher carrying costs; tightening credit standards would affect profits positively as a result of lower carrying costs.

Bad Debt Expenses

The probability, or risk, of acquiring a bad debt increases as credit standards are relaxed. The increase in bad debts associated with relaxation of credit standards raises bad debt expenses and has a negative impact on profits. The opposite effects on bad debt expenses and profits result from a tightening of credit standards.

The basic changes and effects on profits expected to result from the *relaxation* of credit standards are tabulated as follows:

Variable	Direction of change	Effect on profits
Sales volume	Increase	Positive
Investment in accounts receivable	Increase	Negative
Bad debt expenses	Increase	Negative

If credit standards were tightened, the opposite effects would be expected.

Determining Values of Key Variables

The way in which the key credit standard variables are determined can be illustrated by the following example.

EXAMPLE   Binz Tool, a manufacturer of small tools, is currently selling a tool for $10 per unit. Sales (all on credit) for last year were 60,000 units. The variable cost per unit is $6. The firm's total fixed costs are $120,000.

The firm is currently contemplating a *relaxation of credit standards* that is expected to result in a 5 percent increase in unit sales to 63,000 units, an increase in the average collection period from its current level of 30 days to 45 days, and an increase in bad debt expenses from the current level of 1 percent of sales to 2 percent. The firm's required return on equal-risk investments, which is the opportunity cost of tying up funds in accounts receivable, is 15 percent.

To determine whether to implement the proposed relaxation in credit standards, Binz Tool must calculate the effect on the firm's additional profit contribution from sales, the cost of the marginal investment in accounts receivable, and the cost of marginal bad debts.

Additional Profit Contribution from Sales   The additional profit contribution from sales expected from the relaxation of credit standards can be calculated easily. Because fixed costs are unaffected by a change in the sales level, the only cost relevant to a change in sales would be out-of-pocket or variable costs. Sales are expected to increase by 5 percent, or 3,000 units. The profit contribution per unit will equal the difference between the sale price per unit ($10) and the variable cost per unit ($6). The profit contribution per unit will therefore be $4. Thus the total additional profit contribution from sales will be $12,000 (3,000 units × $4 per unit).

Cost of the Marginal Investment in Accounts Receivable   The cost of the marginal investment in accounts receivable can be calculated by finding the difference between the cost of carrying receivables before and after the introduction of the relaxed credit standards. Because our concern is only with the out-of-pocket costs rather than the fixed costs (which are unaffected by this decision), *the relevant cost in this analysis is the variable cost*. The average investment in accounts receivable (A/R)[1] can be calculated using the following formula:

Equation 9.1
Expression for the average investment in accounts receivable

Average investment in accounts receivable

$$= \frac{\text{total variable cost of annual sales}}{\text{turnover of accounts receivable}}$$

where

Turnover of accounts receivable

$$= \frac{360}{\text{average collection period}}$$

---

[1]Throughout the text, A/R will often be used interchangeably with *accounts receivable*.

The total variable cost of annual sales under the proposed and present plans can be found as noted below.

Total variable cost of annual sales:

Under proposed plan: ($6 × 63,000 units) = $378,000

Under present plan: ($6 × 60,000 units) = $360,000

The calculation of the total variable cost for both plans involves the straightforward use of the variable cost per unit of $6. The total variable cost under the proposed plan is $378,000, and under the present plan it is $360,000. Therefore, implementation of the proposed plan will cause the total variable cost of annual sales to increase from $360,000 to $378,000.

The turnover of accounts receivable refers to the number of times each year the firm's accounts receivable are actually turned into cash. In each case it is found by dividing the average collection period into 360—the number of days in a year.[2]

Turnover of accounts receivable:

$$\text{Under proposed plan: } \frac{360}{45} = 8$$

$$\text{Under present plan: } \frac{360}{30} = 12$$

With implementation of the proposed plan, the accounts receivable turnover would drop from 12 to 8.

Substituting the cost and turnover data just calculated into Equation 9.1 for each case, the following average investments in accounts receivable result:

Average investment in accounts receivable:

$$\text{Under proposed plan: } \frac{\$378,000}{8} = \$47,250$$

$$\text{Under present plan: } \frac{\$360,000}{12} = \$30,000$$

The marginal investment in accounts receivable as well as its cost are calculated as follows:

Cost of marginal investment in accounts receivable:

Average investment under proposed plan	$47,250
− Average investment under present plan	30,000
Marginal investment in accounts receivable	$17,250
× Required return on investment	.15
Cost of marginal investment in A/R	$ 2,588

---

[2]The turnover of accounts receivable can also be calculated by *dividing annual sales by accounts receivable.* For the purposes of this chapter, only the formula transforming the average collection period to a turnover of accounts receivable is emphasized.

The cost of investing an additional $17,250 in accounts receivable was found by multiplying this marginal investment by 15 percent (the firm's required return on investment). The resulting value of $2,588 is considered a cost because it represents the maximum amount that could have been earned on the $17,250 had it been placed in the best equal-risk investment alternative available.

Cost of Marginal Bad Debts The cost of marginal bad debts is found by taking the difference between the level of bad debts before and after the relaxation of credit standards, as shown here.

Cost of marginal bad debts:

Under proposed plan:
        (.02 × $10/unit × 63,000 units)   = $12,600

Under present plan:
        (.01 × $10/unit × 60,000 units)   =   6,000

        Cost of marginal bad debts   = $ 6,600

Thus the resulting cost of marginal bad debts is $6,600.

Making the Credit Standard Decision

To decide whether the firm should relax its credit standards, the additional profit contribution from sales must be compared to the sum of the cost of the marginal investment in accounts receivable and the cost of marginal bad debts. If the additional profit contribution is greater than marginal costs, credit standards should be relaxed; otherwise, present standards should remain unchanged. Let us look at an example.

EXAMPLE   The results and key calculations relative to Binz Tool's decision to relax its credit standards are summarized in Table 9.3. The additional profit contribution from the increased sales would be $12,000. This amount exceeds the sum of the cost of the marginal investment in accounts receivable and the cost of marginal bad debts; the firm *should* therefore relax its credits standards as proposed. The net addition to total profits resulting from such an action will be $2,812 per year.

The technique described here for making a credit standard decision is commonly used for evaluating other types of changes in the management of accounts receivable as well. If the firm in the preceding example had been contemplating tightening its credit standards, the cost would have been a reduction in the profit contribution from sales, and the return would have been from reductions in the cost of the marginal investment in accounts receivable and in bad debts. Another application of this analytical technique is demonstrated later in the chapter.

Table 9.3   **The Effects on Binz Tool of a Relaxation of Credit Standards**

Additional profit contribution from sales
  [3,000 units × ($10 − $6)] $12,000

Cost of marginal investment in A/R[a]

  Average investment under proposed plan:
$$\frac{(\$6 \times 63{,}000)}{8} = \frac{\$378{,}000}{8}$$ $47,250

  Average investment under present plan:
$$\frac{(\$6 \times 60{,}000)}{12} = \frac{\$360{,}000}{12}$$ 30,000

    Marginal investment in A/R $17,250

    Cost of marginal investment in A/R
      (.15 × $17,250)   ($2,588)

Cost of marginal bad debts

  Bad debts under proposed plan:
  (.02 × $10 × 63,000) $12,600

  Bad debts under present plan:
  (.01 × $10 × 60,000)   6,000

    Cost of marginal bad debts   ($6,600)

Net profit from implementation of proposed plan $2,812

---

[a]The denominators 8 and 12 in the calculation of the average investment in accounts receivable under the proposed and present plans are the accounts receivable turnovers for each of these plans (360/45 = 8 and 360/30 = 12).

CHANGING CREDIT TERMS

A firm's **credit terms** specify the repayment terms required of all its credit customers.[3] Typically, a type of shorthand is used. For example, credit terms may be stated as *2/10 net 30*. This notation means that the purchaser receives a 2 percent cash discount if the bill is paid within 10 days after the beginning of the credit period; if the customer does not take the cash discount, the full amount must be paid within 30 days after the beginning of the credit period. Credit terms cover three things: (1) the cash discount, if any (in this case 2 percent); (2) the cash discount period (in this case 10 days); and (3) the credit period (in this case 30 days). Changes in any aspect of the firm's credit terms may have an effect on its overall profitability. The positive and negative factors associated with such changes, and quantitative procedures for evaluating them, are presented in this section.

credit terms Terms under which a firm's credit customers must pay their accounts.

---

[3]An in-depth discussion of credit terms as viewed by the customer is presented in Chapter 10. In this chapter our concern is with credit terms from the point of view of the seller.

F I N A N C E   I N   A C T I O N

Packaging and Selling Accounts Receivable

For years, banks have been involved in *securitization*. The loan manager packages a pool of loans and sells it to a pension fund, insurance company, or the public in general. The purchaser receives the interest and principal payments over an extended period of time. Through securitization, the bank obtains cash which can be lent to the next borrower, rather than having to wait to receive principal and interest payments.

Sears Roebuck, among other retailers, does the same thing with the accounts receivable arising from its credit card customers. The receivables themselves are the security for investors, which effectively become the new lenders. In the process, Sears can minimize collection expenditures. Over the 1989–1990 period, Sears raised $5 billion in cash by selling its credit card receivables to investors. They used the cash to earn discounts by paying their suppliers early, rather than waiting until payments were received from their customers.

Securitization has created account manager positions at both the firms packaging the receivables and those buying receivables. Analysis by the purchaser is necessary, regardless of the credit standards of the selling firm. For instance, Chemical Bank recently put together a deal to sell Allied Stores' credit-card receivables, despite Allied's filing for Chapter 11 bankruptcy protection.

Source: "Hunting for gold in the company attic," *Business Month*, September 1990, p. 78.

Cash Discount

When a firm initiates or *increases* a cash discount, the following changes and effects on profits can be expected:

Variable	Direction of change	Effect on profits
Sales volume	Increase	Positive
Investment in accounts receivable due to nondiscount takers paying earlier	Decrease	Positive
Investment in accounts receivable due to new customers	Increase	Negative
Bad debt expenses	Decrease	Positive
Profit per unit	Decrease	Negative

The sales volume should increase because if a firm is willing to pay by day 10, the unit price decreases. The net effect on the accounts receivable investment is difficult to determine because the nondiscount takers paying earlier will reduce the accounts receivable investment, while the new customer accounts will increase this investment. The bad debt expenses should decline since, as customers on the average will pay earlier, the probability of their not paying at all will decrease. Both the decrease in the receivables investment and the decrease in bad debt expenses should result in increased profits. The negative aspect of an increased cash discount is a decreased profit per unit as more customers take the discount and pay the reduced price.

Decreasing or eliminating a cash discount would have opposite effects. The quantitative effects of changes in cash discounts can be evaluated by a method similar to that used earlier to evaluate changes in credit standards.

EXAMPLE   Assume that Binz Tool is considering initiating a cash discount of 2 percent for payment prior to day 10 after a purchase. The firm's current average collection period is 30 days [turnover = (360/30) = 12], credit sales of 60,000 units are made, and the variable cost per unit is $6. The firm expects that if the cash discount is initiated, 60 percent of its sales will be on discount and sales will increase by 5 percent to 63,000 units. The average collection period is expected to drop to 15 days [turnover = (360/15) = 24]. Bad debt expenses are expected to drop from the current level of 1 percent of sales to .5 percent of sales. The firm's required return on equal-risk investments remains at 15 percent.

The analysis of this decision is presented in Table 9.4. The calculations are similar to those presented for Binz's credit standard decision in Table 9.3 except for the final entry, "Cost of cash discount." This cost of $7,560 reflects the fact that *profits will be reduced* as a result of a 2 percent cash discount being taken on 60 percent of the new level of sales. Binz Tool can increase profit by $9,428 by initiating the proposed cash discount. Such an action therefore seems advisable. This type of analysis can also be applied to decisions concerning the elimination or reduction of cash discounts.

Cash Discount Period

The net effect of changes in the cash discount period is quite difficult to analyze due to the nature of the forces involved. For example, if the cash discount period were *increased*, the following changes could be expected:

Variable	Direction of change	Effect on profits
Sales volume	Increase	Positive
Investment in accounts receivable due to nondiscount takers paying earlier	Decrease	Positive
Investment in accounts receivable due to discount takers still getting cash discount but paying later	Increase	Negative
Investment in accounts receivable due to new customers	Increase	Negative
Bad debt expenses	Decrease	Positive
Profit per unit	Decrease	Negative

The problems in determining the exact results of changes in the cash discount period are directly attributable to the three forces affecting the firm's *investment in accounts receivable*. If the firm were to shorten the cash discount period, the effects would be the opposite of those described above.

Table 9.4   **The Effects on Binz Tool of Initiating a Cash Discount**

Additional profit contribution from sales [3,000 units × ($10 − $6)]		$12,000
Cost of marginal investment in A/R		
Average investment under proposed plan: $\frac{(\$6 \times 63,000)}{24} = \frac{\$378,000}{24}$	$15,750	
Average investment under present plan: $\frac{(\$6 \times 60,000)}{12} = \frac{\$360,000}{12}$	30,000	
Marginal investment in A/R	($14,250)	
Cost of marginal investment in A/R (.15 × $14,250)		$ 2,138[a]
Cost of marginal bad debts		
Bad debts under proposed plan: (.005 × $10 × 63,000)	$ 3,150	
Bad debts under present plan: (.01 × $10 × 60,000)	6,000	
Cost of marginal bad debts		$ 2,850[a]
Cost of cash discount[b] (.02 × .60 × $10 × 63,000)		($ 7,560)
Net profit from implementation of proposed plan		$ 9,428

[a]This value is positive since it represents a savings rather than a cost.
[b]This calculation reflects the fact that a 2 percent cash discount will be taken on 60 percent of the new level of sales—63,000 units at $10 each.

Credit Period

Changes in the credit period also affect the firm's profitability. The following effects on profits can be expected from an *increase* in the length of the credit period:

Variable	Direction of change	Effect on profits
Sales volume	Increase	Positive
Investment in accounts receivable	Increase	Negative
Bad debt expenses	Increase	Negative

Increasing the length of the credit period should increase sales, but both the investment in accounts receivable and bad debt expenses are likely to increase as well. Thus the net effect on profits of the sales increase is positive, while the increases in accounts receivable investment and bad debt expenses will negatively affect profits. A decrease in the length of the credit period is likely to have the opposite effect. The credit period decision is analyzed in the same ways as the credit standard decision illustrated in Table 9.3.

COLLECTION POLICY

The firm's **collection policy** is the set of procedures for collecting accounts receivable when they are due. The effectiveness of this policy can be partly evaluated by looking at the level of bad debt expenses. This level depends not only on collection policy but also on the policy on which the extension of credit is based. If one assumes that the level of bad debts attributable to *credit policy* is relatively constant, increasing collection expenditures can be expected to reduce bad debts. This relationship is depicted in Figure 9.2. As the figure indicates, beyond point A, additional collection expenditures will not reduce bad debt losses sufficiently to justify the outlay of funds. Popular approaches used to evaluate credit and collection policies include the *average collection period ratio* (presented in Chapter 4) and *aging accounts receivable*.

collection policy The procedures for collecting a firm's accounts receivable when they are due.

Aging Accounts Receivable

Aging is a technique that indicates the proportion of the accounts receivable balance that has been outstanding for a specified period of time. By highlighting irregularities, it allows the analyst to pinpoint the cause of credit or collection problems. Aging requires that the firm's

aging A technique used to evaluate credit or collection policies by indicating the proportion of the accounts receivable balance that has been outstanding for a specified period of time.

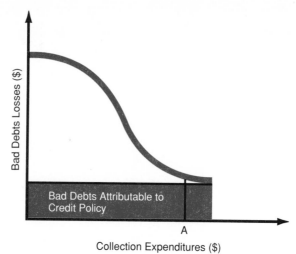

**Figure 9.2   Collection Expenditures
                    and Bad Debt Losses**

By increasing collection expenditures, the firm
can decrease bad debt losses up to a point (A),
beyond which bad debts cannot be economically
reduced. These inescapable bad debts are
attributed to the firm's credit policy.

accounts receivable be broken down into groups based on the time of
origin. This breakdown is typically made on a month-by-month basis,
going back three or four months. Let us look at an example.

EXAMPLE   Assume that Binz Tool extends 30-day credit terms to its
customers. The firm's December 31, 1992, balance sheet
shows $200,000 of accounts receivable. An evaluation of the
$200,000 of accounts receivable results in the following
breakdown:

Days	Current	0–30	31–60	61–90	Over 90	
Month	Dec.	Nov.	Oct.	Sept.	Aug.	Total
Accounts receivable	$60,000	$40,000	$66,000	$26,000	$8,000	$200,000
Percentage of total	30	20	33	13	4	100

Since it is assumed that Binz Tool gives its customers
30 days after the end of the month in which the sale is made

to pay off their accounts, any December receivables still on the firm's books are considered current. November receivables are between zero and 30 days overdue, October receivables still unpaid are 31 to 60 days overdue, and so on.

The table shows that 30 percent of the firm's receivables are current, 20 percent are one month late, 33 percent are two months late, 13 percent are three months late, and 4 percent are more than three months late. While payment seems generally slow, a noticeable irregularity in these data is the high percentage represented by October receivables. This indicates that some problem may have occurred in October. Investigation may find that the problem can be attributed to the hiring of a new credit manager, the acceptance of a new account that has made a large credit purchase it has not yet paid for, or ineffective collection policy. When accounts are aged and such a discrepancy is found, the analyst should determine its cause.

Basic Trade-Offs

The basic trade-offs expected to result from an *increase* in collection efforts are as follows:

Variable	Direction of change	Effect on profits
Sales volume	None or decrease	None or negative
Investment in accounts receivable	Decrease	Positive
Bad debt expenses	Decrease	Positive
Collection expenditures	Increase	Negative

Increased collection efforts should reduce the investment in accounts receivable and bad debt expenses, increasing profits. The costs of this strategy may include lost sales in addition to increased collection expenditures if the level of collection effort is too intense. In other words, if the firm pushes its customers too hard to pay their accounts, they may be angered and may take their business elsewhere. The firm should therefore be careful not to be overly aggressive. The basic collection policy trade-offs can be evaluated quantitatively in a manner similar to that used to evaluate the trade-offs for credit standards and cash discounts.

Types of Collection Techniques

A number of collection techniques are employed. As an account becomes more and more overdue, the collection effort becomes more personal and more strict. The basic techniques are presented in the order typically followed in the collection process.

Letters

After an account receivable becomes overdue a certain number of days, the firm normally sends a polite letter reminding the customer of its obligation. If the account is not paid within a certain period of time after the letter has been sent, a second, more demanding letter is sent. This letter may be followed by yet another letter, if necessary. Collection letters are the first step in the collection process for overdue accounts.

Telephone Calls

If letters prove unsuccessful, a telephone call may be made to the customer to personally request immediate payment. If the customer has a reasonable excuse, arrangements may be made to extend the payment period. A call from the seller's attorney may be used if all other discussions seem to fail.

Personal Visits

This technique is much more common at the consumer credit level, but it may be effectively employed by industrial suppliers. Sending a local salesperson, or a collection person, to confront the customer can be a very effective collection procedure. Payment may be made on the spot.

Using Collection Agencies

A firm can turn uncollectible accounts over to a collection agency or an attorney for collection. The fees for this service are typically quite high; the firm may receive less than 50 cents on the dollar from accounts collected in this way.

Legal Action

Legal action is the most stringent step in the collection process. It is an alternative to the use of a collection agency. Not only is direct legal action expensive, but it may force the debtor into bankruptcy, thereby reducing the possibility of future business without guaranteeing the ultimate receipt of the overdue amount.

INVENTORY MANAGEMENT

Inventory, or goods on hand, is a necessary current asset. Like accounts receivable, inventory represents a significant monetary investment on the part of most firms. For the average manufacturer, it accounts for about 42 percent of *current assets* and about 18 percent of *total assets.*

Chapter 8 illustrated the importance of turning over inventory quickly in order to reduce financing costs. The financial manager generally acts as a "watchdog" and advisor in matters concerning inventory; he or she does not have direct control over inventory but does provide input into the inventory management process.

Inventory Fundamentals

Two aspects of inventory require some elaboration. One is the *types of inventory;* the other concerns differing viewpoints as to the *appropriate level of inventory.*

Types of Inventory

The three basic types of inventory are raw materials, work in process, and finished goods. **Raw materials inventory** consists of items purchased by the firm—usually basic materials such as screws, plastic, raw steel, or rivets—for use in the manufacture of a finished product. If a firm manufactures complex products with numerous parts, its raw materials inventory may consist of manufactured items that have been purchased from another company or from another division of the same firm. **Work-in-process inventory** consists of all items currently in production. These are normally partially finished goods at some intermediate stage of completion. **Finished goods inventory** consists of items that have been produced but not yet sold.

raw materials inventory Items purchased by the firm for use in the manufacture of a finished product.

work-in-process inventory All items currently in production.

finished goods inventory Items that have been produced but not yet sold.

Differing Viewpoints about Inventory Level

Differing viewpoints concerning appropriate inventory levels commonly exist among the finance, marketing, manufacturing, and purchasing managers of a company. Each sector views inventory levels in light of its own objectives. The *financial manager's* general disposition toward inventory levels is to keep them low. The financial manager must police the inventories, making sure that the firm's money is not being unwisely invested in excess resources. The *marketing manager,* on the other hand, would like to have large inventories of each of the firm's finished products. This would ensure that all orders could be filled quickly, eliminating the need for backorders due to stockouts.

The *manufacturing manager's* major responsibility is to make sure that the production plan is correctly implemented and that it results in the desired amount of finished goods. In fulfilling this role, the manufacturing manager would keep raw materials inventories high to avoid production delays and would favor high finished goods inventories by making large production runs for the sake of lower unit production costs. The *purchasing manager* is concerned solely with the raw materials inventories. He or she is responsible for seeing that whatever raw materials are required by production are available in the correct quantities at the desired times and at a favorable price. Without proper control, the purchasing manager may purchase larger quantities of resources than are actually needed in order to get quantity discounts or in anticipation of rising prices or a shortage of certain materials.

F I N A N C E   I N   A C T I O N

Nuts and Bolts of Inventory Management

Unglamorous and low-profile, Illinois Tool Works (ITW) is a noisy, grimy manufacturer of nuts and screws. Its obscurity arises from the fact that it makes an array of items that are a portion of someone else's goods. Yet, ITW holds over 2,400 active U.S. patents and generates over $2 billion in sales.

In such a diverse company efficient inventory management is crucial. Yet, in the early 1970s and early 1980s, ITW stood quietly by as important design patents ran out and consequently faced the low-cost competition of Asian suppliers. Simultaneously, to allow Detroit automobile makers to become more competitive, ITW had to reduce its prices. Since ITW had never before had to lower its prices or compete for business, its plants were highly inefficient.

The prime offender was ITW's home plant in Elgin, Illinois, maker of screws. The plant consisted of six departments representing different phases of the screw-making process: heading, threading, pointing, slotting, heat-treating, and plating. These individual fiefdoms periodically came together in the process of making 2,500 varieties of the screws. In each division, bins full of "work-in-process" took up every available inch of floor space. Even with computer job ordering, some units waited five weeks to move to the next department.

ITW solved this inventory problem three ways. One, it set the manufacturing machines in rows from heading to plating for each item. This technique worked for high-production items, which accounted for 80 percent of sales. Two, ITW isolated and handled low-volume runs in a designated area of the plant. Before, the time spent resetting machines for low-volume runs had reduced output on all machines. Three, ITW set up focused factories. These 25-person units took charge of ordering supplies and packaging. Each unit was able to operate as a cost center, minimizing its total ordering and carrying costs. Despite a sluggish economy, better inventory management strengthened Illinois Tool Works' net income in 1990 when its return on equity was 18 percent.

Source: Ronald Henkoff, "The ultimate nuts and bolts company," *Fortune*, July 16, 1990, pp. 70–73; *Value Line*, January 5, 1991.

Inventory as an Investment

Inventory is an investment in the sense that it requires that the firm tie up its money, thereby forgoing certain other earnings opportunities. In general, the higher a firm's average inventories, the larger the dollar investment and cost required, and vice versa. In evaluating planned changes in inventory levels, the financial manager should consider such changes from a benefit-versus-cost standpoint.

EXAMPLE   Excellent Manufacturing is contemplating making larger production runs in order to reduce the high setup costs associated with the production of its only product, industrial hoists. The total *annual* reduction in setup costs that can be obtained has been estimated at $20,000. As a result of the larger production runs, the average inventory investment is expected to increase from $200,000 to $300,000. If the firm can earn 25 percent per year on equal-risk investments, the *annual* cost of the additional $100,000 ($300,000 − $200,000) inventory investment will be $25,000 (.25 × $100,000). Comparing the annual $25,000 cost of the system with the annual savings of $20,000 shows that the proposal should be rejected since it results in a net annual *loss* of $5,000.

The Relationship between Inventory and Accounts Receivable

The level and the management of inventory and accounts receivable are closely related. Generally in the case of manufacturing firms, when an item is sold, it moves from inventory to accounts receivable and ultimately to cash. Because of the close relationship between inventory and accounts receivable, management of them should not be viewed independently. For example, the decision to extend credit to a customer can result in an increased level of sales, which can be supported only by higher levels of inventory and accounts receivable. The credit terms extended will also affect the investment in inventory and receivables, since longer credit terms may allow a firm to move items from inventory to accounts receivable. Generally there is an advantage to such a strategy, since the cost of carrying an item in inventory is greater than the cost of carrying an account receivable. This is true because the cost of carrying inventory includes, in addition to the required return on the invested funds, the costs of storing, insuring, and otherwise maintaining the physical inventory. This relationship can be shown using a simple example.

EXAMPLE   Most Industries, a producer of PVC pipe, estimates that the annual cost of carrying $1 of merchandise in inventory for a one-year period is 25 cents, whereas the annual cost of carrying $1 of receivables is 15 cents. The firm currently maintains average inventories of $300,000 and an average *investment* in accounts receivable of $200,000. The firm believes that by altering its credit terms, it can cause its customers to purchase in larger quantities on the average, thereby reducing its average inventories to $150,000 and increasing the average investment in accounts receivable to $350,000. The altered credit terms are not expected to generate new business but will result only in a shift in purchasing and payment patterns. The costs of the present and proposed inventory–accounts receivable systems are calculated in Table 9.5.

Table 9.5 shows that by shifting $150,000 of inventory to accounts receivable, Most Industries is able to lower the cost of carrying inventory and accounts receivable from $105,000 to $90,000—a $15,000 ($105,000 − $90,000) addition to profits. This profit is achieved without changing the level of average inventory and accounts receivable investment from its $500,000 total. Rather, the profit is attributed to a shift in the mix of these current assets so that a larger portion of them is held in the form of accounts receivable, which is less costly to hold than inventory.

The inventory–accounts receivable relationship is affected by decisions made in all areas of the firm—finance, marketing, manufacturing, and purchasing. The financial manager should consider the interactions between inventory and accounts receivable when developing strategies and making decisions related to the production-sale process. This interaction is especially important when making credit decisions, since the required as well as actual levels of inventory will be directly affected.

TECHNIQUES FOR MANAGING INVENTORY

Techniques commonly used in managing inventory are (1) the ABC system, (2) the basic economic order quantity (EOQ) model, (3) the reorder point, (4) the materials requirement planning (MRP) system, and (5) the just-in-time (JIT) system. Although these techniques are not strictly financial, it is helpful for the financial manager to understand them.

The ABC System

ABC system Inventory management technique that divides inventory into three categories of descending importance based on the dollar investment in each.

red-line method Inventory management technique in which a reorder is placed when use of inventory items from a bin exposes a red line drawn inside the bin.

A firm using the **ABC system** divides its inventory into three groups, A, B, and C. The *A group* includes those items that require the largest dollar investment. In the typical distribution of inventory items, this group consists of the 20 percent of inventory items that account for 80 percent of the firm's dollar investment. The *B group* consists of the items accounting for the next largest investment. The *C group* typically consists of a large number of items accounting for a relatively small dollar investment. Dividing its inventory into A, B, and C items allows the firm to determine the level and types of inventory control procedures needed. Control of the A items should be most intensive due to the high dollar investment involved; daily monitoring of these inventory levels is appropriate. C items could be controlled by using unsophisticated procedures such as a **red-line method,** in which a reorder is placed when

Table 9.5   **Analysis of Inventory–Accounts Receivable Systems for Most Industries**

		Present		Proposed	
Variable	Cost/ return (1)	Average investment (2)	Cost [(1) × (2)] (3)	Average investment (4)	Cost [(1) × (4)] (5)
Average inventory	25%	$300,000	$ 75,000	$150,000	$37,500
Average receivables	15	200,000	30,000	350,000	52,500
Totals		$500,000	$105,000	$500,000	$90,000

enough inventory has been removed from a bin containing the inventory item to expose a red line that has been drawn around the inside of the bin. The economic order quantity (EOQ) model, discussed next, is appropriate for use in monitoring B items.

The Basic Economic Order Quantity (EOQ) Model

One of the most commonly cited sophisticated tools for determining the optimal order quantity for an item of inventory is the **economic order quantity (EOQ) model.** It takes into account various operating and financial costs and determines the order quantity that minimizes total inventory cost.

economic order quantity (EOQ) model Inventory management technique for determining the optimal order quantity for an item of inventory.

Basic Costs

Excluding the actual cost of the merchandise, the costs associated with inventory can be divided into three broad groups: order costs, carrying costs, and total cost. Each has certain key components and characteristics.

Order Costs **Order costs** include the fixed clerical costs of placing and receiving an order—the cost of writing a purchase order, of processing the resulting paperwork, and of receiving an order and checking it against the invoice. Order costs are normally stated as dollars per order.

order costs The fixed clerical costs of placing and receiving an inventory order.

Carrying Costs **Carrying costs** are the variable costs per unit of holding an item in inventory for a specified time period. These costs are typically stated as dollars per unit per period. Carrying costs include storage costs, insurance costs, the cost of deterioration and obsolescence, and most important, the opportunity, or financial, cost of tying up funds in inventory. A commonly cited rule of thumb suggests that the cost of carrying an item in inventory for one year is between 20 and 30 percent of the cost (value) of the item.

carrying costs The variable costs per unit of holding an item in inventory for a specified period of time.

Total Cost The **total cost** of inventory is defined as the sum of the order and carrying costs. Total cost is important in the EOQ model,

total cost The sum of the order costs and carrying costs of inventory.

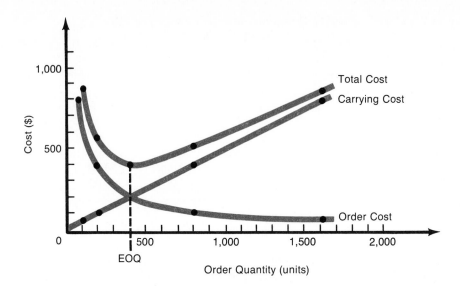

Figure 9.3   **A Graphic Presentation of an EOQ**
The total cost line represents the sum of the order costs and carrying costs for each order quantity. The EOQ, which is the order quantity that minimizes total inventory cost, occurs where the order cost line and carrying cost line intersect.

since the model's objective is to determine the order quantity that minimizes it.

A Graphic Approach
The stated objective of the EOQ model is to find the order quantity that minimizes the firm's total inventory cost. The economic order quantity can be found graphically by plotting order quantities on the *x*, or horizontal, axis and costs on the *y*, or vertical, axis. Figure 9.3 shows the general behavior of these costs. The total cost line represents the sum of the order costs and carrying costs for each order quantity. The minimum total cost occurs at the point labeled EOQ, where the order cost line and the carrying cost line intersect.

A Mathematial Approach
The formula given in Equation 9.2 can be used to determine the firm's EOQ for a given inventory item:

Equation 9.2
Formula for the economic order quantity (EOQ)

$$EOQ = \sqrt{\frac{2 \times S \times O}{C}}$$

where

S = usage in units per period
O = order cost per order
C = carrying cost per unit per period

EXAMPLE   Assume that RLB, Inc., a manufacturer of electronic test equipment, uses 1,600 units of an item annually. Its order cost is $50 per order and carrying cost is $1 per unit per year. Substituting $S = 1,600$, $O = \$50$, and $C = \$1$ into Equation 9.2 yields an EOQ of 400 units:

$$EOQ = \sqrt{\frac{2 \times 1,600 \times \$50}{\$1}} = \sqrt{160,000} = \underline{\underline{400 \text{ units}}}$$

If the firm orders in quantities of 400 units, it will minimize its total inventory cost. The solution is depicted in Figure 9.3.

The Reorder Point

Once the firm has calculated its economic order quantity, it must determine when to place orders. A reorder point is required that considers the lead time needed to place and receive orders. Assuming a constant usage rate for inventory, the **reorder point** can be determined by the following equation:

reorder point The point at which to reorder inventory.

Reorder point = lead time in days × daily usage

Equation 9.3 Expression for the reorder point

For example, if a firm knows that it requires 10 days to place and receive an order, and if it uses 5 units of inventory daily, the reorder point would be 50 units (10 days × 5 units per day). Thus as soon as the firm's inventory level reaches 50 units, an order will be placed for an amount equal to the economic order quantity. If the estimates of lead time and daily usage are correct, the order will be received exactly when the inventory level reaches zero. Because of the difficulty in precisely predicting lead times and daily usage rates, many firms typically maintain **safety stocks,** which are extra inventories that can be drawn down when actual outcomes are greater than expected.

safety stocks Extra inventories that can be drawn down when actual lead times or usage rates are greater than expected.

Materials Requirement Planning (MRP) System

Many companies use a **materials requirement planning (MRP) system** to determine what to order, when to order, and what priorities to assign to ordering materials. MRP uses EOQ concepts to determine how much to order. It simulates, using a computer, each product's bill of materials structure, inventory status, and process of manufacturing. The *bill of materials* structure simply refers to every part or material that goes into making the finished product. For a given production plan, the computer simulates needed materials requirements by comparing production needs to available inventory balances. Based on the time it takes for a product that is in process to move through the various production stages, and the lead time required to get materials, the MRP system determines when orders should be placed for the various items on the bill of materials. The advantage of the MRP system is that it forces the firm to more thoughtfully consider its inventory needs and plan accord-

materials requirement planning (MRP) system Inventory management system that compares production needs to available inventory balances and determines when orders should be placed for various material inputs.

ingly. The objective is to lower the firm's inventory investment without impairing production. If the firm's opportunity cost of capital for investments of equal risk is 25 percent, every dollar of investment released from inventory increases before-tax profits by $.25.

Just-in-Time (JIT) System

just-in-time (JIT) system Inventory management system that minimizes inventory investment by having material inputs arrive at exactly the time they are needed for production.

The **just-in-time (JIT) system** is used to minimize inventory investment. The philosophy is that materials should arrive at exactly the time they are needed for production. Ideally, the firm would have only work-in-process inventory. Since its objective is to minimize inventory investment, a JIT system uses no, or very little, safety stocks. Extensive coordination must exist between the firm, its suppliers, and shipping companies to ensure that material inputs arrive on time. Failure of materials to arrive on time results in a shutdown of the production line until the materials arrive. Likewise, a JIT system requires high quality parts from suppliers. When quality problems arise, production must be stopped until the problems are solved.

The goal of the JIT system is manufacturing efficiency. It uses inventory as a tool for attaining efficiency by emphasizing quality, in terms of both the materials used and their timely delivery. When JIT is working properly it forces process inefficiences to surface and be resolved. A JIT system requires cooperation among all parties involved in the process—suppliers, shipping companies, and the firm's employees. Employees must encourage competitive excellence, continuous improvements, and 100-percent quality items. If they are not committed to these goals, the JIT system will likely be unsuccessful.

 INTERNATIONAL DIMENSION: CREDIT AND INVENTORY MANAGEMENT

Multinationals based in different countries compete for the same global export markets. Therefore, it is essential that they offer attractive credit terms to potential customers. Increasingly, however, the maturity and saturation of developed markets is forcing MNCs to maintain and increase revenues by exporting and selling a higher percentage of their output to developing countries. Given the risks associated with the latter group of buyers, as partly evidenced by their lack of a major (hard) currency, the MNC must use a variety of tools to protect such revenues. In addition to the use of hedging and making certain adjustments in their operations, MNCs should seek the backing of their respective governments in both identifying target markets and extending credit. Multinationals based in a number of Western European nations and those based in Japan currently benefit from extensive involvement of government agencies that provide them with the needed service and financial support suggested here. For U.S.-based MNCs, the international positions of government agencies such as the Export-Import Bank currently do not provide a comparable level of support.

In terms of inventory management, MNCs must consider a number of factors related to both economics and politics. In the former category, in addition to maintaining the appropriate level of inventory in various locations around the world, a multinational firm is compelled to deal with exchange rate fluctuations, tariffs, non-tariff barriers, integration schemes such as the European Economic Community (EC), and other rules and regulations. Politically, inventories could be subjected to wars, expropriations, blockages, and other forms of government intervention.

SUMMARY

1   **Discuss the key aspects of credit selection, including the five C's of credit, obtaining credit information, analyzing credit information, and credit scoring.**   Credit selection includes deciding whether to extend credit to a customer and how much credit to extend. The five C's of credit—character, capacity, capital, collateral, and conditions—are used to guide credit investigations. Credit information can be obtained from a variety of external sources and can be analyzed in a number of ways. An analyst's subjective judgment is an important input to the final decision. At the consumer level impersonal techniques, such as credit scoring, are often used.

2   **Understand how to isolate and measure the key variables and use them to make both credit standard and credit term decisions.**   At the mercantile level, credit standards—the minimum criteria for extension of credit to a customer—must be set by considering the trade-offs between the key variables, which are the profit contribution from sales, the cost of investment in accounts receivable, and the cost of bad debts. Changes in any of the three components of credit terms affect the firm's sales, investment in accounts receivable, bad debt expenses, and profit per unit.

3   **Explain the key features of collection policy, including aging accounts receivable, the basic trade-offs, and the types of collection techniques.**   Collection policy determines the type and degree of effort exercised to collect overdue accounts. In addition to looking at the average collection period ratio, firms often age accounts receivable to evaluate the effectiveness of their credit and collection policies. Generally increased collection expenditures will have little effect on sales volume and will reduce the investment in accounts receivable and bad debt expenses, and vice versa. The basic collection techniques include letters, telephone calls, personal visits, the use of collection agencies, and, as a last resort, legal action.

4   **Understand the types of inventory, differing viewpoints about inventory level, inventory as an investment, and the relationship between inventory and accounts receivable.**   The respective viewpoints held by marketing, manufacturing, and purchasing managers regarding the appropriate levels of various types of inventory (raw materials, work in process, and finished goods) tend to conflict with that of the financial manager. The financial manager views inventory as an investment that consumes dollars and should be maintained at a low level. He or she must consider the interrelationship between inventory and accounts receivable when making decisions related to the production-sale process.

5   **Describe the common techniques for managing inventory, including the ABC system, the basic economic order quantity (EOQ) model, the reorder point, the materials requirement planning (MRP) system, and the just-in-time (JIT) system.   The ABC system determines which inventories require the most attention according to dollar investment. One of the most common techniques for determining optimal order quantities is the economic order quantity (EOQ) model. Once the optimal order quantity has been determined, the firm can set the reorder point, the level of inventory at which an order will be placed. Materials requirement planning (MRP) is a system that can be used to determine when orders should be placed for various items on a firm's bill of materials. Just-in-time (JIT) systems are used to minimize inventory investment by having inputs arrive at exactly the time they are needed for production.

 6   **Identify the key concerns and strategies that multinational companies need to consider in order to effectively manage credit and inventory when exporting and selling in foreign markets.**   Multinational companies (MNCs) must offer competitive credit terms and maintain adequate inventories to provide timely delivery to foreign buyers. Obtaining the backing of foreign governments is helpful to the MNC in effectively managing credit and inventory.

QUESTIONS

9—1   What do the *accounts receivable* of a firm typically represent? What is meant by a firm's *credit policy?*

9—2   What does the *credit selection* activity include? Briefly list, define, and discuss the role of the *five C's of credit* in this process.

9—3   Summarize the basic sources of credit information. What procedures are commonly used to analyze credit information? How do economic considerations affect the depth of credit analysis?

9—4   Describe *credit scoring* and explain why this technique is typically applied to consumer credit decisions rather than to mercantile credit decisions.

9—5   What key variables should be considered when evaluating possible changes in a firm's *credit standards?* What are the basic trade-offs in a *tightening* of credit standards?

9—6   Discuss what is meant by *credit terms.* What are the three components of credit terms? How do credit terms affect the firm's accounts receivable?

9—7   What are the expected effects of a *decrease* in the firm's cash discount on sales volume, investment in accounts receivable, bad debt expenses, and per-unit profits, respectively?

9—8   What are the expected effects of a *decrease* in the firm's credit period? What is likely to happen to sales volume, investment in accounts receivable, and bad debt expenses, respectively?

9—9   What is meant by a firm's *collection policy?* Explain how *aging accounts receivable* can be used to evaluate the effectiveness of both the credit policy and the collection policy.

9—10   Describe the basic trade-offs involved in collection policy decisions, and describe the popular types of collection techniques.

9—11   What is the financial manager's role with respect to the management of inventory? What are likely to be the viewpoints of each of the following managers, respectively, about the levels of the various types of inventory?
         a. Finance
         b. Marketing
         c. Manufacturing
         d. Purchasing

9—12   Explain the relationship between inventory and accounts receivable. Assuming the total investment in inventory and accounts receivable remains constant, what impact would lengthening the credit terms have on the firm's profits? Why?

9—13 Briefly describe each of the following techniques for managing inventory.
   a. ABC system
   b. Reorder point
   c. Materials requirement planning (MRP) system
   d. Just-in-time (JIT) system

9—14 What is the *EOQ model?* To which group of inventory items is it most applicable? What costs does it consider? What financial cost is involved?

PROBLEMS

9—1 **(Credit Scoring)** Dooley Department Store uses credit scoring to evaluate retail credit applications. The financial and credit characteristics considered and weights indicating their relative importance in the credit decision are given in the following table. The firm's credit standards are to accept all applicants with credit scores of 80 or more; to extend limited credit on a probationary basis to applicants with scores of greater than 70 and less than 80; and to reject all applicants with scores below 70.

Financial and credit characteristics	Predetermined weight
Credit references	.25
Education	.15
Home ownership	.10
Income range	.10
Payment history	.30
Years on job	.10

The firm currently needs to process three applications recently received and scored by one of its credit analysts. The scores for each of the applicants on each of the financial and credit characteristics are summarized in the following table:

Financial and credit characteristics	Applicant		
	A	B	C
	Score (0 to 100)		
Credit references	60	90	80
Education	70	70	80
Home ownership	100	90	60
Income range	75	80	80
Payment history	60	85	70
Years on job	50	60	90

a. Use the data presented to find the credit score for each of the applicants.

b. Recommend the appropriate action for each of the three applicants.

9—2   **(Accounts Receivable and Costs)** Wicklow Products currently has an average collection period of 45 days and annual credit sales of $1 million. Assume a 360-day year.

a. What is the firm's average accounts receivable balance?

b. If the variable cost of each product is 60 percent of sales, what is the average *investment* in accounts receivable?

c. If the equal-risk opportunity cost of the investment in accounts receivable is 12 percent, what is the total opportunity cost of the investment in accounts receivable?

9—3   **(Accounts Receivable Changes without Bad Debts)** Small Appliance currently has credit sales of $360 million per year and an average collection period of 60 days. Assume that the price of Small's products is $60 per unit and the variable costs are $55 per unit. The firm is considering an account receivable change that will result in a 20 percent increase in sales and an equal 20 percent increase in the average collection period. No change in bad debts is expected. The firm's equal-risk opportunity cost on its investment in accounts receivable is 14 percent.

a. Calculate the additional profit contribution from new sales that the firm will realize if it makes the proposed change.

b. What marginal investment in accounts receivable will result?

c. Calculate the cost of the marginal investment in accounts receivable.

d. Should the firm implement the proposed change? What other information would be helpful in your analysis?

9—4   **(Accounts Receivable Changes and Bad Debts)** A firm is evaluating an accounts receivable change that would increase bad debts from 2 percent to 4 percent of sales. Sales are currently 50,000 units, the selling price is $20 per unit, and the variable cost per unit is $15. As a result of the proposed change, sales are forecast to increase to 60,000 units.

a. What are bad debts in dollars presently and under the proposed change?

b. Calculate the cost of the marginal bad debts to the firm.

c. Ignoring the additional profit contribution from increased sales, if the proposed change saves $3,500 and causes no change in the average investment in accounts receivable, would you recommend it? Explain.

d. Considering *all* changes in costs and benefits, would you recommend the proposed change? Explain.

e. Compare and discuss your answers in **c** and **d**.

9—5   **(Tightening Credit Standards—Sales and Bad Debt Effects Only)** Cheryl's Menswear feels its credit costs are too high. By tightening its credit standards, bad debts will fall from 5 percent of sales to 2 percent. However, the firm estimates that sales will fall from $100,000 to $90,000 per year. The variable cost per unit is 50 percent of the sale price, and the average investment in receivables is expected to remain unchanged.

a. What cost will the firm face in a reduced contribution to profits from sales?

b. Should the firm tighten its credit standards? Explain your answer.

9—6   **(Relaxation of Credit Standards)** Adair Industries is considering relaxing its credit standards in order to increase its currently sagging sales. As a result of the proposed relaxation, sales are expected to increase by 10 percent from 10,000 to 11,000 units during the coming year, the average collection period is expected to increase from 45 to 60 days, and bad debts are expected to increase from 1 percent to 3 percent of sales. The sale price per unit is $40 and the variable cost per unit is $31. If the firm's required return on equal-risk investments is 25 percent, evaluate the proposed relaxation and make a recommendation to the firm.

9—7   **(Initiating a Cash Discount)** Pritchard Products currently makes all sales on credit and offers no cash discount. The firm is considering a 2 percent cash discount for payment within 15 days. The firm's current average collection period is 60 days, sales are 40,000 units, the selling price is $45 per unit, and the variable cost per unit is $36. The firm expects that the change in credit terms will result in an increase in sales to 42,000 units, that 70 percent of the sales will take the discount, and that the average collection period will fall to 30 days. If the firm's required rate of return on equal-risk investments is 25 percent, should the proposed discount be offered?

9—8   **(Shortening the Credit Period)** Spectradyne, Inc., is contemplating *shortening* its credit period from 40 to 30 days and believes that as a result of this change its average collection period will decline from 45 to 36 days. Bad debt expenses are expected to decrease from 1.5 percent to 1 percent of sales. The firm is currently selling 12,000 units but believes that as a result of the proposed change, sales will decline to 10,000 units. The sale price per unit is $56 and the variable cost per unit is $45. The firm has a required return on equal-risk investments of 25 percent. Evaluate this decision and make a recommendation to the firm.

9—9   **(Lengthening the Credit Period)** Heaton Equipment Company is considering lengthening its credit period from 30 to 60 days. All customers will continue to pay on the net date. The firm currently bills $450,000 for sales and has $345,000 in variable costs. The change in credit terms is expected to increase sales to $510,000. Bad debt expense will increase from 1 percent to 1.5 percent of sales. The firm has a required rate of return on equal-risk investments of 20 percent.
   a. What additional profit contribution from sales will be realized from the proposed change?
   b. What is the cost of the marginal investment in accounts receivable?
   c. What is the cost of the marginal bad debts?
   d. Do you recommend this change in credit terms? Why or why not?

9—10   **(Aging Accounts Receivable)** Cellular Corporation's accounts receivable totaled $874,000 on August 31, 1992. A breakdown of these outstanding accounts on the basis of the month in which the credit sale was initially made is given below. The firm extends 30-day credit terms to its credit customers.

Month of credit sale	Accounts receivable
August 1992	$320,000
July 1992	250,000
June 1992	81,000
May 1992	195,000
April 1992 or before	28,000
Total (August 31, 1992)	$874,000

a. Prepare an aging schedule for Cellular Corporation's August 31, 1992, accounts receivable balance.

b. Using your findings in **a,** evaluate the firm's credit and collection activities.

c. What are some probable causes of the situation discussed in **b?**

9—11   **(Inventory Investment)** Winblad, Inc., is considering leasing a computerized inventory control system in order to reduce its average inventories. The annual cost of the system is $46,000. It is expected that with the system the firm's average inventory will deline by 50 percent from its current level of $980,000. The level of stockouts is expected to be unaffected by this system. The firm can earn 20 percent per year on equal-risk investments.

a. How much of a reduction in average inventory will result from the proposed installation of the computerized inventory control system?

b. How much, if any, annual savings will the firm realize on the reduced level of average inventory?

c. Should the firm lease the computerized inventory control system? Explain why or why not.

9—12   **(Inventory versus Accounts Receivable Costs)** Harbor Manufacturing estimates the annual cost of carrying a dollar of inventory is $0.27, while the annual carrying cost of an equal investment in accounts receivable is $0.17. The firm's current balance sheet reflects its average inventory of $400,000 and average investment in accounts receivable of $100,000. If the firm can convince its customers to purchase in large quantities, the average level of inventory can be reduced by $200,000 and the average investment in receivables increased by the same amount. Assuming no change in annual sales, what addition to profits will be generated from this shift? Explain your answer.

9—13   **(Inventory—The ABC System)** Zap Supply has 16 different items in its inventory. The average number of units held in inventory and the average unit cost for each item are listed below and on page 295. The firm wishes to introduce the ABC system of inventory management. Suggest a breakdown of the items into classifications of A, B, and C. Justify your selection and point out items that could be considered borderline cases.

Item	Average number of units in inventory	Average cost per unit
1	1,800	$ 0.54
2	1,000	8.20
3	100	6.00
4	250	1.20
5	8	94.50
6	400	3.00
7	80	45.00
8	1,600	1.45
9	600	0.95

Item	Average number of units in inventory	Average cost per unit
10	3,000	0.18
11	900	15.00
12	65	1.35
13	2,200	4.75
14	1,800	1.30
15	60	18.00
16	200	17.50

9—14   **(EOQ Analysis)** Lyons Electronics purchases 1,200,000 units per year of one component. Fixed cost per order is $25. Annual carrying cost of the item is 27 percent of its $2 cost.
   a. Determine the EOQ under the following conditions: (1) no changes, (2) order cost of zero, (3) carrying cost of zero.
   b. What do your answers illustrate about the EOQ model? Explain.

9—15   **(Reorder Point)** Ticho Gas and Electric (TG&E) is required to carry a minimum of 20 days' average coal usage, which is 100 tons of coal. It takes 10 days between order and delivery. At what level of coal would TG&E reorder?

9—16   **(EOQ and Reorder Point)** Sabra Co. uses 800 units of a product per year on a continuous basis. The product has a fixed cost of $50 per order, and its carrying cost is $2 per unit per year. It takes 5 days to receive a shipment after an order is placed.
   a. Calculate the EOQ.
   b. Determine the reorder point. (*Note:* Use a 360-day year to calculate daily usage.)

CASE

Evaluating Zen Bakery Product's Proposed Cash Discount

Jack Weinstein, a financial analyst for Zen Bakery Products, has been asked to investigate a proposed change in the firm's credit terms. The company founder and president believes that by offering a 3 percent cash discount to customers who pay by day 20 of the credit period, annual sales (all on credit) will increase from the current level of $4,000,000 to $4,400,000. Jack's investigation indicates that with the cash discount the firm's average collection period will drop from 75 days to 45 days. In addition, bad debts will drop from 2 percent to 1 percent of sales. He estimates that 70 percent of the sales will take the 3 percent cash discount. The firm's variable costs are expected to continue to amount to 80 cents of each $1 of sales. Zen currently requires a 15 percent rate of return on equal-risk investments.

Required

   a. Find the additional annual profit contribution expected from the increase in sales as a result of the proposed cash discount.

b. Determine the reduction of Zen's average investment in accounts receivable and the resulting annual savings attributable to the proposed cash discount. (Assume a 360-day year.)

c. Calculate the annual savings expected to result from the decline in bad debt expenses attributable to the proposed cash discount.

d. Use your findings in **a** through **c** to advise Jack on whether or not the proposed cash discount can be financially justified. Explain your recommendation.

CHAPTER 10

SOURCES OF SHORT-TERM FINANCING

After studying this chapter, you should be able to:

1 Describe the key features of the major sources of spontaneous short-term financing.

2 Analyze credit terms and decide, when the alternative is to borrow funds, whether to take or forgo cash discounts and whether to stretch accounts payable.

3 Discuss the interest rates, basic forms, and key features of unsecured bank sources of short-term loans, and define commercial paper and explain its role in short-term financing.

4 Describe the characteristics, acceptable collateral, and terms of secured short-term loans, and identify the key institutions extending these loans.

5 Explain how accounts receivable and inventory can be used as collateral to secure short-term loans.

6 Discuss how the Eurocurrency market can be used by multinational companies to take advantage of short-term borrowing and investing (lending) opportunities.

" ". . . short-term credit markets are filled with novel financing arrangements and creative ideas . . . "

When Merchant Bankers Go to Niagara Falls, They're Not Always on Vacation

Dominated by discussions of accounts payable, bank loans, and commercial paper, the study of short-term financing may be the last place you would think to look for new ideas and financial innovation. In reality, however, short-term credit markets are filled with novel financing arrangements and creative ideas—especially in the area of small business finance.

Think for a moment about the need of young firms to search for short-term sources of funds. They have neither an established track record nor a strong balance sheet. Many of them face rejection when they turn to traditional sources of short-term financing. Lacking significant accounts receivable or other assets, these firms have little collateral to offer lenders in exchange for loans.

So what can these small businesses do to raise the short-term funds they need? One answer is merchant banking. The Del-Rain Corporation, a tiny manufacturer of portable heaters located in Niagara Falls, N.Y., turned to Trading Alliance Corporation (TAC) to satisfy its recent need for short-term financing during a seasonal lull in sales.

Del-Rain negotiated the sale of its inventory to TAC for 90 percent of its sales value. As part of the deal, TAC received $2.5 million of guaranteed payments from Del-Rain's retail customers who promised to purchase the firm's heaters once the New York weather turned cool. Factors such as Del-Rain's manufacturing capability and product reputation played a major role in TAC's decision to extend credit to the small firm. At the same time, the risk associated with this unusual financing arrangement warranted a high interest rate. Del-Rain effectively paid an interest rate of 34.5 percent—well above the rates charged for traditional short-term loans.

Will Del-Rain continue to use this financing source as it grows? Probably not. By that time, the firm will be able to obtain less expensive sources of financing to meet its short-term needs. In the meantime, TAC's financial backing enabled Del-Rain to survive during a long, hot New York summer, and the first chill of winter brought a warm glow to Del-Rain's income statement and balance sheet.

$\mathcal{S}$ hort-term financing is debt that matures in one year or less and is used to fulfill seasonal and current asset needs. **Secured short-term financing** has specific assets pledged as collateral, whereas **unsecured short-term financing** does not. Both these forms of financing appear on the balance sheet as *current liabilities*—accounts payable, accruals, and notes payable. (*Notes payable* include all negotiated short-term financing.) For convenience, a summary table of the key features of the common sources of short-term financing is included as Table 10.3 in the chapter summary.

secured short-term financing Financing that matures in one year or less and has specific assets pledged as collateral.

unsecured short-term financing Financing that matures in one year or less and has no assets pledged as collateral.

SPONTANEOUS SOURCES

Spontaneous financing arises from the normal operations of the firm. The two major spontaneous sources of short-term financing are *accounts payable* and *accruals*. Each of these sources is unsecured. As the firm's sales increase, accounts payable increases because of increased purchases required to produce at higher levels. The firm's accruals also increase as wages and taxes rise due to greater labor requirements and the increased taxes on the firm's increased earnings. There is normally no explicit cost attached to either of these current liabilities (although they do have certain implicit costs). The firm should take advantage of these often "interest-free" sources of unsecured short-term financing whenever possible.

spontaneous financing Financing that arises from the normal operations of the firm, the two major short-term sources of which are accounts payable and accruals.

Accounts Payable

Accounts payable is the major source of unsecured short-term financing for business firms. Such accounts result from transactions in which merchandise is purchased but no formal note is signed to show the purchaser's liability to the seller. The purchaser, by accepting merchandise, in effect agrees to pay the supplier the amount required in accordance with the terms of sale. The credit terms extended in such transactions are normally stated on the supplier's invoice. The discussion of accounts payable here is presented from the viewpoint of the purchaser rather than the supplier of "trade credit."[1]

Credit Terms
The supplier's credit terms state the credit period, the size of the cash discount offered (if any), the cash discount period, and the date the

---

[1]An account payable of a purchaser is an account receivable on the supplier's books. Chapter 9 highlighted the key strategies and considerations involved in extending credit to customers.

credit period begins. Each of these aspects of a firm's credit terms is concisely stated in such expressions as "2/10 net 30 EOM." These expressions are a kind of shorthand containing the key information about the length of the credit period (30 days), the cash discount (2 percent), the cash discount period (10 days), and the time the credit period begins, which is the end of each month (EOM).

credit period   The number of days until full payment of an account payable is required.

Credit Period   The **credit period** of an account payable is the number of days until payment in full is required. Regardless of whether a cash discount is offered, the credit period associated with any transaction must always be indicated. Credit periods usually range from zero to 120 days. In certain instances longer times are provided. Most credit terms refer to the credit period as the "net period." The word *net* indicates that the full amount of the purchase must be paid within the number of days indicated from the beginning of the credit period. For example, "net 30 days" indicates that the firm must make *full payment* within 30 days of the beginning of the credit period.

cash discount   A percentage deduction from the purchase price if the buyer pays within a specified time shorter than the credit period.

Cash Discount   The **cash discount,** if offered as part of the firm's credit terms, is a percentage deduction from the purchase price if the buyer pays within a specified time shorter than the credit period. Cash discounts normally range from between 1 and 5 percent. A 2 percent cash discount indicates that the purchaser of $100 of merchandise need pay only $98 if payment is made within the specified shorter interval. The purchaser, whose objective is to stretch accounts payable by paying as late as possible, must determine whether it is more advantageous to take the cash discount or to pay at the end of the full credit period. Techniques for analyzing the benefits of each alternative are discussed in a later section.

cash discount period   The number of days after the beginning of the credit period during which the cash discount is available.

Cash Discount Period   The **cash discount period** is the number of days after the beginning of the credit period during which the cash discount is available. Typically the cash discount period is between 5 and 20 days. Often large customers of smaller firms use their position as key customers to take cash discounts far beyond the end of the cash discount period. This strategy, although ethically questionable, is not uncommon.

date of invoice   Indicates that the beginning of the credit period is the date on the invoice for the purchase.

end of month (EOM)   Indicates that the credit period for all purchases made within a given month begins on the first day of the month immediately following.

Beginning of the Credit Period   The beginning of the credit period is stated as part of the supplier's credit terms. One of the most common designations for the beginning of the credit period is the **date of invoice.** Both the cash discount period and the net period are then measured from the invoice date. **End of month (EOM)** indicates that the credit period for all purchases made within a given month begins on the first day of the month immediately following. These terms simplify record keeping on the part of the firm extending credit. The following example may help to clarify the differences between credit period beginnings.

F I N A N C E   I N   A C T I O N

Does This Sound Like a Cash Discount to You?

These days, it's getting harder and harder to distinguish a merchandise trade discount from some other type of financing arrangement. In late 1990, word leaked out in the financial press that French aircraft manufacturer Airbus Industrie and General Electric would lend Northwest Airlines $500 million in exchange for an order for 75 new Airbus A320 jets. Northwest could use the loan proceeds in any way the company desires, and the money would be paid to Northwest up front, prior to the delivery of any aircraft.

The U.S. Government objected to this financing arrangement, because the government-subsidized French aircraft manufacturer maintains a distinct selling advantage over domestic airplane producers such as Boeing and Douglas Aircraft Company. You'd think executives within these domestic firms would also object to Airbus' actions, but as one United Airlines executive noted, Airbus' loans were "just another form of discounting" its payment terms.

It's common practice for all aircraft manufacturers to link purchase orders with substantial financing contracts. In another recent transaction, Airbus arranged the sale of 100 commercial jets to America West Airlines, but America West never bought the planes. Instead, Airbus sold the jets to airplane lessor GPA Group, PLC in Britain, and Airbus arranged $150 million in lease terms for America West. Once again, the lease financing arrangement was used to discount the cost of aircraft acquisition at America West.

Source: Michael O'Neal, "Is Airbus pushing the envelope?" *Business Week,* October 8, 1990, p. 42.

EXAMPLE   The McKinley Company, a producer of computer graphics software, made two purchases from a certain supplier offering credit terms of 2/10 net 30. One purchase was made on September 10 and the other on September 20. The payment dates for each purchase, based on date of invoice and end of month (EOM) credit period beginnings, are given in Table 10.1. The payment dates if the firm takes the cash discount and if it pays the net amount are shown. From the point of view of the recipient of trade credit, a credit period beginning at the end of the month is preferable in both cases: Their purchases can be paid for without penalty at a later date than otherwise would have been possible.

Table 10.1   **Payment Dates for the McKinley Company
Given Various Assumptions**

Beginning of credit period	September 10 purchase		September 20 purchase	
	Discount taken	**Net amount paid**	**Discount taken**	**Net amount paid**
Date of invoice	Sept. 20	Oct. 10	Sept. 30	Oct. 20
End of month (EOM)	Oct. 10	Oct. 30	Oct. 10	Oct. 30

In order to maintain their competitive position, firms within an industry generally offer the same terms. In many cases, stated credit terms are not the terms actually given to a customer. Special arrangements, or "deals," are made to provide certain customers with more favorable terms. The prospective purchaser is wise to look closely at the credit terms of suppliers when making a purchase decision. In many instances, concessions may be available.

Analyzing Credit Terms

The credit terms offered a firm by its suppliers allow it to delay payments for its purchases. Since the supplier's cost of having its money tied up in merchandise after it is sold is probably reflected in the purchase price, the purchaser is already indirectly paying for this benefit. The purchaser should therefore carefully analyze credit terms in order to determine the best trade credit strategy.

Taking the Cash Discount   If a firm is extended credit terms that include a cash discount, it has two options. Its first option is to *take the cash discount*. If a firm intends to take a cash discount, it should pay on the last day of the discount period. There is no cost associated with taking a cash discount.

EXAMPLE   Presti Corporation, operator of a small chain of video stores, purchased $1,000 worth of merchandise on February 27 from a supplier extending terms of 2/10 net 30 EOM. If the firm takes the cash discount, it will have to pay $980 [$1,000 − (.02 × $1,000)] on March 10, thereby saving $20.

Forgoing the Cash Discount   The second option open to the firm is to *forgo the cash discount* and pay on the final day of the credit period. Although there is no direct cost associated with forgoing a cash discount, there is an implicit cost. The **cost of forgoing a cash discount** is the implied rate of interest paid in order to delay payment of an account payable for an additional number of days. This cost can be illustrated by a simple example. The example assumes that if the firm takes a cash discount, payment will be made on the final day of the cash discount

cost of forgoing a cash discount The implied rate of interest paid in order to delay payment of an account payable for an additional number of days.

period, and if the cash discount is forgone, payment will be made on the final day of the credit period.

EXAMPLE   As in the preceding example, Presti Corporation has been extended credit terms of 2/10 net 30 EOM on $1,000 worth of merchandise. If it takes the cash discount on its February 27 purchase, payment will be required on March 10. If the cash discount is forgone, payment can be made on March 30. To keep its money for an extra 20 days (from March 10 to March 30), the firm must forgo an opportunity to pay $980 for its $1,000 purchase. In other words, it will cost the firm $20 to delay payment for 20 days. Figure 10.1 shows the payment options open to the corporation.

To calculate the cost of forgoing the cash discount, the *true purchase price* must be viewed as the discounted cost of the merchandise. For Presti Corporation, this discounted cost would be $980. To delay paying the $980 for an extra 20 days, the firm must pay $20 ($1,000 − $980). The annual percentage cost of forgoing the cash discount can be calculated using Equation 10.1.

$$\text{Cost of forgoing cash discount} = \frac{CD}{100\% - CD} \times \frac{360}{N}$$

Equation 10.1
Formula for finding the cost of forgoing a cash discount

where

CD = the stated cash discount in percentage terms
N = the number of days payment can be delayed by forgoing the cash discount

Substituting the values for CD (2%) and N (20 days) into Equation 10.1 results in an annualized cost of forgoing the

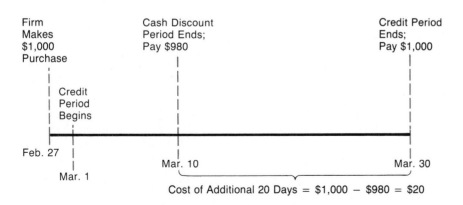

Figure 10.1   Payment Options for Presti Corporation
As a result of its February 27 $1,000 purchase under credit terms of 2/10 net 30 EOM, Presti Corporation can either take the $20 discount and pay $980 on March 10 or forgo the discount and pay the full $1,000 20 days later on March 30.

cash discount of 36.73 percent $[(2\% \div 98\%) \times (360 \div 20)]$. A 360-day year is assumed.

A simple way to *approximate* the cost of a forgone discount is to use the stated cash discount percentage, CD, in place of the first term of Equation 10.1.

Equation 10.2
Formula for approximating the cost of forgoing a cash discount

$$\text{Approximate cost of forgoing cash discount} = CD \times \frac{360}{N}$$

The smaller the cash discount, the closer the approximation to the actual cost of forgoing the cash discount. Using this approximation, the cost of forgoing the cash discount for Presti Corporation is 36 percent $[2\% \times (360 \div 20)]$.

Using the Cost of Forgoing a Cash Discount in Decision Making

The financial manager must determine whether it is advisable to take a cash discount.

EXAMPLE Omst Products, a large building supply company, has four possible suppliers, each offering different credit terms. Except for the differences in credit terms, their products and services are identical. Table 10.2 presents the credit terms offered by suppliers A, B, C, and D, respectively, and the cost of forgoing the cash discounts in each transaction. The approximation method of calculating the cost of forgoing a cash discount (Equation 10.2) has been used to simplify the analysis. The cost of forgoing the cash discount from supplier A is 36 percent; from supplier B, 8 percent; from supplier C, 21.6 percent; and from supplier D, 28.8 percent.

If the firm needs short-term funds, which it could borrow from its bank at an interest rate of 13 percent, and if each of the suppliers (A, B, C, and D) is viewed *separately*, which (if any) of the suppliers' cash discounts will the firm forgo? To answer this question, each supplier's terms must be evaluated as if it were the firm's sole supplier. In dealing with supplier A, the firm will take the cash discount since the cost of forgoing it is 36 percent. The firm will then borrow the funds it requires from its bank at 13 percent interest. In dealing with supplier B, the firm will do better to forgo the cash discount since the cost of this action is less than the cost of borrowing money from the bank (8 percent versus 13 percent). In dealing with either supplier C or supplier D, the firm should take the cash discount since in both cases the cost of forgoing the discount is greater than the 13 percent cost of borrowing from the bank.

The example shows that the cost of forgoing a cash discount is relevant when evaluating a single supplier's credit terms in light of certain *bank borrowing costs*. When comparing various suppliers' credit terms, the cost of forgoing the cash discount may not be the most impor-

Table 10.2   **Cash Discounts and Associated Costs
for Omst Products**

Supplier	Credit terms	Approximate cost of forgoing cash discount
A	2/10 net 30 EOM	36.0%
B	1/10 net 55 EOM	8.0
C	3/20 net 70 EOM	21.6
D	4/10 net 60 EOM	28.8

tant factor in the decision process. Other factors such as the size of the cash discount, the length of the cash discount period, and the length of the credit period may be of primary importance.

Effects of Stretching Accounts Payable

If a firm anticipates *stretching accounts payable*, its cost of forgoing a cash discount is reduced. Stretching accounts payable is sometimes suggested as a reasonable strategy for a firm as long as it does not damage its credit rating. As noted in Chapter 8, although this strategy is financially attractive, it raises an important ethical issue: It may cause the firm to violate the agreement it entered into with its supplier when it purchased merchandise. Clearly, a supplier would not look kindly on a customer who regularly and purposely postponed paying for purchases.

EXAMPLE   Presti Corporation was extended credit terms of 2/10 net 30 EOM. The cost of forgoing the cash discount, assuming payment on the last day of the credit period, was found to be approximately 36 percent $[2\% \times (360 \div 20)]$. If the firm were able to stretch its account payable to 70 days without damaging its credit rating, the cost of forgoing the cash discount would be only 12 percent $[2\% \times (360 \div 60)]$. Stretching accounts payable reduces the implicit cost of forgoing a cash discount.

Accruals

The second spontaneous source of short-term financing for a business is accruals. **Accruals** are liabilities for services received for which payment has yet to be made. The most common items accrued by a firm are wages and taxes. Since taxes are payments to the government, their accrual cannot be manipulated by the firm. However, the accrual of wages can be manipulated to some extent. This is accomplished by delaying payment of wages, thereby receiving an interest-free loan from

accruals Liabilities for services received for which payment has yet to be made.

employees who are paid sometime after they have performed the work. The pay period for employees who earn an hourly rate is often governed by union regulations or by state or federal law. However, in other cases the frequency of payment is at the discretion of the company's management.

EXAMPLE   Chan Company, a large janitorial service company, currently pays its employees at the end of each work week. The weekly payroll totals $400,000. If the firm were to extend the pay period so as to pay its employees one week later throughout an entire year, the employees would in effect be loaning the firm $400,000 for a year. If the firm could earn 10 percent annually on invested funds, such a strategy would be worth $40,000 per year (.10 × $400,000). By delaying payment of accruals in this way, the firm could save this amount of money.

UNSECURED BANK SOURCES

short-term self-liqui-dating loan An unsecured short-term loan in which the use to which the borrowed money is put provides the mechanism through which the loan is repaid.

Banks are a major source of unsecured short-term loans to businesses. Unlike the spontaneous sources of *unsecured short-term financing*, bank loans are negotiated and result from deliberate actions taken by the financial manager. The major type of loan made by banks to businesses is the **short-term self-liquidating loan.** Self-liquidating loans are intended merely to carry the firm through seasonal peaks in financing needs, mainly buildups of accounts receivable and inventory. As receivables and inventories are converted into cash, the funds needed to retire these loans will automatically be generated. In other words, the use to which the borrowed money is put provides the mechanism through which the loan is repaid (hence the term *self-liquidating*). Banks lend unsecured short-term funds in three basic ways: through single-payment notes, lines of credit, and revolving credit agreements. Before we look at these types of loans, it is necessary to lay some groundwork about loan interest rates.

Loan Interest Rates

The interest rate on a bank loan is typically based upon the prime rate of interest and can be a fixed or a floating rate. It should be evaluated using the effective interest rate. There are differing ways to calculate this rate, depending on whether interest is paid when the loan matures or in advance. Each of these aspects of loan interest rates is evaluated below.

prime rate of interest (prime rate) The lowest rate of interest charged by the nation's leading banks on loans to their most reliable business borrowers.

Prime Rate of Interest
The **prime rate of interest (prime rate)** is the lowest rate of interest charged by the nation's leading banks on business loans to their most

important and reliable business borrowers. The prime rate fluctuates with changing supply-and-demand relationships for short-term funds.[2] Banks generally determine the rate charged on loans to various borrowers by adding some type of premium to the prime rate to adjust it for the borrower's "riskiness." The premium may amount to 4 percent or more. Most unsecured short-term notes carry premiums of less than 2 percent. In general, banks do not make short-term unsecured loans to businesses that are believed to be questionable risks.

Fixed- and Floating-Rate Loans

Loans can have either fixed or floating interest rates. On a **fixed-rate loan** the rate of interest is determined at a set increment above the prime rate on the date of the loan and remains unvarying at that fixed rate until maturity. On a **floating-rate loan** the increment above the prime rate is initially established and the rate of interest is allowed to "float," or vary, above prime *as the prime rate varies* until maturity. Generally the increment above the prime rate on a floating-rate loan will be *lower* than on a fixed-rate loan of equivalent risk because the lender bears less risk with a floating-rate loan. The highly volatile nature of the prime rate in recent years, coupled with the widespread use of computers by banks to monitor and calculate loan interest, has been responsible for the *current dominance of floating-rate loans.*

Method of Computing Interest

Once the rate of interest has been established, the method of computing interest is determined. Interest can be paid either when a loan matures or in advance. If interest is paid at maturity, the **effective interest rate** —the actual rate of interest paid—for the period is equal to

$$\frac{\text{Interest}}{\text{Amount borrowed}}$$

Most bank loans to businesses require the interest payment at maturity. When interest is paid in advance, it is deducted from the loan so that the borrower actually receives less money than is requested. Loans on which interest is paid in advance are often called **discount loans.** The *effective interest rate for a discount loan* is calculated as

$$\frac{\text{Interest}}{\text{Amount borrowed} - \text{interest}}$$

Paying interest in advance therefore raises the effective interest rate above the stated interest rate. Let us look at an example.

fixed-rate loan A loan whose rate of interest is determined at a set increment above the prime rate and remains unvarying until maturity.

floating-rate loan A loan whose rate of interest is set at an increment above the prime rate and is allowed to "float" above prime *as the prime rate varies* until maturity.

effective interest rate The actual rate of interest paid on a loan as opposed to the stated rate.

Equation 10.3 Formula for the effective interest rate when interest is paid at maturity

discount loans Loans on which interest is paid in advance by deducting it from the amount borrowed.

Equation 10.4 Formula for the effective interest rate on a discount loan

---

[2]From 1975 through the third quarter of 1978 the prime rate was generally below 9 percent. From the end of 1978 until June of 1985 the prime rate remained above 9.5 percent. In late December 1980 the prime rate reached a record high 21.5 percent. The prime rate slowly dropped from 9.5 percent in June 1985 to 7.5 percent in late August 1986, and in March 1987 it began a slow rise to 9.0 percent by November of 1987. It remained around 9.0 percent until the middle of 1988 when it began to rise, peaking at 11.5 percent in 1989. The prime rate then declined to and remained at about 10.0 percent through the end of 1990. By the middle of 1991 it had declined to 8.5 percent.

EXAMPLE   Booster Company, a manufacturer of athletic apparel, wants to borrow $10,000 at a stated rate of 10 percent interest for one year. If the interest on the loan is paid at maturity, the firm will pay $1,000 (.10 × $10,000) for the use of the $10,000 for the year. Substituting into Equation 10.3, the effective interest rate will therefore be

$$\frac{\$1,000}{\$10,000} = 10.0 \text{ percent}$$

If the money is borrowed at the same *stated* rate but interest is paid in advance, the firm will still pay $1,000 in interest, but it will receive only $9,000 ($10,000 − $1,000). Thus, substituting into Equation 10.4, the effective interest rate in this case is

$$\frac{\$1,000}{\$10,000 - \$1,000} = \frac{\$1,000}{\$9,000} = 11.1 \text{ percent}$$

Paying interest in advance thus makes the effective interest rate (11.1 percent) greater than the stated interest rate (10.0 percent).

Single-Payment Notes

single-payment note
A short-term, one-time loan payable as a single amount at its maturity.

A **single-payment note** can be obtained from a commercial bank by a creditworthy business borrower. This type of loan is usually a "one-shot" deal made when a borrower needs additional funds for a short period. The resulting instrument is a *note*, signed by the borrower. The note states the terms of the loan, which include the length of the loan (the maturity date) and the interest rate charged. This type of short-term note generally has a maturity of 30 days to 9 months or more. The interest charged on the note is generally tied in some fashion to the prime rate of interest. A note may have either a fixed or floating rate. Let us look at an example.

EXAMPLE   Golden Manufacturing, a producer of rotary mower blades, recently borrowed $100,000 from each of two banks— bank A and bank B. The loans were incurred on the same day, when the prime rate of interest was 9 percent. Each loan involved a 90-day note with interest to be paid at the end of 90 days. The interest rate was set at 1½ percent above the prime rate on bank A's fixed-rate note. This means that over the 90-day period, the rate of interest will remain at 10½ percent (9% prime rate + 1½% increment) regardless of fluctuations in the prime rate. The total interest cost on this loan is $2,625 [$100,000 × (10½% × 90/360)]. The effective cost of this loan is 2.625 percent ($2,625/$100,000) for 90 days.

On bank B's floating-rate note the interest rate was set at 1 percent above the prime rate. This means that the rate charged over the 90 days will vary directly *with* the prime rate. Initially the rate will be 10 percent (9% + 1%), but when the prime rate changes, so will the rate of interest on the note. For instance, if after 30 days the prime rate rises to 9.5 percent and after another 30 days drops to 9.25 percent, the firm would be paying 0.833 percent for the first 30 days (10% × 30/360), 0.875 percent for the next 30 days (10.5% × 30/360), and 0.854 percent for the last 30 days (10.25% × 30/360). Its total interest cost would be $2,562 [$100,000 × (0.833% + 0.875% + 0.854%)] resulting in an effective cost of 2.562 percent ($2,562/$100,000) for 90 days.

Clearly, in this case the floating-rate loan would have been less expensive (2.562 percent) than the fixed-rate loan (2.625 percent) due to its generally lower interest rates over the 90-day term of the note.

Lines of Credit

A **line of credit** is an agreement between a commercial bank and a business specifying the amount of unsecured short-term borrowing the bank will make available to the firm over a given period of time. A line of credit agreement is typically made for a period of one year and often places certain constraints on the borrower. A line of credit is *not a guaranteed loan* but indicates that if the bank has sufficient funds available, it will allow the borrower to owe it up to a certain amount of money. The amount of a line of credit is *the maximum amount the firm can owe the bank* at any point in time.

When applying for a line of credit the borrower may be required to submit such documents as its cash budget, its pro forma income statement, its pro forma balance sheet, and its recent financial statements. If the bank finds the customer acceptable, the line of credit will be extended. The major attraction of a line of credit from the bank's point of view is that it eliminates the need to examine the creditworthiness of a customer each time it borrows money. A few characteristics of lines of credit require further explanation.

Interest Rates
The interest rate on a line of credit is normally stated as a floating rate—the *prime rate plus a percent*. If the prime rate changes, the interest rate charged on new *as well as on outstanding* borrowing will automatically change. The amount a borrower is charged in excess of the prime rate depends on its creditworthiness. The more creditworthy the borrower, the lower the interest increment above prime, and vice versa.

Operating Change Restrictions
In a line of credit agreement, a bank may impose **operating change restrictions.** Such restrictions give the bank the right to revoke the line

line of credit   An agreement specifying the amount of unsecured short-term borrowing a bank will make available to a firm over a given period of time.

operating change restrictions   Contractual restrictions that a bank may impose on a firm as part of a line of credit agreement.

F I N A N C E   I N   A C T I O N

Donald Trump's Bridge Loans

Some financing arrangements involve a complicated layering of different types of debt, so that the financial position of the borrower begins to resemble the leaves of an artichoke. Peeling off one layer of debt leads to a second layer, and this second layer leads to yet a third layer. In many cases, short-term bridge loans hold these complex financing arrangements together.

New York real estate financier Donald Trump's financial structure provides a good example of debt layering. In mid-1990, as East Coast real estate values began to fall, Trump's ability to pay his debts took a similar turn for the worse. In order to raise $20 million and prevent default on his New Jersey casino debt, Trump's bankers arranged an eleventh-hour *bridge loan* for $20 million.

This temporary credit arrangement was contingent upon the completion of a broader, long-term credit pact with Trump that called for the extension of $65 million in new financing to support Trump Tower in New York. In addition, this $65 million transaction allowed Trump to defer interest payments on some $2 billion in bank debt. The $20 million bridge loan gave Trump's bankers the necessary time to work out the details for the larger financing transaction, with the proceeds from the $65 million loan used, in part, to repay the temporary bridge loan.

Source: William Goodwin, "Trump's banks seal credit pact with a $20 million bridge loan," *The American Banker*, June 27, 1990, p. 2.

if any major changes occur in the firm's financial condition or operations. The firm is usually required to submit for review periodically (quarterly or semiannually) up-to-date and, preferably, audited financial statements. In addition, the bank typically needs to be informed of shifts in key managerial personnel or in the firm's operations prior to changes taking place. Such changes may affect the future success and debt-paying ability of the firm and thus could alter its credit status. If the bank does not agree with the proposed changes and the firm makes them anyway, the bank has the right to revoke the line-of-credit agreement.

compensating balance A required checking account balance equal to a certain percentage of the borrower's short-term unsecured loan.

Compensating Balances

To ensure that the borrower will be a good customer, many short-term unsecured bank loans often require the borrower to maintain a **compensating balance** in a demand deposit account (checking account). The compensating balance is equal to a certain percentage of the amount borrowed. Compensating balances of 10 to 20 percent are frequently required. They may be required on single-payment notes as well as lines of credit. A compensating balance not only forces the borrower to be a good customer of the bank but may also raise the interest cost to the borrower, thereby increasing the bank's earnings. An example will illustrate.

EXAMPLE   Exact Graphics, a graphic design firm, has borrowed $1 million under a line of credit agreement. It must pay a stated interest rate of 10 percent and maintain a compensating balance of 20 percent of the funds borrowed, or $200,000, in its checking account. Thus it actually receives the use of only $800,000. To use the $800,000 for a year, the firm pays $100,000 (.10 × $1,000,000). The effective interest rate on the funds is therefore 12.5 percent ($100,000 ÷ $800,000), 2.5 percent more than the stated rate of 10 percent.

If the firm normally maintains a balance of $200,000 or more in its checking account, the effective interest rate will equal the stated interest rate of 10 percent because none of the $1 million borrowed is needed to satisfy the compensating balance requirement. If the firm normally maintains a $100,000 balance in its checking account, only an additional $100,000 will have to be tied up, leaving it with $900,000 ($1,000,000 − $100,000) of usable funds. The effective interest rate in this case would be 11.1 percent ($100,000 ÷ $900,000). Thus a compensating balance raises the cost of borrowing *only* if it is larger than the firm's normal cash balance.

Annual Cleanups

To ensure that money lent under a line of credit agreement is actually being used to finance seasonal needs, many banks require an **annual cleanup.** This means that the borrower must have a loan balance of zero—that is, owe the bank nothing—for a certain number of days during the year. Forcing the borrower to carry a zero loan balance for a certain period of time ensures that short-term loans do not turn into long-term loans.

All the characteristics of a line of credit agreement are negotiable to some extent. Today, banks bid competitively to attract large, well-known firms. A prospective borrower should attempt to negotiate a line of credit with the most favorable interest rate, for an optimal amount of funds, and with a minimum of restrictions. Borrowers today frequently pay fees to lenders instead of maintaining deposit balances as compensation for loans and other services provided by the lender. The lender will attempt to get a good return with maximum safety. These negotiations should produce a line of credit suitable to both borrower and lender.

annual cleanup The requirement that for a certain number of days during the year borrowers under a line of credit carry a zero loan balance.

Revolving Credit Agreements

revolving credit agreement A line of credit *guaranteed* to a borrower by a bank for a stated time period and regardless of the scarcity of money.

commitment fee The fee normally charged on a revolving credit agreement.

A **revolving credit agreement** is nothing more than a *guaranteed line of credit*. It is guaranteed in the sense that the bank making the arrangement assures the borrower that a specified amount of funds will be made available regardless of the scarcity of money. The interest rate and other requirements for a revolving credit agreement are similar to those for a line of credit. It is not uncommon for a revolving credit agreement to be for a period greater than one year. Since the bank guarantees the availability of funds to the borrower, a **commitment fee** is normally charged on a revolving credit agreement. This fee often applies to the average unused balance of the agreement. It is normally about .5 percent of the *average unused portion* of the funds. An example will clarify the nature of a commitment fee.

EXAMPLE   The Blount Company, a major real estate developer, has a $2 million revolving credit agreement with its bank. Its average borrowing under the agreement for the past year was $1.5 million. The bank charges a commitment fee of .5 percent. Since the average unused portion of the committed funds was $500,000 ($2 million − $1.5 million), the commitment fee for the year was $2,500 (.005 × $500,000). Of course, Blount also had to pay interest on the actual $1.5 million borrowed under the agreement. Assuming $160,000 interest was paid on the $1.5 million borrowed, the effective cost of the agreement is 10.83 percent [($160,000 + $2,500)/$1,500,000]. Although more expensive than a line of credit, a revolving credit agreement can be less risky from the borrower's viewpoint, since the availability of funds is guaranteed by the bank.

COMMERCIAL PAPER

commercial paper A form of financing consisting of short-term, unsecured promissory notes issued by firms with a high credit standing.

Commercial paper is a form of financing that consists of short-term, unsecured promissory notes issued by firms with a high credit standing. Generally, only quite large firms of unquestionable financial soundness and reputation are able to issue commercial paper. Most commercial paper has maturities ranging from 3 to 270 days. Although there is no set denomination, it is generally issued in multiples of $100,000 or more. A large portion of the commercial paper today is issued by finance companies; manufacturing firms account for a smaller portion of this type of financing. As noted in Chapter 8, businesses often purchase commercial paper, which they hold as marketable securities, to provide an interest-earning reserve of liquidity.

Sale of Commercial Paper

Commercial paper is *directly placed with investors* by the issuer or is *sold by commercial paper dealers*. For performing the marketing function, the commercial paper dealer is paid a fee. Regardless of the method of sale, most commercial paper is purchased from a firm by other businesses, banks, life insurance companies, pension funds, and money market mutual funds.

Interest on Commercial Paper

The interest paid by the issuer of commercial paper is determined by the size of the discount and the length of time to maturity. Commercial paper is sold at a discount from its *par,* or *face, value*, and the actual interest earned by the purchaser is determined by certain calculations. These can be illustrated by the following example.

EXAMPLE   Deems Corporation, a large shipbuilder, has just issued $1 million worth of commercial paper that has a 90-day maturity and sells for $980,000. At the end of 90 days the purchaser of this paper will receive $1 million for its $980,000 investment. The interest paid on the financing is therefore $20,000 on a principal of $980,000. This is equivalent to an annual interest rate for Deems Corporation commercial paper of 8.2 percent [($20,000 ÷ $980,000) × (360 days ÷ 90 days)].

An interesting characteristic of commercial paper is that it *normally* has a yield of 1 to 2 percent below the prime bank lending rate. In other words, firms are able to raise funds through the sale of commercial paper more cheaply than by borrowing from a commercial bank. The reason is that many suppliers of short-term funds do not have the option of making low-risk business loans at the prime rate. They can invest only in marketable securities such as Treasury bills and commercial paper.

Although the cost of borrowing through the sale of commercial paper is usually lower than the prime bank loan rate, a firm needs to maintain a good working relationship with its bank. Therefore even if it is slightly more expensive to borrow from a bank, it may at times be advisable to do so in order to establish the necessary rapport. This strategy ensures that when money is tight, funds can be obtained promptly and at a reasonable interest rate.

SECURED SOURCES

Once a firm has exhausted its unsecured sources of short-term financing, it may be able to obtain additional short-term loans on a secured

secured loan A loan for which the lender requires collateral.

collateral The security offered the lender by the borrower.

security agreement The agreement between the borrower and the lender that specifies the collateral held against a secured loan.

basis. A **secured loan** is a loan for which the lender requires collateral. The **collateral** commonly takes the form of an asset, such as accounts receivable or inventory. The lender obtains a security interest in the collateral through a contract (security agreement) with the borrower. The **security agreement** specifies the collateral held against the loan. In addition, the terms of the loan against which the security is held are attached to, or form part of, the security agreement. They specify the conditions required for the security interest to be removed, along with the interest rate on the loan, repayment dates, and other loan provisions. A copy of the security agreement is filed in a public office within the state—typically a county or state court. Filing provides subsequent lenders with information about which assets of a prospective borrower are unavailable for use as collateral. The filing requirement protects the lender by legally establishing the lender's security interest.

Characteristics of Secured Short-Term Loans

Although many people believe that holding collateral as security reduces the risk of the loan, lenders do not usually view loans in this way. Lenders recognize that by having an interest in collateral they can reduce losses if the borrower defaults, but *as far as changing the risk of default, the presence of collateral has no impact.* A lender requires collateral to ensure recovery of some portion of the loan in the event of default. What the lender wants above all, however, is to be repaid as scheduled. In general, lenders prefer to make less risky loans at lower rates of interest than to be in a position in which they are forced to liquidate collateral.

Collateral and Terms
A number of factors concerning the characteristics desirable in collateral and the basic terms of secured short-term loans need to be examined.

Collateral Lenders of secured short-term funds prefer collateral that has a life, or duration, closely matched to the term of the loan. This assures the lender that the collateral can be used to satisfy the loan in the event of a default. Current assets—accounts receivable and inventories—are the most desirable short-term loan collateral since they normally convert into cash much sooner than do fixed assets. Thus the short-term lender of secured funds generally accepts only liquid current assets as collateral.

percentage advance The percent of the book value of the collateral that constitutes the principal of a secured loan.

Terms Typically, the lender determines the desirable **percentage advance** to make against the collateral. This percentage advance constitutes the principal of the secured loan. It is normally between 30 and 100 percent of the book value of the collateral. It varies not only according to the type and liquidity of collateral but also according to the type of security interest being taken.

The interest rate charged on secured short-term loans is typically *higher* than the rate on unsecured short-term loans. Commercial banks and other institutions do not normally consider secured loans less risky than unsecured loans; they therefore require higher interest rates on them. In addition, negotiating and administering secured loans is more troublesome for the lender than negotiating and administering unsecured loans. The lender therefore normally requires added compensation in the form of a service charge, a higher interest rate, or both. *The higher cost of secured as opposed to unsecured borrowing is due to the greater risk of default and to the increased administration costs involved.* (Remember that firms typically borrow on a secured basis only after exhausting less costly unsecured sources of short-term funds.)

Institutions Extending Secured Short-Term Loans

The primary sources of secured short-term loans to businesses are commercial banks and commercial finance companies. Both institutions deal in short-term loans secured primarily by accounts receivable and inventory. The operations of banks have already been described. **Commercial finance companies** are lending institutions that make *only* secured loans—both short-term and long-term—to businesses. Unlike banks, finance companies are not permitted to hold deposits.

Only when its unsecured and secured short-term borrowing power from the bank is exhausted will a borrower turn to the commercial finance company for additional secured borrowing. Because the finance company generally ends up with higher-risk borrowers, its interest charges on secured short-term loans are usually higher than those of commercial banks. The leading U.S. commercial finance companies include the Commercial Investors Trust (CIT) Corporation and GE Capital Division of General Electric Credit Corporation.

commercial finance companies Lending institutions that make *only* secured loans to businesses.

The Use of Accounts Receivable as Collateral

Two commonly used means of obtaining short-term financing with accounts receivable are pledging accounts receivable and factoring accounts receivable. Actually, only a pledge of accounts receivable creates a secured short-term loan; factoring really entails the *sale* of accounts receivable at a discount. Although factoring is not actually a form of secured short-term borrowing, it does involve the use of accounts receivable to obtain needed short-term funds.

Pledging Accounts Receivable

A **pledge of accounts receivable** is often used to secure a short-term loan. Because accounts receivable are normally quite liquid, they are an attractive form of short-term collateral. Both commercial banks and commercial finance companies extend loans against pledges of accounts receivable.

When a firm approaches a prospective lender to request a loan against accounts receivable, the lender will first evaluate the firm's accounts receivable to determine their desirability as collateral. Next, the

pledge of accounts receivable The use of a firm's accounts receivable as collateral to obtain a short-term loan.

dollar value of the acceptable accounts is adjusted by the lender for expected returns on sales and other allowances. Then, the percentage advanced against the adjusted collateral is determined by the lender based on its overall evaluation of the quality of the acceptable receivables and the expected cost of their liquidation. This percentage represents the principal of the loan. It typically ranges between 50 and 90 percent of the face value of acceptable accounts receivable. Finally, to protect its interest in the collateral the lender will file a **lien,** which is a publicly disclosed legal claim on the collateral.

Pledges of accounts receivable are normally made on a **nonnotification basis.** This means that a customer whose account has been pledged as collateral is not notified of this action. Under the nonnotification arrangement, the borrower still collects the pledged account receivable and the lender trusts that the borrower will remit these payments as they are received. If a pledge of accounts receivable is made on a **notification basis,** the customer is notified to remit payment directly to the lender.

The stated cost of a pledge of accounts receivable is normally 2 to 5 percent above the prime rate of interest offered by banks. In addition to the stated interest rate, a service charge of up to 3 percent may be levied. Although the interest payment is expected to compensate the lender for making the loan, the service charge is needed to cover the administrative costs incurred by the lender.

Factoring Accounts Receivable

Factoring accounts receivable involves their outright sale at a discount to a factor or other financial institution. A **factor** is a financial institution that purchases accounts receivable from businesses. There are 15 to 20 firms currently operating in the United States that deal solely in factoring accounts receivable. Some commercial banks and commercial finance companies also factor accounts receivable. Although not actually the same as obtaining a short-term loan, factoring accounts receivable is similar to borrowing with accounts receivable as collateral. Factoring constitutes approximately one-third of the total financing secured by accounts receivable (including factoring) and inventory in the United States currently.

A factoring agreement normally states the exact conditions, charges, and procedures for the purchase of an account. The factor, like a lender against a pledge of accounts receivable, chooses accounts for purchase, selecting only those that appear to be acceptable credit risks. Where factoring is to be on a continuing basis, the factor will actually make the firm's credit decisions, since this will guarantee the acceptability of accounts. Factoring is normally done on a *notification basis*, and the factor receives payment of the account directly from the customer. In addition, most sales of accounts receivable to a factor are made on a **nonrecourse basis.** This means that the factor agrees to accept all credit risks. Thus if a purchased account turns out to be uncollectible, the factor must absorb the loss.

Typically the factor is not required to pay the firm until the account is collected or until the last day of the credit period, whichever

---

lien A publicly disclosed legal claim on collateral.

nonnotification basis The basis on which a borrower, having pledged an account receivable, continues to collect the account payments without notifying the account customer.

notification basis The basis on which an account customer whose account has been pledged is notified to remit payments directly to the lender.

factoring accounts receivable The outright sale of accounts receivable at a discount in order to obtain funds.

factor A financial institution that specializes in purchasing accounts receivable.

nonrecourse basis The basis on which accounts receivable are sold to a factor with the understanding that the factor accepts all credit risks on the purchased accounts.

occurs first. The factor sets up an account similar to a bank deposit account for each customer. As payment is received or as due dates arrive, the factor deposits money into the seller's account, from which the seller is free to make withdrawals as needed. In many cases, if the firm leaves the money in the account, a *surplus* will exist on which the factor will pay interest. In other instances, the factor may make *advances* to the firm against uncollected accounts that are not yet due. These advances represent a negative balance in the firm's account, on which interest is charged.

Factoring costs include commissions, interest levied on advances, and interest earned on surpluses. The factor deposits in the firm's account the book value of the accounts purchased by the factor, less the commissions. The commissions are typically stated as a 1 to 3 percent discount from the book value of factored accounts receivable. The *interest levied on advances* is generally 2 to 4 percent above the prime rate. It is levied on the actual amount advanced. The interest paid on surpluses or positive account balances left with a factor is generally around .5 percent per month. Although its cost may seem high, factoring has certain advantages that make it quite attractive to many firms. One is the ability it gives the firm to *turn accounts receivable immediately into cash* without having to worry about repayment. Another advantage of factoring is that it ensures a *known pattern of cash flows*. In addition, if factoring is undertaken on a continuous basis, the firm *can eliminate its credit and collection departments*.

The Use of Inventory as Collateral

Inventory is generally second to accounts receivable in desirability as short-term loan collateral. Inventory is attractive as collateral since it normally has a market value greater than its book value, which is used to establish its value as collateral. A lender securing a loan with inventory will probably be able to sell it for at least book value if the borrower defaults on its obligations.

Desirable Characteristics

Raw materials, work in process, or finished goods may all be offered as collateral for a short-term loan; usually only raw materials or finished goods inventories are considered acceptable. The most important characteristic of inventory being evaluated as loan collateral is *marketability*, which must be considered in light of its physical properties. A warehouse of *perishable* items, such as fresh peaches, may be quite marketable, but if the cost of storing and selling the peaches is high, they may not be desirable collateral. *Specialized items*, such as moon-roving vehicles, are not desirable collateral either, since finding a buyer for them could be difficult. When evaluating inventory as possible loan collateral, the lender looks for items with very stable market prices that have ready markets and that lack undesirable physical properties.

Floating Inventory Liens

floating inventory lien A lender's claim on the borrower's general inventory as collateral for a secured loan.

A lender may be willing to secure a loan under a **floating inventory lien,** which is a claim on inventory in general. This arrangement is most attractive when the firm has a stable level of inventory that consists of a diversified group of relatively inexpensive merchandise. Inventories of items such as auto tires, screws and bolts, and shoes are candidates for floating-lien loans. Since it is difficult for a lender to verify the presence of the inventory, the lender will generally advance less than 50 percent of the book value of the average inventory. The interest charge on a floating lien is 3 to 5 percent above the prime rate. Floating liens are often required by commercial banks as extra security on what would otherwise be an unsecured loan. A floating-lien inventory loan may also be available from commercial finance companies.

Trust Receipt Inventory Loans

trust receipt inventory loan An agreement under which the lender advances a portion of the cost of the borrower's salable inventory items in exchange for the borrower's promise to repay the loan, with accrued interest, upon the sale of each item.

A **trust receipt inventory loan** can often be made against relatively expensive automotive, consumer-durable, and industrial equipment that can be identified by serial number. Under this agreement, the borrower keeps the inventory and the lender may advance 80 to 100 percent of its cost. The lender files a *lien* on all the items financed. The borrower is free to sell the merchandise and is trusted to remit the amount lent against each item, along with accrued interest, to the lender immediately after the sale. The lender then releases the lien on the appropriate item. The lender makes periodic checks of the borrower's inventory to make sure that the required amount of collateral is still in the hands of the borrower. The interest charge to the borrower is normally 2 percent or more above the prime rate.

Trust receipt loans are often made by manufacturers' wholly owned financing subsidiaries, known as *captive finance companies*, to their customers. *Floor planning* of automobile or equipment retailers is done under this arrangement. For example, General Motors Acceptance Corporation (GMAC), the financing subsidiary of General Motors, grants these types of loans to its dealers. Trust receipt loans are also available from commercial banks and commercial finance companies.

Warehouse Receipt Loans

warehouse receipt loan An arrangement in which the lender receives control of the pledged inventory collateral, which is warehoused by a designated agent.

A **warehouse receipt loan** is an arrangement whereby a lender receives control of the pledged collateral, which is warehoused (stored) in the lender's possession. After selecting acceptable collateral, the lender hires a warehousing company to act as its agent and take possession of the inventory. The lender may be a commercial bank or a commercial finance company.

Two types of warehousing arrangements are possible: terminal warehouses and field warehouses. A *terminal warehouse* is a central warehouse used to store the merchandise of various customers. Such a warehouse is normally used by the lender when the inventory can be delivered to the warehouse relatively inexpensively. Under a *field warehouse* arrangement, the lender hires a field warehousing firm to set up a warehouse on the borrower's premises or to lease part of the borrower's warehouse in which to store the pledged collateral. Regardless of whether a terminal or field warehouse is established, the warehousing company places a guard over the inventory. Only upon written approval of the lender can any portion of the secured inventory be released.

The actual lending agreement specifically states the requirements for the release of inventory. As in the case of other secured loans, the lender accepts only collateral believed to be readily marketable and advances only a portion—generally 75 to 90 percent—of the collateral's value. The specific costs of warehouse receipt loans are generally higher than those of any other secured lending arrangements due to the need to hire and pay a third party (the warehousing firm) to guard and supervise the collateral. The basic interest charged on warehouse receipt loans is higher than that charged on unsecured loans, generally ranging from 3 to 5 percent above the prime rate. In addition to the interest charge, the borrower must absorb the costs of warehousing by paying the warehouse fee, which is generally between 1 and 3 percent of the amount of the loan. The borrower is normally also required to pay the insurance costs on the warehoused merchandise.

INTERNATIONAL DIMENSION: SHORT-TERM FINANCING

In international operations the usual domestic sources of short-term financing are available to MNCs. Included are accounts payable, accruals, and bank and nonbank sources in each subsidiary's local environment. The Euromarket discussed in Chapter 2 is another possible source of short-term financing. Our emphasis here is on the "foreign" sources.

For a subsidiary of a multinational company, its local economic market is a basic source of both short- and long-term financing. Moreover, the subsidiary's borrowing and lending status can be superior to that of a local firm in the same economy, since the subsidiary can rely on the potential backing and guarantee of its parent MNC. One drawback, however, is that most local markets and local currencies are regulated by local authorities. Thus a subsidiary may ultimately choose to turn to the Euromarket and take advantage of borrowing and investing in an unregulated financial forum.

The Euromarket offers nondomestic financing opportunities for both the short term (Eurocurrency) and the long term (Eurobonds). (Eurobonds are discussed in Chapter 19.) In the case of short-term financing, the forces of supply and demand are among the main factors determining exchange rates in **Eurocurrency markets.** Each currency's normal interest rate is influenced by economic policies pursued by the respective "home" government. For example, the interest rates offered in the Euromarket on the U.S. dollar are greatly affected by the prime rate inside the United States; the dollar's exchange rates with other major currencies are influenced by the supply and demand forces acting in such markets (and in response to interest rates).

Unlike borrowing in the domestic markets, where only one currency and a **nominal interest rate** are involved, financing activities in

Eurocurrency markets The portion of the Euromarket that provides short-term foreign-currency financing to subsidiaries of MNCs.

nominal interest rate (in the international context) The stated interest rate charged on financing when only the MNC parent's currency is involved.

effective interest rate (in the international context) The rate equal to the nominal rate plus any forecast appreciation (or minus any forecast depreciation) of a foreign currency relative to the currency of the MNC parent.

the Euromarket can involve several currencies and both nominal and effective interest rates. **Effective interest rates** are equal to nominal rates plus any forecast appreciation (or minus any depreciation) of a foreign currency relative to the currency of the MNC parent—say, the U.S. dollar. An example will illustrate the issues involved.

EXAMPLE   A multinational plastics company, Overseas Molding, has subsidiaries in Switzerland (local currency, Swiss franc, Sf) and Belgium (local currency, Belgian franc, Bf). Based on each subsidiary's forecast operations, the short-term financial needs (in equivalent U.S. dollars) are as follows:

Switzerland: $80 million excess cash to be invested (lent)
Belgium: $60 million funds to be raised (borrowed)

Based on the available information, the parent firm has provided each subsidiary with the following figures regarding exchange rates and interest rates. (The figures for the effective rates shown are derived by adding the forecast percentage changes to the nominal rates.)

		Currency	
Item	US$	Sf	Bf
Spot exchange rates		Sf 1.44/US$	Bf 34.9/US$
Forecast % change		+2.2%	−1.5%
Interest rates			
Nominal			
Euromarket	7.9%	4.0%	8.7%
Domestic	7.5	3.6	9.2
Effective			
Euromarket	7.9%	6.2%	7.2%
Domestic	7.5	5.8	7.7

From the point of view of a multinational, the effective rates of interest, which take into account each currency's forecast percentage change (appreciation or depreciation) relative to the U.S. dollar, are the main items to be considered for investment and borrowing decisions. (It is assumed here that due to local regulations, a subsidiary is *not* permitted to use the domestic market of *any other* subsidiary.) The relevant question is, where should funds be invested and borrowed?

For investment purposes, the highest available rate of interest is the effective rate for the U.S. dollar in the Euromarket. Therefore, the Swiss subsidiary should invest the $80 million in dollars in the Euromarket. In the case of raising funds, the cheapest source *open* to the Belgian subsidiary is the 6.2 percent in the Sf Euromarket. The subsidiary should therefore raise the $60 million in Swiss francs. These two transactions will result in the most revenues and least costs, respectively.

Several points should be made with respect to the preceding example. First of all, this is a simplified case of the actual workings of the Eurocurrency markets. The example ignores taxes, intersubsidiary investing and borrowing, and periods longer or shorter than a year. Nevertheless, it shows how the existence of many currencies can provide both challenges and opportunities for MNCs. Next, the focus has been solely on accounting values; of greater importance would be the impact of these actions on market value. Finally, it is important to note the following details about the figures presented. The forecast percentage change (appreciation or depreciation) data are regarded as those normally supplied by the MNC's international financial managers. The management may have a *range of forecasts*, from the most likely to the least likely. In addition, the company's management is likely to take a specific position in terms of its response to any remaining foreign exchange exposures. If any action is to be taken, certain amounts of one or more currencies will be borrowed and then invested in other currencies. In doing so, the firm hopes to realize potential gains to offset potential losses associated with the exposures.

SUMMARY

1   **Describe the key features of the major sources of spontaneous short-term financing.**   Spontaneous sources of short-term financing include accounts payable, which are the primary source of short-term funds, and accruals. Accounts payable result from credit purchases of merchandise, and accruals result primarily from wage and tax obligations. The key features of these forms of financing are summarized in part I of Table 10.3.

2   **Analyze credit terms and decide, when the alternative is to borrow funds, whether to take or forgo cash discounts and whether to stretch accounts payable.**   Credit terms may differ with respect to the credit period, cash discount, cash discount period, and beginning of the credit period. The cost of forgoing cash discounts is a factor in deciding whether to take or forgo a cash discount. Cash discounts should be forgone only when a firm in need of short-term funds must pay an interest rate on borrowing that is greater than the cost of forgoing the cash discount. Stretching accounts payable can lower the cost of forgoing a cash discount, thereby increasing the attractiveness of forgoing the discount.

3   **Discuss the interest rates, basic forms, and key features of unsecured bank sources of short-term loans, and define commercial paper and explain its role in short-term financing.**   Banks are the major source of unsecured short-term loans to businesses. The interest rate on these loans is tied to the prime rate of interest by a risk premium and may be fixed or may float. It should be evaluated using the effective interest rate. This rate is calculated differently depending upon whether interest is paid when the loan matures or in advance. Bank loans may take the form of a single-payment note, a line of credit, or a revolving credit agreement. Commercial paper, IOUs issued by firms

Table 10.3   Summary of Key Features of Common Sources of Short-Term Financing

Type of short-term financing	Source	Cost or conditions	Characteristics
I. Spontaneous sources			
Accounts payable	Suppliers of merchandise	No stated cost except when a cash discount is offered for early payment.	Credit extended on open account for 0 to 120 days. The largest source of short-term financing.
Accruals	Employees and government	Free.	Result from the fact that wages (to employees) and taxes (to government) are paid at discrete points in time after the service has been rendered. Hard to manipulate this source of financing.
II. Unsecured bank sources			
Single-payment notes	Commercial banks	Prime plus 0–4% risk premium—fixed or floating rate.	A single-payment loan used to meet a funds shortage expected to last only a short period of time.
Lines of credit	Commercial banks	Prime plus 0–4% risk premium—fixed or floating rate. Often must maintain 10–20% compensating balance and clean up the line.	A prearranged borrowing limit under which funds, if available, will be lent to allow the borrower to meet seasonal needs.
Revolving credit agreements	Commercial banks	Prime plus 0–4% risk premium—fixed or floating rate. Often must maintain 10–20% compensating balance and pay a commitment fee of approximately .5% of the average unused balance.	A line of credit agreement under which the availability of funds is guaranteed. Often for a period greater than one year.
III. Commercial paper	Other businesses, banks, life insurance companies, pension funds, and money market mutual funds	Generally 1–2% below the prime rate of interest.	An unsecured short-term promissory note issued by the most financially sound firms. May be placed directly or sold through commercial paper dealers.

Type of short-term financing	Source	Cost or conditions	Characteristics
IV. Secured sources			
Accounts receivable collateral			
Pledging	Commercial banks and commercial finance companies	2–5% above prime plus up to 3% in fees. Advance 50–90% of collateral value.	Selected accounts receivable are used as collateral. The borrower is trusted to remit to the lender upon collection of pledged accounts. Done on a nonnotification basis.
Factoring	Factors, commercial banks, and commercial finance companies	1–3% discount from face value of factored accounts. Interest levied on advances of 2–4% above prime. Interest earned on surplus balances left with factor of about .5% per month.	Selected accounts are sold—generally without recourse—at a discount. All credit risks go with the accounts. Factor will loan against uncollected accounts that are not yet due. Factor will also pay interest on surplus balances. Typically done on a notification basis.
Inventory collateral			
Floating liens	Commercial banks and commercial finance companies	3–5% above prime. Advance less than 50% of collateral value.	A loan against inventory in general. Made when firm has stable inventory of a variety of inexpensive items.
Trust receipts	Manufacturers' captive financing subsidiaries, commercial banks, and commercial finance companies	2% or more above prime. Advance 80–100% of cost of collateral.	Loan against relatively expensive automotive, consumer-durable, and industrial equipment that can be identified by serial number. Collateral remains in possession of borrower, who is trusted to remit proceeds to lender upon its sale.
Warehouse receipts	Commercial banks and commercial finance companies	3–5% above prime plus a 1–3% warehouse fee. Advance 75–90% of collateral value.	Inventory used as collateral is placed under control of the lender by putting it in a terminal warehouse or a field warehouse. A third party—a warehousing firm—guards the inventory for the lender. Inventory is released only upon written approval of the lender.

with a high credit standing, is directly placed with investors by the issuer or is sold by commercial paper dealers. The key features of the various forms of bank loans as well as commercial paper are summarized in parts II and III, respectively, of Table 10.3.

4   **Describe the characteristics, acceptable collateral, and terms of secured short-term loans, and identify the key institutions extending these loans.** Secured short-term loans are those for which the lender requires collateral—typically, current assets such as accounts receivable or inventory. Only a certain percentage of the book value of acceptable collateral is advanced by the lender. These loans are more expensive than unsecured loans; the presence of collateral does not lower the risk of default, and increased administrative costs result. Both commercial banks and commercial finance companies make secured short-term loans.

5   **Explain how accounts receivable and inventory can be used as collateral to secure short-term loans.** Accounts receivable is generally the most desirable form of short-term loan collateral. Both pledging, which involves the use of accounts receivable as loan collateral, and factoring, which involves the outright sale of accounts receivable at a discount, involve the use of accounts receivable to obtain needed short-term funds. Inventory can be used as short-term loan collateral under a floating lien, a trust receipt arrangement, or a warehouse receipt loan. The key features of these various forms of secured short-term loans are summarized in part IV of Table 10.3.

 6   **Discuss how the Eurocurrency market can be used by multinational companies to take advantage of short-term borrowing and investing (lending) opportunities.** Eurocurrency markets allow multinationals to take advantage of unregulated financial markets to invest (lend) and raise (borrow) short-term funds in a variety of currencies and to protect themselves against foreign exchange risk exposures. The effective rates of interest, which take into account each currency's forecast percentage change relative to the MNC parent's currency, are the main items considered by an MNC when making investment and borrowing decisions. The MNC invests in the currency with the highest effective rate and borrows in the currency with the lowest effective rate.

QUESTIONS

10—1   What are the two key sources of spontaneous short-term financing for a firm? Why are these sources considered spontaneous, and how are they related to the firm's sales? Do they normally have a stated cost?

10—2   Is there a cost associated with taking a cash discount? Is there any cost associated with forgoing a cash discount? How is the decision to take a cash discount affected by the firm's cost of borrowing short-term funds?

10—3   What are *accruals*? What items are most commonly accrued by the firm? How attractive are accruals as a source of financing to the firm?

10—4   What is the primary source of *unsecured* short-term loans to business? When are loans considered short-term self-liquidating loans?

10—5   What is the *prime rate of interest*? How is it relevant to the cost of short-term bank borrowing? What is a *floating-rate loan*? How does the effective interest rate differ between a loan requiring interest payments at *maturity* and another similar loan requiring interest *in advance*?

10—6   What are the basic terms and characteristics of a single-payment note?

10—7   What is a *line of credit?* Describe each of the following features often included in these agreements.
          a. Operating change restrictions
          b. Compensating balance
          c. Annual cleanup

10—8   What is meant by a *revolving credit agreement?* How does this arrangement differ from the line of credit agreement? What is a *commitment fee?*

10—9   How is commercial paper used to raise short-term funds? Who can issue commercial paper? Who buys commercial paper? How is it sold?

10—10   What are the key differences between unsecured and secured forms of short-term borrowing? In what circumstances do firms borrow short-term money on a secured basis?

10—11   In general, what kind of interest rates and fees are levied on secured short-term loans? Why are these rates generally *higher* than the rates on unsecured short-term loans?

10—12   Compare, contrast, and describe the basic features of the following methods of using *accounts receivable* to obtain short-term financing. Be sure to mention the institutions offering each of them.
          a. Pledging accounts receivable
          b. Factoring accounts receivable

10—13   Describe the basic features and compare each of the following methods of using *inventory* as short-term loan collateral.
          a. Floating lien
          b. Trust receipt loan
          c. Warehouse receipt loan

10—14   What is the *Eurocurrency market?* What are the main factors determining exchange rates in that market? Define and differentiate between the *nominal interest rate* and *effective interest rate* in this market.

PROBLEMS

10—1   **(Payment Dates)** Determine when a firm must make payment for purchases made and invoices dated on November 25 under each of the following credit terms.
          a. net 30   **c.** net 45 date of invoice
          b. net 30 EOM   **d.** net 60 EOM

10—2   **(Cost of Forgoing Cash Discounts)** Determine the cost of forgoing cash discounts under each of the following terms of sale.
          a. 2/10 net 30   **e.** 1/10 net 60
          b. 1/10 net 30   **f.** 3/10 net 30
          c. 2/10 net 45   **g.** 4/10 net 180
          d. 3/10 net 45

10—3   **(Cash Discount versus Loan)** Ann Daniels works in the accounts payable department of Penrod Industries. She has attempted to convince her boss to take the discount on the 3/10 net 45 credit terms most suppliers offer, but her boss argues that forgoing the 3 percent discount is less costly than a short-term loan at 14 percent. Prove that either Ann or her boss is incorrect.

10—4   **(Cash Discount Decisions)** Lenly Manufacturing has four possible suppliers, each offering different credit terms. Except for the differences in credit terms, their products and services are virtually identical. The credit terms offered by each supplier are as follows:

Supplier	Credit terms
Q	1/10 net 30 EOM
R	2/20 net 80 EOM
S	1/20 net 60 EOM
T	3/10 net 55 EOM

a. Calculate the *approximate* cost of forgoing the cash discount from each supplier.

b. If the firm needs short-term funds, which are currently available from its bank at 16 percent, and if each of the suppliers is viewed *separately*, which, if any, of the suppliers' cash discounts should the firm forgo? Explain why.

c. The firm could stretch its accounts payable (net period only) by 30 days from supplier T. What impact, if any, would this strategy have on your answer in **b** relative to this supplier?

10—5   **(Changing Payment Cycle)**   Upon accepting the position of chief executive officer and chairman of Reeves Cash Register, David Stanley changed the firm's weekly payday from Monday afternoon to the following Friday afternoon. The firm's weekly payroll was $10 million, and the cost of short-term funds was 13 percent. If the effect of this change was to delay check clearing by one week, what *annual* savings, if any, were realized?

10—6   **(Cost of Bank Loan)**   Quick Enterprises has obtained a $10,000, 90-day bank loan at an annual interest rate of 15 percent, payable at maturity. (*Note:* Assume a 360-day year.)

a. How much interest (in dollars) will the firm pay on the 90-day loan?

b. Find the effective cost of the loan for the 90 days.

10—7   **(Effective Interest Rate)**   A financial institution made a $10,000, one-year discount loan at 10 percent interest requiring a compensating balance equal to 20 percent of the face value of the loan. Determine the effective annual interest rate associated with this loan.

10—8   **(Compensating Balances and Effective Interest Rates)**   LH Industries has a line of credit at First Bank that requires it to pay 11 percent interest on its borrowing and maintain a compensating balance equal to 15 percent of the amount borrowed. The firm has borrowed $800,000 during the year under the agreement. Calculate the effective interest rate on the firm's borrowing in each of the following circumstances.

a. The firm normally maintains no deposit balances at First Bank.

b. The firm normally maintains $70,000 in deposit balances at First Bank.

c. The firm normally maintains $150,000 in deposit balances at First Bank.

10—9   **(Cost of Commercial Paper)**   Commercial paper is usually sold at a discount. PULP has just sold an issue of 90-day commercial paper with a face value of $1 million. The firm has received $978,000.

a. What effective *annual* interest rate will the firm pay for financing with commercial paper?

b. If a brokerage fee of $9,612 was paid from the initial proceeds to an investment banker for selling the issue, what effective annual interest rate will the firm pay?

10—10   **(Accounts Receivable as Collateral)**   Vosburgh Plate and Glass wishes to borrow $80,000 from the Vosburgh National Bank using its accounts receivable to secure the loan. The bank's policy is to accept as collateral any accounts that are normally paid within 30 days of the end of the credit period so long as the average age of the account is not greater than the customer's average payment period. Vosburgh Plate's accounts receivable, their average ages, and the average payment period for each customer are given in the following table. The company extends terms of net 30 days.

a. Calculate the dollar amount of acceptable accounts receivable collateral held by Vosburgh Plate and Glass.

b. The bank reduces collateral by 10 percent for returns and allowances. What is the level of acceptable collateral under this condition?

c. The bank will advance 75 percent against the firm's acceptable collateral (after adjusting for returns and allowances). What amount can Vosburgh Plate and Glass borrow against these accounts?

Customer	Account receivable	Average age of account	Average payment period of customer
A	$20,000	20 days	40 days
B	6,000	40	35
C	22,000	62	50
D	11,000	68	65
E	2,000	14	30
F	12,000	38	50
G	27,000	55	60
H	19,000	20	35

10—11   **(Factoring)**   Freedom Finance factors the accounts of the Mooring Company. All eight factored accounts are listed, with the amount factored, the date due, and the status as of May 30. Indicate the amounts Freedom should have remitted to Mooring as of May 30 and the dates of those remittances. Assume that the factor's commission of 2 percent is deducted as part of determining the amount of the remittance.

Account	Amount	Date due	Status on May 30
A	$200,000	May 30	Collected May 15
B	90,000	May 30	Uncollected
C	110,000	May 30	Uncollected
D	85,000	June 15	Collected May 30
E	120,000	May 30	Collected May 27
F	180,000	June 15	Collected May 30
G	90,000	May 15	Uncollected
H	30,000	June 30	Collected May 30

10—12   **(Inventory Financing)**   Lake Turbine Company faces a liquidity crisis—it needs a loan of $100,000 for 30 days. Having no source of additional unsecured borrowing, the firm must find a secured short-term lender. The firm's accounts receivable are quite low, but its inventory is considered liquid and reasonably good collateral. The book value of the inventory is $300,000, of which $120,000 is finished goods.

(1) Center City Bank will make a $100,000 trust receipt loan against the finished goods inventory. The annual interest rate on the loan is 12 percent on the outstanding loan balance plus a .25 percent administration fee levied against the $100,000 initial loan amount. Because it will be liquidated as inventory is sold, the average amount owed over the month is expected to be $75,000.

(2) First Local Bank is willing to lend $100,000 against a floating lien on the book value of inventory for the 30-day period at an annual interest rate of 13 percent.

(3) North Mall Bank and Trust will loan $100,000 against a warehouse receipt on the finished goods inventory and charge 15 percent annual interest on the outstanding loan balance. A .5 percent warehousing fee will be levied against the average amount borrowed. Because the loan will be liquidated as inventory is sold, the average loan balance is expected to be $60,000.

a. Calculate the dollar cost of each of the proposed plans for obtaining an initial loan amount of $100,000.

b. Which plan do you recommend? Why?

c. If the firm had made a purchase of $100,000 for which it had been given terms of 2/10 net 30, would it increase the firm's profitability to forgo the discount and not borrow as recommended in **b?** Why or why not?

10—13   **(Euromarket Investment and Fund Raising)** A U.S.-based multinational company has two subsidiaries, in Germany (local currency, Deutsche marks, DM) and in Switzerland (local currency, Swiss francs, Sf). Forecasts of business operations indicate the following short-term financing position for each subsidiary (in equivalent U.S. dollars):

Germany: $80 million excess cash to be invested (lent)

Switzerland: $60 million funds to be raised (borrowed)

The management gathered the following data:

| | | Currency | |
Item	US$	DM	Sf
Spot exchange rates		DM 1.69/US$	Sf 1.44/US$
Forecast % change		+3.5%	+2.5%
Interest rates			
Nominal			
Euromarket	8.8%	5.4%	4.2%
Domestic	7.7	4.6	3.2
Effective			
Euromarket			
Domestic			

Determine the effective rates of interest for all three currencies in both the Euromarket and the domestic market; then indicate where the funds should be invested and raised. (*Note:* Assume that due to local regulations, a subsidiary is *not* permitted to use the domestic market of *any other* subsidiary.)

CASE

Analyzing Baldwin Can's Unsecured Short-Term Borrowing Alternatives

Otis Baker, manager of banking relationships at Baldwin Can, wishes to establish a prearranged unsecured short-term borrowing arrangement with the firm's local bank. The bank has offered either a line of credit or a revolving credit agreement. The bank's terms for a line of credit are an interest rate of 3.30 percent above the prime rate, and the borrowing must be reduced to zero for a 30-day period during the year. On an equivalent revolving credit agreement, the interest rate would be 2.80 percent above prime with a commitment fee of .50 percent on the average unused balance. Under both loans, a compensating balance equal to 20 percent of the amount borrowed would be required. The prime rate is currently 8 percent. Both the line of credit and the revolving credit agreement would have borrowing limits of $1,000,000. Otis expects Baldwin on average to borrow $500,000 during the year regardless of which loan agreement it chooses.

Required

    a. Find the effective annual rate of interest under the line of credit.

    b. Find the effective annual rate of interest under the revolving credit agreement. (*Hint:* Compute the ratio of the dollars the firm will pay in interest and commitment fees to the dollars the firm will effectively have use of.)

    c. If the firm does expect to borrow an average of half of the amount available, which arrangement would you recommend to Baldwin? Explain why.

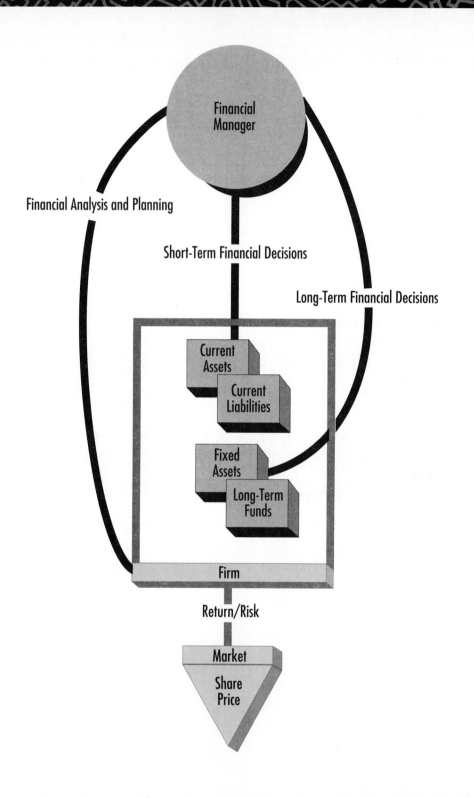

BASIC LONG-TERM FINANCIAL CONCEPTS

CHAPTER 11

TIME VALUE OF MONEY

After studying this chapter, you should be able to:

1 Understand the concept of future value, its calculation for a single amount, and the use of future-value interest tables and business calculators.

2 Calculate the future value of a single amount when interest is compounded more frequently than annually, specifically, semiannually or quarterly.

3 Determine the future value of an annuity using either a future-value interest table for an annuity or a business calculator.

4 Discuss the concept of present value, its calculation for a single amount, the use of present-value interest tables and business calculators, and the relationship of present to future value.

5 Find the present value of a mixed stream of cash flows and an annuity, using present-value interest tables for either a single amount or an annuity, or a business calculator.

6 Describe the procedures involved in (1) determining deposits to accumulate a future sum, (2) loan amortization, (3) finding interest or growth rates, and (4) evaluating perpetuities.

Switzerland: The Land of Expensive Watches, Secret Bank Accounts, and Life Insurance

" " Is Swiss life insurance a better investment than a domestic stock portfolio? That depends . . . . ""

When you think about Switzerland, what export products come to mind? Swiss watches? Perhaps. Swiss bank accounts? Another good guess. Swiss life insurance? Probably not. But American investors are buying Swiss life insurance these days—for some very unconventional reasons.

A $50,000 premium on a Swiss life insurance policy buys an immediate death benefit of $90,000, which is well below the death benefit promised by American life insurers for the same initial premium. The Swiss policy, however, allows the cash value of your investment to grow with reinvested earnings and dividends, and this growth is not taxed by the Swiss government. A small portion of the initial premium is used to cover the policy's basic death benefit, while the balance is invested in a cash-value account that guarantees a minimum 3 percent annual rate of return.

This may sound like a paltry sum, but the story gets more interesting. The policy's return is enhanced by the tax-free reinvestment of dividend income, bringing the annual rate of return up to about 6.5 percent. In addition, the rising value of the Swiss franc relative to the U.S. dollar means that when American investors cash in their life insurance and convert the proceeds to dollars, the francs they receive at the termination of the policy buy more dollars than they did when the policy was first issued.

So how much can you actually earn on your investment? A policy purchased for $210,000 would grow to roughly $670,000 in 10 years, given the tax-free reinvestment of interest and dividends and a 15 percent rate of annual currency appreciation by the Swiss franc. Compounded annually, this represents a 12.3 percent annual rate of return before U.S. taxes. Not bad—especially when you consider that $210,000 invested 10 years ago in a portfolio of stocks resembling the Dow Jones Industrials would be worth only $552,000 today, providing a before-tax rate of return equal to about 10.2 percent.

Is a Swiss life insurance policy a better investment today than a domestic stock portfolio? That depends on your attitude toward risk, your tax rate, and whether you believe the Swiss franc will continue to gain value against the U.S. dollar. But one thing is certain: in order to evaluate different investment alternatives, you need to know how money grows in value through time.

magine that at age 25 you begin making annual cash deposits of $2,000 into a savings account that pays 5 percent annual interest. At the end of 40 years, at age 65, you would have made deposits totaling $80,000 (40 years × $2,000 per year). Assuming you have made no withdrawals, what do you think your account balance would be then? $100,000? $150,000? $200,000? No, your $80,000 would have grown to $242,000! Why? Because the time value of money allowed the deposits to earn interest that was compounded over the 40 years. Because opportunities to earn interest on funds are readily available, the time value of money affects everyone—individuals, businesses, and government.

Financial managers use time-value concepts primarily when making decisions whose costs and benefits occur over a period of future years. The key concepts of *time value* are *future value* and *present value*. Future-value techniques are used to determine the future worth of current investments. Present-value techniques are used to find the current worth of future benefits expected from a given action. Time-value methods are used to calculate the deposits required to accumulate a future sum, to amortize loans by calculating loan payment schedules, to determine interest or growth rates of money streams, and to evaluate perpetuities. In addition, time-value techniques are used to find the internal rate of return—an important concept discussed in Chapter 15.[1]

FUTURE VALUE OF A SINGLE AMOUNT

future value The value of a present amount at a future date, found by applying compound interest over a specified period of time.

The **future value** of a present amount is found by applying compound interest over a specified period of time. Savings institutions advertise compound interest returns at a rate of x percent or x percent compounded annually, semiannually, quarterly, monthly, weekly, daily, or even continuously. The principles of future value are quite simple, regardless of the period of time involved.

----

[1]Many of the computations introduced in this chapter and in subsequent ones can be streamlined using a hand-held business/financial calculator or a personal computer. In addition to describing the use of the financial tables included in this text, this chapter describes the calculator keystrokes for directly calculating table factors as well as for making other financial computations. For convenience, use of one of the least expensive ($15 to $20 at a discount store) and most popular calculators—the Texas Instruments BA-35—is assumed. Keystrokes on other business/financial calculators are similar and are generally clearly explained in the reference guide that accompanies the calculator.

You are strongly urged to use a calculator or personal computer to streamline routine financial calculations *once the basic underlying concepts are understood*. Remember, an ability to solve problems with the aid of a calculator does not necessarily reflect a conceptual understanding of the material—which is the objective of this text. It is therefore important that you make sure you *understand* the underlying concepts before relying on the calculator to streamline required computations. Clearly, with a little practice, both the speed and accuracy of financial computations using a calculator or personal computer can be greatly enhanced.

The Concept of Future Value

We speak of **compounded interest** when we wish to indicate that the amount earned on a given deposit has become part of the principal at the end of a specified period. The term **principal** refers to the amount of money on which the interest is paid. Annual compounding is the most common type. The concept of future value with annual compounding can be illustrated by a simple example.

compounded interest Interest earned on a given deposit that has become part of the principal at the end of a specified period.

principal The amount of money on which interest is paid.

EXAMPLE   If Rich Saver placed $100 in a savings account paying 8 percent interest compounded annually, at the end of one year he will have $108 in the account. This $108 represents the initial principal of $100 plus 8 percent ($8) in interest. The future value at the end of the first year is calculated using Equation 11.1:

Future value at end of year 1 = $100 × (1 + .08) = $108   **Equation 11.1**

If Rich were to leave this money in the account for another year, he would be paid interest at the rate of 8 percent on the new principal of $108. At the end of this second year, there would be $116.64 in the account. This amount would represent the principal at the beginning of year 2 ($108) plus 8 percent of the $108 ($8.64) in interest. The future value at the end of the second year is calculated using Equation 11.2:

Future value at end of year 2 = $108 × (1 + .08) = $116.64   **Equation 11.2**

Substituting the expression between the equal signs in Equation 11.1 for the $108 figure in Equation 11.2 gives us Equation 11.3.

Future value at end of year 2 = $100 × (1 + .08) × (1 + .08)   **Equation 11.3**

$$= \$100 \times (1.08)^2$$

$$= \$116.64$$

The Calculation of Future Value

The basic relationship in Equation 11.3 can be generalized to find the future value after any number of periods. Let

FV_n = the future value at the end of period n

PV = the initial principal, or present value

k = the annual rate of interest paid
   (*Note:* On business calculators i is typically used to represent this rate.)

n = the number of periods—typically years—the money is left on deposit

S M A L L   B U S I N E S S

Small Business Lending in Latin America

While financial managers within large domestic corporations face a variety of challenges, business operators in less-developed Latin American countries deal with substantial problems of their own. In order to create new jobs and generate sales revenue, small foreign businesses must raise funds to invest in their operations. Unfortunately, commercial banks and other providers of credit are difficult to find. Many small businesses lack the credit history and asset base that traditional lenders like to see before they extend credit.

The time value of money is being applied in creative ways to help solve this problem. Accion International, a not-for-profit organization that lends money to small Latin American businesses from its headquarters in Cambridge, Massachusetts, introduced its Bridge Fund to raise funds for international small business operators. Investors deposit $10,000 in an 18-month certificate of deposit issued by Accion, and receive a 5 percent rate of return. Accion then lends money from the Bridge Fund to small businesses at higher interest rates and uses its net return to cover overhead expenses and allow the Fund to grow over time.

At present, the $2 million Bridge Fund has supported 40,000 different loans to tailors, fruit merchants, mechanics, and other small businesses. Moreover, the default experience of the Fund is only 2 percent annually. Even without new investment, if the Fund earns a modest 4 percent net return over the next 10 years, it will grow to almost $3 million. That growth will enable Accion to fund another 4,400 small loans. How can so little money help so many foreign entrepreneurs? In 1990, Accion's average business loan was only $227 to each of the Latin American companies it supported.

Source: Mark Katzman, "Community service: Money talks," *Inc.*, November 1990, p. 144.

Using this notation, a general equation for the future value at the end of period n can be formulated:

Equation 11.4
General formula for future value

$$FV_n = PV \times (1 + k)^n$$

Equation 11.4 can be used to find the future value, FV_n, in an account paying k percent interest compounded annually for n periods if PV dollars were deposited initially. A simple example will illustrate.

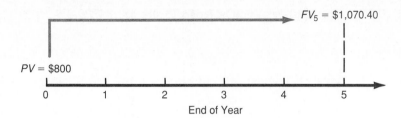

Figure 11.1   Time Line for Future Value of a Single Amount
($800 Initial Principal, Earning 6 Percent Annual Interest,
at End of Five Years)

An initial principal, *PV*, of $800 deposited into an account paying 6 percent annual interest, *k*, will have a future value at the end of 5 years, FV_5, of $1,070.40.

EXAMPLE   Jane Frugal has placed $800 in a savings account paying 6 percent interest compounded annually. She wishes to determine how much money will be in the account at the end of five years. Substituting *PV* = $800, *k* = .06, and *n* = 5 into Equation 11.4 gives the amount at the end of year 5.

$$FV_5 = \$800 \times (1 + .06)^5 = \$800 \times (1.338) = \$1,070.40$$

Jane will have $1,070.40 in the account at the end of the fifth year. This analysis can be depicted diagrammatically on a time line as shown in Figure 11.1.

Future-Value Interest Tables

Solving the equation in the preceding example is quite time-consuming, since one must raise 1.06 to the fifth power. Using future-value interest tables simplifies the calculations. A table for the amount generated by the payment of compound interest on an initial principal of $1 is given as Appendix Table C-1 (at the back of the book). The table provides values for $(1 + k)^n$ in Equation 11.4. This portion of Equation 11.4 is called the **future-value interest factor.** This factor is the multiplier used to calculate at a specified interest rate the future value of a present amount as of a given time. The future-value interest factor for an initial principal of $1 compounded at *k* percent for *n* periods is referred to as $FVIF_{k,n}$:

future-value interest factor The multiplier used to calculate at a specified interest rate the future value of a present amount as of a given time.

$$\text{Future-value interest factor} = FVIF_{k,n} = (1 + k)^n$$

By accessing the table with respect to the annual interest rate, *k*, and the appropriate periods, *n*, the factor relevant to a particular problem can be found.[2]

Equation 11.5
Formula for the future-value interest factor for a single amount

---

[2]Although we commonly deal with years rather than periods, financial tables are frequently presented in terms of periods to provide maximum flexibility.

Table 11.1   The Future-Value Interest Factors for One Dollar, $FVIF_{k,n}$

Period	5%	6%	7%	8%	9%	10%
1	1.050	1.060	1.070	1.080	1.090	1.100
2	1.102	1.124	1.145	1.166	1.188	1.210
3	1.158	1.191	1.225	1.260	1.295	1.331
4	1.216	1.262	1.311	1.360	1.412	1.464
5	1.276	1.338	1.403	1.469	1.539	1.611
6	1.340	1.419	1.501	1.587	1.677	1.772
7	1.407	1.504	1.606	1.714	1.828	1.949
8	1.477	1.594	1.718	1.851	1.993	2.144
9	1.551	1.689	1.838	1.999	2.172	2.358
10	1.629	1.791	1.967	2.159	2.367	2.594

Note: All table values have been rounded to the nearest thousandth. Thus the calculated values may differ slightly from the table values.

A sample portion of Table C-1 is shown in Table 11.1. Because the factors in Table C-1 give the value for the expression $(1 + k)^n$ for various k and n combinations, by letting $FVIF_{k,n}$ represent the appropriate factor from Table C-1 we can rewrite Equation 11.4 as follows:

Equation 11.6
General formula for the future value of a single amount

$$FV_n = PV \times (FVIF_{k,n})$$

The expression indicates that to find the future value, FV_n, at the end of period n of an initial deposit, we have merely to multiply the initial deposit, PV, by the appropriate future-value interest factor from Table C-1. An example will illustrate the use of this table as well as a hand-held business calculator.

EXAMPLE   Jane Frugal, as noted in the preceding example, has placed $800 in her savings account at 6 percent interest compounded annually. She wishes to find out how much would be in the account at the end of five years.
Table Use   The future-value interest factor for an initial principal of $1 on deposit for five years at 6 percent interest compounded annually, $FVIF_{6\%, 5yrs}$, found in Table C-1 (or Table 11.1), is 1.338. Multiplying the initial principal of $800 by this factor in accordance with Equation 11.6 results in a future value at the end of year 5 of $1,070.40.
Calculator Use   The preprogrammed financial functions in the business calculator can be used to calculate the future value directly.[3] First punch in $800 and depress the "PV"

---

[3]The BA-35 calculator, like many other multi-function business calculators, has two preprogrammed functions—financial and statistical. It is therefore important always to make sure that the finance function keys have been activated prior to making financial calculations. On the BA-35 this is done by pressing the "2nd" key followed by the "N" key. "FIN" will appear in the calculator display to confirm the activation of these functions.

key; next punch in 5 and depress the "N" key; then punch in 6 and depress the "%i" key (which is equivalent to k in our notation); and finally, to calculate the future value, depress the "CPT" key and then the "FV" key. The future value of $1,070.58 should appear on the calculator display.

The calculator is more accurate than the use of factors from Table C-1, which have been rounded to the nearest one-thousandth. Thus, a slight difference—in this case $0.18—will frequently exist between the values found using these alternative methods. Clearly, the improved accuracy and ease of calculation tend to favor the use of the calculator when making financial calculations such as this.

Four important observations should be made about the table for the future value of one dollar:

1 ■■■ The factors in the table are those for determining the future value of one dollar *at the end of the given period.*

2 ■■■ *The future-value interest factor for a single amount is always greater than 1.* Only if the interest rate were 0 would this factor equal 1.

3 ■■■ *As the interest rate increases for any given period, the future-value interest factor also increases.* Thus the higher the interest rate, the greater the future value.

4 ■■■ *For a given interest rate, the future value of a dollar increases with the passage of time.* Thus the longer the period of time, the greater the future value.

The relationship between various interest rates, the number of periods interest is earned, and future-value interest factors is illustrated in Figure 11.2. It clearly shows two relationships: (1) The higher the interest rate, the higher the future-value interest factor is. (2) The longer the period of time, the higher the future-value interest factor is. Note that for an interest rate of 0 percent, the future-value interest factor always equals 1.000, and the future value of funds therefore equals their present value.

Compounding More Frequently than Annually

Interest is often compounded more frequently than once a year. Savings institutions compound interest semiannually, quarterly, monthly, weekly, daily, or even continuously. This section discusses semiannual and quarterly compounding and explains how to use both future-value interest tables and a business calculator in these situations.

Semiannual Compounding

Semiannual compounding of interest involves two compounding periods within the year. Instead of the stated interest rate being paid once a year, one-half of the stated interest rate is paid twice a year.

semiannual compounding
Compounding of interest over two periods within the year.

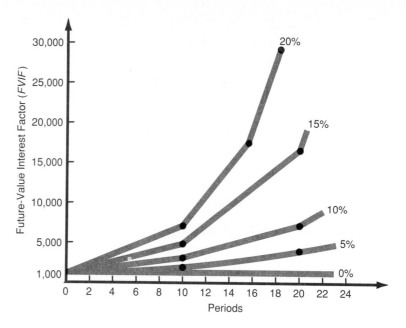

Figure 11.2   Interest Rates, Time Periods, and Future-Value Interest Factors Used to Find the Future Value of One Dollar

The future-value interest factor increases with increases in the interest rate or the period of time funds are left on deposit. At zero percent interest, the future-value interest factor equals 1.000, and for interest rates greater than zero the factor is always greater than 1.000.

EXAMPLE   Rich Saver has decided to invest $100 in a savings account paying 8 percent interest *compounded semiannually*. If he leaves his money in the account for two years, he will be paid 4 percent interest compounded over four periods, each of which is six months long. Table 11.2 shows that at the end of one year, when the 8 percent interest is compounded semiannually, Rich will have $108.16. At the end of two years, he will have $116.99.

Table 11.2   **The Future Value from Investing $100 at 8 Percent Interest Compounded Semiannually over Two Years**

Period	Beginning principal (1)	Future-value interest factor (2)	Future value at end of period [(1) × (2)] (3)
6 months	$100.00	1.04	$104.00
1 year	104.00	1.04	108.16
18 months	108.16	1.04	112.49
2 years	112.49	1.04	116.99

Quarterly Compounding

Quarterly compounding of interest involves four compounding periods within the year. One-fourth of the stated interest rate is paid four times a year.

quarterly compounding Compounding of interest over four periods within the year.

EXAMPLE Rich Saver, after further investigation of his savings opportunities, has found an institution that will pay him 8 percent interest *compounded quarterly*. If he leaves his money in this account for two years, he will be paid 2 percent interest compounded over eight periods, each of which is three months long. Table 11.3 presents the calculations required to determine the amount Rich will have at the end of two years. As the table shows, at the end of one year, when the 8 percent interest is compounded quarterly, Rich will have $108.24. At the end of two years, he will have $117.16.

Table 11.4 presents comparative values for Rich Saver's $100 at the end of years 1 and 2 given annual, semiannual, and quarterly compounding at the 8 percent rate. As the table shows, *the more frequently interest is compounded, the greater the amount of money accumulated.* This is true for any interest rate for any period of time.

Using Table C-1

Table C-1, the table of future-value interest factors for one dollar, can be used to find the future value when interest is compounded m times each year. Instead of indexing the table for k percent and n years, as we do when interest is compounded annually, we index it for $(k \div m)$ percent and $(m \times n)$ periods. The usefulness of the table is usually somewhat limited, since only selected rates for a limited number of periods can be found. The table can commonly be used to calculate the results of semi-

Table 11.3 **The Future Value from Investing $100 at 8 Percent Interest Compounded Quarterly over Two Years**

Period	Beginning principal (1)	Future-value interest factor (2)	Future value at end of period [(1) × (2)] (3)
3 months	$100.00	1.02	$102.00
6 months	102.00	1.02	104.04
9 months	104.04	1.02	106.12
1 year	106.12	1.02	108.24
15 months	108.24	1.02	110.40
18 months	110.40	1.02	112.61
21 months	112.61	1.02	114.86
2 years	114.86	1.02	117.16

Table 11.4   **The Future Value from Investing
$100 at 8 Percent for Years 1 and 2 Given
Various Compounding Periods**

End of year	Compounding period		
	Annual	**Semiannual**	**Quarterly**
1	$108.00	$108.16	$108.24
2	116.64	116.99	117.16

annual ($m = 2$) and quarterly ($m = 4$) compounding. When more frequent compounding is done, the aid of a business calculator or personal computer may be necessary. The following example will clarify the use of the future-value interest factor table as well as a business calculator.

EXAMPLE   In the earlier examples, Rich Saver wished to find the future value of $100 invested at 8 percent compounded both semiannually and quarterly for two years. The number of compounding periods, m, was 2 and 4, respectively, in these cases. The values by which the table for the future value of one dollar is accessed, along with the future-value interest factor in each case, are shown below.

Compounding period	m	Interest rate $(k \div m)$	Periods $(m \times n)$	Future-value interest factor from Table C-1
Semiannual	2	8% ÷ 2 = 4%	2 × 2 = 4	1.170
Quarterly	4	8% ÷ 4 = 2%	4 × 2 = 8	1.172

Table Use   The factor for 4 percent and four periods is used for semiannual compounding, and the factor for 2 percent and eight periods is used for quarterly compounding. Multiplying each of the factors by the initial $100 deposit results in a value of $117.00 (1.170 × $100) for semiannual compounding and a value of $117.20 (1.172 × $100) for quarterly compounding.

Calculator Use   To use the calculator for the semiannual compounding calculation, as noted in the preceding table, the number of periods would be 4 and the interest rate would be 4 percent. First punch in $100 and depress the "PV" key; next punch in 4 and depress the "N" key; then punch in 4 and depress the "%i" key; finally, to calculate the future value, depress the "CPT" key followed by the "FV" key. The future value of $116.99 should appear on the calculator display.

For the quarterly compounding case, the number of periods would be 8 and the interest rate would be 2 percent. First punch in $100 and depress the "PV" key; next punch in 8 and depress the "N" key; then punch in 2 and depress the "%i" key; finally, to calculate the future value, depress the "CPT" key followed by the "FV" key. The future value of $117.17 should appear on the calculator display.

Comparing the values found using the calculator to those based on the use of Table C-1, we see that the calculator values generally agree with those values given in Table 11.4 but are more precise because the table factors have been rounded.

FUTURE VALUE OF AN ANNUITY

An **annuity** is a stream of equal annual cash flows. These cash flows can be *inflows* of returns earned on investments or *outflows* of funds invested in order to earn future returns. The calculations required to find the future value of an annuity on which interest is paid at a specified rate compounded annually can be illustrated by the following example.

annuity A stream of equal annual cash flows.

EXAMPLE Mollie Carr wishes to determine how much money she will have at the end of five years if she deposits $1,000 annually into a savings account paying 7 percent annual interest. The deposits will be made *at the end* of each of the next five years. Table 11.5 presents the calculations required to find the future value of this annuity at the end of year 5. This

Table 11.5   **The Future Value of a $1,000 Five-Year Annuity Compounded at 7 Percent**

End of year	Amount deposited (1)	Number of years compounded (2)	Future-value interest factors from Table C-1 (3)	Future value at end of year [(1) × (3)] (4)
1	$1,000	4	1.311	$1,311
2	1,000	3	1.225	1,225
3	1,000	2	1.145	1,145
4	1,000	1	1.070	1,070
5	1,000	0	1.000	1,000
	Future value of annuity at end of year 5			$5,751

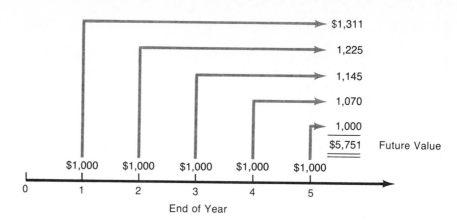

Figure 11.3   Time Line for Future Value of an Annuity
($1,000 End-of-Year Deposit, Earning 7 Percent, at End of 5 Years)
Annual end-of-year deposits, *PMT*, of $1,000 into an account paying 7
percent annual interest, *k*, will have a future value at the end of 5 years,
*FVA*₅, of $5,751.

situation is depicted diagrammatically on a time line in Figure 11.3. As the table and figure show, at the end of year 5 Mollie will have $5,751 in her account. Column 2 of the table indicates that since the deposits are made at the end of the year, the first deposit will earn interest for four years, the second for three years, and so on. The future-value interest factors in column 3 correspond to these interest-earning periods and the 7 percent rate of interest.

Using a Future-Value-of-an-Annuity Table

future-value interest factor for an annuity
The multiplier used to calculate the future value of an annuity at a specified interest rate over a given period of time.

Annuity calculations can be simplified using a **future-value interest factor for an annuity.** This factor is the multiplier used to calculate the future value of an annuity at a specified interest rate over a given period of time. A portion of Appendix Table C-2, which contains future-value interest factors for an annuity, is shown in Table 11.6. The factors included in the table are based on the assumption that every deposit is made at the *end of the period.*[4] The formula for the future-value interest factor for an *n*-year annuity with end-of-year cash flows when interest is compounded annually at *k* percent, $FVIFA_{k,n}$, is[5]

---

[4]The discussions of annuities throughout this text concentrate on the more common form of annuity—the *ordinary annuity,* which is an annuity that occurs at the *end* of each period. An annuity that occurs at the *beginning* of each period is called an *annuity due.* The financial tables for annuities included in this book are prepared for use with ordinary annuities.

[5]This formula merely states that the future-value interest factor for an *n*-year annuity is found by adding the sum of the first $n - 1$ future-value interest factors to 1.000

$$\left(\text{i.e., } FVIFA_{k,n} = 1.000 + \sum_{t=1}^{n-1} FVIF_{k,t}\right).$$

Table 11.6

**The Future-Value Interest Factors
for a One-Dollar Annuity, FVIFA$_{k,n}$**

Period	5%	6%	7%	8%	9%	10%
1	1.000	1.000	1.000	1.000	1.000	1.000
2	2.050	2.060	2.070	2.080	2.090	2.100
3	3.152	3.184	3.215	3.246	3.278	3.310
4	4.310	4.375	4.440	4.506	4.573	4.641
5	5.526	5.637	5.751	5.867	5.985	6.105
6	6.802	6.975	7.153	7.336	7.523	7.716
7	8.142	8.394	8.654	8.923	9.200	9.487
8	9.549	9.897	10.260	10.637	11.028	11.436
9	11.027	11.491	11.978	12.488	13.021	13.579
10	12.578	13.181	13.816	14.487	15.193	15.937

$$FVIFA_{k,n} = \sum_{t=1}^{n} (1 + k)^{t-1}$$

Equation 11.7
Formula for the future-value interest factor for an annuity

Letting FVA_n equal the future value of an n-year annuity, PMT equal the amount to be deposited annually at the end of each year, and $FVIFA_{k,n}$ represent the appropriate *future-value interest factor for an n-year annuity compounded at* k *percent*, the relationship among these variables can be expressed as follows:

$$FVA_n = PMT \times (FVIFA_{k,n})$$

Equation 11.8
General formula for the future value of an annuity

Equation 11.8 along with either Table C-2 or a business calculator can be used to find the future value of an annuity.

EXAMPLE   Mollie Carr, as noted in the preceding example, wishes to find the future value (FVA_n) at the end of five years (n) of an annual *end-of-year deposit* of $1,000 ($PMT$) into an account paying 7 percent annual interest (k) during the next five years.

Table Use The appropriate future-value interest factor for a five-year annuity at 7 percent, $FVIFA_{7\%,\ 5yrs}$, is found in Table C-2 (or Table 11.6) to equal 5.751. Multiplying the $1,000 deposit by this factor in accordance with Equation 11.8 results in a future value for the annuity of $5,751.

Calculator Use Using the calculator, first punch in the $1,000 and depress the "PMT" key; next punch in 5 and depress the "N" key; then punch in 7 and depress the "%i" key; to calculate the future value of this annuity, depress the "CPT" key followed by the "FV" key. Ignoring the minus sign,[6] the future value of the annuity of $5,751 should appear on the calculator display. This is the same value as that obtained using the factor from Table C-2.

 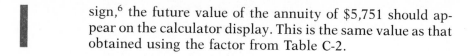

PRESENT VALUE OF A SINGLE AMOUNT

present value The current dollar value of a future amount.

It is often useful to determine the "present value" of a future amount of money. **Present value** is the current dollar value of a future amount—the amount of money that would have to be invested today at a given interest rate over a specified period in order to equal the future amount. Present value, like future value, is based on the belief that a dollar today is worth more than a dollar that will be received at some future date. The actual present value of a dollar depends largely on the investment opportunities of the recipient and the point in time at which the dollar is to be received. This section explores the present value of a single amount.

The Concept of Present Value

discounting cash flows The process of finding present values; the inverse of compounding interest.

The process of finding present values is often referred to as **discounting cash flows.** This process is actually the inverse of compounding interest. It is concerned with answering the question "If I can earn k percent on my money, what is the most I would be willing to pay for an opportunity to receive FV_n dollars n periods from today?" Instead of finding the future value of present dollars invested at a given rate, discounting determines the present value of a future amount, assuming that the decision maker has an opportunity to earn a certain return, k, on the money. This return is variously referred to as the *discount rate, required return, cost of capital,* or *opportunity cost.* These terms will be used interchangeably in this text. The discounting process can be illustrated by a simple example.

EXAMPLE Mr. Cotter has been given an opportunity to receive $300 one year from now. If he can earn 6 percent on his investments in the normal course of events, what is the most he should pay for this opportunity? To answer this question, we must determine how many dollars must be invested at 6 percent today to have $300 one year from now. Letting *PV* equal this unknown amount, and using the same notation as

---

[6]Note that on many calculators, like the BA-35, the calculated future value of an annuity will be preceded by a minus sign. Technically this sign is intended to refer to the fact that this future value (*FVA*) is an outflow or withdrawal from the annuity account, since the amount of the annuity (*PMT*) is treated as an inflow or deposit into the annuity account. For our purposes, the negative sign is not important and therefore should be ignored.

in the compounding discussion, the situation can be expressed as follows:

$$PV \times (1 + .06) = \$300$$

Equation 11.9

Solving Equation 11.9 for PV gives us Equation 11.10:

$$PV = \frac{\$300}{1.06}$$
$$= \$283.02$$

Equation 11.10

which results in a value of $283.02 for PV. In other words, the "present value" of $300 received one year from today, given an opportunity cost of 6 percent, is $283.02. Mr. Cotter should be indifferent to whether he receives $283.02 today or $300.00 one year from now. If he can receive either by paying less than $283.02 today, he should, of course, do so.

A Mathematical Expression for Present Value

The present value of a future amount can be found mathematically by solving Equation 11.4 for PV. In other words, one merely wants to obtain the present value, PV, of some future amount, FV_n, to be received n periods from now, assuming an opportunity cost of k. Solving Equation 11.4 for PV gives us Equation 11.11, which is the general equation for the present value of a future amount.

$$PV = \frac{FV_n}{(1 + k)^n} = FV_n \times \left[\frac{1}{(1 + k)^n} \right]$$

Equation 11.11
General formula for
present value

Note the similarity between this general equation for present value and the equation in the preceding example (Equation 11.10). The use of this equation in finding the present value of a future amount can be illustrated by a simple example.

EXAMPLE Bob Lambert wishes to find the present value of $1,700 that will be received eight years from now. Bob's opportunity cost is 8 percent. Substituting $FV_8 = \$1,700$, $n = 8$, and $k = .08$ into Equation 11.11 yields Equation 11.12.

$$PV = \frac{\$1,700}{(1 + .08)^8}$$

Equation 11.12

To solve Equation 11.12, the term $(1 + .08)$ must be raised to the eighth power. The value resulting from this time-consuming calculation is 1.851. Dividing this value into $1,700 yields a present value for the $1,700 of $918.42. This analysis can be depicted diagrammatically on a time line as shown in Figure 11.4.

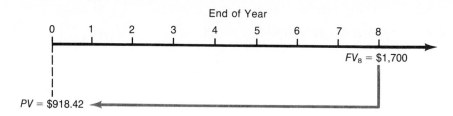

Figure 11.4   Time Line for Present Value of a Single Amount
($1,700 Future Amount, Discounted at 8 Percent, from End of 8 Years)

The present value, PV, of $1,700 to be received at the end of eight years, FV_8, using a discount rate, k, of 8 percent is $918.42.

Present-Value Interest Tables

present-value interest factor The multiplier used to calculate at a specified discount rate the present value of an amount to be received in a future period.

The present-value calculation can be simplified using a **present-value interest factor.** This factor is the multiplier used to calculate at a specified discount rate the present value of an amount to be received in a future period. To further facilitate present-value calculations, tables of present-value interest factors are available. The table for the present-value interest factor, $PVIF_{k,n}$, gives values for the expression $1/(1 + k)^n$ where k is the discount rate and n is the number of periods—typically years—involved.

Equation 11.13
Formula for the present-value interest factor for a single amount

$$\text{Present-value interest factor} = PVIF_{k,n} = \frac{1}{(1 + k)^n}$$

Table C-3 in the Appendix presents present-value interest factors for various discount rates and periods. A portion of Table C-3 is shown in Table 11.7. Since the factors in Table C-3 give the value for the expression $1/(1 + k)^n$ for various k and n combinations, we can, by letting

Table 11.7   **The Present-Value Interest Factors for One Dollar, $PVIF_{k,n}$**

Period	5%	6%	7%	8%	9%	10%
1	.952	.943	.935	.926	.917	.909
2	.907	.890	.873	.857	.842	.826
3	.864	.840	.816	.794	.772	.751
4	.823	.792	.763	.735	.708	.683
5	.784	.747	.713	.681	.650	.621
6	.746	.705	.666	.630	.596	.564
7	.711	.665	.623	.583	.547	.513
8	.677	.627	.582	.540	.502	.467
9	.645	.592	.544	.500	.460	.424
10	.614	.558	.508	.463	.422	.386

PVIF$_{k,n}$ represent the appropriate factor from Table C-3, rewrite Equation 11.11 as follows:

$$PV = FV_n \times (PVIF_{k,n})$$

Equation 11.14
General formula for the present value of a single amount

This expression indicates that to find the present value, *PV*, of an amount to be received in a future period, *n*, we have merely to multiply the future amount, *FV*$_n$, by the appropriate present-value interest factor from Table C-3. An example will illustrate the use of this table as well as a business calculator.

EXAMPLE   Bob Lambert, as noted in the preceding example, wishes to find the present value of $1,700 to be received eight years from now, assuming an 8 percent opportunity cost.
Table Use   The present-value interest factor for 8 percent and 8 years, *PVIF*$_{8\%,8yrs}$, found in Table C-3 (or Table 11.7) is .540. Multiplying the $1,700 future value by this factor in accordance with Equation 11.14 results in a present value of $918.
Calculator Use   Present value can alternately be found using the business calculator's financial functions. First punch in $1,700 and depress the "FV" key; next punch 8 and depress the "N" key; then punch 8 and depress the "%i" key; and finally, to calculate the present value, depress the "CPT" key followed by the "PV" key. The present value, $918.46, should appear on the calculator display.
Note that because of rounding in the calculation in Equation 11.12 and of the factors in Table C-3, the value obtained with the calculator—$918.46—is more accurate, although for purposes of this text these differences are insignificant.

Four additional points with respect to present-value tables are also important:

1 ■■■ The factors in the table are those for determining the present value of one dollar to be *received at the end of the given period.*

2 ■■■ *The present-value interest factor for a single amount is always less than 1.* Only if the opportunity cost were 0 would this factor equal 1.

3 ■■■ *The higher the discount rate for a given period, the smaller the present-value interest factor.* Thus the greater the potential return on an investment, the less an amount to be received in a specified future year is worth today.

4 ■■■ *For a given discount rate, the present value of a dollar decreases with the passage of time.* Thus the longer the period of time, the smaller the present value.

The relationship among various discount rates, time periods, and present-value interest factors is illustrated in Figure 11.5. Everything

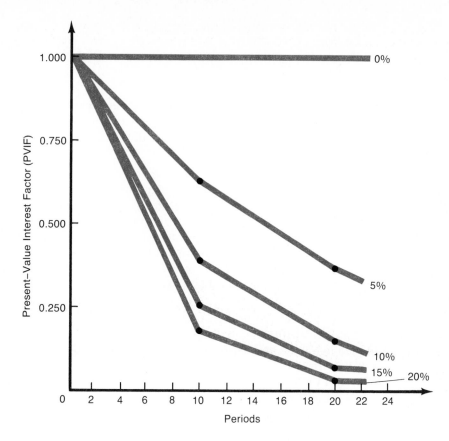

**Figure 11.5   Discount Rates, Time Periods, and Present-Value Interest Factors
Used to Find the Present Value of One Dollar**

The present-value interest factor decreases with increases in the discount
rate or the period of time until the future funds are received. At a zero
percent discount rate the present-value interest factor equals 1.000, and
for discount rates greater than zero the factor is always less than 1.000.

else being equal, the figure clearly shows two relationships: (1) the
higher the discount rate, the lower the present-value interest factor, and
(2) the longer the period of time, the lower the present-value interest
factor. Also note that given a discount rate of 0 percent, the present-
value interest factor always equals 1.000, and the present value of the
funds therefore equals their future value.

Comparing Present Value and Future Value

A few important observations must be made with respect to present
values. One is that the expression for the present-value interest factor
for k percent and n periods, $1/(1 + k)^n$, is the inverse of the future-value
interest factor for k percent and n periods, $(1 + k)^n$. This observation can

F I N A N C E   I N   A C T I O N

The IRS Understands the Time Value of Money, Too

The time value of money represents an important concept in managerial finance. Its significance is not lost on the Internal Revenue Service. Faced with sagging tax revenues and rising government expenditures in 1990, the IRS proposed a modest change in the way that businesses are allowed to deduct recurring expenses like property taxes, state and local income taxes, and insurance premiums.

Before 1991, businesses deducted these expenditures from taxable income as they were incurred, which in many cases was in advance of the date on which they were actually paid. The proposed IRS rule change would require these deductions to be delayed until actual payment occurs or, if deducted early, actual payment must occur within 8½ months of the firm's year-end tax filing date.

It sounds like a minor change. However, it turns out that in the year the rule change takes effect, the change is anything but modest. For a company in the 30 to 40 percent tax bracket, with $1 million in accrued liabilities, the interest income that will be lost on this change in tax regulations amounts to $40,000. If companies are permitted to take tax deductions far in advance of the dates on which payment is actually made, they receive a "time value" tax benefit. The IRS believes this tax benefit is unfair. Don't forget, however, that the $40,000 loss to the corporate taxpayer can represent a $40,000 gain to the IRS, since higher tax payments made by businesses can be invested to earn interest for Uncle Sam.

Source: David Bernstein, "IRS: Businesses pay up now," *CFO Magazine*, November 1990, p. 14.

be confirmed: Divide a present-value interest factor for k percent and n periods, $PVIF_{k,n}$, into 1.0 and compare the resulting value to the future-value interest factor given in Table C-1 for k percent and n periods, $FVIF_{k,n}$. The two values should be equivalent. Because of the relationship between present-value interest factors and future-value interest factors, we can find the present-value interest factors given a table of future-value interest factors, and vice versa. For example, the future-value interest factor from Table C-1 for 10 percent and five periods is 1.611. Dividing this value into 1.0 yields .621, which is the present-value interest factor given in Table C-3 for 10 percent and five periods.

PRESENT VALUE OF CASH FLOW STREAMS

mixed stream A
stream of cash flows that
reflects no particular
pattern.

Quite often in finance there is a need to find the present value of a stream of cash flows to be received in various future periods. Two basic types of cash flow streams are possible: the mixed stream and the annuity. A **mixed stream** of cash flows reflects no particular pattern, whereas, as stated earlier, an *annuity* is a pattern of equal annual cash flows. Since certain shortcuts are possible when finding the present value of an annuity, mixed streams and annuities will be discussed separately.

 ### Present Value of a Mixed Stream

Finding the present value of a mixed stream of cash flows involves two steps. First, determine the present value of each future amount in the manner described in the preceding section. Then add all the individual present values to find the total present value of the stream. An example can be used to illustrate this procedure using Table C-3 or a business calculator.

EXAMPLE   QTD Company, a shoe manufacturer, has been offered an opportunity to receive the following mixed stream of cash flows over the next five years:

Year	Cash flow
1	$400
2	800
3	500
4	400
5	300

If the firm must earn 9 percent, at minimum, on its investments, what is the most it should pay for this opportunity? **Table Use** To solve this problem, we determine the present value of each cash flow discounted at 9 percent for the appropriate number of years. The sum of all these individual values is then calculated to get the present value of the total stream. The present-value interest factors required are obtained from Table C-3. Table 11.8 presents the calculations needed to find the present value of the cash flow stream, which turns out to be $1,904.60.
Calculator Use A calculator could be used to find the present value of each individual cash flow, using the procedure demonstrated earlier; then the present values could be summed to get the present value of the stream of cash flows.

Table 11.8   **The Present Value of a Mixed Stream of Cash Flows**

Year (n)	Cash flow (1)	$PVIF^a_{9\%,n}$ (2)	Present value [(1) × (2)] (3)
1	$400	.917	$ 366.80
2	800	.842	673.60
3	500	.772	386.00
4	400	.708	283.20
5	300	.650	195.00
Present value of mixed stream			$1,904.60

[a]Present-value interest factors at 9 percent are from Table C-3.

Most more-expensive financial calculators have a function that allows you to punch in all cash flows, specify the discount rate, and then directly calculate the present value of the entire cash flow stream. The inexpensive BA-35 business calculator used here does not have that function. Because calculators provide more precise solutions than those based upon the use of rounded table factors, using a calculator to find the present value of QTD Company's cash flow stream will result in a value close but not precisely equal to the $1,904.60 value calculated above.

QTD should not pay more than $1,904.60 for the opportunity to receive these cash flows, since paying $1,904.60 would provide exactly a 9 percent return. This situation is depicted diagrammatically on a time line in Figure 11.6.

Present Value of an Annuity

The present value of an annuity can be found in a manner similar to that used for a mixed stream, but a shortcut is possible.

EXAMPLE   Labco Company, a small producer of plastic toys, is attempting to determine the most it should pay to purchase a particular annuity. The firm requires a minimum return of 8 percent on all investments, and the annuity consists of cash flows of $700 per year for five years. Table 11.9 shows the long way of finding the present value of the annuity, which is the same as the method used for mixed streams. This procedure yields a present value of $2,795.10, which can be interpreted in the same manner as for the mixed cash flow stream in the preceding example. Similarly, this situation is depicted graphically on a time line in Figure 11.7 on page 355.

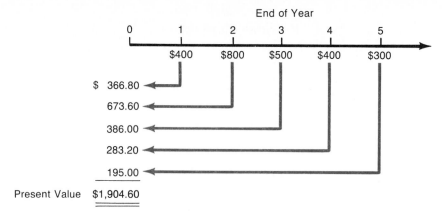

Figure 11.6   **Time Line for Present Value of a Mixed Stream (End-of-Year Cash Flows, Discounted at 9 Percent, over Corresponding Number of Years)**

The $1,904.60 present value of the mixed stream of cash flows occurring at the end of each of the next five years is calculated by finding the sum of the present values of the individual cash flows using the 9 percent discount rate.

Using a Present-Value-of-an-Annuity Table

present-value interest factor for an annuity   The multiplier used to calculate the present value of an annuity at a specified discount rate over a given period of time.

Annuity calculations can be simplified by using a **present-value interest factor for an annuity.** This factor is the multiplier used to calculate the present value of an annuity at a specified discount rate over a given period of time. A portion of Appendix Table C-4, which contains present-value interest factors for an annuity, is shown in Table 11.10. The interest factors in Table C-4 actually represent the sum of the first n present-

Table 11.9   **The Long Method for Finding the Present Value of an Annuity**

Year (n)	Cash flow (1)	$PVIF^a_{8\%,n}$ (2)	Present value [(1) × (2)] (3)
1	$700	.926	$ 648.20
2	700	.857	599.90
3	700	.794	555.80
4	700	.735	514.50
5	700	.681	476.70
	Present value of annuity		$2,795.10

[a]Present-value interest factors at 8 percent are from Table C-3.

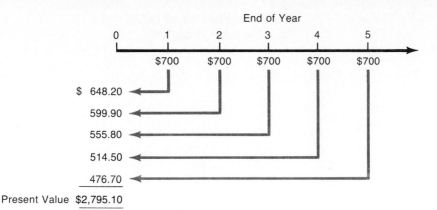

Figure 11.7   **Time Line for Present Value of an Annuity**
                    ($700 End-of-Year Cash Flows, Discounted at 8 Percent, over 5 Years)

The $2,795.10 present value of the annuity cash flow of $700 occurring at
the end of each of the next five years is calculated by finding the sum of
the present values of the individual cash flows using the 8 percent
discount rate.

value interest factors in Table C-3 for a given discount rate. The formula
for the present-value interest factor for an *n*-year annuity with end-of-
year cash flows that are discounted at *k* percent, $PVIFA_{k,n}$, is[7]

$$PVIFA_{k,n} = \sum_{t=1}^{n} \frac{1}{(1 + k)^t}$$

Equation 11.15
Formula for the
present-value interest
factor for an annuity

Letting PVA_n equal the present value of an *n*-year annuity, *PMT*
equal the amount to be received annually at the end of each year, and
$PVIFA_{k,n}$ represent the appropriate value for the *present-value interest
factor for a one-dollar annuity discounted at* k *percent for* n *years*, the
relationship among these variables can be expressed as follows:

$$PVA_n = PMT \times (PVIFA_{k,n})$$

Equation 11.16
General formula for the
present value of an
annuity

The application of this equation using Table C-4 or a business calculator
can be demonstrated by an example.

EXAMPLE   Labco Company, as noted in the preceding example,
wishes to find the present value of a five-year annuity of
$700 assuming an 8 percent opportunity cost.
Table Use The present-value interest factor for an annuity
at 8 percent for five years, $PVIFA_{8\%,5yrs}$, found in Table C-4

---

[7]This formula merely states that the present-value interest factor for an *n*-year annuity
is found by summing the first *n* present-value interest factors at the given rate

$$\left(\text{i.e., } PVIFA_{k,n} = \sum_{t=1}^{n} PVIF_{k,t}\right).$$

Table 11.10   **The Present-Value Interest Factors
for a One-Dollar Annuity,** $PVIFA_{k,n}$

Period	5%	6%	7%	8%	9%	10%
1	.952	.943	.935	.926	.917	.909
2	1.859	1.833	1.808	1.783	1.759	1.736
3	2.723	2.673	2.624	2.577	2.531	2.487
4	3.546	3.465	3.387	3.312	3.240	3.170
5	4.329	4.212	4.100	3.993	3.890	3.791
6	5.076	4.917	4.767	4.623	4.486	4.355
7	5.786	5.582	5.389	5.206	5.033	4.868
8	6.463	6.210	5.971	5.747	5.535	5.335
9	7.108	6.802	6.515	6.247	5.995	5.759
10	7.722	7.360	7.024	6.710	6.418	6.145

(or Table 11.10) is 3.993. Multiplying the $700 annuity by this factor in accordance with Equation 11.16 results in a present value of $2,795.10.

Calculator Use The present value of an annuity can alternatively be found using the business calculator's financial functions. First punch in $700 and depress the "PMT" key; next punch in 5 and depress the "N" key; then punch in 8 and depress the "%i" key; and finally, to calculate the present value of the annuity, depress the "CPT" key followed by the "PV" key. The present value of $2,794.90 should appear on the calculator display.

Note that because of rounding in the calculation in Table 11.9 and of the factors in Table C-4, the value obtained with the calculator—$2,794.90—is more accurate, although for purposes of this text these differences are insignificant.

SPECIAL APPLICATIONS OF TIME VALUE

Future-value and present-value techniques have a number of important applications. Four are presented in this section: (1) the calculation of the deposits needed to accumulate a future sum, (2) the calculation of amortization on loans, (3) the determination of interest or growth rates, and (4) the calculation of the present value of perpetuities.

Deposits to Accumulate a Future Sum

Often an individual may wish to determine the annual deposit necessary to accumulate a certain amount of money so many years hence. Suppose a person wishes to buy a house five years from now and estimates that an initial down payment of $20,000 will be required at that time. She wishes to make equal annual end-of-year deposits in an account paying annual interest of 6 percent. She must determine what size annuity will result in a lump sum equal to $20,000 at the end of year 5. The solution to this problem is closely related to the process of finding the future value of an annuity.

In an earlier section of this chapter, the future value of an n-year annuity, FVA_n, was found by multiplying the annual deposit, PMT, by the appropriate interest factor (from Table C-2), $FVIFA_{k,n}$. The relationship of the three variables has been defined by Equation 11.8, which is rewritten here as Equation 11.17.

$$FVA_n = PMT \times (FVIFA_{k,n})$$

Equation 11.17
General formula for the future value of an n-year annuity

We can find the annual deposit required to accumulate FVA_n dollars, given a specified interest rate, k, and a certain number of years, n, by solving Equation 11.17 for PMT. Isolating PMT on the left side of the equation gives us

$$PMT = \frac{FVA_n}{FVIFA_{k,n}}$$

Equation 11.18
Formula for finding the annual deposit required to accumulate a specified future sum

Once this is done, we have only to substitute the known values of FVA_n and $FVIFA_{k,n}$ into the right side of the equation to find the annual deposit required. An example demonstrates this calculation using Table C-2 as well as a business calculator.

EXAMPLE   In the problem just stated, a person wished to determine the equal annual end-of-year deposits required to accumulate $20,000 at the end of five years given an interest rate of 6 percent.

Table Use   Table C-2 indicates that the future-value interest factor for an annuity at 6 percent for five years, $FVIFA_{6\%,5yrs}$, is 5.637. Substituting $FVA_5 = \$20,000$ and $FVIFA_{6\%,5yrs} = 5.637$ into Equation 11.18 yields an annual required deposit, PMT, of $3,547.99 ($20,000 ÷ 5.637). If $3,547.99 is deposited at the end of each year for five years at 6 percent, at the end of the five years there will be $20,000 in the account.

Calculator Use   Using the calculator, begin by punching in $20,000 and depressing the "FV" key; next punch in 5 and depress the "N" key; then punch 6 and depress the "%i" key; and finally, to calculate the annual deposit, depress the "CPT" key followed by the "PMT" key. The annual deposit amount appearing on the calculator display is $3,547.93 (ignore the minus sign). Note that this value, except for a slight rounding difference, agrees with the value found using Table C-2 above.

Loan Amortization

The term **loan amortization** refers to the determination of the equal annual loan payments necessary to provide a lender with a specified

loan amortization
The determination of the equal annual loan payments necessary to provide a lender with a specified interest return and repay the loan principal over a specified period.

loan amortization schedule   A schedule showing the allocation to interest and principal of each of the equal payments to repay a loan.

interest return and repay the loan principal over a specified period. The loan amortization process involves finding the future payments (over the term of the loan) whose present value at the loan interest rate equals the amount of initial principal borrowed. Lenders use a **loan amortization schedule** to determine these payment amounts as well as to allocate parts of each payment to interest and principal. In the case of home mortgages, these tables are used to find the equal *monthly* payments necessary to amortize, or pay off, the mortgage at a specified interest rate over a 15- to 30-year period.

Amortizing a loan actually involves creating an annuity out of a present amount. For example, an individual may borrow $6,000 at 10 percent and agree to make equal annual end-of-year payments over four years. To find the size of the payments, the lender determines the amount of a four-year annuity discounted at 10 percent that has a present value of $6,000. This process is actually the inverse of finding the present value of an annuity.

Earlier in this chapter the present value, PVA_n, of an n-year annuity of PMT dollars was found by multiplying the annual amount, PMT, by the present-value interest factor for an annuity from Table C-4, $PVIFA_{k,n}$. This relationship, which was originally expressed as Equation 11.16, is rewritten here as Equation 11.19:

Equation 11.19
General formula for the present value of an n-year annuity

$$PVA_n = PMT \times (PVIFA_{k,n})$$

To find the equal annual payment, PMT, required to pay off, or amortize, the loan, PVA_n, over a certain number of years at a specified interest rate, we need to solve Equation 11.19 for PMT. Isolating PMT on the left side of the equation gives us

Equation 11.20
Formula for finding the annual payment required to pay off a loan

$$PMT = \frac{PVA_n}{PVIFA_{k,n}}$$

Once this is done, we have only to substitute the known values of PVA_n and $PVIFA_{k,n}$ into the right side of the equation to find the annual payment required.

EXAMPLE   In the problem stated above, a person wished to determine the equal annual end-of-year payments necessary to amortize fully a $6,000, 10 percent loan over four years. **Table Use**   Table C-4 indicates that the present-value interest factor for an annuity corresponding to 10 percent and four years, $PVIFA_{10\%,4\text{yrs}}$, is 3.170. Substituting $PVA_4 =$ $6,000 and $PVIFA_{10\%,4\text{yrs}} = 3.170$ into Equation 11.20 and solving for PMT yields an annual loan payment of $1,892.74 ($6,000 ÷ 3.170). Thus, to repay the interest and principal on a $6,000, 10 percent, four-year loan, equal annual end-of-year payments of $1,892.74 are necessary. **Calculator Use**   Using the calculator, begin by punching in $6,000 and depressing the "PV" key; next punch in 4 and depress the "N" key; then punch in 10 and depress the "%i" key; and finally, to calculate the annual loan payment, de-

Table 11.11   **Loan Amortization Schedule ($6,000 Principal, 10 Percent Interest, Four-Year Repayment Period)**

End of year	Loan payment (1)	Beginning-of-year principal (2)	Payments		End-of-year principal [(2) − (4)] (5)
			Interest [.10 × (2)] (3)	Principal [(1) − (3)] (4)	
1	$1,892.74	$6,000.00	$600.00	$1,292.74	$4,707.26
2	1,892.74	4,707.26	470.73	1,422.01	3,285.25
3	1,892.74	3,285.25	328.53	1,564.21	1,721.04
4	1,892.74	1,721.04	172.10	1,720.64	—ᵃ

ᵃDue to rounding, a slight difference ($.40) exists between the beginning-of-year-4 principal (in column 2) and the year-4 principal payment (in column 4).

press the "CPT" key followed by the "PMT" key. The annual deposit amount of $1,892.82 appearing on the display, except for a slight rounding difference, agrees with the value found using Table C-4 above.

The allocation of each loan payment to interest and principal can be seen in columns 3 and 4 of the *loan amortization schedule* given in Table 11.11. The portion of each payment representing interest (column 3) declines, and the portion going to principal repayment (column 4) increases over the repayment period. This is typical of amortized loans. With level payments, as the principal is reduced, the interest component declines, leaving a larger portion of each subsequent payment to repay principal.

Interest or Growth Rates

It is often necessary to calculate the compound annual interest or growth rate of a stream of cash flows. In doing this, either future-value or present-value interest factors can be used. The approach using present-value interest tables is described in this section. The simplest situation is one in which a person wishes to find the rate of interest or growth in a cash flow stream.[8] This can be illustrated by the following example using both present-value tables and a business calculator.

---

[8]Since the calculations required for finding interest rates and growth rates, given certain cash flow streams, are the same, this section refers to the calculations as those required to find interest or growth rates.

EXAMPLE   Al Taylor wishes to find the rate of interest or growth of the following stream of cash flows.

Year	Cash flow	
1992	$1,520	} 4
1991	1,440	} 3
1990	1,370	} 2
1989	1,300	} 1
1988	1,250	

With the first year (1988) as a base year, we see that interest has been earned (or growth experienced) for four years.

Table Use   The first step in finding the interest or growth rate is to divide the amount received in the earliest year by the amount received in the latest year. This gives the present-value interest factor for four years, $PVIF_{k,4\text{yrs}}$, which is .822 ($1,250 ÷ $1,520). The interest rate in Table C-3 associated with the factor closest to .822 for four years is the rate of interest or growth rate exhibited by the cash flows. Looking across year 4 of Table C-3 shows that the factor for 5 percent is .823—almost exactly the .822 value. Therefore, the rate of interest or growth rate exhibited by the cash flows given is approximately (to the nearest whole percent) 5 percent.[9]

Calculator Use   Using the calculator, we treat the earliest value as a present value (PV) and the latest value as a future value (FV_n). First punch in the 1988 value of $1,250 and depress the "PV" key; next punch in the 1992 value of $1,520 and depress the "FV" key; then punch in the number of years of growth—4—and depress the "N" key; and finally, to get the interest or growth rate, depress the "CPT" key followed by the "%i" key. The interest or growth rate appearing on the display is 5.01 percent, which is consistent with, but more precise than, the value found using Table C-3 above.

Sometimes one wishes to find the interest rate associated with an equal-payment loan. The procedure for doing so can be demonstrated with an example using both financial tables and a business calculator.

EXAMPLE   Jan Jong can borrow $2,000 to be repaid in equal annual end-of-year amounts of $514.14 for the next five years. She would like to calculate the interest rate on this loan.

---

[9]Rounding of interest or growth rate estimates to the nearest whole percent is assumed throughout this text. To obtain more precise estimates, interpolation would be required.

Table Use   Substituting $PVA_5 = \$2,000$ and $PMT = \$514.14$ into Equation 11.19 and rearranging the equation to solve for $PVIFA_{k,5\text{yrs}}$, we get:

$$PVIFA_{k,5\text{yrs}} = \frac{PVA_5}{PMT} = \frac{\$2,000}{\$514.14} = 3.890$$

Equation 11.21
Formula for finding the present-value interest factor given the initial loan principal and the annual loan payment

The interest rate for five years associated with the factor closest to 3.890 in Table C-4 is 9 percent; therefore, the interest rate on the loan is approximately (to the nearest whole percent) 9 percent.

Calculator Use   Using the calculator, first punch in $514.14 and depress the "PMT" key; next punch in $2,000 and depress the "PV" key; then punch in 5 and depress the "N" key; and finally, to get the interest rate, depress the "CPT" key followed by the "%i" key. The interest rate appearing on the display is 9 percent, which is consistent with, but more precise than, the approximate value found using Table C-4 above.

Perpetuities

A **perpetuity** is an annuity with an infinite life—in other words, an annuity that never stops providing its holder with PMT dollars at the end of each year. It is sometimes necessary to find the present value of a perpetuity. The present value of a PMT-dollar perpetuity discounted at the rate k is defined by Equation 11.22.

perpetuity   An annuity with an infinite life, making continual annual payments

Present value of a PMT-dollar perpetuity discounted at k percent =
$$PMT \times (PVIFA_{k,\infty}) = PMT \times \left(\frac{1}{k}\right)$$

Equation 11.22
Formula for finding the present value of a perpetuity

As noted in the equation, the appropriate factor, $PVIFA_{k,\infty}$, is found merely by dividing the discount rate, k (stated as a decimal), into 1. The validity of this method can be seen by looking at the factors in Table C-4 for 8 percent, 10 percent, 20 percent, and 40 percent. As the number of periods (typically years) approaches 50, the value of these factors approaches 12.500, 10.000, 5.000, and 2.500, respectively. Dividing .08, .10, .20, and .50 (for k) into 1 gives factors for finding the present value of perpetuities at these rates of 12.500, 10.000, 5.000, and 2.500. An example will help clarify the application of Equation 11.22.

EXAMPLE   A person wishes to determine the present value of a $1,000 perpetuity discounted at 10 percent. The appropriate present-value interest factor can be found by dividing 1 by .10. As prescribed by Equation 11.22, the resulting factor, 10, is then multiplied by the annual perpetuity cash inflow of $1,000 to get the present value of the perpetuity, which is $10,000. In other words, the receipt of $1,000 every year for an indefinite period is worth only $10,000 today if a person can earn 10 percent on investments. The reason is that if the person had $10,000 and earned 10 percent interest on it each year, $1,000 a year could be withdrawn indefinitely without affecting the initial $10,000, which would never be drawn upon.

SUMMARY

1   **Understand the concept of future value, its calculation for a single amount, and the use of future-value interest tables and business calculators.** Future value relies on compounded interest to measure the value of future amounts. When interest is compounded, the initial principal or deposit in one period, along with the interest earned on it, becomes the beginning principal of the following period, and so on. The key time-value definitions, formulas, and equations relating to both future value and present value are summarized in Table 11.12. Financial tables as well as a hand-held business calculator can be used to greatly streamline the application of many of these formulas and equations.

2   **Calculate the future value of a single amount when interest is compounded more frequently than annually, specifically, semiannually or quarterly.** Interest can be compounded annually, semiannually, quarterly, monthly, weekly, daily, or even continuously. The more frequently interest is compounded, the larger the future amount that will be accumulated. This is true for any interest rate for any period of time. Semiannual compounding involves using one-half of the stated interest rate for twice the number of periods; quarterly compounding involves using one-fourth of the stated interest rate for four times the number of periods; and so on.

3   **Determine the future value of an annuity using either a future-value interest table for an annuity or a business calculator.** The future value of an annuity, which is a pattern of equal annual cash flows, can be found using the future-value interest factor for an annuity. The product of the annual amount of the annuity and the future-value interest factor for the appropriate rate of interest and number of time periods is the future value of the annuity. Alternatively, a business calculator can be used to quickly calculate the future value of an annuity. The interest-factor formula and basic equation for the future value of an annuity are summarized in Table 11.12.

4   **Discuss the concept of present value, its calculation for a single amount, the use of present value interest tables and business calculators, and the relationship of present value to future value.** When finding the present value of a future amount, we determine what amount of money today would be equivalent to the given future amount, considering the fact that we can earn a certain return on the current money. The present value of a single amount can be found using either the present-value interest factor for one dollar or a business calculator. Present value represents the inverse of future value. The interest factor formula and basic equation for the present value of a single amount are given in Table 11.12.

5   **Find the present value of a mixed stream of cash flows and an annuity, using present-value interest tables for either a single amount or an annuity, or a business calculator.** Occasionally it is necessary to find the present value of a stream of cash flows. For mixed streams, the individual present values must be found and summed. In the case of an annuity, the present value can be found by using the present-value interest factor for an annuity. For annu-

Table C-1 — Future-Value Interest Factors for One Dollar Compounded at k Percent for n Periods:

$$FVIF_{k,n} = (1 + k)^n$$

Period	1%	2%	3%	4%	5%	6%	7%	8%	9%	10%	11%	12%	13%	14%	15%	16%	20%	25%	30%	35%
1	1.010	1.020	1.030	1.040	1.050	1.060	1.070	1.080	1.090	1.100	1.110	1.120	1.130	1.140	1.150	1.160	1.200	1.250	1.300	1.350
2	1.020	1.040	1.061	1.082	1.102	1.124	1.145	1.166	1.188	1.210	1.232	1.254	1.277	1.300	1.322	1.346	1.440	1.562	1.690	1.822
3	1.030	1.061	1.093	1.125	1.158	1.191	1.225	1.260	1.295	1.331	1.368	1.405	1.443	1.482	1.521	1.561	1.728	1.953	2.197	2.460
4	1.041	1.082	1.126	1.170	1.216	1.262	1.311	1.360	1.412	1.464	1.518	1.574	1.630	1.689	1.749	1.811	2.074	2.441	2.856	3.321
5	1.051	1.104	1.159	1.217	1.276	1.338	1.403	1.469	1.539	1.611	1.685	1.762	1.842	1.925	2.011	2.100	2.488	3.052	3.713	4.484
6	1.062	1.126	1.194	1.265	1.340	1.419	1.501	1.587	1.677	1.772	1.870	1.974	2.082	2.195	2.313	2.436	2.986	3.815	4.827	6.053
7	1.072	1.149	1.230	1.316	1.407	1.504	1.606	1.714	1.828	1.949	2.076	2.211	2.353	2.502	2.660	2.826	3.583	4.768	6.275	8.172
8	1.083	1.172	1.267	1.369	1.477	1.594	1.718	1.851	1.993	2.144	2.305	2.476	2.658	2.853	3.059	3.278	4.300	5.960	8.157	11.032
9	1.094	1.195	1.305	1.423	1.551	1.689	1.838	1.999	2.172	2.358	2.558	2.773	3.004	3.252	3.518	3.803	5.160	7.451	10.604	14.894
10	1.105	1.219	1.344	1.480	1.629	1.791	1.967	2.159	2.367	2.594	2.839	3.106	3.395	3.707	4.046	4.411	6.192	9.313	13.786	20.106
11	1.116	1.243	1.384	1.539	1.710	1.898	2.105	2.332	2.580	2.853	3.152	3.479	3.836	4.226	4.652	5.117	7.430	11.642	17.921	27.144
12	1.127	1.268	1.426	1.601	1.796	2.012	2.252	2.518	2.813	3.138	3.498	3.896	4.334	4.818	5.350	5.936	8.916	14.552	23.298	36.644
13	1.138	1.294	1.469	1.665	1.886	2.133	2.410	2.720	3.066	3.452	3.883	4.363	4.898	5.492	6.153	6.886	10.699	18.190	30.287	49.469
14	1.149	1.319	1.513	1.732	1.980	2.261	2.579	2.937	3.342	3.797	4.310	4.887	5.535	6.261	7.076	7.987	12.839	22.737	39.373	66.784
15	1.161	1.346	1.558	1.801	2.079	2.397	2.759	3.172	3.642	4.177	4.785	5.474	6.254	7.138	8.137	9.265	15.407	28.422	51.185	90.158
16	1.173	1.373	1.605	1.873	2.183	2.540	2.952	3.426	3.970	4.595	5.311	6.130	7.067	8.137	9.358	10.748	18.488	35.527	66.541	121.71
17	1.184	1.400	1.653	1.948	2.292	2.693	3.159	3.700	4.328	5.054	5.895	6.866	7.986	9.276	10.761	12.468	22.186	44.409	86.503	164.31
18	1.196	1.428	1.702	2.026	2.407	2.854	3.380	3.996	4.717	5.560	6.543	7.690	9.024	10.575	12.375	14.462	26.623	55.511	112.45	221.82
19	1.208	1.457	1.753	2.107	2.527	3.026	3.616	4.316	5.142	6.116	7.263	8.613	10.197	12.055	14.232	16.776	31.948	69.389	146.19	299.46
20	1.220	1.486	1.806	2.191	2.653	3.207	3.870	4.661	5.604	6.727	8.062	9.646	11.523	13.743	16.366	19.461	38.337	86.736	190.05	404.27
21	1.232	1.516	1.860	2.279	2.786	3.399	4.140	5.034	6.109	7.400	8.949	10.804	13.021	15.667	18.821	22.574	46.005	108.42	247.06	545.76
22	1.245	1.546	1.916	2.370	2.925	3.603	4.430	5.436	6.658	8.140	9.933	12.100	14.713	17.861	21.644	26.186	55.205	135.53	321.18	736.78
23	1.257	1.577	1.974	2.465	3.071	3.820	4.740	5.871	7.258	8.954	11.026	13.552	16.626	20.361	24.891	30.376	66.247	169.41	417.53	994.65
24	1.270	1.608	2.033	2.563	3.225	4.049	5.072	6.341	7.911	9.850	12.239	15.178	18.788	23.212	28.625	35.236	79.496	211.76	542.79	1342.8
25	1.282	1.641	2.094	2.666	3.386	4.292	5.427	6.848	8.623	10.834	13.585	17.000	21.230	26.461	32.918	40.874	95.395	264.70	705.63	1812.8
30	1.348	1.811	2.427	3.243	4.322	5.743	7.612	10.062	13.267	17.449	22.892	29.960	39.115	50.949	66.210	85.849	237.37	807.79	2619.9	8128.4
35	1.417	2.000	2.814	3.946	5.516	7.686	10.676	14.785	20.413	28.102	38.574	52.799	72.066	98.097	133.17	180.31	590.66	2465.2	9727.6	36448.
40	1.489	2.208	3.262	4.801	7.040	10.285	14.974	21.724	31.408	45.258	64.999	93.049	132.78	188.88	267.86	378.72	1469.7	7523.2	36118.	*
45	1.565	2.438	3.781	5.841	8.985	13.764	21.002	31.920	48.325	72.888	109.53	163.99	244.63	363.66	538.75	795.43	3657.2	22959.	*	*
50	1.645	2.691	4.384	7.106	11.467	18.419	29.456	46.900	74.354	117.39	184.56	289.00	450.71	700.20	1083.6	1670.7	9100.2	70065.	*	*

*FVIF > 99,999.

Table C-2 — Future-Value Interest Factors for a One-Dollar Annuity Compounded at k Percent for n Periods:

$$FVIFA_{k,n} = \sum_{t=1}^{n} (1 + k)^{t-1}$$

Period	1%	2%	3%	4%	5%	6%	7%	8%	9%	10%	11%	12%	13%	14%	15%	16%	20%	25%	30%	35%
1	1.000	1.000	1.000	1.000	1.000	1.000	1.000	1.000	1.000	1.000	1.000	1.000	1.000	1.000	1.000	1.000	1.000	1.000	1.000	1.000
2	2.010	2.020	2.030	2.040	2.050	2.060	2.070	2.080	2.090	2.100	2.110	2.120	2.130	2.140	2.150	2.160	2.200	2.250	2.300	2.350
3	3.030	3.060	3.091	3.122	3.152	3.184	3.215	3.246	3.278	3.310	3.342	3.374	3.407	3.440	3.472	3.506	3.640	3.813	3.990	4.172
4	4.060	4.122	4.184	4.246	4.310	4.375	4.440	4.506	4.573	4.641	4.710	4.779	4.850	4.921	4.993	5.066	5.368	5.766	6.187	6.633
5	5.101	5.204	5.309	5.416	5.526	5.637	5.751	5.867	5.985	6.105	6.228	6.353	6.480	6.610	6.742	6.877	7.442	8.207	9.043	9.954
6	6.152	6.308	6.468	6.633	6.802	6.975	7.153	7.336	7.523	7.716	7.913	8.115	8.323	8.535	8.754	8.977	9.930	11.259	12.756	14.438
7	7.214	7.434	7.662	7.898	8.142	8.394	8.654	8.923	9.200	9.487	9.783	10.089	10.405	10.730	11.067	11.414	12.916	15.073	17.583	20.492
8	8.286	8.583	8.892	9.214	9.549	9.897	10.260	10.637	11.028	11.436	11.859	12.300	12.757	13.233	13.727	14.240	16.499	19.842	23.858	28.664
9	9.368	9.755	10.159	10.583	11.027	11.491	11.978	12.488	13.021	13.579	14.164	14.776	15.416	16.085	16.786	17.518	20.799	25.802	32.015	39.696
10	10.462	10.950	11.464	12.006	12.578	13.181	13.816	14.487	15.193	15.937	16.722	17.549	18.420	19.337	20.304	21.321	25.959	33.253	42.619	54.590
11	11.567	12.169	12.808	13.486	14.207	14.972	15.784	16.645	17.560	18.531	19.561	20.655	21.814	23.044	24.349	25.733	32.150	42.566	56.405	74.696
12	12.682	13.412	14.192	15.026	15.917	16.870	17.888	18.977	20.141	21.384	22.713	24.133	25.650	27.271	29.001	30.850	39.580	54.208	74.326	101.84
13	13.809	14.680	15.618	16.627	17.713	18.882	20.141	21.495	22.953	24.523	26.211	28.029	29.984	32.088	34.352	36.786	48.496	68.760	97.624	138.48
14	14.947	15.974	17.086	18.292	19.598	21.015	22.550	24.215	26.019	27.975	30.095	32.392	34.882	37.581	40.504	43.672	59.196	86.949	127.91	187.95
15	16.097	17.293	18.599	20.023	21.578	23.276	25.129	27.152	29.361	31.772	34.405	37.280	40.417	43.842	47.580	51.659	72.035	109.69	167.29	254.74
16	17.258	18.639	20.157	21.824	23.657	25.672	27.888	30.324	33.003	35.949	39.190	42.753	46.671	50.980	55.717	60.925	87.442	138.11	218.47	344.90
17	18.430	20.012	21.761	23.697	25.840	28.213	30.840	33.750	36.973	40.544	44.500	48.883	53.738	59.117	65.075	71.673	105.93	173.64	285.01	466.61
18	19.614	21.412	23.414	25.645	28.132	30.905	33.999	37.450	41.301	45.599	50.396	55.749	61.724	68.393	75.836	84.140	128.12	218.05	371.51	630.92
19	20.811	22.840	25.117	27.671	30.539	33.760	37.379	41.446	46.018	51.158	56.939	63.439	70.748	78.968	88.211	98.603	154.74	273.56	483.97	852.74
20	22.019	24.297	26.870	29.778	33.066	36.785	40.995	45.762	51.159	57.274	64.202	72.052	80.946	91.024	102.44	115.38	186.69	342.95	630.16	1152.2
21	23.239	25.783	28.676	31.969	35.719	39.992	44.865	50.422	56.764	64.002	72.264	81.698	92.468	104.77	118.81	134.84	225.02	429.68	820.20	1556.5
22	24.471	27.299	30.536	34.248	38.505	43.392	49.005	55.456	62.872	71.402	81.213	92.502	105.49	120.43	137.63	157.41	271.03	538.10	1067.3	2102.2
23	25.716	28.845	32.452	36.618	41.430	46.995	53.435	60.893	69.531	79.542	91.147	104.60	120.20	138.30	159.27	183.60	326.23	673.63	1388.4	2839.0
24	26.973	30.421	34.426	39.082	44.501	50.815	58.176	66.764	76.789	88.496	102.17	118.15	136.83	158.66	184.17	213.98	392.48	843.03	1806.0	3833.7
25	28.243	32.030	36.459	41.645	47.726	54.864	63.248	73.105	84.699	98.346	114.41	133.33	155.62	181.87	212.79	249.21	471.98	1054.8	2348.8	5176.4
30	34.784	40.567	47.575	56.084	66.438	79.057	94.459	113.28	136.31	164.49	199.02	241.33	293.19	356.78	434.74	530.31	1181.9	3227.2	8729.8	23221.
35	41.659	49.994	60.461	73.651	90.318	111.43	138.23	172.31	215.71	271.02	341.58	431.66	546.66	693.55	881.15	1120.7	2948.3	9856.7	32422.	*
40	48.885	60.401	75.400	95.024	120.80	154.76	199.63	259.05	337.87	442.58	581.81	767.08	1013.7	1342.0	1779.0	2360.7	7343.7	30089.	*	*
45	56.479	71.891	92.718	121.03	159.70	212.74	285.74	386.50	525.84	718.88	986.61	1358.2	1874.1	2590.5	3585.0	4965.2	18281.	91831.	*	*
50	64.461	84.577	112.79	152.66	209.34	290.33	406.52	573.76	815.05	1163.9	1668.7	2400.0	3459.3	4994.3	7217.5	10435.	45496.	*	*	*

*FVIFA > 99,999.

© 1992 HarperCollins*Publishers*, Inc.

Table C-3 — Present-Value Interest Factors for One Dollar Discounted at k Percent for n Periods:

$$PVIF_{k,n} = 1/(1 + k)^n$$

Period	1%	2%	3%	4%	5%	6%	7%	8%	9%	10%	11%	12%	13%	14%	15%	16%	17%	18%	19%	20%	25%	30%	35%
1	.990	.980	.971	.962	.952	.943	.935	.926	.917	.909	.901	.893	.885	.877	.870	.862	.855	.847	.840	.833	.800	.769	.741
2	.980	.961	.943	.925	.907	.890	.873	.857	.842	.826	.812	.797	.783	.769	.756	.743	.731	.718	.706	.694	.640	.592	.549
3	.971	.942	.915	.889	.864	.840	.816	.794	.772	.751	.731	.712	.693	.675	.658	.641	.624	.609	.593	.579	.512	.455	.406
4	.961	.924	.888	.855	.823	.792	.763	.735	.708	.683	.659	.636	.613	.592	.572	.552	.534	.516	.499	.482	.410	.350	.301
5	.951	.906	.863	.822	.784	.747	.713	.681	.650	.621	.593	.567	.543	.519	.497	.476	.456	.437	.419	.402	.328	.269	.223
6	.942	.888	.837	.790	.746	.705	.666	.630	.596	.564	.535	.507	.480	.456	.432	.410	.390	.370	.352	.335	.262	.207	.165
7	.933	.871	.813	.760	.711	.665	.623	.583	.547	.513	.482	.452	.425	.400	.376	.354	.333	.314	.296	.279	.210	.159	.122
8	.923	.853	.789	.731	.677	.627	.582	.540	.502	.467	.434	.404	.376	.351	.327	.305	.285	.266	.249	.233	.168	.123	.091
9	.914	.837	.766	.703	.645	.592	.544	.500	.460	.424	.391	.361	.333	.308	.284	.263	.243	.225	.209	.194	.134	.094	.067
10	.905	.820	.744	.676	.614	.558	.508	.463	.422	.386	.352	.322	.295	.270	.247	.227	.208	.191	.176	.162	.107	.073	.050
11	.896	.804	.722	.650	.585	.527	.475	.429	.388	.350	.317	.287	.261	.237	.215	.195	.178	.162	.148	.135	.086	.056	.037
12	.887	.789	.701	.625	.557	.497	.444	.397	.356	.319	.286	.257	.231	.208	.187	.168	.152	.137	.124	.112	.069	.043	.027
13	.879	.773	.681	.601	.530	.469	.415	.368	.326	.290	.258	.229	.204	.182	.163	.145	.130	.116	.104	.093	.055	.033	.020
14	.870	.758	.661	.577	.505	.442	.388	.340	.299	.263	.232	.205	.181	.160	.141	.125	.111	.099	.088	.078	.044	.025	.015
15	.861	.743	.642	.555	.481	.417	.362	.315	.275	.239	.209	.183	.160	.140	.123	.108	.095	.084	.074	.065	.035	.020	.011
16	.853	.728	.623	.534	.458	.394	.339	.292	.252	.218	.188	.163	.141	.123	.107	.093	.081	.071	.062	.054	.028	.015	.008
17	.844	.714	.605	.513	.436	.371	.317	.270	.231	.198	.170	.146	.125	.108	.093	.080	.069	.060	.052	.045	.023	.012	.006
18	.836	.700	.587	.494	.416	.350	.296	.250	.212	.180	.153	.130	.111	.095	.081	.069	.059	.051	.044	.038	.018	.009	.005
19	.828	.686	.570	.475	.396	.331	.277	.232	.194	.164	.138	.116	.098	.083	.070	.060	.051	.043	.037	.031	.014	.007	.003
20	.820	.673	.554	.456	.377	.312	.258	.215	.178	.149	.124	.104	.087	.073	.061	.051	.043	.037	.031	.026	.012	.005	.002
21	.811	.660	.538	.439	.359	.294	.242	.199	.164	.135	.112	.093	.077	.064	.053	.044	.037	.031	.026	.022	.009	.004	.002
22	.803	.647	.522	.422	.342	.278	.226	.184	.150	.123	.101	.083	.068	.056	.046	.038	.032	.026	.022	.018	.007	.003	.001
23	.795	.634	.507	.406	.326	.262	.211	.170	.138	.112	.091	.074	.060	.049	.040	.033	.027	.022	.018	.015	.006	.002	.001
24	.788	.622	.492	.390	.310	.247	.197	.158	.126	.102	.082	.066	.053	.043	.035	.028	.023	.019	.015	.013	.005	.002	.001
25	.780	.610	.478	.375	.295	.233	.184	.146	.116	.092	.074	.059	.047	.038	.030	.024	.020	.016	.013	.010	.004	.001	.001
30	.742	.552	.412	.308	.231	.174	.131	.099	.075	.057	.044	.033	.026	.020	.015	.012	.009	.007	.005	.004	.001	*	*
35	.706	.500	.355	.253	.181	.130	.094	.068	.049	.036	.026	.019	.014	.010	.008	.006	.004	.003	.002	.002	*	*	*
40	.672	.453	.307	.208	.142	.097	.067	.046	.032	.022	.015	.011	.008	.005	.004	.003	.002	.001	.001	.001	*	*	*
45	.639	.410	.264	.171	.111	.073	.048	.031	.021	.014	.009	.006	.004	.003	.002	.001	.001	.001	*	*	*	*	*
50	.608	.372	.228	.141	.087	.054	.034	.021	.013	.009	.005	.003	.002	.001	.001	.001	*	*	*	*	*	*	*

*PVIF = .000 when rounded to three decimal places.

Table C-4 — Present-Value Interest Factors for a One-Dollar Annuity Discounted at k Percent for n Periods:

$$PVIFA_{k,n} = \sum_{t=1}^{n} 1/(1 + k)^t$$

Period	1%	2%	3%	4%	5%	6%	7%	8%	9%	10%	11%	12%	13%	14%	15%	16%	17%	18%	19%	20%	25%	30%	35%
1	.990	.980	.971	.962	.952	.943	.935	.926	.917	.909	.901	.893	.885	.877	.870	.862	.855	.847	.840	.833	.800	.769	.741
2	1.970	1.942	1.913	1.886	1.859	1.833	1.808	1.783	1.759	1.736	1.713	1.690	1.668	1.647	1.626	1.605	1.585	1.566	1.547	1.528	1.440	1.361	1.289
3	2.941	2.884	2.829	2.775	2.723	2.673	2.624	2.577	2.531	2.487	2.444	2.402	2.361	2.322	2.283	2.246	2.210	2.174	2.140	2.106	1.952	1.816	1.696
4	3.902	3.808	3.717	3.630	3.546	3.465	3.387	3.312	3.240	3.170	3.102	3.037	2.974	2.914	2.855	2.798	2.743	2.690	2.639	2.589	2.362	2.166	1.997
5	4.853	4.713	4.580	4.452	4.329	4.212	4.100	3.993	3.890	3.791	3.696	3.605	3.517	3.433	3.352	3.274	3.199	3.127	3.058	2.991	2.689	2.436	2.220
6	5.795	5.601	5.417	5.242	5.076	4.917	4.767	4.623	4.486	4.355	4.231	4.111	3.998	3.889	3.784	3.685	3.589	3.498	3.410	3.326	2.951	2.643	2.385
7	6.728	6.472	6.230	6.002	5.786	5.582	5.389	5.206	5.033	4.868	4.712	4.564	4.423	4.288	4.160	4.039	3.922	3.812	3.706	3.605	3.161	2.802	2.508
8	7.652	7.326	7.020	6.733	6.463	6.210	5.971	5.747	5.535	5.335	5.146	4.968	4.799	4.639	4.487	4.344	4.207	4.078	3.954	3.837	3.329	2.925	2.598
9	8.566	8.162	7.786	7.435	7.108	6.802	6.515	6.247	5.995	5.759	5.537	5.328	5.132	4.946	4.772	4.607	4.451	4.303	4.163	4.031	3.463	3.019	2.665
10	9.471	8.983	8.530	8.111	7.722	7.360	7.024	6.710	6.418	6.145	5.889	5.650	5.426	5.216	5.019	4.833	4.659	4.494	4.339	4.192	3.570	3.092	2.715
11	10.368	9.787	9.253	8.760	8.306	7.887	7.499	7.139	6.805	6.495	6.207	5.938	5.687	5.453	5.234	5.029	4.836	4.656	4.486	4.327	3.656	3.147	2.752
12	11.255	10.575	9.954	9.385	8.863	8.384	7.943	7.536	7.161	6.814	6.492	6.194	5.918	5.660	5.421	5.197	4.988	4.793	4.611	4.439	3.725	3.190	2.779
13	12.134	11.348	10.635	9.986	9.394	8.853	8.358	7.904	7.487	7.103	6.750	6.424	6.122	5.842	5.583	5.342	5.118	4.910	4.715	4.533	3.780	3.223	2.799
14	13.004	12.106	11.296	10.563	9.899	9.295	8.745	8.244	7.786	7.367	6.982	6.628	6.302	6.002	5.724	5.468	5.229	5.008	4.802	4.611	3.824	3.249	2.814
15	13.865	12.849	11.938	11.118	10.380	9.712	9.108	8.560	8.061	7.606	7.191	6.811	6.462	6.142	5.847	5.575	5.324	5.092	4.876	4.675	3.859	3.268	2.825
16	14.718	13.578	12.561	11.652	10.838	10.106	9.447	8.851	8.313	7.824	7.379	6.974	6.604	6.265	5.954	5.668	5.405	5.162	4.938	4.730	3.887	3.283	2.834
17	15.562	14.292	13.166	12.166	11.274	10.477	9.763	9.122	8.544	8.022	7.549	7.120	6.729	6.373	6.047	5.749	5.475	5.222	4.990	4.775	3.910	3.295	2.840
18	16.398	14.992	13.754	12.659	11.690	10.828	10.059	9.372	8.756	8.201	7.702	7.250	6.840	6.467	6.128	5.818	5.534	5.273	5.033	4.812	3.928	3.304	2.844
19	17.226	15.679	14.324	13.134	12.085	11.158	10.336	9.604	8.950	8.365	7.839	7.366	6.938	6.550	6.198	5.877	5.584	5.316	5.070	4.843	3.942	3.311	2.848
20	18.046	16.352	14.878	13.590	12.462	11.470	10.594	9.818	9.129	8.514	7.963	7.469	7.025	6.623	6.259	5.929	5.628	5.353	5.101	4.870	3.954	3.316	2.850
21	18.857	17.011	15.415	14.029	12.821	11.764	10.836	10.017	9.292	8.649	8.075	7.562	7.102	6.687	6.312	5.973	5.665	5.384	5.127	4.891	3.963	3.320	2.852
22	19.661	17.658	15.937	14.451	13.163	12.042	11.061	10.201	9.442	8.772	8.176	7.645	7.170	6.743	6.359	6.011	5.696	5.410	5.149	4.909	3.970	3.323	2.853
23	20.456	18.292	16.444	14.857	13.489	12.303	11.272	10.371	9.580	8.883	8.266	7.718	7.230	6.792	6.399	6.044	5.723	5.432	5.167	4.925	3.976	3.325	2.854
24	21.244	18.914	16.936	15.247	13.799	12.550	11.469	10.529	9.707	8.985	8.348	7.784	7.283	6.835	6.434	6.073	5.746	5.451	5.182	4.937	3.981	3.327	2.855
25	22.023	19.524	17.413	15.622	14.094	12.783	11.654	10.675	9.823	9.077	8.422	7.843	7.330	6.873	6.464	6.097	5.766	5.467	5.195	4.948	3.985	3.329	2.856
30	25.808	22.396	19.601	17.292	15.373	13.765	12.409	11.258	10.274	9.427	8.694	8.055	7.496	7.003	6.566	6.177	5.829	5.517	5.235	4.979	3.995	3.332	2.857
35	29.409	24.999	21.487	18.665	16.374	14.498	12.948	11.655	10.567	9.644	8.855	8.176	7.586	7.070	6.617	6.215	5.858	5.539	5.251	4.992	3.998	3.333	2.857
40	32.835	27.356	23.115	19.793	17.159	15.046	13.332	11.925	10.757	9.779	8.951	8.244	7.634	7.105	6.642	6.233	5.871	5.548	5.258	4.997	3.999	3.333	2.857
45	36.095	29.490	24.519	20.720	17.774	15.456	13.606	12.108	10.881	9.863	9.008	8.283	7.661	7.123	6.654	6.242	5.877	5.552	5.261	4.999	4.000	3.333	2.857
50	39.196	31.424	25.730	21.482	18.256	15.762	13.801	12.233	10.962	9.915	9.042	8.304	7.675	7.133	6.661	6.246	5.880	5.554	5.262	4.999	4.000	3.333	2.857

© 1992 HarperCollins*Publishers*, Inc.

Table 11.12   **Summary of Key Definitions, Formulas,
                            and Equations for Time Value of Money**

Variable definitions

FV_n = future value or amount at the end of period n

PV = initial principal, or present value

k = annual rate of interest

n = number of periods—typically years—over which money earns a return

t = period number index

FVA_n = future value of an n-year annuity

PMT = amount deposited or received annually at the end of each year

PVA_n = present value of an n-year annuity

Interest factor formulas

Future value of a single amount

$$FVIF_{k,n} = (1 + k)^n$$ [Eq. 11.5; factors in Table C-1]

Future value of an (ordinary) annuity

$$FVIFA_{k,n} = \sum_{t=1}^{n} (1 + k)^{t-1}$$ [Eq. 11.7; factors in Table C-2]

Present value of a single amount

$$PVIF_{k,n} = \frac{1}{(1 + k)^n}$$ [Eq. 11.13; factors in Table C-3]

Present value of an annuity

$$PVIFA_{k,n} = \sum_{t=1}^{n} \frac{1}{(1 + k)^t}$$ [Eq. 11.15; factors in Table C-4]

Basic equations

Future value (single amount): $FV_n = PV \times (FVIF_{k,n})$ [Eq. 11.6]

Future value (annuity): $FVA_n = PMT \times (FVIFA_{k,n})$ [Eq. 11.8]

Present value (single amount): $PV = FV_n \times (PVIF_{k,n})$ [Eq. 11.14]

Present value (annuity): $PVA_n = PMT \times (PVIFA_{k,n})$ [Eq. 11.16]

ities, the product of the annual amount of the annuity and the present-value interest factor for the appropriate rate of interest and number of time periods is the present value of the annuity. The interest factor formula and basic equation for the present value of an annuity are summarized in Table 11.12.

6   **Describe the procedures involved in (1) determining deposits to accumulate a future sum, (2) loan amortization, (3) finding interest or growth rates, and (4) evaluating perpetuities.** The annual deposit needed to accumulate a given future sum can be found by solving the equation for the future value of an annuity for the annual payment. A loan can be amortized into equal annual payments by solving the equation for the present value of an annuity for the annual payment. Interest or growth rates can be estimated by finding the unknown interest rate in the equation for the present value of either a single amount or an annuity. The present value of a perpetuity—an infinite-lived annuity—can be found by dividing the annual payment by the appropriate discount rate.

QUESTIONS

11—1   How is the *compounding process* related to the payment of interest on savings? What is the general equation for the future value, FV_n, in period n if PV dollars are deposited in an account paying k percent annual interest?

11—2   What effect would (a) a *decrease* in the interest rate or (b) an *increase* in the holding period of a deposit have on its future value? Why?

11—3   What effect does compounding interest more frequently than annually have on the future value generated by a beginning principal? Why?

11—4   Explain how one can conveniently determine the future value of an annuity that provides a stream of end-of-period cash inflows.

11—5   What is meant by the phrase "the present value of a future amount"? How are present-value and future-value calculations related?

11—6   What is the equation for the present value, PV, of a future amount, FV_n, to be received in period n assuming that the firm requires a minimum return of k percent? How is this equation different from the equation for the future value of one dollar?

11—7   What effect do *increasing* (a) required return and (b) time periods have on the present value of a future amount? Why?

11—8   How can present-value tables be used to find the present value of a mixed stream of cash flows? How can the calculations required to find the present value of an annuity be simplified?

11—9   How can the size of the equal annual end-of-year deposits necessary to accumulate a certain future sum in a specified future period be determined? How might one of the financial tables discussed in this chapter aid in this calculation?

11—10   Describe the procedure used to amortize a loan into a series of equal annual payments. What is a *loan amortization schedule*?

11—11   Which financial table(s) would be used to find (a) the growth rate associated with a stream of cash flows and (b) the interest rate associated with an equal-payment loan? How would each of these be calculated?

11—12   What is a *perpetuity*? How might the present-value interest factor for such a stream of cash flows be determined?

PROBLEMS

11—1   **(Future-Value Calculation)** *Without tables*, use the basic formula for future value along with the given interest rate, k, and number of periods, n, to calculate the future-value interest factor in each of the following cases. Compare the calculated value to the table value in Appendix Table C-1.

Case	Interest rate, k (%)	Number of periods, n
A	12	2
B	6	3
C	9	2
D	3	4

11—2   **(Future-Value Tables)**   Use the future-value interest factors in Appendix Table C-1 in each of the following cases to estimate, to the nearest year, how long it would take an initial deposit, assuming no withdrawals,
a. To double.
b. To quadruple.

Case	Interest rate (%)
A	7
B	40
C	20
D	10

11—3   **(Future Values)**   For each of the following cases, calculate the future value of the single cash flow deposited today that will be available at the end of the deposit period if the interest is compounded annually at the rate specified over the given period.

Case	Single cash flow ($)	Interest rate (%)	Deposit period (years)
A	200	5	20
B	4,500	8	7
C	10,000	9	10
D	25,000	10	12
E	37,000	11	5
F	40,000	12	9

11—4   **(Single-Payment Loan Repayment)**   A person borrows $200 to be repaid in eight years with 14 percent annually compounded interest. The loan may be repaid at the end of any earlier year with no prepayment penalty.
a. What amount would be due if the loan is repaid at the end of year 1?
b. What is the repayment at the end of year 4?
c. What amount is due at the end of the eighth year?

11—5   **(Changing Compounding Frequency)**   Using annual, semiannual, and quarterly compounding periods, calculate the future value if $5,000 is initially deposited
a. At 12 percent for five years.
b. At 16 percent for six years.
c. At 20 percent for ten years.

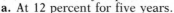

11—6   **(Comparing Compounding Periods)**   Rose Levin wishes to determine the future value at the end of two years of a $15,000 deposit made today into an account paying an annual rate of interest of 12 percent.

a. Find the future value of Rose's deposit assuming interest is compounded:
(1) Annually.
(2) Semiannually.
(3) Quarterly.

b. Compare your findings in **a** and use them to demonstrate the relationship between compounding frequency and future value.

11—7 **(Future Value of an Annuity)** For each of the following cases, calculate the future value of the annuity at the end of the deposit period, assuming that the annuity cash flows occur at the end of each year.

Case	Amount of annuity ($)	Interest rate (%)	Deposit period (years)
A	2,500	8	10
B	500	12	6
C	30,000	20	5
D	11,500	9	8
E	6,000	14	30

11—8 **(Future Value of a Mixed Stream)** For each of the following mixed streams of cash flows, determine the future value at the end of the final year if deposits are made at the *beginning of each year* into an account paying annual interest of 12 percent, assuming no withdrawals are made during the period.

	Cash flow stream		
Year	A	B	C
1	$ 900	$30,000	$1,200
2	1,000	25,000	1,200
3	1,200	20,000	1,000
4		10,000	1,900
5		5,000	

11—9 **(Present-Value Calculation)** *Without tables*, use the basic formula for present value along with the given opportunity cost, k, and number of periods, n, to calculate the present-value interest factor in each of the following cases. Compare the calculated value to the table value.

Case	Opportunity cost, k (%)	Number of periods, n
A	2	4
B	10	2
C	5	3
D	13	2

11—10 **(Present Values)** For each of the following cases, calculate the present value of the cash flow, discounting at the rate given and assuming that the cash flow will be received at the end of the period noted.

Case	Single cash flow ($)	Discount rate (%)	End of period (years)
A	7,000	12	4
B	28,000	8	20
C	10,000	14	12
D	150,000	11	6
E	45,000	20	8

11—11 **(Present Value)** Terry Murphy has been offered a future payment of $500 three years from today. If his opportunity cost is 7 percent compounded annually, what value would he place on this opportunity?

11—12 **(Present Value)** An Ohio state savings bond can be converted to $100 at maturity six years from purchase. If the state bonds are to be competitive with U.S. Savings Bonds, which pay 8 percent annual interest (compounded annually), at what price will the state sell its bonds? Assume no cash payments on savings bonds prior to redemption.

11—13 **(Present Value—Mixed Streams)** Given the following mixed streams of cash flows:

Year	Cash flow stream A	B
1	$ 50,000	$ 10,000
2	40,000	20,000
3	30,000	30,000
4	20,000	40,000
5	10,000	50,000
Totals	$150,000	$150,000

  a. Find the present value of each stream using a 15 percent discount rate.
  b. Compare the calculated present values and discuss them in light of the fact that the undiscounted total cash flows amount to $150,000 in each case.

11—14 **(Present Value—Mixed Streams)** Find the present value of the following streams of cash flows. Assume that the firm's opportunity cost is 12 percent.

A		B		C	
Year	Amount	Year	Amount	Year	Amount
1	−$2,000	1	$10,000	1–5	$10,000/yr.
2	3,000	2–5	5,000/yr.	6–10	8,000/yr.
3	4,000	6	7,000		
4	6,000				
5	8,000				

 11—15 **(Relationship between Future Value and Present Value)** Using *only* the following information:

Year (t)	Cash flow ($)	Future-value interest factor at 5 percent ($FVIF_{5\%,\ t}$)
1	800	1.050
2	900	1.102
3	1,000	1.158
4	1,500	1.216
5	2,000	1.276

a. Determine the *present value* of the mixed stream of cash flows using a 5 percent discount rate.

b. How much would you be willing to pay for an opportunity to buy this stream, assuming that you can at best earn 5 percent on your investments?

c. What effect, if any, would a 7 percent rather than 5 percent opportunity cost have on your analysis? (Explain verbally.)

 11—16 **(Present Value of an Annuity)** For each of the following cases, calculate the present value of the annuity, assuming that the annuity cash flows occur at the end of each year.

Case	Amount of annuity ($)	Interest rate (%)	Period (years)
A	12,000	7	3
B	55,000	12	15
C	700	20	9
D	140,000	5	7
E	22,500	10	5

 11—17 **(Cash Flow Investment Decision)** Jerry Carney has an opportunity to purchase any of the following investments. The purchase price, amount of the single cash inflow, and its year of receipt are given below for each investment. Which purchase recommendations would you make, assuming that Mr. Carney can earn 10 percent on his investments?

Investment	Price ($)	Single cash inflow ($)	Year of receipt
A	18,000	30,000	5
B	600	3,000	20
C	3,500	10,000	10
D	1,000	15,000	40

11—18 **(Deposits to Accumulate Future Sums)** For each of the cases given below, determine the amount of the equal annual end-of-year deposit that would be required to accumulate the given sum at the end of the specified period, assuming the stated annual interest rate.

Case	Sum to be accumulated ($)	Accumulation period (years)	Interest rate (%)
A	5,000	3	12
B	100,000	20	7
C	30,000	8	10
D	15,000	12	8

11—19 **(Accumulating a Growing Future Sum)** A retirement home at Marineworld Estates now costs $85,000. Inflation is expected to cause this price to increase at 6 percent per year over the 20 years before J. R. Rogers retires. How large an equal annual end-of-year deposit must be made each year into an account paying an annual rate of 10 percent in order for Rogers to have the cash to purchase a home at retirement?

11—20 **(Loan Amortization)** Determine the equal annual end-of-year pay- ment required each year over the life of the following loans in order to repay them fully during the stated term of the loan.

Loan	Principal ($)	Interest rate (%)	Term of loan (years)
A	12,000	8	3
B	60,000	12	10
C	75,000	10	30
D	4,000	15	5

11—21 **(Loan Amortization Schedule)** Val Hawkins borrowed $15,000 at a 14 percent annual rate of interest to be repaid over three years. The loan is amortized into three equal annual end-of-year payments.
a. Calculate the annual end-of-year loan payment.
b. Prepare a loan amortization schedule showing the interest and principal breakdown of each of the three loan payments.

c. Explain why the interest portion of each payment declines with the passage of time.

11—22   **(Growth Rates)** You are given the following series of cash flows:

| | Cash flows | | |
Year	A	B	C
1	$500	$1,500	$2,500
2	560	1,550	2,600
3	640	1,610	2,650
4	720	1,680	2,650
5	800	1,760	2,800
6		1,850	2,850
7		1,950	2,900
8		2,060	
9		2,170	
10		2,280	

a. Calculate the compound growth rate associated with each cash flow stream.
b. If year 1 values represent initial deposits in a savings account paying annual interest, what is the rate of interest earned on each account?
c. Compare and discuss the growth rates and interest rates found in **a** and **b**, respectively.

11—23   **(Rate of Return)** Carlos Cordero has $1,500 to invest. His investment counselor suggests an investment that pays no explicit interest but will return $2,000 at the end of three years.
a. What annual rate of return will Mr. Cordero earn with this investment?
b. Mr. Cordero is considering another investment, of equal risk, which earns a return of 8 percent. Which investment should he take, and why?

11—24   **(Rate of Return—Annuity)** What is the rate of return on an investment of $10,606 if the company expects to receive $2,000 each year for the next ten years?

11—25   **(Loan Rates of Interest)** David Pearson has been shopping for a loan to finance the purchase of his new car. He has found three possibilities that seem attractive and wishes to select the one having the lowest interest rate. The information available with respect to each of the three $5,000 loans follows.

Loan	Principal ($)	Annual payment ($)	Term (years)
A	5,000	1,352.81	5
B	5,000	1,543.21	4
C	5,000	2,010.45	3

  a. Determine the interest rate that would be associated with each of the loans.
  b. Which loan should Mr. Pearson take?

11—26   **(Perpetuities)** Given the following data, determine for each of the following perpetuities:

Perpetuity	Annual amount ($)	Discount rate (%)
A	20,000	8
B	100,000	10
C	3,000	6
D	60,000	5

  a. The appropriate present-value interest factor.
  b. The present value.

11—27   **(Annuity and Perpetuity)** You have decided to endow your favorite university with a scholarship in honor of your successful completion of managerial finance. It is expected that it will cost $6,000 per year to attend the university into perpetuity. You expect to give the university the endowment in 10 years and will accumulate it by making annual (end-of-year) deposits into an account. The rate of interest is expected to be 10 percent for all future time periods.
  a. How large must the endowment be?
  b. How much must you deposit at the end of each of the next 10 years to accumulate the required amount?

CASE

JMR's Retirement Program

JMR Corporation wishes to accumulate funds to provide a retirement annuity for its Vice President of Research—Andrea McNutt. Ms. McNutt by contract will retire at the end of exactly 12 years. Upon retirement she is entitled to receive an annual end-of-year payment of $42,000 for exactly 20 years. If she dies prior to the end of the 20-year period, the annual payments will pass to her heirs. During the 12-year "accumulation period," JMR Corporation wishes to fund the annuity by making equal annual end-of-year deposits into an account earning 9 percent interest. Once the 20-year "distribution period" begins, JMR plans to move the accumulated monies into an account earning a guaranteed 12 percent per year. At the end of the distribution period, the account balance will equal zero. Note that the first deposit will be made at the end of year 1 and the first distribution payment will be received at the end of year 13. (*Hint:* It may be helpful to draw a time line of cash flows before solving this problem.)

Required

    a. How large a sum must JMR Corporation accumulate by the end of year 12 in order to provide the 20-year $42,000 annuity?

    b. How large must JMR's equal annual end-of-year deposits into the account be over the 12-year accumulation period in order to fully fund Ms. McNutt's retirement annuity?

    c. How much would JMR have to deposit annually during the accumulation period if it could earn 10 percent rather than 9 percent during the accumulation period?

CHAPTER 12

RISK, RETURN, AND VALUATION

CHAPTER OBJECTIVES

After studying this chapter, you should be able to:

1 Describe basic risk and return concepts, including risk aversion, risk of a single asset, risk and time, and risk of a portfolio.

2 Understand the relationship between risk and return as presented by the capital asset pricing model (CAPM).

3 Discuss the key inputs and basic model used in the valuation process.

4 Apply the basic valuation model to bonds and preferred stocks, and evaluate the relationship between required returns and bond values.

5 Perform basic common stock valuation using both the zero and constant growth models and popular estimation approaches, and relate decision making to common stock value.

6 Describe the two risks—foreign exchange and political—requiring special consideration by the multinational company, and explain how MNCs manage them.

❛❛ When your hottest property is being courted . . . , the importance of financial deliberations can reach new heights. ❜❜

The Risks of Janet Jackson to PolyGram

Estimating a project's future cash flows and risks is difficult when dealing with bricks and mortar. The most important assets in many organizations, however, are the individuals the firm relies upon for revenues. Compound this dilemma with the "popular today, has-been tomorrow" nature of the music industry and you get an impression of the problems faced when trying to value entertainment projects. When your hottest property is being courted by all of the major record labels, the importance of financial deliberations can reach new heights.

Such was the situation at PolyGram N.V. when its contract with superstar Janet Jackson was up for grabs. Traded on the Amsterdam and New York stock exchanges, PolyGram was valued at $3 billion in early 1991. Though largely unknown, the company is the world's third-largest recording company. Its strength is its domination in the classical recording industry, with artists such as tenor Lucianno Pavarotti and the New York Philharmonic Orchestra. Unfortunately, sales of classical recordings account for only one-tenth of total industry sales.

The European music giant wanted to go global, which meant developing a major U.S. presence. Hence in 1990 PolyGram purchased A&M records for $460 million. Janet Jackson, the sister of Michael Jackson, was A&M's best-selling act. Her *Rhythm Nation 1814* album brought the company $45 million in revenues—a revenue stream sought by such competitors as Sony's CBS Records, Warner Music Group, Britain's Virgin Group, and others.

Although offers to musicians are seldom made public, PolyGram was reportedly offering a guaranteed contract which would provide the firm a return of less than 5 percent on its investment—a rate lower than that of Treasury bills. The required return for normal PolyGram projects would have been about 8 percent.

Although the contract appears to be one that would reduce owner wealth, management felt that the impact of losing Janet Jackson from the PolyGram label would have repercussions beyond the single contract. PolyGram's ability to nurture talent was being questioned because it had charted only 11 gold or platinum records in 1989. The loss of Janet Jackson would have sent a signal to PolyGram's other acts, including Def Leppard, U2, and Sting. Losing any of them would have greatly reduced the diversification in PolyGram's portfolio of pop singers.

n Chapter 1 the goal of the financial manager, and therefore the firm, was specified as owner wealth maximization. For the publicly traded corporation, the financial manager's primary mission is to maximize the price of the firm's common stock. To do this the manager must learn to assess the two key determinants of share price: risk and return. **Valuation** is the process that links risk and return to determine the worth of an asset—bond, preferred stock, common stock, or fixed asset. Valuation relies on the use of the time value techniques presented in Chapter 11. Like investors, financial managers must understand how to value assets in order to determine whether they are a "good buy." Each financial decision presents certain risk and return characteristics, and all major financial decisions must be viewed in terms of expected risk, expected return, and their combined impact on share price.

valuation The process that links risk and return to determine the worth of an asset.

BASIC RISK AND RETURN CONCEPTS

Risk and return concepts can be viewed as they relate to a single asset held in isolation or to a **portfolio**—a collection, or group, of assets. Although portfolio risk is probably more important to the financial manager, the general concept of risk is more readily developed in terms of a single asset.

portfolio A collection, or group, of assets.

Fundamentals

Before developing risk and return concepts, we must define risk, return, and risk aversion.

Risk Defined

In the most basic sense, **risk** can be defined as the chance of financial loss. Assets having greater chances of loss are viewed as more risky than those with lesser chances of loss. More formally, the term *risk* is used interchangeably with *uncertainty* to refer to the *variability of returns associated with a given asset*. For instance, a government bond that guarantees its holder $100 interest after 30 days has no risk, since there is no variability associated with the return. An equivalent investment in a firm's common stock that may earn over the same period anywhere from $0 to $200 is very risky due to the high variability of the return. The more certain the return from an asset, the less variability and therefore the less risk.

risk The chance of financial loss or, more formally, the variability of returns associated with a given asset.

Return Defined

As noted in Chapter 2 (see Equation 2.1), the **return** on an asset is the change in its value plus any cash distribution over a given period of time, expressed as a percentage of its initial value. The return on com-

return The change in value of an asset plus any cash distribution over a given period of time, expressed as a percentage of its initial value.

mon stock is calculated by dividing the sum of any increase (or decrease) in share price and any cash dividends earned over a given period by its initial share price. For example, assume you purchased a share of stock one year ago for $20. If the stock is now selling for $22 per share and during the year you received a $1 cash dividend, your return over the year would be 15 percent {[$2 increase in price ($22 − $20) + $1 cash dividend] ÷ $20 initial price}.

Risk Aversion

risk-averse The attitude toward risk in which an increased return would be required for an increase in risk.

Financial managers generally seek to avoid risk. Most managers are **risk-averse,** since for a given increase in risk they require an increase in return. This behavior is believed consistent with the preference of the owners for whom the firm is being managed. Managers tend to accept only those risks with which they feel comfortable. And they generally tend to be conservative rather than aggressive when accepting risk. Accordingly, *a risk-averse financial manager requiring higher returns for greater risk is assumed throughout this text.*

Risk of a Single Asset

The risk of a single asset is measured in much the same way as the risk of an entire portfolio of assets. Yet it is important to differentiate between these two entities, since certain benefits accrue to holders of portfolios. It is also useful to assess risk from both a behavioral and a quantitative point of view.

Sensitivity Analysis

sensitivity analysis An approach for assessing risk that uses a number of possible return estimates to obtain a sense of the variability among outcomes.

Sensitivity analysis is an approach that uses a number of possible return estimates to obtain a sense of the variability among outcomes. One common method involves the estimation of the pessimistic (worst), the most likely (expected), and the optimistic (best) returns associated with a given asset. In this case the asset's risk can be measured by the **range,** which is found by subtracting the pessimistic (worst) outcome from the optimistic (best) outcome. The greater the range for a given asset, the more variability, or risk, it is said to have.

range A measure of an asset's risk, which is found by subtracting the worst outcome from the best outcome.

EXAMPLE   Alfred Company, a custom golfing-equipment manufacturer, is attempting to choose the better of two alternative investments, A and B. Each requires an initial outlay of $10,000 and each has a *most likely* annual rate of return of 15 percent. To evaluate the riskiness of these assets, management has made *pessimistic* and *optimistic* estimates of the returns associated with each. The three estimates for each asset, along with its range, are given in Table 12.1. Asset A appears to be less risky than asset B since its range of 4 percent (17%–13%) is less than the range of 16 percent (23%–7%) for asset B. The risk-averse financial decision maker would prefer asset A over asset B: A offers the same most likely return as B (15%) but with lower risk (smaller range).

Table 12.1   Assets A and B

	Asset A	Asset B
Initial investment	$10,000	$10,000
Annual rate of return		
Pessimistic	13%	7%
Most likely	15	15
Optimistic	17	23
Range	4%	16%

Probabilities

Probabilities can be used to more precisely assess an asset's risk. The **probability** of a given outcome is the *chance* of it occurring. If an outcome has an 80 percent probability of occurrence, the given outcome would be expected to occur eight out of ten times. If an outcome has a probability of 100 percent, it is certain to occur. Outcomes having a probability of zero will never occur.

probability The *chance that a given outcome will occur.*

EXAMPLE   An evaluation of Alfred Company's past estimates indicates that the probabilities of the pessimistic, most likely, and optimistic outcomes' occurring are 25 percent, 50 percent, and 25 percent, respectively. The sum of these probabilities must equal 100 percent; that is, they must be based on all the alternatives considered.

Probability Distributions

A **probability distribution** is a model that relates probabilities to the associated outcomes. The simplest type of probability distribution is the **bar chart,** which shows only a limited number of outcome–probability coordinates. The bar charts for Alfred Company's assets A and B are shown in Figure 12.1. Although both assets have the same most likely return, the range of return is much more dispersed for asset B than for asset A—16 percent versus 4 percent. If we knew all the possible outcomes and associated probabilities, a **continuous probability distribution** could be developed. This type of distribution can be thought of as a bar chart for a very large number of outcomes. Figure 12.2 on page 379 presents continuous probability distributions for assets A and B. Note in Figure 12.2 that although assets A and B have the same most likely return (15 percent), the distribution of returns for asset B has much greater *dispersion* than the distribution for asset A. Clearly, asset B is more risky than asset A.

probability distribution A model that relates probabilities to the associated outcomes.

bar chart The simplest type of probability distribution showing only a limited number of outcomes and associated probabilities for a given event.

continuous probability distribution A probability distribution showing all the possible outcomes and associated probabilities for a given event.

Standard Deviation

The most common statistical indicator of an asset's risk is the **standard deviation,** σ_k, which measures the dispersion around the *expected* value.

standard deviation, σ_k Statistical indicator of an asset's risk; it measures the dispersion around the *expected* value.

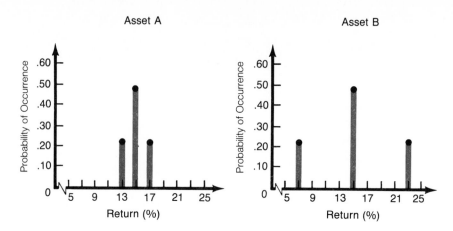

Figure 12.1   Bar Charts for Asset A's and Asset B's Returns
The bar charts show that although Assets A and B have the same most likely return of 15 percent, the range of returns for Asset B has much greater dispersion than that of Asset A. Asset B is therefore more risky.

expected value of a return, $\bar{k}$ The most likely return on a given asset.

The **expected value of a return, $\bar{k}$,** is the most likely return on an asset. This can be calculated using Equation 12.1:

$$\bar{k} = \sum_{i=1}^{n} k_i \times Pr_i$$

Equation 12.1
Formula for calculating the expected return on an asset

where

k_i = return for the ith outcome

Pr_i = probability of occurrence of the ith outcome

n = number of outcomes considered

EXAMPLE   The calculation of the expected values for Alfred Company's assets A and B are presented in Table 12.2. Column 1 gives the Pr_i's and column 2 gives the k_i's, n equaling 3 in each case. The expected value for each asset's return is 15 percent.

The expression for the *standard deviation of returns, σ_k,* is given in Equation 12.2:

$$\sigma_k = \sqrt{\sum_{i=1}^{n} (k_i - \bar{k})^2 \times Pr_i}$$

Equation 12.2
Formula for calculating the standard deviation when various return outcomes, expected returns, and associated probabilities are known

In general, the higher the standard deviation, the greater the risk.

EXAMPLE   Table 12.3 presents the calculation of standard deviations for Alfred Company's assets A and B, based on the data presented earlier. The standard deviation for asset A is 1.41 per-

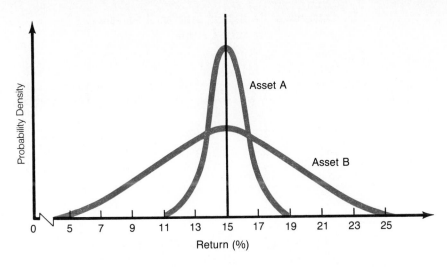

Figure 12.2 Continuous Probability Distributions for Asset A's and Asset B's Returns
The continuous distribution of returns for Asset B has much greater
dispersion than that of Asset A, although both assets have the same most
likely return of 15 percent. Asset B is therefore more risky.

cent, and the standard deviation for asset B is 5.66 percent.
The higher risk of asset B is clearly reflected in its higher
standard deviation.

Coefficient of Variation

The **coefficient of variation, CV,** is a measure of relative dispersion that
is useful in comparing the risk of assets with differing expected returns.
Equation 12.3 gives the expressions for the coefficient of variation:

**coefficient of varia-
tion, CV** A measure of
relative dispersion used
in comparing the risk of
assets with differing ex-
pected returns.

Table 12.2   **Expected Values of Returns for Assets A and B**

Possible outcomes	Probability (1)	Returns (%) (2)	Weighted value (%) [(1) × (2)] (3)
Asset A			
Pessimistic	.25	13	3.25
Most likely	.50	15	7.50
Optimistic	.25	17	4.25
Total	1.00	Expected return	15.00
Asset B			
Pessimistic	.25	7	1.75
Most likely	.50	15	7.50
Optimistic	.25	23	5.75
Total	1.00	Expected return	15.00

Table 12.3   **The Calculation of the Standard Deviation of the Returns for Assets A and B**

			Asset A			
i	k_i	$\bar{k}$	$k_i - \bar{k}$	$(k_i - \bar{k})^2$	Pr_i	$(k_i - \bar{k})^2 \times Pr_i$
1	13%	15%	−2%	4%	.25	1%
2	15	15	0	0	.50	0
3	17	15	2	4	.25	1

$$\sum_{i=1}^{3} (k_i - \bar{k})^2 \times Pr_i = 2\%$$

$$\sigma_{k_A} = \sqrt{\sum_{i=1}^{3} (k_i - \bar{k})^2 \times Pr_i} = \sqrt{2\%} = \underline{\underline{1.41\%}}$$

			Asset B			
i	k_i	$\bar{k}$	$k_i - \bar{k}$	$(k_i - \bar{k})^2$	Pr_i	$(k_i - \bar{k})^2 \times Pr_i$
1	7%	15%	−8%	64%	.25	16%
2	15	15	0	0	.50	0
3	23	15	8	64	.25	16

$$\sum_{i=1}^{3} (k_i - \bar{k})^2 \times Pr_i = 32\%$$

$$\sigma_{k_B} = \sqrt{\sum_{i=1}^{3} (k_i - \bar{k})^2 \times Pr_i} = \sqrt{32\%} = \underline{\underline{5.66\%}}$$

Equation 12.3
Formula for the coefficient of variation

$$CV = \frac{\sigma_k}{\bar{k}}$$

The higher the coefficient of variation, the greater the risk.

EXAMPLE   Substituting the standard deviation values (from Table 12.3) and the expected returns (from Table 12.2) for assets A and B into Equation 12.3, the coefficients of variation for A and B, respectively, are .094 (1.41% ÷ 15%) and .377 (5.66% ÷ 15%). Asset B has the higher coefficient of variation and is therefore more risky than asset A. Since both assets have the same expected return, the coefficient of variation has not provided any more information than the standard deviation.

The real utility of the coefficient of variation is in comparing assets that have *different* expected returns. A simple example will illustrate this point.

EXAMPLE   A firm is attempting to select the less risky of two alternative assets—X and Y. The expected return, standard deviation, and coefficient of variation for each of these assets' returns is given below.

Statistics	Asset X	Asset Y
(1) Expected return	12%	20%
(2) Standard deviation	9%[a]	10%
(3) Coefficient of variation [(2) ÷ (1)]	.75	.50[a]

[a]Preferred asset using the given risk measure.

If the firm were to compare the assets solely on the basis of their standard deviations, it would prefer asset X, since asset X has a lower standard deviation than asset Y (9 percent versus 10 percent). However, comparing the coefficients of variation of the assets shows that management would be making a serious error in choosing asset X over asset Y. The relative dispersion, or risk, of the assets as reflected in the coefficient of variation is lower for Y than for X (.50 versus .75). Clearly, the use of the coefficient of variation to compare asset risk is effective because it also considers the relative size, or expected return, of the assets.

Risk and Time

Risk can be viewed not only with respect to the current time period but also as an *increasing function of time*. Figure 12.3 depicts probability distributions of returns for a 1-year, 10-year, 15-year, and 20-year forecast, assuming each year's expected returns are equal. A band representing ± 1 standard deviation, σ, from the expected return, $\bar{k}$, is indicated in the figure. It can be seen that the *variability of the returns, and therefore the risk, increases with the passage of time*. Generally, the longer-lived an asset investment, the greater its risk. This relationship is due to increasing variability of returns resulting from increased forecasting errors for distant years.

Risk of a Portfolio

The risk of any single proposed asset investment should not be viewed independent of other assets. New investments must be considered in light of their impact on the risk and return of the *portfolio* of assets. The financial manager's goal for the firm is to create an **efficient portfolio,** one that maximizes return for a given level of risk or minimizes risk for a given level of return. The statistical concept of *correlation* underlies the process of diversification that is used to develop an efficient portfolio of assets.

efficient portfolio A portfolio that maximizes return for a given level of risk or minimizes risk for a given level of return.

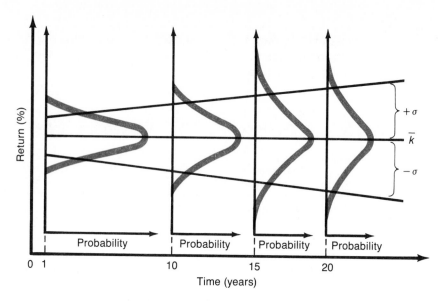

Figure 12.3   **Risk as a Function of Time**

The probability distributions of returns for a 1-year, 10-year, 15-year, and 20-year forecast, assuming each year's expected returns ($\bar{k}$) are equal, show that the variability of returns (σ)—and therefore the risk—increases with the passage of time.

correlation A statistical measure of the relationship between series of numbers representing data of any kind.

positively correlated Two series of numbers that move in the same direction.

negatively correlated Two series of numbers that move in opposite directions.

correlation coefficient A measure of the degree of correlation between two series of numbers.

perfectly positively correlated Two positively correlated series of numbers that have a correlation coefficient of +1.

perfectly negatively correlated Two negatively correlated series of numbers that have a correlation coefficient of −1.

Correlation

Correlation is a statistical measure of the relationship, if any, between series of numbers representing data of any kind, from returns to test scores. If two series move in the same direction, they are **positively correlated**; if the series move in opposite directions, they are **negatively correlated.** The degree of correlation is measured by the **correlation coefficient,** which ranges from +1 for **perfectly positively correlated** series to −1 for **perfectly negatively correlated** series. These two extremes are depicted for series M and N in Figure 12.4. The perfectly positively correlated series move exactly together; the perfectly negatively correlated series move in exactly opposite directions.

Diversification

To reduce overall risk, it is best to combine or add to the portfolio assets that have a negative (or a low positive) correlation. By combining negatively correlated assets, the overall variability of returns, or risk, can be reduced. Figure 12.5 on page 384 shows the effect of combining negatively correlated assets. Assets F and G individually have the same expected return $\bar{k}$. A portfolio containing these negatively correlated assets also has the return, $\bar{k}$, but has less risk (variability) than either of

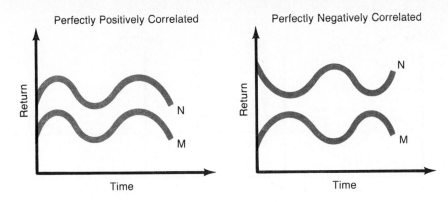

Figure 12.4   The Correlation between Series M and N
The perfectly positively correlated series M and N in the left graph move exactly together. The perfectly negatively correlated series M and N in the right graph move in exactly opposite directions.

the individual assets. Even if assets are not negatively correlated, the lower the positive correlation between them, the lower the resulting risk.[1]

A portfolio that combines two assets having perfectly positively correlated returns *cannot* reduce the portfolio's overall risk below the risk of the least risky asset. Alternatively, a portfolio combining two assets with less than perfectly positive correlation *can* reduce total risk to a level below that of either of the components. In certain situations total risk may be zero. For example, assume you manufacture machine tools. This business is very *cyclical*, having high sales when the economy is expanding and low sales during a recession. If you acquired another machine-tool company, which would have sales positively correlated with those of your firm, the combined sales would continue to be cyclical. Risk would remain the same. As an alternative, however, you could acquire a sewing machine manufacturer which is *countercyclical*. It has low sales during economic expansion and high sales during recession (since consumers are more likely to make their own clothes at such a time). Combination with the sewing machine manufacturer, which has negatively correlated sales, should reduce risk. The low machine tool sales during a recession would be balanced out by high sewing machine sales, and vice versa. A numeric example will provide a better understanding of the role of correlation in the diversification process.

---

[1]Some assets are *uncorrelated*. That is, they are completely unrelated in the sense that there is no interaction between their returns. Combining uncorrelated assets can reduce risk—not as effectively as combining negatively correlated assets, but more effectively than combining positively correlated assets. The correlation coefficient for uncorrelated assets is close to zero and acts as the midpoint between perfect positive and perfect negative correlation.

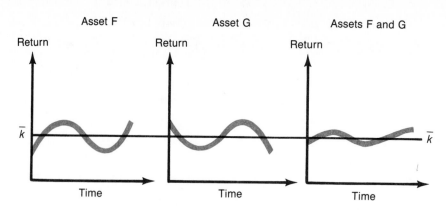

Figure 12.5   Combining Negatively Correlated Assets to Diversify Risk
The risk, or variability of returns, resulting from combining negatively correlated Assets F and G, both having the same expected return, $\bar{k}$, results in a portfolio (shown in the graph at right) with the same level of expected return but less risk.

EXAMPLE   Table 12.4 presents the forecasted returns from three different assets—X, Y, and Z—over the next five years, along with their expected values and standard deviations. Each of the assets has an expected value of return of 12 percent and a standard deviation of 3.16 percent. The assets therefore have equal return and equal risk, although their return patterns are not necessarily identical. A comparison of the return patterns of assets X and Y shows that they are perfectly negatively correlated, since they move in exactly opposite directions over time. A comparison of assets X and Z shows that they are perfectly positively correlated, since they move in precisely the same direction. (*Note:* The returns for X and Z are identical.)

Portfolio XY   By combining equal portions of assets X and Y—the perfectly negatively correlated assets—portfolio XY (shown in Table 12.4) is created. The risk in the portfolio created by this combination, as reflected by its standard deviation, is reduced to 0 percent, while the expected return value remains at 12 percent. Since both assets have the same expected return values, are combined in equal parts, and are perfectly negatively correlated, the combination results in the complete elimination of risk. Whenever assets are perfectly negatively correlated, an optimum combination (similar to the 50–50 mix in the case of assets X and Y) exists for which the resulting standard deviation will equal 0.

Portfolio XZ   By combining equal portions of assets X and Z—the perfectly positively correlated assets—portfolio XZ (shown in Table 12.4) is created. The risk in this portfolio, as reflected by its standard deviation, which remains at 3.16

Table 12.4   **Forecasted Returns, Expected Values, and Standard Deviations for Assets X, Y, and Z and Portfolios XY and XZ**

Year	Assets			Portfolios	
	X	**Y**	**Z**	**XY[a]** (50%X + 50%Y)	**XZ[b]** (50%X + 50%Z)
1993	8%	16%	8%	12%	8%
1994	10	14	10	12	10
1995	12	12	12	12	12
1996	14	10	14	12	14
1997	16	8	16	12	16
Statistics:					
Expected value[c]	12%	12%	12%	12%	12%
Standard deviation[d]	3.16%	3.16%	3.16%	0%	3.16%

[a]Portfolio XY, which consists of 50 percent of asset X and 50 percent of asset Y, illustrates *perfect negative correlation*, since these two return streams behave in completely opposite fashion over the five-year period. Its return values were calculated as follows.

Year	Forecasted return		Portfolio return calculation (3)	Expected portfolio return, k_p (4)
	Asset X (1)	Asset Y (2)		
1993	8%	16%	$(.50 \times 8\%) + (.50 \times 16\%) =$	12%
1994	10	14	$(.50 \times 10) + (.50 \times 14) =$	12
1995	12	12	$(.50 \times 12) + (.50 \times 12) =$	12
1996	14	10	$(.50 \times 14) + (.50 \times 10) =$	12
1997	16	8	$(.50 \times 16) + (.50 \times 8) =$	12

[b]Portfolio XZ, which consists of 50 percent of asset X and 50 percent of asset Z, illustrates *perfect positive correlation*, since these two return streams behave identically over the five-year period. Its return values were calculated using the same method demonstrated in note a above for portfolio XY.

[c]Since the probabilities associated with the returns are not given, the formula given earlier in Equation 12.1 could not be used to calculate expected value, $\bar{k}$. Instead the general formula

$$\bar{k} = \frac{\sum\limits_{i=1}^{n} k_i}{n}$$

where k_i = return i and n = the number of outcomes considered, was used. For portfolio XY:

$$\bar{k}_{xy} = \frac{12\% + 12\% + 12\% + 12\% + 12\%}{5} = \frac{60\%}{5} = \underline{\underline{12\%}}$$

The same formula was applied to find the expected value of return for assets X, Y, and Z, and portfolio XZ.

[d]Since the probabilities associated with the returns are not given, the formula given earlier in Equation 12.2 could not be used to calculate the standard deviations, σ_k. Instead the general formula

$$\sigma_k = \sqrt{\frac{\sum\limits_{i=1}^{n} (k_i - \bar{k})^2}{n - 1}}$$

where k_i = return i, $\bar{k}$ = expected value of return, and n = the number of outcomes considered, was used. For portfolio XY:

$$\sigma_{k_{xy}} = \sqrt{\frac{(12\% - 12\%)^2 + (12\% - 12\%)^2 + (12\% - 12\%)^2 + (12\% - 12\%)^2 + (12\% - 12\%)^2}{5 - 1}}$$

$$= \sqrt{\frac{0\% + 0\% + 0\% + 0\% + 0\%}{4}} = \sqrt{\frac{0\%}{4}} = \underline{\underline{0\%}}$$

The same formula was applied to find the standard deviation of returns for assets X, Y, and Z, and portfolio XZ.

percent, is unaffected by this combination, and the expected return value remains at 12 percent. Whenever perfectly positively correlated assets such as X and Z are combined, the standard deviation of the resulting portfolio cannot be reduced below that of the least risky asset; the maximum portfolio standard deviation will be that of the riskiest asset. Since assets X and Z have the same standard deviation (3.16 percent), the minimum and maximum standard deviations are both 3.16 percent. It is the only value that could be taken on by a combination of these assets. This result can be attributed to the unlikely situation that X and Z are identical assets.

Although detailed statistical explanations can be given for the behaviors illustrated in Table 12.4, the important point is that assets can be combined so that the resulting portfolio has less risk than that of either of the assets independently. And this can be achieved without any loss of return. Portfolio XY in the preceding example illustrated such behavior. The more negative (or less positive) the correlation between asset returns, the greater the risk-reducing benefits of diversification. In no case will creating portfolios of assets result in greater risk than that of the riskiest asset included in the portfolio. It is important to recognize that these relationships apply when considering the addition of an asset to an existing portfolio.

RISK AND RETURN: THE CAPITAL ASSET PRICING MODEL (CAPM)

capital asset pricing model (CAPM) The basic theory that links risk and return for all assets.

The most important aspect of risk is the *overall risk* of the firm as viewed by investors in the marketplace. Overall risk significantly affects investment opportunities—and even more important, the owners' wealth. The basic theory that links together risk and return for all assets is commonly called the **capital asset pricing model (CAPM).** Here we will use CAPM to understand the basic risk-return trade-offs involved in all types of financial decisions.

Types of Risk

To understand the basic types of risk, consider what happens when we begin with a single security (asset) in a portfolio. Then we expand the portfolio by randomly selecting additional securities from, say, the population of all actively traded securities. Using the standard deviation of returns, σ_k, to measure the total portfolio risk, Figure 12.6 depicts the behavior of the total portfolio risk (y-axis) as more securities are added

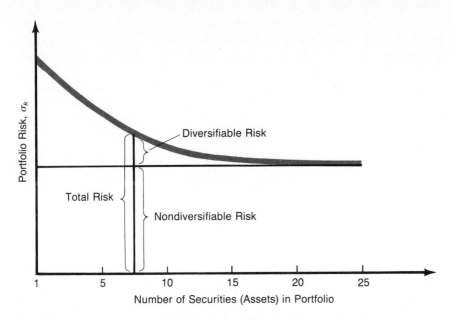

Figure 12.6   **Portfolio Risk and Diversification**

As randomly selected securities (assets) are combined to create a
portfolio, the *total risk* of the portfolio declines until 15 to 20 securities
are included. The portion of the risk eliminated is *diversifiable risk*, while
that remaining is *nondiversifiable risk.*

(x-axis). With the addition of securities, the total portfolio risk declines,
due to the effects of diversification (as explained in the previous section), and tends to approach a limit. Research has shown that most of
the benefits of diversification, in terms of risk reduction, can be gained
by forming portfolios containing 15 to 20 randomly selected
securities.

The **total risk** of a security can be viewed as consisting of two
parts:

Total security risk = nondiversifiable risk + diversifiable risk

Diversifiable risk represents the portion of an asset's risk associated
with random causes that can be eliminated through diversification. It is
attributable to firm-specific events, such as strikes, lawsuits, regulatory
actions, loss of a key account, and so forth. **Nondiversifiable risk** is attributable to market factors that affect all firms, and it cannot be eliminated through diversification. Factors such as war, inflation, international incidents, and political events account for nondiversifiable
risk.

Because, as illustrated in Figure 12.6, any investor can create a
portfolio of assets that will eliminate all, or virtually all, diversifiable
risk, the *only relevant risk is nondiversifiable risk.* Any investor (or firm)
must therefore be concerned solely with nondiversifiable risk; it reflects

total risk The combi-
nation of a security's
nondiversifiable and
diversifiable risk.

Equation 12.4
Formula showing the
two parts of total secu-
rity risk

diversifiable risk
The portion of risk attributable to firm-specific,
random causes; can be
eliminated through diver-
sification.

nondiversifiable risk
The relevant portion of
risk attributable to mar-
ket factors that affect all
firms; cannot be elimi-
nated through diversifi-
cation.

the contribution of an asset to the risk, or standard deviation, of the portfolio. The measurement of nondiversifiable risk is thus of primary importance in selecting those assets possessing the most desired risk-return characteristics.

The Model: CAPM

The capital asset pricing model (CAPM) links together nondiversifiable risk and return for all assets. We will discuss the model in three parts. The first part defines and describes the beta coefficient, which is a measure of nondiversifiable risk. The second part presents an equation of the model itself, and the final part graphically describes the relationship between risk and return.

Beta Coefficient

beta coefficient, b
An *index* of the degree of movement of an asset's return in response to a change in the market return; measures nondiversifiable risk.

market return The return on the market portfolio of all traded securities.

The **beta coefficient, b,** is used to measure nondiversifiable risk. It is an *index* of the degree of movement of an asset's return in response to a change in the *market return*. The beta coefficient for an asset can be found by examining the asset's historical returns relative to the returns for the market. The **market return** is the return on the market portfolio of all traded securities. The return on a portfolio of the stocks in *Standard & Poor's 500 Stock Composite Index* or some similar stock index is commonly used to measure the market return. Beta coefficients can be obtained for actively traded stocks from published sources, such as *Value Line Investment Survey*, or through brokerage firms. Betas for some selected stocks are given in Table 12.5. The beta coefficient for the

Table 12.5   **Beta Coefficients for Selected Stocks (May 31, 1991)**

Stock	Beta	Stock	Beta
Anheuser-Busch	1.00	Liz Claiborne	1.55
Apple Computer	1.25	Merrill Lynch & Company	1.30
Boston Edison	.70	Occidental Petroleum	.90
CBS, Inc.	1.05	Procter & Gamble	1.00
Caesars World	1.45	Seagram Company	1.10
Cascade Natural Gas	.65	Sony Corporation	.80
Delta Air Lines	1.05	Tootsie Roll Industries	1.05
Exxon Corporation	.75	Union Electric	.70
General Motors	1.00	Xerox Corporation	1.20
International Business Machines	.95	Zenith Electronics	1.45

Source: *Value Line Investment Survey* (New York: Value Line, Inc., May 31, 1991).

market is considered to be equal to 1.0; all other betas are viewed in relation to this value. Asset betas may take on values that are either positive or negative, but positive betas are the norm. The majority of beta coefficients fall between 0.5 and 2.0. Table 12.6 provides some selected beta values and their associated interpretations.

The Equation

The *capital asset pricing model (CAPM)*, given in Equation 12.5, uses the beta coefficient, *b*, to measure nondiversifiable risk:

$$k_j = R_F + [b_j \times (k_m - R_F)]$$

where

Equation 12.5
Expression for the capital asset pricing model (CAPM)

k_j = required return on asset *j*

R_F = risk-free rate of return, commonly measured by the return on a U.S. Treasury bill

b_j = beta coefficient or index of nondiversifiable risk for asset *j*

k_m = market return; the return on the market portfolio of assets

The required return on an asset, k_j, is an increasing function of beta, b_j, which measures nondiversifiable risk. In other words, *the higher the risk, the higher the required return, and vice versa.* The model can be broken into two parts: (1) the *risk-free rate*, R_F, and (2) the *risk premium*, $b_j \times (k_m - R_F)$. The $(k_m - R_F)$ portion of the risk premium is called the *market risk premium.* It represents the premium the investor must receive for taking the average amount of risk associated with holding the market portfolio of assets. Let us look at an example.

Table 12.6   **Selected Beta Coefficients and Their Interpretations**

Beta	Comment	Interpretation[a]
2.0		Twice as responsive, or risky, as the market
1.0	Move in same direction as market	Same response or risk as the market (i.e., average risk)
.5		Only half as responsive, or risky, as the market
0		Unaffected by market movement
− .5		Only half as responsive, or risky, as the market
−1.0	Move in opposite direction to market	Same response or risk as the market (i.e., average risk)
−2.0		Twice as responsive, or risky, as the market

[a]A stock that is twice as responsive as the market will experience a 2 percent change in its return for each 1 percent change in the return of the market portfolio, whereas the return of a stock that is half as responsive as the market will change by $\frac{1}{2}$ of 1 percent for each 1 percent change in the return of the market portfolio.

S M A L L   B U S I N E S S

Payco American: Recession Insurance

Most stocks have positive betas. As economic expansion slows down and recedes, earnings and cash flows tend to decline. So do their betas. A couple of firms, however, do quite well in recessions. In early 1991, for example, Payco American was profiting from the recession.

Payco American is a collection agency; it attracts clients as the number of unpaid bills rises. Credit information and collection operations become more valuable as recessions deepen, enhancing the value of Payco's database and collection ability. Benefitting from a gloomy economic forecast, Payco's 1991 earnings and cash flows were expected to increase 27 percent from 1990 levels. Further enhancing Payco's value was its increasing share of the debt-collection business. Consequently, Payco's share price rose approximately 31 percent from November 1990 to January 1991.

Due to its financial strength and counter-cyclical nature, Payco was considered to be a likely takeover target. Acquiring financial managers could offset some of the risk in their other divisions with the revenue stream available from Payco. At a minimum, Payco American was considered attractive to investors seeking a recession-proof investment.

Source: "Tough times, yippee!" *Business Week*, January 14, 1991, p. 58.

EXAMPLE   Herbst Corporation, a growing computer software developer, wishes to determine the required return on an asset—asset Z—that has a beta, b_z, of 1.5. The risk-free rate of return is found to be 7 percent; the return on the market portfolio of assets is 11 percent. Substituting $b_z = 1.5$, $R_F = 7$ percent, and $k_m = 11$ percent into the capital asset pricing model given in Equation 12.5 yields a required return of:

$$k_z = 7\% + [1.5 \times (11\% - 7\%)] = 7\% + 6\% = \underline{\underline{13\%}}$$

The market risk premium of 4 percent (11% −7%), when adjusted for the asset's index of risk (beta) of 1.5, results in a risk premium of 6 percent (1.5 × 4%). This premium, when added to the 7 percent risk-free rate, results in a 13 percent required return. Other things being equal, the higher the beta, the greater the required return, and vice versa.

The Graph: The Security Market Line (SML)

When the capital asset pricing model is depicted graphically, it is called the **security market line (SML).** The SML will, in fact, be a straight line. It reflects for each level of nondiversifiable risk (beta) the required return in the marketplace. In the graph, risk as measured by beta, b, is plotted on the x-axis, and required returns, k, are plotted on the y-axis. The risk-return trade-off is clearly represented by the SML. Let us look at an example.

security market line (SML) The depiction of the capital asset pricing model (CAPM) as a graph that reflects the required return for each level of nondiversifiable risk (beta).

EXAMPLE   In the preceding example for the Herbst Corporation, the risk-free rate, R_F, was 7 percent, and the market return, k_m, was 11 percent. Since the betas associated with R_F and k_m, b_{R_F} and b_m, are by definition 0^2 and 1, respectively, the SML can be plotted using these two sets of coordinates. (That is, $b_{R_F} = 0$, $R_F = 7\%$; and $b_m = 1$, $k_m = 11\%$.) Figure 12.7 presents the security market line that results from plotting the given coordinates. As traditionally shown, the security market line in Figure 12.7 presents the required return associated with all positive betas. The market risk premium of 4 percent (k_m of $11\% - R_F$ of 7%) has been highlighted. With the beta for asset Z, b_z, of 1.5, its corresponding required return, k_z, is 13 percent. Also shown in the figure is asset Z's risk premium of 6 percent (k_z of $13\% - R_F$ of 7%). For assets with betas greater than 1, the risk premium is greater than that for the market; for assets with betas less than 1, the risk premium is less than that for the market.

VALUATION FUNDAMENTALS

As stated at the beginning of this chapter, *valuation* is the process that links risk and return to determine the worth of an asset. It is a relatively simple process that can be applied to expected streams of benefits from bonds, stocks, income properties, oil wells, and so on to determine their worth at a given point in time. To do this, the manager uses the time value of money techniques presented in Chapter 11 and the concepts of risk and return developed earlier in this chapter.

Key Inputs

The key inputs to the valuation process include cash flows (returns), timing, and the discount rate (risk). Each is described briefly below.

---

[2]Since R_F is the rate of return on a risk-free asset, the beta associated with the risk-free asset, b_{R_F}, would equal 0. The 0 beta on the risk-free asset reflects not only its absence of risk but also the fact that the asset's return is unaffected by movements in the market return.

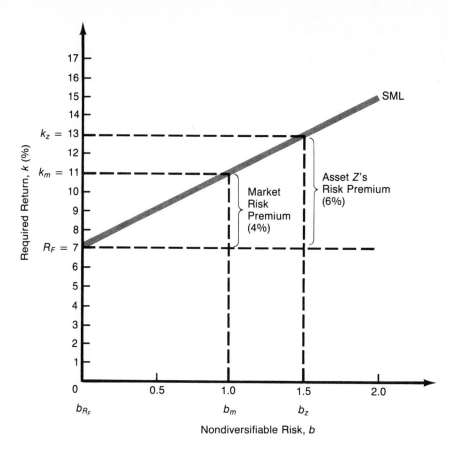

Figure 12.7   The Security Market Line (SML) with Herbst Corporation's Asset Z Data Shown

At a beta of 0, the required return is the risk-free rate of 7 percent, and at a beta of 1.0, the required return is 11 percent (the 7% risk-free rate + a 4% market risk premium). The required return for asset Z, which has a beta of 1.5, is 13 percent (the 7% risk-free rate + a 6% risk premium).

Cash Flows (Returns)

The value of any asset depends on the cash flow(s) it is expected to provide over the ownership period. To have value, an asset does not have to provide an annual cash flow; it can provide an intermittent cash flow or even a single cash flow over the period.

EXAMPLE   Nancy Dorr, the financial analyst for Kemp Industries, a diversified holding company, wishes to estimate the value of three of its assets—common stock in Wortz United, an interest in an oil well, and an original painting by a well-known artist. Her cash flow estimates for each were:

Stock in Wortz United   Expect to receive cash dividends of $300 per year indefinitely.

Oil well Expect to receive cash flow of $2,000 at the end of one year, $4,000 at the end of two years, and $10,000 at the end of four years, when the well is to be sold.

Original painting Expect to be able to sell the painting in five years for $85,000.

Having developed these cash flow estimates, Nancy has taken the first step toward placing a value on each of these assets.

Timing

In addition to making cash flow estimates, we must know the timing of the cash flows.[3] It is customary to specify the timing along with the amounts of cash flow. For example, the cash flows of $2,000, $4,000, and $10,000 for the oil well in the example were expected to occur at the end of years 1, 2, and 4, respectively. In combination, the cash flow and its timing fully define the return expected from the asset.

Discount Rate (Risk)

Risk, as noted earlier, describes the chance that an expected outcome will not be realized. The level of risk associated with a given cash flow can significantly affect its value. In general, the greater the risk of (or the less certain) a cash flow, the lower its value. In terms of present value (see Chapter 11), greater risk can be incorporated into an analysis by using a higher discount rate or required return. Recall that in the capital asset pricing model (CAPM) (see Equation 12.5), the greater the risk as measured by beta, b, the higher the required return, k. In the valuation process, too, the discount rate is used to incoporate risk into the analysis—the higher the risk, the greater the discount rate (required return), and vice versa.

EXAMPLE   Let's return to Nancy Dorr's task of placing a value on the original painting owned by Kemp Industries. Remember that it is expected to provide a single cash flow of $85,000 from its sale at the end of five years. Let's consider two scenarios:

Scenario 1—Certainty A major art gallery has contracted to buy the painting for $85,000 at the end of five years. Because this is considered a certain situation, Nancy views this asset as "money in the bank." She would use the prevailing risk-free rate, R_F, of 9 percent as the discount rate when calculating the value of the painting.

Scenario 2—High Risk The value of original paintings by this artist has fluctuated widely over the past 10 years. Although Nancy expects to be able to get $85,000 for the painting, she realizes that its sale price in five years could range between $30,000 and $140,000. Due to the high uncertainty surrounding the painting's value, Nancy believes a 15 percent discount rate is appropriate.

---

[3]Although cash flows can occur at any time during a year, for computational convenience as well as custom, we will assume they occur at the *end* of the year unless otherwise noted.

The preceding example and the associated estimates of the appropriate discount rate illustrate the role this rate plays in capturing risk. The often subjective nature of such estimates is also clear.

The Basic Valuation Model

Simply stated, the value of any asset is *the present value of all future cash flows it is expected to provide over the relevant time period.* The time period can be as short as one year or as long as infinity. The value of an asset is therefore determined by discounting the expected cash flows back to their present value. A discount rate commensurate with the asset's risk is used. Utilizing the present-value techniques presented in Chapter 11, we can express the value of any asset at time zero, V_0, as

Equation 12.6
Formula for the value of any asset

$$V_0 = \frac{CF_1}{(1 + k)^1} + \frac{CF_2}{(1 + k)^2} + \cdots + \frac{CF_n}{(1 + k)^n}$$

where

V_0 = value of the asset at time zero

CF_t = cash flow expected at the end of year t

k = appropriate discount rate (required return)

n = relevant time period

Using present-value interest factor notation, $PVIF_{k,n}$ from Chapter 11, we can rewrite Equation 12.6 as

Equation 12.7
Formula for the value of any asset using present-value interest factor notation

$$V_0 = [CF_1 \times (PVIF_{k,1})] + [CF_2 \times (PVIF_{k,2})] + \cdots + [CF_n \times (PVIF_{k,n})]$$

Substituting the expected cash flows, CF_t, over the relevant time period, n, and the appropriate discount rate, k, into Equation 12.7, we can determine the value of any asset.

EXAMPLE   Nancy Dorr, using appropriate discount rates and Equation 12.7, calculated the value of each asset as shown in Table 12.7. The Wortz United stock has a value of $2,500; the oil well's value is $9,262; and the original painting has a value of $42,245. Note that regardless of the pattern of the expected cash flow from an asset, the basic valuation equation can be used to determine its value.

BOND AND PREFERRED STOCK VALUES

The basic valuation equation can be customized for use in valuing specific securities—bonds, preferred stock, and common stock. Bonds and preferred stock are similar since they have stated contractual interest and dividend cash flows. The dividends on common stock, on the other

Table 12.7   **Valuation of Kemp Industries' Assets by Nancy Dorr**

Asset	Cash flow, CF		Appropriate discount rate (%)	Valuation
Wortz United stock[a]	$300/year indefinitely		12	$V_0 = \$300 \times (PVIFA_{12\%,\infty})$ $= \dfrac{\$300}{.12} = \underline{\underline{\$2,500}}$
Oil well[b]	Year (t)	CF_t	20	$V_0 = [\$2,000 \times (PVIF_{20\%,1})]$
	1	$ 2,000		$+ [\$4,000 \times (PVIF_{20\%,2})]$
	2	4,000		$+ [\$0 \times (PVIF_{20\%,3})]$
	3	0		$+ [\$10,000 \times (PVIF_{20\%,4})]$
	4	10,000		$= [\$2,000 \times (.833)]$
				$+ [\$4,000 \times (.694)]$
				$+ [\$0 \times (.579)]$
				$+ [\$10,000 \times (.482)]$
				$= \$1,666 + \$2,776$
				$+ \$0 + \$4,820$
				$= \underline{\underline{\$9,262}}$
Original painting[c]	$85,000 at end of year 5		15	$V_0 = \$85,000 \times (PVIF_{15\%,5})$ $= \$85,000 \times (.497)$ $= \underline{\underline{\$42,245}}$

[a]This is a perpetuity (infinite-lived annuity), and therefore Equation 11.22 is applied.
[b]This is a mixed stream of cash flows and therefore requires a number of *PVIFs* as noted.
[c]This is a lump-sum cash flow and therefore requires a single *PVIF*.

hand, are not known in advance. Bond and preferred stock valuation is described in this section. Common stock valuation is discussed in the following section.

Bond Valuation

Bonds are long-term debt instruments used by business and government to raise large sums of money. (Bonds are discussed fully in Chapter 19.) As noted in Chapter 2, most corporate bonds pay interest *semiannually* (every six months) at a stated *coupon interest rate*, have an initial *maturity* of 10 to 30 years, and have a *par*, or *face, value* of $1,000 that must be repaid at maturity. An example will illustrate the point.

EXAMPLE   Stills Company, a large defense contractor, on January 1, 1993, issued a 10 percent coupon interest rate, 10-year bond with a $1,000 par value that pays interest semiannually. Investors who buy this bond receive the contractual right to (1) $100 annual interest (10% coupon interest rate ×

$1,000 par value) distributed as $50 ($\frac{1}{2} \times \$100$) at the end of each six months and (2) the $1,000 par value at the end of the tenth year.

Basic Bond Valuation

The value of a bond is the present value of the payments its issuer is obligated to make from the current time until it matures. The appropriate discount rate would be the required return, k_d, which depends on prevailing interest rates and risk. The basic equation for the value of a bond is given by Equation 12.8:

Equation 12.8
Formula for the value of a bond

Equation 12.8a
Simplified formula for the value of a bond using present-value interest factor notation

$$B_0 = I \times \left[\sum_{i=1}^{n} \frac{1}{(1 + k_d)^t} \right] + M \times \left[\frac{1}{(1 + k_d)^n} \right]$$

$$= I \times (PVIFA_{k_d,n}) + M \times (PVIF_{k_d,n})$$

where

B_0 = the value of the bond at time zero

I = *annual* interest paid in dollars[4]

n = years to maturity

M = par value in dollars

k_d = required return on a bond

Equation 12.8a along with the appropriate financial tables (C-3 and C-4) or a business calculator can be used to calculate bond value.

EXAMPLE   Using the Stills Company data for the January 1, 1993, new issue and *assuming that interest is paid annually* and that the required return is equal to the bond's coupon interest rate, $I = \$100$, $k_d = 10$ percent, $M = \$1,000$, and $n = 10$ years.

Table Use   Substituting the values noted above into Equation 12.8a yields:

$$B_0 = \$100 \times (PVIFA_{10\%,10yrs}) + \$1,000 \times (PVIF_{10\%,10yrs})$$

$$= \$100 \times (6.145) + \$1,000 \times (.386)$$

$$= \$614.50 + \$386.00 = \underline{\$1,000.50}$$

The bond therefore has a value of approximately $1,000.[5]

Calculator Use   Using the calculator, first punch in 10 and depress the "N" key; then punch in the required return, k_d, of 10 and depress the "%i" key; next punch in the annual interest, I, of $100 and depress the "PMT" key; then punch

---

[4]The payment of annual rather than semiannual bond interest is assumed throughout the following discussion. This assumption simplifies the calculations involved while maintaining the conceptual accuracy of the valuation procedures presented.

[5]Note that a slight rounding error ($.50) results here due to the use of the table factors rounded to the nearest thousandth.

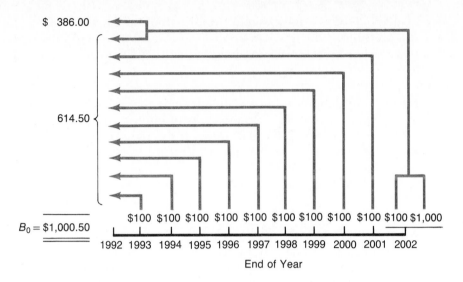

$ 386.00

614.50

$B_0 = \$1,000.50$

$100 $100 $100 $100 $100 $100 $100 $100 $100 $100 $1,000

1992 1993 1994 1995 1996 1997 1998 1999 2000 2001 2002

End of Year

Figure 12.8 Graphic Depiction of Bond Valuation (Stills Company's 10 Percent Coupon Interest Rate, 10-Year Maturity, $1,000 Par, January 1, 1993, Issue Paying Annual Interest; Required Return = 10 Percent)
The $1,000.50 value of the Stills Company bond is found by adding the $614.50 present value (found using the 10 percent required return) of the 10 annual $100 interest payments to the $386.00 present value (also at 10 percent) of the $1,000 par value to be received in 10 years at maturity.

in the maturity value, M, of $1,000 and depress the "FV" key; and to calculate the bond value, depress the "CPT" key followed by the "PV" key. The bond value of exactly $1,000 should appear on the calculator display.

Note that *the bond value calculated in the example above is equal to its par value. This will always be the case when the required return is equal to the coupon interest rate.* The computations involved in finding the bond value are depicted graphically on the time line in Figure 12.8.

Required Returns and Bond Values

Whenever the required return on a bond differs from the bond's coupon interest rate, the bond's value will differ from its par, or face, value. The required return on the bond is likely to differ from the coupon interest rate for either of two reasons: (1) Economic conditions may have changed, causing a shift in the basic cost of long-term funds. Or (2) the firm's risk has changed. Increases in the basic cost of long-term funds or in risk will raise the required return, and vice versa.

Regardless of the exact cause, the important point is that when the required return is greater than the coupon rate of interest, the bond value, B_0, will be less than its par value, M. In this case the bond is said to sell at a **discount**, which will equal $M - B_0$. On the other hand, when the required rate of return falls below the coupon rate of interest, the

discount The amount by which a bond sells at a value less than its par, or face, value.

premium The amount by which a bond sells at a value greater than its par, or face, value.

bond value will be greater than par. In this situation the bond is said to sell at a **premium**, which will equal $B_0 - M$. An example will illustrate this point using Equation 12.8a along with either financial tables or a business calculator.

EXAMPLE   In the preceding example we saw that when the required return equaled the coupon rate of interest, the bond's value equaled its $1,000 par value. If for the same bond the required return were to rise to 12 percent, its value would be found as follows:

Table Use

$$B_0 = \$100 \times (PVIFA_{12\%,10\text{yrs}}) + \$1,000 \times (PVIF_{12\%,10\text{yrs}})$$
$$= \$100 \times (5.650) + \$1,000 \times (.322) = \underline{\$887.00}$$

Calculator Use   First punch in 10 and depress the "N" key; then punch in the required return of 12 and depress the "%i" key; next punch in the annual interest of $100 and depress the "PMT" key; then punch in the maturity value of $1,000 and depress the "FV" key; and to calculate the bond value, depress the "CPT" key followed by the "PV" key. The bond value of $887.00 should appear on the calculator display.

   The bond would therefore sell at a *discount* of $113.00 ($1,000 par value − $887.00 value).

   If, on the other hand, the required return fell to, say, 8 percent, the bond's value would be found as follows:

Table Use

$$B_0 = \$100 \times (PVIFA_{8\%,10\text{yrs}}) + \$1,000 \times (PVIF_{8\%,10\text{yrs}})$$
$$= \$100 \times (6.710) + \$1,000 \times (.463) = \underline{\$1,134.00}$$

Calculator Use   First punch in 10 and depress the "N" key; then punch in the required return of 8 and depress the "%i" key; next punch in the annual interest of $100 and depress the "PMT" key; then punch in the maturity value of $1,000 and depress the "FV" key; and to calculate the bond value, depress the "CPT" key followed by the "PV" key. The bond value of $1,134.20 should appear on the calculator display. Note that this value is more precise than the $1,134 value calculated above, using the rounded financial table factors.

   The bond would therefore sell for a *premium* of about $134 ($1,134.00 value − $1,000 par value). The results of this and earlier calculations for Stills Company's bond values are summarized in Table 12.8.

Preferred Stock Valuation

As noted in Chapter 2, preferred stock promises to pay a fixed periodic dividend. Since preferred stock never matures, its divided payments can be viewed as a perpetuity. Assuming that preferred stock dividends,

FINANCE   IN   ACTION

Georgia-Pacific Attempts to Soothe Lenders' Nerves

Before the RJR Nabisco leveraged buyout was announced, bond-holders held investment-grade debt. After the announcement they owned junk bonds. That event and other similar leveraged buyouts in the 1980s led investors to abandon bond markets and drove up financing costs for even the highest-quality lenders. In order to attract the needed financing for Georgia-Pacific Corporation's acquisition of Great Northern Nekoosa, credit-sensitive notes were used to draw investors back into the high-yield bond market.

Credit sensitive notes protect investors from a sudden decline in issuer credit rating. If the credit rating drops, Georgia-Pacific will pay a higher interest rate. If Georgia-Pacific's credit rating improves, the interest payment will decline. The company essentially assumes some of the bondholder's default risk exposure.

The reduced risk has attracted investors and reduced Georgia-Pacific's original interest rate. Georgia-Pacific's seven-year notes were issued to yield 10 percent. A fixed-rate bond would have cost Georgia-Pacific 10.75 percent. The rate reduction decreases Georgia-Pacific's annual interest expense on the $600 million issue by $4.5 million. Georgia Pacific is gambling that the acquisition of Great Northern Nekoosa will improve its balance sheet, and its credit rating, and allow it to reduce its interest payments to the minimum 9.55 percent.

Source: "Hunting for gold in the company attic," *Business Month*, September 1990, p. 78.

Table 12.8   **Bond Values for Various Required Returns (10 Percent Coupon Interest Rate, 10-Year Maturity, $1,000 Par, Interest Paid Annually)**

Required return, k_d (%)	Bond value, B_0	Status
12	$ 887.00	Discount
10	1,000.00	Par value
8	1,134.00	Premium

D_p, are paid *annually,*[6] and the required return is k_p, the value of preferred stock, PS_0, can be given by Equation 12.9:

Equation 12.9
Formula for the value
of preferred stock

$$PS_0 = D_P \times \left(\frac{1}{k_p}\right) = \frac{D_p}{k_p}$$

Recall from Chapter 11 that in the case of a perpetuity, the present-value interest factor, $PVIFA_{k_p,\infty} = 1/k_p$, must be used. The use of this factor to find the value of preferred stock can be noted in Equation 12.9. An example will show how this is done.

EXAMPLE   Stills Company has an issue of preferred stock outstanding that has a stated annual dividend of $5. The required return on the preferred stock has been estimated to be 13 percent. Substituting $D_p = \$5$ and $k_p = 13\%$ into Equation 12.9 yields a preferred stock value of $38.46 ($5 ÷ .13). Equation 12.9 can be used in this manner to find the value of any perpetuity.

COMMON STOCK VALUATION

Common stockholders expect to be rewarded through the receipt of periodic cash dividends and an increasing—or at least nondeclining—share value. Prospective owners and security analysts also frequently estimate the firm's value. They choose to purchase the stock when they believe it to be *undervalued* (i.e., that its true value is greater than its market price). They sell when they feel it is *overvalued* (i.e., that its market price is greater than its true value).

The Basic Equation

Like bonds and preferred stock, the value of a share of common stock is equal to the present value of all future benefits it is expected to provide. That is, *the value of a share of common stock is equal to the present value of all future dividends it is expected to provide over an infinite time horizon.* By selling stock at a price above that originally paid, a stockholder can earn capital gains in addition to dividends. Yet what the stockholder is really selling is the right to all future dividends. Therefore, from a valuation viewpoint only dividends are relevant. By redefining terms, the basic valuation model in Equation 12.6 can be specified for common stock as given in Equation 12.10:

Equation 12.10
Basic formula for the
value of common stock

$$P_0 = \frac{D_1}{(1 + k_s)^1} + \frac{D_2}{(1 + k_s)^2} + \cdots + \frac{D_\infty}{(1 + k_s)^\infty}$$

---

[6]The payment of annual rather than quarterly dividends is assumed for simplicity. Preferred stock is discussed in detail in Chapter 20.

where

P_0 = value of common stock

D_t = per-share dividend expected at the end of year t

k_s = required return on common stock

The equation can be simplified somewhat by redefining each year's dividend, D_t, in terms of anticipated growth. We will consider two cases here—zero growth and constant growth.

Zero Growth

The simplest approach to dividend valuation, the **zero growth model,** assumes a constant, nongrowing dividend stream. In terms of the notation already introduced,

$$D_1 = D_2 = \cdots = D_\infty$$

Letting D_1 represent the amount of the annual dividend, Equation 12.10 under zero growth would reduce to

$$P_0 = D_1 \sum_{t=1}^{\infty} \frac{1}{(1 + k_s)^t} = D_1 \times (PVIFA_{k_s, \infty}) = \frac{D_1}{k_s}$$

zero growth model
An approach to dividend valuation that assumes a constant, nongrowing dividend stream.

Equation 12.11
Formula for the value of a share of stock assuming zero dividend growth

The equation shows that with zero growth, the value of a share of stock would equal the present value of a perpetuity of D_1 dollars discounted at a rate k_s. Let us look at an example.

EXAMPLE   The dividend of Addison Company, an established textile producer, is expected to remain constant at $3 per share indefinitely. If the required return on its stock is 15 percent, the stock's value is $20 ($3 ÷ .15).

constant growth model   An approach to dividend valuation that assumes dividends will grow at a constant rate that is less than the required return.

Constant Growth

The most widely cited dividend valuation approach, the **constant growth model,** assumes that dividends will grow at a constant rate, g, that is less than the required return, $k_s (g < k_s)$. Letting D_0 represent the most recent dividend, Equation 12.10 can be rewritten as follows:

$$P_0 = \frac{D_0 \times (1 + g)^1}{(1 + k_s)^1} + \frac{D_0 \times (1 + g)^2}{(1 + k_s)^2} + \cdots + \frac{D_0 \times (1 + g)^\infty}{(1 + k_s)^\infty}$$

If we simplify Equation 12.12, it can be rewritten as follows

$$P_0 = \frac{D_1}{k_s - g}$$

Equation 12.12
General formula for the value of a share of stock assuming constant dividend growth

Equation 12.13
Simplified formula for the value of a share of stock under the constant growth, or Gordon, model

The constant growth model in Equation 12.13 is commonly called the **Gordon model.** An example will show how it works.

Gordon model
Common name for the constant growth model.

EXAMPLE   Honee Company, a small cosmetics company, from 1987 through 1992 paid the per-share dividends shown below.

Year	Dividend ($)
1992	1.40
1991	1.29
1990	1.20
1989	1.12
1988	1.05
1987	1.00

The annual growth rate of dividends is assumed to equal the expected constant rate of dividend growth, g. Using Appendix Table C-3 for the present-value interest factor, $PVIF$, and the technique for finding growth rates described in Chapter 11, we find that the annual growth rate of dividends equals 7 percent.[7] The company estimates that its dividend in 1993, D_1, will equal $1.50. The required return, k_s, is assumed to be 15 percent. Substituting these values into Equation 12.13, the value of the stock is

$$P_0 = \frac{\$1.50}{.15 - .07} = \frac{\$1.50}{.08} = \underline{\underline{\$18.75 \text{ per share}}}$$

Assuming that the values of D_1, k_s, and g are accurately estimated, Honee Company's stock value is $18.75.

Popular Approaches

Many popular approaches for measuring value exist, but only one is widely accepted. The popular approaches to valuation include the use of book value, liquidation value, or some type of a price/earnings multiple.

---

[7]The technique involves solving the following equation for g:

$$D_{1992} = D_{1987} \times (1 + g)^5$$

$$\frac{D_{1987}}{D_{1992}} = \frac{1}{(1 + g)^5} = PVIF_{g,5}$$

Two basic steps can be followed. First, dividing the earliest dividend ($D_{1987} = \$1.00$) by the most recent dividend ($D_{1992} = \$1.40$), a factor for the present value of one dollar, $PVIF$, of .714 ($1.00 ÷ $1.40) results. Although six dividends are shown, *they reflect only five years of growth*. Looking across the table at the present-value interest factors, $PVIF$, for five years, the factor closest to .714 occurs at 7 percent (.713). Therefore, the growth rate of the dividends, rounded to the nearest whole percentage, is 7 percent.

Alternatively, using a business calculator, begin by punching in the 1987 value of $1.00 and depress the "PV" key; next punch in the 1992 value of $1.40 and depress the "FV" key; then punch in the number of years of growth—5—and depress the "N" key; and finally, to get the growth rate, depress the "CPT" key followed by the "%i" key. The growth rate of 6.96 percent, which we round to 7 percent, appears on the display.

Book Value

Book value per share is simply the amount per share of common stock to be received if all assets are liquidated for their exact book (accounting) value and if the proceeds remaining after paying all liabilities (including preferred stock) are divided among the common stockholders. This method lacks sophistication and can be criticized on the basis of its reliance on historical balance sheet data. It ignores the firm's expected earnings potential and generally lacks any true relationship to the firm's value in the marketplace. Let us look at an example.

book value per share The amount per share of common stock if all assets are liquidated for their book value and the remaining proceeds after paying all liabilities (including preferred stock) are divided among the common stockholders.

EXAMPLE   Honee Company currently (December 31, 1992) has total assets of $6 million, total liabilities including preferred stock of $4.5 million, and 100,000 shares of common stock outstanding. Its book value per share would therefore be

$$\frac{\$6,000,000 - \$4,500,000}{100,000 \text{ shares}} = \underline{\underline{\$15 \text{ per share}}}$$

Since this value assumes that assets are liquidated for their book value, it may not represent the minimum share value. As a matter of fact, although most stocks sell above book value, it is not unusual to find stocks selling below book value.

Liquidation Value

Liquidation value per share is the *actual* amount per share of common stock to be received if all the firm's assets are sold, liabilities (including preferred stock) are paid, and any remaining money is divided among the common stockholders.[8] This measure is more realistic than book value, but it still fails to consider the earning power of the firm's assets. An example will illustrate.

liquidation value per share The *actual* amount per share of common stock if all assets are sold, liabilities (including preferred stock) are paid, and any remaining money is divided among common stockholders.

EXAMPLE   Honee Company found upon investigation that it would obtain only $5.25 million if it liquidated its assets today. The firm's liquidation value per share would therefore be

$$\frac{\$5,250,000 - \$4,500,000}{100,000 \text{ shares}} = \underline{\underline{\$7.50 \text{ per share}}}$$

Ignoring any expenses of liquidation, this would be the firm's minimum value.

Price/Earnings (P/E) Multiples

The *price/earnings (P/E) ratio*, introduced in Chapter 4, reflects the amount investors are willing to pay for each dollar of earnings. The average P/E ratio in a particular industry can be used as the guide to a

---

[8]In the event of liquidation, creditors' claims must be satisfied first, then those of the preferred stockholders. Anything left goes to common stockholders. A more detailed discussion of liquidation procedures is presented in Chapter 17.

price/earnings multiple approach A technique to estimate the firm's share value; calculated by multiplying the firm's expected earnings per share by the average price/earnings ratio for the industry.

firm's value if it is assumed that investors value the earnings of a given firm the same as they do the "average" firm in that industry. The **price/earnings multiple approach** to value is a popular technique; the firm's expected earnings per share (EPS) are multiplied by the average price/earnings (P/E) ratio for the industry to estimate the firm's share value. The average P/E ratio for the industry can be obtained from a source such as *Standard & Poor's Industrial Ratios*.

The use of P/E multiples is especially helpful in valuing firms that are not publicly traded, whereas the use of the market price may be preferable for a publicly traded firm. In any case, the price/earnings multiple approach is considered superior to the use of book or liquidation values since it considers *expected* earnings. An example will demonstrate the use of price/earnings multiples.

EXAMPLE   Honee Company is expected to earn $2.60 per share next year (1993). This expectation is based on an analysis of the firm's historical earnings trend and expected economic and industry conditions. The average price/earnings ratio for firms in the same industry is 7. Multiplying Honee's expected earnings per share of $2.60 by this ratio gives us a value for the firm's shares of $18.20, assuming that investors will continue to measure the value of the average firm at 7 times its earnings.

Decision Making and Common Stock Value

Valuation equations measure the stock value at a point in time based on expected return (D_1, g) and risk (k_s) data. The decisions of the financial manager, through their effect on these variables, can cause the value of the firm, P_0, to change.

Changes in Expected Return

Assuming that economic conditions remain stable, any management action that would cause current and prospective stockholders to raise their dividend expectations should increase the firm's value. In Equation 12.13 we can see that P_0 will increase for any increase in D_1 or g. Any action of the financial manager that will increase the level of expected returns without changing risk (the required return) should be undertaken, since it will positively affect owners' wealth. An example will illustrate.

EXAMPLE   In an earlier example using the constant growth model, Honee Company was found to have a share value of $18.75. Imagine that on the following day the company announced a major technological breakthrough that would revolutionize its industry. Current and prospective stockholders are not expected to adjust their required return of 15 percent, but they do expect that future dividends will be increased. Specifically, they feel that although the dividend next year,

D_1, will remain at \$1.50, the expected rate of growth will increase from 7 to 9 percent. Substituting $D_1 =$ \$1.50, $k_s =$ .15, and $g = .09$ into Equation 12.13 results in a share value of \$25 [i.e., \$1.50 ÷ (.15 − .09)]. The higher expected future dividends, reflected in the increase in the growth rate, g, caused the increase in value.

Changes in Risk

Although k_s is defined as the required return, it is directly related to the nondiversifiable risk, which can be measured by the beta coefficient. The *capital asset pricing model (CAPM)* given in Equation 12.5 shows this relationship. With the risk-free rate, R_F, and the market return, k_m, held constant, the required return, k_s, depends directly on beta. In other words, any action taken by the financial manager that increases risk will also increase the required return. In Equation 12.13 it can be seen that with all else constant, an increase in the required return, k_s, will reduce share value, P_0, and vice versa. Thus any action of the financial manager that increases risk contributes toward a reduction in value, and vice versa. An example will illustrate.

EXAMPLE   Assume that Honee Company's 15 percent required return resulted from a risk-free rate, R_F, of 9 percent, a market return, k_m, of 13 percent, and a beta, b, of 1.50. Substituting into the capital asset pricing model (Equation 12.5), we get the 15 percent required return, k_s:

$$k_s = 9\% + [1.50 \times (13\% - 9\%)] = \underline{\underline{15\%}}$$

With this return, the value of the firm, P_0, was calculated to be \$18.75 in the earlier example.

Now imagine that the financial manager makes a decision that, without changing expected dividends, increases the firm's beta to 1.75. Assuming that R_F and k_m remain at 9 and 13 percent, respectively, the required return will increase to 16 percent (i.e., $9\% + [1.75 \times (13\% - 9\%)]$). The higher required return will compensate stockholders for the increased risk. Substituting $D_1 =$ \$1.50, $k_s = .16$, and $g = .07$ into the valuation equation, Equation 12.13, results in a share value of \$16.67 [i.e., \$1.50 ÷ (.16 − .07)]. As expected, the owners, by raising the required return (without any corresponding increase in expected return), cause the firm's stock value to decline. Clearly the financial manager's action was not in the owners' best interest.

Combined Effect

A financial decision rarely affects return and risk independently; most decisions affect both factors. In terms of the measures presented, with an increase in risk (beta, b) one would expect an increase in return (D_1 or g, or both), assuming that R_F and k_m remain unchanged. Depending on the size of the changes in these variables, the net effect on value can be assessed.

EXAMPLE   If we assume that the two changes illustrated for Honee Company in the preceding examples occur simultaneously as a result of an action of the financial decision maker, key variable values would be $D_1 = \$1.50$, $k_s = .16$, and $g = .09$. Substituting into the valuation model, we obtain a share price of \$21.43 [i.e., $\$1.50 \div (.16 - .09)$]. Return increased ($g$ from 7 to 9 percent) as did risk (b from 1.50 to 1.75 and therefore k_s from 15 to 16 percent). The net result of the decision is positive: the share price increased from \$18.75 to \$21.43. Assuming that the key variables are accurately measured, the decision appears to be in the best interest of the firm's owners, since it increases their wealth.

INTERNATIONAL DIMENSION: RISK

The concept of risk clearly applies to international investments as well as purely domestic ones. However, MNCs must take into account additional factors including both foreign exchange and political risks.

Foreign Exchange Risks

foreign exchange risk The risk caused by varying exchange rates between two currencies.

Since multinational companies operate in many different foreign markets, portions of their revenues and costs are based on foreign currencies. In order to understand the **foreign exchange risk** caused by varying exchange rates between two currencies, we examine two factors: the relationships that exist among various currencies and the impact of currency fluctuations.

Relationship among Currencies

foreign exchange rate The value of two currencies with respect to each other.

Since the mid-1970s, the major currencies of the world have had a *floating*—as opposed to *fixed*—relationship with respect to the U.S. dollar and to one another. Among the currencies regarded as being major (or "hard") are the British pound (£), the Swiss franc (Sf), the Deutsche mark (DM), the French franc (Ff), the Japanese yen (Y), the Canadian dollar (C$), and, of course, the U.S. dollar (US$). The value of two currencies with respect to each other is their **foreign exchange rate.** It is expressed as follows:

$$US\$ \ 1.00 = SF \ 1.44$$

$$Sf \ 1.00 = US\$ \ .696$$

The usual exchange quotation in international markets is given as Sf 1.44/US$, where the unit of account is the Swiss franc and the unit of currency being priced is one U.S. dollar.

floating relationship The fluctuating relationship of the values of two currencies with respect to each other.

For the major currencies, the existence of a **floating relationship** means that the value of any two currencies with respect to each other is allowed to fluctuate on a daily basis. On the other hand, many of the nonmajor currencies of the world try to maintain a **fixed (or semi-fixed) relationship** with respect to one of the major currencies, a combination (basket) of major currencies, or some type of an international foreign exchange standard.

On any given day, the relationship between any two of the major currencies will contain two sets of figures: One reflects the **spot exchange rate** (the rate on that day), and the other indicates the **forward exchange rate** (the rate at some specified future date). The foreign exchange rates given in Figure 12.9 can be used to illustrate these concepts. For instance, the figure shows that on Thursday, May 16, 1991, the spot rate for the Swiss franc was Sf 1.4370/US$. On that same date the forward (future) rate was Sf 1.4397/US$ for 30-day delivery. In other words, on May 16, 1991, one could take a contract on Swiss francs for 30 days hence at an exchange rate of Sf 1.4397/US$. *Forward delivery rates* are also available for 90-day and 180-day contracts. For all such contracts, the agreements and signatures are completed on, say, May 16, 1991, whereas the actual exchange of dollar and Swiss francs between buyers and sellers will take place on the future date, say 30 days later.

Figure 12.9 can also be used to illustrate the differences between floating and fixed currencies. All the major currencies previously mentioned have spot and forward rates with respect to the U.S. dollar. Moreover, a comparison of the exchange rates prevailing on Thursday, May 16, 1991, versus those on Wednesday, May 15, 1991, indicates that the floating major currencies (or other currencies that also float in relation to the U.S. dollar, such as the Austrian schilling and the Belgian franc) experienced changes in rates. Other currencies, however, such as the United Arab dirham, have very limited movements on a daily basis with respect to either the U.S. dollar or other currencies.

A final point to note is the concept of changes in the value of a currency with respect to the U.S. dollar or another currency. For the floating currencies, changes in the value of foreign exchange rates are called *appreciation* or *depreciation*. For example, referring to Figure 12.9, it can be seen that the value of the French franc has depreciated from Ff 5.7235/US$ on Wednesday to Ff 5.7455/US$ on Thursday. In other words, it takes more francs to buy one dollar. For the fixed currencies, changes in values are called official *revaluation* or *devaluation*, but these terms have the same meanings as appreciation and depreciation, respectively.

Impact of Currency Fluctuations

Multinational companies face foreign exchange risks under both floating and fixed arrangements. The case of the floating currencies can be used to illustrate these risks. Returning to the U.S. dollar–Swiss franc relationship, we note that the forces of international supply and demand as well as internal and external economic and political elements help shape both the spot and the forward rates between these two currencies. Since the MNC cannot control much (or most) of these "outside" elements, the company faces potential changes in exchange rates in the form of appreciation or depreciation. These changes can in turn affect the MNC's revenues, costs, and profits as measured in U.S. dol-

fixed (or semi-fixed) relationship The constant (or relatively constant) relationship of a currency to one of the major currencies, a combination of major currencies, or some type of international foreign exchange standard.

spot exchange rate The rate of exchange between two currencies on any given day.

forward exchange rate The rate of exchange between two currencies at some specified future date.

EXCHANGE RATES

Thursday, May 16, 1991

The New York foreign exchange selling rates below apply to trading among banks in amounts of $1 million and more, as quoted at 3 p.m. Eastern time by Bankers Trust Co. and other sources. Retail transactions provide fewer units of foreign currency per dollar.

Country	U.S. $ equiv. Thurs.	U.S. $ equiv. Wed.	Currency per U.S. $ Thurs.	Currency per U.S. $ Wed.
Argentina (Austral) ...	.0001037	.0001037	9641.06	9643.02
Australia (Dollar)	.7835	.7835	1.2763	1.2763
Austria (Schilling)	.08382	.08428	11.93	11.87
Bahrain (Dinar)	2.6532	2.6532	.3769	.3769
Belgium (Franc)				
Commercial rate	.02867	.02884	34.88	34.68
Brazil (Cruzeiro)	.00379	.00380	263.80	262.87
Britain (Pound)	1.7500	1.7535	.5714	.5703
30-Day Forward	1.7414	1.7447	.5743	.5732
90-Day Forward	1.7269	1.7293	.5791	.5783
180-Day Forward	1.7085	1.7106	.5853	.5846
Canada (Dollar)	.8696	.8703	1.1500	1.1490
30-Day Forward	.8672	.8679	1.1532	1.1522
90-Day Forward	.8632	.8639	1.1585	1.1575
180-Day Forward	.8571	.8579	1.1667	1.1657
Chile (Peso)	.003043	.003044	328.60	328.51
China (Renmimbi)	.189226	.189226	5.2847	5.2847
Colombia (Peso)	.001709	.001709	585.00	585.00
Denmark (Krone)	.1546	.1551	6.4685	6.4477
Ecuador (Sucre)				
Floating rate	.000966	.000966	1035.00	1035.00
Finland (Markka)	.24978	.25157	4.0035	3.9750
France (Franc)	.17405	.17472	5.7455	5.7235
30-Day Forward	.17357	.17421	5.7615	5.7401
90-Day Forward	.17271	.17327	5.7902	5.7715
180-Day Forward	.17153	.17206	5.8298	5.8120
Germany (Mark)	.5903	.5933	1.6940	1.6855
30-Day Forward	.5888	.5918	1.6983	1.6898
90-Day Forward	.5859	.5887	1.7068	1.6986
180-Day Forward	.5817	.5844	1.7190	1.7112
Greece (Drachma)	.005384	.005419	185.75	184.55
Hong Kong (Dollar) ...	.12841	.12835	7.7875	7.7910
India (Rupee)	.04950	.04950	20.20	20.20
Indonesia (Rupiah)	.0005208	.0005208	1920.01	1920.01
Ireland (Punt)	1.5805	1.5885	.6327	.6295
Israel (Shekel)	.4333	.4320	2.3080	2.3150
Italy (Lira)	.0008029	.0008071	1245.50	1239.00
Japan (Yen)	.007281	.007297	137.35	137.05
30-Day Forward	.007268	.007284	137.58	137.28
90-Day Forward	.007250	.007265	137.94	137.65
180-Day Forward	.007229	.007244	138.34	138.04
Jordan (Dinar)	1.5029	1.5029	.6654	.6654
Kuwait (Dinar)	z	z	z	z
Lebanon (Pound)	.001078	.001078	928.00	928.00
Malaysia (Ringgit)	.3635	.3632	2.7510	2.7535
Malta (Lira)	3.0075	3.0075	.3325	.3325
Mexico (Peso)				
Floating rate	.0003333	.0003333	3000.00	3000.00
Netherland (Guilder) .	.5238	.5261	1.9090	1.9007
New Zealand (Dollar) .	.5920	.5897	1.6892	1.6958
Norway (Krone)	.1516	.1524	6.5981	6.5630
Pakistan (Rupee)	.0428	.0428	23.35	23.35
Peru (New Sol)	1.3245	1.3245	.76	.76
Philippines (Peso)	.03693	.03693	27.08	27.08
Portugal (Escudo)	.006770	.006782	147.70	147.46
Saudi Arabia (Riyal) ..	.26667	.26667	3.7500	3.7500
Singapore (Dollar)	.5669	.5669	1.7640	1.7640
South Africa (Rand)				
Commercial rate ...	.3598	.3603	2.7793	2.7758
Financial rate	.3048	.3064	3.2810	3.2640
South Korea (Won) ...	.0013805	.0013805	724.35	724.35
Spain (Peseta)	.009519	.009569	105.05	104.50
Sweden (Krona)	.1642	.1649	6.0895	6.0660
Switzerland (Franc) ..	.6959	.7010	1.4370	1.4265
30-Day Forward	.6946	.6996	1.4397	1.4293
90-Day Forward	.6919	.6969	1.4452	1.4349
180-Day Forward	.6887	.6936	1.4520	1.4418
Taiwan (Dollar)	.037023	.037064	27.01	26.98
Thailand (Baht)	.03905	.03905	25.61	25.61
Turkey (Lira)	.0002563	.0002545	3901.01	3929.01
United Arab (Dirham) ..	.2723	.2723	3.6725	3.6725
Uruguay (New Peso)				
Financial	.000536	.000536	1865.00	1865.00
Venezuela (Bolivar)				
Floating rate	.01847	.01847	54.15	54.15
SDR	1.35068	1.35003	.74037	.74072
ECU	1.21690	1.21382	....	....

Special Drawing Rights (SDR) are based on exchange rates for the U.S., German, British, French and Japanese currencies. Source: International Monetary Fund.

European Currency Unit (ECU) is based on a basket of community currencies. Source: European Community Commission.

z-Not quoted.

Figure 12.9   **Spot and Forward Exchange Rate Quotations**

On each business day the exchange rate between the U.S. dollar and other currencies is reported as a spot rate on either a floating or fixed-rate basis, depending on the currency. For major currencies, forward exchange rates are also reported.

Source: *The Wall Street Journal*, May 17, 1991, p. C10.

lars. For currencies fixed in relation to each other, the risks come from the same set of elements indicated above. Again, these official changes, like the ones brought about by the market in the case of floating currencies, can affect the MNC's operations and its dollar-based financial position.

The risks stemming from changes in exchange rates can be illustrated by an example.

EXAMPLE   MNC, Inc., a multinational manufacturer of dental drills, has a subsidiary in Switzerland that at the end of 1992 has the financial statements shown in Table 12.9. The figures for the balance sheet and income statement are given in the local currency, Swiss franc (Sf). Using the foreign exchange rate of Sf 1.50/US$ for December 31, 1992, MNC has translated the statements into U.S. dollars. For simplicity it is assumed that all the local figures are expected to remain the

Table 12.9   **Financial Statements for MNC, Inc.'s, Swiss Subsidiary**

Assets	Translation of balance sheet 12/31/92		12/31/93
	Sf	US$	US$
Cash	8.00	5.33	6.15
Inventory	60.00	40.00	46.15
Plant and equipment (net)	32.00	21.33	24.61
Total	100.00	66.66	76.91
Liabilities and equity			
Debt	48.00	32.00	36.92
Paid-in capital	40.00	26.66	30.76
Retained earnings	12.00	8.00	9.23
Total	100.00	66.66	76.91

Translation of income statement			
Sales	600.00	400.00	461.53
Cost of goods sold	550.00	366.66	423.07
Operating profits	50.00	33.34	38.46

Note: This example is simplified to show how the balance sheet and income statement are subject to exchange rate fluctuations. For the applicable rules on the translation of foreign accounts, review the discussion of international financial statements presented earlier.

same during 1993. As a result, as of January 1, 1993, the subsidiary expects to show the same Swiss franc figures on 12/31/93 as on 12/31/92. However, due to the change in the value of the Swiss franc relative to the dollar, from Sf 1.50/ US$ to Sf 1.30/US$, the translated dollar values of the items on the balance sheet, along with the dollar profit value on 12/31/93, are higher than those of the previous year. The changes are due only to fluctuations in foreign exchange.

There are additional complexities attached to each individual account in the financial statements. For instance, it is important whether a subsidiary's debt is all in the local currency, in U.S. dollars, or in several currencies. Moreover, it is important which currency (or currencies) the revenues and costs are denominated in. The risks shown so far relate to what is called the **accounting exposure.** In other words, foreign exchange fluctuations affect individual accounts in the financial statements. A different, and perhaps more important, risk element concerns **economic exposure,** which is the potential impact of exchange rate fluctuations on the firm's value. All future revenues and thus net profits can be subject to exchange rate changes. It is then obvious that the *present*

accounting exposure
The risk resulting from the effects of changes in foreign exchange rates on the translated value of a firm's financial statement accounts denominated in a given foreign currency.

economic exposure
The risk resulting from the effects of changes in foreign exchange rates on the firm's value.

value of the net profits derived from foreign operations will have, as a part of its total diversifiable risk, an element reflecting appreciation or depreciation of various currencies.

What can the management of MNCs do about these risks? The actions will depend on the attitude of management toward risk. This attitude, in turn, translates into how aggressively management wants to hedge the company's undesirable positions and exposures. The money markets, the forward (futures) markets, and the foreign currency options markets can be used—either individually or in conjunction with one another—to hedge foreign exchange exposures.

Political Risks

political risk The potential seizure of an MNC's operations in a host country.

macro political risk The subjection of *all* foreign firms to political risk (takeover) by a host country.

micro political risk The subjection of an individual firm, specific industry, or companies from a particular foreign country to political risk (takeover) by the host country.

Another important risk facing MNCs is political risk. **Political risk** refers to the implementation by a host government of specific rules and regulations that can result in the discontinuity or seizure of the operations of a foreign company in that country. Political risk is usually manifested in the form of nationalization, expropriation, or confiscation. In general, the assets and operations of a foreign firm are taken over by the host government, usually without proper (or any) compensation.

Political risk has two basic paths: *macro* and *micro*. **Macro political risk** means that due to political change, revolution, or the adoption of new policies by a host government, *all* foreign firms in the country will be subjected to political risk. In other words, no individual country or firm is treated differently; all assets and operations of foreign firms are taken over wholesale. An example of macro political risk is China in 1949 or Cuba in 1959–1960. **Micro political risk,** on the other hand, refers to the case in which an individual firm, a specific industry, or companies from a particular foreign country will be subjected to takeover. Examples include the nationalization by a majority of the oil-exporting countries of the assets of the international oil companies in their territories.

Although political risk can take place in any country—even in the United States—the political instability of the Third World generally makes the positions of multinational companies most vulnerable there. At the same time, some of the countries in this group have the most promising markets for the goods and services being offered by MNCs. The main question, therefore, is how to engage in operations and foreign investment in such countries and yet avoid or minimize the potential political risk.

Table 12.10 shows some of the approaches that MNCs may be able to adopt to cope with political risk. The negative approaches are generally used by firms in extractive industries. The external approaches are also of limited use. The best policies MNCs can follow are the positive approaches, which have both economic and political aspects.

In recent years MNCs have been relying on a variety of complex forecasting techniques. In these, "international experts," using available historical data, predict the chances for political instability in a host country and the potential effects on MNC operations. Events in Iran and Nicaragua, among others, however, point to the limited use of

Table 12.10   **Approaches for Coping with Political Risks**

Positive approaches		Negative approaches
Prior negotiation of controls and operating contracts		License or patent restrictions under international agreements
Prior agreement for sale	Direct	
Joint venture with government or local private sector		Control of external raw materials
Use of locals in management		Control of transportation to (external) markets
Joint venture with local banks		
Equity participation by middle class	Indirect	Control of downstream processing
Local sourcing		Control of external markets
Local retail outlets		

External approaches to minimize loss

International insurance or investment guarantees

Thinly capitalized firms:

   Local financing

   External financing secured only by the local operation

Source: Rita M. Rodriguez and E. Eugene Carter, *International Financial Management*, 3rd ed. (Englewood Cliffs, NJ: Prentice-Hall, 1984), p. 512.

such techniques and tend to reinforce the usefulness of the positive approaches.

A final point relates to the introduction by most "host" governments in the last two decades of comprehensive sets of rules, regulations, and incentives. Known as **national entry control systems,** they are aimed at regulating inflows of *foreign direct investments* involving MNCs. They are designed to extract more benefits from MNCs' presence by regulating such flows in terms of a variety of factors—local ownership, level of exportation, use of local inputs, number of local managers, internal geographic location, level of local borrowing, and the respective percentages of profits to be remitted and of capital to be repatriated back to parent firms. Host countries expect that as MNCs comply with these regulations, the potential for acts of political risk will decline, thus benefiting MNCs as well.

national entry control systems
Comprehensive rules, regulations, and incentives aimed at regulating inflows of *foreign direct investments* of MNCs and extracting more benefits from their presence.

SUMMARY

1   **Describe basic risk and return concepts, including risk aversion, risk of a single asset, risk and time, and risk of a portfolio.** Risk is the chance of loss, or, more formally, refers to the variability of returns. Return is the change in value plus any cash distributions expressed as a percentage of the initial value. Most financial decision makers are risk-averse. The risk of a single asset is measured in much the same way as the risk of a portfolio, or collection, of

Table 12.11   **Summary of Key Definitions and Formulas for Risk, Return, and Valuation**

Variable definitions

$\bar{k}$ = expected value of a return

k_i = return on the ith outcome

Pr_i = probability of occurrence of the ith return

n = number of outcomes considered

σ_k = standard deviation of returns

CV = coefficient of variation

k_j = required return on asset j

R_F = risk-free rate of return

b_j = beta coefficient or index of nondiversifiable risk for asset j

k_m = market return; the return on the market portfolio of assets

B_0 = bond value

I = annual interest on a bond

k_d = required return on a bond

M = par value of a bond

PS_0 = value of preferred stock

D_P = annual preferred stock dividend

k_P = required return on preferred stock

P_0 = value of common stock

D_t = per-share dividend expected at the end of year t

k_s = required return on common stock

g = constant rate of growth in dividends

Risk and return formulas

Expected value of a return

$$\bar{k} = \sum_{t=1}^{n} k_i \times Pr_i \qquad \text{[Eq. 12.1]}$$

Standard deviation of returns

$$\sigma_k = \sqrt{\sum_{i=1}^{n} (k_i - \bar{k})^2 \times Pr_i} \qquad \text{[Eq. 12.2]}$$

Coefficient of variation

$$CV = \frac{\sigma_k}{\bar{k}} \qquad \text{[Eq. 12.3]}$$

Capital asset pricing model (CAPM)

$$k_j = R_F + [b_j \times (k_m - R_F)] \qquad \text{[Eq. 12.5]}$$

Valuation formulas

Bond value

$$B_0 = I \times \left[\sum_{t=1}^{n} \frac{1}{(1 + k_d)^t} \right] + M \times \left[\frac{1}{(1 + k_d)^n} \right] \text{[Eq. 12.8]}$$

$$= I \times (PVIFA_{k_d,n}) + M \times (PVIF_{k_d,n}) \qquad \text{[Eq. 12.8a]}$$

Preferred stock value

$$PS_0 = \frac{D_p}{k_p} \qquad \text{[Eq. 12.9]}$$

Common stock value

Zero growth: $P_0 = \dfrac{D_1}{k_s}$ [Eq. 12.11]

Constant growth: $P_0 = \dfrac{D_1}{k_s - g}$ [Eq. 12.13]

assets. However holders of portfolios may be able to reduce risk through diversification. Risk is an increasing function of time. The key risk and return definitions and formulas are given in Table 12.11. New investments must be considered in light of their impact on the risk and return of the portfolio of assets. The correlation of asset returns affects the diversification process.

2 **Understand the relationship between risk and return as presented by the capital asset pricing model (CAPM).** Total risk consists of nondiversifiable and diversifiable risk. Nondiversifiable risk is the only relevant risk, since diversifiable risk can be easily eliminated through diversification. Nondiversifiable risk can be measured by the beta coefficient. The capital asset pricing model (CAPM) uses beta to relate an asset's risk relative to the market to the asset's required return. The definitions and formula for CAPM are given in Table 12.11. The graphic depiction of CAPM is the security market line (SML).

3   **Discuss the key inputs and basic model used in the valuation process.** Key inputs to the valuation process include cash flows (returns), timing, and the discount rate (risk). The value, or worth, of any asset is equal to the present value of all future cash flows it is expected to provide over the relevant time period.

4   **Apply the basic valuation model to bonds and preferred stocks, and evaluate the relationship between required returns and bond values.** The value of a bond is the present value of interest payments plus the present value of its par, or face, value. The discount rate used to determine bond value is the required return, which may differ from the bond's coupon interest rate. A bond can sell at a discount, at par, or at a premium, depending upon whether the required return is respectively greater than, equal to, or less than its coupon interest rate. The value of preferred stock is determined by applying the appropriate present-value interest factor for a perpetuity to its annual dividend. The definitions and formulas for finding bond and preferred stock values are given in Table 12.11.

5   **Perform basic common stock valuation using both the zero and constant growth models and popular estimation approaches, and relate decision making to common stock value.** The value of a share of common stock is the present value of all future dividends it is expected to provide over an infinite time horizon. Of the two cases of dividend growth, zero and constant, the more widely cited is the constant growth model. The definitions and formulas for these two cases are given in Table 12.11. Popular approaches for estimating common stock value include book value, liquidation value, and price/earnings (P/E) multiples. Because most financial decisions affect both return and risk, an assessment of their combined effect on value must be part of the financial decision-making process.

6   **Describe the two risks—foreign exchange and political—requiring special consideration by the multinational company, and explain how MNCs manage them.** Operating in international markets involves certain factors that can influence the risk and return characteristics of an MNC. Economic exposure from foreign exchange risk results from the existence of different currencies and the potential impact they can have on the value of foreign operations. The money markets, the forward (futures) markets, and the foreign currency options markets can be used to hedge foreign exchange exposures. Political risks stem mainly from political instability in a number of countries and from the associated implications for the assets and operations of MNCs with subsidiaries located in such countries. Negative, external, and positive approaches can be employed by MNCs to cope with political risk.

QUESTIONS

12—1   Define *risk* as it relates to financial decision making. How can the return on common stock be calculated? Why are financial managers commonly viewed as *risk-averse*?

12—2   How can *sensitivity analysis* be used to assess asset risk? What is one of the most common methods of sensitivity analysis? Define and describe the role of the *range* in sensitivity analysis.

12—3   How does a plot of the *probability distribution* of outcomes allow the decision maker to get a sense of asset risk? What is the difference between a *bar chart* and a *continuous probability distribution*?

12—4   What does the *standard deviation* of a distribution of asset returns indicate? What is the *coefficient of variation*? When is the coefficient of variation preferred over the standard deviation for comparing asset risk?

12—5   Why must assets be evaluated in a portfolio context? What is an *efficient portfolio*? What is *correlation*, and how is it related to the process of diversification?

12—6   What is the relationship of total risk, nondiversifiable risk, and diversifiable risk? Which risk is measured by *beta*? Why would someone argue that nondiversifiable risk is the only relevant risk?

12—7   What is the equation for the *capital asset pricing model (CAPM)*? Explain the meaning of each variable. Assuming a risk-free rate of 8 percent and a market return of 12 percent, draw the *security market line (SML)*.

12—8   What are the three key inputs to the valuation process? Define and specify the general equation for the value of any asset, V_0, in terms of its expected cash flow, CF_t, in each year t, and the appropriate discount rate (required return), k.

12—9   In terms of the required return and the coupon interest rate, what relationship between them will cause a bond to sell (a) at a discount? (b) at a premium? (c) at its par value? Explain.

12—10   Describe the procedure used to estimate the value of preferred stock. Why are preferred stock dividends treated as a perpetuity?

12—11   Describe, compare, and contrast the zero growth and constant growth approaches for estimating the value of common stock.

12—12   Explain each of the three popular approaches—(a) book value, (b) liquidation value, and (c) price/earnings (P/E) multiples—for estimating common stock value. Which of these is considered the best?

12—13   Explain the linkages among financial decisions, return, risk, and stock value. How does the capital asset pricing model (CAPM) fit into this basic framework? Explain.

12—14   Define *spot* and *forward exchange rates*. Define and compare *accounting exposures* and *economic exposures* to exchange rate fluctuations.

12—15   Discuss *macro* and *micro political risk*. Describe some techniques for dealing with political risk.

PROBLEMS

12—1   **(Risk Preference)** Oren Wells, the financial manager for Winston Enterprises, wishes to evaluate three prospective investments—X, Y, and Z. Currently the firm earns 12 percent on its investments, which have a risk index of 6 percent. The three investments under consideration are profiled below in terms of expected return and expected risk. If Oren Wells were risk-averse, which investment, if any, would he select? Explain why.

Investment	Expected return (%)	Expected risk index (%)
X	14	7
Y	12	8
Z	10	9

12—2   **(Risk Analysis)** Babb Products is considering an investment in an expanded product line. Two possible types of expansion are being considered. After investigating the possible outcomes, the company made the following estimates:

	Expansion A	Expansion B
Initial investment	$12,000	$12,000
Annual rate of return		
Pessimistic	16%	10%
Most likely	20	20
Optimistic	24	30

a. Determine the range of the rates of return for each of the two projects.
b. Which project is less risky? Why?
c. If you were making the investment decision, which one would you choose? Why? What does this imply about your feelings toward risk?
d. Assume that expansion B's most likely outcome was 21 percent per year and all other facts remained the same. Does this change your answer to part **c**? Why?

12—3   **(Risk and Probability)** Blue Book Publishers is considering the purchase of one of two microfilm cameras—R or S. Both should provide benefits over a 10-year period. Each requires an initial investment of $4,000. Management has constructed the following table of estimates of probabilities and rates of return for pessimistic, most likely, and optimistic results:

	Camera R		Camera S	
	Amount	Probability	Amount	Probability
Initial investment	$4,000	1.00	$4,000	1.00
Annual rate of return				
Pessimistic	20%	.25	15%	.20
Most likely	25	.50	25	.55
Optimistic	30	.25	35	.25

a. Determine the range for the rate of return for each of the two cameras.
b. Determine the expected value of return for each camera.
c. Which camera is more risky? Why?

12—4   **(Bar Charts and Risk)** David's Sportswear is considering bringing out a line of designer jeans. Currently it is negotiating with two different well-known designers. Because of the highly competitive nature of the industry, the two designs have been given code names. After market research, the firm has established the following expectations about the annual rates of return:

| Market acceptance | Probability | Annual rate of return | |
		Line J	Line K
Very poor	.05	.0075	.010
Poor	.15	.0125	.025
Average	.60	.0850	.080
Good	.15	.1475	.135
Excellent	.05	.1625	.150

Use the table to:
a. Construct a bar chart for each line's annual rate of return.
b. Calculate the expected value of return for each line.
c. Evaluate the relative riskiness for each jean line's rate of return using the bar charts.

12—5   **(Coefficient of Variation)** Ferrous Manufacturing has isolated four alternatives for meeting its need for increased production capacity. The data gathered relative to each of these alternatives is summarized in the following table.

Alternative	Expected return (%)	Standard deviation of return (%)
A	20	7.0
B	22	9.5
C	19	6.0
D	16	5.5

a. Calculate the coefficient of variation for each alternative.
b. If the firm wishes to minimize risk, which alternative would you recommend? Why?

12—6   **(Assessing Return and Risk)** Newby Tool must choose between two asset purchases. The annual rate of return and the related probabilities given below summarize the firm's analysis to this point.

| Project 257 | | Project 432 | |
Rate of return	Probability	Rate of return	Probability
−10%	.01	10%	.05
10	.04	15	.10
20	.05	20	.10
30	.10	25	.15
40	.15	30	.20
45	.30	35	.15
50	.15	40	.10
60	.10	45	.10
70	.05	50	.05
80	.04		
100	.01		

| Asset | Cash flow | | Appropriate discount rate (%) |
	End of year	Amount ($)	
D	1 through 5	1,500	12
	6	8,500	
E	1	2,000	14
	2	3,000	
	3	5,000	
	4	7,000	
	5	4,000	
	6	1,000	

12—19   **(Asset Valuation and Risk)**   Dora Hayes wishes to estimate the value of an asset expected to provide cash inflows of $3,000 per year at the end of years 1 through 4 and $15,000 at the end of year 5. Her research indicates that she must earn 10 percent on low-risk assets, 15 percent on average-risk assets, and 22 percent on high-risk assets.
   a. What is the most Dora should pay for the asset if it is classified as (1) low risk? (2) average risk? or (3) high risk?
   b. If Dora is unable to assess the risk of the asset and wants to be certain she makes a good deal, based on your findings in **a**, what is the most she should pay? Why?
   c. All else being the same, what effect does increasing risk have on the value of an asset? Explain in light of your findings in **a**.

12—20   **(Basic Bond Valuation)**   Redenour Supply has an issue of $1,000-par-value bonds with a 12 percent coupon interest rate outstanding. The issue pays interest annually and has 16 years remaining to its maturity date.
   a. If bonds of similar risk are currently earning a 10 percent rate of return, how much will the Redenour Supply bond sell for today?
   b. Describe the *two* possible reasons that similar-risk bonds are currently earning a return below the coupon interest rate on the Redenour Supply bond.
   c. If the required return were at 12 percent instead of 10 percent, what would the current value of Redenour's bond be? Contrast this finding with your findings in **a** and discuss.

12—21   **(Bond Valuation—Annual Interest)**   Calculate the value of each of the following bonds, all of which pay interest *annually*.

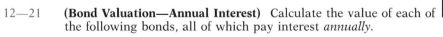

Bond	Par value ($)	Coupon interest rate (%)	Years to maturity	Required return (%)
A	1,000	14	20	12
B	1,000	8	16	8
C	100	10	8	13
D	500	16	13	18
E	1,000	12	10	10

12—22 **(Bond Value and Changing Required Returns)** National Telephone has outstanding a bond issue that will mature to its $1,000 par value in 12 years. The bond has a coupon interest rate of 11 percent and pays interest *annually*.
a. Find the value of the bond if the required return is
  (1) 11 percent
  (2) 15 percent
  (3) 8 percent
b. What two reasons cause the required return to differ from the coupon interest rate?

12—23 **(Preferred Stock Valuation)** Poltak Stamping wishes to estimate the value of its outstanding preferred stock. The preferred issue has an $80 par value and pays an annual dividend of $6.40 per share. Similar-risk preferred stocks are currently earning a 9.3 percent annual rate of return.
a. What is the market value of the outstanding preferred stock?
b. If an investor purchases the preferred stock at the value calculated in **a**, how much would she gain or lose per share if she sells the stock when the required return on similar-risk preferreds has risen to 10.5 percent? Explain.

 12—24 **(Common Stock Valuation—Zero Growth)** Cable Enterprises is a mature firm in the machine tool component industry. The firm's most recent common stock dividend was $2.40 per share. Due to its maturity as well as stable sales and earnings, the firm's management feels that their dividends will remain at the current level for the foreseeable future.
a. If the required return is 12 percent, what is the value of Cable Enterprises' common stock?
b. If the firm's risk as perceived by market participants suddenly increases, causing the required return to rise to 20 percent, what will be the common stock value?
c. Based on your findings in **a** and **b**, what impact does risk have on value? Explain.

  12—25 **(Common Stock Value—Constant Growth)** Use the constant growth valuation model (Gordon model) to find the value of each of the following firms.

Firm	Dividend expected next year ($)	Dividend growth rate (%)	Required return (%)
A	1.20	8	13
B	4.00	5	15
C	.65	10	14
D	6.00	8	9
E	2.25	8	20

 12—26 **(Common Stock Value—Constant Growth)** The Moody Boiler Company has paid the following dividends over the past six years:

Year	Dividend per share ($)
1992	2.87
1991	2.76
1990	2.60
1989	2.46
1988	2.37
1987	2.25

The firm's dividend per share next year is expected to be $3.02.
a. If you can earn 13 percent on similar-risk investments, what is the most you would pay per share for this firm?
b. If you can earn only 10 percent on similar-risk investments, what is the most you would be willing to pay per share?
c. Compare and contrast your findings in **a** and **b** and discuss the impact of changing risk on share value.

12—27   **(Common Stock Value—Both Growth Models)** You are evaluating the potential purchase of a small business currently generating $42,500 of after-tax cash flow ($D_0 = $42,500$). Based on a review of similar-risk investment opportunities, you must earn an 18 percent rate of return on the proposed purchase. Since you are relatively uncertain as to future cash flows, you have decided to estimate the firm's value using two possible cash flow growth rate assumptions.
a. What is the firm's value if cash flows are expected to grow at an annual rate of 0 percent to infinity?
b. What is the firm's value if cash flows are expected to grow at a constant annual rate of 7 percent to infinity?

12—28   **(Book and Liquidation Value)** The balance sheet for the Grannis Mill Company follows.

Balance sheet
Grannis Mill Company
December 31

Assets		Liabilities and equity	
Cash	$ 40,000	Accounts payable	$100,000
Marketable securities	60,000	Notes payable	30,000
Accounts receivable	120,000	Accrued wages	30,000
Inventories	160,000	Total current liabilities	$160,000
Total current assets	$380,000	Long-term debt	$180,000
Land and buildings (net)	$150,000	Preferred stock	$ 80,000
Machinery and equipment	250,000	Common stock (10,000 shares)	360,000
Total fixed assets (net)	$400,000	Total liabilities and	
Total assets	$780,000	stockholders' equity	$780,000

Additional information with respect to the firm is available:

(1) Preferred stock can be liquidated for its book value.

(2) Accounts receivable and inventories can be liquidated at 90 percent of book value.

(3) The firm has 10,000 shares of common stock outstanding.

(4) All interest and dividends are currently paid up.

(5) Land and buildings can be liquidated for 130 percent of their book value.

(6) Machinery and equipment can be liquidated at 70 percent of book value.

(7) Cash and marketable securities can be liquidated at book value.

Given this information, answer the following:

a. What is Grannis Mill's book value per share?

b. What is their liquidation value per share?

c. Compare, contrast, and discuss the values found in **a** and **b**.

 12—29   **(Valuation with Price/Earnings Multiples)** For each of the following firms, use the data given to estimate their common stock value employing price/earnings (P/E) multiples.

Firm	Expected EPS ($)	Price/earnings multiple
A	3.00	6.2
B	4.50	10.0
C	1.80	12.6
D	2.40	8.9
E	5.10	15.0

12—30   **(Management Action and Stock Value)** Blanding Enterprises' most recent dividend was $3 per share, its expected annual rate of dividend growth is 5 percent, and the required return is now 15 percent. A variety of proposals are currently being considered by management in order to redirect the firm's activities. For each of the proposed actions below, determine the resulting impact on share price and indicate the best alternative.

a. Do nothing, which will leave the key financial variables unchanged.

b. Invest in a new machine that will increase the dividend growth rate to 6 percent and lower the required return to 14 percent.

c. Eliminate an unprofitable product line, which will increase the dividend growth rate to 7 percent and raise the required return to 17 percent.

d. Merge with another firm, which will reduce the growth rate to 4 percent and raise the required return to 16 percent.

e. Acquire a subsidiary operation from another manufacturer. The acquisition should increase the dividend growth rate to 8 percent and increase the required return to 17 percent.

12—31   **(Integrative—Risk and Valuation)** RPM Enterprises has a beta of 1.20, the risk-free rate of return is currently 10 percent, and the market return is 14 percent. The company plans to pay a dividend of $2.60 per share in the coming year. It anticipates that its future dividends will increase at an annual rate consistent with that experienced over the 1986 to 1992 period, when the following dividends were paid:

Year	Dividend per share ($)	Year	Dividend per share ($)
1992	2.45	1988	1.82
1991	2.28	1987	1.80
1990	2.10	1986	1.73
1989	1.95		

a. Use the capital asset pricing model (CAPM) to determine the required return on RPM Enterprises' stock.

b. Using the constant growth dividend valuation model and your finding in **a**, estimate the value of RPM Enterprises' stock.

c. Explain what effect, if any, a decrease in beta would have on the value of RPM's stock.

12—32   **(Integrative—Valuation and CAPM)** Pinckney Steel Company wishes to determine the value of Acme Foundry, a firm that it is considering acquiring for cash. Pinckney wishes to use the capital asset pricing model (CAPM) to determine the applicable discount rate to use as an input to the constant growth valuation model. Acme's stock is not publicly traded. After studying the betas of firms similar to Acme that are publicly traded, Pinckney believes that an appropriate beta for Acme's stock would be 1.25. The risk-free rate is currently 9 percent, and the market return is 13 percent. Acme's historical dividend per share for each of the past six years is given below:

Year	Dividend per share ($)
1992	3.44
1991	3.28
1990	3.15
1989	2.90
1988	2.75
1987	2.45

a. Given that Acme is expected to pay a dividend of $3.68 next year, determine the maximum cash price Pinckney should pay for each share of Acme.

b. Discuss the use of the CAPM for estimating the value of common stock, and describe the effect on the resulting value of Acme of:
(1) A decrease in the dividend growth rate of 2 percent from that exhibited over the 1987–1992 period.
(2) A decrease in the beta to 1.

12—33   **(Translation of Financial Statements)** A U.S.-based MNC has a subsidiary in France. The balance sheet and income statement of the subsidiary are shown below. On 12/31/92, the exchange rate is Ff 6.50/US$. Assume that the local (French franc, Ff) figures for the statements remain the same on 12/31/93. Calculate the U.S.–dollar–translated figures for the two ending time periods, assuming that between 12/31/92 and 12/31/93 the French currency has appreciated against the U.S. dollar by 6 percent.

Translation of balance sheet

| | 12/31/92 | | 12/31/93 |
Assets	Ff	US$	US$
Cash	40.00		
Inventory	300.00		
Plant and equipment (net)	160.00		
Total	500.00		

Liabilities and equity

Debt	240.00		
Paid-in capital	200.00		
Retained earnings	60.00		
Total	500.00		

Translation of income statement

Sales	3,000.00		
Cost of goods sold	2,750.00		
Operating profits	250.00		

CASE

Assessing the Value of Elektra Fashions

In 1992, after ten years in business, Jane Easton's casual-wear company, Elektra Fashions, achieved sales of $300 million. The company's historical growth was so spectacular that securities analysts felt it could not keep up the pace. They warned that due to fierce competition, Elektra might experience little or no growth in the future. They estimated that stockholders should expect no growth in future dividends.

Contrary to the conservative security analysts, Ms. Easton felt the company could maintain a constant annual growth rate in dividends per share of 6 percent indefinitely in the future. She based her estimates on an established long-term expansion plan into European and Latin American markets. The risk of the firm as measured by beta was expected to immediately increase from 1.10 to 1.25 as a result of venturing into these markets.

Mark Scott, assistant treasurer of Elektra, was charged with evaluating the firm's current stock price in light of the conservative predictions of the securities analysts and the aggressive predictions of the company founder. He compiled the following company and market data to aid his analysis.

Company data	1992 value
Earnings per share (EPS)	$6.25
Price per share of common stock	$40.00
Book value of common stock equity	$60,000,000
Total common shares outstanding	2,500,000
Common stock dividend per share	$4.00
Market data	**Current value**
Risk-free rate, R_F	6.00%
Market return, k_m	14.00%

Required

   a. What is the firm's current price/earnings (P/E) ratio?

   b. What is the firm's current book value per share?

   c. Use the capital asset pricing model (CAPM) to find the required return on Elektra's stock when beta is equal to (1) 1.10 and (2) 1.25. What effect will the anticipated increase in beta have on Elektra's required return?

   d. Assuming beta is 1.25, find the value of Elektra's stock using (1) the securities analysts' no-growth-in-dividend prediction and (2) Jane Easton's prediction of constant 6 percent annual dividend growth.

   e. Compare the current (1992) stock price with the stock values found in **b** and **d**. Discuss why these values may differ. Which valuation method do you believe more clearly represents the true value of the Elektra stock?

CHAPTER 13

THE COST
OF CAPITAL

CHAPTER OBJECTIVES

After studying this chapter, you should be able to:

1 Understand the basic concept of cost of capital and the reasons why a weighted average is the appropriate cost measurement.

2 Calculate both the cost of long-term debt (bonds), using a popular approximation technique, and the cost of preferred stock.

3 Find the cost of common stock equity and convert it into the cost of retained earnings and the cost of new issues of common stock.

4 Calculate the weighted average cost of capital (WACC) and discuss the alternative weighting schemes.

5 Describe the rationale for and procedures used to determine the weighted marginal cost of capital (WMCC).

6 Explain how the weighted marginal cost of capital (WMCC) can be used with the investment opportunities schedule (IOS) to make the firm's financing/investment decisions.

“ “. . . both Buford
and NatWest share the
risk associated with
changing interest
rates . . . ” ”

Collars, Caps, and the Cost of Debt at Buford Television

When the winds of recession send a shiver through the economy, you expect businesses to conserve resources, rethink expansion plans, and cut costs. Throughout the country, announced inventory reductions and employee layoffs signal the unwelcome arrival of an economic downturn. But the quest to cut costs and conserve cash runs far deeper than most newspapers can report. Effective cost containment practices that spell the difference between corporate survival and financial collapse represent complicated undertakings.

At Buford Television Inc., a small cable television company based in Tyler, Texas, managers are using a financial innovation called a "costless collar" to contain the firm's cost of debt. The collar provides a way to stabilize the firm's interest costs when market interest rates move up or down. It thus gives Buford the ability to forecast its future debt payment costs with reasonable accuracy. How does the collar work? It consists of two components: an interest rate cap and an interest rate floor on the firm's debt. The cap sets the maximum borrowing cost at 10 percent. The floor provides a guaranteed minimum interest rate—7.7 percent—that Buford will pay its bank, National Westminster Bank USA.

Buford's commercial loan agreements with NatWest actually carry a variable interest rate, so that the firm's interest charges depend upon the level of market interest rates. Every three months, Buford's interest payments are reset so that they increase with rising interest rates and decrease with falling rates. The costless collar, however, severely restricts Buford's changing interest costs as market interest rates fluctuate. In late 1990, the base rate on Buford's debt stood at 8.3 percent, and the firm's financial managers were assured that borrowing costs would not rise by more than 1.7 percent, or fall by more than .6 percent, through the end of 1992.

From Buford's perspective, the best part of this interest rate protection is that it requires no explicit payment by the firm. Buford's "payment" to NatWest for the 10 percent interest rate cap is the 7.7 percent interest rate floor. While the cap is valuable to Buford, the floor is valuable to NatWest because it establishes the minimum interest revenue received from Buford. In this case, both Buford and NatWest share the risk associated with changing interest rates, and each firm receives something of value for bearing some of this risk.

$\mathbf{T}$ he cost of capital is an extremely important financial concept. It acts as a major link between the firm's long-term financial decisions (discussed in Part Five) and the wealth of the owners as determined by investors in the marketplace. It is in effect the "magic number" used to decide whether a proposed corporate investment will increase or decrease the firm's stock price. Clearly, only those investments expected to increase stock price would be recommended. Due to its key role in financial decision making, the importance of the cost of capital cannot be overemphasized.

AN OVERVIEW OF THE COST OF CAPITAL

cost of capital The rate of return a firm must earn on its project investments to maintain its market value and attract funds.

The **cost of capital** is the rate of return a firm must earn on its project investments in order to maintain the market value of its stock. It can also be thought of as the rate of return required by the market suppliers of capital in order to attract their funds to the firm. Holding risk constant, the implementation of projects with a rate of return above the cost of capital will increase the value of the firm, and vice versa.

The Basic Concept

The cost of capital is measured at a given point in time. It reflects the cost of funds over the long run, based on the best information available. This view is consistent with the use of the cost of capital to make long-term financial investment decisions. Although firms typically raise money in lumps, the cost of capital should reflect the interrelatedness of financing activities. For example, if a firm raises funds with debt (borrowing) today, it is likely that some form of equity, such as common stock, will have to be used next time. Most firms maintain a deliberate, optimal mix of debt and equity financing. This mix is commonly called a **target capital structure**—a topic that will be discussed in greater detail in Chapter 16. It is sufficient here to say that although firms raise money in lumps, they tend toward some desired *mix of financing* in order to maximize owner wealth.

target capital structure The desired optimal mix of debt and equity financing that most firms attempt to achieve and maintain.

To capture the interrelatedness of financing under a target capital structure, we need a broad view. We need to look at the *overall cost of capital* rather than the cost of the specific source of funds used to finance a given expenditure. The importance of such a view can be illustrated by a simple example.

EXAMPLE   A firm is *currently* faced with an opportunity. Assume the following:

Best project available
Cost = $100,000
Life = 20 years
Return = 7 percent
Cost of least-cost financing source available
Debt = 6 percent

Since it can earn 7 percent on the investment of funds costing only 6 percent, the firm undertakes the opportunity. Imagine that *one week later* a new opportunity is available:

Best project available
Cost = $100,000
Life = 20 years
Return = 12 percent
Cost of least-cost financing source available
Equity = 14 percent

In this instance the firm rejects the opportunity, since the 14 percent cost is greater than the 12 percent return expected.

The firm's actions were not in the best interests of its owners. It accepted a project yielding a 7 percent return and rejected one with a 12 percent return. Clearly, there is a better way. Due to the interrelatedness of financing decisions, the firm must use a combined cost. Over the long run the combined cost would provide for better decisions. By weighting the cost of each source of financing by its target proportion in the firm's capital structure, a *weighted average cost* that reflects the interrelationship of financing decisions can be obtained. Assuming that a 50–50 mix of debt and equity is desired, the weighted average cost in this case would be 10 percent [(.50 × 6% debt) + (.50 × 14% equity)]. Using this cost, the first opportunity would have been rejected (7% return <10% weighted average cost), and the second one would have been accepted (12% return > 10% weighted average cost). Such an outcome would clearly be more desirable.

The Cost of Specific Sources of Capital

This chapter focuses on finding the costs of specific sources of capital and combining them in order to determine and apply the weighted average cost of capital. Our concern is only with the long-term sources of funds available to a business firm, since these sources supply the permanent financing. Long-term financing supports the firm's fixed-asset investments.[1]

---

[1] The role of both long-term and short-term financing in supporting both fixed and current asset investments was addressed in Chapter 7. Suffice it to say that long-term funds are at minimum used to finance fixed assets.

There are four basic sources of long-term funds for the business firm: long-term debt, preferred stock, common stock, and retained earnings. The right-hand side of a balance sheet can be used to illustrate these sources.

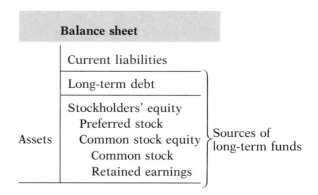

Although not all firms will use each of these methods of financing, each firm is expected to have funds from some of these sources in its capital structure. The *specific cost* of each source of financing is the *after-tax* cost of obtaining the financing *today*. (The cost is not the historically based cost reflected by the existing financing on the firm's books.) Techniques for determining the specific cost of each source of long-term funds are presented on the following pages. Although these techniques tend to develop precisely calculated values, the resulting values are at best *rough approximations* due to the numerous assumptions and forecasts that underlie them. While we round calculated costs to the nearest 0.1 percent throughout this chapter, it is not unusual for practicing financial managers to use costs rounded to the nearest 1 percent due to the fact that these values are merely estimates.

THE COST OF LONG-TERM DEBT (BONDS)

cost of long-term debt (bonds), k_i The after-tax cost today of raising long-term funds through borrowing.

The **cost of long-term debt (bonds), k_i**, is the after-tax cost today of raising long-term funds through borrowing. For convenience we typically assume that the funds are raised through issuance and sale of bonds. In addition, consistent with Chapter 12, we assume that the bonds pay *annual*—rather than *semiannual*—interest.

Net Proceeds

net proceeds Funds actually received from the sale of a security.

flotation costs The total costs of issuing and selling a security.

Most corporate long-term debts are incurred through the sale of bonds. The **net proceeds** from the sale of a bond, or any security, are the funds actually received from the sale. **Flotation costs**—the total costs of issuing and selling a security—reduce the net proceeds from the sale of a bond, whether sold at a premium, at a discount, or at its par (face) value.

EXAMPLE   Debbo Company, a major hardware manufacturer, is contemplating selling $10 million worth of 20-year, 9 percent coupon (stated *annual* interest rate) bonds, each with a par value of $1,000. Since similar-risk bonds earn returns greater than 9 percent, the firm must sell the bonds for $980 to compensate for the lower coupon interest rate. The flotation costs paid to the investment banker are 2 percent of the par value of the bond (2% × $1,000), or $20. The net proceeds to the firm from the sale of each bond are therefore $960 ($980 − $20).

Before-Tax Cost of Debt

The before-tax cost of debt, k_d, for a bond with a $1,000 par value can be approximated using the following equation:

$$k_d = \frac{I + \dfrac{\$1,000 - N_d}{n}}{\dfrac{N_d + \$1,000}{2}}$$

Equation 13.1
Formula for the approximate before-tax cost of debt

where

I = annual interest in dollars

N_d = net proceeds from the sale of debt (bond)

n = number of years to the bond's maturity

EXAMPLE   Substituting the appropriate values from the Debbo Company example into Equation 13.1 results in an approximate before-tax debt cost, k_d, of 9.4 percent. Note that the annual interest, I, is $90 (9% coupon interest rate × $1,000 par value).

$$k_d = \frac{\$90 + \dfrac{\$1,000 - \$960}{20}}{\dfrac{\$960 + \$1,000}{2}} = \frac{\$90 + \$2}{\$980}$$

$$= \frac{\$92}{\$980} = \underline{\underline{9.4\%}}$$

After-Tax Cost of Debt

As indicated earlier, the *specific cost* of financing must be stated on an after-tax basis. Since interest on debt is tax-deductible, a tax adjustment is required. The before-tax debt cost, k_d, can be converted to an after-tax debt cost, k_i, by the following equation:

Equation 13.2
Formula for the after-tax cost of debt

$$k_i = k_d \times (1 - T)$$

The T represents the firm's tax rate.

EXAMPLE   We can use the 9.4 percent before-tax debt cost approximation for Debbo Company, which has a 40 percent tax rate, to demonstrate the after-tax debt cost calculation. Applying Equation 13.2 results in an after-tax cost of debt of 5.6 percent [i.e., 9.4% × (1 − .40)]. Typically, the explicit cost of long-term debt is less than the explicit cost of any of the alternative forms of long-term financing. This is primarily due to the tax-deductibility of interest.

THE COST OF PREFERRED STOCK

Preferred stock represents a special type of ownership interest in the firm. Preferred stockholders must receive their *stated* dividends prior to the distribution of any earnings to common stockholders. Since preferred stock is a form of ownership, the proceeds from the sale of preferred stock are expected to be held for an infinite period of time. A complete discussion of the various characteristics of preferred stock is presented in Chapter 20. However, the one aspect of preferred stock that requires clarification at this point is dividends.

Preferred Stock Dividends

The amount of preferred stock dividends that must be paid each year before earnings can be distributed to common stockholders may be stated in dollars or as a percentage of the stock's par, or face, value.

Dollar Amounts
Most preferred stock dividends are stated as "*x* dollars per year." When dividends are stated this way, the stock is often referred to as "*x*-dollar preferred stock." Thus a $4 preferred stock is expected to pay preferred stockholders $4 in dividends each year on each share of preferred stock owned.

Percentage Amounts
Sometimes preferred stock dividends are stated as an annual percentage rate. This rate represents the percentage of the stock's par, or face, value that equals the annual dividend. For instance, an 8 percent preferred stock with a $50 par value would be expected to pay an annual dividend of $4 a share (.08 × $50 par = $4). Any dividends stated as percentages should be converted to annual dollar dividends before the cost of preferred stock is calculated.

FINANCE   IN   ACTION

Preferred Stock Issues Gain Popularity in the Banking Industry

In some cases, it's not the cost of capital that drives corporate security issuance—it's the availability of capital that determines what type of securities firms decide to issue. In the commercial banking industry, where credit conditions have deteriorated to levels not seen since the period following the Great Depression in 1929, many large bank holding companies are willing to issue whatever securities investors seem willing to purchase.

As the decade of the 1980s drew to a close, a weak economy and volatile corporate earnings battered bank security prices. Institutional investors that traditionally supply debt and equity capital to the banking industry grew wary of these investments. By the early 1990s, bankers began looking toward individual investors to provide new funds. But these investors were also afraid of purchasing the unsecured debt and common stock of banking firms.

The solution? Many banks are currently offering fixed dividend preferred stock to individual investors. These securities pay relatively high dividends and require substantial flotation costs. Individual investors do seem willing to buy these securities in order to capture attractive dividend returns, which in some recent cases have been as high as 15 percent.

In spite of this high cost, Citicorp, Mellon Bank Corp, Manufacturers Hanover Corp., Norwest Corp., and Barnett Banks, Inc. all began issuing preferred stock to individual investors in 1990. With all these firms seeking to sell similar securities at the same time, what do you think will happen to the returns that these securities must offer to attract new investors?

Source: Kelley Holland, "Banks compelled to turn to retail investors," *American Banker*, September 18, 1990, p. 32.

Calculating the Cost of Preferred Stock

The **cost of preferred stock, k_p,** is found by dividing the annual preferred stock dividend, D_p, by the net proceeds from the sale of the preferred stock, N_p. The net proceeds represent the amount of money to be received net of any flotation costs required to issue and sell the stock. For example, if a preferred stock is sold for \$100 per share but \$3 per share flotation costs are incurred, the net proceeds from the sale are \$97. Equation 13.3 gives the cost of preferred stock, k_p, in terms of the

cost of preferred stock, k_p The annual preferred stock dividend divided by the net proceeds from the sale of the preferred stock.

annual dollar dividend, D_p, and the net proceeds from the sale of the stock, N_p:

Equation 13.3
Formula for the cost of preferred stock

$$k_p = \frac{D_p}{N_p}$$

Since preferred stock dividends are paid out of the firm's *after-tax* cash flows, a tax adjustment is not required.

EXAMPLE   Debbo Company is contemplating issuance of an 8.5 percent preferred stock expected to sell for its $87 per share par value. The cost of issuing and selling the stock is expected to be $5 per share. The firm would like to determine the cost of the stock. Since the dividend is stated as a percentage of the stock's $87 par value, the first step in finding this cost is to calculate the dollar amount of preferred dividends. The annual dollar dividend is $7.40 (.085 × $87). The net proceeds from the proposed sale of stock can be found by subtracting the flotation costs from the sale price. This gives a value of $82 per share. Substituting the annual dividend, D_p, of $7.40 and the net proceeds, N_p, of $82 into Equation 13.3 gives the cost of preferred stock, 9.0 percent ($7.40 ÷ $82).

Comparing the 9.0 percent cost of perferred stock to the 5.6 percent cost of long-term debt (bonds) shows that the preferred stock is more expensive. This difference results primarily because the cost of long-term debt—interest—is tax deductible.

THE COST OF COMMON STOCK

The *cost of common stock* is the return required on the stock by investors in the marketplace. There are two forms of common stock financing: (1) retained earnings and (2) new issues of common stock. As a first step in finding each of these costs we must estimate the cost of common stock equity.

cost of common stock equity, k_s The rate at which investors discount the expected dividends of the firm in order to determine its share value.

Finding the Cost of Common Stock Equity

The **cost of common stock equity, k_s,** is the rate at which investors discount the expected dividends of the firm in order to determine its share value. Two techniques for measuring the cost of common stock equity capital are available. One uses the constant growth valuation model; the other relies on the capital asset pricing model (CAPM).

 Using the Constant Growth Valuation (Gordon) Model
The **constant growth valuation model**—the **Gordon model**—was presented in Chapter 12. It is based on the premise that the value of a share

of stock is equal to the present value of all future dividends it is expected to provide over an infinite time horizon. The key expression derived in Chapter 12 and presented as Equation 12.13 is restated in Equation 13.4:

$$P_0 = \frac{D_1}{k_s - g}$$

where

P_0 = value of common stock

D_1 = per-share dividend expected at the end of year 1

k_s = required return on common stock

g = constant rate of growth in dividends

Equation 13.4
Formula for the value of a share of stock under the constant growth, or Gordon, model

Solving Equation 13.4 for k_s results in the following expression for the *cost of common stock equity:*

$$k_s = \frac{D_1}{P_0} + g$$

Equation 13.5
Formula for the cost of common stock equity

Equation 13.5 indicates that the cost of common stock equity can be found by dividing the dividend expected at the end of year 1 by the current price of the stock and adding the expected growth rate. Since common stock dividends are paid from after-tax income, no tax adjustment is required.

constant growth valuation (Gordon) model Assumes that the value of a share of stock equals the present value of all future dividends (assumed to grow at a constant rate) that it is expected to provide over an infinite time horizon.

EXAMPLE   Debbo Company wishes to determine its cost of common stock equity capital, k_s. The market price, P_0, of its common stock is $50 per share. The firm expects to pay a dividend, D_1, of $4 at the end of the coming year, 1993. The dividends paid on the outstanding stock over the past six years (1987–1992) were as follows:

Year	Dividend
1992	$3.80
1991	3.62
1990	3.47
1989	3.33
1988	3.12
1987	2.97

Using the table for the present-value interest factors, *PVIF* (Table C-3) or a business calculator, in conjunction with the technique described for finding growth rates in Chapter 11, we can calculate the annual growth rate of dividends, g. It turns out to be approximately 5 percent (more precisely, 5.05 percent). Substituting $D_1 = \$4$, $P_0 = \$50$, and $g = 5$ percent into Equation 13.5 results in the cost of common stock equity:

$$k_s = \frac{\$4}{\$50} + 5.0\% = 8.0\% + 5.0\% = \underline{\underline{13.0\%}}$$

The 13.0 percent cost of common stock equity capital represents the return required by *existing* shareholders on their investment in order to leave the market price of the firm's outstanding shares unchanged.

Using the Capital Asset Pricing Model (CAPM)

The **capital asset pricing model (CAPM)** was developed and discussed in Chapter 12. It describes the relationship between the required return, or cost of common stock equity capital, k_s, and the nondiversifiable risk of the firm as measured by the beta coefficient, b. The basic CAPM is given in Equation 13.6:

$$k_s = R_F + [b \times (k_m - R_F)]$$

where

Equation 13.6
Formula for the capital asset pricing model (CAPM)

capital asset pricing model (CAPM)
Theory that describes the relationship between the required return and the nondiversifiable risk of the firm as measured by the beta coefficient.

R_F = risk-free rate of return, commonly measured by the return on a U.S. Treasury bill

k_m = market return; the return on the market portfolio of assets

Using CAPM, the cost of common stock equity is the return required by investors as compensation for the firm's nondiversifiable risk, which is measured by beta.

EXAMPLE   Debbo Company, which calculated its cost of common stock equity capital, k_s, using the constant growth valuation model in the preceding example, also wishes to calculate this cost using the capital asset pricing model. From information provided by the firm's investment advisers and its own analyses, it is found that the risk-free rate, R_F, equals 7 percent; the firm's beta, b, equals 1.5; and the market return, k_m, equals 11 percent. Substituting these values into the CAPM (Equation 13.6), the company estimates the cost of common stock equity capital, k_s, as follows:

$$k_s = 7.0\% + [1.5 \times (11.0\% - 7.0\%)] = 7.0\% + 6.0\% = \underline{\underline{13.0\%}}$$

The 13.0 percent cost of common stock equity capital, which is the same as that found using the constant growth valuation model, represents the required return of investors in Debbo Company common stock.

cost of retained earnings, k_r The same as the cost of an equivalent fully subscribed issue of additional common stock, which is measured by the cost of common stock equity, k_s.

The Cost of Retained Earnings

If earnings were not retained, they would be paid out to the common stockholders as dividends. Thus the **cost of retained earnings, k_r,** to the firm is the same as the cost of an *equivalent fully subscribed issue of additional common stock*. This means that retained earnings increase the stockholders' equity in the same way as a new issue of common stock. Stockholders find the firm's retention of earnings acceptable only if they expect it will earn at least their required return on the reinvested funds.

Viewing retained earnings as a fully subscribed issue of additional common stock, we can set the firm's cost of retained earnings, k_r, equal to the cost of common stock equity as given by Equations 13.5 and 13.6.[2]

$$k_r = k_s$$

Equation 13.7
Formula for a firm's cost of retained earnings

It is not necessary to adjust the cost of retained earnings for flotation costs since by retaining earnings the firm raises equity capital without incurring these costs.

EXAMPLE   The cost of retained earnings for Debbo Company was actually calculated in the preceding examples, since it is equal to the cost of common stock equity. Thus k_r equals 13.0 percent. As we will show in the next section, the cost of retained earnings is always lower than the cost of a new issue of common stock, due to the absence of flotation costs when financing projects with retained earnings.

The Cost of New Issues of Common Stock

Our purpose in finding the firm's overall cost of capital is to determine the after-tax cost of *new* funds required for financing projects. Attention must therefore be given to the **cost of a new issue of common stock, k_n.** This cost is determined by calculating the cost of common stock after considering both the amount of underpricing and the associated flotation costs. Normally, in order to sell a new issue it will have to be **underpriced**—sold at a price below the current market price, P_0. In addition, flotation costs paid for issuing and selling the new issue will reduce proceeds.

The cost of new issues can be calculated by determining the net proceeds after underpricing and flotation costs. We use the constant growth valuation model expression for the cost of existing common stock, k_s, as a starting point. If we let N_n represent the net proceeds from the sale of new common stock after allowing for underpricing and flota-

cost of a new issue of common stock, k_n
Cost determined by calculating the cost of common stock after considering both the amount of underpricing and the associated flotation costs.

underpriced   Stock sold at a price below its current market price.

---

[2]Technically, if a stockholder received dividends and wished to invest them in additional shares of the firm's stock, he or she would have to first pay personal taxes on the dividends and then pay brokerage fees prior to acquiring additional shares. Using *pt* as the average stockholder's personal tax rate and *bf* as the average brokerage fees stated as a percentage, the cost of retained earnings, k_r, can be specified as: $k_r = k_s \times (1 - pt) \times (1 - bf)$. Due to the difficulty in estimating *pt* and *bf*, only the simpler definition of k_r given in Equation 13.7 is used here.

tion costs, the cost of the new issue, k_n, can be expressed as follows:

Equation 13.8
Formula for the cost of a new issue of common stock

$$k_n = \frac{D_1}{N_n} + g$$

The net proceeds from sale of new common stock, N_n, will be less than the current market price, P_0. Therefore, the cost of new issues, k_n, will always be greater than the cost of existing issues, k_s, which as noted above is equal to the cost of retained earnings, k_r. The cost of new common stock is normally greater than any other long-term financing cost. Since common stock dividends are paid from after-tax cash flows, no tax adjustment is required.

EXAMPLE   In the example using the constant growth valuation model, we used an expected dividend, D_1, of $4; a current market price, P_0, of $50; and an expected growth rate of dividends, g, of 5 percent to calculate Debbo Company's cost of common stock equity capital, k_s. It was found to be 13.0 percent. To determine its cost of *new* common stock, k_n, Debbo Company has estimated that, on average, new shares can be sold for $47. The $3 per share underpricing is necessary due to the competitive nature of the market. A second cost associated with a new issue is an underwriting fee of $2.50 per share that would be paid to cover the costs of issuing and selling the new issue. The total underpricing and flotation costs per share are therefore expected to be $5.50 ($3.00 per share underpricing plus $2.50 per share flotation).

Subtracting the $5.50 per share underpricing and flotation cost from the current $50 share price, P_0, results in expected net proceeds, N_n, of $44.50 per share ($50.00 − $5.50). Substituting $D_1 = \$4$, $N_n = \$44.50$, and $g = 5$ percent into Equation 13.8 results in a cost of new common stock, k_n, as follows:

$$k_n = \frac{\$4.00}{\$44.50} + 5.0\% = 9.0\% + 5.0\% = \underline{\underline{14.0\%}}$$

Debbo Company's cost of new common stock, k_n, is therefore 14.0 percent. This is the value to be used in the subsequent calculation of the firm's overall cost of capital.

THE WEIGHTED AVERAGE COST OF CAPITAL (WACC)

weighted average cost of capital (WACC), k_a Cost determined by weighting the cost of each specific type of capital by its proportion in the firm's capital structure.

Now that methods for calculating the cost of specific sources of financing have been reviewed, we can present techniques for determining the overall cost of capital. As noted earlier, the **weighted average cost of capital (WACC), k_a**, is found by weighting the cost of each specific type of capital by its proportion in the firm's capital structure. Let us look at the common computational procedures and weighting schemes involved.

Calculating the Weighted Average Cost of Capital (WACC)

The weighted average cost of capital (WACC) can be calculated once the costs of the specific sources of financing have been determined. This calculation is performed by multiplying the specific cost of each form of financing by its proportion in the firm's capital structure and summing the weighted values. As an equation, the weighted average cost of capital, k_a, can be expressed as follows:

$$k_a = (w_i \times k_i) + (w_p \times k_p) + (w_s \times k_{r \text{ or } n})$$

where

    w_i = proportion of long-term debt in capital structure

    w_p = proportion of preferred stock in capital structure

    w_s = proportion of common stock equity in capital structure

    $w_i + w_p + w_s = 1.0$

Equation 13.9
Formula for the weighted average cost of capital (WACC)

Two important points should be noted about Equation 13.9:

1 ■■■ *The sum of weights must equal 1.0.* Simply stated, all capital structure components must be accounted for.

2 ■■■ The firm's common stock equity weight, w_s, is multiplied by either the cost of retained earnings, k_r, or the cost of new common stock, k_n. The specific cost used in the common stock equity term depends on whether the firm's common stock equity financing will be obtained using retained earnings, k_r, or new common stock, k_n.

EXAMPLE   Earlier in the chapter, we found the costs of the various types of capital for Debbo Company to be as follows:

    Cost of debt, k_i = 5.6 percent

    Cost of preferred stock, k_p = 9.0 percent

    Cost of retained earnings, k_r = 13.0 percent

    Cost of new common stock, k_n = 14.0 percent

The company uses the following weights when calculating its weighted average cost of capital.

Source of capital	Weight
Long-term debt	40%
Preferred stock	10
Common stock equity	50
Total	100%

Because the firm expects to have a sizable amount of

Table 13.1   Calculation of the Weighted Average Cost
                                of Capital for Debbo Company

Source of capital	Weight (1)	Cost (2)	Weighted cost [(1) × (2)] (3)
Long-term debt	40%	5.6%	2.2%
Preferred stock	10	9.0	.9
Common stock equity	50	13.0	6.5
Totals	100%		9.6%

Weighted average cost of capital = 9.6%

retained earnings available ($300,000), it plans to use its cost of retained earnings, k_r, as the cost of common stock equity. Debbo Company's weighted average cost of capital is calculated in Table 13.1. The resulting weighted average cost of capital for Debbo is 9.6 percent. In view of this cost of capital and assuming an unchanged risk level, the firm should accept all projects that earn a return greater than or equal to 9.6 percent.

Weighting Schemes

book value weights Weights that use accounting values to measure the proportion of each type of capital in the firm's financial structure.

market value weights Weights that use market values to measure the proportion of each type of capital in the firm's financial structure.

historic weights Either book or market value weights based on *actual* capital structure proportions.

target weights Either book or market value weights based on *desired* capital structure proportions.

Weights can be calculated as *book value* or *market value* and as *historic* or *target*.

Book Value Versus Market Value

Book value weights use accounting values to measure the proportion of each type of capital in the firm's financial structure. **Market value weights** measure the proportion of each type of capital at its market value. Market value weights are appealing, since the market values of securities closely approximate the actual dollars to be received from their sale. Moreover, since the costs of the various types of capital are calculated using prevailing market prices, it seems reasonable to use market value weights. *Market value weights are clearly preferred over book value weights.*

Historic Versus Target

Historic weights can be either book or market value weights based on *actual* capital structure proportions. For example, past as well as current book value proportions would constitute a form of historic weighting. Likewise, past or current market value proportions would represent a historic weighting scheme. Such a weighting scheme would therefore be based on real—rather than desired—proportions. **Target weights** reflect the firm's *desired* capital structure proportions. Like historic weights, they can also be based on either book or market values.

F I N A N C E   I N   A C T I O N

The Dynamics of the Weighted Average Cost of Capital

At times it may be tempting to view the weighted average cost of capital as a static cost to the firm, one that does not fluctuate much from period to period. The trouble is, however, that firms must issue new securities on a fairly regular basis to fund growth and retire maturing debt obligations. In some cases, new funds are needed at the most inopportune times.

Consider the 1991 plight of the commercial banking industry, described in the boxed discussion earlier in this chapter. While many bankers scrambled to issue preferred stock to cover new funding needs in the early 1990s, they also faced another problem: approximately $400 billion in bank debt was maturing or subject to interest rate adjustments in the first quarter of 1991. That forced many banks to issue new debt securities at substantially higher interest rates than the maturing debt, driving up the weighted average cost of capital for many financial institutions. In early 1991, Citicorp alone faced $3.9 billion in maturing long-term debt, while Chemical Banking Corporation and Security Pacific Corporation [now part of Bank of America] faced an additional $2.5 billion in debt obligations to refinance.

What's the best way to cope with the continued need to issue new debt in uncertain credit markets? Many bankers are anticipating future debt maturities well in advance of the actual due date, and issuing new securities before the new funds are needed. Other banks are replacing long-term debt obligations with medium-term notes, hoping that credit conditions for bank securities will improve over the next few years.

If they're right, bankers can refinance these medium-term notes by issuing long-term debt at lower interest rates a few years down the road. Doing so will reduce their weighted average capital costs to more comfortable levels. In the meantime, however, commercial banks face a skeptical investment community demanding substantially higher rates of return on new corporate debt obligations, and a significant increase in their weighted average cost of capital.

Source: Kelley Holland, "Maturing debt puts bankers in a new bind," *American Banker*, September 19, 1990, p. 1.

Firms using target weights establish such proportions on the basis of the "optimal" capital structure they wish to achieve. When one considers the somewhat approximate nature of the calculations, the choice of weights may not be critical. However, from a strictly theoretical point of view the *preferred weighting scheme is target market value proportions*, and these are assumed throughout this chapter.

THE MARGINAL COST AND INVESTMENT DECISIONS

The firm's weighted average cost of capital is a key input to the investment decision-making process. As demonstrated earlier in the chapter, the firm should make only those investments for which the expected return is greater than the weighted average cost of capital. Of course at any given time the firm's financing costs and investment returns will be affected by the volume of financing/investment undertaken. The concepts of a *weighted marginal cost of capital* and an *investment opportunities schedule* provide the mechanisms whereby financing and investment decisions can be made simultaneously at any point in time.

The Weighted Marginal Cost of Capital (WMCC)

weighted marginal cost of capital (WMCC) The firm's weighted average cost of capital (WACC) associated with its next dollar of total new financing.

weighted marginal cost of capital (WMCC) schedule Graph that relates the firm's weighted average cost of capital (WACC) to the level of total new financing.

The weighted average cost of capital may vary at any time depending on the volume of financing the firm plans to raise. *As the volume of financing increases, the costs of the various types of financing will increase, raising the firm's weighted average cost of capital.* The **weighted marginal cost of capital (WMCC)** is simply the firm's weighted average cost of capital (WACC) associated with its next dollar of total new financing. A schedule or graph relating the firm's weighted average cost of capital to the level of total new financing is called the **weighted marginal cost of capital (WMCC) schedule.** The increasing financing costs are attributable to the fact that fund suppliers require greater returns in the form of interest, dividends, or growth as compensation for the increased risk introduced as larger volumes of *new* financing are incurred.

Another factor causing the weighted average cost of capital to increase relates to the use of common stock equity financing. The portion of new financing provided by common stock equity will be taken from available retained earnings until exhausted and then obtained through new common stock financing. Remember that retained earnings are a less expensive form of common stock equity financing than the sale of new common stock. It should be clear, then, that once retained earnings have been exhausted, the weighted average cost of capital will rise with the addition of more expensive new common stock.

EXAMPLE   In the preceding example the weighted average cost of capital (WACC) for Debbo Company was calculated in Table 13.1 using the 13.0 percent cost of retained earnings, k_r, as the cost of common stock equity. Once the $300,000 of available retained earnings is exhausted, the firm must use the more expensive new common stock financing ($k_n = 14.0\%$) to meet its common stock equity needs. Since the target capital structure dictates that common stock equity represent 50 percent of total capital, the $300,000 of retained earnings

Table 13.2   **Calculation of the WACC for Debbo Company
for Greater than $600,000 of Total New Financing**

Source of capital	Weight (1)	Cost (2)	Weighted cost [(1) × (2)] (3)
Long-term debt	40%	5.6%	2.2%
Preferred stock	10	9.0	.9
Common stock equity	50	14.0	7.0
Totals	100%		10.1%

Weighted average cost of capital = 10.1%

will support only $600,000 of *total new financing.* This value is found by dividing the available retained earnings of $300,000 by the common stock equity target proportion of 50 percent ($300,000 ÷ .50 = $600,000). Therefore, when the firm's total new financing increases beyond $600,000 the weighted average cost of capital will rise: the cost of common stock equity increases from the 13.0 percent cost of retained earnings to the 14.0 percent cost of new common stock. Table 13.1 demonstrated the WACC calculation for the first $600,000 of total new financing. The WACC calculation for greater than $600,000 of total new financing is given in Table 13.2.

When the total new financing exceeds $600,000, the WACC rises from 9.6 percent (Table 13.1) to 10.1 percent (Table 13.2). Of course the firm may face other increases in the WACC due to increases in debt, preferred stock, and common stock equity costs as additional new funds are raised. Using calculations similar to those demonstrated above, Debbo Company developed its *weighted marginal cost of capital (WMCC) schedule,* which is summarized in Table 13.3 and graphed in Figure 13.1. It is quite clear from both the tabular and graphic data that the WMCC is an *increasing* function of the amount of total new financing raised.

Table 13.3 **Weighted Marginal Cost of Capital
for Debbo Company**

Range of total new financing	Weighted average cost of capital
$0 to $600,000	9.6%
$600,000 to $1,000,000	10.1
$1,000,000 and above	11.3

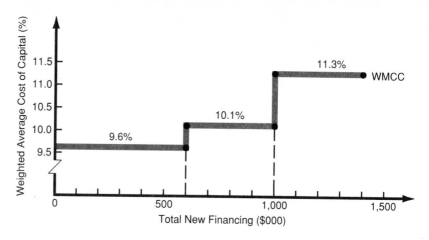

Figure 13.1   Weighted Marginal Cost of Capital (WMCC) Schedule for Debbo Company

Debbo Company's WMCC schedule shows that its weighted average cost of capital (WACC) increases from 9.6% between $0 and $600,000 of total new financing, to 10.1% between $600,000 and $1 million, to 11.3% for above $1 million. The increasing nature of this function is clearly depicted by this schedule.

The Investment Opportunities Schedule (IOS)

investment opportunities schedule (IOS)
A ranking of investment possibilities from best (highest returns) to worst (lowest returns).

At any given time a firm has certain investment opportunities available to it. These opportunities differ with respect to the size of investment anticipated, risk, and return. (For convenience, we assume that all opportunities have equal risk similar to the firm's risk.) The firm's **investment opportunities schedule (IOS)** is a ranking of investment possibilities from best (hightest returns) to worst (lowest returns). As the cumulative amount of money invested in a firm's capital projects increases, its return on the projects will decrease. Generally the first project selected will have the highest return, the next project the second highest, and so on. In other words, the return on investments will *decrease* as the firm accepts additional projects.

EXAMPLE   Debbo Company's current investment opportunities schedule (IOS) lists the best (highest return) to the worst (lowest return) investment possibilities in column 1 of Table 13.4. In column 2 of the table, the initial investment required by each project is shown. In column 3 the cumulative total invested funds required to finance all projects better than and including the corresponding investment opportunity are given. Plotting the project returns against the cumulative investment (column 1 against column 3 in Table 13.4) on a set of total new financing or investment-weighted average cost of capital and return axes results in the firm's

Table 13.4   **Investment Opportunities Schedule (IOS) for Debbo Company**

Investment opportunity	Rate of return (1)	Initial investment (2)	Cumulative investment[a] (3)
A	15.0%	$100,000	$ 100,000
B	14.5	200,000	300,000
C	14.0	400,000	700,000
D	13.0	100,000	800,000
E	12.0	300,000	1,100,000
F	11.0	200,000	1,300,000
G	10.0	100,000	1,400,000

[a]The cumulative investment represents the total amount invested in projects with higher returns plus the investment required for the given investment opportunity.

investment opportunities schedule (IOS). A graph of the IOS for Debbo Company is given in Figure 13.2.

Making Financing/Investment Decisions

As long as a project's rate of return is greater than the weighted marginal cost of new financing, the project should be accepted by the firm. While the return will decrease with the acceptance of more projects, the weighted marginal cost of capital will increase because greater amounts of financing will be required. The firm would therefore *accept projects up to the point where the marginal return on its investment equals its weighted marginal cost of capital.* Beyond that point its investment return will be less than its capital cost. This approach is completely consistent with the firm's owner wealth maximization goal. Returning to the Debbo Company example, we can demonstrate the application of this procedure.

EXAMPLE   Figure 13.2 shows the Debbo Company's WMCC schedule and IOS on the same set of axes. Using these two functions in combination, the firm can determine its optimal capital budget ("X" in the figure). By raising $1.1 million of new financing and investing these funds in projects A, B, C, D, and E, the firm should maximize the wealth of its owners, since the 12.0 percent return on the last dollar invested (in project E) *exceeds* its 11.3 percent weighted average cost. Investment in project F is not feasible because its 11.0 percent return is *less than* the 11.3 percent cost of funds available for investment. The importance of the WMCC and IOS for investment decision making should now be quite clear.

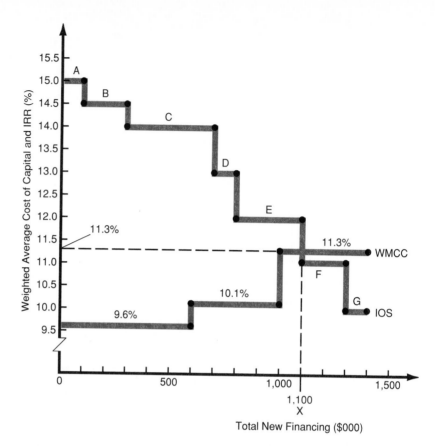

Figure 13.2   **Using the IOS and WMCC to Select Projects**

Debbo Company's investment opportunities schedule (IOS) depicts in descending order its investment possibilities. A total of $1.1 million should be raised and invested in projects A, B, C, D, and E since their marginal returns are in excess of the associated weighted marginal cost of capital (WMCC).

SUMMARY

1   **Understand the basic concept of cost of capital and the reasons why a weighted average is the appropriate cost measurement.** The cost of capital is the rate of return a firm must earn on its investments in order to maintain its market value and attract needed funds. To capture the interrelatedness of financing, an overall or weighted average cost of capital should be used rather than the cost of the specific source used to finance a given expenditure. This approach, by combining the costs of long-term financing sources, results in an average long-run cost that can be used to make long-term investment decisions.

2   **Calculate both the cost of long-term debt (bonds), using a popular approximation technique, and the cost of preferred stock.** The cost of long-term debt (bonds) is the after-tax cost today of raising long-term funds through borrowing. It can be approximated using a formula and a tax-adjustment calculation. The cost of preferred stock is the stated annual dividend expressed as a percentage of the net proceeds from the sale of preferred shares. The key variable definitions and formulas for the before- and after-tax cost of debt and the cost of preferred stock are given in Table 13.5.

Table 13.5   **Summary of Key Variable Definitions and Formulas
for Cost of Capital**

Variable definitions

k_d = before-tax cost of debt
I = annual interest in dollars
N_d = net proceeds from the sale of debt (bond)
n = number of years to the bond's maturity
k_i = after-tax cost of debt
T = firm's tax rate
k_p = cost of preferred stock
D_p = annual preferred stock dividend
N_p = net proceeds from the sale of preferred stock
k_s = required return on common stock
D_1 = per-share dividend expected at the end of year 1
P_0 = value of common stock
g = constant rate of growth in dividends
R_F = risk-free rate of return
b = beta coefficient or measure of nondiversifiable risk
k_m = market return; return on the market portfolio of assets
k_r = cost of retained earnings
k_n = cost of a new issue of common stock
N_n = net proceeds from sale of new common stock
k_a = weighted average cost of capital
w_i = proportion of long-term debt in capital structure
w_p = proportion of preferred stock in capital structure
w_s = proportion of common stock equity in capital structure

Cost of Capital Formulas

Before-tax cost of debt

$$k_d = \frac{I + \dfrac{\$1{,}000 - N_d}{n}}{\dfrac{N_d + \$1{,}000}{2}} \qquad \text{[Eq. 13.1]}$$

After-tax cost of debt

$$k_i = k_d \times (1 - T) \qquad \text{[Eq. 13.2]}$$

Cost of preferred stock

$$k_p = \frac{D_p}{N_p} \qquad \text{[Eq. 13.3]}$$

Cost of common stock equity

Using constant growth valuation model: $k_s = \dfrac{D_1}{P_0} + g$ [Eq. 13.5]

Using capital asset pricing model (CAPM):
$k_s = R_F + [b \times (k_m - R_F)]$ [Eq. 13.6]

Cost of retained earnings   [Eq. 13.7]

$$k_r = k_s$$

Cost of new issues of common stock

$$k_n = \frac{D_1}{N_n} + g \qquad \text{[Eq. 13.8]}$$

Weighted average cost of capital (WACC)

$$k_a = (w_i \times k_i) + (w_p \times k_p) + (w_s \times k_{r \text{ or } n}) \qquad \text{[Eq. 13.9]}$$

3　　**Find the cost of common stock equity and convert it into the cost of retained earnings and the cost of new issues of common stock.** The cost of common stock equity can be calculated using the constant growth valuation model or the capital asset pricing model (CAPM). The cost of retained earnings is equal to the cost of common stock equity. An adjustment in the cost of common stock equity to reflect underpricing and flotation cost is required to find the cost of new issues of common stock. The key variable definitions and formulas for the cost of common stock equity, the cost of retained earnings, and the cost of new issues of common stock are given in Table 13.5.

4　　**Calculate the weighted average cost of capital (WACC) and discuss the alternative weighting schemes.** A firm's weighted average cost of capital (WACC) can be determined by combining the costs of specific types of capital after weighting each cost using historical book or market value weights or target book or market value weights. The theoretically preferred approach uses target weights based on market values. The key variable definitions and formula for the WACC are given in Table 13.5.

5　　**Describe the rationale for and procedures used to determine the weighted marginal cost of capital (WMCC).** A firm's weighted marginal cost of capital (WMCC) reflects the fact that as the volume of financing increases, the costs of the various types of financing will increase, raising the firm's weighted average cost of capital (WACC). The WMCC is the firm's WACC associated with its next dollar of total new financing. The WMCC schedule relates the WACC to each level of total new financing.

6　　**Explain how the weighted marginal cost of capital (WMCC) can be used with the investment opportunities schedule (IOS) to make the firm's financing/investment decisions.** The investment opportunities schedule (IOS) presents a ranking of currently available investments from those with the highest returns to those with the lowest returns. It is used in combination with the weighted marginal cost of capital (WMCC) to find the level of financing/investment that maximizes owners' wealth. With this approach the firm would accept projects up to the point where the marginal return on its investment equals its weighted marginal cost of capital.

QUESTIONS

13—1　　What is the *cost of capital?* What role does it play in making long-term investment decisions? Why is use of a weighted average cost rather than the specific cost recommended?

13—2　　You have just been told, "Since we are going to finance this project with debt, its required rate of return must exceed the cost of debt." Do you agree or disagree? Explain.

13—3　　Why is the cost of capital most appropriately measured on an after-tax basis? What effect, if any, does this have on specific cost components?

13—4　　What is meant by the *net proceeds* from the sale of a bond? In which circumstances is a bond expected to sell at a discount or at a premium?

13—5　　What sort of general approximation can be used to find the before-tax cost of debt? How is the before-tax cost of debt converted into the after-tax cost?

13—6　　How would you calculate the cost of preferred stock? Why do we concern ourselves with the net proceeds from the sale of the stock instead of its sale price?

13—7   What premise about share value underlies the constant growth valu-
            ation (Gordon) model used to measure the cost of common
            stock equity, k_s? What does each component of the equation
            represent?
13—8   If retained earnings are viewed as a fully subscribed issue of addi-
            tional common stock, why is the cost of financing a project with
            retained earnings technically less than the cost of using a new issue
            of common stock?
13—9   Describe the logic underlying the use of *target capital structure
            weights,* and compare and contrast this approach with the use of
            historic weights.
13—10   What is the *weighted marginal cost of capital (WMCC)?* What does the
            WMCC *schedule* represent? Why does this schedule increase?
13—11   What is the *investment opportunities schedule (IOS)?* Is it typically
            depicted as an increasing or decreasing function of the level of in-
            vestment at a given point in time? Why?
13—12   Use a graph to show how the weighted marginal cost of capital
            (WMCC) schedule and the investment opportunities schedule (IOS)
            can be used to find the level of financing/investment that maximizes
            owners' wealth.

PROBLEMS

13—1   **(Concept of Cost of Capital)** Ren Manufacturing is in the process of
            analyzing its investment decision-making procedures. The two proj-
            ects evaluated by the firm during the past month were projects 263
            and 264. The basic variables surrounding each project analysis and
            the resulting decision actions are summarized in the following table.

Basic variables	Project 263	Project 264
Cost	$64,000	$58,000
Life	15 years	15 years
Return	8%	15%
Least-cost financing		
Source	Debt	Equity
Cost (after-tax)	7%	16%
Decision		
Action	Accept	Reject
Reason	8% return > 7% cost	15% return < 16% cost

            a. Evaluate the firm's decision-making procedures, and explain why
               the acceptance of project 263 and rejection of project 264 may not
               be in the owners' best interest.
            b. If the firm maintains a capital structure containing 40 percent
               debt and 60 percent equity, find its weighted average cost using
               the data in the table.
            c. Had the firm used the weighted average cost calculated in **b,** what
               actions would have been taken relative to projects 263 and 264?
            d. Compare and contrast the firm's actions with your findings in **c.**
               Which decision method seems more appropriate? Explain why.

13—2   **(Cost of Debt)**   Currently Krick and Company can sell 15-year, $1,000 par-value bonds paying *annual interest* at a 12 percent coupon rate. As a result of current interest rates, the bonds can be sold for $1,010 each; flotation costs of $30 per bond will be incurred in this process. The firm is in the 40 percent tax bracket.
a. Find the net proceeds from sale of the bond, N_d.
b. Estimate the before-tax cost of debt, k_d.
c. Convert your finding in **b** into the after-tax cost of debt, k_i.

13—3   **(Cost of Debt)**   For each of the following $1,000 par-value bonds, assuming *annual interest* payment and a 40 percent tax rate, calculate the *after-tax* cost.

Bond	Life (years)	Underwriting fee	Discount (−) or premium (+)	Coupon interest rate
A	20	$25	$−20	9%
B	16	40	+10	10
C	15	30	−15	12
D	25	15	Par	9
E	22	20	−60	11

13—4   **(Cost of Preferred Stock)**   The No-Tread Tire Company has just issued preferred stock. The stock has a 12 percent annual dividend and a $100 par value. It was sold at $97.50 per share. In addition, flotation costs of $2.50 per share must be paid.
a. Calculate the cost of the preferred stock.
b. If the firm had sold the preferred stock with a 10 percent annual dividend and a $90 net price, what would its cost have been?

13—5   **(Cost of Preferred Stock)**   Determine the cost for each of the following preferred stocks.

Preferred stock	Par value	Sales price	Flotation cost	Annual dividend
A	$100	$101	$9.00	11%
B	40	38	$3.50	8%
C	35	37	$4.00	$5.00
D	30	26	5% of par	$3.00
E	20	20	$2.50	9%

13—6   **(Cost of Common Stock Equity—CAPM)**   JAM Corporation common stock has a beta, b, of 1.2. The risk-free rate is 6 percent and the market return is 11 percent.
a. Determine the risk premium on JAM common stock.
b. Determine the required return JAM common stock should provide.
c. Determine JAM's cost of common stock equity using the CAPM.

13—7   **(Cost of Common Stock Equity)**   Delico Meat Packing wishes to measure its cost of common stock equity. The firm's stock is currently selling for $57.50. The firm expects to pay a $3.40 dividend at the end of the year (1993). The dividends for the past five years were as follows:

Year	Dividend
1992	$3.10
1991	2.92
1990	2.60
1989	2.30
1988	2.12

After underpricing and flotation costs, the firm expects to net $52 per share on a new issue.
a. Determine the growth rate of dividends.
b. Determine the net proceeds, N_n, the firm actually receives.
c. Using the constant growth valuation model, determine the cost of retained earnings, k_r.
d. Using the constant growth valuation model, determine the cost of new common stock, k_n.

13—8   **(Retained Earnings versus New Common Stock)** Using the data for each firm in the following table, calculate the cost of retained earnings and the cost of new common stock using the constant growth valuation model.

Firm	Current market price per share	Dividend growth rate	Projected dividend per share next year	Underpricing per share	Flotation cost per share
A	$50.00	8%	$2.25	$2.00	$1.00
B	20.00	4	1.00	.50	1.50
C	42.50	6	2.00	1.00	2.00
D	19.00	2	2.10	1.30	1.70

13—9   **(WACC—Book Weights)** Atlanta Tire has on its books the following amounts and specific (after-tax) costs for each source of capital:

Source of capital	Book value	Specific cost
Long-term debt	$700,000	5.3%
Preferred stock	50,000	12.0
Common stock equity	650,000	16.0

a. Calculate the firm's weighted average cost of capital using book value weights.
b. Explain how the firm can use this cost in the investment decision-making process.

13—10   (WACC—Book Weights and Market Weights) The Pure Air Company has compiled the following information:

Source of capital	Book value	Market value	After-tax cost
Long-term debt	$4,000,000	$3,840,000	6.0%
Preferred stock	40,000	60,000	13.0
Common stock equity	1,060,000	3,000,000	17.0
Totals	$5,100,000	$6,900,000	

a. Calculate the weighted average cost of capital using book value weights.
b. Calculate the weighted average cost of capital using market value weights.
c. Compare the answers obtained in **a** and **b**. Explain the differences.

 13—11   (WACC and Target Weights) After careful analysis, Ellwood Company has determined that its optimal capital structure is composed of the following sources and target market value weights:

Source of capital	Target market value weight
Long-term debt	30%
Preferred stock	15
Common stock equity	55
Total	100%

The cost of debt is estimated to be 7.2 percent; the cost of preferred stock is estimated to be 13.5 percent; the cost of retained earnings is estimated to be 16.0 percent; and the cost of new common stock is estimated to be 18.0 percent. All of these are after-tax rates. Currently, the company's debt represents 25 percent, the preferred stock represents 10 percent, and the common stock equity represents 65 percent of total capital based on the market values of the three components. The company expects to have a significant amount of retained earnings available and does not expect to sell any new common stock.

a. Calculate the weighted average cost of capital based on historic market value weights.
b. Calculate the weighted average cost of capital based on target market value weights.

 13—12   (Calculation of Specific Costs and the WACC) Keystone Pump has asked Martin Drywater, its financial manager, to measure the cost of each specific type of capital as well as the weighted average cost of capital. The weighted average cost is to be measured using the following weights: 40 percent long-term debt, 10 percent preferred stock, and 50 percent common stock equity (retained earnings, new common stock, or both). The firm's tax rate is 40 percent on ordinary income.

Debt   The firm can sell for $980 a 10-year, $1,000 par-value bond with a 10 percent *annual* coupon interest rate. A flotation cost of 3 percent of the par value would be required in addition to the discount of $20 per bond.

Preferred stock   Eight percent preferred stock having a par value of $100 can be sold for $65. An additional fee of $2 per share must be paid to the underwriters.

Common stock   The firm's common stock is currently selling for $50 per share. The dividend expected to be paid at the end of the coming year (1993) is $4. Dividend payments in each of the past five years were as follows:

Year	Dividend
1992	$3.75
1991	3.50
1990	3.30
1989	3.15
1988	2.85

It is expected that, to sell, new common stock must be underpriced $5 per share and the firm must also pay $3 per share in flotation costs.
a. Calculate the specific cost of each source of financing. (Assume that $k_r = k_s$.)
b. Assuming the firm plans to pay out all of its earnings as dividends (i.e., retained earnings = $0), calculate its weighted average cost of capital.

13—13   **(Calculation of Specific Costs, WACC, and WMCC)**   Cloak, Inc., is interested in measuring its overall cost of capital. Current investigation has gathered the following data. The firm is in the 40 percent tax bracket.

Debt   The firm can raise an unlimited amount of debt by selling $1,000 par-value, 8 percent coupon interest rate, 20-year bonds on which *annual interest* payments will be made. To sell the issue, an average discount of $30 per bond would have to be given. The firm also must pay flotation costs of $30 per bond.

Preferred stock   The firm can sell 8 percent preferred stock at its $95-per-share par value. The cost of issuing and selling the preferred stock is expected to be $5 per share. An unlimited amount of preferred stock can be sold under these terms.

Common stock   The firm's common stock is currently selling for $90 per share. The firm expects to pay cash dividends of $7 per share next year. The firm's dividends have been growing at an annual rate of 6 percent, and this is expected to continue into the future. The stock will have to be underpriced by $7 per share, and flotation costs are expected to amount to $5 per share. The firm can sell an unlimited amount of new common stock under these terms.

Retained earnings The firm expects to have available a limited amount of retained earnings. Once these retained earnings are exhausted, the firm will use new common stock as the form of common stock equity financing.

a. Calculate the specific cost of each source of financing. (Round answers to the nearest 0.1 percent.)

b. The firm's capital structure weights used in calculating its weighted average cost of capital are given. (Round answers to the nearest 0.1 percent in this part.)

Source of capital	Weight
Long-term debt	30%
Preferred stock	20
Common stock equity	50
Total	100%

(1) Calculate the weighted average cost of capital associated with total financing *up to* the point where retained earnings are exhausted.

(2) Calculate the weighted average cost of capital associated with total financing *after* retained earnings are exhausted and new common stock is used as common stock equity financing.

 13—14 **(Integrative—WACC, WMCC, and IOS)** The H. Grimmer Company has compiled the data given in the following table relative to the current costs of its three basic sources of capital—long-term debt, preferred stock, and common stock equity—for various ranges of total new financing.

Range of total new financing	Cost of given source of capital		
	Debt	Preferred	Common
$0 to $200,000	6%	17%	20%
$200,000 to $500,000	6	17	22
$500,000 to $750,000	7	19	22
$750,000 to $1,000,000	9	19	24
Greater than $1,000,000	9	19	26

The company's capital structure weights used in calculating its weighted average cost of capital are as follows:

Source of capital	Weight
Long-term debt	40%
Preferred stock	20
Common stock equity	40
Total	100%

a. Calculate the weighted average cost of capital (WACC) for each range of total new financing.
b. Using the results in **a,** draw the firm's weighted marginal cost of capital (WMCC) schedule on a set of total new financing or investment (x-axis)-weighted average cost of capital and return (y-axis) axes.
c. Using the following information, draw the firm's investment opportunities schedule (IOS) on the set of axes used in **b.**
d. Which, if any, of the available investments would you recommend the firm accept? Explain your answer.

Investment opportunity	Rate of return	Initial investment
A	19%	$200,000
B	15	300,000
C	22	100,000
D	14	600,000
E	23	200,000
F	13	100,000
G	21	300,000
H	17	100,000
I	16	400,000

CASE

Dude Surfwear's Financing/Investment Decision

Dude Surfwear Company is a growing manufacturer of casual clothing whose stock is traded on the over-the-counter exchange. During 1992 the Los Angeles–based company experienced sharp increases in both sales and earnings. Because of this recent growth, Melissa Jen, the company's treasurer, wants to make sure that available funds are being used to their fullest. Management has set a policy to maintain the current capital structure proportions of 25 percent long-term debt, 10 percent preferred stock, and 65 percent common stock equity for at least the next three years. The firm is in the 40 percent tax bracket.

Dude's division and product managers have presented several competing investment opportunities to Ms. Jen. However, since funds are limited, choices of which projects to accept must be made. The investment opportunities schedule (IOS) is given on the next page.

Investment opportunities schedule (IOS)
Dude Surfwear Company

Investment opportunity	Rate of return	Initial investment
A	21%	$400,000
B	19	200,000
C	24	700,000
D	27	500,000
E	18	300,000
F	22	600,000
G	17	500,000

In order to estimate the firm's weighted average cost of capital (WACC), Ms. Jen contacted a leading investment banking firm which provided the financing cost data given below.

Financing cost data
Dude Surfwear Company

Long-term debt

The firm can raise an unlimited amount of additional debt by selling ten-year, $1,000, 12 percent annual coupon interest rate bonds to net $970 after flotation costs.

Preferred stock

Preferred stock, regardless of the amount sold, can be issued with a $60 par value, 17 percent annual dividend rate, and will net $57 per share after flotation costs.

Common stock equity

The firm expects dividends and earnings per share to be $1.76 and $4.40, respectively, in 1993 and to continue to grow at a constant rate of 15 percent per year. The firm's stock is currently selling for $20 per share. The firm expects to have sufficient retained earnings available to support $2,000,000 in total new financing. Once the retained earnings have been exhausted the firm can raise additional funds by selling new common stock, netting $16 per share after flotation costs.

Required

a. Calculate the after-tax cost of each of Dude Surfwear's sources of financing—long-term debt, preferred stock, retained earnings, and new common stock.

b. Using your findings in **a,** calculate the firm's weighted average cost of capital (WACC) for:
   (1) Total new financing ranging between $0 and $2,000,000.
   (2) Total new financing in excess of $2,000,000.

c. Using your findings from **b** along with the investment opportunities schedule (IOS), draw the firm's weighted marginal cost of capital (WMCC) schedule and IOS on the same set of axes. Make the *x*-axis represent total new financing or investment and the *y*-axis the weighted average cost of capital and return.

d. Which, if any, of the available investments would you recommend the firm accept? Explain your answer.

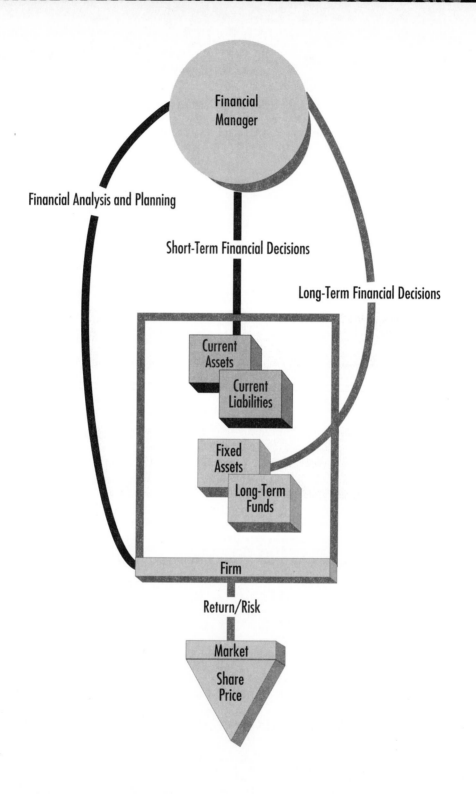

LONG-TERM FINANCIAL DECISIONS

CHAPTER 14

CAPITAL BUDGETING AND CASH FLOW PRINCIPLES

After studying this chapter, you should be able to:

1 Understand the key capital expenditure motives and the steps in the capital budgeting process, beginning with proposal generation and ending with follow-up.

2 Define the basic terminology used to describe projects, funds availability, decision approaches, and cash flow patterns.

3 Discuss the major components of relevant cash flows and differences in the development of expansion- versus replacement-decision cash flows.

4 Calculate the initial investment associated with a proposed capital expenditure given relevant cost, depreciation, and tax data.

5 Determine the operating cash inflows relevant to a capital budgeting proposal using the income statement format.

6 Discuss foreign direct investment, its risks, and the role of U.S.–based multinational companies in it.

Car Washes and Finance

"The new $13 million automated aircraft washing system . . . is a little more complicated than your average car wash . . . ."

Stop and think for a moment about the remarkable longevity of many corporations. Firms like General Electric, IBM, and Mitsubishi are household names throughout the world. Like many others, they have provided generations of customers with a steady flow of new products, generations of employees with a comfortable standard of living, and generations of bond- and stockholders with consistent investment returns. How do they manage to keep up with the rapidly changing marketplace and prosper over long periods of time? Hard work, innovation, and, oh yes, a bit of good, old-fashioned financial analysis.

In some cases, ideas lead to new products that satisfy obvious needs in the marketplace. Japan Airlines (JAL) and Kawasaki Heavy Industries, for example, recently developed an automated "car wash" to scrub jumbo jets between flights. Before 1991, this cleaning chore required four hours of work from a crew of 20 people to hand-wash each airplane, and cost the airlines $2,600 per wash job. The new $13 million automated aircraft washing system requires just five operators, and does the same job in just 80 minutes for $1,300. The new system is a little more complicated than your average car wash, but the general idea is the same. JAL and Kawasaki plan to begin marketing the system to airlines in 1991, and customers are already in line.

The search for new ideas and new products marches constantly forward. But how do corporations determine if their new ideas are commercially viable? How do they know that new products will provide profits in the marketplace, and how do they determine if these profits adequately compensate investors for the risks they bear?

Financial managers use a process known as capital budgeting to answer these questions. Managers classify different projects, estimate the cash flows associated with them, and determine how strong the chances are that a given project will cover its development, production, and selling costs, and increase shareholder wealth. Without capital budgeting, good ideas like the automated aircraft washing system would remain just that—ideas.

capital budgeting
The process of evaluating and selecting long-term investments consistent with the firm's goal of owner wealth maximization.

Capital budgeting is the process of evaluating and selecting long-term investments consistent with the firm's goal of owner wealth maximization. Firms typically make a variety of long-term investments. The most common such investment for the manufacturing firm is in *fixed assets*. These assets are a necessity: without them production would be impossible. Fixed assets are quite often referred to as *earning assets* because they generally provide the basis for the firm's earning power and value. The three major classes of fixed assets are property (land), plant, and equipment. Chapters 18 to 21 address the key issues related to long-term financing of fixed assets. We here concentrate on fixed-asset acquisition without regard to the specific method of financing used.

THE CAPITAL BUDGETING DECISION PROCESS

Long-term investments represent sizable outlays of funds. Consequently, procedures are needed to analyze and select them properly. Attention must be given to the initial outlay and to subsequent cash flows associated with long-term or fixed-asset investments. As time passes, fixed assets may become obsolete or may require an overhaul; at these points, too, financial decisions may be required. This section of the chapter discusses capital expenditure motives and briefly describes the steps in the capital budgeting process.

Capital Expenditure Motives

capital expenditure
An outlay of funds that is expected to produce benefits over a period of time *greater than* one year.

current expenditure
An outlay of funds resulting in benefits received *within* one year.

A **capital expenditure** is an outlay of funds by the firm that is expected to produce benefits over a period of time *greater than* one year. A **current expenditure** is an outlay resulting in benefits received *within* one year. Fixed-asset outlays are capital expenditures, but not all capital expenditures are classified as fixed assets. A $60,000 outlay for a new machine with a usable life of 15 years is a capital expenditure that would appear as a fixed asset on the firm's balance sheet. A $60,000 outlay for advertising that produces benefits over a long period is also a capital expenditure. However, an outlay for advertising would rarely be shown as a fixed asset.

Capital expenditures are made for many reasons. Although the motives may differ, the evaluation techniques are the same. The basic motives for capital expenditures are to expand, replace, or renew fixed assets or to obtain some other less tangible benefit over a long period.

Expansion
Perhaps the most common motive for a capital expenditure is to expand the level of operations—usually through acquisition of fixed assets. A

growing firm often finds it necessary to acquire new fixed assets rapidly. Remember that fixed assets include property (land), plant, and equipment. In other words, the purchase of additional physical facilities, such as additional property or a new factory, is a capital expenditure.

Replacement

As a firm's growth slows and it reaches maturity, most of its capital expenditures will be for the replacement or renewal of obsolete or worn-out assets. This type of capital expenditure does not always result from the outright failure of a piece of equipment or the inability of an existing plant to function efficiently. The need to replace existing assets must be periodically examined by the firm's financial manager. A machine does not break down and say, "Please replace me!" But each time a machine requires a major repair, the firm should evaluate the outlay for the repair in terms of the outlay to replace the machine and the benefits of replacement.

Renewal

The renewal of fixed assets is often an alternative to replacement. Renewal may involve rebuilding, overhauling, or retrofitting an existing machine or facility. For example, an existing drill press could be renewed by replacing its motor and adding a numeric control system. A physical facility could be renewed by rewiring, adding air conditioning, and so on. Firms wishing to improve efficiency may find that both replacing and renewing existing machinery are suitable solutions.

Other Purposes

Some capital expenditures do not result in the acquisition or transformation of tangible fixed assets shown on the firm's balance sheet. Instead, they involve a long-term commitment of funds by the firm in expectation of a future return. These expenditures include outlays for advertising, research and development, management consulting, and new products. Advertising outlays are expected to provide benefits in the form of increased future sales. Research and development outlays are expected to provide future benefits in the form of new product ideas. Management-consulting outlays are expected to provide returns in the form of increased profits from increased efficiency of operation. New products are expected to contribute to a product mix that maximizes overall returns. Other capital expenditure proposals—such as the installment of pollution-control and safety devices mandated by the government—are difficult to evaluate because they provide intangible returns rather than clearly measurable cash flows.

Steps in the Process

The **capital budgeting process** can be viewed as consisting of five distinct but interrelated steps. It begins with proposal generation. This is followed by review and analysis, decision making, implementation, and

capital budgeting process Five distinct but interrelated steps used to evaluate and select long-term investments: proposal generation, review and analysis, decision making, implementation, and follow-up.

follow-up. Each step in the process is important. Major time and effort, however, are devoted to review and analysis and decision making. These are the steps given the most attention in this and the following chapter.

Proposal Generation

Proposals for capital expenditures are made by people at all levels within a business organization. To stimulate a flow of ideas that could result in potential cost savings, many firms offer cash rewards to employees whose proposals are ultimately adopted. Capital expenditure proposals typically travel from the originator to a reviewer at a higher level in the organization. For relatively minor expenditures, the review might be made at the next organizational level. Major expenditure proposals go before a higher-level reviewer or review committee. Clearly, proposals requiring large outlays will be much more carefully scrutinized than less costly ones.

Review and Analysis

Capital expenditure proposals—especially those requiring major outlays—are formally reviewed in the firm. The review will seek to assess a proposal's appropriateness in light of the firm's overall objectives and plans. More important, it will evaluate the proposal's economic validity. The proposed costs and benefits are estimated and then converted into a series of relevant cash flows. To these various capital budgeting techniques are applied in order to measure the investment merit of the potential outlay. In addition, various aspects of the *risk* associated with the proposal are considered. They are either incorporated into the economic analysis or rated and recorded along with the economic measures. Once the economic analysis is completed, a summary report, often with a recommendation, is submitted to the decision maker(s).

Decision Making

The size of proposed capital expenditures can vary significantly. Some expenditures, such as the purchase of a hammer that will provide benefits for three years, are by definition capital expenditures, even if the cost is only $15.[1] The purchase of a new machine costing $60,000 is also a capital expenditure because it is expected to provide long-run returns. The actual dollar outlay and the importance of a capital expenditure determine the organizational level at which the expenditure decision is made.

---

[1] Even though outlays to purchase items such as hammers are known to provide benefits over a period greater than a year, they are treated as current expenditures in the year of purchase. There is a certain dollar limit beyond which outlays are *capitalized* (i.e., treated as a fixed asset) and *depreciated* rather than *expensed*. This dollar limit depends largely on what the U.S. Internal Revenue Service will permit. In accounting, the issue of whether to expense or capitalize an outlay is resolved using the *principle of materiality*. This rule suggests that any outlays deemed material (i.e., large) relative to the firm's scale of operations should be capitalized, whereas others should be expensed in the current period.

Table 14.1   **A Scheme for Delegating Capital Expenditure Decision Authority**

Size of expenditure	Decision-making authority
Over $200,000	Board of directors or top management committee
$100,000–$200,000	President and/or chair of board of directors
$50,000–$100,000	Vice-president in charge of division
$10,000–$50,000	Plant manager
Under $10,000	Persons designated by plant manager

Dollar Outlay   Firms delegate capital-expenditure authority on the basis of certain dollar limits. Generally, the board of directors reserves the right to make final decisions on capital expenditures requiring outlays beyond a certain amount; the authority for making smaller expenditures is given to other organizational levels. An example of a scheme for delegating capital-expenditure decision authority is presented in Table 14.1. As the size of expenditures increases, the decision-making authority moves to higher levels within the organization. Of course, the detail and formality of the economic analysis on which the decision is based tend to increase in rigor with the dollar value of the proposal. The decision to buy a computer network would be much more closely considered than the decision to buy new calculators for the clerical staff.

Importance   Firms operating under critical time constraints with respect to production often find it necessary to provide exceptions to a strict dollar-outlay scheme. In such cases the plant manager is often given the power to make decisions necessary to keep the production line moving, even though the outlays are larger than he or she would normally be allowed to authorize. These exceptions must be allowed due to the high cost of interrupting production. It is wise to put some dollar limit on these critically important expenditures, but it can be set somewhat above the norm for that organizational level.

Implementation

Once a proposal has been approved and funding has been made available,[2] the implementation phase begins. For minor outlays, implementation is relatively routine; the expenditure is made and payment is rendered. For major expenditures, greater control is required to ensure that what has been proposed and approved is acquired at the budgeted costs. Often the expenditures for a single proposal may occur in phases, with each outlay requiring the signed approval of company officers.

---

[2]Capital expenditures are often approved as part of the annual budgeting process, although funding will not be made available until the budget is implemented—frequently as long as six months after approval.

Follow-Up

Follow-up involves monitoring the results during the operating phase of a project. The comparisons of actual costs and benefits with those expected and those of previous projects are vital. When actual outcomes deviate from projected outcomes, action may be required to cut costs, improve benefits, or possibly terminate the project. Follow-up is often ignored in practice, but it is an important activity that can contribute favorably to the firm's overall risk, return, and value.

CAPITAL BUDGETING TERMINOLOGY

An understanding of some basic capital budgeting terminology is necessary before we can develop the concepts, tools, and techniques related to the capital budgeting process. In addition, we present a number of key assumptions used to simplify the discussion in the remainder of this chapter as well as in Chapter 15.

Types of Projects

The firm may be confronted with a number of different types of projects. Depending on the types of projects being considered, different decision-making approaches may be required. The two most common project types are (1) independent and (2) mutually exclusive projects.

Independent Projects

independent projects Projects whose cash flows are unrelated or independent of one another; the acceptance of one *does not eliminate* the others from consideration.

Independent projects are projects whose cash flows are unrelated or independent of one another; the acceptance of one *does not eliminate* the others from further consideration. If a firm has unlimited funds to invest, all the independent projects that meet its minimum investment criteria can be implemented. For example, a firm with unlimited funds may be faced with three acceptable independent projects—(1) installing air conditioning in the plant, (2) acquiring a small supplier, and (3) purchasing a new computer system. Clearly, the acceptance of any one of these projects does not eliminate the others from further consideration; all three could be undertaken if funds are available to do so.

Mutually Exclusive Projects

mutually exclusive projects Projects that compete with one another, so that the acceptance of one *eliminates* the others from further consideration.

Mutually exclusive projects are projects that have the same function and therefore compete with one another. The acceptance of one of a group of mutually exclusive projects *eliminates* from further consideration all other projects in the group. For example, a firm in need of increased production capacity could obtain it by (1) expanding its plant, (2) acquiring another company, or (3) contracting with another company for production. If each of these alternatives meets the firm's minimum acceptance criteria, some technique must be used to determine the "best" one. Clearly, the acceptance of one of these alternatives eliminates the need for either of the others.

ETHICS IN FINANCE

Capital Budgeting and Competitiveness in High-Tech Markets

In most cases, corporations undertake capital budgeting projects in an isolated manner. Firms rarely collaborate with one another in developing new products or manufacturing processes. This tendency to "go it alone" against the competition is beginning to change, however, as American firms seek innovative ways to respond to the threat of foreign competition.

In the 1980s, most U.S. manufacturers of dynamic random access computer chips (DRAMs) were forced out of business when Japanese chip makers dumped DRAM chips in the American market. The practice of dumping, or selling products below cost in foreign markets to gain overseas market share, provided dramatic growth for Japanese chipmakers. In response, 14 worried U.S. electronics companies, working with the financial support of the Department of Defense, formed Sematech, Inc. This research consortium based in Austin, Texas, pools the financial resources of U.S. electronics firms to provide funding for capital budgeting projects across various computer equipment manufacturers. It also directs joint research efforts to accelerate U.S. chip-making technology.

In 1990, Sematech provided $100 million in new funding for individual electronics firms. One recipient of funds, CGA Corporation, introduced a new manufacturing process that prints circuit patterns as thin as 0.5 microns—far thinner than a human hair. This equipment was quickly delivered to Sematech, which has established a production line to turn out new computer chips with 0.5 micron circuit paths. The new chips are constructed entirely in the U.S. using American-built equipment.

Whereas Japanese chipmakers resorted to questionable business tactics in the 1980s to gain a competitive edge on American firms, collaborative capital budgeting practices are providing an innovative way for domestic firms to fight back in the 1990s.

Source: Otis Port, "Sematech may give America's middleweights a fighting chance," *Business Week*, December 10, 1990, p. 186.

The Availability of Funds

The availability of funds for capital expenditures affects the firm's decision environment.

Unlimited Funds
If a firm has **unlimited funds** for investment, making capital budgeting decisions is quite simple. All independent projects that will provide re-

unlimited funds The financial situation in which a firm is able to accept all independent projects that provide an acceptable return.

turns greater than some predetermined level can be accepted. Most firms are not in such a situation. Typically only a certain number of dollars are budgeted for making capital expenditures.

Capital Rationing

capital rationing The financial situation in which a firm has only a fixed number of dollars to allocate among competing capital expenditures.

Most firms operate under **capital rationing.** This means that they have only a fixed number of dollars available for capital expenditures and that numerous projects will compete for these limited dollars. The firm must therefore ration its funds by allocating them to projects that will maximize share value. Procedures for dealing with capital rationing are presented in Chapter 15. The discussions that follow in this chapter assume unlimited funds.

Approaches to Decision Making

Two basic approaches to capital budgeting decisions are available. These approaches are somewhat dependent on whether or not the firm is confronted with capital rationing. They are also affected by the type of project involved. The two are the *accept-reject approach* and the *ranking approach*.

The Accept-Reject Approach

accept-reject approach The evaluation of capital expenditure proposals to determine whether they are acceptable.

The **accept-reject approach** involves evaluating capital expenditure proposals to determine whether they are acceptable. This is a simple approach; it requires merely comparing the projected return of the potential expenditure to the firm's minimum acceptable return. This approach can be used when the firm has unlimited funds, as a preliminary step when evaluating mutually exclusive projects, or in a situation in which capital must be rationed. In these cases only acceptable projects should be considered.

The Ranking Approach

ranking approach The ranking of capital expenditure proposals on the basis of a predetermined measure, such as the rate of return.

The second method, the **ranking approach,** involves ranking proposals on the basis of some predetermined measure, such as the rate of return. The project with the highest return is ranked first, and the project with the lowest return is ranked last. Only acceptable projects should be ranked. Ranking is useful in selecting the "best" of a group of mutually exclusive projects and in evaluating projects with a view to capital rationing.

When the firm is confronted with a number of projects, some of which are mutually exclusive and some of which are independent, it must first determine the best of each group of mutually exclusive alternatives. This reduces the mixed group of projects to a group of independent projects. The best of the acceptable independent projects can then be selected. All acceptable projects can be implemented if the firm has unlimited funds. If capital rationing is necessary, the mix of projects that maximizes the firm's overall value should be accepted. The following example illustrates the evaluation process.

EXAMPLE   California Slimfast, a diet products concern with unlimited funds, wishes to evaluate eight projects—A through H. Projects A, B, and C are mutually exclusive; projects G and H are also mutually exclusive; and projects D, E, and F are independent of the other projects. The projects are listed along with their returns:

Project	Status	Return (%)
A		16
B	Mutually exclusive	19
C		11
D	Independent	15
E	Independent	13
F	Independent	21
G	Mutually exclusive	20
H		17

To evaluate these projects, the firm must first determine the best of the mutually exclusive groups. On the basis of the given return figures, project B would be selected from mutually exclusive projects A, B, and C since it has the highest return of this group. Project G would be preferred to project H since it has the higher return. After the selection of the best of the two groups of mutually exclusive projects, the five remaining independent projects can be ranked on the basis of their respective returns:

Rank	Project	Return (%)
1	F	21
2	G	20
3	B	19
4	D	15
5	E	13

Given that the firm has unlimited funds, and assuming that all projects are acceptable, ranking in this case would not be necessary. California Slimfast could undertake all five projects (F, G, B, D, E). If the firm were operating in an environment of capital rationing, however, ranking would be useful in determining which projects to accept.

Types of Cash Flow Patterns

Cash flow patterns associated with capital investment projects can be classified as *conventional* or *nonconventional*. Another classification is as an *annuity* or a *mixed stream*.

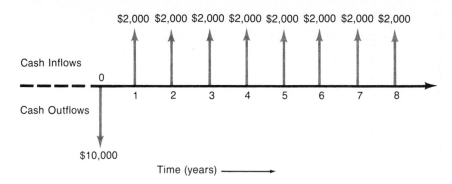

Figure 14.1   **A Conventional Cash Flow Pattern**
This conventional cash flow pattern consists of an initial outflow
($10,000) followed by a series of inflows ($2,000 each year for eight years).

Conventional Cash Flows

**conventional cash
flow pattern** An ini-
tial outflow followed by
a series of inflows.

A **conventional cash flow pattern** consists of an initial outflow followed
by a series of inflows. This pattern is associated with many types of
capital expenditures. For example, a firm may spend $10,000 today and
as a result expect to receive cash inflows of $2,000 each year for the next
eight years. This conventional pattern is diagrammed in Figure 14.1.

Nonconventional Cash Flows

**nonconventional
cash flow patterns**
A pattern in which an
initial outflow is *not* followed by a series of in-
flows.

A **nonconventional cash flow pattern** is any pattern in which an initial
outflow is *not* followed by a series of inflows. For example, the purchase
of a machine may require an initial cash outflow of $20,000 and gener-
ate cash inflows of $5,000 each year for four years. In the fifth year after
purchase, an outflow of $8,000 may be required to overhaul the ma-
chine, after which it generates inflows of $5,000 each year for five years.
This nonconventional pattern is illustrated in Figure 14.2.

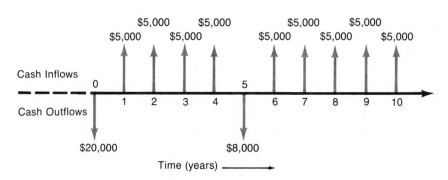

Figure 14.2   **A Nonconventional Cash Flow Pattern**
This nonconventional cash flow pattern consists of an initial outflow
($20,000) followed by a series of inflows ($5,000 each year for four years)
followed by another outflow ($8,000 in year 5) followed by a final series
of inflows ($5,000 each year for five years).

Difficulties often arise in evaluating projects with nonconventional patterns of cash flows. The discussions in the remainder of this chapter and in the following chapter are therefore limited to the evaluation of conventional patterns.

Annuity or Mixed Stream

As pointed out in Chapter 11, an **annuity** is a stream of equal annual cash flows. A series of cash flows exhibiting any pattern other than that of an annuity is a **mixed stream** of cash flows. The cash inflows of $2,000 per year (for eight years) in Figure 14.1 are inflows from an annuity. The unequal pattern of inflows in Figure 14.3 (page 474) represents a mixed stream. As pointed out in Chapter 11, the techniques required to evaluate cash flows are much simpler to use when the pattern of flows is an annuity.

annuity A stream of equal annual cash flows.

mixed stream A series of cash flows exhibiting any pattern other than that of an annuity.

THE RELEVANT CASH FLOWS

To evaluate capital expenditure alternatives, the **relevant cash flows** must be determined. These are the *incremental after-tax cash outflow (investment) and resulting subsequent inflows.* The **incremental cash flows** represent the *additional* cash flows—outflows or inflows—expected to result from a proposed capital expenditure. As noted in Chapter 3, cash flows, rather than accounting figures, are used; it is these flows that directly affect the firm's ability to pay bills and purchase assets. Furthermore, accounting figures and cash flows are not necessarily the same, due to the presence of certain noncash expenditures on the firm's income statement. The remainder of this chapter is devoted to the procedures for measuring the relevant cash flows associated with proposed capital expenditures.

relevant cash flows The *incremental after-tax cash outflow and resulting subsequent inflows* associated with a proposed capital expenditure.

incremental cash flows The *additional* cash flows—outflows or inflows—expected to result from a proposed capital expenditure.

Major Cash Flow Components

The cash flows of any project having the *conventional pattern* include two basic components: (1) an initial investment and (2) operating cash inflows. All projects—whether for expansion, replacement, renewal, or some other purpose—have these components. Figure 14.3 shows the cash flows for a project. Each of the cash flow components is labeled. The **initial investment** is the relevant cash outflow at time zero. For the proposed project it is $50,000. The **operating cash inflows** are the incremental after-tax cash inflows resulting from use of the project during its life. In Figure 14.3, these gradually increase from $4,000 in the first year to $10,000 in the tenth and final year of the project.

initial investment The relevant cash outflow for a proposed project at time zero.

operating cash inflows The incremental after-tax cash inflows resulting from use of a project during its life.

Expansion versus Replacement Cash Flows

The development of relevant cash flows is most straightforward in the case of *expansion decisions.* In this case the initial investment and oper-

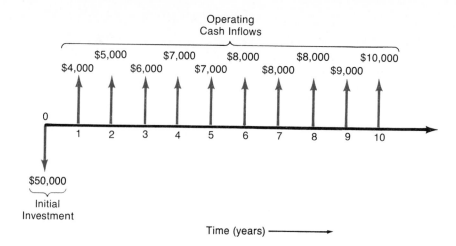

Figure 14.3   **Major Cash Flow Components**

The major cash flow components for this project consist of the initial investment of $50,000 at time zero and the operating cash inflows, which increase from $4,000 in the first year to $10,000 in the tenth and final year.

ating cash inflows are merely the after-tax cash outflow and inflows, respectively, associated with the proposed outlay. The development of relevant cash flows for *replacement decisions* is more complicated; the firm must find the *incremental* cash outflows and inflows that will result from the proposed replacement. To find the initial investment in this case, the firm would subtract from the initial investment needed to acquire the new asset any after-tax cash inflows expected from liquidation of the old asset. The operating cash inflows would be the difference between the operating cash inflows from the new asset and those from the replaced asset.

EXAMPLE   Column 1 of Table 14.2 shows the initial investment and operating cash inflows for an *expansion decision* involving the acquisition of new asset A. As a result of a $13,000 initial investment, the firm expects operating cash inflows of $5,000 in each of the next five years.

If new asset A is being considered as a *replacement* for old asset A, the relevant cash flows would be found by subtracting the expected cash flows attributed to old asset A from the expected cash flows for new asset A. The expected after-tax cash inflows from liquidating old asset A and the expected operating cash inflows from the old asset are shown in column 2 of Table 14.2. If old asset A is liquidated, $3,000 of after-tax cash inflows would result initially. In years one through five, $3,000, $2,500, $2,000, $1,500 and $1,000 of expected operating cash inflows would be eliminated. Therefore the relevant cash flows resulting from the replacement decision would be the difference in expected cash flows between new asset A and old asset A, as shown in column 3 of the table.

Table 14.2   **Expansion and Replacement Cash Flows**

| | Expansion | Replacement | |
	New asset A (1)	Old asset A (2)	Relevant cash flows [(1) − (2)] (3)
Initial investment	$13,000	$3,000[a]	$10,000
Year	Operating cash inflows		
1	$ 5,000	$3,000	$ 2,000
2	5,000	2,500	2,500
3	5,000	2,000	3,000
4	5,000	1,500	3,500
5	5,000	1,000	4,000

[a]After-tax cash inflows expected from liquidation of old asset A, which will be replaced by new Asset A.

Actually, all capital budgeting decisions can be viewed as replacement decisions. Expansion decisions are merely replacement decisions in which all cash flows from the old asset are zero. In light of this fact, the following discussions emphasize replacement decisions.

FINDING THE INITIAL INVESTMENT

The term *initial investment* as used here refers to the relevant cash outflow to be considered when evaluating a prospective capital expenditure. Since our discussion of capital budgeting is concerned only with investments exhibiting conventional cash flows, the initial investment occurs at *time zero*—the time the expenditure is made. To calculate the initial investment, we subtract all cash inflows occurring at time zero from all cash outflows occurring at time zero.

A number of basic variables must be considered when determining the initial investment associated with a capital expenditure: (1) the cost of the new asset, (2) the installation costs (if any), (3) the proceeds (if any) from the sale of an old asset, and (4) the taxes (if any) resulting from the sale of an old asset. The basic format for determining the initial investment is given in Table 14.3.

Table 14.3   **The Basic Format for Determining Initial Investment**

Cost of new asset
+ Installation costs
− Proceeds from sale of old asset
± Taxes on sale of old asset
Initial investment

The Cost of a New Asset

cost of a new asset
The net outflow required to acquire a new asset.

The **cost of a new asset** is the net outflow its acquisition requires. If there are no installation costs and the firm is not replacing an existing asset, the purchase price of the asset is equal to the initial investment. Each capital expenditure decision should be checked to make sure installation costs have not been overlooked.

Installation Costs

installation costs
Any added costs necessary to place an asset into operation.

Installation costs are any added costs necessary to place an asset into operation. They are considered part of the firm's capital expenditure. The Internal Revenue Service (IRS) requires the firm to add installation costs to the purchase price of an asset in order to determine its depreciable value. This value is depreciated over a period of years.

Proceeds from the Sale of an Old Asset

proceeds from the sale of an old asset
The net cash inflow resulting from the sale of an existing asset.

If a new asset is intended to replace an existing asset that is being sold, the **proceeds from the sale of an old asset** are the net cash inflows it provides. The proceeds from the sale of the old asset are reduced by any costs incurred in the process of removing the old asset. Proceeds received from the sale of an old asset decrease the firm's initial investment in the new asset.

Taxes

Taxes must be considered in calculating the initial investment whenever a new asset replaces an old asset that has been sold.[3] The proceeds from the sale of the replaced asset are normally subject to some type of tax. The amount of tax depends on the relationship between the sale price, initial purchase price, and book value of the asset being replaced. An understanding of (1) book value and (2) basic tax rules is necessary to determine the taxes on the sale of an asset.

book value   The strict accounting value of an asset.

Book Value
The **book value** of an asset is its strict accounting value. It can be calculated using the following equation:

Equation 14.1
Formula for book value

Book value = installed cost of asset − accumulated depreciation

EXAMPLE   Kontra Industries, a small electronics company, acquired a machine tool with an installed cost of $100,000 two years ago. The asset was being depreciated under ACRS using a five-

---

[3] A brief discussion of the tax treatment of ordinary and capital gains income was presented in Chapter 2.

year recovery period.[4] Table 3.6 (page 74), shows that under ACRS for a five-year recovery period, 20 percent and 32 percent of the installed cost would be depreciated in years 1 and 2, respectively. In other words, 52 percent (20% + 32%) of the $100,000 cost, or $52,000 (.52 × $100,000), would represent the accumulated depreciation at the end of year 2. Substituting into Equation 14.1, we get:

$$\text{Book value} = \$100,000 - \$52,000 = \$48,000$$

The book value of Kontra's asset at the end of year 2 is therefore $48,000.

Basic Tax Rules

Four potential tax situations can occur when selling an asset. These situations differ, depending upon the relationship between the asset's sale price, its initial purchase price, and its book value. The three key forms of taxable income and their associated tax treatments are defined and summarized in Table 14.4. The assumed tax rates used throughout

Table 14.4   **Tax Treatment on Sales of Assets**

Form of taxable income	Definition	Tax treatment	Assumed tax rate
Capital gain	Portion of the sale price that is in excess of the initial purchase price.	Regardless of how long the asset has been held, the total capital gain is taxed as ordinary income.	40%
Recaptured depreciation	Portion of the sale price that is in excess of book value and represents a recovery of previously taken depreciation.	All recaptured depreciation is taxed as ordinary income.	40%
Loss on sale of asset	Amount by which sale price is *less than* book value.	If asset is depreciable and used in business, loss is deducted from ordinary income.	40% of loss is a tax savings
		If asset is *not* depreciable or is *not* used in business, loss is deductible only against capital gains.	40% of loss is a tax savings

[4]For a review of ACRS, see Chapter 3. Under the *Tax Reform Act of 1986* most manufacturing machinery and equipment has a seven-year recovery period as noted in Table 3.5. Using this recovery period results in eight years of depreciation, which unnecessarily complicates examples and problems. To simplify, *machinery and equipment are treated as five-year assets in this and the following chapters.*

this text are noted in the final column of the same table. The four possible tax situations resulting in one or more forms of taxable income are:

1 ■■■ The asset is sold for more than its initial purchase price.

2 ■■■ The asset is sold for more than its book value but less than its initial purchase price.

3 ■■■ The asset is sold for its book value.

4 ■■■ The asset is sold for less than its book value.

An example will illustrate.

recaptured depreciation   The portion of the sale price that is above book value and below the initial purchase price.

EXAMPLE   The old asset purchased two years ago for $100,000 by Kontra Industries has a current book value of $48,000. What will happen if the firm now decides to sell the asset and replace it? The tax consequences associated with sale of the asset depend upon the sale price. Let us consider each of the four possible situations.

The sale of the asset for more than its initial purchase price If Kontra sells the old asset for $110,000, it realizes a capital gain of $10,000 (the amount by which the sale price exceeds the initial purchase price of $100,000) which is taxed as ordinary income.[5] The firm also experiences ordinary income in the form of **recaptured depreciation,** which is the portion of the sale price that is above book value and below the initial purchase price. In this case there is recaptured depreciation of $52,000 ($100,000 − $48,000). The taxes on the total gain of $62,000 are calculated as follows:

	Amount (1)	Rate (2)	Tax [(1) × (2)] (3)
Capital gain	$10,000	.40	$ 4,000
Recaptured depreciation	52,000	.40	20,800
Totals	$62,000		$24,800

These taxes should be used in calculating the initial investment in the new asset, using the format in Table 14.3. In effect, the taxes raise the amount of the firm's initial investment in the new asset by reducing the proceeds from the sale of the old asset.

---

[5]The *Tax Reform Act of 1986* requires corporate capital gains to be treated as ordinary income. However, the structure for corporate capital gains is retained under the law for use in the likely event of future tax revisions. Therefore, this distinction is made throughout the text discussions.

The sale of the asset for more than its book value but less than its initial purchase price If Kontra sells the old asset for $70,000, which is less than its original purchase price but more than its book value, there is no capital gain. However, the firm still experiences a gain in the form of recaptured depreciation of $22,000 ($70,000 − $48,000), which is taxed as ordinary income. Since the firm is assumed to be in the 40 percent tax bracket, the taxes on the $22,000 gain are $8,800. This amount in taxes should be used in calculating the initial investment in the new asset.

The sale of the asset for its book value If the asset is sold for $48,000, its book value, the firm breaks even. Since *no tax results from selling an asset for its book value,* there is no effect on the initial investment in the new asset.

The sale of the asset for less than its book value If Kontra sells the asset for $30,000, an amount less than its book value, it experiences a loss of $18,000 ($48,000 − $30,000). If this is a depreciable asset used in the business, the loss may be used to offset ordinary operating income. If the asset is *not* depreciable or *not* used in the business, the loss can be used only to offset capital gains. In either case the loss will save the firm $7,200 ($18,000 × .40) in taxes. And, if current operating earnings or capital gains are not sufficient to offset the loss, the firm may be able to apply these losses to prior or future years' taxes.[6]

Calculating the Initial Investment

It should be clear that a variety of tax and other considerations enter into the initial investment calculation. The following example illustrates how the basic variables described in the preceding discussion are used to calculate the initial investment according to the format in Table 14.3.

EXAMPLE Norman Company, a large diversified manufacturer of aircraft components, is trying to determine the initial investment required to replace an old machine with a new, much more sophisticated model. The proposed machine's purchase price is $380,000, and an additional $20,000 will be required to install it. It will be depreciated under ACRS using a five-year recovery period. The old machine was purchased three years ago at a cost of $240,000. It was being depreciated under ACRS using a five-year recovery period. The firm has found a buyer willing to pay $280,000 for the

---

[6]The tax law provides detailed procedures for tax loss *carrybacks* and *carryforwards*. Application of such procedures to capital budgeting is beyond the scope of this text, and they are therefore ignored in subsequent discussions.

old machine and remove it at the buyer's expense. Both ordinary income and capital gains are taxed at a rate of 40 percent.

The only component of the initial investment calculation that is difficult to obtain is taxes. Since the firm is planning to sell the old machine for $40,000 more than its purchase price, it will realize a *capital gain of $40,000*. The book value of the old machine can be found using the depreciation percentages from Table 3.6 (page 74) of 20 percent, 32 percent, and 19 percent for years 1 through 3, respectively. The resulting book value is $69,600 ($240,000 − [(.20 + .32 + .19) × $240,000]). An *ordinary gain of $170,400* ($240,000 − $69,600) in recaptured depreciation is also realized on the sale. The total taxes on the gain are $84,160 [($40,000 + $170,400) × .40]. Substituting these taxes along with the purchase price and installation cost of the new machine and the proceeds from the sale of the old machine into the format in Table 14.3 results in an initial investment of $204,160. This amount represents the net cash outflow required at time zero:

Cost of new machine	$380,000 \] Depreciable
+ Installation costs	20,000 \] outlay
− Proceeds from sale of old machine	280,000
+ Taxes on sale of old machine	84,160
Initial investment	$204,160

FINDING THE OPERATING CASH INFLOWS

The benefits expected from a capital expenditure are measured by its *operating cash inflows*, which are *incremental after-tax cash inflows*. In this section we use the income statement format to develop clear definitions of the terms *after-tax*, *cash inflows*, and *incremental*.

Interpreting the Term *After-Tax*

Benefits expected to result from proposed capital expenditures must be measured on an after-tax basis. The firm will not have the use of any benefits until it has satisfied the government's tax claims, and these claims depend on the firm's taxable income. Thus, the deduction of taxes *prior to* making comparisons between proposed investments is necessary for consistency. Consistency is required when evaluating capital expenditure alternatives, since the intention is to compare like benefits.

S M A L L   B U S I N E S S

Capital Budgeting in the Kansas Oil Patch

How can you evaluate a capital budgeting project accurately when the initial project investment and the cash inflows from the project are completely unknown? If this sounds like an impossible problem, you wouldn't want the job Larry Childress has. As the owner of Petex, Inc., a small oil exploration firm drilling in the northwest corner of Kansas, Childress faces this financial dilemma every working day.

While business in the Kansas oil patch is down from the mid-1980s oil boom, it continues to provide a modest living for a few hearty souls like Childress. Every time Childress identifies a new drilling location, he's betting his company that there is oil about a mile below his boots. Since 1983, he has established a solid track record in finding new oil: out of 75 new wells, 30 have become "producers."

As CEO of Petex, Childress brings little more to the drilling site than his Ford Bronco and an old briefcase. An independent operator, Petex owns no drilling equipment or Kansas real estate. Childress leases mineral rights from local landowners and hires a drilling contractor to punch a hole through 5,000 feet of Kansas bedrock.

At $6.00 per foot, Petex owes the drilling firm about $24,000 before things even begin to get interesting. Once the potential well reaches a depth of 4,000 feet, the drill bit nears the payoff zone where oil may be located. At this point, Childress—together with the geologists he hires on a contract basis—must decide whether to drill deeper, or abandon the hole as a "duster." Peering deep into the earth, Childress makes a quick decision to spend the $80,000 to $100,000 necessary to continue the well. At that point he doesn't know whether oil lurks just beyond the tip of the drill, or if another mile of bedrock separates the drill from a worthless puddle of salt water.

This is real life in the oil business. Although Childress is formally trained as a geophysical engineer, he's also an astute financial manager—though far from the Wall Street offices of corporate financiers. Staring deep into the Kansas ground, Childress carefully evaluates the costs and potential payoffs of digging deeper. As oil prices fell from $35 a barrel to below $20 in early 1991, only one thing was certain: if he gave the signal to continue drilling, there had better be oil beneath his boots.

Source: James R. Chiles, "There are new signs of energy out in the Kansas oil patch," *Smithsonian*, March 1991, p. 36.

Interpreting the Term *Cash Inflows*

All benefits expected from a proposed project must be measured on a cash flow basis. Cash inflows represent dollars that can be spent, not merely "accounting profits" (which are not necessarily available for paying the firm's bills). A simple technique for converting after-tax net profits into operating cash inflows was illustrated in Chapter 3. The basic calculation requires adding any *noncash charges* deducted as expenses on the firm's income statement back to net profits after taxes. Probably the most common noncash charge found on income statements is depreciation. It is the only noncash charge that will be considered in this section. The following example shows how after-tax operating cash inflows can be calculated for a present and a proposed project.

EXAMPLE   Norman Company's estimates of its revenue and expenses (excluding depreciation), with and without the proposed capital expenditure described in the preceding example, are given in Table 14.5. Note that both the expected usable life of the proposed machine and the remaining usable life of the present machine are five years. The amount to be depreciated with the proposed machine is calculated by summing the purchase price of $380,000 and the installation costs of $20,000. Since the new machine is to be depreciated under ACRS using a five-year recovery period, 20, 32, 19, 12, 12, and 5 percent would be recovered in years 1 through 6, respectively. (See Chapter 3 and Table 3.6 on page 74 for more

Table 14.5 **Norman Company's Revenue and Expenses (Excluding Depreciation) for Proposed and Present Machines**

Year	Revenue (1)	Expenses (excl. depr.) (2)
With proposed machine		
1	$2,520,000	$2,300,000
2	2,520,000	2,300,000
3	2,520,000	2,300,000
4	2,520,000	2,300,000
5	2,520,000	2,300,000
With present machine		
1	$2,200,000	$1,990,000
2	2,300,000	2,110,000
3	2,400,000	2,230,000
4	2,400,000	2,250,000
5	2,250,000	2,120,000

Table 14.6   **Depreciation Expense for Proposed and Present Machines for Norman Company**

Year	Cost (1)	Applicable ACRS depreciation percentages (from Table 3.6) (2)	Depreciation [(1) × (2)] (3)
With proposed machine			
1	$400,000	20%	$ 80,000
2	400,000	32	128,000
3	400,000	19	76,000
4	400,000	12	48,000
5	400,000	12	48,000
6	400,000	5	20,000
Totals		100%	$400,000
With present machine			
1	$240,000	12% (year-4 depreciation)	$ 28,800
2	240,000	12 (year-5 depreciation)	28,800
3	240,000	5 (year-6 depreciation)	12,000
4	Since the present machine is at the end of the third year of its cost recovery at the time the analysis is performed, it has only the final three years of depreciation (years 4, 5, and 6) yet applicable.		0
5			0
6			0
		Total	$ 69,600ᵃ

ᵃThe total $69,600 represents the book value of the present machine at the end of the third year, as calculated in the preceding example.

detail.)[7] The resulting depreciation on this machine for each of the six years, as well as the remaining three years of depreciation on the old machine, is calculated in Table 14.6.[8]

The operating cash inflows in each year can be calculated using the income statement format shown in Table 14.7. Substituting the data from Tables 14.5 and 14.6 into this format and assuming a 40 percent tax rate, we get Table 14.8. It demonstrates the calculation of operating cash inflows for each year for both the proposed and the present machines. Since the proposed machine will be depreciated over six years, the analysis must be performed over the six-year period in order to fully capture the tax effect of depreci-

[7]As noted in Chapter 3, it takes $n + 1$ years to depreciate an n-year class asset under the provisions of the *Tax Reform Act of 1986*. Therefore, ACRS percentages are given for each of six years for use in depreciating an asset with a five-year recovery period.

[8]It is important to recognize that although both machines will provide five years of use, the proposed new machine will be depreciated over the six-year period, whereas the present machine—as noted in the preceding example—has been depreciated over three years and therefore has only its final three years (years 4, 5, and 6) of depreciation (i.e., 12, 12, and 5 percent, respectively, under ACRS) remaining.

Table 14.7   **Calculation of Operating Cash Inflows Using an Income Statement Format**

Revenue
− Expenses (excluding depreciation)
Profits before depreciation and taxes
− Depreciation
Net profits before taxes
− Taxes
Net profits after taxes
+ Depreciation
Operating cash inflows

ation in year 6 for the new asset. The resulting operating cash inflows are shown in column 8 of the table. The year-6 cash inflow for the proposed machine of $8,000 results solely from the tax benefit of the year-6 depreciation deduction.

Interpreting the Term *Incremental*

The final step in estimating the operating cash inflows to be used in evaluating a proposed project is to calculate the *incremental (relevant)* cash inflows. Incremental operating cash inflows are needed, since our concern is *only* with how much more or less operating cash will flow into the firm as a result of the proposed project.

EXAMPLE   Table 14.9 demonstrates the calculation of Norman Company's incremental (relevant) operating cash inflows for each year. The estimates of operating cash inflows developed in Table 14.8 are given in columns 1 and 2. The column 2 values represent the amount of operating cash inflows that Norman Company will receive if it does not replace the present machine. If the proposed machine replaces the present machine, the firm's operating cash inflows for each year will be those shown in column 1. Subtracting the operating cash inflows with the present machine from the operating cash inflows with the proposed machine in each year results in the incremental operating cash inflows for each year, shown in column 3 of Table 14.9. These cash flows represent the amounts by which each respective year's cash inflows will increase as a result of replacing the present machine with the proposed machine. For example, in year 1, Norman Company's cash inflows would increase by $26,480 if the proposed project were undertaken. Clearly, these are the relevant inflows to be considered when evaluating the benefits of making a capital expenditure for the proposed machine.

Table 14.8   Calculation of Operating Cash Inflows for Norman Company's Proposed and Present Machines

Year	Revenue[a] (1)	Expenses (excl. depr.)[b] (2)	Profits before depreciation and taxes [(1) − (2)] (3)	Depreciation[c] (4)	Net profits before taxes [(3) − (4)] (5)	Taxes [.40 × (5)] (6)	Net profits after taxes [(5) − (6)] (7)	Operating cash inflows [(4) + (7)] (8)
With proposed machine								
1	$2,520,000	$2,300,000	$220,000	$ 80,000	$140,000	$56,000	$ 84,000	$164,000
2	2,520,000	2,300,000	220,000	128,000	92,000	36,800	55,200	183,200
3	2,520,000	2,300,000	220,000	76,000	144,000	57,600	86,400	162,400
4	2,520,000	2,300,000	220,000	48,000	172,000	68,800	103,200	151,200
5	2,520,000	2,300,000	220,000	48,000	172,000	68,800	103,200	151,200
6	0	0	0	20,000	−20,000	−8,000	−12,000	8,000
With present machine								
1	$2,200,000	$1,990,000	$210,000	$ 28,800	$181,200	$72,480	$108,720	$137,520
2	2,300,000	2,110,000	190,000	28,800	161,200	64,480	96,720	125,520
3	2,400,000	2,230,000	170,000	12,000	158,000	63,200	94,800	106,800
4	2,400,000	2,250,000	150,000	0	150,000	60,000	90,000	90,000
5	2,250,000	2,120,000	130,000	0	130,000	52,000	78,000	78,000
6	0	0	0	0	0	0	0	0

[a]From column 1 of Table 14.5.
[b]From column 2 of Table 14.5.
[c]From column 3 of Table 14.6.

Table 14.9   Incremental (Relevant) Operating Cash Inflows
for Norman Company

Year	Operating cash inflows		
	Proposed machine[a] (1)	Present machine[a] (2)	Incremental (relevant) [(1) − (2)] (3)
1	$164,000	$137,520	$26,480
2	183,200	125,520	57,680
3	162,400	106,800	55,600
4	151,200	90,000	61,200
5	151,200	78,000	73,200
6	8,000	0	8,000

[a]From column 8 of Table 14.8.

SUMMARIZING THE RELEVANT CASH FLOWS

The two cash flow components—the initial investment and the operating cash inflows—together represent a project's *relevant cash flows*. These cash flows can be viewed as the incremental after-tax cash flows attributable to the proposed project. They represent, in a cash flow sense, how much better or worse off the firm will be if it chooses to implement the proposal.

EXAMPLE   The relevant cash flows for Norman Company's proposed replacement expenditure can now be presented. They are shown graphically in Figure 14.4. As the figure shows, the relevant cash flows follow a conventional pattern (an initial outflow followed by a series of inflows). Techniques for analyzing this pattern to determine whether to undertake a proposed capital investment are discussed in Chapter 15.

INTERNATIONAL DIMENSION: LONG-TERM INVESTMENTS

foreign direct investment (FDI) An MNC's transfer of capital, managerial, and technical assets from its home country to a host country.

Multinational firms make long-term investments by transferring money and other assets from their home country to a host country. **Foreign direct investment (FDI)** is the transfer, by a multinational firm, of capital, managerial, and technical assets from its home country to a host country. The equity participation on the part of an MNC can vary. A 100 percent participation results in a wholly-owned foreign subsidiary. Less than 100 percent participation leads to a joint-venture project with foreign participants. Unlike short-term, foreign portfolio investments undertaken by individuals and companies (e.g., internationally diversified mutual funds), FDI involves equity participation, managerial control,

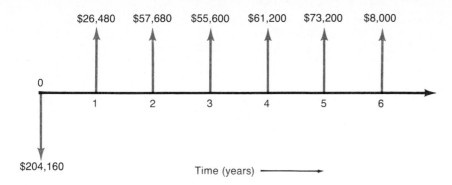

Figure 14.4   Norman Company's Relevant Cash Flows with the Proposed Machine
The relevant cash flows for Norman Company's proposed machine investment display a conventional pattern. An initial investment of $204,160 is followed by operating cash inflows of $26,480, $57,680, $55,600, $61,200, $73,200, and $8,000 in years 1 through 6, respectively.

and day-to-day operational activities on the part of MNCs. Therefore, FDI projects will be subject not only to business, financial, inflation, and foreign exchange risks (as would foreign portfolio investments) but also to the additional element of political risk.

For a number of decades, U.S.–based MNCs had dominated the international scene in terms of both the *flow* and *stock* of FDI. The total FDI stock of U.S.–based MNCs, for instance, increased from $7.7 billion in 1929 to over $232.5 billion at the end of 1985. Since the 1970s, though, their global presence has been challenged by MNCs based in Japan, Western Europe, and other developed and developing nations. In fact, even the "home" market of U.S. multinationals is being challenged by foreign firms. For instance, in 1960, FDI into the United States amounted to only 11.5 percent of American investment overseas. By the end of 1990, the book value of FDI into the United States, at US$404 billion, equaled nearly 96 percent of the comparable figure, of US$421 billion, for U.S. FDI abroad.

SUMMARY

1   **Understand the key capital expenditure motives and the steps in the capital budgeting process, beginning with proposal generation and ending with follow-up.**   Capital budgeting is the process used to evaluate and select capital expenditures consistent with the goal of owner wealth maximization. The key motives for capital expenditures are to expand, replace, or renew fixed assets or to obtain some less tangible benefit. The capital budgeting process contains five distinct but interrelated steps: proposal generation, review and analysis, decision making, implementation, and follow-up.

2   **Define the basic terminology used to describe projects, funds availability, decision approaches, and cash flow patterns.**   Capital expenditure projects may be independent or mutually exclusive. Typically, firms have only limited funds for capital investments and must ration them among carefully selected projects. To make investment decisions when proposals are mutually exclusive or when capital must be rationed, projects must be ranked. Otherwise, accept-reject decisions must be made. Conventional cash flow patterns consist of an initial outflow followed by a series of inflows; any other pattern is nonconventional. These patterns can be either annuities or mixed streams.

3   **Discuss the major components of relevant cash flows and differences in the development of expansion- versus replacement-decision cash flows.** The relevant cash flows necessary for making capital budgeting decisions are the initial investment and the operating cash inflows associated with a given proposal. For replacement decisions, these flows are found by determining the difference between the cash flows associated with the new asset and the old asset. Expansion decisions are viewed as replacement decisions in which all cash flows from the old asset are zero.

4   **Calculate the initial investment associated with a proposed capital expenditure given relevant cost, depreciation, and tax data.** The initial investment is the initial outflow required, taking into account the cost (including installation) of the new asset, proceeds from the sale of the old asset, and taxes on the sale of the old asset. The book value of an asset is its strict accounting value, which is used to determine what, if any, taxes are owed as a result of selling an asset. Any of three forms of taxable income—capital gain, recaptured depreciation, or a loss—can result from sale of an asset. The form of taxable income that applies depends upon whether it is sold (1) for more than its initial purchase price, (2) for more than book value but less than initially paid, (3) for book value, or (4) for less than book value.

5   **Determine the operating cash inflows relevant to a capital budgeting proposal using the income statement format.** The operating cash inflows are the incremental after-tax operating cash inflows expected to result from implementing a proposal. The income statement format, which involves adding depreciation back to net profits after taxes, gives the operating cash inflows associated with the present and proposed projects. The relevant (incremental) cash inflows, which are used to evaluate the proposed project, are found by subtracting the operating cash inflows associated with the present project from those of the proposed project.

 6   **Discuss foreign direct investment, its risks, and the role of U.S.–based multinational companies in it.** Foreign direct investment (FDI) involves an MNC's transfer of capital, managerial, and technical assets from its home country to a host country. FDI projects are subject to business, financial, inflation, foreign exchange, and political risks. The FDI of U.S.–based multinational companies has grown dramatically, although in recent years its global presence has been challenged by companies in Japan, Western Europe, and others. In addition, during recent years FDI into the U.S. has surpassed U.S. FDI abroad.

QUESTIONS

14—1   What is *capital budgeting?* How do capital expenditures relate to the capital budgeting process? Do all capital expenditures involve fixed assets? Explain.

14—2   What are the basic motives described in the chapter for making capital expenditures? Discuss, compare, and contrast them.

14—3   Briefly describe each of the steps involved in the capital budgeting process.

14—4   Define and differentiate between each of the following sets of capital budgeting terms.
   a. Independent versus mutually exclusive projects
   b. Unlimited funds versus capital rationing

    c. Accept-reject versus ranking approaches
    d. Conventional versus nonconventional cash flow patterns
    e Annuity versus mixed stream cash flows

14—5   Why is it important to evaluate capital budgeting projects on the basis of *incremental after-tax cash flows?* How can expansion decisions be treated as replacement decisions? Explain.

14—6   Describe each of the following components of the initial investment and explain how the initial investment is calculated using them.
    a. Cost of new asset
    b. Installation costs
    c. Proceeds from sale of old asset
    d. Taxes on sale of old asset

14—7   What is the *book value* of an asset, and how is it calculated? Describe the three key forms of taxable income and their associated tax treatments.

14—8   What four tax situations may result from the sale of an asset that is being replaced? Describe the tax treatment in each situation.

14—9   Referring to the framework for calculating initial investment given in this chapter, explain how a firm would determine the *depreciable value* of the new asset.

14—10   How is the *Accelerated Cost Recovery System (ACRS)* used to depreciate an asset? How does depreciation enter into the operating cash inflow calculation?

14—11   Given the revenues, expenses (excluding depreciation), and depreciation associated with a present asset and a proposed replacement for it, how would the incremental (relevant) operating cash inflows associated with the decision be calculated?

14—12   Diagram and describe the two elements representing the *relevant cash flows* for a conventional capital budgeting project.

14—13   What is *foreign direct investment (FDI)?* Describe the past and current global role of U.S.–based MNCs in FDI.

PROBLEMS

14—1   **(Classification of Expenditures)** Given the following list of outlays, indicate whether each would normally be considered a capital or a current expenditure. Explain your answers.
    a. An initial lease payment of $5,000 for electronic point-of-sale cash register systems.
    b. An outlay of $20,000 to purchase patent rights from an inventor.
    c. An outlay of $80,000 for a major research and development program.
    d. An $80,000 investment in a portfolio of marketable securities.
    e. A $300 outlay for an office machine.
    f. An outlay of $2,000 for a new machine tool.
    g. An outlay of $240,000 for a new building.
    h. An outlay of $1,000 for a marketing research report.

14—2   **(Basic Terminology)** A firm is considering the following three separate situations.

    Situation A: Build either a small office building or a convenience store on a parcel of land located in a high-traffic area. Adequate funding is available, and both projects are known to be acceptable. The office building will require an initial investment of $620,000 and is expected to provide operating cash inflows of $40,000 per year for 20 years. The convenience store is expected to cost $500,000 and provide a growing stream of operating cash inflows over its 20-year life. The initial operating cash inflow is $20,000 and will increase by 5 percent each year.

Situation B: Replace a machine with a new one requiring a $60,000 initial investment and providing operating cash inflows of $10,000 per year for the first five years. At the end of year 5, a machine overhaul costing $20,000 is required. After it is completed, expected operating cash inflows are $10,000 in year 6; $7,000 in year 7; $4,000 in year 8; and $1,000 in year 9, at the end of which the machine will be scrapped.

Situation C: Invest in any or all of the four machines whose relevant cash flows are given in the following table. The firm has $500,000 budgeted to fund these machines, all of which are known to be acceptable. Initial investment for each machine is $250,000.

	Operating cash inflows			
Year	Machine 1	Machine 2	Machine 3	Machine 4
1	$ 50,000	$70,000	$65,000	$90,000
2	70,000	70,000	65,000	80,000
3	90,000	70,000	80,000	70,000
4	−30,000	70,000	80,000	60,000
5	100,000	70,000	−20,000	50,000

For each situation or project, indicate:
a. Whether the *situation* is independent or mutually exclusive.
b. Whether the availability of funds is unlimited or if capital rationing exists.
c. Whether accept-reject or ranking decisions are required.
d. Whether each *project's* cash flows are conventional or nonconventional.
e. Whether each *project's* cash flow pattern is an annuity or mixed stream.

14—3   **(Expansion versus Replacement Cash Flows)**   Nick Stamas, Inc., has estimated the cash flows over the five-year lives for two projects, A and B. These cash flows are summarized below.

	Project	
	Project A	Project B
Initial investment	$40,000	$12,000[a]
Year	Operating cash inflows	
1	$10,000	$6,000
2	12,000	6,000
3	14,000	6,000
4	16,000	6,000
5	10,000	6,000

[a]After-tax cash inflows expected from liquidation.

a. If project A were actually a *replacement* for project B and the $12,000 initial investment shown for B was the after-tax cash inflows expected from liquidating it, what would be the relevant cash flows for this replacement decision?

b. How can an *expansion decision* such as project A be viewed as a special form of a replacement decision? Explain.

14—4   **(Relevant Cash Flow Pattern Fundamentals)** For each of the following projects, determine the *relevant cash flows,* classify the cash flow pattern, and diagram the pattern.

a. A project requiring an initial investment of $120,000 that generates annual operating cash inflows of $25,000 for the next 18 years. In each of the 18 years, maintenance of the project will require a $5,000 cash outflow.

b. A new machine having an installed cost of $85,000. Sale of the old machine will yield $30,000 after taxes. Operating cash inflows generated by the replacement will exceed the operating cash inflows of this old machine by $20,000 in each year of a six-year period.

c. An asset requiring an initial investment of $2 million that will yield annual operating cash inflows of $300,000 for each of the next ten years. Operating cash outlays will be $20,000 for each year except year 6, when an overhaul requiring an additional cash outlay of $500,000 will be required.

14—5   **(Book Value)** Find the book value for each of the assets below, assuming that ACRS depreciation is being used. (*Note:* See Table 3.6 on page 74 for the applicable depreciation percentages.)

Asset	Installed cost	Recovery period	Elapsed time since purchase
A	$ 950,000	5 years	3 years
B	40,000	3 years	1 year
C	96,000	5 years	4 years
D	350,000	5 years	1 year
E	1,500,000	7 years	5 years

14—6   **(Book Value and Taxes on Sale of Assets)** Waters Manufacturing purchased a new machine three years ago for $80,000. It is being depreciated under ACRS with a five-year recovery period using the percentages given in Table 3.6 on page 74. Assume 40 percent ordinary and capital gains tax rates.

a. What is the book value of the machine?

b. Calculate the firm's tax liability if it sells the machine for the following amounts: $100,000; $56,000; $23,200; $15,000.

14—7   **(Tax Calculations)** For each of the following cases, describe the various taxable components of the funds received through sale of the asset and determine the total taxes resulting from the transaction. Assume 40 percent ordinary and capital gains tax rates. The asset was purchased for $200,000 two years ago and is being depreciated under ACRS using a five-year recovery period. (See Table 3.6 on page 74 for the applicable depreciation percentages.)

a. The asset is sold for $220,000.

b. The asset is sold for $150,000.

c. The asset is sold for $96,000.

d. The asset is sold for $80,000.

14—8   **(Initial Investment—Basic Calculation)** M. Higgins, Inc., is considering the purchase of a new grading machine to replace an existing one. The existing machine was purchased three years ago at an installed cost of $20,000. It was being depreciated under ACRS using a five-year recovery period. (See Table 3.6 on page 74 for the applicable depreciation percentages.) The existing machine is expected to have a usable life of at least five more years. The new machine would cost $35,000 and require $5,000 in installation costs. It would be depreciated using a five-year recovery period under ACRS. The existing machine can currently be sold for $25,000 without incurring any removal costs. The firm pays 40 percent taxes on both ordinary income and capital gains. Calculate the *initial investment* associated with the proposed purchase of a new grading machine.

14—9   **(Initial Investment at Various Sale Prices)**   Bolton Castings Corporation is considering replacing one machine with another. The old machine was purchased three years ago for an installed cost of $10,000. The firm is depreciating the machine under ACRS using a five-year recovery period. (See Table 3.6 on page 74 for the applicable depreciation percentages.) The new machine costs $24,000 and requires $2,000 in installation costs. Assume the firm is subject to a 40 percent tax rate on both ordinary income and capital gains. In each of the following cases, calculate the initial investment for the replacement.

a. Bolton Castings Corporation (BCC) sells the old machine for $11,000.

b. BCC sells the old machine for $7,000.

c. BCC sells the old machine for $2,900.

d. BCC sells the old machine for $1,500.

14—10   **(Depreciation)**   A firm is evaluating the acquisition of an asset that costs $64,000 and requires $4,000 in installation costs. If the firm depreciates the asset under ACRS using a five-year recovery period (see Table 3.6 on page 74 for the applicable depreciation percentages), determine the depreciation charge for each year.

14—11   **(Incremental Operating Cash Inflows)**   A firm is considering renewing its equipment to meet increased demand for its product. The cost of equipment modifications will be $1.9 million plus $100,000 in installation costs. The firm will depreciate the equipment modifications under ACRS using a five-year recovery period. (See Table 3.6 on page 74 for the applicable depreciation percentages.) Additional sales revenue from the renewal should amount to $1.2 million per year, and additional operating expenses and other costs (excluding depreciation) will amount to 40 percent of the additional sales. The firm has an ordinary tax rate of 40 percent. (*Note:* Answer the following questions for each of the next *six* years.)

a. What incremental earnings before depreciation and taxes will result from the renewal?

b. What incremental earnings after taxes will result from the renewal?

c. What incremental operating cash inflows will result from the renewal?

14—12   **(Incremental Operating Cash Inflows—Expense Reduction)**   Tex-Tube Corporation is considering replacing a machine. The replacement will reduce operating expenses (i.e., increase revenues) by $16,000 per year for each of the five years the new machine is expected to last. Although the old machine has zero book value, it can be used for five more years. The depreciable value of the new machine is $48,000. The firm will depreciate the machine under ACRS using a five-year recovery period (see Table 3.6 on page 74 for the applicable depreciation percentages) and is subject to a 40 percent tax rate on ordinary income. Estimate the incremental operating cash inflows generated by the replacement. (*Note:* Be sure to consider the depreciation in year 6.)

14—13 **(Incremental Operating Cash Inflows)** Fenton Tool Company has been considering purchasing a new lathe to replace a fully depreciated lathe that will last five more years. The new lathe is expected to have a five-year life and depreciation charges of $2,000 in year 1; $3,200 in year 2; $1,900 in year 3; $1,200 in both year 4 and year 5; and $500 in year 6. The firm estimates the revenues and expenses (excluding depreciation) for the new and the old lathes as shown in the following table. The firm has a 40 percent tax rate on ordinary income.

	New lathe		Old lathe	
Year	Revenue	Expenses (excl. depr.)	Revenue	Expenses (excl. depr.)
1	$40,000	$30,000	$35,000	$25,000
2	41,000	30,000	35,000	25,000
3	42,000	30,000	35,000	25,000
4	43,000	30,000	35,000	25,000
5	44,000	30,000	35,000	25,000

a. Calculate the operating cash inflows associated with each lathe. (*Note:* Be sure to consider the depreciation in year 6.)
b. Calculate the incremental (relevant) operating cash inflows resulting from the proposed lathe replacement.
c. Diagram the incremental operating cash inflows calculated in question **b.**

14—14 **(Relevant Cash Flows for a Marketing Campaign)** Maltin Tube, a high-quality aluminum tube manufacturer, has maintained stable sales and profits over the past 10 years. While the market for aluminum tubing has been expanding by 3 percent per year, Maltin has been unsuccessful in sharing this growth. In order to increase its sales, the firm is considering an aggressive marketing campaign which centers on regularly running ads in all relevant trade journals and exhibiting products at all major regional and national trade shows. The campaign is expected to require an *annual* tax-deductible expenditure of $150,000 over the next five years. Sales revenue, as noted in the income statement for 1992 shown below, totaled $20,000,000. If the proposed marketing campaign is not initiated, sales are expected to remain at this level in each of the next five years, 1993–1997. With the marketing campaign, sales for each of the next five years are expected to rise to the levels shown in the following table; cost of goods sold is expected to remain at 80 percent of sales; general and administrative expense (exclusive of any marketing campaign outlays) is expected to remain at 10 percent of sales; and annual depreciation expense is expected to remain at $500,000. Assuming a 40 percent tax rate, find the relevant cash flows over the next five years associated with the proposed marketing campaign.

Income statement
Maltin Tube
for the year ended December 31, 1992

Sales revenue		$20,000,000
Less: Cost of good sold (80%)		16,000,000
Gross profits		$ 4,000,000
Less: Operating expenses		
General and administrative expense (10%)	$2,000,000	
Depreciation expense	500,000	
Total operating expense		2,500,000
Net profits before taxes		$ 1,500,000
Less: Taxes (rate = 40%)		600,000
Net profits after taxes		$ 900,000

Sales forecast
Maltin Tube

Year	Sales revenue
1993	$20,500,000
1994	21,000,000
1995	21,500,000
1996	22,500,000
1997	23,500,000

    14—15   **(Relevant Cash Flows)** Blake Company is considering replacing an existing piece of machinery with a more sophisticated machine. The old machine was purchased three years ago at a cost of $50,000. This amount was being depreciated under ACRS using a five-year recovery period. The machine has five years of usable life remaining. The new machine being considered will cost $76,000 and requires $4,000 in installation costs. The new machine would be depreciated under ACRS using a five-year recovery period. The old machine can currently be sold for $55,000 without incurring any removal costs. The firm pays 40 percent taxes on both ordinary income and capital gains. The revenues and expenses (excluding depreciation) associated with the new and the old machine for the next five years are given in the table below. (Table 3.6 on page 74 contains the applicable ACRS depreciation percentages.)

	New machine		Old machine	
Year	Revenue	Expenses (excl. depr.)	Revenue	Expenses (excl. depr.)
1	$750,000	$720,000	$674,000	$660,000
2	750,000	720,000	676,000	660,000
3	750,000	720,000	680,000	660,000
4	750,000	720,000	678,000	660,000
5	750,000	720,000	674,000	660,000

a. Calculate the initial investment associated with replacement of the old machine by the new one.

b. Determine the incremental operating cash inflows associated with the proposed replacement. (*Note:* Be sure to consider the depreciation in year 6.)

c. Diagram the relevant cash flows found in **a** and **b** associated with the proposed replacement decision.

14—16   **(Integrative—Determining Relevant Cash Flows)**   Sentry Company is contemplating the purchase of a new high-speed widget grinder to replace the existing grinder. The existing grinder was purchased two years ago at an installed cost of $60,000. It was being depreciated under ACRS using a five-year recovery period. The existing grinder is expected to have a usable life of five more years. The new grinder would cost $105,000 and require $5,000 in installation costs. It has a five-year usable life and would be depreciated under ACRS using a five-year recovery period. The existing grinder can currently be sold for $70,000 without incurring any removal costs. The firm pays 40 percent taxes on both ordinary income and capital gains. The estimated *profits before depreciation and taxes* over the five years for both the new and existing grinder are given below. (Table 3.6 on page 74 contains the applicable ACRS depreciation percentages.)

	Profits before depreciation and taxes	
Year	New grinder	Existing grinder
1	$43,000	$26,000
2	43,000	24,000
3	43,000	22,000
4	43,000	20,000
5	43,000	18,000

a. Calculate the initial investment associated with the replacement of the existing grinder by the new one.

b. Determine the incremental operating cash inflows associated with the proposed grinder replacement. (*Note:* Be sure to consider the depreciation in year 6.)

c. Diagram the relevant cash flows associated with the proposed grinder replacement decision.

14—17   **(Integrative—Determining Relevant Cash Flows)**   East Coast Drydock is considering replacing an existing hoist with one of two newer, more efficient pieces of equipment. The existing hoist is three years old, cost $32,000, and is being depreciated under ACRS using a five-year recovery period. Although the existing hoist has only three years (years 4, 5, and 6) of depreciation remaining under ACRS, it has a remaining usable life of five years. Hoist A, one of the two possible replacement hoists, costs $40,000 to purchase and $8,000 to install. It has a five-year usable life and will be depreciated under ACRS using a five-year recovery period. The other hoist, B, costs $54,000 to purchase and $6,000 to install. It also has a five-year usable life and will be depreciated under ACRS using a five-year recovery period.

The projected *profits before depreciation and taxes* with each alternative hoist and the existing hoist are given in the following table. The existing hoist can currently be sold for $18,000 and will not incur any removal costs. The firm is subject to a 40 percent tax rate on both ordinary income and capital gains. (Table 3.6 on page 74 contains the applicable ACRS depreciation percentages.)

| Year | Profits before depreciation and taxes | | |
	With hoist A	With hoist B	With existing hoist
1	$21,000	$22,000	$14,000
2	21,000	24,000	14,000
3	21,000	26,000	14,000
4	21,000	26,000	14,000
5	21,000	26,000	14,000

a. Calculate the initial investment associated with each alternative.
b. Calculate the incremental operating cash inflows associated with each alternative. (*Note:* Be sure to consider the depreciation in year 6.)
c. Diagram the relevant cash flows associated with each alternative.

 14—18   **(Integrative—Determining Relevant Cash Flows)** Doormaster Products Company expects its *net profits after taxes* for the next five years to be as shown in the following table.

Year	Net profits after taxes
1	$100,000
2	150,000
3	200,000
4	250,000
5	320,000

Consideration is currently being given to the renewal or replacement of Doormaster's *only* depreciable asset, a machine originally costing $30,000 and having a current book value of zero. It can now be sold for $20,000. (*Note:* Because the firm's only depreciable asset is fully depreciated—its book value is zero—its expected net profits after taxes equal its operating cash inflows.) The firm is subject to a 40 percent tax on both ordinary income and capital gains. The company uses ACRS depreciation. (See Table 3.6 on page 74 for the applicable depreciation percentages.) The two alternatives being considered are described below.

Alternative 1: Renew the existing machine at a total depreciable cost of $90,000. The renewed machine would have a five-year usable life and be depreciated under ACRS using a five-year recovery period. Renewing the machine would result in the following projected *profits before depreciation and taxes:*

Year	Profits before depreciation and taxes
1	$198,500
2	290,800
3	381,900
4	481,900
5	581,900

Alternative 2: Replace the existing machine with a new machine costing $100,000 and requiring installation costs of $10,000. The new machine would have a five-year usable life and be depreciated under ACRS using a five-year recovery period. The firm's projected *profits before depreciation and taxes,* if it acquires the machine, are as follows:

Year	Profits before depreciation and taxes
1	$235,500
2	335,200
3	385,100
4	435,100
5	551,100

a. Calculate the initial investment associated with each alternative.
b. Calculate the incremental operating cash inflows associated with each alternative. (*Note:* Be sure to consider the depreciation in year 6.)
c. Diagram the relevant cash flows associated with each alternative.

CASE

Finding Lakeshore Press's Investment Cash Flows

Lakeshore Press (LP) is a medium-sized commercial printer of promotional advertising brochures, booklets, and other direct-mail pieces. The firm is currently having trouble competing effectively due to its existing inefficient presses. The general manager has proposed the purchase of one of two large six-color presses designed for long, high-quality runs. The purchase of a new press would enable LP to reduce its cost of labor and therefore the price to the client, putting the firm in a more competitive position.

The first step in analzying the alternative new presses involves determining their relevant cash flows. The key financial characteristics of the old press and the two proposed presses are summarized below.

Old press: Originally purchased three years ago at an installed cost of $400,000, the old press is being depreciated under ACRS using a five-year recovery period. It has a remaining economic life of five years. It can be sold today to net $420,000 before taxes.

Press A: This highly automated press can be purchased for $830,000 and will require $40,000 in installation costs. It will be depreciated under ACRS using a five-year recovery period.

Press B: This press is not as sophisticated as press A. It costs $640,000 and requires $20,000 in installation costs. It will be depreciated under ACRS using a five-year recovery period.

The firm estimates that its *profits before depreciation and taxes* with the old press and with press A or press B for each of the five years would be as shown below.

Profits before Depreciation and Taxes for Lakeshore Press's Investment Alternatives

Year	Old press	Press A	Press B
1	$120,000	$250,000	$210,000
2	120,000	270,000	210,000
3	120,000	300,000	210,000
4	120,000	330,000	210,000
5	120,000	370,000	210,000

The firm is subject to a 40 percent tax rate on both ordinary income and capital gains. (Table 3.6 on page 74 contains the applicable ACRS depreciation percentages.)

Required

    a. Determine the initial investment for each of the two proposed presses.

    b. Find the operating cash inflows for each of the two proposed presses.

    c. Using your results from **a** and **b**, diagram the relevant cash flows associated with each alternative.

CHAPTER 15

CAPITAL BUDGETING TECHNIQUES: CERTAINTY AND RISK

CHAPTER OBJECTIVES

After studying this chapter, you should be able to:

1 Calculate, interpret, and evaluate the two most popular unsophisticated capital budgeting techniques—average rate of return and payback period.

2 Apply the sophisticated capital budgeting techniques—net present value (NPV), profitability index (PI), and internal rate of return (IRR)—to relevant cash flows to choose acceptable as well as preferred capital expenditures.

3 Discuss whether the net present value or the internal rate of return technique is better, and describe basic approaches for choosing projects under capital rationing.

4 Recognize the basic approaches—sensitivity and scenario analysis, statistical approaches, decision trees, and simulation—for dealing with project risk.

5 Understand the calculation and practical aspects of the two basic risk-adjustment techniques—certainty equivalents (CEs) and risk-adjusted discount rates (RADRs).

6 Describe the difficulties associated with measuring the amount invested in a foreign project, its resulting cash flows, and the associated risk when making long-term investment decisions in an international setting.

Targeting Consumer Vices for Profit

"... capital budgeting techniques apparently indicate that cigarette and brewery projects will generate positive effects on share value."

For years the adverse health effects of drinking alcoholic beverages and smoking have been well known. Yet, many businesses depend upon consumers who drink and smoke. The ethical issue is obvious: Are projects designed to increase profits from greater sales of alcohol and cigarettes acceptable? Some firms have found such projects more palatable if the customers are located abroad. The unification of East and West Germany, as well as the economic integration of Europe in 1992, presented many companies with opportunities to increase foreign sales of their products.

Philip Morris purchased the largest East German cigarette operation as soon as it was put on the auction block. Not to be outdone, RJR Nabisco quickly purchased East Germany's third-largest local brand. RJR also began selling its Camel, Winston, and Salem brands in East Germany.

American breweries are also finding that Europe may be a profitable region for investment. Though local breweries were the norm for centuries, the 1992 deadline for European economic integration has seen many big breweries acquiring small breweries.

Top brewers have taken different routes to the eventual goal of being a respected name on the European continent. Budweiser has licensed its beer to a British brewmaster that sells products on the continent under the Bud name. (Budejovicky Budvar, a Czech brewery, was already distributing a beer called Budweiser.) Philip Morris teamed up with a small Belgian brewery to produce and sell Miller Special Premium. Coors, taking the least risky approach, simply sells its beers in those nations with lenient shipping regulations.

Several factors, however, have diminished the projected positive impact on the value of North American brewers entering the $3.8 billion eastern Europe market. One is the low value of the United States dollar, which makes European breweries costly now. Cultural clash also makes the potential return risky. Distribution systems tie pubs and supermarkets to breweries. Ancient purity laws create hurdles. Traditional tastes also differ from the lagers produced by U.S. breweries.

However, capital budgeting techniques apparently indicate that cigarette and brewery projects will generate positive effects on share values. If investors do not rebel against the source of these profits, the prices of these so-called "sin-stocks" should rise.

The relevant cash flows developed in Chapter 14 must be analyzed to assess whether a project is acceptable or to rank projects. A number of techniques are available for performing such analyses. The preferred approaches integrate time value procedures, risk, return, and valuation concepts, and the cost of capital. They enable the financial manager to select capital expenditures that are consistent with the firm's goal of maximizing owners' wealth. The focus of this chapter is on the use of these techniques to evaluate capital expenditure proposals for decision-making purposes. Initially it is assumed that the firm has unlimited funds and that all projects' cash flows have the same level of risk. Since very few decisions are actually made under such conditions, these simplifying assumptions are relaxed in the discussions of capital rationing and risk presented later in the chapter. Here we begin with a look at both unsophisticated and sophisticated capital budgeting techniques.

UNSOPHISTICATED CAPITAL BUDGETING TECHNIQUES

Unsophisticated capital budgeting techniques do *not* explicitly consider the time value of money by discounting cash flows to find present value. There are two basic unsophisticated techniques for determining the acceptability of capital expenditure alternatives. One is to calculate the average rate of return; the other is to find the payback period.

    We shall use the same basic problem to illustrate the application of all the techniques described in this chapter. The problem concerns Blano Company, a medium-sized metal fabricator. The firm is currently contemplating two projects—project A, requiring an initial investment of $42,000, and project B, requiring an initial investment of $45,000. The projected profits after taxes and incremental (relevant) operating cash inflows for the two projects are presented in Table 15.1.[1] The average profits after taxes and average cash inflows for each project are also included. The projects exhibit conventional cash flow patterns, which are assumed throughout the text.

> **unsophisticated capital budgeting techniques** Methods that do *not* explicitly consider the time value of money.

Average Rate of Return

The average rate of return is a popular technique used to evaluate proposed capital expenditures. Its appeal stems from the fact that the aver-

---

[1]For simplification, five-year-lived projects with five years of cash inflows are used throughout this chapter. Projects with usable lives equal to the number of years of cash inflows are also included in the end-of-chapter problems. Recall from Chapter 14 that under the *Tax Reform Act of 1986* ACRS depreciation results in $n + 1$ years of depreciation for an n-year class asset. This means that in actual practice projects will commonly have at least one year of cash flow beyond their recovery period.

Table 15.1   Capital Expenditure Data for Blano Company

Year	Project A		Project B	
	Profits after taxes	Cash inflows	Profits after taxes	Cash inflows
Initial investment	$42,000		$45,000	
1	$7,700	$14,000	$21,250	$28,000
2	4,760	14,000	2,100	12,000
3	5,180	14,000	550	10,000
4	5,180	14,000	550	10,000
5	5,180	14,000	550	10,000
Averages	$5,600	$14,000	$ 5,000	$14,000

average rate of return For a given project, the annual accounting rate of return expected on the average investment.

age rate of return is typically calculated from available accounting data (profits after taxes). The most common definition of the **average rate of return** for a given project is as follows:

Equation 15.1 Formula for the average rate of return

$$\text{Average rate of return} = \frac{\text{average profits after taxes}}{\text{average investment}}$$

average profits after taxes The total after-tax profits expected over the project's life divided by the number of years of the project's life.

Average profits after taxes are found by adding up the after-tax profits expected over the project's total life and dividing the total by the number of years of life. In the case of an annuity, the average after-tax profits are equal to any year's profits. The **average investment** is found by dividing the initial investment by 2. The average rate of return can be interpreted as the annual accounting rate of return expected on the average investment.

average investment The initial investment divided by 2.

The Decision Criterion

The decision criterion when average rate of return is used to make accept-reject decisions is as follows: *If the average rate of return is greater than the minimum acceptable average rate of return, accept the project; if the average rate of return is less than the minimum acceptable average rate of return, reject the project.*

EXAMPLE The average profits expected for projects A and B (given in Table 15.1) are $5,600 and $5,000, respectively. The average investment for project A is $21,000 ($42,000 ÷ 2) and for project B is $22,500 ($45,000 ÷ 2). Dividing the average profits after taxes by the average investment results in the average rate of return for each project:

$$\text{Project A: } \frac{\$\ 5,600}{\$21,000} = 26.67\%$$

$$\text{Project B: } \frac{\$\ 5,000}{\$22,500} = 22.22\%$$

If Blano's minimum acceptable average rate of return is 24 percent, then project A would be accepted and project B rejected. If the minimum return is 28 percent, both projects would be rejected. If the projects were being ranked for profitability, project A would be preferred over project B because it has a higher average rate of return (26.67% versus 22.22%).

Pros and Cons of the Average Rate of Return

The most favorable aspect of using the average rate of return to evaluate projects is its ease of calculation. The only input required is projected profit, a figure that should be easily obtainable.

There are three major weaknesses of this approach, however. The key conceptual weakness is the inability to specify the appropriate average rate of return in light of the wealth maximization goal. The second weakness stems from the use of accounting profits rather than cash flow as a measure of return. (This weakness can be overcome by using average cash inflows in the numerator in Equation 15.1.) The third major weakness is that this method ignores the time factor in the value of money. The indifference to the time factor can be illustrated by the following example.

EXAMPLE   Each of the three projects for which data are given in Table 15.2 has an average rate of return of 40 percent. Although the average rates of return are the same for all three projects, the financial manager would *not* be indifferent to them. He or she would prefer project Z to project Y and project Y to project X because project Z has the most favorable profit flow pattern, project Y has the next most favorable flow pattern, and project X has the least attractive flow pattern. Clearly the financial manager prefers to receive profits sooner than later.

Table 15.2   **Calculation of the Average Rate of Return for Three Alternative Capital Expenditure Projects**

	Project X	Project Y	Project Z
(1) Initial investment	$20,000	$20,000	$20,000
(2) Average investment [(1) ÷ 2]	$10,000	$10,000	$10,000
Year	Profits after taxes		
1	$2,000	$4,000	$6,000
2	3,000	4,000	5,000
3	4,000	4,000	4,000
4	5,000	4,000	3,000
5	6,000	4,000	2,000
(3) Average profits after taxes	$4,000	$4,000	$4,000
(4) Average rate of return [(3) ÷ (2)]	40%	40%	40%

C A R E E R S   I N   F I N A N C E

Waiting for the Payback at Midwest Express

For decades, Kimberly-Clark frequently flew its managers between the Neenah, Wisconsin, headquarters and plants located across the nation. These executives lost valuable time waiting for connections, complained about airline food, and found it difficult to do paperwork while en route. A related problem was getting clients to Kimberly-Clark's headquarters.

In 1969, Kimberly-Clark began offering customized travel services to corporate clients. The firm's managers, however, had to wait until 1982 before Kimberly-Clark began its own corporate shuttle service. Much to the astonishment of Timothy Hoeksema, soon-to-be-president of Midwest Express, other firms and individuals called Kimberly-Clark asking for rides on their shuttles.

Deregulation, air fare wars, and industry megamergers were undesirable risks and not part of the business plan for the maker of Kleenex, Kotex, Huggies, and Depend. Hoeksema, however, convinced Kimberly-Clark that he could pay back the cost of aircraft and related expenditures in three years. Following the University of Chicago graduate's "Best Care in the Air" motto, Midwest offers a 90 percent on-time record, seats that are 30 percent wider than those on commercial flights, and fresh lobster and wine with dinners. The reputation of the airline has attracted businesses to Midwest's charter service, which carries Air Jordan and the Chicago Bulls, the Milwaukee Bucks, and the Milwaukee Brewers.

Customer satisfaction, however, is less important than stockholder wealth maximization at Kimberly-Clark. Its Midwest Express unit paid back project costs by the end of the second year. Subsequent purchases have allowed Midwest Express to expand passenger bookings four-fold and earn a profit each year. These profits greatly exceed the costs incurred in carrying Kimberly-Clark's executives to their next meeting.

Source: Brian Moskal, "Midwest Express rides on old formula," *Industry Week*, October 1, 1990, pp. 57–59.

Payback Period

Payback periods are another commonly used criterion for evaluating proposed investments. The **payback period** is the exact amount of time required for the firm to recover its initial investment as calculated from *cash inflows.* In the case of an *annuity,* the payback period can be found by dividing the initial investment by the annual cash inflow. For a *mixed stream,* the yearly cash inflows must be accumulated until the initial investment is recovered.

payback period The exact amount of time required for a firm to recover its initial investment in a project as calculated from *cash inflows.*

The Decision Criterion

The decision criterion when payback is used to make accept-reject decisions is as follows: *If the payback period is less than the maximum acceptable payback period, accept the project; if the payback period is greater than the maximum acceptable payback period, reject the project.*

EXAMPLE   The data for Blano Company's projects A and B presented in Table 15.1 can be used to demonstrate the calculation of the payback period. For project A, which is an annuity, the payback period is 3.0 years ($42,000 initial investment ÷ $14,000 annual cash inflow). Since project B generates a mixed stream of cash inflows, the calculation of the payback period is not quite as clear-cut. In year 1, the firm will recover $28,000 of its $45,000 initial investment. At the end of year 2, $40,000 ($28,000 from year 1 + $12,000 from year 2) will be recovered. At the end of year 3, $50,000 ($40,000 from years 1 and 2 + $10,000 from year 3) will be recovered. Since the amount received by the end of year 3 is greater than the initial investment of $45,000, the payback period is somewhere between two and three years. Only $5,000 ($45,000 − $40,000) must be recovered during year 3. Actually, $10,000 is recovered, but only 50 percent of this cash inflow ($5,000 ÷ $10,000) is needed to complete the payback of the initial $45,000. The payback period for project B is therefore 2.5 years (2 years + 50 percent of year 3).

If Blano's maximum acceptable payback period were 2.75 years, project A would be rejected and project B would be accepted. If the maximum payback period were 2.25 years, both projects would be rejected. If the projects were being ranked, project B would be preferred over project A since it has a shorter payback period (2.5 years versus 3.0 years).

Pros and Cons of Payback Periods

The payback period is a more accurate measure than the average rate of return because it considers cash flows rather than accounting profits. The payback period is also a superior measure (compared to the average rate of return) in that it gives *some* implicit consideration to the timing of cash flows and therefore to the time value of money. Because it can be viewed as a measure of *risk exposure,* many firms use the payback period as a decision criterion or as a supplement to sophisticated decision techniques. The longer the firm must wait to recover its invested funds, the greater the possibility of a calamity, and vice versa. Therefore, the shorter the payback period, the lower the firm's exposure to such risk.

Table 15.3 **Calculation of the Payback Period
for Two Alternative Investment Projects**

	Project X	Project Y
Initial investment	$10,000	$10,000
Year	**Cash inflows**	
1	$5,000	$3,000
2	5,000	4,000
3	1,000	3,000
4	100	4,000
5	100	3,000
Payback period	2 years	3 years

The major weakness of payback is that, like the average rate of return, this method cannot specify the appropriate payback period in light of the wealth maximization goal. The reason it cannot is that it is not based upon discounting cash flows to determine whether they add to the firm's value. Instead, the appropriate payback period is merely a subjectively determined maximum acceptable period of time over which a project's cash flows must break even (i.e., just equal the initial investment). A second weakness is that this approach fails to take *fully* into account the time factor in the value of money. By measuring how quickly the firm recovers its initial investment, it only implicitly considers the timing of cash flows. A third weakness is the failure to recognize cash flows that occur *after* the payback period. This weakness can be illustrated by an example.

EXAMPLE   Data for two investment opportunities—X and Y—are given in Table 15.3. The payback period for project X is two years; for project Y it is three years. Strict adherence to the payback approach suggests that project X is preferable to project Y. However, if we look beyond the payback period, we see that project X returns only an additional $1,200 ($1,000 in year 3, $100 in year 4, and $100 in year 5), whereas project Y returns an additional $7,000 ($4,000 in year 4 and $3,000 in year 5). Based on this information, it appears that project Y is preferable to X. The payback approach ignores the cash inflows in years 3, 4, and 5 for project X and in years 4 and 5 for project Y.

SOPHISTICATED CAPITAL BUDGETING TECHNIQUES

Sophisticated capital budgeting techniques give explicit consideration to the time value of money. These techniques include net present value, the profitability index, and the internal rate of return. They all discount the firm's cash flows using the cost of capital, which was discussed in detail in Chapter 13. The terms *discount rate* and *opportunity cost* are used interchangeably with *cost of capital* to refer to the minimum return that must be earned on a project in order to leave the firm's market value unchanged.

sophisticated capital budgeting techniques   Methods that give explicit consideration to the time value of money.

Net Present Value (NPV)

The **net present value (NPV),** as noted in Equation 15.2, is found by subtracting a project's initial investment from the present value of its cash inflows discounted at a rate equal to the firm's cost of capital:

$$NPV = \text{present value of cash inflows} - \text{initial investment}$$

Equation 15.2
Formula for net present value (NPV)

net present value (NPV)   The present value of a project's cash inflows minus its initial investment.

The Decision Criterion

The decision criterion when NPV is used to make accept-reject decisions is as follows: *If NPV is greater than $0, accept the project; if NPV is less than $0, reject the project.* If NPV is greater than zero, the firm will earn a return greater than its cost of capital. Such action should enhance the wealth of the firm's owners.

EXAMPLE   The net present value (NPV) approach can be illustrated using the Blano Company data presented in Table 15.1. If the firm has a 10 percent cost of capital, the net present values for projects A (an annuity) and B (a mixed stream) can be calculated as in Table 15.4. These calculations are based on the techniques presented in Chapter 11 using the appropriate present-value table factors.[2] The results show that the net present values of projects A and B are, respectively, $11,074 and $10,914. Both projects are acceptable, since the net present value of each is greater than zero. If the projects were being ranked, project A would be considered superior to B since it has a higher net present value ($11,074 versus $10,914) than that of B.

Profitability Index (PI)

The **profitability index (PI),** as noted in Equation 15.3, is calculated by dividing the present value of a project's cash inflows by its initial investment.

$$PI = \frac{\text{present value of cash inflows}}{\text{initial investment}}$$

profitability index (PI)   The present value of a project's cash inflows divided by its initial investment.

Equation 15.3
Formula for the profitability index (PI)

---

[2]Alternatively, a hand-held business calculator such as the Texas Instruments BA-35 could have been used to streamline these calculations as described in Chapter 11. Most of the more sophisticated (and more expensive) financial calculators are pre-programmed to find NPVs. With these calculators you merely punch in all cash flows along with the cost of capital or discount rate and depress the "NPV" key to find the net present value. Using such a calculator, the resulting values for projects A and B are $11,071 and $10,924, respectively.

Table 15.4   **The Calculation of NPVs for Blano Company's Capital Expenditure Alternatives**

Project A	
Annual cash inflow	$14,000
× Present value annuity interest factor, *PVIFA*[a]	3.791
Present value of cash inflows	$53,074
− Initial investment	42,000
Net present value (NPV)	$11,074

		Project B	
Year	Cash inflows (1)	Present-value interest factor, *PVIF*[b] (2)	Present value [(1) × (2)] (3)
1	$28,000	.909	$25,452
2	12,000	.826	9,912
3	10,000	.751	7,510
4	10,000	.683	6,830
5	10,000	.621	6,210
		Present value of cash inflows	$55,914
		− Initial investment	45,000
		Net present value (NPV)	$10,914

[a]From Table C-4, for 5 years and 10 percent.
[b]From Table C-3, for given year and 10 percent.

The Decision Criterion

The decision criterion when the PI is used to make accept-reject decisions is as follows: *If the PI is greater than 1, accept the project; if the PI is less than 1, reject the project.* When the PI is greater than 1, the net present value is greater than $0. Therefore the NPV and the PI approaches give the same accept-reject decisions. The acceptance of projects having PIs greater than 1 will enhance or maintain the wealth of the firm's owners.

EXAMPLE Profitability indexes for Blano Company can be easily determined using the present values calculated in Table 15.4. The PIs for projects A and B are, respectively, 1.26 ($53,074 ÷ $42,000) and 1.24 ($55,914 ÷ $45,000). Since both PIs are greater than 1, both projects are acceptable. Ranked on a PI basis, project A is preferable to project B. Project A returns $1.26 present value for each dollar invested, whereas B returns only $1.24. This ranking is the same as that obtained using *NPVs*. However, *it is not unusual to get conflicting rankings using these two techniques.*

Internal Rate of Return (IRR)

The **internal rate of return (IRR)** is the discount rate that equates the present value of cash inflows with the initial investment associated with a project. The IRR, in other words, is the discount rate that equates the NPV of an investment opportunity with zero (since the present value of cash inflows equals the initial investment). The calculation of the IRR is no easy chore.

internal rate of return (IRR)   The discount rate that equates the present value of cash inflows with the initial investment associated with a project, thereby making NPV = $0.

The Decision Criterion
The criterion when the IRR is used to make accept-reject decisions is as follows: *If the IRR is greater than the cost of capital, accept the project; if the IRR is less than the cost of capital, reject the project.* This criterion guarantees that the firm earns at least its required return. Such an outcome should enhance the market value of the firm and therefore the wealth of its owners.

Calculating the IRR
The IRR can be found either by using trial-and-error techniques or with the aid of a sophisticated financial calculator or a computer.[3] Calculating the IRR for an annuity is considerably easier than calculating it for a mixed stream of operating cash inflows. The steps involved in calculating the IRR in each case are given in Table 15.5. These steps are illustrated by the following example.

EXAMPLE   The two-step procedure given in Table 15.5 for finding the IRR of an *annuity* can be demonstrated using Blano Company's project A cash flows in Table 15.1.

Step 1:   Dividing the initial investment of $42,000 by the annual cash inflow of $14,000 results in a payback period of 3.000 years ($42,000 ÷ $14,000 = 3.000).

Step 2:   According to Table C-4, the *PVIFA* factors closest to 3.000 for five years are 3.058 (for 19 percent) and 2.991 (for 20 percent). The value closest to 3.000 is 2.991; therefore, the IRR for project A, to the nearest 1 percent, is *20 percent*. The actual value, which is between 19 and 20 percent, could be found using

---

[3]The Texas Instruments BA-35 calculator—the business calculator used throughout this text—can be used to find the IRR of an annuity, but it lacks a function for finding the IRR of a mixed stream of cash flows. Most of the more sophisticated (and more expensive) financial calculators are pre-programmed to find IRRs. With these calculators you merely punch in all cash flows and depress the "IRR" key to find the internal rate of return. Computer software, like the *Basic Managerial Finance (BMF) Disk* described in Appendix B and various spreadsheet programs such as *Lotus 1–2–3*, are also available for calculating IRRs.

Table 15.5   Steps for Calculating the Internal Rates of Return (IRRs) of Annuities and Mixed Streams

For An Annuity

Step 1: Calculate the payback period for the project.[a]

Step 2: Use Table C-4 (the present-value interest factors for a $1 annuity, *PVIFA*) to find, for the life of the project, the factor closest to the payback value. The discount rate associated with that factor is the internal rate of return (IRR) to the nearest 1 percent.

For A Mixed Stream[b]

Step 1: Calculate the average annual cash inflow.

Step 2: Divide the average annual cash inflow into the initial investment to get an "average payback period" (or present-value interest factor for a $1 annuity, *PVIFA*). The average payback is needed to estimate the IRR for the average annual cash inflow.

Step 3: Use Table C-4 (*PVIFA*) and the average payback period in the same manner as described in step 2 for finding the IRR of an annuity. The result will be a *very rough* approximation of the IRR, based on the assumption that the mixed stream of cash inflows is an annuity.

Step 4:[c] Adjust subjectively the IRR obtained in step 3 by comparing the pattern of average annual cash inflows (calculated in step 1) to the actual mixed stream of cash inflows. If the actual cash flow stream seems to have higher inflows in the earlier years than the average stream, adjust the IRR up. If the actual cash inflows in the earlier years are below the average, adjust the IRR down. The amount of adjustment up or down typically ranges from 1 to 3 percentage points depending upon how much the actual cash inflow stream's pattern deviates from the average annual cash inflows. For small deviations, an adjustment of around 1 percentage point may be best; for large deviations, adjustments of around 3 percentage points are generally appropriate. If the average cash inflows seem fairly close to the actual pattern, make no adjustment in the IRR.

Step 5: Using the IRR from step 4, calculate the net present value of the mixed-stream project. Be sure to use Table C-3 (the present-value interest factors for $1, *PVIF*), treating the estimated IRR as the discount rate.

Step 6: If the resulting NPV is greater than zero, subjectively raise the discount rate; if the resulting NPV is less than zero, subjectively lower the discount rate. The greater the deviation of the resulting NPV from zero, the larger the subjective adjustment. Typically, adjustments of 1 to 3 percentage points are used for relatively small deviations; larger adjustments are required for relatively large deviations.

Step 7: Calculate the NPV using the new discount rate. Repeat step 6. Stop as soon as two *consecutive* discount rates that cause the NPV to be positive and negative, respectively, have been found. Whichever of these rates causes the NPV to be closer to zero is the IRR to the nearest 1 percent.

---

[a]The payback period calculated actually represents the interest factor for the present value of an annuity (*PVIFA*) for the given life discounted at an unknown rate. Once determined, that rate represents the IRR for the project.
[b]Note that subjective estimates are suggested in steps 4 and 6. After working a number of these problems, a "feel" for the appropriate subjective adjustment, or "educated guess," may result.
[c]The purpose of this step is to provide a more accurate first estimate of the IRR. This step can be skipped.

interpolation, a calculator,[4] or a computer; it is 19.87 percent. (Note: For our purposes, values rounded to the nearest 1 percent will suffice.) Project A with an IRR of 20 percent is quite acceptable,

---

[4]The procedure for using a business calculator to find the unknown interest rate on an equal-payment loan described in Chapter 11 can be used to find the IRR for an annuity. When applying this procedure, we treat the life of the annuity the same as the term of the loan, the initial investment the same as the loan principal, and the annual cash inflows the same as the annual loan payments. The resulting solution is the IRR for the annuity rather than the interest rate on the loan.

since this IRR is above the firm's 10 percent cost of capital (20 percent IRR > 10 percent cost of capital).

The seven-step procedure in Table 15.5 for finding the internal rate of return of a *mixed stream* of cash inflows can be illustrated using Blano Company's project B cash flows given in Table 15.1.

Step 1:   Summing the cash inflows for years 1 through 5 results in total cash inflows of $70,000. That amount, when divided by the number of years in the project's life, results in an average annual cash inflow of $14,000 [($28,000 + $12,000 + $10,000 + $10,000 + $10,000) ÷ 5].

Step 2:   Dividing the initial outlay of $45,000 by the average annual cash inflow of $14,000 (calculated in step 1) results in an "average payback period" (or present value of an annuity factor, *PVIFA*) of 3.214 years.

Step 3:   In Table C-4, the factor closest to 3.214 for five years is 3.199, the factor for a discount rate of 17 percent. The starting estimate of the IRR is therefore 17 percent.

Step 4:   Since the actual early-year cash inflows are greater than the average cash inflows of $14,000, a *subjective* increase of 2 percent is made in the discount rate. This makes the estimated IRR 19 percent.

Step 5:   With the present-value interest factors (*PVIF*) for 19 percent and the correct year from Table C-3, the net present value of the mixed stream is calculated as follows:

Year (t)	Cash inflows (1)	$PVIF_{19\%,t}$ (2)	Present value at 19% [(1) × (2)] (3)
1	$28,000	.840	$23,520
2	12,000	.706	8,472
3	10,000	.593	5,930
4	10,000	.499	4,990
5	10,000	.419	4,190
	Present value of cash inflows		$47,102
	− Initial investment		45,000
	Net present value (NPV)		$ 2,102

Steps 6 and 7: Since the net present value of $2,102, calculated in step 5, is greater than zero, we need to try another discount rate. Since the NPV deviates by only about 5 percent from the $45,000 initial investment, let's try a 2 percentage point increase to 21 percent.

Year (t)	Cash inflows (1)	$PVIF_{21\%,t}$ (2)	Present value at 21% [(1) × (2)] (3)
1	$28,000	.826	$23,128
2	12,000	.683	8,196
3	10,000	.564	5,640
4	10,000	.467	4,670
5	10,000	.386	3,860
		Present value of cash inflows	$45,494
		− Initial investment	45,000
		Net present value (NPV)	$ 494

These calculations indicate that the NPV of $494 for an IRR of 21 percent is reasonably close to, but still greater than, zero. Thus a higher discount rate should be tried. Since we are so close, let's try a 1 percentage point increase to 22 percent. As the following calculations show, the net present value using a discount rate of 22 percent is −$256.

Year (t)	Cash inflows (1)	$PVIF_{22\%,t}$ (2)	Present value at 22% [(1) × (2)] (3)
1	$28,000	.820	$22,960
2	12,000	.672	8,064
3	10,000	.551	5,510
4	10,000	.451	4,510
5	10,000	.370	3,700
		Present value of cash inflows	$44,744
		− Initial investment	45,000
		Net present value (NPV)	−$ 256

Since 21 and 22 percent are consecutive discount rates that give positive and negative net present values, we can stop the trial-and-error process.

The IRR we are seeking is the discount rate for which the NPV is closest to zero. For this project, 22 percent causes the NPV to be closer to zero than 21 percent, so 22 percent is the IRR we shall use. If we had used interpolation, a financial calculator, or a computer, the IRR would be 21.66 percent; as indicated earlier, for our purposes the IRR rounded to the nearest 1 percent will suffice. Therefore, the IRR of project B is approximately *22 percent*.

Project B is acceptable since its IRR of approximately 22 percent is greater than Blano Company's 10 percent cost of capital. This is the same conclusion reached using the NPV and PI as criteria. It is interesting to note that the IRR suggests that project B is preferable to A, which has an IRR of approximately 20 percent. This conflicts with the rankings of the projects obtained using *NPV and PI*. Such conflicts are not unusual; *there is no guarantee that these three techniques (NPV, PI, and IRR) will rank projects in the same order. However, all methods should reach the same conclusion about the acceptability or nonacceptability of projects.*

Comparison of NPV and IRR

Of the three sophisticated capital budgeting techniques, net present value (NPV) and internal rate of return (IRR) deserve the greatest attention. *For conventional projects, both techniques will always generate the same accept-reject decision, but differences in their underlying assumptions can cause them to rank projects differently.* To understand the differences and preferences surrounding these techniques, we need to look at conflicting rankings and consider the question of which approach is better.

Conflicting Rankings

The possibility of *conflicting rankings* of projects by NPV and IRR should be clear from the Blano Company example. Ranking is an important consideration when projects are mutually exclusive or when capital rationing is necessary. When projects are mutually exclusive, ranking enables the firm to determine the best project from a financial viewpoint. When capital rationing is necessary, ranking projects may not determine the group of projects to accept, but it will provide a logical starting point.

Conflicting rankings using NPV and IRR result from *differences in the magnitude and timing of cash flows*. Although these two factors explain conflicting rankings, the underlying cause is the implicit assumption concerning the reinvestment of **intermediate cash inflows**—cash inflows received prior to the termination of a project. NPV assumes that intermediate cash inflows are reinvested at the cost of capital, whereas IRR assumes that intermediate cash inflows are invested at a rate equal to the project's IRR.

conflicting rankings Conflicts in the ranking given a project by NPV and IRR, resulting from differences in the magnitude and timing of cash flows.

intermediate cash inflows Cash inflows received prior to the termination of a project.

Which Approach Is Better?

On a purely theoretical basis, NPV is the better approach to capital budgeting. Its theoretical superiority is based on a number of factors. Most important is the fact that the use of NPV assumes that any intermediate cash inflows are reinvested at the firm's cost of capital. The use of IRR assumes reinvestment at the often high rate specified by the IRR. The cost of capital tends to be a reasonable estimate of the rate at which the firm could actually reinvest intermediate cash inflows. Thus the use of NPV with its more conservative and more realistic reinvestment rate is in theory preferable. In addition, certain mathematical properties may cause a project with nonconventional cash flows to have zero or more than one IRR; this problem does not occur with the NPV approach.

Evidence suggests that in spite of the theoretical superiority of NPV, *financial managers prefer to use IRR.* In general, business people prefer *rates of return* rather than actual *dollar returns*. Because interest rates, profitability, and so on are most often expressed as annual rates of return, the use of IRR makes sense to financial decision makers. They tend to find NPV more difficult to use because it does not really measure benefits *relative to the amount invested*. The widespread use of IRR should not be viewed as reflecting a lack of sophistication on the part of financial decision makers, however. A variety of methods and techniques are available for avoiding the pitfalls of IRR.

CAPITAL RATIONING

Like individuals, firms commonly find a greater number of acceptable projects than they have the funds to undertake. The objective of *capital rationing* is to select the group of projects that provides the *highest overall net present value* and does not require more dollars than are budgeted. As a prerequisite to capital rationing, the best of any mutually exclusive projects must be chosen and placed in the group of independent projects. Two basic approaches to project selection under capital rationing are discussed here.

Internal Rate of Return Approach

internal rate of return approach An approach to capital rationing that involves graphing project IRRs in descending order against the total dollar investment.

The **internal rate of return approach** involves graphing IRRs in descending order against the total dollar investment. This graph, which was discussed in some detail in Chapter 13, is called the *investment opportunities schedule* (IOS). By drawing the cost of capital line and then imposing a budget constraint, the financial manager can determine the group of acceptable projects. The problem with this technique is that it does not guarantee the maximum dollar return to the firm. It merely provides a satisfactory solution to capital rationing problems.

EXAMPLE   Gould Company, a fast-growing plastics company, is confronted with six projects competing for its fixed budget of $250,000. The initial investment and IRR for each project are as follows:

Project	Initial investment	IRR
A	$ 80,000	12%
B	70,000	20
C	100,000	16
D	40,000	8
E	60,000	15
F	110,000	11

The firm has a cost of capital of 10 percent. Figure 15.1 presents the investment opportunities schedule (IOS) resulting from ranking the six projects in descending order based on IRRs. According to the schedule, only projects B, C, and E should be accepted. Together, they will absorb $230,000 of the $250,000 budget. Project D is not worthy of consideration since its IRR is less than the firm's 10 percent cost of capital. The drawback of this approach, however, is that

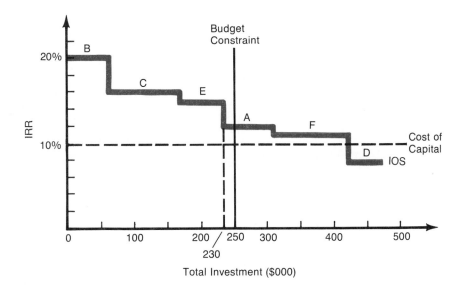

Figure 15.1   Investment Opportunities Schedule (IOS) for Gould Company Projects
Under the IRR approach to capital rationing, Gould Company's $250,000 budget constraint would permit acceptance of only projects B, C, and E in spite of the fact that projects A and F have IRRs greater than the 10 percent cost of capital.

SMALL BUSINESS

An Absence of Small Business Capital Budgeting

The capital budgeting question in Fortune 500 companies is frequently which of the firm's potential projects provide positive net present values. The question in small businesses is often whether or not to do any capital spending. Every quarter the National Federation of Independent Business queries its 2,140 members regarding their planned capital outlays over the subsequent three to six months. The results of the survey, published in *Business Week* and other financial media, frequently provide an indicator of upcoming economic conditions. At the onset of deteriorating economic conditions, small businesses have a tendency to go beyond rationing and eliminate capital spending altogether.

Even during economic expansions, most small businesses do not actively engage in capital spending. The highest percentage of surveyed small businesses planning to undertake capital expenditures during any quarter over the 1981–1990 period was 36 percent. Over the same time period, the lowest percentage of small businesses indicating that they planned to expand during the following three to six months was 24 percent.

Fears of recession, banking system jitters, and war in the Middle East were just a few of the factors reducing the likelihood of capital spending by small businesses in early 1991. Just 27 percent of small business owners planned to make capital expenditures during the first quarter of 1991. This was the lowest level since 1982 and represented a decrease of 9 percentage points from the 36 percent reached in the first quarter of 1989.

Source: "Small business tightens up on capital spending," *Business Week,* December 24, 1990, p. 73.

there is no guarantee that the acceptance of projects B, C, and E will maximize *total dollar returns* and therefore owners' wealth.

Net Present Value Approach

net present value approach An approach to capital rationing that is based on the use of present values to determine the group of projects that will maximize owners' wealth.

The **net present value approach** is based on the use of present values to determine the group of projects that will maximize owners' wealth. With it, the financial manager ranks projects on the basis of IRRs or PIs

Table 15.6   **Rankings for Gould Company Projects**

Project	Initial investment	IRR	Present value of inflows at 10%	
B	$ 70,000	20%	$112,000	
C	100,000	16	145,000	
E	60,000	15	79,000	
A	80,000	12	100,000	
F	110,000	11	126,500	Cutoff point
D	40,000	8	36,000	(IRR < 10%)

(profitability indexes) and then evaluates the present value of the benefits from each potential project. The goal is to *determine the combination of projects with the highest overall present value.* This is the same as maximizing net present value, because whether the entire budget is used or not, it is viewed as the total initial investment. The portion of the firm's budget that is not used does not increase the firm's value. At best, the unused money can be invested in marketable securities or returned to the owners in the form of cash dividends. In either case the wealth of the owners is not likely to be enhanced.

EXAMPLE   The group of projects described in the preceding example is ranked in Table 15.6 on the basis of IRRs. The present value of the cash inflows associated with the projects is also included in the table. Projects B, C, and E, which together require $230,000, yield a present value of $336,000. However, if projects B, C, and A were implemented, the total budget of $250,000 would be used and the present value of the cash inflows would be $357,000. This is greater than the return expected from selecting the projects on the basis of the highest IRRs. Implementing B, C, and A is preferable, because they maximize the present value for the given budget. *The firm's objective is to use its budget to generate the highest present value of inflows.* Assuming that any unused portion of the budget does not gain or lose money, the total NPV for projects B, C, and E would be $106,000 ($336,000 − $230,000), whereas for projects B, C, and A, the total NPV would be $107,000 ($357,000 − $250,000). Selection of projects B, C, and A will therefore maximize NPV.

APPROACHES FOR DEALING WITH RISK

In the discussion of capital budgeting, **risk** refers to the chance that a project will prove unacceptable (i.e., NPV < $0, PI < 1, or IRR < cost of capital) or, more formally, to the degree of variability of cash flows.

risk (in capital budgeting) The chance that a project will prove unacceptable or, more formally, the degree of variability of cash flows.

Projects with a small chance of being acceptable and a broad range of expected cash flows are more risky than projects having a high chance of being acceptable and a narrow range of expected cash flows. In the conventional capital budgeting projects assumed here, risk stems almost entirely from *cash inflows*, since the initial investment is generally known with relative certainty. Using the basic risk concepts presented in Chapter 12, we present here some approaches for dealing with risk in capital budgeting: sensitivity and scenario analysis, statistical approaches, decision trees, and simulation.

Sensitivity and Scenario Analysis

sensitivity analysis An approach that uses a number of possible values for a given variable in order to assess its impact on a firm's return.

Two approaches for dealing with project risk to capture the variability of cash inflows and NPVs are sensitivity analysis and scenario analysis. **Sensitivity analysis,** as noted in Chapter 12, uses a number of possible values for a given variable, such as cash inflows, to assess its impact on the firm's return, measured here by NPV. This technique is often useful in getting a feel for the variability of return in response to changes in a key variable. In capital budgeting, one of the most common sensitivity approaches is to estimate the NPVs associated with pessimistic (worst), most likely (expected), and optimistic (best) cash inflow estimates. The *range* can be determined by subtracting the pessimistic-outcome NPV from the optimistic-outcome NPV.

EXAMPLE   Treadwell Tire Company, a tire retailer, is considering investing in either of two mutually exclusive projects, A and B. Each requires a $10,000 initial outlay and is expected to provide equal annual cash inflows over their 15-year lives. The firm's financial manager made pessimistic, most likely, and optimistic estimates of the cash inflows for each project. The cash inflow estimates and resulting NPVs in each case are summarized in Table 15.7. The ranges of cash inflows is $1,000 for project A and $4,000 for project B. More important, the range of NPVs is $7,606 for project A and $30,424 for project B. It is clear that project A is less risky than project B. The risk-averse decision maker will take project A, thereby eliminating the possibility of loss.

scenario analysis An approach that evaluates the impact on return of simultaneous changes in a number of variables.

Scenario analysis is similar to sensitivity analysis but broader in scope. It is used to evaluate the impact of various circumstances on the firm's return. Rather than isolating the effect of a change in a single variable, scenario analysis is used to evaluate the impact on return of simultaneous changes in a number of variables. Decision makers can study the effects on return of changes in variables such as cash inflows, cash outflows, and the cost of capital, resulting from differing assumptions about economic and competitive conditions. For example, the firm could evaluate the impact of both high inflation (scenario 1) and low inflation (scenario 2) on a project's NPV. Each scenario will affect the firm's cash inflows, cash outflows, and cost of capital, thereby re-

Table 15.7   Sensitivity Analysis
of Treadwell's
Projects A and B

	Project A	Project B
Initial investment	$10,000	$10,000
	Annual cash inflows	
Outcome		
Pessimistic	$1,500	$ 0
Most likely	2,000	2,000
Optimistic	2,500	4,000
Range	$1,000	$4,000
	Net present values[a]	
Outcome		
Pessimistic	$1,409	−$10,000
Most likely	5,212	5,212
Optimistic	9,015	20,424
Range	$7,606	$30,424

[a]These values were calculated using the corresponding annual cash inflows. A 10 percent cost of capital
and a 15-year life for the annual cash inflows were
used.

sulting in different levels of NPV. The decision maker can use these NPV
estimates to roughly assess the risk involved with respect to the level of
inflation. The widespread availability of computer-based spreadsheet
programs (such as *Lotus 1–2–3*) has greatly enhanced the ease and popularity of use of scenario as well as sensitivity analysis.

Statistical Approaches

The use of the standard deviation and coefficient of variation to measure the risk of a single asset held in isolation were presented in Chapter
12. These measures can be applied to cash inflow or net present value
(NPV) data in order to measure project risk statistically. The following
example illustrates the calculation of these statistics using NPV data.

EXAMPLE   Treadwell Tire Company estimated the probabilities of
the pessimistic, most likely, and optimistic NPV outcomes
for projects A and B shown in Table 15.8. To find the standard deviation of each project, the first step is to calculate
the *expected net present value of each project*. The *expected*
NPV, $\overline{\text{NPV}}$, can be calculated using Equation 12.1 from
Chapter 12, rewritten as

Table 15.8   **NPVs and Associated Probability Estimates
for Treadwell's Projects A and B**

i	Outcome$_i$	NPV$^a{}_i$	Probability, $Pr^b{}_i$
Project A			
1	Pessimistic	$ 1,409	.25
2	Most likely	5,212	.50
3	Optimistic	9,015	.25
Project B			
1	Pessimistic	−$10,000	.25
2	Most likely	5,212	.50
3	Optimistic	20,424	.25

[a]From Table 15.7.
[b]Values estimated subjectively, based on past experience.

Equation 15.4
Formula for the expected net present value

$$\overline{NPV} = \sum_{i=1}^{n} NPV_i \times Pr_i$$

where

NPV_i = NPV for the ith outcome
Pr_i = probability of occurrence of the ith NPV
n = number of outcomes considered

Substituting the data from Table 15.8, we can calculate the expected NPV for each project:

$$\overline{NPV}_A = \$1,409(.25) + \$5,212(.50) + \$9,015(.25)$$
$$= \$352.25 + \$2,606.00 + \$2,253.75 = \underline{\$5,212}$$
$$\overline{NPV}_B = -\$10,000(.25) + \$5,212(.50) + \$20,424(.25)$$
$$= -\$2,500 + \$2,606 + \$5,106 = \underline{\$5,212}$$

Note that both projects have expected NPVs of $5,212 which also equals their most likely estimates.

Once the expected NPV, $\overline{NPV}$, has been calculated, the *standard deviation of* NPV, σ_{NPV}, can be found using Equation 12.2 from Chapter 12, rewritten as

Equation 15.5
Formula for the standard deviation of NPV

$$\sigma_{NPV} = \sqrt{\sum_{i=1}^{n} (NPV_i - \overline{NPV})^2 \times Pr_i}$$

The calculation of the standard deviation of NPV for projects A and B using Equation 15.5 is given in Table 15.9. It can be seen that project B's standard deviation of $10,756 is much higher than project A's standard deviation of $2,689. Project B is therefore clearly more risky than project A.

The *coefficient of variation*, CV, is an especially useful statistic for comparing the risk of projects of differing sizes.

Table 15.9   **Calculation of the Standard Deviation of NPV for Treadwell's Projects A and B**

i	NPV_i	$\overline{NPV}$	$NPV_i - \overline{NPV}$	$(NPV_i - \overline{NPV})^2$	Pr_i	$(NPV_i - \overline{NPV})^2 \times Pr_i$
			Project A			
1	$1,409	$5,212	−$3,803	$14,462,809	.25	$3,615,702
2	5,212	5,212	0	0	.50	0
3	9,015	5,212	3,803	14,462,809	.25	3,615,702

$$\sum_{i=1}^{3} (NPV_i - \overline{NPV})^2 \times Pr_i = \$7,231,404$$

$$\sigma_{NPV_A} = \sqrt{\sum_{i=1}^{3} (NPV_i - \overline{NPV})^2 \times Pr_i} = \sqrt{\$7,231,404} = \underline{\$2,689}$$

i	NPV_i	$\overline{NPV}$	$NPV_i - \overline{NPV}$	$(NPV_i - \overline{NPV})^2$	Pr_i	$(NPV_i - \overline{NPV})^2 \times Pr_i$
			Project B			
1	−$10,000	$5,212	$15,212	$231,400,000	.25	$ 57,850,000
2	5,212	5,212	0	0	.50	0
3	20,424	5,212	15,212	231,400,000	.25	57,850,000

$$\sum_{i=1}^{3} (NPV_i - \overline{NPV})^2 \times Pr_i = \$115,700,000$$

$$\sigma_{NPV_B} = \sqrt{\sum_{i=1}^{3} (NPV_i - \overline{NPV})^2 \times Pr_i} = \sqrt{\$115,700,000} = \underline{\$10,756}$$

Since projects A and B have the same expected NPV, the coefficient of variation does not really improve the comparison. Applying Equation 12.3 from Chapter 12 to the NPV data, the coefficient of variation of NPV, CV_{NPV}, is defined as

$$CV_{NPV} = \frac{\sigma_{NPV}}{\overline{NPV}}$$

Substituting σ_{NPV} and $\overline{NPV}$ for projects A and B into Equation 15.6 yields

$$CV_{NPV_A} = \frac{\sigma_{NPV_A}}{\overline{NPV}_A} = \frac{\$2,689}{\$5,212} = \underline{.516}$$

$$CV_{NPVB} = \frac{\sigma_{NPV_B}}{\overline{NPV}_B} = \frac{\$10,756}{\$5,212} = \underline{2.064}$$

Equation 15.6
Formula for the coefficient of variation of NPV

Clearly project B, with a coefficient of variation of NPV of 2.064, is more risky than project A, which has a CV of .516.

Decision Trees

decision trees
Diagrams that map the various investment decision alternatives and payoffs as well as their probabilities of occurrence.

Decision trees are diagrams that map the various investment decision alternatives and payoffs as well as their probabilities of occurrence. Their name derives from their resemblance to the branches of a tree (see

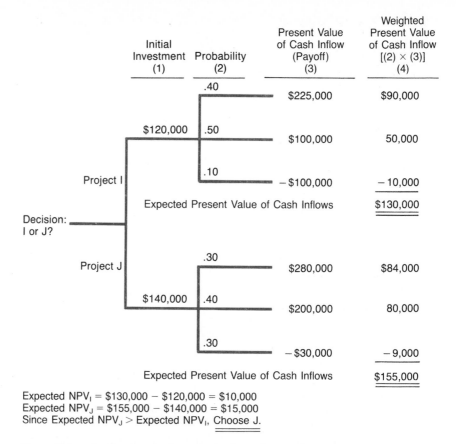

	Initial Investment (1)	Probability (2)	Present Value of Cash Inflow (Payoff) (3)	Weighted Present Value of Cash Inflow [(2) × (3)] (4)
		.40	$225,000	$90,000
	$120,000	.50	$100,000	50,000
Project I		.10	−$100,000	−10,000
		Expected Present Value of Cash Inflows		$130,000
		.30	$280,000	$84,000
Project J	$140,000	.40	$200,000	80,000
		.30	−$30,000	−9,000
		Expected Present Value of Cash Inflows		$155,000

Decision: I or J?

Expected NPV$_I$ = $130,000 − $120,000 = $10,000
Expected NPV$_J$ = $155,000 − $140,000 = $15,000
Since Expected NPV$_J$ > Expected NPV$_I$, Choose J.

Figure 15.2   Decision Tree for Convy, Inc.'s, Choice Between Projects I and J
The $10,000 expected NPV of project I ($130,000 expected present value of cash inflows − $120,000 initial investment) is less than the $15,000 expected NPV of project J ($155,000 expected present value of cash inflows − $140,000 initial investment). Project J is therefore preferred.

Figure 15.2). Decision trees rely on estimates of the probabilities associated with the outcomes (payoffs) of competing courses of action. The payoffs associated with each course of action are weighted by the associated probability; the weighted payoffs for each course of action are summed; and the expected value of each course of action is then determined. The alternative providing the highest expected value would be preferred.

EXAMPLE   Convy, Inc., a manufacturer of picture frames, wishes to choose between two equally risky projects, I and J. To make this decision, Convy's management has gathered the necessary data, which are depicted in the decision tree in Figure 15.2. Project I requires an initial investment of $120,000; a resulting expected present value of cash inflows of $130,000 is shown in column 4. Project I's expected net present value, which is calculated below the decision tree, is therefore

$10,000. Since the $15,000 expected net present value of project J, which is determined in a similar fashion, is greater than that for project I, project J would be preferred.

Simulation

Simulation is a statistically based approach used in capital budgeting to get a feel for risk by applying predetermined probability distributions and random numbers to estimate risky outcomes. By tying the various cash flow components together in a mathematical model and repeating the process numerous times, the financial manager can develop a probability distribution of project returns. Figure 15.3 presents

simulation A statistically based approach used to get a feel for risk by applying predetermined probability distributions and random numbers to estimate risky outcomes.

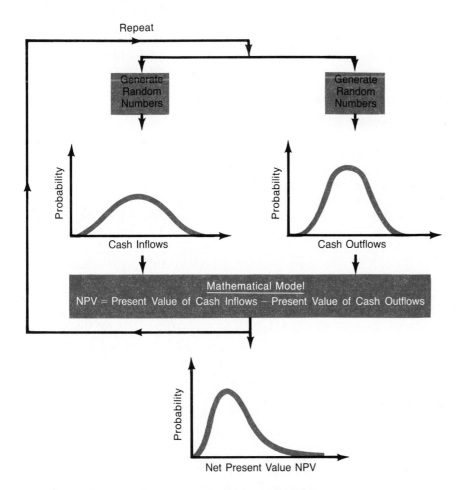

Figure 15.3   Flowchart of a Net Present Value Simulation
The basic NPV simulation uses random numbers with the probability distributions to determine cash inflows and cash outflows. These are substituted into the mathematical model to determine NPV. This process is repeated a large number of times in order to create a probability distribution of NPV.

a flowchart of the simulation of the net present value of a project. The process of generating random numbers and using the probability distributions for cash inflows and outflows allows the decision maker to determine values for each of these variables. Substituting these values into the mathematical model results in an NPV. By repeating this process perhaps a thousand times, a probability distribution of net present values is created.

Although only gross cash inflows and outflows are simulated in Figure 15.3, more sophisticated simulations using individual inflow and outflow components, such as sales volume, sale price, raw material cost, labor cost, maintenance expense, and so on, are quite common. From the distribution of returns, regardless of how they are measured (NPV, IRR, and so on), the decision maker can determine not only the expected value of the return but also the probability of achieving or surpassing a given return. The use of computers has made the simulation approach feasible. The output of simulation provides an excellent basis for decision making; it allows the decision maker to view a continuum of risk-return trade-offs rather than a single-point estimate.

RISK-ADJUSTMENT TECHNIQUES

The approaches for dealing with risk presented so far allow the financial manager to get a "feel" for project risk. Unfortunately, they do not provide a straightforward basis for evaluating risky projects. We will now illustrate the two major risk-adjustment techniques using the net present value (NPV) decision method.[5] The NPV decision rule of accepting only those projects with NPVs greater than $0 will continue to hold. The basic equation for NPV was presented earlier in Equation 15.2. Since the initial investment, which occurs at time zero, is known with certainty, a project's risk is embodied in the present value of cash inflows.

There are two ways to adjust the present value of cash inflows for risk: (1) the cash inflows themselves can be adjusted, or (2) the discount rate can be adjusted. Here we describe and compare the two techniques—the cash inflow adjustment process using *certainty equivalents*, and the discount rate adjustment process using *risk-adjusted discount rates*. In addition, we discuss the practical aspects of certainty equivalents and risk-adjusted discount rates.

Certainty Equivalents (CEs)

certainty equivalents (CEs) Risk-adjustment factors that represent the percent of estimated cash inflow that investors would be satisfied to receive *for certain* rather than the cash inflows that are *possible* each year.

The theoretically preferred approach for risk adjustment is the use of **certainty equivalents (CEs).** They represent the percent of estimated

[5]The IRR could just as well have been used, but since NPV is theoretically preferable, it is used instead.

cash inflow that investors would be satisfied to receive *for certain* rather than the cash inflows that are *possible* for each year. A project under consideration is therefore adjusted for risk in two steps: by first converting its expected cash inflows to certain amounts using the certainty equivalents and by then discounting the cash inflows at the risk-free rate, R_F. The **risk-free rate (R_F)** is the rate of return one would earn on a virtually riskless investment such as a U.S. Treasury bill. It is used to discount the certain cash inflows and should not be confused with a risk-adjusted discount rate. (If a risk-adjusted rate were used, the risk would in effect be counted twice.) Although the process described here of converting risky cash inflows to certain cash inflows is somewhat subjective, the technique is theoretically sound.

risk-free rate (R_F)
The rate of return on a virtually riskless investment.

EXAMPLE   Blano Company wishes to consider risk in the analysis of two projects, A and B. The basic data for these projects were initially presented in Table 15.1, and the analysis of the projects using net present value and assuming the projects had equivalent risks was presented in Table 15.4. Ignoring risk differences and using net present value, we saw earlier that at the firm's 10 percent cost of capital, project A was preferred over project B; its NPV of $11,074 was greater than B's NPV of $10,914. Assume, however, that on further analysis the firm found that project A was actually more risky than project B. To consider the differing risks, the firm estimated the certainty equivalents for each project's cash inflows for each year. Columns 2 and 7 of Table 15.10 show the estimated values for projects A and B, respectively. Multiplying the risky cash inflows (given in columns 1 and 6) by the corresponding certainty equivalent factors (CEs) (columns 2 and 7, respectively) gives the certain cash inflows for projects A and B shown in columns 3 and 8, respectively.

Upon investigation, Blano's management estimated the prevailing risk-free rate of return, R_F, to be 6 percent. Using that rate to discount the certain cash inflows for each of the projects results in the net present values of $4,541 for project A and $10,141 for project B. (The calculated values using a business calculator are $4,544 and $10,151 for projects A and B, respectively.) Note that as a result of the risk adjustment, project B is now preferred. The usefulness of the certainty equivalent approach for risk adjustment should be quite clear; the only difficulty lies in the need to make subjective estimates of the certainty equivalents.

Risk-Adjusted Discount Rates (RADRs)

A more practical approach for risk adjustment involves the use of *risk-adjusted discount rates (RADRs)*. Instead of adjusting the cash inflows for risk, as was done in the certainty equivalent approach, this ap-

Table 15.10   **Analysis of Blano Company's Projects A and B Using Certainty Equivalents**

			Project A		
Year (t)	Cash inflows (1)	Certainty equivalent factors[a] (2)	Certain cash inflows [(1) × (2)] (3)	$PVIF_{6\%,t}$ (4)	Present value [(3) × (4)] (5)
1	$14,000	.90	$12,600	.943	$11,882
2	14,000	.90	12,600	.890	11,214
3	14,000	.80	11,200	.840	9,408
4	14,000	.70	9,800	.792	7,762
5	14,000	.60	8,400	.747	6,275
			Present value of cash inflows		$46,541
			− Initial investment		42,000
			Net present value (NPV)		$ 4,541

			Project B		
Year (t)	Cash inflows (6)	Certainty equivalent factors[a] (7)	Certain cash inflows [(6) × (7)] (8)	$PVIF_{6\%,t}$ (9)	Present value [(8) × (9)] (10)
1	$28,000	1.00	$28,000	.943	$26,404
2	12,000	.90	10,800	.890	9,612
3	10,000	.90	9,000	.840	7,560
4	10,000	.80	8,000	.792	6,336
5	10,000	.70	7,000	.747	5,229
			Present value of cash inflows		$55,141
			− Initial investment		45,000
			Net present value (NPV)		$10,141

[a]These values were estimated by management; they reflect the risk managers perceive in the cash inflows.
Note: The basic cash flows for these projects were presented in Table 15.1, and the analysis of the projects using NPV and assuming equal risk was presented in Table 15.4.

risk-adjusted discount rate (RADR)
The rate of return that must be earned on a given project in order to compensate the firm's owners adequately.

proach adjusts the discount rate. The **risk-adjusted discount rate (RADR)** is the rate of return that must be earned on a given project in order to compensate the firm's owners adequately—i.e., maintain or improve the firm's share price. The higher the risk of a project, the higher the RADR and therefore the lower the net present value for a given stream of cash inflows.

Using the coefficient of variation (CV) as a measure of project risk, the firm can develop a **market risk-return function**—a graph of the dis-

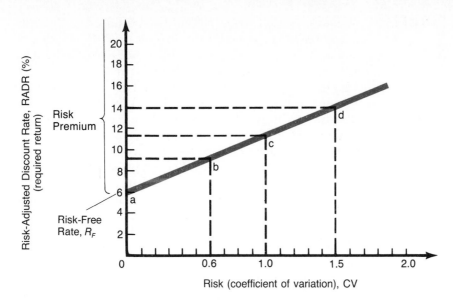

Figure 15.4   **A Market Risk-Return Function**
The market risk-return function shows the risk-adjusted discount rate,
RADR, or required return associated with each level of risk measured by
the coefficient of variation, CV. At CVs of 0 (no risk), 0.6, 1.0, and 1.5,
the RADRs are approximately 6 percent (risk-free rate, R_F), 9 percent,
11 percent, and 14 percent, respectively.

count rates associated with each level of project risk. An example of
such a function is given in Figure 15.4. It relates the risk-adjusted discount rate, RADR, to the project risk as measured by the coefficient of
variation, CV. This function is similar to the capital asset pricing model
(CAPM) presented in Chapter 12. The risk-return function in Figure 15.4
indicates that project cash inflows associated with a riskless event
(CV = 0) should be discounted at a 6 percent rate. This rate of return
therefore represents the risk-free rate, R_F (point a in the figure). For all
levels of risk greater than certainty (CV > 0), the associated required
rate of return is indicated. Points b, c, and d indicate that rates of return
of approximately 9, 11, and 14 percent will be required on projects with
coefficients of variation of 0.6, 1.0, and 1.5, respectively.

Figure 15.4 is a *market risk-return function*. This means that investors will discount cash inflows with the given levels of risk at the corresponding rates. Therefore, in order not to damage its market value, the
firm must use the correct discount rate for evaluating a project. If a firm
discounts a risky project's cash inflows at too low a rate and accepts the
project, the firm's market price may drop as investors recognize that the
firm itself has become more risky. The amount by which the required discount rate for a project exceeds the risk-free rate is called the
risk premium. It of course increases with increasing project risk. A simple example will clarify the use of the risk-adjusted discount rate in
evaluating capital budgeting projects.

**market risk-return
function** A graph of
the discount rates associated with each level of
project risk.

risk premium The
amount by which the
required discount rate
for a project exceeds the
risk-free rate.

EXAMPLE   Blano Company wishes to use the risk-adjusted discount rate approach to determine, according to NPV, whether to implement project A or project B. In addition to the data presented earlier, Blano's management has estimated the coefficient of variation for project A as 1.5 and for project B as 1.0. According to Figure 15.4, the RADR for project A is approximately 14 percent; for project B, it is approximately 11 percent. Due to the riskier nature of project A, its risk premium is 8 percent (14% − 6%); for project B the risk premium is 5 percent (11% − 6%). The net present value of each project, using its RADR, is calculated in Table 15.11. (The calculated values using a business calculator are $6,063 and $9,798 for projects A and B, respectively.) The results clearly show that project B is preferable; its risk-adjusted net present value (NPV) of $9,802 is greater than the $6,062 risk-adjusted NPV for project A. This is the same conclusion that resulted using certainty equivalents in the preceding example. As noted earlier (see Table 15.4), when the discount rates are not adjusted for risk, project A would be preferred to project B. The usefulness of risk-adjusted discount rates should now be clear; the real difficulty of this approach lies in estimating the market risk-return function.

Table 15.11   **Analysis of Blano Company's Projects A and B Using Risk-Adjusted Discount Rates**

Project A	
Annual cash inflow	$14,000
× $PVIFA_{14\%,5 \text{ yrs}}$	3.433
Present value of cash inflows	$48,062
− Initial investment	42,000
Net present value (NPV)	$ 6,062

	Project B		
Year (t)	Cash inflows (1)	$PVIF_{11\%,t}$ (2)	Present value [(1) × (2)] (3)
1	$28,000	.901	$25,228
2	12,000	.812	9,744
3	10,000	.731	7,310
4	10,000	.659	6,590
5	10,000	.593	5,930
		− Present value of cash inflows	$54,802
		− Initial investment	45,000
		Net present value (NPV)	$ 9,802

Note: Using Figure 15.4 and the coefficients of variation of 1.5 and 1.0 for projects A and B, respectively, a discount rate of 14 percent is used for project A and 11 percent for B.

CE versus RADR in Practice

Certainty equivalents (CEs) are theoretically superior to risk-adjusted discount rates (RADRs) for project risk adjustment. However, because of the complexity of developing CEs, *RADRs are more often used in practice.* Their popularity stems from two major facts: (1) They are consistent with the general disposition of financial decision makers toward rates of return. (2) They are easily estimated and applied. The first reason is clearly a matter of personal preference. The second is based on the computational convenience and well-developed procedures involved in the use of RADRs. In practice, risk is often subjectively categorized rather than related to a continuum of RADRs associated with each level of risk, as illustrated by the market risk-return function in Figure 15.4. Firms often establish a number of *risk classes,* with an RADR assigned to each. Each project is then subjectively placed in the appropriate risk class, and the corresponding RADR is used to evaluate it. This is sometimes done on a division-by-division basis. Each division is given its own set of risk classes and associated RADRs, similar to those in Table 15.12. The use of *divisional costs of capital* and associated risk classes allows the large multidivisional firm to incorporate differing levels of divisional risk into the capital budgeting process. At the same time it recognizes differences in the levels of individual project risk. An example will help to illustrate the general use of risk classes and RADRs.

Table 15.12   **Blano Company's Risk Classes and RADRs**

Risk Class	Description	Risk-adjusted discount rate, RADR
I	*Below-average risk:* Projects with low risk. Typically involve routine replacement without renewal of existing activities.	8%
II	*Average risk:* Projects similar to those currently implemented. Typically involve replacement or renewal of existing activities.	10%
III	*Above-average risk:* Projects with higher than normal, but not excessive, risk. Typically involve expansion of existing or similar activities.	14%
IV	*Highest risk:* Projects with very high risk. Typically involve expansion into new or unfamiliar activities.	20%

EXAMPLE   Assume that the management of Blano Company decided to use a more subjective but practical RADR approach to analyze projects. Each project was placed in one of four risk classes according to its perceived risk. The classes were ranged from I for the lowest-risk projects to IV for the highest-risk projects. Associated with each class was an RADR appropriate to the level of risk of projects in the class. A brief description of each class, along with the associated RADR, is given in Table 15.12. It shows that lower-risk projects tend to involve routine replacement or renewal activities; higher-risk projects involve expansion, often into new or unfamiliar activities.

The financial manager of Blano has assigned project A to Class III and project B to Class II. The cash flows for project A would therefore be evaluated using a 14 percent RADR; project B's would be evaluated using a 10 percent RADR.[6] The net present value of project A at 14 percent was calculated in Table 15.11 to be $6,062. The NPV for project B at a 10 percent RADR was found in Table 15.4 to be $10,914. Clearly, with RADRs based on the use of risk classes, project B is preferred over project A. As noted earlier, this result is contrary to the findings in Table 15.4, where no attention was given to the differing risk of projects A and B.

INTERNATIONAL DIMENSION: INVESTMENT CASH FLOWS AND DECISIONS

Several factors unique to the international setting need to be examined when making long-term investment decisions. First, elements relating to a parent company's *investment* in a subsidiary and the concept of taxes must be considered. For example, in the case of manufacturing investments, questions may arise as to the value of the equipment a parent firm may contribute to the subsidiary. Is the value based on the market conditions in the parent country or the local host economy? In general, the market value in the host country is the relevant "price."

The existence of different taxes—as pointed out in Chapter 2—can complicate measurement of the *cash flows* to be received by the parent because different definitions of taxable income can arise. There are still other complications when it comes to measuring the actual cash flows. From a parent firm's viewpoint, the cash flows are those repatriated from the subsidiary. In some countries, however, such cash flows may be totally or partially blocked. Obviously, depending on the life of the project in the host country, the returns and net present values (NPVs) associated with such projects can significantly vary from the subsid-

---

[6]Note that the 10 percent RADR for project B using the risk classes in Table 15.12 differs from the 11 percent RADR found earlier for project B using the market risk-return function. This difference is attributable to the less precise nature of the use of risk classes.

iary's and the parent's point of view. For instance, for a project of only five years' duration, if all yearly cash flows are blocked by the host government, the subsidiary may show a "normal" or even superior return and NPV, although the parent may show no return at all. On the other hand, for a project of longer life, even if cash flows are blocked for the first few years, the remaining years' cash flows can contribute toward the parent's returns and NPV.

Finally, there is the issue of *risk* attached to international cash flows. The three basic types of risk categories are (1) business and financial risks, (2) inflation and foreign exchange risks, and (3) political risks. The first category relates to the type of industry the subsidiary is in as well as its capital structure (see Chapter 16). As for the other two categories, we have already discussed both the risks of having investments, profits, and assets/liabilities in different currencies (see Chapters 3 and 12) as well as the potential impact of political risks and how MNCs can combat them (see Chapter 12).

The important point to note here is that the presence of such risks will influence the discount rate to be used in evaluating international cash flows. The basic rule, however, is that the *local cost of equity capital* (applicable to the local business and financial environments within which a subsidiary operates) is the starting discount rate to which risks stemming from foreign exchange and political factors can be added, and from which benefits reflecting the parent's lower capital costs may be subtracted.

SUMMARY

1   **Calculate, interpret, and evaluate the two most popular unsophisticated capital budgeting techniques—average rate of return and payback period.**   The average rate of return measures the annual accounting rate of return expected on the average investment. Its ease of calculation is appealing although it lacks any link to the wealth maximization goal, fails to consider cash flows, and ignores the time value of money. The payback period measures the amount of time required by the firm to recover its initial investment. Shorter paybacks are preferred. Its appeal lies in its consideration of cash flows, the implicit consideration given to timing, and its ability to measure risk exposure. The weaknesses of the payback period include its lack of linkage to the wealth maximization goal, failure to explicitly consider time value, and the fact that it ignores cash flows that occur after the payback period. The key formulas and decision criteria for the average rate of return and the payback period are summarized in Table 15.13.

2   **Apply the sophisticated capital budgeting techniques—net present value (NPV), profitability index (PI), and internal rate of return (IRR)—to relevant cash flows to choose acceptable as well as preferred capital expenditures.**   Sophisticated capital budgeting techniques use the cost of capital to consider the time factor in the value of money. They include net present value (NPV), the profitability index (PI), and the internal rate of return (IRR). All of these techniques provide the same accept-reject decisions for a given project but often conflict when ranking projects. The key formulas and decision criteria for NPV, PI, and IRR are summarized in Table 15.13.

Table 15.13   **Summary of Key Formulas/Definitions and Decision Criteria for Capital Budgeting Techniques**

Technique	Formula/definition	Decision criteria
Unsophisticated		
Average rate of return	$$\frac{\text{average profits after taxes}}{\text{average investment}}$$	*Accept* if greater than the minimum acceptable average rate of return; *reject* if less than the minimum acceptable average rate of return.
Payback period	For annuity: $\dfrac{\text{initial investment}}{\text{annual cash inflow}}$ For mixed stream: Calculate cumulative cash inflows on year-to-year basis until the initial investment is recovered.	*Accept* if less than the maximum acceptable payback period; *reject* if greater than the maximum acceptable payback period.
Sophisticated		
Net present value (NPV)	present value of cash inflows— initial investment	*Accept* if greater than $0; *reject* if less than $0.
Profitability index (PI)	$$\frac{\text{present value of cash inflows}}{\text{initial investment}}$$	*Accept* if greater than 1; *reject* if less than 1.
Internal rate of return (IRR)	The discount rate that equates the present value of cash inflows with the initial investment thereby causing NPV = $0.	*Accept* if greater than the cost of capital; *reject* if less than the cost of capital.

3   **Discuss whether the net present value or the internal rate of return technique is better, and describe basic approaches for choosing projects under capital rationing.** On a purely theoretical basis, NPV is preferred over IRR, since NPV assumes reinvestment of intermediate cash inflows at the cost of capital and does not exhibit the mathematical problems often occurring when calculating IRRs for nonconventional cash flows. In practice the IRR is more commonly used by major firms because it is consistent with the general preference of business people toward rates of return. The two basic approaches for choosing projects under capital rationing are the internal rate of return approach and the net present value approach. Of the two, the net present value approach better achieves the objective of using the budget to generate the highest present value of inflows.

4   **Recognize the basic approaches—sensitivity and scenario analysis, statistical approaches, decision trees, and simulation—for dealing with project risk.** Risk in capital budgeting is concerned with either the chance that a project will prove unacceptable or, more formally, the degree of variability of cash flows. Sensitivity analysis and scenario analysis are two approaches for dealing with project risk to capture the variability of cash inflows and NPVs. Statistical approaches for measuring project risk include the standard deviation and the coefficient of variation. A decision tree relies on estimates of probabilities associated with the outcomes of competing courses of action to determine the expected values used to select a preferred action. Simulation, which results in a probability distribution of project returns, usually requires a computer and allows the decision maker to understand the risk-return trade-offs involved in a proposed investment.

5   **Understand the calculation and practical aspects of the two basic risk-adjustment techniques—certainty equivalents (CEs) and risk-adjusted discount rates (RADRs).** Certainty equivalents (CEs) are used to adjust the risky cash inflows to certain amounts, which are discounted at a risk-free rate in order to find the NPV. The risk-adjusted discount rate (RADR) technique involves a market-based adjustment of the discount rate used to calculate NPV. CEs are the theoretically superior risk-adjustment technique. RADRs are more commonly used in practice because decision makers prefer rates of return and find them easier to estimate and apply.

6 **Describe the difficulties associated with measuring the amount invested in a foreign project, its resulting cash flows, and the associated risk when making long-term investment decisions in an international setting.**   The amount invested by a parent company in its foreign subsidiary is often open to question, although the market value of the investment in the host country is frequently viewed as the relevant "price." Measuring the investment cash flows can be subject to a variety of factors, including local taxes in host countries, host-country regulations that may block the return of the multinational company's cash flow, the usual business and financial risks, risks stemming from inflation and different currency and political actions by host governments, and the application of a local cost of capital.

QUESTIONS

15—1   What is the *average rate of return*? What weaknesses are associated with its use in evaluating a proposed capital expenditure? How can a tie in the rankings be resolved using this technique?

15—2   What is the *payback period*? How is it calculated? What weaknesses are commonly associated with the use of the payback period to evaluate a proposed investment?

15—3   What is the one characteristic that sophisticated capital budgeting techniques have in common that the unsophisticated techniques do not? What are the names commonly used to describe the rate at which cash flows are discounted in order to find present values?

15—4   What is the formula for finding the *net present value (NPV)* of a project with conventional cash flows? What is the acceptance criterion for NPV?

15—5   How is the *profitability index (PI)* calculated? What is its acceptance criterion? Is this measure consistent with the use of NPV? Explain.

15—6   What is the *internal rate of return (IRR)* on an investment? How is it determined? What is its acceptance criterion?

15—7   Do the net present value (NPV), profitability index (PI), and internal rate of return (IRR) always agree with respect to accept-reject decisions? With respect to ranking decisions? Explain.

15—8   What causes conflicts in the ranking of projects using net present value (NPV) and internal rate of return (IRR)? Explain how, on a purely theoretical basis, the assumption concerning the reinvestment of intermediate cash inflows tends to favor the use of net present value (NPV) over internal rate of return (IRR).

15—9   In practice, which of the two major capital budgeting techniques— net present value (NPV) or internal rate of return (IRR)—is preferred? Explain the rationale for this preference in light of the fact that it is inconsistent with theory.

15—10   What is *capital rationing*? Is it unusual for a firm to ration capital? Compare and contrast the *internal rate of return approach* and *net present value approach* to capital rationing. Which is better? Why?

15—11   Define *risk* in terms of the cash inflows from a project. Briefly describe each of the following, and explain how each can be used to deal with project risk:
a. Sensitivity and scenario analysis
b. Statistics
c. Decision trees
d. Simulation

15—12   Describe the underlying logic and basic procedures involved in using (1) *certainty equivalents* (*CEs*) and (2) *risk-adjusted discount rates* (*RADRs*) in the risk-adjustment process.

15—13   Compare and contrast certainty equivalents (CEs) and risk-adjusted discount rates (RADRs) from both a theoretical and a practical point of view. In practice, how are *risk classes* often used to apply RADRs? Explain.

15—14   Indicate how net present value (NPV) can differ if measured from the parent's point of view or from that of the foreign subsidiary when cash flows may be blocked by local authorities.

PROBLEMS

15—1   **(Average Rate of Return)** A firm is considering the acquisition of an asset that requires an initial investment of $10,000 and will provide after-tax profits of $1,000 per year for five years. The firm has a minimum acceptable average rate of return of 25 percent.
a. Calculate the average rate of return.
b. Should the firm accept the project? Why?

15—2   **(Payback Period)** Lee Corporation is considering a capital expenditure that requires an initial investment of $42,000 and returns after-tax cash inflows of $7,000 per year for 10 years. The firm has a maximum acceptable payback period of eight years.
a. Determine the payback period for this project.
b. Should the company accept the project? Why, or why not?

15—3   **(Average Rate of Return, Cash Inflows, and Payback)** Dandy's Sporting Equipment Company is evaluating a new machine. The initial investment of $20,000 will be depreciated under ACRS using a recovery period of five years. The machine will generate profits after taxes of $3,000 per year for each of the five years of its usable life.
a. Determine the average rate of return for the machine, using the most common formula.
b. Determine the after-tax cash inflows associated with the machine for years 1 through 6. (*Note:* Although no profits are given for year 6, the depreciation in year 6 will create cash inflow. See Equation 3.1 on page 69 and Table 3.6 on page 74.)
c. Determine the payback period for the machine.

15—4   **(Payback Comparisons)** Dallas Tool has a five-year maximum acceptable payback period. The firm is considering the purchase of a new machine and must choose between two alternative ones. The first machine requires an initial investment of $14,000 and will generate annual after-tax cash inflows of $3,000 for each of the next seven years. The second machine requires an initial investment of $21,000 and will provide an annual cash inflow after taxes of $4,000 for 20 years.
a. Determine the payback period for each machine.
b. Comment on the acceptability of the machines, assuming they are independent projects.
c. Which machine should the firm accept? Why?
d. Do the machines in this problem illustrate any of the criticisms of using payback? Discuss.

15—5   **(NPV for Varying Required Returns)** Cheryl's Beauty Aids is evaluating a new fragrance-mixing machine. The asset requires an initial investment of $24,000 and will generate after-tax cash inflows of

$5,000 per year for eight years. For each of the required rates of return listed, (1) calculate the net present value (NPV), (2) indicate whether to accept or reject the machine, and (3) explain your decision.
a. The cost of capital is 10 percent.
b. The cost of capital is 12 percent.
c. The cost of capital is 14 percent.

15—6 **(Net Present Value—Independent Projects)** Using a 14 percent cost of capital, calculate the net present value for each of the independent projects given in the following table and indicate whether or not each is acceptable.

	Project A	Project B	Project C	Project D	Project E
Initial investment	$26,000	$500,000	$170,000	$950,000	$80,000
Year			Cash inflows		
1	$4,000	$100,000	$20,000	$230,000	$ 0
2	4,000	120,000	19,000	230,000	0
3	4,000	140,000	18,000	230,000	0
4	4,000	160,000	17,000	230,000	20,000
5	4,000	180,000	16,000	230,000	30,000
6	4,000	200,000	15,000	230,000	0
7	4,000		14,000	230,000	50,000
8	4,000		13,000	230,000	60,000
9	4,000		12,000		70,000
10	4,000		11,000		

15—7 **(Average Rate of Return, Payback, and NPV)** MacAllister Products has three projects under consideration. The cash flows for each of them are given in the following table. The firm has a 16 percent cost of capital.

	Project A	Project B	Project C
Initial investment	$40,000	$40,000	$40,000
Year		Cash inflows	
1	$13,000	$ 7,000	$19,000
2	13,000	10,000	16,000
3	13,000	13,000	13,000
4	13,000	16,000	10,000
5	13,000	19,000	7,000

a. *Using the cash inflows*, calculate the average rate of return for each project. Which project is preferred using this method?
b. Calculate each project's payback period. Which project is preferred using this method?

c. Calculate each project's net present value (NPV). Which project is preferred using this method?

d. Comment on your findings in **a, b,** and **c** and recommend the best project. Explain your recommendation.

15—8   **(NPV and PI)** Calculate the net present value (NPV) and profitability index (PI) for the following 20-year projects. Comment on the acceptability of each. Assume that the firm has an opportunity cost of 14 percent.

a. Initial investment is $10,000; cash inflows are $2,000 per year.

b. Initial investment is $25,000; cash inflows are $3,000 per year.

c. Initial investment is $30,000; cash inflows are $5,000 per year.

15—9   **(NPV, PI, and Maximum Return)** A firm can purchase a fixed asset for a $13,000 initial investment. If the asset generates an annual after-tax cash inflow of $4,000 for four years:

a. Determine the net present value (NPV) of the asset, assuming that the firm has a 10 percent cost of capital. Is the project acceptable?

b. Determine the profitability index (PI) assuming that the firm has a 10 percent cost of capital. Is the project acceptable?

c. Determine the maximum required rate of return (closest whole-percentage rate) the firm can have and still accept the asset. Discuss this finding in light of your responses to **a** and **b**.

15—10   **(NPV and PI—Mutually Exclusive Projects)** Jackson Enterprises is considering the replacement of one of its old drill presses. Three alternative replacement presses are under consideration. The relevant cash flows associated with each are given in the following table. The firm's cost of capital is 15 percent.

	Press A	Press B	Press C
Initial investment	$85,000	$60,000	$130,000
Year	**Cash inflows**		
1	$18,000	$12,000	$50,000
2	18,000	14,000	30,000
3	18,000	16,000	20,000
4	18,000	18,000	20,000
5	18,000	20,000	20,000
6	18,000	25,000	30,000
7	18,000	—	40,000
8	18,000	—	50,000

a. Calculate the net present value (NPV) of each press.

b. Calculate the profitability index (PI) for each press.

c. Using both NPV and PI, evaluate the acceptability of each press. Do the two techniques agree with respect to each press?

d. Rank the presses from best to worst using each technique, NPV and PI. Do the rankings agree? Explain your findings.

15—11   **(Internal Rate of Return)** For each of the following projects, calculate the internal rate of return (IRR), and indicate for each project the maximum cost of capital the firm could have and find the IRR acceptable.

	Project A	Project B	Project C	Project D
Initial investment	$90,000	$490,000	$20,000	$240,000
Year	Cash inflows			
1	$20,000	$150,000	$7,500	$120,000
2	25,000	150,000	7,500	100,000
3	30,000	150,000	7,500	80,000
4	35,000	150,000	7,500	60,000
5	40,000	—	7,500	—

15—12   **(IRR—Mutually Exclusive Projects)** Paulus Corporation is attempting to choose the better of two mutually exclusive projects available for expanding the firm's warehouse capacity. The relevant cash flows for the projects are given. The firm's cost of capital is 15 percent.

	Project X	Project Y
Initial investment	$50,000	$325,000
Year	Cash inflows	
1	$100,000	$140,000
2	120,000	120,000
3	150,000	95,000
4	190,000	70,000
5	250,000	50,000

a. Calculate the IRR to the nearest whole percent for each of the projects.
b. Assess the acceptability of each project based on the IRRs found in **a**.
c. Which project is preferred, based on the IRRs found in **a**?

15—13   **(IRR, Investment Life, and Cash Inflows)** Cincinnati Machine Tool (CMT) accepts projects earning more than the firm's 15 percent cost of capital. CMT is currently considering a 10-year project that provides annual cash inflows of $10,000 and requires an initial investment of $61,450. (*Note:* All amounts are after taxes.)
a. Determine the IRR of this project. It is acceptable?
b. Assuming that the cash inflows continue to be $10,000 per year, how many *additional years* would the flows have to continue to make the project acceptable (i.e., have an IRR of 15 percent)?
c. With the given life, initial investment, and cost of capital, what is the minimum annual cash inflow the firm should accept?

15—14   **(NPV, PI, and IRR)** Lilo Manufacturing Enterprises has prepared the following estimates for a long-term project it is considering. The initial investment will be $18,250, and the project is expected to yield after-tax cash inflows of $4,000 per year for seven years. The firm has a 10 percent cost of capital.

a. Determine the net present value (NPV) of the project.
b. Determing the profitability index (PI) for the project.
c. Determine the internal rate of return (IRR) for the project.
d. Would you recommend that Lilo accept or reject the project? Explain your answer.

15—15   **(ARR, Payback, NPV, PI, and IRR)**   Bruce Read Enterprises is attempting to evaluate the feasibility of investing $95,000 in a piece of equipment having a five-year life. The firm has estimated the *profits after taxes* and *cash inflows* associated with the proposal as follows:

Year	Profits after taxes	Cash inflows
1	$ 5,000	$20,000
2	3,000	25,000
3	9,000	30,000
4	14,000	35,000
5	19,000	40,000

The firm has a 12 percent cost of capital.

a. Calculate the average rate of return (ARR) for the proposed investment.
b. Calculate the payback period for the proposed investment.
c. Calculate the net present value (NPV) for the proposed investment.
d. Calculate the profitability index (PI) for the proposed investment.
e. Calculate the internal rate of return (IRR), rounded to the nearest whole percent, for the proposed investment.
f. Evaluate the acceptability of the proposed investment using NPV, PI, and IRR. What recommendation would you make relative to implementation of the project? Why?

15—16   **(NPV, IRR, and Conflicting Rankings)**   Candor Enterprises is considering two mutually exclusive projects. The firm, which has a 12 percent cost of capital, has estimated its cash flows as shown in the following table.

	Project A	Project B
Initial investment	$130,000	$85,000
Year	Cash inflows	
1	$25,000	$40,000
2	35,000	35,000
3	45,000	30,000
4	50,000	10,000
5	55,000	5,000

a. Calculate the NPV of each project and assess its acceptability.
b. Calculate the IRR of each project and assess its acceptability.
c. Evaluate and discuss the rankings of the two projects based on your findings in **a** and **b**.

15—17   **(All Techniques—Mutually Exclusive Investment Decision)**   Easi Chair Company is attempting to select the best of three mutually exclusive projects. The initial investment and after-tax cash inflows associated with each project are given in the following table.

Cash flows	Project A	Project B	Project C
Initial investment	$60,000	$100,000	$110,000
Cash inflows, years 1–5	$20,000	$ 31,500	$ 32,500

   a. Calculate the average rate of return (ARR) for each project using the *cash inflows* rather than the after-tax profits.
   b. Calculate the payback period for each project.
   c. Calculate the net present value (NPV) of each project, assuming that the firm has a cost of capital equal to 13 percent.
   d. Calculate the internal rate of return (IRR) for each project.
   e. Assuming that the cost of capital is 13 percent, which project would you recommend? Explain why.

15—18   **(All Techniques—Mutually Exclusive Projects)**   The following two projects of equal risk are being considered for the purchase of new equipment. The firm's cost of capital is 13 percent. The cash flows for each project are given in the following table.

	Project A	Project B
Initial investment	$80,000	$50,000
Year	Cash inflows	
1	$15,000	$15,000
2	20,000	15,000
3	25,000	15,000
4	30,000	15,000
5	35,000	15,000

   a. Use the firm's *cash inflows* rather than after-tax profits to calculate the average rate of return (ARR) for each project.
   b. Calculate each project's payback period.
   c. Calculate the net present value (NPV) for each project.
   d. Calculate the profitability index (PI) for each project.
   e. Calculate the internal rate of return (IRR) for each project.
   f. Summarize the preferences dictated by each measure and indicate which project you would recommend if the firm has (1) unlimited funds and (2) capital rationing.

15—19   **(Integrative—Complete Investment Decision)**   Hot Springs Press is considering the purchase of a new printing press. The total installed cost of the press would be $2.2 million. This outlay would be partially offset by the sale of an existing press. The old press has zero book value, cost $1 million 10 years earlier, and can be sold currently for $1.2 million before taxes. As a result of the new press, sales in each of the next five years are expected to increase by $1.6 million, but product costs (excluding depreciation) will represent 50 percent of sales. The new press will be depreciated under ACRS using a five-year recovery period (see Table 3.6 on page 74). The firm is subject to a 40 percent tax rate on both ordinary income and capital gains. Hot Springs Press's cost of capital is 11 percent.

a. Determine the initial investment required by the new press.
b. Determine the operating cash inflows attributable to the new press. (*Note:* Be sure to consider the depreciation in year 6.)
c. Determine the payback period.
d. Determine the net present value (NPV) and the internal rate of return (IRR) related to the proposed new press.
e. Make a recommendation to accept or reject the new press and justify your answer.

 15—20   **(Capital Rationing—IRR and NPV Approaches)** Bromley and Sons is attempting to select the best of a group of independent projects competing for the firm's fixed capital budget of $4.5 million. The firm recognizes that any unused portion of this budget will earn less than its 15 percent cost of capital, thereby resulting in a present value of inflows that is less than the initial investment. The firm has summarized the key data to be used in selecting the best group of projects in the following table.

Project	Initial investment	IRR	Present value of inflows at 15%
A	$5,000,000	17%	$5,400,000
B	800,000	18	1,100,000
C	2,000,000	19	2,300,000
D	1,500,000	16	1,600,000
E	800,000	22	900,000
F	2,500,000	23	3,000,000
G	1,200,000	20	1,300,000

a. Use the *internal rate of return (IRR) approach* to select the best group of projects.
b. Use the *net present value (NPV) approach* to select the best group of projects.
c. Compare, contrast, and discuss your findings in **a** and **b**.
d. Which projects should the firm implement? Why?

15—21   **(Capital Rationing—NPV Approach)** A firm with a 13 percent cost of capital must select the optimal group of projects from those in the table, given its capital budget of $1 million.

Project	Initial investment	NPV at 13% cost of capital
A	$300,000	$ 84,000
B	200,000	10,000
C	100,000	25,000
D	900,000	90,000
E	500,000	70,000
F	100,000	50,000
G	800,000	160,000

a. Calculate the *profitability index (PI)* associated with each project.

b. Select the optimal group of projects using the PIs from **a** to prepare an initial ranking. Keep in mind that unused funds are costly.

15—22   **(Sensitivity Analysis)**   Renaissance Pharmaceutical is in the process of evaluating two mutually exclusive additions to their processing capacity. The firm's financial analysts have developed pessimistic, most likely, and optimistic estimates of the annual cash inflows associated with each project. These estimates are given in the following table.

	Project A	Project B
Initial investment	$8,000	$8,000
Outcome	Annual cash inflows	
Pessimistic	$ 200	$ 900
Most likely	1,000	1,000
Optimistic	1,800	1,100

a. Determine the range of annual cash inflows for each of the two projects.

b. Assume that the firm's cost of capital is 10 percent and that both projects have 20-year lives. Construct a table similar to that above for the NPVs for each project. Include the *range* of NPVs for each project.

c. Do **a** and **b** provide consistent views of the two projects? Explain.

d. Which project would you recommend? Why?

15—23   **(Expected NPV and Risk)**   Using the net present values (NPVs) and associated probabilities for projects X and Y summarized in the table below,

a. Calculate and compare the expected NPVs of the projects.

b. Compare the riskiness of the two projects.

Project X		Project Y	
NPV ($)	Probability	NPV ($)	Probability
−15,000	.01	−20,000	.00
0	.03	−10,000	.02
15,000	.03	0	.04
25,000	.05	10,000	.06
30,000	.15	20,000	.08
35,000	.50	30,000	.15
40,000	.15	40,000	.35
45,000	.05	50,000	.20
55,000	.03	60,000	.05
70,000	.00	70,000	.03
		80,000	.01
		90,000	.01
		100,000	.00

15–24   **(Statistical Evaluation of NPV)** A clothing manufacturer is considering a new line. The following table summarizes the net present values (NPVs) and associated probabilities for various outcomes for the two lines being considered.

| | | Net present value | |
Market outcome	Probability	Line S	Line T
Very poor	.05	−$ 6,000	$ 500
Poor	.15	2,000	4,500
Average	.60	8,500	8,000
Good	.15	15,000	12,500
Excellent	.05	23,000	16,500

a. Calculate the expected NPV for each line.
b. Calculate the range of NPVs for each line.
c. Calculate the standard deviation of NPV, σ_{NPV}, for each line.
d. Calculate the coefficient of variation of NPV, CV_{NPV}, for each line.
e. Using the statistics developed in **a** through **d**, evaluate the risk and return of the lines. Which do you prefer? Why?

15—25   **(Decision Trees)** The Ouija Board-Games Company can bring out one of two new games this season. The *Signs Away* game has a higher initial cost but also has a higher expected return. *Monopolistic Competition*, the alternative, has a slightly lower initial cost but also a lower expected return. The present values and probabilities associated with each game are listed in the following table.

Game	Initial investment	Present value of cash inflows	Probabilities
Signs Away	$140,000		1.00
		$320,000	.30
		220,000	.50
		− 80,000	.20
Monopolistic Competition	$120,000		1.00
		$260,000	.20
		200,000	.45
		− 50,000	.35

a. Construct a decision tree to analyze the games.
b. Which game would you recommend (following a decision-tree analysis)?
c. Has your analysis captured the differences in project risk? Explain.

15—26   **(Simulation)** Wales Castings has compiled the following information on a capital expenditure proposal:
(1) The projected cash *inflows* are normally distributed with a mean of $36,000 and a standard deviation of $9,000.

(2) The projected cash *outflows* are normally distributed with a mean of $30,000 and a standard deviation of $6,000.

(3) The firm has an 11 percent cost of capital.

(4) The probability distributions of cash inflows and cash outflows are not expected to change over the project's 10-year life.

a. Describe how the preceding data could be used to develop a simulation model for finding the net present value of the project.

b. Discuss the advantages of using a simulation to evaluate the proposed project.

15—27 **(Certainty Equivalents—Accept-Reject Decision)** Pleasantville Ball Valve has constructed a table, shown below, that gives expected cash inflows and certainty equivalent factors for these cash inflows. These measures are for a new machine that lasts five years and requires an initial investment of $95,000. The firm has a 15 percent cost of capital, and the risk-free rate is 10 percent.

Year	Cash inflows	Certainty equivalent factors
1	$35,000	1.0
2	35,000	.8
3	35,000	.6
4	35,000	.6
5	35,000	.2

a. What is the net present value (unadjusted for risk)?

b. What is the certainty equivalent net present value?

c. Should the firm accept the project? Explain.

d. Management has some doubts about the estimate of the certainty equivalent for year 5. There is some evidence that it may not be any lower than for year 4. What impact might this have on the decision you recommended in **c**? Explain.

15—28 **(Certainty Equivalents—Mutually Exclusive Decision)** JAN Ventures, Inc., is considering investing in either of two mutually exclusive projects, C and D. The firm has a 14 percent cost of capital, and the risk-free rate is currently 9 percent. The initial investment, expected cash inflows, and certainty equivalent factors associated with each of the projects are presented in the following table.

	Project C		Project D	
Initial investment	$40,000		$56,000	
Year	Cash inflows	Certainty equivalent factors	Cash inflows	Certainty equivalent factors
1	$20,000	.90	$20,000	.95
2	16,000	.80	25,000	.90
3	12,000	.60	15,000	.85
4	10,000	.50	20,000	.80
5	10,000	.40	10,000	.80

a. Find the net present value (unadjusted for risk) for each project. Which is preferred using this measure?
b. Find the certainty equivalent net present value for each project. Which is preferred using this risk-adjustment technique?
c. Compare and discuss your findings in **a** and **b**. Which, if either, of the projects would you recommend that the firm accept? Explain.

15—29   **(Risk-Adjusted Discount Rates—Basic)** P. Ladew, Inc., is considering investment in one of three mutually exclusive projects, E, F, and G. The firm's cost of capital is 15 percent, and the risk-free rate, R_F, is 10 percent. The firm has gathered the following basic cash flow and risk index data for each project.

	Project (j)		
	E	**F**	**G**
Initial investment	$15,000	$11,000	$19,000
Year	**Cash inflows**		
1	$6,000	$6,000	$ 4,000
2	6,000	4,000	6,000
3	6,000	5,000	8,000
4	6,000	2,000	12,000
Risk index (RI_j)	1.80	1.00	0.60

a. Find the net present value (NPV) of each project using the firm's cost of capital. Which project is preferred in this situation?
b. The firm uses the following equation to determine the risk-adjusted discount rate, $RADR_j$, for each project j.

$$RADR_j = R_F + [RI_j \times (k - R_F)]$$

where

$$R_F = \text{risk-free rate of return}$$
$$RI_j = \text{risk index for project } j$$
$$k = \text{cost of capital}$$

Substitute each project's risk index into this equation to determine its RADR.
c. Use the RADR for each project to determine its risk-adjusted NPV. Which project is preferable in this situation?
d. Compare and discuss your findings in **a** and **c**. Which project would you recommend that the firm accept?

15—30   **(Integrative—Certainty Equivalents and Risk-Adjusted Discount Rates)** After a careful evaluation of investment alternatives and opportunities, Joely Company has determined the best estimate of the market risk-return function as shown in the following table.

Risk index	Appropriate discount rate
0.0	7.0% (risk-free rate, R_F)
0.2	8.0
0.4	9.0
0.6	10.0
0.8	11.0
1.0	12.0
1.2	13.0
1.4	14.0
1.6	15.0
1.8	16.0
2.0	17.0

The firm is faced with two mutually exclusive projects, A and B. The following are the data the firm has been able to gather about the projects:

	Project A	Project B
Initial investment	$20,000	$30,000
Project life	5 years	5 years
Annual cash inflow	$ 7,000	$10,000
Risk index	0.2	1.4

	Certainty equivalents factors	
Year	Project A	Project B
0	1.00	1.00
1	0.95	0.90
2	0.90	0.80
3	0.90	0.70
4	0.85	0.70
Greater than 4	0.80	0.60

All the firm's cash inflows have already been adjusted for taxes.
a. Evaluate the projects using *certainty equivalents*.
b. Evaluate the projects using *risk-adjusted discount rates*.
c. Discuss your findings in **a** and **b** and explain why the two approaches are alternative techniques for considering risk in capital budgeting.

15—31   **(Risk Classes and RADR)**   Attila Industries is attempting to select the best of three mutually exclusive projects, X, Y, and Z. Though all the projects have five-year lives, they possess differing degrees of risk. Project X is in Class V, the highest-risk class; project Y is in Class II, the below-average-risk class; and project Z is in Class III, the average-risk class. The basic cash flow data for each project and the risk classes and risk-adjusted discount rates (RADRs) used by the firm are given in the following tables.

	Project X	Project Y	Project Z
Initial investment	$180,000	$235,000	$310,000
Year		**Cash inflows**	
1	$80,000	$50,000	$90,000
2	70,000	60,000	90,000
3	60,000	70,000	90,000
4	60,000	80,000	90,000
5	60,000	90,000	90,000

Risk Classes and RADRs

Risk class	Description	Risk-adjusted discount rate, *RADR*
I	Lowest risk	10%
II	Below-average risk	13
III	Average risk	15
IV	Above-average risk	19
V	Highest risk	22

a. Find the risk-adjusted NPV for each project.
b. Which, if any, project would you recommend the firm undertake?

CASE

Norwich Tool's Lathe Investment Decision

Norwich Tool, a large machine shop, is considering replacing one of its lathes with either of two new lathes—lathe A or lathe B. Lathe A is a highly automated, computer-controlled lathe; lathe B is a less expensive lathe that uses standard technology. In order to analyze these alternatives, Mario Jackson, a financial analyst, prepared estimates of the initial investment, profits after taxes, and incremental (relevant) cash inflows associated with each lathe. These are summarized in the following table.

	Lathe A		Lathe B	
Initial investment	$660,000		$360,000	
Year	Profits after taxes	Cash inflows	Profits after taxes	Cash inflows
1	$ 5,000	$128,000	$ 5,000	$ 88,000
2	10,000	182,000	15,000	120,000
3	20,000	166,000	10,000	96,000
4	65,000	168,000	20,000	86,000
5	210,000	450,000	100,000	207,000

Note that Mario planned to analyze both lathes over a five-year period. At the end of that time the lathe would be sold, thus accounting for the large fifth-year cash inflow.

One of Mario's major dilemmas centered on the risk of the two lathes. He felt that although the two lathes had similar risk, lathe A had a much higher chance of breakdown and repair due to its sophisticated and not fully proven solid state electronic technology. Because he was unable to effectively quantify this possibility, Mario decided to apply the firm's 13 percent cost of capital when analyzing the lathes. Norwich Tool required all projects to earn a minimum average rate of return of 15 percent and to have a maximum payback period of 4.0 years.

Required

   a. Use the following unsophisticated capital budgeting techniques to assess the acceptability and relative ranking of each lathe.
   (1) Average rate of return
   (2) Payback period

   b. Assuming equal risk, use the following sophisticated capital budgeting techniques to assess the acceptability and relative ranking of each lathe.
   (1) Net present value (NPV)
   (2) Profitability index (PI)
   (3) Internal rate of return (IRR)

   c. Summarize the preferences indicated by the techniques used in a and b and indicate which lathe you would recommend, if either, if the firm has (1) unlimited funds or (2) capital rationing.

   d. Repeat part b assuming that Mario decided that, due to its greater risk, lathe A's cash inflows should be evaluated using a 15 percent cost of capital.

   e. What, if any, effect does recognition of lathe A's greater risk in d have on your recommendation in c?

CHAPTER 16

CAPITAL STRUCTURE AND DIVIDEND POLICY

CHAPTER OBJECTIVES

After studying this chapter, you should be able to:

1 Understand capital structure, including the basic types of capital, external assessment of capital structure, and the concept of an optimal capital structure.

2 Discuss the graphic presentation, risk considerations, and basic shortcoming of using the EBIT–EPS approach to compare capital structures.

3 Describe cash dividend payment procedures, dividend reinvestment plans, the relevance of dividend policy and related arguments, and the key factors that affect dividend policy.

4 Describe and evaluate the three basic types of dividend policies—constant-payout-ratio, regular, and low-regular-and-extra.

5 Contrast the basic features, objectives, and procedures for paying other forms of dividends, including stock dividends, stock splits, and stock repurchases.

6 Explain how international capital markets, international diversification, and country factors cause the capital structures of multinational companies to differ from those of purely domestic firms.

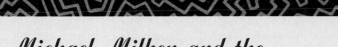

Michael Milken and the Art of Zen

((. . . knowing how far you can go, and stopping there, requires wisdom.))

Zen, the sect of Buddhism that aims at enlightenment by direct intuition through meditation, teaches that going far requires skill and courage. It also teaches that knowing how far you can go, and stopping there, requires wisdom. If only Michael Milken, the junk bond king of the 1980s, had heard this inner call, he might not be facing ten years in prison *and* $600 million dollars in fines.

Despite all of the press coverage of the financial falls of E. F. Hutton, Charles Keating, Alan Bond, Saatchi, and others, they are all outweighed by the Drexel Burnham Lambert catastrophe. Drexel's fall resulted from its efforts to clean up the junk bond mess left by Milken. The junk bond collapse, in turn, has its roots in some brilliant original ideas that were displaced by greed.

A key activity of financial managers is that of managing the firm's capital structure, the mix of long-term debt and equity. Debt can provide resources that are not available through equity financing alone. The steps whereby Milken may have conceived of the leap from genuine financing to takeover financing were:

1. Companies were being denied debt financing because size ruled out their "investment grade" status, even though they were able to make the required interest payments.
2. The investment grade barrier could be crossed by offering higher-than-usual interest rates.
3. High-yield junk bonds, which historically had low default rates, were the very thing that investment institutions needed to attract savers.
4. The same high-yielding bonds could do even more for corporate raiders, by securing debt on the basis of assets possessed if the deal succeeded.
5. Merchant bankers could pocket extravagant fees for selling this debt to the public.

Drexel Burnham suddenly had more ill-secured debt than it could sell. High interest rates gave way to arm twisting and more. With the collapse of Drexel Burnham, reason regained its domination, lending support to the Zen axiom, "Let no opportunity pass by, but think twice before acting."

C apital structure and dividend policy are important long-term financial decision areas. Both are deeply rooted in financial theory and play an important role in maximizing shareholder wealth. The firm's **capital structure**—the mix of long-term debt and equity maintained by the firm—can significantly affect its value by affecting risk and return. Poor capital structure decisions can result in a high cost of capital, thereby making more investments unacceptable. Effective decisions can lower the cost of capital, resulting in more acceptable investments that will add to owners' wealth.

As noted in Chapter 12, expected cash dividends are the key return variable from which owners and investors determine share price. In each period, any earnings that remain after satisfying obligations to creditors, the government, and preferred stockholders can be retained by the firm, paid out as cash dividends, or divided between retained earnings and cash dividends. Retained earnings can be invested in assets that will help the firm expand or maintain its present rate of growth. On the other hand, the owners of the firm generally desire some current return on their equity investment—the payment of a cash dividend, which reduces the amount of earnings retained. Here we first discuss the important aspects of capital structure and then consider dividend policy.

capital structure The mix of long-term debt and equity maintained by the firm.

THE FIRM'S CAPITAL STRUCTURE

Capital structure is one of the most complex areas of financial decision making due to its interrelationship with other financial decision variables. In order to achieve the firm's goal of owner wealth maximization, the financial manager must be able to assess the firm's capital structure and understand its relationship to risk, return, and value. This and the following two sections link together the concepts presented in Chapters 4, 5, 12, and 13.

Types of Capital

capital The long-term funds of the firm; all items on the right-hand side of the firm's balance sheet, excluding current liabilities.

The term **capital** denotes the long-term funds of the firm. All of the items on the right-hand side of the firm's balance sheet, excluding current liabilities, are sources of capital. The simplified balance sheet below illustrates the basic breakdown of total capital into its two components—debt capital and equity capital.

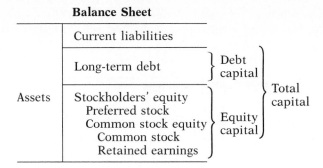

Debt capital includes all of the firm's long-term borrowing. The various types and characteristics of long-term debt will be discussed in detail in Chapter 19. Remember from Chapter 13 that the cost of debt is less than the cost of other forms of financing. The relative inexpensiveness of debt capital is due to the fact that the lenders take the least risk of any long-term contributors of capital. Their risk is less than that of others because (1) they have a higher priority of claim against any earnings or assets available for payment, (2) they have a far stronger legal pressure against the company to make payment than do preferred or common stockholders, and (3) the tax-deductibility of interest payments lowers the debt cost to the firm substantially.

debt capital All long-term borrowing done by the firm.

Equity capital consists of the long-term funds provided by the firm's owners, the stockholders. Unlike borrowed funds that must be repaid at a specified future date, equity capital is expected to remain in the firm for an indefinite period of time. The two basic sources of equity capital are (1) preferred stock and (2) common stock equity, which includes common stock and retained earnings. As demonstrated in Chapter 13, common stock is typically the most expensive form of equity, followed by retained earnings and preferred stock, respectively. The characteristics of retained earnings are briefly discussed as part of the dividend presentation later in this chapter; preferred and common stock are discussed further in Chapter 20.

equity capital The long-term funds provided by the firm's owners, the stockholders.

Our concern here is the relationship between debt and equity capital. Key differences between these two types of capital are summarized in Table 16.1. It should be clear that due to its secondary position rela-

Table 16.1   **Key Differences between Debt and Equity Capital**

Characteristic	Type of capital	
	Debt	Equity
Voice in management[a]	No	Yes
Claims on income and assets	Senior to equity	Subordinate to debt
Maturity	Stated	None
Tax treatment	Interest deduction	No deduction

[a]In default, debtholders and preferred stockholders *may* receive a voice in management; otherwise, only common stockholders have voting rights.

tive to debt, suppliers of equity capital take greater risk and therefore must be compensated with higher expected returns than suppliers of debt capital.

External Assessment of Capital Structure

In Chapter 5 we saw that *financial leverage* results from the use of fixed-payment financing, such as debt and preferred stock, to magnify return and risk. Debt ratios, which measure the firm's degree of financial leverage, were presented in Chapter 4. A direct measure of the degree of indebtedness is the *debt ratio:* The higher this ratio, the greater the firm's financial leverage. The measures of the firm's ability to meet fixed payments associated with debt include the *times interest earned ratio* and the *fixed-payment coverage ratio.* These ratios provide indirect information on leverage. The smaller these ratios, the less able the firm is to meet payments as they come due. In general, low debt-payment ratios are associated with high degrees of financial leverage. The more risk a firm is willing to take, the greater will be its financial leverage. In theory, the firm should maintain financial leverage consistent with a capital structure that maximizes owners' wealth.

An acceptable degree of financial leverage for one industry or line of business can be highly risky in another, due to differing operating characteristics between industries or lines of business. Table 16.2 presents the debt and times interest earned ratios for selected industries and lines of business. Significant industry differences can be seen in these data. For example, the debt ratio for electronic computer manufacturers is 55.0 percent, whereas for auto retailers it is 79.2 percent. Of course, differences in debt positions are also likely to exist *within* an industry or line of business.

THE OPTIMAL CAPITAL STRUCTURE

A firm's capital structure is closely related to its cost of capital. Many debates over whether an "optimal" capital structure exists are found in the financial literature. This controversy began in the late 1950s and is not yet resolved. Those who believe that an optimal capital structure exists follow the **traditional approach.** Those who believe such a structure does *not* exist are supporters of the **M and M approach,** named for its initial proponents, Franco Modigliani and Merton H. Miller.

To provide some insight into what is meant by an optimal capital structure, we will examine the basic financial relationships associated with the traditional approach.[1] It is generally believed that *the value of*

traditional approach
The theory that an optimal capital structure exists, and that the value of the firm is maximized when the cost of capital is minimized.

M and M approach
Named for its initial proponents, Modigliani and Miller, the theory that an optimal capital structure does *not* exist.

---

[1]You may wonder why attention is given only to the traditional approach and not to the Modigliani and Miller approach. The chief reason is that the M and M model is algebraically somewhat rigorous, and it is more important at this level to become familiar with the key concepts that affect managerial decisions than to delve deeply into the theory of finance. Business people tend to believe the traditional as opposed to the M and M approach.

Table 16.2   Debt Ratios for Selected Industries
and Lines of Business (Fiscal Years Ended 6/30/89 through 3/31/90)

Industry or line of business	Debt ratio	Times interest earned ratio
Manufacturing industries		
Books: publishing and printing	65.3%	1.8 X
Dairy products	63.1	2.5
Electronic computers	55.0	3.7
Fertilizers	59.1	2.5
Iron and steel foundries	65.2	2.5
Jewelry and precious metals	60.8	2.1
Motor vehicles	68.4	1.9
Wines, distilled liquors, and liqueurs	64.1	1.9
Women's dresses	54.4	3.9
Wholesaling industries		
Furniture	67.1	2.3
General groceries	68.8	2.3
Hardware and paints	60.1	2.7
Men's and boys' clothing	67.2	2.3
Petroleum and petroleum products	65.6	2.2
Retailing industries		
Autos, new and used	79.2	1.3
Department stores	57.6	1.7
Radio, television, and consumer electronics	69.6	2.5
Restaurants	71.2	2.0
Shoes	63.2	2.0
Service industries		
Accounting, auditing, and bookkeeping	53.5	4.8
Advertising agencies	74.7	3.6
Auto repair—general	62.8	2.4
Insurance agents and brokers	81.4	2.4
Physicians	68.0	2.0
Travel agencies	67.4	5.6

Source: *RMA Annual Statement Studies, 1990* (fiscal years ended 6/30/89 through 3/31/90)
(Philadelphia: Robert Morris Associates, 1990). Copyright © 1990 by Robert Morris Associates.

the firm is maximized when the cost of capital is minimized. Using a modification of the simple zero growth valuation model (see Equation 12.11 in Chapter 12), we can define the value of the firm, *V*, by Equation 16.1, where EBIT equals earnings before interest and taxes, *T* is the tax rate, EBIT $\times$ (1 − *T*) represents the after-tax operating earnings available to debt and equity holders, and k_a is the weighted average cost of capital:

Equation 16.1
Formula for the value
of the firm

$$V = \frac{\text{EBIT} \times (1 - T)}{k_a}$$

Clearly, if we assume that EBIT is constant, the value of the firm, V, is maximized by minimizing the weighted average cost of capital, k_a.

Cost Functions

Figure 16.1(a) plots three cost functions—the after-tax cost of debt, k_i; the cost of equity, k_s; and the weighted average cost of capital, k_a—as a function of financial leverage measured by the debt ratio (debt-to-total assets). The *cost of debt*, k_i, remains low due to the tax subsidy (interest is tax-deductible) but slowly increases with increasing leverage in order to compensate lenders for increasing risk. The *cost of equity*, k_s, is above the cost of debt. It increases with increasing financial leverage, but generally more rapidly than the cost of debt. The increase in the cost of equity occurs because, in order to compensate for the higher degree of financial risk, the stockholders require a higher return as leverage increases.

The *weighted average cost of capital*, k_a, results from a weighted average of the firm's debt and equity capital. At a debt ratio of zero, the firm is 100 percent equity-financed. As debt is substituted for equity and as the debt ratio increases, the weighted average cost of capital declines because the debt cost is less than the equity cost ($k_i < k_s$). As the debt ratio continues to increase, the increased debt and equity costs eventually cause the weighted average cost of capital to rise [after point M in Figure 16.1(a)]. This behavior results in a U-shaped, or saucer-shaped, weighted average cost of capital function, k_a.

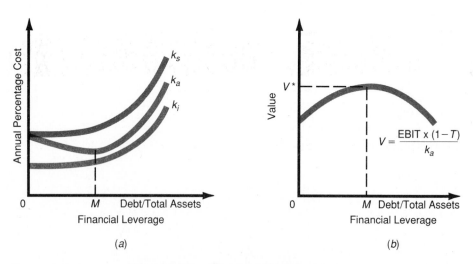

(a)   (b)

Figure 16.1   Capital Costs and the Optimal Capital Structure
(a) As financial leverage increases, the cost of debt, k_i, remains constant and then rises, while the cost of equity, k_s, always rises. The resulting weighted average cost of capital, k_a, is U-shaped or saucer-shaped causing the optimal capital structure to occur at its minimum, M. (b) At the optimal capital structure, M, the value of the firm is maximized at V^*.

F I N A N C E   I N   A C T I O N

Sharing Risk, Not Control, at R. H. Macy

R. H. Macy, the heavily indebted retailer, received an infusion of $150 million in late 1990. The money was used to buy back some of Macy's high-yield junk bonds that had been issued in the process of a management-led leveraged buyout. As a result of the 1986 buyout, Macy had been financed with $300 million of equity and $3 billion of debt. Although the firm had persistently paid its bills promptly, forecasts of weak sales for the November–December Christmas selling season had led shareholders to worry that Macy would be unable to pay interest on its debt.

The announcement of the cash infusion was timed to give suppliers reason for shipping to the retailer. Bankers had informed apparel makers that they were no longer willing to accept accounts receivable issued by Macy. Hence, the generally small apparel makers would be assuming the risk of shipping goods to Macy. The infusion was designed to indicate that funds would be available for payment of accounts receivable.

Two thirds of the infusion, or $100 million, was committed by Macy's four largest shareholders, including General Electric's General Capital Corporation. Sounding upbeat, Macy Chairman Edward Finkelstein indicated that the injection illustrated the commitment of Macy's largest shareholders. However, he left it to a spokesman to announce that Macy's management would not be buying any of the new equity. As a result of the transfer of the issues to current shareholders, management's share of the firm declined by about one third. Nonetheless, Macy management would still control the company's board of directors by being able to select members to 9 of 15 seats.

Source: George Anders, "Macy holders' injection of $100 million," *The Wall Street Journal*, November 2, 1990, pp. A3 & B2.

A Graphic View of the Optimal Structure

Since the maximization of value, V, is achieved when the overall cost of capital, k_a, is at a minimum (see Equation 16.1), the **optimal capital structure** is therefore that at which the weighted average cost of capital, k_a, is minimized. In Figure 16.1(*a*) the point M represents the minimum weighted average cost of capital—the point of optimal financial leverage and hence of optimal capital structure for the firm. As shown in Figure 16.1(*b*), at that point, M, the value of the firm is maximized at V^*. Generally, the lower the firm's weighted average cost of capital, the

optimal capital structure The capital structure at which the weighted average cost of capital is minimized, thereby maximizing the firm's value.

greater the difference between the return on a project and this cost, and therefore the greater the owners' return. These increased returns of course contribute to an increase in the firm's value.

THE EBIT–EPS APPROACH TO CAPITAL STRUCTURE

EBIT–EPS approach
An approach for selecting the capital structure that maximizes earnings per share (EPS) over the expected range of earnings before interest and taxes (EBIT).

The graphic comparison of financing plans on a set of EBIT–EPS axes was briefly described in Chapter 5. Here, a similar EBIT–EPS approach is used to evaluate alternative capital structures. The **EBIT–EPS approach** to capital structure involves selecting the capital structure that maximizes earnings per share (EPS) over the expected range of earnings before interest and taxes (EBIT). Here the main emphasis is on the effects of various capital structures on *owners' returns*. Since one of the key variables affecting the market value of the firm's shares is its earnings, EPS can be conveniently used to analyze alternative capital structures.

Presenting a Financing Plan Graphically

To analyze the effects of a firm's capital structure on the owners' returns, we consider the relationship between earnings before interest and taxes (EBIT) and earnings per share (EPS). A constant level of EBIT is assumed in order to isolate the impact on returns of the financing costs associated with alternative capital structures (financing plans). EPS is used to measure the owners' returns, which are expected to be closely related to share price.

The Data Required
To graph a financing plan, we need to know at least two EBIT–EPS coordinates. The approach for obtaining coordinates can be illustrated by the following example.

EXAMPLE   The current capital structure of JSG Company, a soft drink manufacturer, is as shown:

Current capital structure	
Long-term debt	$ 0
Common stock equity (25,000 shares @ $20)	500,000
Total capital (assets)	$500,000

Note that JSG's capital structure currently contains only common stock equity; the firm has no debt or preferred stock. If for convenience we assume the firm has no current liabilities, its debt ratio (total liabilities ÷ total assets) is currently 0 percent ($0 ÷ $500,000); it therefore has *zero* financial leverage. Assume the firm is in the 40 percent tax bracket.

EBIT–EPS coordinates for JSG's current capital structure can be found using the technique presented in Chapter 5. Since the EBIT–EPS graph is a straight line, any two EBIT values can be used to find coordinates. Here we arbitrarily use values of $100,000 and $200,000.

EBIT (assumed)	$100,000	$200,000
− Interest (rate × $0 debt)	0	0
Earnings before taxes	$100,000	$200,000
− Taxes (.40)	40,000	80,000
Earnings after taxes	$ 60,000	$120,000
EPS	$\dfrac{\$60,000}{25,000 \text{ sh.}} = \$2.40$	$\dfrac{\$120,000}{25,000 \text{ sh.}} = \$4.80$

The two EBIT–EPS coordinates resulting from these calculations are (1) $100,000 EBIT and $2.40 EPS and (2) $200,000 EBIT and $4.80 EPS.

Plotting the Data

The two sets of EBIT–EPS coordinates developed for JSG Company's current zero leverage (debt ratio = 0 percent) situation can be plotted on a set of EBIT–EPS axes, as shown in Figure 16.2. Since our concern is

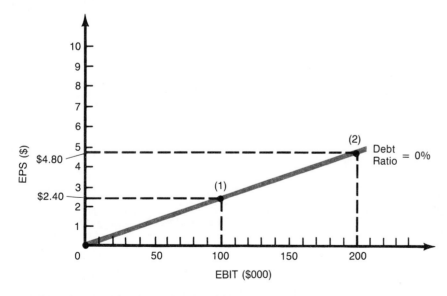

Figure 16.2 Graphic Presentation of JSG Company's Zero Leverage Financing Plan
Plotting the two coordinates (1) $100,000 EBIT and $2.40 EPS and (2) $200,000 EBIT and $4.80 EPS on the EBIT–EPS axes results in a straight line representing JSG Company's zero leverage (debt ratio = 0 percent) financing plan. The figure shows the level of EPS for each level of EBIT.

only with positive levels of EPS, the graph has not been extended below the *x*-axis. The figure shows the level of EPS expected for each level of EBIT.

Comparing Alternative Capital Structures

The graphic display of financing plans (similar to Figure 16.2) can be used to compare alternative capital structures. The following example illustrates this procedure.

EXAMPLE JSG Company, whose current zero leverage capital structure was described in the preceding example, is contemplating shifting its capital structure to either of two leveraged positions. In order to maintain its $500,000 of total capital, JSG's capital structure will be shifted to greater leverage by issuing debt and using the proceeds to retire an equivalent amount of common stock. The two alternative capital structures result in debt ratios of 30 percent and 60 percent, respectively. The basic information on the current and two alternative capital structures is summarized in Table 16.3.

Using the data in Table 16.3, we can calculate the coordinates needed to plot the 30 percent and 60 percent debt capital structures. For convenience, using the same $100,000 and $200,000 EBIT values used earlier to plot the current capital structure, we get the following:

	Capital structure			
	30% Debt		**60% Debt**	
EBIT (assumed)	$100,000	$200,000	$100,000	$200,000
− Interest (Table 16.3)	15,000	15,000	49,500	49,500
Earnings before taxes	$ 85,000	$185,000	$ 50,500	$150,500
− Taxes (.40)	34,000	74,000	20,200	60,200
Earnings after taxes	$ 51,000	$111,000	$ 30,300	$ 90,300
EPS	$\frac{\$51,000}{17,500 \text{ sh.}} = \$2.91$	$\frac{\$111,000}{17,500 \text{ sh.}} = \$6.34$	$\frac{\$30,300}{10,000 \text{ sh.}} = \$3.03$	$\frac{\$90,300}{10,000 \text{ sh.}} = \$9.03$

The two sets of EBIT–EPS coordinates developed above, along with those developed earlier for the current zero-leverage capital structure, are summarized in Table 16.4. They are used to plot the 30 percent and 60 percent capital structures (along with the 0 percent structure) on the EBIT–EPS axes in Figure 16.3. An analysis of the figure

Table 16.3   **Basic Information on JSG Company's Current and Alternative Capital Structures**

Capital structure debt ratio (1)	Total assets[a] (2)	Debt [(1) × (2)] (3)	Equity [(2) − (3)] (4)	Interest rate on debt[b] (5)	Annual interest [(3) × (5)] (6)	Shares of common stock outstanding [(4) ÷ $20][c] (7)
0% (current)	$500,000	$ 0	$500,000	0 %	$ 0	25,000
30	500,000	150,000	350,000	10	15,000	17,500
60	500,000	300,000	200,000	16.5	49,500	10,000

[a]Because for convenience the firm is assumed to have no current liabilities, total assets equals total capital of $500,000.
[b]The interest rate on all debt increases with increases in the debt ratio due to the greater leverage and risk associated with higher debt ratios.
[c]The $20 value represents the book value of common stock equity.

shows that over certain ranges of EBIT, each capital structure reflects superiority over the others in terms of maximizing EPS. The zero-leverage capital structure (debt ratio = 0 percent) would be superior to either of the other capital structures for levels of EBIT between $0 and $50,000. Between $50,000 and $95,500 of EBIT, the capital structure associated with a debt ratio of 30 percent would be preferred. At a level of EBIT in excess of $95,500 the capital structure associated with a debt ratio of 60 percent would provide the highest earnings per share.[2]

Considering Risk in EBIT–EPS Analysis

When interpreting EBIT–EPS analysis, the financial analyst must consider the risk of each capital structure alternative. Graphically, the risk

Table 16.4   **EBIT–EPS Coordinates for JSG Company's Selected Capital Structures**

Capital structure debt ratio	EBIT	
	$100,000	$200,000
	Earnings per share (EPS)	
0%	$2.40	$4.80
30	2.91	6.34
60	3.03	9.03

---

[2]An algebraic technique can be used to find the *indifference points* between the capital structure alternatives. Due to its relative complexity, this technique is not presented. Instead, emphasis here is given to the visual estimation of these points from the graph.

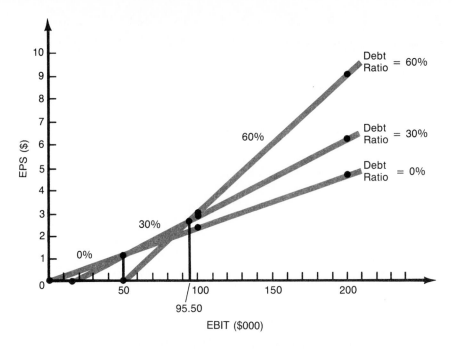

Figure 16.3 A Graphic Comparison of Selected Capital Structures for JSG Company
The zero leverage capital structure (debt ratio = 0 percent) maximizes
EPS when EBIT is between $0 and $50,000. Between $50,000 and $95,500
of EBIT, the capital structure with the 30 percent debt ratio is preferred.
For EBIT in excess of $95,500, the capital structure with the 60 percent
debt ratio maximizes EPS.

of each capital structure can be viewed in light of the *financial breakeven
point* (EBIT-axis intercept) and the *degree of financial leverage* reflected
in the slope of the capital structure line. The higher the financial breakeven point and the steeper the slope of the capital structure line, the
greater the financial risk. Further assessment of risk can be performed
using ratios. With increased financial leverage, as measured using the
debt ratio, we would expect a corresponding decline in the firm's ability
to make scheduled interest payments, as measured using the times interest earned ratio.

EXAMPLE   Reviewing the three capital structures plotted for JSG
Company in Figure 16.3, we can see that as the debt ratio
increases, so does the financial risk of each alternative. Both
the financial breakeven point and the slope of the capital
structure lines increase with increasing debt ratios. If we
use the $100,000 EBIT value, the times interest earned ratio
(EBIT ÷ interest) for the zero-leverage capital structure is
infinity ($100,000 ÷ $0). For the 30 percent debt case it is
6.67 ($100,000 ÷ $15,000). For the 60 percent debt case it is
2.02 ($100,000 ÷ $49,500). Since lower times interest earned
ratios reflect higher risk, these ratios support the earlier

conclusion that the risk of the capital structures increases with increasing financial leverage. The capital structure for a debt ratio of 60 percent is more risky than that for a debt ratio of 30 percent, which in turn is more risky than the capital structure for a debt ratio of 0 percent.

Basic Shortcoming of EBIT–EPS Analysis

The most important point to recognize when using EBIT–EPS analysis is that this technique tends to concentrate on *maximizing earnings rather than maximizing owners' wealth.* Although there may be a positive relationship between these two objectives, the use of an EPS-maximizing approach ignores risk. Because risk increases with increases in financial leverage, the maximization of EPS does *not* assure owners' wealth maximization. To select the best capital structure, the financial manager must integrate both return (EPS) and risk (via the required return, k_s) into a valuation framework consistent with the capital structure theory presented earlier. Although more sophisticated approaches that consider both return and risk are available, their complexity puts them beyond the scope of this basic text.

DIVIDEND FUNDAMENTALS

Dividend policy, like capital structure, can significantly affect the firm's share price. Dividends represent a source of cash flow to stockholders and provide them with information about the firm's current and future performance. Because **retained earnings**—earnings not distributed as dividends—are a form of *internal* financing, the dividend decision can significantly affect the firm's *external* financing requirements. In other words, if the firm needs financing, the larger the cash dividend paid, the greater the amount of financing that must be raised externally. Such financing would be obtained through borrowing or through the sale of preferred or common stock. To provide an understanding of the fundamentals of dividend policy, we discuss the procedures for paying cash dividends, dividend reinvestment plans, the relevance of dividend policy, and the key factors affecting dividend policy.

retained earnings Earnings not distributed as dividends; a form of *internal* financing.

Cash Dividend Payment Procedures

The payment of cash dividends to corporate stockholders is decided by the firm's board of directors. The directors normally hold a quarterly or semiannual dividend meeting at which they evaluate the past period's financial performance and future outlook. They then determine whether and in what amount dividends should be paid. The payment date of the cash dividend, if one is declared, must also be established.

Amount of Dividends

Whether dividends should be paid and, if they are, how large they should be are important decisions that depend largely on the firm's dividend policy. Most firms pay some cash dividends each period. The amount is generally fixed, although significant increases or decreases in earnings may justify changing it. Most firms have a set policy with respect to the amount of the periodic dividend, but the firm's directors can change this amount at the dividend meeting.

Relevant Dates

If the directors of the firm declare a dividend, they will also indicate the record and payment dates associated with the dividend. Typically, the directors issue a statement indicating their dividend decision, the record date, and the payment date. This statement is generally quoted in *The Wall Street Journal*, *Barron's*, and other financial news media.

date of record (dividends) The date, set by the firm's directors, on which all persons whose names are recorded as stockholders will at a specified future time receive a declared dividend.

holders of record Owners of the firm's shares on the *date of record*.

ex dividend Period beginning four *business days* prior to the date of record during which a stock will be sold without the right to receive the current dividend.

payment date The actual date on which the firm will mail the dividend payment to the holders of record.

Record Date   All persons whose names are recorded as stockholders on the **date of record,** which is set by the directors, will at a specified future time receive a declared dividend. These stockholders are often referred to as **holders of record.** Due to the time needed to make bookkeeping entries when a stock is traded, the stock will begin selling **ex dividend** four *business days* prior to the date of record. A simple way to determine the first day on which the stock sells ex dividend is to subtract four from the date of record; if a weekend intervenes, subtract six days. Purchasers of a stock selling ex dividend do not receive the current dividend.

Payment Date   The payment date is also set by the directors. It is generally set a few weeks after the record date. The **payment date** is the actual date on which the firm will mail the dividend payment to the holders of record. An example will clarify the various dates and accounting entries.

EXAMPLE   At the quarterly dividend meeting of Junot Company, a distributor of office products, held June 10, the directors declared an $.80 per share cash dividend for holders of record on Monday, July 1. The firm had 100,000 shares of common stock outstanding. The payment date for the dividend was August 1. Before the dividend was declared, the key accounts of the firm were as follows:

Cash	$200,000	Dividends payable	$ 0
		Retained earnings	1,000,000

When the dividend was announced by the directors, $80,000 of the retained earnings ($.80 per share × 100,000 shares) was transferred to the dividends payable account. The key accounts thus became:

Cash	$200,000	Dividends payable	$ 80,000
		Retained earnings	920,000

Junot Company's stock sold ex dividend for four *business days* prior to the date of record, which was June 25. This date was found by subtracting six days (since a weekend intervened) from the July 1 date of record. Purchasers of Junot's stock on June 24 or earlier received the rights to the dividends; those purchasing the stock on or after June 25 did not. When the August 1 payment date arrived, the firm mailed dividend checks to the holders of record as of July 1. This produced the following balances in the key accounts of the firm:

Cash	$120,000	Dividends payable	$ 0
		Retained earnings	920,000

The net effect of declaration and payment of the dividend was to reduce the firm's total assets (and stockholders' equity) by $80,000.

Dividend Reinvestment Plans

A growing number of firms offer **dividend reinvestment plans.** These plans enable stockholders to use dividends to acquire shares—even fractional shares—at little or no transaction (brokerage) cost. Especially popular between 1982 and 1985 were the plans of public utilities, such as electric companies, telephone companies, and natural gas distributors, because participating shareholders received a special tax break that ended December 31, 1985. Today, cash dividends from all plans (or the value of the stocks received through a dividend reinvestment plan) are taxed as ordinary income. In addition, when the acquired shares are sold, if the proceeds are in excess of the original purchase price, the capital gain will also be taxed as ordinary income.

Dividend reinvestment plans can be handled by a company in either of two ways. Both allow the stockholder to elect to have dividends reinvested in the firm's shares. In one approach, a third-party trustee is paid a fee to buy the firm's *outstanding shares* in the open market on behalf of the shareholders who wish to reinvest their dividends. This type of plan benefits participating shareholders; it allows them to use their dividends to purchase shares generally at a lower transaction cost than they would otherwise pay. The second approach involves buying *newly issued shares* directly from the firm without paying any transaction costs. This approach allows the firm to raise new capital while permitting owners to reinvest their dividends, frequently at about 5 percent below the current market price. Clearly, the existence of dividend reinvestment plans may enhance the appeal of a firm's shares.

dividend reinvestment plans Plans that enable stockholders to use dividends to acquire full or fractional shares at little or no transaction (brokerage) cost.

The Relevance of Dividend Policy

Over the past 30 or so years the results of a great deal of research concerning dividend policy have been reported in the financial literature. Although this research has provided some interesting arguments and insights about dividend policy, the key questions have yet to be resolved—Does dividend policy matter? What effect does dividend policy have on share price? Is there a model that can be used to evaluate alternative dividend policies in view of share value? Here we begin by describing the residual theory of dividends. It is used as a backdrop for discussion of the key arguments in support of dividend irrelevance and then those in support of dividend relevance.

The Residual Theory of Dividends

residual theory of dividends A theory that the dividend paid by a firm should be the amount left over after all acceptable investment opportunities have been undertaken.

One school of thought—the **residual theory of dividends**—suggests that the dividend paid by a firm should be viewed as a *residual*—the amount left over after all acceptable investment opportunities have been undertaken. According to this approach, as long as the firm's equity need is in excess of the amount of retained earnings, no cash dividend would be paid. If an excess of retained earnings exists, the residual amount would then be distributed as a cash dividend. This view of dividends tends to suggest that the required return of investors, k_s, is *not* influenced by the firm's dividend policy—a premise that in turn suggests that dividend policy is irrelevant.

Dividend Irrelevance Arguments

The residual theory of dividends suggests that dividends are irrelevant—that they represent an earnings residual rather than an active decision variable that affects the firm's value. The major advocates of this view are Franco Modigliani and Merton H. Miller (commonly referred to as M and M). They argue that the firm's value is determined solely by the earning power and risk of its assets (investments) and that the manner in which it splits its earnings stream between dividends and internally retained (and reinvested) funds does not affect this value.

informational content The information provided by the dividends of a firm with respect to future earnings, which causes owners to bid up (or down) the price of the firm's stock.

However, some studies have shown that large dividend changes affect share price in the same direction—increases in dividends result in increased share price, and vice versa. In response, M and M argue that these effects are attributable not to the dividend itself but rather to the **informational content** of dividends with respect to future earnings. As a result, an increase in dividends would cause investors to bid up the share price, and a decrease in dividends would cause a decrease in share price.

clientele effect The argument that a firm will attract shareholders whose preferences with respect to the payment and stability of dividends correspond to the payment pattern and stability of the firm itself.

M and M further argue that a **clientele effect** exists: A firm will attract shareholders whose preferences with respect to the payment and stability of dividends correspond to the payment pattern and stability of the firm itself. In other words, investors desiring stable and predictable dividends as a source of income would hold the stock of firms that pay about the same dividend amount each period; investors preferring to earn capital gains would be more attracted to growing firms that reinvest a large portion of their earnings, which results in a fairly unstable pattern of dividends. Since the shareholders get what they expect, M and M argue that the value of their firm's stock is unaffected by dividend policy.

In summary, M and M and other dividend irrelevance proponents argue that—all else being equal—an investor's required return, k_s, and therefore the value of the firm, are unaffected by dividend policy for the following reasons:

1 ▪▪▪ The firm's value is determined solely by the earning power and risk of its assets.

2 ▪▪▪ If dividends do affect value, they do so solely because of their informational content, which signals management's earnings expectations.

3 ▪▪▪ A clientele effect exists which causes a firm's shareholders to receive the dividends that they expect.

These views of M and M with respect to dividend irrelevance are consistent with the residual theory which focuses on making the best investment decisions in order to maximize share value. The proponents of dividend irrelevance conclude that since dividends are irrelevant to a firm's value, the firm does not need to have a dividend policy.

Dividend Relevance Arguments

The key argument in support of dividend relevance is attributed to Myron J. Gordon and John Lintner, who suggest that stockholders prefer current dividends and that there is, in fact, a direct relationship between the dividend policy of the firm and its market value. Fundamental to this proposition is their **bird-in-the-hand argument.** It suggests that investors are generally risk averters and attach less risk to current as opposed to future dividends or capital gains. Simply stated, "a bird in the hand is worth two in the bush." Current dividend payments are therefore believed to reduce investor uncertainty, causing investors to discount the firm's earnings at a lower rate, k_s, thereby—all else being equal—placing a higher value on the firm's stock. Conversely, if dividends are reduced or not paid, investor uncertainty will increase, raising the required return, k_s, and lowering the stock's value.

bird-in-the-hand argument The belief, in support of dividend relevance arguments, that current dividend payments ("a bird in the hand") reduce investor uncertainty and result in a higher value for the firm's stock.

Although many other arguments and counter-arguments relating to the question of dividend relevance have been put forward, researchers have yet to develop a model that can be used to evaluate alternative policies in view of share value. In practice, however, the actions of financial managers and stockholders alike tend to support the belief that dividend policy affects stock value. Since our concern centers on the day-to-day behavior of business firms, the remainder of this chapter is consistent with the belief that dividends *are relevant*—that each firm must develop a dividend policy that fulfills the goals of owners and maximizes their wealth as reflected in the firm's share price.

Factors Affecting Dividend Policy

Before discussing the basic types of dividend policies, we should consider the factors involved in formulating dividend policy. These include legal constraints, contractual constraints, internal constraints, the firm's growth prospects, owner considerations, and market considerations.

Legal Constraints

Most states prohibit corporations from paying out as cash dividends any portion of the firm's "legal capital," which is measured by the par value of common stock. Other states define legal capital to include not only the par value of the common stock but also any paid-in capital in excess of par. These "capital impairment restrictions" are generally established to provide a sufficient equity base to protect creditors' claims. An example will clarify the differing definitions of capital.

EXAMPLE   The stockholders' equity account of Moeller Flour Company, a large grain processor, is presented below.

Moeller Flour Company's stockholders' equity	
Common stock at par	$100,000
Paid-in capital in excess of par	200,000
Retained earnings	140,000
Total stockholders' equity	$440,000

In states where the firm's legal capital is defined as the par value of its common stock, the firm could pay out $340,000 ($200,000 + $140,000) in cash dividends without impairing its capital. In states where the firm's legal capital includes all paid-in capital, the firm could pay out only $140,000 in cash dividends.

An earnings requirement limiting the amount of dividends to the sum of the firm's present and past earnings is sometimes imposed. In other words, the firm cannot pay more in cash dividends than the sum of its most recent and past retained earnings. However, *the firm is not prohibited from paying more in dividends than its current earnings.*[3]

EXAMPLE   Assume Moeller Flour Company, from the preceding example, in the year just ended has $30,000 in earnings available for common stock dividends. An analysis of the

---

[3]A firm having an operating loss in the current period could still pay cash dividends as long as sufficient retained earnings were available and, of course, as long as it had the cash with which to make the payments.

stockholders' equity account above indicates that the firm has past retained earnings of $140,000. Thus it could legally pay dividends of up to $170,000.

If a firm has overdue liabilities or is legally insolvent or bankrupt (if the fair market value of its assets is less than its liabilities), most states prohibit its payment of cash dividends. In addition, the Internal Revenue Service prohibits firms from accumulating earnings in order to reduce the owners' taxes. A firm's owners must pay income taxes on dividends when received, but the owners are not taxed on capital gains in market value until the stock is sold. A firm may retain a large portion of earnings in order to delay the payment of taxes by its owners. If the IRS can determine that a firm has accumulated an excess of earnings in order to allow owners to delay paying ordinary income taxes, it may levy an **excess earnings accumulation tax** on any retained earnings above $250,000—the amount currently exempt from this tax for all firms except personal service corporations.

excess earnings accumulation tax The tax levied by the IRS on retained earnings above $250,000, when it has determined that the firm has accumulated an excess of earnings in order to allow owners to delay paying ordinary income taxes.

Contractual Constraints

Often the firm's ability to pay cash dividends is constrained by certain restrictive provisions in a loan agreement. Generally, these constraints prohibit the payment of cash dividends until a certain level of earnings has been achieved. Or they may limit the amount of dividends paid to a certain dollar amount or percentage of earnings. Constraints on dividend payments help to protect creditors from losses due to insolvency on the part of the firm. The violation of a contractual constraint is generally grounds for a demand of immediate payment by the funds supplier affected.

Internal Constraints

The firm's ability to pay cash dividends is generally constrained by the amount of excess cash available. Although it is possible for a firm to borrow funds to pay dividends, lenders are generally reluctant to make such loans since they produce no tangible or operating benefits that will help the firm repay the loan. Although a firm may have high earnings, its ability to pay dividends may be constrained by a low level of liquid assets (cash and marketable securities).

EXAMPLE   The Moeller Flour Company's stockholders' equity account presented earlier indicates that if the firm's legal capital is defined as all paid-in capital, the firm can pay $140,000 in dividends. If the firm has total liquid assets of $50,000 ($20,000 in cash + marketable securities worth $30,000) and $35,000 of this is needed for operations, the maximum cash dividend the firm can pay is $15,000 ($50,000 − $35,000).

Growth Prospects

The firm's financial requirements are directly related to the degree of asset expansion anticipated. If the firm is in a growth stage, it may need all the funds it can get to finance capital expenditures. A growing firm also requires funds to maintain and improve its assets. High-growth firms typically find themselves constantly in need of funds. Their financial requirements may be characterized as large and immediate. Firms exhibiting little or no growth may, nevertheless, periodically need funds to replace or renew assets.

A firm must evaluate its financial position from the standpoint of profitability and risk in order to develop insight into its ability to raise capital externally. It must determine not only its ability to raise funds but also the cost and speed with which financing can be obtained. Generally, a large, mature firm has adequate access to new capital, whereas the funds available to a rapidly growing firm may not be sufficient to support its numerous acceptable projects. A growth firm is likely to have to depend heavily on internal financing through retained earnings to take advantage of profitable projects; it is likely to pay out only a very small percentage of its earnings as dividends. A more stable firm that needs long-term funds only for planned outlays is in a better position to pay out a large proportion of its earnings, especially if it has ready sources of financing.

Owner Considerations

In establishing a dividend policy, the firm's primary concern should be to maximize owners' wealth. Although it is impossible to establish a policy that will maximize each owner's wealth, the firm must establish a policy that has a favorable effect on the wealth of the *majority* of owners.

One consideration is the *tax status of a firm's owners*. If a firm has a large percentage of wealthy stockholders who are in a high tax bracket, it may decide to pay out a *lower* percentage of its earnings in order to allow the owners to delay the payment of taxes until they sell the stock. Of course, when the stock is sold, if the proceeds are in excess of the original purchase price, the capital gain will be taxed as ordinary income. Lower-income shareholders, however, who need dividend income, will prefer a *higher* payout of earnings.

A second consideration is the *owners' investment opportunities*. A firm should not retain funds for investment in projects yielding lower returns than the owners could obtain from external investments of equal risk. The firm should evaluate the returns expected on its own investment opportunities and, using present-value techniques, determine whether greater returns are obtainable from external investments such as government securities or other corporate stocks. If it appears that the owners would have better opportunities externally, the firm should pay out a higher percentage of its earnings. If the firm's investment opportunities are at least as good as similar-risk external investments, a lower payout is justifiable.

A final consideration is the *potential dilution of ownership*. If a firm pays out a higher percentage of earnings, new equity capital will have to be raised with common stock. The result may be the dilution of both control and earnings for the existing owners. By paying out a low percentage of its earnings, the firm can minimize such possibility of dilution.

Market Considerations

Since the wealth of the firm's owners is reflected in the market price of the firm's shares, an awareness of the market's probable response to certain types of policies is helpful in formulating a suitable dividend policy. Stockholders are believed to value a *fixed or increasing level of dividends* as opposed to a fluctuating pattern of dividends. In addition, stockholders are believed to value a policy of *continuous dividend payment.* Since regularly paying a fixed or increasing dividend eliminates uncertainty about the frequency and magnitude of dividends, the earnings of the firm are likely to be discounted at a lower rate. This should result in an increase in the market value of the stock and therefore increased owners' wealth.

A final market consideration is the *informational content* of dividends. Shareholders often view the firm's dividend payment as an indicator of future success. A stable and continuous dividend conveys to the owners that the firm is in good health and that there is no reason for concern. If the firm skips a dividend payment in a given period due to a loss or to very low earnings, shareholders are likely to react unfavorably. The nonpayment of the dividend creates uncertainty about the future, and this uncertainty is likely to result in lower stock value. Owners and investors generally construe a dividend payment during a period of losses as an indication that the loss is merely temporary.

TYPES OF DIVIDEND POLICIES

The firm's **dividend policy** represents a plan of action to be followed whenever the dividend decision must be made. The dividend policy must be formulated with two basic objectives in mind: maximizing the wealth of the firm's owners and providing for sufficient financing. These two objectives are interrelated. They must be fulfilled in light of a number of factors—legal, contractual, internal, growth, owner-related, and market-related—that limit the policy alternatives. Three of the more commonly used dividend policies are described below. A particular firm's cash dividend policy may incorporate elements of each.

dividend policy The firm's plan of action in regard to the declaration of dividends.

Constant-Payout-Ratio Dividend Policy

One type of dividend policy occasionally adopted by firms is the use of a constant payout ratio. The **dividend payout ratio,** calculated by dividing the firm's cash dividend per share by its earnings per share, indicates the percentage of each dollar earned that is distributed to the owners in the form of cash. With a **constant-payout-ratio dividend policy,** the firm establishes that a certain percentage of earnings will be paid to owners in each dividend period. The problem with this policy is that if the firm's earnings drop or if a loss occurs in a given period, the dividends may be low or even nonexistent. Since dividends are often considered an indicator of the firm's future condition and status, the firm's stock price may thus be adversely affected by this type of action.

dividend payout ratio Indicates the percentage of each dollar earned that is distributed to the owners in the form of cash.

constant-payout-ratio dividend policy A dividend policy based on the payment of a certain percentage of earnings to owners in each dividend period.

An example will clarify the problems stemming from a constant-payout-ratio policy.

EXAMPLE   Nader Industries, a miner of potassium, has a policy of paying out 40 percent of earnings in cash dividends. In periods when a loss occurs, the firm's policy is to pay no cash dividends. Nader's earnings per share, dividends per share, and average price per share for the past six years were as follows:

Year	Earnings/share	Dividends/share	Average price/share
1992	$-0.50	$0.00	$42.00
1991	3.00	1.20	52.00
1990	1.75	0.70	48.00
1989	-1.50	0.00	38.00
1988	2.00	0.80	46.00
1987	4.50	1.80	50.00

Dividends increased in 1989–1990 and in 1990–1991 and decreased in 1987–1988, 1988–1989, and 1991–1992. The data show that in years of decreasing dividends the firm's stock price dropped; when dividends increased, the price of the stock increased. Nader's sporadic dividend payments appear to make its owners uncertain about the returns they can expect from their investment in the firm and therefore tend to generally depress the stock's price. Although a constant-payout-ratio dividend policy is used by some firms, it is *not* recommended.

Regular Dividend Policy

regular dividend policy A dividend policy based on the payment of a fixed-dollar dividend in each period.

Another type of dividend policy, the **regular dividend policy,** is based on the payment of a fixed-dollar dividend in each period. The regular dividend policy provides the owners with generally positive information, indicating that the firm is okay and thereby minimizing their uncertainty. Often, firms using this policy will increase the regular dividend once a *proven* increase in earnings has occurred. Under this policy, dividends are almost never decreased.

EXAMPLE   The dividend policy of Norman Oil Company, an oil exploration company, is to pay annual dividends of $1.00 per share until per-share earnings have exceeded $4.00 for three consecutive years. The annual dividend is then raised to $1.50 per share and a new earnings plateau is established. The firm does not anticipate decreasing its dividend unless its liquidity is in jeopardy. Norman's earnings per share, dividends per share, and average price per share for the past 12 years were as follows:

Year	Earnings/share	Dividends/share	Average price/share
1992	$4.50	$1.50	$47.50
1991	3.90	1.50	46.50
1990	4.60	1.50	45.00
1989	4.20	1.00	43.00
1988	5.00	1.00	42.00
1987	2.00	1.00	38.50
1986	6.00	1.00	38.00
1985	3.00	1.00	36.00
1984	0.75	1.00	33.00
1983	0.50	1.00	33.00
1982	2.70	1.00	33.50
1981	2.85	1.00	35.00

Regardless of the level of earnings, Norman Oil paid dividends of $1.00 per share through 1989. In 1990 the dividend was raised to $1.50 per share, since earnings of $4.00 per share had been achieved for three years. In 1990 the firm would also have had to establish a new earnings plateau for further dividend increases. Norman Oil Company's average price per share exhibited a stable, increasing behavior in spite of a somewhat volatile pattern of earnings.

Often, a regular dividend policy is built around a **target dividend-payout ratio.** Under this policy the firm attempts to pay out a certain percentage of earnings, but rather than let dividends fluctuate, it pays a stated dollar dividend and adjusts it toward the target payout as proven increases in earnings occur. For instance, Norman Oil Company appears to have a target payout ratio of around 35 percent. The payout was about 35 percent ($1.00 ÷ $2.85) when the dividend policy was set in 1981, and when the dividend was raised to $1.50 in 1990 the payout ratio was about 33 percent ($1.50 ÷ $4.60).

Low-Regular-and-Extra Dividend Policy

Some firms establish a **low-regular-and-extra dividend policy,** paying a low regular dividend, supplemented by an additional dividend when earnings warrant it. If earnings are higher than normal in a given period, the firm may pay this additional dividend, which will be designated an **extra dividend.** By designating the amount by which the dividend exceeds the regular payment as an extra dividend, the firm avoids giving shareholders false hopes. The use of the "extra" designation is

target dividend-payout ratio   A policy under which the firm attempts to pay out a certain percentage of earnings as a stated dollar dividend, which it adjusts toward a target payout as proven earnings increases occur.

low-regular-and-extra dividend policy   A dividend policy based on paying a low regular dividend, supplemented by an additional dividend when earnings warrant it.

extra dividend   An additional dividend optionally paid by the firm if earnings are higher than normal in a given period.

especially common among companies that experience cyclical shifts in earnings.

By establishing a low regular dividend that is paid each period, the firm gives investors the stable income necessary to build confidence in the firm, and the extra dividend permits them to share in the "earnings" if the firm experiences an especially good period. Firms using this policy must raise the level of the regular dividend when proven increases in earnings have been achieved. The extra dividend should not be a regular event, or it becomes meaningless. The use of a target dividend-payout ratio in establishing the regular dividend level is advisable.

OTHER FORMS OF DIVIDENDS

A number of other forms of dividends are available to the firm. In this section we will discuss two other methods of paying dividends—stock dividends and stock repurchases—as well as a closely related topic, stock splits.

Stock Dividends

stock dividend The payment to existing owners of a dividend in the form of stock.

A **stock dividend** is the payment to existing owners of a dividend in the form of stock. Often, firms pay stock dividends as a replacement for or a supplement to cash dividends. Although stock dividends do not have a real value, stockholders may perceive them to represent something they did not have before and therefore to have value.

Accounting Aspects

In an accounting sense, the payment of a stock dividend is a shifting of funds between capital accounts rather than a use of funds. When a firm declares a stock dividend, the procedures with respect to announcement and distribution are the same as those described earlier for a cash dividend. The accounting entries associated with the payment of stock dividends vary depending upon whether or not it is a **small (ordinary) stock dividend**—a stock dividend representing less than 20 to 25 percent of the common stock outstanding at the time the dividend is declared. Because small stock dividends are most common, the accounting entries associated with them are illustrated in the following example.

small (ordinary) stock dividend A stock dividend that represents less than 20 to 25 percent of the common stock outstanding at the time the dividend is declared.

EXAMPLE   The current stockholders' equity on the balance sheet of Wieta Company, a distributor of prefabricated cabinets, is as follows:

Preferred stock	$ 300,000
Common stock (100,000 shares at $4 par)	400,000
Paid-in capital in excess of par	600,000
Retained earnings	700,000
Total stockholders' equity	$2,000,000

If Wieta declares a 10 percent stock dividend and the market price of its stock is $15 per share, $150,000 of retained earnings (10% × 100,000 shares × $15 per share) will be capitalized. The $150,000 will be distributed between common stock and paid-in capital in excess of par accounts based on the par value of the common stock. The resulting account balances are as follows:

Preferred stock	$ 300,000
Common stock (110,000 shares at $4 par)	440,000
Paid-in capital in excess of par	710,000
Retained earnings	550,000
Total stockholders' equity	$2,000,000

Since 10,000 new shares (10% × 100,000) have been issued and the prevailing market price is $15 per share, $150,000 ($15 per share × 10,000 shares) has been shifted from retained earnings to the common stock and paid-in capital accounts. A total of $40,000 ($4 par × 10,000 shares) has been added to common stock, and the remaining $110,000 [($15 − $4) × 10,000 shares] has been added to the paid-in capital in excess of par. The firm's total stockholders' equity has not changed; funds have only been *redistributed* among stockholders' equity accounts.

The Shareholder's Viewpoint

The shareholder receiving a stock dividend receives nothing of value. After the dividend is paid, the per-share value of the shareholder's stock will decrease in proportion to the dividend in such a way that the market value of his or her total holdings in the firm will remain unchanged. The shareholder's proportion of ownership in the firm will also remain the same, and as long as the firm's earnings remain unchanged, so will his or her share of total earnings. A continuation of the preceding example will clarify this point.

EXAMPLE Mr. X owned 10,000 shares of the Wieta Company's stock. The company's most recent earnings were $220,000, and earnings are not expected to change in the near future. Before the stock dividend, Mr. X owned 10 percent (10,000 shares ÷ 100,000 shares) of the firm's stock, which was selling for $15 per share. Earnings per share were $2.20 ($220,000 ÷ 100,000 shares). Since Mr. X owned 10,000 shares, his earnings were $22,000 ($2.20 per share × 10,000 shares). After receiving the 10 percent stock dividend, Mr. X has 11,000 shares, which again is 10 percent (11,000 shares ÷ 110,000 shares) of the ownership. The market price of the stock can be expected to drop to $13.64 per share [$15 × (1.00 ÷ 1.10)]. Thus the market value of Mr. X's holdings will be $150,000 (11,000 shares × $13.64 per share).

This is the same as the initial value of his holdings (10,000 shares × $15 per share). The future earnings per share will drop to $2 ($220,000 ÷ 110,000 shares), since the same $220,000 in earnings must now be divided among 110,000 shares. Since Mr. X still owns 10 percent of the stock, his share of total earnings is still $22,000 ($2 per share × 11,000 shares). In summary, if the firm's earnings remain constant and total cash dividends do not increase, a stock dividend will result in a lower per-share market value for the firm's stock.

The Company's Viewpoint

Stock dividends are more costly to issue than cash dividends, but the advantages generally outweigh these costs. Firms find the stock dividend a means of giving owners something without having to use cash. Generally, when a firm is growing rapidly and needs internal financing to perpetuate this growth, a stock dividend is used. As long as the stockholders recognize that the firm is reinvesting its earnings in a manner that should tend to maximize future earnings, the market value of the firm should at least remain unchanged. If the stock dividend is paid so that cash can be retained to satisfy past-due bills, a decline in market value may result.

Stock Splits

stock split A method commonly used to lower the market price of a firm's stock by increasing the number of shares belonging to each shareholder.

Although not a type of dividend, *stock splits* have an effect on a firm's share price similar to that of stock dividends. A **stock split** is a method commonly used to lower the market price of a firm's stock by increasing the number of shares belonging to each shareholder. Quite often, a firm believes that its stock is priced too high and that lowering the market price will enhance trading activity. Stock splits are often made prior to new issues of a stock to enhance the marketability of the stock and stimulate market activity.

A stock split has no effect on the firm's capital structure. It commonly increases the number of shares outstanding and reduces the stock's per-share par value. In other words, when a stock is split, a specified number of new shares are exchanged for a given number of outstanding shares. In a 2-for-1 split, two new shares are exchanged for each old share; in a 3-for-2 split, three new shares are exchanged for each two old shares, and so on.

EXAMPLE   Brandt Company, a forest products concern, had 200,000 shares of $2 par-value common stock and no preferred stock outstanding. Since the stock is selling at a high market price, the firm has declared a 2-for-1 stock split. The total before- and after-split stockholders' equity is given below.

Before split	
Common stock (200,000 shares at $2 par)	$ 400,000
Paid-in capital in excess of par	4,000,000
Retained earnings	2,000,000
Total stockholders' equity	$6,400,000

After 2-for-1 split	
Common stock (400,000 shares at $1 par)	$ 400,000
Paid-in capital in excess of par	4,000,000
Retained earnings	2,000,000
Total stockholders' equity	$6,400,000

The insignificant effect of the stock split on the firm's books is obvious.

Stock can be split in any way desired. Sometimes a **reverse stock split** is made: a certain number of outstanding shares are exchanged for one new share. For example, in a 1-for-2 split, one new share is exchanged for two old shares; in a 2-for-3 split, two new shares are exchanged for three old shares, and so on. Reverse stock splits are initiated when a stock is selling at too low a price to appear respectable.

reverse stock split   A method used to raise the market price of a firm's stock by exchanging a certain number of outstanding shares for one new share of stock.

It is not unusual for a stock split to cause a slight increase in the market value of the stock. This is attributable to the informational content of stock splits and the fact that *total* dividends paid commonly increase slightly after a split.

Stock Repurchases

Over the past 5 to 10 years, firms have increased their repurchasing of outstanding common stock in the marketplace. The practical motives for **stock repurchase** include obtaining shares to be used in acquisitions, having shares available for employee stock option plans, or merely retiring shares. Here we focus on the repurchase of shares for retirement, since this motive for repurchase is similar to the payment of cash dividends.

stock repurchase   The repurchasing by the firm of outstanding shares of its common stock in the marketplace.

Accounting Entries

The accounting entries that result when common stock is repurchased are a reduction in cash and the establishment of a contra capital account called "treasury stock," which is shown as a deduction from stockholders' equity. The label **treasury stock** is used to indicate the presence of repurchased shares on the balance sheet. The repurchase of stock can be viewed as a cash dividend, since it involves the distribution of cash to the firm's owners, who are the sellers of the shares.

treasury stock   The label used on the firm's balance sheet to designate repurchased shares of stock; shown as a deduction from stockholders' equity.

E T H I C S   I N   F I N A N C E

Motives for the Buyback of Diasonics

Diasonics, a maker of X-ray and ultrasound equipment, bought 14.5 million shares of its own stock on the open market between June 1990 and January 1991. As a result the total number of shares outstanding fell 19 percent. Such an active, yet unannounced, buyback program was catching the attention of many investors in early 1991. Each of these investors had their own explanation for Diasonics' buyback.

Some investors believed Diasonics was simply using its excess cash obtained from selling its Magnetic Resonance Imaging unit for a net of $70 million. Since 14.5 million shares were purchased at an average price of $2.25, this theory has support. Management may have been sharing the value of the sale with its shareholders without the consequences of paying tax on a cash distribution.

Other investors did not believe management was being benevolent. Some insist that the purpose of reducing the number of outstanding shares was to increase management control. At the extreme, a couple investors believed that management was considering a leveraged buyout. By taking many shares off the market, the management's voting control increased. At a minimum, the repurchase increased the value of the shares management holds in their personal portfolios.

Others were projecting a takeover by either a Japanese or European company. Foreign sales account for 50 percent of Diasonics' revenue. Earnings per share had risen from a loss of 29 cents in 1989 to a profit of 20 cents in 1990. Furthermore, 1991 earnings were expected to be 35 cents per share. Earnings at this level, given Diasonics' risk, suggested to others that the stock was worth $4.70. Hence, the best project option was stock repurchase.

Of course, a Diasonics representative stated that he was unaware of any plans for a management-led leveraged buyout or acquisition by foreign companies. The motives for Diasonics' buyback remained unclear.

Source: "Why the buybacks of Diasonics?", *Business Week*, February 4, 1991, p. 80.

Viewed as a Cash Dividend

When common stock is repurchased for retirement, the underlying motive is to distribute excess cash to the owners. As a result of any repurchase the owners receive cash for their shares. Generally as long as earnings remain constant, the repurchase of shares reduces the number of outstanding shares, raising the earnings per share and therefore the market price per share. In addition, certain owner tax benefits may result from stock repurchases. The repurchase of common stock results in a type of reverse dilution, since the earnings per share and the market price of stock are increased by reducing the number of shares outstanding. The net effect of the repurchase is similar to the payment of a cash dividend. A simple example will clarify this point.

EXAMPLE   Farrell Company, a national sportswear chain, has released the following financial data:

Earnings available for common stockholders	$1,000,000
Number of shares of common outstanding	400,000
Earnings per share ($1,000,000 ÷ 400,000)	$2.50
Market price per share	$50
Price/earnings (P/E) ratio ($50 ÷ $2.50)	20

The firm is contemplating using $800,000 of its earnings either to pay cash dividends or to repurchase shares. If the firm pays cash dividends, the amount of the dividend would be $2 per share ($800,000 ÷ 400,000 shares). If the firm pays $52 per share to repurchase stock, it could repurchase approximately 15,385 shares ($800,000 ÷ $52 per share). As a result of this repurchase, 384,615 shares (400,000 shares − 15,385 shares) of common stock would remain outstanding. Earnings per share (EPS) would rise to $2.60 ($1,000,000 ÷ 384,615). If the stock still sold at 20 times earnings (P/E = 20), applying the price/earnings (P/E) multiples approach presented in Chapter 12, its market price would rise to $52 per share ($2.60 × 20). In both cases the stockholders would receive $2 per share—a $2 cash dividend in the dividend case or a $2 increase in share price ($50 per share to $52 per share) in the repurchase case.

The advantages of stock repurchases are an increase in per-share earnings and certain owner tax benefits. The tax advantage stems from the fact that if the cash dividend is paid, the owners will have to pay ordinary income taxes on it, whereas the $2 increase in the market value of the stock due to the repurchase will not be taxed until the owner sells the stock. Of course, when the stock is sold, if the proceeds are in excess of the original purchase price, the capital gain will be taxed as ordinary income. The IRS allegedly watches firms that regularly repurchase stock and levies a penalty if it believes the repurchases have been made to delay the payment of taxes by the stockholders. Enforcement in this area appears to be relatively lax.

INTERNATIONAL DIMENSION: CAPITAL STRUCTURE

Both theory and research findings indicate that the capital structures of multinational companies differ from those of purely domestic firms. Furthermore, differences are also observed among the capital structures of MNCs domiciled in various countries. Several factors tend to influence the capital structures of MNCs. Each is briefly discussed below.

International Capital Markets

MNCs, unlike smaller-size domestic firms, have access to the Euromarket (see Chapter 2) and the variety of financial instruments available there (see Chapters 10, 19, and 20). Due to their access to the international bond and equity markets, MNCs may have lower costs of various sources of long-term financing. This results in differences between the capital structures of these MNCs and purely domestic companies. Similarly, MNCs based in different countries and regions, such as those domiciled in the United States, Japan, and Western Europe, may have access to different currencies and markets, resulting in variances in capital structures for these multinationals.

International Diversification

It is well-established that MNCs, in contrast to domestic firms, can achieve further risk reduction in their cash flows by diversifying internationally. International diversification, in turn, may lead to varying degrees of debt versus equity. The research findings on debt ratios are mixed. Some studies have found MNCs' debt proportions to be higher than those of domestic firms. Other studies have concluded the opposite. They cite imperfections in certain foreign markets, political risk factors, and complexities in the international financial environment as causes of higher costs of debt for MNCs.

Country Factors

A number of studies have concluded that certain factors unique to each host country can cause differences in capital structures. These factors include legal, tax, political, social, and financial aspects, as well as the overall relationship between the public and private sectors. Owing to such factors, differences have been found not only among MNCs based in various countries but also among the foreign affiliates of an MNC. However, since no one capital structure is ideal for all MNCs, each multinational has to consider a set of global and domestic factors when deciding on the appropriate capital structure for both the overall corporation and its affiliates.

SUMMARY

1   **Understand capital structure, including the basic types of capital, external assessment of capital structure, and the concept of an optimal capital structure.** A firm's capital structure is determined by the mix of long-term debt and equity it uses in financing its operations. Debt and equity capital differ with respect to voice in management, claims on income and assets, maturity, and tax treatment. Capital structure can be externally assessed using the debt ratio, times interest earned ratio, and the fixed-payment coverage ratio. Under the traditional approach to capital structure, as financial leverage increases, the cost of debt remains constant and then rises, whereas the cost of equity always rises. The optimal capital structure is that for which the weighted average cost of capital is minimized, thereby maximizing share value.

2   **Discuss the graphic presentation, risk considerations, and basic shortcoming of using the EBIT–EPS approach to compare capital structures.** The EBIT–EPS approach can be used to evaluate various capital structures in light of the returns they provide the firm's owners and their degree of financial risk. Under the EBIT–EPS approach, the preferred capital structure would be the one expected to provide maximum EPS over the firm's expected range of EBIT. Graphically, this approach reflects risk in terms of the financial break-even point and the slope of the capital structure line. The major shortcoming of EBIT–EPS analysis is that by ignoring risk it concentrates on maximization of earnings rather than maximization of owners' wealth.

3   **Describe cash dividend payment procedures, dividend reinvestment plans, the relevance of dividend policy and related arguments, and the key factors that affect dividend policy.** The cash dividend decision is normally a quarterly decision made by the corporate board of directors which establishes the record date and payment date. Because the dividend decision affects the level of retained earnings, it can significantly affect the firm's external financing requirements. Some firms offer dividend reinvestment plans that allow stockholders to acquire shares in lieu of cash dividends, often at an attractive price. A company offering such a plan can either have a trustee buy outstanding shares on behalf of participating shareholders, or it can issue new shares to any participants.

The residual theory suggests that dividends should be viewed as the residual earnings left after all acceptable investment opportunities have been undertaken. Dividend irrelevance, which supports the residual theory, is argued by Modigliani and Miller using a perfect world wherein information content and clientele effects exist. Gordon and Lintner argue dividend relevance based upon the uncertainty-reducing effect of dividends, supported by their bird-in-the-hand argument. The actions of financial managers and stockholders alike tend to support the belief that dividend policy is relevant—it affects stock value. Certain legal, contractual, and internal constraints as well as growth prospects, owner considerations, and certain market considerations affect a firm's dividend policy.

4   **Describe and evaluate the three basic types of dividend policies—constant-payout-ratio, regular, and low-regular-and-extra.** With a constant-payout-ratio dividend policy, the firm pays a fixed percentage of earnings out to the owners each period. The problem with this policy is that dividends move up and down with earnings, and no dividend is paid when the firm experiences a loss. Under a regular dividend policy, the firm pays a fixed-dollar dividend each period; it increases the amount of the dividend only after a proven increase in earnings has occurred. The regular dividend policy is appealing because it provides the owners with generally positive information, indicating the firm is okay and thereby minimizing their uncertainty. The low-regular-and-extra dividend policy is similar to the regular dividend policy, except that it pays an "extra dividend" in periods when the firm's earnings are higher than normal. By establishing a low regular dividend that is paid each period, the firm using this policy gives investors stable predictable income and pays a bonus when the firm experiences an especially good period. The regular and the low-regular-and-extra dividend policies are generally preferred over the constant-payout-ratio dividend policy because of the uncertainty-reducing effect of their stable patterns of dividends.

5 ████   **Contrast the basic features, objectives, and procedures for paying other forms of dividends, including stock dividends, stock splits, and stock repurchases.** Occasionally firms may pay stock dividends as a replacement for or supplement to cash dividends. The payment of stock dividends involves a shifting of funds between capital accounts rather than a use of funds. Stock splits are sometimes used to enhance trading activity by lowering or raising the market price of the firm's stock by increasing or decreasing, respectively, the number of shares belonging to each shareholder. A stock split has no effect on the firm's capital structure. Stock repurchases can be made in lieu of cash dividend payments in order to retire outstanding shares and delay the payment of taxes. Whereas both stock dividends and stock repurchases can be viewed as dividend alternatives, stock splits are merely used to deliberately adjust the market price of shares. Only stock repurchases involve the actual outflow of cash—both stock dividends and stock splits involve accounting adjustments in the capital accounts.

6 ████   **Explain how international capital markets, international diversification, and country factors cause the capital structures of multinational companies to differ from those of purely domestic firms.** The capital structures of MNCs differ from those of purely domestic firms. A number of factors influence the capital structure of MNCs: their access to the Euromarket and the variety of financial instruments available there, their ability to achieve greater risk reduction in their cash flows by diversifying internationally, and the impact of legal, tax, political, social, and financial factors unique to each host country. In addition, differences in capital structures also exist among the capital structures of MNCs domiciled in various countries.

QUESTIONS

16—1   What is a firm's *capital structure?* How do *debt* and *equity* capital differ?

16—2   What ratios can be used to assess the degree of financial leverage in the firm's capital structure?

16—3   Under the traditional approach to capital structure, what happens to the cost of debt, the cost of equity, and the weighted average cost of capital as the firm's financial leverage increases from zero? Where is an *optimal capital structure* under this approach, and what is its relationship to the firm's value at that point?

16—4   Explain the *EBIT–EPS approach* to capital structure. Include in your explanation a graph indicating the financial breakeven point; label the axes. Is this approach consistent with maximization of value? Explain.

16—5   How do the date of record and the holders of record relate to the payment of cash dividends? What does the term *ex dividend* mean? Who sets the dividend payment date?

16—6   What is a *dividend reinvestment plan?* What benefit is available to plan participants? Describe the two ways companies can handle such plans.

16—7   Describe the *residual theory of dividends.* Would following this approach lead to a stable dividend? Is this approach consistent with dividend relevance? Explain.

16—8   Describe, compare, and contrast the basic arguments relative to the irrelevance or relevance of dividend policy given by:
a. Franco Modigliani and Merton H. Miller (M and M)
b. Myron J. Gordon and John Lintner

16—9   Briefly describe each of the following factors affecting dividend pol-
         icy:
         a. Legal constraints
         b. Contractual constraints
         c. Internal constraints
         d. Growth prospects
         e. Owner considerations
         f. Market considerations
16—10   What are (a) a constant-payout-ratio dividend policy, (b) a regular
         dividend policy, and (c) a low-regular-and-extra dividend policy?
         What are the effects of these policies?
16—11   What is a *stock dividend?* If it is more costly to issue stock than to pay
         cash dividends, why do firms issue stock dividends?
16—12   What is a *stock split?* What is a *reverse stock split?* Compare a stock
         split with a stock dividend.
16—13   What is the logic behind *repurchasing shares* of common stock to
         distribute excess cash to the firm's owners? How might this raise the
         per-share earnings and market price of outstanding shares?
16—14   Briefly discuss some of the international factors that cause the capi-
         tal structures of MNCs to differ from those of purely domestic firms.

PROBLEMS

16—1   **(Various Capital Structures)**   Zachary Corporation currently has $1
         million in total assets and is totally equity-financed. It is contem-
         plating a change in capital structure. Compute the amount of debt
         and equity that would be outstanding if the firm were to shift to one
         of the following debt ratios: 10, 20, 30, 40, 50, 60, and 90 percent.
         (*Note:* The amount of total assets would not change.) Is there a limit
         to the debt ratio's value?

16—2   **(EBIT and EPS)**   Western Oil Corporation has a current capital
         structure consisting of $250,000 of 16 percent (annual interest) debt
         and 2,000 shares of common stock. The firm pays taxes at the rate of
         40 percent on ordinary income.
         a. Using EBIT values of $80,000 and $120,000, determine the associ-
             ated earnings per share (EPS).
         b. Graph the firm's current capital structure on a set of EBIT–EPS
             axes.

16—3   **(EBIT–EPS and Capital Structure)**   Parker Petroleum is consider-
         ing two capital structures. The key information follows. Assume a
         40-percent tax rate.

Source of capital	Structure A	Structure B
Long-term debt	$100,000, annual interest at 16% coupon rate	$200,000, annual interest at 17% coupon rate
Common stock	4,000 shares	2,000 shares

         a. Calculate two EBIT–EPS coordinates for each of the structures
             by selecting any two EBIT values and finding their associated
             EPS.
         b. Plot the two capital structures on a set of EBIT–EPS axes.

c. Indicate over what EBIT range, if any, each structure is preferred.
d. Discuss the leverage and risk aspects of each structure.
e. If the firm is fairly certain its EBIT will exceed $75,000, which structure would you recommend? Why?

16—4   **(EBIT–EPS and Capital Structure)** Wonder Diaper is considering two possible capital structures, A and B, shown below. Assume a 40 percent tax rate.

Source of capital	Structure A	Structure B
Long-term debt	$75,000, annual interest at 16% coupon rate	$50,000, annual interest at 15% coupon rate
Common stock	8,000 shares	10,000 shares

a. Calculate two EBIT–EPS coordinates for each of the structures by selecting any two EBIT values and finding their associated EPS.
b. Graph the two capital structures on the same set of EBIT–EPS axes.
c. Discuss the leverage and risk associated with each of the structures.
d. Over what range of EBIT would each structure be preferred?
e. Which structure would you recommend if the firm expects its EBIT to be $35,000? Explain.

16—5   **(Integrative—EBIT–EPS and Alternative Capital Structures)** Triple D Corporation wishes to analyze five possible capital structures—0, 15, 30, 45, and 60 percent debt ratios. The firm's total assets of $1 million are assumed constant. Its common stock is valued at $25 per share, and the firm is in the 40 percent tax bracket. The following additional data has been gathered for use in analyzing the five capital structures under consideration.

Capital structure debt ratio	Interest rate on debt
0%	0.0%
15	8.0
30	10.0
45	13.0
60	17.0

a. Calculate the amount of debt, the amount of equity, and the number of shares of common stock outstanding for each of the capital structures being considered.
b. Calculate the annual interest on the debt under each of the capital structures being considered. (*Note:* The interest rate given is applicable to *all* debt associated with the corresponding debt ratio.)
c. Calculate EPS associated with $150,000 and $250,000 of EBIT for each of the five capital structures.

d. Using the EBIT–EPS data developed in **c**, plot the five capital structures on the same set of EBIT–EPS axes.

e. Evaluate the relative degrees of leverage of the plans and discuss the range of EBIT (from the graph in **d**) over which each capital structure is preferred.

f. What is the major problem with the use of EBIT–EPS analysis to select the best capital structure? Explain.

16—6 **(Dividend Payment Procedures)**   Dayton Widget, at its quarterly dividend meeting, declared a cash dividend of $1.10 per share for holders of record on Monday, July 10. The firm has 300,000 shares of common stock outstanding and has set a payment date of July 31. Prior to the dividend declaration, the firm's key accounts were as follows:

Cash	$500,000	Dividends payable	$ 0
		Retained earnings	2,500,000

a. Show the entries after the meeting adjourned.

b. When is the ex dividend date?

c. After the July 31 payment date, what values would the key accounts have?

d. What effect, if any, will the dividend have on the firm's total assets?

16—7 **(Dividend Constraints)**   The Boulder Company's stockholders' equity account is as follows:

Common stock (400,000 shares at $4 par)	$1,600,000
Paid-in capital in excess of par	1,000,000
Retained earnings	1,900,000
Total stockholders' equity	$4,500,000

The earnings available for common stockholders from this period's operations are $100,000, which have been included as part of the $1.9 million retained earnings.

a. What is the maximum dividend per share the firm can pay? (Assume that legal capital includes *all* paid-in capital.)

b. If the firm has $160,000 in cash, what is the largest per-share dividend it can pay without borrowing?

c. Indicate the accounts and changes, if any, that will result if the firm pays the dividends indicated in **a** and **b**.

d. Indicate the effects of an $80,000 cash dividend on stockholders' equity.

16—8 **(Dividend Constraints)**   A firm has $800,000 in paid-in capital, retained earnings of $40,000 (including the current year's earnings), and 25,000 shares of common stock outstanding. In the current year it has $29,000 of earnings available for the common stockholders.

a. What is the most the firm can pay in cash dividends to each common stockholder? (Assume that legal capital includes *all* paid-in capital.)

b. What effect would a cash dividend of $.80 per share have on the firm's balance sheet entries?

c. If the firm cannot raise any new funds from external sources, what do you consider the key constraint with respect to the magnitude of the firm's dividend payments? Why?

16—9 **(Alternative Dividend Policies)**   A firm has had the earnings per share over the past 10 years shown in the following table.

Year	Earnings per share
1992	$4.00
1991	3.80
1990	3.20
1989	2.80
1988	3.20
1987	2.40
1986	1.20
1985	1.80
1984	−0.50
1983	0.25

a. If the firm's dividend policy was based on a constant payout ratio of 40 percent for all years with positive earnings and a zero payout otherwise, determine the annual dividend for each year.

b. If the firm had a dividend payout of $1.00 per share, increasing by $.10 per share whenever the dividend payout fell below 50 percent for two consecutive years, what annual dividend did the firm pay each year?

c. If the firm's policy was to pay $.50 per share each period except when earnings per share exceed $3.00, when an extra dividend equal to 80 percent of earnings beyond $3.00 would be paid, what annual dividend did the firm pay each year?

d. Discuss the pros and cons of each dividend policy described in **a** through **c**.

16—10   **(Alternative Dividend Policies)** Given the following earnings per share over the period 1985–1992, determine the annual dividend per share under each of the policies set forth in **a** through **d**.

Year	Earnings per share
1992	$1.40
1991	1.56
1990	1.20
1989	−0.85
1988	1.05
1987	0.60
1986	1.00
1985	0.44

a. Pay out 50 percent of earnings in all years with positive earnings.

b. Pay $.50 per share and increase to $.60 per share whenever earnings per share rise above $.90 per share for two consecutive years.

c. Pay $.50 per share except when earnings exceed $1.00 per share, when there would be an extra dividend of 60 percent of earnings above $1.00 per share.

d. Combine policies in **b** and **c**. When the dividend is raised (in **b**), raise the excess dividend base (in **c**) from $1.00 to $1.10 per share.

e. Compare and contrast each of the dividend policies described in **a** through **d**.

16—11   **(Stock Dividend—Firm)**   TFS has the stockholders' equity account, given here. The firm's common stock has a current market price of $30 per share.

Preferred stock	$100,000
Common stock (10,000 shares at $2 par)	20,000
Paid-in capital in excess of par	280,000
Retained earnings	100,000
Total stockholders' equity	$500,000

a. Show the effects on TFS of a 5 percent stock dividend.

b. Show the effects of (1) a 10 percent and (2) a 20 percent stock dividend.

c. In light of your answers to **a** and **b**, discuss the effects of stock dividends on stockholders' equity.

16—12   **(Cash versus Stock Dividend)**   Nimms Steel has a stockholders' equity account as given. The firm's common stock currently sells for $4 per share.

Preferred stock	$ 100,000
Common stock (400,000 shares at $1 par)	400,000
Paid-in capital in excess of par	200,000
Retained earnings	320,000
Total stockholders' equity	$1,020,000

a. Show the effects on the firm of a $.01, $.05, $.10, and $.20 per-share *cash* dividend.

b. Show the effects on the firm of a 1 percent, 5 percent, 10 percent, and 20 percent *stock* dividend.

c. Compare the effects in **a** and **b**. What are the significant differences in the two methods of paying dividends?

16—13   **(Stock Dividend—Investor)**   Dana Bond currently holds 400 shares of Mountain Grown Coffee. The firm has 40,000 shares outstanding. The firm most recently had earnings available for common stockholders of $80,000, and its stock has been selling for $22 per share. The firm intends to retain its earnings and pay a 10 percent stock dividend.

a. How much does the firm currently earn per share?

b. What proportion of the firm does Dana Bond currently own?

c. What proportion of the firm will Ms. Bond own after the stock dividend? Explain your answer.

d. At what market price would you expect the stock to sell after the stock dividend?

e. Discuss what effect, if any, the payment of stock dividends will have on Ms. Bond's share of the ownership and earnings of Mountain Grown Coffee.

16—14   **(Stock Dividend—Investor)** The Mission Company has outstanding 50,000 shares of common stock currently selling at $40 per share. The firm most recently had earnings available for common stockholders of $120,000, but it has decided to retain these funds and is considering either a 5 percent or a 10 percent stock dividend in lieu of a cash dividend.

   a. Determine the firm's current earnings per share.

   b. If Jack Frost currently owns 500 shares of the firm's stock, determine his proportion of ownership currently and under each of the proposed stock dividend plans. Explain your findings.

   c. Calculate and explain the market price per share under each of the stock dividend plans.

   d. For each of the proposed stock dividends, calculate the earnings per share after payment of the stock dividend.

   e. How much would the value of Jack Frost's holdings be under each of the plans? Explain.

   f. As Mr. Frost, would you have any preference with respect to the proposed stock dividends? Why or why not?

16—15   **(Stock Split—Firm)** U.S. Oil Company's current stockholders' equity account is as follows:

Preferred stock	$ 400,000
Common stock (600,000 shares at $3 par)	1,800,000
Paid-in capital in excess of par	200,000
Retained earnings	800,000
Total stockholders' equity	$3,200,000

   a. Indicate the change, if any, expected if the firm declares a 2-for-1 stock split.

   b. Indicate the change, if any, expected if the firm declares a 1-for-1½ *reverse* stock split.

   c. Indicate the change, if any, expected if the firm declares a 3-for-1 stock split.

   d. Indicate the change, if any, expected if the firm declares a 6-for-1 stock split.

   e. Indicate the change, if any, expected if the firm declares a 1-for-4 *reverse* stock split.

16—16   **(Stock Split—Firm)** Grande Company is considering a 3-for-2 stock split. It currently has the stockholders' equity position shown below. The current stock price is $120 per share. The most recent period's earnings available for common is included in retained earnings.

Preferred stock	$ 1,000,000
Common stock (100,000 shares at $3 par)	300,000
Paid-in capital in excess of par	1,700,000
Retained earnings	10,000,000
Total stockholders' equity	$13,000,000

   a. What effects on Grande Company would result from the stock split?

   b. What change in stock price would you expect to result from the stock split?

   c. What is the maximum cash dividend *per share* the firm could pay on common stock before and after the stock split? (Assume that legal capital includes *all* paid-in capital.)

    d. Contrast your answers to **a** through **c** with the circumstances surrounding a 50 percent stock dividend.

    e. Explain the differences between stock splits and stock dividends.

16—17   **(Stock Repurchase)**   The following financial data on the Victor Stock Company are available:

Earnings available for common stockholders	$800,000
Number of shares of common outstanding	400,000
Earnings per share ($800,000 ÷ 400,000)	$2
Market price per share	$20
Price/earnings (P/E) ratio ($20 ÷ $2)	10

The firm is currently contemplating using $400,000 of its earnings to pay cash dividends of $1 per share or repurchasing stock at $21 per share.

    a. Approximately how many shares of stock can the firm repurchase at the $21-per-share price using the funds that would have gone to pay the cash dividend?

    b. Calculate earnings per share (EPS) after the repurchase. Explain your calculations.

    c. If the stock still sells at 10 times earnings, how much will the market price be after the repurchase?

    d. Compare and contrast the pre- and post-repurchase earnings per share.

    e. Compare and contrast the stockholders' position under the dividend and repurchase alternatives. What are the tax implications under each alternative?

CASE

Evaluating McGraw Industries'
Capital Structure and Dividend Policy

McGraw Industries, an established manufacturer of printing equipment, expects its sales to remain flat for the next three to five years due to both a weak economic outlook and an expectation of little new printing technology development over that period. Based on this scenario, the firm's management has been instructed by its board to institute programs that will allow it to operate more efficiently, earn high profits, and, most importantly, maximize share value. In this regard, the firm's chief financial officer (CFO), Ron Lewis, has been charged with evaluating the firm's capital structure and dividend policy. Although Lewis feels certain that the firm's current policy of paying out 60 percent of each year's earnings in dividends is appropriate, he believes that the current capital structure, which contains 10 percent debt and 90 percent equity, may lack adequate financial leverage. In order to evaluate the firm's capital structure, Lewis has gathered the data summarized below on the current capital structure (10% debt ratio) and two alternative capital structures—A (30% debt ratio) and B (50% debt ratio).

Source of capital	Capital structure[a]		
	Current (10% debt)	A (30% debt)	(50% debt)
Long-term debt	$1,000,000	$3,000,000	$5,000,000
Coupon interest rate[b]	9%	10%	12%
Common stock	100,000 shares	78,000 shares	56,000 shares

[a]These structures are based upon maintaining the firm's current level of $10,000,000 of total financing.
[b]Interest rate applicable to *all* debt.

Lewis expects the firm's earnings before interest and taxes (EBIT) to remain at its current level of $1,200,000. The firm has a 40 percent tax rate.

Required

a. Use the current level of EBIT to calculate the times interest earned ratio for each capital structure. Evaluate the current and two alternative capital structures using the times interest earned and debt ratios.

b. Prepare a single EBIT–EPS graph showing the current and two alternative capital structures.

c. Based on the graph in **b**, which capital structure will maximize McGraw's earnings per share at its expected level of EBIT of $1,200,000? Why might this not be the best capital structure?

d. Based on your analyses in **a, b,** and **c,** which capital structure would you recommend? Why?

e. What impact would your recommendation in **d** have on the firm's dividend policy?

f. Evaluate the firm's current dividend policy. Might an alternative policy be more appropriate? Explain.

CHAPTER 17

MERGERS, LBOs, DIVESTITURES, AND FAILURE

CHAPTER OBJECTIVES

After studying this chapter, you should be able to:

1 Understand merger fundamentals, including basic terminology, motives for merging, and types of mergers.

2 Describe the objectives and procedures used in leveraged buyouts (LBOs) and divestitures.

3 Demonstrate the procedures used to analyze and negotiate mergers, including valuing the target company, stock swap transactions, the merger negotiation process, and holding companies.

4 Understand the types and major causes of business failure and the use of voluntary settlements to sustain or liquidate the failed firm.

5 Explain bankruptcy legislation and the procedures involved in reorganizing or liquidating a bankrupt firm.

6 Discuss the growth of and special factors relating to international mergers and joint ventures.

" The bank's rescue began with a retrenchment . . . with the goal of being the premier consumer bank on the West Coast. *""*

Divestiture and Expansion at BankAmerica

While other banks in the mid-1980s were earning high fees from interstate banking, high-flying real estate deals, and risky leveraged buyouts, BankAmerica was fighting for its life. Nonperforming Third World debt and bloated expenses required much of BankAmerica's available capital. Many felt BankAmerica was destined for ruin or takeover.

The bank's rescue began with a retrenchment. CEO A. W. Ted Clausen replaced the objective of being a nationally-recognized money-center bank with the goal of being the premier consumer bank on the West Coast. Clausen sold many of the bank's businesses including Charles Schwab (a discount brokerage business). It cut nonperforming loans to under 4 percent of the total loan portfolio. At this point, BankAmerica's performance ranking was twice that of New York money-center banks.

Depreciating real estate and LBO failures changed the bank's financial destiny. While East Coast money-center rivals were struggling for survival, BankAmerica's strong retail business provided excess cash. The excess cash allowed it to obtain many insolvent savings banks and S&Ls at bargain prices. Seven acquisitions and 250 branches were added in 1990 alone. The $400 million cost of the $7 billion dollars in core deposits was easily paid by BankAmerica.

Given BankAmerica's success, one might have expected its stock to be selling at all-time highs. Actually, it declined 21 percent in 1990. In part, the drop may have been a consequence of investor concern about both the focus and location of BankAmerica's most recent expansions. Over $10 billion in home loans were issued when real estate prices had been at their peak. Falling home prices and the recessionary economy could raise the number of nonperforming loans, especially since many of the new units were located in the hard-hit Southwest. The geographic distribution of these locations, removed from the bank's headquarters, would make necessary new management systems to ensure success.

These concerns were then overshadowed by BankAmerica's announcement in late 1991 of its merger with Los Angeles–based Security Pacific. The merger will make BankAmerica the dominant West Coast bank and return it to the numbr two position among America's largest banks. It appears that BankAmerica is meeting its goals, and its past experiences may help it prosper in the current expansion.

Mergers, LBOs, divestitures, and failure are important areas of long-term financial decision making. Although decisions in these areas are typically made much less frequently than capital budgeting, capital structure, and dividend decisions, their outcomes can significantly affect a firm's value. Mergers are sometimes used by firms to expand externally by acquiring control of another firm. While the overriding objective for a merger should be to improve (and hopefully maximize) the firm's share value, a number of more immediate motivations frequently exist. These include diversification, tax considerations, and increasing owner liquidity. Sometimes mergers are pursued in order to acquire needed assets rather than the going concern. Although the "merger mania" of the 1980s has cooled somewhat, brisk merger activity continues to take place today. Unfortunately not all firms are able to sustain themselves indefinitely; many fail each year. In some instances they can be reorganized voluntarily or under bankruptcy law with the cooperation of outsiders. If reorganization is not feasible, voluntary or legal procedures can be used to liquidate the firm in an orderly fashion. It is important that the financial manager understand the fundamental aspects of both mergers and business failure. Here we first discuss mergers, LBOs, and divestitures, followed by a brief review of business failure.

MERGER FUNDAMENTALS

In this section we discuss merger fundamentals—terminology, motives, and types. In the following sections we'll briefly describe the related topics of leveraged buyouts and divestitures and review the procedures used to analyze and negotiate mergers.

Basic Terminology

The high level of merger activity occurring over the last 10 to 15 years has resulted in the coining of numerous new terms to describe various actions, strategies, participants, and techniques. In the broadest sense, activities involving expansion or contraction of a firm's operations or changes in its asset or financial (ownership) structure are called **corporate restructuring.** The topics addressed in this chapter—mergers, LBOs, and divestitures—are some of the most common forms of corporate restructuring. Below we define some basic merger terminology; other terms are introduced and defined as needed in subsequent discussions.

corporate restructuring The activities involving expansion or contraction of a firm's operations or changes in its asset or financial (ownership) structure.

merger The combination of two or more firms, in which the resulting firm maintains the identity of one of the firms, usually the larger one.

Mergers, Consolidations, and Holding Companies

A **merger** occurs when two or more firms are combined and the resulting firm maintains the identity of one of the firms. Usually the assets

consolidation The combination of two or more firms to form a completely new firm.

holding company A corporation that has voting control of one or more other corporations.

subsidiaries The companies controlled by a holding company.

acquiring company The firm in a merger transaction that attempts to acquire another firm.

target company The firm in a merger transaction that the acquiring company is pursuing.

friendly merger A merger transaction endorsed by the target firm's management, approved by its stockholders, and easily consummated.

tender offer A formal offer to purchase a given number of shares of a firm's stock at a specified price.

hostile merger A merger transaction not supported by the target firm's management, forcing the acquiring company to try to gain control of the firm by buying shares in the marketplace.

strategic merger A merger transaction undertaken to achieve economies of scale.

and liabilities of the smaller firm are merged into those of the larger firm. **Consolidation,** on the other hand, involves the combination of two or more firms to form a completely new firm. The new corporation normally absorbs the assets and liabilities of the companies from which it is formed. Due to the similarity of mergers and consolidations, the term *merger* is used throughout this chapter to refer to both. A **holding company** is a corporation that has voting control of one or more other corporations. Having control in large, widely held companies generally requires ownership of between 10 and 20 percent of the outstanding stock. The companies controlled by a holding company are normally referred to as its **subsidiaries.** Control of a subsidiary is typically obtained by purchasing (generally for cash) a sufficient number of shares of its stock.

Acquiring versus Target Companies

The firm in a merger transaction that attempts to acquire another firm is commonly called the **acquiring company.** The firm that the acquiring company is pursuing is referred to as the **target company.** Generally the acquiring company identifies, evaluates, and negotiates with the management and/or shareholders of the target company. Occasionally the management of a target company initiates its acquisition by seeking to be acquired.

Friendly versus Hostile Takeovers

Mergers can occur on either a friendly or a hostile basis. Typically, after isolating the target company, the acquirer initiates discussions with its management. If the target management is receptive to the acquirer's proposal it may endorse the merger and recommend shareholder approval. If the stockholders approve the merger, the transaction is typically consummated through either a cash purchase of shares by the acquirer or through an exchange of the acquirer's stock, bonds, or some combination for the target firm's shares. This type of negotiated transaction is known as a **friendly merger.** If, on the other hand, the takeover target's management does not support the proposed takeover due to any of a number of possible reasons, it can fight the acquirer's actions. In this case the acquirer can attempt to gain control of the firm by buying sufficient shares of the target firm in the marketplace. This is typically accomplished using a **tender offer,** which is a formal offer to purchase a given number of shares of a firm's stock at a specified price. This type of unfriendly transaction is commonly referred to as a **hostile merger.** Clearly, hostile mergers are more difficult to consummate because the target firm's management acts to deter the acquisition. Regardless, hostile takeovers are sometimes successful.

Strategic versus Financial Mergers

Mergers are undertaken for either strategic or financial reasons. **Strategic mergers** involve merging firms in order to achieve various economies of scale by eliminating redundant functions, increasing market share, improving raw material sourcing and finished product distribution, and so on. In these mergers the operations of the acquiring and target firms are combined in order to achieve economies and thereby cause the performance of the merged firm to exceed that of the pre-merged firms. Recent examples of strategic mergers include the mergers of AT&T (telecommunication services) and NCR (computers), Bristol Meyers and Squibb (both drug firms), and Procter & Gamble (consumer products) and Noxell (cosmetics). An interesting variation of the strategic merger involves the purchase of specific product lines (rather than the whole company) for strategic reasons. Recent examples include the Colgate-Palmolive (consumer products) purchase of the Softsoap Liquid line from Minnetonka Labs and Shaw Industries' (textiles) purchase of the carpet division of Armstrong World Industries.

Financial mergers, on the other hand, are based upon the acquisition of companies that can be restructured in order to improve their cash flow. These mergers involve the acquisition of the target firm by an acquirer, which may be another company or a group of investors—often the firm's existing management. The objective of the acquirer is to drastically cut costs and sell off certain unproductive or noncompatible assets in order to increase the firm's cash flows. The increased cash flows are used to service the sizable debt typically incurred to finance these transactions. Financial mergers are not based on the firm's ability to achieve economies of scale, but rather on the acquirer's belief that through restructuring, the firm's hidden value can be unlocked. The ready availability of expensive, high-risk (junk) bond financing throughout the 1980s fueled the financial merger mania during that period. Examples of financial mergers include the takeover of RJR Nabisco by Kohlberg Kravis Roberts (KKR), Campeau Corporation's (real estate) acquisition of Allied Stores and Federated Department Stores, and Merv Griffin's acquisition of Resorts International (hotels/casinos) from Donald Trump. With the collapse of the junk bond market in the early 1990s, financial mergers have fallen on relatively hard times. The heavy debt burdens involved in many of the glamour financial mergers of the 1980s have caused many of these deals, such as the Allied Stores/Federated Department Stores and Resorts International mergers, to be in or near bankruptcy in the early 1990s. As a result, the strategic merger, which does not rely as heavily on debt, tends to dominate today.

financial merger A merger transaction undertaken to restructure the acquired company in order to improve its cash flow and unlock its hidden value.

Motives for Merging

Firms merge in order to fulfill certain objectives. The overriding goal for merging is the maximization of the owners' wealth as reflected in the acquirer's share price. Specific motives include growth or diversification, synergy, fund raising, increased managerial skill or technology, tax considerations, increased ownership liquidity, and defense against takeover. These motives should be pursued when they are believed consistent with owner wealth maximization.

Growth or Diversification
Companies that desire rapid growth in *size* or *market share* or diversification in *the range of their products* may find that a merger can be used to fulfill this objective. Instead of going through the time-consuming

S M A L L   B U S I N E S S

Small Businesses as Liquid Assets

Steve McDonnell knew little about meat when he bought Jugtown Mountain Smokehouse in 1987. He had plenty of business experience though. McDonnell figured that even a family-owned, specialty-meats producer could provide opportunities for a growth-oriented individual. New meat-processing equipment and an updated computer system were installed. Capital budgeting determined that the projects with the highest net present value consisted of meats emphasizing low-fat products such as smoked turkey. Cost accounting and other working capital techniques were also employed. As a result, sales rose from roughly $300,000 in 1987 to $1.4 million in 1990.

McDonnell then began to expand his business. To reduce competition, he sought acquisition of his major competitor. Beyond reducing price competition, the acquisition reduced distribution costs per unit since both firms were servicing the same outlets. Another expansion included acquiring a company that specializes in European-style meats. Steve McDonnell views small firms as assets held within a larger portfolio. Self-admittedly afraid to manage a start-up, acquisition is his mode of expansion.

McDonnell is not the classic entrepreneur with an idea waiting to be cultivated. The objective of such an entrepreneur is to build a company using techniques learned in business schools and practiced in commerce. As the ranks of experienced and available managers have swelled in response to America's largest corporations slashing white-collar payrolls, entrepreneurs are being displaced by growth-oriented business managers like Steve McDonnell. The rules of business expansion have consequently changed. Small businesses are often viewed as liquid assets, capable of being bought, sold, and combined in a variety of ways. Businesses are being viewed less as bricks and mortar and more as a collection of skills and assets.

Source: John Case, "Buy now—avoid the rush," *INC.*, February 1991, pp. 36–45.

process of internal growth or diversification, the firm may achieve the same objective in a short period of time by merging with an existing firm. In addition, such a strategy is often less costly than the alternative of developing the necessary production capability and capacity. If a firm that wants to expand operations in existing or new product areas can find a suitable going concern, it may avoid many of the risks associated with the design, manufacture, and sale of additional or new products. Moreover, when a firm expands or extends its product line by acquiring another firm, it also removes a potential competitor.[1]

Synergy

The *synergy* of mergers is the economies of scale resulting from the merged firms' lower overhead. Synergy is said to be present when a whole is greater than the sum of the parts ("1 plus 1 equals 3"). The economies of scale that generally result from a merger lower the combined overhead, thereby increasing earnings to a level greater than the sum of the earnings of each of the independent firms. Synergy is most obvious when firms merge with other firms in the same line of business, since many redundant functions and employees can thereby be eliminated. Staff functions, such as purchasing and sales, are probably most greatly affected by this type of combination.

Fund Raising

Often firms combine to enhance their fund-raising ability. A firm may be unable to obtain funds for its own internal expansion but able to obtain funds for external business combinations. Quite often one firm may combine with another that has high liquid assets and low levels of liabilities. The acquisition of this type of "cash-rich" company immediately increases the firm's borrowing power by decreasing its financial leverage. This result should allow funds to be raised externally at lower cost.

Increased Managerial Skill or Technology

Occasionally a firm will have good potential that it finds itself unable to develop fully due to deficiencies in certain areas of management or an absence of needed product or production technology. If the firm cannot hire the management or develop the technology it needs, it might combine with a compatible firm that has the needed managerial personnel or technical expertise. Of course any merger, regardless of the specific motive for it, should contribute to the maximization of owners' wealth.

Tax Considerations

Quite often tax considerations are a key motive for merging. In such a case the tax benefit generally stems from the fact that one of the firms has a **tax loss carryforward.** This means that the company's tax loss can be applied against a limited amount of future income of the merged firm over the shorter of either 15 years or until the total tax loss has

tax loss carryforward In a merger, the tax loss of one of the firms that can be applied against a limited amount of future income of the merged firm over the shorter of either 15 years or until the total tax loss has been fully recovered.

---

[1]Certain legal constraints on growth exist—especially where the elimination of competition is expected. The various antitrust laws, which are closely enforced by the Federal Trade Commission (FTC) and the Justice Department, prohibit business combinations that eliminate competition, especially when the resulting enterprise would be a monopoly.

been fully recovered.[2] Two situations could actually exist. A company with a tax loss could acquire a profitable company in order to utilize the tax loss. In this case the acquiring firm would boost the combination's after-tax earnings by reducing the taxable income of the acquired firm. A tax loss may also be useful when a profitable firm acquires a firm that has such a loss. In either situation, however, the merger must be justified not only on the basis of the tax benefits but also on grounds consistent with the goal of owner wealth maximization. Moreover, the tax benefits described can be used only in mergers. They cannot be used in the formation of holding companies, since only in the case of mergers are operating results reported on a consolidated basis. An example will clarify the use of the tax loss carryforward.

EXAMPLE   Maxwell Company, a wheel bearing manufacturer, has a total of $450,000 in tax loss carryforwards resulting from operating tax losses of $150,000 a year in each of the past three years. To use these losses and to diversify its operations, C.B. Company, a molder of plastics, has acquired Maxwell through a merger. C.B. expects to have *earnings before taxes* of $300,000 per year. We assume that these earnings are realized, that they fall within the annual limit legally allowed for application of the tax loss carryforward resulting from the merger (see footnote 2 below), that the Maxwell portion of the merged firm just breaks even, and that C.B. is in the 40 percent tax bracket. The total taxes paid by the two firms and their after-tax earnings without and with the merger are calculated as shown in Table 17.1.

With the merger the total tax payments are less— $180,000 (total of line 7) versus $360,000 (total of line 2). With the merger the total after-tax earnings are more— $720,000 (total of line 8) versus $540,000 (total of line 3). The merged firm is able to deduct the tax loss either for 15 years subsequently or until the total tax loss has been fully recovered, whichever period is shorter. In this example the shorter is at the end of year 2.

Increased Ownership Liquidity

The merger of two small firms or a small and a larger firm may provide the owners of the small firm(s) with greater liquidity. This is due to the higher marketability associated with the shares of larger firms. Instead of holding shares in a small firm that has a very "thin" market, the owners will receive shares that are traded in a broader market and can thus be liquidated more readily. The ability to convert shares into cash

---

[2]The *Tax Reform Act of 1986*, in order to deter firms from combining solely to take advantage of tax loss carryforwards, initiated an annual limit on the amount of taxable income against which such losses can be applied. The annual limit is determined by formula and is tied to the pre-merger value of the corporation with the loss. While not fully eliminating this motive for combination, the act makes it more difficult for firms to justify combinations solely on the basis of tax loss carryforwards.

Table 17.1   Total Taxes and After-Tax Earnings for C.B. Company
without and with Merger

Total taxes and after-tax earnings without merger

	Year			Total for 3 years
	1	2	3	
(1) Earnings before taxes	$300,000	$300,000	$300,000	$900,000
(2) Taxes [.40 × (1)]	120,000	120,000	120,000	360,000
(3) Earnings after taxes [(1) − (2)]	$180,000	$180,000	$180,000	$540,000

Total taxes and after-tax earnings with merger

(4) Earnings before losses	$300,000	$300,000	$300,000	$900,000
(5) Tax loss carryforward	300,000	150,000	0	450,000
(6) Earnings before taxes [(4) − (5)]	$ 0	$150,000	$300,000	$450,000
(7) Taxes [.40 × (6)]	0	60,000	120,000	180,000
(8) Earnings after taxes [(4) − (7)]	$300,000	$240,000	$180,000	$720,000

quickly is welcome. And owning shares for which market price quotations are readily available provides owners with a better sense of the value of their holdings. Especially in the case of small, closely held firms, the improved liquidity of ownership obtainable through merger with an acceptable firm may have considerable appeal.

Defense against Takeover

Occasionally when a firm becomes the target of an unfriendly takeover, it will as a defense acquire another company. Such a strategy typically works like this: The original target firm takes on additional debt in order to finance its defensive acquisition; because of the debt load, the target firm becomes too large and too highly levered financially to be of any further interest to its suitor. To be effective, a defensive takeover must create greater value for shareholders than they would have realized had the firm been merged with its suitor. An example of such a defense was the 1987 acquisition of Holt, Rinehart and Winston (publishing) from CBS, Inc. (broadcasting) by Harcourt Brace Jovanovich, HBJ (publishing, insurance, theme parks) in order to ward off its suitor, Robert Maxwell (British takeover specialist). In order to service the huge debt incurred in this transaction, HBJ subsequently sold its Sea World theme parks to Anheuser-Busch Co. (alcoholic beverages), but continued to experience serious financial difficulty. In late 1991, after much negotiation, HBJ was acquired by General Cinema. In retrospect it appears that HBJ's defense was its downfall. Clearly the use of a merger as a takeover defense, while effectively deterring the takeover, can result in subsequent financial difficulty, and possibly failure.

Types of Mergers

horizontal merger A merger of two firms *in the same line of business.*

vertical merger A merger in which a firm acquires *a supplier or a customer.*

congeneric merger A merger in which one firm acquires another firm *in the same general industry* but neither in the same line of business nor a supplier or customer.

conglomerate merger A merger combining firms in *unrelated businesses.*

The four types of mergers are the (1) horizontal merger, (2) vertical merger, (3) congeneric merger, and (4) conglomerate merger. A **horizontal merger** results when two firms *in the same line of business* are merged. An example would be the merger of two machine-tool manufacturers. This form of merger results in the expansion of a firm's operations in a given product line and at the same time eliminates a competitor. A **vertical merger** occurs when a firm acquires *a supplier or a customer.* For example, the merger of a machine-tool manufacturer with its supplier of castings would be a vertical merger. The economic benefit of this type of merger stems from the firm's increased control over the acquisition of raw materials or the distribution of finished goods.

A **congeneric merger** is achieved by acquiring a firm *in the same general industry* but neither in the same line of business nor a supplier or customer. An example is the merger of a machine-tool manufacturer with a manufacturer of industrial conveyor systems. The benefit of this type of merger is the resulting ability to use the same sales and distribution channels to reach customers of both businesses. A **conglomerate merger** involves the combination of firms in *unrelated businesses.* The merger of a machine-tool manufacturer with a chain of fast-food restaurants would be an example of this kind of merger. The key benefit of the conglomerate merger is its ability to *reduce risk* by merging firms with different seasonal or cyclical patterns of sales and earnings.

LBOs AND DIVESTITURES

Before addressing the mechanics of merger analysis and negotiation, we will cover two topics that are closely related to mergers—LBOs and divestitures. An LBO is a method of structuring a financial merger, whereas divestiture involves the sale of a firm's assets.

Leveraged Buyouts (LBOs)

leveraged buyout (LBO) An acquisition technique involving the use of a large amount of debt to purchase a firm.

A popular technique widely used during the 1980s to make acquisitions is the **leveraged buyout (LBO).** It involves the use of a large amount of debt to purchase a firm. LBOs are a clear-cut example of a *financial merger* undertaken to create a high-debt private corporation with improved cash flow and value. Typically 90 percent or more of the purchase price of an LBO is financed with debt. A large part of the borrowing is secured by the acquired firm's assets. The lenders, due to the high risk, take a portion of the firm's equity. Expensive, high-risk (junk) bonds have been routinely used to raise the large amounts of debt needed to finance LBO transactions. Of course, the purchasers in an LBO expect to use the improved cash flow to service the large amount of junk bond and other debt incurred in the buyout. The acquirers in LBOs are other firms or groups of investors that frequently include key members of the acquired firm's existing management.

An attractive candidate for acquisition through leveraged buyout should possess three basic attributes:

1 ■■■ It must have a good position in its industry with a solid profit history and reasonable expectations for growth.

2 ■■■ The firm should have a relatively low level of debt and a high level of "bankable" assets that can be used as loan collateral.

3 ■■■ It must have stable and predictable cash flows that are adequate to meet interest and principal payments on the debt and provide adequate working capital.

Of course, a willingness on the part of existing ownership and management to sell the company on a leveraged basis is also needed.

The leveraged buyout of Gibson Greeting Cards by a group of investors and managers headed by William Simon, former secretary of the treasury, is the classic example of a highly successful LBO. In the early 1980s Simon's group, Wesray, purchased Gibson from RCA for $81 million. The group put up $1 million and borrowed the remaining $80 million, using the firm's assets as collateral. Within three years after Gibson had been acquired, Wesray had publicly sold 50 percent of the company for $87 million. Wesray still owned 50 percent of Gibson and had earned $87 million on a $1 million investment. While success of this magnitude is indeed not typical, it does point out the potential rewards from the use of LBOs to finance acquisitions.

More recent examples of LBOs include the largest ever, the $24.5 billion buyout of RJR Nabisco by KKR; Campeau Corporation's buyouts of Allied Stores and Federated Department Stores; and the management buyout of Topps Co. (baseball cards, Bazooka bubble gum). Topps was subsequently taken public, resulting in sizable profits for the buyout group. Less fortunate was KKR's buyout of Seaman Furniture; like Campeau Corporation, KKR defaulted on this transaction. Today, with a number of highly publicized LBOs at or near default on the debt (primarily high-risk junk bonds) incurred to finance the buyout, the jury remains out on the success of the numerous LBOs of the 1980s. Coupled with the collapse of the high-risk (junk) bond market in early 1990, the future level of LBO activity is expected to be greatly diminished from its frenzied pace of the 1980s.

Divestitures

It is important to recognize that companies often achieve external expansion by acquiring an **operating unit**—plant, division, product line, subsidiary, etc.—of another company. In such a case, the seller generally believes that the value of the firm would be enhanced by converting the unit into cash or some other more productive asset. The selling of some of a firm's assets is called **divestiture.** Unlike selling assets in the case of business failure, the motive for divestiture is often positive: to

operating unit A part of a business, such as a plant, division, product line, or subsidiary, that contributes to the actual operations of the firm.

divestiture The selling of some of a firm's assets, for various strategic motives.

generate cash for expansion of other product lines; to get rid of a poorly performing operation; to streamline the corporation; to restructure the corporation's business consistent with its strategic goals.

There are a variety of methods by which firms divest themselves of operating units. One involves the *sale of a product line to another firm*. Examples include Dow Jones & Co.'s (newspaper publishing) sale of Richard D. Irwin (publishing) to Times Mirror (newspapers) in order to concentrate on its business publishing, and Clorox Company's (soap and cleaning products) sale of its Lucite/Olympic Paint business in order to focus entirely on its supermarket-distributed products. These outright sales can be accomplished on a cash or stock-swap basis using the procedures described later in this chapter. A second method that has become quite popular in recent years involves the *sale of the unit to existing management*. This sale is often achieved through the use of a leveraged buyout (LBO). Sometimes divestiture is achieved through a **spin-off** which results in an operating unit becoming an independent company. A spin-off is accomplished by issuing shares in the unit being divested on a pro rata basis to the parent company's shareholders. Such an action allows the unit to be separated from the corporation and to trade as a separate entity. An example is the spin-off of Crystal Brands (textile and apparel manufacturing) by General Mills (foods). Like outright sale, this approach achieves the divestiture objective although it does not bring additional cash or stock to the parent company. The final and least popular approach to divestiture involves *liquidation of the operating unit's individual assets*.

Regardless of the method used to divest a firm of an unwanted operating unit, the goal typically is to create a more lean and focused operation. This, in turn, will enhance the efficiency as well as the profitability of the enterprise and create maximum value for shareholders. Recent divestitures seem to suggest that many operating units are worth much more to others than to the firm itself. Comparisons of post- and pre-divestiture market values have shown that the "breakup value" of many firms is significantly greater than their combined value. As a result of market valuations, divestiture often creates value in excess of the cash or stock received in the transaction. Unlike LBOs, the use of divestitures in corporate restructuring is expected to remain popular.

spin-off A form of divestiture in which an operating unit becomes an independent company by issuing shares in it on a pro rata basis to the parent company's share-holders.

ANALYZING AND NEGOTIATING MERGERS

This portion of the chapter describes the procedures used to analyze and negotiate mergers. Initially, we'll consider valuing the target company and using stock swap transactions to acquire companies. Next, we'll look at the merger negotiation process. Finally, we'll discuss the major advantages and disadvantages of holding companies.

Valuing the Target Company

Once the acquiring company isolates a target company it wishes to acquire, it must estimate the target's value. The value would then be used, along with a proposed financing scheme, to negotiate the transaction—on a friendly or hostile basis. The value of the target would be estimated using the valuation techniques presented in Chapter 12 and applied to long-term investment decisions in Chapters 14 and 15. Similar capital budgeting techniques would be applied whether the target firm is being acquired for its assets or as a going concern.

Acquisitions of Assets

Occasionally a firm is acquired not for its income-earning potential but as a collection of assets (generally fixed assets) that are needed by the acquiring company. The price paid for this type of acquisition depends largely on which assets are being acquired. Consideration must also be given to the value of any tax losses. To determine whether the purchase of assets is financially justified, the acquirer must estimate both the costs and benefits of the target assets. This is a capital budgeting problem (see Chapters 14 and 15) since an initial cash outlay is made to acquire assets and, as a result, future cash inflows are expected.

EXAMPLE   PR Company, a major manufacturer of electric transformers, is interested in acquiring certain fixed assets of Zoom Company, an industrial electronics company. Zoom, which has tax loss carryforwards from losses over the past five years, is interested in selling out, but it wishes to sell out entirely, not just get rid of certain fixed assets. A condensed balance sheet for Zoom Company follows.

Balance Sheet Zoom Company			
Assets		**Liabilities and stockholders' equity**	
Cash	$ 2,000	Total liabilities	$ 80,000
Marketable securities	0	Stockholders' equity	120,000
Accounts receivable	8,000	Total liabilities and	
Inventories	10,000	stockholders'	$200,000
Machine A	10,000	equity	
Machine B	30,000		
Machine C	25,000		
Land and buildings	115,000		
Total assets	$200,000		

PR Company needs only machines B and C and the land and buildings. However, it has made some inquiries and has arranged to sell the accounts receivable, inventories, and machine A for $23,000. Since there is also $2,000 in cash, PR will get $25,000 for the excess assets. Zoom wants $20,000 for the entire company, which means that PR will have to pay the firm's creditors $80,000 and its owners $20,000. The actual outlay required by PR after liquidating

Table 17.2   **Net Present Value of Zoom Company's Assets**

Year(s)	Cash inflow (1)	Present value factor at 11% (2)	Present value [(1) × (2)] (3)
1–5	$14,000	3.696[a]	$51,744
6	12,000	0.535[b]	6,420
7	12,000	0.482[b]	5,784
8	12,000	0.434[b]	5,208
9	12,000	0.391[b]	4,692
10	12,000	0.352[b]	4,224
		Present value of inflows	$78,072
		Less: Cash outlay required	75,000
		Net present value[c]	$ 3,072

[a]The present-value interest factor for an annuity, *PVIFA*, with a five-year life discounted at 11 percent obtained from Table C-4.
[b]The present-value interest factor, *PVIF*, for $1 discounted at 11 percent for the corresponding year obtained from Table C-3.
[c]Using a business calculator the net present value is $3,063.

the unneeded assets will be $75,000 [($80,000 + $20,000) − $25,000]. In other words, to obtain the use of the desired assets (machines B and C and the land and buildings) and the benefits of Zoom's tax losses, PR must pay $75,000. The *after-tax cash inflows* expected to result from the new assets and applicable tax losses are $14,000 per year for the next five years and $12,000 per year for the following five years. The desirability of this asset acquisition can be determined by calculating the net present value of this outlay using PR Company's 11 percent cost of capital, as shown in Table 17.2. *Since the net present value of $3,072 is greater than zero, PR's value should be increased by acquiring Zoom Company's assets.*

Acquisitions of Going Concerns

Acquisitions of target companies that are going concerns are best analyzed using capital budgeting techniques similar to those described for asset acquisitions. The basic difficulty in applying the capital budgeting approach to the acquisition of a going concern is the *estimation of cash flows* and certain *risk considerations*. The methods of estimating expected cash flows from an acquisition are similar to those used in estimating capital budgeting cash flows. Typically, *pro forma income statements* reflecting the postmerger revenues and costs attributable to the target company are prepared (see Chapter 6). They are then adjusted to reflect the expected cash flows over the relevant time period. Whenever a firm considers acquiring a target company that has different risk behaviors, it should adjust the cost of capital appropriately prior to applying the appropriate capital budgeting techniques (see Chapter 15). An example will clarify this procedure.

EXAMPLE   Edge Company, a major media company, is contemplating the acquisition of Wall Company, a small independent film producer that can be purchased for $60,000. Edge currently has a high degree of financial leverage, which is reflected in its 13 percent cost of capital. Because of the low financial leverage of the Wall Company, Edge estimates that its overall cost of capital will drop to 10 percent after the acquisition. Since the effect of the less risky capital structure resulting from the acquisition of Wall Company cannot be reflected in the expected cash flows, the postmerger cost of capital (10 percent) must be used to evaluate the cash flows expected from the acquisition. The postmerger cash flows attributable to the target company are forecast over a 30-year time horizon. These estimated cash flows (all inflows) are $5,000 for years 1 through 10; $13,000 for years 11 through 18; and $4,000 for years 19 through 30. The net present value (i.e., value) of the target company, Wall Company, is calculated in Table 17.3.

Since the net present value of the target company of $2,357 is greater than zero, the merger is acceptable. It is interesting to note that, had the effect of the changed capital structure on the cost of capital not been considered, the ac-

Table 17.3   **Net Present Value
of the Wall Company Acquisition**

Year(s)	Cash inflow (1)	Present value factor at 10%[a] (2)	Present value [(1) × (2)] (3)
1–10	$ 5,000	6.145	$30,725
11–18	13,000	(8.201 − 6.145)[b]	26,728
19–30	4,000	(9.427 − 8.201)[b]	4,904
	Present value of inflows		$62,357
	Less: Cash purchase price		60,000
	Net present value[c]		$ 2,357

[a]Present-value interest factors for annuities, *PVIFA*, obtained from Table C-4.
[b]These factors are found using a shortcut technique that can be applied to annuities for periods of years beginning at some point in the future. By finding the appropriate interest factor for the present value of an annuity given for the last year of the annuity and subtracting the present-value interest factor of an annuity for the year immediately preceding the beginning of the annuity, the analyst can obtain the appropriate interest factor for the present value of an annuity beginning sometime in the future. You can check this shortcut by using the long approach and comparing the results.
[c]The net present value using a business calculator is $2,364.

quisition would have been found unacceptable since the net present value *at a 13 percent cost of capital* is −$11,864, which is less than zero. (The calculated value using a business calculator is −$11,868.)

Stock Swap Transactions

stock swap transaction An acquisition method in which the acquiring firm exchanges its shares for shares of the target company according to a predetermined ratio.

Once the value of the target company is determined, the acquirer must develop a proposed financing package. The simplest, but probably least common case, would be a pure cash purchase. Beyond this extreme case there are virtually an infinite number of financing packages. They use various combinations of cash, debt, preferred stock, and common stock. Here we look at the other extreme—**stock swap transactions** in which the acquisition is paid for using an exchange of common stock. The acquiring firm exchanges its shares for shares of the target company according to a predetermined ratio. The *ratio of exchange* of shares is determined in the merger negotiations. This ratio affects the various financial yardsticks that are used by existing and prospective shareholders to value the merged firm's shares. With the demise of LBOs, the use of stock swaps to finance mergers has grown in popularity during the past few years.

Ratio of Exchange

ratio of exchange The ratio of the amount *paid* per share of the target company to the per-share market price of the acquiring firm.

When one firm swaps its stock for the shares of another firm, the firms must determine the number of shares of the acquiring firm to be exchanged for each share of the target firm. The first requirement, of course, is that the acquiring company have sufficient shares available to complete the transaction. Often a firm's repurchase of shares (which was discussed in Chapter 16) is necessary to obtain sufficient shares for such a transaction. The acquiring firm generally offers more for each share of the target company than the current market price of its publicly traded shares. The actual **ratio of exchange** is merely the ratio of the amount *paid* per share of the target company to the per-share market price of the acquiring firm. It is calculated in this manner since the acquiring firm pays the target firm in stock, which has a value equal to its market price. An example will clarify the calculation.

EXAMPLE   Bigge Company, a leather products concern, whose stock is currently selling for $80 per share, is interested in acquiring Tiny Company, a producer of belts. To prepare for the acquisition, Bigge has been repurchasing its own shares over the past three years. Tiny's stock is currently selling for $75 per share, but in the merger negotiations, Bigge has found it necessary to offer Tiny $110 per share. Since Bigge does not have sufficient financial resources to purchase the firm for cash, and it does not wish to raise these funds, Tiny has agreed to accept Bigge's stock in exchange for its shares. As stated, Bigge's stock currently sells for $80 per share, and it must pay $110 per share for Tiny's stock. Therefore the ratio of exchange is 1.375 ($110 ÷ $80). This means that Bigge Company must exchange 1.375 shares of its stock for each share of Tiny's stock.

Effect on Earnings per Share

Ordinarily the resulting earnings per share differ from the premerger earnings per share for both the acquiring firm and the target firm. They depend largely on the ratio of exchange and the premerger earnings per share of each firm. It is best to view the initial and long-run effects of the ratio of exchange on earnings per share (EPS) separately.

Initial Effect   When the ratio of exchange is equal to 1 and both the acquiring and the target firm have the *same* premerger earnings per share, the merged firm's earnings per share will initially remain constant. In this rare instance, both the acquiring and the target firm would also have equal price/earnings (P/E) ratios. In actuality the earnings per share of the merged firm are generally above the premerger earnings per share of one firm and below the premerger earnings per share of the other, after making the necessary adjustment for the ratio of exchange. These differences can be illustrated by a simple example.

EXAMPLE   Bigge Company is contemplating acquiring Tiny Company by swapping 1.375 shares of its stock for each share of Tiny's stock. The current financial data related to the earnings and market price for each of these companies are given in Table 17.4. Although Tiny's stock currently has a market price of $75 per share, Bigge has offered it $110 per share. As seen in the preceding example, this results in a ratio of exchange of 1.375.

To complete the merger and retire the 20,000 shares of Tiny Company stock outstanding, Bigge will have to issue or use treasury stock totaling 27,500 shares (1.375 × 20,000 shares). Once the merger is completed, Bigge will have 152,500 shares of common stock (125,000 + 27,500) outstanding. If the earnings of each of the firms remain constant, the merged company will be expected to have earn-

Table 17.4   **Bigge Company and Tiny Company Financial Data**

Item	Bigge Company	Tiny Company
(1) Earnings available for common stock	$500,000	$100,000
(2) Number of shares of common stock outstanding	125,000	20,000
(3) Earnings per share [(1) ÷ (2)]	$4	$5
(4) Market price per share	$80	$75
(5) Price/earnings (P/E) ratio [(4) ÷ (3)]	20	15

Table 17.5   **Summary of the Effects on Earnings per Share of a Merger between Bigge Company and Tiny Company at $110 per Share**

	Earnings per share	
Stockholders	**Before merger**	**After merger**
Bigge Company	$4.00	$3.93[a]
Tiny Company	5.00	5.40[b]

[a] $\dfrac{\$500,000 + \$100,000}{125,000 + (1.375 \times 20,000)} = \$3.93$

[b] $\$3.93 \times 1.375 = \$5.40$

ings available for the common stockholders of $600,000 ($500,000 + $100,000). The earnings per share of the merged company should therefore equal approximately $3.93 per share ($600,000 ÷ 152,500 shares).

It would appear at first that Tiny Company's shareholders have sustained a decrease in per-share earnings from $5 to $3.93. But since each share of Tiny Company's original stock is equivalent to 1.375 shares of the merged company, the equivalent earnings per share are actually $5.40 ($3.93 × 1.375). In other words, as a result of the merger Bigge Company's original shareholders experience a decrease in earnings per share from $4 to $3.93 to the benefit of Tiny Company's shareholders, whose earnings per share increase from $5 to $5.40. These results are summarized in Table 17.5.

The postmerger earnings per share for owners of the acquiring and target companies can be explained by comparing the price/earnings (P/E) ratio paid by the acquiring company with its initial P/E ratio. This relationship is summarized in Table 17.6. By paying more than its current value per dollar of earnings to acquire each dollar of earnings (P/E paid > P/E of acquiring company), the acquiring firm transfers the claim on a portion of its premerger earnings to the owners of the target firm. Therefore, on a postmerger basis the target firm's EPS increases and the acquiring firm's EPS decreases. Note that this outcome is *almost always* the case. The acquirer typically pays a 50 percent, on average, premium above the target firm's market price, thereby resulting in the P/E paid being much above its own P/E. Examples include Bristol-Myers paying 26 times Squibb's EPS when its own P/E was 16, and Procter & Gamble paying 27 times Noxell's EPS when its own P/E was only 17. If the acquiring company were to pay less than its current value per dollar of earnings to acquire each dollar of earnings (P/E paid < P/E of acquiring company), the opposite effects would result. The P/E ratios associated with the Bigge-Tiny merger can be used to explain the effect of the merger on earnings per share.

Table 17.6   **Effect of Price/Earnings (P/E) Ratios on Earnings per Share (EPS)**

Relationship between P/E paid and P/E of acquiring company	Effect on EPS	
	Acquiring company	Target company
P/E paid > P/E of acquiring company	Decrease	Increase
P/E paid = P/E of acquiring company	Constant	Constant
P/E paid < P/E of acquiring company	Increase	Decrease

EXAMPLE   Bigge Company's P/E ratio is 20, while the P/E ratio paid for Tiny Company's earnings was 22 ($110 ÷ $5). Since the P/E paid for Tiny Company was greater than the P/E for Bigge Company (22 versus 20), the effect of the merger was to decrease the EPS for original holders of shares in Bigge Company (from $4.00 to $3.93) and to increase the effective EPS of original holders of shares in Tiny Company (from $5.00 to $5.40).

Long-Run Effect   The long-run effect of a merger on the earnings per share of the merged company depends largely on whether the earnings of the merged firm grow. Often, although a decrease in the per-share earnings of the stock held by the original owners of the acquiring firm is expected initially, the long-run effects of the merger on earnings per share are quite favorable. What, then, enables the acquiring company to experience higher future EPS than it would have without the merger? The key factor is that the earnings attributable to the target company's assets grow at a faster rate than those resulting from the acquiring company's premerger assets. An example will clarify this point.

EXAMPLE   In 1992 Bigge Company acquired Tiny Company by swapping 1.375 shares of its common stock for each share of Tiny Company. Other key financial data and the effects of this exchange ratio were discussed in the preceding examples. The total earnings of Bigge Company were expected to grow at an annual rate of 3 percent without the merger; Tiny Company's earnings were expected to grow at a 7 percent annual rate without the merger. The same growth rates are expected to apply to the component earnings streams with the merger.[3] Table 17.7 shows the future effects on EPS for Bigge Company without and with the proposed Tiny Company merger, based on these growth rates.

Table 17.7 indicates that the earnings per share without the merger will be greater than the EPS with the merger for the years 1992 through 1994. After 1994, however, the

---

[3]Frequently, due to synergy, the combined earnings stream is greater than the sum of the individual earnings streams. This possibility is ignored here.

Table 17.7

**Effects of Earnings Growth
on EPS for Bigge Company
without and with the Tiny Company Merger**

Year	Without merger		With merger	
	Total earnings[a]	Earnings per share[b]	Total earnings[c]	Earnings per share[d]
1992	$500,000	$4.00	$600,000	$3.93
1993	515,000	4.12	622,000	4.08
1994	530,450	4.24	644,940	4.23
1995	546,364	4.37	668,868	4.39
1996	562,755	4.50	693,835	4.55
1997	579,638	4.64	719,893	4.72

[a]Based on a 3 percent annual growth rate.
[b]Based on 125,000 shares outstanding.
[c]Based on 3 percent annual growth in Bigge Company's earnings and 7 percent annual growth in Tiny Company's earnings.
[d]Based on 152,500 shares outstanding [125,000 shares + (1.375 × 20,000 shares)].

EPS will be higher than they would have been without the merger as a result of the faster earnings growth rate of Tiny Company (7% versus 3%). Although a few years are required for this difference in the growth rate of earnings to pay off, it can be seen that in the future Bigge Company will receive an earnings benefit as a result of merging with Tiny Company at a 1.375 ratio of exchange. The relationships in Table 17.7 are graphed in Figure 17.1. The long-run earnings advantage of the merger is clearly depicted by this graph.

Effect on Market Price per Share

The market price per share does not necessarily remain constant after the acquisition of one firm by another. Adjustments occur in the marketplace in response to changes in expected earnings, the dilution of ownership, changes in risk, and certain other operating and financial changes. Using the ratio of exchange, we can calculate a **ratio of exchange in market price.** It indicates the market price per share of the acquiring firm *paid* for each dollar of market price per share of the target firm. This ratio, the *MPR*, is defined by Equation 17.1:

ratio of exchange in market price The ratio of the market price per share of the acquiring firm *paid* to each dollar of market price per share of the target firm.

Equation 17.1
Formula for the ratio of exchange in market price

$$MPR = \frac{MP_{\text{acquiring}} \times RE}{MP_{\text{target}}}$$

where

MPR = market price ratio of exchange

$MP_{\text{acquiring}}$ = market price per share of the acquiring firm

MP_{target} = market price per share of the target firm

RE = ratio of exchange

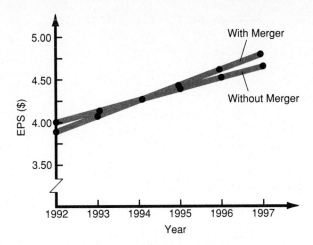

Figure 17.1   Future EPS without and with
**   the Bigge-Tiny Merger**
The earnings per share (EPS) for Bigge Company in
the period from 1992 through 1994 will be lower
with the proposed Tiny Company merger than
without it. After 1994 the postmerger EPS will be
greater with than without the proposed merger.

The following example can be used to illustrate the calculation of
this ratio.

EXAMPLE   In the Bigge-Tiny example, the market price of Bigge
Company's stock was $80 and that of Tiny Company's was
$75. The ratio of exchange was 1.375. Substituting these val-
ues into Equation 17.1 yields a ratio of exchange in market
price of 1.47 [($80 × 1.375) ÷ $75]. This means that $1.47 of
the market price of Bigge Company is given in exchange for
every $1.00 of the market price of Tiny Company.

The ratio of exchange in market price is normally always greater
than 1. This fact indicates that to acquire a firm, a premium above its
market price must be paid by the acquirer. Even so, the original owners
of the acquiring firm may still gain because the merged firm's stock
may sell at a price/earnings ratio above the individual premerger ratios.
This results due to the improved risk and return relationship perceived
by shareholders and other investors.

EXAMPLE   The financial data developed earlier for the Bigge-Tiny
merger can be used to explain the market price effects of a
merger. If the earnings of the merged company remain at
the premerger levels, and if the stock of the merged company sells at an assumed multiple of 21 times earnings, the
values in Table 17.8 can be expected. In spite of the fact that
Bigge Company's earnings per share decline from $4.00 to

Table 17.8   **Postmerger Market Price of Bigge Company Using a P/E Ratio of 21**

Item	Merged company
(1) Earnings available for common stock	$600,000
(2) Number of shares of common stock outstanding	152,500
(3) Earnings per share [(1) ÷ (2)]	$3.93
(4) Price/earnings (P/E) ratio	21
(5) Expected market price per share [(3) × (4)]	$82.53

$3.93 (see Table 17.5), the market price of its shares will increase from $80.00 (see Table 17.4) to $82.53 as a result of the merger.

Although the kind of behavior exhibited in this example is not unusual, the financial manager must recognize that only with proper management of the merged enterprise can its market value be improved. If the merged firm cannot achieve sufficiently high earnings in view of its risk, there is no guarantee that its market price will reach the forecast value. Nevertheless, a policy of acquiring firms with low P/Es can produce favorable results for the owners of the acquiring firm. Acquisitions are especially attractive when the acquiring firm's stock price is high, since fewer shares must be exchanged to acquire a given firm.

The Merger Negotiation Process

investment bankers
Financial institutions hired by the prospective participants in a merger to find suitable partners and assist in negotiations.

Mergers are often handled by **investment bankers**—financial institutions hired by the acquirer to find suitable target companies and assist in negotiations. A firm seeking a potential acquisition can hire an investment banker to find firms meeting its requirements. Once a target company is selected, the investment banker negotiates with its management or investment banker. Frequently, when management wishes to sell the firm or a division of the firm, it will hire an investment banker to seek out potential buyers.

If attempts to negotiate with the management of the target company break down, the acquiring firm, often with the aid of its investment banker, can make a direct appeal to shareholders by using *tender offers* (as explained below). The investment banker is typically compensated with a fixed fee, a commission tied to the transaction price, or with a combination of fees and commissions. Frequently, particularly in LBOs, the investment banker will take an equity position in the target company.

Many observers attribute the frenzied merger activity of the 1980s largely to the aggressive actions of investment bankers who initiated most of the transactions that took place. The huge fees extracted by

CAREERS IN FINANCE

Father-Son Power Struggle Leads to Sale of HBJ

One of the most perilous times in any business' life is when new management takes the helm. When the departing manager is retiring, there often is a period of adjustment in preparation for the new manager. One might expect there to be less friction than usual when the replacement is a son who has been groomed by his father as replacement.

A stormy father-to-son transition occurred at Harcourt Brace Jovanovich (HBJ) in 1990 and early 1991. The power struggle that ensued following the departure of William Jovanovich ultimately resulted in his son selling HBJ to General Cinema. Many claim Peter Jovanovich simply sold the "mess he had inherited."

The elder Jovanovich had left the HBJ board of directors in May 1990. Shortly thereafter, members received letters and calls claiming that the son was not cut out to run HBJ. William Jovanovich stated that his son was too young and not a good manager.

In November 1990, William forced a showdown by seeking reinstatement as chairman. Two factors, however, weighed against the man who built the firm. One, William Jovanovich had mired HBJ in $3 billion of debt to thwart a hostile takeover attempt. Several assets, including the profitable Sea World parks, had been subsequently sold to pay down the debt. Two, William Jovanovich never presented an explanation of what he would do differently.

After a morning-long debate, HBJ's directors dismissed the request without a vote. Shortly thereafter, General Cinema made an offer to Peter Jovanovich under which the acquiring firm agreed to pay $1.4 billion to buy out investors and creditors. Another reason General Cinema's offer may have been accepted in (early 1991) and the acquisition made (in late 1991) was the belief that General Cinema would leave HBJ's management intact.

Source: Antonia Fins, "The father-son saga at Harcourt Brace," *Business Week*, February 11, 1991, p. 29.

investment bankers, as well as attorneys, from their clients in these transactions in effect fueled the market. Today, with the collapse of the high-risk (junk) bond market and the related demise of LBOs and other forms of purely financial mergers, the investment banking community—especially the segment of investment bankers involved in mergers and acquisitions—is in the midst of a major slowdown. Although the merger business is not expected to disappear, investment banking revenues from mergers and acquisitions are expected to be much smaller in the future than they were in the recent past. (Detailed discussions of all aspects of investment banking are included in Chapter 18.)

Management Negotiations

To initiate the negotiation process, the acquiring firm must make an offer either in cash or based on a stock swap with a specified ratio of exchange. The target company must then review the offer and, in light of alternative offers, accept or reject the terms presented. A desirable merger candidate usually receives more than a single offer. Normally, certain nonfinancial issues must be resolved. These may include the disposition and compensation of the existing management, product-line policies, financing policies, and the independence of the target firm. The key factor, of course, is the per-share price offered in cash or reflected in the ratio of exchange. Although the negotiations are generally based on the expectation of a merger, sometimes they do break down.

Tender Offers

When management negotiations for an acquisition break down, tender offers may be used to negotiate a then "hostile merger" directly with the firm's stockholders. As noted earlier, a *tender offer* is a formal offer to purchase a given number of shares of a firm's stock at a specified price. The offer is made to all the stockholders at a premium above the market price. Occasionally the acquirer will make a **two-tier offer** in which the terms offered are more attractive to those who tender (present) shares early. For example, the acquirer offers to pay $25 per share for the first 60 percent of the outstanding shares tendered, and only $23 per share for the remaining shares. The stockholders are advised of a tender offer through announcements in financial newspapers or through direct communications from the offering firm. Sometimes a tender offer is made in order to add pressure to existing merger negotiations. In other cases the tender offer may be made without warning as an attempt at an abrupt corporate takeover.

Fighting Hostile Takeovers

If the management of a target firm does not favor a merger or considers the price offered in a proposed merger too low, it is likely to take defensive actions to ward off the hostile tender offer. Such actions are generally developed with the assistance of investment bankers and lawyers who, for generally sizable fees, help the firm develop and employ effective **takeover defenses.** Numerous strategies for fighting hostile takeovers were developed during the 1980s. There are obvious strategies such as informing stockholders of the alleged damaging effects of a takeover, acquiring another company, or attempting to sue the acquiring firm on antitrust or other grounds. In addition, many other defenses (some with colorful names) exist—white knight, poison pills, greenmail, leveraged recapitalization, golden parachutes, and shark repellents. We now take a brief look at these strategies.

With the **white knight** strategy, the target firm finds a more suitable acquirer (the "white knight") and prompts it to compete with the

two-tier offer A tender offer in which the terms offered are more attractive to those who tender shares early.

takeover defenses Strategies for fighting hostile takeovers.

white knight A takeover defense in which the target firm finds an acquirer more to its liking than the initial hostile acquirer and prompts the two to compete to take over the firm.

initial hostile acquirer to take over the firm. The basic premise of this strategy is that if being taken over is nearly certain, the target firm ought to attempt to be taken over by the firm deemed most acceptable to its management. Use of a **poison pill** typically involves the creation of securities that give their holders certain rights that become effective when a takeover is attempted. The "pill" allows the shareholders to receive special voting rights or securities that, once issued, cause the firm to be much less desirable to the hostile acquirer. **Greenmail** is a strategy under which the firm repurchases through private negotiation a large block of stock at a premium from one or more shareholders in order to end a hostile takeover attempt by those shareholders. Clearly, greenmail is a form of corporate blackmail by the holders of a large block of shares.

Another hostile takeover defense involves the use of a **leveraged recapitalization.** It involves the payment of a large debt-financed cash dividend. This strategy significantly increases the firm's financial leverage, thereby deterring the takeover attempt. As a further deterrent the recapitalization is often structured to increase the equity and control of the existing management. **Golden parachutes** are provisions in the employment contracts of key executives that provide them with sizable compensation if the firm is taken over. Golden parachutes deter hostile takeovers to the extent that cash outflows required by these contracts are large enough to make the takeover unattractive to the acquirer. Another defense is use of **shark repellents.** These anti-takeover amendments to the corporate charter constrain the firm's ability to transfer managerial control of the firm as a result of a merger. Although this defense could entrench existing management, many firms have had such amendments ratified by shareholders.

Because takeover defenses tend to insulate management from shareholders, the potential for litigation is great when these strategies are employed. Lawsuits are sometimes filed against management by dissident shareholders. In addition, federal and state governments frequently intervene when a proposed takeover is deemed in violation of federal or state law. A number of states have legislation on their books limiting or restricting hostile takeovers within their boundaries. While new takeover defenses will surely be developed in the future, so too will new legislation be passed to regulate merger activity. Lawmakers want to protect the interests not only of stockholders but also of employees, customers, suppliers, creditors, and other "stakeholders" in target firms.

poison pill   A takeover defense in which a firm issues securities that give their holders certain rights that become effective when a takeover is attempted and that make the target firm less desirable to a hostile acquirer.

greenmail   A takeover defense under which a target firm repurchases a large block of stock at a premium from one or more shareholders in order to end a hostile takeover attempt by those shareholders.

leveraged recapitalization   A takeover defense in which the target firm pays a large debt-financed cash dividend, increasing the firm's financial leverage.

golden parachutes   Provisions in the employment contracts of key executives that provide sizable compensation if the firm is taken over.

shark repellents   Anti-takeover amendments to a corporate charter that constrain the firm's ability to transfer managerial control as a result of a merger.

Holding Companies

As defined earlier, a *holding company* is a corporation that has voting control of one or more other corporations. The holding company may need to own only a small percentage of the outstanding shares to have this voting control. In the case of companies with a relatively small number of shareholders, as much as 30 to 40 percent of the stock may be required. In the case of firms with a widely dispersed ownership, 10 to

20 percent of the shares may be sufficient to gain voting control. A holding company wishing to obtain voting control of a firm may use direct market purchases or tender offers to acquire needed shares. Although there are relatively few holding companies and they are far less important than mergers, it is helpful to understand their key advantages and disadvantages.

Advantages of Holding Companies

The primary advantage of holding companies is the *leverage effect*. It permits the firm to control a large amount of assets with a relatively small dollar investment. In other words, the owners of a holding company can *control* significantly larger amounts of assets than they could *acquire* through mergers. The following example illustrates the leverage effect.

EXAMPLE   Hauck Company, a holding company, currently holds voting control of two subsidiaries—company X and company Y. The balance sheets for Hauck Company and its two subsidiaries are presented in Table 17.9. It owns approximately 17 percent ($10 ÷ $60) of company X and 20 percent ($14 ÷ $70) of company Y. It is assumed that these holdings are sufficient for voting control.

The owners of Hauck Company's $12 worth of equity have control over $260 worth of assets (company X's $100 worth and company Y's $160 worth). Thus the owners' equity represents only about 4.6 percent ($12 ÷ $260) of the total assets controlled. From the discussions of ratio analysis, leverage, and capital structure in Chapters 4, 5, and 16, you should recognize that this is quite a high degree of leverage. If an individual stockholder or even another holding company owns $3 of Hauck Company's stock, which is assumed sufficient for its control, it will in actuality control the whole $260 of assets. The investment itself in this case would represent only 1.15 percent ($3 ÷ $260) of the assets controlled.

The high leverage obtained through a holding company arrangement greatly magnifies earnings and losses for the holding company. Quite often a **pyramiding** of holding companies occurs: one holding company controls other holding companies, thereby causing an even greater magnification of earnings and losses. The greater the leverage, the greater the risk involved. The risk-return trade-off is a key consideration in the holding company decision.

Another commonly cited advantage of holding companies is *risk protection*. The failure of one of the companies (such as Y in the preceding example) does not result in the failure of the entire holding company. Since each subsidiary is a separate corporation, the failure of one company should cost the holding company, at maximum, no more than its investment in that subsidiary. Other advantages include the following: (1) Certain state *tax benefits* may be realized by each subsidiary in

pyramiding An arrangement among holding companies wherein one holding company controls others, thereby causing an even greater magnification of earnings and losses.

Table 17.9   Balance Sheets for Hauck Company and Its Subsidiaries

Assets		Liabilities and stockholders' equity	
Hauck Company			
Common stock holdings		Long-term debt	$ 6
Company X	$10	Preferred stock	6
Company Y	14	Common stock equity	12
Total	$24	Total	$24
Company X			
Current assets	$ 30	Current liabilities	$ 15
Fixed assets	70	Long-term debt	25
Total	$100	Common stock equity	60
		Total	$100
Company Y			
Current assets	$ 20	Current liabilities	$ 10
Fixed assets	140	Long-term debt	60
Total	$160	Preferred stock	20
		Common stock equity	70
		Total	$160

its state of incorporation. (2) *Lawsuits* or *legal actions* against a subsidiary will not threaten the remaining companies. (3) It is *generally easy to gain control* of a firm since stockholder or management approval is not generally necessary.

Disadvantages of Holding Companies

A major disadvantage of the holding company arrangement is the *increased risk* resulting from the leverage effect. When general economic conditions are unfavorable, a loss by one subsidiary may be magnified. For example, if subsidiary company X in Table 17.9 experiences a loss, its inability to pay dividends to Hauck Company could result in Hauck Company's inability to meet its scheduled payments.

Another disadvantage is *double taxation*. Prior to paying dividends a subsidiary must pay federal and state taxes on its earnings. Although a 70 percent tax exclusion is allowed on dividends received by one corporation from another, the remaining 30 percent received is taxable. (If the holding company owns between 20 and 80 percent of the stock in a subsidiary, the exclusion is 80 percent; if it owns more than 80 percent of the stock in the subsidiary, 100 percent of the dividends are excluded.) If a subsidiary were part of a merged company, double taxation would *not* exist.

The fact that holding companies are *difficult to analyze* is another disadvantage. Security analysts and investors typically have difficulty understanding holding companies due to their complexity. As a result these firms tend to sell at low multiples of earnings (P/Es). This means that the shareholder value of holding companies may suffer.

A final disadvantage of holding companies is the generally *high cost of administration* resulting from maintaining each subsidiary company as a separate entity. A merger, on the other hand, would likely result in certain administrative economies of scale. The need for coordination and communication between the holding company and its subsidiaries may further elevate these costs.

BUSINESS FAILURE FUNDAMENTALS

A business failure is an unfortunate circumstance. Although the majority of firms that fail do so within the first year or two of life, other firms grow, mature, and fail much later. The failure of a business can be viewed in a number of ways and can result from one or more causes.

Types of Business Failure

A firm may fail because its *returns are negative or low*. A firm that consistently reports operating losses will probably experience a decline in market value. If the firm fails to earn a return greater than its cost of capital, it can be viewed as having failed. Negative or low returns, unless remedied, are likely to result eventually in one of the following more serious types of failure.

technical insolvency Business failure that occurs when a firm is unable to pay its liabilities as they come due.

A second type of failure, **technical insolvency,** occurs when a firm is unable to pay its liabilities as they come due. When a firm is technically insolvent, its assets are still greater than its liabilities, but it is confronted with a *liquidity crisis*. If some of its assets can be converted into cash within a reasonable period, the company may be able to escape complete failure. If not, the result is the third and most serious type of failure, **bankruptcy.** Bankruptcy occurs when a firm's liabilities exceed the fair market value of its assets. A bankrupt firm has a *negative stockholders' equity*.[4] This means that the claims of creditors cannot be satisfied unless the firm's assets can be liquidated for more than their book value. Although bankruptcy is an obvious form of failure, *the courts treat technical insolvency and bankruptcy in the same way*. They are both considered to indicate the financial failure of the firm.

bankruptcy Business failure that occurs when a firm's liabilities exceed the fair market value of its assets.

---

[4]Since on a balance sheet the firm's assets equal the sum of its liabilities and stockholders' equity, the only way a firm that has more liabilities than assets can balance its balance sheet is to have a *negative* stockholders' equity.

Major Causes of Business Failure

The primary cause of business failure is *mismanagement*, which accounts for more than 50 percent of all cases. Numerous specific managerial faults can cause the firm to fail. Overexpansion, poor financial actions, an ineffective sales force, and high production costs can all singly, or in combination, cause the ultimate failure of the firm. Recently a number of major business failures such as those of Allied Stores/Federated Department Stores (Campeau Corporation), America West Airlines, and Southmark Corporation (convenience stores) have resulted from overexpansion. Since all major corporate decisions are eventually measured in terms of dollars, the financial manager may play a key role in avoiding or causing a business failure. It is his or her duty to monitor the firm's financial pulse.

Economic activity—especially economic downturns—can contribute to the failure of a firm. If the economy goes into a recession, sales may decrease abruptly, leaving the firm with high fixed costs and insufficient revenues to cover them. In addition, rapid rises in interest rates during a recession can further contribute to cash flow problems and make it more difficult for the firm to obtain and maintain needed financing. If the recession is prolonged, the likelihood of survival decreases even further.

A final cause of business failure is *corporate maturity*. Firms, like individuals, do not have infinite lives. Like a product, a firm goes through the stages of birth, growth, maturity, and eventual decline. The firm's management should attempt to prolong the growth stage through research, the development of new products, and mergers. Once the firm has matured and has begun to decline, it should seek to be acquired by another firm or liquidate before it fails. Effective management planning should help the firm to postpone decline and ultimate failure.

Voluntary Settlements

When a firm becomes technically insolvent or bankrupt, it may arrange with its creditors a **voluntary settlement,** which enables it to bypass many of the costs involved in legal bankruptcy proceedings. The settlement is normally initiated by the debtor firm. Such an arrangement may enable the firm to continue to exist or to be liquidated in a manner that gives the owners the greatest chance of recovering part of their investment. The debtor, possibly with the aid of a key creditor, arranges a meeting between the firm and all its creditors. At the meeting a committee of creditors is selected to investigate and analyze the debtor's situation and recommend a plan of action. The recommendations of the committee are discussed with both the debtor and the creditors, and a plan for sustaining or liquidating the firm is drawn up.

voluntary settlement
An arrangement between a technically insolvent or bankrupt firm and its creditors, enabling it to bypass many of the costs involved in legal bankruptcy proceedings.

Voluntary Settlement to Sustain the Firm
Normally the rationale for sustaining a firm is a reasonable belief that the firm's recovery is feasible. By sustaining the firm the creditor can

extension An arrangement whereby the firm's creditors receive payment in full, although not immediately.

composition A cash settlement of creditor claims by the debtor firm under which a uniform percentage of each dollar owed is paid.

creditor control An arrangement in which the creditor committee replaces the firm's operating management and operates the firm until all claims have been settled.

continue to receive business from it. A number of strategies are commonly used. An **extension** is an arrangement whereby the firm's creditors receive payment in full, although not immediately. Normally when creditors grant an extension, they agree to require cash payments for purchases until all past debts have been paid. A second arrangement, called **composition,** is a pro rata cash settlement of creditor claims. Instead of receiving full payment of their claims, as in the case of an extension, creditors receive only a partial payment. A uniform percentage of each dollar owed is paid in satisfaction of each creditor's claim. A third arrangement is **creditor control.** In this case the creditor committee may decide that the only circumstance in which maintaining the firm is feasible is if the operating management is replaced. The committee may then take control of the firm and operate it until all claims have been settled. Sometimes, a plan involving some combination of extension, composition, and creditor control results. An example would be a settlement whereby the debtor agrees to pay a total of 75 cents on the dollar in three annual installments of 25 cents on the dollar, while the creditors agree to sell additional merchandise to the firm on 30-day terms if the existing management is replaced by a new management acceptable to them.

Voluntary Settlement Resulting in Liquidation

After the situation of the firm has been investigated by the creditor committee, recommendations have been made, and talks among the creditors and the debtor have been held, the only acceptable course of action may be liquidation of the firm. Liquidation can be carried out in two ways—privately or through the legal procedures provided by bankruptcy law. If the debtor firm is willing to accept liquidation, legal procedures may not be required. Generally, the avoidance of litigation enables the creditors to obtain *quicker* and *higher* settlements. However, all the creditors must agree to a private liquidation in order for it to be feasible.

The objective of the voluntary liquidation process is to recover as much per dollar owed as possible. Under voluntary liquidation, common stockholders, who are the firm's true owners, cannot receive any funds until the claims of all other parties have been satisfied. A common procedure is to have a meeting of the creditors at which they make an **assignment.** This procedure passes the power to liquidate the firm's assets to an adjustment bureau, trade association, or a third party, which is designated the *assignee.* The assignee's job is to liquidate the assets, obtaining the best price possible. The assignee is sometimes referred to as the *trustee,* since it is entrusted with the title to the company's assets and the responsibility to liquidate them efficiently. Once the trustee has liquidated the assets, it distributes the recovered funds to the creditors and owners (if any funds remain for the owners). The final action in a private liquidation is for the creditors to sign a release attesting to the satisfactory settlement of their claims.

assignment A voluntary liquidation procedure by which a firm's creditors pass the power to liquidate the firm's assets to a third party, designated the *assignee* or *trustee.*

REORGANIZATION AND LIQUIDATION IN BANKRUPTCY

If a voluntary settlement for a failed firm cannot be agreed upon, the firm can be forced into bankruptcy by its creditors. As a result of bankruptcy proceedings, the firm may be either reorganized or liquidated.

Bankruptcy Legislation

As already stated, *bankruptcy* in the legal sense occurs when the firm cannot pay its bills or when its liabilities exceed the fair market value of its assets. In either of these situations a firm may be declared legally bankrupt. However, creditors generally attempt to avoid forcing a firm into bankruptcy if it appears to have opportunities for future success.

The governing bankruptcy legislation in the United States today is the **Bankruptcy Reform Act of 1978,** which significantly modified earlier bankruptcy legislation. This law contains nine chapters: eight odd-numbered (1 through 15) and one even-numbered (12). A number of these chapters apply in the instance of failure; the two key ones are Chapters 7 and 11. **Chapter 7** details the procedures to be followed when liquidating a failed firm. This chapter typically comes into play once it has been determined that a fair, equitable, and feasible basis for the reorganization of a failed firm does not exist. (Although a firm may of its own accord choose not to reorganize and may instead go directly into liquidation.) **Chapter 11** outlines the procedures for reorganizing a failed (or failing) firm, whether its petition is filed voluntarily or involuntarily. If a workable plan for reorganization cannot be developed, the firm will be liquidated under Chapter 7.

Bankruptcy Reform Act of 1978 The current governing bankruptcy legislation in the United States.

Chapter 7 The portion of the *Bankruptcy Reform Act of 1978* that details the procedures for liquidating a failed firm.

Chapter 11 The portion of the *Bankruptcy Reform Act of 1978* that outlines the procedures for reorganizing a failed (or failing) firm, whether its petition is filed voluntarily or involuntarily.

Reorganization in Bankruptcy

There are two basic types of reorganization petitions—voluntary and involuntary. Any firm that is not a municipal or financial institution can file a petition for **voluntary reorganization** on its own behalf. **Involuntary reorganization** is initiated by an outside party, usually a creditor. An involuntary petition against a firm can be filed if one of three conditions is met:

1 ▰▰▰ The firm has past-due debts of $5,000 or more.

2 ▰▰▰ Three or more creditors can prove they have aggregate unpaid claims of $5,000 against the firm. If the firm has fewer than 12 creditors, any creditor owed more than $5,000 can file the petition.

3 ▰▰▰ The firm is *insolvent*, which means (a) that it is not paying its debts as they come due, (b) that within the immediately preceding 120 days a third party (a "custodian") was appointed or took

voluntary reorganization A petition filed by a failed firm on its own behalf for reorganizing its structure and paying its creditors.

involuntary reorganization A petition initiated by an outside party, usually a creditor, for the reorganization of a failed firm and payment of its creditors.

possession of the debtor's property, or (c) that the fair market value of the firm's assets is less than the stated value of its liabilities.

Procedures

The procedures for initiation and execution of corporate reorganizations involve five separate steps: filing, appointment, development and approval of a reorganization plan, acceptance of the plan, and payment of expenses.

Filing   A reorganization petition under Chapter 11 must be filed in a federal bankruptcy court. In the case of an involuntary petition, if it is challenged by the debtor, a hearing must be held to determine whether the firm is insolvent. If so, the court enters an "Order for Relief" that formally initiates the process.

debtor in possession (DIP) The term for a firm that files a reorganization petition under Chapter 11 and then develops, if feasible, a reorganization plan.

Appointment   Upon the filing of a reorganization petition, the filing firm becomes the **debtor in possession (DIP)** of the assets. If creditors object to the filing firm being the debtor in possession, they can ask the judge to appoint a trustee.

Reorganization Plan   After reviewing its situation, the debtor in possession submits to the court a plan of reorganization and a disclosure statement summarizing the plan. A hearing is held to determine whether the plan is *fair, equitable,* and *feasible* and whether the disclosure statement contains adequate information. The court's approval or disapproval is based on its evaluation of the plan in light of these standards. A plan is considered *fair and equitable* if it *maintains the priorities* of the contractual claims of the creditors, preferred stockholders, and common stockholders. The court must also find the reorganization plan *feasible,* meaning it must be *workable.* The reorganized corporation must have sufficient working capital, sufficient funds to cover fixed charges, sufficient credit prospects, and sufficient ability to retire or refund debts as proposed by the plan.

Acceptance of the Reorganization Plan   Once approved, the plan, along with the disclosure statement, is given to the firm's creditors and shareholders for their acceptance. Under the Bankruptcy Reform Act, creditors and owners are separated into groups with similar types of claims. In the case of creditor groups, approval by holders of at least two-thirds of the dollar amount of claims as well as a numerical majority of creditors in the group is required. In the case of ownership groups (preferred and common stockholders), two-thirds of the shares in each group must approve the reorganization plan for it to be accepted. Once accepted and confirmed by the court, the plan is put into effect as soon as possible.

Payment of Expenses   After the reorganization plan has been approved or disapproved, all parties to the proceedings whose services were beneficial or contributed to the approval or disapproval of the plan file a statement of expenses. If the court finds these claims accept-able, the debtor must pay these expenses within a reasonable period of time.

Role of the Debtor in Possession (DIP)

Since reorganization activities are largely in the hands of the debtor in possession (DIP), it is useful to understand the DIP's responsibilities. The DIP's first responsibility is the valuation of the firm to determine whether reorganization is appropriate. To do this, the DIP must esti-mate both the *liquidation value* of the enterprise and its value as a *going concern*. If the DIP finds that its value as a going concern is less than its liquidation value, it will recommend liquidation. If the opposite is found to be true, the DIP will recommend reorganization. If the reorga-nization of the firm is recommended by the DIP, a plan of reorganiza-tion must be drawn up.

The key portion of the reorganization plan generally concerns the firm's capital structure. Since most firms' financial difficulties result from high fixed charges, the company's capital structure is generally *recapitalized*, or altered, in order to reduce these charges. Under **recapi-talization,** debts are generally exchanged for equity, or the maturities of existing debts are extended. When recapitalizing the firm, the DIP places a great deal of emphasis on building a mix of debt and equity that will allow the firm to meet its debts and provide a reasonable level of earnings for its owners.

recapitalization The reorganization procedure under which a failed firm's debts are gener-ally exchanged for equity or the maturities of exist-ing debts are extended.

Once the optimal capital structure has been determined, the DIP must establish a plan for exchanging outstanding obligations for new securities. The guiding principle is to *observe priorities*. Senior claims (those with higher legal priority) must be satisfied prior to junior claims (those with lower legal priority). To comply with this principle, senior suppliers of capital must receive a claim on new capital equal to their previous claims. The common stockholders are the last to receive any new securities. (It is not unusual for them to receive nothing.) Security holders do not necessarily have to receive the same type of security they held before; often they receive a combination of securities. Once the debtor in possession has determined the new capital structure and dis-tribution of capital, it will submit the reorganization plan and disclo-sure statement to the court as described.

Liquidation in Bankruptcy

The liquidation of a bankrupt firm usually occurs once the courts have determined that reorganization is not feasible. A petition for reorgani-zation must normally be filed by the managers or creditors of the bank-rupt firm. If no petition is filed, if a petition is filed and denied, or if the reorganization plan is denied, the firm must be liquidated. Three im-portant aspects of liquidation in bankruptcy are the procedures, the priority of claims, and the final accounting.

Procedures

When a firm is decreed bankrupt, the judge may appoint a *trustee* to perform the many routine duties required in administering the bankruptcy. The trustee takes charge of the property of the bankrupt firm and protects the interest of its creditors. A meeting of creditors must be held within 20 and 40 days. At this meeting the creditors are made aware of the prospects for the liquidation. The meeting is presided over by the bankruptcy court clerk. The trustee is then given the responsibility to liquidate the firm, keep records, examine creditors' claims, disburse money, furnish information as required, and make final reports on the liquidation. In essence the trustee is responsible for the liquidation of the firm. Occasionally the court will call subsequent creditor meetings, but only a final meeting for closing the bankruptcy is required.

Priority of Claims

secured creditors
Creditors who have specific assets pledged as collateral and in liquidation received proceeds from the sale of those assets.

unsecured, or general, creditors
Creditors who have a general claim against all the firm's assets other than those specifically pledged as collateral.

It is the trustee's responsibility to liquidate all the firm's assets and to distribute the proceeds to the holders of *provable claims*. The courts have established certain procedures for determining the provability of claims. The priority of claims, which is specified in Chapter 7 of the Bankruptcy Reform Act, must be maintained by the trustee when distributing the funds from liquidation. Any **secured creditors** have specific assets pledged as collateral and in liquidation receive proceeds from the sale of those assets. If these proceeds are inadequate to meet their claim, the secured creditors become **unsecured, or general, creditors** for the unrecovered amount since specific collateral no longer exists. These and all other unsecured creditors will divide up, on a pro rata basis, any funds remaining after all prior claims have been satisfied. If the proceeds from the sale of secured assets are in excess of the claims against them, the excess funds become available to meet claims of unsecured creditors. The complete order of priority of claims is listed in Table 17.10.

In spite of the priorities listed in items 1 through 7, secured creditors have first claim on proceeds from the sale of their collateral. The claims of unsecured creditors, including the unpaid claims of secured creditors, are satisfied next and, finally, the claims of preferred and common stockholders. The application of these priorities by the trustee in bankruptcy liquidation proceedings can be illustrated by a simple example.

EXAMPLE   Dempsey Company, a manufacturer of portable computers, has the balance sheet presented in Table 17.11. The trustee, as was her obligation, has liquidated the firm's assets, obtaining the highest amounts she could get. She managed to obtain $2.3 million for the firm's current assets and $2 million for the firm's fixed assets. The total proceeds from the liquidation were therefore $4.3 million. Obviously, the firm is legally bankrupt, since its liabilities of $5.6 million dollars exceed the $4.3 million fair market value of its assets.

Table 17.10   **Order of Priority of Claims in Liquidation of a Failed Firm**

1. The expenses of administering the bankruptcy proceedings.

2. Any unpaid interim expenses incurred in the ordinary course of business between filing the bankruptcy petition and the entry of an Order for Relief in an involuntary proceeding. (This step is *not* applicable in a voluntary bankruptcy.)

3. Wages of not more than $2,000 per worker that have been earned by workers in the 90-day period immediately preceding the start of bankruptcy proceedings.

4. Unpaid employee benefit plan contributions that were to be paid in the 180-day period preceding the filing of bankruptcy or the termination of business, whichever occurred first. For any employee, the sum of this claim plus eligible unpaid wages (item 3) cannot exceed $2,000.

5. Claims of farmers or fishermen in a grain-storage or fish-storage facility, not to exceed $2,000 for each producer.

6. Unsecured customer deposits, not to exceed $900 each, resulting from purchasing or leasing a good or service from the failed firm.

7. Taxes legally due and owed by the bankrupt firm to the federal government, state government, or to any other governmental subdivision.

8. Claims of secured creditors, who receive the proceeds from the sale of collateral held, regardless of the priorities above. If the proceeds from the liquidation of the collateral are insufficient to satisfy the secured creditors' claims, the secured creditors become unsecured creditors for the unpaid amount.

9. Claims of unsecured creditors. The claims of unsecured, or general, creditors and unsatisfied portions of secured creditors' claims (item 8) are all treated equally.

10. Preferred stockholders, who receive an amount up to the par, or stated, value of their preferred stock.

11. Common stockholders, who receive any remaining funds, which are distributed on an equal per-share basis. If different classes of common stock are outstanding (see Chapter 20), priorities may exist.

The next step is to distribute the proceeds to the various creditors. The only liability not shown on the balance sheet is $800,000 in expenses for administering the bankruptcy proceedings and satisfying unpaid bills incurred between the time of filing the bankruptcy petition and the entry of an Order for Relief. The distribution of the $4.3 million among the firm's creditors is shown in Table 17.12 (page 624). The table shows that once all prior claims on the proceeds from liquidation have been satisfied, the unsecured creditors get the remaining funds. The pro rata distribution of the $700,000 among the unsecured creditors is given in Table 17.13 (page 625). The disposition of funds in the Dempsey Company liquidation should be clear from Tables 17.12 and 17.13. Since the claims of the unsecured creditors have not been fully satisfied, the preferred and common stockholders receive nothing.

Table 17.11   **Balance Sheet for Dempsey Company**

Assets		Liabilities and stockholders' equity	
Cash	$ 10,000	Accounts payable	$ 200,000
Marketable securities	5,000	Notes payable—bank	1,000,000
Accounts receivable	1,090,000	Accrued wages[a]	320,000
Inventories	3,100,000	Unpaid employee benefits[b]	80,000
Prepaid expenses	5,000	Unsecured customer deposits[c]	100,000
Total current assets	$4,210,000	Taxes payable	300,000
Land	$2,000,000	Total current liabilities	$2,000,000
Net plant	1,810,000	First mortgage[d]	$1,800,000
Net equipment	80,000	Second mortgage[d]	1,000,000
Total fixed assets	$3,890,000	Unsecured bonds	800,000
Total	$8,100,000	Total long-term debt	$3,600,000
		Preferred stock (5,000 shares)	$ 400,000
		Common stock (10,000 shares)	500,000
		Paid-in capital in excess of par	1,500,000
		Retained earnings	100,000
		Total stockholders' equity	$2,500,000
		Total	$8,100,000

[a]Represents wages of $800 per employee earned within 90 days of filing bankruptcy for 400 of the firm's employees.
[b]These unpaid employee benefits were due in the 180-day period preceding the firm's bankruptcy filing, which occurred simultaneously with the termination of its business.
[c]Unsecured customer deposits not exceeding $900 each.
[d]The first and second mortgages are on the firm's total fixed assets.

Final Accounting

After the trustee has liquidated all the bankrupt firm's assets and distributed the proceeds to satisfy all provable claims in the appropriate order of priority, he or she makes a final accounting to the bankruptcy court and creditors. Once the court approves the final accounting, the liquidation is complete.

Table 17.12   **Distribution of the Liquidation Proceeds of Dempsey Company**

Proceeds from liquidation	$4,300,000
—Expenses of administering bankruptcy and paying interim bills	$ 800,000
—Wages owed workers	320,000
—Unpaid employee benefits	80,000
—Unsecured customer deposits	100,000
—Taxes owed governments	300,000
Funds available for creditors	$2,700,000
—First mortgage, paid from the $2 million proceeds from the sale of fixed assets	$1,800,000
—Second mortgage, partially paid from the remaining $200,000 of fixed assets proceeds	200,000
Funds available for unsecured creditors	$ 700,000

INTERNATIONAL DIMENSION: MERGERS AND JOINT VENTURES

The motives for domestic mergers—growth or diversification, synergy, fund raising, increased managerial skill or technology, tax considerations, increased ownership liquidity, and defense against takeover—are all applicable to MNCs' international mergers and joint ventures. Several points, nevertheless, need attention.

Beginning in the 1980s, international mergers and joint ventures, especially those involving European firms acquiring assets in the United States, have increased significantly. MNCs based in Western Europe, Japan, and North America have made substantial contributions to this increase. Moreover, a fast-growing group of MNCs has emerged in the past two decades. These are based in the so-called newly-industrializing countries, which include, among others, Brazil, Argentina, Mexico, Hong Kong, Singapore, South Korea, Taiwan, India, and Pakistan. This growth has added further to the number and value of international mergers.

Foreign direct investments (i.e., *new* investments or *mergers*, on the basis of either wholly-owned or joint venture) in the United States have gained popularity in the past few years. Most of the foreign direct investors in the United States come from seven countries: Britain, Canada, France, the Netherlands, Japan, Switzerland, and Germany. The heaviest investments are concentrated in manufacturing, followed by the petroleum and trade/service sectors. Another interesting trend is the current rise in the number of joint ventures between companies based in Japan and firms based elsewhere in the industrialized world, especially U.S.-based MNCs. While Japanese authorities continue their discus-

Table 17.13   **Pro Rata Distribution of Funds among Unsecured Creditors of Dempsey Company**

Unsecured creditors' claims	Amount	Settlement at 25%[a]
Unpaid balance of second mortgage	$ 800,000[b]	$200,000
Accounts payable	200,000	50,000
Notes payable—bank	1,000,000	250,000
Unsecured bonds	800,000	200,000
Totals	$2,800,000	$700,000

[a]The 25 percent rate is calculated by dividing the $700,000 available for unsecured creditors by the $2.8 million owed unsecured creditors. Each is entitled to a pro rata share.
[b]This figure represents the difference between the $1 million second mortgage and the $200,000 payment on the second mortgage from the proceeds from the sale of the collateral remaining after satisfying the first mortgage.

sions and debates with other governments regarding Japan's international trade surpluses as well as perceived trade barriers, mergers and joint ventures continue to take place. In the eyes of some U.S. corporate executives, such business ventures are viewed as a "ticket into the Japanese market" as well as a way to curb a potentially tough competitor.

Developing countries, too, have been attracting foreign direct investments in both horizontal and vertical industries. Meanwhile, during the last two decades a number of these nations have adopted specific policies and regulations aimed at controlling the inflows of foreign investments. A major provision has been the 49 percent ownership limitation applied to MNCs. Of course, international competition among differently based MNCs has been of benefit to some developing countries in their attempts to extract concessions from the multinationals. However, as MNCs have become more reluctant to form joint ventures under the stated conditions, an increasing number of such nations have shown greater flexibility in their recent dealings with MNCs. Furthermore, given the present and the expected international economic and trade status, it is likely that more Third World countries will show even greater flexibility in their agreements with MNCs as they recognize the need for foreign capital and technology.

A final point relates to the existence of international *holding companies*. Places such as Liechtenstein and Panama have long been considered favorable spots for forming holding companies due to their attractive legal, corporate, and tax environments. International holding companies control many business entities in the form of subsidiaries, branches, joint ventures, and other agreements. For international legal reasons (especially tax-related ones), as well as anonymity, such holding companies have become increasingly popular in recent years.

SUMMARY

1 **Understand merger fundamentals, including basic terminology, motives for merging, and types of mergers.** Mergers, including consolidations, result from the combining of firms. Typically the acquiring company pursues and attempts to merge with the target company, either on a friendly or a hostile basis. Mergers are undertaken either for strategic reasons to achieve economies of scale or for financial reasons to restructure the firm to improve its cash flow. The overriding goal of merging is maximization of owners' wealth (share price). Other specific merger motives include growth or diversification, synergy, fund raising, increased managerial skill or technology, tax considerations, increased ownership liquidity, and defense against takeovers. The four basic types of mergers are horizontal, vertical, congeneric, and conglomerate.

2 **Describe the objectives and procedures used in leveraged buyouts (LBOs) and divestitures.** A popular technique for structuring financial mergers during the 1980s was the leveraged buyout (LBO), which involves use of a large amount of debt to purchase a firm. Attractive LBO candidates must have good profits and growth prospects, low debt and a high level of assets that can be used as collateral, and stable and predictable cash flows that can be used to repay the debt and provide adequate working capital.

Divestiture involves the sale of a firm's assets, typically an operating unit, to another firm or existing management, the spin-off of assets into an independent company, or the liquidation of assets. Regardless of the method used, the goal of divestiture is to create a more lean and focused operation that creates maximum value for shareholders.

3   **Demonstrate the procedures used to analyze and negotiate mergers, including valuing the target company, stock swap transactions, the merger negotiation process, and holding companies.**   The value of a target company can be estimated using valuation techniques. Capital budgeting techniques are applied to the relevant cash flows whether the target firm is being acquired for its assets or as a going concern. All proposed mergers with positive net present values would be considered acceptable. In a stock swap transaction in which the acquisition is paid for by an exchange of common stock, a ratio of exchange must be established. Investment bankers are commonly hired by the acquirer to find a suitable target company and assist in negotiations. When the management of the target firm does not favor the merger, it can employ any of a number of takeover defenses. These include a white knight, poison pills, greenmail, leveraged recapitalization, golden parachutes, and shark repellents. A holding company can be created by one firm gaining control of other companies, often by owning as little as 10 to 20 percent of their stock.

4   **Understand the types and major causes of business failure and the use of voluntary settlements to sustain or liquidate the failed firm.**   A firm may fail because it has negative or low returns, because it is technically insolvent, or because it is bankrupt. The major causes of business failure are mismanagement, downturns in economic activity, and corporate maturity. Voluntary settlements are initiated by the debtor and can result in sustaining the firm through an extension, a composition, creditor control of the firm, or a combination of these strategies. If creditors do not agree to a plan to sustain a firm, they may recommend voluntary liquidation, which bypasses many of the legal requirements and costs of bankruptcy proceedings.

5   **Explain bankruptcy legislation and the procedures involved in reorganizing or liquidating a bankrupt firm.**   A failed firm that cannot or does not want to arrange a voluntary settlement can voluntarily or involuntarily file in federal bankruptcy court for reorganization under Chapter 11 or for liquidation under Chapter 7 of the Bankruptcy Reform Act of 1978. Under Chapter 11 the judge will appoint the debtor in possession (DIP). With court supervision the DIP develops, if feasible, a reorganization plan. A firm that cannot be reorganized under Chapter 11 of the bankruptcy law or does not petition for reorganization is liquidated under Chapter 7. The responsibility for liquidation is placed in the hands of a court-appointed trustee, whose responsibilities include the liquidation of assets, the distribution of the proceeds, and a final accounting.

6   **Discuss the growth of and special factors relating to international mergers and joint ventures.**   International mergers and joint ventures, including international holding companies, increased significantly in the last decade. Special factors affecting these mergers relate to various regulations imposed on MNCs by host countries and economic and trade conditions.

QUESTIONS

17—1   Define and differentiate each of the following sets of terms.
    a. Mergers, consolidations, and holding companies
    b. Acquiring versus target company
    c. Friendly versus hostile mergers
    d. Strategic versus financial mergers

17—2   Briefly describe each of the following motives for merging.
    a. Growth or diversification
    b. Synergy
    c. Fund raising
    d. Increased managerial skill or technology
    e. Tax considerations
    f. Increased ownership liquidity
    g. Defense against takeover

17—3   Briefly describe each of the following types of mergers.
    a. Horizontal merger
    b. Vertical merger
    c. Congeneric merger
    d. Conglomerate merger

17—4   What is a *leveraged buyout (LBO)?* What are the three key attributes of an attractive candidate for acquisition using an LBO?

17—5   What is a *divestiture?* What is an *operating unit?* What are four common methods used by firms to divest themselves of operating units?

17—6   Describe the procedures typically used by an acquirer to value a target company, whether it is being acquired for its assets or as a going concern.

17—7   What is the *ratio of exchange?* Is it based on the current market prices of the shares of the acquiring and target firms? Why may a long-run view of the merged firm's earnings per share change a merger decision?

17—8   What role do *investment bankers* often play in the merger negotiation process? What is a *tender offer?* When and how is it used?

17—9   Briefly describe each of the following *takeover defenses* against a hostile merger.
    a. White knight
    b. Poison pill
    c. Greenmail
    d. Leveraged recapitalization
    e. Golden parachutes
    f. Shark repellents

17—10   What are the key advantages and disadvantages cited for the holding company arrangement? What is *pyramiding*, and what are its consequences?

17—11   What are the three types of business failure? What is the difference between *technical insolvency* and *bankruptcy?* What are the major causes of business failure?

17—12   Define an *extension* and a *composition*, and explain how they might be combined to form a voluntary settlement plan to sustain the firm. How is a voluntary settlement resulting in liquidation handled?

17—13   What is the concern of Chapter 11 of the Bankruptcy Reform Act of 1978? How is the *debtor in possession (DIP)* involved in (a) the valuation of the firm, (b) the recapitalization of the firm, and (c) the exchange of obligations using the priority rule?

17—14   What is the concern of Chapter 7 of the Bankruptcy Reform Act of 1978? Under which conditions is a firm liquidated in bankruptcy? Describe the procedures (including the role of the trustee) involved in liquidating the bankrupt firm.

17—15   In which order would the following claims be settled when distributing the proceeds from liquidating a bankrupt firm?
    a. Claims of preferred stockholders
    b. Claims of secured creditors
    c. Expenses of administering the bankruptcy
    d. Claims of common stockholders
    e. Claims of unsecured, or general, creditors
    f. Taxes legally due
    g. Unsecured deposits of customers

    h. Certain eligible wages

    i. Unpaid employee benefit plan contributions

    j. Unpaid interim expenses incurred between the time of filing and the entry of an Order for Relief

    k. Claims of farmers or fishermen in a grain-storage or fish-storage facility

17—16 What are some of the major reasons for the rapid expansion in international business mergers and joint ventures of firms?

PROBLEMS

17—1 **(Tax Effects of Acquisition)** Overtime Watch Company is contemplating the acquisition of SportWatch Company, a firm that has shown large operating tax losses over the past few years. As a result of the acquisition, Overtime believes the total pretax profits of the merger will not change from their present level for 15 years. The tax loss carryforward of SportWatch is $800,000, while Overtime projects annual earnings before taxes to be $280,000 per year for each of the next 15 years. These earnings are assumed to fall within the annual limit legally allowed for application of the tax loss carryforward resulting from the proposed merger (see footnote 2 on page 596). The firm is in the 40 percent tax bracket.

    a. If Overtime does not make the acquisition, what are the company's tax liability and earnings after taxes each year over the next 15 years?

    b. If the acquisition is made, what are the company's tax liability and earnings after taxes each year over the next 15 years?

    c. If SportWatch can be acquired for $350,000 in cash, should Overtime make the acquisition, based on tax considerations? (Ignore present value.)

17—2 **(Tax Effects of Acquisition)** Gourmette Corporation is evaluating the acquisition of Student Prince Hot Dog Stands. Student Prince has a tax loss carryforward of $1.8 million. Gourmette can purchase Student Prince for $2.1 million. It can sell the assets for $1.6 million—their book value. Gourmette expects earnings before taxes in the five years after the merger to be as follows:

Year	Earnings before taxes
1	$150,000
2	400,000
3	450,000
4	600,000
5	600,000

    The expected earnings given above are assumed to fall within the annual limit legally allowed for application of the tax loss carryforward resulting from the proposed merger (see footnote 2 on page 596). Gourmette is in the 40 percent tax bracket.

    a. Calculate the firm's tax payments and earnings after taxes for each of the next five years *without* the merger.

    b. Calculate the firm's tax payments and earnings after taxes for each of the next five years *with* the merger.

    c. What are the total benefits associated with the tax losses from the merger? (Ignore present value.)

    d. Discuss whether you would recommend the proposed merger. Support your decision with figures.

17—3   **(Tax Benefits and Price)** Painted Pants has a tax loss carryforward of $800,000. Two firms are interested in acquiring Painted for the tax loss advantage. Studs Duds has expected earnings before taxes of $200,000 per year for each of the next seven years and a cost of capital of 15 percent. Glitter Threads has expected earnings before taxes for the next seven years as indicated:

Glitter Threads

Year	Earnings before taxes
1	$ 80,000
2	120,000
3	200,000
4	300,000
5	400,000
6	400,000
7	500,000

Both Studs Duds' and Glitter Threads' expected earnings are assumed to fall within the annual limit legally allowed for application of the tax loss carryforward resulting from the proposed merger (see footnote 2 on page 596). Glitter Threads has a cost of capital of 15 percent. Both firms are subject to 40 percent tax rates on ordinary income.

    a. What is the tax advantage of the merger each year for Studs Duds?

    b. What is the tax advantage of the merger each year for Glitter Threads?

    c. What is the maximum cash price each interested firm would be willing to pay for Painted Pants? (*Hint:* Calculate the present value of the tax advantages.)

    d. Use your answers in **a** through **c** to explain why a target company can have different values to different potential acquiring firms.

17—4   **(Asset Acquisition Decision)** Blue Printing Company is considering the acquisition of Multicolor Press at a cash price of $60,000. Multicolor Press has liabilities of $90,000. Multicolor has a large press that Blue needs; the remaining assets would be sold to net $65,000. As a result of acquiring the press, Blue would experience an increase in cash inflow of $20,000 per year over the next 10 years. The firm has a 14 percent cost of capital.

    a. What is the effective or net cost of the large press?

    b. If this is the only way Blue can obtain the large press, should the firm go ahead with the merger? Explain your answer.

    c. If the firm could purchase a press that would provide slightly better quality and $26,000 annual cash inflow for 10 years for a price of $120,000, which alternative would you recommend? Explain your answer.

17—5   **(Cash Acquisition Decision)** Cathcart Oil is being considered for acquisition by Onagonda Oil. The combination, Onagonda believes, would increase its cash inflows by $25,000 for each of the next five years and $50,000 for each of the following five years. Cathcart has high financial leverage, and Onagonda can expect its cost of capital to increase from 12 to 15 percent if the merger is undertaken. The cash price of Cathcart is $125,000.

a. Would you recommend the merger?

b. Would you recommend the merger if Onagonda could use the $125,000 to purchase equipment returning cash inflows of $40,000 per year for each of the next 10 years?

c. If the cost of capital does not change with the merger, would your decision in **b** be different? Explain.

17—6   **(Ratio of Exchange and EPS)** McBell's Public House is attempting to acquire the Moon Bar and Club. Certain financial data on these corporations are summarized as follows:

Item	McBell's Public House	Moon Bar and Club
Earnings available for common stock	$20,000	$8,000
Number of shares of common stock outstanding	20,000	4,000
Market price per share	$12	$24

McBell's has sufficient authorized but unissued shares to carry out the proposed merger.

a. If the ratio of exchange is 1.8, what will be the earnings per share (EPS) based on the original shares of each firm?

b. If the ratio of exchange is 2.0, what will be the earnings per share (EPS) based on the original shares of each firm?

c. If the ratio of exchange is 2.2, what will be the earnings per share (EPS) based on the original shares of each firm?

d. Discuss the principle illustrated by your answers to **a** through **c**.

17—7   **(EPS and Merger Terms)** Dodd Manufacturing Company is interested in acquiring the Talbot Machine Company by swapping 4/10 shares of its stock for each share of Talbot stock. Certain financial data on these companies are given.

Item	Dodd Manufacturing	Talbot Machine
Earnings available for common stock	$200,000	$50,000
Number of shares of common stock outstanding	50,000	20,000
Earnings per share (EPS)	$4.00	$2.50
Market price per share	$50.00	$15.00
Price/earnings (P/E) ratio	12.5	6

Dodd has sufficient authorized but unissued shares to carry out the proposed merger.

a. How many new shares of stock will Dodd have to issue in order to make the proposed merger?

b. If the earnings for each firm remain unchanged, what will the postmerger earnings per share be?

c. How much, effectively, has been earned on behalf of each of the original shares of Talbot stock?

d. How much, effectively, has been earned on behalf of each of the original shares of Dodd stock?

17—8   **(Ratio of Exchange)** Calculate the ratio of exchange (a) of shares and (b) in market price for each of the following cases. What does each ratio signify? Explain.

Case	Current market price per share		Price per share offered
	Acquiring company	Target company	
A	$50	$25	$ 30.00
B	80	80	100.00
C	40	60	70.00
D	50	10	12.50
E	25	20	25.00

17—9   **(Expected EPS—Merger Decision)** O.T. Books wishes to evaluate a proposed merger into Plain Cover Publications. O.T. had 1992 earnings of $200,000, has 100,000 shares of common stock outstanding, and expects earnings to grow at an annual rate of 7 percent. Plain Cover had 1992 earnings of $800,000, has 200,000 shares of common stock outstanding, and expects its earnings to grow at 3 percent per year.

a. Calculate the expected earnings per share (EPS) for O.T. Books for each of the next five years without the merger.

b. What would O.T. Books' stockholders earn in each of the next five years on each of their O.T shares swapped for Plain Cover shares at a ratio of (1) 0.6 and (2) 0.8 shares of Plain Cover for one share of O.T. Books?

c. Graph the pre- and postmerger EPS figures developed in **a** and **b** on a set of year (x-axis)–EPS (y-axis) axes.

d. If you were the financial manager for O.T. Books, what would you recommend from **b**, (1) or (2)? Explain your answer.

17—10   **(EPS and Postmerger Price)** Data for the Vinco Company and Lyle Company are given. Vinco Company is considering merging with Lyle by swapping 1.25 shares of its stock for each share of Lyle stock. Vinco Company expects to sell at the same price/earnings (P/E) multiple after the merger as before it.

Item	Vinco Company	Lyle Company
Earnings available for common stock	$225,000	$50,000
Number of shares of common stock outstanding	90,000	15,000
Market price per share	$45	$50

a. Calculate the ratio of exchange of market prices.
b. Calculate the earnings per share (EPS) and price/earnings (P/E) ratio for each company.
c. Calculate the price/earnings (P/E) ratio used to purchase Lyle Company.
d. Calculate the postmerger earnings per share (EPS) for Vinco Company.
e. Calculate the expected market price per share of the merged firm. Discuss this result in light of your findings in **a.**

17—11   **(Holding Company)** Summa Company holds stock in company A and company B. Simplified balance sheets for the companies are presented below. Summa has voting control over both company A and company B.

Assets		Liabilities and stockholders' equity	
Summa Company			
Common stock holdings		Long-term debt	$ 40,000
		Preferred stock	25,000
Company A	$ 40,000	Common stock equity	35,000
Company B	60,000		
Total	$100,000	Total	$100,000
Company A			
Current assets	$100,000	Current liabilities	$100,000
Fixed assets	400,000	Long-term debt	200,000
Total	$500,000	Common stock equity	200,000
		Total	$500,000
Company B			
Current assets	$180,000	Current liabilities	$100,000
Fixed assets	720,000	Long-term debt	500,000
Total	$900,000	Common stock equity	300,000
		Total	$900,000

a. What percentage of the total assets controlled by Summa Company does its common stock equity represent?
b. If another company owns 15 percent of the common stock of Summa Company and by virtue of this fact has voting control, what percentage of the total assets controlled does the outside company's equity represent?
c. How does a holding company effectively provide a great deal of control for a small dollar investment?
d. Answer questions **a** and **b** in light of the following additional facts.
  (1) Company A's fixed assets consist of $20,000 of common stock in company C. This provides voting control.

(2) Company C, which has total assets of $400,000, has voting control of company D, which has $50,000 of total assets.

(3) Company B's fixed assets consist of $60,000 of stock in both company E and company F. In both cases, this gives it voting control. Companies E and F have total assets of $300,000 and $400,000, respectively.

17—12   **(Voluntary Settlements)** Classify each of the following voluntary settlements as an extension, a composition, or a combination of the two.
a. Paying all creditors 30 cents on the dollar in exchange for complete discharge of the debt.
b. Paying all creditors in full in three periodic installments.
c. Paying a group of creditors with claims of $10,000 in full over two years and immediately paying the remaining creditors 75 cents on the dollar.

17—13   **(Voluntary Settlements)** For a firm with outstanding debt of $125,000, classify each of the following voluntary settlements as an extension, a composition, or a combination of the two.
a. Paying a group of creditors in full in four periodic installments and paying the remaining creditors in full immediately.
b. Paying a group of creditors 90 cents on the dollar immediately and paying the remaining creditors 80 cents on the dollar in two periodic installments.
c. Paying all creditors 15 cents on the dollar.
d. Paying all creditors in full in 180 days.

17—14   **(Voluntary Settlements—Payments)** Limetree Business Forms Company recently ran into certain financial difficulties that have resulted in the initiation of voluntary settlement procedures. The firm currently has $150,000 in outstanding debts and approximately $75,000 in liquidable short-term assets. Indicate, for each plan below, whether the plan is an extension, a composition, or a combination of the two. Also indicate the cash payments and timing of the payments required of the firm under each plan.
a. Each creditor will be paid 50 cents on the dollar immediately, and the debts will be considered fully satisfied.
b. Each creditor will be paid 80 cents on the dollar in two quarterly installments of 50 cents and 30 cents. The first installment is to be paid in 90 days.
c. Each creditor will be paid the full amount of its claims in three installments of 50 cents, 25 cents, and 25 cents on the dollar. The installments will be made in 60-day intervals, beginning in 60 days.
d. A group of creditors with claims of $50,000 will be immediately paid in full; the rest will be paid 85 cents on the dollar, payable in 90 days.

17—15   **(Unsecured Creditors)** A firm has $450,000 in funds to distribute to its unsecured creditors. Three possible sets of unsecured creditor claims are presented. Calculate the settlement, if any, to be received by each creditor in each case.

Unsecured creditors' claims	Case I	Case II	Case III
Unpaid balance of second mortgage	$300,000	$200,000	$ 500,000
Accounts payable	200,000	100,000	300,000
Notes payable—bank	300,000	100,000	500,000
Unsecured bonds	100,000	200,000	500,000
Total	$900,000	$600,000	$1,800,000

17—16   **(Liquidation and Priority of Claims)** Windy Corporation recently failed and was liquidated by a court-appointed trustee who charged $200,000 for her services. Between the time of filing of the bankruptcy petition and the entry of an Order for Relief, a total of $100,000 in unpaid bills was incurred and remain unpaid. The preliquidation balance sheet is shown below.

Assets		Liabilities and stockholders' equity	
Cash	$ 40,000	Accounts payable	$ 200,000
Marketable securities	30,000	Notes payable—bank	300,000
Accounts receivable	620,000	Accrued wages[a]	50,000
Inventories	1,200,000	Unsecured customer deposits[b]	30,000
Prepaid expenses	10,000	Taxes payable	20,000
Total current assets	$1,900,000	Total current liabilities	$ 600,000
Land	$ 300,000	First mortgage[c]	$ 700,000
Net plant	400,000	Second mortgage[c]	400,000
Net equipment	400,000	Unsecured bonds	300,000
Total fixed assets	$1,100,000	Total long-term debt	$1,400,000
Total	$3,000,000	Preferred stock (15,000 shares)	$ 200,000
		Common stock (10,000 shares)	200,000
		Paid-in capital in excess of par	500,000
		Retained earnings	100,000
		Total stockholders' equity	$1,000,000
		Total	$3,000,000

[a]Represents wages of $500 per employee earned within 90 days of filing bankruptcy for 100 of the firm's employees.
[b]Unsecured customer deposits not exceeding $900 each.
[c]The first and second mortgages are on the firm's total fixed assets.

    a. Assume the trustee liquidates the assets for $2.5 million—$1.3 million from current assets and $1.2 million from fixed assets.
      (1) Prepare a table indicating the amount to be distributed to each claimant. Indicate if the claimant is an unsecured creditor.

(2) Prior to satisfying unsecured creditor claims, how much is owed to first-mortgage holders and second-mortgage holders?

(3) Do the firm's owners receive any funds? If so, in what amounts?

b. Assume the trustee liquidates the assets for $1.8 million—$1.2 million from current assets and $600,000 from fixed assets; rework your answers in **a.**

c. Compare, contrast, and discuss your findings in **a** and **b.**

CASE

Analyzing Plants Galore's Proposed Acquisition of PSI

Plants Galore (PG), one of the nation's leading plant wholesalers, is interested in expanding into a related business. Because of PG's strong profitability and cash position, the members of its executive committee began searching for a target company to acquire. Finally, after a few months of research and investigation, they isolated Plant Service, Inc. (PSI) as their prime target. PSI has a significant market share and an excellent reputation in servicing plants under contract with large commercial offices, hotels, zoos, and theme parks.

PG's chief financial officer, Jack Levine, had approached the owner of PSI (which is a closely owned corporation) to determine if a merger offer would be welcomed. The company's owner reacted favorably and subsequently provided financial data including PSI's earnings record and most recent (December 31, 1992) balance sheet. These are presented below.

Plant Service, Inc., earnings record

Year	EPS	Year	EPS
1985	$2.20	1989	$2.85
1986	2.35	1990	3.00
1987	2.45	1991	3.10
1988	2.60	1992	3.30

Plant Service, Inc., balance sheet (December 31, 1992)

Assets		Liabilities and equity	
Cash	$ 2,500,000	Current liabilities	$ 5,250,000
Accounts receivable	1,500,000	Mortgage payable	3,125,000
Inventories	7,625,000	Common stock	15,625,000
Land	7,475,000	Retained earnings	9,000,000
Fixed assets (net)	13,900,000	Total liabilities	
Total assets	$33,000,000	and equity	$33,000,000

Mr. Levine estimated that the incremental cash flow after taxes from the acquisition would be $18,750,000 for years 1 and 2; $20,500,000 for year 3, $21,750,000 for year 4; $24,000,000 for year 5; and $25,000,000 for years 6 through 30. He also estimated that the company should earn a rate of return of at least 16 percent on an investment of this type. Additional financial data Levine gathered for 1992 are summarized in the following table.

PG and PSI financial data (December 31, 1992)

Item	PG	PSI
Earnings available for common stock	$35,000,000	$15,246,000
Number of shares of common stock outstanding	10,000,000	4,620,000
Market price per share	$50	$30[a]

[a]Estimated by Plants Galore.

Required

a. What is the maximum price Plants Galore should offer PSI for a cash acquisition? (*Note:* Assume the relevant time horizon for analysis is 30 years.)

b. (1) What is the ratio of exchange in a stock swap acquisition if PG pays $30 per share of PSI? Explain why.

   (2) What effect will this swap of stock have on the EPS of the original shares of (a) Plants Galore and (b) Plant Service, Inc.? Explain why.

   (3) If the earnings attributed to PSI's assets grow at a much slower rate than those attributed to PG's pre-merger assets, what effect might this have on the EPS of the merged firm over the long run?

c. What other merger proposals could PG make to PSI's owners?

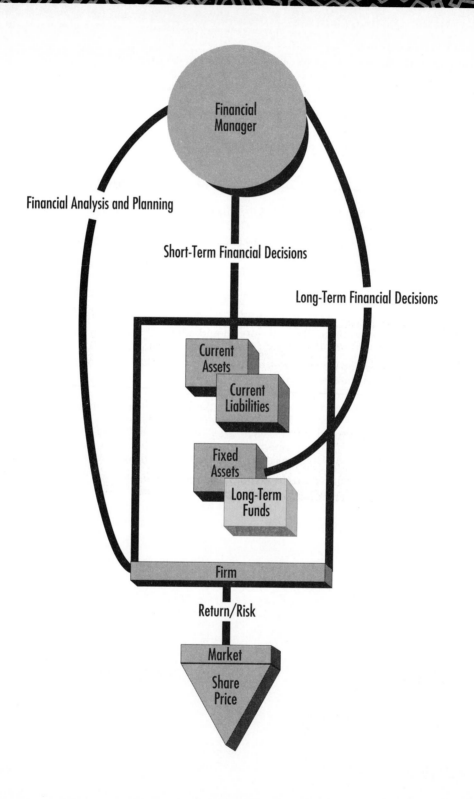

SOURCES OF LONG-TERM FINANCING

CHAPTER 18

INVESTMENT BANKING: ITS ROLE IN RAISING LONG-TERM FUNDS

CHAPTER OBJECTIVES

After studying this chapter, you should be able to:

1 Understand the importance and role of long-term funds, including internal and external sources, the need for external funds, and the methods used to raise external funds.

2 Define venture capital and discuss the role it plays in long-term financing.

3 Describe the role of investment bankers in long-term business financing, the underwriting process, services provided, distribution activities, and investment banker compensation.

4 Explain the key activities of the firm in an initial public offering—selecting an investment banker, the process of going public, and the advantages and disadvantages of going public.

5 Review the restrictions and dilemmas frequently faced by the financial manager when making subsequent public offerings of new common stock.

6 Discuss recent trends in the investment banking industry—the demise of debt-driven takeovers and the rise of financial engineering—and how it is likely to change in the future.

" " . . . the suit is bound to stimulate a lot of companies that are deep in debt to blame Wall Street advisors for their predicament. " "

Investment Banking on Trial

Interco, Inc., a St. Louis-based furniture and shoe company, was under attack in 1988. Steven and Mitchell Rales had launched a hostile takeover bid. The Rales brothers had secretly purchased over $200 million worth of Interco stock and subsequently announced their interest in taking over the firm. Interco turned to the investment banking firm of Wasserstein Perella & Co. for assistance. Although Wasserstein helped Interco thwart the takeover bid, the debt-laden recapitalization plan had disastrous consequences for Interco. Asset sales failed to generate as much cash as anticipated and earnings were short of projections. After staggering under a $2 billion debt load, Interco filed for bankruptcy in January 1991.

As part of its bankruptcy filing, Interco sued Wasserstein for negligence. The suit asked for a minimum of $89.5 million in damages, resulting from Wasserstein's delay in the sale of Interco's Ethan Allen unit. During the delay, the value of bids for Ethan Allen shrunk. Consequently, Interco had trouble paying interest on debt. Shareholders decided that only under the protection from creditors offered by Chapter 11 of the Bankruptcy Reform Act of 1978 would they be able to maintain any ownership position.

Bondholders, as well as stockholders, agreed that quick action was important before suppliers withheld materials, employees felt insecure, or customers questioned product quality. Banks and holders of medium-term notes chose an investment banker, Rothschild Inc., to negotiate with the company on behalf of lenders. Rothschild assisted in arranging for 14 banks to lend Interco $185 million, enabling it to continue operating under bankruptcy-court protection. In return, the banks received half of Interco's stock.

Wasserstein Perella quickly branded Interco's claims as totally without merit. Nevertheless, the suit is bound to encourage many companies that are deep in debt to blame Wall Street advisors for their predicament. Through lawsuits they may obtain enough funding to make the next interest payment.

long-term financing
Financing with an initial maturity of more than one year.

Successful businesses routinely need **long-term financing**—financing with an initial maturity of more than one year. Such financing enables firms to finance corporate growth and the replacement of worn-out equipment and to pay off debts and other obligations as they come due. Frequently these funds are obtained internally by retaining corporate profits rather than paying them out to shareholders as dividends. At other times, managers raise long-term funds externally through the sale of new debt, preferred stock, or common stock. Issuing and selling new securities can be a difficult task. The financial manager must know how to structure the terms of the new issue, how to satisfy the legal and regulatory requirements of security issuance, and how to effectively market and sell new securities to investors. Financial managers often hire investment banking firms to assist in the design and marketing of new security issues to investors. In this chapter we discuss the various ways in which financial managers raise long-term funds, the role of the investment banker, compensating investment bankers, initial and subsequent sales of new common stock, and recent trends in the investment banking industry.

RAISING LONG-TERM FUNDS

Financial managers face a wide variety of choices when they raise long-term funds. They can raise either debt or equity. Debt (discussed in Chapter 19) is an **external source of funds**—it is raised outside of the firm—obtained either through negotiated loans (discussed in Chapter 19 but ignored here) or the sale of bonds. Equity (discussed in Chapter 20) can be obtained either as an **internal source of funds**—funds generated within the firm—from retained earnings or raised externally through the sale of preferred or common stock. Figure 18.1 shows the various sources of internal and external long-term financing that are discussed throughout this chapter.

external sources of funds Funds raised outside the firm from negotiated loans and the sale of bonds and stock.

internal sources of funds Funds generated inside the firm from retained earnings.

When Do Firms Need External Funds?

Most growing firms are unable through internally generated retained earnings to obtain all of the long-term funds needed. These firms must use externally generated funds to fulfill their long-term financing needs. Firms seek more external funding during periods when internally generated funds are in short supply. This typically occurs when the economy enters a recession, business activity slows down, and corporate profits fall. When economic recovery begins at the end of a recessionary period, corporate profits begin to recover, internal sources of funds increase, and corporate use of external funding declines. Because the availability of internal funds varies directly with the business cycle, the

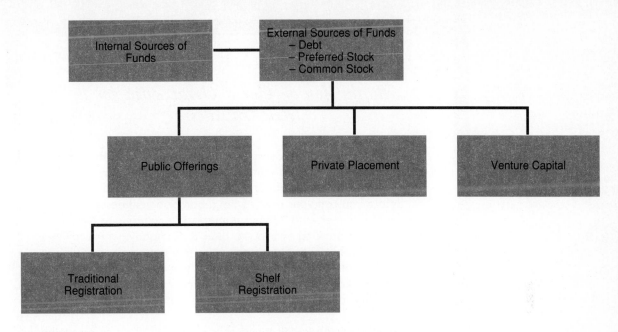

Figure 18.1   **Sources of Long-Term Corporate Financing**

Firms can raise long-term funds internally through retained earnings or externally through the sale of debt, preferred stock, or common stock. External financing may be raised through public offerings or placed directly. Small start-up firms typically must rely on venture capital for their long-term financing.

use of external funds rises when economic activity declines and falls when economic activity increases.

How Do Firms Raise External Funds?

Corporations wishing to raise external funds can do so either through a public offering or a direct placement of the securities. Here we take a brief look at these alternatives for selling new debt or equity.

In a **public offering**, the firm offers its securities for sale to the general public. To do so it must register the securities with the Securities and Exchange Commission (SEC). Most public offerings are underwritten by an **investment banker**—a financial intermediary that "underwrites" the sale of new securities by purchasing them from issuing firms at an arranged price and then reselling them to the general public in the primary capital market. (Recall from Chapter 2 that a *primary market* is the market in which securities are initially issued; in contrast, preowned securities are traded in *secondary markets* such as the New York Stock Exchange.) In addition, the investment banker provides advice and helps the issuing firm meet SEC registration requirements for the new securities.

An alternative to public offerings is direct placement of new securities with selected investors. Under a **private placement**, new securities are sold by the issuer directly to selected groups of investors such as

public offering The sale of a firm's securities to the general public.

investment banker Financial intermediary that purchases new securities from issuing firms and resells them to the general public in the primary capital market.

private placement The sale of new securities directly to selected groups of investors, without SEC registration.

CAREERS   IN   FINANCE

Think You've Got a Great Idea for a New Business?

OK—you've just discovered the best business idea since Edwin Land invented the Polaroid camera, and all you need now is a little start-up capital to begin raking in the bucks. What do you do?

Before you call your friendly neighborhood venture capitalist to pitch your idea, it pays to do your homework. According to New York City investment banking firm D. H. Blair & Company, which reviews over 3,000 new business plans each year, you don't get much time to win the attention, and financing, of most venture capital firms. You need to be well organized and have a business plan that really stands out from the other 2,999 plans sitting with yours in the "in" basket.

So how do you knock their socks off? D. H. Blair suggests the following pointers:

■ Make it simple and brief. Prepare a well-written executive summary to introduce your report. The summary should explain why you think your business will succeed, highlight your financial goals, and demonstrate your skills as a manager.

■ Provide an analysis of your competition. This shows that you have thoroughly studied your market and that you know what you're up against.

■ Detail your management experience, showing that you have the skills, ability, and track record to transform your idea into a successful business.

■ Prepare realistic pro forma financial statements that show how your start-up costs will be paid and how your investors will realize a return on their investment.

What turns off most venture capitalists? According to D. H. Blair, sending a product sample that does not work, delivering a handwritten business plan, having friends write letters of recommendation to vouch for your business skills, and being persistent to the point that you become a pest in the venture capitalist's office are the fastest ways to lose the attention—and financial backing—of firms that fund private placements.

Source: Ellyn E. Spragins, "How to write a business plan that will get you in the door," *Inc.*, November 1990, p. 159.

insurance companies and pension funds. Privately placed securities do *not* require SEC registration. Because these institutional investors are sophisticated enough to request and examine relevant investment information with respect to the issuer and the securities, assistance from the federal government is not necessary. While direct placement allows the issuer to avoid the time and expense of SEC registration, it limits the issuer to a far smaller group of potential investors.

Venture Capital

While established businesses can raise long-term funds with relative ease by issuing debt and equity securities, young corporations have a harder time. They often lack the asset base and credit history needed to publicly sell securities. In addition, these firms frequently cannot afford hiring an investment banking firm to make a direct placement. Thus, young corporations frequently seek financing in the form of venture capital. **Venture capital** is financing invested in a young firm by specialized financial intermediaries known as venture capitalists. Although venture capital firms sometimes provide debt financing, in most cases they obtain common stock ownership in the businesses they finance. They typically finance innovative businesses that operate in rapidly growing segments of the economy and have a good chance of success.

venture capital
Funds invested in a start-up business by specialized financial intermediaries.

Usually, the common stock issued by start-up corporations is not publicly traded, and venture capitalists that hold it therefore face a substantial liquidity risk. Because many young businesses fail before public sale of their common equity can occur, venture capitalists also face a significant risk that they will lose their entire investment in a firm. Historic data show that about 17 percent of all start-up corporations funded by venture capitalists experience total failure. Many more earn negligible or negative returns. Only a small number of ventures earn positive cash returns, but these returns are generally so large that they more than compensate for the losses incurred in connection with failed ventures.

THE ROLE OF THE INVESTMENT BANKER

Some corporations, and even the U.S. government, bring new securities to market without hiring an investment banker to purchase their new debt or equity securities and resell them to the general public. Such securities are termed *nonunderwritten issues*. Most corporations, however, hire an investment banker, such as Merrill Lynch or Goldman, Sachs, to put together an underwritten offering. The investment banking firm underwrites new security issues and provides a variety of related services.

Table 18.1 identifies the largest domestic investment banking firms by rank, showing the number of security issues each firm man-

Table 18.1   **Leading Underwriters for U.S. Securities Offerings in 1990**

Rank	Underwriter	Number of issues	Total underwriting volume (millions)	Percent of total underwriting volume	Average size of issue (millions)
1	Merrill Lynch	726	$55,754.3	17.6%	$76.8
2	Goldman, Sachs	474	40,743.2	12.8	85.9
3	First Boston	524	33,051.4	10.4	63.1
4	Salomon Brothers	375	32,667.1	10.3	87.1
5	Morgan Stanley	325	31,272.4	9.9	96.2
6	Kidder, Peabody	672	22,066.0	7.0	32.8
7	Lehman Brothers	444	20,331.9	6.4	45.8
8	Bear, Stearns	538	20,010.0	6.3	37.2
9	Prudential-Bache	335	13,449.5	4.2	40.1
10	Donaldson, Lufkin & Jenrette	294	6,172.7	1.9	21.0
11	Paine Webber	170	5,984.9	1.9	35.2
12	Dean Witter	24	5,263.7	1.7	219.3
13	J.P. Morgan	98	4,132.6	1.3	42.2
14	Citicorp	77	3,740.5	1.2	48.6
15	Smith Barney, Harris Upham	109	3,406.1	1.1	31.2
	All others combined	863	19,162.8	6.0	22.2
	Total	6,048	$317,209.1	100.0%	$52.4

Source: *Investment Dealers' Digest* (January 7, 1991).

aged in 1990 and the total business volume that these issues represented. Notice that the investment banking industry is highly concentrated. The five largest firms in the industry accounted for 40 percent of all new issues and 61 percent of total underwriting volume in 1990. In addition, note that the largest investment bankers managed the biggest deals. In the investment banking industry, size confers prestige. The largest firms have an extensive network of contacts in the capital market. These contacts are important to nonfinancial corporations seeking to issue new securities, because they mean that the issuer's new securities will achieve the widest possible distribution within the financial community.

Investment Banking Services

The Underwriting Process

price risk The risk that the price of a new security will fall while it is being held by an investment banking firm.

When an investment banker underwrites a new securities issue, it purchases the securities from the issuing firm at a prearranged price and then resells them to other investors. The investment banker bears **price risk** in an underwriting. If the price of the securities falls while they are held by the investment banking firm, it—not the issuing corporation— experiences the loss. Consequently, investment bankers must maintain close contact with the capital markets in order to accurately estimate how a particular issue will be received by investors. It is the investment bankers' knowledge of financial markets, along with their expertise in structuring new offerings and skill in marketing new securities, that explains why most nonfinancial corporations hire them to assist in raising funds externally.

Best Efforts Offerings

As an alternative to underwriting new security issues, investment bankers may agree to take new securities from the issuer and market them on a **best efforts basis.** In this case, the investment banker does not purchase the securities from the issuer for resale to the general public. Instead, the investment banker agrees only to sell as many of the new securities as possible at a preestablished price, acting as an agent for the issuer. Any securities remaining unsold at the conclusion of the offering are simply returned to the issuer; the investment banker bears no underwriting or price risk. This arrangement is frequently used when the issuer is a small, unknown corporation and the investment banker does not wish to be saddled with an inventory of unsold securities at the conclusion of the offering. In addition, very large corporations that believe their newly issued securities will sell quickly in the market often establish best efforts agreements with their investment bankers. These issuers agree to accept the underwriting risk associated with the offering in exchange for a fee reduction from the investment banker.

best efforts basis
Arrangement in which an investment banker agrees to act as an agent to sell as much of a securities issue as possible at a preset price but does not purchase the securities from the issuer for resale.

Other Services Provided by Investment Bankers

Underwriting the public sale of new corporate securities is the major service provided by investment bankers. They also perform a number of other valuable functions related to raising external funds through public offering. Investment bankers use their knowledge and expertise in financial markets to *advise corporate issuers* as to the type of security to offer, the appropriate terms and timing of the issue, and the best financial market in which to sell the issue. They also *assist the firm in preparing and filing the accounting and legal documents necessary for security issuance.* Investment bankers *help issuers price securities* by determining their value. This activity is particularly important. If the offering price is set too high, the new securities will not sell and the investment banker will lose money on the underwriting transaction. If the offering price is set too low, a portion of the firm's value will be transferred from existing stockholders to purchasers of the new shares. In this case, both the management and stockholders of the issuing firm will be dissatisfied with the investment banker's performance.

Investment bankers use their industry contacts with other investment banking firms to *create the widest possible distribution for new issues and maintain an orderly market for them.* Maintaining order in the market means that the investment banker will maintain an inventory of underwritten securities, quote purchase and sales prices on them, and stand ready to buy and sell those securities at the quoted prices for a limited period of time following the original public issue. When a firm announces a new security issue, the announcement often causes a change in the firm's existing stock price because it provides new information to investors outside the firm. The investment banker attempts to *communicate the purpose, intent, and value of the new security offering throughout the investment community* in order to give investors the same information that is available to the firm's management. The investment banker also *places its reputation behind the new issues* it underwrites, thereby strengthening each issue's perceived quality and legitimacy.

The Distribution Process

Investment bankers use a variety of different methods to reduce the price risk they face when underwriting new security issues. While small public issues may be completely controlled by a single investment banker, larger offerings are distributed in the capital market using an **underwriting syndicate**—a group of investment banking firms collectively participates in buying and selling a portion of the new issue.

Syndicated Offerings

In a syndicated offering, the **managing (or lead) underwriter** of the syndicate negotiates with the issuing corporation the terms of the issue, its price, and the fees payable to the investment banking syndicate. Then the managing underwriter invites other investment banking firms to join the syndicate and underwrite a portion of the issue.

Investors can easily determine the membership and organizational structure of an underwriting syndicate from its **tombstone advertisements** published in the financial press. Figure 18.2 shows a tombstone that appeared in *The Wall Street Journal* to announce a 1991 common stock issue by Pac Rim Holding Corporation. The tombstone, which gets its name from the stark, businesslike appearance of the announcement, alerts the investment community of a firm's intentions to issue new securities. Notice that the tombstone provides information concerning the number of shares offered and their issue price. It also lists each investment banker participating in the underwriting syndicate.

The order in which investment banking firms appear in the tombstone is meaningful. At the top, the advertisement identifies the managing underwriters as Salomon Brothers and Wedbush Morgan Securities. Next, national investment banking firms taking a major position in the underwriting are listed in alphabetical order. This listing begins with First Boston Corporation and ends with Wertheim Schroeder & Co. The next section in the list identifies underwriters that purchase a small number of shares in the offering, followed by an alphabetic listing of regional investment banking firms that purchase an even smaller portion of the offering.

Distribution relationships can be quite complex, as the underwriters try to make the new shares widely available through a number of retail brokerage firms. Members of the underwriting syndicate solicit sales from institutional and individual investors, and often form a **selling group** composed of brokerage houses located throughout the U.S.

underwriting syndicate Group of investment banking firms that collectively participates in buying and selling a portion of a new security issue.

managing (or lead) underwriter Underwriter of a syndicate that negotiates the terms of the issue with the issuing corporation.

tombstone advertisements Advertisements for security issues.

selling group Group of brokerage houses who promote a securities issue through their branch offices and retail stockbrokers in their area.

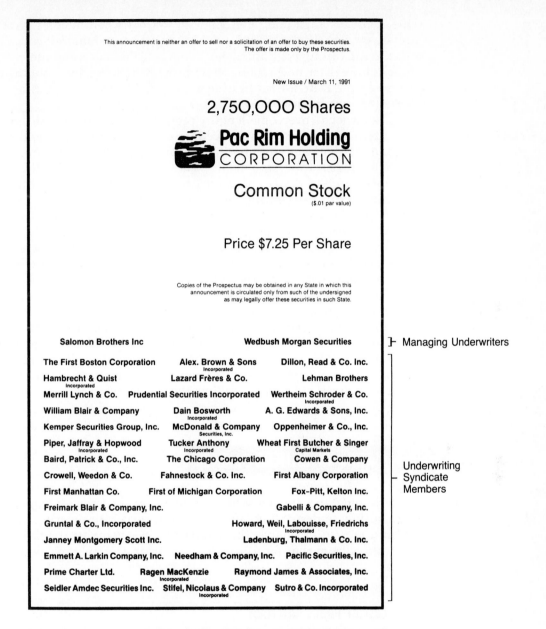

Figure 18.2   Tombstone Advertisement for Pac Rim Holding Corporation

The tombstone for Pac Rim Holding Corporation's common stock offering of March 11, 1991, shows that 2,750,000 shares are offered at $7.25 per share by a large syndicate of underwriters managed by two firms—Salomon Brothers and Wedbush Morgan Securities.

Members of the selling group promote the securities through their branch offices and retail stockbrokers in their particular market area.

Shelf Registration

Corporations issuing new securities often try to "time the market." Their goal is to bring new common stock to market when stock prices are relatively high and new bonds to market when interest rates are relatively low. Under traditional SEC registration requirements, effective market timing is difficult to achieve. It takes at minimum several weeks to register new securities with the SEC. Typically, months pass between the time a firm first decides to issue new securities and the date they are finally sold.

In order to overcome lengthy registration delays, the SEC allows an alternative registration procedure called **shelf registration.** Firms with more than $150 million in outstanding common stock may file a "master registration statement." The statement describes the firm's planned funding needs and forecasts security issues over a two-year horizon. At any time during the two years following the effective date of the shelf registration, the firm, after filing a "short statement," can sell securities already approved under the master statement.

Shelf registration of new securities has become extremely popular. Over one-half of new equity issues in 1990 were covered by shelf registration statements. But does shelf registration allow financial managers to time the market effectively? The evidence is mixed. In some cases, shelf registration reduces the transactions costs of bringing new securities to market, because it minimizes the paperwork necessary to initiate security sales. The shelf registration process does not, however, appear to have a significant impact on reducing the cost of debt and equity capital for new issues. Why? Because even with streamlined registration procedures, it isn't easy to time the market when issuing new securities.

COMPENSATING INVESTMENT BANKERS

Determining the compensation received by investment bankers for structuring, underwriting, and marketing corporate security offerings is quite simple. Of course, the compensation scheme for a public offering differs from that for a private placement. Here we review each of them.

The Cost of Public Offerings

Public security offerings underwritten by a single investment banker or syndicate of investment bankers are purchased from the issuing corporation at a lower price than that at which they are to be resold to the public. This difference represents the investment banker's **gross commission** (or **gross underwriting spread**).

The gross commission is easy to determine by examining the front cover of the **prospectus,** which is a portion of the registration statement filed by the issuer with the SEC that details the firm's operating and financial position. Figure 18.3 shows the front cover of a prospectus describing the terms and conditions associated with the issue of 2,750,000 shares of common stock by Pac Rim Holding Corporation in March 1991. The managing underwriters in this transaction—Salomon

shelf registration
Securities registration procedure that allows a firm to sell securities during a two-year period under a master registration statement filed with the SEC.

gross commission (gross underwriting spread) The difference between the price at which an investment banker sells a securities issue to the public and the price at which it bought the issue from the issuing firm.

prospectus The portion of the registration statement filed by a securities issuer with the SEC that details the firm's operating and financial position.

Prospectus

2,750,000 Shares

Pac Rim Holding
CORPORATION

Common Stock
($.01 par value)

All of the 2,750,000 shares of Common Stock, $.01 par value, offered hereby (the "Shares") are being sold by Pac Rim Holding Corporation (the "Company" or "Pac Rim").

Prior to this offering, there has been no public market for the Common Stock of the Company. See "Underwriting" for a discussion of the factors considered in determining the initial public offering price.

The Common Stock has been approved for quotation on the NASDAQ National Market System under the symbol "PRIM", upon notice of issuance.

See "Investment Considerations" for a discussion of certain factors that should be considered by prospective purchasers of the Shares.

THESE SECURITIES HAVE NOT BEEN APPROVED OR DISAPPROVED BY THE SECURITIES AND EXCHANGE COMMISSION OR ANY STATE SECURITIES COMMISSION NOR HAS THE SECURITIES AND EXCHANGE COMMISSION OR ANY STATE SECURITIES COMMISSION PASSED UPON THE ACCURACY OR ADEQUACY OF THIS PROSPECTUS. ANY REPRESENTATION TO THE CONTRARY IS A CRIMINAL OFFENSE.

	Price to Public	Underwriting Discount	Proceeds to Company(1)
Per Share	$7.25	$.50	$6.75
Total (2)	$19,937,500	$1,375,000	$18,562,500

(1) Before deducting expenses payable by the Company estimated to be $560,000.

(2) The Company has granted the Underwriters an option, exercisable within 30 days hereof, to purchase up to 412,500 additional Shares to cover over-allotments, if any. If the Underwriters exercise such option in full, the total Price to Public, Underwriting Discount and Proceeds to Company will be $22,928,125, $1,581,250 and $21,346,875, respectively. See "Underwriting."

The Shares are offered subject to receipt and acceptance by the Underwriters, to prior sale and to the Underwriters' right to reject any order in whole or in part or to withdraw, cancel or modify the offer without notice. It is expected that delivery of the Shares will be made at the office of Salomon Brothers Inc, One New York Plaza, New York, New York, or through the facilities of The Depository Trust Company, on or about March 15, 1991.

Salomon Brothers Inc   Wedbush Morgan Securities

The date of this Prospectus is March 8, 1991.

Figure 18.3   Front Cover of Prospectus for Pac Rim Holding Corporation's Common Stock Offering

The front cover of the prospectus for Pac Rim Holding Corporation's March 1991 common stock issue indicates that the managing underwriters—Salomon Brothers and Wedbush Morgan Securities— paid $6.75 per share and planned to sell 2,750,000 shares to the public for $7.25 each. They will net a gross commission of $.50 per share for a total of $1,375,000.

Brothers and Wedbush Morgan Securities—paid $6.75 per share for the stock and planned to resell it to the public for $7.25. The gross commission represents $0.50 per share and totals $1,375,000 ($0.50 × 2,750,000 shares).

The distribution of the gross commission depends on the syndicate agreement. In most cases, the gross commission from the underwriting transaction is divided four ways as listed below:

out-of-pocket costs
Costs of a managing underwriter incurred in connection with a securities issue.

1 ■ First, the managing underwriter pays all **out-of-pocket costs** incurred in connection with the issue. These costs include lawyers' fees, accountants' fees, SEC filing fees, printing and engraving costs, postage, and miscellaneous costs.

management fee
Fee paid a managing underwriter for coordinating and sponsoring an underwriting syndicate.

2 ■ Next, the managing underwriter subtracts a **management fee,** which is its payment for coordinating and sponsoring the syndicate. This fee usually equals about 15 percent of the gross commission.

underwriting fee
Fee divided on a pro rata basis among members of an underwriting syndicate.

3 ■ Then the managing underwriter divides the total **underwriting fee** on a pro rata basis among the syndicate participants who purchased securities from the issuing corporation. The underwriting fee also equals about 15 percent of the gross commission.

selling concession
Fee paid to members of an underwriting syndicate based on the number of shares each member sold.

4 ■ Finally, the balance of the gross commission is divided among all members of the syndicate based on the number of shares that each member sold. This represents the **selling concession** paid to members of the selling group that distributed shares in the capital market.

An example can demonstrate the calculation and distribution of the gross commission realized by the managing underwriter.

EXAMPLE   Plath Industries, a diversified producer of building products, recently issued 1,000,000 shares of new common stock through an underwritten offering arranged by Flatbush Securities, Inc. As the managing underwriter for the sale, Flatbush formed a syndicate composed of three other investment banking firms—Alpha Company, Beta Company, and Delta Company—to purchase and resell Plath's common stock to the public. According to the prospectus describing the issue, Flatbush paid Plath $28.00 per share for the new stock, and set the initial offering price at $30.00. Flatbush's out-of-pocket costs for the transaction totaled $450,000. It sold 200,000 shares at $28.70 a share to each of its three partners in the underwriting group and planned to distribute the remaining 400,000 shares directly to the public. The investment bankers earned an underwriting fee of $0.30 from each share and were paid a selling concession of $1.00 per share on each share they sold. The stock was well received in the market, and the syndicate sold out the entire issue in one day.

The *gross commission* in this transaction was $2.00 per share ($30.00 offering price − $28.00 purchase price), or $2,000,000 for the entire issue ($2.00 per share × 1,000,000 shares).

The gross commission would be broken down and divided among syndicate members as noted in Table 18.2. The breakdown of the gross commission developed in Table 18.2 is summarized and evaluated on a percentage basis relative to both the initial offering price and the gross commission in Table 18.3. The table shows that the selling concession accounts for 50 percent of the gross commission. The out-of-pocket costs, management fee, and underwriting fee account for 22.5 percent, 12.5 percent, and 15.0 percent, respectively, of the gross commission.

Table 18.2	**Distribution of the Gross Commission for Plath Industries' Common Stock Offering**		
		Total	**Per share**[a]
1. Out-of-Pocket Costs Paid by Flatbush Securities, Inc.		$ 450,000	$0.45
2. Management Fee		250,000	0.25

[($0.25 per share) × (1,000,000 shares)]. This fee was paid to Flatbush as the lead underwriter. Notice that the total cost paid by Flatbush for each share was $28.45, representing the $28.00 paid to Plath and $0.45 in out-of-pocket costs associated with the issue. Flatbush resold shares to the investment banking syndicate for $28.70 each, earning a management fee of $0.25 on each share [$28.70 − $28.45].

3. Underwriting Fee

Flatbush Securities	$120,000		
Alpha Company	60,000		
Beta Company	60,000		
Delta Company	60,000		
Total		300,000	0.30

Shares resold to selling group for $29.00 ($30.00 price to public − $1 selling concession). Syndicate pays $28.70 for shares. The underwriting fee on each share was therefore $0.30 ($29.00 price to selling group − $28.70 price to syndicate). Flatbush sold 200,000 shares to each of its underwriting partners ($0.30 × 200,000 = $60,000), and retained 400,000 shares for distribution to the public ($0.30 × 400,000 = $120,000).

4. Selling Concession

Flatbush Securities	$400,000		
Alpha Company	200,000		
Beta Company	200,000		
Delta Company	200,000		
Total		1,000,000	1.00

The selling concession was $1.00 per share ($30.00 price to public − $29.00 price to selling group). Flatbush sold 400,000 shares to the public; each of the other three underwriters sold 200,000 shares each.

Gross Commission		$2,000,000	$2.00

[a]Per-share values were calculated by dividing the total cost by 1,000,000—the number of shares issued.

Table 18.3   Analysis of the Gross Commission
                                    for Plath Industries' Common Stock Offering

Component	Value[a]		Percent of initial offering price	Percent of gross commission
	Total	Per share		
Out-of-pocket costs	$ 450,000	$0.45	$0.45/$30 = 1.5%	$0.45/$2 = 22.5%
Management fee	250,000	0.25	0.25/ 30 = 0.9	0.25/ 2 = 12.5
Underwriting fee	300,000	0.30	0.30/ 30 = 1.0	0.30/ 2 = 15.0
Selling concession	1,000,000	1.00	1.00/ 30 = 3.3	1.00/ 2 = 50.0
Total	$2,000,000	$2.00	$2.00/$30 = 6.7%	$2.00/$2 = 100.0%

[a]From Table 18.2

Table 18.4 provides historical data concerning the cost of public
offerings of common stock, preferred stock, and corporate bonds during
the 1973–1989 period. The table separates the underwriting spread
from the out-of-pocket costs. The gross commissions in the table represent the amount paid to investment banking firms. Notice that the *gross
commissions for debt are significantly below the gross commissions for
equity*. This difference is reflected in both the underwriting spread and
the out-of-pocket costs. Clearly, firms issue more debt that equity because it is cheaper to sell new debt securities. In addition, note that the
gross commissions decline for all types of securities as the issue size
increases. This is particularly true of the out-of-pocket costs, which are

Table 18.4   **The Cost of Public Security Offerings as a Percentage of Offering Price, 1973–1989**

Issue size (in millions)	Common stock			Preferred stock			Corporate bonds		
	Under-writing spread[a] (%)	Out-of-pocket costs[b] (%)	Gross commission[c] (%)	Under-writing spread[a] (%)	Out-of-pocket costs[b] (%)	Gross commission[c] (%)	Under-writing spread[a] (%)	Out-of-pocket costs[b] (%)	Gross commission[c] (%)
Under $10.0	8.68	6.16	14.84	8.83	2.65	11.48	4.72	1.46	6.18
10.0 to 24.9	6.41	2.19	8.60	5.62	1.15	6.77	1.89	0.56	2.45
25.0 to 49.9	5.62	1.26	6.88	2.69	0.76	3.45	2.17	0.59	2.76
50.0 to 99.9	5.12	0.89	6.01	1.95	0.31	2.26	1.43	0.31	1.74
100.0 to 199.9	4.74	0.57	5.31	2.65	0.31	2.96	1.07	0.19	1.26
200.0 to 500.0	4.66	0.38	5.04	3.27	0.18	3.45	1.07	0.12	1.19
Over 500	5.87	0.23	6.10	3.50	0.30	3.80	1.78	0.16	1.94
Average	5.87	1.67	7.54	4.07	0.81	4.88	2.02	0.48	2.50

[a]Represents the sum of the management fee, underwriting fee, and selling concession.
[b]Represents the out-of-pocket costs which include lawyers' fees, accountants' fees, SEC filing fees, printing and engraving costs, postage, mailing, and miscellaneous costs.
[c]Represents the sum of the underwriting spread and the out-of-pocket costs given in the two preceding columns.
Source: Securities Data Company, Inc.

much like fixed costs. From a cost standpoint, it is much cheaper for firms to issue a large quantity of securities at infrequent intervals than to issue small quantities of securities on a regular basis.

The Cost of Private Placements

Nonunderwritten issues, private placements, and transactions handled by investment bankers on a best efforts basis involve a slightly different compensation mechanism. Because in these situations investment bankers do not purchase and resell securities, they cannot be compensated on the basis of a price mark-up at the time of public sale. Instead, investment bankers establish a charge based on the advising, marketing, and distribution services they provide. In most cases, advising services carry a fixed charge. Marketing and distribution services are billed according to the number of securities the issuer sells during the time the investment banker is acting as its agent. Thus, these transactions earn investment bankers advisory fees and selling commissions rather than the gross commission earned in public offerings.

THE INITIAL PUBLIC OFFERING (IPO)

In the preceding sections we described how firms raise long-term funds and the role played by investment bankers in that process. Here, we examine the decisions faced by financial managers when they raise external funds through a public stock issue. Typically, start-up businesses rely on private equity investments from their founders, venture capitalists, and other individuals personally known by the firm's founders. As they grow, these businesses may expand their equity base through the accumulation of retained earnings and/or the private placement of additional shares of common stock with interested parties close to the firm. In time, however, many privately held firms reach the point at which further expansion requires the public sale of common stock. When a privately held firm publicly issues common stock for the first time, it is said to be **"going public,"** and its stock issue is called an **initial public offering (IPO).** This section reviews important decisions and procedures that managers of privately held firms encounter when they decide to go public. Note that most of these decisions and procedures are applicable to subsequent sales of securities as well.

going public Offering to the general public common stock previously held by private investors.

initial public offering (IPO) The stock issue of a firm that offers shares to the public for the first time.

Selecting an Investment Banker

A firm that wishes to go public must first select an investment banker to assist with the IPO. It then must determine whether the issue should be underwritten or distributed on a best efforts basis. If the firm finds investment bankers that are willing to underwrite the issue, it will probably hire them to make the offering. An underwritten offering en-

competitive bidding
The process in which a
number of investment
bankers bid for the right
to sell a securities issue
and the highest bid is the
winner.

negotiated offering
The process in which a
securities issuer inter-
views a number of in-
vestment bankers and
selects the one that it
thinks will best meet its
needs at the lowest cost.

sures the firm that it will raise a specified amount of money in exchange for a given number of shares.

Next, the firm must decide whether to hire its investment banker on the basis of *competitive bidding* or a *negotiated offering*. Under **competitive bidding**, the issuer specifies the type of security it intends to sell and invites a number of investment bankers to bid for the issue. The bidder offering the highest price for the issue is awarded it. Competitive bidding is common among registered public utilities. The Public Utility Holding Company Act of 1935 requires these firms to select an investment banker using the competitive bidding process. *Among industrial firms, however, competitive bidding is infrequently used.* Most likely an issuer will use a negotiated offering to select an investment banker. Under a **negotiated offering** the issuer interviews a variety of investment bankers and selects the one that is expected to best meet its needs at the lowest cost. In this case, the issuer negotiates the total underwriting cost of the issue directly with the investment banker.

Does competitive bidding result in lower issuance costs than a negotiated offering? The answer is not completely clear. Research has shown that during periods of relatively stable stock prices, competition among investment bankers results in lower issuance costs. However, when stock prices are volatile competitive bidding leads to greater competition among investment bankers; it thus increases the risk of the issue to the investment banker and raises issuance costs. Negotiated offerings in a volatile market may result in a cost advantage to the issuer by allowing investment bankers to tailor new securities to prevailing market conditions. In addition, negotiated offerings better allow investment bankers to work together in syndicates when bringing new issues to market; syndication helps diversify underwriting risk and thereby can reduce the issuer's underwriting costs. Finally, negotiated offerings involve a smaller time lag between the design of the issue and its being offered for sale. In a volatile market, this time savings can help reduce uncertainty concerning the ultimate selling price of the new issue.

The Process of Going Public

Once the firm has selected an investment banker, the real work begins. First, the firm's board of directors must make sure the corporate charter authorizes the proposed public sale of new common stock. If it doesn't, the corporate charter must be amended (with the approval of shareholders) to authorize the issuance of new common stock. Next, the firm must comply with state and federal regulations governing new stock issues.

Securities Regulation

Prior to 1933, regulation of security sales was left to individual state governments. Because securities regulations were not consistent across all states, however, the federal government stepped into the picture

ETHICS   IN   FINANCE

An Underwriting Disaster at Pru-Bache

When investment banking firms offer new securities to the public, many potential investors feel that the reputation of the offering firm and disclosure requirements enforced by the SEC protect them from shady investments. This protection, however, is sometimes an illusion. Prudential-Bache Securities, Inc., backed by the conservative reputation of the $160 billion Prudential Insurance Corporation of America, sold more than $6 billion in limited partnership investments to over 100,000 investors between 1982 and 1991. Due to the plummeting value of many assets underlying these partnerships and substantial brokerage fees levied against partnership investors, however, these partnerships today are worth less than $3 billion.

To make matters worse, the Pru-Bache executive in charge of selling limited partnership shares between 1979 and 1988 is currently under investigation for possible conflicts of interest involving many limited partnership sales. In some cases, Pru-Bache may have compromised its responsibility to investors in locating and offering for sale the best possible limited partnership investments, because the executive in charge of these investments maintained personal investment dealings with several sponsors of limited partnerships who were selling their securities through Prudential-Bache.

How could such a serious breach of professional ethics occur? Many observers believe that Pru-Bache's senior managers emphasized sales and earnings growth over financial control. Because the firm's limited partnership unit was tremendously profitable, senior corporate officers failed to question the methods used by the unit to generate sales and income.

Investors who purchased limited partnership shares from Pru-Bache, however, are now asking a lot of questions. By early 1991, Pru-Bache investors had filed 100 different lawsuits against the firm, seeking more than $2 billion in damages. The firm's CEO and the executive in charge of the limited partnership unit resigned their positions, leaving behind more than $250 million in cash losses, a variety of unsettled legal claims, and scores of angry investors. While Pru-Bache's limited partnership business increased short-run operating profits at the firm, the long-run impact on shareholder value will be disastrous for Pru-Bache's equity holders.

Source: Chuck Hawkins, "The mess at Pru-Bache," *Business Week,* March 4, 1991, p. 66.

Securities Act of 1933
Federal law that regulates the public sale of new security issues.

Securities Exchange Act of 1934   Federal law that regulates the sale of securities in secondary markets.

registration statement   Statement with information about a new security issue that must be filed with the SEC for approval before public sale of the issue can take place.

with a series of legislative measures after the stock market crash of 1929. The **Securities Act of 1933** currently regulates the public sale of new security issues; the **Securities Exchange Act of 1934** provides federal rules governing the sale of securities in secondary markets—both organized and over-the-counter. The fundamental objective of the 1933 Securities Act is to provide full disclosure of all relevant information to potential investors. *The act does not, however, require the federal government to assess the investment merits of new security issues.* It merely charges the government with ensuring the full disclosure of all relevant information with respect to new security issues, and allows the government to halt the offering of securities that contain false or misleading claims.

The Securities Act of 1933 requires SEC approval for all interstate public offerings in excess of $500,000 that involve securities with a maturity of more than 270 days. Public offerings by railroads, banks, and public utilities are excluded from SEC registration requirements because these firms are regulated by other federal agencies. The **registration statement** filed with the SEC contains financial, legal, and technical information regarding the new issue and the business of the issuer. The registration statement must be filed with the SEC for a minimum of 20 days before approval is granted. The sale of new securities cannot begin until the registration statement is approved.

To complete the registration statement, the issuer must identify the type and terms of the security being offered for sale. At first glance, this might appear to be quite simple. In reality, it can be very difficult. The issuer must specify the key features of the debt or equity offering. Included would be items such as the coupon interest rate, maturity date, and any collateral in the case of a debt issue. Items such as voting rights, planned dividend payments, and expected dilution of earnings per share would be specified for an equity issue.

Market Listing

Once the firm specifies the type of security it plans to sell, it must identify where the securities will trade. The common stock of most small firms trades in the over-the-counter market, since there is not enough interest in it to justify listing it on a regional or national stock exchange. As a firm grows and achieves a wider ownership base, it may decide to apply for listing on a regional stock exchange. For example, a firm based in Los Angeles might decide to list its stock on the Pacific Stock Exchange, while a Chicago firm may list its stock on the Midwest Stock Exchange. Growing still larger, a firm might decide to apply for listing on one of the national exchanges—like the New York Stock Exchange or the American Stock Exchange—or even on a foreign stock exchange located in Hong Kong, London, Sydney, or Tokyo. Of course, listing is not automatic. The firm must apply for listing, meet the specified listing requirements of the given exchange, and pay fees in order to have its stock listed on an organized exchange.

Pricing the Issue

One of the critical functions of the managing underwriter is to price the new security. When a firm's stock is offered to the public for the first time, this job can be particularly difficult. Without existing shares trading in the market, the investment banker has few reference points to suggest how the market will value the new shares. As a consequence, the managing underwriter uses a variety of stock valuation models, such as the constant growth dividend valuation model introduced in Chapter 12, to price the new shares at their market value.

Preparing Documents

Next the firm begins the document preparation process. Public offerings require submission of a registration statement to the SEC. While the federal government reviews the registration statement, the issuer can circulate among potential investors a *prospectus*. The cover of Pac Rim Holding Corporation's 58-page common stock prospectus is shown in Figure 18.3. As noted earlier, a prospectus is the portion of the registration statement that has important operating and financial data. In order to circulate the prospectus during this period, a **"red herring"**—a statement indicating the tentative nature of the offer—must be printed in red ink on its cover. After the registration statement receives SEC approval, the red herring will be removed and the prospectus will become final. Note that the new security can be offered for sale if the prospectus is made available to all interested parties.

red herring A statement printed in red ink on the cover of a prospectus indicating the tentative nature of a securities offering before its approval by the SEC.

Selling the Issue

After the registration statement is approved, the underwriter or underwriting syndicate purchases the new securities from the issuing firm and begins to sell them to the general public. The underwriters closely monitor the price that retail buyers are paying for the new stock. It is essential that the demand for, and therefore the price of, the stock remain strong. Any weakness in demand for the stock will cause a price decline and reduce the underwriters' gross commission. If the retail price begins to move below the initial offering price printed on the prospectus, the underwriters may reverse direction and begin purchasing shares in the open market. This activity, called **market stabilization,** usually lasts up to two or three days following the initial offering. For new issues that are particularly difficult to sell, however, the stabilization period can last as long as 30 days. This activity is legal as long as its intent is disclosed in the registration statement filed with the SEC. Market stabilization is in the best interest of both the issuer and the underwriters; it reduces the underwriters' risk, thereby justifying payment of a higher price to the issuer by the underwriters.

market stabilization The purchase by underwriters of a security they are attempting to sell if the retail price of the shares moves below the initial offering price.

Once the underwriters' inventory of shares is completely exhausted, their job is still not finished. The managing underwriter in particular will continue to monitor the aftermarket behavior of the security's price for periods extending up to one year. The investment banker's reputation and future underwriting business are significantly affected by its track record in correctly pricing and marketing new securities issues. Hence, the managing underwriter watches the price movement of the new stock and through its trading activities tries to make sure that the issue is neither significantly overvalued nor undervalued.

Advantages and Disadvantages of Going Public

Given all the work it takes to arrange a public offering, one might wonder why any firm would decide to go public. A look at the advantages associated with going public will help explain the motives for doing so. Because investors can easily resell publicly traded securities in secondary markets, they offer *greater liquidity* to current and prospective stockholders. When a firm's securities are publicly held, it *can more readily issue additional securities* to raise more funds. This gives the firm wider access to a larger pool of financing. This is largely attributed to the greater market awareness resulting from public trading. In addition it is *easy to determine the market value of the firm's shares* when they are publicly traded. In contrast, privately held firms have more difficulty determining the market value of their shares, because they are not regularly exchanged by investors in a competitive marketplace. Another advantage is the *listing prestige* often resulting from having shares listed on a major stock exchange. For example, a firm whose shares are listed on the NYSE can publicize that its shares trade in the same market as the largest, best-known U.S. corporations. Finally, a public stock issue *allows the founders to sell their shares to the public and use the proceeds to diversify their investment portfolios.* It in effect creates a convenient mechanism that allows the founders to "cash out" if they so choose.

While going public has many advantages, it is not the best course of action for all small firms. There are a number of drawbacks to the public sale of stock. The out-of-pocket and underwriting *costs associated with public security sales are significant.* Firms can avoid, or at least reduce, these costs by using private placements to raise external funds. Another disadvantage is that SEC registration for public sale *requires firms to publicly disclose a great deal of operating and financial information.* Publicly held firms must make quarterly and annual financial statements available to the SEC, all shareholders, and the general public. These disclosures not only provide competitors with potentially useful information but also are costly. Another concern is that if investors focus on the short-term operating results of publicly held firms, *managers may operate these businesses to enhance short-run profits at the expense of long-run value.* For example, managers might postpone or forego major expenditures on research and development as well as equipment renovation, even where these projects would increase the long-run value of the firm, in order to increase short-run profits. While this criticism is controversial, it may be valid for stocks that are publicly traded but not widely followed by professional investors. Public trading also *exposes the firm to the risk of a hostile takeover* by a corporate outsider that accumulates a controlling interest in the firm. Clearly, this possibility may result in a change in management and a loss of control by the firm's founders. Even if a firm does not become vulnerable to a hostile takeover, public sale will result in the *dilution of ownership.* This occurs because when the owner-managers of a privately held firm take it public, they transfer some ownership rights to outside investors, thus reducing their proportionate ownership rights and control of the firm.

Given the advantages and disadvantages of going public, it is not surprising that some firms choose public offerings, while others select private placements. Interestingly, the trend in recent years is toward increasing use of private placements and diminished use of public offerings. This is particularly true for new common stock issues. For example, between 1985 and 1989 the percentage of new debt issues that were privately placed grew from about 28 percent to 39 percent. During the same period the percent of new common stock issues that were privately placed increased from about 30 percent to 50 percent. This trend can be attributed to the high cost of public offerings, the disadvantages of going public cited above, and an increased willingness on the part of institutional investors to purchase new corporate debt and equity securities through private placement transactions.

BEYOND THE IPO: SELLING ADDITIONAL COMMON STOCK

If the managing underwriter does a good job of managing an IPO, the new stock will for a time trade in the market at very close to its initial offering price. When this happens, the issuer is typically satisfied with the services provided by the underwriter and will likely use the same investment banker to manage future offerings of additional equity. Here we examine some of the activities involved in subsequent public offerings of new common stock.

Corporate Charter Restrictions

When a firm wishes to sell additional common stock, it must first make sure that it has enough **authorized shares** to support the issue. A firm's corporate charter defines the number of authorized shares that it can issue. The firm cannot sell more shares than the charter authorizes without obtaining approval from its owners through a shareholder vote. Authorized shares become **outstanding shares** when they are sold to the public. If the firm repurchases any of its outstanding shares, these shares are recorded as *treasury stock* and shown as a deduction from stockholders' equity on the firm's balance sheet. **Issued shares** is the number of shares of common stock that has been put into circulation; it represents the sum of outstanding shares and treasury stock.

authorized shares
The number of shares of common stock that a firm's corporate charter allows without further stockholder approval.

outstanding shares
The number of shares of common stock sold to the public.

issued shares The number of shares of common stock that has been put into circulation; outstanding shares plus treasury stock.

EXAMPLE Golden Enterprises, a producer of medical pumps, has the following stockholders' equity account on December 31, 1992.

Stockholders' equity	
Common stock—$0.66⅔ par value:	
Authorized 35,000,000 shares; issued 15,900,000 shares	$10,600,000
Paid-in capital in excess of par	6,400,000
Retained earnings	31,000,000
	$48,000,000
Less: Cost of treasury stock (1,000,000 shares)	4,000,000
Total stockholders' equity	$44,000,000

If Golden decides to sell additional common stock, how many shares can it sell without gaining approval from its shareholders? Note that the firm has 35 million authorized shares, 15.9 million issued shares, and 1.0 million shares of treasury stock. Thus, 14.9 million shares are outstanding (15.9 million issued shares − 1.0 million shares of treasury stock), and Golden can issue 20.1 million additional shares (35.0 million authorized shares − 14.9 million outstanding shares) without seeking shareholder approval to amend its corporate charter. This total includes the treasury shares currently held by Golden, which the firm can always reissue to the public without obtaining shareholder approval for their sale.

Dilemmas Facing the Financial Manager

If a corporation has enough authorized shares to support the sale of additional stock, it follows a sequence of activities similar to an IPO in order to bring new stock to market. This means using the same process as the one described above for an initial public offering. In addition, subsequent public offerings of new common stock create a few dilemmas for financial managers.

Timing the Sale

When selling new common stock, financial managers try to time the sale in order to get the highest possible price for the shares. If stock markets are *efficient* (i.e., stock prices are close to their true values), however, such actions are futile. Although financial managers may occasionally time equity sales to occur at peak pricing periods in the market, they will not be able to do so on a consistent basis.

Although the stock market is reasonably efficient, evidence suggests that some periods are better than others for issuing new stock. For example, it is not a good idea to offer new shares near the expiration date of options contracts written on a firm's common stock (discussed in Chapter 21). Stock prices can behave unpredictably during these periods. Second, it may be better to offer stocks that have historically paid high dividends before, rather than after, their ex dividend dates. Share prices tend to drop when common stock goes ex dividend due to tax factors associated with cash dividends. Finally, it is usually a good idea to sell new issues when the demand for new stock is relatively high and the supply of new issues is relatively low. This means that financial managers are better off bringing new shares to market when investor optimism is high, and they are better off postponing new issues when numerous firms are actively trying to publicly sell new issues of common stock.

Underpricing the Issue

When publicly held firms issue new shares of common stock, they often set the initial offering price slightly below the market price of the firm's outstanding common stock. This provides some insurance that all of the new stock offered will be absorbed by the market. If the offering price is set too low, however, the value of the new shares will quickly rise in the first few days after it is issued. This presents a problem for the issuer: it suggests that the new stock was underpriced at the time it was issued. If so, the issuer has sold valuable securities to its new shareholders at a price below their true worth. As a result, the firm's cost of common stock equity (see Chapter 13) will increase, and the wealth of its current owners will decline as a result of a drop in share price. A transfer of wealth will effectively result; the new shareholders will gain by receiving more value than they paid for, and the existing shareholders' shares will drop correspondingly in value.

Market Impact of Public Offering

When a publicly held corporation announces its plans to issue additional stock, the price of the firm's outstanding shares typically drops. Investors believe that the firm's managers feel the stock is overvalued and have therefore chosen to finance with common stock rather than debt. It may also occur because investors do not have the same information as the firm's managers regarding its investment opportunities. Shareholders may feel that the new stock issue will lower earnings per share, because the announced increase in the number of outstanding shares exceeds the growth in earnings they expect. Unless managers can convince them otherwise, these shareholders will not view the new equity issue as good news. Some may even sell their shares, which would hurt the market for them shortly after the firm announces its intent to sell new shares. Clearly, the financial manager must carefully and effectively communicate to its shareholders and the investment community positive information about the firm's motivations, plans, and expectations for the sale of additional common stock.

RECENT TRENDS IN THE INVESTMENT BANKING INDUSTRY

Investment banking is an extremely dynamic industry. Investment bankers vigorously compete with one another to attract new clients and win new underwriting business. They take advantage of changes in eco-

junk bonds
Low-rated, high-risk debt securities used to finance corporate takeovers.

corporate raider
Corporate outsider that uses junk bond financing to gain control of a firm and then uses the firm's operating cash flows or assets to repay the debt.

nomic conditions, regulation, and social attitudes to bring innovative new securities to market. During the 1980s, many investment bankers used deregulation within the financial services industry, changes in tax laws, and the growing public acceptance of debt-financed hostile take-overs to gain new business underwriting high-risk debt securities known as **junk bonds.** These takeovers were structured as leveraged buyouts (LBOs) in which corporate outsiders raised substantial amounts of money by issuing junk bonds through a few investment banking firms. They then used the proceeds to acquire controlling equity interests in firms that they believed were undervalued. (See Chapter 17 for a discussion of leveraged buyouts.) Once the outsider, or **corporate raider,** gained control of the firm, it planned to use the firm's operating cash flows to repay the debt that financed the takeover. If operating cash flows were inadequate to meet the interest and principal payments on the debt, corporate raiders believed they could always sell some of the acquired firm's assets to other investors and use the sale proceeds to reduce their heavy debt burdens.

The Demise of Debt-Driven Takeovers

Initially, many hostile takeovers proceeded according to the plan noted above. Many investors profited: junk bond underwriters captured huge underwriting profits; shareholders of firms acquired in hostile take-overs realized substantial capital gains; corporate raiders made fortunes through speculative and short-term investments; and junk bond-holders realized sizeable returns on their investments while apparently taking little risk. Each new deal involved bigger numbers and more leverage—it seemed like the party would never end. However, toward the end of the 1980s, it did. Economic growth slowed to a crawl, and in mid-1990 the domestic economy officially entered a recession. With little economic growth to stimulate corporate sales, the operating cash flows of highly-leveraged firms plummeted. Without the cash flow needed to meet the excessive debt burdens, managers of newly acquired firms sold assets in order to raise cash. In a recessionary economy, however, few new buyers came forward to buy the assets. Many bond issues entered default when corporations could no longer make required interest and principal payments on these debts.

At the same time, the demise of the savings and loan industry and the growing crisis among commercial banks and insurance companies took many institutional purchasers of junk bonds out of the market. With savings and loans posting record losses in the late 1980s, the government passed the *Financial Institutions Reform, Recovery, and Enforcement Act of 1989* to salvage federal deposit insurance programs as well as the remains of the savings and loan industry. This legislation prohibited federally insured financial institutions from owning junk bonds. It also ordered savings and loans to sell their existing junk bond investments over a relatively short period of time. In addition, commercial bank regulators tightened federal regulations governing loans to highly-leveraged borrowers.

These changes resulted in fewer individual and institutional investors seeking to buy junk bonds, and therefore significantly reduced the volume of funds flowing into the junk bond market. With little new money entering the market and a growing list of junk bond defaults, the value of existing junk bonds sank dramatically. Financial institutions and investment bankers who were holding large portfolios of junk bonds watched in horror. Their asset values collapsed and the value of their equity turned negative. Drexel, Burnham, Lambert, the largest underwriter of junk bond issues in the 1980s, filed for bankruptcy in early 1990. At the same time, many savings and loans and insurance companies holding large junk bond portfolios faced financial ruin.

What did we learn from the excessive use of leverage in the 1980s? First, risk and return are closely linked. In order to achieve higher returns, investors must take larger risks. In addition, leverage can be addictive. Naive investors and financial managers frequently overlooked the risks contained in highly-leveraged transactions and focused instead on the attractive returns they would earn through the use of debt financing. In the end, however, it was the risk—not the high expected returns—that they remembered. While the *prudent use* of debt financing is good for stockholders, bondholders, financial managers, and investment bankers, the lesson of the 1980s is that the *excessive use* of debt can really hurt all of them.

The Rise of Financial Engineering

How will investment bankers survive and prosper in the 1990s, given the collapse of their junk bond underwriting business? While it is true that many corporations will reduce their use of debt financing in coming years, the market for new debt issues will not completely disappear. In addition, investment bankers will continue developing new and innovative financing arrangements that meet the needs of firms seeking to raise external funds and provide risk-return characteristics that attract investors.

The process of bringing innovative financial products and procedures to market is known as **financial engineering.** Financial engineering includes the introduction of new consumer investments such as IRA and Keogh accounts, the creation of new securities such as money market preferred stock, the development of new procedures such as shelf registration, and the identification of innovative solutions to corporate finance problems such as the creation and sale of junk bond portfolios.

A variety of factors explain the motives for financial engineering within the investment banking industry. First, investment bankers must constantly monitor and respond to changes in tax laws and securities regulation. These changes create opportunities to design new securities that save corporate borrowers money and provide attractive returns for investors. Second, environmental changes often signal the need for innovative financing arrangements. Increased interest rate movements in the 1980s offered investment bankers an opportunity to design securities that exploit as well as minimize the risk of interest

financial engineering
The process of bringing new innovative financial products and procedures to market.

rate changes. A number of these securities were soon introduced to help borrowers and lenders cope with rapidly changing interest rates. Finally, the competition between investment banking firms encourages financial engineering. The firms that develop innovative securities and new solutions to corporate financing problems can use these products and services to solicit business from new clients, thereby gaining market share and a reputation for financial innovation.

Investment Banking in the Future

With the eventual entry of commercial banks into the investment banking industry sometime in the 1990s, competition among investment bankers will surely accelerate. Increased competition means more financial engineering, and hence a steady flow of new financial products and procedures. What will future innovations look like, and how will we know they are significant innovations when we see them? In general, any innovation that enhances shareholder value is likely to succeed. This can be accomplished in a variety of ways.

First, if investment bankers can develop new securities that are less costly to the issuer than existing securities with similar terms, they will create shareholder value. The lower cost will lower the firm's cost of capital (see Chapter 13) and (assuming constant earnings) will increase the firm's value (see Chapter 12). Second, if investment bankers can develop products and procedures that reduce the riskiness of payment streams made by issuing corporations to investors, they will create shareholder value. Lower risk means that investors will accept lower returns, the issuers' cost of capital will be reduced, and (again assuming constant earnings) shareholder value will increase. Third, if investment bankers can develop ways for corporations to build fixed asset portfolios less expensively than individual investors can build portfolios of fixed assets, then shareholder value will increase. Corporations will issue securities backed by their fixed assets, and because it will be cheaper for investors to buy these securities than assemble their own portfolios of fixed assets, new investment dollars will flow to the firm at a reasonable cost. Once again, the lower-cost financing resulting from this innovation will create shareholder value.

There are a number of other techniques that investment bankers will use in the 1990s to create shareholder value. Underwritten instruments with lower transaction costs help build value, so investment bankers will search for new financing arrangements that require lower underwriting spreads. Securities that reduce the issuer's tax liability create shareholder value, so investment bankers will carefully examine the tax code to identify new ways to engineer securities that minimize corporate taxes. Finally, new issues that convey more information to investors concerning the strength of the issuer create value, because these securities reduce the information gap between a firm's managers and outside investors. Equal access to information will reduce a costly barrier to the investor's understanding of the firm's condition and outlook, and will increase the value of the firm.

SUMMARY

1   **Understand the importance and role of long-term funds, including internal and external sources, the need for external funds, and the methods used to raise external funds.** Businesses routinely need long-term funds to finance corporate growth and the replacement of worn-out equipment and to pay off debts and other obligations as they come due. The internal source of funds is funds generated within the firm from retained earnings. External sources of funds are raised outside of the firm through negotiated loans or the sale of bonds, preferred stock, or common stock. Firms use external funds to finance growth when their internally generated funds are inadequate to meet their long-term financing need. Firms typically raise external funds through either a public offering or a private placement of new debt or equity securities.

2   **Define venture capital and discuss the role it plays in long-term financing.** Venture capital is financing invested in a young business by specialized financial intermediaries known as venture capitalists. Venture capital firms finance young businesses that are not sufficiently established to publicly sell securities. Although they sometimes provide debt financing, in most cases venture capital firms obtain common stock ownership in the corporations they finance. The two major risks facing venture capitalists are the liquidity risk attributable to the inability to sell the stock of the company they have financed and the risk that the start-up firm being financed will fail.

3   **Describe the role of investment bankers in long-term business financing, the underwriting process, services provided, distribution activities, and investment banker compensation.** Investment bankers are financial intermediaries that underwrite the sale of new securities by purchasing them from issuing firms and reselling them to the general public in the primary capital market. They bear the price risk in the underwriting process. As an alternative, investment bankers may market securities on a best efforts basis. Investment bankers also advise issuers, prepare and file registration documents, help issuers price securities, distribute new securities and maintain an orderly market for them, communicate relevant information to the investment community, and place their reputation behind the issue. Investment bankers usually distribute securities through syndicated underwritten offerings. They are compensated with a gross commission on underwritten issues and a fee paid on a per share basis for nonunderwritten issues, direct placements, and best efforts sales.

4   **Explain the key activities of the firm in an initial public offering—selecting an investment banker, the process of going public, and the advantages and disadvantages of going public.** In an IPO, the firm must select an investment banker either on the basis of competitive bidding or a negotiated offering. With the help of the investment banker, the firm will then obtain authorization to issue new common stock to the public, identify the market in which the securities will trade, price the new security, submit documents to and obtain approval from the SEC, and sell the securities to the general public. The advantages of going public include greater liquidity of the firm's equity, enhanced ability of the firm to issue additional securities, ease of market value determination, prestige of being a listed company, and ability of the founders to diversify their investment portfolios. Disadvantages include the cost of public sale, need to publicly disclose business information, possible short-run profit focus of management, risk of hostile takeover, and dilution of ownership.

5   **Review the restrictions and dilemmas frequently faced by the financial manager when making subsequent public offerings of new common stock.** When a publicly held firm wishes to sell additional equity it must first make sure that a sufficient number of authorized and unissued shares are available. If not, it will have to obtain shareholder approval for issuance of additional shares. The dilemmas faced by the financial manager when making subsequent public offerings of common stock include timing the sale to get the highest possible price, avoiding excessive underpricing that would reduce the wealth of current owners, and effectively communicating to its shareholders positive information about the motives for the offering.

6   **Discuss recent trends in the investment banking industry—the demise of debt-driven takeovers and the rise of financial engineering—and how it is likely to change in the future.**   During the 1980s, investment bankers prospered by underwriting an increasing quantity of high-risk debt securities—junk bonds—that were issued to finance takeovers. A slowdown in the rate of economic growth, the demise of the savings and loan industry, and the growing crisis among commercial banks and insurance companies brought on the collapse of the junk bond market. Also, many highly debt-financed firms, as a result of diminished cash flows, found themselves unable to make payments on their debts. In the 1990s, investment bankers will face increased competition. To survive, they will focus on financial engineering, the introduction of innovative financial products and procedures intended to reduce the cost of capital and increase the issuer's shareholder value. The new financial products and procedures will be aimed at lowering financing costs—directly, through risk reduction, or by lowering transactions costs—in order to enhance shareholder value.

QUESTIONS

18—1   Define and differentiate between *internal* and *external* sources of funds. When do firms typically raise external funds?

18—2   How does a *public offering* differ from a *private placement?*

18—3   What is *venture capital?* What are the two key risks borne by venture capitalists?

18—4   What is the role of an investment banker? How do investment bankers bear *price risk* when *underwriting* new security issues?

18—5   How does a *best efforts basis* offering differ from an underwriting of a new security issue?

18—6   Describe some of the key services that investment bankers provide to firms issuing new securities.

18—7   Describe the role of an *underwriting syndicate* in the distribution of a new security issue. What is the significance of the order in which investment banking firms are listed in a *tombstone advertisement?* What is a *selling group?*

18—8   What is *shelf registration?* How does this procedure work? What benefit does this procedure provide to the corporation?

18—9   What are the components of the investment banker's *gross commission?* How are these components allocated among members of an *underwriting syndicate?*

18—10   What is an *initial public offering (IPO)?* Why might a privately held firm decide to go public?

18—11   Describe, compare, and contrast the use of *competitive bidding* and the use of a *negotiated offering* to hire an investment banker.

18—12   What role does the *Securities Act of 1933* play in protecting investors? Does SEC approval of a security issue indicate that it is a good investment? Describe the roles of the *registration statement, prospectus,* and *red herring* as they relate to SEC registration.

18—13   List and briefly describe the key advantages and disadvantages commonly cited for going public.

18—14   Briefly discuss each of the following dilemmas that frequently face a corporation that has adequate authorized shares and wishes to sell additional common stock.
   a. Timing the sale of the new shares
   b. Underpricing the new shares
   c. Anticipating the market impact of the offering
18—15   **a.** Describe the following two recent trends in the investment banking industry:
   (1) Demise of *debt-driven takeovers*
   (2) Rise in *financial engineering*
   b. Discuss the future of investment banking.

PROBLEMS

18—1   **(Underwriting Spread)**   Nimbus Securities, an investment banking firm, has been invited by Tasty Kleen Foods, Inc., to bid on Tasty Kleen's planned $12 million common stock issue. Tasty Kleen's managers will accept no less than $37 per share for the firm's new stock, and Nimbus believes the stock will sell for $40 per share in the market. Nimbus estimates that its out-of-pocket costs for this issue will be $300,000. Given the information in Table 18.4, can Nimbus expect to earn an "average" underwriting spread if it bids $37 for Tasty Kleen's stock and resells it for $40? Why or why not?

18—2   **(Managing Underwriter's Compensation)**   Bradford and Company is the managing underwriter for a new common stock offering by Dave's Diving Boards, Inc. Bradford will buy Dave's stock for $25 a share, and it will be resold to the public for $29.40 per share. If Bradford offers the stock through an underwriting syndicate, members of the syndicate will acquire shares for $27.35 each. If Bradford uses a selling group to help market the new shares, it will sell the stock for $28.15 per share to members of the selling group. Bradford expects out-of-pocket costs for the issue to total $1.75 per share.
   a. Calculate Bradford's total compensation per share, net of out-of-pocket costs, if it sells the shares directly to the public.
   b. Calculate Bradford's total compensation per share, net of out-of-pocket costs, if it forms an underwriting syndicate to sell the stock but does not use a selling group to help market new shares.
   c. Calculate Bradford's total compensation per share, net of out-of-pocket costs, if it underwrites the entire issue without the assistance of an underwriting syndicate but does assemble a selling group to help market new shares.

18—3   **(Distribution of Underwriting Compensation)**   Barney and Smith, Inc. was the managing underwriter for Wellington Computers' recent initial public offering of common stock. According to the terms outlined in the prospectus covering this issue, Barney and Smith paid Wellington $75.00 per share for three million shares of stock and set the initial offering price at $79.00 per share. Barney and Smith sold 1 million of Wellington's new shares directly to the public, and divided the remaining 2 million shares equally among the four other members of the underwriting syndicate (500,000 shares to each member)—A, B, C, and D Companies. Each of these members of the underwriting syndicate paid Barney and Smith $75.94 per share for their 500,000 shares, and they resold all shares to various retail brokerage firms for $76.75 a share. In total, the four syndicate members used a selling group of 12 retail brokerage firms to sell their 2,000,000 shares to the public. Barney and Smith incurred $1,020,000 in legal, accounting, printing, and postage costs in its role as managing underwriter for the issue.

a. Calculate the gross commission on this underwriting transaction.

b. Allocate the gross commission to the out-of-pocket costs, management fee, underwriting fee, and selling concession associated with the issue.

c. Show how the gross commission is distributed among the managing underwriter, each member of the underwriting syndicate, and the selling group.

18—4   **(Distribution of Underwriter Compensation)** Texas Transistor hired Yount Brothers, a large investment banking firm, to sell 5 million new shares of common stock to the public. The terms of the underwriting agreement specified that Yount would pay Texas Transistor $41 per share and the shares would be offered to the public at $45 each. Yount created an underwriting syndicate consisting of itself as managing underwriter and three other investment banking firms—the X, Y, and Z companies. Each of the four members of the syndicate was responsible for selling 25 percent (1,250,000 shares) of the offering. Yount sold shares to the other three syndicate members for $42.50 each. Yount's out-of-pocket costs for legal, accounting, printing, and postage services related to the offering totaled $2,200,000. The syndicate formed a selling group to sell all shares to the public and sold the stock to the selling group for $43.90 per share. The selling group quickly and completely sold out the offering in a period of three months.

a. Calculate the gross commission on this underwriting transaction.

b. Allocate the gross commission to the out-of-pocket costs, management fee, underwriting fee, and selling concession associated with the issue.

c. Show how the gross commission is distributed among the managing underwriter, each member of the underwriting syndicate, and the selling group.

18—5   **(Economics of Offering Preferred Stock)** Finnerty Appliance Warehouse is planning a new public offering of 250,000 shares of preferred stock in order to finance the planned expansion of its distribution facility. The firm's investment banker, Day and Reeves, Inc., plans to use a zero growth dividend valuation model to price the firm's shares. The investment banker notes that Finnerty's preferred shares will carry a $3 annual dividend. The firm's required return on these securities is 15 percent. Finnerty must raise $4.5 million from the new stock sale to complete its investment plans.

a. Using the zero growth dividend valuation model (Equation 12.11 in Chapter 12), determine the initial public offering price for Finnerty's preferred stock.

b. If Day and Reeves must earn a gross commission of 11.5 percent on this transaction, how much will it offer Finnerty for each share?

c. Based on your findings in **a** and **b,** can Finnerty raise $4.5 million by selling 250,000 shares of preferred stock? If not, how many new shares must the firm issue to finance the planned expansion of its distribution facility?

18—6   **(Investment Banker's Profit with Market Stabilization)** Reynolds and Stewart, a large New York investment banking firm, recently underwrote a 2 million share offering of common stock for Lafferty Automotive. The investment banker purchased the shares for $35 each and resold them to the public for $38.75. Out-of-pocket costs for the issue totaled $775,000. Due to an unexpected vehicle recall shortly after Reynolds and Stewart completed the public offering, however, the price of Lafferty's common stock plummeted. The underwriter was forced to purchase 700,000 shares in the marketplace at an average cost of $37 in order to stabilize Lafferty's stock price. Reynolds and Stewart later resold these shares at an average price of $25. Calculate Reynolds and Stewart's net gain (or loss) from this transaction.

18—7   **(Proposed Initial Public Offering)** Trimex Software is planning the first public common stock sale in the firm's history in order to allow its founders to diversify their investment portfolios. Trimex's investment bankers believe that the firm's shares can be sold to the public at 8 times the firm's current earnings per share, and out-of-pocket costs for the issue will equal 3 percent of the initial offering price. Trimex currently has after-tax earnings of $3 million. The firm's founders will continue to hold their 600,000 shares of stock, and the new public offering involves the sale of 400,000 new shares. The gross commission (ignoring recovery of out-of-pocket costs) will equal 6 percent of the initial offering price. Use this information to answer the following questions:
a. Calculate Trimex's current earnings per share (EPS).
b. Use the price/earnings multiple approach introduced in Chapter 12 to determine the initial offering price for Trimex's common stock.
c. Find the total amount of cash that Trimex will raise from the proposed offering.
d. Assuming after-tax earnings remain unchanged, what will Trimex's EPS be after the initial public offering?
e. What rate of return must Trimex earn on the net proceeds it receives from the public sale of stock in order to avoid earnings dilution?
f. If Trimex's founders believe they can earn a 12 percent annual return on the investment of the funds raised, would you recommend that they proceed with the proposed public offering? Why or why not?

18—8   **(Earnings Dilution from Common Stock Sale)** Tabletop Sub Shops is considering issuing 1 million shares of new common stock. The firm currently has 5 million shares outstanding and reported earnings of $6.25 million in the year just ended. Tabletop expects earnings to grow by 10 percent this year.
a. Calculate Tabletop's earnings per share assuming the firm issues the new stock. Will the new stock dilute Tabletop's earnings per share?
b. If an investment banker will purchase Tabletop's new stock for $10 per share, what rate of return must the firm earn in the coming year on the funds raised in order to maintain its current level of earnings per share?

18—9   **(Authorized and Available Shares)** Landon Corporation's charter authorizes issuance of 2,000,000 shares of common stock. Currently 1,400,000 shares are outstanding and 100,000 shares are being held as treasury stock. The firm wishes to raise $48,000,000 for a plant expansion. Discussions with its investment bankers indicate that the sale of new common stock will net the firm $60 per share.
a. What is the maximum number of new shares of common stock the firm can sell without receiving further authorization from shareholders?
b. Based on the data given above and your finding in **a,** will the firm be able to raise the needed funds without receiving further authorization?
c. What must the firm do to obtain authorization to issue more than the number of shares found in **a?**

CASE

Antioch Food Company's Initial Public Offering

Antioch Food Company is considering its first public sale of stock in order to raise the funds needed to expand into new markets. As a regional distributor of packaged foods and canned goods located in the midwest, the firm plans to begin selling its products in selected urban areas along the east coast. Antioch estimates that its expansion plans will require a $2 million investment. The firm's founders currently hold all of the firm's 500,000 outstanding shares, and the corporate charter currently authorizes the public sale of new common stock.

To help bring its stock to market, Antioch has contacted the regional investment banking firm of Burns and Wellborne to discuss a negotiated offering. Chuck Kole, an analyst with Burns and Wellborne, has been asked to prepare for an upcoming meeting with Antioch's major shareholders. At that meeting Burns and Wellborne plans to present its ideas concerning Antioch's initial public offering.

Antioch is especially eager to learn how Burns and Wellborne would price its new common stock. Antioch has provided a copy of its financial statements for the year just ended. Chuck Kole's research indicates that regional food distributors similar to Antioch are currently selling at 12 times earnings. He has also learned that any dilution of per-share earnings accompanying new stock issues in this industry severely dampens investor interest in them.

Income statement
Antioch Food Company
for the year ended December 31, 1992

Sales revenue		$14,167,500
Less: Cost of sales		8,256,250
Gross profit		$ 5,911,250
Less: Operating expenses		
Depreciation expense	$1,000,000	
Selling expense	2,156,250	
General and administrative expense	1,096,250	
Interest expense	121,250	
Total operating expense		4,373,750
Net profits before taxes		1,537,500
Less: Taxes		538,130
Net profits after taxes		$ 999,370

Balance sheet
Antioch Food Company
December 31, 1992

Assets	
Current assets	
Cash	$ 508,750
Accounts receivable	1,018,750
Inventories	2,266,250
Total current assets	$ 3,793,750
Fixed assets	
Land	$ 1,400,000
Plant and equipment	5,565,000
Other assets	166,250
Total fixed assets	$ 7,131,250
Total assets	$10,925,000

Liabilities and stockholders' equity	
Current liabilities	
Accounts payable	$ 890,000
Notes payable	625,000
Accrued expenses	417,500
Total current liabilities	$ 1,932,500
Long-term debt	$ 1,325,000
Total liabilities	$ 3,257,500
Stockholders' equity	
Common stock	$ 2,812,500
Retained earnings	4,855,000
Total stockholders' equity	$ 7,667,500
Total liabilities and stockholders' equity	$10,925,000

Required

a. Where should Antioch offer its new stock—on a regional stock exchange, a national exchange, or the over-the-counter exchange?

b. What is the initial offering price that Burns and Wellborne will likely recommend for Antioch's shares? (*Hint:* Use the price/earnings multiple approach introduced in Chapter 12 to estimate the initial offering price.)

c. Using the industry data given in Table 18.4, estimate how much Burns and Wellborne would pay to acquire Antioch's shares, and how many new shares must be sold to raise the desired $2 million.

d. Will the new issue create any dilution in Antioch's earnings per share? If so, what rate of return on the funds raised is necessary for Antioch to avoid this earnings dilution?

e. Based upon Antioch's current return on investment (net profits after taxes ÷ total assets), is it reasonable to expect that the firm will earn the return on new investment needed to offset any potential earnings dilution that was calculated in **d?**

f. What kind of registration documents must be filed on Antioch's behalf with the SEC in connection with its proposed public offering?

g. Should Antioch arrange to have its new stock sold on an underwritten or best efforts basis? Why?

CHAPTER 19

LONG-TERM DEBT AND LEASING

CHAPTER OBJECTIVES

After studying this chapter, you should be able to:

1 Describe the basic characteristics of long-term debt financing, including standard debt provisions, restrictive debt provisions, and cost.

2 Understand the characteristics of term (long-term) loan agreements and the various term lenders to business.

3 Discuss the legal aspects of corporate bonds, general features of a bond issue, bond ratings, popular types of bonds, and bond-refunding options.

4 Review the basic types of leases, leasing arrangements, and the lease contract.

5 Analyze the lease-versus-purchase decision, the effects of leasing on future financing, and the advantages and disadvantages of leasing.

6 Describe the use by multinational companies of international bonds, international financial institutions to underwrite them, and various techniques to change the structure of their long-term debts.

"MNC Corporation
. . . took a look at the
original loan agree-
ment with Fellheimer
and began to grow
nervous. "

Loan Collateral Made of Straw

Former Philadelphia bankruptcy attorney Alan Fellheimer owes MNC Corporation, a Maryland banking concern, $11.7 million. Although his loan payments have always been made on time, MNC recently declared that Fellhemier is in technical default on his debt obligation, and the bank has filed a civil suit to force him to repay immediately the loan's outstanding balance.

It all started in 1987, when Fellheimer decided to give up his law practice and begin a new career in the banking business. He purchased $11.7 million in the preferred stock of Equimark Corporation, a Pittsburgh-based bank holding company. Equimark was in sad financial condition at the time of the purchase, but Fellheimer felt that, as chairman, he could turn the bank around.

In order to buy Equimark's stock, Fellheimer turned to the Equitable Bankcorporation for an $11.7 million loan in late 1988. Fellheimer and his wife used the proceeds to purchase $9.5 million in Equimark's preferred stock. In theory, carrying the loan would be painless: Equimark's preferred stock dividends were set to cover the $800,000 quarterly interest payments due on the loan.

Things didn't work out quite according to the plan. Equimark lost a lot of money in the late 1980s. The bank's board of directors voted to replace Fellheimer in late 1990. Not only did he lose his job but he also lost about half of his original investment in Equimark's preferred stock.

Now comes the interesting part of the story. MNC Corporation, which acquired Equitable Bankcorp in 1989, took a look at the original loan agreement with Fellheimer and began to grow nervous. MNC reviewed the collateral for the $11.7 million loan. First was the Equimark preferred stock that Fellheimer had purchased with the loan proceeds. Continuing the search, MNC discovered that Fellheimer had also pledged his interest in a Philadelphia office building against the loan. Appraised at $5.8 million in 1990, the value of this commercial property was dependent upon the rental income paid by the building's tenants. And who leased the majority of office space in Fellheimer's office building? That's right—Equimark, which was still losing money.

Officials at MNC demanded immediate repayment of the $11.7 million loan. Even though it is not currently past-due, when MNC's lending officers disassembled the various financial contracts between Fellheimer, Equimark, and MNC, the bankers realized that the collateral backing the loan was made of straw.

L ong-term debt and leasing are important forms of *long-term financing*. Long-term debt can be obtained with a *term loan*, which is negotiated from a financial institution, or through the sale of *bonds*, which are marketable debt sold to a number of institutional and individual lenders. Long-term debt provides financial leverage and is a desirable component of capital structure since it tends to lower the weighted average cost of capital.[1]

Leasing, like long-term debt, allows the firm to obtain use of, but not ownership of, fixed assets in exchange for a series of contractual, periodic lease payments. The use of leasing has grown in popularity over the past 30 or so years. We begin this chapter with discussions of long-term debt financing followed by a review of leasing.

CHARACTERISTICS OF LONG-TERM DEBT FINANCING

The long-term debts of a business typically have maturities of between 5 and 20 years. When a long-term debt is within one year of its maturity, accountants will show the balance of the long-term debt as a current liability; at that point it becomes a short-term obligation. Similar treatment is given to portions of long-term debts payable in the coming year. These entries are normally labeled "current portion of long-term debt." Here we discuss long-term debt provisions and costs. In subsequent sections we'll turn our attention to term loans and corporate bonds.

Standard Debt Provisions

A number of **standard debt provisions** are included in long-term debt agreements. These provisions specify certain criteria of satisfactory record keeping and reporting, tax payment, and general business maintenance on the part of the borrowing firm. Standard debt provisions do not normally place a burden on the financially sound business. Commonly included standard provisions are listed below.

1 ■■■ The borrower is required to *maintain satisfactory accounting records* in accordance with generally accepted accounting principles (GAAP).

2 ■■■ The borrower is required to periodically *supply audited financial statements* which are used by the lender to monitor the firm and enforce the debt agreement.

standard debt provisions Provisions in long-term debt agreements specifying certain operating criteria, which normally do not place a burden on the financially sound business borrower.

---

[1]Of course, as noted in Chapter 16, the introduction of large quantities of debt into the firm's capital structure can result in high levels of financial risk, which cause the weighted average cost of capital to rise.

3 ■■■ The borrower is required to *pay taxes and other liabilities when due.*

4 ■■■ The borrower is required to *maintain all facilities in good working order,* thereby behaving as a "going concern."

Restrictive Debt Provisions

restrictive covenants
Contractual clauses in long-term debt agreements that place certain operating and financial constraints on the borrower.

Long-term debt agreements, whether resulting from a term loan or a bond issue, normally include certain **restrictive covenants,** contractual clauses that place certain operating and financial constraints on the borrower. Since the lender is committing funds for a long period, it of course seeks to protect itself. Restrictive covenants, coupled with standard debt provisions, allow the lender to monitor and control the borrower's activities in order to protect itself against increases in borrower risk. These covenants remain in force for the life of the debt agreement. The most common restrictive covenants are listed below.

1 ■■■ The borrower is required to *maintain a minimum level of net working capital.* Net working capital below the minimum is considered indicative of inadequate liquidity, a common precursor to loan default and ultimate failure.

2 ■■■ Borrowers are *prohibited from selling accounts receivable* to generate cash. Doing so could cause a long-run cash shortage if proceeds are used to meet current obligations.

3 ■■■ Long-term lenders commonly impose *fixed-asset restrictions* on the firm. These constrain the firm with respect to the liquidation, acquisition, and encumbrance of fixed assets; any of these actions could damage the firm's ability to repay its debt.

subordination   The stipulation in a long-term debt agreement that all subsequent or less important creditors agree to wait until all claims of the *senior debt* are satisfied before having their claims satisfied.

4 ■■■ Many debt agreements *constrain subsequent borrowing* by prohibiting additional long-term debt or by requiring that additional borrowing be *"subordinated"* to the original loan. **Subordination** means that all subsequent or less important creditors agree to wait until all claims of the *senior debt* are satisfied before having their claims satisfied.

5 ■■■ Borrowers may be *prohibited from entering into certain types of leases.* This provision limits additional fixed-payment obligations.

6 ■■■ Occasionally the lender *prohibits combinations* by requiring the borrower to agree not to consolidate, merge, or combine in any way with another firm, since such an action could significantly change the borrower's business and financial risk.

7 ■■■ To prevent liquidation of assets through large salary payments, the lender may *prohibit or limit salary increases for specified employees.*

8 ■■■ The lender may include *management restrictions* requiring the borrower to maintain certain "key employees" without whom the future of the firm would be uncertain.

9 ■■■ Occasionally the lender includes a covenant *limiting the borrower's security investment* alternatives. This restriction protects the lender by controlling the risk and marketability of the borrower's security investments.

10 ■■■ Occasionally a covenant specifically requires the borrower to *spend the borrowed funds on a proven financial need.*

11 ■■■ A relatively common provision *limits the firm's annual cash dividend payments* to a maximum of 50 to 70 percent of its net earnings or a specified dollar amount.

In the process of negotiating the terms of long-term debt, borrower and lender must ultimately agree to acceptable restrictive covenants. A good financial manager will know in advance the relative impact of proposed restrictions. He or she will "hold the line" on those that may have a severely negative or damaging effect. The violation of any standard or restrictive provision by the borrower gives the lender the right to demand immediate repayment of the debt. Generally the lender will evaluate any violation in order to determine whether it is serious enough to jeopardize the loan. On the basis of such an evaluation the lender may demand immediate repayment of the loan, waive the violation and continue the loan, or waive the violation but alter the terms of the initial debt agreement.

Cost of Long-Term Debt

The cost of long-term debt is generally greater than that of short-term borrowing. In addition to standard and restrictive provisions, the long-term debt agreement specifies the interest rate, the timing of payments, and the dollar amount of payments. The major factors affecting the cost, or interest rate, of long-term debt are loan maturity, loan size, and more importantly, borrower risk and the basic cost of money.

Loan Maturity
Generally, long-term loans have higher interest rates than short-term loans. The longer the term of a loan, the less accuracy there is in predicting future interest rates and therefore the greater the lender's risk of missing an opportunity to loan money at a higher rate. In addition, the longer the term, the greater the repayment risk associated with the loan. To compensate for both the uncertainty of future interest rates and the higher probability that the borrower will default, the lender typically charges a higher interest rate on long-term loans.

Loan Size
The size of the loan affects the interest cost of borrowing in an inverse manner. As loan size increases, loan administration costs per dollar bor-

---

E T H I C S   I N   F I N A N C E

A Simple Debt Covenant Creates a Big Mess at FNN

At times, the most carefully planned debt covenants can surprise financial managers with unanticipated consequences. Financial News Network, the 24-hour cable channel for business news, recently faced a disagreement with its auditors over how the firm should account for $28 million in development expenses associated with its ProService. This new service provided stock quote information to brokers and professional traders via cable television.

FNN wanted to spread the $28 million development expense over the life of ProService, but the firm's accountants at Deloitte & Touche took a more conservative stand. The auditors believed that FNN should write off the entire $28 million in the current accounting period. Doing so would lead to a substantial loss in the current fiscal year. According to FNN's existing loan agreements, a financial loss would violate the firm's debt covenants and require FNN to repay $48.5 million in bank debt immediately. Since FNN couldn't afford the $48.5 million payment, the firm decided instead to fire Deloitte & Touche as its independent auditor.

While shooting the messenger seemed like a good idea at the time, it only made things worse for FNN. In April 1991 the firm was forced into bankruptcy, and the following month FNN was purchased by Consumer News and Business Channel, a subsidiary of the General Electric Company. In June 1991 a group of FNN's former shareholders filed suit against Deloitte & Touche, charging that the accounting firm falsely portrayed FNN as profitable between 1988 and 1990, when the firm was, in fact, losing tens of millions of dollars. The SEC also initiated a separate investigation into accounting irregularities at FNN during the 1988–1990 period. While officials at Deloitte & Touche have declared that they were not involved in any wrongdoing, they currently refuse to comment on the trouble at FNN because of the on-going nature of legal proceedings and government investigations against the firm.

Sources: Harris Collingwood, "FNN vs. its bean counters," *Business Week*, October 15, 1990, p. 40; Dennis Kneale, "FNN staffers bid a final farewell to their viewers," *The Wall Street Journal*, May 22, 1991, p. B6; and "Deloitte & Touche is sued by investors," *The Wall Street Journal*, June 5, 1991, p. C6.

---

rowed tend to decrease. On the other hand, the risk to the lender increases, since larger loans result in less diversification. The size of the loan sought by each borrower must therefore be evaluated to determine the net administrative cost-risk trade-off.

Borrower Risk

As noted in Chapter 5, the higher the firm's operating leverage, the greater its business risk. Also, the higher the borrower's debt ratio, the greater its financial risk. (Likewise, the lower the firm's times interest earned ratio or its fixed-payment coverage ratio, the greater its financial risk.) The lender's main concern is with the ability of the borrower to fully repay the loan as prescribed in the debt agreement. The overall assessment of the borrower's business and financial risk, along with information on past payment patterns, is used by the lender in setting the interest rate on any loan.

Basic Cost of Money

The cost of money is the basis for determining the actual interest rate charged. Generally the rate on U.S. Treasury securities with *equivalent maturities* is used as the basic standard for the risk-free cost of money. To determine the actual interest rate to be charged, the lender will add premiums for loan size and borrower risk to this basic cost of money for the given maturity. Alternatively, some lenders use the rate charged on similar-maturity loans to firms believed to have equivalent risk. Instead of having to determine a risk premium, the lender can use the risk premium prevailing in the marketplace for similar loans.

TERM LOANS

A **term (long-term) loan** is a loan with an initial maturity of more than one year, made by a financial institution to a business. These loans generally have maturities of 5 to 12 years; shorter maturities are available, but minimum 5-year maturities are common. Term loans are often made to finance *permanent* working capital needs, to pay for machinery and equipment, or to liquidate other loans.

term (long-term) loan A loan with an initial maturity of more than one year, made by a financial institution to a business.

Characteristics of Term Loan Agreements

The actual **term loan agreement** is a formal contract ranging from a few to a few hundred pages. The following items are commonly specified in the document: the amount and maturity of the loan, payment dates, interest rate, standard provisions, restrictive provisions, collateral (if any), purpose of the loan, action to be taken if the agreement is violated, and stock-purchase warrants. Of these, only payment dates, collateral requirements, and stock-purchase warrants require further discussion.

term loan agreement A formal contract specifying the conditions under which a financial institution has made a long-term loan.

Payment Dates

Term loan agreements generally specify monthly, quarterly, semiannual, or annual loan payments. Generally these equal payments fully repay the interest and principal over the life of the loan. Occasionally a term loan agreement will require periodic payments over the life of the loan followed by a large lump-sum payment at maturity. This so-called **balloon payment** represents the entire loan principal if the periodic payments represent only interest.

balloon payment At the maturity of a loan, a large lump-sum payment.

Collateral Requirements

Term lending arrangements may be unsecured or secured, similar to those for short-term loans. Whether *collateral* is required depends on the lender's evaluation of the borrower's financial condition. Common forms of collateral include machinery and equipment, plant, inventory, pledges of accounts receivable, and pledges of securities. Any collateral required and its disposition under various circumstances are specifically described in the term loan agreement. In addition, the lender will file necessary legal documents which clearly establish its right to seize and liquidate loan collateral if the borrower defaults.

Stock-Purchase Warrants

stock-purchase warrants Instruments that give their holders the right to purchase a certain number of shares of the firm's common stock at a specified price over a certain period of time.

A trend in term lending is for the corporate borrower to give the lender certain financial perquisites in addition to the payment of interest and repayment of principal. **Stock-purchase warrants** are instruments that give their holders the right to purchase a certain number of shares of the firm's common stock at a specified price over a certain period of time. These are used to entice institutional lenders to make long-term loans, possibly under more-than-normally-favorable terms. Stock-purchase warrants are discussed in greater detail in Chapter 21.

Term Lenders

The primary term lenders to business are commercial banks, insurance companies, pension funds, regional development companies, the federal government's Small Business Administration, small business investment companies, commercial finance companies, and equipment manufacturers' financing subsidiaries. Although the characteristics and provisions of term lending agreements made by these lenders are similar, a number of basic differences exist. Table 19.1 summarizes the key characteristics and types of loans made.

CORPORATE BONDS

corporate bond A certificate indicating that a corporation has borrowed a certain amount of money and promises to repay it in the future under clearly defined terms.

A **corporate bond** is a certificate indicating that a corporation has borrowed a certain amount of money from an institution or an individual and promises to repay it in the future under clearly defined terms. Most bonds are issued with maturities of 10 to 30 years and with a par, or face, value of $1,000. The coupon interest rate on a bond represents the percentage of the bond's par value that will be paid annually, typically in two equal semiannual payments. The bondholders, who are the lenders, are promised the semiannual interest payments and, at maturity, repayment of the principal amount (par value).

Legal Aspects of Corporate Bonds

Since a corporate bond issue may be for hundreds of millions of dollars obtained by selling portions of the debt to numerous unrelated persons,

Table 19.1   **Characteristics and Types of Loans Made by Major Term Lenders**

Institution	Characteristics	Types of loans
Commercial bank	Makes some term loans to businesses.	Generally less than 12-year maturity except for real estate. Often participates in large loans made by a group of banks since banks are legally limited[a] in the amount they can loan a single borrower. Loans typically secured by collateral.
Insurance company	Life insurers are most active lenders.	Maturities of 10 to 20 years. Generally to larger firms and in larger amounts than commercial bank loans. Both unsecured and secured loans.
Pension fund	Invests a small portion of its funds in term loans to business.	Generally mortgage loans to large firms. Similar to insurance company loans.
Regional development company	An association generally attached to local or regional governments. Attempts to promote business development in a given area by offering attractive financing deals. Obtains funds from various governmental bodies and through sale of tax-exempt bonds.	Term loans are made at competitive rates.
Small Business Administration (SBA)	An agency of the federal government that makes loans to eligible small and minority-owned businesses.	Joins with private lender and lends or guarantees repayment of all or part of the loan. Most loans are made for less than $750,000, at or below commercial bank interest rates.
Small business investment company (SBIC)	Licensed by the government. Makes both debt and equity investments in small firms.	Makes loans to small firms with high growth potential. Term loans with 5- to 20-year maturities and interest rates above those on bank loans. Generally receives, in addition, an equity interest in the borrowing firm.
Commercial finance company (CFC)	Involved in financing equipment purchases. Often a subsidiary of the manufacturer of equipment.	Makes secured loans for purchase of equipment. Typically installment loans with less-than-10-year maturities at higher-than-bank interest rates.
Equipment manufacturers' financing subsidiary	A type of "captive finance company" owned by the equipment manufacturer.	Makes long-term installment loans on equipment sales. Similar to commercial finance companies.

[a]Commercial banks are legally prohibited from loaning amounts in excess of 15 percent (plus an additional 10 percent for loans secured by readily marketable collateral) of the bank's unimpaired capital and surplus to any one borrower. This restriction is intended to protect depositors by forcing the commercial bank to spread its risk across a number of borrowers.

certain legal arrangements are required to protect purchasers. Bondholders are legally protected primarily through the indenture and the trustee.

Bond Indenture

bond indenture A legal document stating the conditions under which a bond has been issued.

A **bond indenture** is a complex and lengthy legal document stating the conditions under which a bond has been issued. It specifies both the rights of the bondholders and the duties of the issuing corporation. In addition to specifying the interest and principal payments and dates, and containing various standard and restrictive provisions, it frequently contains sinking-fund requirements and, if the bond is secured, provisions with respect to a security interest.

sinking-fund requirement A restrictive provision often included in a bond indenture providing for the systematic retirement of bonds prior to their maturity.

Sinking-Fund Requirements   The standard and restrictive provisions for long-term debt and for bond issues were described in an earlier section of this chapter. However, an additional restrictive provision often included in a bond indenture is a **sinking-fund requirement.** Its objective is to provide for the systematic retirement of bonds prior to their maturity. To carry out this requirement, the corporation makes semiannual or annual payments to a *trustee*, who uses these funds to retire bonds by purchasing them in the marketplace. This process is simplified by inclusion of a *call feature*, which permits the issuer to repurchase bonds at a stated price prior to maturity. The trustee will "call" bonds only when sufficient bonds cannot be purchased in the marketplace or when the market price of the bond is above the stated (call) price.

Security Interest   The bond indenture is similar to a loan agreement in that any collateral pledged against the bond is specifically identified in the document. Usually, the title to the collateral is attached to the indenture, and the disposition of the collateral in various circumstances is specifically described. The protection of bond collateral is crucial to increase the safety and thereby enhance the marketability of a bond issue.

Trustee

trustee A paid third party to a bond indenture, whose job it is to ensure that the issuer does not default on its contractual responsibilities to bondholders.

A **trustee** is a third party to a bond indenture. The trustee can be an individual, a corporation, or, most often, a commercial bank trust department. The trustee, whose services are paid for, acts as a "watchdog" on behalf of the bondholders, making sure that the issuer does not default on its contractual responsibilities. The trustee is empowered to take specified actions on behalf of the bondholders if the terms of the indenture are violated.

General Features of a Bond Issue

Three common features of a bond issue are a conversion feature, a call feature, and stock-purchase warrants. These features provide both the issuer and the purchaser with certain opportunities for replacing, retiring, and (or) supplementing the bond with some type of equity issue.

Conversion Feature

The **conversion feature** of certain so-called *convertible bonds* allows bondholders to change each bond into a stated number of shares of stock. Bondholders will convert their bonds only when the market price of the stock is greater than the conversion price, hence providing a profit for the bondholder. Chapter 21 discusses convertible bonds in detail.

conversion feature A feature of so-called *convertible bonds* that allows bondholders to change each bond into a stated number of shares of stock.

Call Feature

The **call feature** is included in almost all corporate bond issues. It gives the issuer the opportunity to repurchase bonds prior to maturity. The **call price** is the stated price at which bonds may be repurchased prior to maturity. Sometimes the call privilege may be exercised only during a certain period. As a rule, the call price exceeds the par value of a bond by an amount equal to one year's interest. For example, a $1,000 bond with a 10 percent coupon interest rate would be callable for around $1,100 [$1,000 + (10% × $1,000)]. The amount by which the call price exceeds the bond's par value is commonly referred to as the **call premium.** The call feature is generally advantageous to the issuer, since it enables the issuer to retire outstanding debt prior to maturity. Thus when interest rates fall, an issuer can call an outstanding bond and reissue a new bond at a lower interest rate. When interest rates rise, the call privilege will not be exercised, except possibly to meet sinking-fund requirements. Of course, to sell a callable bond the issuer must pay a higher interest rate than on noncallable bonds of equal risk. Bondholders must be compensated for the risk of having the bonds called away from them.

call feature A feature of most corporate bonds that allows the issuer to repurchase bonds at a stated price prior to maturity.

call price The stated price at which a bond may be repurchased, by use of a call feature, prior to maturity.

call premium The amount by which a bond's call price exceeds its par value.

Stock-Purchase Warrants

Like term loans, bonds occasionally have warrants attached as "sweeteners" to make them more attractive to prospective buyers. As noted earlier, a stock-purchase warrant gives its holder the right to purchase a certain number of shares of common stock at a specified price over a certain period of time. An in-depth discussion of stock-purchase warrants is included in Chapter 21.

Bond Ratings

The riskiness of publicly traded bond issues is assessed by independent agencies such as Moody's and Standard & Poor's. Moody's has 9 ratings; Standard & Poor's has 12. These agencies derive their ratings by using financial ratio and cash flow analyses. Table 19.2 summarizes the ratings. There is normally an inverse relationship between the quality or rating of a bond and the rate of return it must provide bondholders. High-quality (high-rated) bonds provide lower returns than lower-quality (low-rated) bonds. This reflects the risk-return trade-off of the lender. When considering bond financing, the financial manager must therefore be concerned with the expected ratings of the firm's bond issue since these ratings can significantly affect salability and cost.

Table 19.2   **Moody's and Standard & Poor's Bond Ratings**

Moody's	Interpretation	Standard & Poor's	Interpretation
Aaa	Prime quality	AAA	Bank investment quality
Aa	High grade	AA	
A	Upper medium grade	A	
Baa	Medium grade	BBB	
Ba	Lower medium grade or speculative	BB	Speculative
B	Speculative	B	
Caa	From very speculative	CCC	
Ca	to near or in default	CC	
C	Lowest grade	C	Income bond
		DDD	In default (rating
		DD	indicates the relative
		D	salvage value)

Source: Moody's Investors Services, Inc., and Standard & Poor's Corporation.

debentures See Table 19.3.

subordinated debentures See Table 19.3.

income bonds See Table 19.3.

mortgage bonds See Table 19.3.

collateral trust bonds See Table 19.3.

equipment trust certificates See Table 19.3.

zero (or low) coupon bonds See Table 19.4.

junk bonds See Table 19.4.

floating rate bonds See Table 19.4.

extendable notes See Table 19.4.

putable bonds See Table 19.4.

Popular Types of Bonds

Bonds can be classified in a variety of ways. Here we break them into traditional and contemporary bonds. Traditional bonds are the basic types that have been around for years. Contemporary bonds are newer, more innovative types of bonds that have been developed and/or become popular in recent years. The traditional types of bonds are summarized in terms of their key characteristics and priority of lenders' claim in Table 19.3. Note that the first three types—**debentures, subordinated debentures,** and **income bonds**—are unsecured; the last three—**mortgage bonds, collateral trust bonds,** and **equipment trust certificates**—are secured.

Table 19.4 summarizes the key characteristics of five contemporary types of bonds—**zero (or low) coupon bonds, junk bonds, floating rate bonds, extendable notes,** and **putable bonds.** These bonds can be either unsecured or secured. Contemporary bonds have been introduced in recent years in response to changing capital market conditions and investor preferences: Zero (or low) coupon bonds are designed to provide tax benefits to both issuer and purchaser; junk bonds were recently widely used to finance mergers and takeovers; both floating rate bonds and extendable notes give purchasers inflation protection; and putable bonds give the bondholder an option to sell the bond at par. These new types of bonds allow the firm to more easily raise funds at a reasonable cost by better meeting the needs of investors. Changing capital market conditions, investor preferences, and corporate financing needs will likely result in development of further innovations in bond financing.

Table 19.3   **Summary of Characteristics and Priority of Claim of Traditional Types of Bonds**

Bond type	Characteristics	Priority of lenders' claim
Debentures	Unsecured bonds that only creditworthy firms can issue. Convertible bonds are normally debentures.	Claims are same as those of any general creditor. May have other unsecured bonds subordinated to them.
Subordinated debentures	Claims are not satisfied until those of the creditors holding certain (senior) debts have been fully satisfied.	Claim is that of a general creditor but not as good as a senior debt claim.
Income bonds	Payment of interest is required only when earnings are available from which to make such payment. Commonly issued in reorganization of a failed or failing firm.	Claim is that of a general creditor. Not in default when interest payments are missed since they are contingent only on earnings being available.
Mortgage bonds	Secured by real estate or buildings. Can be *open-end* (other bonds issued against collateral), *limited open-end* (a specified amount of additional bonds can be issued against collateral), or *closed-end;* may contain an *after-acquired clause* (property subsequently acquired becomes part of mortgage collateral).	Claim is on proceeds from sale of mortgaged assets; if not fully satisfied, holder becomes a general creditor. The *first-mortgage* claim must be fully satisfied prior to distribution of proceeds to *second-mortgage* holders, and so on. A number of mortgages can be issued against the same collateral.
Collateral trust bonds	Secured by stock and (or) bonds that are owned by the issuer. Collateral value is generally 25 to 35 percent greater than bond value.	Claim is on proceeds from stock and (or) bond collateral; if not fully satisfied, holders become general creditors.
Equipment trust certificates	Used to finance "rolling stock"—airplanes, trucks, boats, railroad cars. A trustee buys equipment with funds raised through the sale of trust certificates and then leases the asset to the firm. After the final scheduled lease payment, the firm receives title to the asset. A type of leasing.	Claim is on proceeds from sale of asset; if proceeds do not satisfy outstanding debt, trust certificate holders become general creditors.

Bond-Refunding Options

A firm that wishes to retire or refund a bond prior to maturity has two options. Both require some foresight on the part of the issuer.

Serial Issues
The borrower can issue **serial bonds,** a certain proportion of which matures each year. When serial bonds are issued, a schedule showing the interest rate associated with each maturity is given. An example would be a $30 million, 20-year bond issue for which $1.5 million of the bonds ($30 million ÷ 20 years) mature each year. The interest rates associated with shorter maturities would, of course, differ from the rates associated with longer maturities. Although serial bonds cannot necessarily

serial bonds An issue of bonds of which a certain proportion matures each year.

Table 19.4   **Summary of Characteristics of Contemporary Types of Bonds**

Bond type	Characteristics[a]
Zero (or low) coupon bonds	Issued with no (zero) or a very low coupon (stated) interest rate and sold at a large discount from par. A significant portion (or all) of the investor's return comes from gain in value (i.e., par value minus purchase price). Generally callable at par value. Because the issuer can annually deduct the current year's interest accrual without having to actually pay the interest until the bond matures (or is called), its cash flow each year is increased by the amount of the tax shield provided by the interest deduction.
Junk bonds	Debt rated Ba or lower by Moody's or BB or lower by Standard & Poor's. During the 1980s commonly used by rapidly growing firms to obtain growth capital, most often as a way to finance mergers and takeovers of other firms. High-risk bonds with high yields—typically yielding 3 percent more than the best-quality corporate debt. As a result of a number of major defaults during the early 1990s, the popularity of these bonds has declined greatly.
Floating rate bonds	Stated interest rate is adjusted periodically within stated limits in response to changes in specified money or capital market rates. Popular when future inflation and interest rates are uncertain. Tend to sell at close to par as a result of the automatic adjustment to changing market conditions. Some issues provide for annual redemption at par at the option of the bondholder.
Extendable notes	Short maturities, typically 1 to 5 years, which can be redeemed or renewed for a similar period at the option of their holders. Similar to a floating rate bond. An issue might be a series of 3-year renewable notes over a period of 15 years; every 3 years the notes could be extended for another 3 years, at a new rate competitive with market interest rates prevailing at the time of renewal.
Putable bonds	Bonds that can be redeemed at par (typically $1,000) at the option of their holder either at specific dates such as 3 to 5 years after the date of issue and every 1 to 5 years thereafter, or when and if the firm takes specified actions such as being acquired, acquiring another company, or issuing a large amount of additional debt. In return for the right to "put the bond" at specified times or actions by the firm, the bond's yield is lower than that of a non-putable bond.

[a]The claims of lenders against holders of each of these types of bonds vary depending on their other features. Each of these bonds can be unsecured or secured.

be retired at the option of the issuer, they do permit the issuer to systematically retire the debt.

Refunding Bonds by Exercising a Call

bond-refunding decision The decision facing firms when bond interest rates drop: whether to refund (refinance) existing bonds with new bonds at the lower interest rate.

If interest rates drop following the issuance of a bond, the issuer may wish to refund (refinance) the debt with new bonds at the lower interest rate. If a call feature has been included in the issue, the issuer can easily retire it. This **bond-refunding decision** is not necessarily obvious but can be made using present-value techniques. It is another application of the capital budgeting techniques described in Chapters 14 and 15. Here the firm must find the net present value (NPV) of the bond refunding cash flows. The *initial investment* is the incremental after-tax outflows associated with calling the old bonds and issuing new bonds. The *annual cash flow savings* are the after-tax cash savings expected to result from the reduced debt payments of the new lower-interest bond. These cash flows are the same each year. The resulting cash flow pattern surrounding this decision is *conventional*—an outflow followed by a series of inflows. The bond-refunding decision can be made using the following three-step procedure.

Step 1: *Find the initial investment.* To do so, the firm estimates the incremental after-tax cash outflow required at time zero to call the old bond and issue a new bond in its place.

Step 2: *Find the annual cash flow savings.* This savings is the difference between the annual after-tax debt payments with the old and new bonds. This cash flow stream will be an annuity with a life equal to the maturity of the new bond.

Step 3: *Find the net present value (NPV).* To get this figure, the firm subtracts the initial investment from the present value of annual cash flow savings. The *after-tax cost of debt* is used as the discount rate because the decision involves very low risk.[2] *If the resulting NPV is greater than zero, the proposed refunding is recommended.* Otherwise, it should be rejected.

Application of these bond-refunding decision procedures can be illustrated with a simple example. However, a few tax-related points must be clarified first.

Call Premiums   The amount by which the call price exceeds the par value of the bond is the *call premium*. It is paid by the issuer to the bondholder to buy back outstanding bonds prior to maturity. The call premium is treated as a tax-deductible expense in the year of the call.

Bond Discounts and Premiums   When bonds are sold at a discount or at a premium, the firm is required to amortize (write off) the discount or premium in equal portions over the life of the bond. The amortized discount is treated as a tax-deductible expenditure, whereas the amortized premium is treated as taxable income. If a bond is retired prior to maturity, any unamortized portion of a discount or premium is deducted from or added to pretax income at that time.

Flotation or Issuance Costs   Any costs incurred in the process of issuing a bond must be amortized over the life of the bond. The annual write-off is therefore a tax-deductible expenditure. If a bond is retired prior to maturity, any unamortized portion of this cost is deducted from pretax income at that time.

---

[2]Because the refunding decision involves the choice between retaining an existing debt or substituting a new, lower-cost debt, it is viewed as a low-risk decision that will not significantly affect the firm's financial risk. The low-risk nature of the decision warrants the use of a very low rate, such as the firm's after-tax cost of debt.

EXAMPLE   Lavery Company, a manufacturer of copper pipe, is contemplating calling $30 million of 30-year, $1,000 bonds (30,000 bonds) issued five years ago with a coupon interest rate of 14 percent. The bonds have a call price of $1,140 and initially netted proceeds of $29.1 million due to a discount of $30 per bond. The initial flotation cost was $360,000. The company intends to sell $30 million of 12 percent coupon interest rate, 25-year bonds in order to raise funds for retiring the old bonds. The firm intends to sell the new bonds at their par value of $1,000. The flotation costs on the new issue are estimated to be $440,000. The firm is currently in the 40 percent tax bracket and estimates its after-tax cost of debt to be 8 percent.

Step 1:   *Find the initial investment.*   A number of calculations are required to find the initial investment.
   a. *Call premium*   The call premium per bond is $140 ($1,140 call price − $1,000 par value). Because the total call premium is deductible in the year of the call, its after-tax cost is:

Before tax ($140 × 30,000 bonds)	$4,200,000
Less: Taxes (.40 × $4,200,000)	1,680,000
After-tax cost of call premium	$2,520,000

   b. *Flotation cost of new bond*   This cost was given as $440,000.
   c. *Unamortized discount on old bond*   The $900,000 discount ($30,000,000 par value − $29,100,000 net proceeds from sale) on the old bond was being amortized over 30 years. Because only five of the 30 years' amortization of the discount has been applied, the remaining 25 years of unamortized discount can be deducted as a lump sum, thereby reducing taxes by $300,000 (25/30 × $900,000 × .40).
   d. *Unamortized flotation cost of old bond*   The $360,000 initial flotation cost on the old bond was being amortized over 30 years. Because only five of the 30 years' amortization of this cost has been applied, the remaining 25 years of unamortized flotation cost can be deducted as a lump sum, thereby reducing taxes by $120,000 (25/30 × $360,000 × .40).
Summarizing these calculations in Table 19.5, we find the initial investment to be $2,540,000. This means that Lavery Company must pay out $2,540,000 now in order to implement the proposed bond refunding.

Table 19.5   **Finding the Initial Investment for Lavery Company's
Bond-Refunding Decision**

a. Call premium
  Before tax [($1,140 − $1,000) × 30,000 bonds] $4,200,000
  Less: Taxes (.40 × $4,200,000)   1,680,000
      After-tax cost of call premium $2,520,000
b. Flotation cost of new bond   440,000
c. Tax savings from unamortized discount on
  old bond [25/30 × ($30,000,000 −
  $29,100,000) × .40]   (300,000)
d. Tax savings from unamortized flotation cost
  of old bond (25/30 × $360,000 × .40)   (120,000)
      Initial investment $2,540,000

Step 2:   *Find the annual cash flow savings.*   In order to find
            the annual cash flow savings, we need to make a
            number of calculations.
            a. *Interest cost of old bond*   The after-tax annual
            interest cost of the old bond is:

            Before tax (.14 × $30,000,000) $4,200,000
            Less: Taxes (.40 × $4,200,000)   1,680,000
                After-tax interest cost $2,520,000

            b. *Amortization of discount on old bond*   The
            $900,000 discount ($30,000,000) par value −
            $29,100,000 net proceeds from sale) on the old
            bond was being amortized over 30 years, result-
            ing in an annual write-off of $30,000
            ($900,000 ÷ 30). Because it is a tax-deductible
            noncash charge, the amortization of this dis-
            count results in an annual tax savings of $12,000
            (.40 × $30,000).
            c. *Amortization of flotation cost on old bond*   The
            $360,000 flotation cost on the old bond was
            being amortized over 30 years, resulting in an
            annual write-off of $12,000 ($360,000 ÷ 30).
            Because it is a tax-deductible noncash charge,
            the amortization of the flotation cost results in
            an annual tax savings of $4,800 (.40 × $12,000).
            d. *Interest cost of new bond*   The after-tax annual
            interest cost of the new bond is:

            Before tax (.12 × $30,000,000) $3,600,000
            Less: Taxes (.40 × $3,600,000)   1,440,000
                After-tax interest cost $2,160,000

Table 19.6   **Finding the Annual Cash Flow Savings for Lavery Company's Bond-Refunding Decision**

	Old bond		
a. Interest cost			
Before tax (.14 × $30,000,000)	$4,200,000		
Less: Taxes (.40 × $4,200,000)	1,680,000		
After-tax interest cost		$2,520,000	
b. Tax savings from amortization of discount [($900,000[a] ÷ 30) × .40]		(12,000)	
c. Tax savings from amortization of flotation cost [($360,000 ÷ 30) × .40]		(4,800)	
(1) Annual after-tax debt payments			$2,503,200

	New bond		
d. Interest cost			
Before tax (.12 × $30,000,000)	$3,600,000		
Less: Taxes (.40 × $3,600,000)	1,440,000		
After-tax interest cost		$2,160,000	
e. Tax savings from amortization of flotation cost [($440,000 ÷ 25) × .40]		(7,040)	
(2) Annual after-tax debt payments			2,152,960
Annual cash flow savings [(1) − (2)]			$ 350,240

[a]$30,000,000 par value − $29,100,000 net proceeds from sale

e. *Amortization of flotation cost on new bond* The $440,000 flotation cost on the new bond will be amortized over 25 years, resulting in an annual write-off of $17,600 ($440,000 ÷ 25). Because it is a tax-deductible noncash charge, the amortization of the flotation cost results in an annual tax savings of $7,040 (.40 × $17,600).

These calculations are summarized in Table 19.6. Totaling the first three values (**a,b**, and **c**), we find the annual after-tax debt payments for the old bond to be $2,503,200. Totaling the values for the new bond (**d** and **e**), we find the annual after-tax debt payments for the new bond to be $2,152,960. Subtracting the new bond's annual debt payments from that of the old bond, we find the annual cash flow savings to be $350,240 ($2,503,200 −

Table 19.7   **Finding the Net Present Value of Lavery Company's
                  Bond-Refunding Decision**

Present value of annual cash flow savings (from Table 19.6)	
$350,240 \times PVIFA_{8\%.,25yrs}$	
$350,240 \times 10.675 =$	$3,738,812
Less: Initial investment (from Table 19.5)	2,540,000
Net present value (NPV) of refunding[a]	$1,198,812

Decision: The proposed refunding is *recommended* because the NPV of
refunding of $1,198,812 is greater than $0.

[a]Using a business calculator, the present value of the annual cash flow savings would be
$3,738,734, which would have resulted in a NPV of refunding of $1,198,734.

$2,152,960). This means that implementation of the proposed bond refunding will result in an annual cash flow savings of $350,240.

Step 3:   *Find the net present value (NPV).*   The net present value (NPV) of the proposed bond refunding is calculated in Table 19.7. The present value of the annual cash flow savings of $350,240 at the 8 percent after-tax cost of debt over the 25 years is $3,738,812. Subtracting the initial investment of $2,540,000 from the present value of annual cash flow savings results in a net present value (NPV) of $1,198,812. Because a positive NPV results, *the proposed bond refunding is recommended.*

CHARACTERISTICS OF LEASES

Through **leasing,** a firm can obtain the use of certain fixed assets for which it must make a series of contractual, periodic, tax-deductible payments. The **lessee** is the receiver of the services of the assets under the lease contract; the **lessor** is the owner of the assets. Leasing can take a number of forms. Here we discuss the basic types of leases and leasing arrangements, with special emphasis on the effects of leasing on the lessee corporation. The lease contract is also briefly described.

leasing The process by which a firm can obtain the use of certain fixed assets for which it must make a series of contractual, periodic, tax-deductible payments.

lessee The receiver of the services of the assets under a lease contract.

lessor The owner of assets that are being leased.

Basic Types of Leases

The two basic types of leases available to a business are *operating* and *financial* leases. (Financial leases are often called *capital leases* by accountants.) Each is briefly described below.

Operating Leases

operating lease A *cancelable* contractual arrangement whereby the lessee agrees to make periodic payments to the lessor, often for five or fewer years, for an asset's services; generally the total payments over the term of the lease are *less* than the lessor's initial cost of the leased asset.

An **operating lease** is normally a contractual arrangement whereby the lessee agrees to make periodic payments to the lessor, often for five or fewer years, in order to obtain an asset's services. Such leases are generally *cancelable* at the option of the lessee, who may be required to pay a predetermined penalty for cancellation. Assets leased under operating leases have a usable life *longer* than the term of the lease. Usually, however, they would become less efficient and technologically obsolete if leased for a longer period of years. Computer systems are prime examples of assets whose relative efficiency is expected to diminish with new technological developments. The operating lease is therefore a common arrangement for obtaining such systems, as well as for other relatively short-lived assets such as automobiles.

If an operating lease is held to maturity, the lessee at that time returns the leased asset to the lessor, who may lease it again or sell the asset. Normally the asset still has a positive market value at the termination of the lease. In some instances, the lease contract will give the lessee the opportunity to purchase the leased asset. Generally the total payments made by the lessee to the lessor are *less* than the lessor's initial cost of the leased asset.

Financial (or Capital) Leases

financial (or capital) lease A *noncancelable* lease that obligates the lessee to make payments for the use of an asset over a predefined period of time; the term of the lease is longer than for an operating lease and total payments over the term of the lease are *greater* than the lessor's initial cost of the leased asset.

A **financial (or capital) lease** is a *longer-term* lease than an operating lease. Financial leases are *noncancelable* and therefore obligate the lessee to make payments for the use of an asset over a predefined period of time. Even if the lessee does not require the service of the leased asset, it is contractually obligated to make payments over the life of the lease contract. Financial leases are commonly used for leasing land, buildings, and large pieces of equipment. The noncancelable feature of the financial lease makes it quite similar to certain types of long-term debt. The lease payment becomes a fixed, tax-deductible expenditure that must be paid at predefined dates over a definite period. Like debt, failure to make the contractual lease payments can result in bankruptcy for the lessee.

Another distinguishing characteristic of the financial lease is that the total payments over the lease period are *greater* than the lessor's initial cost of the leased asset. In other words, the lessor must receive more than the asset's purchase price in order to earn its required return on the investment. The emphasis in this chapter is on financial leases, since they result in inescapable long-term financial commitments by the firm.

Leasing Arrangements

direct lease A lease under which a lessor owns or acquires the assets that are leased to a given lessee.

Lessors use three primary techniques for obtaining assets to be leased. The method depends largely on the desires of the prospective lessee. A **direct lease** results when a lessor owns or acquires the assets that are leased to a given lessee. In other words, the lessee did not previously own the assets it is leasing. A second technique commonly used by les-

F I N A N C E   I N   A C T I O N

Using Sale-Leaseback Transactions to Rescue Failing LBOs

In 1989 the market for junk bonds collapsed. Almost overnight, it became difficult to acquire corporations by issuing high-yield debt securities, and almost impossible to dispose of these acquisitions by publicly selling new common stock. Fears of recession, volatility in oil prices, and accelerating inflation meant that few investors were willing to buy the newly-issued shares of highly leveraged companies.

Unfortunately, the 1980s junk bond craze left many firms struggling to make payments on excessive debt loads acquired in connection with previous LBO acquisitions. If these firms are unable to issue new equity to retire their high-cost debt obligations, what will they do in the 1990s?

Lease financing is providing one possible answer, especially for companies that own significant real estate assets. The Shidler Group, a San Francisco firm specializing in corporate real estate transactions, reports that many highly leveraged companies can find cash to make payments and retire debt by using a sale-leaseback arrangement. Under this financing option, the firm sells its real estate to a willing buyer, uses the sale proceeds to retire debt or invest in operations, and then leases back from the new owner the property it needs.

According to Gary Lyon, vice president at Shidler, the sale-leaseback is especially attractive when real estate assets generate paltry investment returns: "If you can return 22 percent on each equity dollar by whatever you do as a corporation, then all those dollars tied up in Wisconsin real estate at 3 percent appreciation cost you 19 percent." There's only one small problem with Mr. Lyon's argument. First you must locate a buyer for your Wisconsin property before you can complete the sale-leaseback transaction.

Source: Stuart Weiss, "Cashing out of LBOs," *CFO Magazine*, November 1990, p. 52.

sale-leaseback arrangement A lease under which the lessee sells an asset for cash to a prospective lessor and then leases back the same asset, making periodic payments for its use.

leveraged lease A lease under which the lessor supplies only about 20 percent of the cost of the asset, while a lender supplies the balance.

sors to acquire leased assets is to purchase assets already owned by the lessee and lease them back. A **sale-leaseback arrangement** is normally initiated by a firm that needs funds for operations. By selling an existing asset to a lessor and then *leasing it back*, the lessee receives cash for the asset immediately while at the same time obligating itself to make fixed periodic payments for use of the leased asset. Leasing arrangements that include one or more third-party lenders are leveraged leases. Unlike direct and sale-leaseback arrangements, under a **leveraged lease** the lessor acts as an equity participant, supplying only about 20 percent of the cost of the asset, and a lender supplies the balance. In recent years leveraged leases have become especially popular in structuring leases of very expensive assets.

A lease agreement normally specifies whether the lessee is responsible for maintenance of the leased assets. Operating leases normally include **maintenance clauses** requiring the lessor to maintain the asset and to make insurance and tax payments. Financial leases almost always require the lessee to pay maintenance and other costs. The lessee is usually given the option to renew a lease at its expiration. **Renewal options,** which grant lessees the right to re-lease assets at expiration, are especially common in operating leases since their term is generally shorter than the usable life of the leased assets. **Purchase options** allow the lessee to purchase the leased asset at maturity, typically for a pre-specified price. Such options are frequently included in both operating and financial leases.

The lessor can be one of a number of parties. In operating lease arrangements, the lessor is quite likely to be the manufacturer's leasing subsidiary or an independent leasing company. Financial leases are frequently handled by independent leasing companies or by the leasing subsidiaries of large financial institutions such as commercial banks and life insurance companies. Life insurance companies are especially active in real estate leasing. Pension funds, like commercial banks, have also been increasing their leasing activities.

maintenance clauses
Provisions common in operating leases that require the lessor to maintain the asset and to make insurance and tax payments.

renewal options
Provisions common in operating leases that grant the lessee the option to re-lease assets at the expiration of the lease.

purchase options
Provisions common in both operating and financial leases that allow the lessee to purchase the leased asset at maturity, typically for a pre-specified price.

The Lease Contract

The key items of the lease contract normally include the term, or duration, of the lease, provisions for its cancellation, lease payment amounts and dates, maintenance and associated cost provisions, renewal options, purchase options, and other provisions specified in the lease negotiation process. Although some provisions are optional, the leased assets, the terms of the agreement, the lease payment, and the payment interval must all be clearly specified in every lease agreement. Furthermore, the consequences of the lessee missing a payment or the violation of any other lease provisions by either the lessee or lessor must be clearly stated in the contract.

LEASING AS A SOURCE OF FINANCING

Leasing is considered a source of financing provided by the lessor to the lessee. The lessee receives the service of a certain fixed asset for a specified period of time, in exchange for which the lessee commits itself to a fixed periodic payment. The only other way the lessee could obtain the services of the given asset would be to purchase it outright, and the outright purchase of the asset would require financing. The following discussions of the lease-versus-purchase decision, the effects of leasing on future financing, and the advantages and disadvantages of leasing explain the role of leasing as a source of financing.

The Lease-versus-Purchase Decision

The **lease-versus-purchase (or lease-versus-buy) decision** is one that commonly confronts firms contemplating the acquisition of new fixed assets. The alternatives available are (1) lease the assets, (2) borrow funds to purchase the assets, or (3) purchase the assets using available liquid resources. Alternatives 2 and 3, although they differ, are analyzed in a similar fashion. Even if the firm has the liquid resources with which to purchase the assets, the use of these funds is viewed as equivalent to borrowing. Therefore, here we need to compare only the leasing and purchasing alternatives.

> **lease-versus-purchase (or lease-versus-buy) decision**
> The decision facing firms needing to acquire new fixed assets: whether to lease the assets or to purchase them, using borrowed funds or available liquid resources.

The lease-versus-purchase decision is made using basic present-value techniques. The following steps are involved in the analysis:

Step 1: *Find the after-tax cash outflows for each year under the lease alternative.* This step generally involves a fairly simple tax adjustment of the annual lease payments. In addition, the cost of exercising a purchase option in the final year of the lease term must frequently be included.

Step 2: *Find the after-tax cash outflows for each year under the purchase alternative.* This step involves adjusting the scheduled loan payment and maintenance cost outlay for the tax shields resulting from the tax deductions due to maintenance, depreciation, and interest.

Step 3: *Calculate the present value of the cash outflows* associated with the lease (from step 1) and purchase (from step 2) alternatives using the *after-tax cost of debt* as the discount rate. The after-tax cost of debt is used since this decision involves very low risk.

Step 4: *Choose the alternative with the lower present value of cash outflows* from step 3. This will be the *least-cost* financing alternative.

Due to the relative complexity of the tax adjustments required to determine the after-tax lease and purchase outflows in steps 1 and 2, only steps 3 and 4 are demonstrated in the following example.

EXAMPLE   Moore Company, a small machine shop, is contemplating acquiring a new machine tool costing $24,000. Arrangements can be made to lease or purchase the machine. The firm is in the 40 percent tax bracket, and its after-tax cost of debt is 6 percent.

>   **Lease:** The firm would obtain a five-year lease requiring annual end-of-year lease payments of $6,000.[3] All maintenance costs would be paid by the lessor, while insurance and other costs would be borne by the lessee. The lessee would exercise its option to purchase the equipment for $4,000 when the lease matures.
>
>   **Purchase:** The firm would finance the purchase of the machine with a 9 percent, five-year loan requiring end-of-year installment payments of $6,170. The machine would be depreciated under ACRS using a five-year recovery period. The firm would pay $1,500 per year for a service contract that covers all maintenance costs; insurance and other costs would be borne by the firm. The firm plans to keep the equipment and use it beyond its five-year recovery period.

Assume that after applying various depreciation, interest, and tax adjustments, the after-tax cash outflows associated with the lease and purchase alternatives were determined as shown, respectively, in columns 1 and 4 of Table 19.8. Applying the appropriate 6 percent present-value interest factors given in columns 2 and 5 to the after-tax cash outflows in columns 1 and 4 results in the present values of lease and purchase cash outflows given in columns 3 and 6, respectively. The sum of the present values of the cash outflows for the leasing alternative is given in column 3 of Table 19.8, and the sum for the purchasing alternative is given in column 6 of Table 19.8. Since the present value of cash outflows for leasing ($18,151) is lower than that for purchasing ($19,539), *the leasing alternative is preferred.* Leasing results in an incremental savings of $1,388 ($19,539 − $18,151) and is therefore the less costly alternative.[4]

Effects of Leasing on Future Financing

Since leasing is considered a type of financing, it affects the firm's future financing. Lease payments are shown as a tax-deductible expense on the firm's income statement. Anyone analyzing the firm's income statement would probably recognize that an asset is being leased, although the actual details of the amount and term of the lease would be unclear. The following sections discuss the lease disclosure requirements established by the Financial Accounting Standards Board (FASB) and the effect of leases on financial ratios.

---

[3] Lease payments are generally made at the beginning of the year. In order to simplify the following discussions, end-of-year payments have been assumed.

[4] Using a business calculator, the present value of the cash outflows for the lease would be $18,154 and for the purchase would be $19,541, resulting in an incremental savings of $1,387.

Table 19.8

A Comparison of the Cash Outflows Associated with Leasing versus Purchasing for Moore Company

End of year	Leasing			Purchasing		
	After-tax cash outflows[a] (1)	Present-value factors[b] (2)	Present value of outflows [(1) × (2)] (3)	After-tax cash outflows[a] (4)	Present-value factors[b] (5)	Present value of outflows [(4) × (5)] (6)
1	$3,600	.943	$3,395	$4,286	.943	$4,042
2	3,600	.890	3,204	3,278	.890	2,917
3	3,600	.840	3,024	4,684	.840	3,935
4	3,600	.792	2,851	5,527	.792	4,377
5	7,600	.747	5,677	5,714	.747	4,268
	Present value of cash outflows		$18,151	Present value of cash outflows		$19,539

[a]Values developed using techniques beyond the scope of this basic text.
[b]From Table C-3, *PVIF*, for 6 percent and the corresponding year.

Lease Disclosure Requirements

After many years of debate and controversy, the *Financial Accounting Standards Board (FASB)* in November 1976 established requirements for the explicit disclosure of certain types of lease obligations on the firm's balance sheet. FASB Standard No. 13, "Accounting for Leases," established criteria for classifying various types of leases and set reporting standards for each class. The standard defines a financial (or capital) lease as one having *any* of the following elements:

1 ▬ The lease transfers ownership of the property to the lessee by the end of the lease term.

2 ▬ The lease contains an option to purchase the property at a "bargain" price. Such an option must be exercisable at a "fair market value."

3 ▬ The lease term is equal to 75 percent or more of the estimated economic life of the property (exceptions exist for property leased toward the end of its usable economic life).

4 ▬ At the beginning of the lease, the present value of the lease payments is equal to 90 percent or more of the fair market value of the leased property.

If a lease meets any of the above criteria, it is shown as a **capitalized lease,** meaning the present value of all its payments is included as an asset and corresponding liability on the firm's balance sheet. If a lease meets none of the above criteria, it is an operating lease and need not be capitalized, but its basic features must be disclosed in a footnote to the financial statements. Standard No. 13, of course, establishes detailed guidelines to be used in capitalizing leases to reflect them as an

capitalized lease A *financial (or capital) lease* that has the present value of all its payments included as an asset and corresponding liability on the firm's balance sheet, as required by FASB Standard No. 13.

asset and corresponding liability on the balance sheet. Subsequent standards have further refined lease capitalization and disclosure procedures. Let us look at an example.

EXAMPLE   Graber Company, a manufacturer of water purifiers, is leasing an asset under a 10-year lease requiring annual end-of-year payments of $15,000. The lease can be capitalized merely by calculating the present value of the lease payments over the life of the lease. However, the rate at which the payments should be discounted is difficult to determine.[5] If 10 percent were used, the present, or capitalized, value of the lease would be $92,175 ($15,000 × 6.145). (The calculated value using a business calculator is $92,169.) The capitalized value would be shown as an asset and corresponding liability on the firm's balance sheet.

Leases and Financial Ratios

Since the consequences of missing a financial lease payment are the same as those of missing an interest or principal payment on debt, a financial analyst must view the lease as a long-term financial commitment of the lessee. As a result of FASB No. 13, the inclusion of financial leases as an asset and corresponding liability (i.e., long-term debt) provides for a balance sheet that more accurately reflects the firm's financial status. It thereby permits various types of financial ratio analyses to be performed directly on the statement by any interested party.

Advantages and Disadvantages of Leasing

Leasing has a number of commonly cited advantages and disadvantages that should be considered when making a lease-versus-purchase decision. Although not all these advantages and disadvantages hold in every case, it is not unusual for a number of them to apply in a given situation.

Advantages

The commonly cited advantages of leasing are as follows:

1 ▨ Leasing allows the lessee, in effect, to *depreciate land*, which is prohibited if the land were purchased. Since the lessee who leases land is permitted to deduct the *total lease payment* as an expense for tax purposes, the effect is the same as if the firm had purchased the land and then depreciated it.

---

[5]The Financial Accounting Standards Board in Standard No. 13 established certain guidelines for the appropriate discount rate to use when capitalizing leases. Most commonly, the rate that the lessee would have incurred to borrow the funds to buy the asset with a secured loan under terms similar to the lease repayment schedule would be used. This simply represents the *before-tax cost of a secured debt*.

2 ■■■ Since it results in the receipt of service from an asset possibly without increasing the assets or liabilities on the firm's balance sheet, leasing may result in *misleading financial ratios*. With the passage of FASB No. 13, this advantage no longer applies to financial leases, although in the case of operating leases it remains a potential advantage.

3 ■■■ The use of sale-leaseback arrangements may permit the firm to *increase its liquidity* by converting an *existing* asset into cash, which can then be used as working capital. A firm short of working capital or in a liquidity bind can sell an owned asset to a lessor and lease the asset back for a specified number of years.

4 ■■■ Leasing provides *100 percent financing*. Most loan agreements for the purchase of fixed assets require the borrower to pay a portion of the purchase price as a down payment. As a result the borrower is able to borrow only 90 to 95 percent of the purchase price of the asset.

5 ■■■ Leasing offers certain *financial advantages when a firm becomes bankrupt* or is reorganized. In such an event, the maximum claim of lessors against the corporation is three years of lease payments, and the lessor of course gets the asset back. If debt is used to purchase an asset, the creditors have a claim equal to the total outstanding loan balance.

6 ■■■ In a lease arrangement, the firm may *avoid the cost of obsolescence* if the lessor fails to accurately anticipate the obsolescence of assets and sets the lease payment too low. This is especially true in the case of operating leases, which generally have relatively short lives.

7 ■■■ A lessee *avoids many of the restrictive covenants* that are normally included as part of a long-term loan. Requirements with respect to minimum net working capital, subsequent borrowing, changes in management, and so on are *not* normally found in a lease agreement.

8 ■■■ In the case of low-cost assets that are infrequently acquired, leasing—especially operating leases—may provide the firm with needed *financing flexibility*. That is, the firm does not have to arrange other financing for these assets and can somewhat conveniently obtain them through a lease.

Disadvantages
The commonly cited disadvantages of leasing are the following:

1 ■■■ A lease does not have a stated interest cost. Thus in many leases the *return to the lessor is quite high;* the firm might be better off borrowing to purchase the asset.

2 ■■■ At the end of the term of the lease agreement, the *salvage value* of an asset, if any, is realized by the lessor. If the lessee had purchased the asset, it could have claimed its salvage value. Of course, an expected salvage value when recognized by the lessor results in lower lease payments.

3 ▬ Under a lease, the lessee is generally *prohibited from making improvements* on the leased property or asset without the approval of the lessor. If the property were owned outright, this difficulty would not arise. Of course, lessors generally encourage leasehold improvements when they are expected to enhance the asset's salvage value.

4 ▬ If a lessee leases (under a financial lease) an *asset that subsequently becomes obsolete*, it still must make lease payments over the remaining term of the lease. This is true even if the asset is unusable.

 ## INTERNATIONAL DIMENSION: LONG-TERM DEBT

As noted in Chapter 16, multinational companies, in conducting their global operations, have access to a variety of international financial instruments. International bonds are among the most widely used, so we will begin by focusing on them. Next, we discuss the role of international financial institutions in underwriting such instruments. Finally, we consider the use of various techniques (such as swaps) by MNCs to change the structure of their long-term debts.

International Bonds

international bond A bond that is initially sold outside the country of the borrower and often distributed in several countries.

foreign bond An international bond sold primarily in the country of the currency of the issue.

Eurobond An international bond sold primarily in countries other than the country of the currency of the issue.

In general, an **international bond** is a bond that is initially sold outside the country of the borrower and often distributed in several countries. When a bond is sold primarily in the country of the currency of the issue, it is called a **foreign bond.** For example, an MNC based in West Germany might float a bond issue in the French capital market underwritten by a French syndicate and denominated in French francs. In the foreign bond category, the Swiss franc continues to be the major choice. Low levels of interest, the general stability of the currency, and the overall efficiency of the Swiss capital markets are among the primary reasons for the ongoing popularity of the Swiss franc.

When an international bond is sold primarily in countries other than the country of the currency in which the issue is denominated, it is called a **Eurobond.** Thus, an MNC based in the United States might float a Eurobond in several European capital markets, underwritten by an international syndicate and denominated in U.S. dollars. The U.S. dollar continues to dominate Eurobond issues, with the Japanese yen gaining popularity. The importance of the U.S. currency in all aspects of international transactions, and thus its importance to MNCs, can explain this continued dominance.

Eurobonds are much more widely used than foreign bonds. These instruments are heavily used by major market participants, including

U.S. corporations. So-called equity-linked Eurobonds (i.e., convertible to equity), especially those offered by a number of high-tech U.S. firms, have found strong demand among Euromarket participants. It is expected that more of these innovative types of instruments will emerge on the international scene in the coming years.

A final point concerns the levels of interest rates in international markets. In the case of foreign bonds, interest rates are usually directly correlated with the domestic rates prevailing in the respective countries. For Eurobonds, several interest rates may be influential. For instance, for a Eurodollar bond, the interest rate will reflect several different rates, most notably the U.S. long-term rate, the Eurodollar rate, and long-term rates in other countries.

The Role of International Financial Institutions

For *foreign bonds,* the underwriting institutions are those that handle bond issues in the respective countries in which such bonds are issued. For *Eurobonds,* a number of financial institutions in the United States, Japan, and Western Europe form international underwriting syndicates. The underwriting costs for Eurobonds are comparable to those for bond flotation in the U.S. domestic market. Although American institutions used to dominate the Eurobond scene, recent economic and financial strengths exhibited by some Japanese and Western European (especially German) financial firms have led to a change in that dominance. Since 1986 a number of Japanese and European firms have held the top positions as managing underwriters of Eurobond issues.

In order to raise funds through international bond issues, many MNCs establish their own financial subsidiaries. Many American-based MNCs, for example, have created subsidiaries in the United States and Western Europe, especially in Luxembourg. Such subsidiaries can be used to raise large amounts of funds in "one move," with the funds redistributed wherever MNCs need them. (Special tax rules applicable to such subsidiaries also make them desirable to MNCs.)

Changing the Structure of Debt

As noted in Chapter 8, *hedging strategies* can be used by MNCs to change the structure/characteristics of their long-term assets and liabilities. For instance, multinationals can use *interest rate swaps* to obtain a desired stream of interest payments (e.g., fixed-rate) in exchange for another (e.g., floating-rate). They can use *currency swaps* to exchange an asset/liability denominated in one currency (e.g., U.S. dollar) for another (e.g., Swiss franc). The use of these tools allows MNCs to gain access to a broader set of markets, currencies, and maturities, thus leading to both cost savings and a means of restructuring the existing assets/liabilities. Such use has experienced significant growth during the last few years, and this trend is expected to continue.

SUMMARY

1   **Describe the basic characteristics of long-term debt financing, including standard debt provisions, restrictive debt provisions, and cost.** Standard and restrictive provisions are included in long-term debt agreements in order to protect the lender. Standard debt provisions do not ordinarily place a burden on a financially sound business. Restrictive covenants tend to place certain operating and financial constraints on the borrower. The cost (interest rate) of long-term debt is normally higher than the cost of short-term borrowing. Major factors affecting the cost of long-term debt are loan maturity, loan size, and more importantly, borrower risk and the basic cost of money.

2   **Understand the characteristics of term (long-term) loan agreements and the various term lenders to business.** The conditions of a term (long-term) loan are specified in the term loan agreement. Term loans generally require periodic installment payments; some require balloon payments at maturity. Term loans may be either unsecured or secured. Some term lenders receive stock-purchase warrants. Term loans can be obtained from a number of major lenders ranging from commercial banks and insurance companies to the federal government's Small Business Administration to the financing subsidiaries of equipment manufacturers. Table 19.1 provides a complete listing of term lenders along with the characteristics and types of loans they make.

3   **Discuss the legal aspects of corporate bonds, general features of a bond issue, bond ratings, popular types of bonds, and bond-refunding options.** All conditions of a bond issue are detailed in the indenture which is enforced by the trustee. A bond issue may include a conversion feature, a call feature, or stock-purchase warrants. Bond ratings by independent agencies indicate the risk of a bond issue. A variety of popular—traditional and contemporary—types of bonds, some unsecured and others secured, are available. Tables 19.3 and 19.4 list them and summarize their key characteristics. Firms sometimes retire or refund (refinance) bonds prior to their maturity. When serial bonds are issued, retirement is on a planned basis. Bonds are refunded (refinanced) when there is a drop in interest rates sufficient to result in a positive net present value from calling the old bonds and replacing them with new lower-interest-rate bonds.

4   **Review the basic types of leases, leasing arrangements, and the lease contract.** A lease, like long-term debt, allows the firm to make contractual, tax-deductible payments in order to obtain the use of fixed assets. Operating leases are generally five or fewer years in term, cancelable, renewable, and provide for maintenance by the lessor. Financial leases are longer term, noncancelable, not renewable, and require the lessee to maintain the asset. A lessor can obtain assets to be leased through a direct lease, a sale-leaseback arrangement, or a leveraged lease. It can be a manufacturer's leasing subsidiary, an independent leasing company, or the leasing subsidiary of a large financial institution. The lease contract normally includes the term (duration) of the lease, provisions for its cancellation, lease payment amounts and dates, maintenance and associated cost provisions, renewal options, purchase options, and other provisions specified in the lease negotiation process.

5   **Analyze the lease-versus-purchase decision, the effects of leasing on future financing, and the advantages and disadvantages of leasing.** A lease-versus-purchase decision can be evaluated by calculating the after-tax cash outflows associated with the leasing and purchasing alternatives. The more desirable alternative is the one that has the lower present value of after-tax cash outflows. FASB Standard No. 13 requires firms to disclose in their financial statements the existence of leases. Financial leases must be capitalized and shown as an asset and corresponding liability on the firm's balance sheet; operating leases must be shown in a footnote to the financial statements. A number of commonly cited advantages and disadvantages should be considered when making lease-versus-purchase decisions.

6   **Describe the use by multinational companies of international bonds, international financial institutions to underwrite them, and various techniques to change the structure of their long-term debts.**   International capital markets provide MNCs with an opportunity to raise long-term debt through the issuance of international bonds in various currencies. Foreign bonds are sold primarily in the country of the currency of issue; Eurobonds are sold primarily in countries other than the country of the currency in which the issue is denominated. Foreign bonds are typically underwritten by firms in the countries in which such bonds are issued, whereas Eurobonds are underwritten by international underwriting syndicates. Hedging, interest rate swaps, and currency swaps can be used by multinational companies to change the structure of their long-term debts.

QUESTIONS

19—1   What are the two key methods of raising long-term debt financing? What motives does the lender have for including certain *restrictive covenants* in a debt agreement? How do these covenants differ from so-called *standard debt provisions?*

19—2   What is the general relationship between the cost of short-term and long-term debt? Why? In addition to loan maturity, what other factors affect the cost, or interest rate, of long-term debt?

19—3   What types of payment dates are generally required in a term (long-term) loan agreement? What is a *balloon payment?*

19—4   What role do commercial banks, insurance companies, pension funds, regional development companies, the Small Business Administration, small business investment companies, commercial finance companies, and equipment manufacturers play in lending long-term funds to businesses?

19—5   What types of maturities, denominations, and interest payments are associated with a typical corporate bond? Describe the role of the *bond indenture* and the *trustee.*

19—6   What does it mean if a bond has a *conversion feature?* A *call feature? Stock-purchase warrants?* How are bonds rated, and why?

19—7   Describe the basic characteristics of each of the following popular types of bonds:
   a. Debentures
   b. Subordinated debentures
   c. Income bonds
   d. Zero (or low) coupon bonds
   e. Junk bonds
   f. Floating rate bonds
   g. Extendable notes
   h. Putable bonds

19—8   Describe, compare, and contrast the basic features of the following secured bonds.
   a. Mortgage bond
   b. Collateral trust bond
   c. Equipment trust certificate

19—9   What two options may be available to a firm that wants to retire or refund an outstanding bond issue prior to maturity? Must these options be provided for in advance of issuance? Why might the issuer wish to retire or refund a bond prior to its maturity?

19—10   Why does the *bond-refunding decision* lend itself to the application of capital budgeting techniques? Describe the three-step procedure used to make these decisions.

19—11   What is *leasing?* Define, compare, and contrast *operating leases* and *financial (or capital) leases*. Describe three methods used by lessors to acquire assets to be leased.

19—12   Describe the four basic steps involved in the *lease-versus-purchase decision* process. Why must present-value techniques be used in this process?

19—13   According to FASB Standard No. 13, under what conditions must a lease be treated as a *capitalized lease* on the balance sheet? How does the financial manager capitalize a lease?

19—14   List and discuss the commonly cited advantages and disadvantages that should be considered when making a lease-versus-purchase decision.

19—15   Describe the difference between *foreign bonds* and *Eurobonds*. Explain how each is sold and discuss the determinant(s) of their interest rates.

PROBLEMS

19—1   **(Bond Discounts or Premiums)** Information about a number of bonds is given below. In each case the firm is in the 40 percent tax bracket and the bond has a $1,000 par value.

Bond	Proceeds per bond	Size of issue	Initial maturity of bond	Years remaining to maturity
A	$ 980	20,000 bonds	25 years	20
B	1,020	14,000 bonds	20 years	12
C	1,000	10,500 bonds	10 years	8
D	950	9,000 bonds	30 years	21
E	1,030	3,000 bonds	30 years	15

a. Indicate whether each bond was sold at a discount, at a premium, or at its par value.
b. Determine the total discount or premium for each issue.
c. Determine the annual amount of discount or premium amortized for each bond.
d. Calculate the unamortized discount or premium for each bond.
e. Determine the after-tax cash flow associated with the retirement now of each of these bonds, using the values developed in **d.**

19—2   **(Cost of a Call)** For each of the callable bond issues in the table, calculate the after-tax cost of calling the issue. Each bond has a $1,000 par value; the various issue sizes and call prices are summarized in the following table. The firm is in the 40 percent tax bracket.

Bond	Size of issue	Call price
A	8,000 bonds	$1,080
B	10,000 bonds	1,060
C	6,000 bonds	1,010
D	3,000 bonds	1,050
E	9,000 bonds	1,040
F	13,000 bonds	1,090

19—3   **(Amortization of Flotation Cost)**   The flotation cost, the initial maturity, and the number of years remaining to maturity are given for a number of bonds. The firm is in the 40 percent tax bracket.

Bond	Flotation cost	Initial maturity of bond	Years remaining to maturity
A	$500,000	30 years	24
B	200,000	20 years	5
C	40,000	25 years	10
D	100,000	10 years	2
E	80,000	15 years	9

   a. Calculate the annual amortization of the flotation cost for each bond.
   b. Determine the tax savings, if any, expected to result from the unamortized flotation cost if the bond were called today.

19—4   **(Bond-Refunding Decision)**   Schuyler Company is contemplating offering a new $30 million bond issue to replace an outstanding $30 million bond issue. The firm wishes to do this to take advantage of the decline in interest rates that has occurred since the initial bond issuance. The old and new bonds are described below. The firm is in the 40 percent tax bracket.
   Old bonds: The outstanding bonds have a $1,000 par value and a 14 percent coupon interest rate. They were issued five years ago with a 25-year maturity. They were initially sold for their par value of $1,000, and the firm incurred $250,000 in flotation costs. They are callable at $1,140.
   New bonds: The new bonds would have a $1,000 par value and a 12 percent coupon interest rate. They would have a 20-year maturity and could be sold at their par value. The flotation cost of the new bonds would be $400,000.
   a. Calculate the tax savings expected from the unamortized portion of the old bonds' flotation cost.
   b. Calculate the annual tax savings from the flotation cost of the new bonds, assuming the 20-year amortization.
   c. Calculate the after-tax cost of the call premium required to retire the old bonds.
   d. Determine the initial investment required to call the old bonds and issue the new bonds.
   e. Calculate the annual cash flow savings, if any, expected from the proposed bond-refunding decision.
   f. If the firm has a 7 percent after-tax cost of debt, find the net present value (NPV) of the bond-refunding decision. Would you recommend the proposed refunding? Why or why not?

19—5   **(Bond-Refunding Decision)**   Lawrence Furniture is considering offering a new $10 million bond issue to replace an outstanding $10 million bond issue. The firm wishes to do this to take advantage of the decline in interest rates that has occurred since the original issue. The two bond issues are described below; the firm is in the 40 percent tax bracket.
   Old bonds: The outstanding bonds have a $1,000 par value and a 17 percent coupon interest rate. They were issued five years ago with a 20-year maturity. They were initially sold at a $20 per-bond discount, and a $120,000 flotation cost was incurred. They are callable at $1,170.

New bonds: The new bonds would have a 15-year maturity, a par value of $1,000, and a 14 percent coupon interest rate. It is expected that these bonds can be sold at par for a flotation cost of $200,000.

a. Calculate the initial investment required to call the old bonds and issue the new bonds.

b. Calculate the annual cash flow savings, if any, expected from the proposed bond-refunding decision.

c. If the firm uses its after-tax cost of debt of 8 percent to evaluate low-risk decisions, find the net present value (NPV) of the bond-refunding decision. Would you recommend the proposed refunding? Explain your answer.

19—6   **(Bond-Refunding Decision—Advanced)** The Korrect Kopy Company is considering using the proceeds from a new $14 million bond issue to call and retire its outstanding $14 million bond issue. The details of both bond issues are outlined below. The firm is in the 40 percent tax bracket.

Old bonds: Korrect's old issue has a coupon interest rate of 14 percent, was issued six years ago, and had a 30-year maturity. The bonds sold at a $15 discount from their $1,000 par value; flotation costs were $120,000; and their call price is $1,140.

New bonds: The new issue is expected to sell at par ($1,000), have a 24-year maturity, and have a flotation cost of $360,000.

a. What is the initial investment required to call the old bonds and issue the new bonds?

b. What are the annual cash flow savings, if any, from the proposed bond-refunding decision if (1) the new bonds have a 12.5 percent coupon interest rate, and (2) the new bonds have a 13 percent coupon interest rate?

c. Construct a table showing the net present value (NPV) of refunding under the two circumstances given in **b**, when (1) the firm has an after-tax cost of debt of 6 percent; and (2) the firm has an after-tax cost of debt of 8 percent.

d. Discuss the set(s) of circumstances (described in **c**) when the refunding would be favorable and when it would not.

19—7   **(Lease-versus-Purchase Decision)**   Action Accounting Service is deciding whether to lease or purchase a new computer. The firm has an after-tax cost of debt of 9 percent and plans to use a 5-year time horizon for comparing the lease and purchase alternatives. The estimated after-tax cash outflows associated with the lease and purchase alternatives are given in the following table.

End of year	After-tax cash outflows	
	Lease	Purchase
1	$3,450	$3,570
2	3,450	3,200
3	3,450	3,470
4	3,450	3,700
5	3,450	3,970

a. Calculate the present value of the lease outflows.

b. Calculate the present value of the purchase outflows.

c. Use your findings in **a** and **b** to recommend either the lease or purchase alternative. Justify your recommendation.

19—8   **(Lease-versus-Purchase Decision)**   Tony Corporation is attempting to determine whether to lease or purchase a new light-duty truck. The firm's after-tax cost of debt is 8 percent, and it plans to use a 3-year time horizon for comparing the lease and purchase alternatives. The estimated after-tax cash outflows for the lease and purchase alternatives are as follows:

End of year	After-tax cash outflows	
	Lease	Purchase
1	$18,400	$16,480
2	16,000	14,340
3	14,600	15,690

a. Calculate the present value of the lease outflows.
b. Calculate the present value of the purchase outflows.
c. Use your findings in **a** and **b** to recommend either the lease or purchase alternative. Justify your recommendation.

19—9   **(Lease-versus-Purchase Decision)**   The Hot Bagel Shop wishes to evaluate two plans, leasing or purchasing, for financing an oven. The firm has a 9 percent after-tax cost of debt and is in the 40 percent tax bracket.
Lease: The shop could lease the oven under a five-year lease requiring annual end-of-year payments of $5,000. All maintenance costs will be paid by the lessor, while insurance and other costs will be borne by the lessee. The lessee will exercise its option to purchase the asset for $4,000 at termination of the lease.
Purchase: The oven costs $20,000 and will have a five-year life. It will be depreciated under ACRS using a five-year recovery period. The total purchase price will be financed by a five-year, 15 percent loan requiring equal annual end-of-year payments of $5,967. The firm will pay $1,000 per year for a service contract that covers all maintenance costs; insurance and other costs will be borne by the firm. The firm plans to keep the equipment and use it beyond its five-year recovery period.

The estimated after-tax cash outflows derived from the lease and purchase data are given in the following table.

End of year	After-tax cash outflows	
	Lease	Purchase
1	$3,000	$3,767
2	3,000	2,985
3	3,000	4,230
4	3,000	5,025
5	7,000	5,296

a. Calculate the present value of the lease outflows.

b. Calculate the present value of the purchase outflows.

c. Use your findings in **a** and **b** to recommend either the lease or purchase alternative. Justify your recommendation.

19—10   **(Capitalized Lease Values)** Given the following lease payments, terms remaining until the leases expire, and discount rates, calculate the capitalized value of each lease. Assume that lease payments are made annually at the end of each year.

Lease	Lease payment	Remaining term	Discount rate
A	$ 40,000	12 years	10%
B	120,000	8 years	12
C	9,000	18 years	14
D	16,000	3 years	9
E	47,000	20 years	11

CASE

Crane Manufacturing's Bond-Refunding-with-Lease Decision

Marilyn Schwartz, chief financial officer of Crane Manufacturing, believes that long-term interest rates are currently lower than they'll be anytime in the next five or so years. With this belief, she has begun investigating whether it might be the right time to offer a new bond issue to replace an outstanding $25 million bond issue. After consulting a number of investment bankers, Marilyn learned that the only way that Crane can successfully market the new bond issue is to convert a currently owned asset into a leased asset. The necessity of doing this is tied to the restrictive covenants in some of the firm's other loan agreements. In order to analyze the appropriateness of a bond refunding, Marilyn gathered data on the old and new bonds and estimated the future cash flows associated with the owned asset and the lease alternative. Crane Manufacturing has a 6 percent after-tax cost of debt and is in the 40 percent tax bracket. The data gathered by Marilyn are presented below.

Bond Refunding
Old bonds: The old bonds were initially issued 10 years ago with a 30-year maturity and a 12¼ percent coupon interest rate. The $1,000-par-value bonds were initially sold for $970, flotation costs were $240,000, and their call price is $1,125.
New bonds: The new issue is expected to sell at its $1,000 par value, have an 11 percent coupon interest rate, have a 20-year maturity, and require $300,000 in flotation costs.

Lease of Currently Owned Asset
The future cash flows associated with the currently owned asset and the lease alternative are summarized below over the assumed relevant five-year time horizon.

End of year	After-tax cash outflows	
	Owned	Leased
1	$10,000	$25,000
2	10,000	25,000
3	15,000	25,000
4	20,000	25,000
5	50,000	40,000

Required

   a. Ignoring the lease requirement, evaluate and make a recommendation relative to the proposed bond refunding.

   b. Determine the incremental savings or cost resulting from converting the owned asset to a leased asset.

   c. Combine your findings in **a** and **b** to make a recommendation as to whether or not Crane Manufacturing should refund the bond under the specified terms and conditions. Justify your recommendation.

CHAPTER 20

PREFERRED AND COMMON STOCK

CHAPTER OBJECTIVES

After studying this chapter, you should be able to:

1 Differentiate between debt and equity capital in terms of ownership rights, claims on income and assets, maturity, and tax treatment.

2 Understand preferred stock fundamentals—the basic rights of preferred stockholders and the features normally included as part of a preferred stock issue.

3 Explain the key advantages and disadvantages of preferred stock financing.

4 Discuss common stock fundamentals, including important aspects of voting rights.

5 Describe stock rights and the key advantages and disadvantages of common stock financing.

6 Review how multinational companies can either sell their shares in international capital markets or through joint ventures in order to raise equity capital abroad.

Hallmark: "When You Want to Send Money—Lend"

"" . . . the Bankruptcy Reform Act of 1978 strengthened the hand of debtors who want to control the business while it lies in bankruptcy court. ""

Univision, the Spanish-language broadcast network, was purchased in mid-1988 by the Hall family of Kansas City, owners of Hallmark, the nation's biggest greeting card company. Half of the purchase was financed with junk bonds that went into default in 1990, when Univision missed an interest payment. Rather than offering to give up equity in a recapitalization plan, the Hall family offered to buy back the junk bonds at a price of less than forty cents per dollar. Management was effectively saying "since we don't have the full amount, why don't you take less?"

In virtually all countries—and in the United States, for most of its history—only after creditors were repaid in full, with interest, did the owner recover some of his or her investment. However, the Bankruptcy Reform Act of 1978 strengthened the hand of debtors who want to control the business while it lies in bankruptcy court. In some instances, bondholders were warned that unless they accepted pennies on the dollar, the managers would strip the company of assets, making the bonds less valuable.

Bondholders at Univision turned to Jack Ackerman, president of the influential investment advisory service BondReview. Mr. Ackerman negotiated an agreement wherein the Univision bondholders received 55 cents on the dollar. Bondholders agreed to the deal because they felt a costly court battle would result in a lower investment recovery.

In other instances, bondholders have used even more aggressive techniques to regain precedence over stockholders in bankruptcy and liquidation. Bondholders gave two former Goldman Sachs bankers the right to turn down a tender offer on their behalf in return for the bankers' promise to throw out Allegheny International's senior management. When Easco Corporation, an aluminum extruding company, offered to buy back bonds at a low price, bondholders led by Equitable Life Insurance offered instead to put up new capital. Bondholders now own seventy percent of Easco's equity. As the $300 billion in junk bonds arising from the leveraged-buyout merger binge of the 1990s is refinanced or paid off, the residual ownership position of owners will probably be reinstated.

A firm needs to maintain an equity base large enough to allow it to take advantage of low-cost debt and build an optimal capital structure (see Chapter 16). Equity capital can be raised *internally* through retained earnings, or *externally* by selling preferred or common stock. Although preferred stock, as noted in the discussion of cost of capital in Chapter 13, is a less costly form of financing than common stock and retained earnings, it is not frequently used. Here we begin with brief discussions of equity capital and preferred stock, and then concentrate our attention on the characteristics, features, and role of common stock.

THE NATURE OF EQUITY CAPITAL

The key differences between debt and equity capital were summarized in Chapter 16 (see specifically Table 16.1). These differences relate to ownership rights, claims on the firm's income and assets, maturity, and tax treatment.

Ownership Rights

Unlike creditors (lenders), holders of equity capital (preferred and common stockholders) are owners of the firm. Holders of equity capital often have voting rights that permit them to select the firm's directors and to vote on special issues. In contrast, debtholders may receive voting privileges only when the firm has violated the conditions of a *term loan agreement* or *bond indenture*.

Claims on Income and Assets

Holders of equity capital have claims on both income and assets that are secondary to the claims of creditors.

Claims on Income
The claims of equity holders on income cannot be paid until the claims of all creditors have been satisfied. These claims include both interest and scheduled principal payments. Once these claims have been satisfied, the firm's board of directors can decide whether to distribute dividends to the owners. Of course, as explained in Chapter 16, a firm's ability to pay dividends may be limited by legal, contractual, or internal constraints.

Claims on Assets

The claims of equity holders on the firm's assets are secondary to the claims of creditors. When the firm becomes bankrupt,[1] assets are sold and the proceeds distributed in this order: to employees and customers, to the government, to secured creditors, to unsecured creditors, and finally to equity holders. Because equity holders are the last to receive any distribution of assets during bankruptcy proceedings, they expect greater compensation in the form of dividends and/or rising stock prices.

Maturity

Unlike debt, equity capital is a permanent form of financing. It does not "mature," and therefore repayment of the initial amount paid in is not required. Since equity does not mature and will be liquidated only during bankruptcy proceedings, the owners must recognize that although a ready market may exist for the firm's shares, the price that can be realized may fluctuate. This potential fluctuation of the market price of equity makes the overall returns to a firm's owners even more risky.

Tax Treatment

As noted in Chapter 2, interest payments to debtholders are treated as tax-deductible expenses on the firm's income statement, whereas dividend payments to preferred and common stockholders are not tax-deductible. The tax-deductibility of interest primarily accounts for the fact that the cost of debt is generally less than the cost of equity (as pointed out in Chapter 13).

PREFERRED STOCK FUNDAMENTALS

Preferred stock gives its holders certain privileges that make them senior to common stockholders. Because of this, firms generally do not issue large quantities of preferred stock. Preferred stockholders are promised a fixed periodic return, which is stated either as a percentage or as a dollar amount. In other words, a 5 percent preferred stock or a $5 preferred stock can be issued. The way the dividend is specified depends on whether the preferred stock has a par value. **Par-value preferred stock** has a stated face value. The annual dividend is stated as a percentage on par-value preferred stock and in dollars on **no-par preferred stock**, which does not have a stated face value. Thus a 5 percent preferred stock with a $100 par value is expected to pay $5 (5% × $100) in divi-

par-value preferred stock   Preferred stock with a stated face value that is used with the specified dividend percentage to determine the annual dollar dividend.

no-par preferred stock   Preferred stock with no stated face value but with a stated annual dollar dividend.

---

[1]The procedures followed when a firm becomes bankrupt were described in Chapter 17.

dends per year, and a $5 preferred stock with no par value is also expected to pay its $5 stated dividend each year.

Most preferred stock has a fixed dividend, but some firms issue **adjustable-rate (or floating-rate) preferred stock (ARPS).** Such stocks have a dividend rate tied to interest rates on specific government securities. Rate adjustments are commonly made quarterly, and typically the rate must be maintained within certain preset limits. The appeal of ARPS is the protection offered investors against sharp rises in interest rates, since the dividend rate on ARPS will rise with interest rates. From the firm's perspective, adjustable-rate preferreds have appeal since they can be sold at an initially lower dividend rate and the scheduled dividend rate will fall if interest rates decline.

A recent innovation in preferred stock financing, first launched in 1986, **payment-in-kind (PIK) preferred stock** usually doesn't pay cash dividends, but rather pays in additional shares of preferred stock. These, in turn, pay dividends in even more preferred stock. Typical dividend rates on PIK preferred stock range from 15 to 18 percent. After a stated time period, generally five or six years, PIK preferreds are supposed to begin paying cash dividends or provide holders with a chance to swap for another, more traditional security. These preferreds are essentially the equivalent of *junk bonds* (see Chapters 18 and 19) and, like them, are issued to finance corporate takeovers. A good deal of uncertainty surrounds PIK preferreds. If the issuer runs into trouble, holders may end up with nothing—little chance of receiving cash dividends and little possibility of legal recourse against the issuer. Because they are primarily used to finance takeovers, PIK preferreds are not viewed as a major corporate financing tool.

Basic Rights of Preferred Stockholders

The basic rights of preferred stockholders with respect to voting, the distribution of earnings, and the distribution of assets are somewhat more favorable than the rights of common stockholders. Because preferred stock is a form of ownership and has no maturity date, its claims on income and assets are secondary to those of the firm's creditors.

Voting Rights

Preferred stock is often considered a *quasi-debt* since, much like interest on debt, it specifies a fixed periodic (dividend) payment. Of course, as ownership, preferred stock is unlike debt in that it has no maturity date. Because their claim on the firm's income is fixed and takes precedence over the claim of common stockholders, preferred stockholders are therefore not exposed to the same degree of risk as common stockholders. They are consequently *not* normally given the right to vote.

Distribution of Earnings

Preferred stockholders are given preference over common stockholders with respect to the distribution of earnings. If the stated preferred stock dividend is *passed* (not paid) by the board of directors, the payment of

---

adjustable-rate (or floating-rate) preferred stock (ARPS)
Preferred stock whose dividend rate is tied to interest rates on specific government securities.

payment-in-kind (PIK) preferred stock
Preferred stock that pays dividends in additional shares of preferred stock rather than cash.

dividends to common stockholders is prohibited. It is this preference in dividend distribution that makes common stockholders the true risk-takers with respect to receipt of periodic returns.

Distribution of Assets

Preferred stockholders are usually given preference over common stockholders in the liquidation of assets as a result of a firm's bankruptcy. However, they must wait until all creditors have been satisfied. The amount of the claim of preferred stockholders in liquidation is normally equal to the par, or stated, value of the preferred stock. The preferred stockholder's preference over the common stockholder places the common stockholder in the more risky position with respect to recovery of investment.

Features of Preferred Stock

A number of features are generally included as part of a preferred stock issue. These features, along with a statement of the stock's par value, the amount of dividend payments, the dividend payment dates, and any restrictive covenants, are specified in an agreement similar to a *term loan agreement* or *bond indenture* (see Chapter 19).

Restrictive Covenants

The restrictive covenants commonly found in a preferred stock issue are aimed at assuring the continued existence of the firm and, most important, regular payment of the stated dividend. These covenants include provisions related to passing dividends, the sale of senior securities, mergers, sales of assets, net working capital requirements, and the payment of common stock dividends or common stock repurchases. The violation of preferred stock covenants usually permits preferred stockholders either to obtain representation on the firm's board of directors or to force the retirement of their stock at or above its par, or stated, value.

Cumulation

Most preferred stock is **cumulative** with respect to any dividends passed. That is, all dividends in arrears must be paid prior to the payment of dividends to common stockholders. If preferred stock is **noncumulative,** passed (unpaid) dividends do not accumulate. In this case only the most recent dividend must be paid prior to paying dividends to common stockholders. Since the common stockholders, who are the firm's true owners, can receive dividends only after the dividend claims of preferred stockholders have been satisfied, it is in the firm's best interest to pay preferred dividends when they are due.[2] The following

cumulative preferred stock   Preferred stock for which all passed (unpaid) dividends in arrears must be paid prior to the payment of dividends to common stockholders.

noncumulative preferred stock   Preferred stock for which passed (unpaid) dividends do not accumulate.

---

[2]Most preferred stock is cumulative since it is difficult to sell noncumulative stock. Common stockholders obviously prefer issuance of noncumulative preferred, since it does not place them in quite as risky a position. But it is often in the best interest of the firm to sell *cumulative* preferred stock due to its lower cost.

example will help clarify the distinction between cumulative and non-cumulative preferred stock.

EXAMPLE   Utley Company, a manufacturer of specialty automobiles, currently has outstanding an issue of $6 preferred stock on which quarterly dividends of $1.50 are to be paid. Due to a cash shortage, the last two quarterly dividends were passed. The directors of the company have been receiving a large number of complaints from common stockholders, who have of course not received any dividends in the past two quarters either. If the preferred stock is cumulative, the company will have to pay its preferred stockholders $4.50 per share ($3.00 of dividends in arrears plus the current $1.50 dividend) prior to paying dividends to its common stockholders. If the preferred stock is noncumulative, the firm must pay only the current $1.50 dividend to its preferred stockholders prior to paying dividends to its common stockholders.

Participation

nonparticipating preferred stock
Preferred stock whose holders receive only the specified dividend payments.

Most issues of preferred stock are **nonparticipating,** which means that preferred stockholders receive only the specified dividend payments. Occasionally, **participating preferred stock** is issued. This type provides for dividend payments based on certain formulas allowing preferred stockholders to participate with common stockholders in the receipt of dividends beyond a specified amount. This feature is included only when the firm considers it absolutely necessary in order to obtain badly needed funds.

participating preferred stock
Preferred stock that offers dividend payments based on formulas allowing preferred stockholders to participate with common stockholders in the receipt of dividends beyond a specified amount.

Call Feature

Preferred stock is generally *callable*, which means that the issuer can retire outstanding stock within a certain period of time at a specified price. The call feature generally cannot be exercised until a period of years has elapsed since the issuance of the stock. The call price is normally set above the initial issuance price but may decrease according to a predetermined schedule as time passes. Making preferred stock callable provides the issuer with a method of bringing the fixed-payment commitment of the preferred issue to an end.

Conversion Feature

conversion feature
A provision permitting the holder of a preferred stock (or bond) to transfer it into a specified number of shares of common stock.

Preferred stock quite often contains a **conversion feature** that permits its transference into a specified number of shares of common stock. Sometimes the conversion ratio, or number of shares of common stock, changes according to a prespecified formula. A detailed discussion of conversion is presented in Chapter 21.

ADVANTAGES AND DISADVANTAGES OF PREFERRED STOCK

It is difficult to generalize about the advantages and disadvantages of preferred stock due to the variety of features that may be incorporated in a preferred stock issue. The attractiveness of preferred stock is also affected by current interest rates and the firm's existing capital structure. Nevertheless, some key advantages and disadvantages are often cited.

Advantages

One commonly cited advantage of preferred stock is its *ability to increase leverage.* Since preferred stock obligates the firm to pay only fixed dividends to its holders, its presence helps to increase the firm's financial leverage. (The effects of preferred stock on a firm's financial leverage were discussed in Chapter 5.) Increased financial leverage will magnifiy the effects of increased earnings on the common stockholders' returns.

A second advantage is the *flexibility* provided by preferred stock. Although preferred stock provides added leverage in much the same way as bonds, it differs from bonds in that the issuer can pass a dividend payment without suffering the consequences that result when an interest or principal payment is missed on a bond. Preferred stock allows the issuer to keep its levered position without running as great a risk of being forced out of business in a lean year as it might if it missed interest or principal payments on actual debt.

A third advantage of preferred stock has been its *use in corporate restructuring—mergers, leveraged buyouts (LBOs), and divestitures.* Often, preferred stock is swapped for the common stock of an acquired firm, with the preferred dividend set at a level equivalent to the historic dividend of the acquired firm. This exchange allows the acquiring firm to state at the time of the acquisition that only a fixed dividend will be paid. All other earnings can be reinvested to perpetuate the growth of the new enterprise. In addition, the owners of the acquired firm will be assured of a continuing stream of dividends equivalent to that which may have been provided prior to the restructuring.

Disadvantages

Three major disadvantages are often cited for preferred stock. One is the *seniority of the preferred stockholder's claim.* Since holders of preferred stock are given preference over common stockholders with respect to the distribution of earnings and assets, the presence of preferred stock in a sense jeopardizes common stockholders' returns. If a firm has preferred stockholders to pay, and if the firm's after-tax earnings are quite variable, its ability to pay at least token dividends to common stockholders may be seriously impaired.

A second disadvantage of preferred stock is cost. The *cost of preferred stock financing is generally higher than that of debt financing.* The reason is that, unlike the payment of interest to bondholders, the payment of dividends to preferred stockholders is not guaranteed. Since preferred stockholders are willing to accept the added risk of purchasing preferred stock rather than long-term debt, they must be compen-

S M A L L   B U S I N E S S

Heaven-Sent Preferred Stockholders

When other sources of capital dry up, many young businesses turn to so-called "angels." These heavenly bodies are investors willing to invest—not lend—their money. "Angels" tend to be wealthy individuals who have business experience and are good at making quick business decisions based on that experience. Finding angels that will not meddle in company affairs is difficult. Yet, "angels" often provide the start-up capital a company needs.

ICOM Simulations is a recent example of a young entrepreneur and "angels" uniting to bring a firm to life. The company designs and sells dazzling computer games. As of February 1991, it was too early to tell if this software company and the "angels'" investment will be successful. However, the firm has one advantage over many other new companies: an experienced angel, known in the finance industry as an "archangel."

William Weaver, a partner in the Chicago law firm of Sachnoff & Weaver, has been orchestrating "angel" investments since the late 1960s. He has a stable of about 25 potential investors who also frequently provide him with leads. After ICOM Simulations came to his attention, Weaver gave entrepreneur Ted Zipnick the chance to present ICOM Simulations to about 15 "angels."

Altogether, 17 of Weaver's "angels" invested $1.9 million. One "angel's" respect for Zipnick's proposal was based on his related expertise. The other "angel" made a very favorable pitch for ICOM on the basis of the firm's board of directors which includes the senior vice-president of Coca-Cola and the CEO of Viacom, the cable television giant.

ICOM Simulations' "angels" received preferred shares for their investment. These preferred shares represent approximately 20 percent of the firm. Zipnick also rewarded the experienced "angel" and Weaver with seats on ICOM's board of directors. Besides having the capital to develop a viable company, the wealthy "angels" do not require periodic dividend payments. Understanding the ups and downs of a new venture, they did not want to strain ICOM's cash flow.

Source: Ellyn Spragins, "Heaven sent," Inc., February 1991, pp. 85–86.

sated with a higher return. Another factor causing the cost of preferred stock to be greater than that of long-term debt is the fact that interest on debt is tax-deductible, whereas preferred stock dividends must be paid from after-tax earnings. Although the lowering of corporate tax rates in recent years has reduced the cost differential between debt and preferred stock, tax-deductibility of interest on debt remains a factor causing preferred stock financing to be more costly than debt.

A third disadvantage of preferred stock is that it is *generally difficult to sell*. Most investors find preferred stock unattractive relative to bonds (due to the issuer's ability to pass dividends) and to common stock (due to its limited return). As a consequence, most preferred stock sold must either have an adjustable rate or be convertible.

COMMON STOCK FUNDAMENTALS

The true owners of business firms are the common stockholders, who invest their money with the expectation of receiving future returns. A common stockholder is sometimes referred to as a *residual owner,* since in essence he or she receives what is left—the residual—after all other claims on the firm's income and assets have been satisfied. As a result of this generally uncertain position, the common stockholder expects to be compensated with adequate dividends and, ultimately, capital gains. Here we discuss the fundamental aspects of common stock: ownership; par value; authorized, outstanding, and issued shares; voting rights; dividends; stock repurchases; and the distribution of earnings and assets.

Ownership

The common stock of a firm can be **privately owned** by a single individual, **closely owned** by a small group of investors, such as a family, or **publicly owned** by a broad group of unrelated individual or institutional investors. Typically, small corporations are privately or closely owned; if their shares are traded, this occurs privately or on the over-the-counter exchange. Large corporations, which are emphasized in the following discussions, are publicly owned, and their shares are generally actively traded on the organized or over-the-counter exchanges, which were briefly described in Chapter 2.

privately owned (stock) All common stock of a firm owned by a single individual.

closely owned (stock) All common stock of a firm owned by a small group of investors such as a family.

publicly owned (stock) Common stock of a firm owned by a broad group of unrelated individual or institutional investors.

Par Value

Common stock may be sold with or without a par value. A **par value** is a relatively useless value arbitrarily placed on the stock in the firm's corporate charter. It is generally quite low, somewhere in the range of $1. Firms often issue stock with **no par value,** in which case they may assign it a value or place it on the books at the price at which it is sold. A low par value may be advantageous in states where certain corporate taxes are based on the par value of stock; if a stock has no par value, the tax may be based on an arbitrarily determined per-share figure. The accounting entries resulting from the sale of common stock can be illustrated by a simple example.

par value A value arbitrarily placed on stock in the firm's corporate charter.

no par value Describes stock issued without a *par value.*

EXAMPLE   Moxie Company, a soft drink manufacturer, has issued 1,000 shares of $2 par-value common stock, receiving proceeds of $50 per share. This results in the following entries on the firm's books:

Common stock (1,000 shares at $2 par)	$ 2,000
Paid-in capital in excess of par	48,000
Common stock equity	$50,000

Sometimes the entry labeled "paid-in capital in excess of par" may be labeled "capital surplus." This value is important because, as noted in Chapter 16, firms are usually prohibited by state law from distributing any paid-in capital as dividends.

Authorized, Outstanding, and Issued Shares

As noted in Chapter 18, the corporate charter states the number of *authorized shares* of common stock. Not all authorized shares will necessarily be *oustanding shares* that are under ownership of the firm's shareholders. Since it is often difficult to amend the charter to authorize the issuance of additional shares, firms generally attempt to authorize more shares than they plan to issue. It is possible for the corporation to have more *issued shares* of common stock than are currently outstanding if it has repurchased stock. Repurchased stock, as noted in Chapter 16, is called *treasury stock*. The amount of treasury stock is therefore found by subtracting the number of outstanding shares from the number of issued shares.

Voting Rights

Generally, each share of common stock entitles the holder to one vote in the election of directors and in other special elections. Votes are generally assignable and must be cast at the annual stockholders' meeting.

In recent years many firms have issued two or more classes of common stock—with unequal voting rights being their key difference. The issuance of different classes of stock has been frequently used as a defense against a *hostile merger* in which an outside group tries to gain voting control of the firm by buying shares in the marketplace. At other times a class of **nonvoting common stock** is issued when the firm wishes to raise capital through the sale of common stock but does not want to give up its voting control. This and other approaches to issuing classes of stock with unequal voting rights result in some **supervoting shares.** By giving their holders more votes per share, supervoting shares allow them to better control the firm's future. An interesting variation of this theme was put in place by J.M. Smucker Co. (food, confectionary). The firm has only one class of stock, which, when it has been held for four years, provides 10 votes per share. Since the Smucker family owns 30

nonvoting common stock   Common stock that carries no voting rights; issued when the firm wishes to raise capital through the sale of common stock but does not want to give up its voting control.

supervoting shares   Stock that carries with it more votes per share than a share of regular common stock.

ETHICS IN FINANCE

Separating Management and Guidance at General Motors

Corporate boards of directors by definition have ultimate authority to guide corporate affairs and make general policy. However, the existing management's ability to solicit stockholder proxy statements at company expense gives corporate management an advantage in selecting their directors. This ability may lead to agency problems, wherein management works for their personal gains at the expense of shareholders.

Under pressure in early 1991, General Motors adopted corporate by-law changes calling for a majority of their board to consist of independent directors. The change was made at the urging of the California Public Employee Retirement System, known as CALPERS. This $57 billion fund is one of the most active of the big pension funds, constantly trying to enhance corporate governance principles. CALPERS and the $47 billion New York State Common Retirement Fund were seeking clarification of the criteria used to evaluate General Motors' chairman.

Two factors caused the adoption of the by-law change by the United States' largest industrial company. First, CALPERS notified GM that it planned to introduce a shareholders proposal calling for a majority of independent directors. Owning 7.2 million shares, CALPERS was in a position to make its request heard. Second, 15 of 20 GM directors were not employees of General Motors. Hence, their positions were not threatened.

The adoption was applauded by attorneys, educators, and other investors who tend to support bigger roles for independent directors on corporate boards. Following GM's lead, ITT Corp., Armstrong World, Sears, and others were also considering similar by-law changes.

Source: James White, "GM bows to California pension fund by adopting by-law on board membership," *The Wall Street Journal*, January 31, 1991, p. A6.

percent of the stock, this procedure, when it was initiated a few years ago, effectively ruled out a hostile merger with the company.

When different classes of common stock are issued on the basis of unequal voting rights, class A common is typically—but not universally—designated as nonvoting and class B common would have voting rights. Generally, higher classes of shares are given preference with respect to the distribution of earnings (dividends) and assets (in liquidation) over the lower-class shares. The lower-class shares in exchange receive more voting rights. In other words, because class A shares are not given voting rights, they are generally given preference over class B shares in terms of the distribution of dividends and assets. Treasury stock, which resides within the corporation, generally *does not* have voting rights. Three aspects of voting require special attention—proxies, majority voting, and cumulative voting.

Proxies

proxy statement A statement giving the votes of a stockholder or stockholders to another party or parties.

Since most small stockholders cannot attend the annual meeting to vote, they may sign a **proxy statement** giving their votes to another party. The solicitation of proxies from shareholders is closely controlled by the Securities and Exchange Commission, to protect against the possibility that proxies will be solicited on the basis of false or misleading information. Existing management generally receives the stockholders' proxies, since it is able to solicit them at company expense. Occasionally, when the ownership of the firm is widely disseminated, outsiders may attempt to gain control by waging a **proxy battle.** They attempt to solicit a sufficient number of votes to unseat the existing management. To win a corporate election, votes from a majority of the shares voted are required. Proxy battles generally occur when the existing management is performing poorly; however, the odds of a nonmanagement group winning a proxy battle are generally slim.

proxy battle The attempt by a nonmanagement group to gain control of the management of a firm by soliciting a sufficient number of proxy votes.

Majority Voting

majority voting system The system whereby, in the election of a board of directors, each stockholder is entitled to one vote for each share of stock owned and can vote all shares for *each* director.

In the **majority voting system,** each stockholder is entitled to one vote for each share of stock owned. The stockholders vote for each position on the board of directors separately, and each stockholder is permitted to vote all of his or her shares for *each* director he or she favors. The directors receiving the majority of the votes are elected. It is impossible for minority interests to select a director, since each shareholder can vote his or her shares for as many of the candidates as he or she wishes. As long as management controls a majority of the votes, it can elect all the directors. An example will clarify this point.

EXAMPLE   Dill Company, a producer of high-quality paper, is in the process of electing three directors. There are 1,000 shares of stock outstanding, of which management controls 60 percent. The management-backed candidates are A, B, and C; the minority candidates are D, E, and F. By voting its 600 shares (60% × 1,000) for *each* of its candidates, management can elect A, B, and C. The minority shareholders, with only 400 votes for each of their candidates, cannot elect any directors. Management's candidates will receive 600 votes each, and other candidates will receive 400 votes each.

Cumulative Voting

cumulative voting system The system under which each share of common stock is allotted a number of votes equal to the total number of corporate directors to be elected and votes can be given to *any* director(s).

Some corporate charters specify the use of a **cumulative voting system** to elect corporate directors. This system gives a number of votes equal to the total number of directors to be elected to each share of common stock. The votes can be given to *any* director(s) the stockholder desires. The advantage of this system is that it provides the minority shareholders with an opportunity to elect at least some directors.

EXAMPLE   Esco Company, a competitor of Dill Company, is also in the process of electing three directors. In this case, however, each share of common stock entitles the holder to three votes, which may be voted in any manner desired. Again, there are 1,000 shares outstanding and management controls 600. It therefore has a total of 1,800 votes (3 × 600), while the minority shareholders have 1,200 votes (3 × 400). In this situation, the majority shareholders can elect only two directors, and the minority shareholders can elect at least one director. The majority shareholders can split their votes evenly among the three candidates (give them 600 votes each); but if the minority shareholders give all their votes to one of their candidates, he or she will win.

A commonly cited formula for determining the number of shares necessary to elect a certain number of directors, *NE*, under cumulative voting is given by Equation 20.1:

$$NE = \frac{O \times D}{TN + 1} + 1$$

Equation 20.1
Formula for the number of shares necessary to elect a certain number of directors under cumulative voting

where

NE = number of shares needed to elect a certain number of directors
 O = total number of shares of common stock outstanding
 D = number of directors desired
TN = total number of directors to be elected

EXAMPLE   Substituting the values in the preceding example for *O* (1,000) and *TN* (3) into Equation 20.1 and letting *D* = 1, 2, and 3 yields values of *NE* equal to 251, 501, and 751. Since the minority stockholders control only 400 shares, they can elect only one director.

The advantage of cumulative voting from the viewpoint of minority shareholders should be clear from the example. However, even with cumulative voting, certain election procedures such as staggered terms for directors can be used to prevent minority representation on a board. Also, the majority shareholders may control a large enough number of shares or the total number of directors to be elected may be small enough to prevent minority representation.

Dividends

The payment of corporate dividends is at the discretion of the board of directors. Most corporations pay dividends quarterly. Dividends may be paid in cash, stock, or merchandise. Cash dividends are the most common; merchandise dividends are the least common. *Stock splits*, which have some similarity to *stock dividends*, are sometimes used to enhance the trading activity of a stock (see Chapter 16).

The common stockholder is not promised a dividend, but he or she comes to expect certain payments based on the historical dividend pattern of the firm. Before dividends are paid to common stockholders, the claims of all creditors, the government, and preferred stockholders must be satisfied. Because of the importance of the dividend decision to the growth and valuation of the firm, a portion of Chapter 16 was devoted to a discussion of dividend policy.

Stock Repurchases

Another characteristic of common stock, alluded to earlier in the discussion of authorized, outstanding, and issued shares, is the repurchase of stock. Firms occasionally repurchase stock in order to change their capital structure or to increase the returns to the owners. The effect of repurchasing common stock is similar to that of the payment of cash dividends to stockholders. The repurchase of stock is popular among firms that are in a very liquid position with no attractive investment opportunities. Since stock repurchases are similar to cash dividend payments, they too were discussed in Chapter 16.

Distribution of Earnings and Assets

As mentioned in previous sections, holders of common stock have no guarantee of receiving any periodic distribution of earnings in the form of dividends. Nor are they guaranteed anything in the event of liquidation. However, one thing they are assured of is that they cannot lose any more than they have invested in the firm. Moreover, the common stockholder can receive unlimited returns through dividends and through the appreciation in the value of his or her holdings. In other words, although nothing is guaranteed, the *possible* rewards for providing risk capital can be considerable and even great.

STOCK RIGHTS AND OTHER CONSIDERATIONS

In addition to common stock fundamentals, stock rights, and the advantages and disadvantages of common stock are important considerations.

Stock Rights

stock rights Allow stockholders to purchase additional shares of stock in direct proportion to their number of owned shares.

Stock rights allow stockholders to purchase additional shares of stock in direct proportion to their number of owned shares. Today, rights are primarily used by smaller corporations whose shares are either *closely* *owned* or *publicly owned* and not actively traded. In these situations rights are an important common stock financing tool without which shareholders would run the risk of losing their proportionate control of the corporation. Rights are rarely used by large publicly owned corporations whose shares are widely held and actively traded. Maintenance of proportionate control in such firms is not a major concern of their shareholders.

Preemptive Rights

Corporate charters sometimes provide common stockholders with **preemptive rights,** which allow them to maintain their *proportionate* ownership in the corporation when new issues are made. Most states permit shareholders to be extended this privilege in the corporate charter. Preemptive rights allow existing shareholders to maintain their voting control and protect against the dilution of their ownership and earnings. **Dilution of ownership** usually results in the dilution of earnings, since each present shareholder will have a claim on a *smaller* part of the firm's earnings than previously. Of course, if total earnings simultaneously increase, the long-run effect may be an overall increase in earnings per share.

From the firm's viewpoint, the use of rights offerings to raise new equity capital may be cheaper than a public offering of stock. An example may help clarify the use of rights.

preemptive rights
Allow common stockholders to maintain their proportionate ownership in the corporation when new issues are made.

dilution of ownership Occurs when a new stock issue results in each present stockholder having a claim on a *smaller* part of the firm's earnings than previously.

EXAMPLE   Dominic Company, a large national advertising firm, currently has 100,000 shares of common stock outstanding and is contemplating issuing an additional 10,000 shares through a rights offering. Each existing shareholder will receive one right per share, and each right will entitle the shareholder to purchase one-tenth of a share of new common stock (10,000 ÷ 100,000). Therefore, 10 rights will be required to purchase one share of the stock. The holder of 1,000 shares of existing common stock will receive 1,000 rights. Since each permits the purchase of one-tenth of a share of new common stock, the holder will be able to purchase 100 shares ($\frac{1}{10}$ × 1,000 shares) of new common stock. If the shareholder exercises the rights, he or she will end up with a total of 1,100 shares of common stock, or 1 percent of the total number of shares outstanding (110,000). Thus the shareholder maintains the same proportion of ownership he or she had prior to the rights offering.

Mechanics of Rights Offerings

When a company makes a rights offering, the board of directors must set a **date of record,** which is the last date on which the recipient of a right must be the legal owner indicated in the company's stock ledger. Due to the time needed to make bookkeeping entries when a stock is traded, stocks usually begin selling **ex rights**—without the rights being attached to the stock—four *business days* prior to the date of record.

date of record (rights) The last date on which the recipient of a right must be the legal owner indicated in the company's stock ledger.

ex rights Period, beginning four *business days* prior to the date of record, during which the stock will be sold without announced rights being attached.

The issuing firm sends rights to *holders of record*, who may exercise their rights, sell them, or let them expire. Rights are negotiable instruments, and many are traded actively enough to be listed on the various securities exchanges. They are exercisable for a specified period of time, generally not more than a few months. The price at which they may be exercised, called the **subscription price,** is set somewhat below the prevailing market price. Since fractions of shares are not always issued, it is sometimes necessary to purchase additional rights or sell extra rights. The value of a right depends largely on the number of rights needed to purchase a share of stock and the amount by which the right's subscription price is below the current market price. If the rights have a very low value and a rights holder owns only a small number of shares, the rights may be allowed to expire.

Management Decisions

A firm's management must make two basic decisions when preparing for a rights offering. The first is the price at which the rights holders can purchase a new share of common stock. The subscription price must be set *below* the current market price, but how far below depends on several things: management's evaluation of the sensitivity of the market demand to a price change, the degree of dilution of ownership and earnings expected, and the size of the offering. Management will consider the rights offering successful if approximately 90 percent of the rights are exercised.

Once management has determined the subscription price, it must determine the number of rights required to purchase a share of stock. Since the amount of funds to be raised is known in advance, the subscription price can be divided into this value to get the total number of shares that must be sold. Dividing the total number of shares outstanding by the total number of shares to be sold will give management the number of rights required to purchase a share of stock.

EXAMPLE   Lorne Company, a closely owned hand-tool manufacturer, intends to raise $1 million through a rights offering. The firm currently has 160,000 shares outstanding, which have been most recently trading for $53 to $58 per share. The company has consulted an investment banking firm, which has recommended setting the subscription price for the rights at $50 per share. It believes that at this price the offering will be fully subscribed. The firm must therefore sell an additional 20,000 shares ($1,000,000 ÷ $50 per share). This means that 8 rights (160,000 ÷ 20,000) will be needed to purchase a new share at $50. Each right will entitle its holder to purchase one-eighth of a share of common stock.

Value of a Right

Theoretically, the value of a right should be the same if the stock is selling *with rights* or *ex rights*. In either case, the market value of a right may differ from its theoretical value.

With Rights   Once a rights offering has been declared, shares will trade with rights for only a few days. Equation 20.2 is used to find the theoretical value of a right when the stock is trading with rights, R_w:

$$R_w = \frac{M_w - S}{N + 1}$$

where

    R_w = theoretical value of a right when stock is selling with rights
   M_w = market value of the stock with rights
     S = subscription price of the stock
     N = number of rights needed to purchase one share of stock

EXAMPLE   Lorne Company's stock is currently selling with rights at a price of $54.50 per share, the subscription price is $50 per share, and 8 rights are required to purchase a new share of stock. According to Equation 20.2, the value of a right is $.50 [($54.50 − $50.00) ÷ (8 + 1)]. A right should therefore be worth $.50 in the marketplace.

Ex Rights   When a share of stock is traded ex rights, meaning that the value of the right is no longer included in the stock's market price, the share price of the stock is expected to drop by the value of a right. Equation 20.3 is used to find the market value of the stock trading ex rights, M_e. The same notation is used as in Equation 20.2:

$$M_e = M_w - R_w$$

The theoretical value of a right when the stock is trading ex rights, R_e, is given by Equation 20.4:

$$R_e = \frac{M_e - S}{N}$$

The use of these equations can be illustrated by returning to the Lorne Company example.

EXAMPLE   According to Equation 20.3, the market price of the Lorne Company stock selling ex rights is $54 ($54.50 − $.50). Substituting this value into Equation 20.4 gives the value of a right when the stock is selling ex rights, which is $.50 [($54.00 − $50.00) ÷ 8]. The theoretical value of the right when the stock is selling with rights or ex rights is therefore the same.

Market Behavior of Rights

As indicated earlier, stock rights are negotiable instruments, often traded on securities exchanges. The market price of a right will generally differ from its theoretical value. The extent to which it will differ depends on how the firm's stock price is expected to behave during the period when the right is exercisable. By buying rights instead of the

Equation 20.2
Formula for the theoretical value of a right when the stock is trading *with rights*

Equation 20.3
Formula for the market value of stock trading ex rights

Equation 20.4
Formula for the theoretical value of a right when the stock is trading ex *rights*

stock itself, investors can achieve much higher returns on their money when stock prices rise.

Advantages and Disadvantages of Common Stock

A number of key advantages and disadvantages of common stock are often cited.

Advantages

The basic advantages of common stock stem from the fact that it is a source of financing that places a *minimum of constraints* on the firm. Since dividends do *not* have to be paid on common stock and their nonpayment does not jeopardize the receipt of payment by other security holders, common stock financing is quite attractive. The fact that common stock has *no maturity*, thereby eliminating a future repayment obligation, also enhances its desirability as a form of financing. Another advantage of common stock over other forms of long-term financing is its *ability to increase the firm's borrowing power*. The more common stock a firm sells, the larger its equity base and therefore the more easily and cheaply long-term debt financing can be obtained.

Disadvantages

The disadvantages of common stock financing include the *potential dilution of earnings*. Clearly, when additional shares are issued, more shares have a claim on the firm's earnings. This often results in a short-run decline in earnings per share (EPS), which in turn can and often does negatively affect the stock's market price. Another disadvantage of common stock financing is its *high cost*. As we saw in Chapter 13, common stock equity is normally the most expensive form of long-term financing. It is expensive because common stock is a riskier security than either debt or preferred stock and because dividends are not tax-deductible.

 INTERNATIONAL DIMENSION: EQUITY CAPITAL

Here we emphasize two major aspects of international equity capital. First, we will look at international capital markets through which multinational companies can raise equity funds. Second, we will focus on the role of equity (versus debt) in the MNCs' foreign direct investment in international joint ventures.

Equity Issues and Markets

One means of raising equity funds for MNCs is to have the parent firm's stock distributed internationally and owned by stockholders of different nationalities. In the 1980s, the world's equity markets became more "internationalized" (i.e., more standardized and thus closer in character to the Eurobond market discussed in Chapter 19). In other words, while distinct *national* stock markets (such as New York, London, and Tokyo) continue to exist and grow, an *international* stock market has also emerged on the global financial scene.

In recent years, the terms **Euro-equity market** and "Euro-equities" have become widely known. While a number of capital markets—including New York, Tokyo, Frankfurt, Zurich, and Paris—play major roles by being hosts to international equity issues, London has become the center of Euro-equity activity. For the year 1989, for instance, the *new issue* volume was close to $12 billion and included 115 offerings. Meanwhile, London's *secondary market* activities in Euro-equities were estimated to have a daily turnover of $2 billion.

As 1992 approaches for the full financial integration of the European Economic Community (EC), some European stock exchanges continue to compete with each other. Others have called for more cooperation in forming a single market capable of competing with New York and Tokyo. From the multinationals' perspective, the most desirable outcome would be to have uniform international rules and regulations with respect to all the major national stock exchanges. Such uniformity would allow MNCs to have unrestricted access to an international equity market paralleling that of the international currency and bond markets.

Euro-equity market
The world capital market, whose center is London, that deals in international equity issues.

Joint Ventures

The basic aspects of foreign ownership of international operations were discussed in Chapter 2. Worth emphasizing here is that certain laws and regulations enacted during the 1960s and 1970s by a number of host countries require MNCs to maintain less than 50 percent ownership in their subsidiaries in most of those countries. For a U.S.-based MNC, for example, establishing foreign subsidiaries in the form of joint ventures means that a certain portion of the firm's total international equity stock is (indirectly) held by foreign owners.

Some of the advantages and disadvantages of joint ventures have previously been highlighted. When establishing a foreign subsidiary, an MNC may wish to have as little equity and as much debt as possible, with the debt coming from local sources in the host country or the MNC itself. Each of these actions can be supported. The host country may allow *more local debt* for a subsidiary than for an MNC; this is a good protective measure in terms of lessening the potential impacts of political risk. In other words, since local sources are involved in the capital structure of a subsidiary, there may be fewer threats from local authorities in the event of changes in government or the enactment of new regulations on foreign business.

In support of the other action—have *more MNC-based debt* in a subsidiary's capital structure—it is true that many host governments are less restrictive, in terms of taxation and actual repatriation, toward intra-MNC interest payments than toward intra-MNC dividend remittances. The parent firm may therefore be in a better position if it has more MNC-based debt than equity in the capital structure of its subsidiaries.

SUMMARY

1   **Differentiate between debt and equity capital in terms of ownership rights, claims on income and assets, maturity, and tax treatment.** Preferred and common stock are external sources of equity (ownership) capital. Holders of common stock have voting rights that permit them to select the firm's directors and vote on special issues; preferred stock and debt capital typically have no voting rights. Preferred and common stockholders have claims on income and assets that are secondary to the claims of creditors, have no maturity date, and do not receive tax benefits similar to those given debtholders.

2   **Understand preferred stock fundamentals—the basic rights of preferred stockholders and the features normally included as part of a preferred stock issue.** Preferred stockholders are given preference over common stockholders with respect to the distribution of earnings and assets. Preferred stock is similar to debt in that though some adjustable-rate (or floating rate) and payment-in-kind (PIK) issues exist, it generally has a fixed annual cash dividend. Because preferred stockholders' claims are given preference over the claims of common stockholders, they do not normally receive voting privileges. Preferred stock issues may have certain restrictive covenants, cumulative dividends, participation in earnings, a call feature, and a conversion feature.

3   **Explain the key advantages and disadvantages of preferred stock financing.** The basic advantages for preferred stock financing include its ability to increase the firm's leverage, the flexibility of the obligation, and its use in corporate restructuring. Disadvantages include the seniority of its claim over that of the common stockholders, its relatively high cost compared to debt financing, and the general difficulty of selling it.

4   **Discuss common stock fundamentals, including important aspects of voting rights.** The common stock of a firm can be privately owned, closely owned, or publicly owned. It can be sold with or without a par value. Not all shares authorized in the corporate charter will be outstanding. If the firm has treasury stock, it will have issued more shares than are outstanding. Some firms issue two or more classes of common stock, with unequal voting rights being their key difference. Proxies can be used to transfer voting rights from one party to another. Either majority voting or cumulative voting may be used by the firm to elect its directors.

5   **Describe stock rights and the key advantages and disadvantages of common stock financing.** Holders of common stock—especially in smaller corporations—may receive stock rights which give them an opportunity to purchase new common stock at a reduced price on a pro rata basis. A certain number of rights is required to purchase the new shares at the reduced price, which causes each right to have a monetary value. Rights may be exercised, sold, purchased, or allowed to expire. Basic advantages of common stock include the minimum of constraints it places on the firm, its lack of a maturity date, and its ability to increase the firm's borrowing power. Disadvantages include the potential dilution of earnings and its high cost.

6   **Review how multinational companies can either sell their shares in international capital markets or through joint ventures in order to raise equity capital abroad.** In the international capital markets the multinational company can have the parent company's stock distributed internationally and owned by stockholders of different nationalities. The stock can trade either in a national stock market or an international stock market—the Euro-equity market, which is centered in London. Many host countries have laws and regulations requiring MNCs to maintain less than 50 percent ownership in their subsidiaries in most of those countries. This causes the U.S.-based MNCs to establish joint ventures, which result in a portion of the firm's total international equity stock being held by foreign owners. To protect against political risk when establishing foreign subsidiaries, it is generally advantageous for the MNC to issue debt (either local or MNC-based) rather than MNC-owned equity.

QUESTIONS

20—1 How do debt and equity capital differ? What are the key differences between them with respect to ownership rights, claims on income and assets, maturity, and tax treatment?

20—2 What is *preferred stock?* What claims do preferred stockholders have with respect to the distribution of earnings (dividends) and assets? What is an *adjustable-rate (or floating-rate) preferred stock (ARPS)?* What is *payment-in-kind (PIK) preferred stock?*

20—3 What are *cumulative* and *noncumulative* preferred stock? Which form is more common? Why?

20—4 What is a *call feature* in a preferred stock issue? When and at what price does the call usually take place? What benefit does the call offer the issuer of preferred stock?

20—5 What are the key advantages and disadvantages of using preferred stock financing as a source of new long-term funds?

20—6 Why is the common stockholder considered the true owner of a firm? What risks do common stockholders take that other suppliers of long-term capital do not?

20—7 What are *proxies?* How are they used? What are *proxy battles,* and why are they initiated? Why is it difficult for minority shareholders to win such battles?

20—8 How do majority and cumulative voting systems differ? Which of these voting systems would be preferred by the minority shareholders? Why?

20—9 What are *stock rights?* What is a right *subscription price?* How is it determined? Given the subscription price, what must the firm know to determine the number of rights to offer?

20—10 Compare the theoretical value of rights when a stock is selling *with rights* with its *ex rights* value. Do these values typically equal their market price? Why?

20—11 What are the key advantages and disadvantages of using common stock financing as a source of new long-term funds?

20—12 What are the long-run advantages of having more *local* debt and less MNC-based equity in the capital structure of a foreign subsidiary?

PROBLEMS

20—1 **(Preferred Dividends)** Pickering, Hardwood, and Rap has an outstanding issue of preferred stock with an $80 par value and an 11 percent annual dividend.

   a. What is the annual dollar dividend? If it is paid quarterly, how much will be paid each quarter?

   b. If the preferred stock is *noncumulative* and the board of directors has passed the preferred dividend for the last three years, how much must be paid to preferred stockholders prior to paying dividends to common stockholders?

c. If the preferred stock is *cumulative* and the board of directors has passed the preferred dividend for the last three years, how much must be paid to preferred stockholders prior to paying dividends to common stockholders?

20—2   **(Preferred Dividends)**   In each case in the following table, how many dollars of preferred dividends per share must be paid to preferred stockholders prior to paying common stock dividends?

Case	Type	Par value ($)	Dividend per share per period	Periods of dividends passed
A	Cumulative	$ 80	$5	2
B	Noncumulative	110	8%	3
C	Noncumulative	100	$11	1
D	Cumulative	60	8.5%	4
E	Cumulative	90	9%	0

20—3   **(Participating Preferred Stock)**   Crumpled Kan Company has outstanding an issue of 3,000 shares of participating preferred stock that has a $100 par value and an 8 percent annual dividend. The preferred stockholders participate fully (on an equal per-share basis) with common stockholders in annual dividends of more than $9 per share for common stock. The firm has 5,000 shares of common stock outstanding.

a. If the firm pays preferred stockholders their dividends and then declares an additional $100,000 in dividends, how much will be the total dividend per share for preferred and common stock, respectively?

b. If the firm pays preferred stockholders their dividends and then declares an additional $40,000 in dividends, what is the total dividend per share for each type of stockholder?

c. If the firm's preferred stock is cumulative and the past two years' dividends have been passed, what dividends will be received by each type of stockholder if the firm declares a *total* dividend of $30,000?

d. Rework **c** assuming that the total dividend payment is $20,000.

e. Rework **a** and **b** assuming that the preferred stock is nonparticipating.

20—4   **(Accounting for Common Stock)**   What accounting entries on the firm's balance sheet would result from the following cases?

a. A firm sells 10,000 shares of $1-par common stock at $13 per share.

b. A firm sells 20,000 shares of $2-par common and receives $100,000.

c. A firm sells 200,000 shares of no-par common stock for $8 million.

d. A firm sells 14,000 shares of common stock for the par value of $5 per share.

20—5   **(Majority versus Cumulative Voting)**   Cobbie's Place, a fast-food franchise, is electing five new directors to its board. The company has 1,000 shares of common stock outstanding. The management, which controls 54 percent of the common shares outstanding, backs candidates A through E; the minority shareholders are backing candidates F through J.

a. If the firm uses a *majority voting system,* how many directors will each group elect?

b. If the firm uses a *cumulative voting system,* how many directors will each group elect?

c. Discuss the differences between these two approaches and the resulting election outcomes.

20—6   **(Majority versus Cumulative Voting)**   Determine the number of directors that can be elected by the *minority shareholders* using (1) majority voting and (2) cumulative voting in each of the following cases.

Case	Number of shares outstanding	Percentage of shares held by minority (%)	Number of directors to be elected
A	140,000	20	3
B	100,000	40	7
C	175,000	30	4
D	880,000	40	5
E	1,000,000	18	9

20—7   **(Number of Rights)**   Indicate (1) how many shares of stock one right is worth and (2) the number of shares a given stockholder, X, can purchase in each of the following cases:

Case	Number of shares outstanding	Number of new shares to be issued	Number of shares held by stockholder X
A	900,000	30,000	600
B	1,400,000	35,000	200
C	800,000	40,000	2,000
D	60,000	12,000	1,200
E	180,000	36,000	1,000

20—8   **(Theoretical Value of Rights)**   Determine the theoretical value of the right when the stock is selling (1) *with rights* and (2) *ex rights* in each of the following cases:

Case	Market value of stock *with rights* ($)	Subscription price of stock ($)	Number of rights needed to purchase one share of stock
A	20.00	17.50	4
B	56.00	50.00	3
C	41.00	30.00	6
D	50.00	40.00	5
E	92.00	82.00	8

20—9   **(Value of a Right)**   Your sister-in-law is a stockholder in a corporation that recently declared a rights offering. In need of cash, she has offered to sell you her rights for 30 cents each. The key data relative to the stock and associated rights are as follows:

Current stock price *with rights*	$37.25/share
Subscription price of stock rights	$36.00/share
Number of rights needed to purchase one share of common stock	4

a. Determine the theoretical value of the rights when the stock is trading *with rights*.
b. Determine the theoretical value of the rights when the stock is trading *ex rights*.
c. Discuss your findings in **a** and **b**. Would it be desirable to accept your sister-in-law's offer?

20—10   **(Sale of Common Equity Using Rights)**   Noonan Energy wishes to raise $5 million in common equity financing using a rights offering. The company has 1,000,000 shares of common stock outstanding that have recently traded for $40 to $43 per share. The firm believes that if the subscription price is set at $40, the shares will be fully subscribed.

a. Determine the number of new shares the firm must sell to raise the desired amount of capital.
b. How many shares will each right entitle a holder of one share to purchase?
c. Rework **a** and **b** assuming that the subscription price is $25.
d. What is the theoretical value of a right if the current market price is $42 *with rights* and the subscription price is $40? Answer for both when the stock is selling *with rights* and *ex rights*.
e. Rework **d** assuming that the subscription price is $25.
f. Which subscription price ($40 or $25) will be more likely to assure complete subscription? Why?

20—11   **(Sale of Common Equity Using Rights)**   Scroll Paper Corporation is interested in raising $600,000 of new equity capital through a rights offering. The firm currently has 300,000 shares of common stock outstanding. It expects to set the subscription price at $25 and anticipates that the stock will sell for $29 *with rights*.

a. Calculate the number of new shares the firm must sell to raise the desired amount of funds.
b. How many rights will be needed to purchase one share of stock at the subscription price?
c. Cogburn Jones holds 48,000 shares of Scroll Paper common stock. If he exercises his rights, how many additional shares can he purchase?
d. Determine the theoretical value of a right when the stock is selling (1) *with rights* and (2) *ex rights*.
e. Approximately how much could Jones get for his rights immediately after the stock goes *ex rights?*
f. If the date of record for Scroll Paper Corporation was Monday, March 15, on what dates would the stock sell (1) *with rights* and (2) *ex rights?*

CASE

Financing Lobo Enterprises'
$23 Million Expansion Program

Lobo Enterprises, located in Albuquerque, New Mexico, is a diversified media company. Its after-tax profits have risen continuously through 1992, 12 years since Lobo first went public. Although a few years ago Lobo reduced its long-term debt from 85 percent to 70 percent of total capital, its equity base remains quite small. The debt carries an average annual interest rate of 11.7 percent before taxes. The debt reduction was partially financed through issuance of $7.7 million of 10 percent (annual dividend) preferred stock. On June 30, 1992, current assets were $55 million, current liabilities totaled $21 million, and net working capital was $34 million. Earnings before interest and taxes (EBIT) for the 1992 fiscal year amounted to $20 million. The firm is in the 40 percent tax bracket.

Currently, the directors must decide upon a method of financing the firm's $23 million expansion program. The directors are primarily interested in an equity financing plan since funds could be obtained without incurring added mandatory interest payments that would result in greater risk. Additional equity would allow Lobo to avoid restrictive covenants often tied to debt financing and would provide a more flexible foundation from which debt could be issued when interest rates fall. The decision, however, could result in lowering earnings per share (EPS) as well as diluting the current stockholder's control of the company. Jonathan Marks, the chief financial officer, presented to the executive committee the capital structure alternatives shown on the following page. He expects additional debt to have a before-tax cost of 11.7 percent, additional preferred stock will pay a 10 percent annual dividend, and EBIT will remain at the $20 million level. The committee must now weigh the advantages, costs, and risks of each plan.

Required

a. Discuss the overall advantages of equity financing for this firm at this time.

b. Discuss the advantages and disadvantages of selling preferred stock.

c. Discuss the advantages and disadvantages of selling common stock. (Be sure to discuss EPS effects.)

d. (1) Marks is also considering a rights offering to raise equity funds. With rights the price of the common stock is $50 per share, the subscription price per share is $43.50, and nine rights are required to purchase a share of stock. Determine the theoretical value of a right.

(2) Discuss the advantages and disadvantages of the proposed rights offering versus the public sale of new common stock.

e. (1) Calculate the (a) debt ratio, (b) times interest earned ratio, and (c) fixed-payment coverage ratio (assuming no principal repayments) for the current as well as each alternative capital structure.

(2) Use your finding in **(1)** to compare and contrast the financial leverage and risk of each alternative capital structure.

f. Recommend how Lobo should finance its $23 million expansion program. Justify your recommendation in light of the alternatives.

Lobo Enterprises' Capital Structure Alternatives

Capital structures	Amount (millions)	Percent of total capital
Current structure		
Long-term debt	$ 53.9	70.0%
Preferred stock	7.7	10.0
Common stock equity (906,000 shares)	15.4	20.0
Total capital	$ 77.0	100.0%
Structure A		
Long-term debt	$ 70.0	70.0%
Preferred stock	10.0	10.0
Common stock equity (998,000 shares)	20.0	20.0
Total capital	$100.0	100.0%
Structure B		
Long-term debt	$ 53.9	53.9%
Preferred stock	7.7	7.7
Common stock equity (1,366,000 shares)	38.4	38.4
Total capital	$100.0	100.0%
Structure C		
Long-term debt	$ 53.9	53.9%
Preferred stock	30.7	30.7
Common stock equity (906,000 shares)	15.4	15.4
Total capital	$100.0	100.0%
Structure D		
Long-term debt	$ 53.9	53.9%
Preferred stock	23.0	23.0
Common stock equity (1,060,000 shares)	23.1	23.1
Total capital	$100.0	100.0%

CHAPTER 21

CONVERTIBLES, WARRANTS, AND OPTIONS

CHAPTER OBJECTIVES

After studying this chapter, you should be able to:

1 Describe the basic types of convertible securities and their general features, including the conversion ratio, conversion period, and conversion (or stock) value.

2 Discuss the key motives for convertible financing, the considerations involved in forcing conversion, and the difficulties associated with overhanging issues.

3 Demonstrate the procedures for determining the straight bond value, conversion (or stock) value, and market value of a convertible bond.

4 Explain the basic characteristics of stock-purchase warrants and compare them with rights and convertibles.

5 Calculate the theoretical value of a warrant and use its market value to determine the warrant premium.

6 Define options and discuss the basics of calls and puts, options markets, options trading, and the role of call and put options in managerial finance.

" The treatment . . .
consisted of issuing
both preferred and
common stock. **"**

Attempting to Cure Citicorp's Ills with Convertible Preferred Stock

As the biggest bank in the United States, Citicorp has long received the kind of attention given by a specialist to his or her patient. A look through the x-ray machine in 1991 would have disclosed a sick corporation. Citicorp's biggest complaint was its commercial loan portfolio. Almost 20 percent of the portfolio—$2.6 billion—was nonperforming. Citicorp was in need of well over one billion dollars.

Recognizing its poor health, Citicorp had slashed expenses through the layoff of 8,000 employees. Efforts were underway to get capital through the sale of its municipal-bond insurance firm. But, no one was willing to meet the $900 million asking price. Citicorp also considered the sale of its huge and profitable credit card business, but feared the cure might cause more harm than good.

Moody's was the first to react to Citicorp's condition. Especially damaging was Moody's rating of Citicorp's existing preferred stock to a level just below investment grade. High-quality junk bonds with a similar rating yielded about 14 percent. Given the amount sought, the cost of boosting the coupon even 1 percent would increase Citicorp's annual interest expense by millions.

The treatment chosen by Citicorp Chairman Reed consisted of issuing both preferred and common stock. The timing could not have been worse: investors were avoiding the ailing banking industry. Citicorp sought financial relief worldwide, without success. Then, after interviewing a number of investment bankers, Citicorp selected Morgan Stanley to help in its recovery.

Morgan Stanley's prescription consisted of privately placing $1.5 billion of callable convertible preferred stock and later selling the common stock. The convertible feature was used to minimize the annual cost of preferred stock. The conversion price was set 15 percent above Citicorp's stock price. The conversion feature was expected to benefit Citicorp in two ways. First, the preferred issue was expected to be priced to yield investors a return of approximately 10 percent (2 percent below Citicorp's outstanding straight preferred stock). Citicorp's annual savings from the lower yield would be about $30 million. Second, after its price rebounded, Citicorp would be able to sell stock at a higher price than it was currently trading in the stock market.

Although a full recovery was still uncertain six months later, Citicorp reported an easing of financing problems, and share prices were up 21 percent.

Chapters 19 and 20 presented the various methods of raising long-term financing externally—term loans, bonds, leasing, preferred stock, and common stock. In addition, three vehicles—the conversion feature, stock-purchase warrants, and options—are available for use by the firm in its long-term financing activities.

The *conversion feature*, which can be part of either a bond or preferred stock, permits the firm's capital structure to be changed without increasing the total financing. *Stock-purchase warrants* can be attached to either a long-term loan or a bond. They permit the firm to raise additional funds at some point in the future by selling common stock, thereby shifting the company's capital structure to a less highly levered position. *Options* are a special type of security that provide the holder with the right to purchase or sell specified assets at a stated price on or before a set expiration date. Here we focus on the characteristics and role in long-term financing of convertibles, warrants, and options.

CHARACTERISTICS OF CONVERTIBLE SECURITIES

A **conversion feature** is an option included as part of a bond or a preferred stock issue that permits its holder to convert the security into a specified number of shares of common stock. The conversion feature typically enhances the marketability of an issue.

conversion feature
An option included as part of a bond or a preferred stock issue that permits its holder to convert the security into a specified number of shares of common stock.

Types of Convertible Securities

Corporate bonds and preferred stocks may be convertible into common stock. The most common type of convertible security is the bond. Convertibles normally have an accompanying *call feature*. This feature permits the issuer to retire or encourage conversion of outstanding convertibles when appropriate.

Convertible Bonds

A **convertible bond** is a bond that at some future time can be converted into a specified number of shares of common stock. It is almost always a *debenture*—an unsecured bond—with a call feature. Because the conversion feature provides the purchaser of a convertible bond with the possibility of becoming a stockholder on favorable terms, convertible bonds are generally a less expensive form of financing than similar-risk nonconvertible or **straight bonds.** The conversion feature adds a degree of speculation to a bond issue, although the issue still maintains its value as a bond. Convertible bonds are normally convertible only for a specified period of years.

convertible bond A bond that at some future time can be converted into a specified number of shares of common stock.

straight bond A bond that has no conversion feature.

Convertible Preferred Stock

convertible preferred stock   Preferred stock that at some future time can be converted into a specified number of shares of common stock.

straight preferred stock   Preferred stock that has no conversion feature.

Convertible preferred stock is preferred stock that at some future time can be converted into a specified number of shares of common stock. It can normally be sold with a lower stated dividend than a similar-risk nonconvertible or **straight preferred stock.** The reason is that the convertible preferred holder is assured of the fixed dividend payment associated with a preferred stock and also may receive the appreciation resulting from increases in the market price of the underlying common stock. Convertible preferred stocks are usually convertible over an unlimited time horizon. Although convertible preferred stock behaves in a fashion similar to convertible bonds, the following discussions will concentrate on the more popular convertible bonds.

General Features of Convertibles

The general features of convertible securities include the conversion ratio, the conversion period, and the conversion (or stock) value.

Conversion Ratio

conversion ratio   The ratio at which a convertible security can be exchanged for common stock.

The **conversion ratio** is the ratio at which a convertible security can be exchanged for common stock. The conversion ratio can be stated in two ways.

1 ▰ Sometimes the conversion ratio is stated by indicating that the security is convertible into a given number of shares of common stock. In this situation the conversion ratio is *given*. To find the **conversion price,** which is the per-share price effectively paid for common stock as the result of conversion, the par value (not the market value) of the convertible security must be divided by the conversion ratio.

conversion price   The per-share price effectively paid for common stock as the result of conversion of a convertible security.

EXAMPLE   Western Company, a manufacturer of denim products, has outstanding a bond with a $1,000 par value and convertible into 25 shares of common stock. The bond's conversion ratio is 25. The conversion price for the bond is $40 per share ($1,000 ÷ 25).

2 ▰ Sometimes, instead of the conversion ratio, the conversion price is given. The conversion ratio can be obtained by dividing the par value of the convertible by the conversion price.

EXAMPLE   Ginsberg Company, a franchisor of seafood restaurants, has outstanding a convertible 20-year bond with a par value of $1,000. The bond is convertible at $50 per share into common stock. The conversion ratio is 20 ($1,000 ÷ $50).

The issuer of a convertible security normally establishes a conversion ratio or conversion price that sets the conversion price per share at the time of issuance above the current market price of the firm's stock. If the prospective purchasers do not expect conversion ever to be feasible, they will purchase a straight security or some other convertible issue. A predictable chance of conversion must be provided for in order to enhance the marketability of a convertible security.

Conversion Period

Convertible securities are often convertible only within or after a certain period of time. Sometimes conversion is not permitted until two to five years have passed. In other instances conversion is permitted only for a limited number of years, say for five or ten years after issuance of the convertible. Other issues are convertible at any time during the life of the security.

Conversion (or Stock) Value

The **conversion (or stock) value** is the value of the convertible measured in terms of the market price of the common stock into which it can be converted. The conversion value can be found simply by multiplying the conversion ratio by the current market price of the firm's common stock.

conversion (or stock) value The value of a convertible security as measured by the market price of the common stock into which it can be converted.

EXAMPLE   Sperling Company, a petroleum processor, has outstanding a $1,000 bond that is convertible into common stock at $62.50 a share. The conversion ratio is therefore 16 ($1,000 ÷ $62.50). Since the current market price of the common stock is $65 per share, the conversion value is $1,040 (16 × $65). Since the conversion value is above the bond value of $1,000, conversion is a viable option for the owner of the convertible security.

Motives for Convertible Financing

Using convertible securities to raise long-term funds can help the firm achieve its cost of capital and capital structure goals (see Chapters 13 and 16, respectively). Specifically, convertibles can be used as a form of deferred common stock financing, as a "sweetener" for financing, and for raising temporarily cheap funds.

Deferred Common Stock Financing

The use of convertible securities provides for future common stock financing. When a convertible security is issued, both issuer and purchaser expect the security to be converted into common stock at some point in the future. If the purchaser did not have this expectation, he or she would not accept the lower interest rate normally associated with convertible issues. Since the security is first sold with a conversion price above the current market price of the firm's stock, conversion is initially not attractive.

The issuer of a convertible alternatively could sell common stock, but only at or below its current market price. By selling the convertible, the issuer in effect makes a *deferred sale* of common stock. As the market price of the firm's common stock rises to a higher level, conversion may occur. By deferring the issuance of new common stock until the market price of the stock has increased, the firm will have to issue fewer shares, thereby minimizing the *dilution of ownership*. This benefit of using convertible securities as a form of deferred common stock financing can be illustrated by the following example.

EXAMPLE   Mitton Manufacturing Company, a producer of lighting fixtures, needs $1 million of new long-term financing. The firm is considering the sale of either common stock or a convertible bond. The current market price of the common stock is $20 per share. To sell the new issue, the stock would have to be underpriced by $1 and sold for $19 per share. This means that approximately 52,632 shares ($1,000,000 ÷ $19 per share) would have to be sold. The alternative would be to issue 30-year, 12 percent (coupon interest rate), $1,000 par-value convertible bonds. The conversion price would be set at $25 per share, and the bond could be sold at par (for $1,000). Thus 1,000 bonds ($1,000,000 ÷ $1,000 per bond) would have to be sold. The firm currently has outstanding 200,000 shares of common stock. Most recently the earnings available for common stock were $500,000 or $2.50 per share ($500,000 ÷ 200,000 shares).

If we assume that the earnings available for common stock will remain at the $500,000 level, the dilution benefit of using a convertible security to defer common stock financing can easily be illustrated. The earnings per share with both common stock financing and a convertible bond are given in the following table.

Financing alternative	Number of shares outstanding	Earnings per share
Common stock	252,632	$1.98
Convertible bond		
Before conversion	200,000	$2.50[a]
After conversion[b]	240,000	$2.08

[a]To simplify this example, the additional interest expense on the convertible bond has been ignored.
[b]Assuming that all bonds are converted.

After conversion of the convertible bond, 40,000 additional shares of common stock are outstanding. The use of the convertible bond has not only resulted in a smaller dilution of earnings per share ($2.08 per share versus $1.98 per share) but also in a smaller number of shares outstanding (240,000 versus 252,632), thereby preserving the voting control of the owners.

A "Sweetener" for Financing

The conversion feature often makes a bond issue more attractive to the purchaser. Since the purchaser is given an opportunity to become a common stockholder and share in the firm's future success, *convertibles can normally be sold with lower interest rates than nonconvertibles.* Therefore, from the firm's viewpoint, including a conversion feature reduces the effective interest cost of debt. The purchaser of the issue sacrifices a portion of his or her interest return for the potential opportunity to become a common stockholder in the future.

Raising Temporarily Cheap Funds

By using convertible bonds, the firm can temporarily raise debt, which is typically less expensive than common stock (see Chapter 13), to finance projects. Once such projects are on line, the firm may wish to shift its capital structure to a less highly levered position. A conversion feature gives the issuer the opportunity, through actions of convertible holders, to shift its capital structure at a future point in time.

Other Considerations

Two other considerations with respect to convertible security issues require discussion—forcing conversion and overhanging issues.

Forcing Conversion

When the price of the firm's common stock rises above the conversion price, the market price of the convertible security will normally rise to a level close to its conversion value. When this happens, many convertible holders will not convert since they already have the market price benefit obtainable from conversion and can still receive fixed periodic interest payments. Because of this behavior, virtually all convertible securities have a *call feature* that enables the issuer to encourage or *"force" conversion.* The call price of the security generally exceeds the security's par value by an amount equal to one year's stated interest on the security. Although the issuer must pay a premium for calling a security, the call privilege is generally not exercised until the conversion value of the security is 10 to 15 percent *above the call price.* This type of premium above the call price helps to assure the issuer that when the call is made, the holders of the convertible will convert it instead of accepting the call price.

EXAMPLE   Armstead Company, a textile distributor, currently has outstanding a 12 percent (coupon interest rate), $1,000 convertible bond. The bond is convertible into 50 shares of common stock at a conversion price of $20 per share ($1,000 ÷ 50 shares) and callable at $1,120. Since the bond is convertible into 50 shares of common stock, calling it would be equivalent to paying each bondholder $22.40 per share ($1120 ÷ 50 shares). If the firm issues the call when the stock

ETHICS   IN   FINANCE

Controlling Convertible Risk at Carnival Cruise Lines

Carnival Cruise Lines, Inc., the world's largest cruise line in terms of number of passengers, took several steps to remain the cruise leader during 1990. Among the steps taken were the acquisition of a resort and a new ship, and the refurbishing of another vessel. To finance these projects, $200 million in cash was raised through an offering of 15-year, zero-coupon convertible bonds.

Since the recreation industry is more sensitive to general economic conditions than the average firm—Carnival's beta was 1.20—investors tend to charge a risk premium even in stable periods. Higher fuel costs and lower-than-expected occupancy rates at the new Crystal Palace suggested that the market might charge Carnival an even higher risk premium. To placate bondholders, Carnival included a convertible zero-coupon provision in the bond indenture.

The Carnival Cruise Line bonds, like other zeros, sold at a deep discount from their par value. However, the discount would have been greater had the bondholders not had the option of converting into common stock at any time prior to the bond's maturity. The yield to maturity on the zeros was less than 10 percent. Furthermore, being a zero-coupon convertible, Carnival Cruise Lines obtained financing without burdening its cash flow with periodic interest payments. Bear, Sterns & Co., who had managed Carnival Cruises' offering, expects many similar varieties of debt-equity issues to be offered during the 1990s.

Source: "What risk? These clever debt instruments can soothe the nerves of today's anxious lenders," *Business Month*, September 1990, p. 78

is selling for $24 per share, a convertible bondholder is likely to take the $1,120 instead of converting the bond even though he or she realizes only $22.40 per share instead of $24. The holder recognizes that the stock price is likely to drop as soon as the conversion occurs. Also, if the holder wishes to sell the stock after conversion, he or she will have to pay brokerage fees and taxes on the transaction.

If the Armstead Company waited until the market price exceeded the call price by 10 to 15 percent—if, say, the call was made when the market price of the stock reached $25—most of the convertible holders would probably convert the bond. The market price of $25 per share would be approximately 11.6 percent above the call price per share of $22.40—high enough to cover any movements in the stock price or brokerage fees and taxes associated with conversion. At least 30 days' advance notice is normally given prior to a call.

Overhanging Issues

There are instances when the market price of a security does not reach a level sufficient to stimulate the conversion of associated convertibles. A convertible security that cannot be forced into conversion using the call feature is called an **overhanging issue.** An overhanging issue can be quite detrimental to a firm. If the firm were to call the issue, the bondholders would accept the call price rather than convert the bonds and effectively pay an excessive price for the stock. In this case not only would the firm have to pay the call premium, but it also would require additional financing to pay for the call itself. If the firm raised these funds through the sale of equity, a large number of shares would have to be issued due to their low market price. This, in turn, could result in the dilution of existing ownership. Another source of financing the call would be the use of debt or preferred stock, but this use would leave the firm's capital structure no less levered than prior to the call. An example can be used to demonstrate the problems associated with an overhanging issue.

overhanging issue
A convertible security that cannot be forced into conversion using the call feature.

EXAMPLE   Armstead Company's 12 percent (coupon interest rate), $1,000 convertible bond described in the preceding example is convertible into 50 shares of common stock at a conversion price of $20 per share, and callable at $1,120. At the $1,120 call price, calling the bonds would be equivalent to paying each bondholder $22.40 per share ($1,120 ÷ 50 shares). If the common stock were selling for less than this amount, say at $21 per share, and the firm wished to force conversion, such an action would be impossible. Calling the bond would *not* force conversion since the bondholders would accept the $1,120 call price rather than the 50 shares of common stock which would be worth only $1,050 ($21 per share × 50 shares). Furthermore, the firm would have to finance the call by selling common stock, additional bonds, or preferred stock. Clearly, this convertible bond is an overhanging issue since the firm cannot force its bondholders to convert to common stock.

DETERMINING THE VALUE OF A CONVERTIBLE BOND

The key characteristic of convertible securities that greatly enhances their marketability is their ability to minimize the possibility of a loss while providing a possibility of capital gains. Here we discuss the three values of a convertible bond: (1) the straight bond value, (2) the conversion (or stock) value, and (3) the market value.

Straight Bond Value

straight bond value
The price at which a convertible bond would sell in the market without the conversion feature.

The **straight bond value** of a convertible bond is the price at which it would sell in the market without the conversion feature. This value is found by determining the value of a nonconvertible bond with similar payments issued by a firm having the same risk. The straight bond value is typically the *floor*, or minimum, price at which the convertible bond would be traded. The straight bond value equals the present value of the bond's interest and principal payments discounted at the interest rate the firm would have to pay on a nonconvertible bond.

EXAMPLE   Rich Company, a southeastern discount store chain, has just sold a $1,000, 20-year convertible bond with a 12 percent coupon interest rate. The bond interest will be paid at the end of each year, and the principal will be repaid at maturity.[1] A straight bond could have been sold with a 14 percent coupon interest rate, but the conversion feature compensates for the lower rate on the convertible. The straight bond value of the convertible is calculated as shown in the table below.

Year(s)	Payments (1)	Present-value interest factor at 14 percent (2)	Present value [(1) × (2)] (3)
1–20	$ 120[a]	6.623[b]	$794.76
20	1,000	.073[c]	73.00
		Straight bond value	$867.76

[a]$1,000 at 12% = $120 interest per year.
[b]Present-value interest factor for an annuity, *PVIFA*, discounted at 14% for 20 years, from Table C-4.
[c]Present-value interest factor for $1, *PVIF*, discounted at 14% for year 20, from Table C-3.

This value, $867.76, is the minimum price at which the convertible bond is expected to sell. (The calculated value using a business calculator is $867.54.) Generally, only in certain instances where the stock's market price is below the conversion price will the bond be expected to sell at this level.

Conversion (or Stock) Value

The *conversion (or stock) value* of a convertible security was defined earlier as the value of the convertible measured in terms of the market

---

[1]Consistent with Chapter 12, we continue to assume the payment of annual rather than semiannual bond interest. This assumption simplifies the calculations involved while maintaining the conceptual accuracy of the procedures presented.

price of the common stock into which the security can be converted. When the market price of the common stock exceeds the conversion price, the conversion (or stock) value exceeds the par value. An example will clarify the point.

EXAMPLE   Rich Company's convertible bond described above is convertible at $50 per share. This means each bond can be converted into 20 shares, since each bond has a $1,000 par value. The conversion values of the bond when the stock is selling at $30, $40, $50, $60, $70, and $80 per share are shown in the following table.

Market price of stock	Conversion value
$30	$ 600
40	800
50 (conversion price)	1,000 (par value)
60	1,200
70	1,400
80	1,600

When the market price of the common stock exceeds the $50 conversion price, the conversion value exceeds the $1,000 par value. Since the straight bond value (calculated in the preceding example) is $867.76, the bond will, in a stable environment, never sell for less than this amount, regardless of how low its conversion value is. If the market price per share were $30, the bond would still sell for $867.76—not $600—because its value as a bond would dominate.

Market Value

The market value of a convertible is likely to be greater than its straight value or its conversion value. The amount by which the market value exceeds its straight or conversion value is called the **market premium.** The closer the straight value is to the conversion value, the larger the market premium. The premium is attributed to the convertible security purchaser's expectations relative to future stock price movements. The general relationship of the straight bond value, conversion value, market value, and market premium for Rich Company's convertible bond is shown in Figure 21.1. The straight bond value acts as a floor for the security's value up to the point X. At that point the stock price is high enough to cause the conversion value to exceed the straight bond value. The market value of the convertible often exceeds both its straight and conversion values, thus resulting in a market premium.

market premium The amount by which the market value of a convertible security exceeds its straight or conversion value.

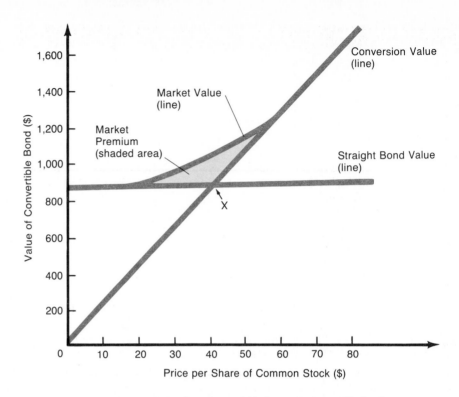

Figure 21.1 The Values and Market Premium for Rich Company's Convertible Bond
The $867.76 straight value of Rich Company's convertible bond acts as a floor for its value up to point X. At that point the stock price is high enough to cause the conversion value to exceed the straight bond value. The market value of the convertible exceeds these values, creating a market premium.

CHARACTERISTICS OF STOCK-PURCHASE WARRANTS

stock-purchase warrant An instrument that gives its holder an option to purchase a certain number of shares of common stock at a specified price over a certain period of time.

Stock-purchase warrants are quite similar to stock rights, which were described in detail in Chapter 20. A **stock-purchase warrant** gives the holder an option to purchase a certain number of shares of common stock at a specified price over a certain period of time. Warrants also bear some similarity to convertibles in that they provide for the injection of additional equity capital into the firm at some future date. Some of the basic characteristics of stock-purchase warrants are discussed here.

Warrants as "Sweeteners"

Warrants are often attached to debt issues as "sweeteners," or added benefits. When a firm makes a large bond issue, the attachment of stock-purchase warrants may add to the marketability of the issue while lowering the required interest rate. As sweeteners, warrants are similar to

CAREERS   IN   FINANCE

Improving Leader Performance with Phantom-Warrants at Clean Cut, Inc.

Clean Cut, Inc., is a 75-employee landscape maintenance business based in Austin, Texas. Employees work in teams headed by a leader who deals with customers and supervises a five-member team. Being a dirty-hands business, these team leaders tend to be lunch-bucket guys with a knack for managing people. Yet, they make the on-site decisions that determine if a job comes in over or under budget.

Management was in search of a reward system that would encourage these managers. Low profit margins and few barriers to entry in the industry, however, limited Clean Cut's options. A profit-sharing plan could provide the needed incentive. But there was the risk that team leaders might take short-cuts to boost profits at the expense of customer service. Over the long term the company's reputation and prospects could suffer. Furthermore, management wanted to maintain complete ownership of the company's stock.

Clean Cut's solution was to offer phantom-warrants to team leaders. Team leaders could use a portion of the profits their crew generated to buy a stake in their own crew's growth. [Since maintenance teams work independently, Clean Cut's management could value the revenue stream of each crew.]

It also was uncommon for individual leaders to have much money available for investment. Consequently, in a paper transaction, Clean Cut essentially lent the desired investment amount to the leader.

Instead of receiving profit-sharing bonuses, leaders invested in a personally controllable percentage of the firm at a fixed price. The value of the leader's position increased if the leader was able to keep clients happy and attract new business. When leaving Clean Cut employment, leaders would sell their position to Clean Cut which would appraise the value of the crew's business and give the leader the percentage he or she had earned through investment of crew profits. These phantom-warrants encouraged leaders to maximize profits but not jeopardize customer service, which was essential to the company's long-term growth.

Source: Tom Richman, "Winning teams," *Inc.,* February 1991, pp. 92–93.

conversion features. Often, when a new firm is raising its initial capital, suppliers of debt will require warrants to permit them to share in whatever success the firm achieves.

Exercise Prices

exercise price (or option price) The price at which holders of warrants can purchase a specified number of shares of common stock.

The price at which holders of warrants can purchase a specified number of shares of common stock is normally referred to as the **exercise price (or option price).** This price is normally set 10 to 20 percent above the market price of the firm's stock at the time of issuance. Until the market price of the stock exceeds the exercise price, holders of warrants would not be advised to exercise them, since they could purchase the stock more cheaply in the marketplace.

Life of a Warrant

Warrants normally have a life of no more than 10 years, although some have infinite lives. While, unlike convertible securities, warrants cannot be called, their limited life stimulates holders to exercise them when the exercise price is below the market price of the firm's stock.

Warrant Trading

A warrant is usually *detachable*, which means that the bondholder may sell the warrant without selling the security to which it is attached. Many detachable warrants are listed and actively traded on organized securities exchanges and on the over-the-counter exchange. The majority of actively traded warrants are listed on the American Stock Exchange. Warrants, as demonstrated in a later section, often provide investors with better opportunities for gain (with increased risk) than the underlying common stock.

Comparison of Warrants and Rights

The similarity between a warrant and a right should be clear. Both result in new equity capital, although the warrant provides for *deferred* equity financing. The life of a right is typically not more than a few months; a warrant is generally exercisable for a period of years. Rights are issued at a subscription price below the prevailing market price of the stock; warrants are generally issued at an exercise price 10 to 20 percent above the prevailing market price.

Comparison of Warrants and Convertibles

The exercise of a warrant shifts the firm's capital structure to a less highly levered position because new common stock is issued without any change in debt. If a convertible bond were converted, the reduction in leverage would be even more pronounced, since common stock would be issued in exchange for a reduction in debt. In addition, the exercise of a warrant provides an influx of new capital; with convertibles the new capital is raised when the securities are originally issued rather than when converted. The influx of new equity capital resulting from the exercise of a warrant does not occur until the firm has achieved a certain degree of success that is reflected in an increased price for its stock. In this instance, the firm conveniently obtains needed funds.

THE VALUE OF WARRANTS

Like a convertible security, a warrant has both a market and a theoretical value. The difference between these values, or the **warrant premium,** depends largely on investor expectations and the ability of investors to get more leverage from the warrants than from the underlying stock.

warrant premium
The difference between the actual market value and the theoretical value of a warrant.

Theoretical Value of a Warrant

The *theoretical value* of a stock-purchase warrant is the amount one would expect the warrant to sell for in the marketplace. Equation 21.1 give the theoretical value of a warrant:

$$TVW = (P_o - E) \times N$$

where

TVW = theoretical value of a warrant

P_o = current market price of a share of common stock

E = exercise price of the warrant

N = number of shares of common stock obtainable with one warrant

The use of Equation 21.1 can be illustrated by the following example.

Equation 21.1
Formula for the theoretical value of a stock-purchase warrant

EXAMPLE   LK Electronics, a major producer of transistors, has outstanding warrants that are exercisable at $40 per share and entitle holders to purchase three shares of common stock. The warrants were initially attached to a bond issue to sweeten the bond. The common stock of the firm is currently selling for $45 per share. Substituting $P_o = \$45$, $E = \$40$, and $N = 3$ into Equation 21.1 yields a theoretical warrant value of $15 [($45 − $40) × 3]. Therefore, LK's warrants should sell for $15 in the marketplace.

Market Value of a Warrant

The market value of a stock-purchase warrant is generally above the theoretical value of the warrant. Only when the theoretical value of the warrant is very high are the market and theoretical values close. The

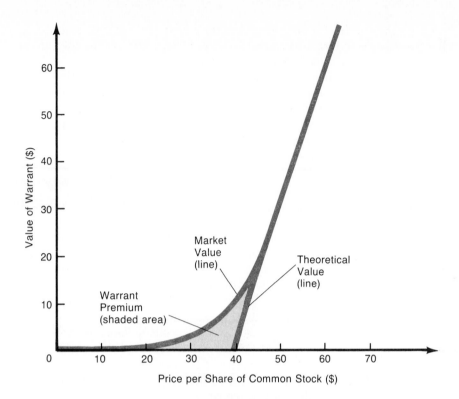

Figure 21.2   **The Values and Warrant Premium
for LK Electronics' Stock-Purchase Warrants**

The theoretical value of LK Electronics' warrants is zero when the
market price of the common stock is below the $40 exercise price, and
greater than zero beyond that point. The market value of the warrant
exceeds the theoretical value, creating a warrant premium.

general relationship between the theoretical and market values of LK
Electronics' warrants is presented graphically in Figure 21.2. The market value of warrants generally exceeds the theoretical value by the
greatest amount when the stock's market price is close to the warrant
exercise price per share.

Warrant Premium

The *warrant premium,* or amount by which the market value of LK Electronics' warrants exceeds the theoretical value of these warrants, is also
shown in Figure 21.2. This premium results from a combination of positive investor expectations and the ability of the investor with a fixed
sum to invest to obtain much larger potential returns (and risk) by trading in warrants rather than the underlying stock. An example will clarify the effect of expected stock price movements and investor leverage
opportunities on warrant market values.

EXAMPLE   John Investor has $2,430 which he is interested in invest-
ing in LK Electronics. The firm's stock is currently selling
for $45 per share, and its warrants are selling for $18 per
warrant. Each warrant entitles the holder to purchase three
shares of LK's common stock at $40 per share. Since the
stock is selling for $45 per share, the theoretical warrant
value, calculated in the preceding example using Equation
21.1, is $15 [($45 − $40) × 3].

The warrant premium is believed to result from positive investor expectations and leverage opportunities. John
Investor could spend his $2,430 in either of two ways. He
could purchase 54 shares of common stock at $45 per share
or 135 warrants at $18 per warrant (ignoring brokerage
fees). If Mr. Investor purchases the stock, its price rises to
$48, and if he then sells the stock, he will gain $162 ($3 per
share × 54 shares). If instead of purchasing the stock he purchases the 135 warrants and the stock price increases by $3
per share, Mr. Investor will make approximately $1,215.
Since the price of a share of stock rises by $3, the price of
each warrant can be expected to rise by $9, since each war-
rant can be used to purchase three shares of common stock.
A gain of $9 per warrant on 135 warrants means a total gain
of $1,215 on the warrants.

The greater leverage associated with trading warrants should be
clear from the preceding example. Of course, since leverage works both
ways it results in greater risk. If the market price fell by $3, the loss on
the stock would be $162, whereas the loss on the warrants would be
close to $1,215. Clearly, the use of warrants by investors is more risky.

OPTIONS

In the most general sense, an **option** can be viewed as an instrument
that gives its holder an opportunity to purchase or sell a specified asset
at a stated price on or before a set *expiration date*. Today the interest in
options centers on common stock options. The development of organized options exchanges has created markets in which to trade these
options, which themselves are securities. Three basic forms of options
are rights, warrants, and calls and puts. Rights were discussed in Chapter 20, and warrants were described in the preceding section.

option An instrument
that gives its holder an
opportunity to purchase
or sell a specified asset
at a stated price on or
before a set *expiration
date*.

Calls and Puts

The two most common types of options are calls and puts. **A call option**
is an option to *purchase* a specified number of shares of a stock (typically 100) on or before some future date at a stated price. Call options
usually have initial lives of one to nine months, occasionally one year.

call option An option
to *purchase* a specified
number of shares of a
stock on or before some
future date at a stated
price.

striking price   The price at which the holder of a call option can buy (or the holder of a put option can sell) a specified amount of stock at any time prior to the option's expiration date.

The **striking price** is the price at which the holder of the option can buy the stock at any time prior to the option's expiration date. This price is generally set at or near the prevailing market price of the stock at the time the option is issued. For example, if the firm's stock is currently selling for $50 per share, a call option on the stock initiated today would likely have a striking price set at $50 per share. To purchase a call option, the investor must pay a specified price of normally a few hundred dollars.

put option   An option to *sell* a given number of shares of a stock on or before some future date at a stated price.

A **put option** is an option to *sell* a given number of shares of a stock (typically 100) on or before a specified future date at a stated striking price. Like the call option, the striking price of the put is close to the market price of the underlying stock at the time of issuance. The lives and costs of puts are similar to those of calls.

How the Options Markets Work

There are two ways of making options transactions. The first involves making a transaction through one of 20 or so call and put options dealers with the help of a stockbroker. The other, more popular mechanism is the organized options exchanges. The dominant exchange is the *Chicago Board Options Exchange (CBOE)*, which was established in 1973. Other exchanges on which options are traded include the American Stock Exchange, the New York Stock Exchange, and several regional stock exchanges. Each exchange provides an organized marketplace in which purchases and sales of both call and put options can be made in an orderly fashion. The options traded on the options exchanges are standardized and are thus considered registered securities. Each option is for 100 shares of the underlying stock. The price at which options transactions can be made is determined by the forces of supply and demand.

Logic of Options Trading

The most common motive for purchasing call options is the expectation that the market price of the underlying stock will rise by more than enough to cover the cost of the option and thereby allow the purchaser of the call to profit.

EXAMPLE   Assume that Sam Peters pays $250 for a three-month *call option* on Altex Corporation, a maker of aircraft components, at a striking price of $50. This means that by paying $250 Sam is guaranteed that he can purchase 100 shares of Altex at $50 per share at any time during the next three months. The stock price must climb $2.50 per share ($250 ÷ 100 shares) to $52.50 per share to cover the cost of the option (ignoring any brokerage fees or dividends). If the stock price were to rise to $60 per share during the period, Sam's net profit would be $750 [(100 shares × $60/share) − (100 shares × \$50/share) − \$250]. Since this return would be earned on a \$250 investment, it illustrates the high potential return on investment that options offer. Of course, had the stock price not risen above \$50 per share, Sam would have lost the \$250 since there would have been no reason to exercise the option. Had the stock price risen to between \$50 and \$52.50 per share, Sam probably would have exercised the option in order to reduce his loss to an amount less than \$250.

Put options are purchased in the expectation that the share price of a given security will decline over the life of the option. Purchasers of puts commonly own the shares and wish to protect a gain they have realized since their initial purchase. By buying a put, they lock in the gain because it enables them to sell their shares at a known price during the life of the option. Investors gain from put options when the price of the underlying stock declines by more than the per-share cost of the option. The logic underlying the purchase of a put is exactly the opposite of that underlying the use of call options.

EXAMPLE   Assume that Dawn Kelly pays \$325 for a six-month *put option* on Allante United, a baked goods manufacturer, at a striking price of \$40. Dawn purchased the put option in expectation that the stock price would drop due to the introduction of a new product line by Allante's chief competitor. By paying \$325 Dawn is assured that she can sell 100 shares of Allante at \$40 per share at any time during the next six months. The stock price must drop by \$3.25 per share (\$325 ÷ 100 shares) to \$36.75 per share to cover the cost of the option (ignoring any brokerage fees or dividends). If the stock price were to drop to \$30 per share during the period, Dawn's net profit would be \$675 [(100 shares × \$40/share) − (100 shares × \$30/share) − \$325]. Since the return would be earned on a \$325 investment, it again illustrates the high potential return on investment that options offer. Of course, had the stock price risen above \$40 per share, Dawn would have lost the \$325 since there would have been no reason to exercise the option. Had the stock price fallen to between \$36.75 and \$40.00 per share, Dawn probably would have exercised the option in order to reduce her loss to an amount less than \$325.

Role of Call and Put Options in Managerial Finance

Although call and put options are extremely popular investment vehicles, they play *no* direct role in the fund-raising activities of the financial manager. These options are issued by investors, not businesses. *They are not a source of financing to the firm.* Corporate pension managers, whose job it is to invest and manage corporate pension funds, may use call and put options as part of their investment activities to earn a return or to protect or lock in returns already earned on securities. The presence of options trading in the firm's stock could—by increasing trading activity—stabilize the firm's share price in the marketplace, but the financial manager has no direct control over this. Buyers of options have neither any say in the firm's management nor any voting rights; only stockholders are given these privileges. Despite the popularity of call and put options as an investment vehicle, the financial manager has very little need to deal with them, especially as part of fund-raising activities.

SUMMARY

1 **Describe the basic types of convertible securities and their general features, including the conversion ratio, conversion period, and conversion (or stock) value.** Corporate bonds and preferred stock may both be convertible into common stock. The conversion ratio indicates the number of shares a convertible can be exchanged for and determines the conversion price. The conversion (or stock) value is the value of the convertible measured in terms of the market price of the common stock into which it can be converted. A conversion privilege may have a limited life.

2 **Discuss the key motives for convertible financing, the considerations involved in forcing conversion, and the difficulties associated with overhanging issues.** The key motives for the use of convertibles are to obtain deferred common stock financing, to "sweeten" bond issues, and to raise temporarily cheap funds. When conversion becomes attractive the firm may use the call feature to encourage or "force" conversion. When conversion cannot be forced, the firm has an overhanging issue. Such an issue can be detrimental to the firm since there is no economically justifiable way to either force conversion or pay the call price to retire the bonds.

3 **Demonstrate the procedures for determining the straight bond value, conversion (or stock) value, and market value of a convertible bond.** The straight bond value of a convertible is the price at which it would sell in the market without the conversion feature. It typically represents the minimum value at which a convertible will trade. The conversion (or stock) value of the convertible is found by multiplying the conversion ratio by the current market price of the underlying common stock. The market value of a convertible generally exceeds both its straight and conversion values, thereby creating a market premium.

4 **Explain the basic characteristics of stock-purchase warrants and compare them with rights and convertibles.** Stock-purchase warrants are often attached to debt issues to "sweeten" them and lower their interest cost. Warrants, like rights, provide their holders with the privilege of purchasing a certain number of shares of common stock at the specified exercise price. Warrants generally have limited lives, are detachable, and may be listed and traded on securities exchanges. Warrants are similar to stock rights, except that the life of a warrant is generally longer than that of a right, and the exercise price of a warrant is initially set above the underlying stock's current market price. Warrants are also similar to convertibles, but exercising them has a less pronounced effect on the firm's leverage and brings in new funds.

5 **Calculate the theoretical value of a warrant and use its market value to determine the warrant premium.** The theoretical value of a warrant is the amount one would expect it to sell for in the marketplace. It is found by multiplying the difference between the current market price of the stock and the exercise price of the warrant by the number of shares of common stock obtainable with one warrant. The market value of a warrant usually exceeds its theoretical value, creating a warrant premium. The premium results from positive investor expectations and the ability of investors to get more leverage from trading warrants than from trading the underlying stock.

6   **Define options and discuss the basics of calls and puts, options markets, options trading, and the role of call and put options in managerial finance.** An option provides its holder with an opportunity to purchase or sell a specified asset at a stated price on or before a set expiration date. Rights, warrants, and calls and puts are all options. Calls are options to purchase common stock, and puts are options to sell common stock. Options exchanges, such as the Chicago Board Options Exchange (CBOE), provide organized marketplaces in which purchases and sales of both call and put options can be made in an orderly fashion. The options traded on the exchanges are standardized and the price at which they trade is determined by the forces of supply and demand. Call and put options do not play a major role in the fund-raising activities of the financial manager.

QUESTIONS

21—1   What is the *conversion feature?* What types of securities typically have this feature?

21—2   What is a *conversion ratio?* How is it related to the *conversion price?* How are conversion periods commonly described?

21—3   Briefly describe each of the following motives for using convertible financing:
   a. Deferred common stock financing
   b. A "sweetener" for financing
   c. Raising temporarily cheap funds

21—4   When the market price of the stock rises above the conversion price, why may a convertible security *not* be converted? How can the *call feature* be used to force conversion in this situation? What is an *overhanging issue?*

21—5   What is meant by the *straight bond value* of a convertible security? How is this value calculated, and why is it often viewed as a floor for the convertible's value?

21—6   What is the *conversion (or stock) value* of a convertible security? How can the conversion value be calculated if you know the conversion ratio and the current market price of the firm's stock?

21—7   Describe the general relationship among the straight bond value, conversion value, market value, and market premium associated with a convertible bond.

21—8   What are *stock-purchase warrants?* What are the similarities and key differences between the effects of warrants and rights on the firm's capital structure and its ability to raise new capital?

21—9   What are the similarities and key differences between the effects of warrants and convertibles on the firm's capital structure and its ability to raise new capital?

21—10   What is the general relationship between the theoretical and market values of a warrant? In what circumstances are these values quite close? What is a *warrant premium?*

21—11   What is an *option?* Define the *striking price* of an option. Are rights and warrants options?

21—12   Define *calls* and *puts*. What is the logic of buying a call and buying a put?

21—13   What role, if any, do call and put options play in the fund-raising activities of the financial manager?

PROBLEMS

21—1   **(Conversion Price)**   Calculate the conversion price for each of the following convertible bonds.
a. A $1,000-par-value bond convertible into 20 shares of common stock.
b. A $500-par-value bond convertible into 25 shares of common stock.
c. A $1,000-par-value bond convertible into 50 shares of common stock.

21—2   **(Conversion Ratio)**   What is the conversion ratio for each of the following bonds?
a. A $1,000-par-value bond convertible into common stock at $43.75 per share.
b. A $1,000-par-value bond convertible into common stock at $25 per share.
c. A $600-par-value bond convertible into common stock at $30 per share.

21—3   **(Conversion Value)**   What is the conversion (or stock) value of each of the following convertible bonds?
a. A $1,000-par-value bond convertible into 25 shares of common stock. The common stock is currently selling at $50 per share.
b. A $1,000-par-value bond convertible into 12.5 shares of common stock. The common stock is currently selling at $42 per share.
c. A $1,000-par-value bond convertible into 100 shares of common stock. The common stock is currently selling at $10.50 per share.

21—4   **(Conversion Value)**   Find the conversion (or stock) value for each of the convertible bonds described in the following table.

Convertible	Conversion ratio	Current market price of stock ($)
A	25	42.25
B	16	50.00
C	20	44.00
D	5	19.50

21—5   **(Convertibles and EPS)**   Chatsworth Ice must decide whether to obtain a needed $2 million of financing by selling common stock at its currently depressed price or selling convertible bonds. The firm's common stock is currently selling for $32 per share; new shares can be sold for $30 per share, an underpricing of $2 per share. The firm currently has 100,000 shares of common stock outstanding. Convertible bonds can be sold for their $1,000 par value and would be convertible at $34. The firm expects its earnings available for common stockholders to be $200,000 each year over the next several years.

a. Calculate the earnings per share (EPS) of common stock resulting from:
(1) The sale of common stock.
(2) The sale of the convertible bonds *prior to conversion.* (Ignore bond interest.)
(3) The sale of convertible bonds *after all bonds have been converted.*
b. Which of the two financing alternatives, stock or convertible bonds, would you recommend the company adopt? Why?

21—6   **(Straight Bond Values)** Calculate the straight bond value for each of the bonds described in the following table.

Bond	Par value ($)	Coupon interest rate (paid annually) (%)	Coupon interest rate on equal-risk straight bond (%)	Years to maturity
A	1,000	10	14	20
B	800	12	15	14
C	1,000	13	16	30
D	1,000	14	17	25

21—7   **(Determining Values—Convertible Bond)** Western Clock Company has an outstanding issue of convertible bonds with a $1,000 par value. These bonds are convertible into 50 shares of common stock. They have a 10 percent annual coupon interest rate and a 20-year maturity. The interest rate on a straight bond of similar risk is currently 12 percent.
a. Calculate the straight bond value of the bond.
b. Calculate the conversion (or stock) values of the bond when the market prices of the common stock are $15, $20, $23, $30, and $45 per share, respectively.
c. For each of the stock prices given in **b**, at what price would you expect the bond to sell? Why?
d. What is the least you would expect the bond to sell for, regardless of the common stock price behavior?

21—8   **(Determining Values—Convertible Bond)** Mrs. Tom's Fish Company has an outstanding issue of 15-year convertible bonds with a $1,000 par value. These bonds are convertible into 80 shares of common stock. They have a 13 percent annual coupon interest rate; the interest rate on straight bonds of similar risk is 16 percent.
a. Calculate the straight bond value of this bond.
b. Calculate the conversion (or stock) values of the bond when the market price is $9, $12, $13, $15, and $20 per share of common stock, respectively.
c. For each of the common stock prices given in **b**, at which price would you expect the bond to sell? Why?
d. Graph the straight value and conversion value of the bond for each common stock price given. Plot the per-share common stock prices on the *x*-axis and the bond values on the *y*-axis. Use this graph to indicate the minimum market value of the bond associated with each common stock price.

21—9   **(Warrant Values)** Joan's Electronics has warrants that allow the purchase of three shares of its outstanding common stock at $50 per share. The common stock price per share and the market value of the warrant associated with that stock price are summarized in the following table.

Common stock price per share	Market value of warrant
$42	$ 2
46	8
48	9
54	18
58	28
62	38
66	48

a. For each of the common stock prices given, calculate the theoretical warrant value.
b. Graph the theoretical and market values of the warrant on a set of per-share common stock price (x-axis)–warrant value (y-axis) axes.
c. If the warrant value is $12 when the market price of common stock is $50, does this contradict or support the graph you have constructed? Explain why or why not.
d. Specify the area of *warrant premium*. Why does this premium exist?
e. If the expiration date of the warrants is quite close, would you expect your graph to look different? Explain.

21—10   **(Common Stock versus Warrant Investment)** Gayle Graham is evaluating the Ever-On Battery Company's common stock and warrants in order to choose the better investment. The firm's stock is currently selling for $50 per share; its warrants to purchase three shares of common stock at $45 per share are selling for $20. Ignoring brokerage fees, Ms. Graham has $8,000 to invest. She is quite optimistic with respect to Ever-On because the firm is close to landing a large government contract.
a. How many shares of stock and how many warrants can Ms. Graham purchase?
b. Suppose Ms. Graham purchased the stock, held it one year, then sold it for $60 per share. Ignoring brokerage fees and taxes, what total gain would she realize?
c. Suppose Ms. Graham purchased the warrants and held them for one year, and the market price of the stock increased to $60 per share. Ignoring brokerage fees and taxes, what would be her total gain if the market value of warrants increased to $45 and she sold out?
d. What benefit, if any, would the warrants provide? Are there any differences in the risk of these two alternative investments? Explain.

21—11   **(Common Stock versus Warrant Investment)** Mark Christian can invest $5,000 in the common stock or the warrants of Kettering Engineering Center, Inc. The common stock is currently selling for $30 per share. Its warrants, which provide for the purchase of two shares of common stock at $28 per share, are currently selling for $7. The stock is expected to rise to a market price of $32 within the next year, so the expected theoretical value of a warrant over the next year is $8. The expiration date of the warrant is one year from the present.

a. If Mr. Christian purchases the stock, holds it for one year, and then sells it for $32, what is his total gain? (Ignore brokerage fees . and taxes.)

b. If Mr. Christian purchases the warrants and converts them to common stock in one year, what is his total gain if the market price of common shares is actually $32? (Ignore brokerage fees and taxes.)

c. Repeat **a** and **b** assuming that the market price of the stock in one year is (1) $30 and (2) $28.

d. Discuss the two alternatives and the trade-offs associated with them.

21—12   **(Options Profits and Losses)**   For each of the following *100-share options*, use the underlying stock price at expiration and other information to determine the amount of profit or loss an investor would have had, ignoring brokerage fees.

Option	Type of option	Cost of option ($)	Striking price per share ($)	Underlying stock price per share at expiration ($)
A	Call	200	50	55
B	Call	350	42	45
C	Put	500	60	50
D	Put	300	35	40
E	Call	450	28	26

21—13   **(Call Option)**   Jack Butler is considering buying 100 shares of Iris, Inc., at $62 per share. Because he has read that the firm will likely soon receive certain large orders from abroad, he expects the price of Iris to increase to $70 per share. As an alternative, Jack is considering purchase of a call option for 100 shares of Iris at a striking price of $60. The 90-day option will cost $600. Ignore any brokerage fees or dividends.

a. What would Jack's profit be on the stock transaction if its price does rise to $70 and he sells?

b. How much would Jack earn on the option transaction if the underlying stock price rises to $70?

c. How high must the stock price rise in order for Jack to break even on the option transaction?

d. Compare, contrast, and discuss the relative profit and risk from the stock and the option transactions.

21—14   **(Put Option)**   Charles Vogel, the pension fund manager for Jayson Industries, is considering purchase of a put option in anticipation of a price decline in the stock of Stick, Inc. The option to sell 100 shares of Stick at any time during the next 90 days at a striking price of $45 can be purchased for $380. The stock of Stick is currently selling for $46 per share.

a. Ignoring any brokerage fees or dividends, what profit or loss would Charles make if he buys the option, and the lowest price of Stick, Inc. stock during the 90 days is $46, $44, $40, $35, respectively?

b. What effect would the fact that the price of Stick, Inc.'s stock slowly rose from its initial $46 level to $55 at the end of 90 days have on Charles's purchase?

c. In light of your findings, discuss the potential risks and returns from using put options to attempt to profit from an anticipated decline in share price.

CASE

I. Walton Company's Choice of Selling Stock or Convertibles

I. Walton Company, a rapidly growing fishing-gear manufacturer, needs to raise $1 million in external funds to finance the acquisition of new manufacturing equipment. After carefully analyzing alternative financing sources, Doris McJohn, the firm's vice-president of finance, has reduced the possibilities to two alternatives. The first involves the sale of common stock at $37 per share, underpriced by $3 relative to the current market price of $40. The second alternative would be to sell $1,000-par-value convertible bonds. These carry a 13 percent annual coupon interest rate and can be sold at par value. The conversion ratio would be 22. The firm currently has 150,000 shares of common stock outstanding. The earnings available for common stockholders are expected to be $600,000 per year for each of the next several years. Armed with this information, Doris plans to evaluate each alternative in terms of its impact on the firm's earnings per share (EPS).

Required

a. Determine the number of shares of common stock outstanding and the earnings per share (EPS) under the common stock financing alternative.

b. Determine the number of shares of common stock outstanding and the earnings per share (EPS) associated with the bond *prior to its conversion* under the convertible bond financing alternative. (Ignore bond interest.)

c. Determine the number of shares outstanding and the earnings per share (EPS) associated with the bond alternative *once all bonds have been converted.*

d. Discuss which of the two alternatives, stock or convertible bonds, is preferable in terms of maximizing earnings per share (EPS). Also discuss the impact of each alternative on voting control.

e. Which alternative should Doris recommend? Why?

CAREER OPPORTUNITIES IN FINANCE

If you have an interest in the dollars and cents of running a business, like to follow the daily ups and downs of the financial markets, have a knack for numbers, and would like to land a job with a salary ranking among the highest of all business graduates, finance might be the career for you. Opportunities for the new graduate are abundant. There are over a million positions in the general field of finance. This appendix focuses on careers in finance—what they are, where to find them, and what they are paying.

WHAT ARE THE JOBS?

There are two basic career paths in finance. The first is *managerial finance*, which involves managing the finance function for businesses in the manufacturing and trade industries. These industries make and sell consumer and commercial products. The second is a career in the *financial services* industry, which creates and sells intangible financial products or services. Banking, securities, real estate, and insurance are all financial service industries.

The job descriptions that follow are divided into two career paths: managerial finance and financial services. A mixture of entry-level positions available to the recent college graduate and advanced positions available after a number of years of work experience or an advanced degree are presented. Although many of the top positions in finance are not available to recent graduates, firms frequently hire new graduates as "assistants" to these positions. A review of the job descriptions below should help you understand the many exciting career opportunities available in finance. (*Note:* One * designates an entry-level position and two **s designate an advanced position.)

CAREER PATH 1: MANAGERIAL FINANCE

A career in managerial finance can lead to the executive suite. Studies of chief executive officers of the nation's largest businesses show that the finance/accounting route is still one of the most common career paths to the executive suite. The majority have risen to the top after an average of 15 years in various financial management positions in the firm. One reason that many CEOs are chosen from financial management may be that the language of business is dollars, and people managing dollars generally have the attention of a firm's top management. Exposure to these top policy makers can speed an effective financial manager's climb in the organization. Today's chief financial officers often rank third in the corporate hierarchy. As a result of rapid changes in and globalization of the business environment, careers in managerial finance are more intellectually challenging than ever before. Many of the positions described here are part of a firm's treasury function.

Financial Analyst*

A financial analyst may be responsible for a variety of financial tasks. Primarily, the analyst is involved in preparing and analyzing the firm's financial plans and budgets. This function requires a close working relationship with the accounting department. Other duties may include financial forecasting, assisting in preparation of pro forma statements, and analyzing other aspects of the firm such as its liquidity, short-term borrowing, fixed assets, and capital structure. The degree of specialization of the analyst's duties is generally dependent upon the size of the firm. Larger firms tend to have specialized analysts, whereas smaller firms assign the analyst a number of areas of responsibility.

Many students headed for a career in managerial finance will begin as a financial, or "budget," analyst, doing financial planning and budgeting. According to the chief financial officers of firms in the *Fortune* 1000, financial planning and budgeting is the biggest career growth area in managerial finance and also the most important and time-consuming managerial finance task.

Salary: Entry-level: $22,000–$28,000
             MBA: $25,000–$45,000
             Manager: $40,000–$60,000

Cash Manager**

The cash manager is responsible for maintaining and controlling the daily cash balances of the firm. In a large company, this involves managing currency risk and coordinating national or international banking relationships, compensating balances, lockbox arrangements, and cash transfers. An understanding of the operating and cash conversion cycles of the firm is essential in projecting the firm's daily cash surplus or deficit. The cash manager is responsible for investing surplus funds in short-term marketable securities or, in the case of a deficit, arranging necessary short-term financing through trade credit, bank notes or lines, accounts receivable or inventory loans, factoring, commercial paper, or other sources. He or she maintains working relationships with the banks providing the firm's cash management and short-term financing services.

Salary: Analyst: $30,000–$43,000
             Manager: $40,000–$75,000

Credit Analyst*/Manager**

The general credit analyst/manager administers the firm's credit policy by analyzing or managing two basic activities: the evaluation of credit applications and the collection of accounts receivable. Routine duties involve analyzing the financial condition of applicants, checking credit histories, and determining the appropriate amount of credit and credit terms to offer applicants. The manager also supervises the collection of current and past-due accounts receivable.

Salary: Analyst: $23,000–$28,000
Manager: $28,000 to $60,000 and up

Capital Budgeting Analyst*/Manager**

The capital budgeting analyst/manager is responsible for the evaluation and selection of proposed projects and for the allocation of funds for these projects. In the evaluation process, the analyst compiles relevant data and makes cash flow projections about proposed projects. The analyst evaluates the project's acceptability based on the firm's return criteria and assesses the project's impact on the firm's asset structure. Upon selection of acceptable projects, the analyst/manager oversees the financial aspects of the implementation of the projects; this job sometimes includes analyzing and arranging the necessary financing.

Salary: Junior analyst: $25,000–$35,000
Manager: $30,000–$60,000

Property Manager (Corporate)**

A property manager is responsible for maximum utilization of the real estate owned or leased by a company. He or she will determine whether surplus or underutilized property should be developed, expanded, upgraded, or sold. Requirements for new office, manufacturing, or warehouse space will be arranged by the property manager, who will lease, develop, or acquire the additional space. The property manager's position has become increasingly important in recent years and is now found at most companies with sales over $100 million.

Salary: Entry level: $20,000–$25,000
Experienced: $28,000–$75,000
(up to $150,000 in large corporations)

CAREER PATH 2: FINANCIAL SERVICES

The financial services industry offers career opportunities in banking, securities, insurance, and real estate. Most of the jobs in the financial services industry can be obtained by qualified candidates upon graduation from college. To be successful in financial services, the graduate must understand the key aspects of financial products and services and also be able to sell them. The majority of entry-level positions in this career path are sales-oriented.

Until recently, the financial services area was the fastest growing area of finance. However, the many changes in these industries have slowed the growth of employment opportunities. Although new job creation is not expected to be as great as in the mid-to-late 1980s, there will still be many interesting and challenging positions available for business graduates.

BANKING

The banking industry is undergoing a period or tremendous change. The high level of merger and acquisition activity, together with major restructuring programs, has reduced the number of positions in the industry. However, desirable positions for business graduates are still available, particularly for those with degrees in finance or accounting, with marketing or management information systems background. Salaries vary according to the size of the bank, with large banks paying more. Many banks have management training programs that provide the entry-level trainee with experience in commercial lending, operations, and retail banking.

Retail Bank Manager*

Retail banking involves the bank's branch offices, which deal directly with the public. The branch manager supervises the programs offered by the bank to its customers—installment loans, mortgages, checking, savings, retirement accounts, and other financial products. Due to the competitive nature of banking since the industry's deregulation, the successful retail banker must aggressively market the bank's new products as well as possess a certain degree of financial savvy. This is one of the fastest growing areas in banking.

Salary: Entry-level: $15,000–$22,000
MBA: $22,000–$30,000
Branch manager: $28,000–$42,000

Loan Officer**

A loan officer evaluates the credit of personal and business loan applicants. Loan officers may specialize in commercial, consumer, or real estate loans. The commercial loan officer develops and monitors the credit relationship between the business customer and the bank. Responsibilities include evaluation of the creditworthiness of the business, negotiating credit terms, monitoring the firm's financial condition, cross-selling the bank's other corporate services, and acting as a financial adviser to smaller firms.

Salary: Entry-level: $25,000–$35,000
Experienced: $30,000–$60,000 and up

Trust Officer**

Trust officers manage portfolios of investments for individuals, foundations, institutions, and corporate pension and profit-sharing plans. The trust officer and his or her staff research, analyze, and monitor both currently held and potential investment vehicles for retention or inclusion in the portfolios they manage.

Salary: $28,000–$52,000

SECURITIES

The securities industry has experienced many changes in recent years due to mergers among brokerage and investment banking firms. Although the growth of employment opportunities is not expected to be as large as in the mid-to-late 1980s, there are still many positions available for finance graduates.

Financial Planner*

The financial planning industry has grown rapidly in recent years as more people seek professional advice on managing their personal finances. The planner advises the client about budgeting, securities, insurance, real estate, taxes, and retirement and estate planning and then devises a comprehensive financial plan to meet the client's objectives. There are two major certification programs for financial planners, each requiring approximately two years of study and several examinations: the Certified Financial Planner (CFP) credential of the International Board of Certified Financial Planners and the Chartered Financial Consultant (ChFC) credential of The American College. The accounting and banking fields also have certification programs.

   The position of financial planner has been included in the securities industry section but could as well have been in the banking, insurance, or real estate sections of this appendix. Eighty percent of all financial planners are employed by the financial services industry and serve as a complement to the sales activity in their firm. The other 20 percent are self-employed and sell advice rather than financial products, such as securities, tax shelters, or insurance.

Salary: Entry-level: $18,000–$25,000
            Experienced: up to $150,000

Stockbroker* or Account Executive*

Stockbrokers or account executives act as agents for people who wish to buy and sell securities. They provide advice to customers on financial matters, supplying the latest stock and bond quotations and latest analyst reports, and respond to customer inquiries. In addition to knowledge of financial analysis and investments, good sales and interpersonal skills are critical for success in this field. Stockbrokers are usually hired by brokerage firms, investment banks, mutual funds, and insurance companies. Job opportunities for brokers are also emerging in traditional financial institutions such as banks and savings and loans. Most brokerage firms offer a training program at the entry level that prepares the stockbroker to take the required standardized licensing examinations. The broker trainee position is among the top entry-level jobs in terms of ultimate salary potential and number of positions available; over one-half of those employed in the securities industry are stockbrokers or securities salespeople. However, the turnover rate for brokers is very high; an estimated 95 percent leave the field within the first two years.

Salary: Trainee: $15,000–$20,000 plus commissions
Experienced broker: $50,000–$100,000 and up, plus commissions

Securities Analyst**

Securities analysts are the financial experts on Wall Street who study stocks and bonds, usually in specific industries. They specialize in a particular firm or industry and understand the economic impact of changes in the competitive, financial, and foreign markets on that firm or industry. They are employed by and act as advisers to securities firms and their customers, fund managers, and insurance companies.

Salary: Junior analyst with MBA: $25,000–$35,000
Experienced analyst: up to $200,000

Investment Banker**

An investment banker acts as a middleman between issuers and buyers of newly issued stocks and bonds. Generally, the investment banker purchases the security issue and then markets it to the public on behalf of corporate and government issuers, bearing all the risk of selling the issue. Advising clients about the various financing strategies available to the firm and developing new financing vehicles in response to specific client needs are important aspects of an investment banker's role. Considerable experience and expertise are necessary to land a job in a Wall Street investment banking firm, but many consider the reward worth the effort.

Salary: Entry-level MBA: $50,000–$75,000
After 10 years' experience: $100,000–$500,000

INSURANCE

In recent years, with the advent of the financial supermarket, insurance companies have begun offering more sophisticated financial products. Many consider their agents to be financial planners, providing advice on a broad range of products. Most major insurance companies have comprehensive training programs and require continuing education to keep abreast of new products.

Insurance Agent*/Broker*

Insurance agents and brokers develop programs to fit customers' needs, interview insurance prospects, help with claims and settlements, and collect premiums. An agent is usually employed by a single insurance company; a broker is independent and represents no particular company but can sell policies from many. Getting a job as an insurance agent is easy; being successful is much more difficult. The turnover rate is similar to that for stockbrokers. Approximately 90 percent of the newly employed in this field leave after two years.

Salary: Trainee: $15,000–$20,000
Experienced agent: $30,000–$75,000

Underwriter**

Underwriters appraise and select the risks their company will insure. This includes the appraisal of the risks of individuals after analyzing insurance applications, reports from loss-control consultants, medical reports, and actuarial studies. Commercial underwriting involves insuring a firm's major fixed assets, such as heavy equipment. When deciding whether an applicant is an acceptable risk, an underwriter may outline the terms of the contract, including the amount of the premium.

Salary: $25,000–$60,000

REAL ESTATE

The real estate field offers a variety of positions to the finance graduate. During the past decade, commercial real estate projects have increased in size, and real estate has become a desirable investment alternative. Institutional investors such as insurance companies and pension funds have become major factors in the industry. Many major real estate developers, operators, and financial institutions with real estate lending departments offer training programs. The outlook for positions in this field is good. However, the real estate market is very cyclical, and opportunities will vary depending on the region of the country.

Mortgage Banker*

Mortgage bankers arrange financing for real estate projects, bringing together the property owner/developer and financing sources. Lenders include insurance companies, pension funds, banks, savings and loans, and major credit companies. The mortgage banker works closely with the borrower to structure the terms of the financing and acts as the borrower's agent to negotiate the financing. The mortgage banker maintains relationships with a large group of financial institutions so that he or she can match each project with an appropriate lender. Mortgage banking companies are generally either privately owned or subsidiaries of bank holding companies.

Salary: Entry-level (analyst): $22,000–$30,000
Experienced: $25,000–$100,000 and up

Property/Real Estate Asset Manager*

Property managers and real estate asset managers are employed by major owners of commercial real estate such as insurance companies, pension fund advisors, and real estate developers. A property manager's objective is to achieve maximum returns on real estate by handling the day-to-day operations of the firm's real estate assets, including negotiating leases with tenants, planning and implementing capital improvement programs, and controlling operating expenses. The real estate asset manager is responsible for one or more portfolios of real estate, overseeing the property managers, and determining the optimum time to sell or refinance.

Salary: Entry level: $21,000–$25,000
Experienced: $32,000–$105,000

Real Estate Agent*/Broker*
(Residential and Commercial)

Most property is sold or leased with the aid of a real estate agent who is generally employed by a broker. Some of the agent's and broker's duties include finding potential buyers and lessees for listed property, showing property, and negotiating sale or lease terms agreeable to both parties. Agents generally specialize in either residential or commercial properties. Commercial brokers work with corporations looking to buy or lease facilities as well as anyone wishing to buy investment properties. Commercial agents analyze property values, income-producing capabilities, and other market conditions to structure acceptable lease or purchase terms. Because many areas of the country have a surplus of office space, demand is strong for successful marketing/leasing agents with a track record of filling vacant space. A broker is generally an independent businessperson experienced in the field of real estate; he or she supports the sales staff, providing office space and a budget for advertising and promoting listed properties. Many real estate agents and brokers are also certified property managers, real estate appraisers, and real estate developers. The demand for commercial and residential real estate brokers is expected to increase in economically developing regions of the country.

Salary: Beginner: $10,000–$25,000 plus commissions
            Experienced: $25,000–$250,000 and up

Real Estate Appraiser*

Appraisers estimate the market value for all types of properties, ranging from small residential parcels to large commercial properties. They may also prepare cost analyses and feasibility studies for proposed projects. Appraisers can work for banks, appraisal firms, insurance companies, and real estate developers; many are independent practitioners. Specialized education is required to become an appraiser. The major credential is the MAI (Member Appraisal Institute) designation, given by the American Institute of Real Estate Appraisers and requiring 5 to 10 years of classes and experience to qualify for the exam. The demand for skilled appraisers, particularly with the MAI designation, is increasing significantly as companies' pension funds and financial institutions with large real estate holdings require current appraisals of asset values.

Salary: Trainee: $25,000–$30,000
            Experienced: $35,000–$75,000
            MAI: $50,000–$103,000

Real Estate Lender*

Real estate lenders generally fall into two categories: construction lenders and permanent lenders. Real estate lending officers focus on lending funds for construction and work primarily for banks. Many banks also provide intermediate-term financing and bridge loans (to cover the period between the end of construction and permanent mortgage financing). Permanent lenders provide long-term mortgage financing, which repays the construction lender, for major real estate projects when construction is complete and certain leasing goals have been reached. All major insurance companies have real estate lending departments.

Salary: Entry-level (analyst): $20,000–$30,000
            Experienced: $35,000–$100,000

WHAT ARE THE JOBS PAYING!

The finance graduate can expect top salary offers among business graduates. According to a survey conducted from July 1990 to March 1991 by the College Placement Council, entry-level job offers for finance majors averaged $25,000, almost 10 percent higher than general business administration majors. The starting salary for MBAs with a nontechnical bachelors degree averaged $33,870. Offers for those with technical undergraduate degrees are typically $5,000 or more higher.

The salaries summarized in Table A.1 are expressed in ranges and are only guidelines. Many factors may affect the salary level for a particular job: the geographic region, the employee's work experience and educational background, and the size of the company.

Table A.1　　**Salaries for Various Career Opportunities in Finance**

Job title	Entry-level salary	Potential salary
Managerial Finance		
Financial analyst	$22,000–$28,000	$ 60,000
Cash manager	——	$ 75,000
Credit analyst	$23,000–$28,000	$ 30,000
Credit manager	$28,000–$40,000	$ 80,000
Capital budgeting analyst	$25,000–$35,000	$ 60,000
Property manager (corporate)	$20,000–$25,000	$ 75,000
Financial Services		
Banking		
Retail bank manager	$15,000–$22,000	$ 42,000
Loan officer	$25,000–$35,000	$ 60,000
Trust officer	$28,000–$30,000	$ 52,000
Securities		
Financial planner	$18,000–$25,000	$150,000
Stockbroker or account executive	$15,000–$20,000	$100,000
Securities analyst	$25,000–$35,000	$200,000
Investment banker	$50,000–$75,000	$500,000
Insurance		
Insurance agent/broker	$15,000–$20,000	$ 75,000
Underwriter	——	$ 60,000
Real Estate		
Mortgage banker	$22,000–$30,000	$100,000
Property/real estate asset manager	$21,000–$25,000	$105,000
Real estate agent/broker	$10,000–$25,000	$250,000
Real estate appraiser	$25,000–$30,000	$103,000
Real estate lender	$20,000–$30,000	$100,000

Source: Salary information for many of these positions was provided by the *Robert Half 1991 Salary Survey*, published by Robert Half International Inc., and the "Huntress 1991 Real Estate Compensation Report," compiled by Huntress Real Estate Executive Search, Kansas City, Mo.

INSTRUCTIONS FOR USING THE *BASIC MANAGERIAL FINANCE (BMF) DISK*

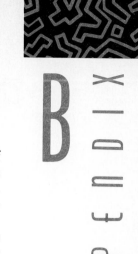

The *Basic Managerial Finance (BMF) Disk* contains two different sets of routines: the *BMF Tutor* and the *BMF Problem-Solver*. These programs are designed for use on IBM PC/XT/AT and compatible microcomputers. All programs are written in Turbo Pascal$_{TM}$ version 5.5 and are extremely user friendly.

The *Tutor* and the *Problem-Solver* routines are arranged in the same order as the text discussions. For convenience, text page references are shown on the screen for each associated computational routine. As noted in the text Preface as well as in Chapter 1, applicability of the software throughout the text and study guide is keyed to related text discussions, end-of-chapter problems, and end-of-part cases by a computer symbol ⬚ for the *Tutor* and by a diskette symbol ⬛ for the *Problem-Solver*. Thus you can integrate the procedures on the disk with the corresponding text discussions.

WHAT IS THE *BMF TUTOR!*

The *BMF Tutor* is a collection of managerial finance problem types constructed by random number generation. It is based on the *Finance Tutor* by Hansen, Bush, and Flowers, also published by HarperCollins. Its purpose is to give you an essentially unlimited number of problems to work so that you can practice until you are satisfied that you understand a concept. The following sequence when using the *Tutor* should produce the best results:

1 ▬▬▬ **Work the problem first yourself.** It is tempting to save time by letting the computer solve the problem for you and then studying the computer's answer. You won't learn much that way. Even if you make mistakes when you try the problem on your own, you will learn from those mistakes.

2 ▬▬▬ **Enter your answer.** The computer will check your answer against the correct answer.

3 ▬▬▬ If you do not get the same answer as the computer, **check your work step-by-step** against the correct solution displayed on the computer screen. Doing so will help you pinpoint your mistakes. Practice each type of problem until you have genuinely mastered it. Don't have false pride about your mastery. When you take the course exams you won't be able to fake your knowledge level. So, don't stop until you know that you have mastered the idea.

The *Tutor* uses randomizing procedures to choose the specific numbers, so it is unlikely that you will ever see a combination of numbers twice. This gives you an effectively unlimited number of practice problems. The only limit is your willingness to practice.

WHAT IS THE *BMF PROBLEM-SOLVER?*

The *BMF Problem-Solver* is a collection of financial computation routines. Its purpose is to aid the student's learning and understanding of managerial finance by providing a fast and easy method for performing the often time-consuming mathematical computations required. It is not the intent of the *BMF Problem-Solver* to eliminate the need for learning the various concepts, but to assist in solving the problems once the appropriate formulas have been studied. The *Problem-Solver* differs from the *Tutor* in that it solves for the answer, given the input data supplied by the user, whereas the *Tutor* supplies the input data and looks to the student to perform the calculations. The *Tutor* should be used to practice application of basic concepts; the *Problem-Solver* should be used to save computational time once the concepts are understood.

HARDWARE REQUIREMENTS

To use the *BMF Disk*, the following equipment is needed:

- An IBM PC or true compatible with MS-DOS® operating system Version 2.1
- At least 256Kb of RAM
- At least one floppy or fixed (hard) disk drive
- Monochrome, Hercules®, CGA, EGA, or VGA card and monitor

CHECKING THE MASTER DISKETTE

The *BMF Disk* comes on a diskette labelled "*BMF* Master Diskette." Some pointers in handling diskettes:

- *Never* put your fingers on the recording window. Always hold the diskette at the label end or by the hub (hole in the center).
- *Never* allow the diskette near a magnetic object or intense heat.
- *Never* apply pressure to the diskette with a ballpoint pen, pencil, or other sharp object. If you want to write something on the label of the diskette, use a soft-tip pen of some kind.
- *Never* bend the diskette.

The *BMF* Master Diskette comes with the following files on it:

```
AUTOEXEC.BAT ................ The automatic execution batch file
                              for floppy disk operation
GITSOFT.EXE ................. The main menu program
```

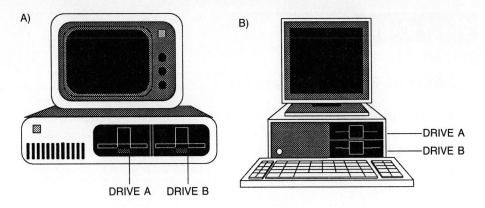

Figure B.1   A) Side-by-Side Disk Arrangement; B) Top-Bottom Disk Arrangement

GITUTOR.EXE .... The *BMF Tutor* program
GITMAN.EXE .... The *BMF Problem-Solver* program
AUTOMATI.C .... Controls automatic detection vs.
                           forced monochrome mode
MONO.BAT .... Sets program to forced monochrome
COLOR.BAT .... Sets program to automatic detection

You should verify through a directory listing that all of these files are on your master diskette. To display a directory listing, place the diskette in diskette drive A (shown in Figure B.1) and type the command:

DIR A:

You should see the following directory listing on your screen:

```
            Volume in drive A has no label
                Directory of A:\
AUTOEXEC    BAT      xxxxxx      dd-dd-dd      tt:ttt
GITSOFT     EXE      xxxxxx      dd-dd-dd      tt:ttt
GITUTOR     EXE      xxxxxx      dd-dd-dd      tt:ttt
GITMAN      EXE      xxxxxx      dd-dd-dd      tt:ttt
AUTOMATI    C        xxxxxx      dd-dd-dd      tt:ttt
MONO        BAT      xxxxxx      dd-dd-dd      tt:ttt
COLOR       BAT      xxxxxx      dd-dd-dd      tt:ttt
         7 Files(s)             xxxxxx bytes free
```

where xxxxxx represents numbers, dd-dd-dd dates, and tt:ttt clock times. Since these will vary with the particular release of the *BMF Disk*, no specific values are given here. If you see these same seven files on your listing, your diskette should be all right. If you do not see this same directory, your diskette is probably defective and should be returned to the publisher as soon as possible.

GETTING STARTED

Copying the *BMF Disk* to a Hard Disk

If a hard disk is available and you wish to run the *BMF Disk* from it, execute the following sequence of steps to place the *BMF Disk* on the hard disk of your computer.

1 ▬ Make certain you are in the root directory by typing the command:

$$CD\backslash \;\;\hookleftarrow$$

(The symbol ↵ means press the **ENTER** or **RETURN** key.)

2 ▬ Create a subdirectory by typing the following command:

$$MD\backslash GITSOFT\hookleftarrow$$

3 ▬ Go to the new subdirectory by typing the following command:

$$CD\backslash GITSOFT\hookleftarrow$$

4 ▬ Place the *BMF* Master Diskette in the floppy disk drive A and type the following command:

$$COPY\; A:*.*\hookleftarrow$$

5 ▬ When the copy operation is completed, store the Master Diskette in a safe place and begin using the *BMF Disk* from your hard disk. Now see the section entitled "Running the *BMF Disk* (Hard Disk)" on page B-6.

Copying the *BMF Disk* to a Floppy Diskette

To execute the *BMF Disk* from a floppy diskette, you need to create a diskette with a copy of the MS-DOS operating system (version 2.1 or later). To do this, place an MS-DOS master diskette (which your instructor may need to supply) in drive A and a blank diskette in drive B. Press the **CTRL** and **ALT** keys simultaneously and without releasing these keys, press the **DEL** key. This will cause the computer to "reboot" to the MS-DOS operating system on your MS-DOS master diskette. Depending on what machine you have, you may be asked to enter the date and the time; you may simply press the **ENTER** or **RETURN** key, or you may enter the actual date and time.

1 ▬ When you see the A> (called the "A prompt") characters on the screen, you should type:

$$FORMAT\; B:\; /S\hookleftarrow$$

(It is important that there be a space between FORMAT and B: and a space between B: and /S.) This will cause the blank diskette in drive B to be prepared to receive the *BMF Disk.* You will first see a message on the screen:

```
Insert new diskette for drive B:
and strike ENTER when ready
```

When you have placed the blank diskette in the B drive and closed the drive door, press the **ENTER** key (on most keyboards this key has the ⏎ symbol on it).

2 ■■■ The computer will next display a message that looks like the following:

```
Head: x Cylinder: xx
```

This is describing the progress of the format operation and will be updated by the computer. You should do nothing but watch at this stage.

3 ■■■ When the format operation is complete, the computer will display another message:

```
Format complete
System transferred
  362496 bytes total disk space
    xxxxx bytes used by the system
  xxxxxx bytes available on disk
```

where xxxxx and xxxxxx are numbers that will vary depending on the version of **MS-DOS** that you use. However, they will always add up to 362496. It is possible that you may occasionally see a slightly different form of the message:

```
362496 bytes total disk space
  xxxxx bytes used by the system
  xxxxx bytes in bad sectors
xxxxxx bytes available on disk
```

If you get this second form of the message, do not use the diskette. Use another diskette and repeat starting at step 1. This message means that the diskette is partially damaged and probably will not have enough space for all of the *BMF Disk* files.

4 ■■■ The format operation will end with the message:

```
Format another (Y/N)?
```

You should press the N key and then press **ENTER**. This will return you to the prompt (A>). Now remove the MS-DOS master diskette from the A drive and put the *BMF* Master Diskette in the A drive. Next, type in the command:

```
COPY *.* B:
```

(It is important that there be a space between COPY and *.* and a space between *.* and B:.) The message

```
copying files
```

will appear on the screen, and the names of the files on the *BMF* Master Diskette will appear on the screen as they are copied. When this is finished, you will see the A prompt (A>) again on the screen.

5 ▮▮▮ Remove the *BMF* Master Diskette from drive A and store it in a safe place. Remove the diskette from drive B and label it "*BMF* Diskette Working Copy." Remember to use a soft-tip pen to do this, never a pencil or hard tip-pen. This is the copy that you should use when you run the *BMF Disk*. Now see the section entitled "Running the *BMF Disk* (Floppy Diskette)" below.

Running the *BMF Disk* (Hard Disk)

To run the *BMF Disk* from a hard disk drive, type the command:

$$CD\backslash GITSOFT\hookleftarrow$$

where the symbol ◁┘ means press the **ENTER** or **RETURN** key. You are now in the subdirectory for the *BMF Disk*. To start the program, type the following command:

$$GITSOFT\hookleftarrow$$

Now skip to the section entitled "Running the *BMF Disk* (Combined)" below.

Running the *BMF Disk* (Floppy Diskette)

To run the *BMF Disk* from a floppy disk drive, place the *BMF* Diskette Working Copy in the floppy disk drive A. Now simultaneously press the **CTRL**, the **ALT**, and the **DEL** keys. When you are asked to enter the date and the time, you may simply press the **ENTER** or **RETURN** key (◁┘) or you may enter the actual date and time. The *BMF Disk* will automatically start running (this is accomplished by the AUTOEXEC.BAT file).

Running the *BMF Disk* (Combined)

As soon as you start the *BMF Disk* running, the screen will clear and the menu screen shown in Figure B.2 will appear. If you press the ↓ key, you will see the large bar move down one line each time you press it. If you press the ↑ key, you will see the large bar move up one line each time you press it. (If you want to select the *BMF Tutor* it is not necessary to move the bar at all.)

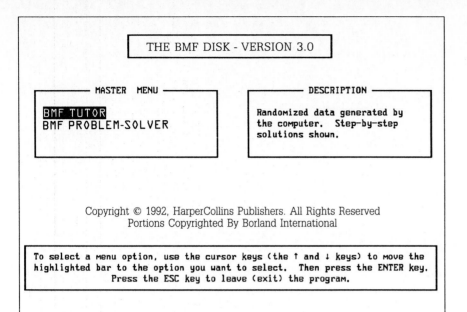

THE BMF DISK - VERSION 3.0

─ MASTER MENU ─

BMF TUTOR
BMF PROBLEM-SOLVER

─ DESCRIPTION ─

Randomized data generated by
the computer. Step-by-step
solutions shown.

Copyright © 1992, HarperCollins Publishers. All Rights Reserved
Portions Copyrighted By Borland International

To select a menu option, use the cursor keys (the ↑ and ↓ keys) to move the
highlighted bar to the option you want to select. Then press the ENTER key.
Press the ESC key to leave (exit) the program.

Figure B.2   ***BMF Disk* Master Menu Screen**

Special Note: If you run the *BMF Disk* on a PC that simulates color
on a monochrome screen, it is possible that the "menu bars" referred to in the instructions may not be visible. If this happens,
press the escape key (ESC) to get to the DOS prompt (A>, B>, or
C>). Then type:

$$MONO \hookleftarrow$$

where $\hookleftarrow$ represents the **ENTER** key. This will rename the
ATUOMATI.C file to the name MONOCHRO.ME. When your pro-
gram sees this, it will be forced to use the monochrome mode, and
you should have no further problem. If at any time you want to
return to automatic detection, get to the DOS prompt and type:

$$COLOR \hookleftarrow$$

After running MONO or COLOR, you can reenter the program by
typing:

$$AUTOEXEC \hookleftarrow$$

If you select the BMF TUTOR option, go to the section "Running
the *BMF Tutor*" (page B-8) for further instruction. If you select BMF
Problem-Solver, go to the section "Running the *BMF Problem-Solver*"
(page B-12) for further instruction.

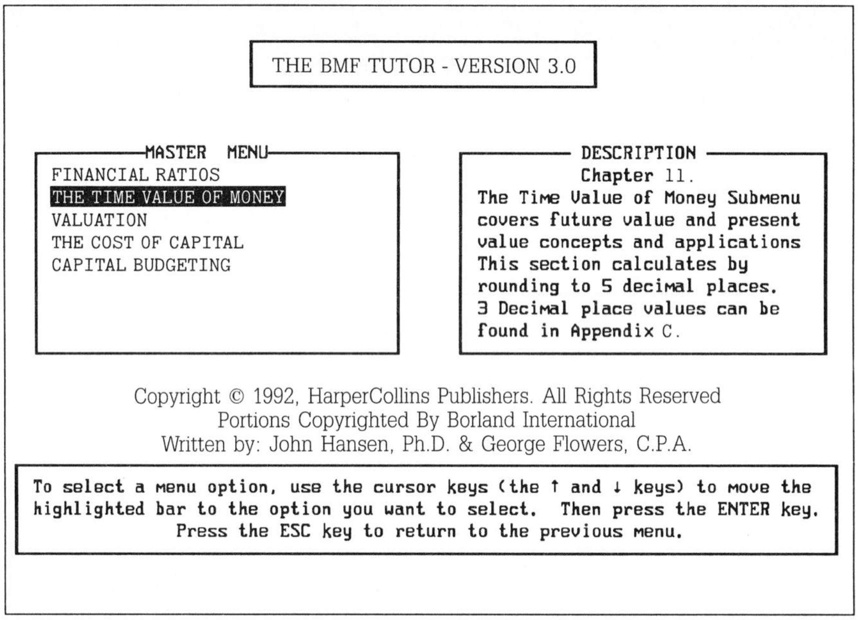

```
┌──────────────────────────────────────────────────────────────────┐
│                  ┌────────────────────────────────┐                │
│                  │  THE BMF TUTOR - VERSION 3.0   │                │
│                  └────────────────────────────────┘                │
│                                                                    │
│   ┌─────MASTER  MENU─────────┐    ┌───── DESCRIPTION ──────┐       │
│   │ FINANCIAL RATIOS         │    │        Chapter 11.     │       │
│   │ THE TIME VALUE OF MONEY  │    │ The Time Value of Money│       │
│   │ VALUATION                │    │ Submenu                │       │
│   │ THE COST OF CAPITAL      │    │ covers future value and│       │
│   │ CAPITAL BUDGETING        │    │ present                │       │
│   │                          │    │ value concepts and     │       │
│   │                          │    │ applications           │       │
│   │                          │    │ This section calculates│       │
│   │                          │    │ by                     │       │
│   │                          │    │ rounding to 5 decimal  │       │
│   │                          │    │ places.                │       │
│   │                          │    │ 3 Decimal place values │       │
│   │                          │    │ can be                 │       │
│   │                          │    │ found in Appendix C.   │       │
│   └──────────────────────────┘    └────────────────────────┘       │
│                                                                    │
│          Copyright © 1992, HarperCollins Publishers. All Rights     │
│          Reserved                                                  │
│          Portions Copyrighted By Borland International             │
│          Written by: John Hansen, Ph.D. & George Flowers, C.P.A.   │
│                                                                    │
│   ┌────────────────────────────────────────────────────────────┐   │
│   │ To select a menu option, use the cursor keys (the ↑ and ↓  │   │
│   │ keys) to move the                                          │   │
│   │ highlighted bar to the option you want to select.  Then    │   │
│   │ press the ENTER key.                                       │   │
│   │ Press the ESC key to return to the previous menu.          │   │
│   └────────────────────────────────────────────────────────────┘   │
│                                                                    │
└──────────────────────────────────────────────────────────────────┘
```

Figure B.3   *BMF Tutor* **Master Menu Screen**

RUNNING THE *BMF TUTOR*

If you select the *BMF Tutor,* the message shown in Figure B.3 will appear on the screen. The menus in the *Tutor* are operated in the same way as the master menu discussed in detail earlier. Each menu option has an individual description that appears in the right-hand window. This description will change as you move the bar up or down in the menu so that the description will always correspond to the option that is highlighted on the left.

To illustrate the use of the menu system, let's look at the time value of money section. If you press the ENTER (↵) key while the highlight bar is on TIME VALUE OF MONEY, you will see a menu screen appear with a listing of the submenu under that topic. If you move the highlight bar to the bottom option, LOAN AMORTIZATION, and press the ENTER (↵) key, the screen in Figure B.4 will appear:

You are now expected to work this problem using the procedures discussed in the textbook. You will find the page number where the relevant subject is discussed—in this case loan amortization, which is found on page 357.

If you wish to have a calculator to work with, you can get one by pressing the F2 key. If you do so, you will see a screen with a simulated calculator in the lower left-hand portion of the screen. To see examples of how to use this calculator, see the section "Using the Pop-Up Calculator" below.

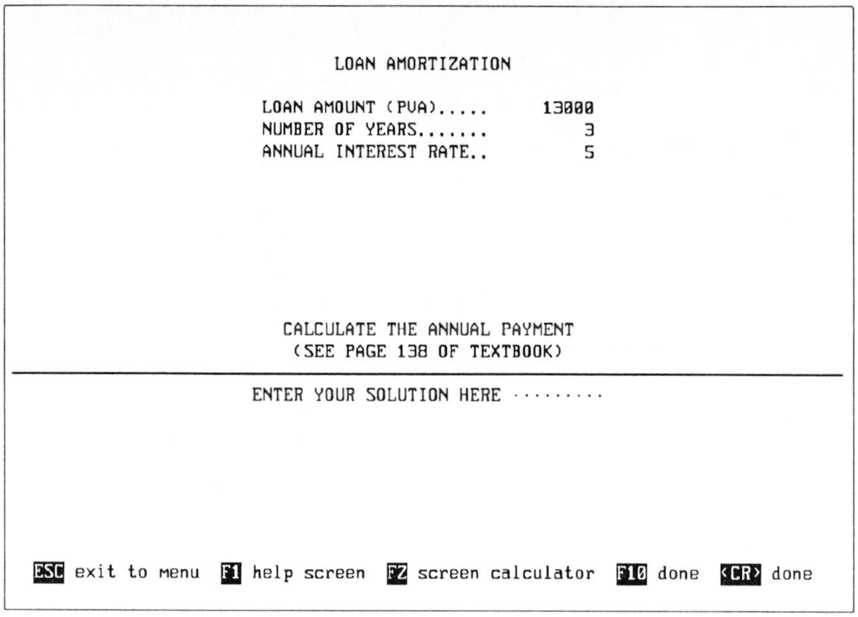

```
                    LOAN AMORTIZATION

           LOAN AMOUNT (PVA).....    13000
           NUMBER OF YEARS.......        3
           ANNUAL INTEREST RATE..        5




           CALCULATE THE ANNUAL PAYMENT
           (SEE PAGE 138 OF TEXTBOOK)
    _____
           ENTER YOUR SOLUTION HERE · · · · · · · ·







  ESC exit to menu  F1 help screen  F2 screen calculator  F10 done  <CR> done
```

Figure B.4   *BMF Tutor* **Calculation Screen**

Once you have worked out the solution to the problem, type in your answer. If you make a mistake, you can use the backspace key, the left (←) and right (→) arrow keys, and the delete (DEL) and insert (INS) keys. This will allow you to correct your answer. When you have successfully entered your answer, press the ENTER (⏎) key.

When you have entered your answer, you will see a screen like the one in Figure B.5. If you have correctly calculated the answer, you may bypass the display of the solution by entering *N* in response to the question of whether or not you want to see the solution.

If you enter *Y*, you will see a screen showing a solution. For all problem types, the solutions are written using the same form as that in the textbook, so if you make a error, you should be able to compare your solution to the steps on the screen to find where you made the error. When you have finished studying the solution, press the ENTER or ESC key and the screen will return to the previous menu.

USING THE POP-UP CALCULATOR

Any time that you press the F2 key while running the *BMF Tutor*, the picture of a calculator will appear on the screen in the lower left-hand corner as shown in Figure B.6. As in the rest of the program, pressing the escape key (ESC) will take you out of the pop-up calculator.

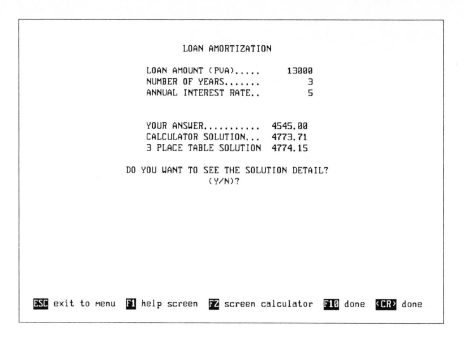

Figure B.5   *BMF Tutor* **Solution Screen**

There are nine command keys associated with the calculator: **=, +, −, *, /, C, P, S,** and **R.** The effect of these command keys is summarized in Table B.1. For the four letter command keys, it does not matter whether you enter an uppercase or a lowercase letter (for example, R or r).

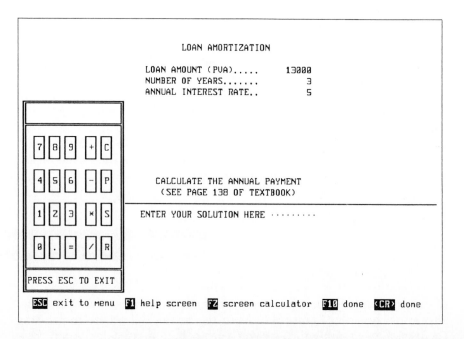

Figure B.6   *BMF Tutor* **Calculation Screen with Pop-Up Calculator**

Table B.1   **Summary of Calculator Command Keys**

Command key	Effect/Operation
=	Causes the calculator to perform the current calculation
+	Addition
−	Subtraction
*	Multiplication
/	Division
C	Clears the display of the calculator
P	Power function raises the previous number to the power of the next number
S	Saves the current display into the calculator memory
R	Recalls the current content of the memory to the display

Using the Command Keys

Four function arithmetic is performed on the pop-up calculator just as it would be on a hand-held calculator. For example, to add 23.7 to 46.2, the following sequence of steps would be executed:

Step 1:   Press the **F2** key to display the pop-up calculator on the screen.

Step 2:   Enter the number *23.7*. (It does not matter whether you use the number on the typewriter part of the keyboard or on the numeric keypad.)

Step 3:   Press the + key.

Step 4:   Enter the second number *46.2*.

Step 5:   Press the = key to display the resulting answer. You should see the number 69.9 appear on the output display.

Similar sequences can be used on the pop-up calculator for subtraction, multiplication, and division.

Power Function
To raise a number to a power, the **P** key must be used. To raise 1.09 to the 7th power, for example, the following sequence would be executed.

Step 1:   Press the **F2** key to display the pop-up calculator on the screen.

Step 2:   Enter the number *1.09*.

Step 3:   Press the **P** key.

Step 4:   Enter the power 7.

Step 5:   Press the = key to display the resulting answer. You should see the number 1.828039 appear on the output display.

Clear Display Function
Just like hand-held calculators, the pop-up calculator allows you to clear the output display. To do this, simply press the **c** key at any time and the calculator will reset.

Save-to-Memory and Recall-to-Display Functions

Sometimes there is a need to save the result of a calculation while another calculation is being performed. Hand-held calculators offer this capability and so does the pop-up calculator. To save a result that is still on the output display, just press the **s** key. When you need to recall the saved result, just press the **R** key.

To illustrate the use of this feature, let's say we want to compute the present-value interest factor for a dollar to be received 5 years from today where the opportunity cost of money is 8 percent per year. The present value interest factor is computed by:

$$\frac{1}{(1.08)^5} = .681 \text{ (rounded to three decimal places)}$$

To perform this calculation on the pop-up calculator, you should perform the following steps:

Step 1:   Press the **F2** key to display the pop-up calculator on the screen.

Step 2:   Enter the number *1.08*.

Step 3:   Press the **P** key.

Step 4:   Enter the power *5*.

Step 5:   Press the = key to display the resulting answer. You should see the number 1.469328 appear on the output display.

Step 6:   Press the **s** key.

Step 7:   Enter the number *1* (the numerator).

Step 8:   Press the / key.

Step 9:   Press the **R** key. At this point you are dividing 1 by the first result.

Step 10: Press the = key to display the resulting answer. You should see the number 0.68058 appear on the output display.

Chaining Operations

The rules for chaining operations on the pop-up calculator are about the same as they are on many hand-held calculators. The key to successful chaining of operations is to remember to press the = key for the previous operation before beginning a new operation. For example, to multiply 23.7 by 46.2 and then divide by 15.3, you should first enter *23.7*, then press the * key, then enter *46.2*, then press the = key, then press the / key, then enter the number *15.3*, and finally press the = key again to get the result 71.5647.

RUNNING THE *BMF PROBLEM-SOLVER*

If you select the *BMF Problem-Solver* at the Master Menu, you will first see a welcome screen. When you press any key, you will see the Main

Menu screen shown in Figure B.7. This menu controls the *BMF Problem-Solver* and is used as the starting point for all of the financial routines. The left side of the screen will have the menu items and the right side will display a brief explanation of the currently highlighted item.

By pressing the **ENTER** or **RETURN** key (⏎), the highlighted routine or its submenu is brought up. If there are no subchoices, the routine will begin; otherwise, a new menu will be displayed, offering the subchoices available for that routine.

For example, if you select "Time Value of Money," a third window opens on the screen showing that you have two further options: "Single Payment/Annuity" or "Mixed Stream." To make a selection, you again move the highlight bar to the line for the option you want (using the cursor movement arrows ↑ and ↓ as before) and press the **ENTER** (⏎) key. If you select the "Single Payment/Annuity" option you will next see a screen that gives you four further options: you can solve for (1) the interest, (2) the number of time periods required, (3) the future value, or (4) the present value. On this screen you must use the ← and → keys to move between options. You should notice that as you press one of those keys, the highlighting around INTEREST shifts to another of the four words. Move the highlighting to the type of calculation you want to do and press the **ENTER** (⏎) key as before.

Once you have answered all the questions, an answer will be displayed. After the answer has been shown, you can either select another option, or you can return to an earlier menu by pressing the **ESC** key until you get back to the master menu. At that point, you can go into the *BMF Tutor* by moving the large bar to that line and pressing the **ENTER** (⏎) key. Or to end the program, press the **ESC** key one more time, and you will leave the program entirely.

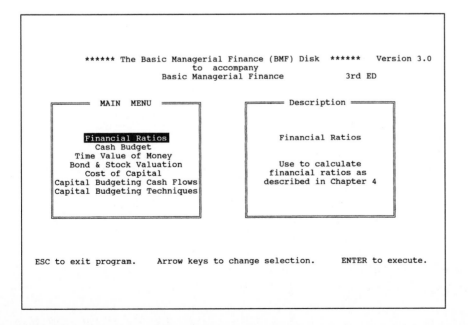

```
****** The Basic Managerial Finance (BMF) Disk ******   Version 3.0
                    to   accompany
             Basic Managerial Finance          3rd ED


    ═══ MAIN   MENU ═══                ═══ Description ═══

                                           Financial Ratios
     ┌─────────────────┐
     │ Financial Ratios│
        Cash Budget                        Use to calculate
     Time Value of Money                 financial ratios as
    Bond & Stock Valuation               described in Chapter 4
       Cost of Capital
  Capital Budgeting Cash Flows
  Capital Budgeting Techniques



  ESC to exit program.    Arrow keys to change selection.    ENTER to execute.
```

Figure B.7   *BMF Problem-Solver* **Main Menu Screen**

FINANCIAL TABLES

Table C-1   Future-Value Interest Factors for One Dollar Compounded at k Percent for n Periods: $FVIF_{k,n} = (1 + k)^n$

Period	1%	2%	3%	4%	5%	6%	7%	8%	9%	10%
1	1.010	1.020	1.030	1.040	1.050	1.060	1.070	1.080	1.090	1.100
2	1.020	1.040	1.061	1.082	1.102	1.124	1.145	1.166	1.188	1.210
3	1.030	1.061	1.093	1.125	1.158	1.191	1.225	1.260	1.295	1.331
4	1.041	1.082	1.126	1.170	1.216	1.262	1.311	1.360	1.412	1.464
5	1.051	1.104	1.159	1.217	1.276	1.338	1.403	1.469	1.539	1.611
6	1.062	1.126	1.194	1.265	1.340	1.419	1.501	1.587	1.677	1.772
7	1.072	1.149	1.230	1.316	1.407	1.504	1.606	1.714	1.828	1.949
8	1.083	1.172	1.267	1.369	1.477	1.594	1.718	1.851	1.993	2.144
9	1.094	1.195	1.305	1.423	1.551	1.689	1.838	1.999	2.172	2.358
10	1.105	1.219	1.344	1.480	1.629	1.791	1.967	2.159	2.367	2.594
11	1.116	1.243	1.384	1.539	1.710	1.898	2.105	2.332	2.580	2.853
12	1.127	1.268	1.426	1.601	1.796	2.012	2.252	2.518	2.813	3.138
13	1.138	1.294	1.469	1.665	1.886	2.133	2.410	2.720	3.066	3.452
14	1.149	1.319	1.513	1.732	1.980	2.261	2.579	2.937	3.342	3.797
15	1.161	1.346	1.558	1.801	2.079	2.397	2.759	3.172	3.642	4.177
16	1.173	1.373	1.605	1.873	2.183	2.540	2.952	3.426	3.970	4.595
17	1.184	1.400	1.653	1.948	2.292	2.693	3.159	3.700	4.328	5.054
18	1.196	1.428	1.702	2.026	2.407	2.854	3.380	3.996	4.717	5.560
19	1.208	1.457	1.753	2.107	2.527	3.026	3.616	4.316	5.142	6.116
20	1.220	1.486	1.806	2.191	2.653	3.207	3.870	4.661	5.604	6.727
21	1.232	1.516	1.860	2.279	2.786	3.399	4.140	5.034	6.109	7.400
22	1.245	1.546	1.916	2.370	2.925	3.603	4.430	5.436	6.658	8.140
23	1.257	1.577	1.974	2.465	3.071	3.820	4.740	5.871	7.258	8.954
24	1.270	1.608	2.033	2.563	3.225	4.049	5.072	6.341	7.911	9.850
25	1.282	1.641	2.094	2.666	3.386	4.292	5.427	6.848	8.623	10.834
30	1.348	1.811	2.427	3.243	4.322	5.743	7.612	10.062	13.267	17.449
35	1.417	2.000	2.814	3.946	5.516	7.686	10.676	14.785	20.413	28.102
40	1.489	2.208	3.262	4.801	7.040	10.285	14.974	21.724	31.408	45.258
45	1.565	2.438	3.781	5.841	8.985	13.764	21.002	31.920	48.325	72.888
50	1.645	2.691	4.384	7.106	11.467	18.419	29.456	46.900	74.354	117.386

Table C-1   **Future-Value Interest Factors for One Dollar Compounded at _k_ Percent for _n_ Periods: $FVIF_{k,n} = (1 + k)^n$ (continued)**

Period	11%	12%	13%	14%	15%	16%	17%	18%	19%	20%
1	1.110	1.120	1.130	1.140	1.150	1.160	1.170	1.180	1.190	1.200
2	1.232	1.254	1.277	1.300	1.322	1.346	1.369	1.392	1.416	1.440
3	1.368	1.405	1.443	1.482	1.521	1.561	1.602	1.643	1.685	1.728
4	1.518	1.574	1.630	1.689	1.749	1.811	1.874	1.939	2.005	2.074
5	1.685	1.762	1.842	1.925	2.011	2.100	2.192	2.288	2.386	2.488
6	1.870	1.974	2.082	2.195	2.313	2.436	2.565	2.700	2.840	2.986
7	2.076	2.211	2.353	2.502	2.660	2.826	3.001	3.185	3.379	3.583
8	2.305	2.476	2.658	2.853	3.059	3.278	3.511	3.759	4.021	4.300
9	2.558	2.773	3.004	3.252	3.518	3.803	4.108	4.435	4.785	5.160
10	2.839	3.106	3.395	3.707	4.046	4.411	4.807	5.234	5.695	6.192
11	3.152	3.479	3.836	4.226	4.652	5.117	5.624	6.176	6.777	7.430
12	3.498	3.896	4.334	4.818	5.350	5.936	6.580	7.288	8.064	8.916
13	3.883	4.363	4.898	5.492	6.153	6.886	7.699	8.599	9.596	10.699
14	4.310	4.887	5.535	6.261	7.076	7.987	9.007	10.147	11.420	12.839
15	4.785	5.474	6.254	7.138	8.137	9.265	10.539	11.974	13.589	15.407
16	5.311	6.130	7.067	8.137	9.358	10.748	12.330	14.129	16.171	18.488
17	5.895	6.866	7.986	9.276	10.761	12.468	14.426	16.672	19.244	22.186
18	6.543	7.690	9.024	10.575	12.375	14.462	16.879	19.673	22.900	26.623
19	7.263	8.613	10.197	12.055	14.232	16.776	19.748	23.214	27.251	31.948
20	8.062	9.646	11.523	13.743	16.366	19.461	23.105	27.393	32.429	38.337
21	8.949	10.804	13.021	15.667	18.821	22.574	27.033	32.323	38.591	46.005
22	9.933	12.100	14.713	17.861	21.644	26.186	31.629	38.141	45.923	55.205
23	11.026	13.552	16.626	20.361	24.891	30.376	37.005	45.007	54.648	66.247
24	12.239	15.178	18.788	23.212	28.625	35.236	43.296	53.108	65.031	79.496
25	13.585	17.000	21.230	26.461	32.918	40.874	50.656	62.667	77.387	95.395
30	22.892	29.960	39.115	50.949	66.210	85.849	111.061	143.367	184.672	237.373
35	38.574	52.799	72.066	98.097	133.172	180.311	243.495	327.988	440.691	590.657
40	64.999	93.049	132.776	188.876	267.856	378.715	533.846	750.353	1051.642	1469.740
45	109.527	163.985	244.629	363.662	538.752	795.429	1170.425	1716.619	2509.583	3657.176
50	184.559	288.996	450.711	700.197	1083.619	1670.669	2566.080	3927.189	5988.730	9100.191

Table C-1   Future-Value Interest Factors for One Dollar Compounded at k Percent for n Periods: $FVIF_{k,n} = (1 + k)^n$ (continued)

Period	21%	22%	23%	24%	25%	26%	27%	28%	29%	30%
1	1.210	1.220	1.230	1.240	1.250	1.260	1.270	1.280	1.290	1.300
2	1.464	1.488	1.513	1.538	1.562	1.588	1.613	1.638	1.664	1.690
3	1.772	1.816	1.861	1.907	1.953	2.000	2.048	2.097	2.147	2.197
4	2.144	2.215	2.289	2.364	2.441	2.520	2.601	2.684	2.769	2.856
5	2.594	2.703	2.815	2.932	3.052	3.176	3.304	3.436	3.572	3.713
6	3.138	3.297	3.463	3.635	3.815	4.001	4.196	4.398	4.608	4.827
7	3.797	4.023	4.259	4.508	4.768	5.042	5.329	5.629	5.945	6.275
8	4.595	4.908	5.239	5.589	5.960	6.353	6.767	7.206	7.669	8.157
9	5.560	5.987	6.444	6.931	7.451	8.004	8.595	9.223	9.893	10.604
10	6.727	7.305	7.926	8.594	9.313	10.086	10.915	11.806	12.761	13.786
11	8.140	8.912	9.749	10.657	11.642	12.708	13.862	15.112	16.462	17.921
12	9.850	10.872	11.991	13.215	14.552	16.012	17.605	19.343	21.236	23.298
13	11.918	13.264	14.749	16.386	18.190	20.175	22.359	24.759	27.395	30.287
14	14.421	16.182	18.141	20.319	22.737	25.420	28.395	31.691	35.339	39.373
15	17.449	19.742	22.314	25.195	28.422	32.030	36.062	40.565	45.587	51.185
16	21.113	24.085	27.446	31.242	35.527	40.357	45.799	51.923	58.808	66.541
17	25.547	29.384	33.758	38.740	44.409	50.850	58.165	66.461	75.862	86.503
18	30.912	35.848	41.523	48.038	55.511	64.071	73.869	85.070	97.862	112.454
19	37.404	43.735	51.073	59.567	69.389	80.730	93.813	108.890	126.242	146.190
20	45.258	53.357	62.820	73.863	86.736	101.720	119.143	139.379	162.852	190.047
21	54.762	65.095	77.268	91.591	108.420	128.167	151.312	178.405	210.079	247.061
22	66.262	79.416	95.040	113.572	135.525	161.490	192.165	228.358	271.002	321.178
23	80.178	96.887	116.899	140.829	169.407	203.477	244.050	292.298	349.592	417.531
24	97.015	118.203	143.786	174.628	211.758	256.381	309.943	374.141	450.974	542.791
25	117.388	144.207	176.857	216.539	264.698	323.040	393.628	478.901	581.756	705.627
30	304.471	389.748	497.904	634.810	807.793	1025.904	1300.477	1645.488	2078.208	2619.936
35	789.716	1053.370	1401.749	1861.020	2465.189	3258.053	4296.547	5653.840	7423.988	9727.598
40	2048.309	2846.941	3946.340	5455.797	7523.156	10346.879	14195.051	19426.418	26520.723	36117.754
45	5312.758	7694.418	11110.121	15994.316	22958.844	32859.457	46897.973	66748.500	94739.937	134102.187
50	13779.844	20795.680	31278.301	46889.207	70064.812	104354.562	154942.687	229345.875	338440.000	497910.125

C-1

Table C-1   Future-Value Interest Factors for One Dollar Compounded at k Percent for n Periods: $FVIF_{k,n} = (1 + k)^n$ (continued)

Period	31%	32%	33%	34%	35%	36%	37%	38%	39%	40%
1	1.310	1.320	1.330	1.340	1.350	1.360	1.370	1.380	1.390	1.400
2	1.716	1.742	1.769	1.796	1.822	1.850	1.877	1.904	1.932	1.960
3	2.248	2.300	2.353	2.406	2.460	2.515	2.571	2.628	2.686	2.744
4	2.945	3.036	3.129	3.224	3.321	3.421	3.523	3.627	3.733	3.842
5	3.858	4.007	4.162	4.320	4.484	4.653	4.826	5.005	5.189	5.378
6	5.054	5.290	5.535	5.789	6.053	6.328	6.612	6.907	7.213	7.530
7	6.621	6.983	7.361	7.758	8.172	8.605	9.058	9.531	10.025	10.541
8	8.673	9.217	9.791	10.395	11.032	11.703	12.410	13.153	13.935	14.758
9	11.362	12.166	13.022	13.930	14.894	15.917	17.001	18.151	19.370	20.661
10	14.884	16.060	17.319	18.666	20.106	21.646	23.292	25.049	26.924	28.925
11	19.498	21.199	23.034	25.012	27.144	29.439	31.910	34.567	37.425	40.495
12	25.542	27.982	30.635	33.516	36.644	40.037	43.716	47.703	52.020	56.694
13	33.460	36.937	40.745	44.912	49.469	54.451	59.892	65.830	72.308	79.371
14	43.832	48.756	54.190	60.181	66.784	74.053	82.051	90.845	100.509	111.119
15	57.420	64.358	72.073	80.643	90.158	100.712	112.410	125.366	139.707	155.567
16	75.220	84.953	95.857	108.061	121.713	136.968	154.002	173.005	194.192	217.793
17	98.539	112.138	127.490	144.802	164.312	186.277	210.983	238.747	269.927	304.911
18	129.086	148.022	169.561	194.035	221.822	253.337	289.046	329.471	375.198	426.875
19	169.102	195.389	225.517	260.006	299.459	344.537	395.993	454.669	521.525	597.625
20	221.523	257.913	299.937	348.408	404.270	468.571	542.511	627.443	724.919	836.674
21	290.196	340.446	398.916	466.867	545.764	637.256	743.240	865.871	1007.637	1171.343
22	380.156	449.388	530.558	625.601	736.781	866.668	1018.238	1194.900	1400.615	1639.878
23	498.004	593.192	705.642	838.305	994.653	1178.668	1394.986	1648.961	1946.854	2295.829
24	652.385	783.013	938.504	1123.328	1342.781	1602.988	1911.129	2275.564	2706.125	3214.158
25	854.623	1033.577	1248.210	1505.258	1812.754	2180.063	2618.245	3140.275	3761.511	4499.816
30	3297.081	4142.008	5194.516	6503.285	8128.426	10142.914	12636.086	15716.703	19517.969	24201.043
35	12719.918	16598.906	21617.363	28096.695	36448.051	47190.727	60983.836	78660.188	101276.125	130158.687
40	49072.621	66519.313	89962.188	121388.437	163433.875	219558.625	294317.937	393684.687	525508.312	700022.688

C-1

Table C-1   Future-Value Interest Factors for One Dollar Compounded at k Percent for n Periods: $FVIF_{k,n} = (1 + k)^n$ (continued)

Period	41%	42%	43%	44%	45%	46%	47%	48%	49%	50%
1	1.410	1.420	1.430	1.440	1.450	1.460	1.470	1.480	1.490	1.500
2	1.988	2.016	2.045	2.074	2.102	2.132	2.161	2.190	2.220	2.250
3	2.803	2.863	2.924	2.986	3.049	3.112	3.177	3.242	3.308	3.375
4	3.953	4.066	4.182	4.300	4.421	4.544	4.669	4.798	4.929	5.063
5	5.573	5.774	5.980	6.192	6.410	6.634	6.864	7.101	7.344	7.594
6	7.858	8.198	8.551	8.916	9.294	9.685	10.090	10.509	10.943	11.391
7	11.080	11.642	12.228	12.839	13.476	14.141	14.833	15.554	16.304	17.086
8	15.623	16.531	17.486	18.488	19.541	20.645	21.804	23.019	24.293	25.629
9	22.028	23.474	25.005	26.623	28.334	30.142	32.052	34.069	36.197	38.443
10	31.059	33.333	35.757	38.337	41.085	44.007	47.116	50.421	53.934	57.665
11	43.793	47.333	51.132	55.206	59.573	64.251	69.261	74.624	80.361	86.498
12	61.749	67.213	73.119	79.496	86.380	93.806	101.813	110.443	119.738	129.746
13	87.066	95.443	104.560	114.475	125.251	136.956	149.665	163.456	178.410	194.620
14	122.763	135.529	149.521	164.843	181.614	199.956	220.008	241.914	265.831	291.929
15	173.095	192.451	213.814	237.374	263.341	291.936	323.411	358.033	396.088	437.894
16	244.064	273.280	305.754	341.819	381.844	426.226	475.414	529.888	590.170	656.841
17	344.130	388.057	437.228	492.219	553.674	622.289	698.859	784.234	879.354	985.261
18	485.224	551.041	625.235	708.794	802.826	908.541	1027.321	1160.666	1310.236	1477.892
19	684.165	782.478	894.086	1020.663	1164.098	1326.469	1510.161	1717.785	1952.252	2216.838
20	964.673	1111.118	1278.543	1469.754	1687.942	1936.642	2219.936	2542.321	2908.854	3325.257
21	1360.188	1577.786	1828.315	2116.445	2447.515	2827.496	3263.304	3762.633	4334.188	4987.883
22	1917.865	2240.455	2614.489	3047.679	3548.896	4128.137	4797.051	5568.691	6457.941	7481.824
23	2704.188	3181.443	3738.717	4388.656	5145.898	6027.078	7051.660	8241.664	9622.324	11222.738
24	3812.905	4517.641	5346.355	6319.656	7461.547	8799.523	10365.934	12197.656	14337.258	16834.109
25	5376.191	6415.047	7645.289	9100.305	10819.242	12847.297	15237.914	18052.516	21362.508	25251.164
30	29961.941	37037.383	45716.496	56346.535	69348.375	85226.375	104594.938	128187.438	156885.438	191751.000

C-2

Table C-2   Future-Value Interest Factors for a One-Dollar Annuity Compounded at k Percent for n Periods: $FVIFA_{k,n} = \sum_{i=1}^{n} (1 + k)^{i-1}$

Period	1%	2%	3%	4%	5%	6%	7%	8%	9%	10%
1	1.000	1.000	1.000	1.000	1.000	1.000	1.000	1.000	1.000	1.000
2	2.010	2.020	2.030	2.040	2.050	2.060	2.070	2.080	2.090	2.100
3	3.030	3.060	3.091	3.122	3.152	3.184	3.215	3.246	3.278	3.310
4	4.060	4.122	4.184	4.246	4.310	4.375	4.440	4.506	4.573	4.641
5	5.101	5.204	5.309	5.416	5.526	5.637	5.751	5.867	5.985	6.105
6	6.152	6.308	6.468	6.633	6.802	6.975	7.153	7.336	7.523	7.716
7	7.214	7.434	7.662	7.898	8.142	8.394	8.654	8.923	9.200	9.487
8	8.286	8.583	8.892	9.214	9.549	9.897	10.260	10.637	11.028	11.436
9	9.368	9.755	10.159	10.583	11.027	11.491	11.978	12.488	13.021	13.579
10	10.462	10.950	11.464	12.006	12.578	13.181	13.816	14.487	15.193	15.937
11	11.567	12.169	12.808	13.486	14.207	14.972	15.784	16.645	17.560	18.531
12	12.682	13.412	14.192	15.026	15.917	16.870	17.888	18.977	20.141	21.384
13	13.809	14.680	15.618	16.627	17.713	18.882	20.141	21.495	22.953	24.523
14	14.947	15.974	17.086	18.292	19.598	21.015	22.550	24.215	26.019	27.975
15	16.097	17.293	18.599	20.023	21.578	23.276	25.129	27.152	29.361	31.772
16	17.258	18.639	20.157	21.824	23.657	25.672	27.888	30.324	33.003	35.949
17	18.430	20.012	21.761	23.697	25.840	28.213	30.840	33.750	36.973	40.544
18	19.614	21.412	23.414	25.645	28.132	30.905	33.999	37.450	41.301	45.599
19	20.811	22.840	25.117	27.671	30.539	33.760	37.379	41.446	46.018	51.158
20	22.019	24.297	26.870	29.778	33.066	36.785	40.995	45.762	51.159	57.274
21	23.239	25.783	28.676	31.969	35.719	39.992	44.865	50.422	56.764	64.002
22	24.471	27.299	30.536	34.248	38.505	43.392	49.005	55.456	62.872	71.402
23	25.716	28.845	32.452	36.618	41.430	46.995	53.435	60.893	69.531	79.542
24	26.973	30.421	34.426	39.082	44.501	50.815	58.176	66.764	76.789	88.496
25	28.243	32.030	36.459	41.645	47.726	54.864	63.248	73.105	84.699	98.346
30	34.784	40.567	47.575	56.084	66.438	79.057	94.459	113.282	136.305	164.491
35	41.659	49.994	60.461	73.651	90.318	111.432	138.234	172.314	215.705	271.018
40	48.885	60.401	75.400	95.024	120.797	154.758	199.630	259.052	337.872	442.580
45	56.479	71.891	92.718	121.027	159.695	212.737	285.741	386.497	525.840	718.881
50	64.461	84.577	112.794	152.664	209.341	290.325	406.516	573.756	815.051	1163.865

Table C-2   Future-Value Interest Factors for a One-Dollar Annuity Compounded at k Percent for n Periods: $FVIFA_{k,n} = \sum\limits_{t=1}^{n} (1 + k)^{t-1}$ (continued)

Period	11%	12%	13%	14%	15%	16%	17%	18%	19%	20%
1	1.000	1.000	1.000	1.000	1.000	1.000	1.000	1.000	1.000	1.000
2	2.110	2.120	2.130	2.140	2.150	2.160	2.170	2.180	2.190	2.200
3	3.342	3.374	3.407	3.440	3.472	3.506	3.539	3.572	3.606	3.640
4	4.710	4.779	4.850	4.921	4.993	5.066	5.141	5.215	5.291	5.368
5	6.228	6.353	6.480	6.610	6.742	6.877	7.014	7.154	7.297	7.442
6	7.913	8.115	8.323	8.535	8.754	8.977	9.207	9.442	9.683	9.930
7	9.783	10.089	10.405	10.730	11.067	11.414	11.772	12.141	12.523	12.916
8	11.859	12.300	12.757	13.233	13.727	14.240	14.773	15.327	15.902	16.499
9	14.164	14.776	15.416	16.085	16.786	17.518	18.285	19.086	19.923	20.799
10	16.722	17.549	18.420	19.337	20.304	21.321	22.393	23.521	24.709	25.959
11	19.561	20.655	21.814	23.044	24.349	25.733	27.200	28.755	30.403	32.150
12	22.713	24.133	25.650	27.271	29.001	30.850	32.824	34.931	37.180	39.580
13	26.211	28.029	29.984	32.088	34.352	36.786	39.404	42.218	45.244	48.496
14	30.095	32.392	34.882	37.581	40.504	43.672	47.102	50.818	54.841	59.196
15	34.405	37.280	40.417	43.842	47.580	51.659	56.109	60.965	66.260	72.035
16	39.190	42.753	46.671	50.980	55.717	60.925	66.648	72.938	79.850	87.442
17	44.500	48.883	53.738	59.117	65.075	71.673	78.978	87.067	96.021	105.930
18	50.396	55.749	61.724	68.393	75.836	84.140	93.404	103.739	115.265	128.116
19	56.939	63.439	70.748	78.968	88.211	98.603	110.283	123.412	138.165	154.739
20	64.202	72.052	80.946	91.024	102.443	115.379	130.031	146.626	165.417	186.687
21	72.264	81.698	92.468	104.767	118.809	134.840	153.136	174.019	197.846	225.024
22	81.213	92.502	105.489	120.434	137.630	157.414	180.169	206.342	236.436	271.028
23	91.147	104.602	120.203	138.295	159.274	183.600	211.798	244.483	282.359	326.234
24	102.173	118.154	136.829	158.656	184.166	213.976	248.803	289.490	337.007	392.480
25	114.412	133.333	155.616	181.867	212.790	249.212	292.099	342.598	402.038	471.976
30	199.018	241.330	293.192	356.778	434.738	530.306	647.423	790.932	966.698	1181.865
35	341.583	431.658	546.663	693.552	881.152	1120.699	1426.448	1816.607	2314.173	2948.294
40	581.812	767.080	1013.667	1341.979	1779.048	2360.724	3134.412	4163.094	5529.711	7343.715
45	986.613	1358.208	1874.086	2590.464	3585.031	4965.191	6879.008	9531.258	13203.105	18280.914
50	1668.723	2399.975	3459.344	4994.301	7217.488	10435.449	15088.805	21812.273	31514.492	45496.094

C-2

Table C-2   **Future-Value Interest Factors for a One-Dollar Annuity Compounded at k Percent for n Periods:** $FVIFA_{k,n} = \sum\limits_{t=1}^{n} (1 + k)^{t-1}$ (continued)

Period	21%	22%	23%	24%	25%	26%	27%	28%	29%	30%
1	1.000	1.000	1.000	1.000	1.000	1.000	1.000	1.000	1.000	1.000
2	2.210	2.220	2.230	2.240	2.250	2.260	2.270	2.280	2.290	2.300
3	3.674	3.708	3.743	3.778	3.813	3.848	3.883	3.918	3.954	3.990
4	5.446	5.524	5.604	5.684	5.766	5.848	5.931	6.016	6.101	6.187
5	7.589	7.740	7.893	8.048	8.207	8.368	8.533	8.700	8.870	9.043
6	10.183	10.442	10.708	10.980	11.259	11.544	11.837	12.136	12.442	12.756
7	13.321	13.740	14.171	14.615	15.073	15.546	16.032	16.534	17.051	17.583
8	17.119	17.762	18.430	19.123	19.842	20.588	21.361	22.163	22.995	23.858
9	21.714	22.670	23.669	24.712	25.802	26.940	28.129	29.369	30.664	32.015
10	27.274	28.657	30.113	31.643	33.253	34.945	36.723	38.592	40.556	42.619
11	34.001	35.962	38.039	40.238	42.566	45.030	47.639	50.398	53.318	56.405
12	42.141	44.873	47.787	50.895	54.208	57.738	61.501	65.510	69.780	74.326
13	51.991	55.745	59.778	64.109	68.760	73.750	79.106	84.853	91.016	97.624
14	63.909	69.009	74.528	80.496	86.949	93.925	101.465	109.611	118.411	127.912
15	78.330	85.191	92.669	100.815	109.687	119.346	129.860	141.302	153.750	167.285
16	95.779	104.933	114.983	126.010	138.109	151.375	165.922	181.867	199.337	218.470
17	116.892	129.019	142.428	157.252	173.636	191.733	211.721	233.790	258.145	285.011
18	142.439	158.403	176.187	195.993	218.045	242.583	269.885	300.250	334.006	371.514
19	173.351	194.251	217.710	244.031	273.556	306.654	343.754	385.321	431.868	483.968
20	210.755	237.986	268.783	303.598	342.945	387.384	437.568	494.210	558.110	630.157
21	256.013	291.343	331.603	377.461	429.681	489.104	556.710	633.589	720.962	820.204
22	310.775	356.438	408.871	469.052	538.101	617.270	708.022	811.993	931.040	1067.265
23	377.038	435.854	503.911	582.624	673.626	778.760	900.187	1040.351	1202.042	1388.443
24	457.215	532.741	620.810	723.453	843.032	982.237	1144.237	1332.649	1551.634	1805.975
25	554.230	650.944	764.596	898.082	1054.791	1238.617	1454.180	1706.790	2002.608	2348.765
30	1445.111	1767.044	2160.459	2640.881	3227.172	3941.953	4812.891	5873.172	7162.785	8729.805
35	3755.814	4783.520	6090.227	7750.094	9856.746	12527.160	15909.480	20188.742	25596.512	32422.090
40	9749.141	12936.141	17153.691	22728.367	30088.621	39791.957	52570.707	69376.562	91447.375	120389.375
45	25294.223	34970.230	48300.660	66638.937	91831.312	126378.937	173692.875	238384.312	326686.375	447005.062

C-2

Table C-2   Future-Value Interest Factors for a One-Dollar Annuity Compounded at k Percent for n Periods: $FVIFA_{k,n} = \sum_{t=1}^{n} (1 + k)^{t-1}$ (continued)

Period	31%	32%	33%	34%	35%	36%	37%	38%	39%	40%
1	1.000	1.000	1.000	1.000	1.000	1.000	1.000	1.000	1.000	1.000
2	2.310	2.320	2.330	2.340	2.350	2.360	2.370	2.380	2.390	2.400
3	4.026	4.062	4.099	4.136	4.172	4.210	4.247	4.284	4.322	4.360
4	6.274	6.362	6.452	6.542	6.633	6.725	6.818	6.912	7.008	7.104
5	9.219	9.398	9.581	9.766	9.954	10.146	10.341	10.539	10.741	10.946
6	13.077	13.406	13.742	14.086	14.438	14.799	15.167	15.544	15.930	16.324
7	18.131	18.696	19.277	19.876	20.492	21.126	21.779	22.451	23.142	23.853
8	24.752	25.678	26.638	27.633	28.664	29.732	30.837	31.982	33.167	34.395
9	33.425	34.895	36.429	38.028	39.696	41.435	43.247	45.135	47.103	49.152
10	44.786	47.062	49.451	51.958	54.590	57.351	60.248	63.287	66.473	69.813
11	59.670	63.121	66.769	70.624	74.696	78.998	83.540	88.335	93.397	98.739
12	79.167	84.320	89.803	95.636	101.840	108.437	115.450	122.903	130.822	139.234
13	104.709	112.302	120.438	129.152	138.484	148.474	159.166	170.606	182.842	195.928
14	138.169	149.239	161.183	174.063	187.953	202.925	219.058	236.435	255.151	275.299
15	182.001	197.996	215.373	234.245	254.737	276.978	301.109	327.281	355.659	386.418
16	239.421	262.354	287.446	314.888	344.895	377.690	413.520	452.647	495.366	541.985
17	314.642	347.307	383.303	422.949	466.608	514.658	567.521	625.652	689.558	759.778
18	413.180	459.445	510.792	567.751	630.920	700.935	778.504	864.399	959.485	1064.689
19	542.266	607.467	680.354	761.786	852.741	954.271	1067.551	1193.870	1334.683	1491.563
20	711.368	802.856	905.870	1021.792	1152.200	1298.809	1463.544	1648.539	1856.208	2089.188
21	932.891	1060.769	1205.807	1370.201	1556.470	1767.380	2006.055	2275.982	2581.128	2925.862
22	1223.087	1401.215	1604.724	1837.068	2102.234	2404.636	2749.294	3141.852	3588.765	4097.203
23	1603.243	1850.603	2135.282	2462.669	2839.014	3271.304	3767.532	4336.750	4989.379	5737.078
24	2101.247	2443.795	2840.924	3300.974	3833.667	4449.969	5162.516	5985.711	6936.230	8032.906
25	2753.631	3226.808	3779.428	4424.301	5176.445	6052.957	7073.645	8261.273	9642.352	11247.062
30	10632.543	12940.672	15737.945	19124.434	23221.258	28172.016	34148.906	41357.227	50043.625	60500.207
35	41028.887	51868.563	65504.199	82634.625	104134.500	131082.625	164818.438	206998.375	259680.313	325394.688

C-2

Table C-2 Future-Value Interest Factors for a One-Dollar Annuity Compounded at k Percent for n Periods: $FVIFA_{k,n} = \sum_{t=1}^{n} (1 + k)^{t-1}$ (continued)

Period	41%	42%	43%	44%	45%	46%	47%	48%	49%	50%
1	1.000	1.000	1.000	1.000	1.000	1.000	1.000	1.000	1.000	1.000
2	2.410	2.420	2.430	2.440	2.450	2.460	2.470	2.480	2.490	2.500
3	4.398	4.436	4.475	4.514	4.552	4.592	4.631	4.670	4.710	4.750
4	7.201	7.300	7.399	7.500	7.601	7.704	7.807	7.912	8.018	8.125
5	11.154	11.366	11.581	11.799	12.022	12.247	12.477	12.710	12.947	13.188
6	16.727	17.139	17.560	17.991	18.431	18.881	19.341	19.811	20.291	20.781
7	24.585	25.337	26.111	26.907	27.725	28.567	29.431	30.320	31.233	32.172
8	35.665	36.979	38.339	39.746	41.202	42.707	44.264	45.874	47.538	49.258
9	51.287	53.510	55.825	58.235	60.743	63.352	66.068	68.893	71.831	74.887
10	73.315	76.985	80.830	84.858	89.077	93.494	98.120	102.961	108.028	113.330
11	104.374	110.318	116.586	123.195	130.161	137.502	145.236	153.383	161.962	170.995
12	148.168	157.651	167.719	178.401	189.734	201.752	214.497	228.007	242.323	257.493
13	209.916	224.865	240.837	257.897	276.114	295.558	316.310	338.449	362.062	387.239
14	296.982	320.308	345.397	372.372	401.365	432.514	465.975	501.905	540.471	581.858
15	419.744	455.837	494.918	537.215	582.980	632.470	685.983	743.819	806.302	873.788
16	592.839	648.288	708.732	774.589	846.321	924.406	1009.394	1101.852	1202.390	1311.681
17	836.903	921.568	1014.486	1116.408	1228.165	1350.631	1484.809	1631.740	1792.560	1968.522
18	1181.034	1309.625	1451.714	1608.626	1781.838	1972.920	2183.667	2415.974	2671.914	2953.783
19	1666.257	1860.666	2076.949	2317.421	2584.665	2881.461	3210.989	3576.640	3982.150	4431.672
20	2350.422	2643.144	2971.035	3338.084	3748.763	4207.926	4721.148	5294.422	5934.402	6648.508
21	3315.095	3754.262	4249.574	4807.836	5436.703	6144.566	6941.082	7836.742	8843.254	9973.762
22	4675.281	5332.047	6077.887	6924.281	7884.215	8972.059	10204.383	11599.375	13177.441	14961.645
23	6593.145	7572.500	8692.375	9971.957	11433.109	13100.195	15001.434	17168.066	19635.383	22443.469
24	9297.332	10753.941	12431.090	14360.613	16579.008	19127.273	22053.094	25409.730	29257.707	33666.307
25	13110.234	15271.582	17777.445	20680.270	24040.555	27926.797	32419.027	37607.387	43594.965	50500.316
30	73075.500	88181.938	106315.250	128058.125	154105.313	185273.000	222540.625	267055.375	320172.750	383500.000

Table C-3   Present-Value Interest Factors for One Dollar Discounted at k Percent for n Periods: $PVIF_{k,n} = \dfrac{1}{(1+k)^n}$

Period	1%	2%	3%	4%	5%	6%	7%	8%	9%	10%
1	.990	.980	.971	.962	.952	.943	.935	.926	.917	.909
2	.980	.961	.943	.925	.907	.890	.873	.857	.842	.826
3	.971	.942	.915	.889	.864	.840	.816	.794	.772	.751
4	.961	.924	.888	.855	.823	.792	.763	.735	.708	.683
5	.951	.906	.863	.822	.784	.747	.713	.681	.650	.621
6	.942	.888	.837	.790	.746	.705	.666	.630	.596	.564
7	.933	.871	.813	.760	.711	.665	.623	.583	.547	.513
8	.923	.853	.789	.731	.677	.627	.582	.540	.502	.467
9	.914	.837	.766	.703	.645	.592	.544	.500	.460	.424
10	.905	.820	.744	.676	.614	.558	.508	.463	.422	.386
11	.896	.804	.722	.650	.585	.527	.475	.429	.388	.350
12	.887	.789	.701	.625	.557	.497	.444	.397	.356	.319
13	.879	.773	.681	.601	.530	.469	.415	.368	.326	.290
14	.870	.758	.661	.577	.505	.442	.388	.340	.299	.263
15	.861	.743	.642	.555	.481	.417	.362	.315	.275	.239
16	.853	.728	.623	.534	.458	.394	.339	.292	.252	.218
17	.844	.714	.605	.513	.436	.371	.317	.270	.231	.198
18	.836	.700	.587	.494	.416	.350	.296	.250	.212	.180
19	.828	.686	.570	.475	.396	.331	.277	.232	.194	.164
20	.820	.673	.554	.456	.377	.312	.258	.215	.178	.149
21	.811	.660	.538	.439	.359	.294	.242	.199	.164	.135
22	.803	.647	.522	.422	.342	.278	.226	.184	.150	.123
23	.795	.634	.507	.406	.326	.262	.211	.170	.138	.112
24	.788	.622	.492	.390	.310	.247	.197	.158	.126	.102
25	.780	.610	.478	.375	.295	.233	.184	.146	.116	.092
30	.742	.552	.412	.308	.231	.174	.131	.099	.075	.057
35	.706	.500	.355	.253	.181	.130	.094	.068	.049	.036
40	.672	.453	.307	.208	.142	.097	.067	.046	.032	.022
45	.639	.410	.264	.171	.111	.073	.048	.031	.021	.014
50	.608	.372	.228	.141	.087	.054	.034	.021	.013	.009

C-3

Table C-3   **Present-Value Interest Factors for One Dollar Discounted at k Percent for n Periods: $PVIF_{k,n} = \dfrac{1}{(1 + k)^n}$ (continued)**

Period	11%	12%	13%	14%	15%	16%	17%	18%	19%	20%
1	.901	.893	.885	.877	.870	.862	.855	.847	.840	.833
2	.812	.797	.783	.769	.756	.743	.731	.718	.706	.694
3	.731	.712	.693	.675	.658	.641	.624	.609	.593	.579
4	.659	.636	.613	.592	.572	.552	.534	.516	.499	.482
5	.593	.567	.543	.519	.497	.476	.456	.437	.419	.402
6	.535	.507	.480	.456	.432	.410	.390	.370	.352	.335
7	.482	.452	.425	.400	.376	.354	.333	.314	.296	.279
8	.434	.404	.376	.351	.327	.305	.285	.266	.249	.233
9	.391	.361	.333	.308	.284	.263	.243	.225	.209	.194
10	.352	.322	.295	.270	.247	.227	.208	.191	.176	.162
11	.317	.287	.261	.237	.215	.195	.178	.162	.148	.135
12	.286	.257	.231	.208	.187	.168	.152	.137	.124	.112
13	.258	.229	.204	.182	.163	.145	.130	.116	.104	.093
14	.232	.205	.181	.160	.141	.125	.111	.099	.088	.078
15	.209	.183	.160	.140	.123	.108	.095	.084	.074	.065
16	.188	.163	.141	.123	.107	.093	.081	.071	.062	.054
17	.170	.146	.125	.108	.093	.080	.069	.060	.052	.045
18	.153	.130	.111	.095	.081	.069	.059	.051	.044	.038
19	.138	.116	.098	.083	.070	.060	.051	.043	.037	.031
20	.124	.104	.087	.073	.061	.051	.043	.037	.031	.026
21	.112	.093	.077	.064	.053	.044	.037	.031	.026	.022
22	.101	.083	.068	.056	.046	.038	.032	.026	.022	.018
23	.091	.074	.060	.049	.040	.033	.027	.022	.018	.015
24	.082	.066	.053	.043	.035	.028	.023	.019	.015	.013
25	.074	.059	.047	.038	.030	.024	.020	.016	.013	.010
30	.044	.033	.026	.020	.015	.012	.009	.007	.005	.004
35	.026	.019	.014	.010	.008	.006	.004	.003	.002	.002
40	.015	.011	.008	.005	.004	.003	.002	.001	.001	.001
45	.009	.006	.004	.003	.002	.001	.001	.001	*	*
50	.005	.003	.002	.001	.001	.001	*	*	*	*

*$PVIF$ is zero to three decimal places.

Table C-3   Present-Value Interest Factors for One Dollar Discounted at k Percent for n Periods: $PVIF_{k,n} = \dfrac{1}{(1+k)^n}$ (continued)

Period	21%	22%	23%	24%	25%	26%	27%	28%	29%	30%
1	.826	.820	.813	.806	.800	.794	.787	.781	.775	.769
2	.683	.672	.661	.650	.640	.630	.620	.610	.601	.592
3	.564	.551	.537	.524	.512	.500	.488	.477	.466	.455
4	.467	.451	.437	.423	.410	.397	.384	.373	.361	.350
5	.386	.370	.355	.341	.328	.315	.303	.291	.280	.269
6	.319	.303	.289	.275	.262	.250	.238	.227	.217	.207
7	.263	.249	.235	.222	.210	.198	.188	.178	.168	.159
8	.218	.204	.191	.179	.168	.157	.148	.139	.130	.123
9	.180	.167	.155	.144	.134	.125	.116	.108	.101	.094
10	.149	.137	.126	.116	.107	.099	.092	.085	.078	.073
11	.123	.112	.103	.094	.086	.079	.072	.066	.061	.056
12	.102	.092	.083	.076	.069	.062	.057	.052	.047	.043
13	.084	.075	.068	.061	.055	.050	.045	.040	.037	.033
14	.069	.062	.055	.049	.044	.039	.035	.032	.028	.025
15	.057	.051	.045	.040	.035	.031	.028	.025	.022	.020
16	.047	.042	.036	.032	.028	.025	.022	.019	.017	.015
17	.039	.034	.030	.026	.023	.020	.017	.015	.013	.012
18	.032	.028	.024	.021	.018	.016	.014	.012	.010	.009
19	.027	.023	.020	.017	.014	.012	.011	.009	.008	.007
20	.022	.019	.016	.014	.012	.010	.008	.007	.006	.005
21	.018	.015	.013	.011	.009	.008	.007	.006	.005	.004
22	.015	.013	.011	.009	.007	.006	.005	.004	.004	.003
23	.012	.010	.009	.007	.006	.005	.004	.003	.003	.002
24	.010	.008	.007	.006	.005	.004	.003	.003	.002	.002
25	.009	.007	.006	.005	.004	.003	.003	.002	.002	.001
30	.003	.003	.002	.002	.001	.001	.001	.001	*	*
35	.001	.001	.001	.001	*	*	*	*	*	*
40	*	*	*	*	*	*	*	*	*	*
45	*	*	*	*	*	*	*	*	*	*
50	*	*	*	*	*	*	*	*	*	*

*$PVIF$ is zero to three decimal places.

C-3

Table C-3   **Present-Value Interest Factors for One Dollar Discounted at k Percent for n Periods:** $PVIF_{k,n} = \dfrac{1}{(1+k)^n}$ (continued)

Period	31%	32%	33%	34%	35%	36%	37%	38%	39%	40%
1	.763	.758	.752	.746	.741	.735	.730	.725	.719	.714
2	.583	.574	.565	.557	.549	.541	.533	.525	.518	.510
3	.445	.435	.425	.416	.406	.398	.389	.381	.372	.364
4	.340	.329	.320	.310	.301	.292	.284	.276	.268	.260
5	.259	.250	.240	.231	.223	.215	.207	.200	.193	.186
6	.198	.189	.181	.173	.165	.158	.151	.145	.139	.133
7	.151	.143	.136	.129	.122	.116	.110	.105	.100	.095
8	.115	.108	.102	.096	.091	.085	.081	.076	.072	.068
9	.088	.082	.077	.072	.067	.063	.059	.055	.052	.048
10	.067	.062	.058	.054	.050	.046	.043	.040	.037	.035
11	.051	.047	.043	.040	.037	.034	.031	.029	.027	.025
12	.039	.036	.033	.030	.027	.025	.023	.021	.019	.018
13	.030	.027	.025	.022	.020	.018	.017	.015	.014	.013
14	.023	.021	.018	.017	.015	.014	.012	.011	.010	.009
15	.017	.016	.014	.012	.011	.010	.009	.008	.007	.006
16	.013	.012	.010	.009	.008	.007	.006	.006	.005	.005
17	.010	.009	.008	.007	.006	.005	.005	.004	.004	.003
18	.008	.007	.006	.005	.005	.004	.003	.003	.003	.002
19	.006	.005	.004	.004	.003	.003	.003	.002	.002	.002
20	.005	.004	.003	.003	.002	.002	.002	.002	.001	.001
21	.003	.003	.003	.002	.002	.002	.001	.001	.001	.001
22	.003	.002	.002	.002	.001	.001	.001	.001	.001	.001
23	.002	.002	.001	.001	.001	.001	.001	.001	.001	*
24	.002	.001	.001	.001	.001	.001	.001	*	*	*
25	.001	.001	.001	.001	.001	*	*	*	*	*
30	*	*	*	*	*	*	*	*	*	*
35	*	*	*	*	*	*	*	*	*	*
40	*	*	*	*	*	*	*	*	*	*
45	*	*	*	*	*	*	*	*	*	*
50	*	*	*	*	*	*	*	*	*	*

*$PVIF$ is zero to three decimal places.

Table C-3   Present-Value Interest Factors for One Dollar Discounted at k Percent for n Periods: $PVIF_{k,n} = \dfrac{1}{(1 + k)^n}$ (continued)

Period	41%	42%	43%	44%	45%	46%	47%	48%	49%	50%
1	.709	.704	.699	.694	.690	.685	.680	.676	.671	.667
2	.503	.496	.489	.482	.476	.469	.463	.457	.450	.444
3	.357	.349	.342	.335	.328	.321	.315	.308	.302	.296
4	.253	.246	.239	.233	.226	.220	.214	.208	.203	.198
5	.179	.173	.167	.162	.156	.151	.146	.141	.136	.132
6	.127	.122	.117	.112	.108	.103	.099	.095	.091	.088
7	.090	.086	.082	.078	.074	.071	.067	.064	.061	.059
8	.064	.060	.057	.054	.051	.048	.046	.043	.041	.039
9	.045	.043	.040	.038	.035	.033	.031	.029	.028	.026
10	.032	.030	.028	.026	.024	.023	.021	.020	.019	.017
11	.023	.021	.020	.018	.017	.016	.014	.013	.012	.012
12	.016	.015	.014	.013	.012	.011	.010	.009	.008	.008
13	.011	.010	.010	.009	.008	.007	.007	.006	.006	.005
14	.008	.007	.007	.006	.006	.005	.005	.004	.004	.003
15	.006	.005	.005	.004	.004	.003	.003	.003	.003	.002
16	.004	.004	.003	.003	.003	.002	.002	.002	.002	.002
17	.003	.003	.002	.002	.002	.002	.001	.001	.001	.001
18	.002	.002	.002	.001	.001	.001	.001	.001	.001	.001
19	.001	.001	.001	.001	.001	.001	.001	.001	.001	*
20	.001	.001	.001	.001	.001	.001	.001	*	*	*
21	.001	.001	.001	*	*	*	*	*	*	*
22	.001	*	*	*	*	*	*	*	*	*
23	*	*	*	*	*	*	*	*	*	*
24	*	*	*	*	*	*	*	*	*	*
25	*	*	*	*	*	*	*	*	*	*
30	*	*	*	*	*	*	*	*	*	*
35	*	*	*	*	*	*	*	*	*	*
40	*	*	*	*	*	*	*	*	*	*
45	*	*	*	*	*	*	*	*	*	*
50	*	*	*	*	*	*	*	*	*	*

*$PVIF$ is zero to three decimal places.

Table C-4   **Present-Value Interest Factors for a One-Dollar Annuity Discounted at *k* Percent for *n* Periods:** $PVIFA_{k,n} = \sum_{t=1}^{n} \dfrac{1}{(1+k)^t}$

Period	1%	2%	3%	4%	5%	6%	7%	8%	9%	10%
1	.990	.980	.971	.962	.952	.943	.935	.926	.917	.909
2	1.970	1.942	1.913	1.886	1.859	1.833	1.808	1.783	1.759	1.736
3	2.941	2.884	2.829	2.775	2.723	2.673	2.624	2.577	2.531	2.487
4	3.902	3.808	3.717	3.630	3.546	3.465	3.387	3.312	3.240	3.170
5	4.853	4.713	4.580	4.452	4.329	4.212	4.100	3.993	3.890	3.791
6	5.795	5.601	5.417	5.242	5.076	4.917	4.767	4.623	4.486	4.355
7	6.728	6.472	6.230	6.002	5.786	5.582	5.389	5.206	5.033	4.868
8	7.652	7.326	7.020	6.733	6.463	6.210	5.971	5.747	5.535	5.335
9	8.566	8.162	7.786	7.435	7.108	6.802	6.515	6.247	5.995	5.759
10	9.471	8.983	8.530	8.111	7.722	7.360	7.024	6.710	6.418	6.145
11	10.368	9.787	9.253	8.760	8.306	7.887	7.499	7.139	6.805	6.495
12	11.255	10.575	9.954	9.385	8.863	8.384	7.943	7.536	7.161	6.814
13	12.134	11.348	10.635	9.986	9.394	8.853	8.358	7.904	7.487	7.013
14	13.004	12.106	11.296	10.563	9.899	9.295	8.745	8.244	7.786	7.367
15	13.865	12.849	11.938	11.118	10.380	9.712	9.108	8.560	8.061	7.606
16	14.718	13.578	12.561	11.652	10.838	10.106	9.447	8.851	8.313	7.824
17	15.562	14.292	13.166	12.166	11.274	10.477	9.763	9.122	8.544	8.022
18	16.398	14.992	13.754	12.659	11.690	10.828	10.059	9.372	8.756	8.201
19	17.226	15.679	14.324	13.134	12.085	11.158	10.336	9.604	8.950	8.365
20	18.046	16.352	14.878	13.590	12.462	11.470	10.594	9.818	9.129	8.514
21	18.857	17.011	15.415	14.029	12.821	11.764	10.836	10.017	9.292	8.649
22	19.661	17.658	15.937	14.451	13.163	12.042	11.061	10.201	9.442	8.772
23	20.456	18.292	16.444	14.857	13.489	12.303	11.272	10.371	9.580	8.883
24	21.244	18.914	16.936	15.247	13.799	12.550	11.469	10.529	9.707	8.985
25	22.023	19.524	17.413	15.622	14.094	12.783	11.654	10.675	9.823	9.077
30	25.808	22.396	19.601	17.292	15.373	13.765	12.409	11.258	10.274	9.427
35	29.409	24.999	21.487	18.665	16.374	14.498	12.948	11.655	10.567	9.644
40	32.835	27.356	23.115	19.793	17.159	15.046	13.332	11.925	10.757	9.779
45	36.095	29.490	24.519	20.720	17.774	15.456	13.606	12.108	10.881	9.863
50	39.196	31.424	25.730	21.482	18.256	15.762	13.801	12.233	10.962	9.915

C-4

Table C-4   Present-Value Interest Factors for a One-Dollar Annuity Discounted at k Percent for n Periods: $PVIFA_{k,n} = \sum_{t=1}^{n} \dfrac{1}{(1+k)^t}$ (continued)

Period	11%	12%	13%	14%	15%	16%	17%	18%	19%	20%
1	.901	.893	.885	.877	.870	.862	.855	.847	8.40	.833
2	1.713	1.690	1.668	1.647	1.626	1.605	1.585	1.566	1.547	1.528
3	2.444	2.402	2.361	2.322	2.283	2.246	2.210	2.174	2.140	2.106
4	3.102	3.037	2.974	2.914	2.855	2.798	2.743	2.690	2.639	2.589
5	3.696	3.605	3.517	3.433	3.352	3.274	3.199	3.127	3.058	2.991
6	4.231	4.111	3.998	3.889	3.784	3.685	3.589	3.498	3.410	3.326
7	4.712	4.564	4.423	4.288	4.160	4.039	3.922	3.812	3.706	3.605
8	5.146	4.968	4.799	4.639	4.487	4.344	4.207	4.078	3.954	3.837
9	5.537	5.328	5.132	4.946	4.772	4.607	4.451	4.303	4.163	4.031
10	5.889	5.650	5.426	5.216	5.019	4.833	4.659	4.494	4.339	4.192
11	6.207	5.938	5.687	5.453	5.234	5.029	4.836	4.656	4.486	4.327
12	6.492	6.194	5.918	5.660	5.421	5.197	4.988	4.793	4.611	4.439
13	6.750	6.424	6.122	5.842	5.583	5.342	5.118	4.910	4.715	4.533
14	6.982	6.628	6.302	6.002	5.724	5.468	5.229	5.008	4.802	4.611
15	7.191	6.811	6.462	6.142	5.847	5.575	5.324	5.092	4.876	4.675
16	7.379	6.974	6.604	6.265	5.954	5.668	5.405	5.162	4.938	4.730
17	7.549	7.120	6.729	6.373	6.047	5.749	5.475	5.222	4.990	4.775
18	7.702	7.250	6.840	6.467	6.128	5.818	5.534	5.273	5.033	4.812
19	7.839	7.366	6.938	6.550	6.198	5.877	5.584	5.316	5.070	4.843
20	7.963	7.469	7.025	6.623	6.259	5.929	5.628	5.353	5.101	4.870
21	8.075	7.562	7.102	6.687	6.312	5.973	5.665	5.384	5.127	4.891
22	8.176	7.645	7.170	6.743	6.359	6.011	5.696	5.410	5.149	4.909
23	8.266	7.718	7.230	6.792	6.399	6.044	5.723	5.432	5.167	4.925
24	8.348	7.784	7.283	6.835	6.434	6.073	5.746	5.451	5.182	4.937
25	8.422	7.843	7.330	6.873	6.464	6.097	5.766	5.467	5.195	4.948
30	8.694	8.055	7.496	7.003	6.566	6.177	5.829	5.517	5.235	4.979
35	8.855	8.176	7.586	7.070	6.617	6.215	5.858	5.539	5.251	4.992
40	8.951	8.244	7.634	7.105	6.642	6.233	5.871	5.548	5.258	4.997
45	9.008	8.283	7.661	7.123	6.654	6.242	5.877	5.552	5.261	4.999
50	9.042	8.304	7.675	7.133	6.661	6.246	5.880	5.554	5.262	4.999

C-4

Table C-4 Present-Value Interest Factors for a One-Dollar Annuity Discounted at k Percent for n Periods: $PVIFA_{k,n} = \sum_{t=1}^{n} \dfrac{1}{(1 + k)^t}$ (continued)

Period	21%	22%	23%	24%	25%	26%	27%	28%	29%	30%
1	.826	.820	.813	.806	.800	.794	.787	.781	.775	.769
2	1.509	1.492	1.474	1.457	1.440	1.424	1.407	1.392	1.376	1.361
3	2.074	2.042	2.011	1.981	1.952	1.923	1.896	1.868	1.842	1.816
4	2.540	2.494	2.448	2.404	2.362	2.320	2.280	2.241	2.203	2.166
5	2.926	2.864	2.803	2.745	2.689	2.635	2.583	2.532	2.483	2.436
6	3.245	3.167	3.092	3.020	2.951	2.885	2.821	2.759	2.700	2.643
7	3.508	3.416	3.327	3.242	3.161	3.083	3.009	2.937	2.868	2.802
8	3.726	3.619	3.518	3.421	3.329	3.241	3.156	3.076	2.999	2.925
9	3.905	3.786	3.673	3.566	3.463	3.366	3.273	3.184	3.100	3.019
10	4.054	3.923	3.799	3.682	3.570	3.465	3.364	3.269	3.178	3.092
11	4.177	4.035	3.902	3.776	3.656	3.544	3.437	3.335	3.239	3.147
12	4.278	4.127	3.985	3.851	3.725	3.606	3.493	3.387	3.286	3.190
13	4.362	4.203	4.053	3.912	3.780	3.656	3.538	3.427	3.322	3.223
14	4.432	4.265	4.108	3.962	3.824	3.695	3.573	3.459	3.351	3.249
15	4.489	4.315	4.153	4.001	3.859	3.726	3.601	3.483	3.373	3.268
16	4.536	4.357	4.189	4.033	3.887	3.751	3.623	3.503	3.390	3.283
17	4.576	4.391	4.219	4.059	3.910	3.771	3.640	3.518	3.403	3.295
18	4.608	4.419	4.243	4.080	3.928	3.786	3.654	3.529	3.413	3.304
19	4.635	4.442	4.263	4.097	3.942	3.799	3.664	3.539	3.421	3.311
20	4.657	4.460	4.279	4.110	3.954	3.808	3.673	3.546	3.427	3.316
21	4.675	4.476	4.292	4.121	3.963	3.816	3.679	3.551	3.432	3.320
22	4.690	4.488	4.302	4.130	3.970	3.822	3.684	3.556	3.436	3.323
23	4.703	4.499	4.311	4.137	3.976	3.827	3.689	3.559	3.438	3.325
24	4.713	4.507	4.318	4.143	3.981	3.831	3.692	3.562	3.441	3.327
25	4.721	4.514	4.323	4.147	3.985	3.834	3.694	3.564	3.442	3.329
30	4.746	4.534	4.339	4.160	3.995	3.842	3.701	3.569	3.447	3.332
35	4.756	4.541	4.345	4.164	3.998	3.845	3.703	3.571	3.448	3.333
40	4.760	4.544	4.347	4.166	3.999	3.846	3.703	3.571	3.448	3.333
45	4.761	4.545	4.347	4.166	4.000	3.846	3.704	3.571	3.448	3.333
50	4.762	4.545	4.348	4.167	4.000	3.846	3.704	3.571	3.448	3.333

C-4

Table C-4   Present-Value Interest Factors for a One-Dollar Annuity Discounted at k Percent for n Periods: $PVIFA_{k,n} = \sum_{t=1}^{n} \dfrac{1}{(1+k)^t}$ (continued)

Period	31%	32%	33%	34%	35%	36%	37%	38%	39%	40%
1	.763	.758	.752	.746	.741	.735	.730	.725	.719	.714
2	1.346	1.331	1.317	1.303	1.289	1.276	1.263	1.250	1.237	1.224
3	1.791	1.766	1.742	1.719	1.696	1.673	1.652	1.630	1.609	1.589
4	2.130	2.096	2.062	2.029	1.997	1.966	1.935	1.906	1.877	1.849
5	2.390	2.345	2.302	2.260	2.220	2.181	2.143	2.106	2.070	2.035
6	2.588	2.534	2.483	2.433	2.385	2.339	2.294	2.251	2.209	2.168
7	2.739	2.677	2.619	2.562	2.508	2.455	2.404	2.355	2.308	2.263
8	2.854	2.786	2.721	2.658	2.598	2.540	2.485	2.432	2.380	2.331
9	2.942	2.868	2.798	2.730	2.665	2.603	2.544	2.487	2.432	2.379
10	3.009	2.930	2.855	2.784	2.715	2.649	2.587	2.527	2.469	2.414
11	3.060	2.978	2.899	2.824	2.752	2.683	2.618	2.555	2.496	2.438
12	3.100	3.013	2.931	2.853	2.779	2.708	2.641	2.576	2.515	2.456
13	3.129	3.040	2.956	2.876	2.799	2.727	2.658	2.592	2.529	2.469
14	3.152	3.061	2.974	2.892	2.814	2.740	2.670	2.603	2.539	2.478
15	3.170	3.076	2.988	2.905	2.825	2.750	2.679	2.611	2.546	2.484
16	3.183	3.088	2.999	2.914	2.834	2.757	2.685	2.616	2.551	2.489
17	3.193	3.097	3.007	2.921	2.840	2.763	2.690	2.621	2.555	2.492
18	3.201	3.104	3.012	2.926	2.844	2.767	2.693	2.624	2.557	2.494
19	3.207	3.109	3.017	2.930	2.848	2.770	2.696	2.626	2.559	2.496
20	3.211	3.113	3.020	2.933	2.850	2.772	2.698	2.627	2.561	2.497
21	3.215	3.116	3.023	2.935	2.852	2.773	2.699	2.629	2.562	2.498
22	3.217	3.118	3.025	2.936	2.853	2.775	2.700	2.629	2.562	2.498
23	3.219	3.120	3.026	2.938	2.854	2.775	2.701	2.630	2.563	2.499
24	3.221	3.121	3.027	2.939	2.855	2.776	2.701	2.630	2.563	2.499
25	3.222	3.122	3.028	2.939	2.856	2.776	2.702	2.631	2.563	2.499
30	3.225	3.124	3.030	2.941	2.857	2.777	2.702	2.631	2.564	2.500
35	3.226	3.125	3.030	2.941	2.857	2.778	2.703	2.632	2.564	2.500
40	3.226	3.125	3.030	2.941	2.857	2.778	2.703	2.632	2.564	2.500
45	3.226	3.125	3.030	2.941	2.857	2.778	2.703	2.632	2.564	2.500
50	3.226	3.125	3.030	2.941	2.857	2.778	2.703	2.632	2.564	2.500

C-4

Table C-4   Present-Value Interest Factors for a One-Dollar Annuity Discounted at k Percent for n Periods: $PVIFA_{k,n} = \sum\limits_{t=1}^{n} \dfrac{1}{(1 + k)^t}$ (continued)

Period	41%	42%	43%	44%	45%	46%	47%	48%	49%	50%
1	.709	.704	.699	.694	.690	.685	.680	.676	.671	.667
2	1.212	1.200	1.188	1.177	1.165	1.154	1.143	1.132	1.122	1.111
3	1.569	1.549	1.530	1.512	1.493	1.475	1.458	1.441	1.424	1.407
4	1.822	1.795	1.769	1.744	1.720	1.695	1.672	1.649	1.627	1.605
5	2.001	1.969	1.937	1.906	1.876	1.846	1.818	1.790	1.763	1.737
6	2.129	2.091	2.054	2.018	1.983	1.949	1.917	1.885	1.854	1.824
7	2.219	2.176	2.135	2.096	2.057	2.020	1.984	1.949	1.916	1.883
8	2.283	2.237	2.193	2.150	2.109	2.069	2.030	1.993	1.957	1.922
9	2.328	2.280	2.233	2.187	2.144	2.102	2.061	2.022	1.984	1.948
10	2.360	2.310	2.261	2.213	2.168	2.125	2.083	2.042	2.003	1.965
11	2.383	2.331	2.280	2.232	2.185	2.140	2.097	2.055	2.015	1.977
12	2.400	2.346	2.294	2.244	2.196	2.151	2.107	2.064	2.024	1.985
13	2.411	2.356	2.303	2.253	2.204	2.158	2.113	2.071	2.029	1.990
14	2.419	2.363	2.310	2.259	2.210	2.163	2.118	2.075	2.033	1.993
15	2.425	2.369	2.315	2.263	2.214	2.166	2.121	2.078	2.036	1.995
16	2.429	2.372	2.318	2.266	2.216	2.169	2.123	2.079	2.037	1.997
17	2.432	2.375	2.320	2.268	2.218	2.170	2.125	2.081	2.038	1.998
18	2.434	2.377	2.322	2.270	2.219	2.172	2.126	2.082	2.039	1.999
19	2.435	2.378	2.323	2.270	2.220	2.172	2.126	2.082	2.040	1.999
20	2.436	2.379	2.324	2.271	2.221	2.173	2.127	2.083	2.040	1.999
21	2.437	2.379	2.324	2.272	2.221	2.173	2.127	2.083	2.040	2.000
22	2.438	2.380	2.325	2.272	2.222	2.173	2.127	2.083	2.040	2.000
23	2.438	2.380	2.325	2.272	2.222	2.174	2.127	2.083	2.041	2.000
24	2.438	2.380	2.325	2.272	2.222	2.174	2.127	2.083	2.041	2.000
25	2.439	2.381	2.325	2.272	2.222	2.174	2.128	2.083	2.041	2.000
30	2.439	2.381	2.326	2.273	2.222	2.174	2.128	2.083	2.041	2.000
35	2.439	2.381	2.326	2.273	2.222	2.174	2.128	2.083	2.041	2.000
40	2.439	2.381	2.326	2.273	2.222	2.174	2.128	2.083	2.041	2.000
45	2.439	2.381	2.326	2.273	2.222	2.174	2.128	2.083	2.041	2.000
50	2.439	2.381	2.326	2.273	2.222	2.174	2.128	2.083	2.041	2.000

C-4

ANSWERS TO SELECTED
END-OF-CHAPTER PROBLEMS

The following list of answers to selected problems and portions of problems is included to provide "check figures" for use in preparing detailed solutions to end-of-chapter problems requiring calculations. For problems that are relatively straightforward, the key answer is given; for more complex problems, answers to a number of parts of the problem are included. Detailed calculations are not shown—only the final and, in some cases, intermediate answers, which should help to confirm whether the correct solution is being developed. Answers to problems involving present and future value were solved using the appropriate tables; calculator solutions are not given. For problems containing a variety of cases for which similar calculations are required, the answers for only one or two cases have been included. The only verbal answers included are simple yes-or-no or "choice of best alternative" responses; answers to problems requiring detailed explanations or discussions are not given.

The problems and portions of problems for which answers have been included were selected randomly; therefore, there is no discernible pattern to the choice of problem answers given. The answers given are based on what are believed to be the most obvious and reasonable assumptions related to the given problem; in some cases, other reasonable assumptions could result in equally correct answers.

2—2 a. Tax liability $19,700
c. Average tax rate 21.3%
2—4 a. Tax on $90,000 = $18,850
2—7 a. Asset X: $250
b. Asset X: $100
2—12 Security C: 5.7% return

2—13 a.

	Actual return
Security A	13.3%
Security E	−2.7%

3—3 Earnings available for common stockholders = $29,000
3—4 b. $22,740
3—8 a. $1.9375 earnings per share
b. Total assets $926,000
3—10 $80,000
3—15 a. (1) Total sources $2,900
3—16 a. (1) Total sources $70,800
4—2 a. Average age of inventory 97.6 days

4—8

	Industry average	Actual 1991	Actual 1992
Current ratio	1.80	1.84	1.04
Average collection period	37 days	36 days	56 days
Debt ratio	65%	67%	61%
Net profit margin	3.5%	3.6%	4.1%
Return on equity	9.5%	8.0%	11.3%

5—3 a. 21,000 units
d. EBIT = $5,250
5—7 a. Q = 8,000 units
D = $508,000 or [($63.50) × (8,000)]
e. DOL = 5.0
5—9 a. EPS = $0.375
5—10 a. DFL = 1.5

5—11   **b.** DFL = 2
         d. EPS at $80,000 = $12.80
5—13   **a.** (1) 175,000 units
             (2) 233,333 units
         d. DTL = 2.40
5—14   **a.** DFL_J = 1.71
         b. DTL_R = 1.25

6—3

	February	March	April
a. Ending cash	$37,000	$67,000	($22,000)
b. Required total financing			$37,000
Excess cash balance	$22,000	$52,000	

         c. Line of credit should be at least $37,000 to cover borrowing needs for the month of April.
6—6   **a.** Net profits after taxes $216,600
            To retained earnings $146,600
         b. Net profits after taxes $227,400
6—8   **a.** Accounts receivable $1,440,000
            Net fixed assets $4,820,000
            Total current liabilities $2,260,000
            External funds required $775,000
            Total assets $9,100,000
6—9   **a.** Net profits after taxes $67,500
         b. Total assets $697,500
            External funds required $11,250
7—1   **a.** (3) Net working capital $2,000
         c. (3) Net working capital $4,000
7—5   **b.** (1) Permanent, monthly average $36,000
            (2) Seasonal, monthly average $10,333
7—6   Annual loan cost $1,200
7—8   **b.** Aggressive $571,667
            Conservative $676,000
7—11   **a.** Aggressive $30,000
            Conservative $35,000
8—1   **a.** OC = 150 days
         b. CCC = 120 days
         c. Financing required = $10,000,000
8—2   **a.** OC = 75 days
         c. Financing required = $97,222
8—4   Plan E is best since it results in largest reduction in the cash cycle.
8—7   **a.** 7 days collection float
         b. $21,450 opportunity cost
8—12   Accept; $180,000 savings versus $100,000 cost
8—13 $22,500 annual savings
9—1   **a.** Credit score Applicant B 81.5
9—2   **b.** Average investment in A/R = $75,000
         c. Total opportunity cost = $9,000
9—4   **b.** Cost of marginal bad debts = $28,000

9—6

Additional profit contribution from sales	$9,000
Cost of marginal investment in accounts receivable	(4,521)
Cost of marginal bad debts	(9,200)
Net loss from changing the policy	($4,721)

9—7   Net profit of the proposal $20,040
9—9   **a.** $14,000 additional profit
         b. $36,432 marginal investment in accounts receivable
            $ 7,286 cost of financing marginal investment in accounts receivable
            $ 3,150 cost of marginal bad debts
9—11   **b.** $52,000 net savings
9—16   **a.** EOQ = 200 units
         b. Reorder point = 12 units
10—1   **c.** January 9
10—2   **a.** 36.73%
         d. 31.81%
         g. 8.82%
10—4   **a.** Q: 18.18%
         b. Q: Borrow
10—5 $1,300,000
10—6   **a.** $375
10—9   **a.** 9.0%
         b. 13.06%
10—11   Total $886,900

10—13

Effective Rates	DM	Sf
Euromarket	8.9%	6.7%
Domestic	8.1	5.7

11—3   A *FV* = $530.60
         D *FV* = $78,450
11—5   **a.** Annual $8,810
            Semiannual $8,955
            Quarterly $9,030
11—8   A $3,862.50
         B $138,450.00
         C $6,956.80
11—11   *PV* = $408
11—13   **a.** A *PV* = $109,890
11—14   C *PV* = $52,410
11—16   E *PV* = $85,297.50
11—19   Future value of retirement home in 20 years = $272,595
         Annual deposit = $4,759.49

11—21

Year	Interest	Principal
2	$1,489.61	$4,970.34

11—24 $PVIFA_{k,\ 5\ yrs.} = 5.303$
$13\% < k < 14\%$
11—27 **b.** $PMT = 3,764.82$

12—2 **a.**

	Expansion	
	A	**B**
Range	8	20

12—6 **a.** Project 257
(1) Range = 1.100
(2) Expected value of return = 0.450
(3) Standard deviation = 0.165378
(4) Coefficient of variation = 0.3675
12—7 Asset F: **a.** Expected return = .04
b. Standard deviation = .1338
c. $CV = 3.345$
12—11 **c.** Asset B because it will have the highest increase in return.
12—13 Case A 8.9%
12—16 **c.** Project C is twice as responsive as the market.
12—18 Asset A $10,870
Asset D $9,717
12—20 **a.** $1,156.88
12—22 **a.** (3) $1,225.96
12—25 Firm B $40.00
Firm D $600.00
12—27 **a.** $236,111
b. $413,409
12—28 **b.** Liquidation value = $30.20 per share
12—30 **b.** $P_0 = \$29.55$
13—1 **b.** 12.4%
13—3 Bond A: $k_d = 9.44\%$; $k_i = 5.66\%$
Bond E: $k_d = 11.84\%$; $k_i = 7.10\%$
13—5 **a.** $k_p = 11.96\%$
13—7 **c.** $k_r = 15.91\%$
d. $k_n = 16.54\%$
13—10 **a.** Weighted cost 8.344%
b. Weighted cost 10.848%
13—13 **a.** $k_i = .0516 \sim 5.2\%$
$k_p = .0844 \sim 8.4\%$
$k_r = 13.8\%$
$k_n = 15.0\%$
b. (1) $k_a = 10.1\%$
(2) $k_a = 10.7\%$
13—14 **a.** WACC, $500,000–$750,000 = 15.40
e. Projects E, C, G, A, and H should be accepted because their respective rates of return exceed the WMCC.
14—1 **a.** Current expenditure
d. Current expenditure
f. Capital expenditure
14—5 Asset A: Book value $275,500
Asset B: Book value $ 26,800
14—7 **a.** Taxes due $49,600
d. Taxes due − $6,400
14—8 Initial investment $22,680

14—9 **a.** Initial investment $18,240
c. Initial investment $23,100
14—11 **a.** Cash inflow Year 3 $584,000
14—14 Incremental cash flow, 1993 = −$60
14—15 **a.** Initial investment $41,200
b.

Year	1	2	3
Incremental operating cash inflows	$13,600	$16,240	$11,080

Year	4	5	6
Incremental operating cash inflows	$11,040	$13,440	$ 1,600

14—16 **a.** Initial investment $56,480
b.

Year	1	2	3
Incremental operating cash inflows	$14,440	$22,600	$18,080

Year	4	5	6
Incremental operating cash inflows	$17,880	$20,280	$ 2,200

14—18 Alternative 1
a. Initial investment $90,000
b.

Year	1	2	3
Incremental operating cash inflows	$26,300	$36,000	$35,980

Year	4	5	6
Incremental operating cash inflows	$43,460	$33,460	$ 1,800

15—1 **a.** 20%
15—4 **a.** Machine 1: 4.67 years
Machine 2: 5.25 years

15—7   **a.** Project A 65%
      Project C 65%
      b. Project A 3.08 years
      Project C 2.39 years

15—9   **a.** NPV = −$320; reject
      b. PI = 0.975; reject

15—11   Project A: 17%
      Project D: 21%

15—14   **a.** NPV = $1,222
      b. PI = 1.067
      c. IRR = 12%

15—16   Project A
      NPV = $15,245
      IRR = 16%

15—19   **a.** Initial investment $1,480,000

      b.

Year	Cash inflow
1	$656,000
2	761,600
3	647,200
4	585,600
5	585,600
6	44,400

      c. 2.1 years
      d. NPV = $959,289
      IRR = 35%

15—20   **d.** B, F, & G should be chosen.

15—24   **a.** Line S: E(NPV) = $8,500
      c. Line S: Standard deviation
      = $5,805.17
      d. Line S: CV = .683

15—27   **a.** NPV = $22,320
      b. NPV = −$5,596

15—29   **a.** Project E: NPV = $2,130
      Project F: NPV = $1,678
      Project G: NPV = $1,144
      c. Project E: NPV = $834
      Project F: NPV = $1,678
      Project G: NPV = $2,138

15—31   **b.** Projects X and Z are acceptable
with positive NPVs while Project Z
with a negative NPV is not. Project
X with the highest NPV should be
undertaken.

16—1

Debt ratio	Debt	Equity
40%	$400,000	$600,000

16—3   **a.** Financial breakeven points:

Structure A	Structure B
$16,000	$34,000

      c. If EBIT is expected to be below
$52,000, Structure A is preferred.
If EBIT is expected to be above
$52,000, Structure B is preferred.
      e. At an EBIT level of $75,000, Structure B is recommended since the
EPS is maximized.

16—5   **a.** Debt ratio 15%; Debt = $150,000,
Equity = $850,000, Number of
shares of common stock = 34,000
      c. Debt ratio 15%; EBIT $250,000,
EPS = $4.20
      Debt ratio 60%; EBIT $250,000,
EPS = $5.55

16—7   **a.** $4.75/share
      b. $0.40/share
      d. Retained earnings (and hence
stockholder's equity) decrease by
$80,000.

16—10   **a.** 1990 = $0.60   **c.** 1990 = $0.62
      b. 1990 = $0.50   **d.** 1990 = $0.62

16—11   **a.** Retained earnings = $85,000
      b. (1) Retained earnings = $70,000
      (2) Retained earnings = $40,000
      c. Stockholders' equity has not
changed. Funds have only been redistributed between the stockholders' equity accounts.

16—13   **a.** EPS = $2
      b. 1%
      c. 1%; stock dividends do not have a
real value.

16—17   **b.** EPS = $2.10
      c. Market price = $21.00 per share

17—1   **a.** Annual tax liability = $112,000
      b. Tax liability: Year 1 = $0
                     Year 2 = $0
                     Year 3 = $16,000
                     Years 4–15 = $112,000/year

17—3   **a.** Total tax advantage = $320,000;
Years 1–4 = $80,000/year
      b. Total tax advantage = $320,000;

Year	Tax advantage
1	$ 32,000
2	48,000
3	80,000
4	120,000
5	40,000
6	0
7	0

      c. Studs Duds: $228,400
      Glitter Threads: $205,288

17—5   **a.** Yes, the NPV = $42,150
      b. Yes, the NPV = $101,000

17—6   **a.** EPS merged firm = $1.029
      b. EPS McBell's = $1.00

c. EPS Moon Bar = ($0.972)(2.2)
    = $2.139

17—8   (1) Ratio of exchange
       (2) Market price
       A: 0.60; 1.20
       D: 0.25; 1.25
       E: 1.00; 1.25

17—10 **a.** 1.125
       b. Vinco Co.: EPS = $2.50,
       P/E = 18 times
       c. 16.89 times

17—15 Case II:
Unpaid balance of 2nd mortgage: $150,000
Accounts payable: $ 75,000
Notes payable: $ 75,000
Unsecured bonds: $150,000

17—16 **a.** (1) 1st mortgage: $700,000
                 2nd mortgage: $400,000
                 Unsecured bonds: $300,000
                 Preferred stock: $200,000
                 Common stock: $ 0
             (2) Zero
       b. (1) 1st mortgage $661,539
                 2nd mortgage $246,154
                 Unsecured bonds $184,615

18—2   **a.** Net to Bradford: $2.65
18—4   **b.** Management fee per share: $1.06
              Underwriting fee per share: $1.40
              Selling concession per share: $1.10
18—5   **b.** Proceeds per share: $17.70
18—7   **c.** Proceeds per share: $36.40
       e. Trimex must earn 13.74% to avoid
              EPS dilution.
18—9   **b.** An additional 200,000 shares are
              required to raise needed funds.
19—1   Bond A: **a** Discount; **b** $400,000;
       c $16,000; **d** $320,000; **e** $128,000
19—3   Bond B: $20,000
19—4   **d.** Initial investment: $2,840,000
       e. Annual cash outflows with old
              bond: $2,516,000
              Annual cash outflows with new
              bond: $2,152,000
       f. Yes, net savings: $1,016,216
19—6   **b.** (2) Annual cash flow savings from
                  new bond: $85,600
       c. (1) 12.5%: PV = $170,980
                  13%;   PV = −$356,120
       d. The reissue is favorable at a 12.5%
              stated interest rate if the discount
              rate is 6%. At a 13% stated interest
              rate the refunding of the bond
              should be rejected. At a discount
              rate of 8%, the refunding of the
              bond should be rejected.

19—8   **a.** PV of lease outflows: $42,342
       b. PV of purchase outflows: $40,008
       c. Since the present value of purchas-
              ing is less than the present value of
              leasing, the purchase is recom-
              mended.

19—10

Lease	Capitalized value
A	$272,560
C	$ 58,203
E	$374,261

20—3   **a.** Preferred dividends = $14.875/share
              Common dividends = $15.875/share
       c. Preferred dividends = $10.00/share
              Common dividends = $0.00/share
20—4   **a.** Common stock
              (10,000 shares @ $1 par) $ 10,000
              Paid in capital in
              excess of par   120,000
              Common stock equity $130,000
20—5   **a.** Majority: A, B, C, D, E:
              (.54)(1,000) = 540
       b. Majority can elect 3, and minority
              can elect 2.
20—8   Case E: (1) With rights, $1.11
                (2) Ex rights $1.11
20—11 **a.** 24,000 shares
       b. 12.5 rights
       c. 3,840 shares
       d. (1) R_w = $0.296
              (2) M_e = $28.704
                  R_e = $0.296
21—1   **a.** Conversion price = $50 per share
21—2   **b.** Conversion ratio = 40 shares
21—3   **c.** Bond value = $1,050
21—5   **a.** (1) EPS = $1.20 per share
              (2) EPS = $2.00 per share
              (3) EPS = $1.26 per share
21—8   **a.** Straight bond value = $832.75
       b. Conversion value at $9.00: $720
       c. Bond value at $9.00: $832.75*
              *The bond will not sell below the
              straight bond value.
21—10 **a.** 160 shares, 400 warrants
       b. 20% return with shares
       c. 125% return with warrants
21—13 **a.** $800 profit
       b. $400
       c. $6/share

GLOSSARY

ABC system Inventory management technique that divides inventory into three categories of descending importance based on the dollar investment in each. (9)

Accelerated Cost Recovery System (ACRS) System used to determine the depreciation of assets for tax purposes. (3)

accept-reject approach The evaluation of capital expenditure proposals to determine whether they are acceptable. (14)

accounting exposure The risk resulting from the effects of changes in foreign exchange rates on the translated value of a firm's financial statement accounts denominated in a given foreign currency. (12)

accrual method Recognizes revenue at the point of sale and recognizes expenses when incurred. (1)

accruals Liabilities for services received for which payment has yet to be made. (10)

ACH (automated clearinghouse) credits Deposits of payroll directly into the payees' (employees') accounts. (8)

ACH (automated clearinghouse) debits Preauthorized electronic withdrawals from the payer's account which are then transferred to the payee's account via a settlement among banks by the automated clearinghouse. (8)

acquiring company The firm in a merger transaction that attempts to acquire another firm. (17)

active investors Persons or institutions with a major equity or debt interest in a firm. (1)

activity ratios Measure the speed with which various accounts are converted into sales or cash. (4)

actual return The percentage return on the initial price or amount invested. (2)

adjustable-rate (or floating-rate) preferred stock (ARPS) Preferred stock whose dividend rate is tied to interest rates on specific government securities. (20)

agency costs The costs borne by stockholders to prevent or minimize agency problems. (1)

agency problem The likelihood that managers may place personal goals ahead of corporate goals. (1)

aggressive financing strategy Strategy by which the firm finances at least its seasonal needs, and possibly some of its permanent needs, with short-term funds and the majority of its permanent needs with long-term funds. (7)

aging A technique used to evaluate credit or collection policies by indicating the proportion of the accounts receivable balance that has been outstanding for a specified period of time. (9)

all-current-rate method The method by which the functional-currency–denominated financial statements of an MNC's subsidiary are translated into the parent company's currency. (3)

annual cleanup The requirement that for a certain number of days during the year borrowers under a line of credit carry a zero loan balance. (10)

annuity A stream of equal annual cash flows. (11, 14)

articles of partnership The written contract used to formally establish a business partnership. (2)

assignment A voluntary liquidation procedure by which a firm's creditors pass the power to liquidate the firm's assets to a third party, designated the *assignee* or *trustee*. (17)

authorized shares The number of shares of common stock that a firm's corporate charter allows without further stockholder approval. (18)

average age of inventory The average length of time inventory is held by the firm. (4)

average collection period The average amount of time needed to collect accounts receivable. (4)

average investment The initial investment divided by 2. (15)

average payment period The average amount of time needed to pay accounts receivable. (4)

average profits after taxes The total after-tax profits expected over the project's life divided by the number of years of the project's life. (15)

average rate of return For a given project, the annual accounting rate of return expected on the average investment. (15)

average tax rate A firm's taxes divided by its taxable income. (2)

balance sheet Summary statement of the firm's financial position at a given point in time. (1, 3)

balloon payment At the maturity of a loan, a large lump-sum payment. (19)

banker's acceptances Short-term, low-risk marketable securities arising from bank guarantees of business transactions. (8)

bankruptcy Business failure that occurs when a firm's liabilities exceed the fair market value of its assets. (17)

Bankruptcy Reform Act of 1978 The current governing bankruptcy legislation in the United States. (17)

bar chart The simplest type of probability distribution showing only a limited number of outcomes and associated probabilities for a given event. (12)

best efforts basis Arrangement in which an investment banker agrees to act as an agent to sell as much of a securities issue as possible at a preset price but does not purchase the securities from the issuer for resale. (18)

beta coefficient, *b* An *index* of the degree of movement of an asset's return in response to a change in the market return; measures nondiversifiable risk. (12)

bird-in-the-hand argument The belief, in support of dividend relevance arguments, that current dividend payments ("a bird in the hand") reduce investor uncertainty and result in a higher value for the firm's stock. (16)

board of directors Group elected by the firm's stockholders and having ultimate authority to guide corporate affairs and make general policy. (2)

bond Long-term debt instrument used by businesses and government to raise large sums of money. (2)

bond indenture A legal document stating the conditions under which a bond has been issued. (19)

bond-refunding decision The decision facing firms when bond interest rates drop: whether to refund (refinance) existing bonds with new bonds at the lower interest rate. (19)

book value The strict accounting value of an asset. (14)

book value per share The amount per share of common stock if all assets are liquidated for their book value and the remaining proceeds after paying all liabilities (including preferred stock) are divided among the common stockholders. (12)

book value weights Weights that use accounting values to measure the proportion of each type of capital in the firm's financial structure. (13)

breadth of a market A characteristic of a ready market, determined by the number of participants (buyers) in the market. (8)

breakeven analysis (cost-volume-profit) analysis Concept used (1) to determine the level of operations necessary to cover all operating costs and (2) to evaluate the profitability associated with various levels of sales. (5)

business risk The risk to the firm of being unable to cover operating costs. (5)

call feature A feature of most corporate bonds that allows the issuer to repurchase bonds at a stated price prior to maturity. (19)

call option An option to *purchase* a specified number of shares of a stock on or before some future date at a stated price. (21)

call premium The amount by which a bond's call price exceeds its par value. (19)

call price The stated price at which a bond may be repurchased, by use of a call feature, prior to maturity. (19)

capital The long-term funds of the firm; all items on the right-hand side of the firm's balance sheet, excluding current liabilities. (16)

capital asset pricing model (CAPM) Theory that describes the relationship between the required return and the nondiversifiable risk of the firm as measured by the beta coefficient. (12, 13)

capital budgeting The process of evaluating and selecting long-term investments consistent with the firm's goal of owner wealth maximization. (14)

capital budgeting process Five distinct but interrelated steps used to evaluate and select long-term investments: proposal generation, review and analysis, decision making, implementation, and follow-up. (14)

capital expenditure An outlay of funds that is expected to produce benefits over a period of time *greater than* one year. (14)

capital gain The amount by which the sale price of an asset exceeds the asset's initial purchase price. (2)

capital market A financial relationship created by institutions and arrangements, allowing suppliers and demanders of *long-term funds* to make transactions. (2)

capital rationing The financial situation in which a firm has only a fixed number of dollars to allocate among competing capital expenditures. (14)

capital structure The mix of long-term debt and equity maintained by the firm. (16)

capitalized lease A *financial (or capital) lease* that has the present value of all its payments included as an asset and corresponding liability on the firm's balance sheet, as required by FASB Standard No. 13. (19)

carrying costs The variable costs per unit of holding an item in inventory for a specified period of time. (9)

cash The ready currency to which all liquid assets can be reduced. (8)

cash breakeven analysis A technique used to find the operating breakeven point when certain noncash charges make up a portion of the firm's fixed operating costs. (5)

cash budget (cash forecast) Financial projection of the firm's short-term cash surpluses or shortages. (6)

cash conversion cycle (CCC) The amount of time the firm's cash is tied up between the payment for production inputs and receipt of payment from the sale of the resulting finished product. (8)

cash disbursements All cash outlays by the firm during a given financial period. (6)

cash discount A percentage deduction from the purchase price if the buyer pays within a specified time shorter than the credit period. (10)

cash discount period The number of days after the beginning of the credit period during which the cash discount is available. (10)

cash method Recognizes revenues and expenses only with respect to actual inflows and outflows of cash. (1)

cash receipts All cash inflows during a given financial period. (6)

certainty equivalents (CEs) Risk-adjustment factors that represent the percent of estimated cash inflow that investors would be satisfied to receive *for certain* rather than the cash inflows that are *possible* each year. (15)

Chapter 11 The portion of the *Bankruptcy Reform Act of 1978* that outlines the procedures for reorganizing a failed (or failing) firm, whether its petition is filed voluntarily or involuntarily. (17)

Chapter 7 The portion of the *Bankruptcy Reform Act of 1978* that details the procedures for liquidating a failed firm. (17)

clearing float The delay between the deposit of a check by the payee and the actual availability of the funds. (8)

clientele effect The argument that a firm will attract shareholders whose preferences with respect to the payment and stability of dividends correspond to the payment pattern and stability of the firm itself. (16)

closely owned (stock) All common stock of a firm owned by a small group of investors such as a family. (20)

coefficient of variation, *CV* A measure of relative dispersion used in comparing the risk of assets with differing expected returns. (12)

collateral The security offered the lender by the borrower. (10)

collateral trust bonds Bonds secured by stock and/or bonds owned by the issuer. (19)

collection float The delay between the time a payer deducts a payment from its checking account ledger and the time the payee actually receives the funds in a spendable form. (8)

collection policy The procedures for collecting a firm's accounts receivable when they are due. (9)

commercial finance companies Lending institutions that make *only* secured loans to businesses. (10)

commercial paper A short-term, unsecured promissory note issued by a corporation with a high credit standing. (8, 10)

commitment fee The fee normally charged on a revolving credit agreement. (10)

common stock Collectively, units of ownership interest, or equity, in a corporation. (2)

common-size income statement An income statement in which each item is expressed as a percentage of sales. (4)

compensating balance A required checking account balance equal to a certain percentage of the borrower's short-term unsecured loan. (10)

competitive bidding The process in which a number of investment bankers bid for the right to sell a securities issue and the highest bid is the winner. (18)

composition A cash settlement of creditor claims by the debtor firm under which a uniform percentage of each dollar owed is paid. (17)

compounded interest Interest earned on a given deposit that has become part of the principal at the end of a specified period. (11)

concentration banking A collection procedure in which payments are made to regionally disbursed collection centers, then deposited in local banks for quick clearing. (8)

conflicting rankings Conflicts in the ranking given a project by NPV and IRR, resulting from differences in the magnitude and timing of cash flows. (15)

congeneric merger A merger in which one firm acquires another firm *in the same general industry* but neither in the same line of business nor a supplier or customer. (17)

conglomerate merger A merger combining firms in *unrelated businesses*. (17)

conservative financing strategy Strategy by which the firm finances all projected funds needs with long-term funds and uses short-term financing only for emergencies or unexpected outflows. (7)

consolidation The combination of two or more firms to form a completely new firm. (17)

constant growth model An approach to dividend valuation that assumes dividends will grow at a constant rate that is less than the required return. (12)

constant growth valuation (Gordon) model Assumes that the value of a share of stock equals the present value of all future dividends (assumed to grow at a constant rate) that it is expected to provide over an infinite time horizon. (13)

constant-payout-ratio dividend policy A dividend policy based on the payment of a certain percentage of earnings to owners in each dividend period. (16)

continuous probability distribution A probability distribution showing all the possible outcomes and associated probabilities for a given event. (12)

contribution margin The percent of each sales dollar that remains after satisfying variable operating costs. (5)

controlled disbursing The strategic use of mailing points and bank accounts to lengthen mail float and clearing float, respectively. (8)

controller The officer responsible for the firm's accounting activities. (1)

conventional cash flow pattern An initial outflow followed by a series of inflows. (14)

conversion feature A feature of so-called *convertible bonds* that allows bondholders to change each bond into a stated number of shares of stock. A similar feature exists in *convertible preferred stock*. (19, 20, 21)

conversion price The per-share price effectively paid for common stock as the result of conversion of a convertible security. (21)

conversion ratio The ratio at which a convertible security can be exchanged for common stock. (21)

conversion (or stock) value The value of a convertible security as measured by the market price of the common stock into which it can be converted. (21)

convertible bond A bond that at some future time can be converted into a specified number of shares of common stock. (21)

convertible preferred stock Preferred stock that at some future time can be converted into a specified number of shares of common stock. (21)

corporate bond A certificate indicating that a corporation has borrowed a certain amount of money and promises to repay it in the future under clearly defined terms. (19)

corporate raider Corporate outsider that uses junk bond financing to gain control of a firm and then uses the firm's operating cash flows or assets to repay the debt. (18)

corporate restructuring The activities involving expansion or contraction of a firm's operations or changes in its asset or financial (ownership) structure. (17)

corporation An intangible business entity created by law. (2)

correlation A statistical measure of the relationship between series of numbers representing data of any kind. (12)

correlation coefficient A measure of the degree of correlation between two series of numbers. (12)

cost of a new asset The net outflow required to acquire a new asset. (14)

cost of a new issue of common stock, k_n Cost determined by calculating the cost of common stock after considering both the amount of underpricing and the associated flotation costs. (13)

cost of capital The rate of return a firm must earn on its project investments to maintain its market value and attract funds. (13)

cost of common stock equity, k_s The rate at which investors discount the expected dividends of the firm in order to determine its share value. (13)

cost of forgoing a cash discount The implied rate of interest paid in order to delay payment of an account payable for an additional number of days. (10)

cost of long-term debt (bonds), k_i The after-tax cost today of raising long-term funds through borrowing. (13)

cost of preferred stock, k_p The annual preferred stock dividend divided by the net proceeds from the sale of the preferred stock. (13)

cost of retained earnings, k_r The same as the cost of an equivalent fully subscribed issue of additional common stock, which is measured by the cost of common stock equity, k_s. (13)

credit analysis The evaluation of credit applicants. (9)

credit period The number of days until full payment of an account payable is required. (10)

credit policy The determination of credit selection, credit standards, and credit terms. (9)

credit scoring The ranking of an applicant's overall credit strength, derived as a weighted average of scores on key financial and credit characteristics. (9)

credit selection The decision whether to extend credit to a customer and how much credit to extend. (9)

credit standards The minimum requirements for extending credit to a customer. (9)

credit terms Terms under which a firm's credit customers must pay their accounts. (9)

creditor control An arrangement in which the creditor committee replaces the firm's operating management and operates the firm until all claims have been settled. (17)

cross-sectional analysis The comparison of different firms' financial ratios at the same point in time. (4)

cumulative preferred stock Preferred stock for which all passed (unpaid) dividends in arrears must be paid prior to the payment of dividends to common stockholders. (20)

cumulative voting system The system under which each share of common stock is allotted a number of votes equal to the total number of corporate directors to be elected and votes can be given to *any* director(s). (20)

current assets Short-term assets, expected to be converted into cash within one year or less. (3)

current expenditure An outlay of funds resulting in benefits received *within* one year. (14)

current liabilities Short-term liabilities, expected to be converted into cash within one year or less. (3)

current ratio A measure of liquidity, calculated by dividing the firm's current assets by its current liabilities. (4)

date of invoice Indicates that the beginning of the credit period is the date on the invoice for the purchase. (10)

date of record (dividends) The date, set by the firm's directors, on which all persons whose names are recorded as stockholders will at a specified future time receive a declared dividend. (16)

date of record (rights) The last date on which the recipient of a right must be the legal owner indicated in the company's stock ledger. (20)

debentures Unsecured bonds that only creditworthy firms can issue, with claims the same as those of any general creditor. (19)

debt capital All long-term borrowing done by the firm. (16)

debt ratio Measures the proportion of total assets financed by the firm's creditors. (4)

debtor in possession (DIP) The term for a firm that files a reorganization petition under Chapter 11 and then develops, if feasible, a reorganization plan. (17)

decision trees Diagrams that map the various investment decision alternatives and payoffs as well as their probabilities of occurrence. (15)

degree of financial leverage (DFL) The numerical measure of the firm's financial leverage. (5)

degree of operating leverage (DOL) The numerical measure of the firm's operating leverage. (5)

degree of total leverage (DTL) The numerical measure of the firm's total leverage. (5)

Depository Institutions Deregulation and Monetary Control Act of 1980 (DIDMCA) Eliminated interest-rate ceilings on all accounts and permitted certain institutions to offer new types of accounts and services. (2)

depository transfer check (DTC) An unsigned check drawn on one of the firm's bank accounts and deposited into its account at a concentration or major disbursement bank. (8)

depreciable life Time period over which an asset is depreciated. (3)

depreciation The systematic charging of a portion of the costs of fixed assets against annual revenues over time. (3)

depth of a market A characteristic of a ready market, determined by its ability to absorb the purchase or sale of a large dollar amount of a particular security. (8)

dilution of ownership Occurs when a new stock issue results in each present stockholder having a claim on a *smaller* part of the firm's earnings than previously. (20)

direct lease A lease under which a lessor owns or acquires the assets that are leased to a given lessee. (19)

direct send A collection procedure in which the payee presents payment checks directly to the banks on which they are drawn. (8)

disbursement float The lapse between the time a firm deducts a payment from its checking account ledger (disburses it) and the time funds are actually withdrawn from its account. (8)

discount The amount by which a bond sells at a value less than its par, or face, value. (12)

discount loans Loans on which interest is paid in advance by deducting it from the amount borrowed. (10)

discounting cash flows The process of finding present values; the inverse of compounding interest. (11)

diversifiable risk The portion of risk attributable to firm-specific, random causes; can be eliminated through diversification. (12)

divestiture The selling of some of a firm's assets, for various strategic motives. (17)

dividend payout ratio Indicates the percentage of each dollar earned that is distributed to the owners in the form of cash. (16)

dividend policy The firm's plan of action in regard to the declaration of dividends. (16)

dividend reinvestment plans Plans that enable stockholders to use dividends to acquire full or fractional shares at little or no transaction (brokerage) cost. (16)

dividends Periodic distributions of earnings to the owners of stock in a firm. (2)

double taxation Occurs when the once-taxed earnings of a corporation are distributed as cash dividends to its stockholders, who are then taxed on these dividends. (2)

Dun & Bradstreet The largest mercantile credit-reporting agency in the United States. (9)

DuPont formula Relates the firm's net profit margin and total asset turnover to its return on investment (ROI). (4)

DuPont system of analysis System used to dissect a firm's financial statements and assess its financial condition. (4)

earnings per share (EPS) The amount earned during the period on each outstanding share of common stock. (1)

EBIT–EPS approach An approach for selecting the capital structure that maximizes earnings per share (EPS) over the expected range of earnings before interest and taxes (EBIT). (16)

economic exposure The risk resulting from the effects of changes in foreign exchange rates on the firm's value. (12)

economic order quantity (EOQ) model Inventory management technique for determining the optimal order quantity for an item of inventory. (9)

effective interest rate The actual rate of interest paid on a loan as opposed to the stated rate. (10)

effective interest rate (in the international context) The rate equal to the nominal rate plus any forecast appreciation (or minus any forecast depreciation) of a foreign currency relative to the currency of the MNC parent. (10)

efficient market Market that allocates funds to their most productive uses as a result of competition among wealth-maximizing investors. (2)

efficient portfolio A portfolio that maximizes return for a given level of risk or minimizes risk for a given level of return. (12)

end of month (EOM) Indicates that the credit period for all purchases made within a given month begins on the first day of the month immediately following. (10)

ending cash The sum of the firm's beginning cash and its net cash flow for the period. (6)

equipment trust certificates Secured bonds used to finance "rolling stock." (19)

equity capital The long-term funds provided by the firm's owners, the stockholders. (16)

equity multiplier The ratio of the firm's total assets to stockholders' equity. (4)

ethics Standards of conduct or moral judgment. (1)

Eurobond An international bond sold primarily in countries other than the country of the currency of the issue. (19)

Eurocurrency markets The portion of the Euromarket that provides short-term foreign-currency financing to subsidiaries of MNCs. (10)

Eurodollar deposits Negotiable deposits of currency not native to the country in which the bank is located. (8)

Euro-equity market The world capital market, whose center is London, that deals in international equity issues. (20)

Euromarket The international financial market that provides for borrowing and lending currencies outside their country of origin. (2)

Europe 1992 The transformation of the European Economic Community (EC) into a single market by year-end 1992. (2)

ex dividend Period beginning four *business days* prior to the date of record during which a stock will be sold without the right to receive the current dividend. (16)

ex rights Period, beginning four *business days* prior to the date of record, during which the stock will be sold without announced rights being attached. (20)

excess cash balance The amount available for investment by the firm if the period's ending cash is greater than the desired minimum cash balance. (6)

excess earnings accumulation tax The tax levied by the IRS on retained earnings above $250,000, when it has determined that the firm has accumulated an excess of earnings in order to allow owners to delay paying ordinary income taxes. (16)

exercise price (or option price) The price at which holders of warrants can purchase a specified number of shares of common stock. (21)

expected return The sum of the forecast change in an investment's value and any expected cash receipts expressed as a percentage of the initial amount invested. (2)

expected value of a return, $\bar{k}$ The most likely return on a given asset. (12)

extendable notes Bonds with short maturities which can be redeemed or renewed for a similar period at a new rate competitive with market interest rates prevailing at the time of renewal. (19)

extension An arrangement whereby the firm's creditors receive payment in full, although not immediately. (17)

external forecast A sales forecast based on the relationships between the firm's sales and certain key external economic indicators. (6)

external funds required ("plug" figure) The amount of external financing needed to bring the pro forma balance sheet into balance under the judgmental approach. (6)

external sources of funds Funds raised outside the firm from negotiated loans and the sale of bonds and stock. (18)

extra dividend An additional dividend optionally paid by the firm if earnings are higher than normal in a given period. (16)

factor A financial institution that specializes in purchasing accounts receivable. (10)

factoring accounts receivable The outright sale of accounts receivable at a discount in order to obtain funds. (10)

FASB No. 52 Statement requiring U.S. MNCs first to convert financial statement accounts of foreign subsidiaries into their *functional currency* and then to translate them into the parent firm's currency using the *all-current-rate method*. (3)

federal agency issues Low-risk securities issued by government agencies but not guaranteed by the U.S. Treasury, having short maturities, and offering slightly higher yields than comparable Treasury issues. (8)

finance The art and science of managing money. (1)

Financial Accounting Standards Board (FASB) The accounting profession's rule-setting body. (3)

financial breakeven point The level of EBIT necessary for the firm to just cover all fixed financial costs. (5)

financial engineering The process of bringing new innovative financial products and procedures to market. (18)

financial institution An intermediary that channels the savings of individuals, businesses, and governments into loans or investments. (2)

financial leverage The potential use of fixed financial costs to magnify the effects of changes in EBIT on the firm's EPS. (4, 5)

financial manager Actively manages the financial affairs of any type of business. (1)

financial markets Provide a forum in which suppliers of funds and demanders of loans and investments can transact business directly. (2)

financial merger A merger transaction undertaken to restructure the acquired company in order to improve its cash flow and unlock its hidden value. (17)

financial (or capital) lease A *noncancelable* lease that obligates the lessee to make payments for the use of an asset over a predefined period of time; the term of the lease is longer than for an operating lease and total payments over the term of the lease are *greater* than the lessor's initial cost of the leased asset. (19)

financial planning process Planning that begins with long-run financial plans that in turn guide short-run plans and budgets. (6)

financial risk The risk to the firm of being unable to cover financial costs. (5)

financial services The area of finance concerned with design and delivery of advice and financial products. (1)

financial supermarket An institution at which the customer can obtain a full array of financial services. (2)

financing flows Cash flows that result from debt and equity financing transactions. (3)

finished goods inventory Items that have been produced but not yet sold. (9)

five C's of credit The five key dimensions—character, capacity, capital, collateral, and conditions—used by credit managers in their analysis of an applicant's creditworthiness. (9)

fixed asset turnover Measures the efficiency with which the firm has been using its *fixed*, or earning, assets to generate sales. (4)

fixed costs Costs that are a function of time, not sales volume. (5)

fixed-payment coverage ratio Measures the firm's ability to meet all fixed-payment obligations. (4)

fixed-rate loan A loan whose rate of interest is determined at a set increment above the prime rate and remains unvarying until maturity. (10)

fixed (or semi-fixed) relationship The constant (or relatively constant) relationship of a currency to one of the major currencies, a combination of major currencies, or some type of international foreign exchange standard. (12)

float Funds dispatched by a payer that are not yet in a form that can be spent by the payee. (8)

floating inventory lien A lender's claim on the borrower's general inventory as collateral for a secured loan. (10)

floating rate bonds Bonds whose stated interest rate is adjusted periodically within stated limits in response to changes in specified money or capital market rates. (19)

floating-rate loan A loan whose rate of interest is set at an increment above the prime rate and is allowed to "float" above prime *as the prime rate varies* until maturity. (10)

floating relationship The fluctuating relationship of the values of two currencies with respect to each other. (12)

flotation costs The total costs of issuing and selling a security. (13)

foreign bond An international bond sold primarily in the country of the currency of the issue. (19)

foreign direct investment (FDI) An MNC's transfer of capital, managerial, and technical assets from its home country to a host country. (14)

foreign exchange rate The value of two currencies with respect to each other. (12)

foreign exchange risk The risk caused by varying exchange rates between two currencies. (12)

forward exchange rate The rate of exchange between two currencies at some specified future date. (12)

friendly merger A merger transaction endorsed by the target firm's management, approved by its stockholders, and easily consummated. (17)

functional currency The currency in which a business entity primarily generates and expends cash and in which its accounts are maintained. (3)

future value The value of a present amount at a future date, found by applying compound interest over a specified period of time. (11)

future-value interest factor The multiplier used to calculate at a specified interest rate the future value of a present amount as of a given time. (11)

future-value interest factor for an annuity The multiplier used to calculate the future value of an annuity at a specified interest rate over a given period of time. (11)

generally accepted accounting principles (GAAP) The practice and procedure guidelines used to prepare and maintain financial records and reports. (3)

going public Offering to the general public common stock previously held by private investors. (18)

golden parachutes Provisions in the employment contracts of key executives that provide sizable compensation if the firm is taken over. (17)

Gordon model Common name for the *constant growth model*. (12)

greenmail A takeover defense under which a target firm repurchases a large block of stock at a premium from one or more shareholders in order to end a hostile takeover attempt by those shareholders. (17)

gross commission (gross underwriting spread) The difference between the price at which an investment banker sells a securities issue to the public and the price at which it bought the issue from the issuing firm. (18)

gross profit margin Indicates the percentage of each sales dollar left after the firm has paid for its goods. (4)

hedging strategies Techniques used to offset the risk of changing relationships between currencies. (8)

historic weights Either book or market value weights based on *actual* capital structure proportions. (13)

holders of record Owners of the firm's shares on the *date of record*. (16)

holding company A corporation that has voting control of one or more other corporations. (17)

horizontal merger A merger of two firms *in the same line of business*. (17)

hostile merger A merger transaction not supported by the target firm's management, forcing the acquiring company to try to gain control of the firm by buying shares in the marketplace. (17)

income bonds Unsecured bonds for which payment of interest is required only when earnings are available for that purpose. (19)

income statement Provides a financial summary of the firm's operating results during a specified period. (3)

incremental cash flows The *additional* cash flows—outflows or inflows—expected to result from a proposed capital expenditure. (14)

independent projects Projects whose cash flows are unrelated or independent of one another; the acceptance of one *does not eliminate* the others from consideration. (14)

indifference point On a graphed comparison of two financing plans, the point at which, for a given EBIT, EPS is the same for both plans. (5)

informational content The information provided by the dividends of a firm with respect to future earnings, which causes owners to bid up (or down) the price of the firm's stock. (16)

initial investment The relevant cash outflow for a proposed project at time zero. (14)

initial public offering (IPO) The stock issue of a firm that offers shares to the public for the first time. (18)

installation costs Any added costs necessary to place an asset into operation. (14)

intercorporate dividends Dividends received by one corporation on common and preferred stock held in other corporations. (2)

interest rate When funds are lent, the cost of borrowing funds. (2)

intermediate cash inflows Cash inflows received prior to the termination of a project. (15)

internal forecast A sales forecast based on a consensus of forecasts through the firm's own sales channels. (6)

internal rate of return (IRR) The discount rate that equates the present value of cash inflows with the initial investment associated with a project, thereby making NPV = $0. (15)

internal rate of return approach An approach to capital rationing that involves graphing project IRRs in descending order against the total dollar investment. (15)

internal sources of funds Funds generated inside the firm from retained earnings. (18)

international bond A bond that is initially sold outside the country of the borrower and often distributed in several countries. (19)

inventory turnover Measures the activity, or liquidity, of a firm's inventory. (4)

investment banker A financial intermediary who purchases securities from corporations and governments and sells them to the public in the *primary market;* also, a firm hired by the prospective participants in a merger to find suitable partners and assist in negotiations. (2, 17, 18)

investment flows Cash flows associated with purchase and sale of both fixed assets and business interests. (3)

investment opportunities schedule (IOS) A ranking of investment possibilities from best (highest returns) to worst (lowest returns). (13)

involuntary reorganization A petition initiated by an outside party, usually a creditor, for the reorganization of a failed firm and payment of its creditors. (17)

issued shares The number of shares of common stock that has been put into circulation; outstanding shares plus treasury stock. (18)

joint venture A partnership under which the participants agree to contribute specified amounts of money and expertise for stated proportions of ownership and profit. (2)

judgmental approach Method for developing the pro forma balance sheet in which the values of certain accounts are estimated while others are calculated, using the firm's external financing as a "plug" figure. (6)

junk bonds Low-rated, high-risk debt securities used to finance corporate takeovers. (18, 19)

just-in-time (JIT) system Inventory management system that minimizes inventory investment by having material inputs arrive at exactly the time they are needed for production. (9)

large private corporation A major corporation whose shares are not publicly traded and that relies heavily on debt as its key source of financing. (1)

lease-versus-purchase (or lease-versus-buy) decision The decision facing firms needing to acquire new fixed assets: whether to lease the assets or to purchase

them, using borrowed funds or available liquid resources. (19)

leasing The process by which a firm can obtain the use of certain fixed assets for which it must make a series of contractual, periodic, tax-deductible payments. (19)

lessee The receiver of the services of the assets under a lease contract. (19)

lessor The owner of assets that are being leased. (19)

letter to stockholders Typically the first element of the annual stockholders' report and the primary communication from management to the firm's owners. (3)

leverage The use of fixed-cost assets or funds to magnify returns to the firm's owners. (5)

leveraged buyout (LBO) An acquisition technique involving the use of a large amount of debt to purchase a firm. (17)

leveraged lease A lease under which the lessor supplies only about 20 percent of the cost of the asset, while a lender supplies the balance. (19)

leveraged recapitalization A takeover defense in which the target firm pays a large debt-financed cash dividend, increasing the firm's financial leverage. (17)

lien A publicly disclosed legal claim on collateral. (10)

limited partnership A partnership in which one or more partners has limited liability as long as at least *one* partner has unlimited liability. (2)

line of credit An agreement specifying the maximum amount of unsecured short-term borrowing a bank will make available to a firm over a given period of time. (9, 10)

liquidation value per share The *actual* amount per share of common stock if all assets are sold, liabilities (including preferred stock) are paid, and any remaining money is divided among common stockholders. (12)

liquidity A firm's ability to satisfy its short-term obligations as they come due. (4)

loan amortization The determination of the equal annual loan payments necessary to provide a lender with a specified interest return and repay the loan principal over a specified period. (11)

loan amortization schedule A schedule showing the allocation to interest and principal of each of the equal payments to repay a loan. (11)

lockbox system A collection procedure under which payers send payments to a nearby post office box from which the firm's bank empties and deposits payment checks in its account several times daily. (8)

long-run (strategic) financial plans Planned long-term financial actions and the anticipated financial impact of those actions. (6)

long-term financing Financing with an initial maturity of more than one year. (18)

long-term funds The sum of the firm's long-term debt and stockholders' equity. (7)

low-regular-and-extra dividend policy A dividend policy based on paying a low regular dividend, supplemented by an additional dividend when earnings warrant it. (16)

M and M approach Named for its initial proponents, Modigliani and Miller, the theory that an optimal capital structure does *not* exist. (16)

macro political risk The subjection of *all* foreign firms to political risk (takeover) by a host country. (12)

mail float The delay between the time a payer mails a

payment and the time the payee receives it. (8)

maintenance clauses Provisions common in operating leases that require the lessor to maintain the asset and to make insurance and tax payments. (19)

majority voting system The system whereby, in the election of a board of directors, each stockholder is entitled to one vote for each share of stock owned and can vote all shares for *each* director. (20)

management fee Fee paid a managing underwriter for coordinating and sponsoring an underwriting syndicate. (18)

managerial finance Concerns the duties of the financial manager in the business firm. (1)

managing (or lead) underwriter Underwriter of a syndicate that negotiates the terms of the issue with the issuing corporation. (18)

marginal analysis States that financial decisions should be made and actions taken only when added benefits exceed added costs. (1)

marginal tax rate The rate at which additional income is taxed. (2)

market premium The amount by which the market value of a convertible security exceeds its straight or conversion value. (21)

market return The return on the market portfolio of all traded securities. (12)

market risk-return function A graph of the discount rates associated with each level of project risk. (15)

market stabilization The purchase by underwriters of a security they are attempting to sell if the retail price of the shares moves below the initial offering price. (18)

market value weights Weights that use market values to measure the proportion of each type of capital in the firm's financial structure. (13)

marketable securities Short-term, interest-earning debt instruments issued by government, business, and financial institutions; frequently used to obtain a return on temporarily idle funds. (2, 8)

materials requirement planning (MRP) system Inventory management system that compares production needs to available inventory balances and determines when orders should be placed for various material inputs. (9)

merger The combination of two or more firms, in which the resulting firm maintains the identity of one of the firms, usually the larger one. (17)

micro political risk The subjection of an individual firm, specific industry, or companies from a particular foreign country to political risk (takeover) by the host country. (12)

mixed stream A stream of cash flows that reflects no particular pattern; any cashflow stream other than that of an annuity. (11, 14)

modified DuPont formula Relates the firm's return on investment (ROI) to its return on equity (ROE) using the *equity multiplier*. (4)

money market A financial relationship created between suppliers and demanders of *short-term funds*. (2)

money market mutual funds Professionally managed portfolios of various popular marketable securities. (8)

mortgage bonds Bonds secured by real estate or buildings. (19)

multinational companies (MNCs) Firms that have in-

ternational assets and operations in foreign markets and draw part of their total revenue and profits from such markets. (1)

mutually exclusive projects Projects that compete with one another, so that the acceptance of one *eliminates* the others from further consideration. (14)

national entry control systems Comprehensive rules, regulations, and incentives aimed at regulating inflows of *foreign direct investments* of MNCs and extracting more benefits from their presence. (12)

near-cash Marketable securities, viewed the same as cash because of their high liquidity. (8)

negatively correlated Two series of numbers that move in opposite directions. (12)

negotiable certificates of deposit (CDs) Negotiable instruments representing specific cash deposits in commercial banks, having varying maturities and yields based on size, maturity, and prevailing money market conditions. (8)

negotiated offering The process in which a securities issuer interviews a number of investment bankers and selects the one that it thinks will best meet its needs at the lowest cost. (18)

net cash flow The mathematical difference between the firm's cash receipts and its cash disbursements in each period. (6)

net present value (NPV) The present value of a project's cash inflows minus its initial investment. (15)

net present value approach An approach to capital rationing that is based on the use of present values to determine the group of projects that will maximize owners' wealth. (15)

net proceeds Funds actually received from the sale of a security. (13)

net profit margin Measures the percentage of each sales dollar remaining after all expenses, including taxes, have been deducted. (4)

net working capital The difference between the firm's current assets and its current liabilities; alternatively, the portion of the firm's current assets financed with long-term funds. (4, 7)

no par value Describes stock issued without a *par value*. (20)

nominal interest rate (in the international context) The stated interest rate charged on financing when only the MNC parent's currency is involved. (10)

noncash charges Expenses deducted on the income statement that do not involve an actual outlay of cash during the period. (3)

nonconventional cash flow patterns A pattern in which an initial outflow is *not* followed by a series of inflows. (14)

noncumulative preferred stock Preferred stock for which passed (unpaid) dividends do not accumulate. (20)

nondiversifiable risk The relevant portion of risk attributable to market factors that affect all firms; cannot be eliminated through diversification. (12)

nonnotification basis The basis on which a borrower, having pledged an account receivable, continues to collect the account payments without notifying the account customer. (10)

nonparticipating preferred stock Preferred stock whose holders receive only the specified dividend payments. (20)

nonrecourse basis The basis on which accounts receivable are sold to a factor with the understanding that the factor accepts all credit risks on the purchased accounts. (10)

nonvoting common stock Common stock that carries no voting rights; issued when the firm wishes to raise capital through the sale of common stock but does not want to give up its voting control. (20)

no-par preferred stock Preferred stock with no stated face value but with a stated annual dollar dividend. (20)

notification basis The basis on which an account customer whose account has been pledged is notified to remit payments directly to the lender. (10)

offshore centers Certain cities or states that have achieved prominence as major centers for Euromarket business. (2)

operating breakeven point The level of sales necessary to cover all operating costs. (5)

operating cash inflows The incremental after-tax cash inflows resulting from use of a project during its life. (14)

operating change restrictions Contractual restrictions that a bank may impose on a firm as part of a line of credit agreement. (10)

operating cycle (OC) The amount of time that elapses from when the firm begins to build inventory to when cash is collected from sale of the resulting finished product. (7, 8)

operating flows Cash flows directly related to production and sale of the firm's products and services. (3)

operating lease A *cancelable* contractual arrangement whereby the lessee agrees to make periodic payments to the lessor, often for five or fewer years, for an asset's services; generally the total payments over the term of the lease are *less* than the lessor's initial cost of the leased asset. (19)

operating leverage The potential use of *fixed operating costs* to magnify the effects of changes in sales on the firm's EBIT. (5)

operating unit A part of a business, such as a plant, division, product line, or subsidiary, that contributes to the actual operations of the firm. (17)

optimal capital structure The capital structure at which the weighted average cost of capital is minimized, thereby maximizing the firm's value. (16)

option An instrument that gives its holder an opportunity to purchase or sell a specified asset at a stated price on or before a set *expiration date*. (21)

order costs The fixed clerical costs of placing and receiving an inventory order. (9)

ordinary income Income earned though the sale of a firm's goods or services. (2)

organized securities exchanges Tangible organizations on whose premises outstanding securities are resold. (2)

out-of-pocket costs Costs of a managing underwriter incurred in connection with a securities issue. (18)

outstanding shares The number of shares of common stock sold to the public. (18)

overdraft system Automatic coverage by the bank of all checks presented against the firm's account, regardless of the account balance. (8)

overhanging issue A convertible security that cannot be forced into conversion using the call feature. (21)

over-the-counter (OTC) exchange Not an organization, but an intangible market for the purchase and sale of

securities not listed by the organized exchanges. (2)

paid-in capital in excess of par The amount of proceeds in excess of the par value received from the original sale of common stock. (3)

par value A per-share value arbitrarily placed on stock in the firm's corporate charter. (3, 20)

participating preferred stock Preferred stock that offers dividend payments based on formulas allowing preferred stockholders to participate with common stockholders in the receipt of dividends beyond a specified amount. (20)

partnership A business owned by two or more persons and operated for profit. (2)

par-value preferred stock Preferred stock with a stated face value that is used with the specified dividend percentage to determine the annual dollar dividend. (20)

payback period The exact amount of time required for a firm to recover its initial investment in a project as calculated from *cash inflows*. (15)

payment date The actual date on which the firm will mail the dividend payment to the holders of record. (16)

payment-in-kind (PIK) preferred stock Preferred stock that pays dividends in additional shares of preferred stock rather than cash. (20)

percentage advance The percent of the book value of the collateral that constitutes the principal of a secured loan. (10)

percent-of-sales method Method for developing the pro forma income statement that expresses the cost of goods sold, operating expenses, and interest expense as a percentage of projected sales. (6)

perfectly negatively correlated Two negatively correlated series of numbers that have a *correlation coefficient* of -1. (12)

perfectly positively correlated Two positively correlated series of numbers that have a *correlation coefficient* of $+1$. (12)

permanent need Financing requirements for the firm's fixed assets plus the permanent portion of the firm's current assets, which remain unchanged over the year. (7)

perpetuity An annuity with an infinite life, making continual annual payments (11)

playing the float A method of consciously anticipating the resulting delay associated with the payment process and using it to keep funds in an interest-earning form for as long as possible. (8)

pledge of accounts receivable The use of a firm's accounts receivable as collateral to obtain a short-term loan. (10)

poison pill A takeover defense in which a firm issues securities that give their holders certain rights that become effective when a takeover is attempted and that make the target firm less desirable to a hostile acquirer. (17)

political risk The potential seizure of an MNC's operations in a host country. (12)

portfolio A collection, or group, of assets. (12)

positively correlated Two series of numbers that move in the same direction. (12)

preauthorized check A check written by the payee against a customer's checking account for a previously agreed-upon amount. (8)

preemptive rights Allow common stockholders to maintain their proportionate ownership in the corporation when new issues are made. (20)

preferred stock A special form of ownership having a fixed periodic dividend that must be paid prior to payment of any common stock dividends. (2)

premium The amount by which a bond sells at a value greater than its par, or face, value. (12)

present value The current dollar value of a future amount. (11)

present-value interest factor The multiplier used to calculate at a specified discount rate the present value of an amount to be received in a future period. (11)

present-value interest factor for an annuity The multiplier used to calculate the present value of an annuity at a specified discount rate over a given period of time. (11)

president or chief executive officer (CEO) Corporate official responsible for managing the firm's day-to-day operations. (2)

price risk The risk that the price of a new security will fall while it is being held by an investment banking firm. (18)

price/earnings multiple approach A technique to estimate the firm's share value; calculated by multiplying the firm's expected earnings per share by the average price/earnings ratio for the industry. (12)

price/earnings (P/E) ratio Reflects the amount investors are willing to pay for each dollar of the firm's earnings. (4)

primary market Financial market in which securities are initially issued. (2)

prime rate of interest (prime rate) The lowest rate of interest charged by the nation's leading banks on loans to their most reliable business borrowers. (10)

principal The amount of money on which interest is paid. (11)

private placement The sale of new securities directly to selected groups of investors, without SEC registration. (18)

privately owned (stock) All common stock of a firm owned by a single individual. (20)

pro forma statements Projected financial statements—income statements and balance sheets. (6)

probability The *chance* that a given outcome will occur. (12)

probability distribution A model that relates probabilities to the associated outcomes. (12)

proceeds from the sale of an old asset The net cash inflow resulting from the sale of an existing asset. (14)

processing float The delay between the receipt of a check by the payee and its deposit in the firm's account. (8)

profitability The relationship between revenues and costs. (7)

profitability index (PI) The present value of a project's cash inflows divided by its initial investment. (15)

prospectus The portion of the registration statement filed by a securities issuer with the SEC that details the firm's operating and financial position. (18)

proxy battle The attempt by a nonmanagement group to gain control of the management of a firm by soliciting a sufficient number of proxy votes. (20)

proxy statement A statement giving the votes of a stockholder or stockholders to another party or parties. (20)

public offering The sale of a firm's securities to the general public. (18)

publicly held corporations Corporations whose stock is traded on either an organized securities exchange or the over-the-counter exchange. (3)

publicly owned (stock) Common stock of a firm owned by a broad group of unrelated individual or institutional investors. (20)

purchase options Provisions common in both operating and financial leases that allow the lessee to purchase the leased asset at maturity, typically for a pre-specified price. (19)

put option An option to *sell* a given number of shares of a stock on or before some future date at a stated price. (21)

putable bonds Bonds that can be redeemed at par at the option of their holder either at specific dates or when and if the firm takes specified actions. (19)

pyramiding An arrangement among holding companies wherein one holding company controls others, thereby causing an even greater magnification of earnings and losses. (17)

quarterly compounding Compounding of interest over four periods within the year. (11)

quick (acid-test) ratio A measure of liquidity, calculated by dividing the firm's current assets minus inventory by current liabilities. (4)

range A measure of an asset's risk, which is found by subtracting the worst outcome from the best outcome. (12)

ranking approach The ranking of capital expenditure proposals on the basis of a predetermined measure, such as the rate of return. (14)

ratio analysis Involves the methods of calculating and interpreting financial ratios in order to assess the firm's performance and status. (4)

ratio of exchange The ratio of the amount *paid* per share of the target company to the per-share market price of the acquiring firm. (17)

ratio of exchange in market price The ratio of the market price per share of the acquiring firm *paid* to each dollar of market price per share of the target firm. (17)

raw materials inventory Items purchased by the firm for use in the manufacture of a finished product. (9)

recapitalization The reorganization procedure under which a failed firm's debts are generally exchanged for equity or the maturities of existing debts are extended. (17)

recaptured depreciation The portion of the sale price that is above book value and below the initial purchase price. (14)

recovery period The appropriate depreciable life of a particular asset as determined by ACRS. (3)

red herring A statement printed in red ink on the cover of a prospectus indicating the tentative nature of a securities offering before its approval by the SEC. (18)

red-line method Inventory management technique in which a reorder is placed when use of inventory items from a bin exposes a red line drawn inside the bin. (9)

registration statement Statement with information about a new security issue that must be filed with the SEC for approval before public sale of the issue can take place. (18)

regular dividend policy A dividend policy based on the payment of a fixed-dollar dividend in each period. (16)

relevant cash flows The *incremental after-tax cash outflow and resulting subsequent inflows* associated with a proposed capital expenditure. (14)

renewal options Provisions common in operating leases that grant the lessee the option to re-lease assets at the expiration of the lease. (19)

reorder point The point at which to reorder inventory. (9)

repurchase agreement An agreement whereby a bank or security dealer sells a firm specific securities and agrees to buy them back at a specific price and time. (8)

required return The cost paid by the demander of funds to the owner of an equity interest in a firm. (2)

required total financing Amount of funds needed by the firm if the ending cash for the period is less than the desired minimum cash balance. (6)

residual theory of dividends A theory that the dividend paid by a firm should be the amount left over after all acceptable investment opportunities have been undertaken. (16)

restrictive covenants Contractual clauses in long-term debt agreements that place certain operating and financial constraints on the borrower. (19)

retained earnings The cumulative total of all earnings retained (not distributed as dividends) and reinvested in the firm since its inception; a form of *internal* financing. (3, 16)

return The change in value of an asset plus any cash distribution over a given period of time, expressed as a percentage of its initial value. (12)

return on equity (ROE) Measures the return earned on the owners' (both preferred and common stockholders') investment in the firm. (4)

return on investment (ROI) Measures the overall effectiveness of management in generating profits with its available assets. (4)

reverse stock split A method used to raise the market price of a firm's stock by exchanging a certain number of outstanding shares for one new share of stock. (16)

revolving credit agreement A line of credit *guaranteed* to a borrower by a bank for a stated time period and regardless of the scarcity of money. (10)

risk The chance of financial loss or, more formally, the variability of returns associated with a given asset, i.e., the chance that actual outcomes may differ from those expected. In a short-term context, the probability that a firm will be unable to pay its bills as they come due. (1, 7, 12)

risk (in capital budgeting) The chance that a project will prove unacceptable or, more formally, the degree of variability of cash flows. (15)

risk premium The amount by which the required discount rate for a project exceeds the risk-free rate. (15)

risk-adjusted discount rate (RADR) The rate of return that must be earned on a given project in order to compensate the firm's owners adequately. (15)

risk-averse Seeking to avoid risk; the attitude toward risk in which an increased return would be required for an increase in risk. (1, 12)

risk-free rate (R_F) The rate of return on a virtually riskless investment. (15)

risk-return trade-off The expectation that for accepting greater risk, investors must be compensated with greater returns. (2)

S corporation A tax-reporting entity whose earnings are taxed not as a corporation but as the incomes of its stockholders, thus avoiding *double taxation*. (2)

safety motive A motive for holding cash or near-cash—to protect the firm against being unable to satisfy unexpected demands for cash. (8)

safety of principal The ease of salability of a security for close to its initial value. (8)

safety stocks Extra inventories that can be drawn down when actual lead times or usage rates are greater than expected. (9)

sale-leaseback arrangement A lease under which the lessee sells an asset for cash to a prospective lessor and then leases back the same asset, making periodic payments for its use. (19)

sales forecast The prediction of the firm's sales over a given period, based on external or internal data. (6)

scenario analysis An approach that evaluates the impact on return of simultaneous changes in a number of variables. (15)

seasonal need Financing requirements for temporary current assets, which vary over the year. (7)

secondary market Financial market in which preowned securities are traded. (2)

secured creditors Creditors who have specific assets pledged as collateral and in liquidation received proceeds from the sale of those assets. (17)

secured loan A loan for which the lender requires collateral. (10)

secured short-term financing Financing that matures in one year or less and has specific assets pledged as collateral. (10)

Securities Act of 1933 Federal law that regulates the public sale of new security issues. (18)

Securities and Exchange Commission (SEC) The federal regulatory body that governs the sale and listing of securities. (3)

Securities Exchange Act of 1934 Federal law that regulates the sale of securities in secondary markets. (18)

securities exchanges The marketplace in which firms can raise funds through the sale of new securities and in which purchasers can resell securities. (2)

security agreement The agreement between the borrower and the lender that specifies the collateral held against a secured loan. (10)

security market line (SML) The depiction of the capital asset pricing model (CAPM) as a graph that reflects the required return for each level of nondiversifiable risk (beta). (12)

selling concession Fee paid to members of an underwriting syndicate based on the number of shares each member sold. (18)

selling group Group of brokerage houses who promote a securities issue through their branch offices and retail stockbrokers in their area. (18)

semiannual compounding Compounding of interest over two periods within the year. (11)

sensitivity analysis An approach for assessing risk that uses a number of possible values for a given variable in order to assess its impact on a firm's return. (12, 15)

serial bonds An issue of bonds of which a certain proportion matures each year. (19)

shark repellents Anti-takeover amendments to a corporate charter that constrain the firm's ability to transfer managerial control as a result of a merger. (17)

shelf registration Securities registration procedure that allows a firm to sell securities during a two-year period under a master registration statement filed with the SEC. (18)

short-run (operating) financial plans Planned short-term financial actions and the anticipated financial impact of those actions. (6)

short-term financial management Management of current assets and current liabilities. (7)

short-term self-liquidating loan An unsecured short-term loan in which the use to which the borrowed money is put provides the mechanism through which the loan is repaid. (10)

simulation A statistically based approach used to get a feel for risk by applying predetermined probability distributions and random numbers to estimate risky outcomes. (15)

single-payment note A short-term, one-time loan payable as a single amount at its maturity. (10)

sinking-fund requirement A restrictive provision often included in a bond indenture providing for the systematic retirement of bonds prior to their maturity. (19)

small (ordinary) stock dividend A stock dividend that represents less than 20 to 25 percent of the common stock outstanding at the time the dividend is declared. (16)

sole proprietorship A business owned by one person and operated for his or her own profit. (2)

sophisticated capital budgeting techniques Methods that give explicit consideration to the time value of money. (15)

speculative motive A motive for holding cash or near-cash—to put unneeded funds to work or to be able to quickly take advantage of unexpected opportunities. (8)

spin-off A form of divestiture in which an operating unit becomes an independent company by issuing shares in it on a pro rata basis to the parent company's shareholders. (17)

spontaneous financing Financing that arises from the normal operations of the firm, the two major short-term sources of which are accounts payable and accruals. (10)

spot exchange rate The rate of exchange between two currencies on any given day. (12)

staggered funding Depositing a certain proportion of a payroll or payment into the firm's checking account on several successive days *following* the actual issuance of checks. (8)

standard debt provisions Provisions in long-term debt agreements specifying certain operating criteria, which normally do not place a burden on the financially sound business borrower. (19)

standard deviation, σ_k Statistical indicator of an asset's risk; it measures the dispersion around the *expected* value. (12)

statement of cash flows Provides a summary of the firm's operating, investment, and financing cash flows, over a certain period. (3)

statement of retained earnings Reconciles the net income earned, and any cash dividends paid, with the change in retained earnings between the start and end of a given year. (3)

stock dividend The payment to existing owners of a dividend in the form of stock. (16)

stock repurchase The repurchasing by the firm of outstanding shares of its common stock in the marketplace. (16)

stock rights Allow stockholders to purchase additional shares of stock in direct proportion to their number of owned shares. (20)

stock split A method commonly used to lower the market price of a firm's stock by increasing the number of shares belonging to each shareholder. (16)

stock swap transaction An acquisition method in which the acquiring firm exchanges its shares for shares of the target company according to a predetermined ratio. (17)

stockholders The true owners of the firm by virtue of their equity in the form of preferred and common stock. (2)

stockholders' report Annual report that summarizes and documents for stockholders the firm's financial activities during the past year. (3)

stock-purchase warrant An instrument that gives its holder an option to purchase a certain number of shares of common stock at a specified price over a certain period of time. (19, 21)

straight bond A bond that has no conversion feature. (21)

straight bond value The price at which a convertible bond would sell in the market without the conversion feature. (21)

straight preferred stock Preferred stock that has no conversion feature. (21)

strategic merger A merger transaction undertaken to achieve economies of scale. (17)

stretching accounts payable Paying the firm's bills as late as possible without damaging its credit rating. (8)

striking price The price at which the holder of a call option can buy (or the holder of a put option can sell) a specified amount of stock at any time prior to the option's expiration date. (21)

subordinated debentures Unsecured bonds whose claims are not satisfied until those of the creditors holding senior debt have been fully satisfied. (19)

subordination The stipulation in a long-term debt agreement that all subsequent or less important creditors agree to wait until all claims of the *senior debt* are satisfied before having their claims satisfied. (19)

subscription price The price, set below the prevailing market price, at which stock rights are exercisable for a specified period of time. (20)

subsidiaries The companies controlled by a holding company. (17)

supervoting shares Stock that carries with it more votes per share than a share of regular common stock. (20)

takeover defenses Strategies for fighting hostile takeovers. (17)

target capital structure The desired optimal mix of debt and equity financing that most firms attempt to achieve and maintain. (13)

target company The firm in a merger transaction that the acquiring company is pursuing. (17)

target dividend-payout ratio A policy under which the firm attempts to pay out a certain percentage of earnings as a stated dollar dividend, which it adjusts toward a target payout as proven earnings increases occur. (16)

target weights Either book or market value weights based on *desired* capital structure proportions. (13)

tax loss carryforward In a merger, the tax loss of one of the firms that can be applied against a limited amount of future income of the merged firm over the shorter of either 15 years or until the total tax loss has been fully recovered. (17)

technically insolvent Describes a firm that is unable to pay its bills as they come due; a form of business failure. (7, 17)

tender offer A formal offer to purchase a given number of shares of a firm's stock at a specified price. (17)

term loan agreement A formal contract specifying the conditions under which a financial institution has made a long-term loan. (19)

term (long-term) loan A loan with an initial maturity of more than one year, made by a financial institution to a business. (19)

term structure of interest rates The relationship between the time to maturity and the interest rate or rate of return on similar-risk securities. (2)

times interest earned ratio Measures the firm's ability to make contractual interest payments. (4)

time-series analysis Evaluation of the firm's financial performance over time using financial ratio analysis. (4)

tombstone advertisements Advertisements for security issues. (18)

total asset turnover Indicates the efficiency with which the firm uses *all* its assets to generate sales. (4)

total cost The sum of the order costs and carrying costs of inventory. (9)

total leverage The potential use of fixed costs, *both operating and financial*, to magnify the effect of changes in sales on the firm's EPS. (5)

total risk The risk to the firm of being unable to cover both operating and financial costs; also, the combination of a security's nondiversifiable and diversifiable risk. (5, 12)

trade-off financing strategy A compromise financing strategy between the aggressive financing strategy and the conservative financing strategy. (7)

traditional approach The theory that an optimal capital structure exists, and that the value of the firm is maximized when the cost of capital is minimized. (16)

transactions motive A motive for holding cash or near-cash—to make planned payments for items needed for operations. (8)

treasurer The officer responsible for the firm's financial activities. (1)

Treasury bills U.S. Treasury obligations issued weekly on an auction basis, having varying maturities, generally under one year, and virtually no risk. (8)

Treasury notes U.S. Treasury obligations with initial maturities of between one and seven years, paying interest at a stated rate semiannually, and having virtually no risk. (8)

treasury stock The label used on the firm's balance sheet to designate repurchased shares of stock; shown as a deduction from stockholders' equity. (16)

trust receipt inventory loan An agreement under which the lender advances a portion of the cost of the borrower's salable inventory items in exchange for the borrower's promise to repay the loan, with accrued interest, upon the sale of each item. (10)

trustee A paid third party to a bond indenture, whose job it is to ensure that the issuer does not default on its contractual responsibilities to bondholders. (19)

two-tier offer A tender offer in which the terms offered are more attractive to those who tender shares early. (17)

underpriced Stock sold at a price below its current market price. (13)

underwriting fee Fee divided on a pro rata basis among members of an underwriting syndicate. (18)

underwriting syndicate Group of investment banking firms that collectively participates in buying and selling a portion of a new security issue. (18)

unitary tax laws Laws in some U.S. states that tax multinationals on a percentage of their *total* worldwide income. (2)

unlimited funds The financial situation in which a firm is able to accept all independent projects that provide an acceptable return. (14)

unlimited liability The condition of a sole proprietorship (or general partnership) allowing the owner's total wealth to be taken to satisfy creditors. (2)

unsecured, or general, creditors Creditors who have a general claim against all the firm's assets other than those specifically pledged as collateral. (17)

unsecured short-term financing Financing that matures in one year or less and has no assets pledged as collateral. (10)

unsophisticated capital budgeting techniques Methods that do *not* explicitly consider the time value of money. (15)

valuation The process that links risk and return to determine the worth of an asset. (12)

variable costs Costs that vary directly with sales and that are a function of volume rather than time. (5)

venture capital Funds invested in a start-up business by specialized financial intermediaries. (18)

vertical merger A merger in which a firm acquires *a supplier or a customer.* (17)

voluntary reorganization A petition filed by a failed firm on its own behalf for reorganizing its structure and paying its creditors. (17)

voluntary settlement An arrangement between a technically insolvent or bankrupt firm and its creditors, enabling it to bypass many of the costs involved in legal bankruptcy proceedings. (17)

warehouse receipt loan An arrangement in which the lender receives control of the pledged inventory collateral, which is warehoused by a designated agent. (10)

warrant premium The difference between the actual market value and the theoretical value of a warrant. (21)

weighted average cost of capital (WACC), k_a Cost determined by weighting the cost of each specific type of capital by its proportion in the firm's capital structure. (13)

weighted marginal cost of capital (WMCC) The firm's weighted average cost of capital (WACC) associated with its next dollar of total new financing. (13)

weighted marginal cost of capital (WMCC) schedule Graph that relates the firm's weighted average cost of capital (WACC) to the level of total new financing. (13)

white knight A takeover defense in which the target firm finds an acquirer more to its liking than the initial hostile acquirer and prompts the two to compete to take over the firm. (17)

wire transfers Telegraphic communications that, via bookkeeping entries, remove funds from the payer's bank and deposit them in the payee's bank. (8)

working capital Current assets, which represent the portion of investment that circulates from one form to another in the ordinary conduct of business. (7)

work-in-process inventory   All items currently in production. (9)

yield   The annual rate of interest earned on a security purchased on a given day and held to maturity. (2)

yield curve   A graph that shows the term structure of interest rates. (2)

zero growth model   An approach to dividend valuation that assumes a constant, nongrowing dividend stream. (12)

zero (or low) coupon bonds   Bonds issued with no (zero) or very low coupon (stated interest) rate and sold at a large discount from par. (19)

zero-balance account   A checking account in which a zero balance is maintained and the firm is required to deposit funds to cover checks drawn on the account only as they are presented for payment. (8)

Sources of Chapter Opening Vignettes

1: *USA Today*, November 23, 1990, p. 1. **2:** Robert Buden, "A 'round peg' squarely focused on oil futures: Michael C. Wilner," *Business Week*, December 31, 1990, p. 128. **3:** David Bernstein, "Electronic tax explosion," *CFO Magazine*, November 1990, p. 12. **4:** Larry Armstrong, "For Kathy Braun, this one's the marathon," *Business Week*, December 17, 1990, p. 98. **5:** Charles S. Major, II, "On course with Jack Nicklaus," *CFO Magazine*, November 1990, p. 71. **6:** D. Strischek, "Lending to quick lube shops," *Journal of Commercial Bank Lending*, September 1990, pp. 40–47. **7:** Jill Andresky Fraser, "Honey, I shrunk the company," *Inc.*, June 1990, pp. 115–116. **8:** Ted Holden, "The era of easy money is over," *Business Week*, October 15, 1990, p. 48. **9:** Jim Ullery, "The ideal collection letter," *Inc.*, February 1991, pp. 59–61. **10:** Ted Moncrieff, "What price salvation?" *CFO Magazine*, October 1990, p. 8. **11:** Don Dunn, "Life insurance that pays off when the dollar is ailing," *Business Week*, October 8, 1990, p. 154. **12:** Peter Furhrman, "Please don't leave us, Janet Jackson," *Forbes*, October 15, 1990, pp. 41–42. **13:** Ellyn E. Spragins, "Collaring interest costs: Caps and floors can protect you from soaring rates," *Inc.*, December 1990, p. 161. **14:** Frederick H. Karayama, "Innovation—Products to Watch: Plane wash," *Fortune*, August 27, 1990, p. 97. **15:** Julio Flynn Siler, "Wooing Jacque and Fritz six-pack," *Business Week*, February 4, 1991, pp. 92–93. **17:** Joan Hamilton, "Will BankAmerica have the last laugh?," *Business Week*, November 26, 1990, pp. 148–50. **18:** Francine Schwadel and George Anders, "Backlash against '80s debt binge seen in Interco's Chapter 11 filing lawsuit," *The Wall Street Journal*, January 28, 1991, p. A4. **19:** Michael Schroeder, "That was crow Alan Fellheimer had for Thanksgiving," *Business Week*, December 3, 1990, p. 34. **20:** Matthew Schifrin, "Enough already!" *Forbes*, May 28, 1990, pp. 129–134. **21:** John Meehan and Leah Nathans Spiro, "Wanted: $5 billion, contact Citicorp," *Business Week*, February 11, 1991, pp. 64–65.

INDEX

BASIC MANAGERIAL FINANCE (BMF) DISK

The *BMF Disk* (enclosed opposite) contains two different sets of routines: the *BMF Tutor* and the *BMF Problem-Solver*. The disk is designed for use on IBM and compatible microcomputers. All programs are written in Turbo Pascal® and are extremely user friendly. Many software products make this claim; you'll see for yourself that the *BMF Disk* really lives up to it.

The *BMF Tutor* is a collection of managerial finance problem types constructed by random number generation. Its purpose is to provide an essentially unlimited number of problems to work, so that users can practice until they are satisfied that they understand a concept. The *BMF Problem-Solver* is a collection of financial computation routines. Its purpose is to provide a fast and easy method for performing the often time-consuming mathematical computations required. The *Tutor* should be used to reinforce application of basic concepts; the *Problem-Solver* should be used to save computational time once the concepts are understood.

The *Tutor* and *Problem-Solver* routines are arranged on the software in the same order as the text discussions, with page reference shown on the screen. Text and problems that utilize the disk are keyed to the text and study guide by a computer symbol, 💻, for the *Tutor* and by a diskette symbol, 💾, for the *Problem-Solver*.

Complete and clear instructions for using the *BMF Disk* are included in Appendix B of the book.